Fodor's 04

SPAIN

Where to Stay and Eat for All Budgets

Must-See Sights and Local Secrets

Ratings You Can Trust

Fodor's Travel Publications New York, Toronto, London, Sydney, Auckland
www.fodors.com

FODOR'S SPAIN 2004
Editor: Diane Mehta

Editorial Production: Linda K. Schmidt, John Whitman
Editorial Contributors: Ignacio Gómez, Mary McLean, George Semler, AnneLise Sorensen
Maps: David Lindroth, *cartographer*; Rebecca Baer and Bob Blake, *map editors*
Design: Fabrizio La Rocca, *creative director*; Guido Caroti, *art director*; Melanie Marin, *senior picture editor*
Production/Manufacturing: Robert B. Shields
Cover Photo (Castile, near Zamora): Michael Busselle/Stone/Getty

COPYRIGHT

ISBN 1-4000-1270-8

ISSN 0071-6545

SPECIAL SALES

Fodor's Travel Publications are available at special discounts for bulk purchases for sales promotions or premiums. Special editions, including personalized covers, excerpts of existing guides, and corporate imprints, can be created in large quantities for special needs. For more information, contact your local bookseller or write to Special Markets, Fodor's Travel Publications, 1745 Broadway, New York, NY 10019. Inquiries from Canada should be directed to your local Canadian bookseller or sent to Random House of Canada, Ltd., Marketing Department, 2775 Matheson Boulevard East, Mississauga, Ontario L4W 4P7. Inquiries from the United Kingdom should be sent to Fodor's Travel Publications, 20 Vauxhall Bridge Road, London SW1V 2SA, England.

AN IMPORTANT TIP & AN INVITATION

Although all prices, opening times, and other details in this book are based on information supplied to us at press time, changes occur all the time in the travel world, and Fodor's cannot accept responsibility for facts that become outdated or for inadvertent errors or omissions. So **always confirm information when it matters,** especially if you're making a detour to visit a specific place. Your experiences—positive and negative—matter to us. If we have missed or misstated something, **please write to us.** We follow up on all suggestions. Contact the Spain editor at editors@fodors.com or c/o Fodor's, 1745 Broadway, New York, NY 10019.

PRINTED IN THE UNITED STATES OF AMERICA

10 9 8 7 6 5 4 3 2 1

DESTINATION SPAIN

Spain was a well-kept secret for much of the 20th century while sequestered within a church-and-military-dominated dictatorship. But once the lid came off this epicurean Pandora's Box, the world discovered a series of cultures and peoples as vibrant and varied as any in the world. Modern Spain landed on its feet and running: you can see it in the various cultural identities, each with its own language, cuisine, and distinct manner of dancing in the streets; you can see it in the landscapes and architecture that change so completely as you move across the country that the land seems to speak for itself; and, most of all, you can see it in the people, whose infectious knack for generosity and pleasure is Iberia's greatest resource. Once you spend some time here you may also start believing that Spaniards know something you don't about enjoying life, expressing moods, and keeping everything in perspective. Have a fabulous trip!

Karen Cure, Editorial Director

CONTENTS

ON THE ROAD WITH FODOR'S

A trip takes you out of yourself. Concerns of life at home completely disappear, driven away by more immediate thoughts—about, say, what marvels will beguile the next day, or where you'll have dinner. That's where Fodor's comes in. We make sure that you know all your options, so that you don't miss something that's around the next bend just because you didn't know it was there. Because the best memories of your trip might have nothing to do with what you came to Spain to see, we guide you to sights large and small across the country. You might set out to see the country's most fascinating small museum, but back at home you find yourself unable to forget that hopping tapas bar or pottery-laden *cerámica* just around the corner from the museum. With Fodor's at your side, serendipitous discoveries are never far away.

Our success in showing you every corner of Spain is a credit to our extraordinary writers. Although there's no substitute for travel advice from a good friend who knows your style, our contributors are the next best thing—the kind of people you would poll for travel advice if you knew them.

Born and raised in Madrid, economist **Ignacio Gómez** spent three years riding the on-line journalism wave in New York and has served as a writer and editor for a Spanish technology and economy Web magazine. His thirst for foreign travel temporarily satisfied, he is concentrating on his master's in Comparative Literature while continuing to unravel his roots.

Journalist **Mary McLean,** from England, and has worked in California, the Middle East and, since 1990, Spain. Mary writes for various magazines and travel publications, including in-flight magazines and guide books. She has covered Portugal, Italy, and various regions of Spain. Mary also contributes to travel-related Web sites. In her spare time she likes nothing better than exploring the wilder regions of the Iberian peninsula, taking along a sketch pad as well her portable computer.

Born and educated in Connecticut, writer and journalist **George Semler** has lived in Spain for the last 30-odd years. During that time he has written on Spain, France, Morocco, Cuba, and the Mediterranean region for *Forbes, Sky, Saveur,* the *International Herald Tribune,* and the *Los Angeles Times* and has published walking guides to Madrid and Barcelona. When not hiking, fly-fishing, or sampling Catalonia's hottest new restaurants, he finds time to work on a magnum opus about the Pyrenees.

Writer and editor **AnneLise Sorensen** has spent several years living in Barcelona, where she has been reconnecting with her Catalan roots. Her updating stint took her from the black-sand beaches of the Canary Islands to the sun-kissed seas of the Costa Blanca; from the Roman ruins of Tarragona to the fragrant orange groves of Valencia; and from Extremadura's wooded valleys and dramatic small towns on the western coast over to the far-flung Balearic Islands off the Mediterranean coast. AnneLise writes for various magazines and travel publications and has contributed to numerous Fodor's guides, including those to San Francisco, Denmark, and Ireland.

ABOUT THIS BOOK

	There's no doubt that the best source for travel advice is a like-minded friend who's just been where you're headed. But with or without that friend, you'll have a better trip with a Fodor's guide in hand. Once you've learned to find your way around its pages, you'll be in great shape to find your way around your destination.
SELECTION	Our goal is to cover the best properties, sights, and activities in their category, as well as the most interesting communities to visit. We make a point of including local food-lovers' hot spots as well as neighborhood options, and we avoid all that's touristy unless it's really worth your time. You can go on the assumption that everything you read about in this book is recommended wholeheartedly by our writers and editors. Flip to On the Road with Fodor's to learn more about who they are. It goes without saying that no property mentioned in the book has paid to be included.
RATINGS	Orange stars ★ denote sights and properties that our editors and writers consider the very best in the area covered by the entire book. These, the best of the best, are listed in the Fodor's Choice section in the front of the book. Black stars ★ highlight the sights and properties we deem Highly Recommended, the don't-miss sights within any region. Fodor's Choice and Highly Recommended options in each region are usually listed on the title page of the chapter covering that region. Use the index to find complete descriptions. In cities, sights pinpointed with numbered map bullets ❶ in the margins tend to be more important than those without bullets.
SPECIAL SPOTS	Pleasures & Pastimes focuses on types of experiences that reveal the spirit of the destination. Watch for Off the Beaten Path sights. Some are out of the way, some are quirky, and all are worth your while. If the munchies hit while you're exploring, look for Need a Break? suggestions.
TIME IT RIGHT	Wondering when to go? Check On the Calendar up front and chapters' Timing sections for weather and crowd overviews and best days and times to visit.
SEE IT ALL	Use Fodor's exclusive Great Itineraries as a model for your trip. (For a good overview of the entire destination, follow those that begin the book, or mix regional itineraries from several chapters.) In cities, Good Walks guide you to important sights in each neighborhood; ⚑ indicates the starting points of walks and itineraries in the text and on the map.
BUDGET WELL	Hotel and restaurant price categories from ¢ to $$$$ are defined in the opening pages of each chapter-expect to find a balanced selection for every budget. For attractions, we always give standard adult admission fees; reductions are usually available for children, students, and senior citizens. Look in Discounts & Deals in Smart Travel Tips for information on destination-wide ticket schemes.
BASIC INFO	Smart Travel Tips lists travel essentials for the entire area covered by the book; city- and region-specific basics end each chapter. To find the best way to get around, see the transportation section; see individual modes of travel ("By Car," "By Train") for details. We assume you'll check Web sites or call for particulars.

ON THE MAPS	Maps throughout the book show you what's where and help you find your way around. Black and orange numbered bullets ❶ ❶ in the text correlate to bullets on maps.
BACKGROUND	In general, we give background information within the chapters in the course of explaining sights as well as in CloseUp boxes and in A Short History in the back of the book. To get in the mood, review the suggestions in Books & Movies. The vocabulary can be invaluable.
FIND IT FAST	Within the book, chapters are arranged in a roughly clockwise direction starting with Madrid, in the center of the country. City chapters cover an entire city and nearby areas; other chapters are divided into small regions, within which towns are covered in logical geographical order and attractive routes and interesting places between towns are flagged as En Route. Heads at the top of each page help you find what you need within a chapter.
DON'T FORGET	Restaurants are open for lunch and dinner daily unless we state otherwise; we mention dress only when there's a specific requirement and reservations only when they're essential or not accepted—it's always best to book ahead. Hotels have private baths, phone, TVs, and air-conditioning. We always list facilities but not whether you'll be charged extra to use them, so when pricing accommodations, find out what's included.

SYMBOLS

Many Listings

- ★ Fodor's Choice
- ★ Highly recommended
- ✉ Physical address
- ✥ Directions
- 📫 Mailing address
- ☎ Telephone
- 📠 Fax
- 🌐 On the Web
- 📧 E-mail
- 🎫 Admission fee
- ⏲ Open/closed times
- ⚑ Start of walk/itinerary
- Ⓜ Metro stations
- 💳 Credit cards

Outdoors

- ⛺ Camping

Hotels & Restaurants

- 🏨 Hotel
- Number of rooms
- Facilities
- Meal plans
- ✕ Restaurant
- Reservations
- Dress code
- Smoking
- BYOB
- ✕🏨 Hotel with restaurant that warrants a visit

Other

- Family-friendly
- Contact information
- ⇨ See also
- Branch address
- ☞ Take note

Bay of Biscay
A Ferrol
A Coruña
Vilalba
Luarca
Gijón
Ribadesella
Santander
Ribadeo
Oviedo
Cangas de Onís
Santiago de Compostela
Lugo
Mieres
PICOS DE EUROPA
Bilbao
Muros
CANTABRIAN MTS.
Pontevedra
Ponferrada
León
Vigo
Ourense
Astorga
Burgos
Tui
Benavente
Palencia
Valladolid
Duero
Zamora
Tordesillas
Salamanca
Adanero
Segovia
SIERRA DE GUA
Avila
Guad
Ciudad Rodrigo
El Escorial
MADR
PORTUGAL
SIERRA DE GREDOS
Toledo
Plasencia
Aranjue
Talavera de la Reina
Tajo
Alcáza San J
Cáceres
Guadalupe
Trujillo
Guadiana
Ciudad Real
Abenójar
Mérida
Badajoz
Almadén
Zafra
Jerez de los Caballeros
SIERRA MORENA
Fregenal de la Sierra
Bailén
Linares
Córdoba
Aroche
Jaén
Baeza
Guadalquivir
Ecija
Seville
Baena
Carmona
Lucena
Granada
Huelva
Antequera
Loja
Gulf of Cadiz
Sanlúcar de Barrameda
Nerja
COSTA DE LA LUZ
Ronda
Jerez de la Frontera
Torremolinos
Málaga
Fuengirola
ATLANTIC OCEAN
Cádiz
Estepona
Marbella
COSTA DEL SOL
Algeciras
Gibraltar
TO CANARY ISLANDS
Strait of Gibraltar
MOROCCO

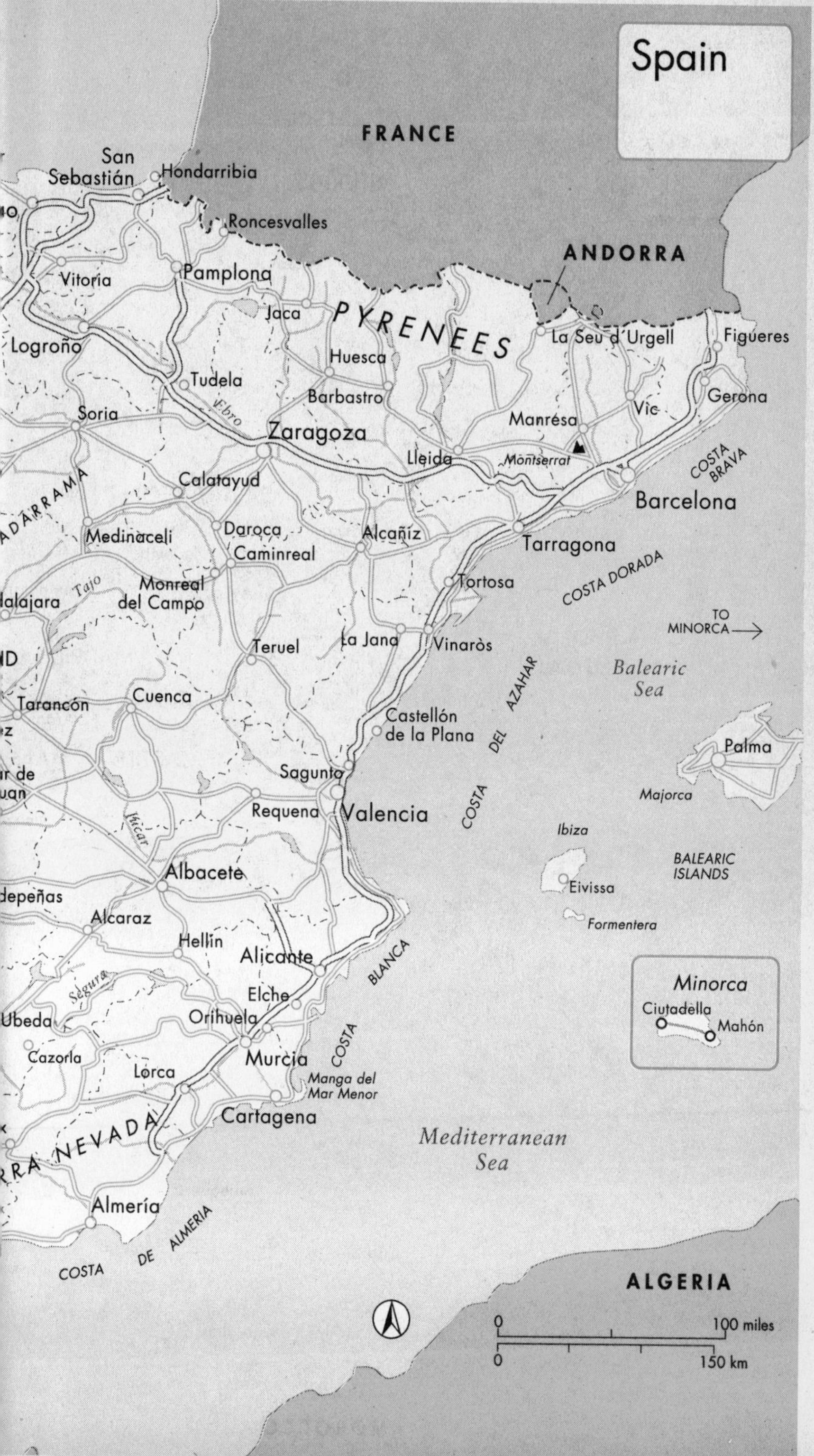
Spain
FRANCE
ANDORRA
PYRENEES
San Sebastián
Hondarribia
Roncesvalles
Vitoria
Pamplona
Jaca
Logroño
Huesca
Tudela
Barbastro
La Seu d'Urgell
Figueres
Gerona
Vic
Manresa
Montserrat
Soria
Ebro
Zaragoza
Lleida
Barcelona
COSTA BRAVA
Calatayud
Medinaceli
Daroca
Caminreal
Alcañíz
Tarragona
Tortosa
COSTA DORADA
Tajo
Monreal del Campo
Teruel
La Jana
Vinaròs
TO MINORCA
Balearic Sea
Tarancón
Cuenca
Castellón de la Plana
COSTA DEL AZAHAR
Palma
Majorca
Sagunto
Valencia
Requena
Júcar
Ibiza
BALEARIC ISLANDS
Eivissa
Formentera
Albacete
Alcaraz
Hellín
Alicante
Elche
Segura
COSTA BLANCA
Orihuela
Minorca
Ciutadella
Mahón
Cazorla
Murcia
Lorca
Manga del Mar Menor
Cartagena
Mediterranean Sea
SIERRA NEVADA
Almería
COSTA DE ALMERÍA
ALGERIA
0
100 miles
0
150 km

Bay of Biscay
Gijón
A Coruña
Oviedo
Santander
VIZCAY
A CORUÑA
LUGO
ASTURIAS
CANTABRIA
Santiago de Compostela
Lugo
Bilba
ÁLAVA
León
GALICIA
Pontevedra
BURGOS
LEON
Burgos
PONTE-VEDRA
Ourense
OURENSE
PALENCIA
Palencia
BURGOS
ZAMORA
Valladolid
Duero
VALLADOLID
Zamora
CASTILE–LEON
SEGOVIA
Salamanca
Segovia
SALAMANCA
Ávila
Guadalaja
MADRID
PORTUGAL
ÁVILA
MADRID
Toledo
Aranjuez
TOLEDO
CÁCERES
Tajo
CASTILE–LA MANC
Cáceres
Trujillo
EXTREMADURA
Alcaz
Guadiana
CIUDAD REAL
Ciudad Real
Badajóz
Valdepeña
BADAJÓZ
CÓRDOBA
Córdoba
JAÉN
Jaén
HUELVA
Guadalquivir
ANDALUSIA
SEVILLE
Huelva
Seville
Granad
Antequera
GRANADA
COSTA DE LA LUZ
Jerez
MÁLAGA
Málaga
ATLANTIC OCEAN
Cádiz
CÁDIZ
COSTA DEL SOL
Gibraltar
KEY
Regions
Provinces
Provincial capitals
MOROCCO

Autonomous Communities & Provinces
EUSKADI (BASQUE COUNTRY)
San Sebastián
FRANCE
GUIPUZCOA
Vitoria
Pamplona
Trevino
NAVARRE
Logroño
LA RIOJA
HUESCA
Huesca
LLEIDA
ANDORRA
GIRONA
Girona
CATALONIA
BARCELONA
COSTA BRAVA
Barcelona
Soria
Ebro
Zaragoza
Lleida
SORIA
ARAGON
ZARAGOZA
Tarragona
TARRAGONA
Tortosa
COSTA DORADA
TO MINORCA
GUADALAJARA
Tajo
TERUEL
Balearic Sea
Teruel
CASTELLÓN
Cuenca
CUENCA
Castellón de la Plana
Palma
Jucar
Valencia
COSTA DEL AZAHAR
Mallorca
Requena
VALENCIA
Ibiza
BALEARIC ISLANDS
Albacete
Eivissa
Formentera
ALBACETE
ALICANTE
Segura
Alicante
COSTA BLANCA
Minorca
Ciutadella
Mahón
MURCIA
Murcia
Lorca
Cartagena
Mediterranean Sea
ALMERÍA
Almería
COSTA DE ALMERIA
ALGERIA
0 50 miles
0 75 km

WHAT'S WHERE

Spain's different geographical and cultural entities are like an all-star team: each player has a significantly different style, strength, and personality. Moist, green Asturias, Galicia, Cantabria, and Euskadi (the Basque Country) are an Iberian Ireland, while Andalusia is a taste of North Africa with a few verdant pockets of its own. Spain's mountains—Alpine fortresses—contrast with Castilla's dramatically dry and minimalist expanse. And Barcelona's colorful Moderniste architecture could hardly be more different from Spain's most characteristic architectural style, the exposed brick Mudéjar hybrid of Moorish and Christian elements. Here's a glimpse of the diverse mix of cultures you can expect from these varied terrains; the geographical organization of the following paragraphs mirrors how this book is arranged.

1 Madrid

Madrid's bright skies and boundless energy make every sight and sound seem larger than life. Although you expect royal palaces to be grand, for instance, Madrid's Palacio Real has 2,800 rooms. The Prado, Reina Sofía, and Thyssen-Bornemisza museums pack 9,000 Spanish and other European masterworks into an art-saturated half mile. Sunday's flea market in El Rastro is as thick with overpriced oddities as with human activity. The cafés in the Plaza Mayor, one of Europe's grandest squares, are perpetually abuzz, and nightlife stretches into the wee hours near Plaza Santa Ana. Indeed, late-night social diversions are the heartbeat of Madrid, distracting locals from sleep even as the rest of the Western world prepares for another day at the grindstone.

2 Old & New Castile

Despite what you may have heard about the rain in Spain falling mainly on the plain, the country's largest such expanse is an arid reach of windy skies and wide vistas. Cut with rocky gorges and fringed with gaunt mountains, this vast plateau is severe, melancholic, and mysterious. It was here that Don Quijote tilted at windmills, and somber Ávila, ringed by its original 11th-century wall, gave rise to the mystical ecstasies of St. Teresa. Austere Toledo, sitting calmly on a battlement-topped granite cliff, inspired El Greco's moody canvases; golden Segovia, with the Roman aqueduct leading to the walled city on a shelf of rock, forms postcard views in every direction. The first sight of Cuenca startles: how do 500-year-old houses cling to the sides of a precipice? Salamanca overwhelms with Renaissance architecture, including one of Spain's largest and most graceful public squares. Valladolid's National Museum of Sculpture has the largest and finest collection of polychrome wood pieces in the world. Medieval Burgos has long been a center of both religious and military activity—symbolized, perhaps, in the person of native son El Cid, the Christian Reconquest's legendary hero. Prosperous León hums with student activity but is best known for its cathedral, with a whopping 125 stained-glass windows.

3 Cantabria, the Basque Country, Navarra & La Rioja

Spain takes on a different character up north—it's greener, cloudier, and more stubbornly independent in spirit. After all, part of the land is Basque, a country within a country, with its own language and culture as well as its own coastline on the Bay of Biscay, one of the most enchanting shores. San Sebastián, near the French border, and the Cantabrian resort Santander, to the west, are seaside showpieces, inviting long, slow walks down elegant promenades, through fashionable lanes, and among restful gardens. La Rioja, a mixture of highlands, plains, and vineyards in and around the Ebro River basin, produces Spain's best wines. Bilbao has experienced a veritable Renaissance with the addition of Frank Gehry's titanium-skinned Guggenheim Museum. Already endowed with an excellent Museum of Fine Arts, renowned Basque restaurants, and various older treasures, Bilbao has become an artistic destination in its own right and may well be Spain's most talked-about city.

4 Galicia & Asturias

To pay homage to St. James, Christian pilgrims once crossed Europe to a corner of Spain so remote it was called *finis terrae* (end of the earth). Santiago de Compostela, their destination, still resonates with mystic importance, especially in and around its magnificent cathedral and on festive St. James Day, July 25. The ancient pilgrimage—the Camino de Santiago—regained popularity as the second millennium drew to a close, but today's pilgrims may or may not hew to the original route. Here in Spain's far northwest, you'll find isolated towns among green hills and sandy beaches beside the Atlantic Ocean and Bay of Biscay; scattered sets of stilted horreos (granaries) with Christian and Celtic symbols; and the solitary, jagged Picos de Europa. Enjoy oysters in Vigo, great seafood and Albariño wines throughout the region, and sample some strong, tangy Picos blue cheeses.

5 The Pyrenees

With its own flora, fauna, and alpine ways of life, Spain's natural border with France is a world unto itself. Cut by more than a dozen steep north–south valleys and four highland domains—Vall de Camprodón, the sunny Cerdanya, Vall d'Aran, and the gently rolling Baztán valley—the Pyrenees are also dotted with such memorable and historic towns as medieval Beget, La Seu d'Urgell, Bellver de Cerdanya, Benasque, Jaca, and Roncesvalles. As a haven from the 8th-century Moorish invasion, the Pyrenees became an unlikely repository of Romanesque art and architecture, as well as a natural preserve of stunning geographical terrain.

6 Barcelona & Northern Catalonia

The poet Federico García Lorca called Barcelona's Rambla the only street in the world he wished would never end. A vivid mass of strollers, market-goers, artists, buskers, vendors, scammers, and vamps, this flow of humanity prepares your eye and imagination for Barcelona's startling and occasionally even bizarre architectural landmarks. The expansive Boquería market breathes new life into the notion of grocery shopping. Antoni Gaudí's sinuous Casa Milà and emphatically unique Sagrada Família church took the late-19th- and early 20th century's Art Nouveau movement into the heart of natural form and design, while the intricate Art Nouveau Palau de la Música takes aesthetic whimsy to the limit. Outside Barcelona are less-explored Catalan towns like medieval Girona, with its important Jewish quarter, and the whitewashed village of Cadaqués on the Costa Brava, a rocky shore shaded with pines and lapped by a lustrous sea.

7 Southern Catalonia & the Levante

The sun rises (*se levanta*) from the Mediterranean to give the citrus-scented, mountain-backed plain near Valencia its name and lend an exotic glow to the city's Christian and Moorish landmarks. The sea yields ingredients for Spain's paella Valenciana and makes a dramatic backdrop for the Roman ruins of cosmopolitan Tarragona. Where the sea meets the Ebro River, 200,000 birds enjoy the tranquillity of the Delta de l'Ebre Natural Park. Farther inland, castles, fortresses, and the mountains of the Sierra de Beceite lure you far off Spain's beaten path.

8 The Southeast

Like Don Quijote moving from one picaresque exploit to another across the vast tracts of La Mancha, today's wanderers find plenty of drama in a still-empty landscape that seems to change with every turn of the road. Rice paddies and fragrant orange groves give way to the palm-fringed port city of Alicante, the fertile plains and dry hills of Murcia, and the craggy lunar landscapes of Almería. Along the way, ceramics are handcrafted from the local white clay in towns like Alicante and rural Albacete; and saffron, red peppers, and dates flavor the region's rice-based cuisine. Modern resorts line the Costa Blanca; inland festivities include Alcoy's annual Moros y Cristianos, which includes reenactments of the Christians' recapture of Alcoy from the Moors in the 13th century. Still, the scenery steals the show, especially on the crowd-free coast of the Cabo de Gata, a haven for rare wildlife and anyone in search of an unspoiled beach.

9 The Balearic Islands

Halfway between France and Africa, these once-remote landfalls off Spain's eastern coast are a playground for northern Europeans, not least because Britain occupied Minorca in the 18th century. Ibiza blasts to life nightly with the anything-goes heat that has come with 20th-century tourism—but even this disco-mad isle, with its summer clubbers, has its quiet coves. Majorca also combines tourist-clogged pockets with undiscovered corners: rugged mountains, abandoned monasteries, and a smattering of Christian and Moorish monuments like the Arab baths in the Balearic capital, Palma. On Minorca you can explore antique Ciutadella and Mahón between trips to the beach. And Formentera, the most purely pastoral island, retains a wild beauty that no man-made attraction can match.

10 The Costa del Sol

Sunseekers from Europe's bleaker climes, crammed into every cranny of this famous strip, make the whole area feel like a hedonistic carnival. The draws? A whopping 320 days of sunshine a year, and endless beaches on which to bask in it. Although Málaga, the provincial capital, is often bypassed in transit, it has historical and maritime appeal. Marbella, a favorite of the rich and famous, adds the seductive charm of a pristine Andalusian old quarter. For more of the same, head into the mountains, where villages like Casares seem wondrously immune to the goings-on along the coast (even as it shimmers below), and the ancient town of Ronda straddles a giant river gorge. East toward Granada, Nerja combines a cliff-bound, gray-sand beach with enormous caves full of natural spires.

11 Granada, Córdoba & Eastern Andalusia

The Moors made an important mark on this corner of their caliphate. Granada's Alhambra is a marvel of patios, arches, and intricate carvings, with the lush Generalife palace gardens next door. Across a gorge is the Moors' old neighborhood, the Albaicín, a grouping of ancient white houses tumbling down a hillside. Córdoba's Mezquita—a mosque with a cathedral in the middle—is sublime, its 850 columns topped with red-and-white-striped arches. Near the mosque, the thick-walled homes in Córdoba's medieval Jewish Quarter, the Judería, all but hide their spectacularly tiled interior courtyards. South of Córdoba, on the way to Granada, the region of Subbética is rich in natural parks and historical and archaeological sites. The historic mining town of Guadix is a good base for exploring Andalusia's many caves, scooped out of the sandstone mountains and often still inhabited. South of Granada, on the slopes of the Sierra Nevada, lie the villages of the Alpujarras, where descendants of transplanted Galicians craft rugs, blankets, baskets, and pottery. Olive groves seem to stretch forever in Andalusia, especially in the province of Jaén. There its green landscape is interrupted by gems like Úbeda and Baeza, which have perfectly preserved Renaissance mansions and churches.

12 Seville & Western Andalusia

Maritime history, heroism, and high adventure seem to linger over the Guadalquivir River's swampy Atlantic delta. Since 1100 BC Cádiz has been port of call for Phoenicians, Carthaginians, and Romans plying the trade routes at the western end of the Mediterranean. It was from Huelva that Columbus set out to discover the New World and at Sanlúcar de Barrameda that Magellan's expedition, with Juan Sebastián Elkano in command, completed the first circumnavigation of the globe. *Y Sevilla!* exclaimed Seville poet Manuel Machado (1874–1947) in his classic "Oda a Andalucía." Indeed, as for Seville—most colorful during its Holy Week festival, Semana Santa—it brims with romance all year round. The city's Giralda tower, massive cathedral, and sumptuous Alcázar recall Moorish caliphs and Christian kings, and elaborate azulejo tiles throughout the city form a cheerful Andalusian motif. Dusty tapas bars and old palaces look unassuming but enchant Sevillanos and travelers alike. Farther south, the fishing town of Sanlúcar de Barrameda serves unbeatable giant shrimp, known as *langostinos,* and in the vast vineyards around Jerez de la Frontera, more than a half million barrels of sherry are maturing at any given time. Gorge on large prawns in Puerto de Santa María, delicious tapas in Seville, and game in season.

13 Extremadura

A journey through the wooded valleys and ocher farmlands of this western region feels a bit like time travel. The land is hushed and haunting. Even in prosperous Cáceres, nothing modern disrupts the Old Quarter, packed with medieval and Renaissance churches and palaces; and in Trujillo, the streets lined with vestigial mansions of Spain's imperial age are nearly deserted. Ancient Mérida, founded in 25 BC, is Spain's richest trove of Roman remains. Out in the mountains, the Jerte Valley and the monastery of Our Lady of Guadalupe make dramatic vantage points.

14 The Canary Islands

Tempered only by cool Atlantic breezes in summer, the balmy sunshine rarely lets up here, and steady winds and perfect waves attract surfers and windsurfers from all over the world to the coast of Lanzarote. Hotels and nightlife abound on Tenerife and Gran Canaria, the largest of the seven islands in this volcanic archipelago. But the islands' natural wonders are unusual among resorts, and Lanzarote's lava-formed water caverns, Los Jameos del Agua, as well as Tenerife's volcanic crater, the Cañadas del Teide, border on the bizarre.

GREAT ITINERARIES

Essential Spain
12 to 16 days

Madrid makes the best starting point for a tour of Spain that aims to cover its main cultural components: Castile (Madrid and the central meseta, or plain), Andalusia (the south), Catalonia (the northeast), and the Basque Country (the north).

MADRID

1 day. The elegant Plaza Mayor is the perfect jumping-off point for a tour of Spain's capital. To the west, see the Plaza de la Villa, Royal Palace, and opera house; to the east visit the Plaza Santa Ana and theater district. Madrid's Paseo del Arte (Art Walk) takes in three major museums, including the Prado. Toledo and Segovia make excellent side trips. ⇨ *Madrid in Chapter 1 and Toledo to Ciudad Real and Segovia and Its Province in Chapter 2.*

CÓRDOBA

1 day. This capital of both Roman and Moorish Spain was a center of Western art and culture in the 8th–11th centuries, to which its stunning mosque bears witness. The medieval Jewish Quarter unfolds in tiny, beckoning alleyways. ⇨ *Córdoba and Environs in Chapter 11.*

SEVILLE

1 day. Seville's Giralda tower, cathedral, bullring, and Barrio de Santa Cruz are visual feasts. Forty minutes south you can sip the world-famous sherries of Jerez de la Frontera, then munch jumbo shrimp on the beach at Sanlúcar de Barrameda. ⇨ *Seville and Environs in Chapter 12.*

GRANADA

1 or 2 days. The hilltop Alhambra palace was conceived by the Moorish caliphs as heaven on earth and still strikes many as exactly that. The nearby Generalife palace has lush formal gardens. Down in the city, see the Royal Chapel, with the tombs of Ferdinand and Isabella; the cathedral; and the magnificent Albaicín, the ancient Moorish quarter. ⇨ *Granada and Environs, the Sierra Nevada, and the Alpujarras in Chapter 11.*

BARCELONA

3 days. There are three key walks in 2,000-year-old Barcelona: the Gothic Quarter; the Eixample, with Art Nouveau buildings by Gaudí and others; and Gaudí's Güell Park and massive, unfinished Sagrada Família church. A stroll on the Rambla and a trip to the Boqueria market are other musts, along with the church of Santa Maria del Mar, the Museu Picasso, and the flamboyant Palau de la Música. Day trips might take you to medieval Girona or Roman Tarragona. ⇨ *Barri Gòtic, The Moderniste Eixample, and Upper Barcelona in Chapter 6.*

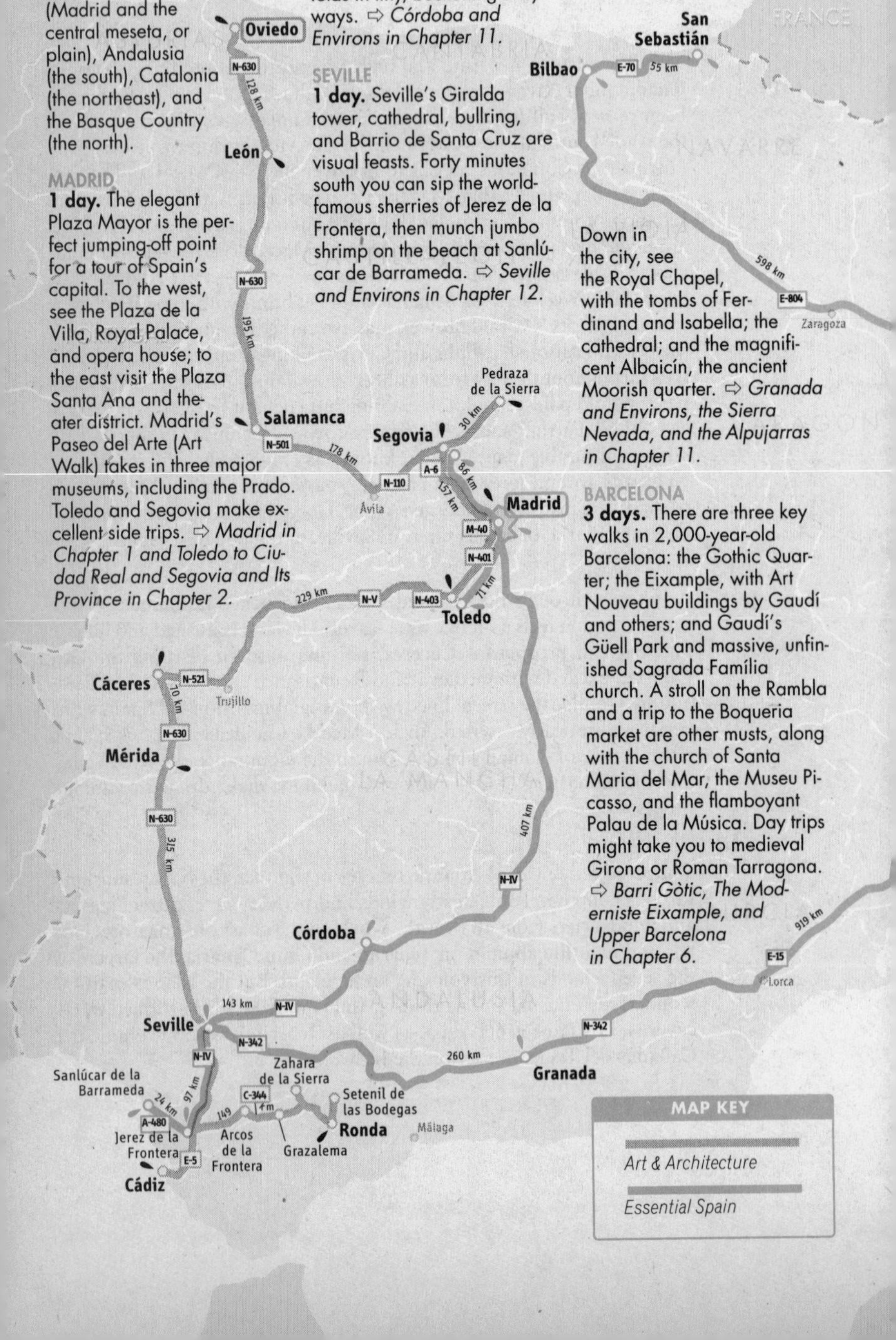

BILBAO

1 or 2 days. Bilbao's Guggenheim Museum is worth a trip for the building itself, and the Museum of Fine Arts has an impressive collection of Basque and Spanish paintings. Restaurants and tapas bars abound. ⇨ *Bilbao and the Basque Coast to Guetaria in Chapter 3.*

THE BASQUE COAST

1 or 2 days. The Basque coast between Bilbao and San Sebastián is lined with beaches, rocky cliffs, and picture-perfect fishing ports. ⇨ *Bilbao and the Basque Coast to Guetaria in Chapter 3.*

SAN SEBASTIÁN

1 or 2 days. San Sebastián is one of Spain's most delicious cities both visually and gastronomically. Belle Epoque buildings nearly encircle the tiny bay, and tapas bars flourish in the old quarter. Duck into a *sidrería* for cider, codfish omelets, and *txuleta de buey* (beefsteak). ⇨ *San Sebastián to Hondarribia in Chapter 3.*

Transportation

Madrid is within five hours of anywhere, and the scenery is relentlessly, well, scenic, since no billboards are permitted on Spanish highways. Overnight trains (on some of which you can transport your car) from Barcelona to Málaga or Sevilla make sense, but the Barcelona to Bilbao drive is now well under five hours. Domestic flights are another option. From Madrid it's a 3-hour drive or a 90-minute ride on the high-speed AVE train to Córdoba, then a 45-minute AVE ride to Seville. Granada is 3 hours from Seville by car, train, or bus. The drive from Granada to Barcelona takes about 7 hours, the flight 70 minutes. The overnight train from Andalusia to Barcelona leaves from Málaga. From Barcelona, a 5-hour drive, an overnight train, or a 1-hour flight to Bilbao lands you in the Basque Country, where a car is your best mode of transport.

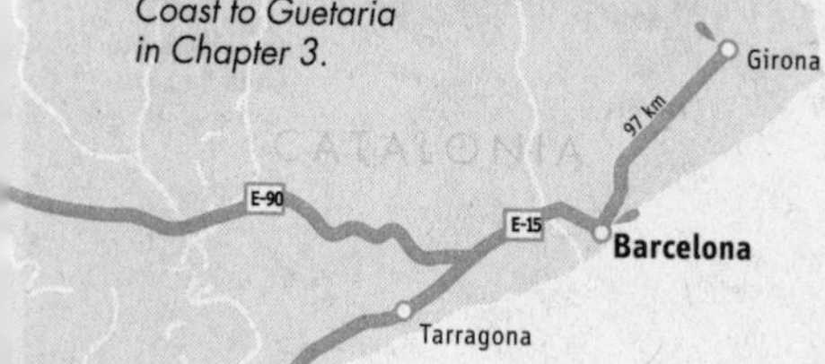

CATALONIA
E-90
E-15
97 km
Girona
Barcelona
Tarragona

Art & Architecture

10 to 12 days

Many of Spain's finest buildings and artworks are far from the capitals of culture and commerce. This north–south tour avoids the behemoths in favor of smaller settings where quiet monuments can speak.

OVIEDO

1 to 2 days. Asturias and the Basque Country are the only parts of Spain that the Moors never conquered. Oviedo, the Asturian capital, is full of rare pre-Romanesque churches, mainly from the 9th century. Other star attractions in Asturias are its 16th-century manor houses—many now inns—the Picos de Europa National Park, and thatch-roof granaries on stilts. ⇨ *Western Asturias in Chapter 4.*

LEÓN

1 day. Crowned by its 13th-century cathedral, with an abundance of stained-glass windows, prosperous León is rich in history and culture. The marvelously preserved 12th-century frescoes in the Royal Pantheon represent some of the finest Romanesque art in Europe. ⇨ *Burgos, León, and the Camino de Santiago in Chapter 2.*

LAGUARDIA

Half day. This 10th-century, walled hilltop town, with panoramic views of the surrounding vineyards, is the capital of La Rioja Alavesa, the part of La Rioja on the north bank of the Ebro river in the Basque province of Alava. The Gothic polychrome doorway to Santa María de los Reyes church is Laguardia's chief treasure. ⇨ *Vitoria and the Rioja Alavesa in Chapter 3.*

SALAMANCA

1 day. This friendly university city is clothed in golden sandstone. The enormous arcaded Plaza Mayor, plateresque university buildings, and adjacent cathedrals add up to an architectural treasury nonpareil. ⇨ *Salamanca and Ciudad Rodrigo in Chapter 2.*

SEGOVIA

1 day. High on the Castilian meseta, medieval Segovia commands stark views, and its charming Plaza Mayor, late-Gothic cathedral, 1st-century Roman aqueduct, and turreted 15th-century Alcázar (fortress) make for an exquisite day and a pleasant overnight. ⇨ *Segovia and Its Province in Chapter 2.*

PEDRAZA DE LA SIERRA

1 day. The handsomely restored village of Pedraza de la Sierra is an exquisite place for a weekend or just for lunch. Try the town specialty, roast lamb, under the wooden arcades bordering the main square. ⇨ *Segovia and Its Province in Chapter 2.*

TOLEDO

1 day. An intellectual nexus of Moors, Christians, and Jews in the Middle Ages, Toledo has a giant cathedral, a Moorish Alcázar, and two synagogues. Tour the 16th-century El Greco home and see his *View and Map of Toledo* and *Burial of Count Orgaz*. Spend the night here to experience the town's haunting quiet and lose yourself (literally) in its labyrinth of streets and alleys. ⇨ *Toledo to Ciudad Real in Chapter 2.*

CÁCERES

1 day. The capital of its province in rural Extremadura and a lively university town, Cáceres has one of Spain's best-preserved old quarters, a Renaissance time warp. ⇨ *Upper Extremadura in Chapter 13.*

MÉRIDA

1 day. Mérida was the capital of Lusitania, the Roman Empire's westernmost province. Its Roman theater, amphitheater, arch, and ruined aqueduct as well as the bridge over the Guadiana are the leading monuments. ⇨ *Lower Extremadura in Chapter 13.*

CÁDIZ

1 day. Founded by Phoenician merchants in about 1100 BC, Cádiz is widely considered Europe's oldest continuously inhabited city but is best known today for its rowdy pre-Lenten Carnival. The 18th-century Oratorio de San Felipe Neri and the cathedral are architectural highlights, and the Museo de Cádiz showcases Zurbarán. ⇨ *Province of Cádiz in Chapter 12.*

RONDA & THE PUEBLOS BLANCOS

2 days. Begin this drive through Andalusia's "white villages" in cliff-top Arcos de la Frontera, to see its whitewashed homes and eclectic church of Santa María de la Asunción. Continue through Zahara de la Sierra, a former Moorish stronghold; colorful, rainy Grazalema; and the cavelike village of Setenil de las Bodegas. Extraordinarily rich in geography, architecture, and legend, Ronda is also the cradle of the art of bullfighting, and its bullring is one of Spain's oldest and most beautiful. ⇨ *Ronda and the Pueblos Blancos in Chapter 10.*

Transportation

You'll need a car to cover this ground efficiently. Trains and buses serve all of these towns, but connections are often indirect, and schedules can be inconvenient.

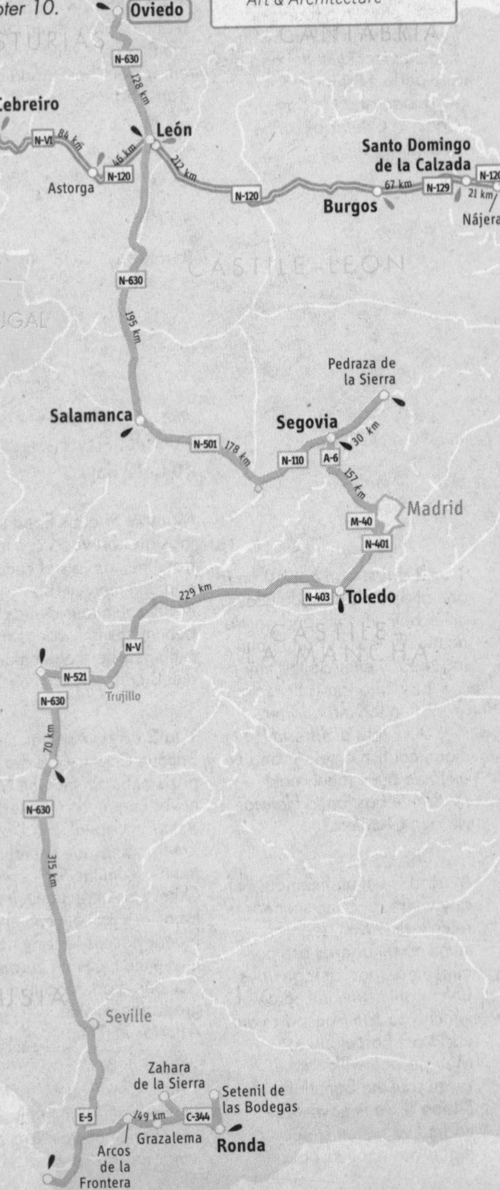

The Camino de Santiago

14 days

The Way of St. James is the most important Christian pilgrimage after those to Jerusalem and Rome. At its peak, in the 12th century, as many as 2 million people walked from all over Europe to the mystical city and cathedral of Santiago de Compostela, in Spain's far

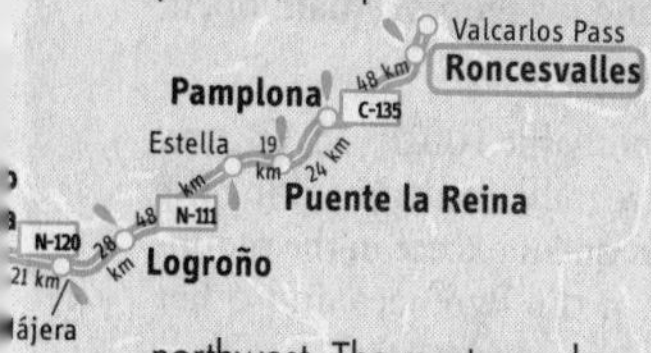

Valcarlos Pass
Roncesvalles
Pamplona
48 km
C-135
Estella
19 km
24 km
N-111
Puente la Reina
N-120
28 km
48 km
21 km
Logroño
Nájera

northwest. The most popular route, the Camino Francés, crosses the Pyrenees near Roncesvalles and alternates between ancient footpath and modern road. Studded with medieval cathedrals, churches, inns, and hospitals, this drive crosses the Basque Pyrenees, the arid Castilian steppe, and the verdant mountains of Galicia.

RONCESVALLES

1 day. The walk across the Pyrenees to Roncesvalles is one of the Camino's most dramatic sections. It's 8 to 10 hours on foot, or an hour by car over the Valcarlos Pass. ⇨ *The Western Pyrenees in Chapter 5.*

PAMPLONA

1 day. Pamplona is the first major Spanish city on the Camino Francés. It's famous for July's running of the bulls but has its share of sacred monuments, including a Gothic cathedral and the churches of San Saturnino and San Nícolas. ⇨ *Pamplona and Southern Navarra in Chapter 3.*

PUENTE LA REINA

1 day. This town's medieval bridge was built for pilgrims in the 11th century. The church of Santiago has a gold sculpture of St. James, and the Church of the Crucifix has a wooden sculpture of Christ on a Y-shaped cross. Just west of Puente la Reina is Estella, a well-placed rest stop with an arcaded square. The Monasterio de Irache dates from the 10th century; next door is a brass faucet that supplies pilgrims with blessed wine. ⇨ *Pamplona and Southern Navarra in Chapter 3.*

LOGROÑO

1 day. Logroño is the capital of La Rioja, Spain's chief wine-making region. Its church of Santiago el Real has a famous equestrian statue honoring Santiago's legendary role in the Christian Reconquest. ⇨ *La Rioja in Chapter 3.*

SANTO DOMINGO DE LA CALZADA

1 day. Once the capital of La Rioja and Navarra, Nájera is known for its monastery of Santa María la Real. Santo Domingo ("of the Causeway") devoted his 11th-century life to the construction of amenities for pilgrims, including the hospital he built here, which is now a parador. Santo Domingo's 14th-century ramparts and cathedral are other draws. ⇨ *La Rioja in Chapter 3.*

BURGOS

2 days. This city's cathedral is one of the greatest in Spain. Of key military significance throughout Spanish history, Burgos has also been a strategic way station on the Camino. In the Monasterio de Las Huelgas Reales is a wooden figure of the saint himself, with a sword said to be used for knighting the princes of Castile into the Order of Santiago. ⇨ *Burgos, León, and the Camino de Santiago in Chapter 2.*

LEÓN

2 days. The stained glass in León's cathedral dazzles. The magnificent 16th-century Hostal de San Marcos was built in the 12th century as a pilgrims' hospital. ⇨ *Burgos, León, and the Camino de Santiago in Chapter 2.*

VILLAFRANCA DEL BIERZO

1 day. The Camino routes from France and Portugal merge in Astorga. This town's main attraction is modern: the Palacio Episcopal, designed by Barcelona's Antoni Gaudí and home to the excellent Museo del Camino, dedicated to the pilgrimage itself. The center of medieval Villafranca del Bierzo is the church of Santiago, whose Puerta del Perdón (Door of Pardon) was designed to grant special dispensation to pilgrims unable to complete their journeys. ⇨ *Burgos, León, and the Camino de Santiago in Chapter 2.*

O CEBREIRO

1 day. Mountaintop O Cebreiro, at Galicia's eastern edge, has a population of 20, but it also has a 9th-century church, a small inn, a hotel, modern-day pilgrims' hostels, and several pallozas—drystone thatched huts that once housed pilgrims. ⇨ *The Camino de Santiago in Chapter 4.*

VILAR DE DONAS

1 day. This stop is named for the elegant women portrayed in the 15th-century frescoes in the town's church. ⇨ *The Camino de Santiago in Chapter 4.*

SANTIAGO DE COMPOSTELA

2 days. The end of the road, Santiago de Compostela is a feast for the senses after the rigors of the pilgrimage. The Plaza del Obradoiro is an explosion of color and humanity and the Puerta de la Gloria on the famous cathedral is truly glorious. The Hotel de los Reyes Católicos, a pilgrims' hospital during the 15th century, is also grand. ⇨ *The Camino de Santiago in Chapter 4.*

Transportation

Traversing the Camino as a true pilgrim—on foot or bike—takes at least a month and leads you into far smaller hamlets than these. Failing that, connecting the dots above requires a car.

WHEN TO GO

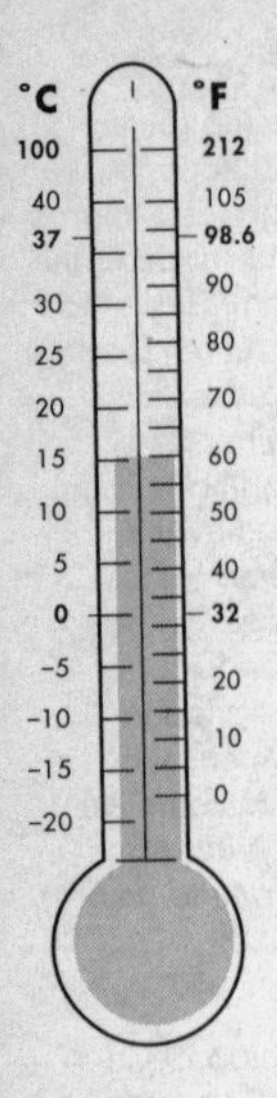

May and October are the optimal times to visit, as the weather is warm and dry. May gives you more hours of daylight, while October offers a chance to enjoy the harvest season, which is especially colorful in the wine regions.

In April you'll see spectacular fiestas, particularly Semana Santa (Holy Week). By then the weather in southern Spain is warm enough to make sightseeing comfortable.

Spain is the number-one destination for European travelers. **To avoid crowds, come before June or after September.** It's worst along the coasts, as the Mediterranean and the Atlantic are too cold for swimming the rest of the year. Spaniards migrate to the beach in August; expect huge traffic jams August 1 and 31. Major cities empty, small shops and some restaurants shut down for the entire month, and museums remain open.

Climate

During summer in Spain, temperatures frequently hit 100°F (38°C), and air-conditioning is not widespread. Winters are mild and rainy along the coasts and bitterly cold elsewhere. Snow is infrequent except in the mountains, where you can ski December–March in the Pyrenees and other resorts near Granada, Madrid, and Burgos.

Forecasts Weather Channel Connection ☎ 900/932–8437, 95¢ per minute from a Touch-Tone phone 🌐 www.weather.com.

The following are average daily maximum and minimum temperatures in Madrid and Barcelona.

MADRID

Jan.	48F	9C	May	70F	21C	Sept.	77F	25C
	36	2		50	10		57	14
Feb.	52F	11C	June	81F	27C	Oct.	66F	19C
	36	2		59	15		50	10
Mar.	59F	15C	July	88F	31C	Nov.	55F	13C
	41	5		63	17		41	5
Apr.	64F	18C	Aug.	86F	30C	Dec.	48F	9C
	45	7		63	17		36	2

BARCELONA

Jan.	55F	13C	May	70F	21C	Sept.	77F	25C
	43	6		57	14		66	19
Feb.	57F	14C	June	77F	25C	Oct.	70F	21C
	45	7		64	18		59	15
Mar.	61F	16C	July	82F	28C	Nov.	61F	16C
	48	9		70	21		52	11
Apr.	64F	18C	Aug.	82F	28C	Dec.	55F	13C
	52	11		70	21		46	8

ON THE CALENDAR

Spain's top seasonal events are listed below. Reserve rooms far in advance for Pamplona's San Fermín, Seville's Holy Week, Valencia's Las Fallas, and Carnival.

WINTER

Dec.	New Year's Eve ticks away at Madrid's Puerta del Sol, where crowds gather to eat one grape on each stroke of midnight.
Jan.	Epiphany (Jan. 6) is a Spanish child's Christmas: youngsters leave their shoes on the doorstep to be filled with gifts from the Three Kings.
Feb.	Carnival dances through Spain just before Lent, most flamboyantly in Cádiz, Sitges, and Santa Cruz de Tenerife.
Mar.	In Valencia, giant papier-mâché figures are torched for Las Fallas. Semana Santa (Holy Week) is the most spectacular feast of all, with Seville staging the most elaborate processions.

SPRING

Apr.	Horseback parades make Seville's Feria de Abril photogenic.
May	The Jerez Horse Fair is a pageant of equestrian events. Barcelona is fragrant on Sant Ponç (May 11), when farmers come into the city to sell their products. In Madrid, San Isídro (May 15) kicks off two weeks of the best bullfighting in Spain.
June	From mid-June to mid-July, Granada's International Festival of Music and Dance brings orchestras, opera companies, and ballet corps to the grounds of the Alhambra. Corpus Christi (June 14) is celebrated with processions, most famously in Toledo. At the Wine War in Haro (La Rioja, June 29) revelers fill bota bags with Rioja and hose each other down (and later drink the remainder).

SUMMER

July	The Fiesta de San Fermín and the accompanying running of the bulls (July 6–13) through the streets of Pamplona unleash wine, bravado, and merriment. Late in the month, Valencia's Moros y Cristianos finds locals reenacting ancient feuds in medieval Moorish and Christian costume. The summer-long Classical Theater Festival presents Greek and Roman dramas in Mérida's 2,000-year-old Roman theater.
Aug.	The International Music and Ballet Festival enlivens the resort town of Santander. El Místeri (Aug. 11–15), in Elche, near Alicante, is Europe's oldest Christian mystery play. A Tomato Battle reddens the town of Buñol, near Valencia, on the last Wednesday of the month. Consuegra, near Toledo, turns another color for the Saffron Rose Festival.

FALL

Sept.	Jerez celebrates harvesttime with Fiestas de Otoño (Autumn Festivals). On September 24, Barcelona celebrates La Mercè with concerts, fireworks, and parades in which people wear giant papier-mâché heads.
Oct.	El Pilar (Oct. 12) gives the children of Zaragoza a chance to dress up in regional costume and cut loose in *jota*-dancing contests.

PLEASURES & PASTIMES

Sea & Sierra

Crisscrossed with mountain ranges and nearly surrounded by water, Spain's unique geographical resources make it ideal for outdoor activities of all kinds. Sailing, boating, and other water sports are popular along the Mediterranean coast, the northern Bay of Biscay, Atlantic Galicia, and in the Balearic Islands. The mountains offer year-round action. Spain has excellent skiing and winter sports facilities. Major resorts include Baqueira-Beret, Port del Compte, Llessui, and Formigal, in the Pyrenees; Sierra Nevada, near Granada; and Navacerrada, Valcoto, and Valdesqui, near Madrid. The Pyrenees offer superior hiking and trekking in Aragon's Ordesa National Park and the Aïguestortes Lago de San Mauricio Park. West of Ávila, the Sierra de Gredos are also popular for climbing and trekking. Hiking is excellent in the Canary Islands, the interior of Spain, and the numerous national parks, from the marshy Doñana to the mountainous Picos de Europa. Golf courses are popping up all over Spain, from Andalusia's Valderrama, considered one of the best in continental Europe, to El Saler, south of Valencia. Marbella has excellent courses, and the Costa Brava and Costa Blanca also have commendable circuits. Clay tennis courts are open and usable year-round throughout Spain, and squash clubs are common. Mountain streams in the Pyrenees and other ranges throughout Spain offer trout and salmon fishing. Spain, with its Arabian roots, is also renowned for its horses: you can see polo matches at country clubs in Madrid and Barcelona or saddle up for a tour of the Alpujarra mountains east of Granada or the climb to the Pyrenean heights in the Cerdanya valley in northern Catalonia. Thousands of pedal-pushers turn out in early summer, when the roads are closed off for Madrid's annual bicycle day. Bicycling in crowded cities is tricky but not impossible, and coastal resorts invariably rent bikes. Perhaps the best part of Spain's outdoor life is that it in no way removes you from, in fact often brings you nearer to, some of the finest architecture and cuisine Iberia has to offer.

An Architectural Cornucopia

Spain's ancient civilization has left an immense national patrimony of architecture to explore, from 12,000-year-old prehistoric caves and Celtic settlements known as *castros* all the way through Roman and Moorish monuments to Romanesque, Gothic, and Renaissance structures, Art Nouveau palaces, and up to Frank Gehry's Guggenheim or Jean Nouvel's skyscraping Torre Agbar in Barcelona. Dazzling churches, chapels, cloisters, convents, mosques, ramparts, aqueducts, palaces, bridges, and castles make Spain a remarkable repository of beautiful buildings. Barcelona and Tarragona's Roman ruins tell the story of the Pax Romana and the encroaching barbarians pushing down from central Europe. The mortarless Roman aqueduct at Segovia is one of the marvels of the world, while the nearby Alcazar fortress with its pinnacles and turrets seems to have fallen out of Richard Burton's exotic classic, *Arabian Nights: Tales from a Thousand and One Nights*. The contrast between Andalusia's Moorish palaces and mosques and the austere Asturian pre-Romanesque churches of the 9th and 10th centuries is all the more startling when you consider that they were constructed at about the same time, though within radically different cultures. Meanwhile the fusion of Christian and Moorish artisans and architects in the 13th and 14th centuries produced the Mudéjar style, Spain's most distinctive and personal architectural form.

The typical village architecture of each of Spain's Autonomous Communities is in itself fascinating in terms of its variety and aesthetics. From the so-called white villages of Andalusia to the slate-roof stone houses of hamlets in the Pyrenees or the brightly painted Basque fishing villages along the Bay of Biscay, Spain is a variegated visual feast with an inexhaustible supply of architectural gems.

Art

Spain's immense collection of artistic treasure owes much to the cultural legacy left by the 781-year Moorish tenure on the Iberian Peninsula. As the so-called "Reconquest" was really a slow process of cohabitation and a gradual reversal of predominance, much knowledge, science, and cultural awareness passed freely from the caliphs and emirs to the counts and kings. When the Spanish Golden Age brought wealth (flowing into the imperial capital of Madrid), Spanish monarchs used it to finance the arts, as well as for defense, cathedrals, and civil projects. Painters from El Greco to Rubens, and writers from Lope de Vega to Cervantes, were drawn to the luminous (and solvent) royal court. For the first time in Europe, the collecting of art became an important symbol of national wealth and power. Madrid's paintings now reside in the Prado, the Centro de Arte Contemporáneo Princesa Sofía, the Museo Thyssen Bornemisza, the Convento de las Descalzas Reales, and other collections around the capital. Leaving Madrid without a look at the Sorolla Museum or the Lázaro Galdiano collection is a mistake. Barcelona, more about architecture than about paintings, is no backwater when it comes to canvases, either. The Picasso Museum is just the icing on a cake consisting of the Romanesque collection at the Museu Nacional d'Art de Catalunya in the Palau Nacional, the Museu d'Art Modern in the Ciutadella, the Museu d'Art Contemporani de Barcelona (Contemporary Art Museum), or the Thyssen-Bornemisza's northern annex in the Monestir de Pedralbes. Bilbao's Guggenheim and, for paintings, the Museo de Bellas Artes, are both excellent. San Sebastián's Chillida Leku shows the work of Eduardo Chillida, Spain's most important 20th-century sculptor, in and around a lovely Basque farmhouse. Valencia's Institut Valencià d'Art Modern is expanding, both in size and in importance. Seville's Museo de Bellas Artes has been billed, as has Bilbao's, as the most important Spanish museum after the Prado. Indeed, Spain probably has more great paintings than you'll ever be able to see.

Itinerant Feasting

Spanish cooking has come into its own over the last 20 years. The Mediterranean diet, with its emphasis on high-quality olive oil, fish, vegetables, garlic, onions, and red wine, is now understood to be not only delicious but health enhancing. Innovative chefs, including Ferrán Adrià and Pedro Subijana, and such masters as Juan Mari Arzak and Santi Santamaría, are making Spain's many regional cuisines famous worldwide, while new stars—Martin Berasategui, Sergi Arola, Fermí Puig, and Carme Ruscalleda Puig—are filling the firmament with new aromas and textures.

Tapas, small morsels or servings of anything from wild, acorn-fed Iberian ham to manchego sheep's cheese, shrimp, or baby octopus, have been Spain's most famous contribution to world dining habits. Nowhere in the world offers more miniature haute cuisine in countless pubs and taverns on any given evening; tapas tasting is a perfect way to take in a town, its people, and its cooking. It's also an ideal means by which to sample the country's many cultures—Galicia's seafood, Castilla's roasts, Valencia's rice dishes, Andalusia's deep fried seafood and Moorish aromas, the Basque Country's fish and general excellence, Catalonia's daring and Dalí-like avant-garde delights. Expect infinite variety and finesse wherever you go; nomadic grazing is a way of life here.

Bullfighting

Modern bullfighting is a ballet performed with a wild and dangerous beast, a combination of pagan religious ritual and spectacle—with life and death as the protagonists. Never to be confused with sport, the bullfight descended from the bull worship of ancient Crete, and evolved into a Spanish art form only in the 18th century. The bullfight is dramatic in the Greek tradition of ineluctable doom; the bull's certain fate is a premonitory glimpse of our own, while for Spain, the *fiesta nacional* is celebrated as one of the few purely Spanish cultural phenomena remaining in an ever more Europeanized modern era.

Bullfights begin with a formal procession of banderilleros, picadors, and the afternoon's three matadors with their respective troupes, or *cuadrillas*. The *lidia* (battle) takes place in four separate acts or movements. First the the matador tests the bull with the large magenta-and-yellow *capote* (big cape). The picadors, on horseback, measure the bull's strength and aggressiveness while weakening his neck and shoulder muscles with a pointed pike or lance. Next, banderilleros place *banderillas,* colorfully wrapped arrows, in the bull's neck to correct tendencies to hook in one direction or another. Finally, using the small cape, the *muleta,* the matador develops the most artistic (and dangerous) part of the performance, the *faena,* concluding by killing the bull with a sword. Matadors may be awarded the bull's ears and/or tail as trophies. Normally, in a single corrida, six bulls are killed by three different matadors.

Corridas (bullfights) are held at exactly 5 (or 6) PM on Sundays, from April to early November. Hemingway made Pamplona's San Fermín festival, with its July 7–15 running of the bulls, famous worldwide, but nowhere is bullfighting better than at Madrid's Las Ventas, where three weeks of daily corridas in May mark the festival of San Isidro. Only Seville, home of Spain's most hallowed bullring, La Maestranza, can compare with (and possibly exceed) Madrid's intensity. During Seville's April Fair, daily corridas spotlight Spain's leading bulls and *toreros.* Valencia hosts top bulls and bullfighters in late July and during Las Fallas, during the first half of March. Ronda's ancient and picturesque bullring is only used for taurine events during festivals in May and September; do not miss a chance to see a bullfight in this historic venue.

FODOR'S CHOICE

Fodor'sChoice ★

The sights, restaurants, hotels, and other travel experiences on these pages are our editors' top picks—our Fodor's Choices. They're the best of their type in the area covered by the book—not to be missed and always worth your time. In the destination chapters that follow, you will find all the details.

LODGING

$$$$ **AC Santo Mauro,** Madrid. This intimate, luxurious, turn-of-the-20th-century mansion has neoclassical architecture and contemporary style.

$$$$ **Alfonso XIII,** Seville. The grand, historical Mudéjar Revival palace, inaugurated by King Alfonso XIII in 1929, has marble floors, wood-panel ceilings, heavy Moorish lamps, stained glass, and ceramic tiles in typical Sevillian colors.

$$$$ **Claris,** Barcelona. The best hotel in town smoothly blends style and tradition, with both 18th-century and contemporary furnishings, a Japanese water garden, and stellar food.

$$$$ **La Residencia,** Deià, Balearic Islands. Princess Diana loved this 16th-century manor house ensconced in olive and citrus groves, with antiques, four-poster beds, and fancy, inventive food.

$$$$ **La Torre del Remei,** Puigcerdà, the Pyrenees. From the champagne upon arrival to the heated bathroom floors, this manor house emphasizes Belle Epoque opulence.

$$$$ **Majestic,** Barcelona. Expect fashionable boulevards outside and stylish rooms inside at this part-modern, part–town house hotel.

$$$$ **Marbella Club,** Marbella, Costa del Sol. Expect to see both international clientele and local patricians here, thanks to handsome bungalow-style rooms, grounds dotted with palms and flowers, and the nearby beach.

$$$$ **Orfila,** Madrid. This elegant 1886 town house on a leafy street was famous for theater performances in the late-19th and early 20th centuries. The restaurant, garden, and tearoom have period furniture; guest rooms are draped with striped and floral silks.

$$$$ **Parador de Granada,** Granada. It doesn't get better than this gorgeous, soul-stirring parador—a former Franciscan monastery—right on the Alhambra property.

$$$$ **Seaside Hotel Palm Beach,** Maspalomas, Canary Islands. Sophisticated, luxurious, a stone's throw from the beach, and a pool encircled by a 1,000-year-old palm oasis make this hotel one of the islands' best bets.

$$$–$$$$ **Condes de Barcelona,** Barcelona. With a pentagonal marble lobby and an original courtyard and columns (1891), plus terraces overlooking an interior garden, this is one of the most popular places in town.

$$$ **Amistad Córdoba,** Córdoba. A cobblestone Mudéjar courtyard and carved-wood ceilings characterize this stylish hotel built around two former 18th-century mansions.

$$$ **Miró Hotel,** Bilbao. This sleek boutique hotel across from the Guggenheim is high-tech, unpretentious, and comfortable, and the breakfast is indulgent.

$$ **Hotel Intur Palacio San Martín,** Madrid. Between the dome-glassed atrium, ornately carved ceilings, spacious rooms, and an unbeatable location across from the celebrated Convent of Descalzas, this place exudes a charming old-world glory.

$$ **Mendigoikoa,** Axpe, the Basque Country. These hillside farmhouses are exquisite, unique hideaways: stunning rooms with glassed-in terraces, and a splendid hillside location.

$$ **Parador de Santillana Gil Blas,** Santillana del Mar, Cantabria. This lovely 16th-century parador has baronial rooms and antique furnishings.

$$ **Parador de Úbeda,** Úbeda, Eastern Andalusia. At this impressive 16th-century ducal palace, the stairway is decked with tapestries and suits of armor and the dining room serves the best meals in town.

$$ **Parador Hotel San Marcos,** León, Castile. This magnificent parador occupies a restored 16th-century monastery built to shelter pilgrims walking the Camino de Santiago. Inside you'll find modern and medieval sections.

$$ **Parador Príncipe de Viana,** Olite, Southern Navarra. This flight-of-fancy castle parador still seems chivalrous and mysterious—grand salons, secret stairways, heraldic tapestries, and the odd suit of armor.

BUDGET LODGING

$ **Jardí,** Barcelona. You can't beat it: chic, inexpensive, with views of a Gothic church and two lovely plazas in the Old City, plus a great breakfast.

ROOMS WITH A VIEW

$$$–$$$$ **Colón,** Barcelona. Joan Miró was a regular here, probably for the spectacular views of the cathedral, if not for the sardana dancing and antiques markets in the plaza in front.

$$$ **Alhambra Palace,** Granada. This neo-Moorish hotel occupies a prime spot: among leafy grounds, at the back of the Alhambra hill. Rooms overlooking the city have incredible views, as does the terrace, a perfect place to watch the sun set over the city.

$$$ **Parador de Jaén,** Jaén, Eastern Andalusia. By all means visit Jaén just to stay here—it's built amid the castle towers and overlooks the mountains. Lofty ceilings, tapestries, baronial shields, and suits of armor underscore the castle motif.

$$$ **Parador de Málaga-Gibralfaro,** Málaga, Costa del Sol. For the best rooms in town, stay at this cozy, gray-stone parador, surrounded by pine trees, with spectacular views of Málaga and the bay.

$$ **La Casa Grande,** Arcos de la Frontera, Western Andalusia. Perched on the edge of the 400-ft cliff is this elegant town house, built in 1729, with a lovely breakfast terrace that overlooks the riverbed below.

RESTAURANTS

$$$$	**Arzak,** San Sebastián. The traditional Basque food at this extremely popular, internationally famous place is jazzed up by the owner's innovations.
$$$$	**El Bullí,** Girona, Costa Brava. Call months ahead for a chair at this seaside getaway with a 12-course menu. It's only open half the year.
$$$$	**El Girasol,** Moraira. Expect imaginative, French-style food at one of the best restaurants in southeastern Spain.
$$$$	**El Racó de Can Fabes,** Sant Celoni (Barcelona outskirts). It's well worth the 45-minute train ride to one of Spain's top four restaurants.
$$$$	**Martín Berasategui,** San Sebastián. Make sure you get to his place just a few miles south of town, and eat whatever the chef feels like preparing for you.
$$$$	**Mugaritz,** San Sebastián. At this farmhouse, surrounded by well-tended herbs and spices, the chef is a master at blending products of the fields and forest with seafood.
$$$$	**Zuberoa,** Oiartzun, the Basque Coast. One of Spain's most celebrated chefs is cooking just a few miles northwest of San Sebastián.
$$$–$$$$	**Ca la Irene,** Vielha, the Pyrenees. Feast on poached foie gras in black truffles and roast wild pigeon in nuts and mint at this rustic little haven, which serves fine mountain cuisine with a French flair.
$$$–$$$$	**Celler de Can Roca,** Girona, Costa Brava. The best restaurant in town is also one of Catalonia's top six eating destinations, perhaps for its oddball blendings: steak tartare with mustard ice cream, and trotters with sea slugs.
$$$–$$$$	**El Caballo Rojo,** Córdoba. The restaurant serves traditional Andalusian dishes and food that reflects the town's Moorish and Jewish heritage—Arab spices, honey, aniseed, and saffron flavors are typical. The dining room, with stained glass and gleaming marble, is as elegant as the food is fine.
$$$–$$$$	**El Chaflán,** Madrid. Juan Pablo Felipe, one of the heralds of Spain's new modern cuisine, is a master of innovation. Come for the annual white truffle sampler week, but anytime you visit you can expect new and sophisticated dishes.
$$$–$$$$	**La Broche,** Madrid. Among the best in town are Sergi Arola's unusual hot-cold, surf-turf dishes. During the course of your meal you can expect to progress from light to dark, fish to foie, seafood to tenderloin.
$$$–$$$$	**Zalacaín,** Madrid. This place introduced nouvelle Basque cuisine to Spain in the 1970s and has since become a classic. From the variety of fungi and game meat to the hard-to-find seafood served, the food here is wonderfully unusual.
$$$	**Poncio,** Sevilla. Dine here for a flawless, distinctive blend of Andalusian and French food.

$$–$$$ **Botín,** Madrid. The *Guinness Book of Records* calls this the world's oldest restaurant (1725), and Hemingway called it the best. Expect excellent roast pig and lamb, in addition to many other popular dishes.

$$–$$$ **Café de París,** Málaga, Costa del Sol. The city-slick sophistication of this restaurant's romantic red-and-mahogany interior is reflected in the excellent meat and fished served here.

$$–$$$ **El Faro,** Cádiz, Western Andalusia. Gonzalo Córdoba's enchanting fishing-quarter restaurant is deservedly known as the best restaurant in the province.

$$–$$$ **El Figón de Pedro,** Cuenca, New Castile. This low-key spot in a lively part of town is run by one of Spain's top restaurateurs, and it's here that you'll discover the excellence of Cuenca's cuisine.

$$–$$$ **Mendigoikoa,** Axpe, the Basque Country. The restaurant in this hideaway hotel—a clutch of hillside farmhouses—is good enough for the King and Queen of Spain. Get Navaz pigeon cooked over coals or the great chunks of beef on the bone.

$$–$$$ **Posada Mayor de Migueloa,** Laguardia, the Basque Country. Dine in style at the tavern in this fabulously done 17th-century palace and hotel. Meats and game of all kinds are plentiful here.

$$ **Txulotxo,** Pasajes San Juan, San Sebastián. You can watch freighters drift by as you devour intensely fresh fish at this fabulous little place.

$–$$ **Casa Ciriaco,** Madrid. As evidenced by the kings, queens, prime ministers, bullfighters, painters, and poets who have dined at this unpretentious restaurant, the home-cooked partridge with broadbeans and the hen in almond sauce are excellent.

$–$$ **La Trucha,** Madrid. This magical, jovial little Andalusian bistro decorated with hanging hams is a place of fun and fine temptations: garlicky trout, crispy squid, smoked-fish delicacies, and pitchers of claret.

BUDGET RESTAURANT

¢–$ **El Fuelle,** Zaragoza. Very fine Aragonese food distinguishes this rustic old-town favorite, decorated with giant bellows, farming tools, and random artifacts.

CHURCHES, MONASTERIES & MOSQUES

Convento de Santa Paula, Seville. This 15th-century Gothic convent has a fine facade and portico, ceramic decoration by Nicolaso Pisano, a chapel with beautiful azulejos and sculptures by Martínez Montañés, and a museum packed with religious objects.

Mezquita, Córdoba. Enter the mosque—one of the loveliest examples of Spanish Muslim architecture—and see 850 columns crowned with red-and-white-stripe arches rise before you in a forest of jasper, marble, granite, and onyx.

Monasterio de San Juan de la Peña, Jaca, the Pyrenees. South of the Aragonese valleys of Hecho and Ansó is this monastery—a site connected to the legend of the Holy Grail and another "cradle" of Christian resistance during the 700-year Moorish occupation of Spain.

Palma's cathedral, Palma de Mallorca, island of Majorca, Balearic Islands. This architectural wonder with a 40-foot-wide rose window and an asymmetrical canopy designed by Gaudí also has a belltower with nine bells—one of which requires six men to ring it.

Sagrada Família, Barcelona. Far from finished at the time of Catalan architect Antoni Gaudí's death in 1926, this mammoth Art Nouveau church continues to grow. Conceived as a veritable bible in stone, the final tower will be completed in 2050.

MUSEUMS & MASTERPIECES

Archbishop's Palace, Astorga. In far-northwestern Castile, a fairytale, neo-Gothic building by Antoni Gaudí houses a museum devoted to the Camino de Santiago pilgrimage.

Centro de Arte Reina Sofía, Madrid. Besides housing Picasso's famous *Guernica,* the modern art collection focuses on Spain's three great modern masters—Pablo Picasso, Salvador Dalí, and Joan Miró.

Guggenheim Museum, Bilbao. Frank Gehry's dramatic assemblage of curves, limestone, glass, titanium, and light houses an equally astonishing collection of 20th-century art.

Museum of Fine Arts, Bilbao. This unbeatable collection includes paintings by El Greco, Goya, Velázquez, Zurbarán, Rivera, and Gauguin, and an excellent section that traces developments in 20th-century Spanish and Basque art alongside those of their better-known European contemporaries.

Museum of Fine Arts, Seville. The fabulous collection includes Murillo, Zurbarán, Valdés Leal, and El Greco; outstanding examples of Seville Gothic art; Baroque religious sculptures in wood; and Sevillian art of the 19th and 20th centuries.

National Museum of Sculpture, Valladolid, Old Castile. It's worth the trek from Madrid to see the expressive, exciting works by three masters of Spanish sculpture—Alonso de Berruguete, Juan de Juni, and Gregorio Fernández.

Prado, Madrid. One of the greatest museums in the world, the Prado holds masterpieces by various Italian and Flemish painters, but its jewels are the works of Spaniards: Goya, Velázquez, and El Greco.

Thyssen-Bornemisza Museum, Madrid. An ambitious collection of 800 paintings traces the development of Western humanism as no other in the world, with examples from every important movement, from the 13th-century Italian Gothic through 20th-century American pop art.

PARKS & GARDENS

Doñana National Park, Western Andalusia. One of Europe's last tracts of true wilderness includes wetlands, 150 species of rare birds, beaches, shifting sand dunes, marshes, and, in addition to the endangered imperial eagle and lynx, countless wildlife.

Ordesa and Monte Perdido National Park, the Pyrenees. Hike in Spain's version of the Grand Canyon. This park spans almost 57,000 acres, and has every outdoor wonder imaginable: waterfalls, caves, forests, alpine meadows, and wildlife.

Timanfaya National Park, Yaiza, the Canary Islands. It doesn't get more exotic: indulge in camel rides among a striking volcanic landscape of cinder cones and lava formations.

QUINTESSENTIAL SPAIN

Albaicín, Granada. Explore this ancient Moorish neighborhood with twisting, cobble alleyways and a dramatic view of the Alhambra's turrets and towers.

Alhambra, Granada. Don't miss Spain's top sight: the remains of this great citadel include a lavishly ornamented palace with patios and cupolas; a summer palace with terraces, fountains, and promenades that wind through magnificent gardens; and a museum of Islamic art.

Judería, Córdoba. A labyrinth of narrow streets and alleyways lined with ancient white houses wind through the heart of the medieval Jewish Quarter.

Moors and Christians festival, Alcoy. The most spectacular fiesta of its kind in Spain takes place inland, in the southeast, on April 23rd—colorful processions and mock battles commemorate the Battle of Alcoy, when St. George's intervention helped liberate the city.

Roman ruins, Mérida. Here you'll find Spain's largest concentration of Roman monuments, including a 64-arch bridge, a fortress, and a Roman amphitheater that once drew crowds to grisly duels between gladiators and wild beasts.

Royal Andalusian School of Equestrian Art, Jerez, Western Andalusia. Don't miss the Thursday performance, when their Cartujana horses—and skilled riders in 18th-century riding costume—demonstrate riding techniques.

Royal Palace, Madrid. Besides its 2,800 wildly opulent rooms, this 18th-century fortress includes a royal library, pharmacy, music museum, and armory with impressive medieval torture tools.

SKI RESORT

$$$–$$$$ **Melia Royal Tanau,** Salardú, the Pyrenees. Ski aficionados, pamper yourselves. Considered the finest skiing hotel in the Pyrenees, this place has every comfort and chair lifts straight up to the slopes.

TOWNS & VILLAGES

Baeza, Eastern Andalusia. Surrounded by hills and olive groves, this historic town has a fine cathedral, Renaissance palaces, and a 16th-century convent that houses a religious masterpiece.

Benasque, the Pyrenees. This mountain hub has ancient churches, manor houses, and palaces, and is base camp for excursions to Aneto, at 11,168 ft the highest peak in the Pyrenees, and Anciles, one of Spain's best-preserved and -restored medieval villages.

Cáçeres, Extremadura. The most beautiful town in the region is a place of contrasts: an old quarter with marvelously preserved medieval and Renaissance palaces, and a bustling nightlife and food scene.

La Seu d'Urgell, the Pyrenees. This mysterious ancient town has a legacy of art and architecture, and streets with dark balconies and porticoes, overhanging galleries, and colonnaded porches. The 12th-century cathedral is the finest in the Pyrenees.

Ronda, Costa del Sol. Spain's oldest town occupies a mountain perch and has a dramatic ravine that divides the twisting streets of the medieval Moorish town from the new section. The father of modern bullfighting, Pedro Romero, supposedly killed 5,600 bulls in the town's bullring.

Salamanca, Old Castile. Explore one of Spain's most architecturally dynamic cities, from the Roman bridge to the many cathedrals and palaces to a fantastically decorated 16th-century cloister in a convent.

San Sebastián, the Basque Coast. This unusually sophisticated city and seaside resort is arched around one of the finest urban beaches in the world, and the food is in a league of its own.

Santillana del Mar, Cantabria. This stunning ensemble of 15th- to 17th-century stone houses is one of Spain's greatest troves of medieval and Renaissance architecture.

Segovia, Old Castile. This breathtaking city on a ridge—once a military town and then a textile center—has a sleepy, arty charm, and is loved by all for its narrow streets, Roman ruins, and beautiful churches.

Toledo, New Castile. Thanks to its labyrinthine streets and the ghost of El Greco, Spain's erstwhile spiritual center—perched on a rocky mount, with steep ocher-color hills rising on either side—remains tinged with a certain mysticism.

Úbeda, Eastern Andalusia. Surrounded by olive groves, this small town happens to be an outstanding enclave of 16th-century architecture.

SMART TRAVEL TIPS

Finding out about your destination before you leave home means you won't squander time organizing everyday minutiae once you've arrived. You'll be more streetwise when you hit the ground as well, better prepared to explore the aspects of Spain that drew you here in the first place. The organizations in this section can provide information to supplement this guide; contact them for up-to-the-minute details, and consult the A to Z sections that end each chapter for facts on the various topics as they relate to Spain's many regions. Happy landings!

ADDRESSES

Apartment addresses in Spain include the street name, building number, floor level, and apartment number. For example, Calle Cervantes 15, 3°, 1a indicates that the apartment is on the *tercero* (third) floor, *primera* (first) door. In older buildings, the first floor is often called the *entresuelo*; one floor above it is *principal* and, above this, the first floor. The top floor of a building is the *ático* (attic). More modern buildings often have no entresuelo or principal. Addresses with the abbreviation s/n mean *sin numero*, or "without number."

AIR TRAVEL

Regular nonstop flights serve Spain from the eastern United States; flying from other North American cities usually involves a stop. Flights from the United Kingdom to Spain are more frequent, cover small cities as well as large ones, and are priced very competitively, particularly if you travel on a low-cost carrier, such as Easy Jet or Go. If you're coming from North America and would like to land in a city other than Madrid or Barcelona, consider flying a British or other European carrier; just know that you may have to stay overnight in London or another European city on your way home. There are no nonstop flights to Spain from Australia or New Zealand. There are numerous daily flights within Spain.

BOOKING

When you book, look for nonstop flights and remember that "direct" flights stop at least once. Try to avoid connecting flights, which require a change of plane. Two airlines may operate a connecting flight jointly, so ask whether your airline operates every segment of the trip; you may find that the carrier you prefer flies you only part of the way. To find more booking tips and to check prices and make online flight reservations, log on to www.fodors.com.

CARRIERS

From North America, American, Continental, US Airways, Air Europa, Spanair, and TWA fly to Madrid; American, Delta, and Iberia fly to Madrid and Barcelona. Within Spain, Iberia is the main domestic airline, but Air Europa and Spanair fly domestic routes at lower prices. Iberia runs a shuttle, the *puente aereo,* between Madrid and Barcelona from around 7 AM to 11 PM; planes depart hourly and more frequently in the morning and afternoon commute hours. You don't need to reserve ahead; you can buy your tickets at the airport ticket counter upon arriving. Terminal C in the Barcelona airport is used exclusively by the shuttle; in Madrid, the shuttle departs from Terminal 3. The Spanish predilection for cigarettes notwithstanding, most airlines serving Spain, including Iberia, don't allow smoking on international or domestic flights.

From North America **Air Europa** ☎ 888/238-7672 🌐 www.air-europa.com. **American** ☎ 800/433-7300 🌐 www.americanairlines.com. **Continental** ☎ 800/231-0856 🌐 www.continental.com. **Delta** ☎ 800/221-1212 🌐 www.delta.com. **Iberia** ☎ 800/772-4642 🌐 www.iberia.com. **Spanair** ☎ 888/545-5757 🌐 www.spanair.com. **TWA** ☎ 800/892-4141 🌐 www.twa.com. **US Airways** ☎ 800/622-1015 🌐 www.usairways.com.

From the U.K. **British Airways** ☎ 0845/773-3377 🌐 www.britishairways.com. **Easy Jet** ☎ 0870/600-0000 🌐 www.easyjet.com. **Iberia** ☎ 0845/601-2854 🌐 www.iberia.com.

Within Spain **Air Europa** ☎ 902/401501. **Iberia** ☎ 902/400500 🌐 www.iberia.com. **Spanair** ☎ 902/131415 🌐 www.spanair.com.

CHECK-IN & BOARDING

Always ask your carrier about its check-in policy. Plan to arrive at the airport about two hours before your scheduled departure time for domestic flights and 2½ to 3 hours before international flights. You may need to arrive earlier if you're flying from one of the busier airports or during peak air-traffic times. To avoid delays at airport-security checkpoints, try not to wear any metal. Jewelry, belt and other buckles, steel-toe shoes, barrettes, and underwire bras are among the items that can set off detectors.

Assuming that not everyone with a ticket will show up, airlines routinely overbook planes. When everyone does show up, airlines ask for volunteers to give up their seats. In return, these volunteers usually get a several-hundred-dollar flight voucher, which can be used toward the purchase of another ticket, and are rebooked on the next flight out. If there are not enough volunteers, the airline must choose who will be denied boarding. The first to get bumped are passengers who checked in late and those flying on discounted tickets, so get to the gate and check in as early as possible, especially during peak periods. Always bring a government-issued photo I.D. to the airport; even when it's not required, a passport is best.

CUTTING COSTS

The least expensive airfares to Spain are priced for round-trip travel and must usually be purchased in advance. Airlines generally allow you to change your return date for a fee; most low-fare tickets, however, are nonrefundable.

If you buy a round-trip transatlantic ticket on **Iberia,** you might want to purchase a Visit Spain pass, good for four domestic flights during your trip. The pass must be purchased before you arrive in Spain, all flights must be booked in advance, and the cost starts at $165 ($290 if you want to include flights to the Canary Islands). On certain days of the week, Iberia also offers *minitarifas* (minifares), which can save you 40% on domestic flights. Tickets must be purchased at least two days in advance, and you must stay over Saturday night.

It's smart to call a number of airlines and check the Internet; when you are quoted a good price, book it on the spot—the same fare may not be available the next day, or even the next hour. Always check different routings and look into using alternate airports. Also, price off-peak flights, which may be significantly less expensive than others. Travel agents, especially low-fare specialists, are helpful.

Consolidators are another good source. They buy tickets for scheduled flights at reduced rates from the airlines, then sell them at prices that beat the best fare available directly from the airlines. Sometimes you can even get your money back if you need to return the ticket. Carefully read the fine print detailing penalties for changes and cancellations, purchase the ticket with a credit card, and confirm your consolidator reservation with the airline.

You can fly as a courier to Spain, though not within Spain. When you do travel this way, you trade your checked-luggage space for a ticket deeply subsidized by a courier service. There are restrictions on when you can book and how long you can stay. Some courier companies list with membership organizations, such as the Air Courier Association and the International Association of Air Travel Couriers; these require you to become a member before you can book a flight. Many airlines, singly or in collaboration, offer discount air passes that allow foreigners to travel economically in a particular country or region. These visitor passes usually must be reserved and purchased before you leave home. Information about passes often can be found on most airlines' international Web pages, which tend to be aimed at travelers from outside the carrier's home country. Also, try typing the name of the pass into a search engine, or search for "pass" within the carrier's Web site.

Consolidators **AirlineConsolidator.com** 888/468-5385 www.airlineconsolidator.com; for international tickets. **Best Fares** 800/576-8255 or 800/576-1600 www.bestfares.com; $59.90 annual membership. **Cheap Tickets** 800/377-1000 or 888/922-8849 www.cheaptickets.com. **Expedia** 800/397-3342 or 404/728-8787 www.expedia.com. **Hotwire** 866/468-9473 or 920/330-9418 www.hotwire.com. **Now Voyager Travel** 45 W. 21st St., 5th floor, New York, NY 10010 212/459-1616 212/243-2711 www.nowvoyagertravel.com. **Onetravel.com** www.onetravel.com. **Orbitz** 888/656-4546 www.orbitz.com. **Priceline.com** www.priceline.com. **Travelocity** 888/709-5983, 877/282-2925 in Canada, 0870/876-3876 in the U.K. www.travelocity.com.

Courier Resources **Air Courier Association/Cheaptrips.com** 800/282-1202 www.aircourier.org or www.cheaptrips.com. **International Association of Air Travel Couriers** 308/632-3273 www.courier.org.

ENJOYING THE FLIGHT

State your seat preference when purchasing your ticket, and then repeat it when you confirm and when you check in. For more legroom, you can request one of the few emergency-aisle seats at check-in, if you are capable of lifting at least 50 pounds—a Federal Aviation Administration requirement of passengers in these seats. Seats behind a bulkhead also offer more legroom, but they don't have underseat storage. Don't sit in the row in front of the emergency aisle or in front of a bulkhead, where seats may not recline.

Ask the airline whether a snack or meal is served on the flight. If you have dietary concerns, request special meals when booking. These can be vegetarian, low-cholesterol, or kosher, for example. It's a good idea to pack some healthful snacks and a small (plastic) bottle of water in your carry-on bag. On long flights, try to maintain a normal routine, to help fight jet lag. At night, get some sleep. By day, eat light meals, drink water (not alcohol), and move around the cabin to stretch your legs. For additional jet-lag tips consult *Fodor's FYI: Travel Fit & Healthy* (available at bookstores everywhere).

FLYING TIMES

Flying time from New York is seven hours; from London, just over two.

HOW TO COMPLAIN

If your baggage goes astray or your flight goes awry, complain right away. Most carriers require that you **file a claim immediately.** The Aviation Consumer Protection Division of the Department of Transportation publishes *Fly-Rights*, which discusses airlines and consumer issues and is available on line.

Airline Complaints **Aviation Consumer Protection Division** U.S. Department of Transportation, C-75, Room 4107, 400 7th St. NW, Washington, DC 20590 202/366-2220 www.dot.gov/airconsumer. **Federal Aviation Administration Consumer Hotline** for inquiries: FAA, 800 Independence Ave. SW, Room 810, Washington, DC 20591 800/322-7873 www.faa.gov.

RECONFIRMING

Check the status of your flight before you leave for the airport. You can do this on your carrier's Web site, by linking to a flight-status checker (many Web booking services offer these), or by calling your carrier or travel agent. Always confirm international flights at least 72 hours ahead of the scheduled departure time.

AIRPORTS

Most flights from the United States and Canada land in, or pass through, Madrid's Barajas (MAD). The other major gateway is Barcelona's El Prat de Llobregat (BCN). From England and elsewhere in Europe, regular flights also land in Málaga (AGP), Alicante (ALC), Palma de Mallorca (PMI), and on Gran Canaria (LPA) and Tenerife (TFN).

Airport Information **Madrid-Barajas** ☎ 91/305-8343. **Barcelona-El Prat de Llobregat** ☎ 93/298-3838.

BIKE TRAVEL

Long distances, an abundance of hilly terrain, and climate (hot summers, rainy winters) make touring Spain by bike less than ideal for all but the fittest bikers. That said, Spain's numerous nature preserves are perfect for mountain biking, especially in spring and fall, and many have specially marked bike paths. It's usually better to rent a bike locally than deal with the logistics of bringing your own. Bikes are not usually allowed on trains, for instance; they must be packed and checked as luggage. At most nature preserves, at least one agency rents mountain bikes and, in many cases, leads guided bike tours. Check with the park's visitor center for details. In addition, rural hotels often make bikes available to guests, sometimes for free.

BIKES IN FLIGHT

Most airlines accommodate bikes as luggage, provided they are dismantled and boxed; check with individual airlines about packing requirements. Some airlines sell bike boxes, which are often free at bike shops, for about $15 (bike bags can be considerably more expensive). International travelers often can substitute a bike for a piece of checked luggage at no charge; otherwise, the cost is about $100. U.S. and Canadian airlines charge $40–$80 each way.

BOAT & FERRY TRAVEL

Regular car ferries connect the United Kingdom with northern Spain. Brittany Ferries sails from Plymouth to Santander, P&O European Ferries from Portsmouth to Bilbao. Trasmediterránea connects mainland Spain to the Balearic and Canary islands. If you want to drive from Spain to Morocco, you can take a car ferry from Málaga, Algeciras, or Tarifa, run by Trasmediterránea or Buquebus; both lines also offer a catamaran service that takes half the time of the standard ferry.

From the U.K. **Brittany Ferries** ☎ 0239/289-2200. **P&O European Ferries** ☎ 0239/230-1000.

In Spain **Buquebus** ☎ 902/414242. **Trasmediterránea** ☎ 902/454645.

BUSINESS HOURS

BANKS & OFFICES

Banks are generally open Monday–Friday 8:30 or 9 until 2 or 2:30. Some banks occasionally open on Saturday 8:30 or 9 until 2 or 2:30. From October to May, savings banks are also open Thursday 4:30–8. Currency exchanges at airports and train stations stay open later; you can also cash traveler's checks at El Corte Inglés department stores until 10 PM (some branches close at 9 PM or 9:30 PM). Most government offices are open weekdays 9–2 only.

MUSEUMS & SIGHTS

Most museums are open from 9:30 to 2 and 4 to 7 six days a week, usually every day but Monday. Schedules are subject to change, particularly between the high and low seasons, so **confirm opening hours before you make plans.** A few large museums, such as Madrid's Prado and Reina Sofía and Barcelona's Picasso Museum, stay open all day, without a siesta.

PHARMACIES

Pharmacies keep normal business hours (9–1:30 and 5–8), but every mid-size town (or city neighborhood) has a duty pharmacy that stays open 24 hours. The location of the duty pharmacy is usually posted on the front door of all pharmacies.

SHOPS

When planning a shopping trip, remember that **almost all shops in Spain close at midday** for at least three hours. The only exceptions are large supermarkets and the department-store chain El Corte Inglés. Stores are generally open from 9 or 10 to 1:30 and from 5 to 8. Most shops are closed on Sunday, and in Madrid and several other places they're also closed Saturday afternoon. Larger shops in tourist areas may stay open Sunday in summer and during the Christmas holiday.

BUS TRAVEL

Within Spain, a mix of private companies provide bus service that ranges from knee-crunchingly basic to luxurious. Fares are lower than the corresponding train fares, and service is more extensive: if you want to reach a town not served by train, you can be sure a bus goes there. Smaller towns don't usually have a central bus depot, so ask the tourist office where to wait for the bus to your destination. Spain's major national long-haul bus line is **Enatcar.** Note that service is less frequent on weekends. For a longer haul, you can travel to Spain by bus from London, Paris, Rome, Frankfurt, Prague, and other major European cities. It's a long journey, but the buses are modern, and the fares are a fraction of what you'd pay to fly.

CLASSES

Most of Spain's larger bus companies have buses with comfortable seats and adequate legroom; on longer journeys (two hours or longer), a movie is shown on board, and earphones are provided. Except for smaller, regional buses that only travel short hops, all buses have a bathroom on board. Nonetheless, most long-haul buses usually stop at least once every two to three hours for a snack and bathroom break. Road and traffic conditions can make or break the journey; Spain's highways, particularly along major routes, are well maintained. That may not be the case in the country's more rural areas, where you could be in for a bumpy ride—sometimes exacerbated by older buses with worn shock absorbers. Enatcar has two luxury classes in addition to its regular line. Supra Clase includes roomy leather seats and on-board meals; also, you have the option of *asientos individuales,* individual seats (with no other seat on either side) that line one side of the bus. The next class is the Eurobus, with comfortable seats and plenty of legroom. The Supra Clase and Eurobus usually cost, respectively, up to one-third and one-fourth more than the regular line.

CUTTING COSTS

If you plan on returning to your initial destination, you can save by buying a round-trip ticket, instead of one-way. Also, some of Spain's smaller, regional bus lines offer multitrip bus passes, which are worthwhile if you plan on making multiple trips between two fixed destinations within the region. Generally, these tickets offer a savings of 20% per journey; you can only buy these tickets in the bus station (not on the bus). The general rule for children is that if they occupy a seat, they pay.

FARES & SCHEDULES

In Spain's larger cities, you can pick up schedule and fare information at the bus station; smaller towns may not have a bus station but just a bus stop. Schedules are sometimes listed at the bus stop; otherwise, call the bus company directly or ask at the tourist office, which can usually supply all schedule and fare information.

PAYING

At the bus station ticket counter, generally all major credit cards (except for American Express) are accepted. If you buy a ticket on the bus, it's cash only. Traveler's checks are almost never accepted.

RESERVATIONS

During peak travel times (Easter, August, and Christmas), it's always a good idea to make a reservation at least three to four days in advance.

From the U.K. **Eurolines/National Express** ☎ 01582/404511 or 0990/143219.

Within Spain **Enatcar** ✉ Estación Sur de Autobuses, Calle Méndez Álvaro, Madrid ☎ 902/422242.

Bus Tours **Marsans** ✉ Gran Vía 59, Madrid ☎ 902/306090. **Pullmantur** ✉ Plaza de Oriente 8, Madrid ☎ 91/541–1805.

CAMERAS & PHOTOGRAPHY

All major brands of film are readily available in Spain, and at reasonable prices. Try to buy film in large stores or photography shops; film sold in smaller outlets may be out of date or stored in poor conditions. To have film developed, **look for shops displaying the Kodak Q-Lab sign,** a guarantee of quality. If you're in a real hurry and happen to be in a large town or resort, you will, of course, find shops that will process film in a few hours. X-ray machines in Spanish airports are said to be film-safe. The *Kodak Guide to Shooting Great Travel Pictures* (available at bookstores everywhere) is loaded with tips.

Photo Help **Kodak Information Center** ☎ 800/242–2424 🌐 www.kodak.com.

EQUIPMENT PRECAUTIONS

Don't pack film and equipment in checked luggage, where it is much more susceptible to damage. X-ray machines used to view checked luggage are extremely powerful and therefore are likely to ruin your film. Try to **ask for hand inspection of film,** which becomes clouded after repeated exposure to airport X-ray machines, and **keep videotapes and computer disks away from metal detectors.** Always **keep film, tape, and computer disks out of the sun.** Carry an extra supply of batteries, and **be prepared to turn on your camera, camcorder, or laptop** to prove to airport security personnel that the device is real.

VIDEOS

Video systems in Spain are on the PAL system (used in Britain and much of continental Europe, though not France). Tapes for other systems are hard to find, so take a good supply with you.

CAR RENTAL

Avis, Hertz, Budget, and National (partnered in Spain with the Spanish agency Atesa) have branches at major Spanish airports and in large cities. Smaller, regional companies and wholesalers offer lower rates. All agencies have a range of models, but virtually all cars in Spain have a manual transmission—**if you don't want a stick shift, reserve weeks in advance and specify automatic transmission,** then call to reconfirm your automatic car before you leave for Spain. Rates in Madrid begin at the equivalents of U.S. $65 a day and $300 a week for an economy car with air-conditioning, manual transmission, and unlimited mileage. Add to this a 16% tax on car rentals. While you should always rent the size car that makes you feel safest, a small car, aside from saving you money, is prudent for the tiny roads and parking spaces in many parts of Spain.

Major Agencies **Alamo** ☎ 800/522-9696 🌐 www.alamo.com. **Avis** ☎ 800/331-1084, 800/879-2847 in Canada, 0870/606-0100 in the U.K., 02/9353-9000 in Australia, 09/526-2847 in New Zealand 🌐 www.avis.com. **Budget** ☎ 800/527-0700, 0870/156-5656 in the U.K. 🌐 www.budget.com. **Dollar** ☎ 800/800-6000, 0124/622-0111 in the U.K., where it's affiliated with Sixt, 02/9223-1444 in Australia 🌐 www.dollar.com. **Hertz** ☎ 800/654-3001, 800/263-0600 in Canada, 0870/844-8844 in the U.K., 02/9669-2444 in Australia, 09/256-8690 in New Zealand 🌐 www.hertz.com. **National Car Rental** ☎ 800/227-7368, 0870/600-6666 in the U.K. 🌐 www.nationalcar.com.

Local Agencies **Avis** ☎ 902/135531 🌐 www.avis.com. **Budget** ☎ 901/201212 🌐 www.budget.com. **Europcar** ☎ 902/105030 🌐 www.europcar.es. **Hertz** ☎ 902/402405 🌐 www.hertz.es. **National/Atesa** ☎ 902/100101 🌐 www.atesa.com.

Wholesalers **Auto Europe** ☎ 207/842-2000 or 800/223-5555 📠 207/842-2222 🌐 www.autoeurope.com. **Europe by Car** ☎ 212/581-3040 or 800/223-1516 📠 212/246-1458 🌐 www.europebycar.com. **Destination Europe Resources** (DER) ✉ 9501 W. Devon Ave., Rosemont, IL 60018 ☎ 800/782-2424 🌐 www.der.com. **Kemwel** ☎ 800/678-0678 📠 207/842-2124 🌐 www.kemwel.com.

INSURANCE

When driving a rented car you are generally responsible for any damage to or loss of the vehicle. Collision policies that car-rental companies sell for European rentals typically do not cover stolen vehicles. Before you rent—and purchase collision or theft coverage—see what coverage you already have under the terms of your personal auto-insurance policy and credit cards.

REQUIREMENTS & RESTRICTIONS

Your own driver's license is valid in Spain, but you may want to get an International Driver's Permit for extra assurance, as having one may save you a problem with local authorities. Permits are available from the American or Canadian Automobile Association, or, in the United Kingdom, from the Automobile Association or Royal Automobile Club. Note that while anyone over 18 with a valid license can drive in Spain, some rental agencies will not rent cars to drivers under 21.

SURCHARGES

Before you pick up a car in one city and leave it in another, **ask about drop-off charges or one-way service fees,** which can be substantial. Note, too, that some rental agencies charge extra if you return the car before the time specified in your contract. To avoid a hefty refueling fee, **fill the tank just before you turn in the car,** but be aware that gas stations near the rental outlet may overcharge. It's almost never a deal to buy the tank of gas that's in the car when you rent it; the understanding is that you'll return it empty, but some fuel usually remains.

CAR TRAVEL

Driving is the best way to see Spain's rural areas. The main cities are connected by a network of excellent four-lane *autovías* (freeways) and *autopistas* (toll freeways; "toll" is *peaje*), which are designated with the letter A and have speed limits of up to 120 kph (74 mph). The letter N indicates a *carretera nacional* (basic national route), which may have four or two lanes. Smaller towns and villages are connected by a network of secondary roads maintained by regional, provincial, and local governments. Spain's major routes bear heavy traffic, especially during holidays. Drive with care: the roads are shared by a potentially perilous mixture of local drivers, Moroccan immigrants traveling between North Africa and northern Europe, and non-Spanish vacationers, some of whom are accustomed to driving on the left side of the road. Be prepared, too, for heavy truck traffic on national routes, which, in the case of two-lane roads, can have you creeping along for hours.

EMERGENCY SERVICES

The rental agencies Hertz and Avis have 24-hour breakdown service. If you belong to an auto club (AAA, CAA, or AA), you can get emergency assistance from the Spanish counterpart, RACE.

Local Auto Clubs RACE ✉ José Abascal 10, Madrid ☎ 900/200093.

GASOLINE

Gas stations are plentiful, and most of those on major routes and in big cities are open 24 hours. On less-traveled routes, gas stations are usually open 7 AM–11 PM. If a gas station is closed, it's required by law to post the address and directions to the nearest open station. Most stations are self-service, though prices are the same as those at full-service stations. You punch in the amount of gas you want (in euros, not in liters), unhook the nozzle, pump the gas, and then pay. At night, however, you must pay before you fill up. Most pumps offer a choice of gas, including leaded, unleaded, and diesel, so **be careful to pick the right one** for your car. All newer cars in Spain use *gasolina sin plomo* (unleaded gas), which is available in two grades, 95 and 98 octane. *Super,* regular 97-octane leaded gas, is gradually being phased out. Prices vary little among stations and were at press time €.82 a liter for leaded, 97 octane; €.76 a liter for *sin plomo* (unleaded; 95 octane), and €.89 a liter for unleaded, 98 octane. Credit cards are widely accepted.

ROAD CONDITIONS

Spain's highway system now includes some 6,000 km (3,600 mi) of beautifully maintained superhighways. Still, you'll find some stretches of major national highways that are only two lanes wide, where traffic often backs up behind slow, heavy trucks. *Autopista* tolls are steep but as a result are often less crowded than the free highways. If you spring for the autopistas, you'll find that many of the rest stops are nicely landscaped and have cafeterias with good food. Most Spanish cities have notoriously long morning and evening rush hours. Traffic jams are especially bad in and around Barcelona and Madrid. If possible, **avoid the morning rush, which can last until noon, and the evening rush, which lasts from 7 to 9.**

ROAD MAPS

Detailed road maps are readily available at major bookstores and gas stations.

RULES OF THE ROAD

Spaniards drive on the right. Horns are banned in cities, but that doesn't keep people from blasting away. Children under 10 may not ride in the front seat, and seat belts are compulsory everywhere. Speed limits are 50 kph (31 mph) in cities, 100 kph (62 mph) on N roads, 120 kph (74 mph) on the *autopista* or *autovía,* and, unless otherwise signposted, 90 kph (56 mph) on other roads. Spanish highway police are particularly vigilant about speeding and illegal passing. Fines start at €90, and police are empowered to demand payment from non-Spanish drivers on the spot. Although local drivers, especially in cities like Madrid, will park their cars just about anywhere, you should **park only in legal spots.** Parking fines are steep, and your car might well be towed, resulting in fines, hassle, and wasted time.

CHILDREN IN SPAIN

Children are greatly indulged in Spain. You'll see kids accompanying their parents everywhere, including bars and restaurants. Shopkeepers often offer kids *caramelos* (sweets), and even the coldest waiters tend to be friendlier when you have a youngster with you, and you won't be shunted into a remote corner. However, you won't find high chairs, or children's menus; kids are expected to eat what their parents do, so it's perfectly acceptable to ask for an extra plate and share your food. Be prepared for late bedtimes, especially in summer—it's common to see toddlers playing cheerfully outdoors until midnight. Because children are expected to be with their parents at all times, few hotels provide baby-sitting services; but those that don't can often refer you to an independent baby-sitter (*canguro*). For advice about traveling with children consult *Fodor's FYI: Travel with Your Baby* (available in bookstores everywhere). If you decide to rent a car, **arrange for a car seat when you reserve.**

EATING & DRINKING

Visiting children may turn up their noses at some of Spain's regional specialties. Although kids seldom get their own menus, most restaurants are happy to provide kids with simple dishes—plain grilled chicken, steak, or fried potatoes. *Pescadito frito* (batter-fried fish) is one Spanish dish that most kids do seem to enjoy. If all else fails, chains like McDonald's, Burger King, and Pizza Hut are well represented in the major cities and popular resorts. Spain's two leading fast food chains, Pans y Company and Bocatta, serve *bocadillos* (baguette-style sandwiches), salads, and fries, and both offer kid's menus and specials, sometimes with prizes and toys.

FLYING

If your children are two or older, **ask about children's airfares.** As a general rule, infants under two not occupying a seat fly at greatly reduced fares or even for free. But if you want to guarantee a seat for an infant, you have to pay full fare. Consider flying during off-peak days and times; most airlines will grant an infant a seat without a ticket if there are available seats. When booking, **confirm carry-on allowances** if you're traveling with infants. In general, for babies charged 10% to 50% of the adult fare you are allowed one carry-on bag and a collapsible stroller; if the flight is full, the stroller may have to be checked or you may be limited to less.

Experts agree that it's a good idea to use safety seats aloft for children weighing less than 40 pounds. Airlines set their own policies: if you use a safety seat, U.S. carriers usually require that the child be ticketed, even if he or she is young enough to ride free, because the seats must be strapped into regular seats. And even if you pay the full adult fare for the seat, it may be worth it, especially on longer trips. Do **check your airline's policy about using safety seats during takeoff and landing.** Safety seats are not allowed everywhere in the plane, so get your seat assignments as early as possible.

When reserving, **request children's meals or a freestanding bassinet** (not available at all airlines) if you need them. But note that bulkhead seats, where you must sit to use the bassinet, may lack an overhead bin or storage space on the floor.

LODGING

Most hotels in Spain allow children under a certain age to stay in their parents' room at no extra charge, but others charge for them as extra adults. **Find out the cutoff age for children's discounts.**

SIGHTS & ATTRACTIONS

Places that are especially appealing to children are indicated by a rubber-duckie icon (☺) in the margin. Museum admissions and bus and metro rides are generally free for children up to age five.

SUPPLIES & EQUIPMENT

Disposable diapers (*pañales*), formula (*leche maternizada*), and bottled baby foods (*papillas*) are readily available at supermarkets and pharmacies.

COMPUTERS ON THE ROAD

A few of Spain's newer hotels, mainly in the major cities, provide data ports for Internet access in guest rooms. If you need to bring your computer, *see* Electricity. Virtually every town with more than two traffic lights has at least one cybercafé, most with hourly rates under €3.

CONSUMER PROTECTION

Whether you're shopping for gifts or purchasing travel services, pay with a major credit card whenever possible, so you can cancel payment or get reimbursed if there's a problem (and you can provide documentation). If you're doing business with a particular company for the first time, contact your local Better Business Bureau and the attorney general's offices in your state and (for U.S. businesses) the company's home state as well. Have any complaints been filed? Finally, if you're buying a package or tour, always **consider travel insurance** that includes default coverage (⇨ Insurance).

BBBs Council of Better Business Bureaus ✉ 4200 Wilson Blvd., Suite 800, Arlington, VA 22203 ☎ 703/276-0100 🖷 703/525-8277 🌐 www.bbb.org.

CRUISE TRAVEL

Barcelona is the cruise capital of Spain, and the point of departure for many Mediterranean cruises. Other popular ports of call are Gibraltar, Málaga, Alicante, and Palma de Mallorca. Among the many cruise lines that call at Spain are Royal Caribbean, Holland America Line, Renaissance Cruises, the Norwegian Cruise Line, and Princess Cruises. To learn how to plan, choose, and book a cruise-ship voyage, check out Cruise How-to's on www.fodors.com and consult *Fodor's FYI: Plan & Enjoy Your Cruise* (available in bookstores everywhere).

CUSTOMS & DUTIES

When shopping abroad, **keep receipts** for all purchases. Upon reentering the country, **be ready to show customs officials what you've bought.** Pack purchases together in an easily accessible place. If you think a duty is incorrect, appeal the assessment. If you object to the way your clearance was handled, note the inspector's badge number. In either case, first ask to see a supervisor. If the problem isn't resolved, write to the appropriate authorities, beginning with the port director at your point of entry.

IN SPAIN

From countries that are not part of the European Union, visitors age 15 and over may *enter* Spain duty-free with up to 200 cigarettes or 50 cigars, up to 1 liter of alcohol over 22 proof, and up to 2 liters of wine. Dogs and cats are admitted as long as they have up-to-date vaccination records from their home country.

IN AUSTRALIA

Australian residents who are 18 or older may bring home A$400 worth of souvenirs and gifts (including jewelry), 250 cigarettes or 250 grams of cigars or other tobacco products, and 1,125 ml of alcohol (including wine, beer, and spirits). Residents under 18 may bring back A$200 worth of goods. Members of the same family traveling together may pool their allowances. Prohibited items include meat products. Seeds, plants, and fruits need to be declared upon arrival.

Australian Customs Service Regional Director, Box 8, Sydney, NSW 2001 ☎ 02/9213-2000 or 1300/363263, 02/9364-7222 or 1800/803-006 quarantine-inquiry line 🖷 02/9213-4043 🌐 www.customs.gov.au.

IN CANADA

Canadian residents who have been out of Canada for at least seven days may bring in C$750 worth of goods duty-free. If you've been away fewer than seven days but more than 48 hours, the duty-free allowance drops to C$200. If your trip lasts 24 to 48 hours, the allowance is C$50. You may not pool allowances with family members. Goods claimed under the C$750 exemption may follow you by mail; those claimed under the lesser exemptions must accompany you. Alcohol and tobacco products may be included in the seven-day and 48-hour exemptions but not in the 24-hour exemption. If you meet the age requirements of the province or territory through which you reenter Canada, you may bring in, duty-free, 1.5 liters of wine *or* 1.14 liters (40 imperial ounces) of liquor *or* 24 12-ounce cans or bottles of beer or ale. Also, if you meet the local age requirement for tobacco products, you may bring in, duty-free, 200 cigarettes and 50 cigars. Check ahead of time with the Canada Customs and Revenue Agency or the Department of Agriculture for policies regarding meat products, seeds, plants, and fruits.

You may send an unlimited number of gifts (only one gift per recipient, however) worth up to C$60 each duty-free to Canada. Label the package UNSOLICITED GIFT—VALUE UNDER $60. Alcohol and tobacco are excluded.

Canada Customs and Revenue Agency ✉ 2265 St. Laurent Blvd., Ottawa, Ontario K1G 4K3 ☎ 800/461-9999, 204/983-3500, 506/636-5064 🌐 www.ccra.gc.ca.

IN NEW ZEALAND

All homeward-bound residents may bring back NZ$700 worth of souvenirs and gifts; passengers may not pool their allowances, and children can claim only the concession on goods intended for their own use. For those 17 or older, the duty-free allowance also includes 4.5 liters of wine or beer; one 1,125-ml bottle of spirits; and either 200 cigarettes, 250 grams of tobacco, 50 cigars, *or* a combination of the three up to 250 grams. Meat products, seeds, plants, and fruits must be declared upon arrival to the Agricultural Services Department.

New Zealand Customs ✉ Head office: The Customhouse, 17–21 Whitmore St., Box 2218, Wellington ☎ 09/300-5399 or 0800/428-786 🌐 www.customs.govt.nz.

IN THE U.K.

If you are a U.K. resident and your journey was wholly within the European Union, you probably won't have to pass through customs when you return to the United Kingdom. If you plan to bring back large quantities of alcohol or tobacco, check EU limits beforehand. In most cases, if you bring back more than 200 cigars, 3200 cigarettes, 10 liters of spirits, 110 liters of beer, and/or 90 liters of wine, you have to declare the goods upon return.

HM Customs and Excise ✉ Portcullis House, 21 Cowbridge Rd. E, Cardiff CF11 9SS ☎ 0845/010-9000 or 0208/929-0152, 0208/929-6731 or 0208/910-3602 complaints 🌐 www.hmce.gov.uk.

IN THE U.S.

U.S. residents who have been out of the country for at least 48 hours may bring home, for personal use, $800 worth of foreign goods duty-free, as long as they haven't used the $800 allowance or any part of it in the past 30 days. This exemption may include 1 liter of alcohol (for travelers 21 and older), 200 cigarettes, and 100 non-Cuban cigars. Family members from the same household who are traveling together may pool their $800 personal exemptions. For fewer than 48 hours, the duty-free allowance drops to $200, which may include 50 cigarettes, 10 non-Cuban cigars, and 150 ml of alcohol (or 150 ml of perfume containing alcohol). The $200 allowance cannot be combined with other individuals' exemptions, and if you exceed it, the full value of all the goods will be taxed. Antiques, which the U.S. Bureau of Customs and Border Protection defines as objects more than 100 years old, enter duty-free, as do original works of art done entirely by hand, including paintings, drawings, and sculptures. This doesn't apply to folk art or handicrafts, which are in general dutiable.

You may also send packages home duty-free, with a limit of one parcel per addressee per day (except alcohol or tobacco products or perfume worth more than $5). You can mail up to $200 worth of goods for personal use; label the package PERSONAL USE and attach a list of its contents and their retail value. If the package contains your used personal belongings, mark it AMERICAN GOODS RETURNED to avoid paying duties. You may send up to $100 worth of goods as a gift; mark the package UNSOLICITED GIFT. Mailed items do not affect your duty-free allowance on your return.

To avoid paying duty on foreign-made high-ticket items you already own and will take on your trip, register them with Customs before you leave the country. Consider filing a Certificate of Registration for laptops, cameras, watches, and other digital devices identified with serial numbers or other permanent markings; you can keep the certificate for other trips. Otherwise, bring a sales receipt or insurance form to show that you owned the item before you left the United States.

U.S. Bureau of Customs and Border Protection ✉ for inquiries and equipment registration, 1300 Pennsylvania Ave. NW, Washington, DC 20229 🌐 www.customs.gov ☎ 202/354-1000 ✉ for complaints, Customer Satisfaction Unit, 1300 Pennsylvania Ave. NW, Room 5.5D, Washington, DC 20229.

DISABILITIES & ACCESSIBILITY

Unfortunately, Spain has made only modest advances in making traveling easy for visitors with disabilities. The Prado and some newer museums, like Madrid's Reina Sofía and Thyssen-Bornemisza, have wheelchair-accessible entrances or elevators. In Granada, the palacios and most of the gardens of the Alhambra are wheelchair accessible. Most of the churches, castles, and monasteries on any itinerary will involve a lot of walking, often on uneven terrain.

RESERVATIONS

When discussing accessibility with an operator or reservations agent, **ask hard questions.** Are there any stairs, inside *or* out?

Are there grab bars next to the toilet *and* in the shower/tub? How wide is the doorway to the room? To the bathroom? For the most extensive facilities meeting the latest legal specifications, **opt for newer accommodations.** If you reserve through a toll-free number, consider also calling the hotel's local number to confirm the information from the central reservations office. Get confirmation in writing when you can.

Complaints **Aviation Consumer Protection Division** (⇨ Air Travel) for airline-related problems. **Departmental Office of Civil Rights** ✉ for general inquiries, U.S. Department of Transportation, S-30, 400 7th St. SW, Room 10215, Washington, DC 20590 ☎ 202/366-4648 📠 202/366-9371 🌐 www.dot.gov/ost/docr/index.htm. **Disability Rights Section** ✉ NYAV, U.S. Department of Justice, Civil Rights Division, 950 Pennsylvania Ave. NW, Washington, DC 20530 ☎ ADA information line 202/514-0301, 800/514-0301, 202/514-0383 TTY, 800/514-0383 TTY 🌐 www.ada.gov. **U.S. Department of Transportation Hotline** ☎ for disability-related air-travel problems, 800/778-4838 or 800/455-9880 TTY.

TRAVEL AGENCIES

In the United States, the Americans with Disabilities Act requires that travel firms serve the needs of all travelers. Some agencies specialize in working with people with disabilities.

Travelers with Mobility Problems **Access Adventures** ✉ 206 Chestnut Ridge Rd., Scottsville, NY 14624 ☎ 585/889-9096 ✉ dltravel@prodigy.net, run by a former physical-rehabilitation counselor. **CareVacations** ✉ No. 5, 5110-50 Ave., Leduc, Alberta, Canada, T9E 6V4 ☎ 780/986-6404 or 877/478-7827 📠 780/986-8332 🌐 www.carevacations.com, for group tours and cruise vacations. **Flying Wheels Travel** ✉ 143 W. Bridge St., Box 382, Owatonna, MN 55060 ☎ 507/451-5005 📠 507/451-1685 🌐 www.flyingwheelstravel.com.

Travelers with Developmental Disabilities **Sprout** ✉ 893 Amsterdam Ave., New York, NY 10025 ☎ 212/222-9575 or 888/222-9575 📠 212/222-9768 🌐 www.gosprout.org.

DISCOUNTS & DEALS

Barcelona and Madrid both have multi-attraction passes. Turisme de Barcelona sells 24-, 48-, and 72-hour versions of the very worthwhile Barcelona Card. For €14, €20, €23, you get unlimited travel on all public transport as well as discounts at 27 museums, 10 restaurants, 14 leisure sites, and 20 stores. Other services include walking tours of the Gothic Quarter, an airport shuttle, a bus to Tibidabo, and the Tombbus, which connects key shopping areas. In Madrid, for €28, €42, or €55 for 1, 2, or 3 days, you get free entry to 40 museums (with no standing in lines to buy tickets) and monuments, all public transport, a tourist bus called Madrid Visión, and a thematic tour through the Madrid de los Austrias (the area around Plaza Mayor), as well as discounts in stores, movies, theaters, restaurants, and parks. You can buy the card at municipal and regional tourist offices, on Madrid Visión buses and its kiosk next to the Prado Museum on Felipe IV, and online via the Madrid Card Web site.

Turisme de Barcelona ✉ Pl. de Catalunya 17 bis, Eixample ☎ 906/301282. **Madrid Tourist Office** ✉ Plaza Mayor 3 ✉ Duque de Medinaceli, 2 ☎ 915/882900 🌐 www.munimadrid.es 🌐 www.madridcard.com.

DISCOUNT RESERVATIONS

To save money, look into discount reservations services with Web sites and toll-free numbers, which use their buying power to get a better price on hotels, airline tickets, even car rentals. When booking a room, always **call the hotel's local toll-free number** (if one is available) rather than the central reservations number—you'll often get a better price. Always ask about special packages or corporate rates.

When shopping for the best deal on hotels and car rentals, look for guaranteed exchange rates, which protect you against a falling dollar. With your rate locked in, you won't pay more, even if the price goes up in the local currency.

Airline Tickets **Air 4 Less** ☎ 800/AIR4LESS; low-fare specialist.

Hotel Rooms **Accommodations Express** ☎ 800/444-7666 or 800/277-1064 🌐 www.accommodationsexpress.com. **Hotels.com** ☎ 800/246-8357 or 214/369-1246 🌐 www.hotels.com. **International Marketing & Travel Concepts** ☎ 800/790-4682 🌐 www.imtc-travel.com. **Steigenberger Reservation Service** ☎ 800/223-5652 🌐 www.srs-worldhotels.com. **Travel Interlink** ☎ 800/888-5898 🌐 www.travelinterlink.com. **Turbotrip.com** ☎ 800/473-7829 🌐 www.turbotrip.com.

PACKAGE DEALS

Don't confuse packages and guided tours. When you buy a package, you travel on your own, just as though you had planned the trip yourself. Fly/drive packages, which combine airfare and car rental, are often a good deal. In cities, ask the local visitor's bureau about hotel packages that include tickets to major museum exhibits or other special events. If you buy a rail/drive pass, you may save on train tickets and car rentals. All Eurailpass holders get a discount on Eurostar fares through the Channel Tunnel and often receive reduced rates for buses, hotels, ferries, and car rentals.

EATING & DRINKING

Spaniards love to eat out, and restaurants in Spain have evolved dramatically, thanks to a favorable economic climate and burgeoning tourism. A new generation of Spanish chefs—some with international reputations—has transformed classic dishes to suit contemporary tastes, drawing on some of the freshest ingredients in Europe. The restaurants included in this book are the best in each price range. Restaurants are identified by a crossed knife-and-fork icon (✕); establishments with a ✕▣ symbol are hotels with restaurants that stand out for their cuisine and are open to nonguests.

MEALS & SPECIALTIES

Most restaurants in Spain do not serve breakfast (*desayuno*); for coffee and carbohydrates, head to a bar or *cafetería*. Outside major hotels, which serve morning buffets, breakfast in Spain is usually limited to coffee and toast or a roll. Lunch (*comida* or *almuerzo*) traditionally consists of an appetizer, a main course, and dessert, followed by coffee and perhaps a liqueur. Between lunch and dinner the best way to snack is to sample some *tapas* (appetizers) at a bar; normally you can choose from quite a variety. Dinner (*cena*) is somewhat lighter, with perhaps only one course.
In addition to an à la carte menu, most restaurants offer a daily fixed-price menu (*menú del día*), consisting of two courses, coffee, and dessert at a very attractive price. If your server does not suggest the menú del día when you're seated, ask for it—"Hay menú del día, por favor?" Restaurants in many of the larger tourist areas will have the menú del día posted outside.

Spain has many cuisines representing its distinct regional cultures. Spain's most famous dish, paella, originated in Valencia but is prevalent throughout the country. Basque and Catalan cooking are considered the finest in Spain—Basque cuisine centers on fresh fish and meat dishes, while Catalan cooking revolves around vegetables and interesting sauces. Galician cuisine is a bit simpler but centers on equally fresh fish and shellfish. The roasts of central Castile are renowned, as are the fried fish and the cold soups—gazpacho and the almond-based *ajo blanco*—of Andalusia. The classic dish in Madrid and many other parts of Spain is the *cocido*, a hearty stew eaten in two parts: the soup, then the solids.

MEALTIMES

Mealtimes in Spain are later than elsewhere in Europe, and later still in Madrid. Lunch starts around 2 or 2:30 (closer to 3 in Madrid), dinner between 8 and 10 (9 and 11 in Madrid). In areas with heavy tourist traffic, some restaurants open a bit earlier. Unless otherwise noted, the restaurants listed in this guide are open daily for lunch and dinner.

PAYING

Credit cards are widely accepted in Spanish restaurants. If you pay by credit card and you want to leave a small tip above and beyond the service charge, leave the tip in cash.

RESERVATIONS & DRESS

Reservations are always a good idea: we mention them only when they're essential or not accepted. For top restaurants, book as far in advance as you can, and confirm when you arrive in Spain. We mention dress only when men are required to wear a jacket or a jacket and tie.

WINE, BEER & SPIRITS

Apart from its famous wines, Spain produces many brands of lager, the most popular of which are San Miguel, Cruzcampo, Aguila, Mahou, and Estrella. Jerez de la Frontera is Europe's largest producer of brandy and is a major source of sherry. Catalonia produces most of the world's *cava* (sparkling wine). Spanish law prohibits the sale of alcohol to persons under 16.

HEALTH CONCERNS

At the end of 2000, the first cases of bovine spongiform encephalopathy (BSE, or "mad cow disease") were detected among Spanish cattle, raising questions about the safety of eating beef in Spain. Cattle is subject to testing, and local health authorities have declared it safe to eat Spanish beef and veal, but dishes containing brains or cuts including the spinal cord should be avoided.

ELECTRICITY

To use electric equipment from the United States, **bring a converter and adapter.** Spain's electrical current is 220 volts, 50 cycles alternating current (AC); wall outlets take Continental-type plugs, with two round prongs. If your appliances are dual-voltage you'll need only an adapter. Don't use 110-volt outlets, marked FOR SHAVERS ONLY, for high-wattage appliances such as hair dryers. Most laptop computers operate equally well on 110 and 220 volts, so they require only an adapter.

EMBASSIES

In Madrid **Australia** ✉ Plaza Descubridor Diegos de Ordas 3 ☎ 91/441-9300. **Canada** ✉ Calle Nuñez de Balboa 35, ☎ 91/423-3250. **New Zealand** ✉ Plaza Lealtad 2 ☎ 91/523-0226. **United Kingdom** ✉ C. Fernando el Santo 16 ☎ 91/319-0200. **United States** ✉ C. Serrano 75 ☎ 91/587-2200.

EMERGENCIES

The pan-European **emergency phone number** (☎ 112) is operative in some parts of Spain but not all. If it doesn't work, dial the emergency numbers below for national police, local police, fire department, or medical services. On the road, there are emergency phones marked SOS at regular intervals on *autovías* (freeways) and *autopistas* (toll highways). If your documents are stolen, contact both the local police and your embassy. If you lose a credit card, phone the issuer immediately (⇨ Money Matters).

National police ☎ 091. **Local police** ☎ 092. **Fire department** ☎ 080. **Medical service** ☎ 061.

ENGLISH-LANGUAGE MEDIA

In cities and major resorts, you'll have no trouble finding newspapers and magazines in English. U.K. newspapers are available on the day of publication. From the United States, you'll see major news magazines, such as *Time,* along with *USA Today* and the *International Herald Tribune*. The *Tribune* includes a news section about Spain in English, provided by *El Pais*.

BOOKS

Major airports sell books in English, including the latest paperback best-sellers. Bookshops in Madrid, Barcelona, Costa del Sol towns, Alicante, and the Canary Islands also sell English-language books.

NEWSPAPERS & MAGAZINES

Several major cities and resorts in Spain have local English-language publications, including Madrid (the monthly *Broadsheet*); Barcelona (the monthly *Barcelona Metropolitan*); Alicante (the weekly *Costa Blanca News, Post,* and *Entertainer*); Málaga (the weekly *Sur, Entertainer,* and *Costa del Sol News* and the monthly magazines *Essential* and *Absolute Marbella*); Majorca (the *Majorca Daily Bulletin*); and the Canary Islands (the biweekly *Island Connections, Island Sun, Paper,* and *Tenerife News*). Distributed throughout the country is the UK-published monthly *Spain,* with articles on travel, lifestyle, property, and gastronomy.

TELEVISION

Spain is served by two state-owned national channels, two private networks, regional channels in some parts of Spain, and local channels serving individual towns. Many hotels have satellite service, which usually includes at least one news channel in English (CNN, BBC World, or Sky News).

ETIQUETTE & BEHAVIOR

The Spanish are very tolerant of foreigners and their different ways, but you should always behave with courtesy. Be respectful when visiting churches: casual dress is fine if it's not gaudy or unkempt. Spaniards do object to men going bare-chested anywhere other than the beach or poolside and generally do not look kindly on public displays of drunkenness. When addressing Spaniards with whom you are not well acquainted, use the formal *usted* rather than the familiar *tu*. For more on language, *see* Language.

BUSINESS ETIQUETTE

Spanish office hours can be confusing to the uninitiated. Some offices stay open more or less continuously from 9 to 3, with a very short lunch break. Others open in the morning, break up the day with a long lunch break of two–three hours, then reopen at 4 or 5 until 7 or 8. Spaniards enjoy a certain notoriety for their lack of punctuality, but this has changed dramatically in recent years: you are expected to show up for meetings on time. Smart dress is the norm.

Spaniards in international fields tend to conduct business with foreigners in English. If you speak Spanish, address new colleagues with the formal *usted* and the corresponding verb conjugations, then follow the lead in switching to the familiar *tu* once a working relationship has been established.

GAY & LESBIAN TRAVEL

Since the end of Franco's dictatorship, the situation for gays and lesbians in Spain has improved dramatically: the paragraph in the Spanish civil code that made homosexuality a crime was repealed in 1978. Violence against gays does occur, but it's generally restricted to the rougher areas of very large cities. In summer, the beaches of the Balearics (especially Ibiza), the Costa del Sol (Torremolinos and Benidorm), and the Costa Brava (Sitges and Lloret del Mar) are gay and lesbian hot spots. Playa del Inglés and Maspalomas, in the Canary Islands, are popular in winter.

Gay- & Lesbian-Friendly Travel Agencies **Different Roads Travel** ✉ 8383 Wilshire Blvd., Suite 520, Beverly Hills, CA 90211 ☎ 323/651-5557 or 800/429-8747 (Ext. 14 for both) 🖷 323/651-3678 ✉ lgernert@tzell.com. **Kennedy Travel** ✉ 130 W. 42nd St., Suite 401, New York, NY 10036 ☎ 212/840-8659 or 800/237-7433 🖷 212/730-2269 🌐 www.kennedytravel.com. **Now, Voyager** ✉ 4406 18th St., San Francisco, CA 94114 ☎ 415/626-1169 or 800/255-6951 🖷 415/626-8626 🌐 www.nowvoyager.com. **Skylink Travel and Tour** ✉ 1455 N. Dutton Ave., Suite A, Santa Rosa, CA 95401 ☎ 707/546-9888 or 800/225-5759 🖷 707/636-0951; serving lesbian travelers.

Local Resources **Gai Inform** ✉ Fuencarral 37, 28004 Madrid ☎ 91/523-0070. **Teléfono Rosa** ✉ C. Finlandia 45, Barcelona ☎ 900/601601.

GUIDEBOOKS

Plan well and you won't be sorry. Guidebooks are excellent tools—and you can take them with you. You may want to check out color-photo-illustrated *Fodor's Exploring Spain,* which is thorough on culture and history. For more regional and city coverage, try *Fodor's Barcelona to Bilbao* or pocket-size *Citypack Barcelona* and *Citypack Madrid,* which include foldout maps. All are available at on-line retailers and bookstores everywhere.

HEALTH

Sunburn and sunstroke are real risks in summertime Spain. On the hottest sunny days, even if you're not normally bothered by strong sun, you should cover yourself up, carry sunblock lotion, drink plenty of fluids, and limit sun time for the first few days. If you require medical attention for any problem, ask your hotel's front desk for assistance or go to the nearest public **Centro de Salud** (day hospital); in serious cases, you'll be referred to the regional hospital. Medical care is good in Spain, but nursing is perfunctory, as relatives are expected to stop by and look after inpatients' needs. In some popular destinations, such as the Costa del Sol, there are volunteer English interpreters on hand. Spain was recently documented as having the highest number of AIDS cases in Europe. If you're applying for a work permit you'll be asked for proof of HIV-negative status.

MEDICAL PLANS

No one plans to get sick while traveling, but it happens, so **consider signing up with a medical-assistance company.** Members get doctor referrals, emergency evacuation or repatriation, hot lines for medical consultation, cash for emergencies, and other assistance. You won't need this in most parts of Spain, but if you're in a very remote area, you may want to consider it.

Medical-Assistance Companies **International SOS Assistance** 🌐 www.internationalsos.com ✉ 8 Neshaminy Interplex, Suite 207, Trevose, PA 19053 ☎ 215/245-4707 or 800/523-6586 🖷 215/244-9617 ✉ Landmark House, Hammersmith Bridge Rd., 6th floor, London, W6 9DP ☎ 20/8762-8008 🖷 20/8748-7744 ✉ 12 Chemin Riantbosson, 1217 Meyrin 1, Geneva, Switzerland ☎ 22/785-6464 🖷 22/785-6424 ✉ 331 N. Bridge Rd., 17-00, Odeon Towers, Singapore 188720 ☎ 6338-7800 🖷 6338-7611.

EATING & DRINKING

The major health risk in Spain is *diarrea,* or traveler's diarrhea, caused by eating contaminated fruit or vegetables or drinking contaminated water. So **watch what you eat.** Avoid ice, uncooked food, and unpasteurized milk and milk products, and **drink only bottled water** or water that has been boiled for several minutes, even when brushing your teeth. Mild cases may respond to Imodium (known generically as loperamide) or Pepto-Bismol, both of which can be purchased over the counter. In Spain, ask for *un antidiarreico,* which is the general term for antidiarrheal medicine; Fortasec is a well-known brand. You don't need a doctor's prescription to buy it. Drink plenty of purified water or tea—chamomile (*manzanilla*) is a good folk remedy. In severe cases, rehydrate yourself with a salt-sugar solution (½ teaspoon salt (*sal*) and 4 tablespoons sugar (*azúcar*) per quart of water.

OVER-THE-COUNTER REMEDIES

Over-the-counter remedies are available at any *farmacia* (pharmacy), recognizable by the large green crosses outside. Some will look familiar, such as *aspirina* (aspirin), while other medications are sold under various brand names. If you regularly take a nonprescription medicine, take a sample box or bottle with you, and the Spanish pharmacist will provide you with its local equivalent.

HOLIDAYS

Spain's national holidays include January 1, January 6 (Epiphany), Good Friday, Easter, May 1 (May Day), August 15 (Assumption), October 12 (National Day), November 1 (All Saints'), December 6 (Constitution), December 8 (Immaculate Conception), and December 25.

In addition, each region, city, and town has its own holidays honoring political events and patron saints. Madrid holidays include May 2 (Madrid Day), May 15 (St. Isidro), and November 9 (Almudena). Barcelona celebrates April 23 (St. George), September 11 (Catalonia Day), and September 24 (Mercy).

If a public holiday falls on a Tuesday or Thursday, remember that **many businesses also close on the nearest Monday or Friday** for a long weekend called a *puente* (bridge). If a major holiday falls on a Sunday, businesses close on Monday.

INSURANCE

The most useful travel-insurance plan is a comprehensive policy that includes coverage for trip cancellation and interruption, default, trip delay, and medical expenses (with a waiver for preexisting conditions).

Without insurance you'll lose all or most of your money if you cancel your trip, regardless of the reason. Default insurance covers you if your tour operator, airline, or cruise line goes out of business. Trip-delay covers expenses that arise because of bad weather or mechanical delays. Study the fine print when comparing policies.

If you're traveling internationally, a key component of travel insurance is coverage for medical bills incurred if you get sick on the road. Such expenses aren't generally covered by Medicare or private policies. U.K. residents can buy a travel-insurance policy valid for most vacations taken during the year in which it's purchased (but check preexisting-condition coverage). British and Australian citizens need extra medical coverage when traveling overseas. Always **buy travel policies directly from the insurance company**; if you buy them from a cruise line, airline, or tour operator that goes out of business you probably won't be covered for the agency or operator's default, a major risk. Before making any purchase, **review your existing health and home-owner's policies** to find what they cover away from home.

Travel Insurers In the U.S.: **Access America** ✉ 6600 W. Broad St., Richmond, VA 23230 ☎ 800/284-8300 🖷 804/673-1491 or 800/346-9265 🌐 www.accessamerica.com. **Travel Guard International** ✉ 1145 Clark St., Stevens Point, WI 54481 ☎ 715/345-0505 or 800/826-1300 🖷 800/955-8785 🌐 www.travelguard.com.

In the U.K.: **Association of British Insurers** ✉ 51 Gresham St., London EC2V 7HQ ☎ 020/7600-3333 🖷 020/7696-8999 🌐 www.abi.org.uk. In Canada: **RBC Insurance** ✉ 6880 Financial Dr., Mississauga, Ontario L5N 7Y5 ☎ 800/565-3129 🖷 905/813-4704 🌐 www.rbcinsurance.com. In Australia: **Insurance Council of Australia** ✉ Insurance Enquiries and Complaints, Level 3, 56 Pitt St., Sydney, NSW 2000 ☎ 1300/363683 or 02/9251-4456 🖷 02/9251-4453 🌐 www.iecltd.com.au. In New Zealand: **Insurance Council of New Zealand** ✉ Level 7, 111-115 Customhouse Quay, Box 474, Wellington ☎ 04/472-5230 🖷 04/473-3011 🌐 www.icnz.org.nz.

LANGUAGE

Although Spaniards exported their language to all Central and South America, you may be surprised to find that Spanish is not the principal language in all of Spain. The Basques speak Euskera; in Catalonia, you'll hear Catalan; in Galicia, Gallego; and in Valencia, Valenciano. Although almost everyone in these regions also speaks and understands Spanish, local radio and television stations may broadcast in these languages, and road signs may be printed (or spray-painted over) with the preferred regional language. Spanish is referred to as Castellano, or Castilian.

Fortunately, **Spanish is fairly easy to pick up, and your efforts to speak it will be graciously received.** Learn at least the following basic phrases: *buenos días* (hello—until 2 PM), *buenas tardes* (good afternoon—until 8 PM), *buenas noches* (hello—after dark), *por favor* (please), *gracias* (thank you), *adiós* (good-bye), *sí* (yes), *no* (no), *los servicios* (the toilets), *la cuenta* (bill/check), *habla inglés?* (do you speak English?), *no comprendo* (I don't understand). For other helpful expressions, *see* the Spanish Vocabulary at the end of this guide.

If your Spanish breaks down, you should have no trouble finding people who speak English in major cities and coastal resorts, but you won't necessarily be able to count on the bus driver or the passerby on the street. Those who do speak English may speak the British variety, so don't be surprised if you're told to queue (line up) or take the lift (elevator) to the loo (toilet). Many guided tours at museums and historic sites are in Spanish; ask about the language that will be spoken before you sign up.

LANGUAGES FOR TRAVELERS

A phrase book and language-tape set can help get you started. *Fodor's/Living Language Spanish for Travelers* is available at bookstores everywhere. Living Language also sells more comprehensive language programs: *Spanish Complete Course, Ultimate Spanish, All Audio Spanish,* and *Spanish Without the Fuss.*

LANGUAGE PROGRAMS

A number of private schools in Spain offer Spanish-language courses of various durations for foreigners. **Don Quijote** is one network with schools in several locations around Spain. The international network **Inlingua** has 30 schools in Spain. Some Spanish universities, including Salamanca and Málaga, have longer-term Spanish programs, usually covering two months or more. In New York, the state-run **Instituto Cervantes,** devoted to promoting Spanish language and culture, teaches both in its offices worldwide and can advise you on other courses in Spain.

Language Programs **Don Quijote** ✉ C. Placentinos 2, Salamanca 37998 ☎ 923/268860. **Inlingua International** ✉ Belpstrasse 11, Berne CH-3007, Switzerland ☎ 4131/388-7777. **Instituto Cervantes** ✉ 122 E. 42nd St., Suite 807, New York, NY 10168 ☎ 212/689-4232.

LODGING

Most of Spain's private hotels are modern high-rises, though more and more innkeepers are restoring historic properties. By law, hotel prices must be posted at the reception desk and should indicate whether or not the value-added tax (IVA; 7%) is included. Breakfast is normally *not* included. Note that high-season rates prevail not only in summer but also during Holy Week and local fiestas. The lodgings we review are the cream of the crop in each price category. We always list the facilities available, but we don't specify whether they cost extra; so when pricing accommodations, always ask what's included and what's not.

APARTMENT & VILLA RENTALS

If you want a home base that's roomy enough for a family and comes with cooking facilities, **consider a furnished rental.** These can save you money, especially if you're traveling with a group. Home-exchange directories sometimes list rentals as well as exchanges.

International Agents **Hideaways International** ✉ 767 Islington St., Portsmouth, NH 03802 ☎ 603/430-4433 or 800/843-4433 🖷 603/430-4444 🌐 www.hideaways.com, membership $129. **Hometours International** ✉ 1108 Scottie La., Knoxville, TN 37919 ☎ 865/690-8484 or 866/367-4668 🌐 http://thor.he.net/~hometour/. **Interhome** ✉ 1990 N.E. 163rd St., Suite 110, North Miami Beach, FL 33162 ☎ 305/940-2299 or 800/882-6864 🖷 305/940-2911 🌐 www.interhome.us. **Villas and Apartments Abroad** ✉ 370 Lexington Ave., Suite 1401, New York, NY 10017 ☎ 212/897-5045 or 800/433-3020 🖷 212/897-5039 🌐 www.ideal-villas.com.**Villas International** ✉ 4340 Redwood Hwy., Suite D309, San Rafael, CA 94903 ☎ 415/499-9490 or 800/221-2260 🖷 415/499-9491 🌐 www.villasintl.com.

CAMPING

Camping in Spain is not a wilderness experience. The country has more than 500 campgrounds, and many have excellent facilities, including hot showers, restaurants, swimming pools, tennis courts, and even nightclubs. In summer, especially August, the best campgrounds fill with Spanish families, who move in with their entire households: pets, grandparents, even the kitchen sink and stove. You can pick up an official list of all Spanish campgrounds at the tourist office. It can be hard to find a site for independent camping outside established campgrounds. For safety reasons, you cannot camp next to roads, on riverbanks, or on the beach, nor can you set up house in urban areas, nature parks (outside designated camping areas), or within 1 km (½ mi) of any established campsite. To camp on a private farm, seek the owner's permission.

HOME EXCHANGES

If you would like to exchange your home for someone else's, **join a home-exchange organization,** which will send you its updated listings of available exchanges for a year and will include your own listing in at least one of them. It's up to you to make specific arrangements.

Exchange Clubs **Intervac U.S.** ✉ 30 Corte San Fernando, Tiburon, CA 94920 ☎ 800/756-4663 ⎙ 415/435-7440 ⊕ www.intervacus.com; $105 yearly for a listing, on-line access, and a catalog; $50 without catalog.

HOSTELS

No matter what your age, you can save on lodging costs by staying at hostels. In some 4,500 locations in more than 70 countries around the world, Hostelling International (HI), the umbrella group for a number of national youth-hostel associations, offers single-sex, dorm-style beds and, at many hostels, rooms for couples and family accommodations. Membership in any HI national hostel association, open to travelers of all ages, allows you to stay in HI-affiliated hostels at member rates; one-year membership is about $28 for adults (C$35 for a two-year minimum membership in Canada, £13.50 in the U.K., A$52 in Australia, and NZ$40 in New Zealand); hostels charge about $10–$30 per night. Members have priority if the hostel is full; they're also eligible for discounts around the world, even on rail and bus travel in some countries.

Organizations **Hostelling International–USA** ✉ 8401 Colesville Rd., Suite 600, Silver Spring, MD 20910 ☎ 301/495-1240 ⎙ 301/495-6697 ⊕ www.hiayh.org. **Hostelling International–Canada** ✉ 400-205 Catherine St., Ottawa, Ontario K2P 1C3 ☎ 613/237-7884 or 800/663-5777 ⎙ 613/237-7868 ⊕ www.hihostels.ca. **YHA England and Wales** ✉ Trevelyan House, Dimple Rd., Matlock, Derbyshire DE4 3YH, U.K. ☎ 0870/870-8808 ⎙ 0870/770-6127 ⊕ www.yha.org.uk. **YHA Australia** ✉ 422 Kent St., Sydney, NSW 2001 ☎ 02/9261-1111 ⎙ 02/9261-1969 ⊕ www.yha.com.au. **YHA New Zealand** ✉ Level 3, 193 Cashel St., Box 436, Christchurch ☎ 03/379-9970 or 0800/278-299 in NZ ⎙ 03/365-4476 ⊕ www.yha.org.nz.

HOTELS

The Spanish government classifies hotels with one to five stars. While quality is a factor, **the rating is technically only an indication of how many facilities the hotel offers.** For example, a three-star hotel may be just as comfortable as a four-star hotel but may lack a swimming pool. Similarly, Fodor's price categories ($–$$$$) indicate room rates only, so you might find a well-kept $$$ inn more charming than the famous $$$$ property down the street.

All hotel entrances are marked with a blue plaque bearing the letter H and the number of stars. The letter R (standing for *residencia*) after the letter H indicates an establishment with no meal service. The designations *fonda* (F), *pensión* (P), *casa de huéspedes* (CH), and *hostal* (Hs) indicate budget accommodations. In most cases, especially in smaller villages, rooms in such buildings will be basic but clean; in large cities, they can be downright dreary. Note that a hostal and *hostel* are not the same thing; while both are budget options, a hostal should be perceived as a less expensive hotel, though not as inexpensive as a dorm room–style hostel.

Spain's major private hotel groups include the Sol Meliá, Tryp, and Hotusa. The NH chain, which is concentrated in major cities, appeals to business travelers. Dozens of reasonably priced beachside high-rises along the various coasts cater to package tours.

There is a growing trend in Spain toward small country hotels. Estancias de España is an association of more than 40 independently owned hotels in restored palaces, monasteries, mills, and post houses, generally in rural Spain; contact them for a free directory. Similar associations serve individual regions.

Although a single room (*habitación sencilla*) is usually available, singles are often on the small side. Solo travelers might prefer to pay a bit extra for single occupancy of a double room (*habitación doble uso individual*). Make sure you request a double bed if you want one—if you don't ask, you may end up with two singles. All hotels listed have private bathrooms unless otherwise noted.

RESERVING A ROOM

Major Spanish Chains **NH Hoteles** ☎ 902/115116 🌐 www.nh-hoteles.es. **Sol Meliá** ☎ 902/144444 🌐 www.solmelia.com. **Tryp** ☎ 901/116199 🌐 www.trypnet.es.

Small Hotels **AHRA** (Andalusian Association of Rural Hotels) ✉ C. Cristo Rey 2, 23400 Úbeda, Jaén ☎ 953/755867 🌐 www.hotelesruralesandaluces.org. **Estancias de España** ✉ Menéndez Pidal 31-bajo izq., 28036 Madrid ☎ 91/345-4141 🌐 www.estancias.com. **Hosterías y Hospederías Reales** (hotels in Castile-La Mancha) ✉ Frailes 1, 13320 Villanueva de los Infantes, Ciudad Real ☎ 902/202010.

International Chains **Best Western** ☎ 800/528-1234 🌐 www.bestwestern.com. **Choice** ☎ 800/424-6423 🌐 www.choicehotels.com.**Holiday Inn** ☎ 800/465-4329 🌐 www.sixcontinentshotels.com. **Hyatt Hotels & Resorts** ☎ 800/233-1234 🌐 www.hyatt.com. **Inter-Continental** ☎ 800/327-0200 🌐 www.intercontinental.com. **Marriott** ☎ 800/228-9290 🌐 www.marriott.com. **Le Meridien** ☎ 800/543-4300 🌐 www.lemeridien-hotels.com.**Radisson** ☎ 800/333-3333 🌐 www.radisson.com. **Ritz-Carlton** ☎ 800/241-3333 🌐 www.ritzcarlton.com. **Sheraton** ☎ 800/325-3535 🌐 www.starwood.com/sheraton. **Westin Hotels & Resorts** ☎ 800/228-3000 🌐 www.starwood.com/westin.

PARADORS

The Spanish government runs more than 80 paradors—upmarket hotels in historic buildings or near significant sites. Some are in castles on a hill with sweeping views; others are in monasteries or convents filled with artistic treasures; still others are in modern buildings on choice beachfront, alpine, or pastoral property. Rates are reasonable, considering that most paradors have four- or five-star amenities; and the premises are invariably immaculate and tastefully furnished, often with antiques or reproductions. The paradors offer 35% discounts to senior citizens 60 and over, usually in May and June, though the months may vary. Those who are 30 and under also qualify for special discounted deals (with the buffet breakfast included in the price), generally from May to December. Each parador has a restaurant serving regional specialties, and you can stop in for a meal or a drink without spending the night. Breakfast, however, is an expensive buffet, so if you just want coffee and a roll, you'll do better to walk down the street to a local café. Because paradors are extremely popular with foreigners and Spaniards alike, **make reservations well in advance.**

In Spain: **Paradores de España** ✉ Central de Reservas, Requena 3, 28013 Madrid ☎ 91/516-6666 🌐 www.parador.es. In the United States: **Marketing Ahead** ✉ 433 5th Ave., New York, NY 10016 ☎ 212/686-9213 or 800/223-1356. In the United Kingdom: **Keytel International** ✉ 402 Edgeware Rd., London W2 1ED ☎ 0207/402-8182.

RURAL LODGINGS

A growing number of *casas rurales* (country houses similar to B&Bs) offer pastoral lodging either in guest rooms or in self-catering cottages. Comfort and conveniences vary widely; it's best to book this type of accommodation through one of the appropriate regional associations. Ask the local tourist office about casas rurales in your chosen area.

MAIL & SHIPPING

Spain's postal system, the *correos,* does work, but delivery times can vary widely. An airmail letter to the United States may take anywhere from four days to two weeks; delivery to other destinations is equally unpredictable. Sending your letters by priority mail ("*urgente*") ensures speedier arrival.

OVERNIGHT SERVICES

When time is of the essence, or when you're sending valuable items or documents overseas, you can use a courier (*mensajero*). The major international agencies, such as Federal Express and UPS, have representatives in Spain; the biggest Spanish courier service is Seur. MRW is another local courier that provides express delivery worldwide.

Major Services **DHL** ☎ 902/122424. **Federal Express** ☎ 900/100871. **MRW** ☎ 900/300400. **Seur** ☎ 902/101010. **UPS** ☎ 900/102410.

POSTAL RATES

Airmail letters to the United States and Canada cost €.75 up to 20 grams. Letters to the United Kingdom and other EU countries cost €.50 up to 20 grams. Letters within Spain are €.25. Postcards carry the same rates as letters. You can buy stamps at post offices and at licensed tobacco shops.

RECEIVING MAIL

Because mail delivery in Spain can often be slow and unreliable, it's best to have your mail sent to American Express. Mail can also be held at a Spanish post office; have it addressed to **Lista de Correos** (the equivalent of Poste Restante) in a town you'll be visiting. Postal addresses should include the name of the province in parentheses, e.g., Marbella (Málaga).

MONEY MATTERS

Spain is no longer a budget destination, but prices still compare slightly favorably with those elsewhere in Europe. Coffee in a bar generally costs €.75 (standing) or €.90 (seated). Beer in a bar: €.95 standing, €1 seated. Small glass of wine in a bar: around €1. Soft drink: €1–€1.40 a bottle. Ham-and-cheese sandwich: €1.80–€2.70. Two-kilometer (1-mi) taxi ride: €2.40, but the meter keeps ticking in traffic jams. Local bus or subway ride: €.85–€1.20. Movie ticket: €3–€4.80 Foreign newspaper: €2.

ATMS

You'll find ATMs in every major city in Spain, as well as most smaller cities. Any ATM you find will be part of the Cirrus and/or Plus networks. Make sure your PIN code (pronounced *peen*) is four digits, which is required in Spain. Also make sure you know the numerical equivalents of the letters, because at some banks the keyboard is reverse from the American keyboard. For example, the 1, 2, 3, 4, etc., that you find on the keyboard will be 9, 8, 7, 6, etc., in Spain.

CREDIT CARDS

Throughout this guide, the following abbreviations are used: **AE**, American Express; **DC**, Diners Club; **MC**, MasterCard; and **V**, Visa.

Reporting Lost Cards **American Express** ☎ 900/941413. **Diners Club** ☎ 901/101011. **Master Card** ☎ 900/974445. **Visa** ☎ 900/971231.

CURRENCY

On January 1, 2002, the European monetary unit, the euro (€), went into circulation in Spain and the other countries that have adopted it (Austria, Belgium, Finland, France, Germany, Greece, Ireland, Italy, Luxembourg, the Netherlands, and Portugal). Euro notes come in denominations of 5, 10, 20, 50, 100, 200, and 500; coins are worth 1 cent of a euro, 2 cents, 5 cents, 10 cents, 20 cents, 50 cents, 1 euro, and 2 euros. At press time, exchange rates were favorable for most English-speaking travelers: €1.03 to the U.S. dollar, €.64 to the pound sterling, €1.59 to the Canadian dollar, €.55 to the Australian dollar, €.47 to the New Zealand dollar, and €.10 to the South African rand.

CURRENCY EXCHANGE

For the most favorable rates, **change money through banks.** Although ATM transaction fees may be higher abroad than at home, ATM rates are excellent because they're based on wholesale rates offered only by major banks. You won't do as well at exchange booths in airports or rail and bus stations, in hotels, in restaurants, or in stores. To avoid lines at airport exchange booths, get a bit of local currency before you leave home.

Exchange Services **International Currency Express** ✉ 427 N. Camden Dr., Suite F, Beverly Hills, CA 90210 ☎ 888/278-6628 orders 📠 310/278-6410 🌐 www.foreignmoney.com. **Thomas Cook Currency Services** ☎ 800/287-7362 orders and retail locations 🌐 www.us.thomascook.com.

TRAVELER'S CHECKS

Do you need traveler's checks? Probably not. If you're going to rural areas and small towns, always go with cash; traveler's checks are best used in cities, but ATMs have become so prevalent that you're better off using them to get small amounts of cash when you need it. It's true, however, that because lost or stolen checks can usually be replaced within 24 hours, carrying traveler's checks is more of a guarantee.

PACKING

Pack light. Although baggage carts are free and plentiful in most Spanish airports, they're rare in train and bus stations.

Spaniards tend to dress up more than Americans or the British. Summer is hot nearly everywhere; visits in winter, fall, and spring call for warm clothing and, in winter, boots. It makes sense to wear casual, comfortable clothing and shoes for sightseeing, but you'll want to **dress up a bit in large cities, especially for fine restaurants and nightclubs.** American tourists are easily spotted for their sneakers—if you want to blend in, wear leather shoes. On the beach, anything goes; it's common to see females of all ages wearing only bikini bottoms, and many of the more remote beaches allow nude sunbathing. Regardless of your style, **bring a cover-up** to wear over your bathing suit when you leave the beach.

In your carry-on luggage, **pack an extra pair of eyeglasses or contact lenses and enough of any medication** you take to last a few days longer than the entire trip. You may also ask your doctor to write a spare prescription using the drug's generic name, as brand names may vary from country to country. In luggage to be checked, **never pack prescription drugs, valuables, or undeveloped film.** And don't forget to carry with you the addresses of offices that handle refunds of lost traveler's checks. Check *Fodor's How to Pack* (available at on-line retailers and bookstores everywhere) for more tips.

To avoid customs and security delays, carry medications in their original packaging. Don't pack any sharp objects in your carry-on luggage, including knives of any size or material, scissors, and corkscrews, or anything else that might arouse suspicion. To avoid having your checked luggage chosen for hand inspection, don't cram bags full. The U.S. Transportation Security Administration suggests packing shoes on top and placing personal items you don't want touched in clear plastic bags.

CHECKING LUGGAGE

You're allowed to carry aboard one bag and one personal article, such as a purse or a laptop computer. Make sure what you carry on fits under your seat or in the overhead bin. Get to the gate early, so you can board as soon as possible, before the overhead bins fill up.

Baggage allowances vary by carrier, destination, and ticket class. On international flights, you're usually allowed to check two bags weighing up to 70 pounds (32 kilograms) each, although a few airlines allow checked bags of up to 88 pounds (40 kilograms) in first class. Some international carriers don't allow more than 66 pounds (30 kilograms) per bag in business class and 44 pounds (20 kilograms) in economy. On domestic flights, the limit may be 50 pounds (23 kilograms) per bag. Most airlines won't accept bags that weigh more than 100 pounds (45 kilograms) on domestic or international flights. Check baggage restrictions with your carrier before you pack.

Airline liability for baggage is limited to $2,500 per person on flights within the United States. On international flights it amounts to $9.07 per pound or $20 per kilogram for checked baggage (roughly $640 per 70-pound bag) and $400 per passenger for unchecked baggage. You can buy additional coverage at check-in for about $10 per $1,000 of coverage, but it often excludes a rather extensive list of items, shown on your airline ticket.

Before departure, **itemize your bags' contents** and their worth, and label the bags with your name, address, and phone number. (If you use your home address, cover it so potential thieves can't see it readily.) Include a label inside each bag and **pack a copy of your itinerary.** At check-in, **make sure each bag is correctly tagged** with the destination airport's three-letter code. Because some checked bags will be opened for hand inspection, the U.S. Transportation Security Administration recommends that you leave luggage unlocked or use the plastic locks offered at check-in. TSA screeners place an inspection notice inside searched bags, which are re-sealed with a special lock.

If your bag has been searched and contents are missing or damaged, file a claim with the TSA Consumer Response Center as soon as possible. If your bags arrive damaged or fail to arrive at all, file a written report with the airline before leaving the airport.

Complaints **U.S. Transportation Security Administration Consumer Response Center** ☎ 866/289-9673 🌐 www.tsa.gov.

PASSPORTS & VISAS

When traveling internationally, **carry your passport** even if you don't need one (it's always the best form of I.D.) and **make two photocopies of the data page** (one for someone at home and another for you, carried separately from your passport). If you lose your passport, promptly call the nearest embassy or consulate and the local police.

U.S. passport applications for children under age 14 require consent from both parents or legal guardians; both parents must appear together to sign the application. If only one parent appears, he or she must submit a written statement from the other parent authorizing passport issuance for the child. A parent with sole authority must present evidence of it when applying; acceptable documentation includes the child's certified birth certificate listing only the applying parent, a court order specifically permitting this parent's travel with the child, or a death certificate for the nonapplying parent. Application forms and instructions are available on the Web site of the U.S. State Department's Bureau of Consular Affairs (www.travel.state.gov).

ENTERING SPAIN

Visitors from the United States, Australia, Canada, New Zealand, and the United Kingdom need a valid passport to enter Spain. Australians who wish to stay longer than a month also need a visa, available from the Spanish embassy in Canberra.

PASSPORT OFFICES

The best time to apply for a passport or to renew is in fall and winter. Before any trip, check your passport's expiration date, and, if necessary, renew it as soon as possible.

Australian Citizens **Passports Australia** 131-232 www.passports.gov.au.

Canadian Citizens **Passport Office** to mail in applications: 200 Promenade du Portage, Hull, Québec J8X 4B7 819/994-3500 or 800/567-6868 www.ppt.gc.ca.

New Zealand Citizens **New Zealand Passports Office** 0800/22-5050 or 04/474-8100 www.passports.govt.nz.

U.K. Citizens **U.K. Passport Service** 0870/521-0410 www.passport.gov.uk.

U.S. Citizens **National Passport Information Center** 900/225-5674 or 900/225-7778 TTY (calls are 55¢ per minute for automated service or $1.50 per minute for operator service), 888/362-8668 or 888/498-3648 TTY (calls are $5.50 each) www.travel.state.gov.

REST ROOMS

Spain has some public rest rooms, including, in larger cities, small coin-operated booths. Your best option, however, is to use the facilities in a bar or cafeteria, remembering that it's customary to order a drink in such cases. Gas stations have rest rooms, but you usually have to request the key to use them.

SAFETY

Petty crime is a huge problem in Spain's most popular tourist destinations. The most frequent offenses are pickpocketing (particularly in Madrid and Barcelona) and theft from cars (all over the country). **Never, ever leave anything valuable in a parked car,** no matter how friendly the area feels, how quickly you'll return, or how invisible the item seems once you lock it in the trunk. Thieves can spot rental cars a mile away, and they work very efficiently. In airports, laptop computers are choice prey. Except when traveling between the airport or train station and your hotel, don't wear a money belt or a waist pack, both of which peg you as a tourist. (If you do use a money belt while traveling, do not reach into it once you're in public.) Distribute your cash and any valuables (including your credit cards and passport) between a deep front pocket or an inside jacket or vest pocket. When walking the streets, particularly in large cities, carry as little cash as possible. Men should carry their wallet in the front pocket; women who need to carry purses should strap them across the front of their bodies. Another alternative is to carry money or important documents in both of your front pockets. Leave the rest of your valuables in the safe at your hotel. On the beach, in cafés and restaurants (particularly in the well-touristed areas), and in Internet centers, always keep your belongings on your lap or tied to your person in some way. Additionally, be cautious of any odd or unnecessary human contact, verbal or physical, whether it's a tap on the shoulder, someone spilling their drink at your table, and so on. Thieves often work in twos, so while one is attracting your attention, the other could be swiping your wallet.

LOCAL SCAMS

In Córdoba, beware of small groups of three teenage boys, known as jumpers, who may sneak up behind you, place an arm against your windpipe until you lose consciousness, and steal your money.

WOMEN IN SPAIN

If you carry a purse, choose one with a zipper and a thick strap that you can drape across your body; adjust the length so that the purse sits in front of you at or above hip level. (Don't wear a money belt or a waist pack.) Store only enough money in the purse to cover casual spending. Distribute the rest of your cash and any valuables between deep front pockets, inside jacket or vest pockets, and a concealed money pouch.

The traditional Spanish custom of the *piropo* (a shouted "compliment" to women walking down the street) is fast disappearing, though women traveling alone may still encounter it on occasion. The piropo is harmless, if annoying, so simply ignore it.

SENIOR-CITIZEN TRAVEL

Although there are few early-bird specials or movie discounts in Spain, senior citizens generally enjoy discounts at museums. Spanish social life encompasses all ages—it's very common to see senior citizens next to young couples or families in late-night cafés.

To qualify for age-related discounts, **mention your senior-citizen status up front** when booking hotel reservations (not when checking out) and before you're seated in restaurants (not when paying the bill). Be sure to have identification on hand. When renting a car, ask about promotional car-rental discounts, which can be cheaper than senior-citizen rates.

Educational Programs **Elderhostel** ✉ 11 Ave. de Lafayette, Boston, MA 02111-1746 ☎ 877/426-8056, 978/323-4141 international callers, 877/426-2167 TTY 📠 877/426-2166 🌐 www.elderhostel.org. **Interhostel** ✉ University of New Hampshire, 6 Garrison Ave., Durham, NH 03824 ☎ 603/862-1147 or 800/733-9753 📠 603/862-1113 🌐 www.learn.unh.edu.

SHOPPING

Spain has plenty to tempt the shopper, from simple souvenirs to high-quality regional crafts. Clothing is highly fashionable, if expensive. Shoes and leather accessories are as chic as you'll find. Many of the best buys are food items; just check customs restrictions in your home country before purchasing edibles. Spanish wines make lovely souvenirs. Spain's major department store is **El Corte Inglés,** with branches in all major cities and towns.

SMART SOUVENIRS

Spain's leather is highly esteemed for its top quality and reasonable prices. Shoe lovers, especially, are spoiled for choice in Spain, where there are many fashionable shoe stores with high-quality leather shoes at decent prices, particularly in Madrid and Barcelona. For more traditional footwear, pick up a pair of *alpargatas,* better known internationally by their French name, *espadrilles.* Originally farmers' shoes, these canvas shoes with rope soles are comfortable and cheap (you can pick up a basic pair for as little as €7), and come in many colors. Spain's Riojan wines are world-renowned—and after one sip of a pungent Riojan red, you'll understand why. You can buy Riojan wines all over Spain, though the best prices are, of course, in the region of La Rioja itself. Spain's wines are matched by its superb cured ham (*jamón serrano*). Many ham shops sell vacuum-sealed packets of sliced, cured ham, which packs easily and makes for tasty souvenirs to take home. Note, too, that every region in Spain has its souvenir specialties, from damascene (metalwork inlaid with gold or silver) from Toledo to Moderniste-inspired crafts and mementos from Barcelona.

SPORTS & THE OUTDOORS

Spain's fair weather is conducive to outdoor sports virtually year-round, though in summer you should restrict physical activity to early morning or late afternoon. Spain has more golf courses than any other country in Europe and is also kind to hikers, water-sports enthusiasts, and, believe it or not, skiers. Spain's sports federations and local tourist offices can be helpful.

GOLF

Spain's best golf courses are on the Mediterranean coast, especially the Costa del Sol. Greens fees can be on the high side (they're cheaper in summer), but many hotels linked to golf courses offer all-inclusive deals.

Real Federación Española de Golf ✉ Capitán Haya 9, 28020 Madrid ☎ 91/555-2682 🌐 www.golfspainfederacion.com.

HIKING

Spain's national parks and regional nature preserves are perfect for hiking and rock climbing. The parks' visitor centers and local outing clubs usually have plenty of information.

Federación Española de Montañismo ✉ C. Floridablanca 75, 08015 Barcelona ☎ 93/426-4267.

SKIING

Not everyone thinks of sunny Spain as a skier's destination, but it's the second most mountainous country in Europe (after Switzerland) and has an impressive 28 ski centers. The best slopes are in the Pyrenees; there's also good skiing in the Sierra Nevada, near Granada.

Federación Española de Deportes de Invierno (Spanish Winter Sports Federation) ✉ Arroyo Fresno 3A, 28035 Madrid ☎ 91/376-9930. **Recorded ski report** ☎ 91/350-2020 in Spanish.

WATER SPORTS

With 1,900 km (1,200 mi) of coastline, Spain has no shortage of water sports. Yacht harbors dot the Mediterranean coast. The coast near Tarifa, on Spain's southernmost tip, constitutes the windsurfing capital of mainland Europe, and surfing is good on the northern coast and, especially, the shores of the Canary Islands. Spain's best dive sites are Granada province and the Cabo de Gata (near Almería); regional tourist offices can direct you to the local diving clubs.

Federación de Actividades Subacuáticas (Underwater Activities Federation) ✉ Santaló 15, 08021 Barcelona ☎ 93/200-6769. **Real Federación Española de Vela** (Royal Spanish Sailing Federation) ✉ Luís de Salazar 9, 28002 Madrid ☎ 91/519-5008 🌐 www.rfev.es.

STUDENTS IN SPAIN

Students can often get discounts on admission to museums and other sights. Remember to bring your valid student ID with you.

I.D.s & Services **STA Travel** ✉ 10 Downing St., New York, NY 10014 ☎ 212/627-3111 or 800/777-0112 🖷 212/627-3387 🌐 www.sta.com. **Travel Cuts** ✉ 187 College St., Toronto, Ontario M5T 1P7, Canada ☎ 416/979-2406, 800/592-2887, 866/246-9762 in Canada 🖷 416/979-8167 🌐 www.travelcuts.com.

TAXES

VALUE-ADDED TAX

Value-added tax, similar to sales tax, is called IVA in Spain (pronounced "*ee*-vah"; for *impuesto sobre el valor añadido*). It is levied on both products and services, such as hotel rooms and restaurant meals. When in doubt about whether tax is included, ask, "*Está incluido el IVA*"?

The IVA rate for hotels and restaurants is 7%, regardless of their number of stars or forks. A special tax law for the Canary Islands allows hotels and restaurants there to charge 4% IVA. Menus will generally say at the bottom whether tax is included (*IVA incluido*) or not (*más 7% IVA*).

Whereas food, pharmaceuticals, and household items are taxed at the lowest rate, most consumer goods are taxed at 16%. A number of shops, particularly large stores and boutiques in holiday resorts, participate in Global Refund (formerly Europe Tax-Free Shopping), a VAT refund service that makes getting your money back relatively hassle-free. On purchases of more than €90, you're entitled to a refund of the 16% tax. **Ask for the Global Refund form** (called a Shopping Cheque) in participating stores. You show your passport and fill out the form; the vendor then mails you the refund, or—often more convenient—you **present your original receipt to the VAT office at the airport** when you leave Spain. (In both Madrid and Barcelona, the office is near the duty-free shops. Save time for this process, as lines can be long.) Customs signs the original and refunds your money on the spot in cash (euros) or sends it to the central office to process a credit-card refund. Credit-card refunds take a few weeks.

V.A.T. Refunds **Global Refund** ✉ 99 Main St., Suite 307, Nyack, NY 10960 ☎ 800/566-9828 🖷 845/348-1549 🌐 www.globalrefund.com.

TELEPHONES

Spain's phone system is perfectly efficient. Direct dialing is the norm. The main operator is Telefónica. Note that only cell phones conforming to the European GSM standard will work in Spain.

AREA & COUNTRY CODES

The country code for Spain is 34. Phoning home: country codes are 1 for the United States and Canada, 44 for the United Kingdom, 61 for Australia, and 64 for New Zealand.

DIRECTORY & OPERATOR ASSISTANCE

For general information in Spain, dial 1003. International operators, who generally speak English, are at 025.

INTERNATIONAL CALLS

International calls are awkward from coin-operated pay phones because of the many coins needed; and they can be expensive from hotels, as the hotel often adds a hefty surcharge. Your best bet is to use a public phone that accepts phone cards (⇨ Phone Cards, *below*) or go to the local telephone office, the *locutorio:* every town has one, and major cities have several. The locutorios near the center of town are generally more expensive; farther from the center, the rates are sometimes as much as one-third less. You converse in a quiet, private booth, and you're charged according to the meter. If the call ends up costing around €3 or more, you can usually pay with Visa or MasterCard.

To make an international call yourself, dial 00, then the country code, then the area code and number.

Madrid's main telephone office is at Gran Vía 28. There's another at the main post office, and a third at Paseo Recoletos 43, just off Plaza Colón. In Barcelona you can phone overseas from the office at Carrer de Fontanella 4, off Plaça de Catalunya.

Before you leave home, **find out your long-distance company's access code in Spain.**

LOCAL & LONG-DISTANCE CALLS

All area codes begin with a 9. To call within Spain—even locally—dial the area code first. Numbers preceded by a 900 code are toll-free; those starting with a 6 are going to a cellular phone. Note that calls to cell phones are significantly more expensive than calls to regular phones.

LONG-DISTANCE SERVICES

AT&T, MCI, and Sprint access codes make calling long-distance relatively convenient, but you may find the local access number blocked in many hotel rooms. First ask the hotel operator to connect you. If the hotel operator balks, ask for an international operator, or dial the international operator yourself. One way to improve your odds of getting connected to your long-distance carrier is to travel with more than one company's calling card (a hotel may block Sprint, for example, but not MCI). If all else fails, call from a pay phone.

General Information **AT&T ☎ 800/222-0300. MCI WorldCom ☎ 800/444-4444. Sprint ☎ 800/793-1153.**

Access Codes **AT&T ☎ 900/990011. MCI ☎ 900/990014. Sprint ☎ 900/990013.**

PHONE CARDS

To use a newer pay phone you need a special phone card (*tarjeta telefónica*), which you can buy at any tobacco shop or newsstand, in various denominations. Some such phones also accept credit cards, but phone cards are more reliable.

PUBLIC PHONES

You'll find pay phones in individual booths, in special telephone offices (*locutorios*), and in many bars and restaurants. Most have a digital readout so you can see your money ticking away. If you're calling with coins, you need at least €.15 to call locally, €.45 to call another province. Simply insert the coins and wait for a dial tone. (With older models, you line coins up in a groove on top of the dial and they drop down as needed.) Note that rates are reduced on the weekends and after 8 PM Monday–Friday.

TIME

Spain is on Central European Time, one hour ahead of Greenwich Mean Time, six hours ahead of Eastern Standard Time. Like the rest of the European Union, Spain switches to daylight saving time on the last weekend in March and switches back on the last weekend in October.

TIPPING

Service staff expect to be tipped, and you can be sure that your contribution will be appreciated. On the other hand, if you experience bad or surly service, don't feel obligated to leave a tip.

Restaurant checks do not list a service charge on the bill, but consider the tip included. If you want to leave a small tip in addition to the bill, **do not tip more than 10% of the bill,** and leave less if you eat tapas or sandwiches at a bar—just enough to round out the bill to the nearest €1. Tip cocktail servers €.30–€.50 a drink, depending on the bar.

Tip taxi drivers about 10% of the total fare, plus a supplement for a long ride or extra help with luggage. Note that rides from airports carry an official surcharge plus a small handling fee for each piece of luggage.

Tip hotel porters €.50 a bag, and the bearer of room service €.50. A doorman who calls a taxi for you gets €.50. If you stay in a hotel for more than two nights, tip the maid about €.50 per night. The concierge should receive a tip for any additional help he or she provides.

Tour guides should be tipped about €2, ushers in theaters or at bullfights €.15–€.20, barbers €.50, and women's hairdressers at least €1 for a wash and style. Rest-room attendants are tipped €.15.

TOURS & PACKAGES

Because everything is prearranged on a prepackaged tour or independent vacation, you spend less time planning—and often get it all at a good price.

BOOKING WITH AN AGENT

Travel agents are excellent resources. But it's a good idea to collect brochures from several agencies, as some agents' suggestions may be influenced by relationships with tour and package firms that reward them for volume sales. If you have a special interest, **find an agent with expertise in that area**; the American Society of Travel Agents (ASTA) has a database of specialists worldwide.

Make sure your travel agent knows the accommodations and other services of the place being recommended. Ask about the hotel's location, room size, beds, and whether it has a pool, room service, or programs for children, if you care about these. Has your agent been there in person or sent others whom you can contact?

Do some homework on your own, too: local tourism boards can provide information about lesser-known and small-niche operators, some of which may sell only direct.

BUYER BEWARE

Each year consumers are stranded or lose their money when tour operators—even large ones with excellent reputations—go out of business. So **check out the operator.** Ask several travel agents about its reputation, and try to **book with a company that has a consumer-protection program.** (Look for information in the company's brochure.) In the United States, members of the National Tour Association and the United States Tour Operators Association are required to set aside funds to cover payments and travel arrangements in the event that the company defaults. It's also a good idea to choose a company that participates in the American Society of Travel Agents' Tour Operator Program; ASTA will act as mediator in any disputes between you and your tour operator.

Remember that the more your package or tour includes, the better you can predict the ultimate cost of your vacation. Make sure you know exactly what is covered, and **beware of hidden costs.** Are taxes, tips, and transfers included? Entertainment and excursions? These can add up.

Tour-Operator Recommendations **American Society of Travel Agents** (⇨ Travel Agencies). **National Tour Association** (NTA) ✉ 546 E. Main St., Lexington, KY 40508 ☎ 859/226-4444 or 800/682-8886 📠 859/226-4404 🌐 www.ntaonline.com. **United States Tour Operators Association** (USTOA) ✉ 275 Madison Ave., Suite 2014, New York, NY 10016 ☎ 212/599-6599 or 800/468-7862 📠 212/599-6744 🌐 www.ustoa.com.

TRAIN TRAVEL

International overnight trains run from Madrid to Lisbon and from Barcelona to Paris (both 11½ hours). A daytime train runs from Barcelona to Grenoble and Geneva (10 hours).

Spain's wonderful high-speed train, the 290-kph (180-mph) AVE, travels between Madrid and Seville (with a stop in Córdoba) in less than three hours at prices starting around €62 each way. The fast Talgo service is also efficient. However, the rest of the state-run rail system—known as RENFE—remains below par by European standards. Local train travel can be tediously slow, and most long-distance trips run at night. Although overnight trains have comfortable sleeper cars, first-class fares that include a sleeping compartment are comparable to airfares.

If you purchase a round-trip ticket on AVE or any of RENFE's Grandes Lineas, which are its faster, long-distance trains (including the Talgo) while in Spain, you'll get a 20% discount. You have up to 60 days to use the return portion of your ticket. If you buy a same-day round-trip ticket on the AVE, a 25% discount applies. On regional trains, you receive a 10% discount on round-trip tickets, and you have up to 15 days to use the return portion. Note that even if you just buy a one-way ticket to your destination, you can still receive the round-trip discount if you present your ticket stub at the train station when buying your return (provided your return is within the allotted time frame, either 15 or 60 days.)

For routes with convenient schedules, trains are the most economical way to go.

First- and second-class seats are reasonably priced, and you can get a bunk in a compartment with five other people for a supplement of about €27.

You can buy train tickets in advance at the train station, which is what most Spaniards do. The lines can be long, so give yourself plenty of time if you plan on buying same-day tickets. For popular train routes, you will need to reserve tickets more than a few days in advance; call RENFE to inquire. The ticket clerks at the stations rarely speak English, so if you need need help or advice in planning a more complex train journey you may be better off going to a travel agency that displays the blue-and-yellow RENFE sign. The price is the same. For shorter, regional train trips, you can often buy your tickets directly from machines in the main train stations. Note that if your itinerary is set in stone and has little room for error, you can buy RENFE tickets through Rail Europe before you leave home.

Commuter trains and most long-distance trains forbid smoking, though some long-distance trains have smoking cars.

CUTTING COSTS

If you're coming from the United States or Canada and are planning extensive train travel, **check Rail Europe for rail passes.** If Spain is your only destination, consider a **Spain Flexipass.** Prices begin at $155 for three days of second-class travel within a two-month period and $200 for first class. Other passes cover more days and longer periods. The **Iberic Saverpass,** which offers a discount for two or more people traveling together in Spain and Portugal, starts at $200. The **Spain 'n France Pass** starts at $252 for four days of second-class travel within a two-month period and $292 for first class.

Spain is one of 17 European countries in which you can use the Eurailpass, which buys you unlimited first-class rail travel in all participating countries for the duration of the pass. If you plan to rack up the miles, get a standard pass. These are available for 15 days ($572), 21 days ($740), one month ($918), two months ($1,298), and three months ($1,606). If your needs are more limited, look into a Europass, which costs less than a Eurailpass and buys you a limited number of travel days, in a limited number of countries (France, Germany, Italy, Spain, and Switzerland), during a specified time period.

In addition to the Eurailpass and Europass, Rail Europe sells the Eurail Youthpass (you must be younger than age 26), the Eurail Saverpass (discount for two or more persons traveling together), a Eurail Flexipass (a certain number of travel days within a set period), the Euraildrive Pass (four days of rail plus two days of car rentals), and the Eurail Selectpass Drive (three days of rail plus two days of car rentals). Whichever you choose, remember that you must **buy your pass before you leave** for Europe.

Many travelers assume that rail passes guarantee them seats on the trains they wish to ride: not so. You need to **reserve seats in advance** even if you're using a rail pass. Seat reservations are required on some trains, particularly high-speed trains, and are wise on any train that might be crowded. You'll also need a reservation if you want a sleeping berth.

FARES & SCHEDULES

Train Information **RENFE** ☎ 902/240202 www.renfe.es.
Rail Passes **CIT Tours Corp.** ☎ 800/248-8687 www.cit-tours.com. **DER Tours** ☎ 800/782-2424. **Rail Europe** ☎ 877/456-7245 or 800/361-7245 www.raileurope.com.

FROM THE U.K.

Train services to Spain from the United Kingdom are not as frequent, fast, or affordable as flights, and you have to change trains—and stations—in Paris. Allow 2 hours for the changing process, then 13 hours for the trip from Paris to Madrid. It's worth paying extra for the Talgo express or Puerta del Sol express to avoid changing trains again at the Spanish border. If you're under 26 years old, Eurotrain has excellent deals.

Eurotrain ✉ 52 Grosvenor Gardens, London SW1W OAG, U.K. ☎ 0207/730-8832. **Transalpino** ✉ 71-75 Buckingham Palace Rd., London SW1W ORE, U.K. ☎ 0207/834-9656.

TRANSPORTATION AROUND SPAIN

After France, Spain is the largest country in Western Europe, so seeing any more than a fraction of the country involves considerable domestic travel. If you want the freedom of straying from your fixed itinerary to follow whims as they come, driving is the best choice. The roads are generally fine, although traffic can be heavy on major routes, trucks can clog minor routes, and parking is a problem in cities.

Spain is well served by domestic flights, though of course these cost more than ground options. Train service between the largest cities is fast, efficient, and punctual, but trains on secondary regional routes can be slow and involve frequent changes of train (⇨ Train Travel). In such cases, buses are far more convenient (⇨ Bus Travel).

TRAVEL AGENCIES

A good travel agent puts your needs first. Look for an agency that has been in business at least five years, emphasizes customer service, and has someone on staff who specializes in your destination. In addition, **make sure the agency belongs to a professional trade organization.** The American Society of Travel Agents (ASTA)—the largest and most influential in the field with more than 20,000 members in some 140 countries—maintains and enforces a strict code of ethics and will step in to help mediate any agent-client disputes involving ASTA members if necessary. ASTA (whose motto is "Without a travel agent, you're on your own") also maintains a Web site that includes a directory of agents. (If a travel agency is also acting as your tour operator, *see* Buyer Beware *in* Tours and Packages.)

Local Agent Referrals **American Society of Travel Agents** (ASTA) ✉ 1101 King St., Suite 200, Alexandria, VA 22314 ☎ 703/739-2782 or 800/965-2782 24-hr hot line 📠 703/739-3268 ⊕ www.astanet.com. **Association of British Travel Agents** ✉ 68-71 Newman St., London W1T 3AH ☎ 020/7637-2444 📠 020/7637-0713 ⊕ www.abtanet.com. **Association of Canadian Travel Agents** ✉ 130 Albert St., Suite 1705, Ottawa, Ontario K1P 5G4 ☎ 613/237-3657 📠 613/237-7052 ⊕ www.acta.ca. **Australian Federation of Travel Agents** ✉ Level 3, 309 Pitt St., Sydney, NSW 2000 ☎ 02/9264-3299 📠 02/9264-1085 ⊕ www.afta.com.au. **Travel Agents' Association of New Zealand** ✉ Level 5, Tourism and Travel House, 79 Boulcott St., Box 1888, Wellington 6001 ☎ 04/499-0104 📠 04/499-0786 ⊕ www.taanz.org.nz.

VISITOR INFORMATION

Before you go, consult the Tourist Office of Spain in your home country or on the World Wide Web. The site ⊕ www.okspain.org provides a basic introduction; the Spain-based ⊕ www.tourspain.es is more sophisticated.

Tourist Offices **Chicago** ✉ Water Tower Pl., 845 N. Michigan Ave., Suite 915-East, Chicago, IL 60611 ☎ 312/642-1992. **Los Angeles** ✉ 8383 Wilshire Blvd., Suite 960, Beverly Hills, CA 90211 ☎ 213/658-7188. **Miami** ✉ 1221 Brickell Ave., Suite 1850, Miami, FL 33131 ☎ 305/358-1992. **New York** ✉ 666 5th Ave., 35th floor, New York, NY 10103 ☎ 212/265-8822. **Canada** ✉ 2 Bloor St. W, Suite 3402, Toronto, Ontario M4W 3E2 ☎ 416/961-3131. **United Kingdom** ✉ 22-23 Manchester Sq., London W1M 5AP, U.K. ☎ 0207/486-8077.

Government Advisories **U.S. Department of State** ✉ Overseas Citizens Services Office, Room 4811, 2201 C St. NW, Washington, DC 20520 ☎ 202/647-5225 interactive hot line or 888/407-4747 ⊕ www.travel.state.gov; enclose a cover letter with your request and a business-size SASE. **Consular Affairs Bureau of Canada** ☎ 800/267-6788 or 613/944-6788 ⊕ www.voyage.gc.ca. **U.K. Foreign and Commonwealth Office** ✉ Travel Advice Unit, Consular Division, Old Admiralty Building, London SW1A 2PA ☎ 020/7008-0232 or 020/7008-0233 ⊕ www.fco.gov.uk/travel. **Australian Department of Foreign Affairs and Trade** ☎ 02/6261-1299 Consular Travel Advice Faxback Service ⊕ www.dfat.gov.au. **New Zealand Ministry of Foreign Affairs and Trade** ☎ 04/439-8000 ⊕ www.mft.govt.nz.

WEB SITES

Do check out the World Wide Web when planning your trip. You'll find everything from weather forecasts to virtual tours of famous cities. Be sure to **visit Fodors.com** (⊕ www.fodors.com), a complete travel-planning site. You can research prices and book plane tickets, hotel rooms, rental cars, vacation packages, and more. In addition, you can post your pressing questions in the Travel Talk section. Other planning tools include a currency converter and weather reports, and there are loads of links to travel resources.

For more information on Spain, visit the Tourist Office of Spain at ⊕ www.tourspain.es and see ⊕ www.okspain.es, ⊕ www.cyberspain.com, or ⊕ www.red2000.com/spain. For a virtual brochure on Spain's paradors, go to ⊕ www.parador.es.

MADRID

1

FODOR'S CHOICE

AC Santo Mauro hotel, Chamberí
Botín restaurant, Centro
Casa Ciriaco restaurant, Centro
Centro de Arte Reina Sofía, Atocha
El Chaflán restaurant, Chamartín
Hotel Intur Palacio San Martín, Centro
La Broche restaurant, Chamberí
La Trucha restaurant, Santa Ana
Orfila hotel, Chamberí
Prado Museum, Retiro
Royal Palace, Centro
Thyssen-Bornemisza Museum
Zalacaín restaurant, Chamartín

HIGHLY RECOMMENDED

RESTAURANTS
Casa Paco, Centro
El Bocaíto tapas bar, Madrid
El Cenador del Prado, Retiro
La Gamella, Retiro
La Terraza—Casino de Madrid, Sol
Taberna Bilbao, La Latina
Viuda de Vacas, La Latina

HOTELS
Hostal Villar, Santa Ana
Tryp Ambassador, Opera
Villa Real, Prado
Westin Palace, Prado

SIGHTS
Cava Baja, La Latina

Revised by George Semler
Updated by Ignacio Gómez

SWASHBUCKLING MADRID CELEBRATES itself and life in general around the clock. After spending much of the 20th century sequestered at the center of a totalitarian regime, Madrid has burst back onto the world stage with an energy redolent of its 16th-century golden age, when painters and playwrights swarmed to the flame of Spain's brilliant royal court. A vibrant crossroads for Iberia and the world's Hispanic peoples and cultures, the Spanish capital has an infectious appetite for art, music, and epicurean pleasure.

After the first gulp of icy mountain air, the next thing likely to strike you is the vast, cerulean, cumulus-clouded sky immortalized in the paintings of Velázquez. "*De Madrid al cielo*" ("from Madrid to heaven") goes the saying, and the heavens seem just overhead at the center of the 2,120-ft-high Castilian plateau. "High, wide, and handsome" might aptly describe this sprawling conglomeration of ancient red-tile rooftops punctuated by redbrick Mudéjar churches and gray-slate roofs and spires left by the 16th-century Habsburg monarchs who made Madrid the capital of Spain in 1561.

Then there are the paintings, the artistic legacy of one of the greatest global empires ever assembled. King Carlos I (1500–58), who later became emperor Carlos V, inherited most of Europe between 1516–1519, and amassed art from all corners of his empire—which is how the early masters of the Flemish, Dutch, Italian, French, German, and Spanish schools found their way to Spain's palaces. The collection was eventually placed in the Prado Museum, part of the grand Madrid built in the 18th century by the Bourbon king Carlos III—known as the Rey-Alcalde, or King-Mayor, for his preoccupation with municipal (rather than global) projects such as the Royal Palace, the Parque del Retiro, and the Paseo del Prado. Among the Prado, the contemporary Reina Sofía museum, the eclectic yet comprehensive Thyssen-Bornemisza collection, and Madrid's smaller artistic repositories—the Real Academia de Bellas Artes de San Fernando, the Convento de las Descalzas Reales, the Sorolla Museum, the Lázaro Galdiano Museum, and still others—there are more paintings in Madrid than anyone can reasonably hope to contemplate in a lifetime.

Modern-day Madrid spreads eastward into the 19th-century grid of the Barrio de Salamanca and sprawls northward through the neighborhoods of Chamberí and Chamartín. But the Madrid to explore carefully on foot is right in the center: the oldest one, between the Royal Palace and Madrid's midtown forest, the Parque del Buen Retiro. These neighborhoods will introduce you to the city's finest resources—its people and their electricity, whether at play in bars or at work in finance or the media and film industries, all in what Madrid's Oscar Wilde, Ramón Gomez de la Serna, called "*la rompeolas de las Españas,*" the breakwater of Spain's many peoples and cultures.

As the highest capital in Europe, Madrid is hot in summer and freezing in winter, with temperate springs and autumns. Especially in winter—when steamy café windows beckon you inside for a hot *caldo* (broth) and the blue skies are particularly bright—Madrid *is* the next best place to heaven. Moreover, it's ideally placed for cherished getaways to dozens of Castilian hamlets and to Toledo, Segovia, and El Escorial.

About the Restaurants

Madrid has attracted generations of courtiers, diplomats, and tradesmen, all of whom have brought tastes and styles from other parts of the Iberian peninsula and the world. The city's best restaurants have traditionally specialized in Basque cooking, though contemporary Mediter-

If you have **2 days**

On the first morning, see the masterworks in the Museo del Prado and tour the Paseo del Prado between Atocha train station and Plaza Colón, past the fountains at Fuente de Neptuno and the Plaza de la Cibeles. Have lunch in or near Plaza Santa Ana. Then cut through the Puerta del Sol to see Madrid's Times Square on your way to the Plaza Mayor. Cut behind the glass-and-iron Mercado de San Miguel and through tiny Calle Puñonrostro to Plaza de la Villa on your way to the church of San Nícolas de las Servitas and then the Plaza de Oriente, where you can tour the Palacio Real and the Teatro Real. If it's summer, take in the sunset from a terrace table at El Ventorrillo at the south end of Calle Bailén's Viaducto. Later, visit the tapas bars along Cava de San Miguel.

On day two, see Picasso's *Guernica* and other works at the Centro de Arte Reina Sofía. Have lunch on Cava Baja, in La Latina. Explore the Museo Thyssen-Bornemisza for an overview of Western art, and take a sunset stroll in the Parque del Buen Retiro before dinner.

If you have **4 days**

Follow the itinerary above, then on day three, taxi or hike up the Paseo de la Castellana to the Museo Sorolla and the Museo Lázaro Galdiano (closed until early 2004). Take in the 16th-century Convento de las Descalzas Reales and the Convento de la Encarnación on the fourth day.

---

ranean interpretations from Catalonia and even Asian fusion restaurants have begun to rock the city's culinary canons. Madrid's many seafood specialists capitalize on the abundant fresh produce trucked in nightly from the Atlantic and the Mediterranean coasts.

Madrid's own cuisine is based on the roasts and thick soups and stews of Castile, Spain's high central *meseta* (plain). Roast suckling pig and lamb are standard Madrid feasts, as are baby goat and chunks of beef from Ávila. *Cocido madrileño* and *callos a la madrileña* are local specialties. Cocido is a hearty winter meal of broth, garbanzo beans, vegetables, potatoes, sausages, pork, and hen. The best cocidos are simmered in earthenware crocks over coals and served in three courses: broth, beans, and meat. Cocido anchors the midday winter menu in the most elegant restaurants as well as the humblest holes-in-the-wall. Callos are a simpler concoction of veal tripe stewed with tomatoes, onions, hot paprika, and garlic. *Jamón serrano* (cured ham)—a specialty from the livestock lands of Teruel, Extremadura, and Andalusia—has become a Madrid staple; wanderers are likely to come across a *museo del jamón* (literally, ham museum), where legs of the dried delicacy dangle in store windows or in bars. For top-quality free-range, acorn-fed, native Iberian ham ask for *jamón ibérico de bellota*. For faster dining, try *bocadillo de tortilla* (potato omelet sandwich) or a *cazuelita* (small earthenware bowl) of anything from wild mushrooms to *riñones al jerez* (lamb or veal kidneys stewed in sherry).

The house wine in basic Madrid restaurants is often a sturdy, uncomplicated Valdepeñas from La Mancha. Serious dining is normally accompanied by a Rioja or a more powerful, complex Ribera de Duero, the latter from northern Castile. Ask your waiter's advice; a smooth Rioja, for example, may not be up to the task of accompanying a cocido or a roast suckling pig. After dinner, try the anise-flavor liqueur (*anís*) produced outside the nearby village of Chinchón.

WHAT IT COSTS In Euros					
	$$$$	$$$	$$	$	¢
AT DINNER	over €25	€18–€25	€12–€18	€8–€12	under €8

Prices are for per person for a main course at dinner.

About the Hotels

Try bargaining at the pricier properties: weekend discounts of up to 30% are widely available. You can also find *hostal* rooms, often on the upper floors of apartment buildings with shared or private baths, for €30 or less. Because these cheap lodgings are often full and don't take reservations, only a few are listed here—you simply have to try your luck door-to-door. Many are in the old city between the Prado and the Puerta del Sol; start your quest around Plaza Santa Ana.

WHAT IT COSTS In Euros					
	$$$$	$$$	$$	$	¢
FOR 2 PEOPLE	over €225	€150–€225	€80–€150	€50–€80	under €50

Prices are for two people in a standard double room in high season, excluding tax.

EXPLORING MADRID

The real Madrid is not to be found along its major arteries such as Gran Vía and the Paseo de la Castellana. To find the quiet, intimate streets and squares that give the city its true character, duck into the warren of villagelike byways in the downtown area 2½ km (1½ mi square) extending from the Royal Palace to the Parque del Retiro and from Plaza de Lavapiés to the Glorieta de Bilbao. Broad *avenidas,* twisting medieval alleys, grand museums, stately gardens, and tiny, tile taverns are all jumbled together, creating an urban texture so rich that walking is really the only way to soak it in. Sadly, petty street crime has become a serious problem in Madrid, and tourists are frequent targets. Be on your guard, and try to blend in: keep cameras concealed, avoid flamboyant map reading, and secure bags and purses. The Japanese embassy has complained to Madrid authorities that tourists who appear East Asian seem to be at particular risk.

Numbers in the text correspond to numbers in the margin and on the Madrid, Side Trips from Madrid, and El Escorial maps.

Old Madrid

The narrow streets of old Madrid wind back through the city's history to its beginnings as an Arab fortress. Madrid's historic quarters are not so readily apparent as the ancient neighborhoods of Toledo and Segovia, nor are they so grand, but make time to explore their quiet, winding alleys.

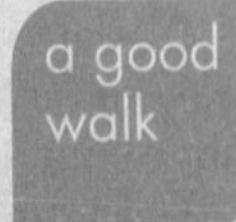

Start in the **Plaza Mayor** ① ⚑. Looking up at the playfully erotic mural on the Casa de la Panadería (Bakery House, named for its former role as Madrid's medieval bread dispensary), exit under the arch to the far left and walk down Ciudad Rodrigo; then turn left. Across the street is the restored San Miguel market; down Cava de San Miguel (under Plaza Mayor), on both sides of the street, you'll find plenty of rustic, if

Art Museums Madrid's greatest daytime attractions are its three world-class art museums, the Prado, the Reina Sofía, and the Thyssen-Bornemisza, all within 1 km (½ mi) of each other along the leafy Paseo del Prado, sometimes called the Paseo del Arte. The Prado has the world's foremost collections of Goya, El Greco, and Velázquez, topping off hundreds of other 14th- to 19th-century masterpieces. The Reina Sofía focuses on modern art, especially Dalí, Miró, and Picasso, whose famous *Guernica* hangs here; it also shows contemporary Spanish artists, such as Jorge Oteiza, Eduardo Chillida, Antoni Tàpies, and Antonio Lopez, as well as postmodern temporary exhibits. The Thyssen-Bornemisza encompasses the entire history of Western art, with collections of impressionist and German expressionist works.

Madrid's lesser-known museums are especially intimate and rewarding. The collections in the Convento de Las Descalzas Reales and the Real Academia de Bellas Artes de San Fernando are superb. The Museo Sorolla displays the paintings of Spain's foremost impressionist painter, Joaquín Sorolla (1863–1923), in his former home, and the Museo Lázaro Galdiano, a 10-minute walk across the Castellana, has a collection of decorative items and paintings by Goya, Zurbarán, Ribera, Murillo, El Greco, and Hieronymus Bosch's superb *San Juan Bautista*.

Bullfighting Bullfighting is an artistic spectacle, not to be confused with sport. For those not squeamish about the sight of six dying bulls every Sunday afternoon from April to early November, it offers all the excitement of a major stadium event. Nowhere in the world is bullfighting better than at Madrid's Las Ventas on Calle Alcalá in Salamanca. The sophisticated audience follows taurine matters closely, and the uninitiated might be baffled by their reactions: cheers and hoots can be hard to distinguish, and it can take years to understand what prompts the wrath of such a hard-to-please crowd. Tickets can be purchased at the ring or, for a 20% surcharge, at one of the agencies on Calle Victoria, just off the Puerta del Sol. Most *corridas* start in late afternoon, and the best fights of all—the world's top displays of bullfighting—come during the three weeks of consecutive daily events that mark the feast of San Isidro, in May. Tickets can be tough to get through normal channels, but are always available from scalpers on Calle Victoria and at the stadium. You can bargain, but even Spaniards pay prices of perhaps 10 times the face value—up to €120 or more.

Music Madrid's musical offerings range from Bach organ recitals in the Catedral de la Almudena to flamenco performances with dinner at Casa Patas. In between there are world-class groups playing in intimate chapels, churches and convents, the Auditorio Nacional, the Teatro Real opera house, the auditorium at the Academia Real de Bellas Artes de San Fernando, and other venues. Ongoing is a classical series organized by the Juan March Foundation. Architecture is never better appreciated than when set to music; check listings for musical events held in spaces you wouldn't otherwise be able to glimpse (old churches, palatial homes).

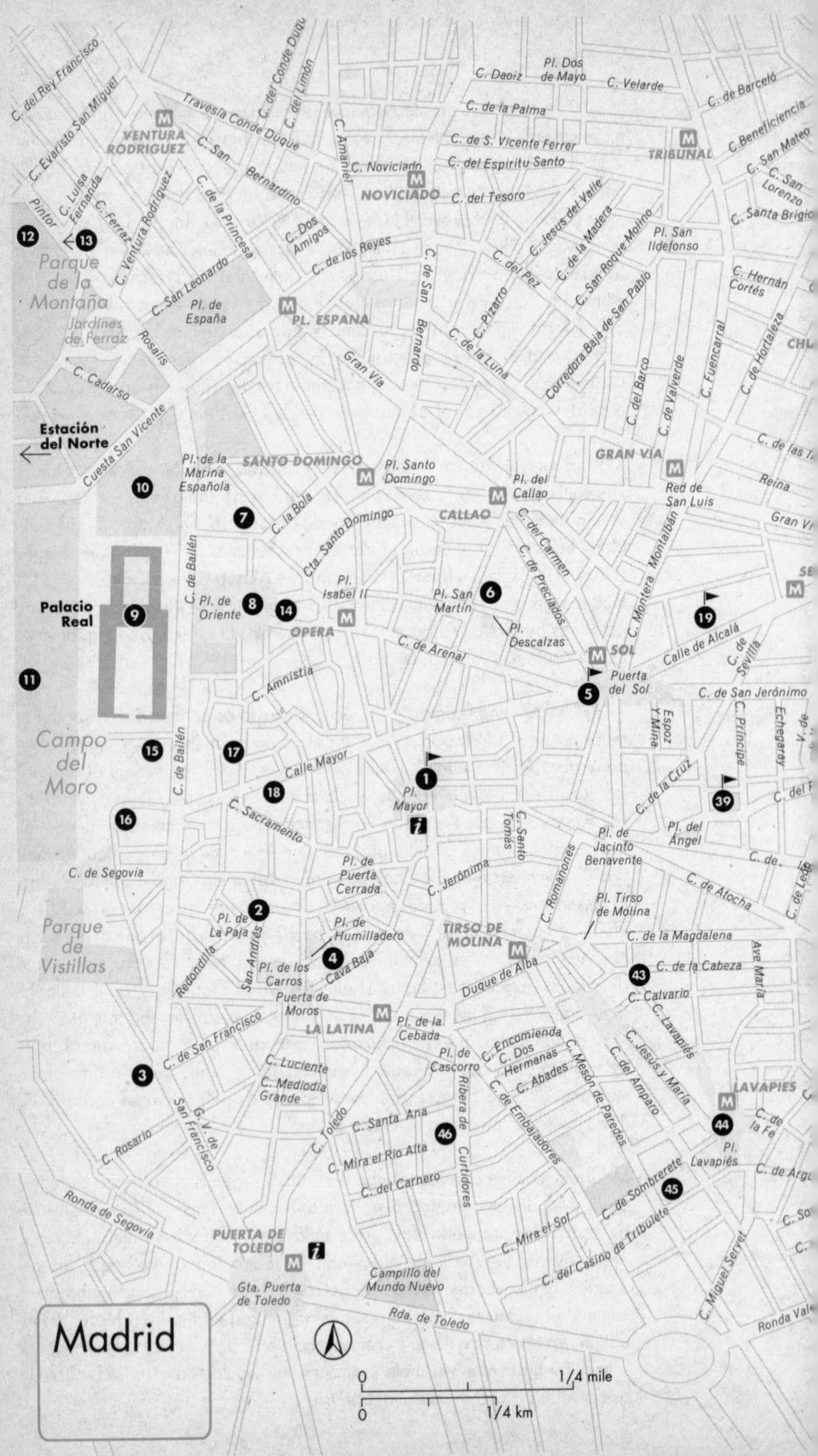
Madrid
C. del Rey Francisco
C. Evaristo San Miguel
Pintor
C. Luisa Fernanda
C. Ferraz
C. Ventura Rodríguez
VENTURA RODRIGUEZ
Travesía Conde Duque
C. San Bernardino
C. de la Princesa
C. del Conde Duque
C. del Limón
C. Amaniel
C. Noviciado
NOVICIADO
C. Dos Amigos
C. de los Reyes
C. San Leonardo
Pl. de España
PL. ESPAÑA
Parque de la Montaña
Jardines de Ferraz
Rosalís
C. Cadarso
Estación del Norte
Cuesta San Vicente
C. Daoiz
Pl. Dos de Mayo
C. Velarde
C. de la Palma
C. de S. Vicente Ferrer
C. del Espíritu Santo
C. del Tesoro
TRIBUNAL
C. de Barceló
C. Beneficiencia
C. San Mateo
C. San Lorenzo
C. Santa Brígida
C. Jesús del Valle
C. de la Madera
C. San Roque Molino
Pl. San Ildefonso
C. Hernán Cortés
C. del Pez
C. Pizarro
C. de San Bernardo
C. de la Luna
Corredora Baja de San Pablo
C. del Barco
C. de Valverde
C. Fuencarral
C. de Hortaleza
Gran Vía
GRAN VIA
C. de las I
Reina
Red de San Luis
Gran Vi
Pl. de la Marina Española
SANTO DOMINGO
Pl. Santo Domingo
Pl. del Callao
CALLAO
C. la Bola
Cta. Santo Domingo
C. del Carmen
C. de Preciados
C. Montera
Montalbán
C. de Bailén
Palacio Real
Pl. de Oriente
Pl. Isabel II
OPERA
Pl. San Martín
Pl. Descalzas
C. de Arenal
SOL
Puerta del Sol
Calle de Alcalá
C. de Sevilla
C. de San Jerónimo
C. Amnistía
Campo del Moro
Calle Mayor
Pl. Mayor
Espoz Y Mina
C. Príncipe
Echegaray
C. de la Cruz
C. Sacramento
C. Santo Tomás
Pl. de Jacinto Benavente
Pl. del Ángel
C. de Segovia
Pl. de Puerta Cerrada
C. Jerónima
C. Romanones
C. de Atocha
Pl. Tirso de Molina
Pl. de La Paja
Pl. de Humilladero
TIRSO DE MOLINA
C. de la Magdalena
Parque de Vistillas
Redondilla
San Andrés
Pl. de los Carros
Cava Baja
Duque de Alba
C. de la Cabeza
Ave María
C. Calvario
C. Lavapiés
Puerta de Moros
LA LATINA
Pl. de la Cebada
C. de San Francisco
C. Luciente
C. Mediodía Grande
Pl. de Cascorro
C. Encomienda
C. Dos Hermanas
C. Abades
C. Mesón de Paredes
C. del Amparo
C. Jesús y María
LAVAPIES
C. de la Fe
G. V. de San Francisco
C. Rosario
C. Toledo
C. Santa Ana
C. Mira el Río Alta
C. del Carnero
Ribera de Curtidores
C. de Embajadores
Pl. Lavapiés
C. de Sombrerete
Ronda de Segovia
PUERTA DE TOLEDO
C. Mira el Sol
C. del Casino de Tribulete
C. Miguel Servet
Gta. Puerta de Toledo
Campillo del Mundo Nuevo
Rda. de Toledo
Ronda Vale
0
1/4 mile
0
1/4 km

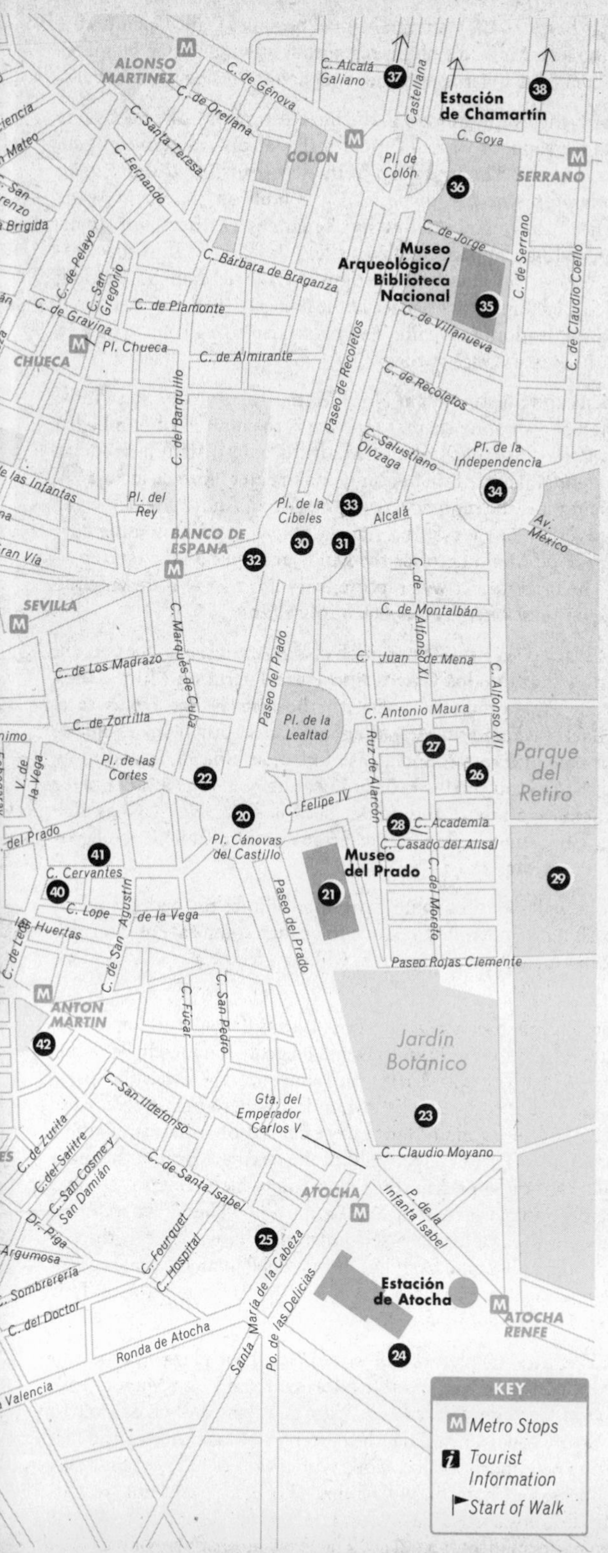

Arab Wall 16
Banco de España 32
Basílica de San Francisco el Grande 3
Campo del Moro 11
Cárcel de la Inquisición. 43
Casa de America 33
Casa de Cervantes 40
Casa de Lope de Vega 41
Casón del Buen Retiro. 26
Catedral de la Almudena. 15
Cava Baja 4
Centro de Arte Reina Sofía . . . 25
Cine Doré 42
Convento de la Encarnación 7
Convento de las Descalzas Reales. 6
Corrala 45
El Rastro 46
Estación de Atocha 24
Fuente de Neptuno 20
Jardín Botánico 23
Jardines Sabatini 10
Museo Arqueológico 35
Museo del Ejército 27
Museo del Prado. 21
Museo Lázaro Galdiano. 38
Museo Sorolla. 37
Museo Thyssen-Bornemisza . . 22
Palacio de Comunicaciones 31
Palacio Real 9
Parque del Retiro 29
Plaza Colón. 36
Plaza de la Cibeles 30
Plaza de la Paja. 2
Plaza de la Villa 18
Plaza de Oriente 8
Plaza Lavapiés. 44
Plaza Mayor 1
Plaza Santa Ana 39
Puerta de Alcalá 34
Puerta del Sol 5
Real Academia de Bellas Artes de San Fernando 19
San Jerónimo el Real. 28
San Nicolás de las Servitas . . . 17
Teatro Real 14
Teleférico 13
Templo de Debod 12

touristy, tapas bars. As Cava de San Miguel becomes Calle Cuchilleros, Botín is on the left, Madrid's oldest restaurant and a onetime Hemingway haunt. Curvy Cuchilleros was once a moat just outside the city walls.

The plaza with the bright murals at the intersection of Calle Segovia is called **Puerta Cerrada,** or Closed Gate, for the (always closed) city gate that once stood here. The mural up to the left reads, "*Fui sobre agua edificada; mis muros de fuego son*" ("I was built on water; my walls are made of fire"), a reference to the city's origins as a fortress with abundant springs and its ramparts made of silex, the kind of flint that creates sparks. Across the square to the right is Calle del Nuncio, leading to the Palacio de la Nunciatura (Palace of the Nunciat), which once housed the Pope's ambassadors to Spain. The palace isn't open, but you can peek inside the Renaissance garden.

Nuncio widens and on your left at No. 17 is the Taberna de Cien Vinos; sample some Spanish wine there. Opposite is the church of San Pedro el Viejo (St. Peter the Elder), one of Madrid's oldest, with a Mudéjar tower. Bear right and enter Príncipe Anglona to enter **Plaza de la Paja** 2. Down on the right is the ramped Costanilla de San Andrés, which leads to Calle Segovia and a view of the viaduct above. Look down the narrow Calle Príncipe Anglona to see the Mudéjar tower on the church of San Pedro. The brick tower was reportedly built in 1354 following the Christian reconquest of Algeciras, near Gibraltar.

At the top of Plaza de la Paja is the church of San Andrés; past the church, turn right after Plaza de los Carros into Plaza Puerta de Moros, then down Carrera San Francisco to visit the **Basílica de San Francisco el Grande** 3. Backtrack and turn left after San Andrés down **Cava Baja** 4, packed with bars and restaurants. Casa Lucio, at No. 35, is said to be a favorite of King Juan Carlos I; Casa Lucas at No. 30 is a great place to have imaginative tapas; and Julián de Tolosa at No. 18 has fine Basque fare. Continue across Puerta Cerrada and up Calle Cuchilleros to return to Plaza Mayor.

TIMING This two-hour walk requires some short uphill climbs through the winding streets. Allow ample time for stops to absorb some café and terrace life—especially in summer, when heat will be a factor.

What to See

3 **Basílica de San Francisco el Grande.** In 1760, Carlos III built this impressive basilica on the site of a Franciscan convent, allegedly founded by St. Francis of Assisi in 1217. The dome, 108 ft in diameter, is the largest in Spain, even larger than that of St. Paul's in London, where its 19 bells were cast in 1882. The seven main doors were carved of American walnut by Casa Juan Guas. Three chapels adjoin the circular church, the most famous being that of **San Bernardino de Siena,** which contains a Goya masterpiece depicting a preaching San Bernardino. The figure standing on the right, not looking up, is a self-portrait of Goya. The 16th-century Gothic choir stalls came from La Cartuja del Paular, in rural Segovia province. ✉ *Pl. de San Francisco, La Latina* ☎ *91/365–3400* 🎫 *Free* ⏲ *Tues.–Fri. 11–12:30 and 4–6:30.*

★ 4 **Cava Baja.** The narrow, picturesque streets south of Plaza Mayor and across Calle Segovia are well worth exploring: from Plaza Mayor, walk to Plaza Puerta Cerrada where Calle Segovia begins and cross over to Cava Baja. Stroll down Cava Baja, the epicenter of fashionable and historic La Latina neighborhood, crowded with a variety of excellent tapas bars (Casa Lucas, La Chata, and El Tempranillo, etc.), traditional restaurants (Julián de Tolosa, Casa Lucio), and even a low-key flamenco night bar with live performances (La Soleá). The lively atmosphere of the Cava

Baja spills over into nearby streets and squares, including Almendro, Cava Alta, Plaza del Humilladero and Plaza de la Paja. ✉ *Across Calle Segovia La Latina.*

need a break?

You'll find **Café del Nuncio** (on Costanilla del Nuncio s/n, in Plaza Mayor, on the corner of Calle Segovia) to be a relaxing place for a coffee or beer, especially against the backdrop of classical music here.

❷ **Plaza de la Paja.** At the top of the hill, on Costanilla San Andrés, the Plaza de la Paja was the most important square in medieval Madrid. The plaza's jewel is the **Capilla del Obispo** (Bishop's Chapel), built between 1520 and 1530; this was where peasants deposited their tithes, called *diezmas*—literally, one-tenth of their crop. The stacks of wheat on the chapel's ceramic tiles refer to this tradition. Architecturally, the chapel marks a transition from the blockish Gothic period, which gave the structure its basic shape, to the Renaissance, the source of the decorations. Go inside to see the intricately carved polychrome altarpiece by Francisco Giralta, with scenes from the life of Christ. Opening hours are erratic; try to visit during mass or on feast days. The chapel is part of the complex of the domed church of **San Andrés**, built for the remains of Madrid's male patron saint, San Isidro Labrador. Isidro was a peasant who worked fields belonging to the Vargas family. The 16th-century **Vargas palace** forms the eastern side of the Plaza de la Paja. According to legend, St. Isidro worked little but had the best-tended fields thanks to many hours of prayer. When Señor Vargas came out to investigate the phenomenon, Isidro made a spring of sweet water spurt from the ground to quench his master's thirst. Because St. Isidro's power had to do with water, his remains were traditionally paraded through the city in times of drought. ✉ *Plaza de la Paja, Centro.*

⚑ ❶ **Plaza Mayor.** Austere, grand, and often surprisingly quiet compared to the rest of Madrid, this arcaded square has seen it all: autos-da-fé (trials of faith, i.e., public burnings of heretics); the canonization of saints; criminal executions; royal marriages, such as that of Princess María and the King of Hungary in 1629; bullfights (until 1847); masked balls; fireworks; and all manner of other events and celebrations. It still hosts fairs, bazaars, and performances.

Measuring 360 ft by 300 ft, Madrid's Plaza Mayor is one of the largest and grandest public squares in Europe. It was designed by Juan de Herrera, the architect to Felipe II and designer of the El Escorial monastery, northwest of Madrid. Construction of the plaza lasted just two years and was finished in 1620 under Felipe III, whose equestrian statue stands in the center. The inauguration ceremonies included the canonization of four Spanish saints: Teresa of Ávila, Ignatius of Loyola, Isidro (Madrid's male patron saint), and Francis Xavier.

This space was once occupied by a city market, and many of the surrounding streets retain the names of the trades and foodstuffs once headquartered there. Nearby are Calle de Cuchilleros (Knifemakers' Street), Calle de Lechuga (Lettuce Street), Calle de Fresa (Strawberry Street), and Calle de Botoneros (Buttonmakers' Street). The plaza's oldest building is the one with the brightly painted murals and the gray spires, called Casa de la Panadería (Bakery House) in honor of the bread shop over which it was built. Opposite is the Casa de la Carnicería (Butcher Shop), now a police station.

The plaza is closed to motorized traffic, making it a pleasant place to sit at one of the sidewalk cafés, watching alfresco artists, street musicians, and Madrileños from all walks of life. Sunday morning brings a stamp and coin market. Around Christmas the plaza fills with stalls selling trees, ornaments, and nativity scenes, as well as all types of practical jokes and tricks for December 28, Día de los Inocentes—a Spanish version of April Fool's Day. ✉ *Plaza Mayor, Centro.*

Central Madrid

The 1-km (½-mi) stretch between the Royal Palace and the Puerta del Sol is loaded with historic sites.

Begin at the **Puerta del Sol** 5 ⚑, the center of Madrid. If you stand with your back to the clock, Calle Arenal is the second street from the far left leaving the plaza: walk down Arenal and turn right into Plaza Celenque. Up on your left, at the corner with Calle Misericordia, is the **Convento de las Descalzas Reales** 6. Follow Misericordia and turn left into the charming Plaza de San Martín to return to Calle Arenal. Turn right and walk down to Plaza Isabel II; then cross the plaza to your right and walk to the end of the short Calle de Arrieta, at which point you'll face the **Convento de la Encarnación** 7. Turn left here into Calle Pavia (off Calle San Quintin) and you'll enter the **Plaza de Oriente** 8.

Here you have a choice of going directly to the **Palacio Real** 9, to your right, or visiting its gardens (1 km [½ mi] farther on) and/or taking a cable-car ride. For the latter, cross Calle Bailén and walk to the right: you'll have a view across the formal **Jardines Sabatini** 10 to the Casa de Campo park and the Guadarrama Mountains. Walk up Bailén, avoiding the overpass, and turn left down Cuesta de San Vicente, then left into Paseo Virgin del Puerto for the entrance to the gardens and the **Campo del Moro** 11. To see the Egyptian **Templo de Debod** 12, cross the overpass to Calle Ferraz and follow the Parque del Oeste on the left. Farther along Paseo de Pintor Rosales, in the park, is the **Teleférico** 13 (cable car) to the Casa de Campo, which grants panoramic views of Madrid. Opposite the Royal Palace on the Plaza de Oriente is the **Teatro Real** 14. Walking down Bailén with the palace on your right, you can enter its huge courtyard and admire the view from atop the escarpment. Alongside the palace is the **Catedral de la Almudena** 15. Walk past the cathedral and turn right onto Calle Mayor: on your left, on Cuesta de la Vega, are the remains of Madrid's **Arab Wall** 16.

Walk back east up Calle Mayor, crossing Bailén. Turn left onto Calle San Nicolás to see the church of **San Nicolás de los Servitas** 17. Return to Calle Mayor and press ahead: on your right you'll see the **Plaza de la Villa** 18, with Madrid's city hall on the right. Farther up Mayor, bear right on Plaza Morenas and enter the **Plaza Mayor** 1 through the arch. The Andalusian Torre de Oro bar on the left displays gory pictures of bullfights, not for the squeamish. On the far side, at No. 33, is the restaurant El Soportal, which gives the plaza's best free tapas with each drink order. (Beware of prices at the other restaurants, especially if you sit outside.) Exit the plaza to the left of El Soportal and head down Calle de Postas and back to the Puerta del Sol. Proceed up the right side of Sol, past the headquarters of the regional government, and in winter consider having a traditional *caldo* (broth) in the charming old shop at the restaurant Lhardy on Carrera de San Jerónimo.

TIMING Without side trips to the palace gardens or the cable car, you can cover this ground in two hours. Set aside an additional morning or afternoon to visit the Royal Palace.

What to See

16 **Arab Wall.** The remains of the Moorish military outpost that became the city of Madrid are visible on Calle Cuesta de la Vega. The sections

of wall here protected a fortress built in the 9th century by Emir Mohammed I. In addition to being an excellent defensive position, the site had plentiful water and was called *Mayrit,* Arabic for "source of life" and the likely origin of the city's name. All that remains of the *medina*—the old Arab city that formed within the walls of the fortress—is the neighborhood's crazy quilt of streets and plazas, which probably follow the same layout they followed more than 1,100 years ago. The park **Emir Mohammed I,** alongside the wall, hosts concerts and plays in the summer. ✉ *C. Cuesta de la Vega, Centro.*

11 **Campo del Moro** (Moors' Field). Below the Sabatini Gardens, but accessible only by an entrance on the far side, is the Campo del Moro. Enjoy the clusters of shady trees, winding paths, and the long lawn leading up to the Royal Palace. Even without considering the riches inside, the palace's immense size (it's twice as large as Buckingham Palace) inspires awe. ✉ *Paseo Virgen del Puerto s/n, Centro.*

15 **Catedral de la Almudena.** The first stone of the cathedral (which adjoins the Royal Palace to the south) was laid in 1883 by King Alfonso XII, and the end result was consecrated by Pope John Paul II in 1993. The building was intended to be Gothic in style, with needles and spires, but funds ran low, the design was simplified by Fernando Chueca Goltia into the existing, more austere classical form. The cathedral has the remains of Madrid's patron saint, San Isidro (St. Isidore), and a wooden statue of Madrid's female patron saint, the Virgin of Almudena, reportedly discovered after the 1085 Christian reconquest of Madrid. Legend has it that a divinely inspired woman named María led authorities to a grain storage vault (in Arabic, *almudeyna*) in the old wall of the Alcázar, now part of the cathedral's foundation, where the statue was found framed by two lighted candles. ✉ *C. Bailén 10, Centro* ☎ *91/542–2200* 🎫 *Free* ⏲ *Daily 9–9.*

7 **Convento de la Encarnación** (Convent of the Incarnation). Once connected to the Royal Palace by an underground passageway, this Augustinian convent was founded in 1611 by the wife of Felipe III. It has several artistic treasures, including a reliquary, which holds among sacred bones a vial containing the dried blood of St. Pantaleón, which is said to liquefy every year on July 27. The ornate church has superb acoustics for medieval and Renaissance choral music; check city listings for concerts. A €6 ticket allows for a combined visit of both this and the Convento de las Descalzas Reales. ✉ *Plaza de la Encarnación 1, Opera* ☎ *91/454–8800 tourist information office* 🎫 *€3.60* ⏲ *Tues.–Thurs. and Sat. 10:30–12:45 and 4–5:45, Fri. 10:30–12:45, Sun. 11–1:45.*

6 **Convento de las Descalzas Reales** (Convent of the Royal Discalced, or Barefoot, Nuns). This 16th-century building was restricted for 200 years to women of royal blood. Its plain, brick-and-stone facade hides paintings by Zurbarán, Titian, and Brueghel the Elder, as well as a hall of sumptuous tapestries crafted from drawings by Peter Paul Rubens. The convent was founded in 1559 by Juana of Austria, whose daughter shut herself up here rather than endure marriage to Felipe II. A handful of nuns (not necessarily royal) still live here, cultivating their own vegetables in the convent's garden. The (required) tour is conducted in Spanish only. ✉ *Plaza de las Descalzas Reales 3, Centro* ☎ *91/454–8800* 🎫 *€5* ⏲ *Tues.–Thurs. and Sat. 10:30–12:45 and 4–5:45, Fri. 10:30–12:45, Sun. 11–1:45.*

10 **Jardines Sabatini** (Sabatini Gardens). The formal gardens to the north of the Royal Palace are crawling with stray cats, but they're a pleasant place to rest or watch the sun set. ✉ *C. Bailén s/n, Centro.*

9 **Palacio Real.** The Royal Palace was commissioned in the early 18th century by the first of Spain's Bourbon rulers, Felipe V, on the same strategic site where Madrid's first Alcázar (Moorish fortress) was built in the 9th. Before you enter, admire the classical French architecture on the graceful **Patio de Armas.** King Felipe was obviously inspired by his childhood days at Versailles with his grandfather Louis XIV. Look for the stone statues of Inca prince Atahualpa and Aztec king Montezuma, perhaps the only tributes in Spain to these pre-Colombian American rulers. Notice how the steep bluff drops westward to the Manzanares River—on a clear day, this vantage point also commands a view of the mountain passes leading into Madrid from Old Castile, and you'll see why the Moors picked this particular spot for a fortress.

Fodor's Choice ★

Inside, 2,800 rooms compete with each other for over-the-top opulence. A nearly two-hour guided tour in English winds a mile-long path through the palace. Highlights include the **Salón de Gasparini,** King Carlos III's private apartments, with swirling, inlaid floors and curlicued, ceramic wall and ceiling decoration, all glistening in the light of a 2-ton crystal chandelier; the **Salón del Trono,** a grand throne room with the royal seats of King Juan Carlos and Queen Sofía; and the **banquet hall,** the palace's largest room, which seats up to 140 people for state dinners. No monarch has lived here since 1931, when Alfonso XIII was deposed following a republican electoral victory. The current king and queen live in the far simpler Zarzuela Palace on the outskirts of Madrid, using this palace only for official occasions.

Also visit the **Biblioteca Real** (Royal Library), with a first edition of Cervantes's *Don Quijote*; the **Museo de Música** (Music Museum), where five stringed instruments by Stradivarius form the world's largest collection; the **Armería Real** (Royal Armory), with historic suits of armor and frightening medieval torture implements; and the **Real Oficina de Farmacía** (Royal Pharmacy), with vials and flasks used to mix the king's medicines. When planning a visit here, note that the Royal Palace is closed during official receptions. ✉ *C. Bailén s/n, Centro* ☎ *91/454–8800* 🎫 *€7, guided tour €8* ⏲ *Apr.–Sept., Mon.–Sat. 9–6, Sun. 9–3; Oct.–Mar., Mon.–Sat. 9:30–5, Sun. 9:30–2.*

8 **Plaza de Oriente.** The stately plaza in front of the Royal Palace is surrounded by massive stone statues of various Spanish monarchs from Ataulfo to Fernando VI. These sculptures were meant to be mounted on the railing on top of the palace, but Queen Isabel of Farnesio, one of the first royals to live in the palace, had them removed because she was afraid their enormous weight would bring the roof down. (Well, that's what she *said* . . . according to palace insiders, the queen wanted the statues removed because her own likeness had not been placed front and center.) The statue of **King Felipe IV** in the plaza's center was the first equestrian bronze ever cast with a rearing horse. The pose comes from a Velázquez painting of the king with which the monarch was so smitten that in 1641 he commissioned an Italian artist, Pietro de Tacca, to turn it into a sculpture. De Tacca enlisted Galileo's help in configuring the statue's weight so it wouldn't tip over. For most Madrileños, the Plaza de Oriente is forever linked with Francisco Franco. The *generalísimo* liked to speak from the roof of the Royal Palace to his followers as they crammed into the plaza below. Even now, on the November anniversary of Franco's death, the plaza fills with supporters, most of whom are old-timers, though the event occasionally has drawn swastika-waving skinheads from other European countries in a chilling fascist tribute. ✉ *Plaza de Oriente, Centro.*

18 **Plaza de la Villa.** Madrid's town council has met in this medieval-looking complex since the Middle Ages, and it's now the city hall. Just two blocks west of the Plaza Mayor on Calle Mayor, it was once called Plaza de San Salvador for a church that used to stand here. The oldest building is the **Casa de los Lujanes,** on the east side—it's the one with the Mudéjar tower. Built as a private home in the late 15th century, the house carries the Lujanes crest over the main doorway. Also on the plaza's east end is the brick-and-stone **Casa de la Villa,** built in 1629, a classic example of Madrid design with its clean lines and spire-topped corner towers. Connected by an overhead walkway, the **Casa de Cisneros** was commissioned in 1537 by the nephew of Cardinal Cisneros. It's one of Madrid's rare examples of the Flamboyant Plateresque style, which has been likened to splashed water—a liquid exuberance wrought in stone. ✉ *C. Mayor, Centro* ⏲ *Free guided tour in Spanish Mon. at 5.*

5 **Puerta del Sol.** Crowded with people and exhaust, Sol is the nerve center of Madrid's traffic. The city's main subway interchange is below, and buses fan out from here. A brass plaque in the sidewalk on the south side of the plaza marks Kilometer 0, the spot from which all distances in Spain are measured. The restored 1756 French-neoclassical building near the marker now houses the offices of the regional government, but during Franco's reign it was the headquarters of his secret police, and it's still known folklorically as the Casa de los Gritos (House of Screams). Across the square is a bronze statue of Madrid's official symbol, a bear with a *madroño* (strawberry tree), and a statue of King-Mayor Carlos III on horseback. ✉ *Puerta del Sol, Centro.*

17 **San Nicolás de las Servitas** (Church of St. Nicholas of the Servitas). This church tower is one of the oldest buildings in Madrid. There is some debate over whether it once formed part of an Arab mosque. It was more likely built after the Christian reconquest of Madrid in 1085, but the brickwork and the horseshoe arches are evidence that it was crafted by either Moorish workers (Mudéjars) or Spaniards well versed in the style. Inside, exhibits detail the Islamic history of early Madrid. ✉ *Near Plaza de San Nicolás, Centro* ☎ *91/559–4064* 🎫 *Donation suggested* ⏲ *Tues.–Sun. 6:30 PM–8:30 PM or by appointment.*

14 **Teatro Real** (Royal Theater). Built in 1850, this neoclassical theater was long a cultural center for Madrileño society. A major restoration project has left it replete with golden balconies, plush seats, and state-of-the-art stage equipment for operas and ballets. Upstairs there's an elegant restaurant that's worth a look. ✉ *Plaza de Isabel II, Centro* ☎ *91/516–0660* 🌐 *www.teatro-real.com.*

13 **Teleférico.** Kids love this cable car, which takes you from just above the Rosaleda gardens in the Parque del Oeste to the center of Casa de Campo. Be warned that the walk from where the cable car drops you off to the zoo and the amusement park is at least 2 km (1 mi), and you'll have to ask directions; it's easier to ride out, turn around, and come back. ✉ *Estación Terminal Teleférico, Paseo de Pintor Rosales (at C. Marques de Urquijo), Centro* ☎ *91/541–7450* 🎫 *€2.80 one-way, €4 round trip* ⏲ *Apr.–Sept., daily noon–dusk; Oct.–Mar., weekends noon–dusk.*

12 **Templo de Debod.** This authentic 4th-century BC Egyptian temple was donated to Spain in gratitude for its technical assistance with the construction of the Aswan Dam. It's near the site of the former Montaña barracks, where Madrileños bloodily crushed the beginnings of a military uprising in 1936. The western side of the small park around the temple is without a doubt the best place to watch Madrid's famously outstanding sunset. ✉ *Hill in Parque de la Montaña, near Estación del Norte,*

Centro 91/765–1008 Free Oct.–Mar., Tues.–Fri. 10–1:35 and 4:30–6, weekends 10–1:30; Apr.–Sept., Tues.–Fri. 10–1:30 and 6–7:45, weekends 10–1:30.

The Art Walk

Madrid's three art museums are all within walking distance of one another via the Paseo del Prado. The Paseo was designed by King-Mayor Carlos III as a leafy nature walk with glorious fountains and a botanical garden for respite in scorching summers. As you walk east down Carrera de San Jerónimo toward the Paseo del Prado, consider that this was the route followed by Ferdinand and Isabella more than 500 years ago toward the church of San Jerónimo el Real. The *Paseo del Arte* (art pass) allows you to visit the three museums for €7.66. You can buy it at any of the three museums.

a good walk

Exit the Puerta del Sol onto Calle de Alcalá, and you'll find on your left the **Real Academia de Bellas Artes de San Fernando** 19. Take the next right, past the elegant bank buildings, onto Calle Sevilla and turn left at Plaza Canalejas—where La Violeta, at No. 6, sells violet-flavor sweets—onto Carrera de San Jerónimo. (If you cross the plaza onto Calle Príncipe, you'll reach the Plaza Santa Ana tapas area.) Walk down San Jerónimo to Plaza de las Cortés.

The granite building on the left, its stairs guarded by bronze lions, is the Congreso, lower house of Las Cortés, Spain's parliament. Walk past the landmark Westin Palace on the right to the **Fuente de Neptuno** 20 in the wide Paseo del Prado—the **Museo del Prado** 21 is across the boulevard to the right. On your left is the **Museo Thyssen-Bornemisza** 22, and across the plaza on the left is the elegant Ritz hotel, alongside the obelisk dedicated to all those who have died for Spain. Either tackle one or both of these museums now, or continue strolling.

Turning right and walking south on Paseo del Prado, you'll see the **Jardín Botánico** 23 on the left and eventually **Estación de Atocha** 24, a railway station said to resemble the overturned hull of a ship. It's worth a quick visit for its humid indoor park with tropical trees, benches, paths, and a restaurant. Across the traffic circle, the immense pile of painted tiles and winged statues houses Spain's Ministry of Agriculture. The **Centro de Arte Reina Sofía** 25, site of Picasso's *Guernica,* is in the building with the exterior glass elevators, best accessed by walking up Calle Atocha from the station and taking the first left. Retracing your steps to the Fuente de Neptuno, turn right and walk between the Ritz and the Prado. Straight ahead you'll see the **Casón del Buen Retiro** 26, on its left the **Museo del Ejército** 27, and farther on the cloister of the church of **San Jerónimo el Real** 28 and the vast **Parque del Retiro** 29.

Back at the fountain again, turn left and walk up the left side of Paseo del Prado (or, even better, the leafy central promenade) past the Museo Thyssen-Bornemisza to the **Plaza de la Cibeles** 30, surrounded by the **Palacio de Comunicaciones** 31, the **Banco de España** 32, and the **Casa de América** 33. Turn right at Cibeles, walk up Calle Alcalá, and you'll see Madrid's unofficial symbol: the **Puerta de Alcalá** 34, and, again, the Parque del Retiro. About 100 yards north of Cibeles, on the Paseo de Recoletos, you'll see a grand yellow mansion on the right—now a bank headquarters, this was once the home of the Marquis of Salamanca, who at the turn of the 20th century built the exclusive shopping and residential neighborhood (northeast of here) that now bears his name. Continue north for the **Museo Arqueológico** 35, which adjoins the National Library, and the **Plaza Colón** 36. If you're an art buff, press on to the **Museo Sorolla** 37 and **Museo Lázaro Galdiano** 38.

TIMING With a visit to the Reina Sofía and the Parque del Retiro, you can do this walk in three to four hours. Set aside a morning or an afternoon *each* to return to the Prado and Thyssen-Bornemisza.

What to See

32 **Banco de España.** This massive 1884 building, Spain's central bank, takes up an entire block. It is said that part of the nation's gold reserves are held in great vaults that stretch under the Plaza de la Cibeles traffic circle all the way to the fountain. (Some reserves are also stored in Fort Knox, in the U.S.) The bank is not open to visitors, but if you can dodge traffic well enough to reach the median strip in front of it, you can take a fine photo of the fountain and the palaces with the Puerta de Alcalá arch in the background. ✉ *Paseo del Prado s/n, at Plaza de la Cibeles, Centro.*

33 **Casa de América.** A cultural center and art gallery focusing on Latin America, the Casa is in the allegedly haunted Palacio de Linares, built by a man who made his fortune in the New World and returned to a life of incestuous love and strange deaths. ✉ *Paseo de Recoletos 2, Centro* ☎ *91/595–4800* 🎫 *Free* ⏲ *Tues.–Fri. 11–8, Sat. 11–7, Sun. 11–2.*

26 **Casón del Buen Retiro.** This Prado annex is just a five-minute walk from the museum and is free with a Prado ticket. The building, once a ballroom, and the formal gardens in the Retiro are all that remain of Madrid's second royal complex, which filled the entire neighborhood until the early 19th century. On display are 19th-century Spanish paintings and sculpture, including works by Sorolla and Rusiñol. A regal restoration of the complex will yield brand-new halls devoted to 17th- and 19th-century Spanish art. At press time these halls were closed for renovation. ✉ *C. Alfonso XII s/n, Retiro* ☎ *91/330–2867* ⏲ *Tues.–Sat. 9–7, Sun. 9–2.*

25 **Centro de Arte Reina Sofía** (Queen Sofía Art Center). Madrid's museum of modern art is in a converted hospital whose classical granite austerity is somewhat relieved (or ruined, depending on your point of view) by the playful pair of glass elevator shafts on its facade. The museum is currently undergoing renovation (but remains open). When completed, in early 2004, the museum will have three new buildings: a library, an auditorium, and a temporary exhibition center. The collection focuses on Spain's three great modern masters—Pablo Picasso, Salvador Dalí, and Joan Miró—and has contributions from Juan Gris, Jorge Oteiza, Pablo Gargallo, Julio Gonzalez, Eduardo Chillida, and Antoni Tàpies. Take the elevator to the second floor to see the heavy hitters, then to the fourth floor for the rest of the permanent collection, which includes both Spanish and international artists. The other floors have traveling exhibits. The exhibition rooms are numbered 1–45, beginning chronologically with the turn-of-the-20th-century birth of Spain's modern movement on the second floor and continuing to contemporary artists such as Eduardo Chillida in Rooms 42 and 43 on the fourth floor. The free English-language guide-booklet is excellent, as are the plastic-covered notes available at each display.

Fodor'sChoice ★

The museum's showpiece is Picasso's ***Guernica,*** in the center hall on the second floor. Surrounded by studies for its many individual elements, the huge black-and-white canvas depicts the horror of the Nazi Condor Legion's bombing of the ancient Basque town of Guernica in 1937, during the Spanish Civil War. The work—in tone and structure a 20th-century version of Goya's *The 3rd of May*—is something of a national shrine. *Guernica* did not reach Madrid until 1981, as Picasso had stipulated in his will that the painting only return to Spain after democracy was restored.

The room in front of *Guernica* has **surrealist** works, with six canvases by Miró. Room 10 belongs to Salvador Dalí hung in three *ámbitos* (areas). The first has the young artist experimenting with different styles, as in his cubist self-portrait and his classical landscape *Paisaje de Cadaqués*; the second shows the evolving painter of the Buñuel portrait and portraits of the artist's sister; and the third includes the full-blown surrealist work for which Dalí is best known, *The Great Masturbator* (1929) and *The Enigma of Hitler* (1939), with its broken, dripping telephone.

The rest of the museum is devoted to more recent art, including the massive sculpture *Toki Egin*, by Eduardo Chillida (who died in 2002), considered among Spain's greatest sculptors, and five paintings by Barcelona artist Antoni Tàpies, whose works use such materials as wrinkled sheets and straw. ✉ *Santa Isabel 52, Atocha* ☎ *91/467–5062* 🌐 *museoreinasofia.mcu.es* 🎫 *€3, free Sat. after 2:30 and all day Sun.* ⏲ *Mon. and Wed.–Sat. 10–9, Sun. 10–2:30.*

24 **Estación de Atocha.** Madrid's Atocha railroad station, a steel-and-glass hangar, was built in the late 19th century by Alberto Palacio Elissague, the same architect who became famous for his work with Ricardo Velázquez in the creation of the Palacio de Cristal (Crystal Palace) in Madrid's Retiro park. The immense space was filled in the late 20th century with a tropical rain forest. For many years closed, and nearly torn down during the '70s, Atocha was restored and refurbished by Spain's internationally acclaimed architect, Rafael Moneo. ✉ *Paseo de Atocha s/n, Retiro* ☎ *91/420–9875.*

20 **Fuente de Neptuno** (Neptune's Fountain). At Plaza Canovas del Castillo, midway between the Palace and Ritz hotels and the Prado and Thyssen-Bornemisza museums, this fountain is at the hub of Madrid's Paseo del Arte. It was a rallying point for Atlético de Madrid soccer triumphs (counterpoint to Real Madrid's celebrations at the Fuente de la Cibeles up the street). It's been quiet here for the past few years, with Atlético mired in second division (a concept comparable to the New York Mets' slipping down to the minors). With Atlético's return to first division in spring of 2002, the Fuente de Neptuno reassumed its pivotal role in Madrid life. ✉ *Plaza Canovas del Castillo, Centro.*

23 **Jardín Botánico** (Botanical Garden). Just south of the Prado Museum, the gardens provide a pleasant place to stroll or sit under the trees. True to the wishes of King Carlos III, they hold many plants, flowers, and cacti from around the world. ✉ *Plaza de Murillo 2, Retiro* ☎ *91/420–3017* 🎫 *€1.50* ⏲ *Summer, daily 10–9; winter, daily 10–6.*

35 **Museo Arqueológico** (Museum of Archaeology). The museum shares its neoclassical building with the **Biblioteca Nacional** (National Library). The biggest attraction here is a replica of the prehistoric cave paintings in Altamira, Cantabria, located underground in the garden. (Access to the real thing is highly restricted.) Inside the museum, look for *La Dama de Elche*, a bust of a wealthy, 5th-century BC Iberian woman, and notice that her headgear is a rough precursor to the mantillas and hair combs still associated with traditional Spanish dress. The ancient Visigothic votive crowns are another highlight, discovered in 1859 near Toledo and believed to date back to the 8th century. ✉ *C. Serrano 13, Salamanca* ☎ *91/577–7912* 🌐 *www.man.es* 🎫 *€3, free Sat. after 2:30 and all day Sun.* ⏲ *Museum Tues.–Sat. 9:30–8:30, Sun. 9:30–2:30.*

27 **Museo del Ejército** (Army Museum). A real treat for arms-and-armor buffs, this place is right on the museum mile. Among the 27,000 items on view are a sword that allegedly belonged to the Spanish hero El Cid; suits of armor; bizarre-looking pistols with barrels capable of holding scores of

bullets; Moorish tents; and a cross carried by Christopher Columbus. It's an unusually entertaining collection. ✉ *Mendez Nuñez 1, Retiro* ☎ *91/522–8977* 🎫 *€1* ⏲ *Tues.–Sun. 10–2.*

21 **Museo del Prado** (Prado Museum). When the Prado was commissioned by King-Mayor Carlos III, in 1785, it was meant to be a natural-science museum. The king wanted the museum, the adjoining botanical gardens, and the elegant Paseo del Prado to serve as a center of scientific enlightenment. By the time the building was completed in 1819, its purpose had changed to exhibiting the art gathered by Spanish royalty since the time of Ferdinand and Isabella. The museum is adding a massive new wing, designed by Rafael Moneo, that will resurrect long-hidden works by Zurbarán and Pereda and more than double the number of paintings on display from the permanent collection. (At press time, the wing was still undergoing renovation.)

Fodor'sChoice ★

The Prado's jewels are its works by the nation's three great masters: Francisco Goya, Diego Velázquez, and El Greco. The museum also holds masterpieces by Flemish, Dutch, German, French, and Italian artists, collected when their lands were part of the Spanish Empire. The museum benefited greatly from the anticlerical laws of 1836, which forced monasteries, convents, and churches to forfeit many of their artworks for public display.

Enter the Prado via the Goya entrance, with steps opposite the Ritz hotel, or by the less-crowded Murillo door opposite the Jardín Botánico. The layout varies (grab a floor plan), but the first halls on the left, coming from the Goya entrance (7A to 11 on the second floor, or *planta primera*), are usually devoted to **17th-century Flemish painters**, including Peter Paul Rubens (1577–1640), Jacob Jordaens (1593–1678), and Antony van Dyck (1599–1641).

Room 12 introduces you to the meticulous brushwork of **Velázquez** (1599–1660) in his numerous portraits of kings and queens. Look for the magnificent *Las Hilanderas* (*The Spinners*), evidence of the artist's talent for painting light. The Prado's most famous canvas, Velázquez's *Las Meninas* (*The Maids of Honor*), combines a self-portrait of the artist at work with a mirror reflection of the king and queen in a revolutionary interplay of space and perspectives. Picasso was obsessed with this work and painted several copies of it in his own abstract style, now on display in the Picasso Museum in Barcelona.

The south ends of the second and top floors (*planta primera* and *planta segunda*) are reserved for **Goya** (1746–1828), whose works span a staggering range of tone, from bucolic to horrific. Among his early masterpieces are portraits of the family of King Carlos IV, for whom he was court painter—one glance at their unflattering and imbecilic expressions, especially in the painting *The Family of Carlos IV*, reveals the loathing Goya developed for these self-indulgent, reactionary rulers. His famous side-by-side canvases, *The Clothed Maja* and *The Nude Maja*, may represent the young duchess of Alba, whom Goya adored and frequently painted. No one knows whether she ever returned his affection. The adjacent rooms house a series of idyllic scenes of Spaniards at play, painted as designs for tapestries.

Goya's paintings took on political purpose starting in 1808, when the population of Madrid rose up against occupying French troops. *The 2nd of May* portrays the insurrection at the Puerta del Sol, and its even more terrifying companion piece, *The 3rd of May*, depicts the nighttime executions of patriots who had rebelled the day before. The garish light effects in this work typify the romantic style, which favors drama over detail, and make it one of the most powerful indictments of violence ever committed to canvas.

Goya's "black paintings" are dark, disturbing works, completed late in his life, that reflect his inner turmoil after losing his hearing and his deep embitterment over the bloody War of Independence. These are copies of the monstrous hallucinatory paintings Goya made with marvelously free brush strokes on the walls of his house by southern Madrid's Manzanares River, popularly known as *La Quinta del Sordo* (the deaf one's villa). Having grown gravely ill in his old age, Goya was deaf, lonely, bitter, and despairing; his terrifying *Saturn Devouring One of his Sons* communicates the ravages of age and time.

Near the Goya entrance, the Prado's ground floor (*planta baja*) is filled with 15th- and 16th-century Flemish paintings, including the bizarre presurrealist masterpiece *Garden of Earthly Delights,* by Hieronymus Bosch (circa 1450–1516). Next come Rooms 60A, 61A, and 62A, filled with the passionately spiritual works of **El Greco** (Doménikos Theotokópoulos, 1541–1614), the Greek-born artist who lived and worked in Toledo. El Greco is known for his mystical, elongated forms and faces. His style was quite shocking to a public accustomed to strictly representational images. Two of his greatest paintings, *The Resurrection* and *The Adoration of the Shepherds,* are on view here. Before you leave, stop in the 14th- to 16th-century Italian rooms to see Titian's *Portrait of Emperor Charles V* and Raphael's exquisite *Portrait of a Cardinal.* ✉ *Paseo del Prado s/n, Retiro* ☎ *91/330–2800* 🌐 *www.museoprado.mcu.es* 🎫 *€3, free Sat. after 2:30 and all day Sun.* ⏲ *Tues.–Sun. 9–7.*

need a break?

La Dolores (Plaza de Jesús 4, Santa Ana) is an atmospheric old ceramic-tile bar that's the perfect place for a beer or glass of wine and a plate of olives. It's a great alternative to the Prado's basement cafeteria and is just across the Paseo, then one block up on Calle Lope de Vega.

38 **Museo Lázaro Galdiano.** A 10-minute walk across the Castellana from the Museo Sorolla, the stately mansion of writer and editor José Lázaro Galdiano (1862–1947) has both decorative items and paintings by Bosch, El Greco, Murillo, and Goya, among others, this is a remarkable collection of five centuries of Spanish, Flemish, English, and Italian art. Bosch's *St. John the Baptist* and the many Goyas are the stars of the show, with El Greco's *San Francisco de Assisi* and Zurbarán's *San Diego de Alcalá* close behind. It's closed for renovation until early 2004. ✉ *Serrano 122, Salamanca* ☎ *91/561–6084* 🎫 *€3* ⏲ *Tues.–Sun. 10–2.*

37 **Museo Sorolla.** Spain's most famous impressionist painter, Joaquín Sorolla (1863–1923), lived and worked here for most of his life. Entering this diminutive but cozy domain is a little like stepping into a Sorolla painting, as it's filled with the artist's best-known works, most of which shimmer with the bright Mediterranean light and color of his native Valencia. Because the house and garden were also designed by Sorolla, you leave with an impression of the world as seen through this painter's exceptional eye. ✉ *General Martinez Campos 37, Chamberí* ☎ *91/310–1584* 🎫 *€3, free Sun. and holidays* ⏲ *Tues.–Sat. 9:30–3, Sun. 10–3.*

22 **Museo Thyssen-Bornemisza.** The newest of Madrid's three major art centers, the "Thyssen" occupies spacious galleries washed in salmon pink and filled with natural light in the late-18th-century Villahermosa Palace, finished in 1771. This ambitious collection of 800 paintings traces the history of Western art with examples from every important movement,

Fodor's Choice ★

from the 13th-century Italian Gothic through 20th-century American pop art. The works were gathered from the 1920s to the 1980s by Swiss industrialist Baron Hans Heinrich Thyssen-Bornemisza and his father. At the urging of his wife, Carmen Cervera (a former Miss Spain), the baron donated the entire collection to Spain in 1993. Critics have described these paintings as the minor works of major artists and the major works of minor artists, but, be that as it may, the collection traces the development of Western humanism as no other in the world.

One of the high points here is Hans Holbein's *Portrait of Henry VIII* (purchased from the late Princess Diana's grandfather, who used the money to buy a new Bugatti sports car). American artists are also well represented; look for the Gilbert Stuart portrait of George Washington's cook, and note how closely the composition and rendering resemble the artist's famous painting of the Founding Father himself. Two halls are devoted to the impressionists and postimpressionists, including many works by Pissarro and a few each by Renoir, Monet, Degas, van Gogh, and Cézanne. Find Pissarro's *Saint-Honoré Street in the Afternoon, Effect of Rain* for a jolt of mortality, or Renoir's *Woman with a Parasol in a Garden* for a sense of bucolic beauty lost. Picasso's *Harlequin with a Mirror* is a self-portrait of a spurned (by Sara Murphy, it is said) lover, while Dalí's *Dream Caused by the Flight of a Bee Around a Pomegranate a Second before Awakening* will take you back to Hieronymus Bosch's *Garden of Earthly Delights,* 300 yards and half a millennium away in the Prado.

Within 20th-century art, the collection is strong on dynamic and colorful German expressionism, with some soothing works by Georgia O'-Keeffe and Andrew Wyeth along with Hoppers, Bacons, Rauschenbergs, and Lichtensteins. Last but not least, the temporary exhibits are often fascinating. ✉ *Paseo del Prado 8, Centro* ☎ *91/369–0151* 🌐 *www.museothyssen.org* 🎫 *€6.60* ⏲ *Tues.–Sun. 10–7.*

31 **Palacio de Comunicaciones.** This ornate building on the southeast side of Plaza de la Cibeles is Madrid's main post office. ✉ *Plaza de Cibeles, Centro* ☎ *902/197197* ⏲ *Weekdays 8:30 AM–10 PM, Sat. 8:30–8 (after 2 PM, entrance by calle Monteleón), Sun. 8:30–1.*

29 **Parque del Retiro** (literally, the Retreat). Once the private playground of royalty, Madrid's crowning park is a vast expanse of green encompassing formal gardens, fountains, lakes, exhibition halls, children's play areas, outdoor cafés, and a **Puppet Theater,** featuring free slapstick routines that even non–Spanish speakers will enjoy. Shows take place on Saturday at 1 and on Sunday at 1, 6, and 7. The park is especially lively on weekends, when it fills with street musicians, jugglers, clowns, gypsy fortune-tellers, and sidewalk painters along with hundreds of Spanish families out for a walk. The park hosts a book fair in May and occasional flamenco concerts in summer. From the entrance at the Puerta de Alcalá, head straight toward the center and you'll find the **Estanque** (lake), presided over by a grandiose equestrian statue of King Alfonso XII, erected by his mother. Just behind the lake, north of the statue, is one of the best of the park's many cafés. If you're feeling nautical, you can rent a boat and work up an appetite rowing around the lake.

The 19th-century **Palacio de Cristal** (Crystal Palace), southeast of the Estanque, was built to house exotic plants from the Philippines, a Spanish possession at the time. This airy marvel of steel and glass sits on a base of decorative tile. Next door is a small lake with ducks and swans. At the south end of the park, along the Paseo del Uruguay, is the **Rosaleda** (rose garden), an English garden bursting with color and heavy with floral scents for most of the summer. West of the Rosaleda, look for a statue called the **Ángel Caído** (Fallen Angel), which Madrileños claim is the only one in the world depicting the prince of darkness before (during, actually) his fall from grace. ✉ *Puerta de Alcalá, Retiro.*

36 **Plaza Colón.** Named for Christopher Columbus, this plaza has a statue of the explorer (identical to the one in Barcelona's port) looking west from a high tower in the middle of the square. Beneath the plaza is the **Centro Cultural de la Villa** (☎ 91/480–0300), a performing-arts facility. Behind Plaza Colón is **Calle Serrano,** the city's premier shopping street (think Gucci, Prada, and Loewe). Stroll in either direction on Serrano for some window-shopping. ✉ *Plaza Colón, Centro.*

need a break?

El Espejo (Paseo de Recoletos 31, Centro) comprises two classy bars near the Plaza Colón—one in a Belle Epoque setting on a side street, the other in a pavilion of glass and wrought iron in the middle of the Paseo de Recoletos. Sit on the shady terrace or in the air-conditioned, stained-glass bar and rest your feet while sipping a coffee or a beer.

30 **Plaza de la Cibeles.** A tree-lined walkway runs down the center of Paseo del Prado to the grand Plaza de la Cibeles, where the famous Fuente de la Cibeles (Fountain of Cybele) depicts the nature goddess driving a chariot drawn by lions. Even more than the officially designated bear and arbutus tree, this monument, beautifully lit at night, has come to symbolize Madrid—so much so that during the civil war, patriotic Madrileños risked life and limb to sandbag it as Nationalist aircraft bombed the city. ✉ *Plaza de la Cibeles, Centro.*

34 **Puerta de Alcalá.** This triumphal arch was built by Carlos III in 1778 to mark the site of one of the ancient city gates. You can still see the bomb damage inflicted on the arch during the civil war. ✉ *C. de Alcalá s/n, Retiro.*

19 **Real Academia de Bellas Artes de San Fernando** (St. Ferdinand Royal Academy of Fine Arts). Designed by Churriguera in the waning baroque years of the early 18th century, this little-known museum showcases 500 years of Spanish painting, from Ribera and Murillo to Sorolla and Zuloaga. The tapestries along the stairways are stunning. The same building houses the **Instituto de Calcografía** (Prints Institute), which sells limited-edition prints from original plates engraved by Spanish artists, including Goya. Check listings for classical and contemporary concerts in the small upstairs concert hall. ✉ *Alcalá 13, Sol* ☎ *91/524–0864* 🎫 *€3, free Wed.* ⏲ *Tues.–Fri. 9–7, Sat.–Mon. 9–2:30.*

28 **San Jerónimo el Real.** Ferdinand and Isabella used this church and cloister as a *retiro,* or place of meditation—hence the name of the nearby park. The building was devastated in the Napoleonic Wars, then rebuilt in the late 19th century. ✉ *Moreto 4, behind Prado museum, Retiro* ☎ *91/420–3578* ⏲ *Daily 9–1:30 and 5–8:30.*

Castizo Madrid

The Spanish word *castizo* means "authentic," and *los Madrileños castizos* are the Spanish equivalent of London's cockneys. There are few "sights" in the usual sense on this route; instead, you wander through some of Madrid's most traditional and lively neighborhoods. Within these are a growing number of immigrants and the attendant employment problems. Purse-snatching and petty crime are not uncommon, so think twice about this walk if you don't feel streetwise.

a good walk

Begin at the **Plaza Santa Ana** 39 ▶, hub of the theater district in the 17th century and now a center of nocturnal activity, not all of it desirable. The plaza's notable buildings include, at the lower end, the Teatro Español. Walk up to the sunny Plaza del Ángel (next to the Reina Victoria hotel) and turn down Calle de Las Huertas, past the ancient olive tree and plant nursery behind the San Sebastián church—once the church cemetery, this was the final resting place for poets such as Lope de Vega and Quevedo. Walk down Huertas to No. 18, Casa Alberto, an ancient (still excellent) bar and restaurant as well as the house where Miguel de Cervantes was living when he finished his last novel, *Viaje al Parnaso*. Continue to Calle León, named for a lion kept here long ago by a resident Moor. A short walk to your left brings you to the corner of Calle Cervantes. As the plaque on the wall overhead attests, *Don Quijote's* author died on April 23, 1616, in what is now called the **Casa de Cervantes** 40. Down the street, at No. 11, is the **Casa de Lope de Vega** 41, where the "Spanish Shakespeare," Fray Felix Lope de Vega Carpio, lived and worked.

A right from Calle Cervantes onto Calle Quevedo takes you past the Basque *sidrería* (cider house) Zerain—where you can catch cider in your glass as it spurts directly from the barrel—down to the corner across from the convent and church of the Trinitarias Descalzas (Discalced, or Barefoot, Trinitarians, a cloistered order of nuns). Miguel de Cervantes is buried inside with his wife and daughter. Turn right on Calle Lope de Vega to return to Calle León, and walk left back to Calle Huertas. One block to the left on Huertas, turn right onto Calle Amor de Dios and walk to its end, the busy Calle Atocha; across the street is the church of San Nicolás. The predecessor of this plain, modern church was burned in 1936, but the site is historic: like many churches during that turbulent period, the original building fell to the wrath of working-class crowds who felt victimized by centuries of clerical oppression. To the left of the church, walk down Pasaje Doré, where, if it's early in the day, you'll pass through the Anton Martín market, a colorful assortment of stalls typical of most Madrid neighborhoods.

Turn right on Calle Santa Isabel, by the **Cine Doré** 42, and take your first left on Calle de la Rosa, which after a jog to the right becomes Calle de la Cabeza. You'll pass the restaurant Casa Lastra. On the southwest corner with Calle Lavapiés is the site of the **Cárcel de la Inquisición** 43. Turn left here: this is the beginning of the Barrio Lavapiés, Madrid's old Judería (Jewish Quarter). Like Moors, Jews were forced to live outside the city walls after the Christian reconquest hit Madrid in 1085, and this was one of the suburbs they founded. Known as Lavapiés (literally, "wash-feet") after the medieval custom of bathing one's feet before entering the *aljama* (ghetto), this hillside neighborhood is a quintessentially grass-roots working-class Madrid barrio, rife with artists, immigrants, students, and aspiring actors, though gentrification is beginning to creep in; the streets have been recobbled, and lighting improved. Holding your belongings tightly and your camera out of sight, explore side streets off Calle Lavapiés; then continue down and south until you reach the heart of the neighborhood, **Plaza Lavapiés** 44. Café Barbieri, on the plaza's Northeastern corner and more than one hundred years old, is a good option if you need a break.

Leave the plaza heading west on Calle Sombrerete. After two blocks you'll reach the intersection of Calle Mesón de Paredes, on which corner you'll see a beautifully preserved example of a popular Madrid architecture, the **Corrala** 45. Life in this type of balconied apartment building is very public, with laundry flapping in the breeze, babies crying, and old women gossiping over the railings. Neighbors once shared common kitchen and bath facilities on the patio. Work your way west, crossing Calle de Embajadores into the neighborhood known as **El Rastro** 46, with streets of small family stores selling furniture, antiques, and a cornucopia of used junk (some of it greatly overpriced). On Sunday, El Rastro becomes a flea market, and Calle de Ribera de Curtidores, the steep main drag, is closed to traffic and jammed with outdoor booths, shoppers, and pickpockets.

TIMING Allow at least three hours. The Anton Martín market comes to life every weekday morning, while the streets surrounding the Plaza Santa Ana are more interesting after dark, as they pack some of Madrid's best tapas bars and nightspots. El Rastro can be saved for a Sunday morning if you decide to join the milling throng at the flea market.

What to See

43 **Cárcel de la Inquisición** (Inquisition Jail). Unmarked by any historical plaque, the former jail is now a large tapas bar, the **Taberna de Lavapiés**, named for the old Jewish Quarter. Here Jews, Moors, and others designated unrepentant heathens or sinners bent to the inquisitors' whims; the prison later became a Cárcel de la Corona (Crown Prison) for the incarceration of wayward soldiers, priests, and nuns. Ask a bartender if you can see the original, two-story medieval patio out back—it's tiny, but highly evocative. ☒ *Southeast corner of C. Cabeza and C. Lavapiés, Lavapiés* ☎ *91/369–3218* ⊙ *Daily 9 AM–2 AM.*

40 **Casa de Cervantes.** A plaque marks the private home where Miguel de Cervantes Saavedra, author of *Don Quijote de la Mancha,* committed his final words to paper: "*Puesto ya el pie en el estribo, con ansias de la muerte . . .*" ("One foot already in the stirrup and yearning for death . . ."). The Western world's first runaway best-seller, and still one of the most widely translated and read books in the world, Cervantes' spoof of a knightly novel playfully but profoundly satirized Spain's rise and decline while portraying man's dual nature in the pragmatic Sancho Panza and the idealistic Don Quijote, ever in search of wrongs to right. ☒ *C. Cervantes and C. León, Santa Ana.*

41 **Casa de Lope de Vega.** Considered the Shakespeare of Spanish literature, Fray Felix Lope de Vega Carpio (1562–1635), a contemporary and adversary of Cervantes, wrote some 1,800 plays and enjoyed great success during his lifetime. His former home is now a museum with period furnishings, offering an intimate look into a bygone era: everything here, from the whale-oil lamps and candles to the well in the tiny garden and the pans used to warm the bedsheets, brings you closer to the great dramatist. Don't miss the Latin inscription over the door: PARVA PROPIA MAGNA / MAGNA ALIENA PARVA (small but mine big / big but someone else's small). ☒ *C. Cervantes 11, Santa Ana* ☎ *91/429–9216* *€2, free Sat.* ⊙ *Sept.–July, weekdays 9:30–2, Sat. 10–2.*

need a break?

Drop into *Taberna de Antonio Sánchez* (Mesón de Paredes 13, Lavapiés) Madrid's oldest tavern, for a glass of wine and some tapas, or just a peek. The dark walls (lined with bullfighting paintings), zinc bar, and pulley system used to lift casks of wine from the cellar look much the same as they did when the place first opened in 1830. Meals are also served in a dining room in the back. Specialties include *rabo de buey* (bull's-tail stew) and *morcillo al horno* (beef stew).

42 **Cine Doré.** A rare example of Art Nouveau architecture in Madrid, the hip Cine Doré shows movies from the Spanish National Film Archives and eclectic foreign films. Show times are listed in newspapers under

"*Filmoteca.*" The lobby, trimmed with smart pink neon, has a sleek café-bar and a good bookshop. ✉ *C. Santa Isabel 3, Lavapiés* ☎ *91/369-1125* ⏲ *Tues.–Sun.; hrs vary depending on show times.*

45 **Corrala.** This structure is not unlike the rowdy outdoor areas, known as *corrales,* used as Madrid's early makeshift theaters; they were usually installed in a vacant lot between two apartment buildings, and families with balconies overlooking the action rented out seats to wealthy patrons of the arts. There's a plaque here to remind you that the setting for the famous 19th-century *zarzuela* (light opera) *La Revoltosa* was a corrala like this one. City-sponsored musical-theater events are occasionally held here in summer. The ruins across the street were once the **Escolapíos de San Fernando,** one of several churches and parochial schools that fell victim to anti-Catholic sentiments during the civil war. ✉ *C. Mesón de Paredes and C. Sombrerete, Lavapiés.*

46 **El Rastro.** Named for the *arrastre* (dragging) of animals in and out of the slaughterhouse that once stood here and, specifically, the *rastro* (blood trail) left behind, this site explodes into a rollicking flea market every Sunday morning from 10 to 2. For serious browsing and bargaining, any *other* morning is a better time to turn up treasures such as old iron grillwork, a marble tabletop, or a gilt picture frame, but Sundays bring out truly bizarre bric-a-brac ranging from stolen earrings to sent postcards to thrown-out love letters. Even so, people-watching is the best part. ✉ *Ribera de los Curtidores s/n, Centro.*

44 **Plaza Lavapiés.** The heart of the historic Jewish barrio, this plaza remains a neighborhood hub. To the left is the Calle de la Fe (Street of Faith), which was called Calle Sinagoga until the expulsion of the Jews in 1492. The church of **San Lorenzo** at the end was built on the site of the razed synagogue. Legend has it that Jews and Moors who chose baptism over exile were forced to walk up this street barefoot to the ceremony to demonstrate their new faith. ✉ *Top of C. de la Fe, Lavapiés.*

39 **Plaza Santa Ana.** This plaza was the heart of the theater district in the 17th century—the golden age of Spanish literature—and is now the center of Madrid's thumping nightlife. A statue of 17th-century playwright Pedro Calderón de la Barca faces the **Teatro Español.** Rebuilt in 1980 following a fire, the theater stands on the site where plays were performed as early as the 16th century in a corrala. Opposite the theater, the **Villa Rosa,** with a facade of ceramic tile, is a popular nightspot. The **Gran Hotel Reina Victoria** was not always so upscale but has always been favored by bullfighters, including Manolete. Off to the side of the hotel is the diminutive **Plaza del Ángel,** with one of Madrid's best jazz clubs, the Café Central. Back on Plaza Santa Ana is one of Madrid's most famous cafés, the former Hemingway hangout **Cervecería Alemana,** still catnip to writers, poets, and beer drinkers. ✉ *Plaza de Santa Ana s/n, Centro.*

TAPAS BARS & CAFÉS

The best tapas areas are in La Latina, Chueca, Sol, Santa Ana, Salamanca, and Lavapiés. La Latina is arguably Madrid's trendiest neighborhood and has a large concentration of good tapas bars, especially in Plaza de la Paja and on Cava Baja, Cava Alta, and Almendro streets. Chueca is sophisticated, colorful and lively. In Santa Ana, a very touristy enclave, avoid the bars in the main plaza, which are always crowded and usually pricier, and get into the ones on the side streets. The bars in the Salamanca neighborhood are more sober and traditional, but the food is often excellent.

Tapas Bars

★ **El Bocaíto.** This place has three dining areas and more than 130 tapas on the menu, including 15–20 types of *tostas* (toast topped with prawns, egg and garlic, paté with caviar, cockles, etc.), and surely the best *pescaito frito* (deep fried whitebait) in the city. ✉ *Libertad 6, Chueca* ☎ *91/532–1219* ⏲ *Closed Sat. morning, Sun., and Aug.*

El Abuelo. This historic place, which has barely changed since it was founded at the beginning of the 20th century, is famous for serving only two tapas (grilled shrimp and shrimp sautéed with garlic), usually accompanied by the house's homemade red wine, and for doing them better than anyone. ✉ *Victoria 12, Sol* ☎ *91/521–2319.*

Casa Lucas. Some of the favorites at this small, cozy bar with a short but creative selection of homemade tapas include the *Carinena* (grilled pork sirloin with caramelized onion) or the *Madrid* (scrambled eggs with onion morcilla and pine seeds in a tomato base). ✉ *Cava Baja 30, La Latina* ☎ *91/365–0804* ⏲ *No lunch Wed.*

Juana la Loca. This newcomer serves plenty of sophisticated and unusual tapas that can be as pricey as they are delightful (do *not* miss the tortilla de patatas). If you drop by the bar during the weekend, go early: the tapas will be at their freshest. On weekdays, order by the menu. ✉ *Plaza Puerta de Moros 4, La Latina* ☎ *91/364–0525* ⏲ *Closed Mon.*

La Bardemcilla. This homey bar belongs to Javier Bardem's family—note the actor's family pictures on the walls. There are plenty of tables, and a good selection of wines and tapas. Highlights include the grilled vegetables and *huevos estrellados.* There's also a fixed price lunch for less than €10. ✉ *Augusto Figueroa 47, Chueca* ☎ *91/521–4256* ⏲ *No lunch Sat.*

La Dolores. Usually crowded and noisy, this bar serves one of the best draft beers in Madrid. It has also a decent selection of pricey tapas, which you can enjoy at one of the few tables in the back. ✉ *Plaza de Jesús 4, Santa Ana* ☎ *91/429–2243.*

Taberna de Cien Vinos. If you are a wine buff, don't leave La Latina without stopping at this bar; you can have the dish of the day (usually beans or marmitako—a thick tuna and potato soup—in winter and a cold soup in summer) as you down one their many Spanish wines available by the glass. ✉ *Nuncio 17, La Latina* ☎ *91/365–4704.*

El Cervantes. Clean, comfortable and very popular among locals, this place serves plenty of hot and cold tapas. A good choice here is the *pulpo a la gallega* (octopus with potatoes, olive oil, and paprika). You may also want to go for the tapas sampler. ✉ *Plaza de Jesús 7, Santa Ana* ☎ *91/429–6093.*

Estay. A two-floor bar and restaurant with functional furnishings, this place has quickly become a landmark among the city's bourgeois crowd. The tapas menu is plentiful and diverse. Specialties include the *tortilla Espanola con atun y lechuga* (Spanish omelette with tuna fish and lettuce), and the *rabas* (fried calamari). They have a dish of the day for €10, and a few tapas samplers. ✉ *Hermosilla 46, Salamanca* ☎ *91/578–0470* ⏲ *Closed Sun.*

La Biotza. This trendy place with a slightly industrial look is a favorite among Madrileños working and living in the Salamanca neighborhood. Expect an inexpensive fixed price lunch menu and a good assortment of tapas and raciones. Show up early, around 1:30 PM, or be prepared to wait. ✉ *Claudio Coello 27, Salamanca* ☎ *91/781–0313.*

Cafés

Delic. This warm and inviting café is a hangout for Madrid's trendy and fashionable crowd. Besides the *patatitas con mousse de parmesano*

TAPAS, A MOVEABLE FEAST

N**EXT TO PAINTINGS,** *Madrid's tapas may be the city's most creative and irresistible attraction. Originally a lid used to tapar (cover or close) a glass of wine, a tapa is a kind of hors d'oeuvre that often comes free with a drink. (The term supposedly came from pieces of ham or cheese laid across glasses of wine—to keep flies out and to keep stagecoach drivers sober.) The history of tapas goes back to the 781-year (7th- to 15th-century) Moorish presence on the Iberian Peninsula. The Moors brought with them exotic ingredients, such as saffron, almonds, and peppers. They introduced sweets and pastries, and created refreshingly cold almond- and vegetable-based soups, still popular today. The Moorish taste for small and varied delicacies has in fact become Spain's best-known culinary innovation.*

Often miniature versions of classic Spanish dishes, tapas allow you to sample different kinds of food and wine with minimal alcohol poisoning, especially on a tapeo, the Spanish version of a pub crawl: you walk off your wine and tapas as you move from bar to bar. Most restaurants have tapas bars where you can test the food without committing to a sit-down meal. Here are a few standards to watch for: croquetas *(deep fried fritters with bechamel),* tortilla de patata *(Spanish omelette),* chorizo *(hard pork sausage),* gambas *(shrimp grilled or cooked in parsley, oil, and garlic),* patatas bravas *(potatoes in spicy sauce), and* boquerones en vinagre *(fresh anchovies marinated in salt and vinegar). The best place to start a tapa tour is in and around Plaza Santa Ana or Cava Baja in the La Latina neighborhood.*

(potatoes with a Parmesan cheese mousse) and zucchini cake, homesick travelers will find carrot cake, brownies, and pumpkin pie among the varied, if eclectic, selections. ✉ *Costanilla de San Andrés 14 (Plaza de la Paja), La Latina* ☎ *91/364–5450* ⊙ *Closed Mon.*

Cafe Gijón. Madrid's most famous literary café has hosted highbrow *tertulias*, discussion groups that meet regularly to hash out the political and artistic issues of the day, since the 19th century. ✉ *Paseo de Recoletos 21, Chamberí* ☎ *91/521–5425.*

El Jardin Secreto. This place has a romantic and exotic setting, with eclectic furniture and lamps (both for sale), savory chocolates, and a generous selection of tasty pastries. It's the perfect place to sip infusions and unwind. ✉ *C/de Conde Duque 2, Centro* ☎ *91/364–5450.*

Café del Círculo ("La Pecera"). Spacious and elegant with large velvet curtains, marble floors, painted ceilings, and sculptures scattered throughout, this café inside the famous art center, Círculo de Bellas Artes, feels more like a private club than a café; expect a bustling intellectual crowd. ✉ *Marqués de Casa Riera 2, Centro* ☎ *91/522–5092.*

Café de Oriente. This landmark has a magnificent view of the Royal Palace and its front yard. Divided into two sections—the left one serves tapas and raciones and the the right one serves more elaborate food—the café also has a splendid terrace that's open when the sun is out. ✉ *Plaza de Oriente 2, Centro* ☎ *91/547–1564.*

Café Libertad. More than just a café, this old staple of Madrid is a music and poetry venue—almost every famous songwriter, musician, and poet has passed through this decadent and charming hangout. ✉ *C/de la Libertad 8, Chueca* ☎ *91/532–1150* 🌐 *www.libertad8cafe.com.*

Chocolatería San Ginés. Gastronomical historians suggest that the practice of dipping explains the reason for Spaniard's lasting fondness for hot, thick chocolate. Only a few of the old places where this hot drink was served exclusively (with crisp *churros*), such as this *chocolaterí*, remain standing. Open from 6 PM to 7 AM, it has also the undistinguished privilege of being the last stop of the bleary-eyed after a night out. ✉ *Pasadizo de San Ginés (enter by Arenal 11), Sol* ☎ *91/365–6546* ⊗ *Closed Mon.*

WHERE TO EAT

Madrileños tend to eat their meals even later than in other parts of Spain, and that's saying something. Restaurants open for lunch at 1:30 and fill up by 3, during which time most offer a *menú del día* (daily fixed-price special) that includes a main course, dessert, wine, and coffee. Dinnertime begins at 9, but reservations for 11 are common, and a meal can be a wonderfully lengthy (up to three hours) affair. If you face hunger meltdown several hours before dinner, make the most of the early evening tapas hour. Dress in most Madrid restaurants and tapas bars is casual but stylish. Compared with Barcelona, the pricier places are a bit more formal; men often wear jackets and ties, and women often wear skirts.

$$$$ ✕ **Casa Benigno.** A specialist in Mediterranean cuisine, this hideaway in northeastern Madrid is best known for its rice dishes, including *arroz a la banda* (rice with pre-shelled seafood) and the best (and most expensive) paella in town. King Juan Carlos is a regular. Accompany the culinary inventions with your choice of olive oil from a truly encyclopedic selection. Owner-creator Don Norberto takes gracious care of international diners, suggesting wines from all over the Iberian Peninsula and guiding you through the casual, understated premises. ✉ *Benigno Soto 9, Chamartín* ☎ *91/416–9357* *Reservations essential* ▭ *AE, DC, MC, V* ⊗ *Closed Mon., Aug., Holy Week, and Christmas wk. No lunch Sat. or dinner Sun.*

$$$$ ✕ **Horcher.** Once Madrid's best restaurant, this place is now widely considered little more than an overpriced reminder of its former glory. Nevertheless, the faithful continue to fill this shrine to fine dining. Wild boar, venison, and roast duck are standard fare. Fish and meat stroganoff, pork chops with sauerkraut, and *baumkuchen* (a chocolate-covered fruit and cake dessert) reflect the restaurant's Germanic roots. The dining room is decorated with rust-color brocade and antique Austrian porcelain; an ample selection of French and German wines rounds out the menu. ✉ *Alfonso XII 6, Retiro* ☎ *91/522–0731* *Reservations essential* *Jacket and tie* ▭ *AE, DC, MC, V* ⊗ *Closed Sun. and Aug. No lunch Sat.*

$$$$ ✕ **Santceloni.** Santi Santamaria's Madrid branch of his Racó de Can Fabes just outside of Barcelona has proved an immediate and major success in the Spanish capital. Along with Juan Mari Arzak and Ferrán Adriá, one of the reigning troika of Spanish chefs, Santamaria may be the best of all. Lighter and more original than Arzak, less playful and bizarre than Adriá, Santamaria serves up exquisite combinations of Mediterranean ingredients accompanied by a comprehensive and daring wine list. ✉ *Paseo de la Castellana 57, Chamberí* ☎ *91/210–8840* *Reservations essential* ▭ *AE, DC, MC, V* ⊗ *Closed Sun. and Aug. No lunch Sat.*

$$$$ ✕ **Viridiana.** This place has a relaxed, somewhat cramped bistro feel, its black-and-white scheme punctuated by prints from Luis Buñuel's classic anticlerical film (for which the place is named). Iconoclast chef Abraham Garcia says "market-based" is too narrow a description for his creative menu, which changes every two weeks. Some standard dishes include: *foie ahumado con chutney de manzanas* (smoked foie with an apple chutney) and *huevos sobre mousse de hongos* (eggs on a mushroom mousse). Or try the superb duck pâté drizzled with sherry and served with Sauternes or Tokay wine. ✉ *Juan de Mena 14, Retiro* ☎ *91/531–1039* ✍ *Reservations essential* ▭ *AE, DC, MC, V* ⊗ *Closed Sun. and Holy Week.*

$$$–$$$$ ✕ **Asador Frontón I.** Fine meat and fish are the headliners here. Uptown, Asador Frontón II is swankier, but this downtown original is more charming. Appetizers include *anchoas frescas* (fresh grilled anchovies) and *pimientos rellenos con bacalao* (peppers stuffed with cod). The huge *chuletón* (T-bone steak), seared over charcoal and sprinkled with sea salt, is for two or more; order *cogollo de lechuga* (lettuce hearts) to accompany. The *kokotxas de merluza* (hake jowls) are supremely light and aromatic. ✉ *Tirso de Molina 7 (entrance on Jesus y Maria, 1), Lavapiés* ☎ *91/369–1617* ✉ *Pedro Muguruza 8, Chamartín* ☎ *91/345–3696* ✍ *Reservations essential* ▭ *AE, DC, MC, V* ⊗ *No dinner Sun.*

$$$–$$$$ Fodor'sChoice ★ ✕ **El Chaflán.** Juan Pablo Felipe, one of the heralds of Spain's new modern cuisine, has converted what was once a venue for traditional Cantabrian cuisine into a temple of sophistication. The soothing pastel tones, indirect colored lighting, and minimalist atmosphere evoke comfort and style. The open kitchen gives you a view of the master chef at work, and the skylight creates a cheery lunch atmosphere. The dishes and the sampler menu (once a year, and for one week, all the sampler dishes carry white truffle as one of the main ingredients) change constantly and reflect the chef's innovative style. The seasonal highlights include the chef's unique gazpacho (not the traditionally red soup, but a transparent golden gelatin obtained from a mix of tomato water, olive oil, and vinegar, with cumin bread, pepper, and ham on top), and the exceptionally creamy mushroom risotto. ✉ *Avda. de Pio XII 34, Chamartín* ☎ *91/345–0450* ▭ *AE, DC, MC, V* ⊗ *Closed Sun. and 2 wks in Aug. No lunch Sat.*

$$$–$$$$ Fodor'sChoice ★ ✕ **La Broche.** Sergi Arola, a Ferrán Adriá disciple, has vaulted directly to the apex of Madrid dining. The minimalist dining room allows you to concentrate on the hot-cold, surf-turf counterpoints of the seasonal menu. (Surf-turf has become a hallmark of the chef's style; playing with food temperature is also a distinctive trait.) The *menú de degustación* permits Sergi and his staff to run you through the gastronomic color wheel, generally progressing from light to dark, fish to foie, seafood to tenderloin. Try a peppery Priorat (a Miserere, for example) with your beef or venison. ✉ *Miguel Angel 29, Chamberí* ☎ *91/399–3437* ✍ *Reservations essential* ▭ *AE, DC, MC, V* ⊗ *Closed weekends and Easter wk.*

★ $$$–$$$$ ✕ **La Terraza—Casino de Madrid.** This rooftop terrace just off Puerta del Sol is in one of Madrid's oldest, most exclusive clubs (the *casino,* a club for gentlemen, not gamblers). The food is inspired and overseen by Ferrán Adriá, who runs his own famous restaurant, El Bullí, near Roses in Catalonia. Francisco Roncero's creations closely follow Adriá's trademarks: try any of the light and tasty mousses and foams or indulge in the unique tapas—experiments of flavor, texture, and temperature. There's also a sampler menu. ✉ *Alcalá 15, Sol* ☎ *91/521–8700* ✍ *Reservations essential* ▭ *AE, DC, MC, V* ⊗ *Closed Sun. and Aug. No lunch Sat.*

$$$–$$$$ ✕ **La Trainera.** With its nautical theme and maze of little dining rooms, this informal restaurant is all about fresh seafood—the best money can buy. Crab, lobster, shrimp, mussels, and a dozen other types of shellfish are served by weight in *raciones* (large portions). Although many Spanish diners share several plates of these shellfish as their entire meal, the grilled hake, sole, or turbot makes an unbeatable second course. To accompany the legendary *carabineros* (giant scarlet shrimp), skip the listless house wine and go for a bottle of Albariño, from the southern Gali-

cian coast. ✉ *Lagasca 60, Salamanca* ☎ *91/576–8035* ▭ *AE, MC, V* ⊗ *Closed Sun. and Aug.*

$$$–$$$$ ✕ **Lhardy.** Serving Madrid specialties for more than 150 years, Lhardy looks about the same as it must have on day one, with its dark-wood paneling, brass chandeliers, and red-velvet chairs. Most people come for the traditional *cocido a la madrileña* and *callos a la madrileña.* Game, sea bass, and soufflés are also available. Dining rooms are upstairs; the ground-floor entry doubles as a delicatessen and stand-up coffee bar that fills on chilly winter mornings with shivering souls sipping steaming-hot *caldo* (broth) from silver urns. ✉ *Carrera de San Jerónimo 8, Sol* ☎ *91/522–2207* ▭ *AE, DC, MC, V* ⊗ *Closed Aug. No dinner Sun.*

$$$–$$$$ Fodor'sChoice ★ ✕ **Zalacaín.** This place introduced nouvelle Basque cuisine to Spain in the 1970s and has since become a Madrid classic. It is particularly known for using the best and freshest seasonal products available, as well as for having the best service in town. From the variety of fungi and game meat to the hard-to-find seafood served, the food here tends to be unusual—you won't find many of these sorts of ingredients, or dishes, elsewhere. The restaurant has a deep-apricot color scheme that is made more dramatic by dark wood and gleaming silver. Inside, you'll feel like you're in a rather exclusive villa. ✉ *Alvarez de Baena 4, Chamartín* ☎ *91/561–4840* ✍ *Reservations essential* 👔 *Jacket and tie* ▭ *AE, DC, V* ⊗ *Closed Sun., Aug., and 1 wk at Easter. No lunch Sat.*

$$$ ✕ **Julián de Tolosa.** This rustic, designer-decorated spot is famous for *alubias pintas* (red kidney beans) from the Basque town of Tolosa. The *bellota* (acorn-fed) ham here is fine-sliced and unctuous, while the two-person chuletón is excellent. The *pimientos de piquillo* (roasted sweet red peppers) come to the table sizzling and may just be the best in the world. Try a Basque *txakolí* (tart, young white wine) with your first course and a Ribera de Duero later. Let maître d' and owner Angela talk you into a diminutive flask of *pacharán,* the famous Basque sloe-berry liqueur, over coffee. ✉ *Cava Baja 18, Centro* ☎ *91/365–8210* ✍ *Reservations essential* ▭ *AE, DC, MC, V* ⊗ *Closed Sun.*

$$–$$$ Fodor'sChoice ★ ✕ **Botín.** The *Guinness Book of Records* calls this the world's oldest restaurant (1725), and Hemingway called it the best. The latter claim may be a bit over the top, but the restaurant *is* excellent and extremely charming (and so successful that the owners opened a "branch" in Miami, Florida). There are four floors of tile, wood-beam dining rooms, and, if you're seated upstairs, you'll pass ovens dating back centuries. Musical groups called *tunas* often drop in to meander among the hordes. Specialties are *cochinillo* (roast pig) and *cordero* (roast lamb). It's rumored Goya washed dishes here before he made it as a painter. ✉ *Cuchilleros 17, off Plaza Mayor, Centro* ☎ *91/366–4217* ▭ *AE, DC, MC, V.*

★ **$$–$$$** ✕ **Casa Paco.** This Castilian tavern wouldn't have looked out of place two or three centuries ago. Squeeze past the old, zinc-top bar, crowded with Madrileños downing shots of Valdepeñas red wine, and into the tile dining rooms. Feast on thick slabs of red meat, sizzling on plates so hot that it continues to cook at your table. The Spanish consider overcooking a sin, so expect looks of dismay if you ask for your meat well done (*bien hecho*). You order by weight, so remember that a *medio kilo* is more than a pound. To start, try the *pisto manchego* (the La Mancha version of ratatouille) or the Castilian *sopa de ajo* (garlic soup). ✉ *Puerta Cerrada 11, Centro* ☎ *91/366–3166* ✍ *Reservations essential* ▭ *AE, DC, MC, V* ⊗ *Closed Sun. and Aug.*

$$–$$$ ✕ **Ciao.** Always noisy and packed, Madrid's best Italian restaurant serves homemade pastas, such as tagliatelle with wild mushrooms and *panzarotti* stuffed with spinach and ricotta. These are popular as inexpensive main courses; but the kitchen also turns out saltinbocca and veal scallopini, accompanied by a good selection of Italian wines. Mirrored walls and sleek black furniture convincingly evoke fashionable Milan. A Chamberí location, run by the owner's sons and daughter, also serves pizza. ✉ *Argensola 7, Centro* ☎ *91/308–2519* ✉ *Apodaca 20, Chamberí* ☎ *91/447–0036* ✍ *Reservations essential* ▭ *AE, DC, MC, V* ⊙ *Closed Sept. and Sun. No lunch Sat.*

★ $$–$$$ ✕ **El Cenador del Prado.** The name means "The Prado Dining Room," and the settings include a boldly painted dining area and plant-filled conservatory, as well as a separate baroque salon (a sitting area, mainly occupied by large groups). The innovative menu has French and Asian touches, as well as exotic Spanish dishes. The house specialty is *patatas a la importancia* (sliced potatoes fried in a sauce of garlic, parsley, and clams); other options include black rice with baby squid and prawns, and sirloin on a pear pastry puff. For dessert try the *bartolillos* (custard-filled pastries). ✉ *C. del Prado 4, Retiro* ☎ *91/429–1561* ▭ *AE, DC, MC, V* ⊙ *Closed Sun. and 1 wk in Aug. No lunch Sat.*

$$–$$$ ✕ **El Landó.** This castizo restaurant with dark-wood-panel walls and lined with bottles of wine serves classic Spanish food. On the staircase that leads to the main dining area are pictures of famous celebrities (including many Americans) who have eaten at this typically noisy landmark. Specialities of the house are *huevos estrellados* (fried eggs with potatoes and sausage), grilled meats, a good selection of fish (sea bass, haddock, grouper) with many different sauces, and steak tartare. As you sit down for your meal, you'll be immediately served a plate of bread with tomato and Spanish ham. ✉ *Plaza Gabriel Miró 8, La Latina* ☎ *91/366–7681* ✍ *Reservations essential* ▭ *AE, DC, MC, V* ⊙ *Closed Sun. and Aug.*

$$–$$$ ✕ **La Ancha.** The traditional Spanish menu includes some of the best lentils, meat cutlets, and croquettes in Madrid, as well as more elaborate dishes, such as the juicy *tortilla con almejas* (Spanish omelet with clams). Both locations belong to the same family and are unpretentious inside but are outstanding in terms of quality. The original Prícipe de Vergara location has a tented patio for the summer; the newer one behind the Congress is often filled with politicians. ✉ *Prícipe de Vergara 204, Chamartín* ☎ *91/563–8977* ✉ *Zorrilla 7, Centro* ☎ *91/429–8186* ▭ *AE, DC, MC, V* ⊙ *Closed Sun. and 1 wk. in Aug.; Zorrilla branch closed 3 wks in Aug.*

$$–$$$ ✕ **La Bola.** First opened as a *botellería* (wine shop) in 1802, La Bola developed slowly into a tapas bar and eventually into a full-fledged restaurant. The traditional setting is the draw: the bar is original and the cozy dining nooks, decorated with polished wood, Spanish tile, and lace curtains, are charming. The restaurant still belongs to the founding family, with the seventh generation currently in training. The house specialty is *cocido a la madrileña* (a hearty meal of broth, garbanzo beans, vegetables, potatoes, and pork). ✉ *C. Bola 5, Ópera* ☎ *91/547–6930* ▭ *No credit cards* ⊙ *No dinner Sun.*

★ $$–$$$ ✕ **La Gamella.** Some of the American-born former chef Dick Stephens's dishes–Caesar salad, hamburger, steak tartare–are still on the reasonably priced menu at this perennially popular dinner spot. The new selections are a fusion of Asian, Mediterranean, and American dishes. The sophisticated rust-red dining room, batik tablecloths, oversize plates, and attentive service remain the same. The lunchtime menú del día is a great value. ✉ *Alfonso XII 4, Retiro* ☎ *91/532–4509* ▭ *AE, DC, MC, V* ⊙ *Closed Sun. and last 2 wks in Aug. No lunch Sat.*

$$–$$$ ✕ **La Paloma.** With a soft and elegant interior with light blue walls, marble floors, linen tablecloths, and upholstered armchairs, this spot perfectly fits into its bourgeois environment. In this split-level restaurant, chef Segundo Alonso pays great attention to detail, taking care that his modern Spanish dishes can compete with any in Madrid's priciest restau-

rants. It's best known for game meats and a variety of mushrooms in season. Other dishes to try include *erizos de mar gratinados* (toasted sea urchins with quail eggs) and *ensalada templada de carabineros* (warm artichoke and scarlet shrimp salad). ✉ *Jorge Juan 39, Salamanca* ☎ *91/576–8692* ▭ *AE, DC, MC, V* ⊗ *Closed Sun. and Aug.*

$$–$$$ ✕ **Pedro Larumbe.** This restaurant is literally the pinnacle of the ABC shopping center between Paseo de la Castellana and Calle Serrano. Dining quarters include a summer roof terrace and an Andalusian patio. Chef-owner Pedro Larumbe is known for his presentations of such contemporary dishes as *foie-gras y piña caramelizada* (foie gras and caramelized pineapple) and *bacalao al pil-pil verde de cilantro* (codfish cooked with oil, garlic and cilantro sauce, and eggplant). The dessert buffet is an art exhibit. A good wine list complements the fare. ✉ *Pàseo de la Castellana 34, at C. Serrano 61, Salamanca* ☎ *91/575–1112* ▭ *AE, DC, MC, V* ⊗ *Closed Sun., Easter wk, and 2 wks in Aug. No lunch Sat.*

$$–$$$ ✕ **Sacha.** Playful sketches decorate the walls of this cozy, French bistro-like restaurant, filled with oversize antique furniture. The cuisine is provincial Spanish—with a touch of imagination. The *lasaña de changurro* (large crab lasagna), *arroz con setas y perdiz* (rice with mushrooms and partridge), and *emperador suculento* (swordfish on a fried tomato base) are some of the house specialties. ✉ *Juan Hurtado de Mendosa 11,* ☎ *91/345–5952* ✍ *Reservations essential* ▭ *AE, DC, MC, V* ⊗ *Closed Sun.*

$$ ✕ **Champagnería Gala.** Hidden on a back street not far from Calle Atocha and the Reina Sofía museum, this cheerful Mediterranean restaurant is usually packed, thanks to the choice of paellas, *fideuas* (paellas with noodles instead of rice), risottos, and hearty bean stews—all served with salad, dessert, and a wine jar. The front dining area is modernly festive; the back room incorporates trees and plants in a glassed-in patio. ✉ *Moratín 22, Santa Ana* ☎ *91/429–2562* ✍ *Reservations essential* ▭ *No credit cards.*

$–$$ Fodor's Choice ★ ✕ **Casa Ciriaco.** At Madrid's most traditional restaurant, host to a long list of Spain's illustrious, from royalty to philosophers and painters and bullfighters, expect simple home cooking in an unpretentious environment. You'll get a flagon of Valdepeñas or a split of a Rioja reserva to accompany the *perdiz con judiones* (partridge with broad beans). The *pepitoria de gallina* (hen in an almond sauce) is another favorite. ✉ *C. Mayor 84, Centro* ☎ *91/559–5066* ▭ *AE, MC, V* ⊗ *Closed Wed. and Aug.*

$–$$ ✕ **Casa Lastra.** Established in 1926, this Asturian tavern is popular with Lavapiés locals. The rustic, half-tile walls strung with relics from the Asturian countryside include wooden clogs, cow bells, sausages, and garlic. Specialties include *fabada* (Asturian white-beans stewed with sausage), *fabas con almejas* (white beans with clams), and *queso de cabrales,* mega-aromatic cheese made in the Picos de Europa. Great hunks of crisp bread and hard Asturian cider complement a hearty meal; desserts include tangy baked apples. It has an inexpensive fixed-price daily lunch menu weekdays. ✉ *Olivar 3, Lavapiés* ☎ *91/369–0837* ▭ *AE, MC, V* ⊗ *Closed Wed. and July. No dinner Sun.*

$–$$ Fodor's Choice ★ ✕ **La Trucha.** This Andalusian deep-fry specialist, decorated with hanging hams and garlic, is one of the happiest places in Madrid. The staff is jovial, and the house specialty, *trucha a la truchana* (crisped trout stuffed with ample garlic and diced *jabugo,* ham) is a work of art. Other star entrées are *chopitos* (baby squid), *pollo al ajillo* (chunks of chicken in crisped garlic), and *espárragos trigueros* (wild asparagus). *Jarras* (pitchers) of chilled Valdepeñas, a young Beaujolais-like claret, seem to function as laughing gas in this magic little bistro. The Nuñez de Arce branch, just down from the Hotel Reina Victoria, is usually less crowded. ✉ *Manuel Fernandez y Gonzalez 3, Santa Ana* ☎ *91/429–3778* ✉ *Nuñez* *de Arce 6, Santa Ana ☎ 91/532–0890 ▭ AE, MC, V ⊙ Closed Sun. and Mon. Nuñez de Arce branch also closed Aug.*

$–$$ ✕ **La Vaca Verónica.** In the golden-age literary quarter, this romantic little hideaway is gathering a following for its *carne a la brasa* (meat cooked over coals), *pescado a la sal* (fish cooked in a shell of salt), homemade pastas with various seafood dressings, and terrific salads. The pasta *a los carabineros* (with scarlet shrimp) is said to be seducing everyone from Penelope Cruz to Alie Nicholas. ✉ *Moratín 38, Santa Ana* ☎ *91/429–7827* ▭ *AE, DC, MC, V* ⊙ *No lunch Sat.*

★ $–$$ ✕ **Taberna Bilbao.** Run by a couple, this popular tavern—highly praised by local restaurant owners and restaurant goers—is something between a tapas bar and a restaurant. It has three small dining areas, floor and walls of red Italian marble, plain wooden furniture, and a menu that is representative of Basque cuisine. Try any of the fish or mushroom *revueltos* (scrambled eggs), the *habas* (broad beans), or the *bacalao* (cod). And order a glass of *txakolí* (tart, young Basque white wine). ✉ *Costanilla de San Andrés 8 (Plaza de la Paja), La Latina* ☎ *91/365–6125* ✍ *Reservations essential* ▭ *AE, DC, MC, V* ⊙ *Closed Mon.*

$–$$ ✕ **Taberna Carmencita.** This old Madrid favorite is now part of priest-restaurateur Patxo de Lezama's sprawling gastronomic empire (which extends to Washington, D.C.). The ceramic-tile tavern retains much of the atmosphere it had in the mid-20th century, when Carmencita herself cared for customers as though they were long-lost children. Try the *chipirones en su tinta* (squid in its ink) and *sopa de pescado* (fish soup), or go for the €21 sampler menu. The restaurant is just north of the Gran Vía–Calle Alcalá intersection. ✉ *Libertad 16, Centro* ☎ *91/531–6612* ▭ *AE, DC, MC, V* ⊙ *Closed Sun. No lunch Sat.*

★ $–$$ ✕ **Viuda de Vacas.** This rustic, two-floor restaurant—in a building that's more than 200 years old—is one of the pioneers upon which the La Latina neighborhood has built its reputation as a gastronomic enclave. Simplicity is key, from the furnishings, which still preserve some of the old tiles, to the traditional, high quality food—cooked in a coal kitchen. This place is a perennial favorite for all ages. Highlights include *calabacines gratinados* (grilled zucchini), *rabo de toro* (bull's tail), and *bacalao abras* (cod with fried onions and fries). ✉ *Cava Alta 23, La Latina* ☎ *91/366–5847* ▭ *DC, MC, V* ⊙ *Closed Thurs. and 10 days in Sept. No dinner Sun.*

¢–$ ✕ **La Finca de Susana.** A huge, diverse crowd comes here in search of grilled vegetables, oven-cooked bacalao with spinach, and caramelized duck. Not irrelevant is the fact that this is one of the best bargains in the city. It has a loft-like interior with hardwood floors and is decorated with warm tones. At the end of the dining room is a huge bookcase lined with wine bottles. Arrive by 1:30 for lunch and 8:30 for dinner or be prepared to wait. ✉ *C/Arlabán 4, Centro* ☎ *91/369–3557* ✍ *Reservations not accepted* ▭ *MC, V.*

¢–$ ✕ **La Galette.** This quaint place will satisfy both vegetarians and non-vegetarians. In the evening it's candlelit, and baroque music plays in the background. Specialties include apple *croquetas* (deep fried fritters filled with apple and bechamel), spinach with tofu, onion soup, and cream of zucchini. ✉ *C/Conde de Aranda 11, Salamanca* ☎ *91/576–0641* ▭ *AE, DC, MC, V.*

¢–$ ✕ **La Musa.** The trendy, elegant vibe, and the creative and inexpensive menu of unique salads and tapas (try the *bomba,* a potato filled with meat or vegetables in a spinach sauce, or the huge meat and vegetable brochettas) draw a stylish young crowd. The original Malasaña location offers a breakfast menu during the week, and a smaller lunch and dinner menu. The newer, bigger, and more sophisticated Plaza de la Paja location opens only on the weekends for breakfast and has a more ex-

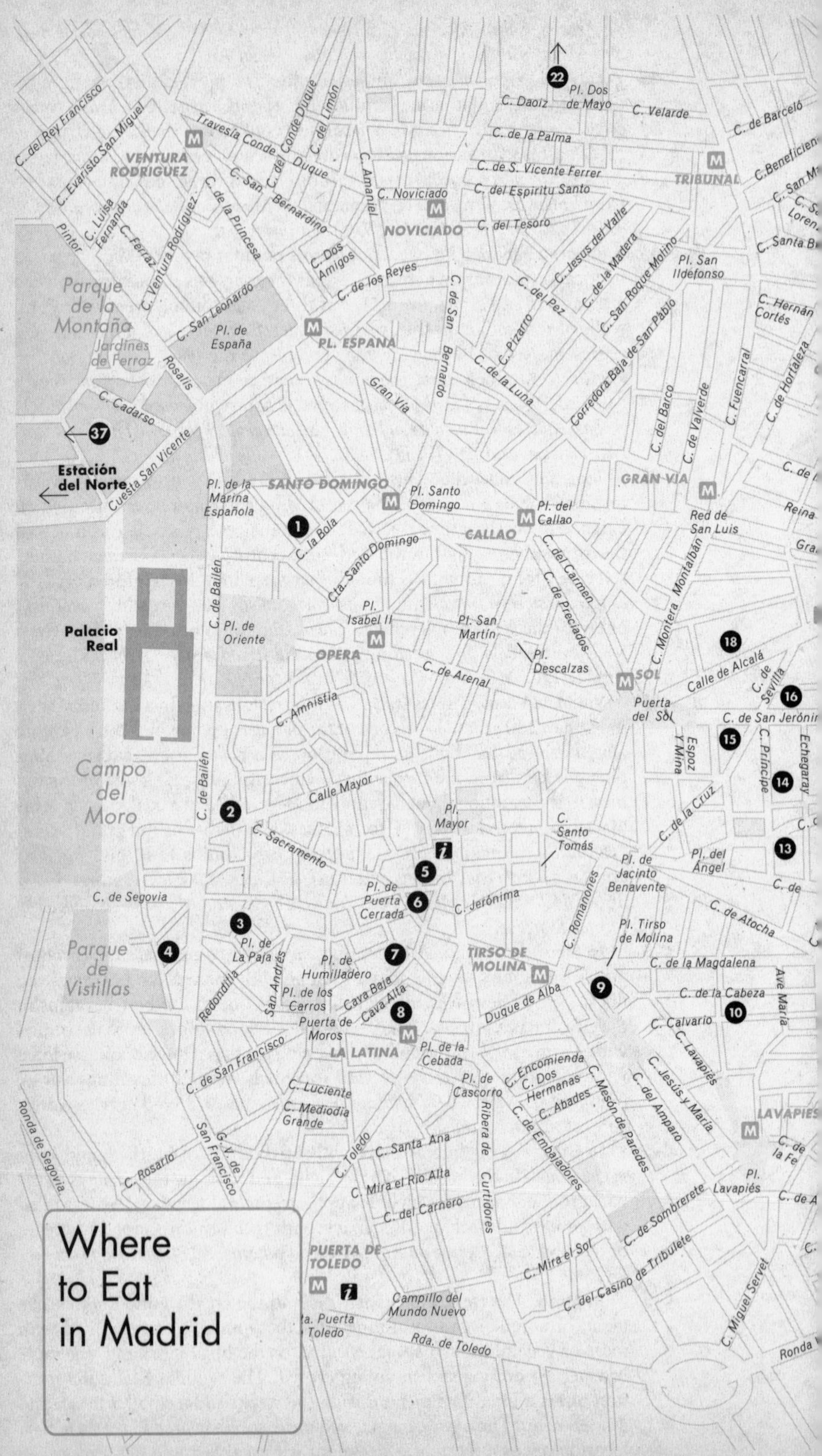
Where to Eat in Madrid
Pl. Dos de Mayo
C. Daoiz
C. Velarde
C. de Barceló
C. de la Palma
C. de S. Vicente Ferrer
C. del Espiritu Santo
TRIBUNAL
C. Beneficiencia
C. del Tesoro
C. Noviciado
NOVICIADO
C. del Rey Francisco
C. Evaristo San Miguel
VENTURA RODRIGUEZ
Travesía Conde Duque
C. del Conde Duque
C. del Limón
C. Amaniel
C. San Bernardino
C. de la Princesa
C. Luisa Fernanda
C. Ferraz
Pintor
C. Ventura Rodríguez
C. Dos Amigos
C. de los Reyes
C. de San Bernardo
C. del Pez
C. Jesus del Valle
C. de la Madera
C. San Roque Molino
Pl. San Ildefonso
C. Santa Bárbara
C. Hernán Cortés
Parque de la Montaña
Jardines de Ferraz
C. San Leonardo
Pl. de España
PL. ESPANA
Rosalis
Gran Via
C. Pizarro
C. de la Luna
Corredora Baja de San Pablo
C. del Barco
C. de Valverde
C. Fuencarral
C. de Hortaleza
C. Cadarso
37
Estación del Norte
Cuesta San Vicente
Pl. de la Marina Española
SANTO DOMINGO
Pl. Santo Domingo
Pl. del Callao
CALLAO
GRAN VIA
Red de San Luis
Reina
C. la Bola
Cta. Santo Domingo
C. del Carmen
C. de Preciados
C. Montera
Montalbán
C. de Bailén
Pl. de Oriente
Pl. Isabel II
OPERA
Pl. San Martín
Pl. Descalzas
C. de Arenal
SOL
Puerta del Sol
Calle de Alcalá
C. de Sevilla
C. de San Jerónimo
Palacio Real
C. Amnistía
Espoz Y Mina
C. Príncipe
Echegaray
Campo del Moro
Calle Mayor
Pl. Mayor
C. Sacramento
C. Santo Tomás
C. de la Cruz
Pl. de Jacinto Benavente
Pl. del Angel
C. de Segovia
Pl. de Puerta Cerrada
C. Jerónima
C. Romanones
C. de Atocha
Parque de Vistillas
Pl. de La Paja
Pl. de Humilladero
TIRSO DE MOLINA
Pl. Tirso de Molina
C. de la Magdalena
Redondilla
San Andrés
Pl. de los Carros
Cava Baja
Cava Alta
Puerta de Moros
LA LATINA
Duque de Alba
C. de la Cabeza
C. Calvario
Ave María
C. Lavapiés
Pl. de la Cebada
Pl. de Cascorro
C. Encomienda
C. Dos Hermanas
C. Abades
C. Mesón de Paredes
C. Jesús y María
C. del Amparo
C. de San Francisco
C. Luciente
C. Mediodia Grande
Ribera de Curtidores
C. de Embajadores
LAVAPIES
C. de la Fe
Ronda de Segovia
C. Rosario
San Francisco
G. V. de
C. Toledo
C. Santa Ana
C. Mira el Río Alta
C. del Carnero
Pl. Lavapiés
C. de Sombrerete
PUERTA DE TOLEDO
Campillo del Mundo Nuevo
C. Mira el Sol
C. del Casino de Tribulete
C. Miguel Servet
Rda. de Toledo
Ronda

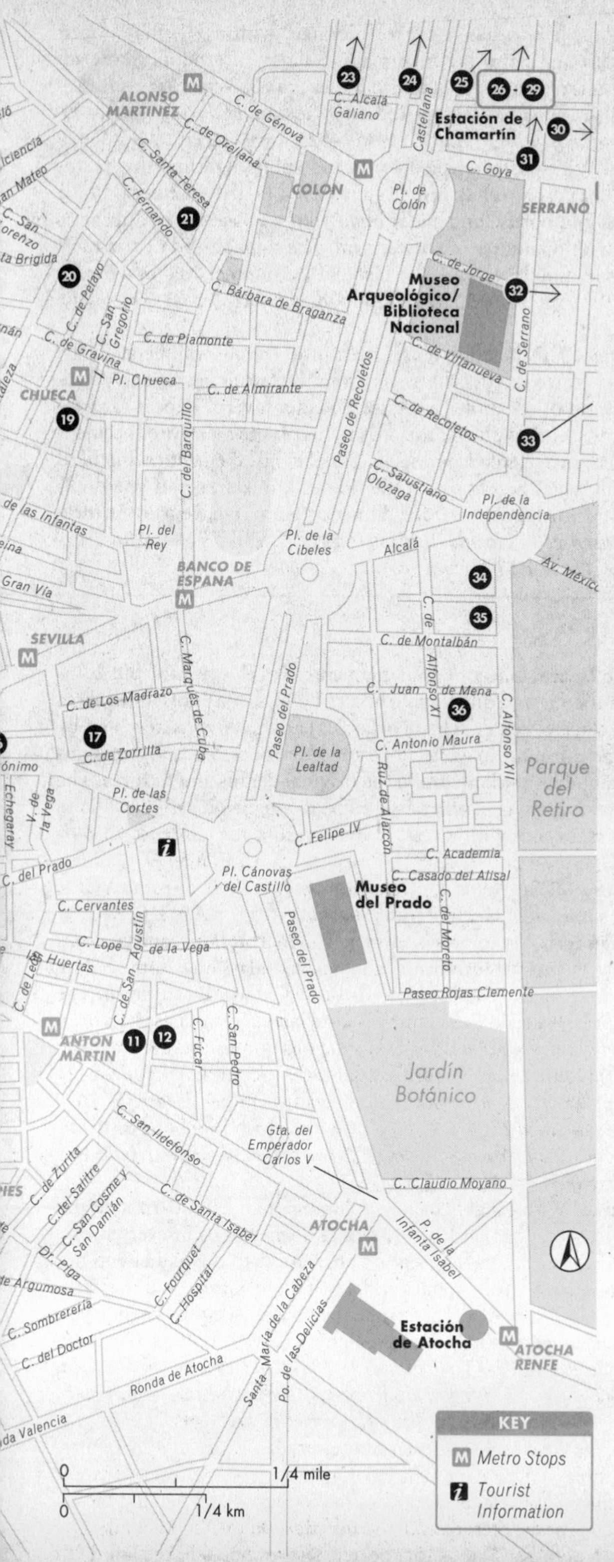

Asador Frontón I **9**
Botín **5**
Casa Benigno **27**
Casa Ciriaco. **2**
Casa Lastra **10**
Casa Mingo. **37**
Casa Paco **6**
Champagnería Gala **11**
Ciao. **21**
El Cenador del Prado. **13**
El Chaflán **25**
El Landó **4**
Horcher. **34**
Julián de Tolosa. **7**
La Ancha **17**
La Bola **1**
La Broche **23**
La Finca de Susana **16**
La Galette **33**
La Gamella **35**
La Musa **22**
La Paloma **32**
La Taberna Bilbao **29**
La Terraza–Casino de Madrid **18**
La Trainera **30**
La Trucha. **14**
La Vaca Verónica **12**
Lhardy. **15**
Nabucco **20**
Pedro Larumbe **26**
Sacha **24**
Santceloni. **28**
Taberna Bilbao **3**
Taberna Carmencita **19**
Viridiana. **36**
Viuda de Vacas **8**
Zalacaín **29**

pansive menu; it also has a cocktail lounge, with a DJ, that's open Thursday through Saturday nights and Sunday afternoon. Show up early or expect to wait. ✉ *C/Manuela Malasaña 18, Malasaña* ✍ *Reservations not accepted* ☎ *91/448–7558* ✉ *Costanilla de San Andres 12 (Plaza de la Paja), La Latina* ☎ *91/354–0255* ▭ *AE, DC, MC, V.*

¢–$ ✕ **Nabucco.** With pastel-washed walls and subtle lighting, this pizzeria and trattoria is a trendy but elegant haven in gritty Chueca. Fresh bread sticks and butter (and garlic olive oil if you ask for it) appear at your table within minutes of your arrival. The spinach and ricotta ravioli is heavenly, and the pizza is also tasty. In the summer, ask for a breezy seat facing the patio. ✉ *Hortaleza 108, Chueca* ☎ *91/310–0611* ▭ *AE, MC, V.*

¢ ✕ **Casa Mingo.** This bustling place, built into a stone wall beneath the Estación del Norte (across the street from the hermitage of San Antonio de la Florida), resembles an Asturian cider tavern. Expect to share long tables with other diners; the only items on the menu are succulent roast chicken, cheese, salad, and sausages, all to be taken with *sidra* (hard cider). Small tables are set up on the sidewalk in summer. If you don't come early (1 for lunch, 8:30 for dinner), you may have to wait for a table. ✉ *Paseo de la Florida 2, Moncloa* ☎ *91/547–7918* ✍ *Reservations not accepted* ▭ *No credit cards.*

WHERE TO STAY

$$$$ **AC Santo Mauro.** Once the Canadian embassy, this turn-of-the-20th-century mansion is now an intimate luxury hotel, an oasis of calm a short walk from the city center. The neoclassical architecture is accented by contemporary furniture in white, gray, and black hues. Some of the rooms in the main building still maintain the original details and fixtures. The top-notch restaurant is in what used to be the mansion's library. Views vary; request a room with a terrace overlooking the gardens. ✉ *Zurbano 36, Chamberí 28010* ☎ *91/319–6900* 🖷 *91/308–5477* 🌐 *www.ac-hotels.com* ⇨ *51 rooms* ♁ *Restaurant, coffee shop, in-room VCRs, pool, gym, sauna, bar, meeting room, parking (fee)* ▭ *AE, DC, MC, V.*

Fodor's Choice ★

$$$$ **Gran Meliá Fénix.** An impressive lobby with marble floors and columns decorated with antique furniture, and a stained-glass blue dome ceiling define the style of this completely refurbished Madrid institution. The hotel overlooks Plaza de Colón on the Castellana and is a mere hop from the posh shops of Calle Serrano. Its spacious rooms are decorated in reds and golds and are amply furnished; flowers abound. Ask for a room facing the Plaza de Colón; otherwise, the view is rather dreary. ✉ *Hermosilla 2, Salamanca 28001* ☎ *91/431–6700* 🖷 *91/576–0661* 🌐 *www.solmelia.com* ⇨ *216 rooms, 9 suites* ♁ *Café, hair salon, bar, baby-sitting, parking (fee)* ▭ *AE, DC, MC, V.*

$$$$ **Hotel Bauzá.** With a highly balanced combination of modern style and elegance, this hotel has dark wood floors, hi-fi stereos in every room, and other details that make it a good alternative to the higher end hotels. The rooms have functional yet distinctive furniture, and the bathrooms are beautifully tiled. The restaurant serves Mediterranean fusion food and has great views of the commercial Goya street. ✉ *Goya 79, Salamanca 28001* ☎ *91/435–7545* 🖷 *91/431–0943* 🌐 *www.hotelbauza.com* ⇨ *167 rooms, 3 suites, 7 apartments* ♁ *Restaurant, health club, bar, library, meeting room, parking (fee)* ▭ *AE, DC, MC, V.*

$$$$ **Orfila.** This elegant 1886 town house, hidden away in a leafy little residential street not far from Plaza Colón, has every comfort of a larger hotel, but more intimate, personalized surroundings. Originally the in-town residence of the literary and aristocratic Gomez-Acebo family, Orfila 6 was an address famous for theater performances in the late 19th

Fodor's Choice ★

and early 20th centuries. The restaurant, garden, and tearoom have period furniture; guest rooms are draped with stripe and floral silks. ✉ *Orfila 6, Chamberí 28010* ☎ *91/702–7770* 📠 *91/702–7772* 🌐 *www.hotelorfila.com* *28 rooms, 4 suites* *Restaurant, health club, bar, meeting room, parking (fee)* 💳 *AE, DC, MC, V.*

$$$$ **Ritz.** Alfonso XIII, about to marry Queen Victoria's granddaughter, encouraged the construction of this hotel, the most exclusive in Spain, for his royal guests. Opened in 1910 by the king himself (who personally supervised construction), the Ritz is a monument to the Belle Epoque, its salons furnished with rare antiques, hand-embroidered linens from Robinson & Cleaver, and handwoven carpets. Most rooms have views of the Prado. The restaurant, Goya, is famous (though pricey), and Sunday brunch is a feast served to the soothing strains of harp music. Weekend tea and supper are accompanied by chamber music from February to May. ✉ *Plaza de la Lealtad 5, Prado 28014* ☎ *91/701–6767* 📠 *91/701–6776* 🌐 *www.ritz.es* *167 rooms* *Restaurant, in-room data ports, in-room fax, hair salon, health club, massage, bar, parking (fee)* 💳 *AE, DC, MC, V.*

★ **$$$$** **Tryp Ambassador.** On an old street between Gran Vía and the Royal Palace, the Ambassador occupies the renovated 19th-century palace of the Dukes of Granada. A magnificent front door and a graceful three-story staircase recall the building's aristocratic past; the rest has been transformed into elegant, somewhat soulless lodgings favored by executives. Large guest rooms have sitting areas and mahogany furnishings, and floral fabrics. The greenhouse restaurant, filled with plants and songbirds, is especially pleasant on cold days. ✉ *Cuesta Santo Domingo 5 and 7, Opera 28013* ☎ *91/541–6700* 📠 *91/559–1040* 🌐 *www.solmelia.com* *182 rooms* *Restaurant, bar, airport shuttle, parking (fee)* 💳 *AE, DC, MC, V.*

$$$$ **Villa Magna.** The concrete facade here gives way to an interior furnished with 18th-century antiques. Prices are robust, but it's hard to find flourishes such as a champagne bar and—in the largest suite in Madrid—a white baby-grand piano. All rooms have large desks, and all bathrooms have fresh flowers. One restaurant, Le Divellec, has walnut paneling and the feel of an English library, and you can dine on its garden terrace in season. The other restaurant, the Tse-Yang, is Madrid's most exclusive for Chinese food. ✉ *Paseo de la Castellana 22, Salamanca 28046* ☎ *91/587–1234* 📠 *91/431–2286* 🌐 *www.madrid.hyatt.com* *164 rooms, 18 suites* *2 restaurants, hair salon, health club, massage, 2 bars, baby-sitting, business services, car rental, parking (fee)* 💳 *AE, DC, MC, V.*

★ **$$$$** **Villa Real.** For a medium-size hotel that combines elegance, modern amenities, friendly service, *and* a great location, look no further: the Villa Real faces Spain's parliament and is convenient to almost everything, particularly the Prado and Thyssen-Bornemisza museums. The simulated 19th-century facade gives way to an intimate lobby with modern furnishings. Many rooms are split-level, with a small sitting area. Some suites have whirlpool baths. ✉ *Plaza de las Cortés 10, Prado 28014* ☎ *91/420–3767* 📠 *91/420–2547* 🌐 *www.derbyhotels.es* *94 rooms, 20 suites* *Restaurant, in-room data ports, hair salon, sauna, bar, meeting room, parking (fee)* 💳 *AE, DC, MC, V.*

★ **$$$$** **Westin Palace.** Built in 1912, Madrid's most famous grand hotel is a Belle Epoque creation of Alfonso XIII and has hosted the likes of Dalí, Brando, Hayworth, and Madonna. Guest rooms are high-tech and generally impeccable; banquet halls and lobbies have been beautified and the facade restored. The Art Nouveau stained-glass dome over the lounge remains exquisitely original, while guest room windows are double-glazed against street noise. The suites are no less luxurious than

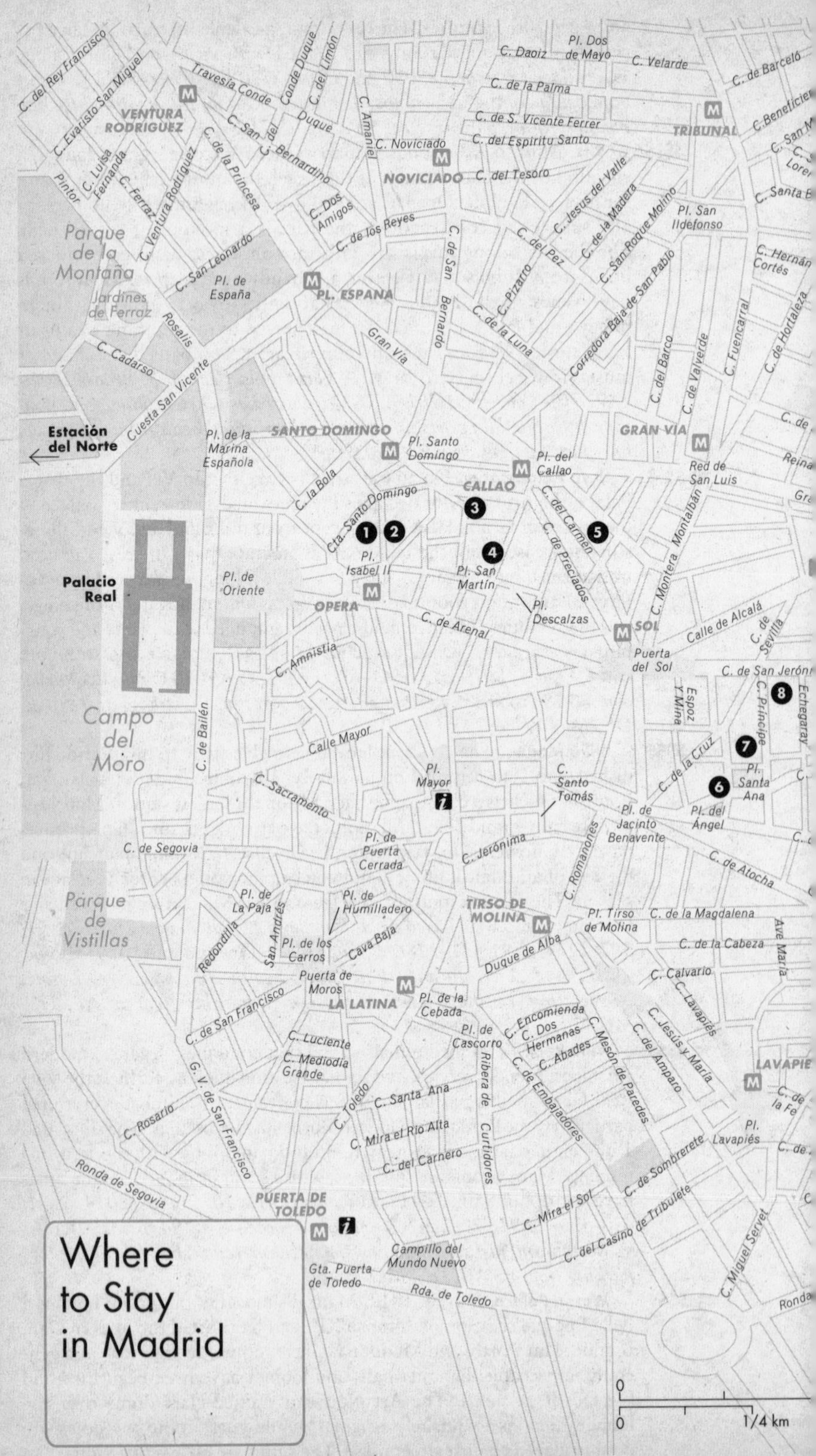

Where to Stay in Madrid
Estación del Norte
Palacio Real
Parque de la Montaña
Campo del Moro
Parque de Vistillas
VENTURA RODRÍGUEZ
NOVICIADO
TRIBUNAL
PL. ESPAÑA
SANTO DOMINGO
CALLAO
GRAN VÍA
OPERA
SOL
TIRSO DE MOLINA
LA LATINA
PUERTA DE TOLEDO
LAVAPIÉS
Gran Vía
Calle Mayor
Calle de Alcalá
Puerta del Sol
Pl. Mayor
Pl. de Oriente
Pl. Isabel II
Pl. Santa Ana
C. de Atocha
Rda. de Toledo
0
1/4 km

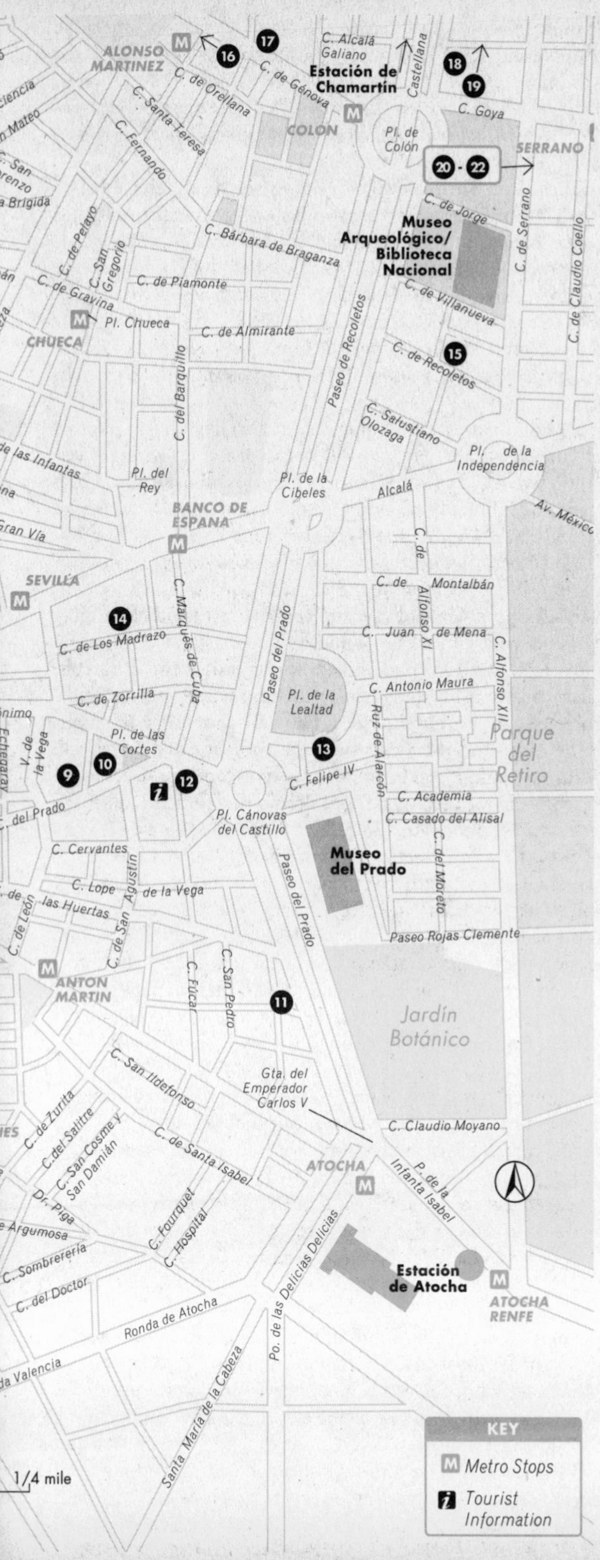

AC Santo Mauro 16
Hotel Bauzá 22
H H Campomanes 2
Gran Meliá Fénix 18
Inglés 8
Hostal Villar 7
Hotel Intur Palacio San Martín 4
Hotel Preciados 3
Jardín de Recoletos 15
Liabeny 5
Mora 11
NH Lagasca 20
Orfila 17
Ramón de la Cruz 21
Reina Victoria 6
Ritz 13
Suecia 14
Suite Prado 9
Tryp Ambassador 1
Villa Magna 19
Villa Real 10
Westin Palace 12

the opulent public spaces with Bang & Olufsen CD players, spacious bathrooms, double sinks, hot tubs, and separate shower stalls. ✉ *Plaza de las Cortés 7, Prado 28014* ☎ *91/360–8000* 📠 *91/360–8100* 🌐 *www.palacemadrid.com* *465 rooms, 45 suites* *2 restaurants, café, in-room data ports, gym, sauna, bar, business services, meeting room, parking (fee)* 💳 *AE, DC, MC, V.*

$$$ **Hotel Preciados.** In a 19th-century building on the quieter edge of one of Madrid's main shopping areas, this hotel is both charming and convenient. The rooms are modern and sophisticated—with hardwood floors and opaque glass closets. Some of the "double superiors" (slightly more expensive) have slanted ceilings and a skylight in the bathroom. ✉ *C/Preciados 37, Centro 28013* ☎ *91/454–4400* 📠 *91/454–4401* 🌐 *www.preciadoshotel.com* *73 rooms, 5 suites* *Restaurant, café, bar, meeting room, parking (fee), in-room data ports* 💳 *AE, DC, MC, V.*

$$$ **NH Lagasca.** In the heart of the elegant Salamanca neighborhood, this newish hotel combines large, brightly decorated rooms with an unbeatable location two blocks from Madrid's main shopping street, Calle Serrano. The marble lobbies border on the coldly functional, but they're fine as a meeting place. ✉ *Lagasca 64, Salamanca 28001* ☎ *91/575–4606* 📠 *91/575–1694* 🌐 *www.nh-hotels.com* *100 rooms* *Restaurant, bar, meeting room, parking (fee)* 💳 *AE, DC, MC, V.*

$$$ **Reina Victoria.** Long a Madrid favorite (particularly with bullfighters), this gleaming white Victorian building across Plaza Santa Ana from the Teatro Español was modernized at the end of the 20th century. The taurine theme is most evident in the bar, where stuffed bulls' heads peer curiously over your shoulder. The best rooms are the highest, for both the quiet and the views over the rooftops or theater. On Friday and Saturday night it can be impossible to escape the street noise below, and the coffee in the breakfast room should be avoided at all costs. ✉ *Plaza Santa Ana 14, Santa Ana 28012* ☎ *91/531–4500* 📠 *91/522–0307* *195 rooms* *Bar, meeting rooms* 💳 *AE, DC, MC, V.*

$$$ **Suecia.** The chief attraction here is location. The hotel is right next to the super-chic Círculo de Bellas Artes (an arts society–café–film–theater complex). The large lobby, which includes a café, is often bustling. Guest rooms are trendy, with contemporary art and futuristic light fixtures, but a little worn. ✉ *Marqués de Riera 4, Centro 28014* ☎ *91/531–6900* 📠 *91/521–7141* 🌐 *www.hotelsuecia.com* *119 rooms, 9 suites* *2 restaurants, bar, baby-sitting, parking (fee)* 💳 *AE, DC, MC, V.*

$$$ **Suite Prado.** Popular with Americans on short stays, this stylish apartment hotel is near the Prado, the Thyssen-Bornemisza, and the Plaza Santa Ana tapas area. The attractive attic studios on the fourth floor have sloped ceilings with wood beams; there are larger suites downstairs. All apartments are brightly decorated and have marble baths and basic kitchens. Breakfast is served daily upon request, by a friendly staff. ✉ *Manuel Fernández y González 10, Santa Ana 28014* ☎ *91/420–2318* 📠 *91/420–0559* 🌐 *www.suiteprado.com* *18 suites* *Kitchenettes, parking (fee)* 💳 *AE, DC, MC, V.*

$$–$$$ Fodor's Choice ★ **Hotel Intur Palacio San Martín.** In an unbeatable location and across from one of Madrid's most celebrated monuments (the Convent of Descalzas), this hotel, once the old U.S. embassy and later a luxurious residential building crowded with noblemen, still exudes a kind of glory. The entrance leads to a dome-glassed atrium that serves as a tranquil sitting area. The hotel has preserved an antique elevator, and many of the ceilings are carved and ornate. The rooms are spacious and carpeted; request one facing the big plaza. ✉ *Plaza de San Martín 5, Centro 28013* ☎ *91/701–5000* 📠 *91/701–5010* 🌐 *www.intur.com* *93* *rooms* ♿ *Restaurant, café, meeting rooms, parking (fee)* ▭ *AE, DC, MC, V.*

$$–$$$ **Jardín de Recoletos.** This sleek apartment hotel offers great value in a quiet street close to Plaza Colón and upmarket Calle Serrano. The large lobby has marble floors and a stained-glass ceiling and adjoins a café and restaurant. The commodious rooms, with light-wood trim and beige and yellow furnishings, include sitting and dining areas. "Superior" rooms and two-room suites have hydromassage baths and large terraces. Book well in advance. ✉ *Gil de Santivañes 6, Salamanca 28001* ☎ *91/781–1640* 📠 *91/781–1641* *36 rooms, 7 suites* ♿ *Restaurant, café, in-room data ports, kitchenettes, in-room VCRs, parking (fee)* ▭ *AE, DC, MC, V.*

$$ **HH Campomanes.** More than just a good deal, this new, modern, and stylish hotel is right in the city center, steps away from the major sites and nightlife. Although somewhat small and limited in services, its bold modern style—white, gray, and black tones—and friendly service are a breath of fresh air from the options of traditional and neoclassic hotels in Madrid. ✉ *Campomanes 4, Centro 28013* ☎ *91/548–8548* 📠 *91/559–1288* 🌐 *www.hhcampomanes.com* *30 rooms, 2 suites* ♿ *Café, laundry* ▭ *AE, DC, MC, V.*

$$ **Inglés.** Virginia Woolf was among the first luminaries to discover this place, which is smack in the middle of the old city's bar-and-restaurant district. Since Woolf's time, the Inglés has attracted more than its share of less-celebrated artists and writers. Rather drab and deteriorated now, it's best if you're looking for location and value rather than luxury. (Rundown suites cost what you'd pay for a standard double.) The balconies overlooking Calle Echegaray give you an unusual aerial view of the medieval quarter, all red tiles and ramshackle gables. ✉ *Echegaray 8, Santa Ana 28014* ☎ *91/429–6551* 📠 *91/420–2423* *58 rooms* ♿ *Cafeteria, gym, bar, parking (fee)* ▭ *AE, DC, MC, V.*

$$ **Liabeny.** Although unassuming in style and a bit outdated, this 1960s hotel near a plaza (and several department stores) between Gran Vía and Puerta del Sol has large and comfortable rooms with floral fabrics and big windows. Interior and top-floor rooms are the quietest. ✉ *Salud 3, Centro 28013* ☎ *91/531–9000* 📠 *91/532–5306* 🌐 *www.liabeny.es* *222 rooms* ♿ *Restaurant, café, 2 bars, meeting room, parking (fee)* ▭ *AE, DC, MC, V.*

$–$$ **Ramón de la Cruz.** If you don't mind a 10-minute metro ride (to Manuel Becerra) from the city center, this medium-size hotel is a find. Rooms are large, with modern bathrooms, and the stone-floor lobby is spacious. ✉ *Don Ramón de la Cruz 94, Salamanca 28006* ☎ *91/401–7200* 📠 *91/402–2126* 🌐 *www.hotelramondelacruz.com* *103 rooms* ♿ *Cafeteria, meeting room* ▭ *MC, V.*

$ **Mora.** You'll find this cheery hotel with a sparkling, faux-marble lobby and bright, carpeted hallways across the Paseo del Prado from the Botanical Garden. Guest rooms are modestly decorated but large and comfortable; those on the street side have great views of the gardens and the Prado, and double-pane windows keep them fairly quiet. For breakfast and lunch, the attached café is excellent, affordable, and popular with locals. ✉ *Paseo del Prado 32, Centro 28014* ☎ *91/420–1569* 📠 *91/420–0564* *62 rooms* ♿ *Café* ▭ *AE, DC, MC, V.*

★ ¢ **Hostal Villar.** Rooms, which go from single to quadruple with or without bathrooms (those facing the busy calle Príncipe are among the ones without bathroom), are reasonably large, clean, and comfortably decorated, with matching bedspreads and curtains. The bathrooms are rather small. However, the service at this bargain hostal, just a step away from Plaza de Santa Ana, is friendly and attentive. ✉ *Príncipe 18, Santa Ana 28012* ☎ *91/531–6600* 📠 *91/521–5073* *46 rooms* ▭ *MC, V.*

NIGHTLIFE & THE ARTS

The Arts

As Madrid's reputation as a vibrant, contemporary arts center has grown, artists and performers have arrived in droves. Consult the weekly *Guía del Ocio* (published Monday) or daily listings in the leading newspaper, *El País,* both of which are understandable even if you don't read much Spanish. The Festival de Otoño (Autumn Festival), from late September to late November, blankets the city with pop concerts, poetry readings, flamenco, and ballet and theater from world-renowned companies. Other annual events include world-class bonanzas of film, contemporary art, and jazz, salsa, rock, and African music, all at very reasonable prices. Seats for the classical performing arts are best purchased through your hotel concierge or at the hall itself. **El Corte Inglés** (☎ 902/400222) sells tickets for major pop concerts. **FNAC** (✉ Preciados 28, Sol ☎ 91/595–6100) sells tickets to musical events. **Tele-Entradas** (☎ 902/101212) is a central ticket broker.

Concerts & Dance

Convento de la Encarnación and the Real Academia de Bellas Artes de San Fernando host concerts. The modern **Auditorio Nacional de Música** (✉ Príncipe de Vergara 146, Salamanca ☎ 91/337–0100 🌐 www.auditorionacional.mcu.es) is Madrid's main concert hall, with spaces for both symphonic and chamber music. The resplendent **Teatro Real** (✉ Plaza de Isabel II, Opera ☎ 91/516–0660) hosts opera.

The subterranean **Centro Cultural de la Villa** (✉ Plaza de Colón, Salamanca ☎ 91/480–0300 information, 902/10–1212 tickets) has an eclectic program ranging from gospel and blues to flamenco and Celtic dance. The **Fundación Juan March** (✉ Castello 77, Salamanca ☎ 91/435–4240) offers chamber music Monday and Saturday at noon, and Wednesday at 7:30 PM.

The **Círculo de Bellas Artes** (✉ Marqués de Casa Riera 2, Centro ☎ 91/522–5092 🌐 www.circulobellasartes.com), at the junction between Gran Vía and Alcalá, has concerts, theater, dance performances, art exhibitions, and other arts events. The **Centro Conde Duque** (✉ Conde Duque 11, Centro ☎ 91/588–5834) is best known for its summer live music concerts (flamenco, jazz, pop), but it also has exhibitions. **La Casa Encendida** (✉ Ronda de Valencia 2, Lavapies ☎ 91/506–3875 🌐 www.lacasaencendida.com) is an exhibition space with movie festivals, art shows, dance performances, and weekend events for children.

Film

Of Madrid's 65 movie theaters, only nine show foreign films, generally in English, with original sound tracks and Spanish subtitles. These are listed in newspapers and in the *Guía de Ocio* under "v. o."—*versión original,* i.e., undubbed. Your best bet for catching a new release is the **Ideal Yelmo Cineplex** (✉ Doctor Cortezo 6, Centro ☎ 902/124134). The excellent, classic v. o. films at the **Filmoteca Cine Doré** (✉ Santa Isabel 3, Lavapiés ☎ 91/369–1125) change daily. **Alphaville** (✉ Martín de los Heros 14, Centro ☎ 91/5593836) is a leading v. o. theater right off Plaza de España. **Renoir Plaza de España** (✉ Martín de los Heros 12, Centro ☎ 91/541–4100) offers v. o. films. **Princesa** (✉ Princesa 3, Centro ☎ 91/541–4100) is a good option for original-version films.

Flamenco

Spain's best flamenco habitat is Andalusia, but if you won't be traveling south, here are a few possibilities. Note that prices for dinner and a show tend to be very high; you can save money by dining elsewhere and arriving in time for the show. Drinks are usually extra.

Café de Chinitas. It's expensive, but the flamenco here is the best in Madrid. Reserve in advance; shows often sell out. Performances are at 10:30 PM Monday–Saturday. ✉ *Torrija 7, Opera* ☎ *91/559–5135.*

Casa Patas. Along with tapas, this well-known space offers good, relatively pure (according to the performers) flamenco. Prices are more reasonable than elsewhere. Shows are at 10:30 PM Monday–Thursday, at midnight Friday–Sunday. ✉ *Canizares 10, Lavapiés* ☎ *91/369–0496.*

Corral de la Morería. Dinner à la carte and well-known visiting flamenco stars accompany the resident dance troupe. Since Morería opened its doors in 1956, celebrities such as Frank Sinatra and Ava Gardner have left their autographed photos for the walls. Shows are daily, from 10:45 PM to 2 AM. ✉ *Morería 17 (on C. Bailén; cross bridge over C. Segovia and turn right), Centro* ☎ *91/365–8446.*

Las Carboneras. One of Madrid's prime flamenco showcases—and less commercial than the traditional and better known tablaos—Las Carboneras presents young artists on their way up as well as more established stars on tour. Shows are staged nightly from 10:30 PM to 2 AM. ✉ *Plaza del Conde de Miranda 1, Centro* ☎ *91/542–8677.*

Theater

English-language plays are rare. When they do come to town, they're staged at any of a dozen venues. One theater you won't need Spanish for is the **Teatro de la Zarzuela** (✉ Jovellanos 4, Centro ☎ 91/524–5400), which specializes in the traditional Spanish operetta known as *zarzuela,* a kind of bawdy comedy. The **Teatro Español** (✉ Príncipe 25, Santa Ana ☎ 91/429–6297) keeps 17th-century Spanish classics alive.

Nightlife

Nightlife—or *la marcha*—reaches legendary heights in Madrid. It has been said that Madrileños rarely sleep, largely because they spend so much time in bars—not drunk, but socializing in the easy, sophisticated way that's unique to this city. This is true of old as well as young, and it's not uncommon for children to play on the sidewalks past midnight while multigenerational families and friends convene over coffee or cocktails at an outdoor café. The streets best known for their social scenes, however, do attract a younger clientele; these include Huertas, Moratín, Segovia, Victoria, and the areas around the Plaza Santa Ana and the Plaza de Anton Martín. The adventurous may want to explore the scruffier bar district around the Plaza Dos de Mayo, in the Malasaña area, where trendy, smoke-filled hangouts line both sides of Calle San Vicente Ferrer. A few blocks east are the haunts of Chueca, where tattoo studios and street-chic boutiques break up the endless alleys of gay and lesbian bars, techno discos, and after-hours clubs.

Cabaret

Berlin Cabaret (✉ Costanilla de San Pedro 11, Centro ☎ 91/366–2034 ⏲ Closed Sun.) professes to provide cabaret as it was performed in Berlin in the '30s. Combining magic, chorus girls, and ribaldry, it draws an eccentric crowd for vintage café theater. On Fridays and Saturdays the fun lasts until daybreak.

Discos

Madrid's oldest and hippest disco for all-night dancing to an international music mix is **El Sol** (✉ C. Jardines 3, Centro ☎ 91/532–6490), open 'til 5:30 AM. There's live music around midnight Thursday–Saturday. **Ave Nox** (✉ Lagasca 31, Salamanca ☎ 91/576–9715 ⏲ Closed

Sun.) is a torrid music bar–disco in a converted chapel with vaulted ceiling, choir loft, and all. **Joy Eslava** (✉ C. Arenal 11, Sol ☎ 91/366–3733), a downtown disco in a converted theater, is an old standby. **Palacio de Gaviria** (✉ Arenal 9, Sol ☎ 91/526–6069) is a maze of rooms turned into a disco, mainly for foreigners.

Pachá (✉ Barceló 11, Centro ☎ 91/447–0128 ⏲ Closed Mon.–Wed.) is always energetic. **Fortuny** (✉ Fortuny 34, Chamberí ☎ 91/319–0588) attracts a celebrity crowd, especially in summer, when the lush outdoor patio opens. Put on your best dancing shoes: the door is ultraselective. Salsa has become a fixture in Madrid; check out the most spectacular moves at **Azúcar** (✉ Paseo Reina Cristina 7, Atocha ☎ 91/501–6107). **Clamores** (✉ Albuquerque 14, Chamberí ☎ 91/445–7938 ⏲ Closed after 11 PM Sun.) plays live music until 2:30 AM. **Suristan** (✉ La Cruz 7, Santa Ana ☎ 91/532–3909 ⏲ Closed Sun. and Mon.) is a world music venue that turns into a disco. The dancing doesn't start until late. **Golden Boite** (✉ Duque de Sesto 54, Retiro ☎ 91/573–8775) is always hot from midnight on, until things wear out. For funky rhythms, try **Stella** (✉ C/Arlabán 7, Centro ☎ 91/531–6378 ⏲ Closed Sun.–Wed.). On Thursday it's called Mondo (electronic & house music); on Friday and Saturday it's The Room—a wilder scene. Show up late.

Bars & Nightclubs

Jazz, rock, flamenco, and classical music are all popular in Madrid's many small clubs.

Café Central. Madrid's best-known jazz venue is chic, and the musicians are often internationally known. Performances are usually from 10 PM to midnight. ✉ *Plaza de Ángel 10, Santa Ana* ☎ *91/369–4143.*

El Clandestino. This bar-café is a hidden hot spot with a local following. Jam sessions on two floors alternate mellow jazz with house and ambient music. ✉ *Barquillo 34, Centro* ☎ *91/521–5563* ⏲ *Closed Sun.*

Del Diego. Arguably Madrid's trendiest cocktail bar, it's frequented by a variety of crowds from movie directors to movie-goers. ✉ *Calle de la Reina 12, Centro* ☎ *91/523–3106* ⏲ *Closed Sun.*

Café Jazz Populart. Blues, jazz, Brazilian music, reggae, and salsa start at 11 PM. ✉ *Huertas 22, Santa Ana* ☎ *91/429–8407.*

Museo Chicote. Another landmark, recently refurbished and regaining popularity. This cocktail bar and lounge is also said to have been one of Hemingway's haunts. ✉ *Gran Vía 12, Centro* ☎ *91/532–6737* ⏲ *Closed Sun. night.*

Los Gabrieles. This building has remarkable tile walls—advertisements from the turn of the 20th century, when this was a high-class brothel. On the same street are other night hang-outs worth a look. ✉ *Echegaray 17, Santa Ana* ☎ *91/429–6261* ⏲ *Closed Sun.*

Honky Tonk. This bar has live performances and is open daily 9–5 (no, not *that* 9-to-5). The classic night scene attracts people of all ages. ✉ *Covarrubias 42, Chamberí* ☎ *91/445–6191.*

Larios Café. Cuban restaurant, bar, and disco, this ultrachic art deco scene is a great place to sip a mojito, any day of the week. The dance floor is open Thursday–Saturday night. ✉ *Silva 4, Centro* ☎ *91/547–9394.*

Oliver. Here you'll find two bars in one: daily there's an upstairs lounge and restaurant; late at night there's a full-fledged Chueca disco in the brick-lined basement cavern. ✉ *Almirante 12, Centro* ☎ *91/521–7379* ⏲ *Closed Sun. and Mon.*

Café de la Palma. With a bar in the front, a music venue for intimate concerts and a chill-out room in the back, and a café in the center room, this is a must if you're in the Malasaña neighborhood. ✉ *La Palma 62, Malasãna* ☎ *91/5225031.*

Star's Café. This mix of artsy café, fairly priced Mediterranean restaurant, bar, and groovy disco (the dance floor is open Friday and Saturday from midnight on) epitomizes the spirit of the eclectic neighborhood. ✉ *Marques de Valdeiglesias 5, Chueca* ☎ *91/522–2712* ⊗ *Closed Sat. No lunch Sun.*

Torero. Come if you imagine yourself to be among the ultrachic—the bouncer allows only those judged to be *gente guapa* (beautiful people) to enter. The bottom floor, open only from Thursday to Saturday night, is a huge exposed-brick, vaulted room. The upper floor is open Tuesday–Saturday. ✉ *Cruz 26, Santa Ana* ☎ *91/523–1129* ⊗ *Closed Sun. and Mon.*

El Viajero. The name of this tri-level café, bar, and restaurant, the top of which is an irresistible and popular terrace, means "The Traveler." It's decorated with antique knickknacks from around the world, and is painted in striking colors. ✉ *Plaza de la Cebada 11, La Latina* ☎ *91/366–9064* ⊗ *Closed Sun. night and Mon.*

SPORTS & THE OUTDOORS

Participant Sports

Golf

Eleven golf courses surround Madrid and more are on the way. The successes of Seve Ballesteros, José María Olazabal, and Sergio García have created a new surge of golf interest in Spain. Most golf clubs require a proof of membership. Playing golf at La Herrería Club's 18-hole course in the shadow of the monolithic Monastery of San Lorenzo del Escorial is one of Spain's great golfing experiences. **Golf Olivar de la Hinojosa** (✉ Av. Dublín s/n, Barajas ☎ 91/721–1889), in Campo de las Naciones outside town, is open to the public with two courses (one 18 holes, one 9) and golf lessons. They have a fixed all-week greens fee of €37.50. **La Herrería Club** (✉ Ctra. Robledo de Chavela s/n, Escorial ☎ 91/890–5111 🌐 www.golflaherreria.com), in San Lorenzo de Escorial, is open to the public. Their greens fee is € 50 during the week and almost double that on weekends.

Jogging

Your best bet for jogging is the Parque del Retiro, where a path circles the park and others weave under trees and through formal gardens. The Casa de Campo is crisscrossed by numerous, sunnier trails.

Swimming

Madrid has an antidote to the dry, sometimes intense heat of the summer months—a superb system of clean, popular, well-run municipal swimming pools (admission about €3.40). The biggest and best pool—fitted with a comfortable, tree-shaded restaurant—is in the **Casa de Campo** (✣ take the metro to Lago (in the Moncloa neighborhood) and walk up the hill a few yards ☎ 91/463–0050). A central option is **La Latina** (✉ Plaza de la Cebada s/n, La Latina ☎ 91/365–8031), which is public and right next to the neighborhood's market. An especially good option in the summer is **Piscina Canal Isabel II** (✉ Plaza Juan Zorrila, entrance off Av. de Filipinas, Chamartín ☎ no phone). It has grass, diving boards, and a wading pool for kids.

Tennis

There are public courts in the **Casa de Campo** (✉ Moncloa ☎ 91/464–9617) and on the Avenida de Vírgen del Puerto, behind the Palacio Real.

Spectator Sports

Soccer

Spain's number-one sport is known locally as *fútbol.* Madrid has three major teams, Real Madrid, Atlético Madrid, and Rayo Vallecano. For tickets, either call a week in advance to reserve and pick them up at the stadium or stand in line at the stadium of your choice. The **Estadio Santiago Bernabeu** (✉ Paseo de la Castellana 140, Chamartín ☎ 91/398–4300), which seats 75,000, is home to Real Madrid, winner of a staggering eight European Champion's Cups over the last 50 years. Atlético Madrid plays at the **Estadio Vicente Calderón** (✉ Virgen del Puerto 67, Arganzuela ☎ 91/366–4707 or 91/364–0888), on the edge of the Manzanares river south of town. Rayo Vallecano plays at **Estadio del Rayo** (✉ Arroyo del Olivar 49, Vallecas ☎ 91/478–2253).

SHOPPING

Madrid has far more to offer than Lladró porcelain and bullfighting posters—Spain has become one of the world's centers for design of every kind. You'll have no trouble finding traditional crafts, such as ceramics, guitars, and leather goods (albeit not at countryside prices), but at this point the city is more like Rodeo Drive than the bargain bin. Known for contemporary furniture and decorative items as well as chic clothing, shoes, and jewelry, Spain's capital has become stiff competition for Barcelona. Keep in mind that many shops, especially the small and family run, close during lunch hours, on Sundays, and on Saturday afternoons. Shops generally accept most major credit cards.

Department Stores

El Corte Inglés. Spain's largest department store carries the best selection of everything, from auto parts to groceries to designer fashions. *✉ Preciados 3, Sol ☎ 91/531–9619, 901/122122 general information, 902/400222 ticket sales ✉ Goya 76 and 87, Salamanca ☎ 91/432–9300 ✉ Princesa 56, Centro ☎ 91/454–6000 ✉ Serrano 47, Salamanca ☎ 91/432–5490 ✉ Raimundo Fernández Villaverde 79, Chamartín ☎ 91/418–8800.*

Zara. For those with young tastes and slim pocketbooks (picture hip clothes that you'll throw away in about six months), Zara has the latest looks for men, women, and children. *✉ Centro Comercial ABC, Serrano 61, Salamanca ☎ 91/575–6334 ✉ Gran Vía 34, Centro ☎ 91/521–1283 ✉ Princesa 63, Centro ☎ 91/543–2415 ✉ Conde de Peñalver 4, Salamanca ☎ 91/435–4135.*

Shopping Districts

Madrid has three main shopping areas. The first, around the Puerta del Sol, includes the major department stores (El Corte Inglés, the French music-and-book chain FNAC, etc.), and mid-range shops along the streets nearby. The second area, far more elegant and expensive, is in the northwestern Salamanca district, bounded roughly by Serrano, Juan Bravo, Jorge Juan (and its blind alleys), and Velázquez; the shops in Goya extend as far as Alcalá. These streets, just off the Plaza de Colón (particularly Calle Serrano and Calle Ortega y Gasset), have the widest selection of smart boutiques and designer fashions—think Prada, Armani, and Donna Karan New York, as well as renowned Spanish designers, such as Sybilla and Josep Font-Luz Diaz. Finally, for hipper clothes Chueca is your best stop. Wander around calles Fuencarral, Hortaleza, Almirante, and Piamonte.

Madrid's newest mall is a four-decker: the **Centro Comercial ABC** (✉ Paseo de la Castellana 34, at Serrano 61, Salamanca), named for the daily newspaper founded on the premises in the 19th century. The building has an ornate tile facade; inside, a large café is surrounded by shops, including leather stores and hairdressers. The fourth-floor restaurant has a rooftop terrace. **El Jardín de Serrano** (✉ Goya 6-8, next to Prada, Salamanca), a smaller mall with an exclusive selection of high end brands including jewelry, fashions for men and women, and shoes.

Flea Market

On Sunday morning, Calle de Ribera de Curtidores is closed to traffic and jammed with outdoor booths selling everything under the sun—its weekly transformation into **El Rastro.** The crowds grow so thick that it takes a while just to advance a few feet amid the hawkers and gawkers. Pickpockets abound here. Hang on to your purse and wallet, and be especially careful if you choose to bring a camera. The flea market sprawls into most of the surrounding streets, with certain areas specializing in particular products. Many of the goods are wildly overpriced. But what goods! The Rastro has everything from antique furniture to exotic parrots and cuddly puppies; from pirated cassette tapes of flamenco music to key chains emblazoned with symbols of the CNT, Spain's old anarchist trade union. Practice your Spanish by bargaining with the vendors over paintings, colorful Gypsy oxen yokes, heraldic iron gates, new and used clothes, and even hashish pipes. They may not lower their prices, but sometimes they'll throw in a handmade bracelet or a stack of postcards to sweeten the deal.

Plaza General Vara del Rey has some of the Rastro's best antiques, and the streets beyond—Calles Mira el Río Alta and Mira el Río Baja—have some truly magnificent junk and bric-a-brac. The market shuts down shortly after 2 PM, in time for a street party to start in the area known as La Latina, centered on the bar El Viajero in Plaza Humilladero.

Off the Ribera are two *galerías,* courtyards with higher-quality, higher-priced antiques shops. All the shops (except for the street vendors) are open during the week.

need a break? If you find yourself anywhere near the top of the Rastro, you can stop into **Bar Santurce** at C. Amazonas 14 in the neighborhood of Lavapiés for sardines, spicy green peppers, and calamari.

Specialty Stores

Books

Casa del Libro (✉ Maestro Victoria 3, Centro ☎ 91/521–4898), not far from the Puerta del Sol, has an impressive collection of English-language books, including city guides and translated Spanish classics. It's also a good source for maps, cookbooks, and gifts. Its discount store around the corner, on calle Salud 17, sells English classics. **Booksellers** (✉ José Abascal 48, Chamberí ☎ 91/442–8104), just off the upper Castellana near the Hotel Miguel Angel, has a large selection of books in English. For travel books, including English-language books about Madrid, seek out **Tierra de Fuego** (✉ C. del Pez 21, Centro ☎ 91/521–3962) in the Barrio de Maravillas, two blocks north of the central Gran Vía. Established in 1950, **La Tienda Verde** (✉ Maudes 23 and 38, Chamberí ☎ 91/535–3810 🌐 www.tiendaverde.org) is perfect for outdoor enthusiasts planning hikes, mountain-climbing expeditions, spelunking trips, and so forth; they have detailed maps and Spanish-language guidebooks.

Boutiques & Fashion

The free magazine, *InfoShopping* (in English and Spanish), distributed at tourist offices and upscale hotels, is a great resource, and provides detailed lists of both young and established Spanish fashion designers, as well as major international stores. You will find lots of Spanish designers' stores along Claudio Coello, Lagasca, and the first few blocks of Serrano. **Adolfo Domínguez** (✉ Serrano 96, Salamanca, and six other locations ☎ 91/576–7053) is one of Spain's best-known designers, with lines for both men and women. Prominent young designer **Jesús del Pozo** (✉ Almirante 9, Salamanca ☎ 91/531–3646) caters to both sexes; his boutique is an excellent, if pricey, place to try on some classic Spanish style. Since the turn of the 20th century **Seseña** (✉ De la Cruz 23, Sol ☎ 91/531–6840) has outfitted international celebrities in wool and velvet capes, some lined with red satin. **Sybilla** (✉ Jorge Juan 12, Salamanca ☎ 91/578–1322) is the studio of Spain's best-known female designer, whose fluid dresses and hand-knit sweaters have made her a favorite with Danish supermodel Helena Christensen.

Next to Sybilla is **Roberto Torretta** (✉ Jorge Juan 12 [at the end of one of the two cul-de-sacs] Salamanca ☎ 91/435–7989), another designer with a celebrity following and with a great talent for mixing materials.

The Madrileño designer **Pedro del Hierro** (✉ Serrano 24 Salamanca ☎ 91/575–6906) has built himself a good reputation for his sophisticated yet uncomplicated clothes for both sexes.

Purificación García (✉ Serrano 28 Salamanca ☎ 91/435–8013) is also a good choice for women searching for contemporary all-day wear.

The three young female designers working for **Homeless** (✉ Serrano 16 Salamanca ☎ 91/781–0612) are gaining a growing acceptance among the younger crowds with their hip and fashionable clothes. Even funkier are the collections, all by young Spanish designers (Josep Font, Ailanto, Miriam Orcaiz, etc.), displayed at the small boutique **The Deli Room** (✉ Santa Bárbara 4 Centro ☎ 91/5211983), located in a narrow short street off Fuencarral.

Ceramics

Antigua Casa Talavera (✉ Isabel la Católica 2, Centro ☎ 91/547–3417) is the best of Madrid's many ceramics shops. Despite the name, the finest ware sold here is from Manises, near Valencia, but the blue-and-yellow Talavera ceramics are also excellent. **Cántaro** (✉ Flor Baja 8, Centro ☎ 91/547–9514) sells handmade ceramics. **Cerámica El Alfar** (✉ Claudio Coello 112, Salamanca ☎ 91/411–3587) has pottery from around Spain. **Sagardelos** (✉ Zurbano 46, Chamberí ☎ 91/310–4830), specializing in modern Spanish ceramics from Galicia, has breakfast sets, coffee pots, and objets d'art.

Crafts & Design

Casa Julia (✉ Almirante 1, Centro ☎ 91/522–0270) is an artistic showcase, with two floors of tasteful antiques, paintings by up-and-coming artists, and furniture in experimental designs. It's a great place to hunt for nontraditional souvenirs. **El Arco** (✉ Plaza Mayor 9, Centro ☎ 91/365–2680) has contemporary handicrafts from all over Spain, including modern ceramics, handblown glassware, jewelry, and leather items—as well as a whimsical collection of pendulum clocks.

Fans

Casa de Diego (✉ Puerta del Sol 12, Sol ☎ 91/522–6643), established in 1853, stocks fans, umbrellas, and classic Spanish walking sticks with ornamented silver handles. The British royal family buys autograph fans here—white kidskin fans for signing on special occasions.

Food & Wine

The Club Gourmet sections in stores sell Spanish wines, olive oils, and food. Right in the middle of Salamanca's shopping area you'll find **Mantequerías Bravo** (✉ C. Ayala 24, Salamanca ☎ 91/576–7641), which has Spanish wines, olive oils, cheeses, and hams. **Lavinia** (✉ José Ortega y Gasset 16, Salamanca ☎ 91/426–0604 ⊕ www.lavinia.es) claims to be the largest wine store in Europe. It has a large selection of bottles, books, and bar accessories. The upscale chain **Mallorca** (✉ Velázquez 59, Salamanca ☎ 91/431–9909 ✉ Serrano 6, Salamanca ☎ 91/577–1859 ✉ Centro Comercial, Goya 6, Salamanca ☎ 91/431–5555) sells prepared meals, cocktail canapés, chocolates, and wines, and has tapas counters. Just across from eateries Los Gabrieles and La Trucha, behind Plaza Santa Ana, **Mariano Aguado** (✉ C. Echegaray 19, Santa Ana ☎ 91/429–6088) is a charming 150-year-old wine store with a quaint ceiling mural and a broad range of fine wines and spirits.

Hats

Founded in 1894, **Casa Yustas** (✉ Plaza Mayor 30, Sol ☎ 91/366–5084) has headgear ranging from the old three-corner, patent-leather hats of the Guardia Civil to fashionable ladies' hats to Basque berets to black Andalusian *sombreros de mayoral.* Designed as hands-free umbrellas for the rainy Cantabrian coast, Basque berets are much wider than those worn by the French and make excellent gifts.

Leather Goods

On a street full of bargain shoe stores (*muestrarios*), **Caligae** (✉ Augusto Figueroa 27, Salamanca ☎ 91/531–5343) is probably the best of the bunch. Posh **Loewe** (✉ Serrano 26 and 34, Salamanca ☎ 91/577–6056 ✉ Gran Vía 8, Centro ☎ 91/532–7024 ✉ Westin Palace, Centro ☎ 91/429–8530) has ultra–high-quality designer purses, accessories, and clothing made of butter-soft leather in dyed, jewel-like colors. Prices can hit the stratosphere. **Tenorio** (✉ Plaza de la Provincia 6, Centro ☎ No phone) is where you'll find one dedicated shoemaker who makes country boots (similar to cowboy boots) typically worn in the Spanish countryside, to order. The workmanship should last a lifetime. The hitch is that he needs five to six months to complete a pair. The boots start at €1,200.

Music

José Ramirez (✉ C. La Paz 8, Centro ☎ 91/531–4229) has provided Spain and the rest of the world with guitars since 1882, and his store includes a museum of antique instruments. Prices for new ones start at €90, though the top concert models are closer to €6,000. **Real Música** (✉ Carlos III 1, Centro ☎ 91/547–3009), around the corner from the Teatro Real, is a music lover's dream, with books, CDs, sheet music, memorabilia, guitars, and a knowledgeable staff.

SIDE TRIPS

El Escorial

50 km (31 mi) northwest of Madrid.

Felipe II was one of history's most deeply religious and forbidding monarchs—not to mention one of its most powerful—and the great granite monastery that he had constructed in a remarkable 21 years (1563–84) is an enduring testament to his character. Outside Madrid in the foothills
46 of the Sierra de Guadarrama, the **Real Monasterio de San Lorenzo de El Escorial** (Royal Monastery of St. Lawrence of Escorial) is severe, recti-

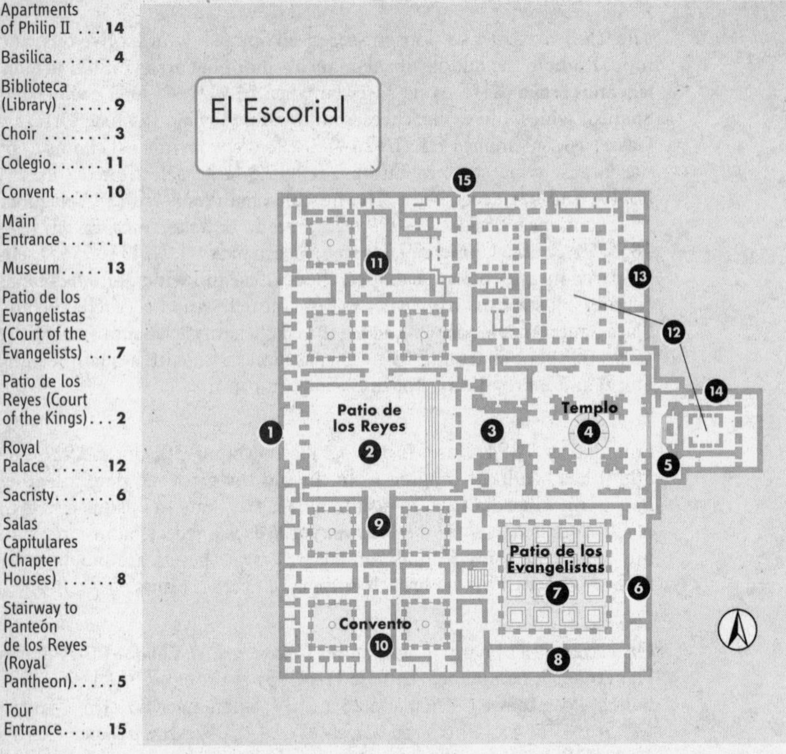

linear, and unforgiving—one of the most gigantic yet simple architectural monuments on the Iberian Peninsula.

Felipe built the monastery in the village of San Lorenzo de El Escorial to commemorate Spain's crushing victory over the French at Saint-Quentin on August 10, 1557, and as a final resting place for his all-powerful father, the Holy Roman Emperor Carlos V. He filled the place with treasures as he ruled the largest empire the world has ever seen, knowing all the while that a marble coffin awaited him in the pantheon deep below. The building's vast rectangle, encompassing 16 courts, is modeled on the red-hot grille upon which St. Lawrence was martyred—appropriate enough, since August 10 was that saint's day. (It's also said that Felipe's troops accidentally destroyed a church dedicated to St. Lawrence during the battle and he sought to make amends.) Some years ago a Spanish psychohistorian theorized that the building is shaped like a prone woman and is thus an unintended emblem of Felipe's sexual repression. Lo and behold, this thesis provoked several newspaper articles and a rash of other commentary.

El Escorial is easily reached by car, train, bus, or organized tour from Madrid; simply inquire at a travel agency or the appropriate station. The building and its adjuncts—a palace, museum, church, and more—can take hours or even days to tour. Easter Sunday's candlelit midnight mass draws crowds, as does the summer tourist season.

The monastery was begun by Juan Bautista de Toledo but finished in 1584 by Juan de Herrera, who would eventually give his name to a major Spanish architectural school. It was completed just in time for Felipe to die here, gangrenous and tortured by the gout that had plagued him for years, in the tiny, sparsely furnished bedroom that resembled a monk's

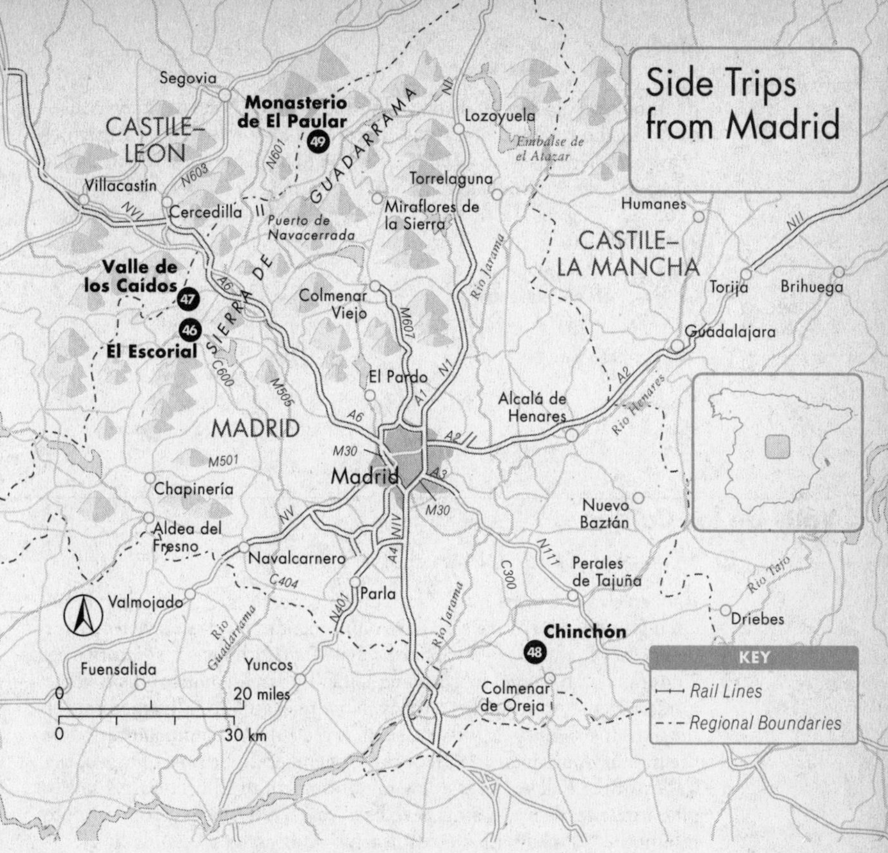

cell more than the resting place of a great monarch. It is in this bedroom—which looks out, through a private entrance, into the royal chapel—that one most appreciates the man's spartan nature. Spain's later Bourbon kings, such as Carlos III and Carlos IV, had clearly different tastes, and their apartments, connected to Felipe's by the Hall of Battles, are far more luxurious.

Perhaps the most interesting part of the entire Escorial is the **Panteón de los Reyes** (Royal Pantheon), which contains the body of every king since Carlos I save three—Felipe V (buried at La Granja), Ferdinand VI (in Madrid), and Amadeus of Savoy (in Italy). The body of Alfonso XIII, who died in Rome in 1941, was brought to El Escorial in January 1980. The rulers' bodies lie in 26 sumptuous marble and bronze sarcophagi that line the walls (three of which are empty, awaiting future rulers). Only those queens who bore sons later crowned lie in the same crypt; the others, along with royal sons and daughters who never ruled, lie nearby, in the **Panteón de los Infantes.** Many of the royal children are in a single circular tomb made of Carrara marble.

Another highlight is the monastery's surprisingly lavish and colorful **library,** with ceiling paintings by Michelangelo disciple Pellegrino Tibaldi (1527–96). The imposing austerity of El Escorial's facades makes this chromatic explosion especially powerful; try to save it for last. The library houses 50,000 rare manuscripts, codices, and ancient books, including the diary of St. Teresa of Ávila and the gold-lettered, illuminated Codex Aureus. Tapestries woven from cartoons by Goya, Rubens, and El Greco cover almost every inch of wall space in huge sections of the building, and extraordinary canvases by Velázquez, El Greco, David, Ribera, Tintoretto, Rubens, and other masters, collected from around the monastery, are now displayed in the **Museos Nuevos** (New Museums). In the **basilica,** don't miss the fresco above the choir, depicting heaven, or Titian's fresco *The Martyrdom of St. Lawrence,* which shows the saint being roasted alive. ✉ *San Lorenzo de El Escorial* ☎ *91/890–5905* *€7, guided tour €8* ⏲ *Apr.–Sept., Tues.–Sun. 10–6; Oct.–Mar., Tues.–Sun. 10–5.*

need a break?

Ideal in summer is the outdoor terrace at **Charolés** (Floridablanca 24, ☎ 91/890–5975), where imaginative seasonal dishes (especially grilled meats) round out a menu of northern-Spanish favorites. Just don't expect picnic prices. For a more contemporary spot with a younger crowd, and a good selection of grilled meats and salads, a cheaper and nearby option is the cozy bistro, **La Cañada Real** (Florida Blanca 30, ☎ 91/890–2703).

Valle de los Caídos

47 *13 km (8 mi) north of El Escorial on C600.*

Ranked as a not-to-be-missed visit until the death of Generalísimo Francisco Franco in 1975, this massive monument to fascisms's victory over democracy in the 1936–39 Spanish Civil War (Catholicism's victory over Communism to some) has become something of an anachronism in the modern democratic Spain of today. Now relegated to rallying point for the extreme right on key dates, such as the July 18 commemoration of the military uprising of 1936 or the November 20 death of Franco, the Valley of the Fallen is just a few minutes north of El Escorial. A lovely pine forest leads up to a massive basilica carved out of a solid granite mountain. Topped with a cross nearly 500 ft high (accessible by elevator), the basilica holds the tombs of both General Franco and José Antonio Primo de Rivera, founder of the fascist Spanish Falange. It was built with the forced labor of postwar Republican prisoners and dedicated, rather disingenuously, to all who died in the three-year conflict. Tapestries of the Apocalypse add to the generally terrifying air inside as every footstep resounds off the polished marble floors and stone walls. An eerie midnight mass is held here on Easter Sunday, the granite peak lit by candlelight. ☎ *91/890–5611* *Basilica €5* ⏲ *Apr.–Sept., Tues.–Sun. 10–6; Oct.–Mar., Tues.–Sun. 10–5.*

Chinchón

48 *54 km (33 mi) southeast of Madrid, off N-III on C300.*

A true Castilian town, the picturesque village of Chinchón seems a good four centuries removed. It makes an ideal day trip, especially if you save time for lunch at one of its many rustic restaurants; the only problem is that swarms of Madrileños have the same idea, so it's often hard to get a table at lunchtime on weekends.

The high point of Chinchón is its charming **Plaza Mayor,** an uneven circle of ancient three- and four-story houses embellished with wooden balconies resting on granite columns. It's something like an open-air Elizabethan theater, but with a Spanish flavor—in fact, the entire plaza is converted to a bullring from time to time, with temporary bleachers erected in the center and seats on the privately owned balconies rented out for splendid views. (Tickets for these rare fights are hard to come by.)

The commanding **Iglesia de la Asunción** (Church of the Assumption), overlooking the plaza, is known for its Goya mural, *The Assumption of the Virgin.*

Along the C300 near the N-III highway, you'll pass through the **Valle del Jarama,** scene of one of the bloodiest battles of the Spanish Civil War. American volunteers in the Abraham Lincoln Brigade, which fought with the democratically elected Spanish Republican government against Franco's military insurgency, were mauled here in a baptism of fire. Folk singer Pete Seeger immortalized the battle with "There's a valley in Spain called Jarama . . ." The trenches are still visible, and bits of rusty military hardware can still be found in the fields.

Where to Eat

The town's arcaded plaza is ringed by charming balconied restaurants serving hearty Castilian fare, particularly roasts and charcoal-grilled meat. Wherever you dine, try the local *anís,* a licorice-flavor spirit; and if you come to Chinchón in April, look for merriment occasioned by the Fiesta del Anís y del Vino (Anise and Wine Festival). On winter weekends, Madrileños in droves come for the superb cocido at the **Parador de Chinchón** (☒ Av. Generalísimo 1 ☎ 91/894–0836). **Mesón de la Virreina** (☒ Plaza Mayor 28 ☎ 91/894–0015), on the square's northeast corner, is a perfect perch for sipping gazpacho or a glass of Chinchón anís. Call ahead for a table at **Café de la Iberia** (☒ Plaza Mayor 17 ☎ 91/894–0998), which has a balcony as well as a cozy interior. **Mesón Las Cuevas del Vino** (☒ Benito Hortelano 13 ☎ 91/894–0206) is a rambling tavern with roaring fireplaces and immense antique wine and olive-oil amphoras scattered around a giant olive press.

Monasterio de El Paular & Lozoya Valley

49 *100 km (62 mi) north of Madrid.*

Rising from Spain's great central *meseta* (plain), the Sierra de Guadarrama looms northwest of Madrid like a dark, jagged shield separating Old and New Castile. Snowcapped for much of the year, the mountains are indeed rough-hewn in many spots, particularly on their northern face, but there is a dramatic exception—the Lozoya Valley.

About 100 km (62 mi) north of the capital, this valley of pines, poplars, and babbling brooks is a cool, green retreat from the often searing heat of the plain. Madrileños repair here for a picnic or a simple drive, rarely joined by foreign travelers, to whom the area is virtually unknown.

You'll need a car to make this trip, and the drive is a pleasant one. Take the A6 northwest from Madrid and exit at signs for the Navacerrada Pass on the N601. As you climb toward the 6,100-ft mountain pass, you'll come to a road bearing off to the left toward Cercedilla. (This little village, a popular base for hikes, is also accessible by train.) Just above Cercedilla, an old Roman road leads up to the ridge of the Guadarrama, where an ancient fountain, known as Fuenfría, long provided the spring water that fed the Roman aqueduct of Segovia. The path traced by this cobble road is very close to the route Hemingway had his hero Robert Jordan take in *For Whom the Bell Tolls* and eventually takes you near the bridge that Jordan blew up in the novel.

If you continue past the Cercedilla road, you'll come to a ski resort at the highest point of the Navacerrada Pass. Take a right here on C604 and you'll follow the ridge of the mountains for a few miles before descending into the **Lozoya Valley.** The valley is filled with picnic spots along the Lozoya River, including several campgrounds. To end the excursion, take C604 north a few miles to Rascafría, and then turn right on a smaller road marked for Miraflores de la Sierra. In that town you'll turn right again, following signs for Colmenar Viejo, and then pick up a short expressway back to Madrid.

Built by King Juan I in 1390, **Monasterio de El Paular** (☎ 91/869–1425) was the first Carthusian monastery in Castile, but it has been neglected since the Disentailment of 1836, when religious organizations gave their artistic treasures to the state. Fewer than a dozen Benedictine monks still live here, eating and praying exactly as their predecessors did centuries ago. One of them gives tours every day at noon, 1, and 5 (on Thursday there's no 5 o'clock tour). The monastery is on your left as you approach the floor of the Lozoya Valley. The monastery is attached to **Hotel Santa María de El Paular** (☎ 91/869–1011 📠 91/869–1006), a cozy mountain refuge run by the same Westin chain that owns the Palace Hotel in Madrid.

MADRID A TO Z

To research prices, get advice from other travelers, and book travel arrangements, visit www.fodors.com.

AIR TRAVEL

Several major airlines have regular flights from the United States, and others serve London and other European capitals daily. Shopping among Madrid travel agencies will probably get you a lower fare than those available abroad, especially to and from Great Britain.

AIRPORTS

Madrid is served by Madrid Barajas Airport, 12 km (7 mi) east of the city.

Aeropuerto de Madrid Barajas ☎ 902/353570, 91/305-8343, 91/305-8344, 91/305-8345.

AIRPORT TRANSFERS

The speediest transfer is the Line 8 metro, running every few minutes (daily from 6:30 AM to 1 AM) between Nuevos Ministerios (where you can check your luggage) and Barajas Airport; it costs €1.10 and takes 12 minutes.

For a mere €3 there's a convenient bus to the central Plaza Colón, where you can catch a taxi to your hotel. Buses leave every 15 minutes between 4:45 AM and 2 AM (slightly less often very early or late in the day). Watch your belongings, as the underground Plaza Colón bus station is a favorite haunt of purse snatchers and con artists.

In bad traffic, the 15-minute taxi ride to Madrid can take the better part of an hour, but it makes sense if you have a lot of luggage. Taxis normally wait outside the airport terminal near the clearly marked bus stop; expect to pay up to €15, more in heavy traffic, plus nominal holiday, airport, and/or late-night surcharges. Make sure the driver is on the meter—off-the-meter "deals" almost always cost more. Finally, some hotels offer shuttle service in vans; check with yours when you reserve.

BIKE TRAVEL

Bicycle travel in Madrid is notably absent, perhaps because traffic is too intense or because bicycles don't make enough noise to respectfully contribute to the din. In any case, it's not a good idea.

BUS TRAVEL TO & FROM MADRID

Madrid has no central bus station; buses are generally less popular than trains (though they can be faster). Most of southern and Eastern Spain is served by the Estación del Sur. From the Estación de Avenida de América two companies, Continental Auto and Alsa (which also has buses departing from the south station), serve mostly the North and the East, respectively. Buses for much of the rest of the peninsula, including

Cuenca, Extremadura, Salamanca, and Valencia, depart from the Auto Res station. There are several smaller stations, however, so inquire at travel agencies for the one serving your destination.

The La Sepulvedana bus company serves Segovia, Ávila, and La Granja. Herranz goes to El Escorial (it leaves from the Intercambiador de Moncloa, i.e., the Moncloa bus station) and from there to the Valle de los Caídos. La Veloz has service to Chinchón.

Bus Companies **Alsa** ✉ Avenida de América 9, Salamanca ☎ 902/422242 🌐 www.alsa.es Ⓜ Avenida de América. **Herranz** ✉ Intercambiador de Moncloa Moncloa ☎ 91/896-9028 Ⓜ Moncloa. **Continental Auto** ✉ Avenida de América 9, Salamanca ☎ 91/745-6300 🌐 www.continental-auto.es Ⓜ Avenida de América. **La Sepulvedana** ✉ Paseo de la Florida 11, near Estación del Norte, Moncloa ☎ 91/530-4800. **La Veloz** ✉ Mediterraneo 49, Atocha ☎ 91/409-7602 Ⓜ Conde de Casal.

Bus Stations **Auto Res** ✉ Fernández Shaw 1, Atocha ☎ 902/020999 🌐 www.auto-res.net Ⓜ Conde de Casal. **Estación del Sur** ✉ Méndez Álvaro s/n, Atocha ☎ 91/468-4200 🌐 www.estaciondeautobuses.com Ⓜ Méndez Álvaro.

BUS TRAVEL WITHIN MADRID

Red city buses run from about 6 AM to midnight and cost €1.10 per ride. After midnight, buses called *búhos* ("night owls") run out to the suburbs from Plaza de Cibeles for the same price. Signs at every stop list all other stops by street name, but they're hard to comprehend if you don't know the city well. Pick up a free route map from EMT kiosks on the Plaza de Cibeles or the Puerta del Sol, where you can also buy a 10-ride ticket called a Metrobus (€5.20) that's also valid for the metro. If you speak Spanish, call for information (☎ 91/406–8810). Drivers will generally make change for anything up to a €10 note. If you've bought a 10-ride ticket, step just behind the driver and insert it in the ticket-punching machine until the mechanism rings.

CAR RENTAL

Nearly every international agency is represented in Madrid, whether in town or at Barajas Airport. It's best to reserve a car before you arrive in Spain; *See* Car Rental *in* Smart Travel Tips for toll-free numbers both at home and in Spain.

CAR TRAVEL

Felipe II made Madrid the capital of Spain because it was at the very center of his peninsular domains, and to this day many of the nation's highways radiate from Madrid like the spokes of a wheel. Originating at Kilometer 0—marked by a brass plaque on the sidewalk of the Puerta del Sol—these highways include the A6 (Segovia, Salamanca, Galicia); N-1 (Burgos and the Basque Country); the N-II (Guadalajara, Barcelona, France); the N-III (Cuenca, Valencia, the Mediterranean coast); the N-4 (Aranjuez, La Mancha, Granada, Seville); the N401 (Toledo); and the N-V (Talavera de la Reina, Portugal). The city is surrounded by the M30 (the inner ring road) and M40 (the outer ring road), from which most of these highways are easily picked up. Driving in Madrid is best avoided. Parking is nightmarish, traffic is heavy almost all the time, and the city's daredevil drivers can be frightening. August is an exception; the streets are then largely emptied by the mass exodus of Madrileños on vacation.

CHILDREN IN MADRID

If you have children who can sit still long enough for a performance, Madrid has a few good picks. The Teatro de Titeres en el Retiro (Puppet Theater in the Retiro) plays in the Retiro Park from October to May on weekends and holidays. Cuarta Pared (Fourth Wall) stages plays for children, and Teatro Lope de Vega often has productions for young audiences. Teatro de la Zarzuela has matinées for kids. If mobility is an issue, Teleférico runs cable cars out over the Casa de Campo. Pista de Hielo (Ice Rink) offers public skating sessions and figure skating classes. For day trips to Warner Bros. Movie World theme park (15 mi south of Madrid), try Julià Tours or take the train from the Atocha station. To go to the Zoo-Aquarium at Casa de Campo take the subway to Príncipe Pío and then bus number 33 to the Zoo.

Cuarta Pared ✉ Ercilla 17, Centro. **Julià Tours** ✉ Gran Vía 68, Centro ☎ 91/559-9605 🌐 www.juliatours.es. **Teatro Lope de Vega** ✉ Gran Vía 57, Centro. **Teatro de la Zarzuela** ✉ Jovellanos 4, Centro. **Teleférico** ✉ Paseo Pintor Rosales s/n, Centro ☎ 91/541-7450 ⏲ Open Oct.–May, weekends noon–8; June–Sept., daily 11–8. **Pista de Hielo** ✉ Agustín de Foxá s/n, Chamartín ☎ 91/315-6308 ⏲ Open Thurs. and Fri. 5:30–10, weekends 11:30–2 and 5:30–10. **Warner Bros. Movie World Park** ✉ Carretera de Andalucía km. 22 ☎ 91/521-3780 🌐 www.warnerbrospark.com. **Zoo-Aquarium** ✉ Casa de Campo s/n ☎ 91/512-3780 🌐 www.zoomadrid.com.

DISCOUNTS & DEALS

For €28, €42, or €55 for 1, 2, or 3 days, you get free entry to 40 museums (with no standing in lines to buy tickets) and monuments, all public transport, a tourist bus called Madrid Visión, and a thematic tour through the Madrid de los Austrias (the area around Plaza Mayor), as well as discounts in stores, movies, theaters, restaurants, and parks. You can buy the card at municipal and regional tourist offices, on Madrid Visión buses and at its kiosk next to the Prado Museum on Felipe IV, and on-line via the Madrid Card Web site.

Madrid Shopping Tours runs a bus around town for determined shoppers. For €25 on Tuesday through Thursday you can see the city's retail districts and nearby factory outlets on a guided tour and get discounts to boot. You must reserve a spot at least one day in advance. The tour runs from 10 to 6; call for pickup locations.

Madrid Tourist Office ✉ Plaza Mayor 3 ☎ 91/588-2900 ✉ Duque de Medinaceli, 2 ☎ 915/882900 🌐 www.munimadrid.es 🌐 www.madridcard.com. **Madrid Shopping Tour** ☎ 91/316-0657 📠 91/316-0842 🌐 www.madridshoppingtour.com.

EMBASSIES

Australia ✉ Plaza del Descubridor Diego de Ordás 3, Chamberí ☎ 91/441-9300. **Canada** ✉ C. Nuñez de Balboa 35, Salamanca ☎ 91/423-3250. **New Zealand** ✉ Plaza de Lealtad 2, Centro ☎ 91/523-0226. **United Kingdom** ✉ C. Fernando el Santo 19, Chamberí ☎ 91/700-8200. **United States** ✉ C. Serrano 75, Salamanca ☎ 91/577-4000.

EMERGENCIES

In any emergency, call ☎ 112; an operator will redirect you to the appropriate number. Emergency pharmacies are required to be open 24 hours a day on a rotating basis; pharmacy windows and the major daily newspapers list pharmacies open round-the-clock that day. The Madrid Police has a special phone service in several languages for tourists: ☎ 902/102112. Your complaint will be sent to the nearest police station where the crime took place, and you will have two days to drop by the station and sign the report.

Doctors & Dentists **English-speaking-doctor referrals** ✉ Conde de Aranda 7, Salamanca ☎ 91/435-1823.

Emergency Services **Ambulancias Cruz Roja** (Red Cross Ambulances) ☎ 91/522-2222 are on call 24 hours a day. **Ambulancias SAMUR** (Red Cross Ambulances) ☎ 092 are always available.

Hospitals **Hospital La Paz** ✉ Paseo de la Castellana 261, Chamartín ☎ 91/358-2600. **Hospital Ramon y Cajal** ✉ Carretera de Colmenar, Km 9, Chamartín ☎ 91/336-8000. **Hospital 12 de Octubre** ✉ Carretera de Andalucía, Km 5.4, Carabanchel ☎ 91/390-8000.

ENGLISH-LANGUAGE MEDIA

The *International Herald Tribune,* as well as major British dailies are available at dawn in Madrid. *The Broadsheet* and *In Madrid* (🌐 www.in-madrid.com) are local Madrid magazines with listings and suggestions about what to do and where to go for English-speaking residents and visitors.

LODGING

Madrid B&B arranges short-term lodging in private apartments, some hosted and some unhosted.

Madrid B&B ✉ 437 J St., Suite 210, San Diego, CA 92101 ☎ 800/872-2632, 619/531-1179 in the U.S. 📠 619/531-1686 🌐 www.madridbandb.com.

MAIL & SHIPPING

Madrid's main post office, the Palacio de Comunicaciones, is at the intersection of Paseo de Recoletos and Calle de Alcalá, just one long block north of the Prado Museum. There are also innumerable Internet cafés and services throughout the city; Easyeverything and BBIGG are the two largest ones. Work Center offers printing, scanning, faxing, digital printing, and other office services on a 24/7 basis. Ask shopkeepers and bartenders for the nearest on-line venue.

Post Office **Palacio de Comunicaciones** ✉ Plaza de Cibeles s/n, Centro ☎ 902/197197 ⏲ Open weekdays 8:30 AM–10 PM, Sat. 8:30–8 (after 2 PM, enter by C. Monteleón), Sun. 10–1.

Internet Cafés **Easyeverything** ✉ Montera 10, Sol, open 24 hrs. **BBIGG** ✉ Alcalá 21, Centro, open daily 10 AM–midnight (2 AM on the weekends). **Work Center** ✉ Alberto Aguilera 1 (Plaza de San Bernardo), Centro ☎ 91/121-7600.

METRO TRAVEL

The metro is quick, frequent, and, at €1.10 no matter how far you travel, cheap. Even cheaper is the 10-ride Metrobus ticket, or *billete de diez,* which costs €5.20, is also valid for buses, and is accepted by automatic turnstiles (lines at ticket booths can be long). The system is open from 6 AM to 1:30 AM, though a few entrances close earlier. There are 10 metro lines, and system maps in stations detail their color-coded routes. Note the end station of the line you need, and follow signs to the correct corridor. Exits are marked SALIDA.

SIGHTSEEING TOURS

Your hotel can arrange standard city tours in either English or Spanish; most offer Madrid Artístico (including the Royal Palace and the Prado), Madrid Panorámico (a basic half-day tour), Madrid de Noche (including a flamenco or nightclub show), and the Sunday-only Panorámico y Toros (a brief city overview followed by a bullfight). The Plaza Mayor tourist office leads tours of Madrid's old quarters in English every Saturday morning, departing from the office at 10. The same office has a leaflet detailing the popular Spanish-language bus and walking tours run by the *ayuntamiento* (city hall) under the rubric "Descubre Madrid"; you then buy tickets at the Patronato de Turismo or by calling ☎ 902/221–622. The walking tours depart most mornings; theme options include Literary Madrid, baroque Madrid, and Religious Monuments. For half- and one-day trips to sites outside Madrid, including Toledo, El Escorial, and Segovia, contact Julià Tours.

Trapsatur runs the Madrid Visión tourist bus, which makes a 1½-hour circuit of the city with recorded commentary in English. No reservation is needed; just show up at Puerta del Sol 5, Gran Vía 32, or at the front of the Prado Museum. Buses depart every 20–30 minutes, starting at 10 (9:30 in summer). A day pass, which allows you to get on and off

Madrid Metro

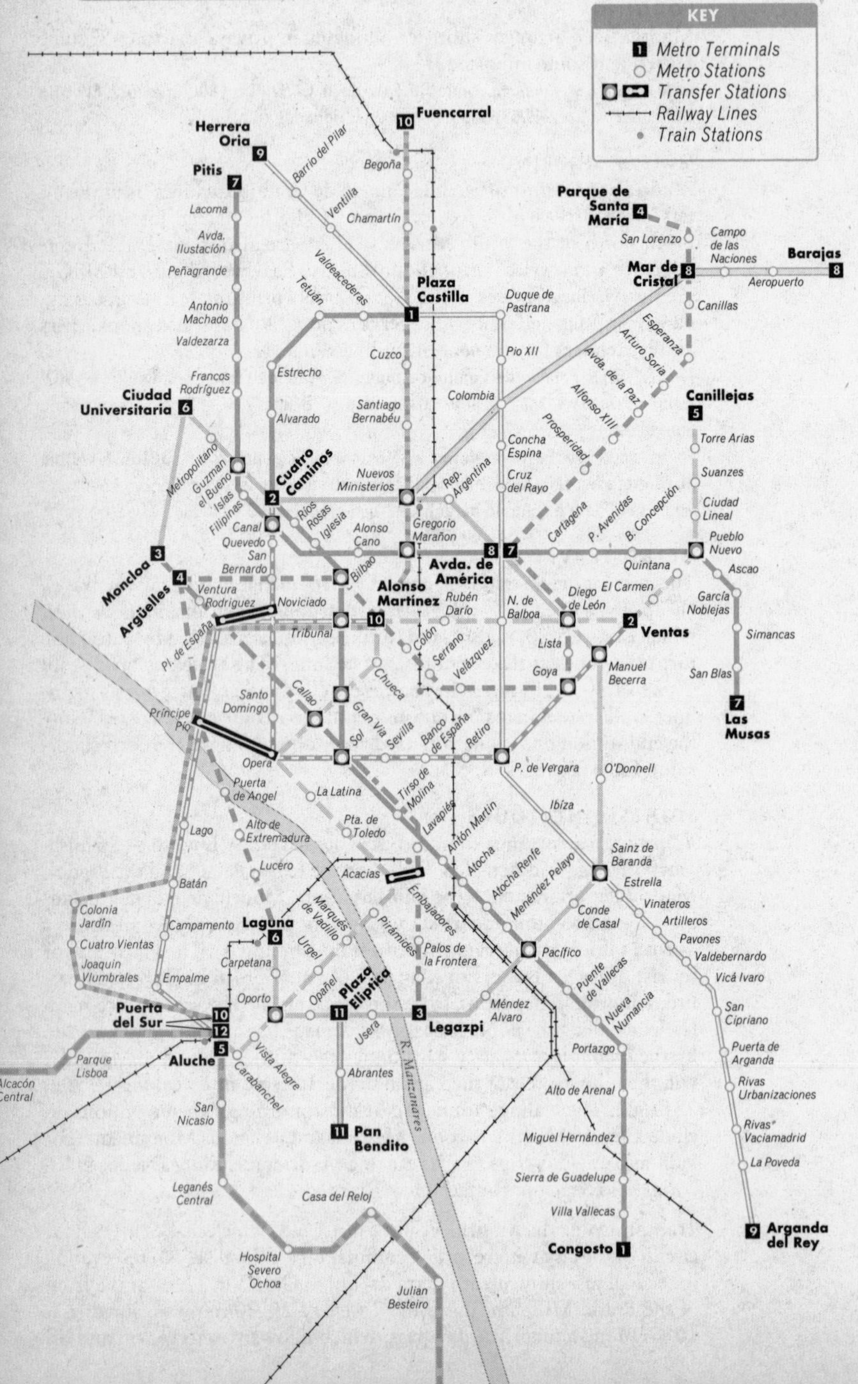

at various attractions, is €13. Contact the Asociación Profesional de Informadores to hire a personal guide.

Asociación Profesional de Informadores ✉ C. Ferraz 82, Moncloa ☎ 91/542-1214 or 91/541-1221 🌐 www.apit.es. **Ayuntamiento** ✉ City Hall, C. Mayor 69, Centro ☎ 91/588-2900. **Julià Tours** ✉ Gran Vía 68, Centro ☎ 91/559-9605 🌐 www.juliatours.es. **Patronato de Turismo** ✉ C. Mayor 69, Centro ☎ 91/588-2906. **Plaza Mayor tourist office** ✉ Plaza Mayor 3, Centro ☎ 91/588-2900. **Sol Pentours** ✉ Gran Vía 26, Centro ☎ 902/303903. **Madrid Visión** ☎ 91/779-1888; Trapsatur.

TAXIS

Taxis are one of Madrid's few truly good deals. They work under three different tariff schemes. Tariff 1 is valid in the city center from 6 AM to 10 PM; meters start at €1.45 and add €.67 per kilometer (½ mi). Supplemental charges include €4 to or from the airport, and €2 from bus and train stations. Tariff 2 is from 10 PM to 6 AM in the city center (and from 6 AM to 10 PM in the suburbs) and the meter runs faster and charges more per kilometer. Tariff 3 runs at night beyond the city limits. Note: you will find all tariffs listed on the taxi window.

Taxi stands are numerous, and taxis are easily hailed in the street—except when it rains, at which point they're exceedingly hard to come by. Available cabs display a LIBRE sign during the day, a green light at night. Spaniards do not tip cabbies, but if you're inspired, €.50 is about right for shorter rides; you can go as high as 10% for a trip to the airport. You can call a cab through Tele-Taxi, Radioteléfono Taxi, or Radio Taxi Gremial.

Taxis & Shuttles **Radio Taxi Gremial** ☎ 91/447-5180. **Radioteléfono Taxi** ☎ 91/547-8200. **Tele-Taxi** ☎ 91/371-2131.

TRAIN TRAVEL

For train schedules and reservations, go to any of Madrid's major train stations, visit a travel agent, or call RENFE toll-free. You can charge tickets to your credit card and even have them delivered to your hotel. Madrid has three main train stations: Chamartín, Atocha, and Norte, the last primarily for commuter trains. Remember to confirm which station you need when arranging a trip. Generally speaking, Chamartín, near the northern tip of Paseo de la Castellana, serves points north and west, including Barcelona, San Sebastián, Burgos, León, Oviedo, La Coruña, and Salamanca, as well as France and Portugal. Atocha, at the southern end of Paseo del Prado, serves towns near Madrid, including El Escorial, Segovia, and Toledo, and southern and eastern cities such as Seville, Málaga, Córdoba, Valencia, and Castellón. Atocha also sends AVE (high-speed) trains to Córdoba, Seville, Zaragosa, and Lleida.

Train Information **Estación de Atocha** ☎ 91/328-9020. **Estación Chamartín** ☎ 91/315-9976. **RENFE** ☎ 902/240202 🌐 www.renfe.es/ingles.

TRAVEL AGENCIES

Scattered throughout Madrid, travel agencies are generally the best way to get tickets, cheap deals, and information without hassles. The major agents below are in central locations. Madrid & Beyond is a British-run agency that can make all your travel and lodging arrangements in Madrid, other historic cities, and some lovely rural areas.

American Express ✉ Plaza de las Cortés 2 ☎ 91/743-7740 🌐 www.americanexpress.es. **Carlson Wagons-Lits/Viajes Ecuador** ✉ Paseo de la Castellana 96 ☎ 91/563-1202 🌐 www.viajesecuador.net. **Madrid & Beyond** ✉ Gran Vía 59-8D ☎ 91/758-0063 📠 91/542-4391. **Pullmantur** ✉ Plaza de Oriente 8 ☎ 91/541-1807.

VISITOR INFORMATION

Madrid has four regional tourist offices. The best is at Duque de Medinaceli 2 (near the Westin Palace), open Monday–Saturday 9–7 and Sunday 9–3. The others are at Barajas Airport, open daily 8–8; the Chamartín train station, open Monday–Saturday 8–8 and Sunday 9–3; and the remote Mercado de la Puerta de Toledo, open Monday–Saturday 9–7 and Sunday 9–3. The city tourist office on the Plaza Mayor is good for little save a few pamphlets; it's open Monday–Saturday 10–8, and Sunday 10–2.

City Tourist Office **Plaza Mayor 3** ☎ 91/588–1636 🌐 www.munimadrid.es.

Regional Tourist Offices **Duque de Medinaceli 2** ☎ 91/429–4951 🌐 www.madrid.org. **Barajas** ☎ 91/305–8656. **Chamartín** ☎ 91/315–9976 🌐 www.madrid.org. **Mercado de la Puerta de Toledo** ✉ Glorieta Puerta de Toledo, 3rd floor, Lavapiés ☎ 91/364–1876 🌐 www.madrid.org.

OLD AND NEW CASTILE

2

FODOR'S CHOICE

Archbishop's Palace, Astorga
El Figón de Pedro restaurant in Cuenca
National Museum of Sculpture, Valladolid
Parador Hotel San Marcos, León
Salamanca, a hilltop riverside university town
Segovia and its Roman and medieval monuments
Toledo, the austere Gothic home of El Greco

HIGHLY RECOMMENDED

RESTAURANTS
Casa Ojeda, Burgos
El Molino de la Losa, Ávila
Mesón de Cándido, Segovia
Mesón de José María, Segovia
Virrey Palafox, El Burgo de Osma

HOTELS
Hostal del Cardenal, Toledo
Hotel Palacio de los Velada, Ávila
Hotel Real Monasterio San Zoilo, Carrión de los Condes
Parador de Almagro
Parador de Sigüenza
Posada San José, Cuenca
Rector, Salamanca

SIGHTS
Burgos's cathedral sculpted in Flamboyant Gothic style
Casas Colgadas, Museum of Spanish Abstract Art in Cuenca
Corral de Comedias theater in Almagro
León's soaring Gothic cathedral with stained-glass
San Isidoro el Real sandstone basilica in León

By Michael Jacobs
Updated by AnneLise Sorensen

FOR ALL THE VARIETY in the towns and countryside around Madrid, there is an underlying unity in Castile—essentially an endless *meseta* (plain) of gray, bronze, and green, divided by mountains just north of the capital. The region is more accurately labeled Old and New Castile, the former (Castilla y León) north of Madrid, the latter (Castilla–La Mancha) south—known as "New" because it was captured from the Moors a bit later. Whereas southern Spaniards are traditionally peace-loving, Castilians have been a race of soldiers. The very name of the region (in effect, *la región castilla,* the region of castles) refers to the great east–west line of castles and fortified towns built in the 12th century between Salamanca and Soria. Segovia's Alcázar, Ávila's fully intact city walls, and other military installations are among Castile's greatest monuments, and some are also splendid hotels.

Stone, a dominant element in the Castilian countryside, gives the region much of its character. Gaunt mountain ranges frame the horizons; gorges and rocky outcrops break up flat expanses; and the fields around Ávila and Segovia are littered with giant boulders. Castilian villages are built predominantly of granite, and their solid, formidable look contrasts markedly with the whitewashed walls of most of southern Spain. Over the centuries, poets—most notably Antonio Machado, whose experiences at Soria in the early 20th century inspired his haunting *Campos de Castilla* (*Fields of Castile*)—and others have characterized Castile as austere and melancholy. There is a distinct, chilly beauty in the stark lines and soothing colors of these breezy expanses.

Faced with the austerity of the Castilian environment, some inhabitants have taken refuge in the spirit and imagination. Ávila is associated with two renowned mystics, St. Teresa and her disciple St. John of the Cross, and Toledo was the main home of one of the most spiritual of all Western painters, El Greco. Escape into fantasy is best illustrated by Cervantes's hero Don Quijote, in whose imagination even the dreary expanse of La Mancha became magical. Many of the region's architects were similarly fanciful: Castile in the 15th and 16th centuries was the center of the plateresque, an ornamental stone-carving style of extraordinary intricacy, named for its resemblance to silverwork. Developed in Toledo and Valladolid, it reached its climax in the university town of Salamanca.

Burgos was the 11th-century capital of Castile and the native city of El Cid ("Lord Conqueror"), Spain's legendary hero of the Christian Reconquest. Franco's wartime headquarters were established at Burgos during the Spanish Civil War (1936–39), possibly as much for symbolic as for strategic reasons. Even today the army and the clergy seem to set the tone in this somber city. León is a provincial capital and prestigious university town. Northwest of León, the medieval Camino de Santiago (Way of St. James) leads Christian pilgrims out of Castile and into Galicia as they wend their way toward Santiago de Compostela.

About the Restaurants

Castilian food is hearty stuff. Classic Castilian dishes are *cordero* (lamb) and *cochinillo* (suckling pig) roasted in a wood oven. Throughout Castile, prize dishes include *perdiz en escabeche,* the marinated partridge of Soria, and *perdiz estofada a la Toledana,* the stewed partridge of Toledo. Castile's most complex and exotic cuisine is perhaps that of Cuenca; here a Moorish influence appears in such dishes as *gazpacho pastor,* a hot terrine made with a mix of game, topped with grapes.

The mountainous districts of Salamanca, particularly the villages of Guijuelo and Candelario, are renowned for their hams and sausages. As the Spanish saying goes, "*Del cerdo se aprovecha todo*" ("All parts of the

It's possible (not ideal) to see Aranjuez, Ávila, Segovia, and Toledo on day trips from Madrid. If you have a car, spend at least four days in this area, staying in Toledo, Segovia, and Salamanca, and passing through Ávila. To see the region's main sights requires another four to six days, with overnight stays in Cuenca, Sigüenza, Soria, Zamora, Burgos, and León.

If you have **4 days**

Start in **Toledo** 1–15, Spain's intellectual and spiritual capital. Spend a full day visiting El Greco's former stomping grounds; then spend the night; move east the next day to **Aranjuez** 16, the summer retreat of the Bourbon monarchy. Farther south, check out Don Quijote's windmills at **Consuegra** 17 and the medieval town of **Almagro** 18, with its unique 16th-century theater. Consider spending a night in Almagro's 17th-century parador; then, hit Madrid's ring roads by 10 AM to avoid the rush hour and head north of Madrid on the N-VI to sublime **Segovia** 31–41, spending a night there. On your fourth day, catch the fountain display in the gardens of the **Palacio Real de la Granja** 42 before returning to Madrid via the spectacular Navacerrada mountain pass.

If you have **6 days**

Spend a day wandering **Toledo** 1–15, and spend the night; then head north to **Segovia** 31–41 for the second day and night. See the medieval **Castillo de Coca** 45 on your way to **Ávila** 46. Continue on to **Salamanca** 50–62 for the third night and spend the next day soaking up the architecture. Head north to **Burgos** 67–72 for the night and the next day. See the monastery at Santo Domingo de Silos, or the closer San Pedro de Cardeña, and spend the night in one of the two. Finally, take the Camino de Santiago pilgrimage route and linger in **León** 79–87.

---

pig are there to be enjoyed"), a philosophy embraced by many Castilian restaurants. A typical dish in the area of El Bierzo, near León, is *botillo*—pig's tail, ribs, and cheeks stuffed into pig's stomach. Bean dishes are specialties of the villages El Barco (Ávila) and La Granja (Segovia), while *trucha* (trout) and *cangrejos de río* (river crab) are common in Guadalajara.

Among the region's sweets are the *yemas* (sugared egg yolks) of Ávila, *almendras garrapiñadas* (candied almonds) of Alcalá de Henares, *mazapán* (marzipan) of Toledo, and *ponche Segovia* (Segovian egg toddy). *Manchego* cheeses (from La Mancha) are staples throughout Spain, and Aranjuez is known for its strawberries and asparagus.

Much of Spain's cheap wine also comes from La Mancha, home of the largest vineyard in the world. Far better in quality are those from the Duero Valley, around Valladolid. Look for the Marqués de Riscal whites from Rueda and the Vega Sicilia reds from Ribera del Duero; Peñafiel is the center of the Ribera region. An excellent, if extremely sweet, Castilian liqueur is Cuenca's *resolí,* made from aquavit, coffee, vanilla, orange peel, and sugar, and often sold in bottles in the shape of Cuenca's Casas Colgadas (Hanging Houses). The province of León produces a sparkling rosé wine called Bierzo, similar to the acidic Galician Ribeiro.

WHAT IT COSTS In Euros					
	$$$$	$$$	$$	$	¢
AT DINNER	over €20	€15–€20	€10–€15	€6–€10	under €6

Prices are per person for a main course at dinner.

About the Hotels

Spain's most stylish hotels are usually paradors. Most of the oldest, most attractive Castilian paradors are in quieter towns, such as Almagro, Ávila, Chinchón, Cuenca, León, and Sigüenza; the paradors in Toledo, Segovia, Salamanca, and Soria are modern buildings, albeit with magnificent views and, in the case of Segovia, wonderful indoor and outdoor swimming pools. Of course, there are pleasant alternatives to paradors, such as Ávila's Palacio de Valderrábanos (a 15th-century palace next to the cathedral), Segovia's Infanta Isabel, Salamanca's Rector, and Cuenca's Posada San José, a 16th-century convent.

WHAT IT COSTS In Euros					
	$$$$	$$$	$$	$	¢
FOR 2 PEOPLE	over €180	€100–€180	€60–€100	€40–€60	under €40

Prices are for two people in a standard double room in high season, excluding tax.

Exploring Old & New Castile

Castile is a large chunk of Spain, and the region could occupy any traveler for weeks. Old Castile lies to the north and west of Madrid; New Castile is to the south and east of Madrid. South of Madrid is ancient Toledo, once home to El Greco, and Aranjuez, with its impressive Royal Palace. Farther south is Consuegra, dominated by hilltop windmills, and the elegant city of Almagro. In Southeast Castile, the Rivers Huecar and Jucar cut through a rugged countryside, out of which rises Cuenca, built into craggy cliffs. North of Madrid is medieval Segovia with its famed Roman aqueduct, and the fairy tale-like Castillo de Coca. Northwest of Madrid are the spectacular peaks of the Sierra de Gredos and the walled city of Ávila. Further northwest is Salamanca, dominated by luminescent sandstone buildings and home to one of Spain's oldest universities. In the northern reaches of Castile are the ancient Castilian capitals of Burgos and Leon, each with inspiring Gothic cathedrals. If you're driving, Old Castile can be combined with later ventures to the Basque country or Galicia, while New Castile can lead you on to Extremadura, Andalusia, or the Mediterranean coast.

Numbers in the text correspond to numbers in the margin and on the Old and New Castile, Segovia, Salamanca, Toledo, and Burgos maps.

Timing

The best time to tour central Spain is between May and October, when the weather is sunny. July and August can be brutally hot, especially south of Madrid. November–February can get cold, especially in the Sierra de Guadarrama, north and west of Madrid. During the pre-Lenten Carnival, León and nearby La Bañeza are popular party centers. The last week of April, in the cloister at León's San Isidoro, the town councilors and ecclesiastical authorities bow to each other to the delight of onlookers; this recalls an ancient dispute over the distribution of power between the clergy and the civil authorities.

TOLEDO TO CIUDAD REAL

The contrast between the towns of Toledo and nearby Aranjuez could hardly be more marked. Toledo is a study in austerity, its introverted, gold-tone houses daring you to know them better. Here you can explore the mighty Gothic cathedral and the Tránsito Synagogue; contemplate El Greco's most famous painting, *The Burial of Count Orgaz*; or just roam the winding lanes. Aranjuez has the sumptuous Palacio Real. Consuegra, present in any picture of Don Quijote's windmills, is also the saffron capital of La Mancha. Farther south is historic Almagro, a hub during La Mancha's Age of Chivalry.

2

Toledo

1–15 *71 km (44 mi) southwest of Madrid.*

Fodor's Choice ★

Toledo was long the spiritual capital of Spain. Perched atop a rocky mount, with steep ocher-color hills rising on either side, Toledo remains tinged with a certain mysticism. If you approach from Madrid, your first glimpse of Toledo will be its northern gates and battlements. The rock on which Toledo stands, bounded on three sides by the Río Tajo (River Tagus), was inhabited in prehistoric times, and there was already an important Iberian settlement here when the Romans came in 192 BC. The Romans built a fort on the highest point of the rock—where you now see the Alcázar, the dominant building in Toledo's skyline—and this was later remodeled by the Visigoths, who transformed the town into their capital by the middle of the 6th century AD. In the early 8th century, the Moors arrived.

The Moors strengthened Toledo's reputation as a great center of religion and learning. Unusual tolerance was extended to those who continued to practice Christianity (the so-called Mozarabs), as well as to the town's exceptionally large Jewish population. Today the Moorish legacy is evident in Toledo's strong crafts tradition, the mazelike arrangement of the streets, and the predominance of brick rather than stone. For the Moors, beauty was a quality to be savored within rather than displayed on the surface, and it is significant that even Toledo's cathedral—one of the most richly endowed in Spain—is hard to see from the outside, largely obscured by the warren of houses around it. Long after the departure of the Moors, Toledo remained secretive.

Alfonso VI, aided by El Cid, captured Toledo in 1085 and styled himself emperor of Toledo. Under the Christians, the town's strong intellectual life was maintained, and Toledo became famous for its school of translators, who spread to the West a knowledge of Arab medicine, law, culture, and philosophy. Religious tolerance continued, and during the rule of Peter the Cruel (so named because he allegedly had members of his own family murdered to advance himself), a Jewish banker, Samuel Levi, became the royal treasurer and one of the wealthiest and most important men in town. By the early 15th century, however, hostility toward both Jews and Arabs had grown as Toledo developed more and more into a bastion of the Catholic Church.

As Florence had the Medici and Rome the papacy, so Toledo had its long line of cardinals, most notably Mendoza, Tavera, and Cisneros. Under these patrons of the arts, Renaissance Toledo emerged as a center of humanism. Economically and politically, however, Toledo began to decline in the 16th century. The expulsion of the Jews from Spain in 1492, as part of the Spanish Inquisition, had serious economic consequences for Toledo. When Madrid became the permanent center of the Spanish court in 1561, Toledo's political importance eroded, and the expulsion from Spain of the converted Arabs (Moriscos) in 1601 led to the departure of most of Toledo's artisan community. The years the painter El Greco spent in Toledo—from 1572 to his death in 1614—were those of the town's decline. Its transformation into a major tourist center began in the late 19th century, when the works of El Greco came to be widely appreciated after years of neglect. Today, Toledo is prosperous and conservative, expensive, and silent at night. Yet Spain has no other town of this size with such a concentration of monuments and works of art.

a good walk

The eastern end of the Tagus gorge, along Calle de Circunvalación, is a good place to park your car (except in the middle of the day, when buses line up) and look down over almost all of historic Toledo. For quicker access to your car after a long day's walk, drive into the city and park by the Alcázar.

A complete tour starts at the **Puente de Alcántara** 1 ⚑. If you skirt the city walls traveling northwest, a long walk past the Puerta de Bisagra on Calle Cardenal Tavera brings you to the **Hospital de Tavera** 2. If you enter the city wall, walk west and pass the **Museo de la Santa Cruz** 3 to emerge in the **Plaza de Zocodover** 4. Due south of here, on Calle Cuesta de Carlos V, is the **Alcázar** 5; a short walk northwest on Calle Nueva brings you to the **Mezquita del Cristo de la Luz** 6. From the southwestern corner of the Alcázar, a series of alleys descends to the east end of the **cathedral** 7. Make your way around the southern side of the building, passing the mid-15th-century Puerta de los Leones. Emerging into the small square in front of the cathedral's west facade, you'll see the stately *ayuntamiento* (town hall) to your right, begun by the young Juan de Herrera and completed by El Greco's son, Jorge Manuel Theotokópoulos.

Near the Museo de los Concilios, on Calle de San Clemente, take in the richly sculpted portal by Covarrubias on the Convento de San Clemente; across the street is the church of **San Román** 8. Almost every wall in this part of town belongs to a convent, and the empty streets make for contemplative walks. This was a district loved by the Romantic poet Gustavo Adolfo Bécquer, author of *Rimas* (*Rhymes*), the most popular collection of Spanish verse before García Lorca's *Romancero Gitano*. Bécquer's favorite corner was the tiny square in front of the 16th-century convent church of **Santo Domingo** 9, a few minutes' walk north of San Román, below the Plazuela de Padilla.

Backtrack, following Calle de San Clemente through the Plaza de Valdecaleros to Calle de Santo Tomé, to get to the church of **Santo Tomé** 10. Downhill from Santo Tomé, off Calle de San Juan de Díos, is the **Casa de El Greco** 11. (Follow the signs, as this is a tricky labyrinth to navigate.) Next door to the Casa de El Greco is the 14th-century **Sinagoga del Tránsito** 12, financed by Samuel Levi, and the accompanying Museo Sefardí. From the synagogue, turn right up Calle de Reyes Católicos. A few steps past the town's other synagogue, **Santa María la Blanca** 13, is the late-15th-century church of **San Juan de los Reyes** 14. The town's western extremity is the **Puente de San Martín** 15.

TIMING Toledo's winding streets and steep hills can be exasperating, especially when you're looking for a specific sight. Take the entire day to absorb the town's medieval trappings, and expect to get a little lost.

What to See

5 **Alcázar.** The name means "fortress" in Arabic and alludes to the Moorish citadel that stood here from the 10th century to the Reconquest. The building's south facade, its most severe, is the work of Juan de Herrera,

of El Escorial fame. The east facade incorporates a large section of battlements. The finest facade is the northern, one of many Toledan works by Alonso de Covarrubias, who did more than any other architect to introduce the Renaissance style here.

Inside are a military headquarters and a large museum—one of Spain's few remaining homages to Francoism, hung with tributes from various right-wing military groups and figures from around the world. The Alcázar's architectural highlight is Covarrubias's Italianate courtyard, which, like most other parts of the building, was largely rebuilt after the civil war, when the Alcázar was besieged by the Republicans. Though the Nationalists' ranks were depleted, they managed to hold on to the building. Franco later turned the Alcázar into a monument to Nationalist bravery; the office of the Nationalist general who defended the building, General Moscardó, has been left exactly as it was after the war, complete with peeling ceiling paper and mortar holes. Also visit the dark cellars, which evoke living conditions at the time of the siege. More cheerful is a ground-floor room full of beautifully crafted swords, a Toledan specialty introduced by Moorish silversmiths. At the top of the grand staircase, which apparently made even Charles V "feel like an emperor," are rooms displaying a vast collection of toy soldiers. At press time, part of the Alcázar's interior was closed for the gradual installation of Spain's Museo del Ejercito (Military Museum), formerly in Madrid. ✉ *Cuesta Carlos V s/n* ☎ *925/221673* 💶 *€1.20* ⏲ *Tues.–Sun. 9:30–2.*

⓫ **Casa de El Greco** (El Greco's House). This house is on the property that belonged to Peter the Cruel's treasurer, Samuel Levi. El Greco once lived in a house owned by Levi, but it's pure conjecture that the artist lived here. The interior, decorated in the late 19th century to resemble a "typ-

CloseUp

EL GRECO: THE TITAN OF TOLEDO

"CRETE GAVE HIM HIS LIFE, and brushes; Toledo, a better land, where he begins with Death to attain Eternity." With these words, the Toledan poet, Fray Hortensio Paravicino, paid homage to his friend El Greco—and to the symbiotic connection between El Greco and his adopted city of Toledo. El Greco's intensely individual and expressionist style—elongated and sometimes distorted figures, charged colors, and a haunting mysticism—was seen as strange and disturbing, and his work remained largely neglected until the late 19th century, when he found wide acclaim and joined the ranks of Velazquez and Goya as one of the Old Masters of Spanish painting.

Born Domenikos Theotokopoulos on the island of Crete, El Greco ("The Greek") received his artistic education and training in Italy, then moved to Spain around 1577, lured in part by the prospect of painting frescoes for the royal monastery of El Escorial. King Philip II, however, rejected El Greco's work for being too unusual. It was in Toledo that El Greco came into his own, creating many of his greatest works and honing his singular style and vision. He remained here until his death in 1614.

The master painter immortalized the city and its citizens. In his masterpiece The Burial of Count Orgaz, *which hangs in Toledo's Chapel of Santo Tomé, El Greco pays tribute to Toledan society. The burial onlookers, beneath a vibrant heaven swarming with angels, include many of El Greco's distinguished contemporaries, their white 16th-century ruff collars framing their angular, ascetic faces. Perhaps the most famous rendering of Toledo is El Greco's dramatic* View of Toledo, *in which Toledo's cityscape crackles with a sinister energy underneath a stormy sky.*

ical" house of El Greco's time, is a fake, albeit pleasant one. The museum next door has a few of El Greco's paintings, including a panorama of Toledo with the Hospital of Tavera in the foreground. ✉ *Samuel Levi s/n* ☎ *925/224046* 💳 *€1.20, free Sat. afternoon and Sun. morning* ⊙ *Tues.–Sat. 10–2 and 4–6, Sun. 10–2.*

❼ **Cathedral.** Jorge Manuel Theotokópoulos was responsible for the cathedral's Mozarabic chapel, the elongated dome of which crowns the right-hand side of the west facade. The rest of this facade is mainly early 15th-century and has a depiction of the Virgin presenting her robe to Toledo's patron saint, the Visigothic Ildefonsus. Enter the cathedral from the 14th-century cloisters to the left of the west facade. The primarily 13th-century architecture was inspired by the Gothic cathedrals of France, such as Chartres, but the squat proportions give it a Spanish feel, as do the wealth and weight of the furnishings and the location of the elaborate choir in the center of the nave. Immediately to your right as you enter the building is a beautifully carved plateresque doorway by Covarrubias, marking the entrance to the Treasury. The latter houses a small Crucifixion by the Italian painter Cimabue and an extraordinarily intricate late-15th-century monstrance by Juan del Arfe, a silversmith of German descent; the ceiling is an excellent example of Mudéjar workmanship.

From here, walk around to the ambulatory, off the right side of which is a chapter house with a strange and quintessentially Spanish mixture of Italianate frescoes by Juan de Borgoña. In the middle of the ambulatory is an example of Baroque illusionism by Narciso Tomé, known as the *Transparente,* a blend of painting, stucco, and sculpture. Finally, off the northern end of the ambulatory, you'll come to the sacristy and several El Grecos, including *El Espolio* (Christ Being Stripped of his Raiment). One of El Greco's earliest works in Toledo, it offended the Inquisition, which accused the artist of putting Christ on a lower level than some of the onlookers. El Greco was thrown into prison, where his career might have ended had he not by this time formed friendships with some of Toledo's more moderate clergy. Before leaving the sacristy, look up at the colorful and spirited late-Baroque ceiling painting by the Italian Luca Giordano. ✉ *Arco de Palacio 2* ☎ *925/222241* 🎟 *€4.80* 🕓 *Mon.–Sat. 10:30–6:30, Sun. 3–6.*

2

❷ **Hospital de Tavera.** You'll find this hospital, Covarrubias's last work, outside the walls beyond Toledo's main northern gate, Covarrubias's imposing Puerta de Bisagra. Unlike the former Hospital of Santa Cruz, this complex is unfinished and slightly dilapidated, but it is nonetheless full of character and has the evocatively ramshackle **Museo de Duque de Lema** in its southern wing. The most important work in the museum's miscellaneous collection is a painting by the 17th-century artist José Ribera. The hospital's monumental chapel holds El Greco's *Baptism of Christ* and the exquisitely carved marble tomb of Cardinal Tavera, the last work of Alonso de Berruguete. Descend into the crypt to experience some bizarre acoustical effects. ✉ *Cardenal Tavera 2* ☎ *925/220451* 🎟 *€3* 🕓 *Daily 10–1:30 and 3:30–6.*

❻ **Mezquita del Cristo de la Luz** (Mosque of Christ of the Light). A gardener will open the gate and show you around this mosque-chapel, in a park above the northern ramparts; if the gardener's not around, inquire at the house opposite. Originally a tiny Visigothic church, the chapel was transformed into a mosque during the Moorish occupation, and the Islamic arches and vaulting survive—making this the most important relic of Moorish Toledo. The chapel got its name when the horse of Alfonso VI, riding into Toledo in triumph in 1085, fell to its knees out front (a white stone marks the spot); it was then discovered that a candle had burned continuously behind the masonry throughout the time that the so-called Infidels had been in power. The first mass of the Reconquest was said here, and later a Mudéjar apse was added (now shielded by glass). After you've seen the chapel, the gardener will take you across the ramparts to climb to the top of the Puerta del Sol, a 12th-century Mudéjar gatehouse. 🎟 *Tip gardener* 🕓 *Any reasonable hr.*

❸ **Museo de la Santa Cruz.** In a beautiful Renaissance hospital with a stunning classical-plateresque facade, the museum, unlike Toledo's other sights, is open all day (limited hours Monday) without a break. The light and elegant interior has changed little since the 16th century, the main difference being that works of art have replaced the hospital beds; among the displays is El Greco's *Assumption* of 1613, the artist's last known work. A small **Museo de Arqueología** (Museum of Archaeology) is in and around the hospital's delightful cloister, off which is a beautifully decorated staircase by Alonso de Covarrubias. ✉ *Cervantes 3* ☎ *925/221036* 🎟 *free* 🕓 *Mon.–Sat. 10–6:30, Sun. 10–2.*

❹ **Plaza de Zocodover.** Toledo's main square was built in the early 17th century as part of an unsuccessful attempt to impose a rigid geometry on the chaotic Moorish ground plan. Nearby, you'll find **Calle del Comercio**, the town's narrow and lively pedestrian thoroughfare, lined with bars and shops and shaded in the summer months by awnings suspended from the roofs of tall houses.

🚩 ❶ **Puente de Alcántara.** Here is the town's oldest bridge, Roman in origin. Next to the bridge is a heavily restored castle built after the Christian capture of 1085 and, above this, a vast and depressingly severe military academy, a typical example of Fascist architecture under Franco. The bridge is off the city's eastern peripheral road, just north of the Puente Nuevo.

15 **Puente de San Martín.** A pedestrian bridge on the western edge of the town, the Puente de San Martín dates from 1203 and has splendid horseshoe arches.

14 **San Juan de los Reyes.** In western Toledo, this convent church was erected by Ferdinand and Isabella to commemorate their victory at the Battle of Toro in 1476 and was intended to be their burial place. The building is largely the work of architect Juan Guas, who considered it his masterpiece and asked to be buried here himself. In true plateresque fashion, the white interior is covered with inscriptions and heraldic motifs. ✉ *Reyes Católicos 17* ☎ *925/223802* 🎫 *€1.20* 🕓 *Apr.–Oct., daily 10–7; Nov.–Mar., daily 10–6.*

8 **San Román.** A virtually unspoiled part of Toledo hides this early 13th-century Mudéjar church with extensive remains of frescoes inside. It has been deconsecrated and is now the **Museo de los Concilios y de la Cultura Visigótica,** with statuary, manuscript illustrations, and jewelry. ✉ *C. de San Clemente s/n* ☎ *925/227872* 🎫 *free* 🕓 *Tues.–Sat. 10–2 and 3:30–6, Sun. 10–2.*

need a break?

If the convolutions of Toledo's maze exhaust you, unwind at **Palacio Sancara** (Alfonso X El Sabio 6). Around the corner from the church of San Román, off Plaza Juan de Mariana, this Arabian café-bar has plush couches, low tables, soothing classical music, and colorful tapestries.

13 **Santa María la Blanca.** Founded in 1203, Toledo's second synagogue is nearly two centuries older than the more-elaborate Tránsito. The white interior has a forest of columns supporting capitals of enchanting filigree workmanship. Stormed in the early 15th century by a Christian mob led by St. Vincent Ferrer, the synagogue was later used as a carpenter's workshop, a store, a barracks, and a refuge for reformed prostitutes. ✉ *Reyes Católicos 4* ☎ *925/227257* 🎫 *€1.50* 🕓 *Daily 10–1:45 and 3:30–6 (7 in summer).*

9 **Santo Domingo.** A few minutes' walk north of San Román is this 16th-century convent church, where you'll find the earliest of El Greco's Toledo paintings as well as the crypt where the artist is believed to be buried. The friendly nuns at the convent will show you around an odd little museum that includes documents bearing El Greco's signature. ✉ *Pl. Santo Domingo el Antiguo s/n* ☎ *925/222930* 🎫 *€1.20* 🕓 *Mon.–Sat. 11–1:30 and 4–7, Sun. 4–7 (weekends only in winter).*

10 **Santo Tomé.** Topped with a Mudéjar tower, this chapel was specially built to house El Greco's most famous painting, *The Burial of Count Orgaz,* and remains devoted to that purpose. The painting portrays the benefactor of the church being buried with the posthumous assistance of St. Augustine and St. Stephen, who have miraculously appeared at the funeral to thank him for all the money he gave to religious institutions named after them. Though the count's burial took place in the 14th century, El Greco painted the onlookers in contemporary costumes and included people he knew; the boy in the foreground is one of El Greco's sons, and the sixth figure on the left is said to be the artist himself. To avoid crowds in summer, try to come here as soon as the building opens. ✉ *Pl. del Conde 4* ☎ *925/256098* 🌐 *www.santotome.org* 🎫 *€1.20* 🕓 *Mar.–mid-Oct., daily 10–6:45; mid-Oct.–Feb., daily 10–5:45.*

12 **Sinagoga del Tránsito.** Financed by Samuel Levi, this 14th-century rectangular synagogue is plain on the outside, but the inside walls are covered with intricate Mudéjar decoration, as well as Hebraic inscriptions glorifying God, Peter the Cruel, and Levi himself. It is said that Levi imported cedars from Lebanon for the building's construction, à la Solomon when he built the First Temple in Jerusalem. Adjoining the main hall is the **Museo Sefardí**, a small museum of Jewish culture in Spain. ✉ *Samuel Levi s/n* ☎ *925/223665* 🎫 *€2.40, free Sat. afternoon and Sun.* ⏲ *Tues.–Sat. 10–2 and 4–6, Sun. 10–2.*

If you're traveling with children, look to Toledo's **Tren Imperial**, a fun little tourist train that chugs past many of the sights to see. Tickets are €3.60 for adults and €1.80 for kids, and the train departs from the Plaza de Zocodover. ☎ *925/142274* 🎫 *€3.60 for adults, €1.80 for kids* ⏲ *Tours daily at 11, and night tours Fri.–Sun.*

Where to Stay & Eat

$$–$$$ ✕ **Asador Adolfo.** Steps from the cathedral but discreetly hidden away, this restaurant has an old, intimate interior whose wood-beam ceiling was painted in the 14th century. The emphasis is on fresh produce and traditional Toledan food. The *tempura de flor de calabacín* (zucchini-blossom tempura in saffron sauce) is a tasty starter; a flavorful entrée is the *solomillo de cerdo* (pork loin with wild mushrooms and black truffles). Finish with a Toledan specialty, *delicias de mazapán* (marzipan delights). ✉ *Granada 6* ☎ *925/227321* *Reservations essential* ▭ *AE, DC, MC, V* ⏲ *Closed Mon. No dinner Sun.*

$$–$$$ ✕ **Cason López.** A vaulted foyer leads to a patio with marble statues, twittering caged birds, a fountain, and abstract religious paintings; in the dining room, carved wood abounds. The market-based Castilian and Continental menu might include garlic-ravioli soup, braised rabbit with sesame sauce and mashed potatoes, or cod with manchego cheese, onions, and olive oil. Try the almond *mazapán* (marzipan) cake topped with cream cheese. Reservations are wise. ✉ *Sillería 3* ☎ *925/254774* ▭ *AE, DC, MC, V* ⏲ *No dinner Sun.*

$$–$$$ ✕ **Hierbabuena.** Here you can dine on an enclosed Moorish patio with plenty of natural light, at tables covered with crocheted tablecloths. The food is just as inviting, and prices surprisingly reasonable. The menu changes with the season; possibilities include artichokes stuffed with seafood and steak with blue-cheese sauce. ✉ *Callejón de San José 17* ☎ *925/223924* ▭ *AE, DC, MC, V* ⏲ *No dinner Sun.*

$–$$ ✕ **Restaurant Maravilla.** Partridge or quail and seafood dishes stand out at this quaint and modestly priced spot. ✉ *Pl. Barrio Rey 7* ☎ *925/228582 or 925/228317* ▭ *AE, DC, MC, V.*

★ $$ ✕ **Hostal del Cardenal.** Built in the 18th century as a summer palace for Cardinal Lorenzana, this quiet and beautiful hotel has rooms with antique furniture. Some rooms overlook the hotel's enchanting wooded garden, which lies at the foot of the town's walls. The restaurant, popular with tourists, has a long-standing reputation; the dishes are mainly local, and in season you'll find delicious asparagus and strawberries from Aranjuez. ✉ *Paseo Recaredo 24, 45004* ☎ *925/224900* 📠 *925/222991* 🌐 *www.hostaldelcardenal.com* *27 rooms* *Restaurant* ▭ *AE, DC, MC, V.*

$$$ **Hotel Alfonso VI.** Besides being smack in the middle of the historic district, this hotel has great views of the city from its summer terrace. The rooms are modern, clean, and inviting; the restaurant is done in the ubiquitous Mudéjar style and serves delicious food. ✉ *General Moscardó 2, 45001* ☎ *925/222600* 📠 *925/214458* 🌐 *www.hotelalfonsovi.com* *83 rooms* *Restaurant* ▭ *AE, DC, MC, V.*

$$$ **Parador de Toledo.** This modern building on Toledo's outskirts has an unbeatable panorama of the town. The architecture and furnishings nod to the traditional Toledan style, emphasizing brick and wood. *Cerro del Emperador s/n, 45001 925/221850 925/225166 www.parador.es 76 rooms Pool AE, DC, MC, V.*

$$ **Hotel Pintor El Greco.** Next door to the painter's house–museum, this friendly hotel occupies what was once a 17th-century bakery. The modern interior is warm and clean, with tawny colors and antique touches, like exposed-brick vaulting. *Alamillos del Transito 13, 45002 925/285191 925/215819 www.hotelpintorelgreco.com 33 rooms AE, DC, MC, V.*

Shopping

The Moors established silverwork, damascene (metalwork inlaid with gold or silver), pottery, embroidery, and marzipan traditions here, and next to Toledo's church of San Juan de los Reyes a turn-of-the-20th-century art school keeps these crafts alive. As for embroidery, the finest in the province comes from **Oropesa** and **Lagartera.** For inexpensive pottery, try to stop at the large roadside emporia on the outskirts of town, on the main road to Madrid. Most of the Toledo region's pottery is made in Talavera la Reina, 76 km (47 mi) west of Toledo, and a worthy stop is **Museo Ruiz de Luna.** Here the development of Talavera's world-famous ceramics is chronicled with 1,500 tiles, bowls, vases, and plates dating back to the 15th century, and you can watch artisans throw local clay. *Pl. de San Augustín 925/800149 Museum €.60 Tues.–Sat. 10–2 and 4–6:30, Sun. 10–2.*

Aranjuez

16 *47 km (29 mi) south of Madrid, 35 km (22 mi) northwest of Toledo.*

Once the site of a Habsburg hunting lodge on the banks of the Tajo, Aranjuez became a favorite summer residence of the Bourbons in the 18th century—they built a palace and other buildings, designed gardens, and planted woods. In the 19th century, Aranjuez developed into a popular retreat for Madrileños. Today, the town retains a faded elegance. Children might enjoy the **tourist train** (925/142274 €4 for adults, €2 for kids) that trundles around town.

Aranjuez's **Palacio Real** (Royal Palace) reflects French grandeur. The high point of the opulent interior is a room covered entirely with porcelain; there are also numerous elaborate clocks and a museum of period costumes. Shaded riverside gardens full of statues and fountains invite pleasant relaxation after the palace tour. *Pl. de Parejas 91/891–0740 Palace €4.80, gardens free Palace May–Sept., Tues.–Sun. 10–6:15; Oct.–Apr., Tues.–Sun. 10–5:15. Gardens May–Sept., daily 8:30–6:30; Oct.–Apr., daily 8:30–8:30.*

The charming **Casa del Labrador** (Farmer's Cottage), a small palace at the eastern end of Aranjuez, was built by Charles IV in 1804 and has a jewel-like interior bursting with color and crowded with delicate objects. *Casa del Labrador 91/891–0305 €3 May–Sept., Tues.–Sun. 10–6:15; Oct.–Apr., Tues.–Sun. 10–5:15.*

Between the Royal Palace and the Casa del Labrador is the **Casa de Marinos** (Sailors' House), where—if ongoing refurbishment is finished—you'll see a gondola that belonged to Philip V and other decorated pleasure boats that once plied the river. *Casa de Marinas, 91/891–2453 €3 May–Sept., Tues.–Sun. 10–6:15 Oct.–Apr., Tues.–Sun. 10–5:15.*

Consuegra

17 *78 km (48 mi) south of Aranjuez, 125 km (78 mi) south of Madrid (Km 119 on N-IV).*

This small, historic town is dominated by a spectacular hilltop castle and 11 white-wall **windmills.** You can drive straight up to the first windmill, **El Bolero** (restored to house the local tourist office), and walk upstairs to see the intricate 16th-century machinery. In October, the fields all around Consuegra are purple with **saffron crocuses** (*Crocus Sativus*). These flowers appear overnight, and the three female stigmas must be hand-picked from each one immediately—each flower produces only once. The stamens are then dried over braziers in private homes to become "red gold" worth €1,800 per kilogram. The process—which requires 4,000 crocuses to make 2 grams (0.7 ounce) of saffron—has been used for 700 years. Consuegra's **Fiesta de la Rosa del Azafrán** (Saffron Festival), complete with competitions and saffron-based foods, is held here the last week of October.

Moors and Christians once did battle for the 10th-century **Castillo de Consuegra,** and during the second week in August the town reenacts their medieval conflict twice a day. In the 12th century the castle housed the Knights of St. John of Jerusalem, and here you can imagine that most notorious knight of all, Don Quijote, tilting at the windmills. The ramparts have classic views of the plains of La Mancha, with the town and saffron fields below. ☎ *925/475731 tourist office* ✉ *€1.80* ⊙ *Nov.–Mar., weekdays 9–2 and 3:30–6, Sat. 10–2 and 3:30–6, Sun. 10:30–2 and 3:30–6; Apr.–Oct., weekdays 9–2 and 4:30–7, Sat. 10–2 and 4:30–7, Sun. 10:30–2 and 4:30–7.*

en route

Return to the N-IV and take the Daimiel exit and bypass to visit **Las Tablas de Daimiel,** a wetland wildlife reserve threatened by drought and farm irrigation. In addition to its rare flora and fauna, the park attracts migrating birds March–April and October–November. The longest of the three marked walks takes an hour, and observation towers aid in viewing; residents include red-crested pochards, broad-billed shoveler ducks, great crested gledes, purple herons, and marsh harriers. ✉ *N430 toward Ciudad Real, 12 km (8 mi) west of Daimiel* ☎ *926/693118* ⊙ *Park and visitor center daily 8:30–dusk.*

Almagro

18 *190 km (118 mi) south of Madrid, 65 km (40 mi) south of Consuegra.*

The center of this noble town contains the only preserved medieval theater in Europe. The theater stands beside the ancient **Plaza Mayor,** where 85 Roman columns form two facing colonnades supporting green-frame 16th-century buildings. Near the plaza are granite mansions embellished with the heraldic shields of their former owners and a splendid parador in a restored 17th-century convent.

★ The **Corral de Comedias** theater stands almost as it was built in the 16th century, with wooden balconies on four sides and the stage at one end of the open central patio. During the golden age of Spanish theater—the time of playwrights Calderón de la Barca, Cervantes, and Lope de Vega—touring actors came to Almagro, which then prospered from mercury mines and lace making. The Corral hosts an international theater festival each July. ✉ *Pl. Mayor 18* ☎ *926/861539* ⊙ *Tues.–Fri. 10–2 and 4–7 (10–2 and 6–9 July–Aug.), Sat. 10–2 and 4–6 (10–2 and 6–8 July–Aug.), Sun. 11–2 and 4–6 (11–2 and 6–8 July–Aug.)* ☞ *Festival*

Old & New Castile
Villafranca del Bierzo
Ponferrada
Castillo de los Polvazares
León
see detail map
Ourense
GALICIA
Astorga
Orbigo Bridge
La Bañeza
CASTILE–LEON
Verín
Donado
Puebla de Sanabria
Benavente
Mayorga
Medina de Rioseco
60 miles
90 km
Alcañices
Zamora
Toro
Valladolid
Tordesillas
Embalse de Almendra
El Cubo de Tierra del Vino
Salamanca
see detail map
Medina del Campo
Vitigudino
CASTILE–LEON
Vecinos
Peñaranda de Bracamonte
Ciudad Rodrigo
PORTUGAL
El Cabaco
Miranda del Castañar
El Barco de Ávila
Sierra de Gredos
Villanueva de la Sierra
Jarandilla
Arenas de San Pedro
Plasencia
Coria
EXTREMADURA
Navalmoral de la Mata
Oropesa
Talavera de la Reina
Casar de Cáceres
Valdelacasa de Tajo
Arroyo de la Luz
Aliseda
San Vicente de Alcántara
Trujillo
Guadalupe
EXTREMADURA
Albuquerque
Montánchez
Valdecaballeros
La Roca de la Sierra
Miajadas
Montijo
Badajoz
Don Benito
Puebla de Alcocer

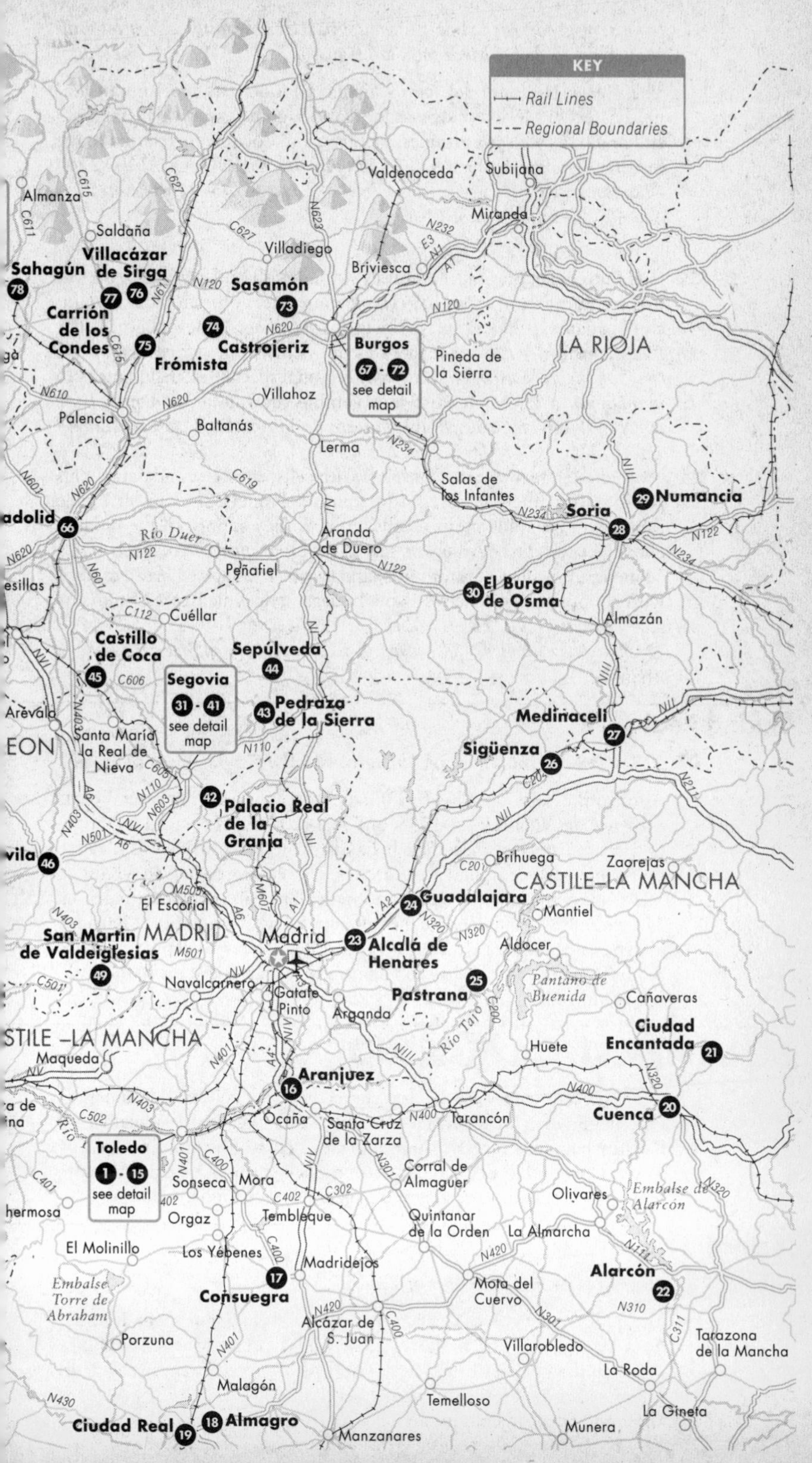
KEY
Rail Lines
Regional Boundaries
Almanza
Saldaña
Villacázar de Sirga
Sahagún
Carrión de los Condes
Frómista
Sasamón
Castrojeriz
Villadiego
Briviesca
Valdenoceda
Subijana
Miranda
Burgos
67 - 72
see detail map
Pineda de la Sierra
LA RIOJA
Palencia
Villahoz
Baltanás
Lerma
Salas de los Infantes
Soria
Numancia
adolid
Río Duero
Peñafiel
Aranda de Duero
El Burgo de Osma
Almazán
esillas
Cuéllar
Castillo de Coca
Sepúlveda
Segovia
31 - 41
see detail map
Pedraza de la Sierra
Arévalo
EON
Santa María la Real de Nieva
Medinaceli
Sigüenza
Palacio Real de la Granja
vila
Brihuega
Zaorejas
CASTILE–LA MANCHA
Guadalajara
El Escorial
Mantiel
San Martin de Valdeiglesias
MADRID
Madrid
Alcalá de Henares
Aldocer
Navalcarnero
Getafe
Pinto
Arganda
Pastrana
Pantano de Buenida
Cañaveras
STILE –LA MANCHA
Maqueda
Río Tajo
Huete
Ciudad Encantada
Aranjuez
Ocaña
Santa Cruz de la Zarza
Tarancón
Cuenca
Toledo
1 - 15
see detail map
Sonseca
Mora
Corral de Almaguer
hermosa
Orgaz
Tembleque
Quintanar de la Orden
Olivares
Embalse de Alarcón
La Almarcha
El Molinillo
Los Yébenes
Madridejos
Alarcón
Embalse Torre de Abraham
Consuegra
Mota del Cuervo
Alcázar de S. Juan
Porzuna
Villarobledo
Tarazona de la Mancha
Malagón
La Roda
Temelloso
La Gineta
Ciudad Real
Almagro
Manzanares
Munera

tickets: by credit card, Tele-Entrada, 902/101212; with cash, after mid-May, Palacio de los Medrano, San Agustín 7.

The **Museo Nacional del Teatro** displays models of the Roman amphitheaters in Mérida (Extremadura) and Sagunto (near Valencia), both still in use, as well as costumes, pictures, and documents relating to the history of Spanish theater. ✉ *Callejón del Villar 4* ☎ *926/882244* 🌐 *museoteatro.mcu.es* ⏲ *Tues.–Fri. 10–2 and 4–7 (6–9 July), Sat. 11–2 and 4–6 (6–8 July), Sun. 11–2.*

Where to Stay & Eat

$$–$$$ ✕ **El Corregidor.** Several old houses stuffed with antiques make up this fine restaurant and tapas bar. The menu centers on rich local fare, including game, fish, and spicy Almagro aubergines, a local delicacy. The €22 *menú de degustación* (taster's menu) yields seven savory tapas, while the €24 *menu Manchego* showcases regional specialties, including *pisto manchego,* a La Mancha-style vegetable ratatouille, and *ravioli de cordero* (lamb-stuffed ravioli.) ✉ *Jerónimo Ceballos 2* ☎ *926/860648* 💳 *AE, DC, MC, V* ⏲ *Closed Mon.*

★ $$$ ✕🏨 **Parador de Almagro.** Complete with cells, cloisters, and patios, this parador is a finely restored 17th-century Franciscan convent. Some rooms still resemble monks' cells, even as they supply all the modern conveniences. The restaurant serves fabulous *pisto manchego* (a La Mancha equivalent of ratatouille) and *migas,* fried spiced bread crumbs with chopped pork. There's also a bodega-style wine bar. ✉ *Ronda de San Francisco 31, 13270 Almagro* ☎ *926/860100* 📠 *926/860150* 🌐 *www.parador.es* 🛏 *54 rooms* 🏊 *Restaurant, pool, bar* 💳 *AE, DC, MC, V.*

Ciudad Real

⑲ *22 km (14 mi) southwest of Almagro, 116 km (72 mi) south of Toledo.*

Alfonso the Wise founded this university town, now the capital of its province, as Villa Real in 1255, and in 1420 Juan II decreed it a bona-fide *ciudad* (city). Since then it has become progressively less regal. Only one of its original gate arches, the **Puerta de Toledo**—built in 1328—remains, and the extensive city wall has disappeared altogether. The cathedral, **Santa María del Prado,** does have a magnificent Baroque altarpiece by Giraldo de Merlo. Ciudad Real's present claim to fame is that it's one of the few stops on Spain's first high-speed train, the AVE, between Madrid and Seville.

SOUTHEAST OF MADRID

Dramatic landscapes are the draw here: the rocky countryside and magnificent gorges of the Rivers Huécar and Júcar make for spectacular views. Cuenca has an impressive museum devoted to abstract art. Nearby towns like Ciudad Encantada, with its rock formations, and Alarcón, which has a medieval castle, make pleasant excursions.

Cuenca

⑳ *167 km (104 mi) southeast of Madrid.*

The quaint, old town of Cuenca is one of the strangest in Spain. It's built on a sloping, curling finger of rock whose precipitous sides plunge down to the gorges of the Huécar and Júcar rivers. Because the town ran out of room to expand, some medieval houses hang right over the abyss and are now a unique architectural attraction: the Casas Colgadas

(Hanging Houses). The old town's dramatic setting grants spectacular gorge views, and its cobble streets, cathedral, churches, bars, and taverns contrast starkly with the modern town, which sprawls beyond the river gorges. Though somewhat isolated, Cuenca makes a good overnight stop if you're traveling between Madrid and Valencia. The lower half of the old town is a maze of tiny streets, any of which will take you up to the Plaza del Carmen. From here the town narrows and a single street, Calle Alfonso VIII, continues the ascent to the Plaza Mayor, which you reach after passing under the arch of the town hall. Calle San Pedro shoots off from the northern side of Plaza Mayor; just off Calle San Pedro, clinging to the western edge of Cuenca, is the tiny **Plaza San Nicolás,** a pleasingly dilapidated square. Nearby, the unpaved Ronda del Júcar hovers over the Júcar gorge and commands remarkable views of the mountainous landscape.

The best views are from the square in front of the **castle,** at the very top of Cuenca, where the town tapers out to the narrowest of ledges. Here, gorges are on either side of you, while old houses sweep down toward a distant plateau in front. The castle itself, which served as the town prison for many years, is now a hotel. ✉ *C. San Pedro 60.*

The **Museo Diocesano de Arte Sacro** (Diocesan Museum of Sacred Art) is in what were once the cellars of the Bishop's Palace. The beautifully clear display includes a jewel-encrusted, Byzantine diptych of the 13th century; a Crucifixion by the 15th-century Flemish artist Gerard David; and two small El Grecos. From the Plaza Mayor, take Calle Obispo Valero and follow signs toward the Casas Colgadas. ✉ *Obispo Valero 1* ☎ *969/224210* 🎫 *€1.80* ⏲ *Oct.–May, Tues.–Sat. 11–2 and 4–6, Sun. 11–2; June–Sept., Tues.–Sat. 11–2 and 5–8, Sun. 11–2.*

★ Cuenca's most famous buildings, the **Casas Colgadas** (Hanging Houses), form one of Spain's finest and most curious museums, the **Museo de Arte Abstracto Español** (Museum of Spanish Abstract Art). Projecting over the town's eastern precipice, these houses originally formed a 15th-century palace; it later served as a town hall before falling into disrepair in the 19th century. In 1927, the cantilevered balconies that had once hung over the gorge were rebuilt, and finally, in 1966, the painter Fernando Zóbel decided to create inside the houses the world's first museum devoted exclusively to abstract art. The works he gathered are almost all by the remarkable generation of Spanish artists who grew up in the 1950s and were essentially forced to live abroad during the Franco regime: the major names include Carlos Saura, Eduardo Chillida, Muñoz, Millares, Antoni Tàpies, and Zóbel. ✉ *Canónigos s/n* ☎ *969/212983* 🌐 *www.march.es* 🎫 *€3* ⏲ *Tues.–Fri. 11–2 and 4–6, Sat. 11–2 and 4–8, Sun. 11–2:30.*

The **Puente de San Pablo,** an iron footbridge over the Huécar gorge, was built in 1903 for the convenience of the Dominican monks of San Pablo, who live on the other side. If you've no fear of heights, cross the narrow bridge to take in the vertiginous view of the river below and the equally thrilling panorama of the Casas Colgadas. A path from the bridge descends to the bottom of the gorge, landing you by the bridge that you crossed to enter the old town.

Where to Stay & Eat

$$–$$$ FodorśChoice ★ ✕ **El Figón de Pedro.** Owner Pedro Torres Pacheco is one of Spain's most famous restaurateurs and has done much to promote the excellence of Cuenca's cuisine. This pleasantly low-key spot in the lively heart of the modern town serves such local specialties as *ajo arriero* (a paste made with pounded salt cod and served with toasted bread), and *morteruelo,* a warm pâté made from the livers of game (including rabbit and partridge) and served with garlic bread. For dessert, try the *alaju,* a Moorish sweet made with honey, bread crumbs, almonds, and orange water. Wash down your meal with *resolí,* Cuenca's liqueur made from orange, coffee, and spices. ✉ *Cervantes 13* ☎ *969/226821* ▭ *AE, DC, MC, V* ⊗ *No dinner Sun.*

$$–$$$ ✕ **Mesón Casas Colgadas.** Run by the same management as El Figón de Pedro, this place offers much the same local fish and game but in a more pretentious manner. The white, ultramodern dining room is next to the Museum of Abstract Art in the spectacularly situated Casas Colgadas. ✉ *Canónigos s/n* ☎ *969/223509* *Reservations essential* ▭ *AE, DC, MC, V* ⊗ *No dinner Mon.*

$–$$ ✕ **Las Brasas.** Meats cooked over wood coals and hearty bean concoctions excel here. Both the cooking and the fire, visible from the bar, will make your meal comforting and festive. The owners use vegetables from their own garden to make a delicious *pucherete* (white bean soup). Castilian accents include wood floors and dark wood furniture. ✉ *Alfonso VIII 105* ☎ *969/213821* ▭ *DC, MC, V* ⊗ *Closed Wed. and July.*

$$$ **Parador de Cuenca.** In the gorge beneath the Casas Colgadas is this exquisitely restored 16th-century monastery. Rooms are furnished in a lighter and more luxurious style than the norm for Castilian houses of this vintage. ✉ *Paseo Hoz de Huécar s/n, 16001* ☎ *969/232320* *969/232534* 🌐 *www.parador.es* *63 rooms* *Restaurant, tennis court, pool, bar* ▭ *AE, DC, MC, V.*

$$–$$$ **Cueva del Fraile.** Seven kilometers (4½ mi) out of town on the Buenache road, this luxurious hotel occupies a 16th-century building ensconced in dramatic surroundings. The rooms have reproduction traditional furniture, stone floors, and in some cases wood ceilings. ✉ *Ctra. Cuenca–Buenache, 16001* ☎ *969/211571* *969/256047* 🌐 *www.hotelcuevadelfraile.com* *62 rooms* *Tennis court, pool, meeting room* ▭ *AE, DC, MC, V* ⊗ *Closed Jan.*

★ **$$** **Posada San José.** Tastefully installed in a 16th-century convent in Cuenca's old town, the *posada* is a hanging house clinging to the top of the Huécar gorge, which most rooms overlook. The furnishings are traditional, and the mood is friendly and intimate thanks to the owners, Antonio Cortinas and his American wife, Jennifer. Reserve well in advance. ✉ *Julián Romero 4, 16001* ☎ *969/211300* *969/230365* 🌐 *www.posadasanjose.com* *29 rooms, 22 with bath* *Cafeteria, bar; no a/c* ▭ *AE, DC, MC, V.*

¢–$ **Hostal Canovas.** Mere paces from Plaza España, in the heart of the new town, this tasteful abode is one of Cuenca's best bargains. The entrance is a bit shabby, and there's no lobby to speak of, but the inviting rooms more than compensate with hardwood floors, gold-trimmed burgundy fabrics, and decorative white moldings. The owners, brothers Edilio and Paulino, spent more than two years restoring the run-down 1878 building. ✉ *Fray Luis de León 38, 16001* ☎ *969/213973* 🌐 *www.servinet.net/canovas* *17 rooms* ▭ *AE, MC, V.*

Ciudad Encantada

㉑ *35 km (22 mi) north of Cuenca.*

The "Enchanted City" comprises a series of large and fantastic mushroomlike rock formations erupting in a landscape of pines. If you like to explore on foot, this natural phenomenon is well worth a visit; a footpath can guide you through striking outcrops with names like El Tobagón (The Toboggan) and Mar de Piedras (Sea of Stones).

Alarcón

22 *69 km (43 mi) south of Cuenca.*

This fortified village on the edge of the great plains of La Mancha stands on a high spur of land encircled almost entirely by a bend of the River Júcar. Alarcón's **castle** dates from the 8th century, and in the 14th century it came into the hands of the *infante* (child prince) Don Juan Manuel, who wrote a collection of classic moral tales. Today the castle is one of Spain's finest paradors. If you're not driving, a bus to Motilla will leave you a short taxi ride away (call 969/331797 for a cab). ✉ *Av. Amigos de los Castillos 3.*

Where to Stay & Eat

$$$ **Parador de Alarcón.** As a place to indulge in medieval fantasies, this 8th- and 12th-century gorge-top castle can't be beat. The structure is of Moorish origin, and the interior has a military motif and only 13 rooms, all of them quite small except the turret room. The rooms in the corner towers have as their windows the narrow slots once used to shoot arrows; others have window niches where the women of the household did their needlework. Dinner is served in an arched baronial hall with shields, armor, and a gigantic fireplace. ✉ *Av. Amigos de los Castillos 3, 16213* ☎ *969/330315* 🖷 *969/330303* 🌐 *www.parador.es* *13 rooms* *Restaurant* *AE, DC, MC, V.*

NORTHEAST OF MADRID

They're off the main tourist tracks, but the provinces of Guadalajara and Soria have a lot to offer and are easily accessible by train. The rail from Madrid to Zaragoza passes through every town in this section, allowing a manageable excursion of two to three days. If you have a car, you can extend this trip with a countryside detour.

Alcalá de Henares

23 *30 km (19 mi) east of Madrid.*

Alcalá's past fame was due largely to its university, founded in 1498 by Cardinal Cisneros. In 1836 the university was moved to Madrid, hastening Alcalá's decline. The civil war destroyed much of the town's artistic and architectural heritage. Nevertheless, enough survives of old Alcalá to suggest what it must have been like during its golden age. On one side of the university square is the **Convento de San Diego,** where Clarissan nuns make and sell *almendras garrapiñadas* (candy-coated almonds), a town specialty. The other side adjoins the large and arcaded **Plaza de Cervantes,** Alcalá's animated center. Off the plaza runs the arcaded Calle Mayor.

Alcalá's principal monument is the enormous **Universidad de Alcalá de Henares,** built between 1537 and 1553 by the great Rodrigo Gil de Hontañón. Although this is one of Spain's earliest and most important Italian Renaissance buildings, most Italian architects of the time would probably have shrieked in terror at its main facade. The use of the classical order is all wrong; the main block is out of line with the two that flank it; and the whole is crowned by a heavy and elaborate gallery. All of this is typically Spanish, as is the prominence given to the massive crest of Cardinal Cisneros and to the ironwork, both of which form integral parts of the powerful overall design. Inside are three patios, of which the most impressive is the first, comprising three superimposed arcades. A guided tour includes a delightfully decorated room where exams were once held, and the Chapel of San Ildefonso, with its richly sculpted Renaissance mausoleum of Cardinal Cisneros. ✉ *Pl. San Diego s/n* ☎ *91/885–4000* *Guided tour €3* ⏲ *Weekdays 9–9, weekends 11–2 and 4–7 (5–8 in winter).*

Miguel de Cervantes was born in a house on Calle Mayor in 1547; a charming replica, **Casa de Cervantes,** built in 1955, contains a small Cervantes museum. ✉ *C. Mayor 48* ☎ *91/889–9654* *Free* ⏲ *Tues.–Sun. 10:15–1:30 and 4–6:30.*

Where to Eat

$$$ ✕ **Hostería del Estudiante.** In one of the first buildings acquired by Spain's parador chain (but with no accommodation), this restaurant is set around a 15th-century cloister and has wood-beam ceilings, a large fireplace, and glass-and-tin lanterns. Complementing this simplicity is good Castilian food, which centers on *asados castellanos* (Castilian-style roast meats). The lamb is renowned, as is the *postre de* Alcalá (an almond puff pastry). ✉ *Los Colegios 3* ☎ *91/888–0330* *AE, DC, MC, V.*

Guadalajara

24 *17 km (10 mi) northeast of Alcalá, 55 km (34 mi) northeast of Madrid.*

In this quiet, affluent provincial capital, many Madrid commuters own the villas with terra-cotta roofs that sprawl down the slopes of the Guadalajara hills. Guadalajara was severely damaged in the civil war, but its **Palacio del Infantado** (Palace of the Prince's Territory) still stands and is one of the most important Spanish palaces of its period. Built between 1461 and 1492 by Juan Guas, the palace is a bizarre and potent mixture of Gothic, classical, and Mudéjar influences. The main facade is rich; the lower floors are studded with diamond shapes; and the whole is crowned by a complex Gothic gallery supported on a frieze pitted with intricate Moorish cellular work (the honeycomb motif). Inside is a fanciful and exciting courtyard. The ground floor holds a modest provincial art gallery. ✉ *Pl. de los Caídos 1* *Free* ⏲ *Tues.–Sat. 10:30–2 and 4:15–7, Sun. 10:30–2.*

en route

East of Guadalajara extends the Alcarria, a high plateau crossed by rivers forming verdant valleys. It was made famous in the 1950s by one of the great classics of Spanish travel literature, Camilo José Cela's *Journey to the Alcarria,* in which Cela evoked the backwardness and remoteness of an area barely an hour from Madrid. Even today you can feel far removed from the modern world here.

Pastrana

25 *42 km (26 mi) southeast of Guadalajara.*

High on a hill, Pastrana's narrow lanes merge into the landscape. This is a pretty village of Roman origin, once the capital of a small duchy. The tiny museum attached to Pastrana's **Colegiata** (collegiate church) displays a glorious series of Gothic tapestries; to see it, stop into the tourist office and they'll dispatch someone to unlock the door for you. ✉ *Tourist office: Pl. del Dean 5,* ☎ *949/370672* *€1.80* ⏲ *Tourist office June–Sept., Mon.–Thurs. 10–2; Oct.–May, Mon.–Thurs. and Sun. 10–2, Fri. 4–8, Sat. 10–2 and 4–8.*

Sigüenza

26 *86 km (53 mi) northeast of Guadalajara.*

Sigüenza has splendid architecture and one of the most beautifully preserved cathedrals in Castile. Begun around 1150 and not completed until the early 16th century, Sigüenza's remarkable **cathedral** is an anthology of Spanish architecture from the Romanesque period to the Renaissance. The sturdy western front is forbidding, but hides a wealth of ornamental and artistic masterpieces. Go directly to the sacristan (the sacristy is at the north end of the ambulatory) for a guided tour (which is obligatory if you're visiting the cathedral). The sacristy is an outstanding Renaissance structure, covered in a barrel vault designed by the great Alonso de Covarrubias; its coffering is studded with hundreds of sculpted heads, which stare at you disarmingly. The tour then takes you into the late-Gothic cloister, off which is a room lined with 17th-century Flemish tapestries. You will also have illuminated for you (in the north transept) the ornate, late-15th-century sepulchre of Dom Fadrique of Portugal, an early example of the classical plateresque. The cathedral's high point is the Chapel of the Doncel (to the right of the sanctuary), with the tomb of Don Martín Vázquez de Arca, commissioned by Isabella, to whom Don Martín served as *doncel* (page) before dying young at the gates of Granada in 1486. The reclining Don Martín is lifelike, an open book in his hands and a wistful melancholy in his eyes. ✉ *Pl. Mayor* 🎟 *€3* ⏲ *Tues.–Sun. 9:30–1:30 and 4:30–7. Guided visits Tues.–Sat. at 11, noon, 4:30, and 5:30; guided visits Sun. at noon and 5:30.*

In a refurbished early 19th-century house next to the cathedral's west facade, the **Museo Diocesano de Arte Sacro** (Diocesan Museum of Sacred Art) contains a prehistoric section and much religious art from the 12th to 18th century. ✉ *Pl. Mayor* 🎟 *€2* ⏲ *Tues.–Sun. 11–2 and 4–7.*

The south side of the cathedral overlooks the arcaded **Plaza Mayor,** a harmonious Renaissance square commissioned by Cardinal Mendoza. The small palaces and cobble alleys around here mark the virtually intact old quarter. Along Calle Mayor you'll find the palace that belonged to the doncel's family. An enchanting **castle,** overlooking wild, hilly countryside from above Sigüenza, is now a parador. Founded by the Romans but rebuilt at various later periods, most of the structure went up in the 14th century, when it became a residence for the queen of Castile, Doña Blanca de Borbón—banished here by her husband, Peter the Cruel. ✉ *C. Mayor.*

Where to Stay

★ $$ **Parador de Sigüenza.** This mighty 12th-century fortress has hosted royalty for centuries, from Ferdinand and Isabella right up to the present king, Juan Carlos. Some rooms have four-poster beds and balconies overlooking the wild landscape. The excellent dining room makes a leisurely lunch essential; your choices might include roast kid, pheasant, or cod with truffles and cheese. ✉ *Pl. del Castillo, 19250* ☎ *949/390100* 📠 *949/391364* 🌐 *www.parador.es* *81 rooms* *Restaurant, meeting room, parking (fee)* 💳 *AE, DC, MC, V.*

Medinaceli

27 *32 km (20 mi) northeast of Sigüenza.*

The preserved village of Medinaceli commands an exhilarating position on the top of a long, steep ridge. Dominating the skyline is a Roman triumphal arch from the 2nd or 3rd century AD, the only surviving triple archway of this period in Spain. (The arch's silhouette is now featured on road signs to national monuments throughout the country.) The surrounding village, once the seat of one of Spain's most powerful dukes, was virtually abandoned by its inhabitants by the end of the 19th century, and if you come here during the week you'll find yourself in a near ghost town. Many Madrileños have weekend houses here, and several Americans are also in part-time residence. The place is undeniably beautiful, with extensive views, picturesquely overgrown houses, and unpaved lanes leading directly into wild countryside. The former palace of the dukes of Medinaceli is currently undergoing restoration, and Roman excavations are being carried out in one of the squares.

Soria

28 *74 km (46 mi) north of Medinaceli, 234 km (145 mi) northeast of Madrid.*

This provincial capital prospered for centuries as a center of sheep farming, but it has been marred by modern development and is often beset by cold, biting winds. Still, its situation in the wooded Duero valley is splendid, and it has a number of fascinating Romanesque buildings.

Soria has strong connections with Antonio Machado. The Seville-born poet lived a bohemian life in Paris for many years, but he eventually returned to Spain and taught French in Soria from 1909 to 1911. A large bronze head of Machado is displayed outside the **school** where he taught, and his former classroom contains a tiny collection of memorabilia. It was in Soria that Machado fell in love with and married his landlady's 16-year-old daughter, Leonor. When his young bride died only two years later, he felt he could no longer stay in a town so full of her memories. He moved on to Baeza, in his native Andalusia, and then went to Segovia, where he spent his last years in Spain (he died early in the civil war, shortly after escaping to France). His most successful work, the *Campos de Castilla,* was greatly inspired by Soria and Leonor; both the town and the woman haunted him until his death.

The main roads to Soria converge onto the wide, modern promenade El Espolón, where you'll find the **Museo Numantino** (Museum of Numancia). Founded in 1919, the museum has local archaeological finds, and few other museums in Spain are laid out quite as well or as spaciously. The collections are rich in prehistoric and Iberian items, and one section on the top floor is dedicated to the important Iberian-Roman settlement at nearby Numancia. ⊠ *Paseo de El Espolón 8* ☎ *975/221428* 🎟 *€1.20, free weekends* ⏲ *July–Aug., Mon.–Sat. 9–2 and 5–9, Sun. 9–2; June and Sept., Tues.–Sat. 9–2 and 5-9, Sun. 9–2; Oct.–May, Tues.– Sat. 9–8:30, Sun. 9–2.*

The late-12th-century church of **Santo Domingo** (⊠ C. Aduana Vieja) has a richly carved, Romanesque west facade. The imposing, 16th-century **Palacio de los Condes de Gomara** (Palace of the Counts of Gomara; ⊠ C. Estudios) is now a law court. Dominating the hill just south of the River Dueron is Soria's **parador** (⊠ Parque del Castillo), which shares a park with the ruins of the town's castle. Machado loved the town and valley views from this hill. Calle de Santiago, which leads to the parador, passes the church and cemetery of El Espino, where Machado's wife, Leonor, is buried. Just before the River Dueron is the **cathedral** (⊠ Santa Apolonia), a late-Gothic hall church attached to a Romanesque cloister.

Across the River Duero from Soria is the deconsecrated church of **San Juan de Duero,** once the property of the Knights Hospitalers. Outside the church are the curious ruins of a Romanesque cloister, with a rare

Spanish example of interlaced arching. The church itself, now maintained by the Museo Numantino, is a small museum of Romanesque art and architecture. ✉ *Piso de las Ánimas s/n* ☎ *975/230218* 🎟 *€.60* ⏲ *June–Aug., daily 10–2 and 5–9; Sept.–Oct., Tues.–Sat. 10:30–2 and 4–7, Sun. 10–2; Nov.–Mar., Tues.–Sat. 10–2 and 3:30–6, Sun. 10–2; Apr.–May, Tues.–Sat. 10–2 and 4–7, Sun. 10–2.*

Take an evocative, half-hour walk along the Duero to the **Ermita de San Saturio**; you'll follow a path (accessible by car) lined by poplars. The hermitage was built in the 18th century above a cave where the Anchorite St. Saturio fasted and prayed. You can climb up to the building through the cave. 🎟 *Free* ⏲ *Tues.–Sat. 10:30–2 and 4:30–6:30, Sun. 10:30–2.*

Where to Stay & Eat

$$–$$$ ✕ **Mesón Castellano.** The most traditional restaurant in town, this cozy establishment has a large, open fire over which succulent *chuletón de ternera* (veal chops) are cooked. Another house specialty is *migas pastoriles* (soaked bread crumbs fried with peppers and bacon), a local dish. ✉ *Pl. Mayor 2* ☎ *975/213045* 💳 *AE, DC, MC, V.*

$$ 🏨 **Parador de Soria.** On a hilltop surrounded by trees and parkland, this modern parador has excellent views of the hilly Duero Valley. Antonio Machado came often to this site for inspiration. ✉ *Parque del Castillo, 42005* ☎ *975/240800* 📠 *975/240803* 🌐 *www.parador.es* *34 rooms* *Restaurant, bar* 💳 *AE, DC, MC, V.*

Numancia

29 *7 km (4½ mi) north of Soria.*

The bleak hilltop ruins of Numancia, an important Iberian settlement, are just a few minutes by car from Soria. Viciously besieged by the Romans in 135–134 BC, Numancia's inhabitants chose death rather than surrender. Most of the foundations that have been unearthed date from the time of the Roman occupation. 🎟 *€.60* ⏲ *Winter, Tues.–Sat. 10–2 and 4–6, Sun. 10–2; summer, Tues.–Sat. 10–2 and 5–9, Sun. 10–2.*

El Burgo de Osma

30 *56 km (35 mi) west of Soria.*

El Burgo de Osma is an attractive medieval and Renaissance town dominated by a Gothic cathedral and a Baroque bell tower. Many of its historic buildings have been tastefully restored.

Where to Stay & Eat

★ $–$$ ✕ **Virrey Palafox.** The white walls, wood-beam ceiling, and furnishings inside this modern building are traditional Castilian, and the long dining room has a nonsmoking section, a rarity in Spain. Virrey Palafox is a well-known family enterprise. Produce is fresh and seasonal, vegetables are homegrown, and there is excellent local game year-round. The house specialty is fish, in particular *merluza Virrey* (hake stuffed with eels and salmon). On the last weekend in January and every weekend in February and March, a pig is slaughtered and a marvelous banquet is held. Admission is €36; try to reserve in advance. ✉ *Universidad 7* ☎ *975/341311* 💳 *AE, DC, MC, V* ⏲ *Closed Mon. and late Dec.–mid-Jan. No dinner Sun.*

$$ 🏨 **Virrey II.** Under the same management as the Virrey Palafox, this pleasant hotel adjoins the 16th-century Convent of San Agustín. Constructed with traditional materials, the hotel's rooms, most of which overlook the plaza, have marble floors, stone walls, and tastefully simple decoration. ✉ *Pl. Mayor 2, 42300* ☎ *975/340890* 📠 *975/340855* 🌐 *www.*

logiccontrol.es/virreypalafox ⇒ *52 rooms* ♿ *Dining room, meeting room* ▭ *AE, DC, MC, V.*

SEGOVIA & ITS PROVINCE

The area north of Madrid is dotted with rich and varied history, from the Roman aqueduct in exquisite Segovia to the 16th-century village of Pedraza de la Sierra. Either town makes a pleasant place to spend the night. Other towns worth a visit include Sepúlveda and Castillo de Coca, for their medieval monuments, and La Granja, where the impressive gardens grow even more spectacular when the fountains are turned on, creating an effect to rival that of Versailles.

Segovia

31–41 Fodor'sChoice ★

87 km (54 mi) north of Madrid.

Breathtaking Segovia—on a ridge in the middle of a gorgeously stark, undulating plain—is defined by its Roman and medieval monuments, its excellent cuisine, its embroideries and textiles, and its sense of well-being. An important military town in Roman times, Segovia was later established by the Moors as a major textile center. Captured by the Christians in 1085, it was enriched by a royal residence, and in 1474 the half sister of Henry IV, Isabella the Catholic (married to Ferdinand of Aragón), was crowned queen of Castile here. By that time Segovia was a bustling city of about 60,000 (there are 53,000 today), but its importance soon diminished as a result of its taking the (losing) side of the Comuneros in the popular revolt against the emperor Charles V. Though the construction in the 18th century of a royal palace in nearby La Granja revived the town's fortunes somewhat, it never recovered its former vitality. Early in the 20th century, Segovia's sleepy charm came to be appreciated by artists and writers, among them painter Ignacio Zuloaga and poet Antonio Machado. Today the streets swarm with tourists from Madrid, and you may want to think twice about trying to experience Segovia in summer.

If you approach Segovia on N603, the first building you see is the cathedral, which seems to rise directly from the fields. Between you and Segovia lies, in fact, a steep and narrow valley, which shields the old town from view. Only when you descend into the valley do you begin to see the old town's spectacular position, rising on top of a narrow rock ledge shaped like a ship. As soon as you reach the modern outskirts, turn left onto the Paseo E. González and follow the road marked **Ruta Panorámica**—you'll soon descend on the narrow and winding Cuesta de los Hoyos, which takes you to the bottom of the wooded valley that dips to the south of the old town. Above, you can see the Romanesque church of San Martín to the right; the cathedral in the middle; and on the far left, where the rock ledge tapers, the turrets, spires, and battlements of Segovia's castle, known as the Alcázar.

a good walk

Driving and parking are problematic on the narrow streets of old Segovia, so it's best to leave the car behind. Beginning at the church of **San Millán** 31 ⚑, go up Avenida de Fernández Ladreda until you come to the Plaza del Azoguejo, once the town center and marketplace. Directly in front of you are the arches of the grand **Acueducto Romano** 32. Turn away from the aqueduct, exit the plaza from the northwest corner, and head up the pedestrian shopping street Calle Cervantes. Continue up the same street, now called Calle de Juan Bravo, and veer off to the left onto Herrería for a look at the late-Gothic **Palacio de Aspiroz/ Palacio de los Condes de Alpuente** 33, covered with Segovian *esgrafiado*

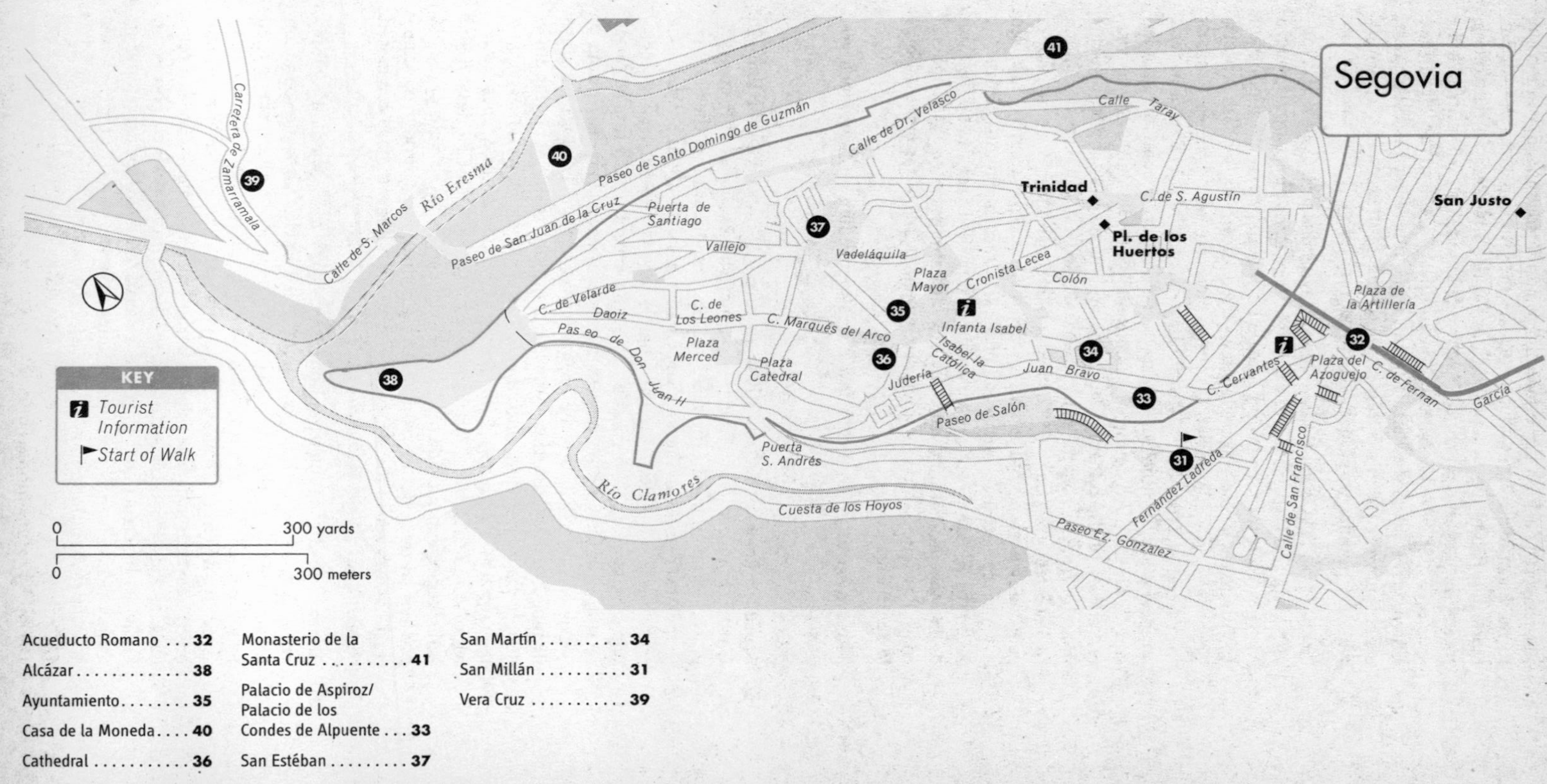
Segovia
KEY
Tourist Information
Start of Walk
0
300 yards
0
300 meters
Carretera de Zamarramala
Calle de S. Marcos
Río Eresma
Paseo de San Juan de la Cruz
Paseo de Santo Domingo de Guzmán
Calle de Dr. Velasco
Calle Taray
Trinidad
Pl. de los Huertos
C. de S. Agustín
San Justo
Puerta de Santiago
Vallejo
Vadeláquila
Plaza Mayor
Cronista Lecea
Colón
C. de Velarde
Daoiz
C. de Los Leones
C. Marqués del Arco
Infanta Isabel
Pas eo de Don Juan II
Plaza Merced
Plaza Catedral
Judería
Isabel la Católica
Juan Bravo
Paseo de Salón
C. Cervantes
Plaza del Azoguejo
C. de Fernan García
Plaza de la Artillería
Calle de San Francisco
Fernández Ladreda
Paseo Ez. Gonzalez
Puerta S. Andrés
Río Clamores
Cuesta de los Hoyos
Acueducto Romano . . . 32
Alcázar 38
Ayuntamiento. 35
Casa de la Moneda. . . . 40
Cathedral 36
Monasterio de la Santa Cruz 41
Palacio de Aspiroz/ Palacio de los Condes de Alpuente . . . 33
San Estéban 37
San Martín 34
San Millán 31
Vera Cruz 39

plasterwork. Back on Calle Juan Bravo and farther ahead, you'll come to the Plaza Martín, on which rises another Romanesque church, **San Martín** 34. Just to the west of the church is the Biblioteca y Archivo Historical (Library and Historical Archive), housed in a 17th-century stone structure that served as Segovia's jail until 1933. Off to the left of Juan Bravo, across from the Plaza Martín, is the refreshing Paseo de Salón, a small promenade at the foot of the town's southern walls. This walk was very popular with Spain's 19th-century queen, Isabel II.

At the Plaza del Corpus, where Juan Bravo splits into Calle de La Judería Vieja and Isabel la Católica, a right turn leads directly to the Plaza Mayor. A left turn leads up Calle de La Judería Vieja into the former Jewish quarter, where Segovia's Jews lived as early as the 13th century. Turn right on Calle de San Frutos, which runs along the east side of the cathedral; from here a short alley leads to the lively Plaza Mayor, an ideal place for lunch or an early evening drink. Facing the arcaded square are the 17th-century **ayuntamiento** 35 (town hall) and the eastern corner of the **cathedral** 36, its flying buttresses a favorite vantage point for storks. From the plaza, take Calle de Valdeláguila to the church of **San Estéban** 37. Calle de Los Leones, lined with tourist shops, slopes gently down from San Estéban toward the western extremity of the old town's ridge. At the western end of the square is the famous **Alcázar** 38. From the Alcázar, you can see the church of **Vera Cruz** 39 and the **Casa de la Moneda** (former Mint) 40. A walk along the city's peripheral road, Paseo de Santo Domingo de Guzmán, leads to the **Monasterio de la Santa Cruz** 41.

TIMING This walk can be done in a few hours, depending on how much you linger.

What to See

32 **Acueducto Romano.** Segovia's Roman aqueduct ranks with the Pont du Gard in France as one of the greatest surviving examples of Roman engineering. Spanning the dip that stretches from the walls of the old town to the lower slopes of the Sierra de Guadarrama, it's about 2,952 ft long and rises in two tiers—above what is now the Plaza del Azoguejo, whose name means "highest point"—to a height of 115 ft. The raised section of stonework in the center originally carried an inscription, of which only the holes for the bronze letters remain. The massive granite blocks are held together by neither mortar nor clamps, but the aqueduct has been standing since the end of the first century AD. The only damage it has suffered is the demolition of 35 of its arches by the Moors, and these were later replaced on the orders of Ferdinand and Isabella. Steps at the side of the aqueduct lead up to the walls of the old town. Because pollution from the freeway that passes through the aqueduct has weakened the structure, the road underneath has been closed to traffic. ✉ *Pl. del Azoguejo.*

38 **Alcázar.** Possibly dating from Roman times, this castle was considerably expanded in the 14th century, remodeled in the 15th, altered again toward the end of the 16th, and completely redone after being gutted by a fire in 1862, when it was used as an artillery school. The exterior, especially when seen from the Ruta Panorámica, is certainly imposing, but the castle is little more than a pseudo-medieval sham. The last remnant of the original structure is the keep through which you enter. Crowned by crenellated towers that seem to have been carved out of icing, the keep can be climbed for superb views; the rest of the interior is a bit disappointing. ✉ *Pl. de la Reina Victoria Eugenia* ☎ *921/460759* 🌐 *www.alcazardesegovia.com* 💳 *€3.10* ⏲ *May–Sept., daily 10–7; Oct.–Apr., Mon.–Thurs. 10–6, Fri.–Sun. 10–7.*

35 **Ayuntamiento.** The 17th-century town hall stands on the active **Plaza Mayor.** It's closed to the public, but it's a great place to sit and watch the world go by. ✉ *Pl. Mayor.*

40 **Casa de la Moneda** (Mint). All Spanish coinage was struck here from 1455 to 1730. The mint is closed for reconstruction, but the exterior is worth a look. ✉ *C. de la Moneda s/n, just south of River Eresma.*

36 **Cathedral.** Begun in 1525 and completed 65 years later, the cathedral was intended to replace an earlier one near the Alcázar, destroyed during the revolt of the Comuneros against Charles V. It's one of the country's last great examples of the Gothic style. The designs were drawn up by the leading late-Gothicist Juan Gil de Hontañón but executed by his son Rodrigo, in whose work can be seen a transition from the Gothic to the Renaissance style. The interior, illuminated by 16th-century Flemish windows, is light and uncluttered, the one distracting detail being the wooden, neoclassical choir. You enter through the north transept, which is marked MUSEO; turn right, and the first chapel on your right has a lamentation group in wood by the Baroque sculptor Gregorio Fernández. Across from the entrance, on the southern transept, is a door opening into the late-Gothic cloister—this and the elaborate door leading into it were transported from the old cathedral and are the work of architect Juan Guas. Under the pavement immediately inside the cloisters are the tombs of Juan and Rodrigo Gil de Hontañón; that these two lie in a space designed by Guas is appropriate, for the three men together dominated the last phase of the Gothic style in Spain. Off the cloister, a small museum of religious art, installed partly in the first-floor chapter house, has a white-and-gold 17th-century ceiling, a late example of Mudéjar *artesonado* work. ✉ *Marqués del Arco 1* ☎ *921/462205* 🎫 *Cathedral, cloister, and museum €2* ⏲ *Apr.–Sept., Mon.–Sat. 9–6:30, Sun. 9–2:30; Oct.–Mar., Mon–Sat. 9–5:30, Sun. 9–2:30.*

41 **Monasterio de la Santa Cruz.** Built in the 13th century, this church was established by St. Dominick of Guzmán, founder of the Dominican order, and rebuilt in the 15th century by Ferdinand and Isabella. Now it's a private university, La Universidad Sec, and during the academic year, you can see the attractive interior, Gothic with plateresque and Renaissance touches. ✉ *Cardenal Zúñiga s/n* ☎ *921/471997.*

33 **Palacio de Aspiroz/Palacio de los Condes de Alpuente** (Palace of the Counts of Alpuente). This late-Gothic palace is covered with a type of plasterwork known as *esgrafiado,* incised with regular patterns; the style was most likely introduced by the Moors and is characteristic of Segovian architecture. The building is now used for city administrative offices and is no longer open to the public. ✉ *Pl. del Platero Oquendo.*

37 **San Estéban.** The third of Segovia's major Romanesque monuments is this porticoed church. Though the interior has a Baroque facing, the exterior has kept some splendid capitals, as well as an exceptionally tall and attractive tower. Due east of the church square is the **Capilla de San Juan de Dios,** next to which is the former pension where the poet Antonio Machado spent his last years in Spain. The family who looked after Machado still owns the building and will show you the poet's room on request, with its paraffin stove, iron bed, and round table. The church is open for mass only. ✉ *Pl. de San Estéban* ⏲ *Mass daily 8–10 AM and 7–9 PM.*

34 **San Martín.** This Romanesque church stands in an attractive little plaza of the same name. ✉ *Pl. San Martín* ☎ *921/443402* ⏲ *Open for mass only* ⏲ *Mass daily 8–10 AM and 7–9 PM.*

31 **San Millán.** A perfect example of the Segovian Romanesque, this 12th-century church is perhaps the finest in town apart from the cathedral. The exterior is notable for its arcaded porch, where church meetings were once held. The virtually untouched Romanesque interior is dominated by massive columns, whose capitals carry such carved scenes as the Flight into Egypt and the Adoration of the Magi. The vaulting on the crossing shows the Moorish influence on Spanish medieval architecture. ✉ *Av. Fernández Ladreda 26, 5-min walk outside town walls* ⏲ *Open for mass only, daily 8–10* AM *and 7–9* PM.

39 **Vera Cruz.** Made of the local warm-orange stone, this isolated Romanesque church was built in 1208 for the Knights Templar. Like other buildings associated with this order, it has 12 sides, inspired by the Church of the Holy Sepulchre in Jerusalem. Your trip pays off in full when you climb the bell tower and see all of Segovia profiled against the Sierra de Guadarrama, capped with snow in winter. ✉ *Ctra. de Zamarramala s/n, on northern outskirts of town, off Cuestra de los Hoyos* ☎ *921/431475* *€1.50* ⏲ *May–Sept., Tues.–Sun. 10:30–1:30 and 3:30–7; Oct. and Dec.–Apr., Tues.–Sun. 10:30–1:30 and 3:30–6:30.*

Where to Stay & Eat

$$–$$$ ✕ **Casa Duque.** Founded in 1895 and still in the family, this restaurant has an intimate interior, with homey wood beams and a plethora of fascinating *objets*. It's similar to Mesón de Cándido, but Duque has fewer tourists. Roasts are the specialty, but the *judiones de La Granja Duque*—enormous white haricot beans from nearby La Granja, served with sausages—are also excellent. ✉ *Cervantes 12* ☎ *921/462487* *Reservations essential* *AE, DC, MC, V.*

★ $$–$$$ ✕ **Mesón de Cándido.** It's way more than just a restaurant. Cándido began life as an inn around the 18th century and was declared a national monument in 1941. Tucked beside the aqueduct, it has a medley of small, irregular dining rooms decorated with memorabilia. Amid the dark-wood beams and Castilian knickknacks hang photos of the celebrities who have dined here, from Hemingway to Princess Grace of Monaco. Cándido's son now runs the place. First-time visitors are virtually obliged to eat the cochinillo (piglet) or *cordero* (baby lamb), roasted in a wood-fire oven. The trout is also renowned. ✉ *Pl. de Azoguejo 5* ☎ *921/425911* *Reservations essential* *AE, DC, MC, V.*

★ $$–$$$ ✕ **Mesón de José María.** With a lively bar, this Mesón (traditional tavern-restaurant) is hospitable, and its passionately dedicated owner is devoted to maintaining traditional Castilian specialties while concocting innovations of his own. The menu changes constantly according to what's in season. The large, old-style, brightly lit dining room is often packed, and the waiters are uncommonly friendly. Although it's a bit touristy, it's equally popular with locals. ✉ *Cronista Lecea 11* ☎ *921/466017* *AE, DC, MC, V.*

$$$ ✕ **Parador de Segovia.** Architecturally one of the most interesting of Spain's modern paradors (if you like naked concrete), this low building is set on a hill overlooking the city; it's a very long walk to the city center. The rooms are cold in appearance, but from the large windows the panorama of Segovia and its aqueduct are spectacular. The restaurant serves Segovian and international dishes, such as *lomo de merluza al aroma de estragón* (hake fillet with tarragon and shrimp). ✉ *Ctra. de Valladolid (2 km [1 mi] from Segovia), 40003* ☎ *921/443737* *921/437362* 🌐 *www.parador.es* *113 rooms* *Restaurant, 2 pools (1 indoor), sauna, meeting room* *AE, DC, MC, V.*

$$ **Infanta Isabel.** You'll get great views of the cathedral from this hotel, perched on the Plaza Mayor—with an entrance on a charming, if congested, pedestrian shopping street. Rooms are light and feminine, with

wrought-iron beds and little round tables; those on the plaza have floor-length shutters and small verandas. ✉ *Pl. Mayor 12, 40001* ☎ *921/461300* 🖷 *921/462217* 🌐 *www.hotelinfantaisabel.com* *37 rooms* *Restaurant* *AE, DC, MC, V.*

$ **Las Sirenas.** If you stay here not only will you be just steps from the Plaza Mayor, above Segovia's nicest shops, but you'll have the benefit of a prime downtown location, a pillared marble lobby, and, from the best rooms, splendid balcony views of the church of San Millán. Sensuous and classical accents include statues of mermaids at the foot of a curving staircase and Greek vases on antique bedside tables. Drawbacks are the tiny showers and slightly faded furnishings, but this is a hard value to beat. ✉ *C. Juan Bravo 30, 40001* ☎ *921/462663* 🖷 *921/462657* *39 rooms* *Bar* *AE, DC, MC, V.*

Shopping

After Toledo, the province of Segovia is Castile's most important for crafts. Glass and crystal are specialties of La Granja, while ironwork, lace, and embroidery are famous in Segovia itself. You can buy good lace from the Gypsies in Segovia's Plaza del Alcázar, but be prepared for some strenuous bargaining, and never offer more than half the opening price. For genuine crafts, go to **San Martín 4** (✉ Pl. San Martín 4), an excellent antiques shop. **Calle Daiza,** leading to the Alcázar, overflows with touristy ceramic, textile, and gift shops.

Palacio Real de la Granja

42 *11 km (7 mi) southeast of Segovia on N601.*

The major attraction in Segovia's immediate vicinity, the Royal Palace of La Granja stands in the town of La Granja de San Ildefonso, on the northern slopes of the Sierra de Guadarrama. (*Granja* means "farm.") Its site was once occupied by a hunting lodge and a shrine to San Ildefonso, administered by Hieronymite monks from the Segovian monastery of El Parral. Commissioned by the Bourbon king Philip V in 1719, the palace has sometimes been described as the first great building of the Spanish Bourbon dynasty. The Italian architects who finished it in 1739—Juvarra and Sachetti—were responsible for the imposing garden facade, a late-Baroque masterpiece anchored throughout its length by a giant order of columns. The interior has been badly gutted by fire; the highlight is the collection of 15th- to 18th-century tapestries in a special museum. It's the **gardens** that are most notable—here, terraces, ornamental ponds, lakes, classical statuary, woods, and Baroque fountains dot the mountainside. On Wednesday, Saturday, and Sunday evenings in the summer (6–7 PM May–Sept.), the fountains are turned on, one by one, creating an exciting spectacle. The starting time has been known to change on a whim; call ahead. ☎ *921/470020* *Palace €4.81, gardens free* ⏲ *Palace Oct.–Mar., Tues.–Sat. 10–1:30 and 3–5, Sun. 10–2; Apr.-Sept., Tues.–Sun. 10–6. Garden daily 10–sunset.*

Pedraza de la Sierra

43 *30 km (19 mi) northeast of Segovia.*

Though it's been commercialized and overprettified in recent years, Pedraza is still a striking 16th-century village. Crowning a rocky outcrop and completely encircled by its walls, it is perfectly preserved, with wonderful views of the Guadarrama mountains. In the center of the village is the attractive, irregularly shaped Plaza Mayor, lined with rustic wooden porticoes and dominated by a Romanesque bell tower. Pedraza's romantic factor spikes on the first two Saturdays of July for the

Conciertos de las Velas (Candle Concerts) when the artificial lights in Pedraza are switched off and the entire town is bathed in the flickering glow of over 35,000 candles, placed along the streets and in the Plaza Mayor. In the evening (at 10 PM) classical music concerts take place in the Plaza Mayor and the castle. Concert tickets must be bought at least a month in advance. Contact the **Fundación Villa de Pedraza** (✉ *C. Real 15 40172 Pedraza* ☎ *921/509960*) or the Segovia tourist office for tickets to the Candle Concerts in July.

At the top of Pedraza de la Sierra is the Renaissance **Castillo Pedraza de la Sierra,** a 14th-century stone castle that the painter Ignacio Zuloaga bought as a private home in the early 20th century. Two sons of the French king Francis I were held hostage here after the Battle of Pavia, together with their majordomo, the father of the Renaissance poet Pierre de Ronsard. Note that visiting times are valid except when Zuloaga's heirs are in residence. ☎ *921/509825* €4 ⏲ *Wed.–Sun. 11–2 and 4–6.*

Where to Stay & Eat

$$–$$$ ✕ **El Yantar de Pedraza.** With wooden tables and beamed ceilings, this traditional restaurant is famous for roast meats. Right on the main square, it's the place to come for that most celebrated Pedrazan specialty—*corderito lechal en horno de leña* (baby lamb roasted in a wood oven). ✉ *Pl. Mayor* ☎ *921/509842* ▭ *AE, DC, MC, V* ⏲ *Closed Mon. No dinner, except first two Sat. in July.*

$$–$$$ **El Hotel de La Villa.** Heavy wooden beams everywhere, a roaring fire in the salon, and an elegant dining room make this Pedraza's chicest place to spend the night. A medieval Moorish oven for roasting lamb is in a corner of the restaurant. The bedrooms are an exquisite combination of heavy Castilian rustic and light postmodern design. ✉ *C. Calzada 5, 40172* ☎ *921/508651* 🖷 *921/508653* 🌐 *www.elhoteldelavilla.com* *35 rooms, 3 suites* *Restaurant, minibars, cable TV, bar, meeting rooms* ▭ *AE, DC, MC, V.*

$$ **La Posada de Don Mariano.** Originally a farmer's home, this picturesque old building has intimate guest rooms filled with rustic furniture and antiques. The restaurant, Enebro, serves cochinillo and a good selection of red meat. ✉ *C. Mayor 14, 40172* ☎🖷 *921/509886* *18 rooms* *Restaurant, bar; no a/c* ▭ *AE, DC, MC, V.*

Sepúlveda

44 *24 km (15 mi) north of Pedraza de la Sierra, 60 km (37 mi) northeast of Segovia.*

A walled village with a commanding position, Sepúlveda has a charming main square, but its main attraction is the 11th-century **El Salvador,** the oldest Romanesque church in Segovia's province. It has a crude but amusing example of the porches found in later Segovian buildings: the carvings on its capitals, probably by a Moorish convert, are fantastical and have little to do with Christianity. ✉ *Cerro de Somosierra.*

Castillo de Coca

45 *52 km (32 mi) northwest of Segovia.*

Perhaps the most famous medieval sight near Segovia—worth a detour between Segovia and Ávila or Valladolid—is the Castillo de Coca. Built in the 15th century for Archbishop Alonso de Fonseca I, the castle is a turreted structure of plaster and red brick, surrounded by a deep moat. It looks like a stage set for a fairy tale, and indeed, it was intended not as a defense but as a place for the notoriously pleasure-loving Archbishop Fonseca to hold riotous parties. The interior, now occupied by a forestry school, has been modernized, with only fragments of the original decoration preserved. Note that opening hours are erratic; call ahead if possible. ☎ *921/586622* ✉ *€2.25* ⊙ *May–Aug., weekdays 10:30–1 and 4:30–7, weekends 11–1 and 4–6; Sept.–Apr., weekdays 10:30–1 and 4:30–6, weekends 11–1 and 4–6. Closed 1st Tues. of month.*

ÁVILA & THE SIERRA DE GREDOS

The mountains of the Sierra de Gredos are a fitting backdrop and counterpoint for Ávila's spectacular medieval walls. In Ávila you can trace the history of the mystic and musical St. Teresa, who lived much of her life here, and in the Gredos mountains you can hike and ski. Other sights include the attractive villages near Arenas de San Pedro and the ancient stone bulls of San Martín de Valdeiglesias.

Ávila

46 *107 km (66 mi) northwest of Madrid.*

In the middle of a windy plateau littered with giant boulders, Ávila can look wild and sinister. Modern development on its outskirts partially obscures Ávila's surrounding **walls,** which, restored in parts, look as they did in the Middle Ages. Begun in 1090, shortly after the town was reclaimed from the Moors, the walls were completed in only nine years—accomplished by the daily employment of an estimated 1,900 men. With nine gates and 88 cylindrical towers bunched together, they are unique to Spain in form, unlike the Moorish defense architecture that the Christians adapted elsewhere. They're most striking when seen from outside the town; for the best view on foot, cross the Adaja River, turn right on the Carretera de Salamanca, and walk uphill about 250 yards to a monument of four pilasters surrounding a cross. When you ultimately leave Ávila, look back on your way out.

The walls reflect Ávila's importance during the Middle Ages. Populated by Alfonso VI mainly with Christians from Asturias, the town came to be known as Ávila of the Knights because of its many nobles. Decline set in at the beginning of the 15th century, with the gradual departure of the nobility to the court of Charles V in Toledo. Ávila's fame later on was due largely to St. Teresa. Born here in 1515 to a noble family of Jewish origin, Teresa spent much of her life in Ávila, leaving a legacy of various convents and the ubiquitous *yemas* (candied egg yolks), originally distributed free to the poor but now sold for high prices to tourists. Ávila today is well preserved, but the mood is slightly sad, austere, and desolate. The quietude is dispelled only for the week beginning October 8, when Ávila celebrates the Fiestas de la Santa Teresa with lighted decorations, parades, and singing in the streets as well as religious observances.

The battlement apse of the **cathedral** forms the most impressive part of the walls. The apse was built mainly in the late 12th century, but the construction of the rest of the cathedral continued until the 18th century. Entering the town gate to the right of the apse, you'll reach the sculpted north portal (originally the west portal, until it was moved in 1455 by the architect Juan Guas) by turning left and walking a few steps. The present west portal, flanked by 18th-century towers, is notable for the crude carvings of hairy male figures on each side; known as "wild men," these figures appear in many Castilian palaces of this period, but their significance is disputed.

The Transitional Gothic interior, with its granite nave, is heavy and severe. The Lisbon earthquake of 1755 deprived the building of its Flemish stained glass, so the main note of color appears in the beautiful mottled stone in the apse, tinted yellow and red. Elaborate, plateresque choir stalls built in 1547 complement the powerful high altar of circa 1504 by painters Juan de Borgoña and Pedro Berruguete. On the wall of the ambulatory, look for the early 16th-century marble sepulchre of Bishop Alonso de Madrigal, a remarkably lifelike representation of the bishop seated at his writing table. Known as "El Tostado" (the Toasted One) for his swarthy complexion, the bishop was a tiny man of enormous intellect, the author of 54 books. When on one occasion Pope Eugenius IV ordered him to stand—mistakenly thinking him to still be on his knees—the bishop indicated the space between his eyebrows and hairline, retorting, "A man's stature is to be measured from here to here!" ✉ *Pl. de la Catedral s/n* ☎ *920/211641* 🎫 *€2.50* ⏲ *June–Aug., weekdays 10–7, Sat. 10–6:30, Sun. noon–6; Sept.–May, weekdays 10–5, Sat. 10–6, Sun. noon–5.*

The 15th-century **Mansión de los Deanes** (Deans' Mansion) houses the cheerful **Museo de Ávila,** a provincial museum full of local archaeology and folklore. It's a few minutes' walk to the east of the cathedral apse. ✉ *Pl. de Nalvillos 3* ☎ *920/211003* 🎫 *€1.20, free weekends* ⏲ *Tues.–Sat. 10–2 and 4:30–7:30, Sun. 10:30–2.*

In the **Convento de San José** (or de Las Madres), four blocks east of the cathedral on Calle Duque de Alba, is the **Museo Teresiano,** with musical instruments used by St. Teresa and her nuns at Christmas. Teresa herself specialized in percussion. ✉ *Las Madres 4* ☎ *920/222127* 🎫 *€1* ⏲ *Summer, daily 10–1:30 and 4–7; fall–spring, daily 10–1:30 and 3–6.*

North of Ávila's cathedral, on Plaza de San Vincente, is the much-venerated Romanesque **Basílica de San Vicente** (Basilica of St. Vincent), founded on the supposed site where St. Vincent was martyred in 303 with his sisters Sts. Sabina and Cristeta. The west front, shielded by a narthex, has damaged but expressive Romanesque carvings depicting the death of Lazarus and the parable of the rich man's table. The sarcophagus of St. Vincent forms the centerpiece of the basilica's Romanesque interior; the extraordinary, Asian-looking canopy above the sarcophagus is a 15th-century addition paid for by the Knights of Ávila. ✉ *Pl. de San Vicente s/n* ☎ *920/255230* 🎫 *€1.20* ⏲ *Daily 10–1:30 and 4–6:30.*

The elegant chapel of **Mosen Rubi** (circa 1516) is illuminated by Renaissance stained glass by Nicolás de Holanda. Try to persuade the nuns in the adjoining convent to let you inside. ✉ *C. de Lopez Nuñez.*

At the west end of the town walls, next to the river in a farmyard nearly hidden by poplars, is the small, Romanesque **Ermita de San Segundo** (Hermitage of St. Secundus). Founded on the site where the remains of St. Secundus (a follower of St. Peter) were reputedly discovered, the hermitage has a realistic marble monument to the saint, carved by Juan de Juni. You may have to ask for the key in the adjoining house. ✉ *Av. de Madrid s/n, toward Salamanca* 🎫 *60* ⏲ *Summer, daily 10–1 and 3:30–6; fall–spring, daily 11–1 and 4–5.*

Inside the south wall on Calle Dama, the **Convento de Santa Teresa** was founded in the 17th century on the site of the saint's birthplace. Teresa's famous written account of an ecstatic vision in which an angel pierced her heart would influence many Baroque artists, most famously the Italian sculptor Giovanni Bernini. The convent has a small museum with relics—including one of Teresa's fingers; you can also see the small and rather gloomy garden where she played as a child. ✉ *Pl. de la Santa s/n* ☎ *920/211030* 🎫 *Museum €2* ⏲ *Daily 10–1:30 and 3:30–5:30* ⏲ *Closed Mon. Oct.–Easter.*

The **Museo del Convento de la Encarnación** is where St. Teresa first took orders and was then based for more than 30 years. Its museum has an interesting drawing of the crucifixion by her disciple St. John of the Cross, as well as a reconstruction of the cell she used when she was a prioress here. The convent is outside the walls in the northern part of town. ✉ *Paseo de la Encarnación s/n* ☎ *920/211212* 💰 *€1.20* ⏲ *May–Sept., weekdays 9:30–1 and 4–7, Sat. 10–1:30 and 4–6; Oct.–Apr., weekdays 9:30–1:30 and 3:30–6, Sat. 10–1:30 and 4–6.*

2

The most interesting architectural monument on Ávila's outskirts is the **Monasterio de Santo Tomás.** A good 10-minute walk from the walls among housing projects, it's not where you would expect to find one of the most important religious institutions in Castile. The monastery was founded by Ferdinand and Isabella with the financial assistance of the notorious Inquisitor-General Tomás de Torquemada, who is buried in the sacristy. Further funds were provided by the confiscated property of converted Jews who ran afoul of the Inquisition. Three decorated cloisters lead to the church; inside, a masterly high altar (circa 1506) by Pedro Berruguete overlooks a serene marble tomb by the Italian artist Domenico Fancelli. One of the earliest examples of the Italian Renaissance style in Spain, this influential work was built for Prince Juan, the only son of Ferdinand and Isabella, who died at 19 while a student at the University of Salamanca. After Juan's burial here, his heartbroken parents found themselves unable to return; in happier times, they had often attended mass here, seated in the upper choir behind a balustrade exquisitely carved with their coats of arms; you can reach the choir from the upper part of the Kings' Cloister. The **Museum of Eastern Art** has works collected from Dominican missions in Vietnam. The museum is currently closed for renovations and will reopen in late 2003 or early 2004. ✉ *Pl. de Granada 1* ☎ *920/220400* 💰 *Cloister €1, museum €1.80* ⏲ *Cloister daily 10–1 and 4–8, museum Tues.–Sun. 11–1 and 4–6.*

Where to Stay & Eat

★ $$–$$$ ✕ **El Molino de la Losa.** Nearly straddling the serene Adaja River, with one of the best views of the town walls, El Molino is in a 15th-century mill, the working mechanism of which has been well preserved and provides much distraction for those seated in the animated bar. Lamb is roasted in a medieval wood oven, and trout comes from the river; try the beans from nearby El Barco (*judías de El Barco*). The garden has a small playground for children. ✉ *Bajada de la Losa 12* ☎ *920/211101 or 920/211102* 💳 *AE, MC, V* ⏲ *Closed Mon.*

$$ ✕ **Las Cancelas.** Locals flock to this little tavern for the €12 menú del día, saving it from a tourist aesthetic. Push your way through the loud tapas bar to the dining room, where wooden tables are heaped with combination platters of roast chicken, french fries, sunny-side-up eggs, and chunks of home-baked bread. The local T-bone steak, *chuletón de Ávila,* is enormous. The succulent cochinillo, much ordered by the regulars, bursts with flavor. ✉ *Cruz Vieja 6* ☎ *920/212249* 💳 *AE, DC, MC, V* ⏲ *Closed last 2 wks in Jan.*

$–$$ ✕ **Mesón del Rastro.** In a wing of the medieval Palacio Abrantes, this restaurant has an attractive Castilian interior with exposed stone walls and beams, low lighting, and dark-wood furniture. Try the lamb and El Barco beans; also worthwhile is the *caldereta de cabrito* (goat stew). The place suffers somewhat from its popularity with tour buses, and service is sometimes slow and impersonal. ✉ *Pl. Rastro 1* ☎ *920/211218* 💳 *AE, DC, MC, V.*

★ $$$ 🏨 **Hotel Palacio de los Velada.** Ávila's top hotel occupies a beautifully restored 16th-century palace in the heart of the city, right beside the cathedral. (It's ideal if you like to relax between sightseeing jaunts.) Upscale locals gather in the bar and the lovely Mediterranean courtyard, and the restaurant is acclaimed. Rooms are modern and comfortable. ✉ *Pl. de la Catedral 10, 05001* ☎ *920/255100* 📠 *920/254900* 🌐 *www.veladahoteles.com* *145 rooms* *Restaurant, bar, pub, meeting room* *AE, DC, MC, V.*

$$$ **Parador de Ávila.** A largely rebuilt medieval castle attached to the town walls, Ávila's parador has the advantage of a garden, from which you can sometimes climb up onto the ramparts. The interior is unusually warm, done mostly in tawny tones, and the public rooms are convivial. Guest rooms have terra-cotta tile floors and leather chairs, and their bathrooms are spacious, gleamingly modern, and fashionably designed. ✉ *Marqués de Canales de Chozas 2, 05001* ☎ *920/211340* 📠 *920/226166* 🌐 *www.parador.es* *61 rooms* *Restaurant, café, bar, meeting room* *AE, DC, MC, V.*

$ **Hostal Alcántara.** This small hostel has modest, clean rooms and is just a two-minute walk from the cathedral. ✉ *Estéban Domingo 11, 05001* ☎ *920/225003* *9 rooms* *AE, DC, MC, V.*

Sierra de Gredos

79 km (49 mi) southwest of Ávila.

The C502 from Ávila follows a road dating from Roman times, when it was used for the transport of oil and flour from Ávila in exchange for
47 potatoes and wood. In winter, the **Sierra de Gredos** (4,435 ft) gives the region a majestic, snowy backdrop. You can enjoy extensive views from the peak; soon after descending you'll see a perfectly preserved stretch of the Roman road, zigzagging down into the valley and crossing the modern road every now and then. Today it's used by hikers, as well as by shepherds transporting their flocks to lower pastures in early December.

Where to Stay

$$ **Parador de Gredos.** Built in 1926 on a site chosen by Alfonso XIII, this was the first parador in Spain. Though modern (it was enlarged in 1941 and again in 1975), the stone architecture has a sturdy look and blends well with the magnificent surroundings. Rooms are standard parador, with heavy, dark furniture and light walls, and more than half have excellent views of the Sierra. It's an ideal base for a hiking or climbing jaunt. ✉ *Ctra. Barraco–Béjar, Km 43, 05635 Navarredonda de Gredos* ☎ *920/348048* 📠 *920/348205* 🌐 *www.parador.es* *76 rooms* *Restaurant, tennis court, bar* *AE, DC, MC, V.*

Sports & the Outdoors

HIKING & MOUNTAINEERING The Sierra de Gredos is Castile's best area for hiking and mountaineering. You can base yourself at the parador or at one of six mountain huts with limited accommodations and facilities. For information contact the **Federación Española de Montañismo** (Spanish Mountaineering Federation; ☎ 93/426–4267) in Barcelona.

HORSEBACK RIDING Near the Gredos Parador, **Turactiv Gredos** (✉ Barajas ☎ 608/920892) offers guides and equipment for horseback riding, canoeing, fishing and archery. You can go riding at **Hípica de Bohoyo** (✉ Bohoyo ☎ 920/341118).

SKIING Skiing is popular in both the Sierra de Gredos and the Guadarrama resorts of La Pinilla (Segovia), Navacerrada (Madrid), Valdesqui (Madrid), and Valcotos (Madrid). You can call **ATUDEM** (☎ 91/350–2020) for conditions, but it's better to call the slope you're considering. Call the **Federación Madrileña de Deportes de Invierno** (Madrid Federation of Winter Sports; ☎ 91/547–0101) for general skiing information in the Sierra de Gredos region.

Arenas de San Pedro

48 *143 km (89 mi) southwest of Madrid.*

This medieval town is surrounded by pretty villages, such as Mombeltrán, Guisando, and Candeleda, where wooden balconies are decorated with flowers. A colorful sight in Candeleda are wicker baskets filled with pimientos for sale. Guisando, incidentally, has nothing to do with the famous stone bulls of that name, 60 km (37 mi) to the east.

2

San Martín de Valdeiglesias

49 *73 km (45 mi) west of Madrid.*

Just 6 km (4 mi) before San Martín, on the right side of the road, is a stone inscription in front of a hedge; this marks the site where, in 1468, Isabella the Catholic was acknowledged by the assembled Castilian nobility as rightful successor to Henry IV. The **Toros de Guisando,** or stone bulls, date from the 6th century BC, and are thought to have been used as land markers on the frontier of a Celto-Iberian tribe. Just three of many such bulls once scattered around the Castilian countryside (they take their name from the nearby Cerro Guisando, or Guisando Hill), they're now a symbol of the Spanish Tourist Board. To see these taurine effigies, head back east from Arenas on the C501; it's a pleasant drive through countryside bordered to the north by the Gredos range. ✉ *Near Cerro Guisando, 6 km/4 mi before San Martín, on right side of road—on the other side of the hedge with the stone inscription.*

SALAMANCA & CIUDAD RODRIGO

Salamanca's radiant sandstone buildings, immense Plaza Mayor, and hilltop riverside perch make it one of the most attractive and beloved cities in Spain. Today, as it did centuries ago, the university predominates, providing an intellectual flavor, a stimulating arts scene, and nightlife to match. About an hour from here are the preserved medieval walls of Ciudad Rodrigo, an interesting town with fewer tourists.

Salamanca

50–62 *205 km (127 mi) northwest of Madrid.*

Fodor'sChoice ★

If you approach from Madrid or Ávila, you'll first see Salamanca rising on the northern banks of the wide and winding River Tormes. In the foreground is its sturdy, 15-arch Roman bridge; above this soars the combined bulk of the Old and New cathedrals. Piercing the skyline to the right is the Renaissance monastery and church of San Estéban. Behind San Estéban and the cathedrals, and largely out of sight from the river, extends a stunning series of palaces, convents, and university buildings that culminates in the Plaza Mayor. Despite considerable damage over the centuries, Salamanca remains one of Spain's greatest cities architecturally, a showpiece of the Spanish Renaissance. It is the warmth of golden sandstone, which seems to glow throughout the city, that you will remember above all things.

Already an important settlement in Iberian times, Salamanca was captured by Hannibal in 217 BC and later flourished as a major Roman station on the road between Mérida and Astorga. Converted to Christianity by at least the end of the 6th century, it later passed back and forth between Christians and Moors and began to experience prolonged stability only after the Reconquest of Toledo in 1085. The town's later importance was due largely to its university, which grew out of a college founded around 1220 by Alfonso IV of León.

Salamanca thrived in the 15th and early 16th centuries, and the number of students at its university rose to almost 10,000. Its greatest royal benefactor was Isabella, who generously financed both the magnificent New Cathedral and the rebuilding of the university. A dual portrait of Isabella and Ferdinand was incorporated into the facade of the main university building to commemorate her patronage. Nearly all of Salamanca's other outstanding Renaissance buildings bear the five-star crest of the all-powerful and ostentatious Fonseca family. The most famous Fonseca, Alonso de Fonseca I, was the archbishop of Santiago and then of Seville; he was also a notorious womanizer and one of the patrons of the Spanish Renaissance.

Both Salamanca and its university began to decline in the early 17th century, corrupted by ultraclericalism and devastated by a flood in 1626. Some of the town's former glory was recovered in the 18th century, with the construction of the Plaza Mayor by the native Churrigueras, who were among the most influential architects of the Spanish Baroque. The town suffered in the Peninsular War of the early 19th century and was marred by modern development initiated by Franco after the civil war; but the university has regained its status as one of the most prestigious in Europe. Come on a weekend to witness the social scene.

Salamanca was elected as a European City of Culture for 2002 by the European Union, and the ambitious €60 million project spawned several properties, listed below.

A major theatre complex, capacity 1,400, is the **Centro de Artes Escénicas** (✉ Av. de la Aldehuela s/n, Prosperidad). The **Centro de Arte de Salamanca** (✉ Av. de la Aldehuela, Prosperidad) is a 4,600-square-ft modern art gallery. An indoor stadium, **Edificio Multiusos,** (✉ Av. de los Cipreses, Garrido) holds 6,000 spectators for sporting events or concerts. A museum and research center, **Museo de Historia de la Automoción** (✉ Pl. del Mercado Viejo s/n ☎ 923/260293 ⊙ Tues.–Fri. 10–2 and 4–8, weekends 10–8), focuses on motorized vehicles and displays the library and vintage car collection of Demetrio Gómez Planche.

During 2002, work started on an archaeological museum based on the ruins of the 10th- to 13th-century San Vicente Convent, in the ancient center of the city, **Parque Arqueológico de San Vicente** (✉ Cerro de San Vicente, City Center). The museum is slated to open at the end of 2003. The **Sala de Exposiciones de Santa Domingo** (✉ Pl. de Concilio de Trento, by Convento de San Estéban) is a 350-square-ft municipal art gallery with a garden for sculpture. The 732-seat theater, **Teatro Liceo** (✉ Pl. del Liceo, City Center), 40 yards from the Plaza Mayor, was recently renovated.

a good walk

In terms of both chronology and parking space, the well-preserved **Puente Romano** 50 ▶ makes a good starting point. This is a quiet part of town with a strong rural character; in the summer, Gypsies camp here, picnicking and playing music while they exercise their horses. After crossing the bridge, bear to the right and look for the modernist building Casa Lis, which serves as the **Museo Art Nouveau y Art Deco** 51. Afterward, make your way up to the old and new **cathedrals** 52, built side by side. Across the Plaza Anaya is the neoclassical Colegio de Anaya. If you face the New Cathedral from the plaza, the back of the main building of the **universidad** 53 is ahead and to your right, facing the cathedral's west facade. Walk between the two down Calle Cardenal Plá y Deniel, turn right on Calle de Calderón de la Barca, then right again on Calle de Los Libreros, and you'll come into the enchanting quadrangle known as the

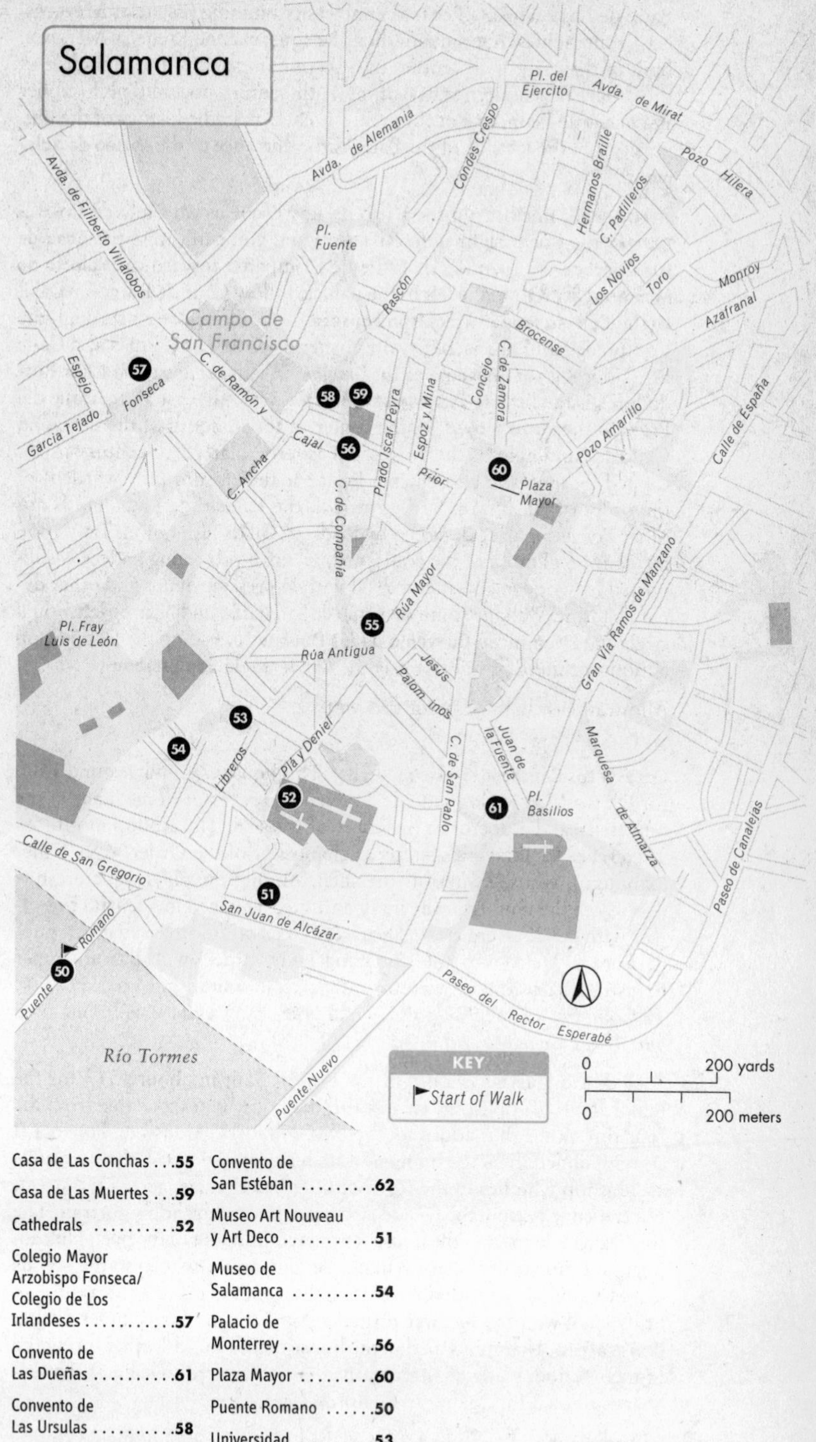
Salamanca
Pl. del Ejercito
Avda. de Mirat
Avda. de Alemania
Condes Crespo
Hermanos Braille
C. Padilleros
Pozo Hilera
Avda. de Filiberto Villalobos
Pl. Fuente
Los Novios
Toro
Monroy
Azafranal
Rascón
Brocense
Campo de San Francisco
Espejo
Fonseca
Garcia Tejado
C. de Ramón y Cajal
C. de Zamora
Concejo
Espoz y Mina
Prado Iscar Peyra
Pozo Amarillo
Calle de España
C. Ancha
Prior
C. de Compañía
Plaza Mayor
Rúa Mayor
Gran Vía Ramos de Manzano
Pl. Fray Luis de León
Rúa Antigua
Jesús
Palom inos
Juan de la Fuente
Marquesa de Almarza
Libreros
Pla y Deniel
C. de San Pablo
Pl. Basilios
Paseo de Canalejas
Calle de San Gregorio
San Juan de Alcázar
Puente Romano
Paseo del Rector Esperabé
Río Tormes
Puente Nuevo
KEY
Start of Walk
0
200 yards
0
200 meters
50
51
52
53
54
55
56
57
58
59
60
61

Patio de Las Escuelas. The main university building (Escuelas Mayores) is to your right, while surrounding the square is the Escuelas Menores, built in the early 16th century as a secondary school. In the middle of the square is a modern statue of the 16th-century poet and philosopher Fray Luis de León, one of the greatest teachers in the history of the university. On the far side of the Patio is the entrance to the **Museo de Salamanca** 54.

If you walk north from the Patio de Las Escuelas on Calle de Los Libreros, then bear right onto Rua Antigua, you can't miss the **Casa de Las Conchas** 55. Turn left at Calle de Compañía toward the **Palacio de Monterrey** 56. Off to the left of the palace, follow Calle de Ramón y Cajal to the **Colegio Mayor Arzobispo Fonseca** 57. Walk back east through the Campo de San Francisco. On the corner of Calle Las Ursulas and Calle Bordadores is the **Convento de Las Ursulas** 58. Farther ahead on Calle Bordadores is the bizarre **Casa de Las Muertes** 59. Walk east along Calle del Prior to the **Plaza Mayor** 60, the center of town. South of the plaza, on Calle de San Pablo, is the Torre del Clavero, a late-15th-century tower topped by fantastic battlements built for the *clavero* (key warden) of the order of Alcántara. Farther down, the Palacio de La Salina is another Fonseca palace designed by Rodrigo Gil de Hontañón. Try to pop inside for a glimpse of the courtyard, where a projecting gallery is supported by wooden consoles carved with expressive nudes and other dynamic forms. Walking south on Calle de San Pablo and bearing left, you'll circle the Dominican **Convento de las Dueñas** 61. Facing the Dueñas, up a monumental flight of steps, is the **Convento de San Estéban** 62.

TIMING Allow at least half a day for this walk.

What to See

55 **Casa de Las Conchas** (House of Shells). This house was built around 1500 for Dr. Rodrigo Maldonado de Talavera, a professor of medicine at the university and a doctor at the court of Isabella. The scallop motif was a reference to Talavera's status as chancellor of the Order of St. James (Santiago), whose symbol is the shell. Among the playful plateresque details are the lions over the main entrance, engaged in a fearful tug-of-war with the Talavera crest. The interior has been converted into a public library. Duck into the charming courtyard, which has an upper balustrade carved with virtuoso intricacy in imitation of basketwork. ✉ *Compañía 2* ☎ *923/269317* 💰 *Free* ⏲ *Weekdays 9–9, Sat. 9–2 and 4–7, Sun. 10–2 and 4–7.*

59 **Casa de Las Muertes** (House of the Dead). Built in about 1513 for the majordomo of Alonso de Fonseca II, the house takes its name from the four tiny skulls that adorn its top two windows. Alonso de Fonseca II commissioned them to commemorate his deceased uncle, the licentious archbishop who lies in the Convento de Las Ursulas, across the street. For the same reason, the facade also bears the archbishop's portrait. The small square in front of the house was a favorite haunt of the poet, philosopher, and university rector Miguel de Unamuno, whose statue stands here. Unamuno supported the Nationalists under Franco at the outbreak of the civil war, but he later turned against them. Placed under virtual house arrest, Unamuno died in the house next door in 1938. During the Franco period, students often daubed his statue red to suggest that his heart still bled for Spain. ✉ *C. Bordadores.*

52 **Cathedrals.** For a complete tour of the old and new buildings' exterior (a 10-minute walk), circle the complex counterclockwise. Nearest the river stands the Catedral Vieja (Old Cathedral), built in the late 12th century, one of the most interesting examples of the Spanish Romanesque.

Because the dome of the crossing tower has strange, plumelike ribbing, it is known as the Torre del Gallo (Rooster's Tower). The much larger **Catedral Nueva** (New Cathedral) dates mainly from the 16th century, though some parts, including the dome over the crossing and the bell tower attached to the west facade, had to be rebuilt after the Lisbon earthquake of 1755. Work began in 1513 under the direction of the distinguished late-Gothic architect Juan Gil de Hontañón, and as at Segovia's cathedral, Juan's son Rodrigo took over the work after his father's death in 1526. The New Cathedral's north facade (which contains the main entrance) is ornamental enough, but the west facade is dazzling in its sculptural complexity. Try to come here in late afternoon, when the sun shines on it.

The interior of the New Cathedral is as light and harmonious as that of Segovia's cathedral, but larger. Here you are treated to a triumphant Baroque effusion designed by the Churrigueras. The wooden choir seems almost alive with anxiously active cherubim and saints. From a door in the south aisle, steps descend into the Old Cathedral, where boldly carved capitals supporting the vaulting are accented by foliage, strange animals, and touches of pure fantasy. Then comes the dome, which seems to owe much to Byzantine architecture; it's a remarkably light structure raised on two tiers of arcaded openings. Not the least of the Old Cathedral's attractions are its furnishings, including sepulchres from the 12th and 13th centuries and a magnificent, curved high altar comprising 53 colorful and delicate scenes by the mid-15th-century artist Nicolás Florentino. In the apse above, Florentino painted an astonishingly fresh Last Judgment fresco.

From the south transept of the Old Cathedral, a door leads into the cloister, begun in 1177. From about 1230 until the construction of the main university building in the early 15th century, the chapels around the cloister served as classrooms for the university students. In the Chapel of St. Barbara, on the eastern side, theology students answered the grueling questions meted out by their doctoral examiners. The chair in which they sat is still there, in front of a recumbent effigy of Bishop Juan Lucero, on whose head the students would place their feet for inspiration. Also attached to the cloister is a small cathedral museum with a 15th-century triptych of St. Catherine by Salamanca's greatest native artist, Fernando Gallego. ✉ *Plá y Deniel s/n* ☎ *923/217476* 🎟 *New Cathedral free, Old Cathedral €3* ⏲ *New Cathedral Mon.–Sat. 9–6, Sun. 9:30–2; Old Cathedral Mon.–Sat. 10–5:30, Sun. 10–2.*

57 **Colegio Mayor Arzobispo Fonseca/Colegio de Los Irlandeses** (Irish College). This small college was founded by Alonso de Fonseca II in 1521 to train young Irish priests. It is now a residence hall for guest lecturers at the university. This part of town was the most severely damaged during the Peninsular War of the early 19th century and still has a slightly derelict character. The interior, however, is a treat. To the right immediately inside the college is a late-Gothic chapel, and beyond it lies one of the most classical and genuinely Italianate of Salamanca's many courtyards. ✉ *Fonseca 4* ☎ *923/294570* 🎟 *€1.80* ⏲ *Daily 10–2 and 4–7.*

61 **Convento de Las Dueñas** (Convent of the Dames). Founded in 1419, this convent hides a 16th-century cloister that is the most fantastically decorated in Salamanca, if not in the whole of Spain. The capitals of its two superimposed Salamantine arcades are crowded with a baffling profusion of grotesques that can absorb you for hours. As you're wandering through, take a moment to look down. The interlocking diamond pattern on the ground floor of the cloister is decorated with the knobby vertebrae of goats and sheep. It's an eerie yet perfect accompaniment

to all the grinning disfigured heads sprouting from the capitals looming above you. There's another reason to come here: the nuns make and sell excellent sweets. ✉ *Pl. Concilio de Trento* ☎ *923/215442* 💶 *€1.50* ⏲ *Apr.–Oct., Mon–Sat. 10:30–1 and 4:30–7, Sun. 11–1 and 4:30–7; Nov.–Mar., Mon.–Sat. 10:30–1 and 4:30–5:30, Sun. 11–1 and 4:30–5:30.*

58 **Convento de Las Ursulas** (Convent of the Ursulines). Archbishop Alonso de Fonseca I lies here, in a splendid marble tomb created by Diego de Siloe during the first half of the 16th century. ✉ *Las Ursulas 2* ☎ *923/219877* 💶 *€1* ⏲ *Daily 11–1 and 4:30–6. Closed last Sun. of month.*

need a break?

Unwind at **La Regenta** (Espoz y Mina 19–20), a warm, plush, Baroque-style café-bar that shines like a beacon of (flickering candle) light in the thronged heart of town. Heavy green-and-gold curtains block most of the street noise, making the Plaza Mayor, a half a block off, a distant memory. Try a *café al caramelo* (coffee with caramel). In the evening you can order creative and potent cocktails with names like "Kiss Me Boy" and "Sangre de Toro" (Bull's Blood).

62 **Convento de San Estéban** (Convent of St. Stephen). The convent's monks, among the most enlightened teachers at the university, were the first to take Columbus's ideas seriously and helped him gain his introduction to Isabella (hence his statue in the nearby Plaza de Colón, back toward Calle de San Pablo). The complex was designed by one of San Estéban's monks, Juan de Alava. The door to the right of the west facade leads you into a gloomy cloister with Gothic arcading, interrupted by tall, spindly columns adorned with classical motifs. From the cloister, you enter the church at its eastern end. The interior is unified and uncluttered but also dark and severe. The one note of color is provided by the ornate and gilded high altar of 1692, a Baroque masterpiece by José Churriguera. The most exciting part of San Estéban, though, is the massive west facade, a thrilling plateresque work in which sculpted figures and ornamentation are piled up to a height of more than 98 ft. ✉ *Pl. Concilio de Trento* ☎ *923/215000* 💶 *€1.20* ⏲ *Daily 9–1 and 4–8 (4–6 in winter).*

51 **Museo Art Nouveau y Art Deco.** The museum is in the Casa Lis, a modernist building from the end of the 19th century. On display are 19th-century paintings and glass, as well as French and German china dolls, Viennese bronze statues, furniture, jewelry, enamels, and jars. ✉ *Gibraltar 14* ☎ *923/121425* 🌐 *www.museocasalis.org* 💶 *€2.10* ⏲ *May–Oct., Tues.–Fri. 11–2 and 5–9, weekends 11–9; Nov.–Mar., Tues.–Fri. 11–2 and 4–7, weekends 11–8.*

54 **Museo de Salamanca** (also Museo de Bellas Artes). Consisting mainly of minor 17th- and 18th-century paintings, this museum, also known as the Museo de Bellas Artes (Museum of Fine Arts), is interesting for its 15th-century building, which belonged to Isabella's physician, Alvárez Abarca. ✉ *Patio de Escuelas Menores 2* ☎ *923/212235* 💶 *€1.20, free weekends* ⏲ *Tues.–Sat. 10–2 and 4–7, Sun. 10–2.*

56 **Palacio de Monterrey.** Built after 1538 by Rodrigo Gil de Hontañón, the Monterrey Palace was meant for an illegitimate son of Alonso de Fonseca I. As in Rodrigo's other local palaces, the building is flanked by towers and has an open arcaded gallery running the whole length of the upper level. Such galleries—which in Italy you would expect to see on the ground floor—are common in Spanish Renaissance palaces and were intended to provide privacy for the women of the house and cool the floor below during the summer. The palace is privately owned and not open to visitors, but you can stroll around it. ✉ *Compañía s/n.*

60 **Plaza Mayor.** Built in the 1730s by Alberto and Nicolás Churriguera, Salamanca's Plaza Mayor is one of the largest squares in Spain, and many find it the most beautiful. Its northern side is dominated by the lavishly elegant, pinkish **ayuntamiento** (city hall). The square and its arcades are popular gathering spots for most of Salamancan society, and the many surrounding cafés make this the perfect spot for a coffee break. At night, the plaza swarms with students meeting "under the clock" on the plaza's north side. *Tunas* (strolling musicians in traditional garb) often meander among the cafés and crowds, playing for smiles and applause rather than tips.

50 **Puente Romano** (Roman Bridge). Next to the bridge is an Iberian stone bull, and opposite the bull is a statue commemorating Lazarillo de Tormes, the young hero of the eponymous (but anonymous) 16th-century work that is one of the masterpieces of Spanish literature.

53 **Universidad.** Parts of the university's walls, like those of the cathedral and other structures in Salamanca, are covered with large, ocher lettering recording the names of famous university graduates. The earliest names are said to have been written in the blood of the bulls killed to celebrate the successful completion of a doctorate.

The **Escuelas Mayores** (Major Schools) dates to 1415, but it was not until more than 100 years later that an unknown architect provided the building with its gloriously elaborate frontispiece. Immediately above the main door is the famous double portrait of Isabella and Ferdinand, surrounded by ornamentation that plays on the yoke-and-arrow heraldic motifs of the two monarchs. The double-eagle crest of Charles V, flanked by portraits of the emperor and empress in classical guise, dominates the middle layer of the frontispiece. Perhaps the most famous rite of passage for new students is to find the carved frog that squats atop a skull at the very top left of the frontispiece. Legend has it that if you spot the frog on your first try, you'll pass all your exams and have a successful university career; for this reason, it's affectionately called *la rana de la suerte* (the lucky frog). It can be hard to pin down the elusive amphibian; if you're not having any luck, pop inside to the ticket booth, where they've kindly posted a detail of the frontispiece for precisely this purpose. You'll then see the beloved frog all over town, on sweatshirts, magnets, pins, jewelry, and postcards.

The interior of the Escuelas Mayores, drastically restored in parts, comes as a slight disappointment after the splendor of the facade. But the *aula* (lecture hall) of Fray Luis de León, where Cervantes, Calderón de la Barca, and numerous other luminaries of Spain's golden age once sat, is of particular interest. Cervantes carved his name on one of the wooden pews up front. After five years' imprisonment for having translated the *Song of Songs* into Spanish, Fray Luis returned to this hall and began his lecture, "As I was saying yesterday . . ."

Your ticket to the Escuelas Mayores also admits you to the nearby **Escuelas Menores** (Minor Schools), built in the early 16th century as a secondary school preparing candidates for the university proper. Passing through a gate crowned with the double-eagle crest of Charles V, you'll come to a green, on the other side of which is a modern building with a fascinating ceiling fresco of the zodiac, originally in the library of the Escuelas Mayores. A fragment of a much larger whole, this painting is generally attributed to Fernando Gallego. ☎ *923/294550* 🎫 *€4, free Mon. 9:30–1:30* ⊙ *Weekdays 9:30–1:30 and 4–7:30, Sat. 9:30–1:30 and 4–7, Sun. 10–2 and 4–7.*

Where to Stay & Eat

$$–$$$ ✕ **Chez Victor.** Try this chic restaurant for a break from traditional Castilian food. Chef-owner Victoriano Salvador learned his trade in France and adapts French cuisine to Spanish taste, with whimsical touches all his own. Sample the traditional *carrillada de buey braseada con jengibre* (cheek of beef braised in ginger) or the more Continental *hojaldre de verduras y foie con salsa de trufas* (puff pastry filled with leeks and julienned carrots in a truffle sauce). Desserts are outstanding, especially the chocolate ones. ✉ *Espoz y Mina 26* ☎ *923/213123* ▭ *AE, DC, MC, V* ⊙ *Closed Mon. and Aug. No dinner Sun.*

$$–$$$ ✕ **El Candil Viejo.** Beloved by locals for its superb, no-nonsense Castilian fare, this tavern is an old favorite with professors in pinstripes and students on dates. Aside from a simple salad, the menu consists of meat, meat, and more meat, including pork, lamb, kid, sausage, and fantastic *marucha* steak. The homemade sausages are especially good. For tapas, try the *farinato* sausage, made from pork, onion, eggs and bread crumbs, or the *picadillo,* similar but spicier with pepper, garlic, and tomato. ✉ *Ventura Ruiz Aguilera 14–16* ☎ *923/217239* ▭ *AE, DC, MC, V* ⊙ *Closed 3 wks in Jan.*

$$ ✕ **La Hoja.** Tucked into a dark passageway off Plaza Mayor, the restaurant has a glass facade, high ceilings, butter-yellow walls, and minimalist art—all signs of a very different kind of Castilian dining experience. Young chef-owner Alberto López Oliva prepares an innovative menu of traditional fare with a twist. *Manitas, manzana, y langostinas al aroma de Módena* are pig trotters with prawns and apple slices, all in Módena vinegar; *perdiz al chocolate con berza* is partridge cooked in chocolate and served with cabbage. ✉ *Pasaje Coliseum 19* ☎ *923/264028* ▭ *AE, MC, V* ⊙ *Closed Tues. and second half of Feb. and Aug.*

$–$$ ✕ **Río de la Plata.** Off Calle de San Pablo, this tiny basement restaurant has been in business since 1958 and retains an old-fashioned character. The gilded yet quiet interior is a pleasant change of scenery, and the fireplace and local crowd provide warmth. The food is simple but carefully prepared, with good-quality fish and meat. ✉ *Pl. Peso 1* ☎ *923/219005* ▭ *AE, MC, V* ⊙ *Closed Mon. and July.*

¢–$ ✕ **Bambú.** At peak times, it's standing room only at this jovial basement tapas bar that caters to students on a budget. The floor may be littered with napkins and you might have to shout to be heard, but it's the generous tapas and big sloppy *bocadillos* (submarine-style sandwiches) that draw the crowds. Although paella is usually the exclusive domain of pricy paella restaurants, here (during lunch) you can enjoy a *ración* of paella, ladled out from a large *caldero* (shallow pan.) Another bonus: even if you just order a drink, you'll be served a liberal helping of the "tapa of the day." ✉ *C. Prior 4* ☎ *923/26092* ▭ *MC, V.*

¢–$ ✕ **El Grillo Azul.** A rare sight in Spain, this vegetarian restaurant—the only one in Salamanca—has an adventurous menu of heaping dishes that easily trump any of the limp salads and vegetarian "options" you'll find at other restaurants. The kitchen takes chances, blending a variety of tastes in every mouthful. Dig into the*arroz basmati con calabacín, zanahorias, y piñones* (basmati rice topped with zucchini, carrots, and pine nuts) or an ample omelette stuffed with almonds and mushrooms. ✉ *C. El Grillo 1* ☎ *923/219233* ▭ *AE, DC, MC, V* ⊙ *Closed Mon. No dinner Sun.*

$$$ 🏨 **AC Palacio de San Estéban.** Near the cathedrals, this five-star hotel is in a former part of the 17th-century Convento de San Estéban. The rooms are modern, finished in cream and white with dark wood trim. ✉ *Arroyo de San Antonio de Salamanca s/n, 37008* ☎ *923/262296* 📠 *917/244263* 🌐 *www.ac-hoteles.com* ⇆ *51 rooms* 👍 *Restaurant, coffee shop, gym, bar, laundry service, business services, meeting room, parking (fee), no-smoking rooms* ▭ *AE, DC, MC, V.*

$$$ **Gran Hotel.** The grande dame of Salamanca's hotels offers stylish Baroque lounges and refurbished yet old-fashioned oversize rooms, just steps from the Plaza Mayor. *Pl. Poeta Iglesias 3, 37001 923/213500 923/213500 www.helcom.es/granhotel 136 rooms Restaurant, bar AE, DC, MC, V.*

$$$ **Palacio del Castellanos.** In an immaculately restored 15th-century palace, this hotel has an exquisite interior patio and an equally beautiful restaurant, as well as a lovely terrace overlooking San Estéban. Rooms are done in peach and white, with wooden bed frames, and have modern, white-tile bathrooms. *San Pablo 58, 37008 923/261818 923/261819 www.nh-hoteles.com 62 rooms Restaurant AE, DC, MC, V.*

★ **$$$** **Rector.** From the stately entrance to the high-ceiling guest rooms, this lovely hotel is a true European experience. The sitting areas, hallways, and breakfast room are all spotless, spacious, warm, and quiet, and the owners and staff will devote themselves to your every whim. Take advantage of their willingness to tell you all about Salamanca. You'll feel like you're staying with family. *Paseo Rector Esperabé 10 923/218482 923/214008 www.hotelrector.com 14 rooms Bar AE, DC, MC, V.*

$$ **San Polo.** Built on the foundations of the old Romanesque church by the same name—the ruins of which you can see through windows in the foyer and hall—the hotel is near the city center and has a friendly staff. The smallish rooms have light ocher tones, with white curtains. *Arroyo de Santo Domingo 1–3, 37008 923/211177 www.hotelsanpolo.com 36 rooms, 1 suite Restaurant, bar, parking (fee) AE, DC, MC, V.*

$ **Hostal Plaza Mayor.** You can't beat the location of this great little *hostal,* just steps from the Plaza Mayor. Rooms are small but modern; the only drawback is the noise level on weekends, when student *tunas* sing ballads at the plaza's crowded cafés until the wee hours. Reservations are advisable, as rooms fill up fast. *Pl. del Corrillo 20, 37008 923/262020 923/217548 19 rooms Restaurant MC, V.*

¢ **Hostal Peña de Francia.**Overlooking the old town's main drag, this family-run place near the *Puente Romano* (Roman Bridge) offers cheap sleeps in basic, freshly scrubbed rooms with bright bedspreads and functional wooden furniture. There's a downside: most rooms receive little outside light, but you'll hardly notice if you just come here to crash at the end of a long day (and night.) C. *San Pablo 96, 37001 923/216687 6 rooms, 2 without bath No credit cards No air-conditioning, no room phones.*

Nightlife

Particularly in summer, Salamanca sees perhaps the greatest influx of foreign students of any city in Spain—by day they study Spanish, and by night they fill Salamanca's bars and clubs to capacity. **Mesón Cervantes** (entrance on the southeast corner of the Plaza Mayor), an upstairs tapas bar, draws crowds to its balcony for a drink and an unparalleled view of the action. Bask in the romantic glow emanating from stained glass lamps in the Baroque-style **Posada de las Almas** (Plaza San Boal s/n), the preferred cocktail-and-conversation nightspot for stylish students. Wrought-iron chandeliers hang from the high wooden-beam ceilings, harp-strumming angels top elegant pillars, and one entire wall of shelves showcases colorful doll's houses. After 11, a well-dressed twenty- and thirtysomething crowd comes to dance at **Camelot** (Rua Bordadores 3), an ancient stone-wall warehouse in one corner of the 16th-century Convento de Las Ursulas. For good wine, heaping portions of tapas, and live music, try the **Café Principal** (Rua Mayor 9). An unusual disco is in a boat on the river, **Barco Ciudad de Salamanca Gogó** (⊠ Paseo Fluvial, beside the Enrique Estéban bridge). After-hours types end (if not spend) the night at **Café Moderno** (⊠ Gran Vía 75), tucking into *chocolate con churros* at daybreak. Try your luck at the **Casino Salamanca**, housed in a glitzily refurbished turn-of-the-century factory on the Tormes River, near the *Puente Romano* (Roman bridge.) You'll need your passport to enter. ⊠ *C. La Pesca 5* ☎ *923/281628* ⊕ *www.grupocomar.com* ⊙ *Sun.–Thurs. 4 PM–4 AM; Fri.–Sat. 4 PM–5 AM.*

Shopping

On Sunday mornings, the **Rastro** flea market is held in Avenida de Aldehuela. Special buses leave from Plaza de España. For unusual gifts, including eclectic pottery, ironwork, paintings, and hand-stitched linens, browse through **Indiana** (⊠ Meléndez 2–4 ☎ 923/264243). The husband-and-wife team in tiny **Artesanía Duende** (⊠ C. San Pablo 33 ☎ 923/213622) have been creating and selling unique wooden crafts for decades. Their music boxes, thimbles, photo frames, and other items are beautifully carved or stenciled with local themes, from the *bailes charros*, Salamanca's regional dance, to the floral designs embroidered on the hems of provincial dresses. For fine leatherwork, try **Salón Campero** (⊠ Pl. Corrillo 5).

Sports & the Outdoors

GOLF There are two golf courses near Salamanca. **Campo de Golf de Salamanca** (⊠ Monte de Zarapicos, Zarapicos ☎ 923/329102 ⎙ 923/329105 ⊕ www.golfysol.com) is 18 km (12 mi) from Salamanca on the C-517 and is more of a country club, also offering swimming pools, horseback riding, tennis, a gym, and a social club and bar. Three kilometers (2 miles) from Salamanca is **Golf Villa Mayor** (⊠ Villamayor ☎ 923/160068 ⊕ www.villamayorgolf.com).

Ciudad Rodrigo

63 *88 km (54 mi) southwest of Salamanca.*

Surveying the fertile valley of the River Agueda, the small town of Ciudad Rodrigo has numerous well-preserved palaces and churches and makes an excellent overnight stop on the way from Spain to Portugal. The **cathedral** combines the Romanesque and Transitional Gothic styles and has a great deal of fine sculpture. Look closely at the early 16th-century choir stalls, elaborately carved with entertaining grotesques by Rodrigo Alemán. The cloister has carved capitals, and the cypresses in its center lend tranquillity. The cathedral's outer walls are still scarred by cannonballs fired during the Peninsular War. ⊠ *Pl. de Herrasti* *Cathedral free, museum €1.50* ⊙ *Daily 10–1 and 4–6.*

A major Salamanca monument is its fortified medieval **castle**, part of which has been turned into a parador. From here you can climb onto the town's battlements. ⊠ *Pl. del Castillo.*

Where to Stay & Eat

$–$$ ✕ **Mayton.** Backed with wood beams and bursting with a wonderfully eccentric collection of antiques ranging from mortars and pestles to Portuguese yokes and old typewriters, this restaurant has a charming interior. In contrast to the busy furnishings, the cooking is simple; specialties include fish, seafood, goat, and lamb. ⊠ *La Colada 9* ☎ *923/460720* ▭ *AE, DC, MC, V* ⊙ *No dinner Mon.*

$$$ **Parador de Ciudad Rodrigo.** In part of the magnificent castle built by Enrique II of Trastamara to stand guard over the Agueda Valley, this parador is a series of small, white rooms along the castle's sturdy, gen-

tly sloping outer walls. The parador's stately entrance is topped by a beautifully preserved medieval stone arch, part of the former castle entrance. Room 10 is particularly special: it has original vaulting. Some rooms, as well as the restaurant, overlook a beautiful garden that runs down to the River Agueda. ✉ *Pl. Castillo 1, 37500* ☎ *923/460150* 📠 *923/460404* 🌐 *www.parador.es* *35 rooms* *Restaurant, bar* 💳 *AE, DC, MC, V.*

PROVINCE OF ZAMORA & CITY OF VALLADOLID

2

Zamora is a densely fertile province divided by the River Duero into two distinct zones: the "land of bread," to the north, and the "land of wine," to the south. The area is most interesting for its Romanesque churches, the finest of which are in Zamora and Toro. The city of Valladolid, in contrast, is less scenic, but it has the National Museum of Sculpture and plenty of interesting history.

Zamora

64 *248 km (154 mi) northwest of Madrid.*

Zamora, on a bluff above the Duero, is not conventionally beautiful, as its many attractive monuments are isolated from one another by ramshackle 19th- and 20th-century development. The town does have lively, old-fashioned character, making it a pleasant place to pause. In Zamora's medieval town center is the Romanesque church of **San Juan** (✉ South side of Pl. Mayor ⏲ open for mass only), remarkable for its elaborate rose window. At the end of Calle Reina is one of Zamora's surviving medieval gates, and near here is the Romanesque church of **Santa María.** ✉ *North of Pl. Mayor.*

Zamora is famous for its Holy Week celebrations. The **Museo de Semana Santa** (Holy Week Museum) houses the sculptures paraded around the streets in processions during that time. Of relatively recent vintage, these works have an appealing provincial quality—for instance, a Crucifixion group filled with what appears to be the contents of a hardware store, including bales of rope, a saw, a spade, and numerous nails. The museum is in an unsightly modern building next to the church of Santa María. ✉ *Pl. de Santa María la Nueva* 🎫 *€2.70* ⏲ *Mon.–Sat. 10–2 and 5–8, Sun. 10–2.*

Zamora's **cathedral** is in a hauntingly beautiful square at the highest and westernmost point of the old town. Most of the building is Romanesque, but the exterior is most remarkable for its dome, which is flanked by turrets, articulated by spiny ribs, and covered in overlapping stones. The interior is notable for its early 16th-century carved choir stalls. The austere, late-16th-century cloister has a small museum, with an intricate *custodia* (monstrance, or receptacle for the Host) by Juan de Arce and some badly displayed but intriguing Flemish tapestries from the 15th and 16th centuries. ✉ *Pl. Catedral* 🎫 *€1.80* ⏲ *Mar.–Sept., Tues.–Sun. 10–2 and 5–8; Oct.–Feb., Tues.–Sun. 10–2 and 4:30–6:30.*

Surrounding Zamora's cathedral to the north is an attractive park incorporating the heavily restored **castle,** begun in the 11th century. Now a municipal school, it is open to visitors only when classes are in session. Calle Trascastillo, descending south from the cathedral to the river, affords views of the fertile countryside to the south and the town's old **Roman bridge.** ✉ C. *Trascastillo.*

Where to Stay

$$ **Parador de Zamora.** This restored 15th-century palace is central yet quiet, with a distinctive patio courtyard adorned with coats of arms and classical medallions of historical and mythological figures. The views are excellent, and the staff is friendly and resourceful. ✉ *Pl. Viriato 5, 49001* ☎ *980/514497* 🖷 *980/530063* 🌐 *www.parador.es* *52 rooms* *Restaurant, pool, bar* 💳 *AE, DC, MC, V.*

Toro

65 *33 km (20 mi) east of Zamora, 272 km (169 mi) northwest of Madrid.*

Above a loop of the River Duero and commanding extensive views over the vast plain to the south, Toro was once a provincial capital. In 1833 it was absorbed into Zamora's province—a loss of status that worked in some ways to its advantage. Zamora developed into a thriving modern town, but Toro slumbered and preserved its old appearance. The town is crowded with Romanesque churches, of which the most important is the **Colegiata,** begun in 1160. The protected west portal, or Portico de La Gloria, has a colorfully painted, perfectly preserved statuary from the early 13th century. The Serbian-Byzantine dome is also prominent. In the sacristy is an anonymous 15th-century painting of the Virgin, a touching work in the so-called Hispano-Flemish style. It's titled *The Virgin of the Fly* because of the fly painted on the Virgin's robe, a rather unusual detail. ✉ *Pl. de la Colegiata* *€1* ⏲ *Summer, Tues.–Sun. 10–1 and 5–8; winter, Tues.–Sun. 10–2 and 4:30–6:30; Mon. open for mass only.*

Valladolid

66 *96 km (60 mi) east of Zamora, 193 km (120 mi) northwest of Madrid.*

Modern Valladolid, capital of Castile–León, is a sprawling industrial center in the middle of a flat stretch of Castilian terrain. The surrounding countryside has a desolate, wintry sort of beauty, its vast, brittle fields unfolding grandly toward the horizon, punctuated here and there with swaths of green. The city has an important place in Spain's history: Ferdinand and Isabella were married here, Philip II was born and baptized here, and Philip III made Valladolid the capital of Spain for six years.

Fodor'sChoice ★

From the bus station, train station, or wherever you park your car, hop a taxi to the **Museo Nacional de Escultura** (National Museum of Sculpture), at the northernmost point in the old town. The late-15th-century Colegio de San Gregorio, in which the main museum is housed, is a masterpiece with playful, naturalistic detail. The facade is especially fantastic, with ribs in the form of pollarded trees, sprouting branches, and—to complete the forest motif—a row of wild men bearing mighty clubs. Across the walkway from the main museum is a Renaissance palace that houses temporary exhibitions. The main museum is arranged in rooms off an elaborate, arcaded courtyard. Its collections do for Spanish sculpture what those in the Prado do for Spanish painting—the only difference is that most people have heard of Velázquez, El Greco, Goya, and Murillo, whereas few are familiar with Alonso de Berruguete, Juan de Juni, and Gregorio Fernández, the three artists represented here.

Attendants and directional cues encourage you to tour the museum in chronological order. Begin on the ground floor, with Alonso de Berruguete's remarkable sculptures from the dismantled high altar in Valladolid's church of San Benito (1532). Berruguete, who trained in Italy under Michelangelo, is the most widely appreciated of Spain's postmedieval sculptors. He strove for pathos rather than realism, and his works have an extraordinarily expressive quality. The San Benito altar was the most important commission of his life, and the fragments here allow you to scrutinize his powerfully emotional art. In the museum's elegant chapel (which you normally see at the end of the tour) is a Berruguete retable from 1526, his first known work; on either side kneel gilded bronze figures by the Italian-born Pompeo Leoni.

Many critics of Spanish sculpture feel that decline set in with the late-16th-century artist Juan de Juni, who used glass for eyes and pearls for tears. Juni's many admirers, however, find his works intensely exciting, and they are in any case the highlights of the museum's upper floor. Dominating Castilian sculpture of the 17th century was the Galician-born Gregorio Fernández, in whose works the dividing line between sculpture and theater becomes tenuous. Respect for Fernández has been diminished by the number of vulgar imitators his work has spawned, but at Valladolid you can see his art at its best. The enormous, dramatic, and moving sculptural groups assembled in the last series of rooms (on the ground floor near the entrance) form a suitably spectacular climax to this fine collection. ✉ *Cadenas San Gregorio 1* ☎ *983/250375* 🌐 *pymes.tsai.es/museoescultura* 🎫 *€2.40, free Sat. 4–6 and Sun.* ⏲ *Tues.–Sat. 10–2 and 4–6, Sun. 10–2.*

At the corner of Calle Angustias is a brick mansion, the **birthplace of Philip II.** The late-15th-century church of **San Pablo** (✉ Pl. de San Pablo) has an overwhelmingly elaborate facade. Though the foundations of Valladolid's **cathedral** were laid in late-Gothic times, the building owes much of its appearance to designs executed in the late 16th century by Juan de Herrera, the architect of the Escorial. Further work was carried out by Alberto de Churriguera in the early 18th century. The Juni altarpiece is the one bit of color in an otherwise visually chilly place. ✉ *Pl. de la Universidad 1* ☎ *983/304362* 🎫 *Cathedral free, museum €2.50* ⏲ *Tues.–Fri. 10–1:30 and 4:30–7, weekends 10–2.*

The main **university building** (✉ Pl. de la Universidad) sits opposite the garden just south of the cathedral. The exuberant and dynamic late-Baroque frontispiece is by Narciso Tomé, creator of the remarkable *Transparente* in Toledo's cathedral. Valladolid's Calle Librería leads south from the main building to the magnificent **Colegio de Santa Cruz** (✉ Pl. Colegio de Santa Cruz), a large university college begun in 1487 in the Gothic style and completed in 1491 by Lorenzo Vázquez in a tentative, pioneering Renaissance mode. Inside is a harmonious courtyard. The house where Christopher Columbus died, in 1506, is now the **Museo de Colón** (Columbus Museum) with a well-arranged collection of objects, models, and explanatory panels illuminating the explorer's life and times. ✉ *Colón s/n* ☎ *983/291353* 🎫 *Free* ⏲ *Tues.–Sat. 10–2 and 5–7, Sun. 10–2.*

An interesting remnant of Spain's golden age is the tiny house where the writer Miguel de Cervantes lived from 1603 to 1606. A haven of peace set back from a noisy thoroughfare, **Casa de Cervantes** (Cervantes's House) is best reached by taxi. It was furnished in the early 20th century in a pseudo-Renaissance style by the Marquis of Valle-Inclan—the creator of the El Greco Museum in Toledo. ✉ *Rastro 7* ☎ *983/308810* 🎫 *€2.40, free Sun.* ⏲ *Tues.–Sat. 9:30–3:30, Sun. 10–3.*

Where to Stay & Eat

$–$$ ✕ **La Fragua.** In a modern building with a traditional Castilian interior of white walls and wood-beam ceilings, Valladolid's most famous and stylish restaurant counts members of the Spanish royal family among its guests. Specialties include meat roasted in a wood oven and such imaginative dishes as *rape Castellano Gran Mesón* (breaded monkfish with clams and peppers) and *lengua empiñonada* (tongue coated in pine nuts). The cozy downstairs bar serves a fine *vino de la casa* (house wine) and a delectable selection of tapas. ✉ *Paseo Zorrilla 10* ☎ *983/338785* ▭ *AE, DC, MC, V* ⊗ *Closed Aug. No dinner Sun.*

$–$$ ✕ **La Parrilla de San Lorenzo.** The restaurant—named for St. Lawrence, who burned to death over a grill (*parrilla*)—is in a 16th-century monastery, to which nobles once sent their children for proper upbringing. Hearty Castilian fare includes *lechazo* (young, milk-fed lamb) cooked in an *horno de leña* (wood oven). Seafood dishes might include *bonito a la forma convento* ("convent-style" bonito tuna, marinated in coarse sea salt and olive oil). Each dining hall is more opulent than the last—stone arches span several, and the walls are variously adorned with gilded mirrors, iron shields, and backlit stained-glass religious images. ✉ *Pedro Niño 1* ☎ *983/335088* ▭ *AE, MC, V* ⊗ *No dinner Sun.*

$$$ **Olid Meliá.** This hotel sits on a modern block in the midst of one of Valladolid's oldest and most attractive districts. The building was erected in the early 1970s, and the rooms have blond-wood furniture. For a splurge book a room with a sauna or hot tub. The first two floors have a pristine, marble elegance. ✉ *Pl. de San Miguel 10, 47003* ☎ *983/357200* *983/336828* 🌐 *www.solmelia.com* *211 rooms* *Restaurant, cafeteria, some hot tubs, bar, meeting room* ▭ *AE, DC, MC, V.*

Nightlife

Valladolid is a university town with a dynamic nightlife. The cafés on the Plaza Mayor are the best places to people-watch as evening falls. Tapas are good in the Zona Santa María la Antigua and on the adjacent Calle Marqués and Calle Paraíso. The modern Zona Paco Suárez is popular with students. More fashionable and less rowdy are the Zona Cantarranas and hidden hot spots around the Plaza del Salvador. For tasty Castilian tapas, make for the boisterous **Bar El Corcho** (✉ Correo 2 ☎ 983/330861), just off the Plaza Mayor. With exposed brick walls, sawdust scattered liberally on the floor, and pig haunches and copper pots hanging over the marble-top bar, it's standing room only every night of the week. The house specialty is *tostada de gambas,* toasted French bread heaped with shrimp and drizzled with olive oil. The perennially popular **Disco Bagur** (✉ C. de la Pasión 13), off Plaza Mayor, is a hopping dance spot.

off the beaten path

Valladolid is close to two famous wine-growing regions, **RUEDA** – for whites and **RIBERA DEL DUERO** – for *tintos* (reds). Wine buffs can enjoy an easy day's excursion from Valladolid, visiting bodegas and the **MUSEO DEL VINO** (Wine Museum; ☎ 983/881199) – in the splendid 220-yard-long 11th-century castle at **PEÑAFIEL** – The wine museum is open Tuesday–Friday 11:30–2:30 and 4:30–7:30, until 8:30 on weekends. Admission to the castle and museum is €5; €12 includes tasting. Leave the city heading east to Renedo and follow the country road via Villabañez and Valbueno (the famous **VEGA SICILIA** – bodega, Sir Winston Churchill's favorite) along the Río Duero to Peñafiel. Return by the N122.

BURGOS, LEÓN & THE CAMINO DE SANTIAGO

Burgos and León are ancient Castilian capitals with lively centers and two of the grandest Gothic cathedrals in Spain. West of Burgos, the N120 to León crosses the ancient Way of St. James, dotted with lovely old churches, tiny hermitages, ruined monasteries, and medieval villages in gently undulating fields. The snowcapped peaks of the Picos de Europa mark the northwestern horizon. West of León, you can actually follow the well-worn Camino as it approaches Galicia and the very last stops on a pilgrimage route that began all the way back in France or Portugal. Wending its way toward the giant cathedral in Santiago de Compostela, this Castilian leg of the Camino passes through medieval towns and quiet valleys as the terrain gets greener, wetter, and hillier.

Burgos

67–72 *240 km (149 mi) north of Madrid.*

On the banks of the Arlanzón River is this small city with some of Spain's most outstanding medieval architecture. The first signs of Burgos, if you approach on the N-I from Madrid, are the spiky twin spires of its cathedral, rising above the main bridge. Burgos's second glory is its heritage as the city of El Cid, the part-historical, part-mythical hero of the Christian Reconquest of Spain. The city has been known for centuries as a center of both militarism and religion, and even today you'll see more nuns on its streets than almost anywhere else in Spain. Burgos was born as a military camp in 884—a fortress built on the orders of the Christian king Alfonso III, who was having a hard time defending the upper reaches of Old Castile from the constant forays of the Arabs. It quickly became vital in the defense of Christian Spain, and its identity as an early outpost of Christianity was sealed with the founding of the Royal Convent of Las Huelgas, in 1187. Burgos also became an important station on the Camino de Santiago and thus a place of rest and sustenance for Christian pilgrims throughout the Middle Ages.

★ 67 Start your walk at the **cathedral,** the city's high point, which contains such a wealth of art and other treasures that jealous burghers actually lynched their civil governor in 1869 for trying to take an inventory of it. The proud Burgalese apparently feared that the poor man was angling to remove the treasures. Most of the outside of the cathedral is sculpted in the Flamboyant Gothic style. The cornerstone was laid in 1221, and the two 275-ft towers were completed by the middle of the 14th century, though the final chapel was not finished until 1731. There are 13 chapels, the most elaborate of which is the hexagonal Condestable Chapel. You'll find the **tomb of El Cid** (1026–99) and his wife, Ximena, under the transept. El Cid (whose real name was Rodrigo Díaz de Vivar) was a mercenary warrior revered for his victories over the Moors; the medieval *Song of My Cid* transformed him into a Spanish national hero.

At the other end of the cathedral, high above the West Door, is the **Reloj de Papamoscas** (Flycatcher Clock), so named for the sculptured bird that opens its mouth as the mechanism marks each hour. The grilles around the choir have some of the finest wrought-iron work in central Spain, and the choir itself has 103 delicately carved walnut stalls, no two alike. The 13th-century stained-glass windows that once shed a beautiful, filtered light were destroyed in 1813, one of many cultural casualties of Napoléon's retreating troops. ✉ *Pl. del Rey San Fernando* ☎ *947/204712* 🎫 *Museum and cloister €3.60* ⏲ *Mon.–Sat. 9:30–1 and 4–7, Sun. 9:30–11:45 and 4–7.*

Across the Plaza del Rey San Fernando from the cathedral is the city's
68 main gate, the **Arco de Santa María**; walk through toward the river and
look above the arch at the 16th-century statues of the first Castilian judges;
El Cid; Spain's patron saint James; and King Charles I.

69 The Arco de Santa María fronts the city's loveliest promenade, the **Espolón.** The walkway follows the riverbank and is shaded with luxuri-
70 ant black poplars. The **Casa del Cordón,** a 15th-century palace, is where
the Catholic Monarchs received Columbus after his second voyage to
the New World. It's now a bank. ✉ *Pl. de Calvo Sotel.*

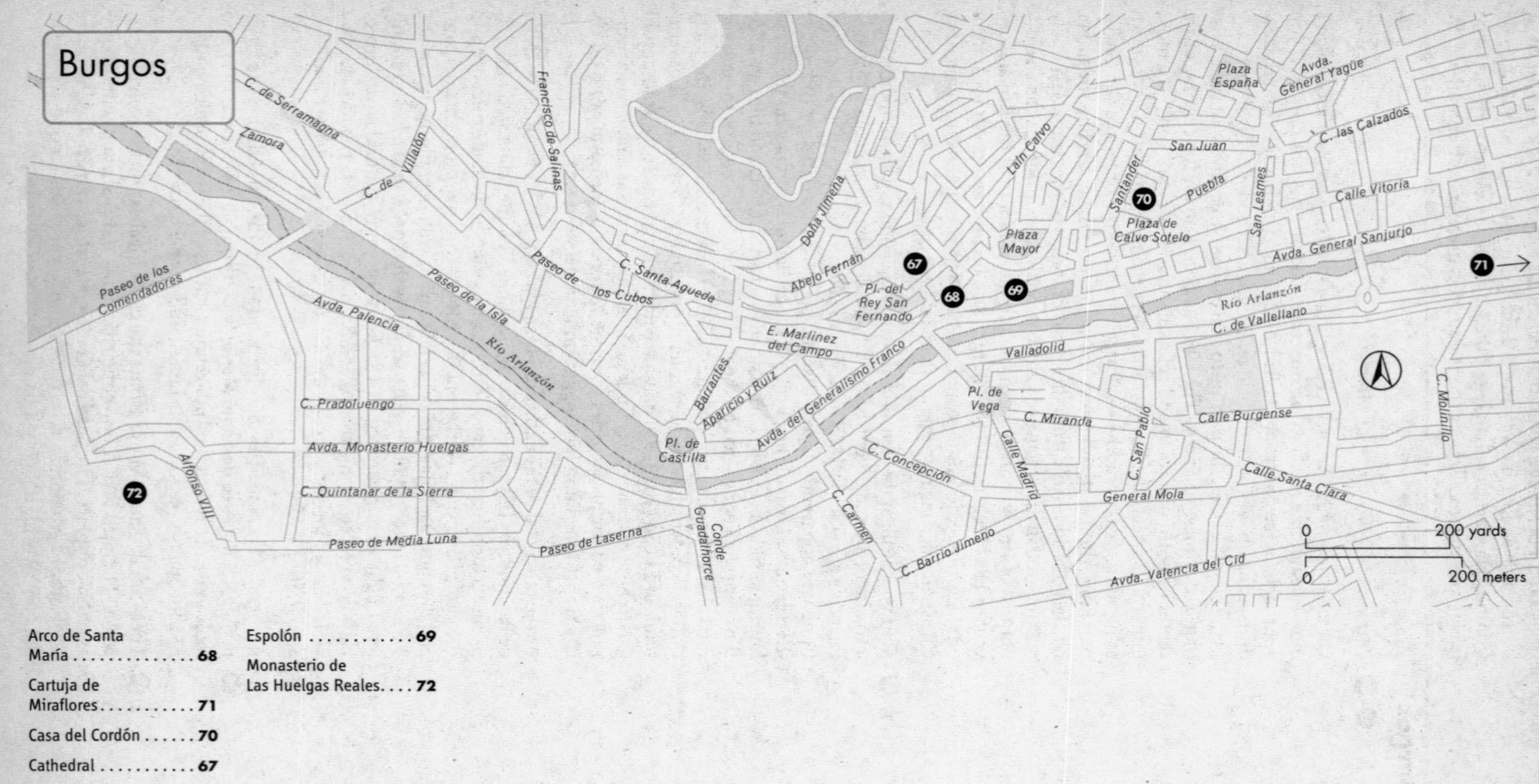

Arco de Santa María 68

Cartuja de Miraflores 71

Casa del Cordón 70

Cathedral 67

Espolón 69

Monasterio de Las Huelgas Reales. . . . 72

71 Founded in 1441, the **Cartuja de Miraflores** is a florid Gothic charterhouse, its Isabelline church has an altarpiece by Gil de Siloe, said to be gilded with the first gold brought back from the New World. To get there, follow signs from the city's main gate. *3 km (2 mi) east of Burgos, at end of a poplar- and elm-lined drive. Free Church open for mass Mon.–Sat. 9 AM, Sun. 7:30 and 10:15 AM; main building Mon.–Sat. 10:15–3 and 4–6, Sun. 11:20–12:30, 1–3, and 4–6.*

72 On the western edge of town—a long walk—is the **Monasterio de Las Huelgas Reales,** still run by nuns. Founded in 1187 by King Alfonso VIII, the convent has a royal mausoleum. All but one of the royal coffins were desecrated by Napoléon's soldiers, the one that survived contained clothes that form the basis of the convent's textile museum. *1½ km (1 mi) southwest of town, along Paseo de la Isla and left across Malatos Bridge 947/201630 €4.80, free Wed. for EU citizens Tues.–Sat. 10–1:15 and 3:45–5:45, Sun. 10:30–2:15.*

Where to Stay & Eat

$$–$$$ ★ **Casa Ojeda.** Across from the Casa del Cordón, this popular restaurant is known for inspired renditions of Burgos classics, especially roast lamb. *C. Vitoria 5 947/209052 AE, DC, MC, V.*

$$$ **Mesón del Cid.** Once a 15th-century printing press, this family-run hotel and restaurant has been hosting travelers and serving Burgalese food for four generations. Guest rooms, which face the cathedral, are done in traditional Castilian style. The dining rooms have hand-hewn beams and views of the cathedral. The *pimientos rellenos* (peppers stuffed with meat) are excellent, as is the *sopa de Doña Jimena* (garlic soup with bread and egg). *Pl. Santa María 8, 48383 947/205971 947/269460 www.minotel.com 40 rooms Restaurant, cafeteria, bar, free parking AE, DC, MC, V.*

Nightlife

Thanks to a university student population, Burgos has a lively *vida nocturna.* House wines and *cañas* (small glasses of beer) flow freely at the crowded tapas bars along Calles Laín Calvo and San Juan, near the Plaza Mayor. Calle Puebla, a small, dark street off Calle San Juan, also gets constant revelers, who pop into Café Principal, La Rebotica, and Spils Cervecería for a quick drink and morsel before moving on to the next hangout. When you order a drink at any Burgos bar, the bartender plunks down a free *pinchito* (small tapa)—a long-standing tradition. The late-night bar scene centers on **Las Llanas,** two interconnected squares near the cathedral.

Shopping

A good buy is a few bottles of local Ribera de Duero *tinto* wines, now strong rivals to those of Rioja-Alta. Burgos is also known for its cheeses. **Casa Quintanilla** (C. Paloma 17) is a good spot to pick up some *queso de Burgos*, a fresh ricotta-like cheese.

en route

For a sojourn with those masters of the Gregorian chant, the double-platinum monks of *Chant* fame, stop at the Monastery of Santo Domingo de Silos, 58 km (36 mi) southeast of Burgos (947/390068). Single men can stay here for up to eight days. If the monastery is full, try to drop in for a vespers service. Quite close to Burgos (10 km [6 mi]) is the Monastery of San Pedro de Cardeña (947/290033), a lodging that allows couples and even families—possibly thanks to the monastery's importance in the story of El Cid, the medieval Spanish hero who left his wife and children there when banished into exile.

Sasamón

73 *25 km (16 mi) west of Burgos.*

Turn right off the highway and soon you'll be in the village where the 15th-century hilltop church of Santa María la Real, with a magnificent carved portico, stands beside a tree-lined plaza with a tinkling fountain. You can visit on weekdays, 11–2 and 4–6. Pick up keys to the church in the nearby Bar Gloria. On the north side of the village is the tiny Ermita de San Isidro Hermitage. If the hermitage is closed, peer through the small window in the door to see, right in the middle of the aisle, its surreal, 20-ft-tall 16th-century Gothic cross. Carved of stone, it depicts the expulsion of Adam and Eve from paradise.

Castrojeriz

74 *20 km (12 mi) southwest of Sasamón.*

From Sasamón, return to the N120 and cross it to reach Olmillas de Sasamón. After passing a castle on your right, continue south following the CAMINO DE SANTIAGO signs. A few miles after Hontanas, the road passes under an arch of the ruined monastery of **San Anton,** now a farm building. Here you can see two niches by the road where food was once left out for pilgrims. As you approach Castrojeriz, its ruined hilltop **castle** is visible. To see the three local **churches** you may have to call the caretaker, Vicente (☎ 947/377034).

Where to Eat

¢–$ ✕ **La Taberna.** Antonio and María Jesús have restored this 18th-century timber building as a bar and a restaurant with good home cooking, including flavorful *sopa de ajo* (garlic soup). They also operate as a basic *hostal.* ✉ *General Mola 43* ☎ *947/377610* ▭ *No credit cards* ⊗ *Closed Mon.*

Frómista

75 *54 km (33 mi) northwest of Castrojeriz.*

Take the small road south from Castrojeriz to Itero de la Vega and Boadillo del Camino to reach Frómista. Just before you arrive, the road crosses the Canal de Castilla, begun in 1753 with the dubious idea of linking Salamanca with the port of Santander—and never completed. The town of Frómista has four hospices for present-day pilgrims, and its architectural gem is the 1066 church of San Martín. Richly sculpted inside, it was part of a monastery in the 11th century, which might explain the geographical breathing room it still enjoys.

Where to Eat

$–$$ ✕ **Hostería de los Palmeros.** Here in a 17th-century pilgrims' hospital, the kitchen serves good fish, game in season, and baby lamb. Dine on an outdoor terrace or in the rather formal upstairs dining room, with a view of the storks' nests on the church of San Telmo, across the highway. ✉ *Pl. San Telmo 4* ☎ *979/810067* ▭ *AE, DC, MC, V.*

Villalcázar de Sirga

76 *13 km (8 mi) west of Frómista.*

Driving toward Carrión de los Condes, turn right into the village of Villalcázar. The Templar church of Santa María la Blanca has a towering double-arch entrance and the polychrome 13th-century tombs of Felipe, brother of Alfonso X the Wise, and Leonor, his wife.

Carrión de los Condes

77 *7 km (4½ mi) west of Villalcázar de Sirga.*

Drive through this busy town and cross the River Carrión to reach the Real Monasterio San Zoilo on the left. Begun in the 10th century, this former Benedictine monastery has magnificent 16th-century Gothic-Renaissance cloisters and the elaborate tombs of the *condes* (counts) of Carrión. You can visit on weekdays 10:30–2 (plus 4–8 between June and August) and on weekends 10:30–2 and 4–8 year-round.

Where to Stay

★ $ **Hotel Real Monasterio San Zoilo.** This former Benedictine monastery dates back to the 10th century, and its spectacular entrance leads to impressive public rooms with exposed bricks and timbers. The vast refectory can seat 330. One floor up is the restaurant Las Vigas, which serves decent Castilian fare at tables set below a forest of medieval beams (*vigas*). The large rooms are well furnished, and the "Habitación del Conde" suite is especially grand. ✉ *34120 Carrión de los Condes, Palencia* ☎ *979/880049* 🖷 *979/881090* 🌐 *www.sanzoilo.com* *33 rooms, 4 suites* *Restaurant, bar, meeting room* ▭ *AE, DC, MC, V.*

Sahagún

78 *44 km (27 mi) west of Carrió de los Condes, 63 km (39 mi) east of León.*

The road winds into Sahagún past rolling fields of wheat. The town was allegedly founded by Charlemagne after he conquered the Moors by the nearby River Cea, and Sahagún is in fact a center of Mudéjar craftsmanship, as evidenced in the brick bell towers and trilobed apses of the 12th-century churches of San Tirso and San Lorenzo. Nuns in the Monasterio de Santa Cruz usually allow visitors to see the treasures, which include a beautifully carved medieval silver casket.

Where to Eat

$–$$ ✕ **Luis.** With a long bar overlooking the narrow Plaza Mayor, this popular, family-run restaurant cooks local produce with flair. At €10, the *puerros de Sahagún rellenos de mariscos* (Sahagún leeks stuffed with shellfish) are highly recommended, and there's a good selection of salads. Breakfast, lunch, and dinner are served daily. ✉ *Pl. Mayor 4* ☎ *987/782058* ▭ *AE, MC, V.*

León

79–87 *333 km (207 mi) northwest of Madrid, 216 km (134 mi) west of Burgos.*

The ancient capital of the group of provinces known as Castilla y León (Castile and León) sits on the banks of the Bernesga River in the high plains of Old Castile. Historians say that the name of the city, which was founded as a permanent camp for the Roman legions in AD 70, has nothing to do with the proud lion that has been its emblem for centuries but is instead a corruption of the Roman word *legio* (legion).

The capital of Christian Spain was moved to León from Oviedo in 914 as the Reconquest spread southward, launching the city's richest era. Walls went up around the old Roman town, and you can still see parts of the 6-ft-thick ramparts in the middle of the modern city. Today, León is a wealthy provincial capital and prestigious university town. The wide avenues of western León are lined with boutiques, while the twisting alleys of the half-timbered old town hide the bars, bookstores, and *chocolaterías* most popular with students. As you're wandering the old town, look down occasionally and you just might notice small brass scal-

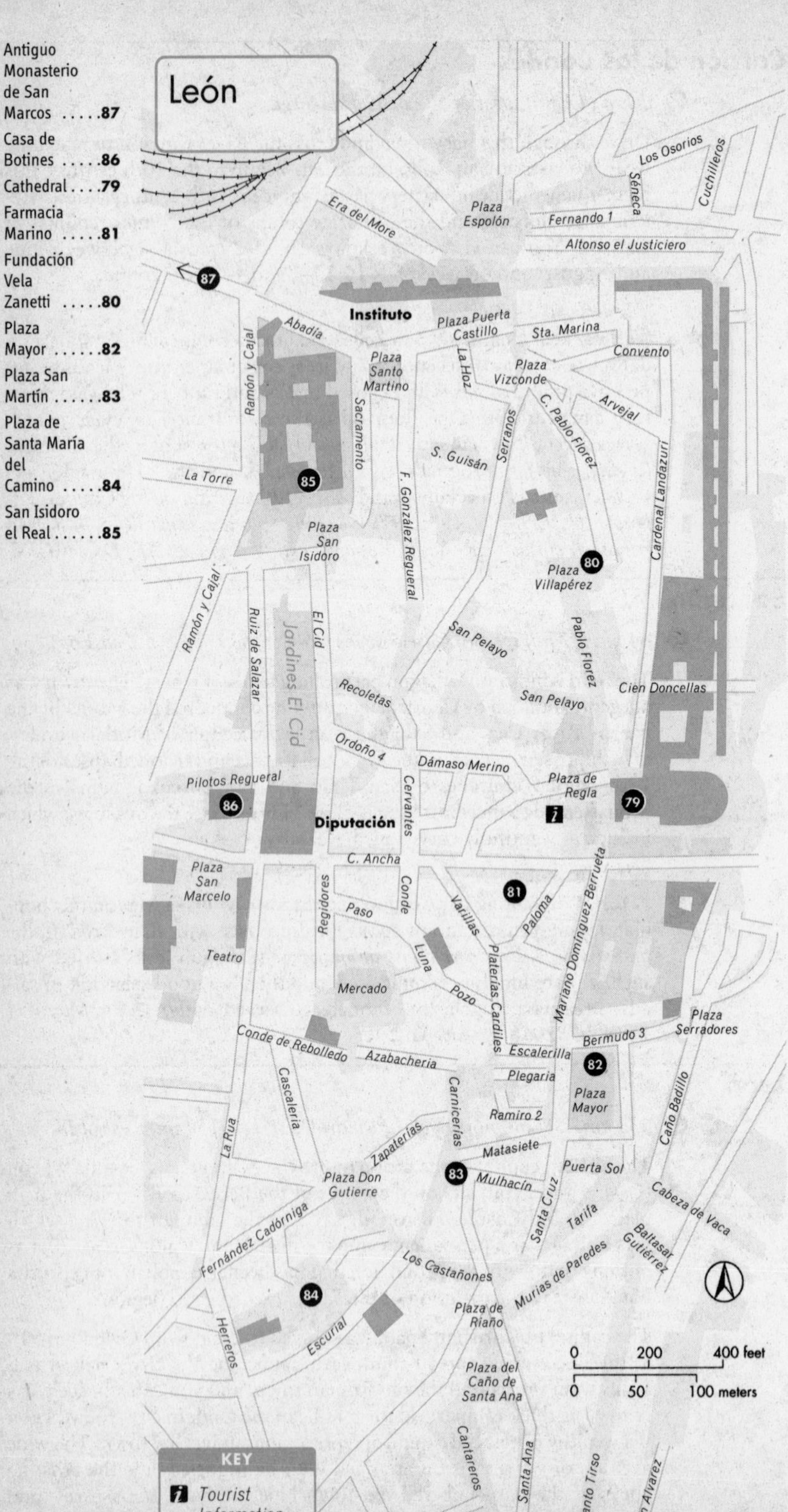
León
Los Osorios
Cuchilleros
Séneca
Plaza Espolón
Fernando 1
Altonso el Justiciero
Era del More
Instituto
Abadía
Plaza Puerta Castillo
Sta. Marina
Convento
Plaza Santo Martino
La Hoz
Plaza Vizconde
Arvejal
C. Pablo Florez
Ramón y Cajal
Sacramento
S. Guisán
Serranos
Cardenal Landazuri
La Torre
F. González Regueral
Plaza San Isidoro
Plaza Villapérez
Ruiz de Salazar
El Cid
Jardines El Cid
San Pelayo
Pablo Florez
Cien Doncellas
Recoletas
San Pelayo
Ordoño 4
Dámaso Merino
Plaza de Regla
Pilotos Regueral
Cervantes
Diputación
C. Ancha
Plaza San Marcelo
Regidores
Conde
Varillas
Paloma
Mariano Domínguez Berrueta
Paso
Luna
Platerías
Teatro
Mercado
Pozo
Cardiles
Plaza Serradores
Bermudo 3
Conde de Rebolledo
Azabachería
Escalerilla
Plegaria
Plaza Mayor
Cascalería
Carnicerías
Ramiro 2
Caño Badillo
La Rúa
Zapaterías
Matasiete
Puerta Sol
Plaza Don Gutierre
Mulhacín
Santa Cruz
Cabeza de Vaca
Tarifa
Baltasar Gutiérrez
Fernández Cadórniga
Los Castañones
Murias de Paredes
Plaza de Riaño
Herreros
Escurial
Plaza del Caño de Santa Ana
0 200 400 feet
0 50 100 meters
Cantareros
Santa Ana
Santo Tirso
Juan Alvarez
KEY
Tourist Information

lop shells set into the street. The scallop is the symbol of St. James; the shells were installed by the town government to mark the path for modern-day pilgrims.

★ 79 León is proudest of its soaring Gothic **cathedral,** on the Plaza de Regla, whose soaring upper reaches are built with more windows than stone. Flanked by two aggressively square towers, the facade has three arched, weatherworn doorways, the middle one adorned with slender statues of the apostles. Begun in 1205, the cathedral has 125 long, slender stained-glass windows; dozens of decorative small ones; and three giant, spectacular rose windows. On sunny days, the glass casts bejeweled shafts of light on the beautifully spare, pale-sandstone interior; the windows themselves depict abstract floral patterns as well as various biblical and medieval scenes. A glass door to the choir gives an unobstructed view of nave windows and the painted altarpiece, framed with gold leaf. The cathedral also contains the sculpted tomb of King Ordoño II, who moved the capital of Christian Spain to León. The **museum** has giant medieval hymnals, textiles, sculptures, wood carvings, and paintings. Look for the carved-wood Mudéjar archive, with a letter of the alphabet above each door: it's one of the world's oldest file cabinets. ✉ *Pl. de Regla* ☎ *987/875770* 🎟 *Museum €3* ⏲ *Cathedral weekdays 8:30–1:30 and 4–7, Sat. 9:30–1:30 and 4–7. Museum July–Sept., weekdays 9:30–1:30 and 4–7, Sat. 9:30–1:30 and 4–7; Oct.–June, Mon.–Sat. 9:30–1 and 4–6:30.*

80 Hidden away just north of the cathedral is the **Fundación Vela Zanetti,** a contemporary, wood-and-windows art museum inside a 15th-century mansion. Zanetti was a 20th-century Castilian artist with a fondness for warm tones and a special interest in human rights. Some of his portraits recall El Greco. Art lovers will find this unknown museum a pleasant surprise. ✉ *C. Pablo Flórez s/n* ☎ *987/244121* 🎟 *Free* ⏲ *Tues.–Fri. 10–1:30 and 5–8, weekends 5:50–8:30.*

81 Down the street from the cathedral, the **Farmacia Marino,** opened in 1827,
is a glimpse into a Spanish drugstore of yore. The ceiling and walls are
richly carved, and the latter include a niche for each apothecary jar. (✉ Av.
82 Generalísimo Franco). The arcaded **Plaza Mayor,** in the heart of the old
town, is surrounded by simple half-timber houses. On Wednesday and
Saturday, the plaza bustles with farmers selling produce and cheeses. Many
farmers still wear wooden shoes called *madreñas,* which are raised on
three heels, two in front and one in back. They were designed to walk
on mud in this usually wet part of Spain. Most of León's tapas bars are
83 in the 12th-century **Plaza San Martín.** This area is called the Barrio
Húmedo, or Wet Neighborhood, for the large amount of wine spilled
here late at night.

84 Southwest of the Plaza San Martín is the **Plaza de Santa María del Camino,** which, as the plaque here points out, used to be called Plaza del Grano (Grain Square) and hosted the local corn and bread market. Also here is the church of **Santa María del Camino,** where pilgrims stop on their way west to Santiago de Compostela. The curious allegorical fountain in the middle depicts two chubby angels clutching a pillar, symbolizing León's two rivers and the capital.

★ 85 The sandstone basilica of **San Isidoro el Real,** on Calle Cid, was built into the side of the city wall in 1063 and rebuilt in the 12th century. The **Panteón de los Reyes** (Royal Pantheon), adjoining the basilica, has been called the Sistine Chapel of Romanesque art for the vibrant 12th-century frescoes on its pillars and ceiling. The pantheon was the first building in Spain to be decorated with scenes from the New Testament. Look for the agricultural calendar painted on one archway, showing which farming task should be performed each month. Twenty-three kings and queens were once buried here, but their tombs were destroyed by French troops during the Napoléonic Wars. Treasures in the adjacent **Museo de San Isidoro** include a jewel-encrusted agate chalice, a richly illustrated handwritten Bible, and many polychrome wood statues of the Virgin Mary. ✉ *Pl. de San Isidoro 4* ☎ *987/229608* *Basilica free, Royal Pantheon and museum €2.40* ⏲ *July-Aug., Mon.–Sat. 9–8, Sun. 9–2; Sept.–June, Mon.–Sat. 9–1:30 and 4–7, Sun. 9–2.*

86 Just south of the old town is the **Casa de Botines,** a multigabled, turreted, granite behemoth designed at the end of the 19th century by that controversial Catalan Antoni Gaudí. It now houses a bank. ✉ *Off Ruiz de Salazar.*

87 Fronted by a large, airy pedestrian plaza, the sumptuous **Antiguo Monasterio de San Marcos** is now a luxury hotel, the Parador Hostal San Marcos. Originally a home for knights of the Order of St. James, who patrolled the Camino de Santiago, and a pit stop for weary pilgrims, the monastery you see today was begun in 1513 by the head of the order, King Ferdinand, who felt that knights deserved something better. Finished at the height of the Renaissance, the plateresque facade is a majestic swath of small sculptures (many depicting knights and lords) and careful ornaments. Inside are an elegant staircase and a cloister full of medieval statues. Have a drink in the bar—its tiny windows are the original defensive slits. The building also houses León's **Museo Arqueológico,** famous for its 11th-century ivory Carrizo crucifix. ✉ *Pl. de San Marcos* ☎ *987/245061 or 987/236405* *Museum €1.20* ⏲ *Tues.–Sat. 10–2 and 5–8:30, Mon. 10–2.*

If you're traveling with children, note that León has a long **park** on the banks of the Bernesga River, with playground equipment every 100 ft or so.

Bars & Cafés

Most of León's liveliest hangouts are clustered in the Plaza Mayor and Plaza San Martín, with the former drawing couples and families and the latter a university crowd. The streets are packed with tapas bars.

In the **Plaza Mayor,** you might want to start your crawl at Universal, Mesón de Don Quijote, Casa Benito, or Bar La Plaza Mayor. In the **Plaza San Martín,** the Latino Bar at No. 10 serves a glass of house wine and your choice of one of four generous tapas for just €.50 a gift. Have a *pinchito* (tidbit) at cozy Prada a Tope, which serves the local Bierzo wine out of a big barrel. Other Plaza San Martín haunts are Rancho Chico, Nuevo Racimo de Oro, and La Bicha.

Where to Stay & Eat

$–$$ ✕ **Adonias.** Enter the bar and go up one flight to this green, softly lit dining room, furnished with rustic tables and colorful ceramics. The cuisine is based on such regional foodstuffs as cured hams, roast peppers, and chorizo. Try the grilled sea bream or the roast suckling pig, and if you have room, the homemade banana pudding with chocolate sauce. ✉ *Santa Nonia 16* ☎ *987/206768* ▭ *AE, DC, MC, V* ⏲ *Closed Sun.*

$–$$ ✕ **Casa Pozo.** This longtime favorite is across from City Hall on the historic Plaza de San Marcelo. Past the small bar, the bright dining rooms are furnished with heavy Castilian furniture. Owner Gabriel del Pozo Alvarez—called Pin—supervises the busy kitchen while his son, also called Pin, is maître d'. Specialties include roast lamb, river crabs with clams, cod with pimiento and olive oil, and deep-fried hake. ✉ *Pl. de San Marcelo 15* ☎ *987/223039* ▭ *AE, DC, MC, V* ⏲ *Sun.*

$–$$ ✕ **Nuevo Racimo de Oro.** Upstairs in a ramshackle 12th-century tavern in the heart of the old town, this cozy restaurant specializes in roast lamb cooked in a wood-fire clay oven. The spicy *sopa de ajo leonese* (garlic soup) is a classic, and *solomillo Racimo al hojaldre* (veal in puff pastry) makes a tasty entrée. Worth trying is *Tarta de San Marcos,* a lemon cake served with whipped cream. ✉ *Pl. San Martín 8* ☎ *987/214767* ▭ *AE, DC, MC, V* ⏲ *Closed Wed. Oct.–May. No dinner Sun.*

$$$ Fodor's Choice ★ ✕🏨 **Parador Hotel San Marcos.** This magnificent parador occupies a restored 16th-century monastery built by King Ferdinand to shelter pilgrims walking the Camino de Santiago; the bridge beside it has helped pilgrims cross the River Bernesga for centuries. The huge, ornamental, plateresque facade also fronts a church and museum of archaeology (which is in the Antiguo Monasterio de San Marcos). Hallways and guest rooms have antiques, high-quality reproductions, and some nice contemporary art. One wing is modern; if you want a more medieval look, ask for a room in the old section. The elegant dining room offers 10 hot and cold regional appetizers for €13. ✉ *Pl. de San Marcos 7, 24001* ☎ *987/237300* 📠 *987/233458* 🌐 *www.parador.es* *230 rooms* *2 restaurants, pool, hair salon, bar, parking (fee)* ▭ *AE, DC, MC, V.*

$$ 🏨 **Hotel Paris.** Rooms here are comfortable, and the classic basement *mesón* (tavern) snuggles up to the stone of a Roman wall. The hotel is on the modern thoroughfare heading east from Plaza Santo Domingo, halfway between the cathedral and the new town. ✉ *Ancha 18, 24003* ☎ *987/238600* 📠 *987/271572* 🌐 *www.hotelparis.lesein.es* *55 rooms* *Restaurant, café, bar, meeting rooms* ▭ *AE, DC, MC, V.*

Shopping

FURNITURE & CRAFTS

For fine funky gifts, visit **Tricosis** (✉ C. Mulhacín 3 ☎ 987/202953), a gallery opened by art students from the universities of Leon and Gijón, where colorful papier-mâché and experimental media form outstanding lamps, candleholders, vases, and frames.

Lovers of home furnishings will enjoy browsing in **Armoan** (✉ Av. Ramón y Cajal 4 ☎ 987/249203), an exquisitely tasteful European collection. Among the smaller—read: more portable—items are clever, soothing prints and artful lamps. In Villar de Mazarife, 22 km (14 mi) west of León toward Astorga, **Monseñor** (✉ Camino de León 21) paints adaptations of Roman archaeological finds and makes tile reproductions of the frescoes in the Royal Pantheon.

FOOD

Tasty regional treats include roasted red peppers, potent brandy-soaked cherries, and candied chestnuts. You can buy these in food shops all over the city. You can shop while having tapas at **Prada a Tope** (✉ Pl. San Martín 1), where they're packaged by the house. The shop **Cuesta Castañón** (✉ Castoñones 2), near Plaza San Martín, has a great selection of wines, cured meats, cookies, preserves, and bottled delicacies, not to mention books on related topics. Friendly owner José María González lets you sample the stock.

At **Hojaldres Alonso** (✉ Ancha 7), near the cathedral, you can browse through the shelves of local goodies (candied nuts, preserves), all produced at their factory in nearby Astorga, and then head to the café in the back. The focus here is on the baked goods, particularly the *hojaldres* (puff pastries) and *torrijas,* a Castilian version of French toast. The café is a favorite among locals who come for their early evening *merienda* (usually between 6 and 8), Spain's answer to the afternoon tea.

en route

Leaving León, follow signs to the N120 and head southwest. Stop to admire the 13th-century Orbigo Bridge, 23 km (14 mi) outside the city, where the knight Quiñones made his stand. Legend has it that Quiñones was the toughest *hombre* on the Camino; in 1434, he staked out his turf on this 24-arch bridge and for a month challenged every other knight who policed the route. You are now on the Way of

St. James itself, marked with large scallop signs for drivers and small ones for those who make the journey on foot or bicycle.

Astorga

88 *46 km (29 mi) southwest of León.*

Astorga, where the pilgrimage roads from France and Portugal merge, once had 22 **hospitals** to lodge and care for ailing travelers. The only one left today is next to the cathedral. The **cathedral** itself is a huge 15th-century building with four statues of St. James. The **Museo de la Catedral** displays 10th- and 12th-century chests, religious silverware, and paintings and sculptures by various Astorgans. ✉ *Pl. de la Catedral* ☎ *987/615429* *€1.50* ⊙ *Oct.–Dec. and Feb., daily 11–2 and 3:30–6:30; Mar.–Sept., daily 10–2 and 4–8.*

Fodor's Choice ★ Just opposite Astorga's cathedral is the fairy-tale, neo-Gothic **Palacio Episcopal** (Archbishop's Palace), designed for a Catalan cleric by Antoni Gaudí in 1889. Visiting the palace the last week of August, during Astorga's Fiesta de Santa María, is a treat for the senses; fireworks explode in the sky casting rainbows of light over Gaudí's ornate, mystical towers. No expense was spared in creating this building, site of the **Museo del Camino** (Museum of the Way). The collection has folk items, such as the standard pilgrim costume—heavy black cloak, staff hung with gourds, and wide-brimmed hat bedecked with scallop shells—as well as contemporary Spanish art. ✉ *Adjacent to Astorga cathedral* ☎ *987/616882* *€2.40* ⊙ *Apr.–Sept., daily 10–2 and 4–8; Oct.–Mar., daily 11–2 and 3:30–6:30.*

Where to Stay & Eat

$$ ✕ **La Peseta.** Family-run since 1865, this place persists in good home cooking, especially the four-dish marathon *cocido maragato,* a sort of serial country stew. There's a 19-room hostel upstairs. ✉ *Pl. de San Bartolomé 3* ☎ *987/617275* ▭ *AE, DC, MC, V* ⊙ *Closed last 2 wks in Oct. and Jan. No dinner Sun. or Tues.*

$–$$ ✕ **Parillada Serrano.** Popular with locals, and occasionally serving the likes of game, wild mushrooms, and pork during special gastronomic weeks, this mesón serves both contemporary cuisine and traditional roasts of baby lamb. ✉ *Portería 2* ☎ *987/617866* ▭ *AE, MC, V* ⊙ *Closed last 2 wks in June. No dinner Mon.*

$$ **Astur Plaza.** This gleaming, well-run hotel is near Astorga's city hall. The yellow guest rooms have dark-brown furnishings, and ample light shines in from large windows. The lounge is glassed in; the large bar and Los Hornos restaurant have beam ceilings and exposed brick walls. ✉ *Pl. de España 2 and 3, 24700* ☎ *987/618900* *987/618949* *www.asturplaza.com* *35 rooms, 5 suites* *Restaurant, bar, parking (fee)* ▭ *AE, MC, V.*

Castillo de los Polvazares

89 *51 km (32 mi) west of León, 5 km (3 mi) northwest of Astorga.*

A short walk or 15-minute drive from Astorga is Castillo de los Polvazares, a 17th-century village built on the site of a fortified Roman settlement. The city's 30-odd residents live in stone houses emblazoned with crests above their green doorways. Walk down the stone streets and look for storks' nests on top of the village church. Castillo de los Polvazares is in León's Maragatería region, whose people are believed to be a mixture of the ancient Celts and Phoenicians. These doughty traders resisted the Roman invasion of the Iberian Peninsula and reached the height of their prowess as muleteers in the 18th and 19th centuries (hence the wide doorways around town), transporting gold from the Americas to the royal court in Madrid.

Ponferrada

90 *115 km (71 mi) west of León, 64 km (40 mi) west of Astorga on N-VI.*

In a hilly region with fertile valleys, Ponferrada is a mining and industrial center that gets its name from an iron toll bridge built by a local bishop in the 1100s. The tall, slim turrets of the 13th-century **Castillo de los Templarios** (Templars' Castle) on the western edge of town has sweeping views of the countryside and may once have been used by the Knights of the Order of St. James to police the route. Restoration is in progress. ✉ *Florez Osorio 4* 🎫 *€1.50* ⏲ *Apr.–May, Tues.–Sat. 10–2 and 4:30–8, Sun. 10–2; June–mid-Sept., Tues.–Sun. 10:30–2 and 5–9; mid-Sept.–Mar., Tues.–Sat. 10:30–2 and 4–6, Sun. 11–2.*

off the beaten path

Leave Ponferrada heading west on the N-VI (toward A Coruña), and take the Las Médulas/Puente de Domingo exit to the N536 toward Carucedo. Turning right here, you can either follow the signs to a viewpoint at Orellán or go to the village of **LAS MEDULAS** – From the latter, you can explore the Roman gold mines 21 km (13 mi) west of Ponferrada, where jagged red cliffs rise out of oak and chestnut woods, and great pits lead to deep tunnels, canals, and caves. Bring a flashlight.

Villafranca del Bierzo

91 *135 km (84 mi) west of León, 20 km (12 mi) west of Ponferrada.*

After crossing León's grape-growing region, where the slightly acidic Bierzo wine is produced, you'll arrive in this medieval village, dominated by a massive and still-inhabited feudal fortress. Villafranca was a destination in itself for some of Santiago's pilgrims: visit the Romanesque church of Santiago to see the Puerta del Perdón (Door of Pardon), a sort of spiritual consolation prize for exhausted worshipers who couldn't make it over the mountains. Stroll the streets and seek out the onetime home of the infamous Grand Inquisitor Torquemada. On the way out, buy wine at any of three local bodegas.

Where to Stay & Eat

$$ ✕🏨 **Villafranca del Bierzo.** This modern, two-story hotel overlooks the Bierzo valley. Rooms have heavy wood furniture, shuttered windows, and large baths. Dine on fresh Bierzo trout, *surtido de verduras naturales* (mixed fresh vegetables), or *tournedo con higos agridulces* (a plump, juicy steak wrapped in bacon and served with marinated figs and wild mushrooms). Try the local Bierzo wine, made from the Mencia grape. ✉ *Calvo Sotelo s/n, 24500* ☎ *987/540175* 📠 *987/540010* 🌐 *www.parador.es* 🛏 *40 rooms* 👍 *Restaurant, bar, meeting room* 💳 *AE, DC, MC, V.*

OLD & NEW CASTILE A TO Z

To research prices, get advice from other travelers, and book travel arrangements, visit www.fodors.com.

AIR TRAVEL

The only international airport in Castile is Madrid's Barajas. Salamanca, León, and Valladolid have domestic airports.

ℹ Airport Information **Madrid** ✉ Aeropuerto de Barajas ☎ 91/3058343 🌐 www.aena.es/madrid-barajas. **León** ✉ Aeropuerto de León ☎ 987/877718. **Salamanca** ✉ Aeropuerto de Matacán ☎ 923/329600. **Valladolid** ✉ Aeropuerto de Valladolid ☎ 983/415400 🌐 www.aena.es.

BIKE TRAVEL

Taking bikes on Spanish intercity trains is problematic, and the very expensive alternative is to courier them. Most of Old and New Castile is the central Spain meseta bisected by mountains, with more mountains west of León province and north of Burgos; the area is generally flat, but extremely hot in summer. Although mad Spaniards do, it is not advisable to cycle on freeways. For bike rentals contact local tourist offices or check with rural hotels.

BUS TRAVEL

Bus connections between Madrid and Castile are excellent. There are several stations and stops; buses to **Toledo** (1 hour) leave every half hour from the Estación del Sur, while buses to **Segovia** (1½ hours) leave every hour from La Sepulvedana's headquarters. Larrea sends buses to **Segovia** and **Ávila** from the Méndez Alvaro Metro stop. Alsa travels to **León** (4½ hours) and **Valladolid** (2¼ hours), while Auto Res serves **Cuenca** (2¾ hours) and **Salamanca** (3 hours). Buses to **Soria** (3 hours), **El Burgo de Osma** (2½ hours), and **Burgos** (3½ hours) are run by Continental Auto.

From Burgos, buses head north to the Basque Country; from León, you can press on to Asturias. Services *between* towns are not as frequent as those to and from Madrid—if you're traveling between, say, Cuenca and Toledo, you'll find it quicker to return to Madrid and make your way from there. Reservations are rarely necessary; if demand exceeds supply, additional buses are usually called into service.

Bus Companies **Alsa** ☎ 902/422242 🌐 www.alsa.es. **Auto Res** ✉ Pl. Conde de Casal 6, Madrid ☎ 902/020999. **Continental Auto** ✉ Intercambiador Autobuses, Av. de América, Madrid ☎ 91/745-6300. **La Sepulvedana** ✉ Paseo de la Florida 11, Madrid ☎ 91/304800. **Larrea** ☎ 91/539-0005.

Bus Stations **Madrid: Estación del Sur** ✉ Méndez Alvaro s/n ☎ 91/468-4200. **Burgos** ✉ C. Miranda s/n ☎ 947/288855. **León** ✉ Paseo Ingeniero Saenz de Miera s/n ☎ 987/211000.

CAR RENTAL

Car rental prices are generally more reasonable outside of Toledo and Madrid. You will find outlets in Toledo, Ciudad Real, Segovia, Ávila, Salamanca, Valladolid, Burgos, and León. Try to arrange your rental before leaving home, as you'll likely save money. Spain's leading car rental agency is Atesa, which works in tandem with National.

Major National Agencies **Avis** ☎ 902/135531 🌐 www.avis.com. **Europcar** ☎ 902/105030 🌐 www.europcar.es. **Hertz** ☎ 902/402405 🌐 www.hertz.es. **National/Atesa** ☎ 902/100101 🌐 www.atesa.com.

Avila **Hertz** ✉ Poligono Las Hervencias, Parcela 3 ☎ 920/226035. **National/Atesa** ✉ Av. José Antonio s/n ☎ 920/255902.

Burgos **Avis** ✉ Maestro Justo Del Rio 2-4 ☎ 947/220606. **Hertz** ✉ Progreso 5 ☎ 947/275228. **National/Atesa** ✉ Ctra. Madrid-Irun, Km. 243, C. Rugauto ☎ 947/471837.

Cuenca **Europcar** ✉ Pl. de la Constitución 10 ☎ 969/233924. **National/Atesa** ✉ Estación de Ferrocarril San Cristobal ☎ 981/231242.

León **Alamo** ✉ Pl. de San Marcos ☎ 987/233297 🌐 www.alamo.com. **Avis** ✉ Aeropuerto de León ☎ 606/992924 ✉ Paseo de la Sagasta 34B ☎ 987/270075. **Europcar** ✉ Aeropuerto de León ☎ 987/300089. **Hertz** ✉ Pl. de San Marcos 6 ☎ 987/243905. **National/Atesa** ✉ Pl. San Marcos 2 ☎ 987/233297.

Salamanca **Alamo** ✉ Av. los Communeros ☎ 923/187998. **Avis** ✉ Paseo de Canalejas 49 ☎ 923/269753. **Europcar** ✉ Hotel NH, Palacio de Castellanos, San Pablo 58-64 ☎ 983/307461. **Hertz** ✉ Av. de Portugal 131 ☎ 923/243134. **National/Atesa** ✉ Av. de los Comuneros 30-32 ☎ 923/187998.

Segovia **Avis** ✉ José Zorrilla 123 ☎ 921/422584. **Hertz** ✉ Vía Roma 4 ☎ 921/440381.
Toledo **Avis** ✉ Venancio González 9 ☎ 925/214535. **Europcar** ✉ Aeropuerto de Alvedro ☎ 981/187285 ✉ Av. de Arteixo 21 ☎ 981/143536. **Hertz** ✉ Estación de Tren, Paseo de la Rosa 1 ☎ 925/253889.
Valladolid **Alamo** ✉ Aeropuerto de Valladolid ☎ 983/415429 ✉ Carrion Peru 9 ☎ 983/390337. **Avis** ✉ Aeropuerto de Valladolid ☎ 983/415530 ✉ Estación de Tren Campo Grande, Recondo, s/n ☎ 983/292222. **Europcar** ✉ Aeropuerto de Valladolid ☎ 983/415430 ✉ Estación Campo Grande Recondo s/n ☎ 983/307461. **Hertz** ✉ Aeropuerto de Valladolid ☎ 983/560256 ✉ Panaderos 25, ☎ 983/000222. **National/Atesa** ✉ Aeropuerto de Valladolid ☎ 983/415429.

CAR TRAVEL

Major roads with long stretches of divided highway—the N–I, II, III, IV, V, and Vl—radiate out from Madrid, making outlying towns easy to reach. If possible, avoid returning to Madrid on these roads at the end of a weekend or a public holiday. Side roads vary in quality, but they give rise to one of the great pleasures of driving around the Castilian countryside—constant surprise encounters with architectural monuments and wild and spectacular vistas.

EMERGENCIES

Emergencies: Fire, Police or Ambulance ☎ 112. **Guardia Civil** ☎ 062. **Insalud** (public health service) ☎ 061. **Policía Local** (local police) ☎ 092. **Policía Nacional** (national police) ☎ 091. **Servicio Marítimo** (Air-Sea Rescue) ☎ 902/202202. **Información Toxicológica** (poisoning) ☎ 915/620420.

LODGING

APARTMENT & VILLA RENTALS

While short-term city rentals are rare, rural tourism feeds a healthy rental market. Madrid and Beyond is a good British-run agency offering packages for individual visitors. The tourist offices in Salamanca and Toledo also have lodging information.

Local Agents **Madrid and Beyond** ✉ Gran Via 59, 28013 Madrid ☎ 91/7580063 🖷 91/5424391 🌐 www.madridandbeyond.com.

SPORTS & THE OUTDOORS

FISHING

The most common fish in Castile's rivers are trout, pike, black bass, and blue carp. The main trout rivers are the Eresma, Alto Duero, Júcar, Jarama, Manzanares, Tajo, and Tormes.

Consejería de Medio Ambiente ✉ Princesa 3 ☎ 91/580-1653 🌐 www.cma.junta-andalucia.es. **La Asociación Madrileña de Pesca** ☎ 91/320-9054.

GOLF

There are golf courses in or near Salamanca, León, Alcalá de Henares, and numerous smaller towns around Madrid.

Real Federación Española de Golf ✉ Capitán Haya 9, 28020 Madrid ☎ 91/555-2682.

TAXIS

All cities and most towns have public taxi services, sometimes several. They must show a license number and at the rear of the vehicle are the letters "SP" (*Servicio Público*). They usually have a sign on the roof reading "Taxi" and a sign on the windshield that reads either "*Libre*" in green or "*Ocupado*" in red. If a green light on the roof is lit, this means the car is for hire (libre). Taxis operate on meters within designated urban centers and fees are negotiable for further distances. The meter starts at a set figure, about €1.50, but should not be turned on until you start your journey. Drivers may charge more for extra luggage, for night and holiday services, and for going to and coming from airports or train stations. Give a tip based on service, with a minimum of 50 centimos.

TOURS

Local tourist offices can advise you on city tours and private guides. Be wary of local guides in Ávila and Toledo, however; they can be ruthless in trying to impose their services. If you hire one, do not buy goods in the shops he takes you to—the prices are likely inflated, as the guide gets a kickback. In summer, the tourist offices of Segovia, Toledo, and Aranjuez organize Trénes Turísticos (miniature tourist trains) that glide past all the major sights; contact the local tourist office for schedules, or call ☎ 925/142274 for information. Prospect Music & Art Tours Ltd. leads a special art tour of Castile. The best of Britain's cultural-tour specialists is Martin Randall, whose excellent five-day trip includes Madrid and Toledo. Equiberia leads horseback tours ranging from 1 to 10 days, a unique way to experience the gorges, fields, and forests of the Sierra de Guadarrama.

Fees & Schedules **Equiberia** ☎ 920/348338. **Martin Randall Travel** ✉ 10 Barley Mow Passage, Chiswick, London W4 4PH, U.K. ☎ 020/8742-3355 📠 020/8742-7766. **Prospect Music & Art Tours Ltd.** ✉ 36 Manchester St., London W1M 5PE, U.K. ☎ 020/7486-5704 📠 020/7486-5868.

TRAIN TRAVEL

Though it's often faster to travel by bus, all the main towns in Old and New Castile are accessible by train from Madrid. Several make feasible day trips: there are commuter trains from Madrid to Segovia (2 hours), Alcalá de Henares (45 minutes), Guadalajara (1 hour), and Toledo (1½ hours). Trains to Toledo depart from Madrid's Atocha station; trains to Salamanca, Burgos, and León depart from Chamartín; and both stations serve Ávila, Segovia, El Escorial, and Sigüenza, though Chamartín may have more frequent service. The one important town that's accessible only by train is Sigüenza. Trains from Segovia only go to Madrid, but you can change at Villalba for Avila and Salamanca.

Train Information **RENFE** ☎ 902/240202 🌐 www.renfe.es.

VISITOR INFORMATION

The central Castilian tourist office is in Madrid, near Plaza de las Cortes. Salamanca has a regional office for Old Castile (Castile-León), and Toledo's only tourist office covers New Castile (Castile–La Mancha). Local tourist offices have town maps.

Tourist Information **Madrid** ✉ Duque de Medinaceli 2 ☎ 91/429-4951. **Salamanca** ✉ Casa de las Conchas, Rúa Mayor s/n ☎ 923/268571. **Toledo** ✉ Puerta de Bisagra s/n ☎ 925/220843.

Local Tourist Offices **Alcalá de Henares** ✉ Callejón de Santa María ☎ 91/889-2694. **Almagro** ✉ Bernardas 2 ☎ 926/860717. **Aranjuez** ✉ Pl. San Antonio 9 ☎ 91/891-0427. **Astorga** ✉ Glorieta Eduardo de Castro 5 ☎ 987/618222. **Ávila** ✉ Pl. de la Catedral 4 ☎ 920/211387. **Burgos** ✉ Pl. Alonso Martínez 7 ☎ 947/203125. **Ciudad Real** ✉ Av. Alarcos 31 ☎ 926/212925. **Ciudad Rodrigo** ✉ Puerta de Amayuelas 5 ☎ 923/460561. **Consuegra** ✉ Molino de Viento/Bolero Windmill ☎ 925/475731. **Cuenca** ✉ Pl. Mayor 1 ☎ 969/232119. **Guadalajara** ✉ Pl. de los Caídos 6 ☎ 949/211626. **León** ✉ Pl. de Regla 3 ☎ 987/237082. **Ponferrada** ✉ Gil y Carrasco 4, next to castle ☎ 987/424236. **Salamanca** ✉ Pl. Mayor 14 ☎ 923/218342. **Segovia** ✉ Pl. Mayor 10 ☎ 921/460334. **Sigüenza** ✉ Paseo de la Alameda s/n ☎ 949/347007. **Soria** ✉ Pl. Ramón y Cajal s/n ☎ 975/212052. **Toledo** ✉ Puerta de Bisagra s/n ☎ 925/220843. **Valladolid** ✉ Santiago 19 ☎ 983/351801. **Zamora** ✉ C. Santa Clara 20 ☎ 980/531845.

CANTABRIA, THE BASQUE COUNTRY, NAVARRA & LA RIOJA

3

FODOR'S CHOICE

Arzak, Basque restaurant in San Sebastián
Guggenheim Museum Bilbao
Martín Berasategui, restaurant in San Sebastián
Mendigoikoa, farmhouse and restaurant in Axpe
Miró Hotel in Bilbao
Mugaritz, restaurant in San Sebastián
Museum of Fine Arts, Bilbao
Parador de Santillana Gil Blas, Santillana del Mar
Parador Príncipe de Viana, Olite
Posada Mayor de Migueloa, palace and tavern in Laguardia
Santillana del Mar, a stunning ensemble of stone houses
Txulotxo, restaurant in Pasajes de San Juan
Zuberoa, restaurant in San Sebastián

HIGHLY RECOMMENDED

RESTAURANTS
El Portalón, Vitoria
Guria, Bilbao
Kaia Kaipe, Guetaria
Urepel, San Sebastián

HOTELS
Carlton, Bilbao
Gran Hotel Domine, Bilbao
Hotel María Cristina, San Sebastián
Las Brisas, Santander
Lopez de Haro, Bilbao
Parador de Argómaniz

SIGHTS
Playing-Card Museum, Vitoria
Town of Santander

By George Semler

NORTHERN SPAIN IS A MOIST AND MISTY land of green hills, low russet rooflines, and colorful fishing villages. Santander, once the main seaport for Old Castile on the Bay of Biscay, is in a mountainous zone wedged between the Basque Country and, to the west, Asturias. Santander and the entire Cantabrian region are cool summer refuges for Madrileños, with sandy beaches, high sierra (including part of the Picos de Europa mountains), and tiny highland towns. The semiautonomous Basque Country, with its steady drizzle (onomatopoetically called the *sirimiri*), damp verdant landscape, and rugged coastline, is a distinct national and cultural entity within the Spanish state. The Navarra is considered Basque in the Pyrenees and just Navarran in its southern reaches, along the Ebro River. La Rioja, tucked between the Sierra de la Demanda (a small-to-mid-size mountain range that separates La Rioja from the central Castilian steppe) and the Ebro River, is Spain's premier wine country.

Called the País Vasco in Castilian Spanish, and Euskadi in the linguistically mysterious, non–Indo-European Basque language called Euskera, the Basque region is more a country within a country, or a nation within a state (the semantics are much debated). The Basques are known to love competition—it has been said that they will bet on anything that has numbers on it and moves (horses, dogs, runners, weightlifters—anything). Such traditional rural sports as chopping mammoth tree trunks, lifting boulders, and scything grass reflect the Basques' attachment to the land and to farm life as well as an ingrained enthusiasm for feats of strength and endurance. Even poetry and gastronomy become contests in Euskadi, as *bertsolaris* (amateur poets) improvise duels of sharp-witted verse, and male-only gastronomic societies compete in cooking contests to see who can make the best *sopa de ajo* (garlic soup) or *marmitako* (tuna stew).

The Basque Country has longtime connections with both Britain and the United States. Bilbao and its province, Vizcaya, provided iron for Britain's industrial revolution, and Elko, Nevada, is a longtime hub for emigrant Basque shepherds. An agricultural and fishing region before industry made it a center of productivity, the Basque Country has long sent waves of immigrants to the New World.

The much-reported Basque independence movement is made up of a small but radical sector of the political spectrum. The underground organization known as ETA, or Euskadi Ta Askatasuna (Basque Homeland and Liberty), has killed about 900 people in more than 30 years of terrorist activity. Conflict waxes and wanes, but the problem is extremely unlikely to affect travelers.

About the Restaurants

Basque food in and around San Sebastián and Bilbao combines the fish of the Atlantic with a love of sauces that is rare south of the Pyrenees—a result, no doubt, of Euskadi's proximity to France. The now 20-year-old *nueva cocina vasca* (new Basque cooking) movement has introduced exciting elements. San Sebastián specialties include *chuleta de buey* (garlicky beefsteak grilled over coals), and firm, flaky *besugo a la parrilla* (sea bream grilled over coals), also wallowing in golden chips of crisped garlic. Around Bilbao, *bacalao al pil-pil* is ubiquitous—cod-flank fillets cooked in a boiled emulsion of garlic and gelatin from the cod itself, so that the oil makes a popping noise ("pil-pil") and a white sauce is created. Other favorites are *kokotxas* (nuggets of cod jaw) and *pimientos de piquillo* (sweet red peppers stuffed with tuna or cod).

Cantabria's cooking is part mountain fare, such as roast kid and lamb or *cocidos* (bean stews) in the highlands, and part seafood on the coast.

If you have 3 days

If you're coming from Madrid or Burgos, drive through the Picos de Europa to Santander 2. Pop over to **Santillana del Mar** 3 to see the museum on the paintings in the nearby Altamira Caves. The next day, follow the Basque coast to **Bilbao** 8–16 for a morning visit to the Guggenheim; move on to **San Sebastián** 28 and lunch in the fishing port of **Guetaria** 27. Drive through **Pamplona** 31 and Navarra on your third day, approaching from the north if you're continuing across Spain, from the west (and then north) if you're France bound.

If you have 6 days

Coming from Madrid or Burgos, drive through the mountains on your way to the coast. Stop in **Santillana del Mar** 3 and then detour west to **Comillas** 4 and **San Vicente de la Barquera** 5. In **Santander** 2, check out the beach scene and wander around the Plaza Porticada. On day two, explore **Laredo** 6 and **Castro-Urdiales** 7. Stop in **Bilbao** 8–16 to see the Guggenheim Museum and other top sights. Devote your third day to the Basque Coast from Bilbao to San Sebastián, picking and choosing among **Bermeo** 19, **Elanchove** 23, **Lequeitio** 24, **Ondárroa** 25, and **Guetaria** 27, each of which outdoes the other in activity, color, and cuisine. Spend day four in sybaritic **San Sebastián** 28. Spend your fifth day in **Pamplona** 31 and the province of Navarra, from which you can continue through southern Navarra to the Basque capital, **Vitoria** 35. Tour La Rioja on day six: drive through **Laguardia** 36 and **Haro** 38 to the provincial capital, **Logroño** 37.

If you have 10 days

Spend one day exploring the mountains between Burgos and Santander: tour La Liébana valley around **Potes** 1 or drive through the highland town of Reinosa and down N611 along the River Saja, past semi-abandoned villages such as Bárcena Mayor. Spend the night near the Altamira Caves, ideally in the parador at **Santillana del Mar** 3. The next morning, detour west to **Comillas** 4 and **San Vicente de la Barquera** 5; then drive to **Santander** 2 and settle in for the day. If it's summer, see what's going on at the university. On day three, explore **Laredo** 6 and **Castro-Urdiales** 7 on your way to **Bilbao** 8–16 for the night. Tour the Guggenheim on the morning of day four; then head up the Basque coast for a night and a day in the fishing villages between **Bermeo** 19 and Zarauz. Visit the **Santuario de San Ignacio de Loyola** 26; take a walk around Zumaya; walk up the Urola River estuary to one of the quayside restaurants (Bedua is the best); *or* have lunch in **Guetaria** 27 after walking over from Zumaya through Askizu. Devote day six to **San Sebastián** 28. Day seven is a chance to see tiny **Pasajes de San Juan** 29; spend that night in a caserío such as the Artzu, which overlooks the ocean and the town of **Hondarribia** 30, which you can see on day eight. If you're inspired, ride the launch to Hendaye, France. Overnight back at the Parador El Emperador before heading up the Bidasoa River into the foothills of the Pyrenees. Explore upper Navarra and **Pamplona** 31 on day nine. If you're here during San Fermín, consider trying a smaller and saner version of this fiesta in the village of Lesaka. Finally, tour **Vitoria** 35 and taste wines in **Laguardia** 36 and **Haro** 38 on the way to **Logroño** 37.

Soropotun is Santander's stew of bonito, potatoes, and vegetables. Navarra is famous for beef, lamb, and vegetable dishes, including *menestra de verduras* (a stew of artichokes, green beans, peas, lettuce, potatoes, onion, and chunks of cured ham). La Rioja is known for meaty stews and roasts in the mountains and vegetable dishes in the Ebro River basin.

The local Basque wine, *txakolí,* is a young, white brew made from tart green grapes, a refreshing accompaniment to both seafood and meats. La Rioja, south of the Basque Country, produces the finest wines in Spain; purists insisting on Basque wine with their Basque cuisine could choose a Rioja Alavesa, from the north side of the Ebro. Navarra also produces some fine vintages, especially rosés and reds—and in such quantity that some churches in Allo, Peralta, and other towns were actually built with a mortar mixed with wine instead of water.

Food isn't cheap in the Basque Country, but some of Europe's finest cuisine is served here in settings that range from the traditional hewn beams and stone walls of old farmhouses to contemporary international restaurants. Don't miss any chance to go to a *sidrería,* a cider house (in Astigarraga, near San Sebastián, there are no fewer than 17) where *tortilla de bacalao* (cod omelet) and thick chuletas de buey provide the traditional ballast for copious draughts of hard apple cider.

WHAT IT COSTS In Euros

	$$$$	$$$	$$	$	¢
AT DINNER	over €20	€15–€20	€10–€15	€6–€10	under €6

Prices are per person for a main course at dinner.

About the Hotels

The largely industrial and well-to-do north is an expensive part of Spain, which is reflected in room rates. San Sebastián is particularly pricey, and Pamplona rates double or triple during the San Fermín fiesta in July. Reserve ahead for Bilbao, where the Guggenheim Museum is filling hotels, and nearly everywhere else in summer. Another lodging option is the Agroturismo lodging network, which often offers rooms in a Basque *caserío* (farmhouse). Check with local tourist offices for details.

WHAT IT COSTS In Euros

	$$$$	$$$	$$	$	¢
FOR 2 PEOPLE	over €180	€100–€180	€60–€100	€40–€60	under €40

Prices are for two people in a standard double room in high season, excluding tax.

Exploring Cantabria, the Basque Country, Navarra & La Rioja

Northern Spain's Bay of Biscay area, at the western end of the Pyrenees and the border with France, is where the Cantabrian Cordillera and the Pyrenees nearly meet. The moist green foothills of the Basque Country and, to the west, Cantabria, gently fill this space between the otherwise unbroken chain of mountains that rises from the Iberian Peninsula's easternmost point at northern Catalonia's Cap de Creus and ends at western Galicia's Fisterra, or Finisterre, land's end. Navarra—part Basque and part Castilian-speaking Navarrese—lies just southeast and inland of the Basque country, with the backdrop of the Pyrenees rising up to the north. La Rioja, below Navarra, nestles in the Ebro River valley under

Beaches

Santander has excellent sandy beaches, and the beach at Laredo, between Santander and Bilbao, is one of Spain's best and least known. Between Bilbao and San Sebastián, the beach at Lequeitio is particularly beautiful, and the smaller beaches at Zumaya, Guetaria, and Zarauz are usually quiet. San Sebastián's best beach, La Concha, which curves around the bay along with the city itself, is scenic and clean, but packed in the summer; Ondarreta, at the western end of La Concha, is often less crowded. Surfers gather at Zurriola on the northern side of the Urumea River. Hondarribia, the last stop before the French border, has a vast expanse of fine sand along the Bidasoa estuary.

Fiestas

Pamplona's feast of **San Fermín** (July 6–14) was made famous by Ernest Hemingway in *The Sun Also Rises* and remains best known for its running of the bulls. Bilbao's **Semana Grande** (Grand Week), in early August, is notorious for the largest bulls of the season and a fine series of street concerts. The coastal town of Lequeitio, east of Bilbao, is famous for its unusual **Fiestas de San Antolín,** in which men dangle (on September 5) from the necks of dead geese strung on a cable over the inlet. Closer to San Sebastián, in the first week of August, the fishing village of **Guetaria** celebrates Juan Sebastián Elkano's completion of Magellan's voyage around the world every other year. San Sebastián hosts a renowned **international film festival** in late September and celebrates its saint's day on January 19–20 with **La Tamborrada,** when 100-odd platoons of chefs and Napoleonic soldiers parade hilariously through the streets. San Vicente de la Barquera honors its patron saint with a famous maritime procession for **La Folía,** April 21. La Rioja's famous **Batalla del Vino** (Wine Battle), a free-for-all honoring the fruit of the vine, takes place in Haro on June 29. Vitoria's weeklong **Fiesta de la Virgen Blanca** (Festival of the White Virgin) celebrates the city's patron saint with bullfights and general carousing beginning on August 4.

Hiking

Well-marked footpaths wend from the Cordillera Cantábrica to the Pyrenees and along the Basque coast, connecting towns, scaling mountains, and ambling from one fishing village to another. The air, color, and scenery far exceed anything you'll experience in a car. Try the walks around Zumaya, or the walk over Jaizkibel between San Sebastián and the French border. The GR11 trail crosses the Pyrenees of Navarra, while the Camino de Santiago pilgrimage route crosses Navarra and La Rioja on its way west.

Sports

Basques are as passionate about sports as they are about food, and you need not participate to catch the action. If you do want to get up and about, there's excellent sailing, surfing, windsurfing, and trout or Atlantic-salmon fishing in various parts of this rich terrain. Pelota—any number of ball games played against a wall—is the Basque national sport. Most towns have a local *frontón* (backboard or wall), where games normally start at 4 or 4:30 PM. Other Basque rural sports (*herrikirolak*) include the tug-of-war and log-chopping, ram-butting, and scything competitions. The most idiosyncratic contest is the *harrijasotazailes,* the raising of huge rocks by practiced stone lifters. You'll also find *Jai-alai* (a generic term for ball games from handball to *cesta punta,* played with wicker gloves), *trainera* (whale-boat regattas), and horse races. Athletic de Bilbao has traditionally been the Basque fútbol giant, with San Sebastián's Real Sociedad just behind, though recently roles have been reversed. Pamplona, Vitoria, and Santander also field first division soccer teams.

---

the Sierra de la Demanda to the south, and stretches east and downriver to Calahorra and the edge of Spain's central meseta.

Numbers in the text correspond to numbers in the margin and on the Cantabria, the Basque Country, Navarra & La Rioja and the Bilbao maps.

Timing

May–June and September–October are the best times to enjoy good weather and avoid the tourist crush, which peaks in August. The Basque Country is rainy, especially in winter; summer is temperate.

CANTABRIA

Historically part of Old Castile, the province of Cantabria was called Santander until 1984, when it became an Autonomous Community. The most direct route from Burgos to Santander is the slow but scenic N623 through the Cordillera Cantábrica, past the Ebro reservoir. For a memorable glimpse of Cantabria's section of the Picos de Europa mountains, however, drive through La Liébana valley via Palencia and Potes, reaching the coast at San Vicente de la Barquera.

Potes

❶ *51 km (31 mi) south of San Vicente de la Barquera, 115 km (69 mi) west of Santander, 173 km (104 mi) north of Palencia.*

Known for its fine cheeses made of milk from cows, goats, and sheep, La Liébana is a highland domain well worth exploring. Named for and sprinkled with ancient bridges, the town of Potes surrounds you with the stunning 9th-century **monasteries** of Santo Toribio de Liébana, Lebeña, and Piasca. The gorges of the Desfiladero de la Hermida pass are 3 km (2 mi) north, and the rustic town of Mogrovejo is on the way to the vertiginous cable car at Fuente Dé, 25 km (15 mi) west of Potes. As you approach **Fuente Dé** by car or foot, you'll see a wall of gray stone rising 6,560 ft straight into the air. Visible at the top is the tiniest of huts: your destination. To get there, you entrust your life to a little red-and-white funicular (€8 round-trip). Once at the top, you're hiking along the Ávila Mountain pasturelands, rich in native wildlife, between the central and eastern massifs of the Picos. There's an official entrance to Picos de Europa National Park up here.

Where to Stay & Eat

$–$$ ✕ **El Bodegón.** Simple, friendly, and cozy, this spot serves a fine *cocido montañes* (mountain stew of sausage, garbanzo beans, and vegetables). *✉ San Roque 4 ☎ 942/730247 ▭ AE, DC, MC, V ⊗ Closed Mon.*

$ 🏨 **Casa Cayo.** You can see this relaxing refuge's attractive brown balconies from the main bridge in town. The Casa has a wide terrace overlooking the river, and a lovely salon with a fireplace for chilly nights in winter or summer. The rooms retain a rustic mountain aesthetic, with wood floors and exposed beams overhead. *✉ Cántabra 6, 39570 ☎ 942/730150 📠 942/730119 ⇆ 16 rooms ▭ AE, DC, MC, V.*

Santander

★ ❷ *390 km (242 mi) north of Madrid, 154 km (96 mi) north of Burgos, 116 km (72 mi) west of Bilbao.*

Santander is one of the great ports on the Bay of Biscay. It's surrounded by beaches that are by no means isolated, but lack the sardinelike package-tour feel of so many Mediterranean resorts. A fire destroyed most of the old town in 1941, so the rebuilt city looks relatively modern; and although it has traditionally been a conservative stronghold loyal to the Spanish state (in contrast to its Basque neighbors), Santander is lively, especially in summer, when its university and music-and-dance festival fill the city with students and performers from abroad. Portus Victoriae, as Santander was then called, was a major port in the 1st- to 4th-century Roman Hispania Ulterior (and even earlier under the aboriginal Cántabros). Commercial life accelerated between the 13th and 16th centuries, but the waning of Spain's naval power and a series of plagues during the reign of Felipe II caused Santander's fortunes to plummet in the late 16th century. Its economy revived after 1778, when Seville's monopoly on trade with the Americas was revoked and Santander entered fully into commerce with the New World. In 1910 the Palacio de la Magdalena was built by popular subscription as a gift to Alfonso XIII and his queen, Victoria Eugenia, lending Santander prestige as one of Spain's royal watering spots.

Santander benefits from promenades and gardens, most of them facing the bay. Walk east along the Paseo de Pereda, the main boulevard, to the Puerto Chico, a small yacht harbor. Past the Puerto Chico, follow Avenida Reina Victoria, and you'll come to the tree-lined park paths above the first of the city's beaches, Playa de la Magdalena. Walk onto the Península de la Magdalena to the Palacio de la Magdalena, today the summer seat of the University of Menéndez y Pelayo, which conducts Spanish-language and -culture courses for foreigners. Beyond the Magdalena Peninsula, wealthy locals have built mansions facing the long stretch of shoreline known as El Sardinero, Santander's best beach. The heart of El Sardinero is the Belle Epoque **Gran Casino del Sardinero,** an elegant casino and restaurant worth a quick visit even if gaming tables hold no charms for you. A white building fronted with red awnings and set in a park among sycamores, the casino lies at the center of the vacationer's Santander, surrounded by expensive hotels and several fine restaurants. ✉ *Plaza de Italia s/n* ☎ *942/276054* 🎫 *Free* 🕒 *8 PM–4 AM; slot machines open at 5 PM.*

In the old city, the center of life is the **Plaza Porticada,** officially called the Plaza Velarde. In August this unassuming little square is the seat of Santander's star event, the outdoor International Festival of Music and Dance. The blockish **Catedral de Santander** marks the transition between Romanesque and Gothic. Though largely rebuilt in the neo-Gothic style after serious damage in the 1941 fire, the cathedral retained its 12th-century crypt. The chief attraction here is the tomb of Marcelino Menéndez y Pelayo (1856–1912), Santander's most famous literary figure. The cathedral is across Avenida de Calvo Sotelo from the Plaza Porticada. ✉ *Somorrostro s/n* ☎ *942/226024* 🎫 *Free* 🕒 *Weekdays 10–1 and 4–7:30, weekends 8–2 and 4:30–8.*

The **Museo Municipal de Bellas Artes** (Municipal Museum of Fine Arts) has works by Flemish, Italian, and Spanish artists. Goya's portrait of absolutist king Fernando VII is worth seeking out; the smirking face of the lion at the king's feet clues you in to Goya's feelings toward his patron. The same building holds the **Biblioteca Menéndez y Pelayo** (☎ 942/

Bay of Biscay
Bay of Santander
San Vicente de la Barquera
Santillana del Mar
Santander
Comillas
Altamira Caves
Camargo
Ajo
Laredo
Colindres
Castro-Urdiales
Cabenzon de la Sal
Potes
CANTABRIA
Arenas de Iguña
Ontaneda
N634
N611
N623
C6318
Algorta
Baracaldo
Bilbao
8 - 16 see detail map
Reinosa
P. del Ebro
Villasante
Cilleruelo
Amurrio
Villarcayo
N625
Berberana
Valdenoceda
Oña
C629
0
20 miles
30 km
Masa
Villadiego
Briviesca
N1
A1
Santo Domingo de la Calzada
Belorado
Melgar
N120
Burgos
Rubena
CASTILE–LEON
N620
Cuevas de S. Clemente
N234
Canales de la Sierra
C110
Salas de los Infantes
Lerma
Arlanza
KEY
Regions
Rail Lines
TO MADRID
Navaleno

Cantabria, the Basque Country, Navarra & La Rioja

234534), a library with some 50,000 volumes, and the writer's study, kept as it was in his day. ✉ *C. Rubio s/n* ☎ *942/239485* 🎟 *Free* ⏱ *Museum Tues.–Fri. 10–1 and 5–8, Sat. 10–1. Library weekdays 9–2 and 4–9:30, Sat. 9–1:30.*

Where to Stay & Eat

$$–$$$ ✕ **Zacarías.** Whether you want tapas or dinner in full, try out this popular place, known for northern Spanish specialties. Owner and chef Zacarías Puente-Herboso is a well-known food writer and an authority on Cantabrian recipes. Sample the *maganos encebollados* (calamari and caramelized onion) or the *alubias rojas estofadas* (red beans stewed with sausage). ✉ *General Mola 41* ☎ *942/212333* 💳 *AE, DC, MC, V.*

$$ ✕ **Bodega del Riojano.** The paintings on wine-barrel ends that decorate this restaurant have given it the sobriquet Museo Redondo (Round Museum). The building dates back to the 16th century, when it was a wine cellar, and this incarnation lives on in dark-wood beams and tables. The menu changes daily and seasonally, but the fish of the day is always a sure bet. Desserts are homemade. ✉ *Río de la Pila 5* ☎ *942/216750* 💳 *AE, DC, MC, V* ⏱ *No dinner Sun. Oct.–May.*

★ $$–$$$ 🏨 **Las Brisas.** Jesús García and his wife, Teresa, run this 80-year-old mansion as an upscale, cottage-style hotel by the sea. Each room or apartment is different, from dollhouse alcoves to an odd but attractive family duplex apartment. The basement bar and breakfast room are especially cozy. You're a short walk from the beach, and many of the rooms have fine views out to sea. ✉ *C. la Braña 14, 39005* ☎ *942/270991 or 942/275011* 📠 *942/281173* 🌐 *www.brisas.spain.com* ⇆ *13 rooms, 12 apartments* △ *Bar* 💳 *AE, DC, MC, V.*

$$–$$$ 🏨 **México.** Don't be put off by the modest exterior. The personal touch still counts in this family-run inn, and the breakfast room is elegant, with Queen Anne chairs, inlaid porcelain rosettes, and oak wainscoting. The rooms are pleasant, with high ceilings and glassed-in balconies. Reserve in advance, as word of this good deal has gotten around. ✉ *Calderón de la Barca 3, 39002* ☎ *942/212450* 📠 *942/229238* 🌐 *www.hotel-mexico.com* ⇆ *30 rooms* △ *Restaurant, bar* 💳 *MC, V.*

Nightlife & the Arts

Santander's big event is its International Festival of Music and Dance, which attracts leading artists throughout August. Many festival concerts are staged in the Plaza Porticada; others are held in monasteries, palaces, and churches. Collect information at the tourist office or at seasonal box offices in the Plaza Porticada and the Jardines de Pereda park. Santander's **Teatro Coliseum** (✉ Plaza de los Remedios 1 ☎ 942/211460) is a movie theater that becomes a theater proper in summer.

Shopping

Santander is known for ceramics. There are several touristy retailers on Calle Arrabal, downtown, but **La Muralla,** (✉ No. 17 ☎ 942/160301), is known locally as the best.

Santillana del Mar

❸ *29 km (18 mi) west of Santander.*

Fodor's Choice ★

This stunning ensemble of 15th- to 17th-century stone houses is one of Spain's greatest troves of medieval and Renaissance architecture. The town is built around the **Colegiata,** Cantabria's finest Romanesque structure, with a 17th-century altarpiece, the tomb of local martyr Santa Juliana, and sculpted capitals depicting biblical scenes. The adjoining Regina Coeli convent has a **Museo Diocesano** (☎ 942/598105) with liturgical art. ✉ *Av. Le Dorat 2* ☎ *942/818004* 🎟 *Colegiata and museum each €3* ⏲ *Daily 10–1 and 4–7 (closed Wed. Oct.–May).*

The world-famous **Altamira Caves,** 3 km (2 mi) southwest of Santillana del Mar, have been called the Sistine Chapel of Prehistoric Art for the beauty of their drawings, believed to be some 20,000 years old. First uncovered in 1875, the caves illustrate humans' love of beauty and their technical skill—especially in the use of rock forms to accentuate perspective. Visitors must now apply two or three years in advance to be among the 25 people allowed into the caves each day; if you're a preternaturally early planner, write to the address below with the number and names of the people in your group, and the date you hope to visit. The adjoining **museum** and another cave with rock formations are open to all. ✉ *Centro de Investigación de Altamira, 39330 Santillana del Mar, Cantabria* ☎ *942/818005.*

Where to Stay & Eat

$$$ Fodor'sChoice ★ **Parador de Santillana Gil Blas.** Built in the 16th century, this lovely parador is in the erstwhile summer home of the Barreda-Bracho family. Rooms are baronial, with rich drapes and antique furnishings. The dining hall serves good local fare and is elegant, if less than intimate. ✉ *Pl. Ramón Pelayo 8, 39330* ☎ *942/818000* 📠 *942/818391* *54 rooms* *Restaurant, bar, parking (fee)* 💳 *AE, DC, MC, V.*

$–$$ **Casona Solar de Hidalgos.** The library, the roomy attic apartment, the antique furniture, and the creaky wooden floors all add to the charm of this 16th-century manor house (*casona*) in the heart of Spain's finest Renaissance town. ✉ *Santo Domingo 5, 39330* ☎ *942/818387* 📠 *942/818387* 🌐 *www.solardehidalgos.com* *12 rooms* *Bar* 💳 *AE, DC, MC, V.*

off the beaten path

PUENTE VIESGO – If you can't sit through the Altamira Caves' 700-day cooling-off period, try Puente Viesgo. In 1903, this 16th-century hamlet in the Pas Valley excavated four caves under the 1,150-ft peak of Monte del Castillo, one of which—the Cueva del Castillo—is open to the public. Bison, deer, bulls, and even humanoid stick figures are depicted; the oldest designs are thought to be 35,000 years old. Most arresting are the paintings of 44 (curiously, 35 of them left) hands, reaching out through time. The painters are thought to have blown red pigment around their hands through a hollow bone, leaving the negative image. ✉ *Ctra. N623, Km 28 (from Santander)* ☎ *942/598425* 🎟 *€2* ⏲ *Apr.–Oct., Tues.–Sun. 9–noon and 3–6:30; Nov.–Mar., Wed.–Sun. 9–2.*

Comillas

❹ *49 km (30 mi) west of Santander.*

This astounding pocket of Catalan Art Nouveau architecture in the green hills of Cantabria will make you rub your eyes in disbelief. Why is it here? The Marqués de Comillas, a Catalan named Antonio López y López (1817–83)—the wealthiest and most influential shipping magnate of his time—was a fervent patron of the arts who encouraged the great Moderniste architects to use his native village as a laboratory. Antonio Gaudí's 1883–89 green and yellow-tile villa, El Capricho (a direct cousin of his Casa Vicens in Barcelona), is the main attraction. The town cemetery is filled with Art Nouveau markers and monuments, most notably an immense angel by eminent Catalan sculptor Josep Llimona (1864–1934). Only a small part of the colossal hilltop ex-seminary **Universidad Pontificia,** designed by Catalan Moderniste architect Joan Martorell, is open to the public, and once inside you see cloisters in disrepair. The colorful church is the only treat. ☎ *942/722543* €2 ⊙ *Tues.–Sun. 10:30–1:30 and 3:30–6:30.*

Palacio Sobrellano, once the home of the Marqués de Comillas, has furnishings designed by a young Gaudí. ☎ *942/720339* ⊙ *Wed.–Sun. 10–2 and 4–7 fall–spring; daily 10–2 and 4–7 in summer.*

Where to Eat

$$$–$$$$ ✕ **El Capricho de Gaudí.** A chance to dine in a Gaudí creation is all but an obligation, especially if the visual rush is accompanied by fresh turbot with young garlic or roast lamb from the moist Cantabrian hills. ✉ *Barrio de Sobrellano* ☎ *942/720365* ▭ *AE, DC, MC, V* ⊙ *Closed Jan. 10–Feb. 10 and Mon. Oct.–May. No dinner Sun.*

San Vicente de la Barquera

❺ *64 km (40 mi) west of Santander, 15 km (9 mi) west of Comillas.*

Important as a Roman port long before many other larger, modern shipping centers (such as Santander) were, San Vicente de la Barquera is one of the oldest and most beautiful maritime settlements in northern Spain. The 28 arches of the ancient bridge **Puente de la Maza,** which spans the *ría* (fjord), welcome you to town. Thanks to its exceptional Romanesque portals, the 15th-century church of **Nuestra Señora de los Angeles** (Our Lady of the Angels) is among San Vicente's most memorable sights. Make sure you check out the arcaded porticoes of the **Plaza Mayor** and the view over the town from the Unquera road (N634) just inland. San Vicente celebrates **La Folía** in late April (the name translates roughly as "folly," and the exact date depends not only on Easter but on the high tide) with a magnificent maritime procession: the town's colorful fishing fleet accompanies the figure of La Virgen de la Barquera as she is transported (in part) by boat from her sanctuary outside town to the village church, where she is honored with folk dances and songs before being returned to her hermitage.

Where to Stay & Eat

$–$$ ✕🏨 **Boga-Boga.** This relatively modern building is surrounded by some of San Vicente's most ancient structures, in the center of the *casco viejo* (old town). Rooms are comfortable and unpretentious, although not especially charming. The restaurant specializes in seafood, such as *merluza al boga-boga* (stewed cod) and *cabracho,* an aromatic, dark-meat goat. ✉ *Pl. José Antonio 9, 39540* ☎ *942/710135* 📠 *942/710151* *18 rooms* *Restaurant, café, bar* ▭ *AE, DC, MC, V* ⊙ *Restaurant closed Tues. Oct.–May.*

Laredo

❻ *49 km (30 mi) southeast of Santander (N635 southeast, N634 east).*

You would hardly know it today, but Laredo was a home port of the Spanish Armada and remained Spain's chief northern harbor until the French sacked it in the 18th century and Santander became the regional capital. This little town was thus visited by the Spanish royals, including Isabella the Catholic and Charles I, better known as the Holy Roman Emperor Carlos V. When Charles—the most powerful monarch in European history—stopped by in the mid-16th century, he donated two brass choir desks in the shape of eagles. Charles I's brass choir desks are on display in the parish church of **La Asunción** (Church of the Assumption), in the center of the town's tiny *parte antigua* (old quarter), which you may want to walk through to see mansions with heraldic coats of arms.

Where to Stay & Eat

$$–$$$ **El Risco.** *Risco* is Spanish for "cliff," which is appropriate for this place because it's built into the craggy slope overlooking Laredo. The food combines classical and contemporary Cantabrian fare; try the *pimientos rellenos de cangrejo y de buey de mar* (peppers stuffed with crab and fish). Every room has a spectacular view of the town and cove below. Hotel reservations are essential in summer. ✉ *La Arenosa 2, 39770* ☎ *942/605030* 🖷 *942/605055* 🌐 *www.hotelrisco.com* *25 rooms* *Restaurant, bar* 💳 *AE, DC, MC, V* ⏲ *Restaurant closed Wed. Sept.–June.*

3

Castro-Urdiales

❼ *34 km (21 mi) northwest of Bilbao.*

Behind Laredo, the N634 winds up into the hills, with views of the Bay of Santoña over your shoulder. A short drive, parts of it within sight of the coast, takes you into the fishing village of Castro-Urdiales, believed to be the oldest settlement on the Cantabrian coast. Castro-Urdiales (*castro* was the Celtiberian word for a fortified village) was the region's leading whaling port in the 13th and 14th centuries when it had almost three times today's 13,000 residents. Now it's known mainly for its seafood. Overlooking the town is the mammoth, rose-color jumble of roofs and buttresses of the Gothic **Santa María** church. Behind the Santa María church is the medieval **castle,** to which a modern lighthouse has been appended. Aside from its arcaded **Plaza del Ayuntamiento** and the narrow streets of its **old quarter** (much of which burned on May 11, 1813), the main things to see in Castro-Urdiales are the Santa María church, looming Gothically over the town, the ruins of the fortress converted into a lighthouse beside it, and the harborfront promenade flanked by a row of glass-gallery houses.

en route

The 45-minute drive on the N634 from Castro-Urdiales to Bilbao takes you through some of the sprawling industrial development that mars much of Vizcaya, the westernmost of the three Basque provinces.

Where to Eat

$$–$$$ **Mesón Marinero.** Local fishermen rub elbows with visiting elites at this pearl of a tavern and restaurant. The tapas on the bar will tempt you to forgo the main meal; if you manage not to *tapear* away the dinner hour, you're in for a treat in the second-floor dining room overlooking Castro's weathered fishing port. *Besugo* (sea bream) is unbeatable here. ✉ *La Correría 23* ☎ *942/860005* 💳 *AE, DC, MC, V.*

BILBAO & THE BASQUE COAST TO GUETARIA

Starring Frank Gehry's titanium meteorite, the Museo Guggenheim Bilbao, Bilbao has suddenly become Spain's 21st-century darling. The loop around the coast of Vizcaya and east into neighboring Guipúzcoa province to Guetaria and San Sebastián is a succession of colorful ports, ocher beaches, and green hills.

Bilbao

8–16 *34 km (21 mi) southeast of Castro-Urdiales, 116 km (72 mi) east of Santander, 397 km (247 mi) north of Madrid.*

Time in Bilbao (Bilbo, in Euskera) may soon need to be identified as BG or AG (Before Guggenheim, After Guggenheim). Never has a single monument of art and architecture so radically changed a city—or, for that matter, a nation, and in this case two: Spain and Euskadi. Frank Gehry's stunning museum, Norman Foster's sleek subway system, and the glass Santiago Calatrava footbridge have all helped foment a cultural revolution in the commercial capital of the Basque Country. Greater Bilbao now encompasses almost 1 million inhabitants, nearly half the total population of the Basque Country and the fourth-largest urban population in Spain. Founded in 1300 by Vizcayan noble Diego López de Haro, Bilbao became an industrial center in the mid-19th century, largely due to the abundance of minerals in the surrounding hills. An affluent industrial class grew up here, as did the working-class suburbs (like Portugalete and Baracaldo) that line the Margen Izquierda (Left Bank) of the Nervión estuary.

Bilbao's new attractions get more press, but the city's old treasures still quietly line the banks of the rust-color Nervión River. The Casco Viejo (old quarter)—also known as Siete Calles (Seven Streets)—is a charming jumble of shops, bars, and restaurants on the river's Right Bank, near the Puente del Arenal bridge. Throughout the old quarter are ancient mansions emblazoned with family coats of arms, noble wooden doors, and fine ironwork balconies. Carefully restored after devastating floods in August 1983, this is now an upscale shopping district replete with excellent taverns, restaurants, and nightlife. The most interesting square is the 64-arch Plaza Nueva, where an outdoor market is pitched every Sunday morning. On the Left Bank, the wide, late-19th-century boulevards of the Ensanche neighborhood, such as Gran Vía (the main shopping artery) and Alameda Mazarredo, are the city's more formal face. Bilbao's cultural institutions include, along with the Guggenheim, a major (BG) museum of fine arts, and an opera society (ABAO: Asociacion Bilbaina de Amigos de la Opera) with 7,000 members from all over Spain and parts of southern France. In addition, epicureans have long ranked Bilbao's culinary offerings among the best in Spain. Don't miss a chance to ride the speedy and quiet new trolley line, the Euskotran, opened in early 2003, for a trip along the river from Atxuri station to the Santiago Calatrava bridge just upstream from the Guggenheim.

8 The **Casco Viejo** is folded into an elbow of the Nervión River behind Bilbao's grand, elaborately restored theater. In exploring the Casco Viejo, don't miss the colossal food market **El Mercado de la Ribera** at the edge of the river, the **Palacio Yohn** at the corner of Sant Maria and Perro, and the **Biblioteca Municipal Bidebarrieta** at C. Bidebarrieta 4. Inaugurated in 1890, **Teatro Arriaga** was a symbol of Bilbao's industrial might and cultural vibrancy by the time it burned nearly to the ground in 1914. Styled after the Paris Opéra by architect Joaquín Rucoba (1844–1909), the theater defies easy classification: while its symmetry and formal repetition suggest neoclassicism, its ornamentation defines the Belle Epoque style. Walk around the building to see the stained glass on its back. ✉ *Plaza Arriaga 1* ☎ *94/416–3333.*

9 Stop at Calle Esperanza 6 and take the elevator to the **Basílica de Begoña** overlooking the city. The church's Gothic hulk was begun in 1519 on a spot where the Virgin Mary had supposedly appeared long before.

10 Near the Ayuntamiento Bridge is the riverside ***ayuntamiento*** (city hall), built in 1892.

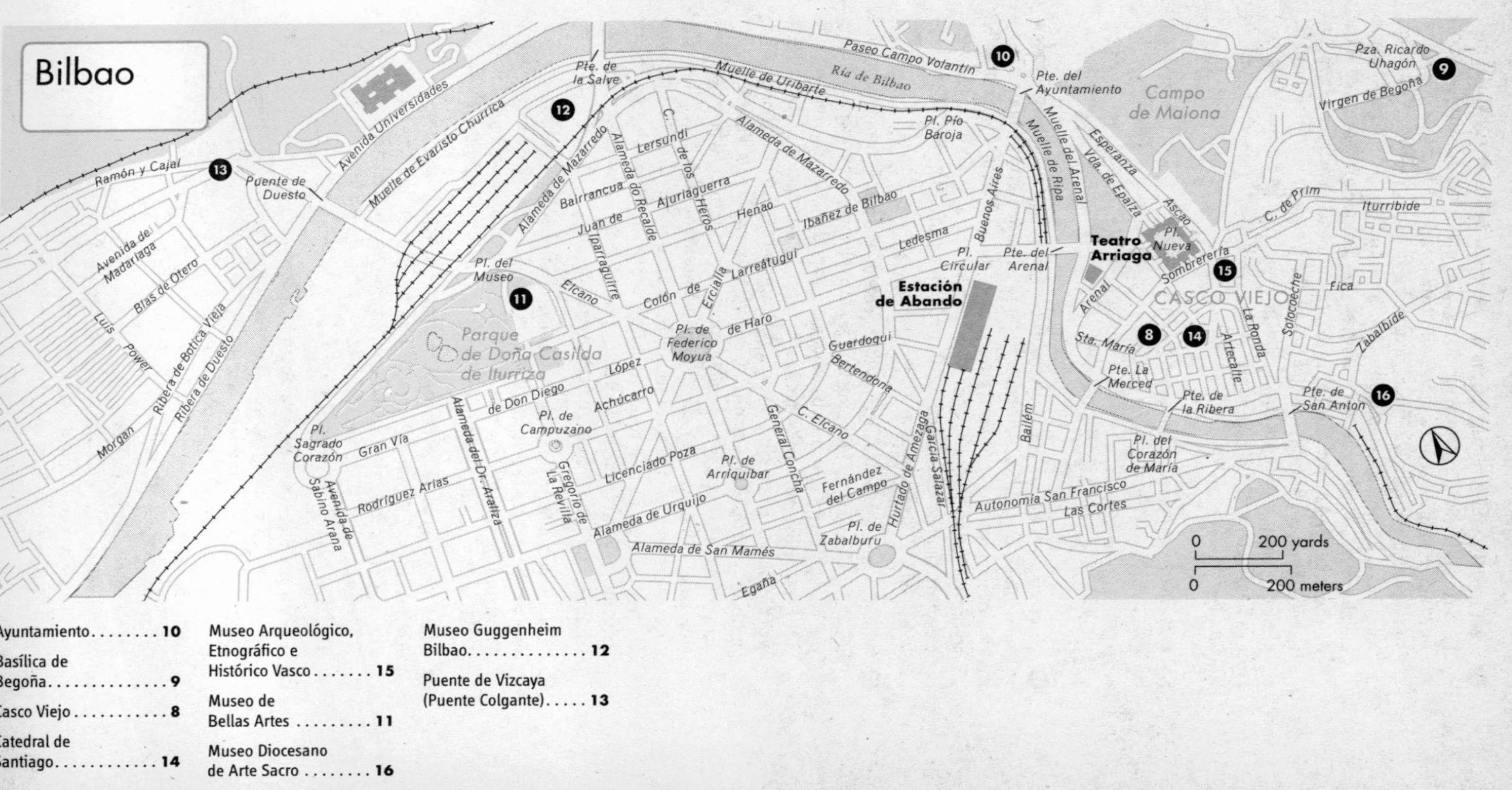

Ayuntamiento **10**

Basílica de Begoña **9**

Casco Viejo **8**

Catedral de Santiago **14**

Museo Arqueológico, Etnográfico e Histórico Vasco **15**

Museo de Bellas Artes **11**

Museo Diocesano de Arte Sacro **16**

Museo Guggenheim Bilbao **12**

Puente de Vizcaya (Puente Colgante) **13**

11 Fodor'sChoice ★ Don't let the Guggenheim eclipse the **Museo de Bellas Artes** (Museum of Fine Arts). Depending on your tastes, you may find the art here more satisfying. The museum's fine collection of Flemish, French, Italian, and Spanish paintings includes works by El Greco, Goya, Velázquez, Zurbarán, Rivera, and Gauguin. One large and excellent section traces developments in 20th-century Spanish and Basque art alongside those of their better-known European contemporaries, such as Léger and Bacon. The building sits on the rim of the pretty Doña Casilda park, about 30 minutes' walk from the old quarter. ✉ *Parque de Doña Casilda Iturriza* ☎ *94/439–6060* *€5, free Wed.* ⏲ *Tues.–Sat. 10–1:30 and 4–7:30, Sun. 10–2.*

need a break?

El Kiosko del Arenal (Paseo del Arenal s/n, under the bandstand in Paseo del Arenal) is an excellent place for a coffee, beer, or tapas. Terrace tables offer views of the river in summer, while underneath the bandstand is a paradigmatic clean, well-lighted place in winter.

12 Fodor'sChoice ★ Covered with a dazzling 30,000 sheets of titanium, the **Museo Guggenheim Bilbao** opened in October 1997 and became Bilbao's main attraction overnight. The enormous atrium, more than 150 ft high, is connected to the 19 galleries by a system of suspended metal walkways and glass elevators. The ground floor is dedicated to large installations. ☎ *94/435–9080* *€9* ⏲ *Tues.–Sun. 10–8.*

13 Down in the Nervión's estuary is the **Puente de Vizcaya**—commonly called the Puente Colgante (Hanging Bridge). A transporter hung from cables, the bridge ferries cars and passengers across the Nervión, uniting two distinct worlds: exclusive, quiet Las Arenas and Portugalete, a much older, working-class town that spawned Dolores Ibarruri, the famous Republican orator of the Spanish Civil War, known as La Pasionaria for her ardor. Portugalete is a 15-minute walk from Santurce, where the quayside Hogar del Pescador serves simple and ample fish specialties. *Besugo* (sea bream) is the traditional choice, but the fresh grilled sardines are hard to surpass. To reach the bridge, take the subway to Areeta, or drive across the Puente de Deusto, turn left on Avenida Lehendakari Aguirre, and follow signs for Las Arenas.

14 **Catedral de Santiago** (St. James's Cathedral). Bilbao's earliest church, this was a pilgrimage stop on the coastal route to Santiago de Compostela. Work on the structure began in 1379, but fire destroyed most of it in 1571; it has a notable outdoor arcade. ✉ *Plaza de Santiago.*

15 The **Museo Arqueológico, Etnográfico e Histórico Vasco** (Museum of Basque Archaeology, Ethnology, and History) is in a stunning 16th-century convent. The collection centers on Basque fishing, crafts, and agriculture. ✉ *C. Cruz 4* ☎ *94/415–5423* *€3, free Thurs.* ⏲ *Tues.–Sat. 10:30–1:30 and 4–7, Sun. 10:30–1.*

16 The **Museo Diocesano de Arte Sacro** (Diocesan Museum of Sacred Art) occupies a carefully restored 16th-century cloister. The inner patio alone, ancient and intimate, is worth the visit. On display are religious silver work, liturgical garments, sculptures, and paintings dating back to the 12th century. ✉ *Pl. de la Encarnación 9* ☎ *94/432–0125* *Free* ⏲ *Tues.–Sat. 10:30–1:30 and 4–7, Sun. 10:30–1.*

Where to Stay & Eat

$$$–$$$$ ✕ **Etxanobe.** This luminous corner of the Euskalduna palace overlooks the Nervión river, the hills of Artxanda above, and Bilbao. Fernando Canales creates sleek, home-grown contemporary cuisine on a par with

THE GLITZY GUGGENHEIM IN BILBAO

*I**F PICASSO'S** Guernica was the 20th century's most famous and embattled painting, Bilbao's Guggenheim may be the most celebrated building of all time. Described by Spanish novelist Manuel Vazquez Montalban as a "meteorite," this eruption of light and titanium paradoxically stationed in Bilbao's muscular industrial context has reinvented this city.*

Perennially chided as the barrio industrial *(industrial quarter) in contrast to San Sebastián's* barrio jardín *(garden quarter), Bilbao has long been perceived as a polluted steel and shipbuilding center by the foul-smelling Nervión estuary.*

The Guggenheim has changed all that. Frank Gehry's gleaming brainchild, alternately hailed as "the greatest building of our time" (architect Philip Johnson), "the best building of the 20th century" (Spain's King Juan Carlos), and "a miracle" (Herbert Muschamp, New York Times*), has sparked a renaissance in the Basque country. In its first year, the Guggenheim attracted 1.4 million visitors, more than what both Guggenheim museums in New York received together in the same period. Revenue in the first year alone exceeded the original investment. Incredibly, the Guggenheim already holds the Spanish record for single-day visits to a museum (9,300), and the crowds are not diminishing.*

The museum itself is as superlative as the hoopla suggests. Gehry's quasi-mechanical tour de force provides an ideal context for the postmodern and futuristic artworks it contains. The smoothly rounded, asymmetrical, ship's-prow–like amalgam of limestone, glass, and titanium ingeniously recalls Bilbao's shipbuilding and steel-manufacturing past while using transparency and reflective materials to create a shimmering, futuristic luminosity. The final section of the Nervión's La Salve bridge is almost part of the structure, rendering the Guggenheim the virtual doorway to Bilbao.

The collection, described by director Thomas Krens as "a daring history of the art of the 20th century," consists of 242 works, 186 from New York's Guggenheim and 50 acquired by the Basque government. Artists whose names are synonymous with the 20th century (Kandinsky, Picasso, Ernst, Braque, Miró, Calder, Malevich) and particularly artists of the '50s and '60s (Pollock, Rothko, De Kooning, Chillida, Tàpies, Iglesias) are joined by contemporary figures (Nauman, Muñoz, Schnabel, Badiola, Barceló, Basquiat). The ground floor is dedicated to large-format and installation work, some of which—like Richard Serra's Serpent*—was created specifically for the space it occupies. Claes Oldenburg's* Knife Ship*, Robert Morris's walk-in* Labyrinth*, and pieces by Beuys, Boltansky, Long, Holzer, and others round out the heavyweight division in and around what is now the largest gallery in the world.*

---

the Basque Country's finest. ✉ *Av. de Abandoibarra 4* ☎ *94/442–1071* ▭ *AE, DC, MC, V* ⊙ *Closed Aug. 1–20; no dinner Sun. and holidays.*

$$$–$$$$ ✕ **Goizeko Kabi.** Here you can choose your own crab or crayfish. The dining rooms are of brick and wood accented by Persian rugs and chairs upholstered with tapestries. Chef Fernando Canales's creations include *láminas de bacalao en ensalada con pimientos rojos asados* (sliced cod in green salad with roasted red peppers) and *hojaldre de verdura a la plancha con manito de cordero* (grilled vegetables in puff pastry with leg of lamb). ✉ *Particular de Estraunza 4 y 6* ☎ *94/442–1129* ⚠ *Reservations essential* ▭ *AE, DC, MC, V* ⊙ *Closed Sun.*

$$$–$$$$ ✕ **Gorrotxa.** Carmelo Gorrotxategui's eclectic menu mixes Basque, French, and Castilian food, from foie gras *con uvas* (with grapes) to lobster Thermidor to chuleta de buey (beef steak). The accents are English, with carpets and wood paneling. ✉ *Alameda Urquijo 30* ☎ *94/443–*

4937 ▭ AE, DC, MC, V ⊙ Closed Sun., Holy Week, 1 wk in July, and 1 wk in Aug.

$$$–$$$$ ✕ **Guggenheim Bilbao.** The museum's restaurant-in-residence has a lot to live up to, and easily succeeds. Famous for his eponymous restaurant outside San Sebastián, Martín Berasategui or his staff will install you at a table overlooking the Nervión and the green heights of Artxanda, then feed you such exciting creations as *pichón de Bresse* (wild pigeon) and *ensalada de bogavante* (lobster salad). ✉ *Av. Abandoibarra 2* ☎ *94/423–9333* ✍ *Reservations essential* ▭ *AE, DC, MC, V* ⊙ *Closed Mon. No dinner Sun. or Tues.*

★ **$$$–$$$$** ✕ **Guria.** Genaro Pildain, born in what he calls "the smallest village in Vizcaya province," is the hands-down dean of Bilbao chefs, a genius of charm and simplicity. Having learned cooking from his mother, Don Genaro has presided over one of Bilbao's finest tables for two decades. Now that Genaro has semi-retired from the day-to-day operation of the restaurant, his partner, Carlos, carries on the same tradition of generosity and hospitality. Everything's impeccable here, from the *crema de puerros con patatas* (cream of potato-and-leek soup) to the *perretxikos de Orduña* (small, wild spring mushrooms). ✉ *Gran Vía 66* ☎ *94/441–5780* ▭ *AE, DC, MC, V* ⊙ *No dinner Sun.*

$$$–$$$$ ✕ **Zortziko.** This place combines an ultramodern kitchen with a building that has been declared a historical monument. Try the *langostinos con risotto de perretxikos* (prawns with wild-mushroom risotto) or the *suprema de pintada asada a la salsa de trufas* (guinea hen in truffle sauce). Chef Daniel García is one of Bilbao's culinary standouts. ✉ *C. Alameda de Mazarredo 17* ☎ *94/423–9743* ✍ *Reservations essential* ▭ *AE, DC, MC, V* ⊙ *Closed Sun., 1 wk at Easter, and late Aug.–mid-Sept.*

$$$ ✕ **El Perro Chico.** This refuge was named for the bridge below Bilbao's Mercado de la Ribera, where a *perro chico* (colloquial name for an ancient coin) was once charged as a toll. From owner Santiago Diez Ponzoa to chef Rafael García Rossi, everyone has a great time here, preparing innovative and thoughtful cuisine without pretense. Try the *pato a la naranja* (duck à l'orange) or the *bacalao con berenjena* (cod with aubergines). ✉ *Aretxaga 2* ☎ *94/415–0519* ▭ *AE, DC, MC, V* ⊙ *Closed Sun. No lunch Mon.*

$$–$$$ ✕ **Berton.** Dinner is served until 11:30 in this sleek, contemporary bistro in the Casco Viejo. Fresh wood tables with a green-tint polyethylene finish and exposed ventilation pipes give the dining room a designer look, while the classic cuisine ranges from Iberian ham to smoked salmon, foie gras, cod, beef, and lamb. ✉ *Jardines 11* ☎ *94/416–7035* ▭ *AE, DC, MC, V* ⊙ *No dinner Sun. and holidays.*

$–$$ ✕ **La Deliciosa.** For carefully prepared fare at friendly prices, this is one of the best values in the Casco Viejo. The *crema de puerros* (cream of leeks) is as good as any in town, and the *dorada al horno* (roast gilthead bream) is fresh from the nearby La Ribera market. ✉ *Jardines 1* ☎ *94/415–0944* ▭ *AE, DC, MC, V.*

$–$$ ✕ **Victor Montes.** A hot point for the daily *tapeo* (tapas tour), this place is always crowded with congenial grazers. The well-stocked counter might offer anything from wild mushrooms to *txistorra* (spicy sausages) to *Idiazabal* (Basque smoked cheese) or, for the adventurous, *huevas de merluza* (hake roe), all taken with splashes of Rioja, txakolí, or cider. ✉ *Pl. Nueva 8* ☎ *94/415–7067* ✍ *Reservations essential* ⊙ *Closed Sun. and Aug. 1–15.*

$ ✕ **Arriaga.** The cider house experience is a must in the Basque country. Cider *al txotx* (flying straight out of the barrel), sausage stewed in apple cider, codfish omelettes, *txuleton de buey* (beef steaks), and Idiazabal cheese with quince jelly are the classic fare. Reserving a table is a good idea, on weekends especially. ✉ *Santa Maria 13* ☎ *94/416–5670* ▭ *AE, DC, MC, V* ⊗ *No dinner Sun.*

¢–$ ✕ **Xukela.** Amid bright lighting and a vivid palette of greens and crimsons, chef Santiago Ruíz Bombin creates some of the tastiest and most eye-watering *pintxos* (morsels on toothpicks) in all of tapa-dom. ✉ *El Perro 2* ☎ *94/415–9772* ▭ *AE, DC, MC, V.*

★ $$$–$$$$ ✕ **Lopez de Haro.** As it's five minutes from the Guggenheim, Bilbao's only five-star hotel is becoming quite a scene. The converted 19th-century building has an English feel and all the comforts your heart desires. Club Náutico, a handy alternative on one of Bilbao's many rainy evenings, serves modern Basque dishes created by Alberto Vélez. ✉ *Obispo Orueta 2, 48009* ☎ *94/423–5500* ⎙ *94/423–4500* 🌐 *www.hotellopezdeharo.com* *49 rooms, 4 suites* *Restaurant, cafeteria, in-room data ports, cable TV, bar, meeting rooms, parking (fee)* ▭ *AE, DC, MC, V.*

★ $$$ **Carlton.** Luminaries who have trod the halls of this grande dame include Orson Welles, Ava Gardner, Ernest Hemingway, Lauren Bacall, and most of Spain's great bullfighters. During the civil war it was the seat of the Republican Basque government; later it housed a number of Nationalist generals. It remains elegant, well attended, and centrally located. ✉ *Pl. Federico Moyúa 2, El Ensanche, 48009* ☎ *94/416–2200* ⎙ *94/416–4628* 🌐 *www.aranzazu-hoteles.com* *148 rooms* *Restaurant, in-room data ports, minibars, cable TV, bar, meeting rooms, parking (fee)* ▭ *AE, DC, MC, V.*

★ $$$ **Gran Hotel Domine.** As much modern design festival as hotel, this Silken chain newcomer (summer 2002) directly across the street from the Guggenheim showcases the conceptual wit of Javier Mariscal, creator of Barcelona's 1992 Olympic mascot Cobi, and the structural knowhow of Bilbao architect Iñaki Aurreroextea. With adjustable windowpanes reflecting Gehry's titanium leviathan and every lamp and piece of furniture reflecting Mariscal's playful whimsy, this is the brightest star in Bilbao's design firmament. Comprehensively equipped and comfortable, it's the next best thing to moving into the Guggenheim. ✉ *Alameda de Mazarredo 61, El Ensanche, 48009* ☎ *94/425–3300* ⎙ *94/425–3301* 🌐 *www.granhoteldominebilbao.com* *131 rooms, 14 suites* *Restaurant, cafeteria, cable TV, minibars, in-room data ports, bar, meeting rooms, parking (fee); no pets* ▭ *AE, DC, MC, V.*

$$$ Fodor'sChoice ★ **Miró Hotel.** Perfectly placed—across from the Guggenheim and one block away from Bilbao's excellent Museo de Bellas Artes—this boutique hotel refurbished by Barcelona fashion designer Toni Miró is relentlessly comfortable and daringly innovative. It's one of the city's sleek new fleet of hotels inspired by the world's most talked-about and architecturally revolutionary art museum. Rooms are quiet, spacious, and ultra-high-tech contemporary. Public rooms are done in blacks and beiges and are simple and unpretentious; the hip downstairs bar is punctuated with canary-yellow walls. Expect a free drink when you arrive, excellent service throughout your stay, and a lavish breakfast with skewered fruit and a fabulous spread that won't leave you hungry. There's also a CD and DVD library, in addition to plenty of books. ✉ *Alameda de Mazarredo 77, El Ensanche, 48001* ☎ *94/661–1880* ⎙ *94/425–5182* 🌐 *www.mirohotelbilbao.com* *45 rooms, 5 suites* *Restaurant, room service, cable TV, minibars, in-room data ports, gym, hot tubs, massage, steam room, bar, lounge, library, laundry service, concierge, Internet, meeting rooms, airport shuttle, parking (fee); no pets* ▭ *AE, DC, MC, V.*

$$–$$$ **Ercilla.** This modern hotel fills with the taurine crowd during Bilbao's Semana Grande in early August, as it's near the bullring and because it has taken over from the Carlton as the place to see and be seen. Im-

peccable rooms, amenities, and service underscore its reputation. This is not an ideal spot for a quiet getaway. ✉ *C. Ercilla 3739, El Ensanche, 48009* ☎ *94/470–5700* 🖷 *94/443–9335* 🌐 *www.hotelercilla.es* ⇨ *338 rooms* ♁ *Restaurant, cafeteria, in-room data ports, minibars, cable TV, bar, parking (fee)* ▭ *AE, DC, MC, V.*

$$–$$$ ▣ **Petit Palace.** This recent addition to the Bilbao hotel fleet is in the Casco Viejo next to the Teatro Arriaga, and has a blended style: centenary limestone blocks, exposed brickwork, hand-hewn beams, and spiral wooden staircases are juxtaposed with clean new surfaces of glass and steel for a contemporary-antique look. The standard rooms and the showers are a tight fit, and the street below gets insane with partying till dawn on weekends, so this place is ideal if you intend to be out all night or you're here early in the week. Fifteen executive rooms have exercise bikes, hot tubs, and computer screens. ✉ *Bidebarrieta 2, Casco Viejo 48005* ☎ *94/415–6411* 🖷 *94/416–1205* 🌐 *www.hthotels.com* ⇨ *64 rooms* ♁ *Breakfast room, in-room data ports, minibars, cable TV, bar, meeting room* ▭ *AE, DC, MC, V.*

$ ▣ **Iturrienea Ostatua** This extraordinarily beautiful, traditional Basque town house in Bilbao's old quarter has charm to spare. It has overhead wooden beams, stone floors, ethnographical and historical objects adorning the walls. The staff is eager to please. The only caveat is nocturnal noise on the front side, especially in summer. Try for a room in the back or bring earplugs. ✉ *Santa María Kalea 14, Casco Viejo, 48005* ☎ *94/416–1500* 🖷 *94/415–8929* ⇨ *21 rooms* ♁ *Breakfast room; no a/c, no pets* ▭ *AE, DC, MC, V.*

Cafés

Bilbao's many coffeehouses and bistros have long provided refuge from the sirimiri and steel mills outside. **Bar los Fueros** (✉ C. de los Fueros 4), as much a watering hole as a café, is one of Bilbao's most authentic enclaves, perfect for an *aperitivo* or a nightcap. The **Café Bulevard** (✉ C. Arenal 3) dates back to 1871. Refuel at the enormous **Café Iruña** (✉ Jardines de Albia), a turn-of-the-20th-century classic. Founded in 1926, **Café La Granja** (✉ Pl. Circular 3), near the Puente del Arenal, is a Bilbao classic for coffee, beer, and *tortilla de patata* (potato omelet). **Café El Tilo** (✉ C. Arenal 1) may be the best in Bilbao, with wooden tables and original frescoes by Basque painter Juan de Aranoa (1901–73). It's open weekdays only. **Café y Té** (✉ Pl. Federico Moyúa 1) has a pleasant marble counter and a rural-urban aesthetic.

Nightlife & the Arts

Bilbao hosts a music festival in August; inquire at the main tourist office on Paseo de Arenal (☎ 94/479–5770), as venues change. The city's abundant nightlife breaks neatly down into ages and zones. Students and anyone else who can pass for being 30ish and under amass on and around Calle Licenciado Poza (known as Pozas; two blocks east of Gran Vía) and the Casco Viejo, where serious *poteo* (tippling) continues until late. Folk dancing sometimes breaks out in the streets. Barring holidays, the first half of the week is quieter. The historic **Teatro Arriaga** (✉ Pl. Arriaga s/n ☎ 94/416–3244) still draws world-class ballet, theater, concerts, opera, and *zarzuela* (comic opera). The bright **Palacio Euskalduna** (✉ Abandoibarra 4 ☎ 944/308372), home of the Orquesta Sinfónica de Bilbao, has all but replaced the Arriaga as Bilbao's prime performing arts venue. Older night owls gather at **Azulito** (✉ Particular de Estraunza 1). **Flash** (✉ C. Telesforo Aranzadi 4, near Hotel Carlton), has dinner, dancing, and cocktails. The **Cotón Club** (✉ Alameda Gregorio de la Revilla 25) has live music followed by dancing. **Magic** (✉ C. Colón de Larreátegui 80) is known for '60s music and clients of roughly the same vintage.

Shopping

Basque *txapelas* (berets) make charming gifts. Best when waterproof, they'll keep you remarkably warm in rain and mist. Look for Elosegui, the best-known brand of txapelas, in the old quarter's **Sombreros Gorostiaga** (✉ C. Victor 9 ☎ 94/416–1276). **Basandere** (✉ C. Iparaguirre 4 ☎ 94/423–6386), near the Guggenheim, has artisanal Basque crafts and foods. **Olañeta** (✉ C. Correo 12 ☎ 94/415–1618), in the Casco Viejo, lovingly restored in stone, wood beams, and brick by antiquer Xabier Olañeta, sells charming ladies' wear.

en route

From Bilbao, drive west down the Nervión to Neguri and Getxo and follow the coast road around through Baquio, Bermeo, and Mundaca to Guernica before proceeding east. Depending on stops for lunch or sprawling on a breezy beach, this can be a two- to six-hour drive, all of it spectacularly scenic. The other choice is to pick up the A8 toll road east to San Sebastián and France, exiting for Guernica (Gernika, in Euskera) and the BI-635 coast road through Vizcaya's hills.

Getxo

17 *13 km (8 mi) northwest of Bilbao, 10 km (6 mi) southwest of Plentzia.*

Getxo, an early watering spot for the elite Bilbao industrial classes, has rambling mansions, five beaches, and an ancient fishing port. Restaurants and hotels along the beaches here make good hideaways—only a 20-minute ride from the center of Bilbao, on the British architect Norman Foster's designer subway line from Bilbao.

San Juan de Gaztelugatxe

18 *12 km (7 mi) west of Bermeo.*

This picturesque hermitage clinging to its rocky promontory over the Bay of Biscay is exactly 231 steps up along a narrow corridor built into the top of a rocky ledge connecting what would otherwise be an island to the mainland. A favorite pilgrimage for Bilbainos on holidays, the Romanesque chapel is said to have been used as a fortress by the Templars in the 14th century. A walk around the bell tower is alleged to cure nightmares and insomnia, as well as to grant wishes.

Where to Stay & Eat

$–$$ **Ostatua Gaztelubegi.** The views from this little hotel and restaurant overlooking the hermitage of San Juan de Gaztelugatxe are some of the most vertiginous of the Basque coast. The bar is always booming, the food, simple Basque cooking from *alubias* to *besugo* (beans to sea bream). ✉ *Ctra. BI-3101, Km 3 (from Bakio), 48130* ☎ *94/619–4924* *7 rooms* *Restaurant, bar, free parking* *MC, V.*

Bermeo

19 *30 km (18 mi) east of Plentzia, 3 km (2 mi) west of Mundaca.*

Bermeo is easy to miss if you don't park and walk through the old part of town to the port. (On your way, inspect the lovely Udaletxea, or town hall, for its sundials in almost perpetual shadow above the fountains, which are dated 1745 at the building's eastern corner.) With the largest fishing fleet in Spain—some 60 long-distance tuna freezer ships of more than 150 tons, and nearly 100 smaller craft that specialize in hake, sea bream, gilthead, and other local species—Bermeo was long famous as a whaling port. In the 16th century, local whalers reportedly were obliged to donate the tongue of every whale to raise money for the church. Bermeo has one of only two wooden-boat shipyards on the northern coast, and the boats in its harbor make a colorful picture. Drive to the top of the windswept hill, where a cemetery overlooks the crashing waves below. Townspeople tend family tombs at sunset.

Bermeo's **Museo del Pescador** is the only museum in the world dedicated to the craft and history of fishermen and the fishing industry, from whales to anchovies. The tower was built by native son Alonso de Ercilla y Zuñiga (1533–94), poet and eminent soldier. Ercilla's "La Araucana," an account of the conquest of Arauco (Chile), is considered one of the best Spanish epic poems. ✉ *Torre de Ercilla* ☎ *946/881171* *Free* ⊙ *Tues.–Sat. 10–1:30 and 4–7:30, Sun. 10–1:30.*

Where to Eat

$–$$ ✕ **Jokin.** You have a good view of the *puerto viejo* (old port) from this cheerful, strategically located restaurant. The fish served comes directly off the boats in the harbor below. Try the *rape Jokin* (anglerfish in a clam and crayfish sauce) or *chipirones en su tinta* (small squid in its own ink) and, for dessert, the *tarta de naranja* (orange cake). ✉ *Eupeme Duna 13* ☎ *94/688–4089* ▭ *AE, DC, MC, V* ⊙ *No dinner Sun.*

Mundaca

20 *45 km (28 mi) northeast of Bilbao.*

Tiny Mundaca (Mundaka, in Euskera) draws surfers from all over the world, especially in winter, when the waves are some of the world's longest. The left-breaking roller that forms off the entrance to the Urdaibai natural preserve at the mouth of the Ría de Guernica is Europe's longest wave. The town is filled with summer homes and houses bearing coats of arms. Architectural sights include the hermitage on the Santa Catalina peninsula and the Renaissance door on the parish church.

Where to Stay & Eat

$–$$ ✕ **Casino José Mari.** Built in 1818 as an auction house for the local fishermen's guild, this building, with wonderful views of Mundaca's beach, is now an eating club. The public is welcome, and it's a prime lunch stop in summer, when you can sit in the glassed-in, upper-floor porch. Very much a local haunt, the club serves excellent fish caught, more often than not, by members. ✉ *Parque Atalaya (center of town)* ☎ *94/687–6005* *Reservations not accepted* ▭ *AE, MC, V.*

$$ **Atalaya.** This 1911 landmark 37 km (22 mi) from Bilbao was converted very tastefully from a private house to a hotel, and has become a big favorite for quick railroad-getaway overnights from Bilbao and the Guggenheim. (The train ride out is spectacular.) Guest rooms are charming and comfortable, and those upstairs have balconies with marvelous views. Room No. 12 is the best in the house. The breakfast room is cheerful and light. ✉ *Paseo de Txorrokopunta 2, 48360* ☎ *94/617–7000* *94/687–6899* *11 rooms* *Restaurant, bar* ▭ *AE, DC, MC, V.*

en route From Mundaca, follow signs for Guernica, stopping at the Mirador de Portuondo—a roadside lookout on the left as you leave town (BI-635, Km 43)—for an excellent view of the estuary.

Guernica

21 *15 km (9 mi) east of Bilbao.*

On Monday, April 26, 1937—market day—Guernica suffered history's second terror bombing against a civilian population (the first, much less

EMBATTLED GUERNICA

WHEN SPAIN'S Second Republic commissioned Picasso to create a work for the Paris 1937 International Exposition, little did he imagine that his grim canvas protesting the bombing of a Basque village would become one of the most famous paintings in history.

The rural market town of Guernica was key to Basque identity since the 14th century. General Francisco Franco knew the strike would be a blow to Basque nationalism. Tuesday, April 26: a busy market day in Guernica. When the raid ended, more than a 1,000 civilians lay dead or dying in the ruins. Not until the 60th anniversary of the event did Germany officially apologize for the bombing.

Picasso's painting had its own struggle. The Spanish Pavilion in the 1937 International Exposition in Paris nearly substituted a more upbeat work, using Guernica as a backdrop. (Artistically, Guernica is considered a cubist remake of Goya's Dos de Mayo, with similar interplay of darkness and fire; gaping, agonized mouths; and an analogous overall organization of pictorial space.) In 1939, Picasso ceded Guernica to New York's Museum of Modern Art on behalf of the democratically elected government of Spain—stipulating that the painting should return only to a democratic Spain. Over the next 30 years, as Picasso's fame grew, so did Guernica's—as a work of art and symbol of Spain's captivity.

When Franco died in 1975, two years after Picasso, negotiations with Picasso's heirs for the painting's return to Spain were already under way. Now on display at Madrid's Centro de Arte Reina Sofía, Guernica is home for good.

famous, was against neighboring Durango, about a month earlier). The planes of the Nazi Luftwaffe were sent with the blessings of General Franco to experiment with saturation bombing of civilian targets and to decimate the traditional seat of Basque autonomy. Since the Middle Ages, Spanish sovereigns had sworn under the ancient **oak tree of Guernica** to respect Basque *fueros* (special local rights—the kind of local autonomy that was anathema to the *generalísimo*'s Madrid-centered "National Movement," which promoted Spanish unity over local identity). More than a thousand people were killed in the bombing, and today Guernica remains a symbol of independence in the heart of every Basque, known to the world through Picasso's famous painting (now in Madrid's Centro de Arte Reina Sofía). The city was destroyed—though the oak tree miraculously emerged unscathed—and has been rebuilt as a modern, unattractive place. One point of interest, however, is the stump of the sacred oak, which finally died several decades ago, in the courtyard of the **Casa de Juntas** (a new oak has been planted alongside the old one)—the object of many a pilgrimage. Nearby is the stunning estuary of the **Ría de Guernica,** a stone's throw from some of the area's most colorful fishing towns.

Where to Stay & Eat

$$–$$$ ✕ **Baserri Maitea.** In the village of Forua 1 km (½ mi) northwest of Guernica, Basseri Maitea is in a stunning 250-year-old Basque caserío. Strings of red peppers and garlic hang from wooden beams in the cathedral-like interior. Entrées include the *pescado del día* (fish of the day) and *cordero de leche asado al horno de leña* (milk-fed lamb roasted in a wood-burning oven). ✉ *BI-635 to Bermeo, Km 2* ☎ *94/625–3408* 💳 *AE, DC, MC, V* ⏲ *No dinner Sun. May–Oct.*

¢–$ 🏨 **Boliña.** Not far from the famous oak in downtown Guernica, the Boliña is pleasant and modern, a good base for exploring the Vizcayan coast.

Rooms are smallish but comfortable. ✉ *Barrenkale 3, 48300* ☎ *94/625–0300* 🖷 *94/625–0304* *16 rooms* *Restaurant, bar* ▭ *AE, DC, MC, V.*

off the beaten path

On the Kortezubi road 5 km (3 mi) from Guernica, the **Cuevas de Santimamiñe** (Santimamiñe Caverns; ✉ Barrio Basondo, Kortezubi ☎ 94/625–2975) have important prehistoric cave paintings. Guided visits are offered weekdays at 10:30, noon, 4, and 5:30, except holidays. On your way out, look for signs for the nearby **Bosque Pintado,** rows of trees vividly painted by Basque artist Agustín Ibarrola, a striking and successful marriage of art and nature.

en route

For the Santimamiñe caves, continue northeast from Guernica toward Kortezubi on the BI-638. For Elanchove (Elantxobe, in Euskera), turn left at Arteaga and follow the BI-3237 around the east side of the Ría de Guernica and the Urdaibai natural preserve. From there, the coast road through Ea and Ipaster leads to Lequeitio, one of the prettiest ports on the Basque coast. But if you long for a taste of Arcadian highlands 30 minutes inland, drive up to Axpe and see Amboto, Vizcaya's mythical limestone mountain.

Axpe

22 *47 km (28 mi) east of Bilbao, 46 km (27 mi) southeast of Guernica.*

The village of Axpe, in the valley of Atxondo, nestles under the limestone heights of Amboto, at 4,777 ft one of the four highest peaks in the Basque Country outside of the Pyrenees. Home of the legendary Basque mother of nature, Mari Urrika or Mari Anbotokodama (María, Our Lady of Amboto), Amboto, with its spectral gray rock face, is a sharp contrast to the soft green meadows running up to the very foot of the mountain. According to Basque scholar and ethnologist José María de Barandiarán in his *Mitología Vasca* (Basque Mythology), Mari was "a beautiful woman, well constructed in all ways except for one foot, which was like that of a goat." Her sons, Mikelatz and Atagorri, are, in Basque mythology, representations of good and evil. To reach Axpe from Bilbao drive east on the A-8/E-70 freeway toward San Sebastián. From Guernica drive south on the BI-635 to the A-6/E-70 freeway, and turn east for San Sebastián. Get off at the Durango exit 40 km (24 mi) from Bilbao and take the BI-632 road for Elorrio. At Apatamonasterio turn right onto the BI-3313 and continue to Axpe.

Where to Stay & Eat

$$ Fodor'sChoice ★ **Mendigoikoa.** This handsome brace of hillside farmhouses is among the province of Vizcaya's most exquisite hideaways. The King and Queen of Spain dined here with the Lehendakari (Basque President) Carlos Garaikoetxea in the early '80s. The lower farmhouse, Mendibekoa (lower mountain), has stunning rooms, restaurant space for breakfast, and a glassed-in terrace overlooking the valley. Mendigoikoa (upper mountain) is the restaurant. With a fire crackling in the far corner of the dining room and the heavy beams overhead, the *pichón de Navaz a la parilla* (Navaz pigeon cooked over coals) or the great chunks of beef on the bone (*txuleta de buey*) are memorable. ✉ *Barrio San Juan 33, 48290 Axpe* ☎ *94/682–0833* 🖷 *94/682–1136* *12 rooms* *Restaurant* ▭ *AE, DC, MC, V.*

Elanchove

23 *27 km (17 mi) from Bermeo.*

The tiny fishing village of Elanchove is surrounded by huge, steep cliffs, with a small breakwater that protects its fleet from the storms of the Bay of Biscay. The view of the port from the upper village is breathtaking. The lower fork in the road leads to the port itself.

Where to Stay & Eat

¢–$ **Casa Rural Arboliz.** On a bluff overlooking the Bay of Biscay about 2 km (1 mi) outside Elanchove on the road to Lequeitio, this rustic inn is removed from the harborside bustle, offering a breath of the country life on the Basque coast. The modern rooms are simple and have balconies overlooking the sea. *Arboliz 12, 48311 Ibarranguelua 94/627–6283 www.euskalnet.net/arboliz 6 rooms Restaurant AE, MC, V.*

¢–$ **Itsasmin.** In the upper village of Elanchove, this place rents simple, cheery rooms and serves home-cooked meals in its diminutive dining room. *Negusia 32 94/627–6174 94/627–6293 15 rooms Restaurant AE, DC MC, V.*

Lequeitio

24 *59 km (37 mi) east of Bilbao, 61 km (38 mi) west of San Sebastián.*

This bright little town is similar to Bermeo but has two wide, sandy beaches right by its harbor. Soaring over the Gothic church of Santa María (open for mass only) is a graceful set of flying buttresses. Lequeitio is famous for its fiestas (September 1–18), which include a gruesome event in which men dangle for as long as they can from the necks of dead geese tied to a cable over the inlet while the cable is whipped in and out of the water by crowds of burly men at either end.

Ondárroa

25 *61 km (38 mi) east of Bilbao, 49 km (30 mi) west of San Sebastián.*

Farther east along the coast from Lequeitio, Ondárroa is a gem of a fishing town. Like its neighbors, it has a major fishing fleet painted various combinations of red, green, and white, the colors of the Ikurriña, the Basque national flag.

en route

Continuing along the coastal road through Motrico and Deva, you'll approach some of the prettiest fishing ports and culinary centers in the Basque Country. Before these, however, as you enter Zumaya, you'll see the turnoff for Azpeitia and the sanctuary of one of Spain's greatest religious figures, St. Ignatius of Loyola. A half-hour trip up the GI-631 takes you to this colossal structure.

Santuario de San Ignacio de Loyola

26 *Cestona: 34 km (21 mi) southwest of San Sebastián.*

The Sanctuary of St. Ignatius of Loyola was erected in honor of Iñigo Lopez de Oñaz y Loyola (1491–1556) after he was sainted as Ignacio de Loyola in 1622 for his defense of the Catholic Church against the tides of Luther's Reformation. The future founder of the Jesuit Order left his life as a courtier to join the army at the age of 26, but after being badly wounded in an intra-Basque battle he returned to his family's ancestral home, underwent a spiritual conversion, and took up theological studies. Almost two centuries later, Roman architect Carlos Fontana designed the basilica that would memorialize the saint. The exuberant, Churrigueresque baroque structure contrasts the austere ways of Iñigo himself, who took vows of poverty and chastity after his conversion. The interior is endowed with polychrome marble, ornate altarwork, and a huge but delicate dome. The fortresslike tower house has the room where Iñigo experienced conversion while recovering from his wound. His reputation as a "soldier of Christ" somewhat belies his teachings, which emphasized mystical union with God, imitation of Christ, human initiative, foreign missionary work, and, especially, the education of youth. Back on the coastal road is **Zumaya**, a cozy little port and summer resort with the fjordlike estuary of the Urola River flowing (back and forth, according to the tide) through town. The **Museo Zuloaga** (☎ 943/862341), on the N634 at the edge of town, has an extraordinary collection of paintings by Goya, El Greco, Zurbarán and others in addition to the Basque impressionist Ignacio Zuloaga himself. It's open Wednesday–Sunday 4–8, and admission is €3.

Where to Stay & Eat

$–$$ ✕ **Bedua.** Locals access this rustic hideaway by boat in the summer. A specialist in *tortilla de patatas con pimientos verdes de la huerta* (potato omelet with homegrown green peppers), Bedua is also known for *tortilla de bacalao* (codfish omelet), *txuleta de buey* (beefsteak), and fish of all kinds, especially *besugo* (sea bream). ✉ *Cestona, Barrio Bedua (3 km [2 mi] up the Urola from Zumaya)* ☎ *943/860551* ▭ *MC, V.*

$–$$ 🏨 **Arocena.** This is one of the many spa hotels to which Europeans flocked at the turn of the 20th century. The hotel has free bus service to the nearby springs, whose medicinal waters are still used to treat liver-related diseases. Rooms facing away from the road have especially fine views of the mountains. The common rooms, including the restaurant and lobby, retain the hotel's Belle Epoque flavor. ✉ *San Juan 12 (10 mins from sanctuary), 20740 Cestona* ☎ *943/147040* 📠 *943/147978* 🌐 *www.hotelarocena.com* ⇨ *109 rooms* ♨ *Restaurant, cable TV, tennis court, pool, health club, bar, playground* ▭ *AE, DC, MC, V.*

Guetaria

27 *22 km (14 mi) west of San Sebastián.*

From Zumaya, the coast road and several good foothpaths lead to Guetaria, known as *la cocina de guipúzcoa,* the kitchen of Guipúzcoa province, for its many restaurants and taverns. Guetaria was the birthplace of Juan Sebastián Elcano (1460–1526), the first circumnavigator of the globe and Spain's most emblematic naval hero. Elcano took over and completed Magellan's voyage after the latter was killed in the Philippines in 1521. The town's galleonlike **church** has sloping wooden floors resembling a ship's deck. **Zarauz,** the next town, has a wide beach and many taverns and cafés.

Where to Stay & Eat

★ $$$–$$$$ ✕ **Kaia Kaipe.** Suspended over Guetaria's colorful fishing port and looking past Zarautz and San Sebastián all the way to Biarritz, this spectacular place puts together exquisite fish soups and serves fresh fish right off the boats you can watch being unloaded below. The town is the home of Txomin Etxaniz, the premier *txakolí* (tart young Basque white wine), and this is the place to drink it. ✉ *General Arnau 4* ☎ *943/140500* ▭ *AE, DC, MC, V.*

$ ✕🏨 **Iribar.** Iribar has been grilling fish and beef over coals outside the church for more than half a century. While Kaia and Kai-pe, in the port, are also excellent places to dine, with views of the harbor's colorful fleet of fishing boats, Iribar is memorable for its family-friendliness and for its delicious fish and beef. ✉ *Kale Nagusia 38* ☎ *943/140406* *4 rooms* *Restaurant, bar* *MC, V.*

en route

Heading east toward San Sebastián, you have a choice of the A8 toll road or the coastal N634 highway. The former is a quick and scenic 44 km (27 mi), but the latter will take you through the village of Orio past a few more tempting inns and restaurants, not the least of which is the Sidrería Ugarte, in Usurbil.

3

SAN SEBASTIÁN TO HONDARRIBIA

Graceful, chic San Sebastián invites you to slow down, stroll the beach, and wander the streets. East of the city, you'll pass through Pasajes, where Lafayette set off to help the colonial forces in the American Revolution. Victor Hugo spent a winter writing here. Just shy of the French border, you'll hit Hondarribia, a quaint and colorful port town.

San Sebastián

28 *100 km (62 mi) east of Bilbao.*

Fodor'sChoice ★

San Sebastián (Donostia, in Euskera) is an unusually sophisticated city arched around one of the finest urban beaches in the world, **La Concha** (The Shell), so named for its almost perfect resemblance to the shape of a scallop shell. The best way to see San Sebastián is to walk around: promenades and pathways lead up the hills that surround the city. The first records of San Sebastián date from the 11th century. A backwater for centuries, the city had the good fortune in 1845 to attract Queen Isabella II, who was seeking relief from a skin ailment in the icy Atlantic waters. Isabella was followed by much of the aristocracy of the time, and San Sebastián became a favored summer retreat for Madrid's well-to-do. The city is laid out with wide streets on a grid pattern, thanks mainly to the 12 different times it has been all but destroyed by fire. The last conflagration came after the French were expelled in 1813; English-Portuguese forces occupied the city, abused the population, and torched the place. Today, San Sebastián is a seaside resort on a par with Nice and Monte Carlo. It becomes one of Spain's most expensive cities in the summer, when French vacationers descend in droves. It is also, like Bilbao, a center of Basque nationalism.

Every corner of Spain champions its culinary identity, but San Sebastián's refined fare is in a league of its own. Many of the city's restaurants—along with scores of private, all-male eating societies—are in the **Parte Vieja** (old quarter), on the east end of the bay beyond the elegant **Casa Consistorial** (City Hall) and formal **Alderdi Eder** gardens. City Hall began as a casino in 1887; after gambling was outlawed early in the 20th century, the town council moved here from the Plaza de la Constitución, the old quarter's main square. The tiny **Isla de Santa Clara,** right in the entrance to the bay, protects the city from Bay of Biscay storms; this makes La Concha one of the calmest beaches on Spain's entire northern coast. A large hill dramatically dominates each side of the entrance to the bay, too. A visit to **Monte Igueldo,** on the western side of the bay, is a must. (You can drive up for a toll of €1 per person or take the *funicular*—cable car—for the same amount round-trip; it runs 10–8 in summer, 11–6 in winter, with departures every 15 minutes.) From the top, you get the remarkable panorama for which San Sebastián is famous: gardens, parks, wide tree-lined boulevards, Belle Epoque buildings, and, of course, the bay itself.

Designed by the world-renowned Spanish architect Rafael Moneo, and situated at the mouth of the Urumea River, the **Kursaal** is San Sebastián's postmodern concert hall, film society, and convention center. The gleaming cubes of glass comprising this bright, rationalist complex were conceived as a perpetuation of the site's natural geography, an attempt to "underline the harmony between the natural and the artificial" and to create a visual stepping stone between the heights of Monte Urgull and Monte Ulía. It has two auditoriums, a gargantuan banquet hall, meeting rooms, exhibition space, and a sibling set of terraces across the estuary. Martín Berasategui, chef at the Guggenheim Bilbao and director of his own restaurant in nearby Lasarte, oversees the dining room. ✉ *Av. de la Zurriola, Gros* ☎ *943/003000* 🎫 *€4* ⏲ *Guided tours daily at 11:30, 12:30, and 1:30.*

Just in from the harbor, in the shadow of Monte Urgull, is the baroque church of **Santa María,** with a stunning carved facade of an arrow-riddled St. Sebastian. The interior is strikingly restful; note the ship above St. Sebastian high on the altar. Looking straight south from the front of Santa María, you can see the facade and spires of the **Catedral Buen Pastor** (Cathedral of the Good Shepherd) across town.

need a break?

Steps from the facade of Santa María, in the heart of the old quarter, have a *chocolate con nata*—thick, dark hot chocolate with real whipped cream—at the tiny café, **Kantoi** (C. Mayor 10, Parte Vieja).

The **Museo de San Telmo** is in a 16th-century monastery behind the Parte Vieja, to the right of the church of Santa María. The former chapel, now a lecture hall, was painted by José María Sert (1876–1945), author of notable works in Barcelona's city hall, London's Tate Gallery, and New York's Waldorf-Astoria hotel. Here, Sert's characteristic tones of gray, gold, violet, and earthy russets enhance the sculptural power of his work, which portrays events from Basque history. The museum displays Basque ethnographic items, such as prehistoric steles once used as grave markers, and paintings by Zuloaga, Ribera, and El Greco. ✉ *Pl. de Ignacio Zuloaga s/n, Parte Vieja* ☎ *943/424970* 🎫 *Free* ⏲ *Tues.–Sat. 10:30–1:30 and 4–8, Sun. 10:30–2.*

San Sebastián is divided by the **Urumea River,** which is crossed by three bridges inspired by late-19th-century French architecture. At the mouth of the Urumea, the incoming surf smashes the rocks with such force that white foam erupts, and the noise is wild and Wagnerian.

off the beaten path

CHILLIDA LEKU – In the Jauregui section of Hernani, 10 minutes south of San Sebastián (suggestively close to both Martín Bersategui's restaurant in Lasarte *and* the cider houses of Astigarraga), the Eduardo Chillida Sculpture Garden and Museum, in a 16th-century farmhouse, is a treat for anyone interested in contemporary art. The late Eduardo Chillida (1924–2002), one of Spain's most prestigious contemporary artists, created the emblematic sculpture *Peine del Viento* (*Wind Comb*), overlooking San Sebastián bay from the foot of Monte Igueldo. ✉ *Caserío Zabalaga, Barrio Jauregui 66, Lasarte* ☎ *943/336006* 🎫 *€5* ⏲ *Closed Tues.*

Where to Stay & Eat

$$$$ ✕ **Akelaré.** On the far side of Monte Igueldo presides Chef Pedro Subijana, one of the most spectacularly experimental chefs in the Basque country. Prepare for tastes of all kinds, from pop rocks in blood sausage to mustard ice cream on tangerine peels. His "straight" dishes are impeccable: try the venison with apple and smoked chestnuts or the *lubina*

(sea bass) with goose barnacles. ✉ *Barrio de Igueldo, Igueldo* ☎ *943/212052 or 943/214086* ⚠ *Reservations essential* ▭ *AE, DC, MC, V* ⊗ *Closed Mon., 1st 2 wks in June, and Dec. No dinner Sun.*

$$$$ Fodor'sChoice ★ ✕ **Arzak.** Renowned chef Juan Mari Arzak's little house at the crest of Alto de Miracruz on the eastern outskirts of San Sebastián is internationally famous, so reserve well in advance. Traditional Basque preparations are enhanced by Arzakian innovations designed to bring out the best in the natural products. The ongoing culinary dialogue between Juan Mari and his daughter Elena is one of the most endearing attractions here. They may not always agree, but it's all in the family and the food just gets better and better. The sauces are perfect and every dish looks beautiful, but the prices even of appetizers (asparagus for €32) are astronomical. Treat yourself to a remarkable dessert of chocolate with pine nuts. Given the name and fame, expect to be rushed through your meal to make room for the next party. ✉ *Alto de Miracruz 21, Alto de Miracruz* ☎ *943/278465* 📠 *943/272753* ⚠ *Reservations essential* ▭ *AE, DC, MC, V* ⊗ *Closed Mon., last 2 wks in June, and 2 wks in Nov. No dinner Sun.*

$$$$ Fodor'sChoice ★ ✕ **Martín Berasategui.** A sure bet here is the *lubina asada con jugo de habas, vainas, cebolletas y tallarines de chipirón* (roast sea bass with juice of fava beans, green beans, baby onions, and cuttlefish shavings), but go with whatever Martín suggests: he can probably tell by looking at you what you really need. The site of San Sebastián's racetrack, Lasarte is 8 km (5 mi) south of San Sebastián. ✉ *Loidi Kalea 4, Lasarte* ☎ *943/366471* ▭ *AE, DC, MC, V* ⊗ *Closed Mon. and mid-Dec.–mid-Jan. No lunch Sat., no dinner Sun.*

$$$$ Fodor'sChoice ★ ✕ **Mugaritz.** This farmhouse in the hills above Rentería 5 mi northeast of San Sebastián is surrounded by spices and herbs tended by chef Andoni Luis Aduriz and his crew. Winner of the 2001 prize for Spain's best dish with his foie-gras over coals with rice and sea lettuce, Aduriz is master at combining products of the fields and forest with seafood. ✉ *Aldura Aldea, Errenteria* ☎ *943/518343* ▭ *AE, DC, MC, V* ⊗ *Closed Easter wk, Dec. 23–Jan. 14, and Mon. No dinner Sun.*

$$$$ ✕ **Panier Fleuri.** Chef Tatus Fombellida, winner of Spain's national gastronomy prize—no mean feat—rules this sober dining room overlooking the crashing surf at the mouth of the Urumea River. Try his *faisán* (pheasant) or the *supremas de lenguado a la florentina* (sole baked with spinach and served with hollandaise sauce) and for dessert the lemon sorbet with champagne. One of the most select wine lists in Spain compliments the food here. ✉ *Paseo de Salamanca 1, Parte Vieja* ☎ *943/424205* ⚠ *Reservations essential* ▭ *AE, DC, MC, V* ⊗ *Closed Wed., last 2 wks in Dec., 3 wks in June, and 1 wk at Christmas. No dinner Sun.*

$$$$ Fodor'sChoice ★ ✕ **Zuberoa.** Six miles northeast of San Sebastian in the village of Oiartzun, Hilario Arbelaitz has long been one of San Sebastián's most celebrated chefs. His original yet simple management of prime raw materials such as spring cuttlefish or woodcock has earned him a spot as one of Spain's top half dozen culinary stars. ✉ *Plaza Bekosoro 1, Oiartzun* ☎ *943/491228* ▭ *AE, DC, MC, V* ⊗ *Closed Dec. 1–15, April 21–May 5; Oct. 15–30; Sun., Wed.*

$$$–$$$$ ✕ **Kursaal.** The food is hit or miss at this bright place wedged between the Urumea River and the Bay of Biscay, where you'll get a lighter, less complex version of Martín Berasategui's concoctions. The corner table is a fine place to be, however, day or night, for a *marmitako* (tuna stew) deconstruction composed of tiger prawns in a pipérade of ricotta, shallots, zucchini, Iberian bacon bits, and chicken broth. The dark, red *pichón de Bresse* (Bresse pigeon) is superb, as is the chestnut soup. ✉ *Zurriola pasealekua 1, Gros* ☎ *943/003162* ▭ *AE, DC, MC, V* ⊗ *Closed Mon. No dinner Sun.*

★ $$$–$$$$ ✕ **Urepel.** The cuisine balances classic and contemporary elements in a felicitous way. The *chicharro al escama dorada* (a skinned, deboned mackerel served under a layer of golden-brown sliced potatoes) is a typical Urepel invention, as is the unbeatable and unusual dish of foie gras wrapped with veal. The appetizer of finely carmelized scallops with caviar is also excellent. There is no head chef; the kitchen staff works as a team, in prototypically Basque egalitarian fashion. ✉ *Paseo de Salamanca 3, Parte Vieja* ☎ *943/424040* ▭ *AE, DC, MC, V* ⏲ *Closed Sun. No dinner Tues.*

$–$$ ✕ **Sidrería Petritegui.** For hearty dining and a certain amount of splashing around in hard cider, make this short excursion east of San Sebastián. Gigantic wooden barrels line the walls, while tables are piled with *tortilla de bacalao* (codfish omelet), *txuleta de buey* (thick chunks of beef), the smoky local sheep's-milk cheese from the town of Idiazabal, and, for dessert, walnuts and *membrillo* (quince jelly). ✉ *Ctra. San Sebastián–Hernani, Km 7, Astigarraga* ☎ *943/457188* ▭ *No credit cards* ⏲ *No lunch weekdays.*

★ $$$$ ▦ **Hotel María Cristina.** The graceful beauty of the Belle Epoque is embodied in San Sebastián's most luxurious hotel, which sits like the queen it's named after on the elegant west bank of the Urumea River. The grandeur continues in salons filled with Oriental rugs, potted palms, and Carrara marble columns, and in bedrooms to match—with gold fixtures and wood wardrobes. Marble bathrooms add still more style. Service is generally excellent, but on occasion, if it's very busy at the desk, you may have to wait a bit. Make sure you request service and directions clearly, and insist on talking to an English-speaking concierge. A piano player pounds out good, often eclectic tunes nightly at the bar. ✉ *Okendo 1, Centro, 20004* ☎ *943/437600 or 900/993539* 🖷 *943/437676* 🌐 *www.westin.com* ⇆ *108 rooms, 28 suites* ♨ *Restaurant, room service, cable TV, massage, in-room data ports, in-room safes, minibars, refrigerators, bar, piano, baby-sitting, laundry service, concierge, Internet, business services, meeting rooms, parking (fee), no-smoking rooms* ▭ *AE, DC, MC, V.*

$$$–$$$$ ▦ **Londres y de Inglaterra.** On the promenade above La Concha, this stately hotel has an old-world aesthetic that informs the bright, formal lobby and continues throughout the hotel. The bar and restaurant face the bay, and the guest rooms with views out to sea are the best in town. ✉ *Zubieta 2, La Concha, 20007* ☎ *943/426989* 🖷 *943/420031* 🌐 *www.hlondres.com* ⇆ *137 rooms, 11 suites* ♨ *Restaurant, tea shop, minibars, cable TV, bar, casino, meeting rooms, parking (fee)* ▭ *AE, DC, MC, V.*

$$$ ▦ **Europa.** Just a block from the beach and a 15-minute walk around La Concha from the booming Parte Vieja, this small Donosti hotel is staffed by savvy professionals eager to help you make the most of your time in town. Rooms are of moderate size but impeccably equipped and comfortable. ✉ *San Martín 52, Centro, 20007* ☎ *943/470880* 🖷 *943/471730* ⇆ *68 rooms* ♨ *Restaurant, minibars, cable TV, bar, parking (fee)* ▭ *AE, DC, MC, V.*

$$–$$$ ▦ **Hotel Parma.** Overlooking the Kursaal and the Zurriola beach at the mouth of the Urumea River, this small but shiny modern hotel is also at the edge of the Parte Vieja, San Sebastián's prime grazing area for tapas and vinos. Some of the cheerfully decorated rooms (though not all) have views northeast out to sea. ✉ *Salamanca Pasealekua 10, Parte Vieja, 20003* ☎ *943/428893* 🖷 *956/777613* 🌐 *www.hotelparma.com* ⇆ *27 rooms* ♨ *Bar* ▭ *AE, DC, MC, V.*

¢–$ ▦ **Aristondo.** Just 15 minutes' drive above San Sebastián on Monte Igueldo, this comfortable farmhouse is a scenic and economical place to stay. Similar *agroturismo* options nearby include **Izen Eder** (☎ 943/580011) and **Pilotegui** (☎ 943/215348). ✉ *San Martín 54 bis, Igueldo, 20007* ☎ *943/215558* 🖷 *943/463914* ⇆ *16 rooms* ▭ *MC, V.*

Nightlife & the Arts

Glitterati descend on San Sebastián for its international film festival in the second half of September. Exact dates vary; ask the tourist office on Calle Fueros (☎ 943/426282) or read the local press for details. The same goes for the late-July jazz festival, which draws many of the world's top performers. At night, look for *copas, potes* (both "drinks"), and general cruising in and around the Parte Vieja. The **Kursaal** (✉ Av. de la Zurriola ☎ 943/003000 ⊕ www.kursaal.org) houses the Orquesta Sinfónica de Euskadi and is the favored venue for ballet, opera, theater, and jazz. There are varied programs of theater, dance, and other events at the beautiful **Teatro Victoria Eugenia** (✉ Reina Regente s/n, Centro ☎ 943/481155 or 943/481160).

Filled with couples and night owls, **Bideluze** (✉ Pl. de Guipúzcoa 14, Centro ☎ 943/460219) is always alive. **Akerbeltz** (✉ Mari Kalea 10, Parte Vieja ☎ 943/460934), at the corner over the port to the left of Santa María del Coro and the Gaztelubide eating society, is a cozy late-night refuge. San Sebastián's top disco is **Bataplan** (✉ Paseo de la Concha s/n, Centro ☎ 943/460439), near the western end of La Concha. **La Rotonda** (✉ Paseo de la Concha 6, Centro ☎ 943/429095), across the street from Bataplan, below Miraconcha, is a top nightspot. **Kabutzia** (✉ Paseo del Muelle s/n, Centro ☎ 943/429725), above the Club Nautico seaward from the Casino, is a busy night haunt. **Discóbolo** (✉ Blvd. Zumardía 27, Centro ☎ 943/217678), near the Parte Vieja, gets pretty incandescent. **Ku** (✉ Ctra. Monte Igueldo s/n, Igueldo ☎ 943/212050), up on the hill, has been going strong for three decades.

Shopping

San Sebastián is nonpareil for stylish home furnishings and clothing. Wander Calle San Martín and the surrounding pedestrian-only streets to see what's in the windows. **Ponsol** (✉ C. Narrica 4, Parte Vieja ☎ 943/420876) is the best place to buy Basque berets, called *boinas*; the Leclerq family has been hatting Donostiarras for three generations. **Bilintx** (✉ C. Fermín Calbetón 21, Parte Vieja ☎ 943/420080) is one of Donosti's best bookstores. Stop into **Maitiena** (✉ Av. Libertad 32, Centro ☎ 943/424721) for a fabulous selection of chocolates.

Tapas Bars

Aloña Berri Bar. Perennial winner of tapa championships, this place across the Urumea River in Gros is well worth the walk. José Ramon Elizondo's miniature creations, from *contraste de pato* (duck à l'orange) to his Moorish-based *bastela de pichón* (pigeon pie), are merely stupendous. Order the excellent *racione* of crisp asparagus coated with burnt garlic. ✉ *C. Bermingham 24, Gros* ☎ *943/290818.*

Astelena. On the northeast corner of Plaza de la Constitución, this *bar de toda la vida* (lifetime favorite bar) is famous for its *pastel de pescado* (fish pudding). ✉ *C. Iñigo 1, Parte Vieja* ☎ *943/425245.*

Bar Ganbara. Near Plaza de la Constitución, morsels here range from shrimp and asparagus to *jamón ibérico* on croissants to anchovies, sea urchins, and wild mushrooms in season. ✉ *C. San Jerónimo 21, Parte Vieja* ☎ *943/422575.*

Bar Ormazabal. You may not have *thought* you were starving, but when you catch a glimpse of the multicolor, polytextured display that goes up on the Ormazabal bar at midday, hunger pangs will kick in. ✉ *C. 31 de Agosto 22, Parte Vieja* ☎ *943/429907.*

Bar San Marcial. Nearly a secret, downstairs in the center of town, this is a very Basque spot with big wooden tables and a monumental bar filled with *cazuelitas* (small earthenware dishes) and tapas of all kinds. ✉ *C. San Marcial 50, Centro* ☎ *943/431827.*

Bergara Bar. Just down the street from Aloñ Berri Bar, on the corner of Artexte and Bermingham, you'll find a good selection of tasty *pintxos.* ✉ *Artexte, 8, Gros.*

Bernardo Etxea. This hangout for locals during the week and everyone else on weekends serves excellent sangria and morsels: fried peppers, octopus, salmon with salsa, and especially fine pimentos with anchovies. ✉ *C. Puerto, 7, Parte Vieja* ☎ *943/422055.*

Casa Vallés. Freshly prepared creations go up on the bar at midday and again in the early evening. Beloved by locals, the bar combines excellent food with great value. ✉ *Reyes Católicos 10, Amara* ☎ *943/452210.*

Casa Vergara. This cozy bar, in front of the Santa María del Coro church, is always filled with reverent tapas devotees; the counter is always piled high with morsels. ✉ *C. Mayor 21, Parte Vieja* ☎ *943/431073.*

Clery. Tucked in next to the frontón court off Calle 31 de Agosto, this terrace restaurant has an intimate inside counter laden with colorful tapas. ✉ *Plaza de la Trinidad 1, Parte Vieja* ☎ *943/423401.*

La Cepa. This booming and boisterous tavern is one of the all-time standards. Everything from the Iberian ham to the little olive, pepper, and anchovy combos called "penalties" will whet your appetite. ✉ *C. 31 de Agosto 7, Parte Vieja,* ☎ *943/426394.*

Pasajes de San Juan

29 *10 km (6 mi) east of San Sebastián.*

General Lafayette set out from Pasajes de San Juan (Pasaia Donibane, in Euskera) to aid the rebels in the American Revolution. There are actually three towns around the commercial port of Rentería: **Pasajes Ancho,** an industrial port; **Pasajes de San Pedro,** a large fishing harbor; and historic **Pasajes de San Juan.** This last is a tiny and unusually gorgeous settlement of 18th- and 19th-century buildings along a single street fronting the bay's outlet to the sea. It's best reached by driving into Pasajes de San Pedro, on the San Sebastián side of the strait, and catching a launch across the mouth of the harbor (about €50, depending on the time of day). Make sure you get good directions for getting here, or take a cab or bus from town.

Where to Eat

$$$ ✕ **Casa Cámara.** Four generations ago, Pablo Cámara turned this old fishing wharf on the narrows into a first-class restaurant. The dining room has lovely views and a central tank from which live lobsters and crayfish are hauled up for your inspection. Try *cangrejo del mar* (spider crab with vegetable sauce) or the superb *merluza con salsa verde* (hake in green sauce). ✉ *Pasajes de San Juan* ☎ *943/523699* ✍ *Reservations essential* ▭ *AE, DC, MC, V* ⊙ *Closed Mon. No dinner Sun.*

$$ Fodor's Choice ★ ✕ **Txulotxo.** Cozy and friendly, this exceptional restaurant sits on stilts at the edge of the Rentería ship passage, perpetually perched in the shadow of the occasional freighter passing only a dozen yards away. The *sopa de pescado* (fish soup), thick and piping hot, is nonpareil, as are the fresh grilled sole and monkfish and the pimento-wrapped *bacalao* (codfish). Make sure you leave some time to stroll around town. ✉ *Pasajes de San Juan* ☎ *943/523952* ⎙ *943/519601* ✍ *Reservations essential* ▭ *AE, DC, MC, V* ⊙ *Closed Tues. No dinner Sun.*

Hondarribia

30 *12 km (7 mi) east of Pasajes.*

Hondarribia (Fuenterrabía, in Castilian Spanish) is the last fishing port before the French border. Lined with fishermen's homes and small fishing boats, the harbor is a beautiful but rather touristy spot. If you have a taste for history, follow signs up the hill to the medieval bastion and onetime castle of Carlos V, now a parador.

Where to Stay & Eat

$$$$ ✕ **Ramón Roteta.** In a beautiful old villa with an informal garden, this restaurant serves excellent food and is an easy choice for anyone staying at the parador. Sample the homemade garlic and shrimp pastries or the rice with vegetables and clams. ✉ *Villa Ainara, C. Irún 2* ☎ *943/641693* ▭ *AE, DC, MC, V* ⊙ *Closed Tues. mid-June–mid-Sept. No dinner Tues. or Sun. mid-Sept.–mid-June.*

$$$–$$$$ ✕ **Alameda.** Hot young Hondarribia star chef Gorka Txapartegi opened this restaurant in 1997 after working with, among others, Martín Berasategui. The elegantly restored house in upper Hondarribia is a delight, as are the seasonally rotated combinations of carefully chosen ingredients from duck to foie gras to vegetables. ✉ *Minasoroeta 1* ☎ *943/642789* ▭ *AE, DC, MC, V* ⊙ *Closed Mon. and 2nd wk in June. No dinner Sun.*

$$ ✕ **La Hermandad de Pescadores.** This "brotherhood" is owned by the local fishermen's guild and serves simple, hearty fare at reasonable prices. Try the sopa de pescado or the *almejas a la marinera* (clams in a thick, garlicky sauce). If you come outside during peak hours (2–4 and 9–11), you'll find space at the long, communal boards. ✉ *C. Zuloaga s/n* ☎ *943/642738* ▭ *AE, DC, MC, V* ⊙ *Closed Wed. No dinner Tues.*

$$–$$$ **Parador El Emperador.** Replete with suits of armor and other chivalric bric-a-brac, this parador is in a superb medieval bastion that dates from the 10th century and housed Carlos V in the 16th century. Many rooms have views of the Bidasoa River and estuary, dotted with colorful fishing boats. Reserve ahead and ask for one of the three "special" rooms, with canopied beds and baronial appointments; they're worth the extra expense. ✉ *Pl. Armas de Castillo, 20005* ☎ *943/645500* *943/642153* *36 rooms* *Restaurant, minibars, cable TV, bar, meeting rooms, parking (fee)* ▭ *AE, DC, MC, V.*

¢ **Caserío "Artzu."** This family barn and house, with its classic low, wide roofline, has been here in one form or another for some 800 years. Just west of the hermitage of Nuestra Señora de Guadalupe, 5 km (3 mi) above Hondarribia, Artzu offers modernized accommodations in an ancient caserío overlooking the junction of the Bidasoa estuary and the Atlantic. Better hosts than this warm, friendly clan are hard to find. ✉ *Barrio Montaña, 20280* ☎ *943/640530* *6 rooms, 1 with bath* *Restaurant, bar* ▭ *No credit cards.*

en route

The fastest route from San Sebastián to Pamplona is the A15 Autovía de Navarra, which cuts through the Leizarán Valley and gets you there in about 45 minutes. Somewhat prettier, if slower and more tortuous, is the 134-km (83-mi) drive on C133, which starts near Hondarribia and follows the Bidasoa River (the border with France) up through Vera de Bidasoa. When C133 meets N121 you can turn left up into the lovely Baztán Valley or right through the Velate pass to Pamplona.

PAMPLONA & SOUTHERN NAVARRA

Bordering the French Pyrenees and populated largely by Basques, Navarra grows progressively less Basque toward its southern and eastern edges. Pamplona, the ancient Navarran capital, draws crowds with its annual feast of San Fermín, but medieval Vitoria, in the Basque province of Alava, is largely undiscovered by tourists. Olite, south of Pamplona, has a storybook castle, and the towns of Puente la Reina and Estella are picturesque stops on the Camino de Santiago.

Pamplona

31 *91 km (56 mi) southeast of San Sebastián.*

Pamplona (Iruña in Euskera) is known worldwide for its running of the bulls, made famous by Ernest Hemingway in his 1926 novel *The Sun Also Rises*. The occasion is the festival of San Fermín, July 6–14, when Pamplona's population triples (along with hotel rates) so reserve rooms months in advance. Tickets to the bullfights (*corridas*), as opposed to the running (*encierro*, meaning "enclosing"), to which access is free, can be difficult to get. Every morning at 7 sharp a skyrocket is shot off, and the bulls kept overnight in the corrals at the edge of town are run through a series of closed-off streets leading to the bullring, a 902-yard dash. Running before them are Spaniards and foreigners feeling festive enough to risk a goring, most wearing the traditional white shirts and trousers with red neckerchiefs and carrying rolled-up newspapers. If all goes well—no bulls separated from the pack, no mayhem—the bulls arrive in the ring in 2½ minutes. The degree of peril in the encierro is difficult to gauge. Serious injuries occur nearly every day; deaths are rare but always a possibility. What's certain is the sense of danger, the mob hysteria, and the exhilaration.

Founded by the Roman emperor Pompey as Pompaelo, or Pameiopolis, Pamplona was successively taken by the Franks, the Goths, and the Moors. In 750, the Pamplonicas put themselves under the protection of Charlemagne and managed to expel the Arabs temporarily. But the foreign commander took advantage of this trust to destroy the city walls, so that when he was driven out once more by the Moors, the Navarrese took their revenge, ambushing and slaughtering the retreating Frankish army as it fled over the Pyrenees through the mountain pass of Roncesvalles in 778. This is the episode depicted in the 11th-century *Song of Roland,* although the French author chose to cast the aggressors as Moors. For centuries after that, Pamplona remained three argumentative towns until they were forcibly incorporated into one city by Carlos III (the Noble, 1387–1425) of Navarra.

Pamplona's **cathedral,** set near the portion of the ancient walls rebuilt in the 17th century, is one of the most important religious buildings in northern Spain, thanks to the fragile grace and gabled Gothic arches of its cloister. Inside are the tombs of Carlos III and his wife, marked by an alabaster sculpture. The **Museo Diocesano** (Diocesan Museum) houses religious art from the Middle Ages and the Renaissance. ✉ *C. Curia s/n* 🎟 *Free* 🕒 *Museum Tues.–Sat. 9–2 and 4–7, Sun. 9–2.*

On Calle Santo Domingo, in a 16th-century building once used as a hospital for pilgrims on their way to Santiago de Compostela, is the **Museo de Navarra,** with a collection of regional archaeological artifacts and historical costumes. ✉ *C. Jaranta s/n* ☎ *948/227831* 🎟 *€3* 🕒 *Tues.–Sat. 9–2 and 5–7, Sun. 9–2.*

RUNNING WITH THE BULLS

*I***N** ***THE SUN ALSO RISES,*** *Hemingway describes the Pamplona encierro (enclosing) in anything but romantic terms. Jake Barnes hears the rocket, steps out on his balcony (at La Perla, still available for a bird's-eye view of the encierro), and watches the crowd run by: men dressed in the traditional San Fermín white with red sashes and neckerchiefs, those behind running faster, "some stragglers who were really running," then the bulls "running together." A perfect encierro: no bulls separated from the pack, no mayhem. "One man fell, rolled to the gutter, and lay quiet." A textbook move, and first-rate observation and reporting. (If the American killed in 1995 had "lay quiet," the bulls would have run by without a pause; the young man, however, tried to get up and was, as a result, gored to death. An experienced runner remains motionless, as fighting bulls respond only to movement.)*

In the next encierro in the novel, a man is gored through and through and dies. The waiter at the Iruña café mutters, "You hear? Muerto. Dead. He's dead. With a horn through him. All for morning fun. . . . " Despite this, generations of young Americans and other internationals have turned this barnyard bull management maneuver into the western world's most famous rite of passage.

The idea is simple: six fighting bulls are guided through the streets by eight to ten cabestros, steers (also known as mansos, meaning "tame"). The bulls are herded through the bullring to the holding pens from which they will emerge to be fought that afternoon. The course covers 848 meters (924 yards) in about three minutes over terrain of surprising variety. The Cuesta de Santo Domingo down to the corrals is the most dangerous part of the run, high in terror and low in elapsed time. The walls are sheer, and the bulls pass quickly. The fear here is that of a bull, as a result of some personal issue or idiosyncrasy, hooking along the wall of the Military Hospital on his way up the hill, forcing runners out in front of the speeding pack in a classic hammer and anvil movement. Mercaderes is next, cutting left for 104 meters by the town hall, then right up Calle Estafeta. The outside of each turn and the centrifugal force of 10,000 kilos of bulls and steers are to be avoided here.

Calle Estafeta is the bread and butter of the run, the longest (425 meters), straightest, and least complicated part of the course. If the classic run, a perfect blend of form and function, is to remain ahead of the horns for as long as possible, fading to the side when overtaken, this is the place to try to do it. The trickiest part of running with the bulls is splitting your vision so that with one eye you keep track of the bulls behind you and with the other you keep from falling over runners ahead of you.

At the end of Estafeta the course descends left through the callejón, the narrow tunnel, into the bullring. The bulls move more slowly here, uncertain of their weak forelegs, allowing runners to stay close and even to touch them as they glide down into the tunnel. The only uncertainty is whether there will be a montón, a pileup, in the tunnel or not. The most dramatic photographs of the encierro have been taken here, as the galloping pack slams through what occasionally turns into a solid wall of humanity. If all goes well—no bulls separated from the pack, no mayhem—the bulls will have arrived in the ring in under three minutes.

Remember that the cardinal crime, punishable by a $1,000 fine, is to attempt to attract the bull, thus removing him from the pack and creating a deadly danger. There have been 13 deaths during this century, the last one on July 13, 1995.

3

Pamplona's most remarkable civil building is the ornate, 18th-century **ayuntamiento,** on the Plaza Consistorial, which over the years has acquired a blackish color that sets off its gilded balconies. Stop in to see the wood-and-marble interior.

need a break?

Pamplona's gentry has been flocking to the ornate, French-style **Café Iruña** (Pl. del Castillo 44) since 1888. Beyond the stand-up bar is a bingo hall (you must be 18 to play). The café is open daily 5 PM–3 AM.

One of Pamplona's greatest charms is the warren of small streets near the **Plaza del Castillo** (especially Calle San Nicolás), which are filled with restaurants, taverns, and bars. Pamplonicas are hardy sorts, well known for their eagerness and capacity to eat and drink. The central **Ciudadela,** an ancient fortress, is a parkland of promenades and pools. Walk through in late afternoon, the time of the *paseo* (traditional stroll), for a taste of everyday life here.

Where to Stay & Eat

$$–$$$ ✕ **Hartza.** Archaic and elegant, this rustic place serves some of the most creative cuisine in Pamplona. Try the *oca con jugo de trufa y manzana* (goose with apple and truffles). ✉ *Juan de Labrit 19* ☎ *948/224568* 💳 *AE, DC, MC, V* ⊗ *Closed Mon., late July–late Aug., and late Dec.–early Jan. No dinner Sun.*

$$–$$$ ✕ **Josetxo.** This warm, elegant family-run restaurant is one of Pamplona's finest. Specialties include *hojaldre de marisco* (shellfish pastry), an *ensalada de langosta* (lobster salad) appetizer, and *muslo de pichón relleno de trufa y foie* (pigeon stuffed with truffles and foie gras). ✉ *Príncipe de Viana 1* ☎ *948/222097* 💳 *AE, DC, MC, V* ⊗ *Closed Sun. except during San Fermín, and Aug.*

$–$$ ✕ **Erburu.** In the heart of the nightlife district, this dark, wood-beam restaurant is a true find, frequented by Pamplonans in the know. Come here to dine or just to sample tapas at the bar. Standouts are the Basque classic *merluza con salsa verde* (hake in green sauce) and any of the dishes made with *alcochofas* (artichokes). ✉ *San Lorenzo 19–21* ☎ *948/225169* 💳 *AE, DC, MC, V* ⊗ *Closed Mon. and last 2 wks in July.*

$–$$ ✕🏨 **Casa Otano.** This friendly, tumultuous hotel and restaurant is simple and well placed, right in the middle of the tapas-and-wine circuit and just a few paces from Pamplona's main square. The restaurant downstairs serves hearty Basque fare. The pace is consistent with the madness that will be raging in the street if you come during San Fermín. ✉ *San Nicolás 5, 31001* ☎ *948/225095* 📠 *948/212012* *15 rooms* *Restaurant, bar* 💳 *AE, DC, MC, V* ⊗ *Closed last 2 wks in July.*

$$$ 🏨 **Los Tres Reyes.** Named for the three kings of Navarra, Aragón, and Castile—who, it was said, could meet at La Mesa de los Tres Reyes, in the Pyrenees, without stepping out of their respective realms—this modern glass-and-stone refuge operates on the same principle: come to Pamplona and find all the comforts of home. ✉ *C. de la Taconera s/n, 31001* ☎ *948/226600* 📠 *948/222930* *168 rooms* *Restaurant, cafeteria, minibars, cable TV, pool, hair salon, health club, bar, piano bar, meeting rooms, car rental, parking (fee)* 💳 *AE, DC, MC, V.*

$$ 🏨 **La Perla.** Hemingway watched his first running of the bulls here, from his balcony over Calle Estafeta. La Perla is the oldest hotel in town, though far from the best. The founder's son was a bullfighter, and the two bulls he killed before retiring preside over the salon. The simple, charming decor is straight out of *The Sun Also Rises*. Prices triple during San Fermín. ✉ *Pl. del Castillo 1, 31001* ☎ *948/227706* 📠 *948/221519* *67 rooms, 45 with bath* *Restaurant, bar* 💳 *AE, DC, MC, V.*

Nightlife & the Arts

The city has a thumping student life year-round. In August, the **Festivales de Navarra** bring theater and other events to Pamplona. There's a varied summer program of concerts, ballet, and zarzuela; contact the **Teatro Gayarre** (✉ Av. Carlos III Noble 1 ☎ 948/220139) for information.

Shopping

Botas are the wineskins from which Basques typically drink at bullfights or during fiestas. The art lies in drinking a stream of wine from a bota held at arm's length—without spilling a drop, if you want to maintain your honor (not to mention your shirt). The neckerchiefs worn for the running of the bulls are sold in various shops, as are *gerrikos,* the wide belts worn by Basque sportsmen during contests of strength, to hold in overstressed organs. You can buy botas in any Basque town, but Pamplona's **Anel** (✉ C. Comedías 7) sells the best brand, Las Tres Zetas—"The Three Zs," written as ZZZ.

For sweets, try **Salcedo** (✉ C. Estafeta 37), open since 1800, which invented and still sells almond-based *mantecadas* (powder cakes), as well as *coronillas* (delightful almond-and-cream concoctions). **Hijas de C. Lozano** (✉ C. Zapatería 11) sells *café y leche* (coffee and milk) toffees that are prized all over Spain.

Olite

32 *41 km (25 mi) south of Pamplona.*

A storybook castle marooned on the plains of Navarra, Olite is an unforgettable glimpse into the life of Spain in the Middle Ages. The 11th-century church of **San Pedro** is interesting for its finely worked Romanesque cloisters and portal. The town's parador is part of a **castle** restored by Carlos III in the French style—ramparts, crenellated battlements, and watchtowers. You can walk the ramparts in the section not occupied by the parador. €2 *Daily 10–2 and 4–5.*

Where to Stay & Eat

$$–$$$ Fodor'sChoice ★ **Parador Príncipe de Viana.** This castle parador is a flight of fancy, named for the grandson of Carlos III, who spent his life here. It's housed in part of Olite's castle complex, and the chivalric tone is well preserved, with grand salons, secret stairways, heraldic tapestries, and the odd suit of armor. ✉ *Pl. de los Teobaldos 2, 31390* ☎ *948/740000* *948/740201* *43 rooms* *Restaurant, minibars, bar, meeting rooms* *AE, DC, MC, V.*

Puente la Reina

33 *31 km (19 mi) west of Olite, 24 km (15 mi) south of Pamplona.*

Puente la Reina (Gares in Euskera) is an important nexus on the Camino de Santiago: the junction of the two pilgrimage routes from northern Europe, one passing through Somport and Jaca and the other through Roncesvalles and Pamplona. A bronze sculpture of a pilgrim marks the spot. The graceful medieval bridge over the river Arga was built for pilgrims by Navarran King Sancho VII el Fuerte (the Strong) in the 11th century. The streets, particularly Calle Mayor, are lined with tiny, ancient houses. The church of **Santiago** (St. James; ✉ C. Mayor) is known for its gold sculpture of the saint. The **Iglesia del Crucifijo** (Church of the Crucifix; ✉ Ctra. de Pamplona s/n) has a notably expressive wooden sculpture of Christ on a Y-shape cross, gift of a 14th-century pilgrim. The octagonal church of **Santa María de Eunate** (5 km [3 mi] east of

Puente la Reina) was once used as a burial place for pilgrims who didn't make it. The church of **San Román** (✣ 6 km [4 mi] west of Puente la Reina), in the restored village of Cirauqui, has an extraordinarily beautiful carved portal.

Where to Stay & Eat

$$ ✕▣ **Mesón del Peregrino.** A renowned haven for weary pilgrims, this rustic stone house north of town is hard to pass up. The rooms are small but charming. Roasts, *menestra de verduras* (Navarran vegetable stew), and hearty bean and sausage–based soups are among the offerings. ✉ *Ctra. Pamplona–Logroño, Km 23, 31100* ☎ *948/340075* ⎙ *948/341190* *13 rooms* *Restaurant, minibars, pool, bar* ▭ *AE, DC, MC, V.*

Estella

34 *19 km (12 mi) south of Puente la Reina, 48 km (30 mi) north of Logroño.*

Once the seat of the Royal Court of Navarra, Estella (Lizarra, in Euskera) is an inspiring stop on the Camino de Santiago. Its heart is the arcaded Plaza San Martín, its chief civic monument the 12th-century **Palacio de los Reyes de Navarra** (Palace of the Kings of Navarra). **San Pedro de la Rúa** (✉ C. San Nicolás s/n) has a beautiful cloister and a stunning carved portal. Across the River Ega from San Pedro, the doorway to the church of **San Miguel** has fantastic relief sculptures of St. Michael the Archangel battling a dragon. The **Iglesia del Santo Sepulcro** (Church of the Holy Sepulchre; ✉ C. Curtidores s/n) has a beautiful fluted portal. **Santa María Jus del Castillo** (✉ C. Curtidores s/n), converted from a synagogue in 1145, is the only vestige of Estella's medieval Jewish quarter. The **Monasterio de Irache** (✉ Ctra. de Logroño, Km 3) dates from the 10th century but was later converted by Cistercian monks to a pilgrims' hospital; next door is the famous brass faucet that supplies pilgrims with free-flowing holy wine.

VITORIA & THE RIOJA ALAVESA

Medieval Vitoria, in the Basque province of Alava, is largely undiscovered by tourists, while the Rioja Alavesa and, in particular, Laguardia rank among the Basque Country's most unforgettable destinations.

Vitoria

35 *93 km (56 mi) west of Pamplona, 115 km (71 mi) southwest of San Sebastián, 64 km (40 mi) southeast of Bilbao.*

Vitoria's standard of living has been rated the highest in Spain, based on such criteria as square meters of green space per inhabitant (14), sports and cultural facilities, and pedestrian-only zones. Capital of the Basque Country, and its second-largest city after Bilbao, Vitoria (Gasteiz, in Euskera) is in many ways Euskadi's least Basque city. Neither a maritime nor a mountain enclave, Vitoria occupies the steppelike *meseta de Alava* (Alava plain) and functions as a modern industrial center with a surprisingly medieval *casco antiguo* (old quarter). Founded by Sancho el Sabio (the Wise) in 1181, the city was built largely of granite rather than sandstone, so Vitoria's oldest streets and squares seem especially dark, weathered, and ancient.

Plaza de la Virgen Blanca, in the southwest corner of old Vitoria, is ringed by noble houses with covered arches and white-trim glass galleries. The monument in the center commemorates the Duke of Wellington's defeat of Napoléon's army here in 1813. For lunch, coffee, or tapas, look to the plaza's top left-hand corner for the Cafeteria de la Virgen Blanca, replete with giant wooden floorboards. The **Plaza de España,** across Virgen Blanca past the monument and the handsome El Victoria café, is an arcaded neoclassical square with the austere elegance typical of formal 19th-century squares all over Spain. The **Plaza del Machete,** overlooking Plaza de España, is named for the sword used by medieval nobility to swear allegiance to the local *fueros,* or special Basque rights and privileges. A jasper niche in the lateral facade of the Gothic church of **San Miguel** (✉ Plaza del Machete) contains the Virgen Blanca (White Virgin), Vitoria's patron saint.

The **Palacio de los Alava Esquivel** (✉ C. de la Soledad) is reached from the Plaza de la Virgen Blanca along Calle de Herrería, which follows the egg-shape outline along the west side of the old city walls. House **No. 27** (✉ across from Cantón Anorbin) has elaborately sculpted engravings over the door and a giant coat of arms on the far corner. The house is past the church of San Pedro Apostol. The 15th-century **Torre de Doña Otxanda** (✉ before C. de las Carnicerías) houses Vitoria's Museo de Ciencias Naturales (Museum of Natural Sciences).

El Portalón (✉ C. de la Correría 151), the ancient brick-and-wood house at the corner across from the museum, a hostelry for 500 years, is an excellent restaurant and wine cellar. The **Museo de la Arqueología** (✉ C. de la Correría) has paleolithic dolmens, Roman art and artifacts, medieval objects, and the famous *stele del jinete* (stele of the horseback rider), an early Basque tombstone. Look at the door nearest the corner in the ocher house at **No. 14** (✉ corner of C. Correría and Cantón Apaizgaitegi): its elaborate coat of arms depicts lions and castles, once painted gold and purple. Equally faded trim spirals around the coat of arms and the corners of the house, while conch shells appear under scrolls below the windows.

The Torre de los Hurtado de Anda is across from the exquisitely sculpted Gothic doorway on the western facade of the **Catedral de Santa María** (✉ C. Fray Zacarías Martinez s/n). Go into the courtyard on the west side of this square; in the far right corner, you'll find the sculpted head of a fish protruding from the grass in front of an intensely sculpted door. Walk through Calle Txikitxoa and up Cantón de Santa María behind the cathedral, noting the tiny accretions that have been added to the back of the apse over the centuries, clinging across corners and filling odd spaces. The lovely plateresque facade of the 16th-century **Palacio de Escoriaza-Esquibel** (✉ C. Fray Zacarías Martinez) overlooks an open space. Don't miss the austere **Palacio Villa Suso** (✉ C. Fray Zacarías Martinez), built in 1538. It's down toward the Plaza del Machete, across from the church of San Miguel. The **Casa del Cordón** (✉ C. Cuchillería), a 15th-century structure with a 13th-century tower, stands at No. 24, identifiable by the Franciscan *cordón* (rope) decorating one of the pointed arches on the facade.

★ The 1525 Palacio de Bendaña is home to one of Vitoria's main attractions, the **Museo Fournier de Naipes** (Playing-Card Museum). In 1868 Don Heraclio Fournier founded a playing-card factory, started amassing cards, and eventually found himself with 15,000 sets, the largest and finest such collection in the world. As you survey rooms of hand-painted cards, the distinction between artwork and game piece quickly gets scrambled. The oldest sets date from the 12th century, making them older than the building, and the story parallels the history of printing. The most unusual and finely painted sets come from Japan, India (the Indian cards are round), and the international practice of tarot. One German set has musical bars that can be combined to form hundreds of different waltzes. By the time you reach the 20th-century rooms, contemporary designs have been debunked as unoriginal. You'll never look at cards the same way again. ✉ *C. Cuchillería 54* ☎ *945/255555* *Free* ⏲ *Tues.–Fri. 10–2 and 4–6:30, Sat. 10–2, Sun. 11–2.*

Parque de la Florida (✉ south of Plaza de la Virgen Blanca) is nice respite during a tour of Vitoria. The **Museo Provincial de Armería** (Provincial Arms Museum; ✉ Paseo Fray Francisco de Vitoria) has prehistoric hatchets, 20th-century pistols, and a sand-table reproduction of the 1813 battle between the Duke of Wellington and the French. The museum is south of the Parque de la Florida. The **Museo de Bellas Artes** (Museum of Fine Arts; ✉ Paseo Fray Francisco de Vitoria) has paintings by Ribera, Picasso, and the Basque painter Zuloaga. Next door is the Palacio Ajuria-Enea, seat of the Basque government.

Where to Stay & Eat

★ **$$–$$$** ✕ **El Portalón.** Between the dark, creaky wood floors and staircases and the ancient beams, pillars, and coats of arms, this famous 15th-century inn turns out food that seems too good to be true. Try the *lomo de cebón asado en su jugo con puré de manzanas* (filet mignon with apple puree) or any of the *merluza* (hake) preparations. ✉ *C. Correría 151* ☎ *945/142755* 💳 *AE, DC, MC, V* ⏲ *Closed Sun., last 3 wks in Aug., and late Dec.–early Jan.*

$–$$ ✕ **Asador Matxete.** In Vitoria's most historic square, this fresh modern space overlooks some of the town's most characteristic wooden galleries, stuck miraculously onto medieval stone buildings. This place, which specializes in meat roasted over coals, is perfect if you want to try a taste of the Castilian *meseta* (plain) at the edge of the Basque Country. ✉ *Plaza del Machete 4–5* ☎ *945/131821* 💳 *AE, DC, MC, V* ⏲ *No dinner Sun.*

★ **$$** ✕🏨 **Parador de Argómaniz.** Some 15 minutes east of Vitoria off the N104 road toward Pamplona, this 17th-century palace has panoramic views over the Alava plains and retains a powerful sense of mystery and romance, with long stone hallways punctuated by imposing antiques. Rooms have polished wood floors and huge, terra-cotta-floor bathrooms; some have glass-enclosed sitting areas and/or hot tubs. The wood-beam dining room on the top (third) floor makes each meal feel like a baronial feast. ✉ *N-I, Km 363, 01192 Argómaniz* ☎ *945/293200* 📠 *945/293287* *53 rooms* *Restaurant, minibars, cable TV, bar, free parking* 💳 *AE, DC, MC, V.*

$$$ 🏨 **Canciller Ayala.** This modern structure is handy for in-town comfort, two minutes from the old quarter next to the lush Parque de la Florida. Rooms are bright, streamlined, and beyond reproach, if unremarkable. ✉ *C. Ramón y Cajal 5, 01007* ☎ *945/130000* 📠 *945/133505* *184 rooms* *Restaurant, minibars, bar, meeting rooms, parking (fee)* 💳 *AE, DC, MC, V.*

en route

Between Vitoria and Logroño, on the north bank of the Ebro River, is the wine-growing Rioja Alavesa region. Either sweep comfortably around on the Madrid road and approach from the west via Haro, Briones (with a lovely medieval bridge), and San Vicente de la Sonsierra, *or* drive south on the slower, curvier A2124 through the Puerto de Herrera pass to the Balcón de La Rioja for a view of the Ebro Valley.

Laguardia

36 *66 km (40 mi) southeast of Vitoria, 17 km (10 mi) west of Logroño.*

Founded in 908 to stand guard, as its name suggests, over Navarra's southwestern flank, Laguardia is on a lofty promontory overlooking the Ebro River and the vineyards of the Rioja Alavesa—La Rioja wine country north of the Ebro in the Basque province of Alava. Flanked by the Sierra de Cantabria, the town rises shiplike, its prow headed north, over the savory sea of surrounding vineyards. Ringed with walls, Laguardia's dense cluster of emblazoned noble facades and stunning patios may have no equal in Spain. Relish the some 50 houses with coats of arms and medieval or Renaissance masonry. The wine cellars and taverns serve excellent local reds, both *vinos del año* (young wines of the year) and *crianzas* (aged three years).

Starting from the 15th-century Puerta de Carnicerías, or Puerta Nueva, the central portal off the parking area on the east side of town, the first landmark is the 16th-century **ayuntamiento,** with its imperial shield of Carlos V. Farther into the square is the current town hall, built in the 19th century. A right down **Calle Santa Engracia** takes you past impressive facades—the floor inside the portal at No. 25 is a lovely stone mosaic, while a walk behind the triple-emblazoned 17th-century facade of No. 19 reveals a stagecoach, floor mosaics, wood beams, an inner porch, and, if you're lucky, the aroma of potato-and-leek soup. Nos. 15 and 9 both have interesting reliefs and masonry. The Puerta de Santa Engracia, with an image of the saint in an overhead niche, opens out to the right, while on the left, at the entrance to Calle Víctor Tapia, house No. 17 bears a coat of arms with the Latin LAUS TIBI (Praise Be to Thee). Laguardia's crown architectural jewel is Spain's only Gothic polychrome portal, on the church of **Santa María de los Reyes.** Protected by a posterior Renaissance facade, the door centers on a lovely, lifelike effigy of La Virgen de los Reyes (Virgin of the Kings), sculpted in the 14th century and painted in the 17th by Juan Francisco de Ribera. Flanking the Virgin are the apostles and biblical scenes.

To the north of the ornate castle and hotel El Collado is the monument to the famous Laguardia composer of fables, Felix María Samaniego (1745–1801), heir to the tradition of Aesop and Lafontaine. Walk around the small, grassy park to the Puerta de Páganos and look right—you'll see Laguardia's oldest civil structure, the late-14th-century **Casa de la Primicia,** at Calle Páganos 78 (so named as the place where fresh fruit was sold). If you walk left of the Casa de la Primicia, past several emblazoned houses to Calle Páganos 13, you'll see the *bodega* (wine cellar) at the Posada Mayor de Migueloa, which is usually in full cry. Go through the corridor to the Posada's Calle Mayor entryway and walk up to the **Juanjo San Pedro** gallery at Calle Mayor 1, filled with antiques and artwork.

Where to Stay & Eat

$$ Fodor's Choice ★ **Posada Mayor de Migueloa.** With a tavern at Calle Páganos 13 and a passageway leading to the stone reception area on Mayor de Migueloa, this 17th-century palace is a beauty. At the tavern, try *patatas a la riojana* (potatoes with chorizo) or *pochas con chorizo y costilla* (beans with sausage and lamb chop). Dinner ranges from beef with foie gras to *mollejas de cordero* (lamb sweetbreads) to *venado con miel y pomelo* (venison with a honey-and-grapefruit sauce). Guest rooms have beautiful, original, rough-hewn ceiling beams. *C. Mayor de Migueloa 20, 01300 945/621175 945/621022 8 rooms Restaurant, bar AE, DC, MC, V Closed mid-Dec.–mid-Jan.*

$–$$ ✕ **Marixa.** Aficionados travel great distances to dine in Marixa's lovely restaurant, known for its excellent roasts, views, and value. The heavy, wooden interior is ancient and intimate, and the cuisine is Vasco-Riojano, combining the best of both worlds. Try the *menestra de riojana verduras,* a mixed-vegetable dish, or the *cordero asado a la parrilla,* lamb roasted over coals. Guest rooms are modern, cheery, and carpeted, with views over the medieval walls of Laguardia to the Ebro Valley beyond. ✉ *C. Sancho Abarca 8, 01300* ☎ *945/600165* *945/600202* *10 rooms* *Restaurant, bar* *AE, DC, MC, V* *Closed mid-Dec.–mid-Jan.*

LA RIOJA

A natural compendium of highlands, plains, vineyards, and the Ebro River basin, La Rioja is Spain's premier producer of wines. The area's quarter of a million inhabitants live mainly along the Ebro, in the cities of Logroño, Haro, and Calahorra, but many of its treasures are in the mountains and river valleys. La Rioja's culture and wines both combine Atlantic and Mediterranean influences, as well as Basque overtones and the arid ruggedness of Iberia's central *meseta.* Drained by the Rivers Oja (hence the name *río oja*), Najerilla, Iregua, Leza, and Cidacos, La Rioja is composed of the Rioja Alta (Upper Rioja), the moist and mountainous western end, and the Rioja Baja (Lower Rioja), the flatter and dryer eastern end, more Mediterranean in climate. Logroño, the capital, lies between the two.

Logroño

37 *92 km (55 mi) southwest of Pamplona on N-III.*

A busy city of 130,000 and a modern industrial center, Logroño retains a lovely old quarter between its two bridges, bordered by the Ebro and the medieval walls. Breton de los Herreros and Muro Francisco de la Mata are the quarter's most characteristic streets. An important wine- and tapa-tasting center, **Calle Laurel** and the neighboring streets are collectively known as *el sendero de los elefantes* (the path of the elephants)—an allusion to *trompas* (trunks), Spanish for a snootful. Each bar is known for a specialty: Bar Soriano for "*champis*" (*champiñones,* mushrooms), Blanco y Negro for *sepia* (cuttlefish), Casa Lucio for *migas de pastor* (bread crumbs with garlic and chorizo) and *embuchados* (crisped, sliced lamb tripe), and La Travesía for *tortillas de patatas* (potato omelets). Order crianza and they'll break out the crystal. A *cosechero,* wine of the year, is served in small shot glasses, while *reserva* (made with specially selected grapes aged three years or more in oak and bottle) will elicit snifters for proper swirling, smelling, and tasting.

Near Logroño, the Roman bridge and the *mirador* (lookout) at **Viguera** are the main sights in the lower Iregua Valley. Santiago (St. James), according to legend, helped the Christians defeat the Moors at the **Castillo de Clavijo,** another panoramic spot. The **Leza (Cañon) del Río Leza** is La Rioja's most dramatic canyon.

Logroño's dominant landmarks are the finest sacred structures in Rioja. The 11th-century church of the **Imperial de Santa María del Palacio** (✉ C. Ruavieja s/n) is known as La Aguja (The Needle) for its pyramid-shape, 45-yard Romanesque-Gothic tower. The church of **Santiago el Real** (Royal St. James; ✉ Plaza de Santiago s/n), reconstructed in the 16th century, is noted for its equestrian statue of the saint (also known as Santiago Matamoros—St. James the Moorslayer), which presides over the main door. **San Bartolomé** (✉ C. San Bartolomé s/n) is a 13th- to 14th-century French Gothic church with an 11th-century Mudéjar tower and an elaborately sculpted 14th-century Gothic doorway. The **Catedral de Santa María de La Redonda** (✉ Plaza de los Portales s/n) is a landmark for its twin baroque towers. Many of Logroño's monuments, such as the elegant **Puente de Piedra** (Stone Bridge), were built as part of the Camino de Santiago pilgrimage route.

Where to Stay & Eat

$$–$$$ ✕ **El Asador de Aranda.** The Castilian rustic feel here suggests how it must have felt to crowd around the fire after a day at the reins of a stagecoach from Barcelona to Madrid. Roast lamb is the specialty, but *alubias* (kidney beans) and *migas de pastor* (bread crumbs with garlic and sausage) are hard to resist. ✉ *Republica Argentina 8* ☎ *941/208125* ▭ *AE, DC, V* ⊙ *No dinner Sun.*

$–$$ ✕ **El Cachetero.** Local fare based on vegetables is the rule here, but you can also tuck away into roast goat or lamb. The cuisine is homespun, its raw materials fresh and seasonally appealing. ✉ *C. Laurel 3* ☎ *941/228463* ▭ *AE, DC, V* ⊙ *Closed Sun. and 1st 2 wks in Aug. No dinner Wed.*

$$$ 🏨 **Herencia Rioja.** This modern hotel near the old quarter has bright and comfortable rooms, a fine restaurant, and a healthy buzz about it. ✉ *Marqués de Murrieta 1, 26005* ☎ *941/210222* 📠 *941/210206* ⇨ *81 rooms, 2 suites* ♨ *Restaurant, cafeteria, gym, bar* ▭ *AE, DC, MC, V.*

$–$$ 🏨 **Marqués de Vallejo.** This family-run hotel is close to, but not overwhelmed by, the food- and wine-tasting frenzy of Calle del Laurel. Rooms are small but intimate, and the best historic sights are nearby. Stash your car in the garage beneath the nearby Plaza del Espolón. ✉ *Marqués de Vallejo 8, 26005* ☎ *941/248333* 📠 *941/240288* ⇨ *30 rooms* ♨ *Cafeteria, bar* ▭ *AE, DC, MC, V.*

La Rioja Alta

The Upper Rioja, the most prosperous part of the wine country, extends from the Ebro River to the Sierra de la Demanda. La Rioja Alta has the most fertile soil, the best vineyards and agriculture, the most impressive castles and monasteries, a ski resort at Ezcaray, and the historical economic advantage of being on the Camino de Santiago. From Logroño, drive 12 km (7 mi) west on the N120 to **Navarrete** to see its noble houses and the baroque altarpiece in Asunción church.

Nájera, 15 km (9 mi) west of Navarrete, was the court of the Kings of Navarra and capital of Navarra and La Rioja until 1076, when La Rioja became part of Castile and the residence of the Castilian royal family. The monastery of **Santa María la Real** (☎ 941/363650), "pantheon of kings," is distinguished by its 16th-century Claustro de los Caballeros (Cavaliers' Cloister), a flamboyant Gothic structure with 24 lacy plateresque Renaissance arches overlooking a grassy patio. The sculpted 12th-century tomb of Doña Blanca de Navarra is the monastery's best-known sarcophagus, and the 67 Flamboyant Gothic choir stalls, dating from 1495, are some of Spain's best.

Santo Domingo de la Calzada, 20 km (12 mi) west of Nájera on the N120, has always been a key stop on the Camino. Santo Domingo was an 11th-century saint who built roads and bridges for pilgrims and founded the pilgrims' hospital that is now the town's parador. The cathedral is a Romanesque-Gothic pile containing the saint's tomb, choir murals, and walnut altarpiece carved by Damià Forment in 1541. The live hen and rooster in a plateresque stone chicken coop commemorate a legendary local miracle in which a pair of roasted fowl came back to life to protest the innocence of a pilgrim hanged for theft. Be sure to stroll through the town's beautifully preserved medieval quarter.

Enter the **Sierra de la Demanda** by heading south 14 km (8½ mi) on LO-810. Your first stop is the town of **Ezcaray,** with its aristocratic houses emblazoned with family crests, of which the **Palacio del Conde de Torremúzquiz** (Palace of the Count of Torremúzquiz) is the most distinguished. Good excursions from here are the Valdezcaray winter-sports center; the source of the River Oja at Llano de la Casa; La Rioja's highest point, at the 7,494-ft Pico de San Lorenzo; and the Romanesque church of Tres Fuentes, at Valgañón. The town of **San Millán de la Cogolla** is southeast of Santo Domingo de la Calzada. Take LO-809 southeast through Berceo to the Monasterio de Yuso, where a 10th-century manuscript on St. Augustine's *Glosas Emilianenses* has notes in what is considered the earliest example of the Spanish language, the vernacular Latin dialect roman paladino. The nearby Visigothic Monasterio de Suso is where Gonzalo de Berceo, recognized as the first Castilian poet, wrote and recited his 13th-century verse in the Castilian tongue, now the language of more than 300 million people.

Where to Stay & Eat

$–$$ ✕ **Echaurren.** This rambling roadhouse in Ezcaray, La Rioja's prime ski resort 61 km (37 mi) southwest of Logrono, is justly famous for fine traditional cuisine, as well as for original and creative recipes. The *patatas a la riojana* (potatoes stewed with peppers and chorizo) alone are well worth the trip. Rooms are modern and the Echaurren family is warm and engaging. ✉ *Héroes del Alcazar 2, 26280 Ezcaray* ☎ *941/354047* 📠 *941/427133* 🌐 *www.echaurren.com* *25 rooms* *Restaurant, bar, parking (fee)* ▭ *AE, DC, MC, V.*

Haro

38 *20 km (12 mi) west of Nájera on the N120, 49 km (29 mi) west of Logroño.*

Haro is the wine capital of La Rioja. The architectural highlight is the Flamboyant Gothic church of **Santo Tomás,** a single-nave church completed in 1564 with an intricately sculpted, reddish-tinge (from the limestone soil of the Rioja Alta) portal on the south side. Ribbed vaulting sweeping down into clustered columns divides the nave, while the richly gilded 60-ft-high organ facade above the choir loft is stunning. Haro's **old quarter** and best taverns, known for their crianzas and tapas, are concentrated in the loop known as La Herradura (The Horseshoe), with Santo Tomás at its curve, and the feet leading up San Martín and Santo Tomás from the open space at the upper left-hand (northeast) corner of Plaza de la Paz. The immense **Palacio de Bendaña** is on the left (east) side of café-lined Plaza de la Paz; you'll see the storks' nest on its cupola belvedere from the far side. Up the left side of the horseshoe, Bar La Esquina, on the left, is the first of many top-notch tapas bars. Bar Los Caños, behind a stone archway at San Martín 5, is built into the vaults and arches of the former church of San Martín. The bar serves an excellent Bikaña crianza and a memorable pintxo of quail egg, anchovy, jalapeño-like pepper, and olive. Haro's century-old **bodegas** (wineries) have been headquartered in the *barrio de la estación* (train-station district) ever since the railroad opened in 1863. Guided tours and tastings, some in English, can be arranged at the facilities themselves or through the tourist office. Haro's June 29 Batalla del Vino (Wine Battle) is an epic wet brawl.

Where to Stay & Eat

$$–$$$ ✕ **Terete.** A favorite with locals, this rustic place has been roasting lamb in wood ovens since 1877 and serves a hearty *minestra de verduras* (vegetable stew). The wine cellar is stocked with some of the Rioja's best.

SPAIN'S WINE COUNTRY

*T**HE EBRO RIVER BASIN** has been an ideal habitat for grapevines since pre-Roman times. Rioja wines were first recognized in official documents in 1102, and exports to Europe flourished over the next several centuries. The phylloxera blight that ruined French vineyards in 1863 brought Spain both the expertise of Bordeaux vintners and an explosion in the demand for Spanish wine.*

With its rich and uneroded soil, river microclimates, ocean moisture, and sun, La Rioja is ideally endowed for high-quality grapes. Shielded from the arid cold of the Iberian meseta *(plain) by the Sierra de la Demanda and from the bitter Atlantic weather by the Sierra de Cantabria, Spain's prime wine country covers an area 150 km (93 mi) long and 50 km (31 mi) wide along the banks of the Ebro. The lighter limestone soils in the 50,000 acres of the Rioja Alta (Upper Rioja) produce the region's finest wines; the vineyards in the 44,000-acre Rioja Baja (Lower Rioja) are composed of alluvial and flood-plain clay in a warmer climate, ideal for the production of great volume.*

The main grape of the Upper Rioja is the Tempranillo—so named for its early (temprano) ripening in mid-September—a dark, thick-skinned grape known for power, stability, and fragrance. Other varieties include the Mazuelo, used for longevity and tannin; and the Graciano, which lends aroma and freshness and makes high-quality wine. The Garnacha, the main grape of the Lower Rioja, is an ideal complement to the more acidic Tempranillo. The Viura, the principal white variety, is fresh and fragrant, while Malvasía grapes stabilize wines that will age in oak barrels.

Rioja wines are categorized according to age. Garantía de Origen is the lowest rank, assuring that the wine comes from where it purports to come from and has been aged for at least a year. A Crianza wine has aged at least three years, with at least one spent in oak. A Reserva is a more carefully selected wine also aged three years, at least one in oak. Gran Reserva is the top category, reserved for extraordinary harvests aged for at least two years in oak and three in the bottle.

Rioja wine is distinguished by the fact that most of it ages for a significant length of time in barrels made of old American oak, as opposed to most French wine, aged for less time in barrels made of new French oak. American oak is more porous, causing faster oxidation of the wine, which means more de facto aging in less time. Thus the average Rioja is deeper and smoother, whereas middle-range French wines are sharper and fruitier. The other difference is economic: a Rioja Reserva can cost under $10.

Wine and ritual overlap everywhere in La Rioja. The first wine of the year is offered to and blessed by the Virgin of Valvanera on the riverbank at the Espolón de Logroño. Haro's Batalla del Vino (Wine Battle) festival is famous throughout Spain. Everything from the harvest and the trimming of the vines to the digging of fermentation pools and the making of baskets, barrels, and botas (wineskins)—even the glassblowing craft employed in bottle manufacture—takes on a magical, almost religious significance.

*For a tour of vineyards and wine cellars, start with **Haro,** filled with world-famous* bodegas *(wineries) and noble architecture. Haro's* barrio de la estación *(train-station district) has all of La Rioja's oldest and most famous bodegas. Call the **Carlos Serres winery** (✉ San Agustín s/n ☎ 941/311308) for a tour of the process. The **Muga bodega** (☎ 941/310498) welcomes tasters at just about any hour. Other visits in the Upper Rioja could include **Fuenmayor,** a wine-making center with an old quarter; **Cenicero,** with several ancient bodegas; **Briones,** a perfectly preserved Renaissance town; **Ollauri,** with a cave bodega, "the Sistine Chapel of the Rioja"; and **Briñas,** with a wine exhibit.*

✉ *C. Lucrecia Arana 17* ☎ *941/310023* ▭ *AE, DC, V* ⏲ *Closed Mon., 1st 2 wks in July, and last 2 wks in Aug.*

$$–$$$ ✕🏨 **Hostería del Monasterio de San Millán.** Declared a World Heritage Site by UNESCO, this magnificent inn occupies a wing of the Monasterio de Yuso. Guest rooms are elegant and somewhat austere, but the comforts are comprehensive. ✉ *San Agustín 2, 26226* ☎ *941/373277* 📠 *941/373266* 🌐 *www.sanmillan.com* *22 rooms* *Restaurant, cafeteria, minibars, bar* ▭ *AE, DC, MC, V.*

$$ ✕🏨 **Los Agustinos.** Haro's best hotel is built into a 14th-century monastery whose cloister (now a pleasant patio) is considered one of the best in La Rioja. Arches, a great hall, and tapestries complete the medieval look. ✉ *San Agustín 2, 26200* ☎ *941/311308* 📠 *941/303148* *60 rooms* *Restaurant, cafeteria, minibars, bar, meeting rooms, parking (fee)* ▭ *AE, DC, MC, V.*

The Highlands

The rivers forming the seven main valleys of the Ebro basin originate in the Sierra de la Demanda, Sierra de Cameros, and Sierra de Alcarama. **Ezcaray** is La Rioja's skiing capital in the **valley of the Rio Oja** just below the slopes at Valdezcaray in the Sierra de la Demanda. The upper **Najerilla Valley** is La Rioja's mountain sanctuary and wildest corner, an excellent hunting and fishing preserve. The Najerilla River, a rich, weed-choked chalk stream, is one of Spain's best trout rivers. Look for the Puente de Hiedra (Ivy Bridge), its heavy curtain of ivy falling to the surface of the water above Anguiano. The **Monasterio de Valvanera,** off C113 near Anguiano, is the sanctuary of the Virgen de Valvanera, a 12th-century Romanesque-Byzantine wood carving of the Virgin and child. **Anguiano** is renowned for its Danza de los Zancos (Dance of the Stilts), held July 22, when dancers on wooden stilts run downhill into the arms of the crowd in the main square. At the valley's highest point are the Mansilla reservoir and the Romanesque **Ermita de San Cristóbal** (Hermitage of St. Christopher).

The upper **Iregua Valley,** off N111, has the prehistoric Gruta de la Paz caves at Ortigosa. The artisans of **Villoslada del Cameros** make the region's patchwork quilts, *almazuelas.* Climb to **Pico Cebollera** for a superb view of the valley. Work back toward the Ebro along the River Leza, through Laguna de Cameros and San Román de Cameros (known for its basket weavers), to complete a tour of the Sierra del Cameros. The upper **Cidacos Valley** leads to the **Parque Jurásico** (Jurassic Park) at Enciso, famous for its dinosaur tracks. The main village in the upper **Alhama Valley** is **Cervera del Rio Alhama,** a center for handmade *alpargatas* (rope-sole shoes). Jews, Moors, and Christians lived here in harmony as long as 400 years after the Christian Reconquest.

Where to Stay & Eat

¢–$ ✕ **La Herradura.** High over the ancient bridge of Anguiano, this roadside restaurant is an excellent place to try the local specialty, *caparrones colorados de Anguiano* (small, red kidney beans stewed with sausage and fatback). Unpretentious and family-run, it's usually filled to the gills with Riojanos and fishermen. The house wine is an impressive Uruñuela *cosechero* (young wine of the year) from the Najerilla Valley. ✉ *Ctra. de Lerma, Km 14, Anguiano* ☎ *941/377151* ▭ *MC, V.*

$ ✕🏨 **Hospedería Nuestra Señora de Valvanera.** Built into the former monks' quarters of a 16th-century monastery that was itself built over a 9th-century hermitage, this is an ideal base, if a little sober in style, for hiking and getting away from it all. The church's 12th-century wood carving of the Virgen of Valvanera is the object of an overnight pilgrimage from Logroño every October 15 in celebration of the harvest. Considered the ultimate factor in the climate so crucial to the development of Rioja's grape, the Virgin is portrayed with a pomegranate (symbolizing fertility) and surrounded by grapevines. ✉ *Monasterio de Valvanera s/n (5 km [3 mi] west of LR-113), 26323* ☎ *941/377044* 🖷 *941/377044* *28 rooms* *Restaurant, cafeteria* ▭ *AE, DC, MC, V.*

¢–$ ✕🏨 **Venta de Goyo.** A favorite with anglers and hunters in season, this cheery spot across from the mouth of the Urbión River (where it meets the Najerilla) has wood-trim bedrooms with check bedspreads and an excellent restaurant specializing in venison, wild boar, partridge, woodcock, and game of all kinds. ✉ *Ctra. LR-113, Km 24.6, 26323 Viniegra de Abajo* ☎ *941/378007* 🖷 *941/378048* *22 rooms* *Restaurant, cafeteria, bar* ▭ *AE, DC, MC, V.*

CANTABRIA, THE BASQUE COUNTRY & LA RIOJA A TO Z

To research prices, get advice from other travelers, and book travel arrangements, visit www.fodors.com.

AIR TRAVEL

Bilbao's airport is 12 km (7 mi) outside the city. Iberia has regular connections from here to Madrid, Barcelona, the United Kingdom, France, and Belgium. There are smaller airports at Santander, Hondarribia (serving San Sebastián), Vitoria, and Pamplona, with twice-daily service to Madrid and Barcelona.

Airport Information **Aeropuerto de Bilbao (Sondika)** ☎ 94/486-9694. **Aeropuerto de Pamplona** ☎ 948/168700. **Aeropuerto de San Sebastián** Hondarribia ☎ 943/643464. **Aeropuerto de Santander** ☎ 942/202100.

BIKE TRAVEL

Bicycle travel in the Basque Country and across the north of Spain is hilly and often wet, but for the iron-hearted, -lunged, -legged, and -bottomed, this is a scenic way to travel and terrific exercise, albeit somewhat perilous on narrow roads often tight for passing motorists.

Bike Maps **Bici Rent Donosti** ✉ Paseo de la Zurriola 22, San Sebastián ☎ 943/279260. **Ciclos Larreki** ✉ Av. de Guipúzcoa s/n, Pamplona ☎ 948/150645. **Comet** ✉ Av. de la Libertad 6, San Sebastián ☎ 943/422351. **Fonfría** ✉ General Dávila 206, Santander ☎ 942/376563.

BOAT & FERRY TRAVEL

Santander is linked year-round to Plymouth, England, by a twice-weekly car ferry run by Brittany Ferries. Travel agencies in Spain and England have details; book at least six weeks in advance in summer, as boats fill up fast. Another such option is the twice-weekly ferry between Bilbao and Portsmouth run by Ferries Golfo de Vizcaya. The trip takes about 24 hours.

Brittany Ferries ✉ Paseo de Pereda 27, 39002 Santander ☎ 942/220000 or 942/214500 ✉ Millbay Docks, Plymouth PL1 3EW, England ☎ 0990/360360. **Ferries Golfo de Vizcaya** ✉ Cosme Etxevarrieta 1, 48009 Bilbao ☎ 944/234477.

BUS TRAVEL

Daily bus service connects the major cities to Madrid; call the bus company Continental Auto for details, or go right to the station at Calle Alenza 20. Bus service between cities and smaller towns is comprehensive, but few have central bus stations; most have numerous bus lines leaving from various points in town.

Bus Company **Continental Auto** ✉ C. Alenza 20, Madrid, ☎ 91/533-0400.

Bus Stations **Bilbao** ✉ Gurtubay 1 ☎ 944/395205. **Logroño** ✉ Av. España 1 ☎ 941/235983. **Pamplona** ✉ C. Conde Oliveto 8 ☎ 948/223854. **San Sebastián** ✉ C. Sancho el Sabio 33 ☎ 943/463974. **Santander** ✉ C. Navas de Tolosa s/n ☎ 942/211995. **Vitoria** ✉ C. de los Herran 27 ☎ 945/258400.

CAR RENTALS

Car rentals are available in the major cities: Bilbao, Pamplona, San Sebastián, Santander, and Vitoria. Cars can also be rented at Hondarribia, the San Sebastián airport.

Agencies **Alquibilbo** ✉ General Eguía 20, Bilbao ☎ 94/441-2012. **A-Rental** ✉ C. Pérez Galdos 24, Bilbao ☎ 94/427-0781. **Avis** ✉ C. Monasterio de la Oliva 29, Pamplona ☎ 948/170036 ✉ Aeropuerto de Pamplona ☎ 948/168763 ✉ Triunfo 2, San Sebastián ☎ 943/461527 ✉ Nicolás Salmerón 3, Santander ☎ 942/227025. **Europcar** ✉ Av. Pio XII 43, Pamplona ☎ 948/172523 ✉ Aeropuerto de Pamplona ☎ 948/312798 ✉ Aeropuerto de Fuenterrabía [Hondarribia], San Sebastián ☎ 943/668530 ✉ Aeropuerto de Santander, Santander ☎ 942/262546.

CAR TRAVEL

Driving is the best way to see this part of Spain, as rural landscapes and small towns are some of the main attractions. Even the remotest points are an easy one-day drive from Madrid, and the north is superbly covered by freeways. From the capital, it's 240 km (149 mi) on the N-I or the A1 toll road to Burgos, after which you can take the N623 to complete the 390 km (242 mi) to Santander. The drive from Madrid to Bilbao is 397 km (247 mi); follow the N-I or A1 past Burgos to Miranda del Ebro, where you pick up the A68.

CONSULATE

United Kingdom **Bilbao** ✉ C. Alameda Urquijo 2, 8th floor ☎ 944/157600 or 944/157722.

EMERGENCIES

Dial 091 for the police.

TAXIS

Taxis normally can be hailed on the street, though from remoter spots such as Pedro Subijana's Akelaré restaurant on Igueldo above San Sebastián, the maître d' will need to call a taxi for you. A taxi stand is called a *parada de taxis*; taxis charge extra for airport dropoffs and pickups as well as for baggage; tipping is entirely optional.

TOURS

Travel agents and tourist offices in the major cities can suggest tours led by local guides and interpreters. Bilbao Paso a Paso conducts fine tours of Bilbao.

Bilbao Paso a Paso ✉ Cocherito de Bilbao 20, Ofic. 5 ☎ 944/730078.

TRAIN TRAVEL

Santander, Bilbao, San Sebastián, Pamplona, Vitoria, and Logroño are served by direct trains from Madrid's Chamartín Station and, with a change or two, virtually every major city in Spain. Trains are not the ideal way to travel within this region, but many cities are connected by RENFE trains. Also, the regional company FEVE runs a delightful narrow-gauge train that winds through stunning landscapes. From San Sebastián, lines west to Bilbao and east to Hendaye depart from Estación de Amara; most long-distance trains use Estación del Norte.

Train Companies **RENFE** ☎ 902/240202 general information ✉ San Sebastián office ✉ C. Camino 1 ☎ 943/426430 ✉ Santander office ✉ Paseo de Pereda 25 ☎ 942/212387 or 942/218567. **Euskotren** ✉ Estación de Atxuri, north of Mercado de la Ribera, Bilbao ☎ 944/338007. **FEVE** ☎ 902/100818.

Train Stations **Bilbao** ✉ Estación del Abando, C. Hurtado de Amezaga ☎ 944/238623 or 944/238636. **Pamplona** ✉ on road to San Sebastián ☎ 948/130202. **Logroño** ✉ Plaza de Europa ☎ 941/240202. **San Sebastián** ✉ Estación de Amara, Plaza Easo 9 ☎ 943/450131 or 943/471852 ✉ Estación del Norte, Av. de Francia ☎ 943/283089 or 943/283599. **Santander** ✉ C. Rodríguez s/n ☎ 942/210211.

VISITOR INFORMATION

Information on all three Basque provinces (Alava, Vizcaya, and Guipúzcoa) is available at the Basque-government building in Vitoria and the tourist office in San Sebastián.

Regional Tourist Offices **Bilbao** ✉ Gran Vía 441 Izquierda ☎ 944/242277. **San Sebastián** ✉ C. Fueros 1 ☎ 943/426282. **Vitoria** ✉ Parque de la Florida ☎ 945/131321.

Local Tourist Offices **Bilbao** ✉ Paseo de Arenal 1 ☎ 944/795760 or 944/165761. **Comillas** ✉ Aldea 6 ☎ 942/720768. **Guernica** ✉ Artekale 5 ☎ 946/255892. **Guetaria** ✉ Parque Aldamar 2 ☎ 943/140957. **Haro** ✉ Pl. Monseñor Florentino Rodriguez ☎ 941/303366. **Hondarribia** Fuenterrabía ✉ Javier Ugarte 6 ☎ 943/645458. **Laguardia** ✉ Pl. San Juan ☎ 945/600845. **Logroño** ✉ C. Miguel Villanueva 10 ☎ 941/291260. **Mundaca** ✉ Txorrokopunta 2 ☎ 946/177201. **Pamplona** ✉ C. Duque de Ahumada 3 ☎ 948/220741. **Potes** ✉ Independencia 30 ☎ 942/730787. **San Sebastián** ✉ C. Reina Regente s/n ☎ 943/481166. **Santander** ✉ Jardines de Pereda ☎ 942/216120 ✉ Plaza de Velarde 5 ☎ 942/310708. **San Vicente de la Barquera** ✉ Generalísimo 20 ☎ 942/710797. **Vitoria** ✉ Edificio Europa, Av. Gasteiz ☎ 945/161598.

GALICIA & ASTURIAS

HIGHLY RECOMMENDED

RESTAURANTS

- Adega O Bebedeiro, A Coruña
- Casa Consuelo, Otur
- Casa Fermín, Oviedo
- Casa Solla, San Salvador de Poio
- El Mosquito, Vigo
- La Máquina, Lugones
- La Penela, A Coruña
- María José, Cambados
- Moncho Vilas, Santiago de Compostela

HOTELS

- Casa Antiga do Monte, Padrón
- Casa-Hotel As Artes, Santiago de Compostela
- Hostal de los Reyes Católicos, Santiago de Compostela
- Hotel de la Reconquista, Oviedo
- Hotel Entrecercas, Santiago de Compostela
- Hotel-Residencia Costa Vella, Santiago de Compostela
- Parador de Baiona, Baiona
- Parador de Cangas de Onís, Cangas de Onís
- Pazo Cibrán, Santiago de Compostela

SIGHTS

- Betanzos
- Museo Provincial, Pontevedra
- Santa María del Naranco, Oviedo
- Santiago de Compostela
- Shrine, Covadonga
- Viveiro

By Deborah Luhrman and Christine Cipriani

Updated by Edward Owen and George Semler

SPAIN'S MOST ATLANTIC region is en route to nowhere, an end in itself. Stretching northwest from the lonesome Castilian plains to the rocky seacoast, Asturias and Galicia incorporate verdant hills and vineyards, gorgeous *rías* (estuaries), and the country's wildest mountains, the Picos de Europa. Northwestern Spain is a series of rainy landscapes, stretching from your feet to the horizon. Ancient granite buildings wear a blanket of moss, and even the stone *horreos* (granaries) are built on stilts above the damp ground. Swirling fog and heavy mist help keep local folk tales of the supernatural alive. The guitar is replaced by the *gaita* (bagpipe), legacy of the Celts' settlements here in the 5th and 6th centuries BC.

4

Though Galicia and Asturias are off the beaten track for many foreigners, they are not undiscovered: Spanish families flock to these cool northern beaches and mountains each summer. Santiago de Compostela, with its cathedral's remains of the apostle James, has drawn pilgrims over the same roads for 900 years, leaving northwestern Spain dotted with churches, shrines, and former hospitals. Asturias, north of the main pilgrim trail, has always maintained a separate identity, isolated by the rocky Picos de Europa. This and the Basque Country are the only parts of Spain never conquered by the Moors, so Asturian architecture shows little Moorish influence. It was from a mountain base at Covadonga that the Christians won their first decisive battle against the Moors and launched the Reconquest of Spain, which, though it took some 700 years, made Spain one of the world's most uniformly Catholic countries.

In the Gallego language, the Castilian Spanish *plaza* (town square) is *praza* and the Castilian *playa* (beach) is *praia*. Closer to Portuguese than to Castilian Spanish, Gallego is the language of choice for nearly all road signs in Galicia.

About the Restaurants

Galicia and Asturias, despite the ecological setback of 2002, remain justly famous for seafood. The quality of the fish is so high that chefs frown on drowning inherent flavors in heavy sauces or pungent seasonings; expect simplicity rather than spice. Fish specialties are *merluza a la gallega,* steamed hake with sweet paprika sauce (Galicia), and *merluza a la sidra,* steamed hake in a tangy Asturian cider sauce (Asturias). Salmon and trout from Asturian rivers are additional treats. The scallop, a symbol of the pilgrimage to Santiago, is popular in Galicia, where you can also find bars serving nothing but wine and *pulpo a feira* (boiled and broiled octopus) or *berberechos* (cockles). Ham lovers should try *lacón con grelos,* a baked shoulder of pork served with sautéed turnip tops. Cheeses are delicious all over northwestern Spain: try the tangy *queso Cabrales* (Asturian blue cheese), the sharp Asturian *afuega'l pitu* (literally, "chokes the rooster," because it's so sharp and so thick), and the Galician *queixo tetilla* (a semisoft cheese in the form of a woman's breast), delicious with *membrillo* (quince jelly) for dessert. Valdeón cheese, from the Picos de Europa village of the same name, is one of the world's finest blue cheeses, made from cow's milk and fat, then "perfumed." This damp region is also known for hearty stews—in Asturias try *fabada* (butter beans and sausage), and in Galicia *caldo gallego* (white beans, turnip greens, chickpeas, cabbage, and potatoes). Savory fish or meat pies called *empanadas* are native to Galicia, as is the famous *lacón con grelos* (cured ham with turnips and chorizo sausage). Asturians enjoy *entrecôte con queso Cabrales,* steak topped with a sauce made of the local blue cheese.

The best Galician wine is the fruity, full-bodied, white Albariño, perfect with seafood and fast being discovered abroad. The acidic Ribeiro wine is often served in a ceramic bowl rather than a glass. Brandy buffs should try Galicia's *queimada* (which superstitious locals claim is a witches' brew), made of potent, grappalike *orujo* mixed with lemon peel and sugar in an earthenware bowl, then set aflame and stirred until the desired amount of alcohol is burned off. Asturias is known for its *sidra* (hard cider), served either carbonated or still. Traditionally, cider is poured from overhead and tossed back *immediately* for full enjoyment of its effervescent flavor. Cider houses generally insist that either you or your waiter pour cider correctly (that is, from overhead to a glass held at knee level) in order to aerate the cider. This process is called the *escancio* (pouring), a much-valued skill around which entire tournaments are held. Give it a try, spilling is allowed.

WHAT IT COSTS In Euros

	$$$$	$$$	$$	$	¢
AT DINNER	over €20	€15–€20	€10–€15	€6–€10	under €6

Prices are for per person for a main course at dinner.

About the Hotels

The state-run parador chain has nine charming lodgings in Galicia alone: three in elegant mansions, two in ancient fortresses, and one in a former convent at Ribas de Sil, near Ourense. The Rusticae chain is giving the paradors a run for their money with a series of graceful and affordable *pazos* (manor houses). Reservations are important between May and October but not essential the rest of the year. Some monasteries provide economical lodging.

WHAT IT COSTS In Euros

	$$$$	$$$	$$	$	¢
FOR 2 PEOPLE	over €180	€100–€180	€60–€100	€40–€60	under €40

Prices are for two people in a standard double room in high season, excluding tax.

Exploring Galicia & Asturias

Approaching Spain's northwest corner, head for Santiago de Compostela along the final stages of the Camino de Santiago before dipping south into the Rías Baixas and west to the beaches along the Atlantic coast north of the Río Miño and the border with Portugal. Then sweep north through the thriving port of A Coruña and move east along the Bay of Biscay to Asturias and Oviedo before again looping south through the lofty Picos de Europa. Be prepared to fall in love with these magical, remote regions. In Gallego they call the feeling *morriña,* a powerful longing for a person or place you've left behind.

Numbers in the text correspond to numbers in the margin and on the Galicia & Asturias and the Santiago de Compostela maps.

Timing

Summer is best for swimming and enjoying water sports. Spring and fall may be the ideal time to explore, as the weather is reasonable and crowds are few. Winter can be rainy to the point of saturation: not for nothing is this region called Green Spain.

THE CAMINO DE SANTIAGO

Santiago de Compostela, alleged final resting place for the apostle St. James, was one of the most important Christian sites in the world in

If you have 5 days

Start in **Santiago de Compostela** 5–10 and spend a day and a half on the cathedral and old town. Drive north the second afternoon to **A Coruña** 23 and devote day three to admiring the glass galleries on the harbor, exploring the old town, and visiting the Torre de Hercules. On day four, head north for some of Spain's loveliest beaches, and stroll around coastal **Viveiro** 27. Crossing into Asturias, stop in **Luarca** 29, a village in a cove, and the lively coastal city of **Gijón** 31. Then drive south to **Oviedo** 30, the provincial capital.

If you have 10 days

Spend a day exploring the Camino villages of Samos, Sarria, Portomarín, **Vilar de Donas** 3, and **Leboreiro** 4 en route to **Santiago de Compostela** 5–10, your base for the next two nights. Over the next two days, visit the cathedral, the old town, and nearby **Pazo de Oca** 11, a Galician manor house, or **Padrón** 12. On day four, drive north to **A Coruña** 23. Head up to the Rías Altas on day five, stopping in picturesque **Betanzos** 24 and **Mondoñedo** 26. Spend a night on the coast, in **Viveiro** 27 or, farther east, **Ribadeo** 28; each have exceptional views. On day six travel to the seaside Asturian towns of **Luarca** 29, Avilés, and **Gijón** 31. On day seven, head inland for a day and night in lively **Oviedo** 30. Finally, drive to nearby **Cangas de Onís** 35 and visit the 8th-century shrine of **Covadonga** 36, then spend two days in Picos de Europa National Park.

---

the Middle Ages. Making the difficult pilgrimage to this remote corner of Spain all but ensured the faithful a place in heaven—perhaps not least because the route was crowded with highway robbers, gallant pilgrim-protecting knights, and innkeepers prospering in the pilgrim trade. There were even souvenir hawkers, providing the scallop shells that pilgrims wore as a symbol of St. James, a fisherman. The main pilgrimage route, the *camino francés,* crosses the Pyrenees from France and heads west across northern Spain, marked by scallop-shell signs. If you drive into Galicia on the N-VI from Castile–León, you enter what might be called the homestretch.

O Cebreiro

1 *32 km (20 mi) northwest of Villafranca del Bierzo.*

From the N-VI at Puerto de Piedrafita, the Camino de Santiago veers left. Climb the steep, narrow road to O Cebreiro, one of the most unusual mountaintop hamlets in Spain. Deserted and haunting outside high season (and often fogged in or snowy to boot), O Cebreiro is a stark settlement built around a 9th-century church. Known for its round, thatched-roof stone huts called **pallozas,** the village has been perfectly preserved and is now an open-air museum showing what life was like in these mountains in the Middle Ages and, indeed, up until a few decades ago. One hut is now a **museum** of the region's Celtic heritage. Higher up, at 3,648 ft, there's a rustic 9th-century **sanctuary.**

Where to Stay

$ **Hostal San Giraldo de Aurillac.** This rural hostel next to the church offers home cooking and a good base for walking the mountains. The Santuario do Cebreiro next door is run by the same establishment as the San Giraldo. ✉ *O Cebreiro, Lugo 27670* ☎ *982/367125* 🖷 *982/367015* *16 rooms* *Restaurant, bar; no a/c* ▭ *MC, V.*

en route

From O Cebreiro the road takes you through **Samos,** with a Benedictine monastery; **Sarria,** a medieval village; and **Portomarín,** on the Miño River, where the Romanesque church was moved—stone by stone—before a new dam flooded the town in 1962.

Lugo

❷ *31 km (19 mi) north of Sarria on C546, 26 km (16 mi) north of Portomarín on LU612.*

Just off the A6 freeway, Galicia's oldest provincial capital is most notable for its 2½-km (1½-mi) **Roman wall.** Built in the year 260, these beautifully preserved ramparts completely surround the pleasant old town. The walkway on top has good views of the circuit. The baroque ***ayuntamiento*** (city hall) has a magnificent rococo facade overlooking the tree-lined Praza Maior (Plaza Mayor). There's a good view of the Río Miño valley from the **Parque Rosalía de Castro,** outside the Roman walls near the cathedral. The large white building on the river is a spa (part of a hotel), where you can visit the remains of the **Roman baths.** Lugo's **cathedral,** open daily 8 AM–8:30 PM, is a mixture of the Romanesque, Gothic, baroque, and neoclassical styles. The **Museo Provincial** (✉ Pl. de la Soledad ☎ 982/242112 🌐 www.museolugo.org) has a large collection of clocks and sundials. It's open weekdays 10:30–2 and 4:30–8:30, Saturday 10:30–2 and 4:30–8, and Sunday 11–2. Admission is free.

Where to Stay & Eat

$$–$$$ ✕ **Mesón de Alberto.** This cozy venue has excellent Galician fare and professional service. The bar and adjoining *bodega* (winery) serve plenty of *raciónes.* (appetizers). The *surtido de quesos Gallegos* provides generous servings of four local cheeses; ask for some *membrillo* (quince jelly) to go with them and the brown, crusty corn bread. The dining room upstairs has an inexpensive set menu. ✉ *Cruz 4* ☎ *982/228310* 💳 *AE, DC, MC, V* ⊗ *Closed Sun.*

$$–$$$ 🏨 **Gran Hotel Lugo.** In a garden near the Praza Maior but outside the city walls, this modern and spacious hotel has comfortable rooms, done in shades of yellow and brown. The rooms overlook either the garden swimming pool or a broad street. ✉ *Avda. Ramón Ferreiro 21, 27002* ☎ *982/224152* 📠 *982/241660* 🌐 *www.gh-hoteles.com* *156 rooms, 12 suites* *Restaurant, pool, parking (fee)* 💳 *AE, DC, MC, V.*

Vilar de Donas

❸ *27 km (17 mi) southwest of Lugo.*

Southwest of Lugo, turn right in Ferradal, pass the picnic ground, and stop at the little **church** in Vilar de Donas to pay tribute to the knights of St. James, whose tombs line the inside walls. The afternoon sun spotlights carved-stone depictions including the horizontal body of Christ. Portraits of the two medieval noblewomen who built the church are mixed with those of the apostles in the 15th-century frescoes on the apse. The church is open for visits April–October, Tuesday–Sunday 11–2 and 3–6; to arrange a visit between November and March contact the verger (☎ 982/153833). Mass is held at 1 PM each Sunday.

Leboreiro

❹ *38 km (23 mi) west of Vilar de Donas.*

West of Vilar de Donas, the countryside flattens out. Just after the sign for Km 42, turn left for Leboreiro, a farming hamlet with simple medieval stone houses surrounding a **Romanesque church.** On the west side

Sunning on the Sand After the 2002 oil spill and the urgent need for reinforcing Galicia's tourist industry to compensate for losses in the fishing sector, the Spanish government and the Galician *Xunta* are vigorously promoting the attractions of the carefully restored northern beaches. When the sun comes out, you can relax on the sand at Llanes, Ribadesella, Cudillero, Santa Ana (by Cadavedo), Luarca, Tapia de Casariego, Muros, Noya, O Grove, the Islas Cies, Boa, and Testal.

Enjoying Fiestas **Carnival,** in February and March, opens the festivities; the town of Laza, in Galicia, is among the prime celebrant of **Os Peliqueiros** (when, charmingly, the townsfolk get flagellated with riding crops). The first week of March, the **Festa do Queixo** (Cheese Festival) in Arzúa, near A Coruña, celebrates food and folklore, including a cheese contest. Viveiro observes **Semana Santa** (Holy Week) with a barefoot procession of flagellants illuminated by hundreds of candles. Local bands and dance troupes perform at the **Festival de Música y Danza** held in Oviedo and Gijón in May. Classical music and dance ensembles come from all over Europe, and street fairs highlight area crafts and cuisine. On June 14, during the feast of **Corpus Christi,** Pontevedra celebrates flowers and the harvest.

The **Rapa das Bestas** (Taming of the Beasts—the breaking of wild horses) takes place the first weekend of July in various locales, including Sabuceda, near Pontevedra, and Mt. Buyo, near Viveiro. **El Día de Santiago** (St. James's Day), July 25, is celebrated in Santiago with processions, fireworks, and the appearance of the dramatic *botafumeiro* (incense burner) at mass in the cathedral. On the first Sunday in August, the **Festa do Vino Albariño** (Albariño Wine Festival) enlivens Cambados with the fruit of the vine. In Gijón, during the last two weeks of August, the **Fiesta de Muestras** (Exposition) transforms Gijón into a street party with bullfights, sports, crafts, concerts, and all-night parties. On August 15, sailors and fishermen in Luarca celebrate **Nuestra Señora del Rosario** (Our Lady of the Rosary) by parading their boats through the harbor. The late September **Procesión de las Mortajas** (Procession of the Shrouded), in Pobra do Carmiñal (A Coruña), dating from the 15th century, carries survivors of illness, bad luck, or bad love around town in open coffins. At O Grove's **Festa do Marisco** (Seafood Festival), the second Sunday in October, crowds feast on lobster, mussels, clams, *percebes* (goose barnacles), spiny *néora* crabs, shrimp, and other delicacies from the sea.

Exploring the Wilderness With so much rugged wilderness, Spain's northwest has become the country's premier outdoor-adventure region. The Picos de Europa and the green hills of Galicia beg to be hiked, trekked, climbed, or just walked; other open-air diversions include horseback riding, canyon rappelling, bungee-jumping, and spelunking. Ribadesella, Asturias, is Spain's white-water capital with its annual August international kayak race on the river Sella from Arriondas to Ribadesella. Atlantic salmon, sea trout, and trout angling provides an excellent pretext for getting to know some of green Spain's finest river valleys and countryside.

Galicia & Asturias
Santiago de Compostela 5 - 10 see detail map
Bay of Biscay
ATLANTIC OCEAN
PORTUGAL
ASTURIAS
GALICIA
CORDILLERA
CANTABRICA
CASTILE-LEON
PICOS DE EUROPA NATIONAL PARK
1 O Cebreiro
2 Lugo
3 Vilar de Donas
4 Leboreiro
11 Pazo de Oca
12 Padrón
13 Fisterra
14 Muros
15 Noia
16 Pontevedra
17 O Grove
18 Cambados
19 Vigo
20 Islas Cies
21 Baiona
22 Tui
23 A Coruña
24 Betanzos
25 Vilalba
26 Mondoñedo
27 Viveiro
28 Ribadeo
29 Luarca
30 Oviedo
31 Gijón
32 Villaviciosa
33 Ribadesella
34 Llanes
35 Cangas de Onís
36 Covadonga
Ortigueira
Sargadelos
Ferrol
Carballo
Guitiriz
Labacolla
Arzúa
Portomarín
Sarriá
Samos
Avilés
Pravia
Cangas de Narcea
Pola de Somiedo
Mieres
Panes
Santander
Villafranca del Bierzo
Castrillo de los Polvazares
La Robla
León
Guardo
Ponferrada
Astorga
Saldaña
Redondela
Ourense
Viana del Bollo
Melón
La Bañeza
Ginzo de Limia
Monterrey
Donado
Puebla de Sanabria
Benavente
Mayorga
Medina de Rioseco
Burgos
TO MADRID
0 30 miles
0 45 km
KEY
Rail Lines
Regional Boundaries

of town, a stretch of the ancient pilgrims' road, paved with granite boulders, and an old bridge are surprisingly intact.

Santiago de Compostela

★ *277 km (172 mi) west of León, 650 km (403 mi) northwest of Madrid.*

A large, lively university makes Santiago one of the most exciting cities in Spain, but its cathedral makes it one of the most impressive. The building is opulent and awesome, yet its towers create a sense of harmony as a benign St. James, dressed in pilgrim's costume, looks down from his perch. The apostle James, who according to 8th- and 9th-century sources preached in northwest Iberia, was beheaded by Herod in AD 44; his remains were placed in a stone boat and steered by the hand of God to the banks of the Galician river Iría Flavia, near Padrón. As the boat approached, a horse on the beach panicked, carrying its rider deep into the water—yet instead of drowning, the pair surfaced with a covering of scallop shells. The scallop remains the symbol of St. James and the Camino. Much later, in 813, religious leaders unearthed a sarcophagus said to contain the remains of the apostle James. ("Santiago" comes from *Sant Iago,* St. James; "Compostela" probably comes from the Latin *campus stellae,* field of stars.) At peak periods in the 12th century, up to 2 million people walked to Santiago each year, putting it in a class with Rome and Jerusalem. Neither the Reformation nor 20th-century secularism managed to kill off the pilgrimage, now a melange of believers, agnostics, and disaffected professionals taking to the hills to hear themselves think. Santiago de Compostela welcomes more than 4½ million visitors a year, with an extra 1 million in Holy Years (such as 2004) when St. James's Day, July 25, falls on a Sunday.

From the **Praza do Obradoiro,** climb the two flights of stairs to the main
5 entrance to Santiago's **cathedral.** The facade is baroque, yet just inside is one of the finest Romanesque sculptures in the world, the **Pórtico de la Gloria.** Completed in 1188 by Maestro Mateo, this is the cathedral's original entrance, its three arches carved with biblical figures from the Apocalypse, the Last Judgment, and Purgatory. On the left are the prophets; in the center, Jesus is flanked by the four Evangelists (Matthew, Mark, Luke, and John) and, above them, the 24 Elders of the Apocalypse playing celestial instruments. Just below Jesus is a serene St. James, poised on a carved column. Look carefully and you'll see five smooth grooves, formed by the millions of pilgrims who have placed their hands here over the centuries. On the back of the pillar, people, especially students preparing for exams, lean forward to touch foreheads with the likeness of Maestro Mateo in the hope that his genius can be shared. In his jeweled cloak, St. James presides over the gold and silver **high altar.** The stairs behind the altar are the cathedral's focal point, surrounded by dazzling baroque decoration, sculpture, and drapery. Here, as the grand finale of their spiritual journey, pilgrims embrace St. James and kiss his cloak. In the crypt beneath the altar lie the alleged remains of St. James and his disciples, St. Theodore and St. Athenasius.

A pilgrims' mass is celebrated every day at noon. On special, somewhat unpredictable occasions, the *botafumeiro* (huge incense burner) is attached to the thick ropes hanging from the ceiling and prepared for a ritual at the end of the pilgrims' mass: as small flames burn inside, eight strong laymen play the ropes to swing the huge vessel in a massive semicircle across the apse. In earlier centuries, this rite served as an air freshener—by the time pilgrims reached Santiago, they smelled, well, ripe. Spanish national television broadcasts this ceremony live on St. James's Day, July 25. A botafumeiro and other cathedral treasures are on dis-

Cathedral **5**

Centro Galego de Arte Contemporánea **8**

Hostal de los Reyes Católicos **7**

Museo de las Peregrinaciones **10**

Museo de Pobo Galego **9**

Pazo de Xelmírez **6**

THE ROAD TO SANTIAGO

ACTS 1:8 STATES "Ye shall be witnesses unto me, unto the uttermost part of the earth". Ninth-century sources have the apostle James (Santiago in Spanish, as in Saint Iago) preaching in northwest Iberia, not far from Fisterra/Finisterre, literally, at that time, "land's end". Beheaded by Herod in AD 44 (Acts:12:2), Santiago's remains, according to legend, were placed in a stone boat and guided by God to the Galician river Iria Flavia, near Padrón. When, as the boat arrived, a horse bolted into deep water (only to emerge, with its rider, covered in scallop shells), the scallop became the symbol of Saint James and the pilgrimage to his tomb in Santiago de Compostela.

At the height of its fame in the 12th century, up to 2 million people made the trek to Santiago each year, nearly as many as to Rome and Jerusalem. As Nancy Louise Frey reports in Pilgrim Stories: On and Off the Road to Santiago, *nearly 30,000 people made the pilgrimage in 1996, 16% declaring no belief in God and only about half of the rest practicing their faith. The modern pilgrimage is a cavalcade of religious believers, agnostics, adventurers, and sundry secular souls in search of peace. While most medieval pilgrims were poor and infirm, today's average trekker is an educated, middle-class, thirtysomething Western European. Most find the Camino a life-changing experience. Now as then, pilgrims can stay for little or no money in special refuges along the route. The main path is the camino francés (the French route), which enters Spain from France at Roncesvalles and hits Santiago 750 km (465 mi) later, a month's walk.*

4

play in the **museums** downstairs and next door. On the right (south) side of the nave is the **Porta das Praterías** (Silversmiths' Door), the only purely Romanesque part of the cathedral's facade. The statues on the portal were cobbled together from various parts of the cathedral. The double doorway opens onto the graceful **Praza das Praterías,** named for the silversmiths' shops that used to line it. The praza's fountain is a popular rest stop in nice weather. ✉ *Praza do Obradoiro* ☎ *981/560527 or 981/583548* 🎫 *Cathedral free, combined museum ticket €4* ⏲ *Cathedral daily 6:30 AM–9 PM; museums July–Oct., Mon.–Sat. 10–2 and 4–8, Sun. 10–2; Nov.–June, Mon.–Sat. 10:30–1:30 and 4–7, Sun. 10:30–1:30.*

The wide **Praza da Quintana** is the haunt of young travelers and folk musicians in summer. The **Porta Santa** (Holy Door) is open only during those years in which St. James's Day falls on a Sunday (such as 2004). The Praza is behind the Santiago cathedral. Stop into the rich 12th-century

❻ **Pazo de Xelmírez** (Palace of Archbishop Xelmírez), an unusual example of Romanesque civic architecture with a cool, clean, vaulted dining hall. The little figures carved on the corbels in this graceful, 100-ft-long space are heart-warmingly lifelike, partaking of food, drink, and music with great medieval gusto. Each one is different; stroll around for a tableau of mealtime merriment. ✉ *Praza do Obradoiro* ☎ *981/572300* 🎫 *€1.20* ⏲ *Easter–Oct., Tues.–Sun. 10–1:30 and 4:30–7:30.*

❼ The **Hostal de los Reyes Católicos** (Hostel of the Catholic Monarchs), facing the cathedral from the left, was built in 1499 by Ferdinand and Isabella to house the pilgrims who slept on Santiago's streets every night. Having lodged and revived travelers for nearly 500 years, it's the oldest refuge in the world and was converted from a hospital to a luxury parador in 1953. The plateresque facade bears a Castilian coat of arms along with Adam, Eve, and various saints; inside, the four arcaded patios have gargoyle rainspouts said to be caricatures of 16th-century townsfolk. There's a small art gallery behind the lobby. Walk-in spectators without room keys risk being asked to leave, but you can tour in the company of an official city guide from the tourist office. ✉ *Praza do Obradoiro 1* ☎ *981/582200* 🎫 *Free* ⏲ *Daily 10–1 and 4–6.*

Santiago's city hall and the president's offices of the regional government of Galicia, La Xunta de Galicia, are in the 18th-century **Pazo de Raxoi** (Rajoy Palace; ✉ Praza do Obradoiro). It's directly opposite the cathedral. Take note of the 16th-century **Colexio de San Xerome** (✉ Praza do Obradoiro), the offices of the rector of the University of Santiago. Its 15th-century entrance was brought from another city college and includes virgins and saints with the Virgin and Child above the door. To visit the cloisters, ask permission from the security guard. Santiago de Compostela packs many old *pazos* (manor houses), convents, and churches that in most towns would receive headline attention. But the best way to spend your remaining time here is simply to walk around the **casco antiguo** (old town), losing yourself in its maze of stone-paved narrow streets and little plazas. The most beautiful pedestrian thoroughfares are Rúa do Vilar, Rúa do Franco, and Rúa Nova—portions of which are covered by arcaded walkways called *soportales,* designed to keep walkers out of the rain.

8 On the north side of town off the Porta do Camino, the **Centro Galego de Arte Contemporánea** (Galician Center for Contemporary Art) is a stark yet elegant modern building that offsets Santiago's ancient feel. Portuguese designer Álvaro Siza built the museum of smooth, angled granite, which mirrors the medieval convent of San Domingos de Bonaval next door. Inside, a gleaming lobby of white Italian marble gives way to white-walled, high-ceiling exhibition halls flooded with light from massive windows and skylights. The museum has a good permanent collection and even better changing exhibits. The museum also hosts concerts and plays. ✉ *Rúa de Valle Inclán s/n* ☎ *981/546629* 🌐 *www.cgac.org* 🎫 *Free* ⏲ *Tues.–Sun. 11–8.*

9 Next door to the Center for Contemporary Art is the **Museo de Pobo Galego** (Galician Folk Museum), in the medieval convent of Santo Domingo de Bonaval. Photos, farm implements, and other displays illustrate various aspects of traditional Galician life. The star attraction is the 13th-century self-supporting spiral granite staircase that still connects three floors. ✉ *Rúa de Bonaval* ☎ *981/583620* 🌐 *www.museodopobo.es* 🎫 *Free* ⏲ *Mon.–Sat. 10–1 and 4–7.*

10 North of Azabachería (follow Ruela de Xerusalén) is the **Museo de las Peregrinaciones** (Pilgrimage Museum), with Camino de Santiago iconography from sculptures and carvings to *azabache* (compact black coal, or jet) items. For an overview of the history of the pilgrimage and the Camino's role in the development of the city itself, this is a key visit. ✉ *Rúa de San Miguel 4* ☎ *981/581558* 🎫 *€2.50* ⏲ *Tues.–Fri. 10–8; Sat. 10:30–1:30, 5–8; Sun. 10:30-1:30.*

Where to Stay & Eat

$$$–$$$$ ✕ **Toñi Vicent.** Galicia's most creative cuisine is concocted in this carefully furnished antiquary. *Marinada de lubina con ensalada amarga, aceite, limón, y eneldo* (marinade of sea bass with bitter salad, olive oil, lemon, and dill) is an example of the meeting of Galicia's finest produce with one of its most inventive chefs. ✉ *Rosalía de Castro 24* ☎ *981/594100* 💳 *AE, MC, V* ⏲ *Closed Dec. 24–Jan. 7, Sept. 1–15, and Sun.*

★ $$$ ✕ **Moncho Vilas.** Owner of the eponymous restaurant reached a zenith when he prepared a banquet for Pope John Paul II (the pontiff visited

Santiago in 1989). Specialties include salmon with clams, *merluza a la gallega* (hake with paprika sauce) or *a la vasca* (in a green sauce), and steak with garlicky potatoes. ✉ *Avda. Villagarcia 21* ☎ *981/598637* ▭ *AE, DC, MC, V* ⊙ *Closed Mon.*

$$–$$$ ✕ **A Barrola.** With lots of polished wood, a niche with wine and travel books, and a terrace, this tavern is a favorite with university faculty. The house salads, mussels with *santiaguiños* (crabmeat), *arroz con bogavante* (rice with lobster), and seafood empanadas are superb. ✉ *Rúa do Franco 29* ☎ *981/577999* ▭ *AE, MC, V* ⊙ *Closed Jan.–Mar. and Mon.*

$$–$$$ ✕ **Don Gaiferos.** One of Santiago's most distinguished restaurants, this timeless tavern next to the church of Santa Maria Salomé serves jumbo prawns stuffed with smoked salmon and white Ribeiro and Albariño wines. The spicy fish stew is enough for two, while the *tarta de almendra* (almond tart) and the bilberry cheesecake are irresistible. ✉ *Rúa Nova 23* ☎ *981/583894* ▭ *AE, DC, MC, V* ⊙ *No dinner Sun. No dinner Mon. Oct.–May.*

$$ ✕ **Carretas.** This casual spot for fresh Galician seafood is around the corner from the parador. Fish dishes abound, but the house specialty is shellfish. For the full experience, order the labor-intensive *variado de mariscos,* a comprehensive platter of langostinos, king prawns, crab, and goose barnacles, complete with shell-cracker. *Salpicón de mariscos* presents the same creatures pre-shelled. ✉ *Rúa de Carretas 21* ☎ *981/563111* ▭ *AE, DC, MC, V* ⊙ *Closed Sun.*

$–$$ ✕ **O Papa Upa.** A decadent assortment of shellfish and the entrecôte Papa Upa, a massive T-bone steak, are specialties. Chase your meal as the locals do—partake in the "rite of burning firewater" with *queimada,* flaming brandy served in a ceramic bowl. ✉ *Rúa da Raiña 18* ☎ *981/566598* ▭ *AE, DC, MC, V.*

★ $$$–$$$$ ✕🏨 **Hostal de los Reyes Católicos.** The mammoth 15th-century baroque doorway gives way to austere courtyards and rooms furnished with antiques, some with canopy beds. Remnants of the 1970s diminish the late-medieval splendor of the building. Libredón, the grand, vaulted dining room, serves top-notch regional fare and is well worth a visit. The tapas bar, Enxebre, is lively and informal. ✉ *Praza do Obradoiro 1, 15705* ☎ *981/582200* 🖷 *981/563094* 🌐 *www.parador.es* 🛏 *137 rooms* 🛎 *2 restaurants, hair salon, bar, car rental, parking (fee)* ▭ *AE, DC, MC, V.*

★ $$ 🏨 **Hotel-Residencia Costa Vella.** This inn snuggles up to Santiago's medieval wall at one of the highest points in the city. The house is classically Galician, but the interior is awash in smooth blond wood and natural light from floor-to-ceiling windows—the better to behold the perfect little garden, stone wall, red-tile rooftops, the baroque convent of San Francisco, and green hills beyond. (Ask for a garden view.) The glass extends to an airy breakfast room and reading area. ✉ *Rúa Porta da Peña 17, 15704* ☎ *981/569530* 🖷 *981/569531* 🌐 *www.santiagohosteleria.com* 🛏 *14 rooms* 🛎 *Bar, lounge* ▭ *MC, V.*

★ $$ 🏨 **Pazo Cibrán.** Charmingly restored, this 18th-century Galician farm mansion is a 20-minute drive from Santiago. Owner Mayka Iglesias maintains six rooms in the main house and five large rooms in the old stable. The antiques-packed living room overlooks gardens with camellias, magnolias, palms, vines, and a bamboo walk. Breakfast is served in the *pazo* itself, with lunch and dinner available in the nearby Casa Roberto. To get here, take the N525 Ourense road from Santiago and turn right at Km 11, after the gas station. ✉ *San Xulián de Sales, 15885* ☎🖷 *981/511515* 🌐 *www.agalicia.com/pazocibran.htm* 🛏 *11 rooms* 🛎 *Breakfast room, library; no TV* ▭ *AE, DC, MC, V.*

★ $–$$ 🏨 **Casa-Hotel As Artes.** This little inn offers sunny quarters at bonanza rates. Each room has at least one stone wall, recessed windows with beveled wood shutters, polished hardwood floors, and a wrought-iron double bed; and each is named after a different artist and decorated accordingly. (The Vivaldi room, for instance, has music-manuscript curtains.) ✉ *Travesía de Dos Puertas 2 (off Rúa San Francisco), 15707* ☎ *981/572590 or 981/555254* 🖷 *981/577823* 🌐 *www.asartes.com* *7 rooms* *Sauna, bar* ▭ *AE, DC, MC, V* ⏲ *Closed Jan.*

★ $–$$ **Hotel Entrecercas.** Just 82 ft from the cathedral, this house was restored to highlight its exposed beams and stonework. There are four doubles and two single rooms, all with bath. The prices include tax and breakfast. Book early for this great location. ✉ *Entrecercas 11 bajo, 15703* ☎ *981/571151* 🖷 *981/571112* *6 rooms* *Cafeteria, bar; no a/c* ▭ *AE, DC, MC, V.*

Tapas Bars

Prada a Tope. This rustic spot just behind the cathedral specializes in products from El Bierzo, either at the bar or in the various dining rooms. ✉ *Troia 10* ☎ *981/581909.*

La Bodeguilla de San Roque. One of Santiago's favorite spots for tapeo and chiquiteo (tapa grazing and hits of wine), this tavern is just a five-minute walk from the cathedral. ✉ *San Roque 13* ☎ *981/564379.*

Adega Abrigadoiro. Just five minutes walk behind the Colegio San Jerónimo, this tapas emporium offers one of the best selections of Galician delicacies in town. ✉ *Carrera del Conde 5* ☎ *981/563–1635.*

O Dezaseis. Specialists in small servings of great products, this traditional favorite near the center is a must on any tapa crawl. ✉ *Rua de San Pedro 16* ☎ *981/577633.*

Cafés

Santiago is one of the best cities in Spain for European-style coffee-nursing in warm surroundings. **Cafe Bar Literarios** (✉ Praza da Quintana 1 ☎ 981/565630) overlooks the plaza with generous windows and outdoor tables. Inside, a deliberately gaudy mural incorporates send-ups of famous paintings. Cozy **Iacobus** (✉ Azibechería 5 ☎ 981/582804 ✉ Caldérería 42 ☎ 981/583415) blends stone walls with contemporary wood trim and light fixtures; look down to see a glass cache of coffee beans in the floor. Popular with students, **A Calderería** (✉ Calderería 26 ☎ 981/572045) juxtaposes contemporary and traditional aesthetics. Try Clip Nougat, ice cream with pistachios and toasted almonds. Once a gathering place for Galician poets, the **Cafe Bar Derby** (✉ Rúa das Orfas 29 ☎ 981/586417) remains a serene place for coffee and pastries.

Nightlife & the Arts

Santiago's nightlife peaks on Thursday night, as many students spend weekends at home with their families. For up-to-date information on concerts, films, and clubs, pick up the student-run magazine *Compostelan* at any newsstand. Also check the monthly paper *Compostela,* available at the main tourist office on Rúa do Vilar, for current goings-on. Bars and seafood-theme tapas joints line the old streets south of the cathedral, particularly **Rúa do Franco, Rúa da Raíña,** and **Rúa do Vilar.** A great first stop, especially if you haven't eaten dinner, is **Rúa de San Clemente,** off the Praza do Obradoiro, where three bars in a row offer two or three plates of tapas free with each drink, an astonishing value.

O Beiro (✉ Rúa da Raiña 3 ☎ 981/581370) is a rustic wine bar with a laid-back professional crowd. Galicia's oldest pub is also one of its most unusual: **Modus Vivendi** (✉ Praza Feixóo 1) is in a former stable. The old stone feeding trough is now a low table, and instead of stairs there are ridged stone inclines designed for the former occupants—horses and cattle. A thirtysomething crowd packs the low-ceiling bar nightly, and on weekends there's live music (jazz, ethnic, Celtic) and sometimes story-telling. Drink to Galicia's Celtic roots and hear live music at **Casa das Crechas** (✉ Vía Sacra 3 ☎ 981/560751), where Celtic wood carvings hang from thick stone walls and playful witches ride their brooms above the bar. **Retablo Concerto** (✉ Rúa Nova 13 ☎ 981/564851) is cozy and has live music. **Iacobus** (✉ Rúa da Senra 24 ☎ 981/585967) is packed around 7 AM for after-hours *chocolate con churros* (thick hot chocolate with strips of fried dough). **Casting** (✉ Alfredo Brañas 5 ☎ 981/595900) is built beneath the glass-bottom pool in the Meliá Araguaney hotel. You must be dressed well to enter.

The tiny **tourist office** (☎ 981/584400) in the middle of Praza de Galicia, south of the old town, is geared specifically toward cultural events at the University of Santiago and elsewhere in Galicia. The modern **Auditorio de Galicia** (✉ Avda. Burgo das Nacións, ☎ 981/573855), north of town, has world-class classical and jazz programs and a fine art gallery. In residence is the Royal Galician Philharmonic, which has hosted Il Giardino Armonico, the Academy of St. Martin-in-the-Fields, and the Leipzig Gewandhaus Orchestra. Players at Santiago's **Teatro Principal** (✉ Rúa Nova 21 ☎ 981/581928) stage plays in Spanish, as well as dance performances and film festivals.

Shopping

Women in the fishing town of Camariñas fashion exquisite lace collars and scarves as well as table linens. The best place to buy their work, and watch some of it being crafted, is **Bolillos** (✉ Rúa Nova 40 ☎ 981/589776). Galicia is known throughout Spain for its distinctive blue-and-white ceramics with bold modern designs, made in Sargadelos and O Castro. Peruse a wide selection at **Sargadelos** (✉ Rúa Nova 16). Look for beautifully crafted jewelry with the black stone *azabache* (jet), a dense form of local lignite coal, at **Antonio Uzal Vázquez** (✉ Abril Ares 8). The boutique founded in 1906 and run by **Augusto Otero** (✉ Casa de Cabildo, Praza de Praterías) has fine handcrafted silver. On a tiny lane off Azabachería, **Noroeste** (✉ Ruela de Xerusalén 0 ☎ 981/577130) sells handmade jewelry.

Pazo de Oca

⓫ *27 km (17 mi) southeast of Santiago.*

The feudal barons who ruled Galicia's peasant society lived in country manor houses like this one, known as *pazos*. Stroll the gardens to the lily pond and lake, where a stone boat stays miraculously afloat. ☎ *986/587435* *€4, free Mon. 9–12:30* *Daily sunrise–sunset.*

Padrón

⓬ *18 km (11 mi) south of Santiago.*

Having grown up beside the Roman port of Iría Flavia, Padrón is where the body of St. James is believed to have washed ashore after its miraculous maritime journey. The town is known for its *pimientos de Padrón,* tiny green peppers fried and sprinkled with sea salt. The fun in eating these is that one in five or so is spicy-hot. Galicia's biggest **food market** is held here every Sunday. Padrón was the birthplace of one of Galicia's heroines, the 19th-century poet Rosalía de Castro. The lovely **Casa-Museo Rosalía de Castro,** where she lived with her husband, a historian, now displays family memorabilia. ✉ *Ctra. de Herbón* ☎ *981/811204* *€1.50* *Tues.–Sat. 10–2 and 4–8; Sun. 10–1:30.*

Where to Stay & Eat

★ $$ ✕ **Casa Antiga do Monte.** Another of the Rusticae chain's unfailingly superb inns, this graceful manor house combines modern comfort and equipment with vintage furniture and Asturian architecture. The crackling fire in the dining room and the 18th-century horreo in the yard add up to perfect rustic comfort. ✉ *Praza do Obradoiro 1, 15705* ☎ *981/812400* 🖷 *981/812401* 🌐 *www.susavilaocio.es* *16 rooms* *Restaurant, bar, pool, gym, parking (fee)* 💳 *AE, DC, MC, V.*

THE COSTA DA MORTE & THE RÍAS BAIXAS

West of Santiago, scenic C543 leads to the coast. Straight west, the shore is windy, rocky, and treacherous—hence its name, the "Coast of Death." The series of wide, quiet estuaries south of here is called the Rías Baixas (Low Estuaries). The hilly drive takes you through a green countryside dappled with vineyards, tiny farms, and Galicia's trademark horreos, most with a cross at one or both ends.

Fisterra

13 *50 km (31 mi) west of Santiago, 75 km (48 mi) southwest of A Coruña.*

There was a time when this lonely, windswept outcrop over raging waters was thought to be the end of the earth—the "*finis terrae.*" (The site's Castilian name is Finisterre.) The known western world sank into the ocean here with a flourish of rocky beaches. All that's left today is a run-down stone *faro* (lighthouse) perched on a cliff; though it's not officially open to the public, you might find the door open. Aside from legends, the only draw in this tiny seaside town is its pleasant (barring storms) main plaza and, off the plaza's southeast corner, the 12th-century church of **Santa Maria das Areas.** Romanesque, Gothic, and baroque elements combine in the impressive but rather gloomy facade. ✉ *Manuel Lago País s/n* *Free* ⏲ *June–Sept., daily 9–2 and 3–6; Oct.–May, daily 10–2 and 4–6.*

Muros

14 *55 km (34 mi) southeast of Fisterra, 65 km (40 mi) southwest of Santiago.*

Muros is a popular summer resort with lovely, arcaded streets framed by Gothic arches. The quiet back alleys of the old town reveal some well-preserved characteristic Galician granite houses. The real action here takes place when fishing boats return to dock from the mussel-breeding platforms that dot the bay. Wander the port on a weekday afternoon during the unloading and mussel-sorting and rinsing. At around 6 PM a siren signals the start of the lonja (fish auction), and anyone is welcome, though you need a special license to buy. Trays upon trays—some spilling over with more than a dozen slimy octopi, or cod with heaving gills—line the floor, which in turn is covered in a sheen of saltwater, jet-black squid ink, and fish blood. The favored footwear is knee-high rubber boots. Nearby Point Louro has good beaches, including Praia de San Francisco and Praia de Area.

Noia

15 *30 km (19 mi) east of Muros, 36 km (22 mi) west of Santiago.*

Tucked deep within the Ría de Muros y Noia, the compact medieval town of Noia nuzzles up to the foot of the Barbanza mountain range.

The Gothic church of **San Martín** rises over the old town's Praza do Tapal, facing resolutely out to sea. In the town center, **La Alameda** is a lovely sculpted park that gives way to a black-, white-, and red-tile pedestrian street lined with palm trees and stone and wrought-iron benches. You can catch glimpses of the ría through the trees; in summer the street fills with terrace cafés. Near Noia are the praias Testal and Boa.

The 14th-century church of **Santa María a Nova** (✉ off Carreiriña do Ferreiro) has many well-preserved medieval tombstones, each carved with a family emblem and the tools or symbols of the buried artisan. One shipbuilder's stone depicts a compass, an anchor, and an axe.

4

Pontevedra

⓰ *59 km (37 mi) south of Santiago, 55 km (34 mi) southeast of Noia.*

At the head of its ría, Pontevedra is the largest city on Spain's northwest coast after A Coruña. You approach through prefab suburbs, but Pontevedra's old quarter is well preserved and largely undiscovered. Speckled with bars, it's lively-to-wild on weekends. The 16th-century seafarers' basilica of **Santa María Mayor,** with a 1541 plateresque facade has lovely, sinuous vaulting and, at the back of the nave, a Romanesque portal. Above the door in the lower part of the basilica is a 16th-century image of Christ with the Virgin and St. John. At the end of the right nave is an 18th-century Christ by the Galician sculptor Ferreiro. ✉ *Avda. de Santa María s/n* ☎ *986/866185* *Free* ⏲ *Daily 9–2 and 5–8:30.*

★ Pontevedra's **Museo Provincial** is in two 18th-century mansions connected by a stone bridge. Displays include some incredible Celtic jewelry, silver from all over the world, and several large model ships. The original kitchen in this building is intact, complete with stone fireplace; nearby, take the tiny, steep wooden stairs down to the reconstructed captain's chamber on the battleship *Numancia,* which limped back to Spain after the Dos de Mayo battle with Peru in 1866. Completing the loop, upstairs in the first building, are Spanish and Italian paintings and some inlay work. ✉ *Praza de Leña* ☎ *986/851455* *€2* ⏲ *Tues.–Sat. 10–2 and 5–8, Sun. 11–2.*

Where to Stay & Eat

★ $$$ ✕ **Casa Solla.** Pepe Solla brings Galicia's bounty to his terrace garden restaurant, 2 km (1 mi) outside of town toward O Grove. Try the sole in Albariño wine sauce, filet mignon in red wine, and, in summer, fresh figs with Cabrales cheese. ✉ *Avda. Sineiro 7 (Crtra. de La Toja Km 2) San Salvador de Poio* ☎ *986/872884* ▭ *AE, DC, MC, V* ⏲ *Closed late Dec.–early Jan; Mon.; no dinner Thurs. or Sun.*

$$–$$$ ✕ **Casa del Barón (Parador de Pontevedra).** A 16th-century manor house built on the foundations of an ancient Roman villa in the heart of the old quarter, this relatively dark parador has a baronial stone stairway winding up from the front lobby. Guest rooms have recessed windows with lace curtains and large wooden shutters; some face a small rose garden. The restaurant, which serves fine Galician food, is full of antique mirrors, candelabras, and portraits. ✉ *Barón 19, 36002* ☎ *986/855800* *986/852195* ⊕ *www.parador.es* *47 rooms* *Restaurant, café, bar, library* ▭ *AE, DC, MC, V.*

en route

As you're driving west on the C550, you'll pass Albariño vineyards, their vines trained along trellises. It's not uncommon, as you tool your way through the small towns around here, to see a donkey helping out with cartage.

O Grove

17 *20 km (12 mi) northwest of Pontevedra, 75 km (47 mi) south of Santiago.*

O Grove (El Grove in Castilian) throws an illustrious shellfish festival the second week of October, but you can enjoy the day's catch in taverns and restaurants year-round. From here you can cross a pretty bridge to the island of **A Toxa** (La Toja), famous for its spas. Legend has it that a man abandoned an ailing donkey here and found it up on all fours, fully rejuvenated, upon his return; the waters are still said to have healing properties. The island's south side has a lovely, fat-palmed, manicured garden anchored on one side by the **Capilla de San Sebastián,** a tiny church covered in cockle shells. Nearby Reboredo is the home of Spain's finest aquarium, **Acquariumgalicia.** ✉ *Punta Moreiras s/n* ☎ *986/731515* 🌐 *www.acquariumgalicia.com* €6 ⏲ *Daily 10–8.*

Where to Stay & Eat

$$–$$$ ✕ **Crisol.** Varied sea creatures greet you from a live tank as you enter this secluded spot, and sure enough, the menu has lobster, shrimp, spider crabs, scallops, and freshly caught fish. If you can't make up your mind, a house stew (*sopa de pescados mixtos*) combines most of the above. Save room for *torta dulce de nueces,* a dense almond cake glazed with honey and powdered sugar. ✉ *Hospital 10–12* ☎ *986/730029* 💳 *AE, DC, MC, V* ⏲ *Closed Mon. and Nov. or Dec.*

$$$$ ✕🏨 **Gran Hotel de La Toja.** Extravagant and exorbitant (for the region), this classic spa hotel is on the breezy island off O Grove, surrounded by pine trees. Guest rooms are simple, their charm slightly faded compared to the grandiose formality of the foyers and salons. Try to book one with a sea view. The dining areas have expansive sea views. ✉ *Isla de la Toja 36991* ☎ *986/730025* 📠 *986/731201* *197 rooms* *Restaurant, 9-hole golf course, tennis court, pool, health club, spa, beach, casino, dance club* 💳 *AE, DC, MC, V.*

Nightlife

The **Casino La Toja** (☎ 986/731000) is steps from the Gran Hotel.

Cambados

18 *34 km (21 mi) north of Pontevedra, 53 km (33 mi) southwest of Santiago.*

This breezy seaside town has a charming, almost entirely residential **old quarter.** The impressive main square, **Praza de Fefiñanes,** is bordered on almost two sides by the imposing 17th-century Pazo de Fefiñanes, now an Albariño bodega.

Where to Stay & Eat

★ $$–$$$ ✕ **María José.** In this privileged spot across from the Parador, the Ribadomar family produces inventive dishes—salads of scallops or large prawns with bacon. Specialties are *arroz de marisco caldoso* (shellfish, stock, and rice), or *mariscada* (fresh seafood). ✉ *San Gregorio 2* ☎ *986/542281* 💳 *MC, V* ⏲ *Closed Mon. and 1st 2 wks in Nov. No dinner Sun. Nov.–June.*

$$–$$$ ✕🏨 **Parador El Albariño.** The bar of this airy parador is large and inviting, with natural light and wooden booths. Rooms are warmly furnished with wrought-iron lamps, area rugs, and full-length wood shutters over small-pane windows. The kitchen's *lenguado al vino albariño* (sole in Albariño wine sauce) is simply divine; be sure to order some local Albariño wine in its purest form. ✉ *Paseo de Cervantes s/n, 36630* ☎ *986/*

542250 🖷 986/542068 🌐 www.parador.es ⇆ 58 rooms ♨ Restaurant, meeting rooms, tennis court, pool ▭ AE, DC, MC, V.

Nightlife

Bar Laya (✉ Praza de Fefiñanes ☎ 986/542436) is easy to spot on the Praza de Fefiñanes, as it's filled with a youngish crowd day and night. Stone walls and close quarters keep the bar lively and inviting. A corner of the bar is given over to a substantial wineshop.

Shopping

Cambados is the hub for Albariño wines, arguably Spain's finest white. **O Casa do Albariño** (✉ Rúa Principe 3 ☎ 986/542236) is a tiny, tasteful emporium of Galician wines and cheeses. Souvenir shops offer Galician witches and the usual kitsch, but **Cucadas** (✉ Praza de Fefiñanes ☎ 986/542511) has a particularly large selection of baskets, copper items, and Camariñas lace.

Vigo

⑲ *90 km (56 mi) south of Santiago, 31 km (19 mi) south of Pontevedra.*

Vigo's formidable port is choked with trawlers and fishing boats and lined with clanging shipbuilding yards. Its sights (or lack thereof) fall far short of its commercial swagger. The city's casual appeal lies a few blocks inland where the port commotion gives way to the narrow, dilapidated streets of the old town. On **Rúa Pescadería,** in the barrio called La Piedra, you'll encounter Vigo's famed *ostreras*—a group of rubber-gloved fisherwomen who have been peddling fresh oysters to passersby for more than 50 years. From 8:30 to 3:30 daily, the ostreras shuck their way through kilos of oysters hauled into port that morning. Healthy rivalry has made them expert hawkers who cheerfully badger all who walk by, occasionally talking up the oyster-as-aphrodisiac. You buy a dozen, the women plate them and plunk a lemon on top, and you can then take your catch into any nearby restaurant and turn it into a meal. A short stroll southwest of the old town brings you to the fishermen's barrio of **El Berbés.** Here the day starts as early as 5 AM with the pungent and cacophonous *lonja* (fish auction), where fishermen sell their morning catch to vendors and restaurants. **Ribera del Berbés,** facing the port, has several seafood restaurants, most with outdoor tables in summer. South of Vigo's old town is the hilltop **Parque del Castro** (✉ between Praza de España and Praza do Rei, beside Avda. Marqués de Alcedo), a quiet, stately park with sandy paths, palm trees, mossy embankments, and stone benches. Climb a series of steps and you'll come to the remains of an old fort and a *mirador* (lookout) with fetching views of Vigo's coastline and the Islas Cies.

Where to Eat

★ $–$$ ✕ **El Mosquito.** Signed photos from the likes of King Juan Carlos and Julio Iglesias cover the walls of this elegant rose- and stone-wall restaurant, open since 1928. The brother-and-sister team of Manolo and Carmiña have been at the helm for the last few decades; their specialties include *lenguado a la plancha* (grilled sole) and *navajas* (razor clams). Try the *tocinillos,* a sugary flan. The restaurant's name refers to an era when wine arrived in wooden barrels: if mosquitoes gathered at the barrel's mouth, it held good wine. *✉ Praza da Pedra 4 ☎ 986/224441 ▭ AE, DC, MC, V ⏲ Closed Sun. and Aug.*

¢–$ ✕ **Bar Cocedero La Piedra.** This jovial tapas bar does a roaring lunch trade with Vigo locals. The chefs serve up heaping plates of *mariscos* (shellfish) at market prices. Wash it all down with Albariño wine. The chummy, elbow-to-elbow crowd sits at round tables covered with functional paper tablecloths. *✉ Rúa Pescadería 3 ☎ 986/223765 ▭ DC, MC, V.*

Shopping

Traditional musical instruments, such as the bagpipes, are studied, displayed, and sold at the **Universidade Popular de Vigo** (✉ Avda. García Barbón 5).

Islas Cies

⓴ *35 km (21 mi) west of Vigo in Atlantic Ocean.*

The Cies Islands are a nature reserve, and was, until the 2002 oil spill, one of the last unspoiled refuges on the Spanish coast. From July to September, about eight boats a day leave from Vigo's harbor, returning later in the day, for the round-trip fare of €12 for adults. The 45-minute ride brings you to fine white-sand beaches. Birds abound, and the only land transportation is your own two feet: it takes about an hour to cross the main island. For camping reservations (required), call **Camping Islas Cies** (☎ 986/438358), open June 15–September 15.

Baiona

㉑ *12 km (8 mi) southwest of Vigo.*

At the southern end of the A–9 freeway and the Ría de Vigo, Baiona (Bayona in Castilian) is a summer haunt of affluent Gallegos. When Columbus's *Pinta* landed here in 1492, Baiona became the first town to receive the news of the discovery of the New World. Once a castle, **Monte Real** is one of Spain's most popular paradors; walk around the battlements for superb views. Inland from Baiona's waterfront Paseo Marítima, a jumble of streets has seafood restaurants and lively cafés and bars. Calle Ventura Misa is one of the main drags. On your way into or out of town, check out Baiona's **Roman bridge.** The best nearby beach is Praia de América, north of town toward Vigo.

Where to Stay & Eat

★ $$$ **Parador de Baiona.** This baronial parador was built inside the walls of a medieval castle on a hilltop fortified since 200 BC. The rooms are plush and some have balconies with ocean views toward the Islas Cies. Try the *entremeses variados* (mixed appetizers) for a sampler of typical seafood, or *parillada de pescados* (grilled swordfish, salmon, and cod). ✉ *Ctra. de Baiona at Monterreal, 36300* ☎ *986/355000* 📠 *986/355076* 🌐 *www.parador.es* *122 rooms* *Restaurant, tennis court, pool, health club, beach, bar, playground* 💳 *AE, DC, MC, V.*

Tui

㉒ *14 km (9 mi) southeast of Baiona, 26 km (16 mi) south of Vigo.*

Leave Vigo on the scenic coastal route C555, which takes you up the banks of the Miño River along the Portuguese border. If time is short, jump on the inland A55: both routes lead to Tui, where steep, narrow streets rich with emblazoned mansions suggest the town's past as one of the seven capitals of the Galician kingdom. Today it's an important border town, from which the mountains of Portugal are visible from the cathedral. Across the river in Portugal, the old fortress town of Vallença contains reasonable shops, bars, restaurants, and a hotel with splendid views of Tui. Tui was crucial during the medieval wars between Castile and Portugal, which explains why the 13th-century **cathedral** looks like a fortress. The cathedral's majestic cloister surrounds a lush formal garden. Consecrated in 1225, the building was remodeled in the 16th century. ✉ *Pl. de San Fernando s/n* ☎ *986/600511* *€2.40* *Daily 10–1 and 5–7.*

Where to Stay & Eat

$$–$$$ ✕🏨 **Parador de Tui.** On the bluffs overlooking the Miño, this granite-and-chestnut hotel has lobbies with rural antiques and paintings by local artists. Guest rooms are furnished with convincing reproductions. Views of the woods surround the dining room, where specialties from the river Miño include Atlantic salmon, lamprey eel, sea trout, and trout. For dessert, try the the *pececitos,* almond-flavor pastries made by local convent nuns. ✉ *Avda. del Portugal s/n, 36700* ☎ *986/600300* 🖷 *986/602163* 🌐 *www.parador.es* *30 rooms* *Restaurant, tennis court, pool, bar, parking (fee)* ▭ *AE, DC, MC, V.*

A CORUÑA & THE RÍAS ALTAS

Galicia's gusty, rainy northern coast has inspired local poets to wax lyrical about raindrops falling continuously on one's head. Don't worry, the sun does shine here, and suffuses town and country with a golden glow. North of A Coruña, the Rías Altas (Upper Estuaries) notch the coast as you head east toward the Cantabrian Sea.

A Coruña

㉓ *57 km (35 mi) north of Santiago.*

One of Spain's busiest ports, A Coruña (La Coruña in Castilian) prides itself on being the most progressive city in the region. The weather can be fierce, wet, and windy—hence the glass-enclosed, white-paned galleries on the houses lining the harbor. To see why sailors once nicknamed A Coruña the Ciudad de Cristal (Crystal City), stroll **Dársena de la Marina,** said to be the longest seaside promenade in Europe. While the congregation of boats is charming, the real sight is across the street: a long, gracefully curved row of houses. Built by fishermen in the 18th century, the houses actually face *away* from the sea—at the end of a long day, these men were tired of looking at the water. Nets were hung from the porches to dry, and fish was sold on the street below. When Galicia's first glass factory opened nearby, someone thought to enclose these porches in glass, like the latticed stern galleries of ocean-going galleons, to keep wind and rain at bay. The resulting **glass galleries** ultimately spread across the harbor and eventually throughout Galicia.

Plaza de María Pita is the focal point of the *ciudad vieja* (old town). Its north side is given over to the neoclassical **Palacio Municipal,** or city hall, built 1908–12 with three Italianate domes. The **monument** in the center, built in 1998, depicts the heroine herself, Maior (María) Pita, holding her lance. When England's notorious Sir Francis Drake arrived to sack A Coruña in 1589, the locals were only half finished building the defensive Castillo de San Antón, and a 13-day battle ensued. When María Pita's husband died, she took up his lance, slew the Briton who tried to plant the Union Jack here, and revived the exhausted Coruñesos, inspiring women to join the battle as well.

The 12th-century church of **Santiago** (✉ Pl. de la Constitución s/n), the oldest church in A Coruña, was the first stop on the *camino inglés* (English route) toward Santiago de Compostela. Originally Romanesque, it's now a hodgepodge, with Gothic arches, a baroque altarpiece, and two 18th-century rose windows. The church smells movingly of age and the sea. The **Colegiata de Santa María** (✉ Pl. de Santa María) is a Romanesque beauty from the mid-13th century, often called Santa María del Campo (St. Mary of the Field) because it was once outside the city walls. The facade depicts the Adoration of the Magi; the celestial figures include St. Peter, holding the keys to heaven. A quirk of this church is that, due to an architectural miscalculation, the roof is too heavy for its supports, so the columns inside lean outward, and the buttresses outside have been thickened. Couples who want to get married in the old town book this poetic church far in advance. At the northeastern tip of the old town is the **Castillo de San Antón** (St. Anthony's Castle), a 16th-century fort. Inside is A Coruña's **Museum of Archaeology,** with remnants of the prehistoric Celtic culture that once thrived in these parts. The collection includes silver artifacts as well as pieces of the Celtic stone forts called *castros.* ☎ *981/189850* 🎫 *€1.80* ⏲ *July–Aug., Tues.–Sat. 10–8:30, Sun. 10–2:30; Sept.–June, Tues.–Sat. 10–7, Sun. 10–2.*

The **Museo de Bellas Artes** (Museum of Fine Arts), housed in a converted convent on the edge of the old town, has French, Spanish, and Italian paintings, and a curious collection of etchings by Goya. ✉ *C. Zalaeta s/n* ☎ *981/223723* 🎫 *€2.50, free weekend afternoons* ⏲ *Tues.–Fri. 10–8, Sat. 10–2 and 4:30–8, Sun. 10–2.*

Across town, on a hill, is the **Casa de las Ciencias** (Science Museum), a hands-on museum where children can learn the principles of physics and technology. ✉ *Parque Santa Margarita* ☎ *981/189848* 🌐 *www.casaciencias.org* 🎫 *Museum €2, planetarium €1.20* ⏲ *Sept.–June, daily 10–7; July–Aug., daily 11–9.*

Much of A Coruña sits on a peninsula, on the tip of which is the **Torre de Hercules**—the oldest still-functioning lighthouse in the world. Originally built during the reign of Trajan, the Roman emperor born in Spain in AD 98, the lighthouse was rebuilt in the 18th century and looks strikingly modern; all that remains from Roman times are inscribed foundation stones. Scale the 245 steps for superb views of the city and coastline—and if you're here in the summer, return at night, when the tower opens for views of city lights along the Atlantic. Lining the approach to the lighthouse are sculptures depicting figures from Galician and Celtic legends. At the base of the structure, a museum displays items dug up during the restoration of the lighthouse and surrounding area. ✉ *Ctra. de la Torre s/n* ☎ *981/202759* 🎫 *€2* ⏲ *Daily 10–6.*

The slate-covered **Domus/Casa del Hombre** (Museum of Mankind) was designed by Japanese architect Arata Isozaki. In the shape of a ship's sail, this museum is dedicated to the study of the human being, and particularly the human body. Exhibits, many of which are interactive, range from a film of a human birth to panels on language. ✉ *C. Santa Teresa 1* ☎ *981/189840* 🎫 *Museum €2, IMAX €6* ⏲ *July–Aug., daily 11–9; Sept.–June, daily 10–7.*

Where to Stay & Eat

$$$ ✕ **Casa Pardo.** Near the port, this chic, double-decker dining room has soft ocher tones, with perfectly matched wood furniture and cool lighting. Try the *rape a la cazuela* (bay leaf–scented monkfish and potatoes drizzled with oil and sprinkled with paprika, baked in a clay casserole). For dessert, there's flaky pastry with cream or chocolate soufflé. ✉ *Novoa Santos 15* ☎ *981/287178* 💳 *AE, DC, MC, V* ⏲ *Closed Sun.*

$$ ✕ **El Coral.** The window is an altar of shellfish, with varieties of mollusks and crustaceans you've probably never seen before. Inside, wood-panel walls, crystal chandeliers, and 12 white-clad tables help create an elegant yet casual experience. Specialties include *turbante de mariscos* (a platter—literally, a "turban"—of steamed and boiled shellfish). ✉ *Callejón de la Estacada 9, at Avda. Marina* ☎ *981/200569* ✍ *Reservations essential* 💳 *AE, DC, MC, V* ⏲ *Closed Sun. Oct.–June.*

★ **$–$$** ✕ **Adega O Bebedeiro.** Despite being steps from the Domus, this tiny restaurant is beloved by locals for its authentic food and low prices. It feels like an old farmhouse, with stone walls, floors, and fireplace; pine tables and stools; dusty wine bottles (*adega* means "wine cellar"); and rustic implements. Appetizers, such as *setas rellenas de marisco y salsa holandesa* (wild mushrooms stuffed with seafood and served with Hollandaise sauce), are followed by various fish at market prices. ✉ *C. Angel Rebollo 34* ☎ *981/210609* ▭ *AE, DC, MC, V* ⊗ *Closed Mon. No dinner Sun., last 2 wks in June, and last 2 wks in Dec.*

★ $–$$ ✕ **La Penela.** Try at least a few crabs or mussels with béchamel—for which this restaurant is locally famous. If shellfish isn't your speed, make sure you sample the equally popular roast veal. Enjoy the smart, contemporary, bottle-green dining room while feasting on fresh fish and sipping some Albariño. The restaurant occupies a corner of the lively Praza María Pita. ✉ *Praza María Pita 12* ☎ *981/209200* ▭ *AE, DC, MC, V* ⊗ *Closed Sun. and Jan. 10–25.*

$$$ **La Toja Finisterre.** This grande dame—where the old town joins the bay—is the oldest of A Coruña's top hotels. A favorite with businesspeople and families, it has large, carpeted rooms with modern wood furnishings and bright upholstery. Ask for a room overlooking the bay. ✉ *Paseo del Parrote 22, 15001* ☎ *981/215200* 🖷 *981/215206* 🌐 *www.hotelfinisterre.com* *92 rooms* *Restaurant, 2 tennis courts, 4 pools, hair salon, health club, bar, playground* ▭ *AE, DC, MC, V.*

$$$ **Tryp Coruña.** It's not charming, per se—fluorescent lighting abounds—but soft blues and nautical prints offset this and reinforce the maritime feel. Convenient to El Corte Inglés and the bus and train stations, this high-rise runs like a well-oiled machine. ✉ *Ramón y Cajal 53, 15001* ☎ *981/242711* 🖷 *981/236728* 🌐 *www.solmelia.com* *181 rooms* *Restaurant, gym, sauna, bar* ▭ *AE, DC, MC, V.*

Nightlife

Begin your evening in the **Plaza de María Pita**—bars, cafés, and tapas bars proliferate off the plaza's western corners and farther inland. **Calles Franja, Riego de Agua, Barrera,** and **Galera** and the **Plaza del Humor** have many bars, some of which serve Ribeiro wine in bowls. Night owls head for the posh and pricey clubs around **Praia del Orzán** (Orzán Beach), particularly along Calle Juan Canalejo. For lower-key late-night entertainment, the old town has cozy taverns where you can grab a nightcap even as the new day dawns. Try **A Roda 2** (✉ Capitán Troncoso 8 ☎ 981/228671) for tapas—octopus in its own ink, garlic garbanzo beans—and a lively evening crowd.

Shopping

Calle Real has boutiques with contemporary fashions. A stroll down **Calle San Andres,** two blocks inland from Calle Real, or **Avenida Juan Flórez,** leading into the newer town, may yield some sartorial treasures. Galicia has actually spawned some of Spain's top designers, notably **Adolfo Dominguez** (✉ C. Real 13 ☎ 981/225142). For traditional berets, try **Luis Tomé Pérez Fábrica de Gorras y Boinas** (✉ Linares Rivas 52 ☎ 981/232014), a hat and cap emporium. For hats and Galician folk clothing, stop into **Sastrería Iglesias** (✉ Rego do Auga 14 ☎ 981/221634)—founded 1864—where artisan José Luis Iglesias Rodrígues sells his textiles. Authentic Galician *zuecos* (hand-painted wooden clogs) are still worn in some villages to navigate mud; the cobbler **José López Rama** (✉ Rúa do Muiño 7 ☎ 981/701068) has a workshop 15 minutes south of A Coruña in the village of Carballo. **Alfares de Buño** (✉ Plazuela de los Angeles 6 ☎ no phone) sells glazed terra-cotta ceramics from Bunho, 40 km (25 mi) west of A Coruña on C552. These crafts are prized by aficionados—to see where they're made, drive out to Bunho itself, where potters work in private studios all over town. Stop into **Alfarería y Cerámica de Buño** (✉ C. Barreiros s/n, Bunho ☎ 981/721658) to see the results. A wide selection of classic blue-and-white pottery is sold at the factory and museum **Cerámicas del Castro** (✉ Ctra. Sada–La Coruña s/n ☎ 981/620200), north of Coruña in the nearby town of Sada.

Betanzos

★ ㉔ · *65 km (40 mi) northeast of Santiago, 25 km (15 mi) east of A Coruña.*

The charming, slightly ramshackle medieval town of Betanzos is still surrounded by parts of its old city wall. It was an important Galician port in the 13th century but is now silted up. The 1292 monastery of **San Francisco** was converted into a church in 1387 by the nobleman Fernán Perez de Andrade, whose magnificent sepulchre, to the left of the west door, has him lying on the backs of a stone bear and boar, with hunting dogs at his feet and an angel receiving his soul by his head. The 15th-century church of **Santa María de Azougue** has 15th-century statues that were stolen in 1981 but subsequently recovered. It's a few steps uphill from the church of San Francisco. The tailors' guild put up the Gothic-style church of **Santiago,** which includes a Door of Glory inspired by the one in Santiago's cathedral. Above the door is a carving of St. James as the Slayer of the Moors.

Shopping

Visit a bagpipe workshop and buy the real thing at **Sellas y Gaitas** (✉ Cerca s/n), open weekdays 10–1 and 5–8.

Vilalba

㉕ *70 km (43 mi) east of A Coruña.*

Known as *Terra Cha* (Flat Land) or the Galician Mesopotamia, Vilalba is the source of several rivers, most notably the Miño, which flows down into Portugal. Hills and knolls add texture to the plain.

Where to Stay & Eat

$$–$$$ ✕🏨 **Parador Condes de Vilalba.** Part of this parador is in a massive 15th-century tower that was once a fortress. A drawbridge leads to the two-story lobby, which is hung with tapestries. The three large octagonal chambers in the tower have beam ceilings, wood floors, traditional hand-carved Spanish furniture, and chandeliers. The restaurant offers empanada *de Rax,* made of beef loin, or the traditional empanada *de atún* (with tuna); for dessert, order the *San Simón,* a cone-shape, birch-smoked cheese served with apples or pears. ✉ *Valeriano Valdesuso s/n, 27800* ☎ *982/510011* 📠 *982/510090* 🌐 *www.parador.es* *48 rooms* *Restaurant, gym, sauna, Turkish baths, bar* 💳 *AE, DC, MC, V.*

Mondoñedo

㉖ *122 km (76 mi) northeast of A Coruña, 52 km (32 mi) northeast of Vilalba.*

Founded in 1156, this town was one of the seven capitals of the kingdom of Galicia from the 16th to early 19th century. The **cathedral,** consecrated in 1248, has a museum, a bishop's tomb with inlaid stone, and medieval murals showing the Slaying of the Innocents and St. Peter. The cathedral dominates the ancient **Plaza Mayor,** where a medieval pageant and market are held the first Sunday in August. The quiet streets and squares are filled with old buildings, monasteries, and churches, and include a medieval Jewish quarter. The shop **El Rey de las Tortas** (✉ Obispo Sarmiento 2) is known for special dessert pies, or *tortas,* made with pastry, sponge cake, vermicelli, and almonds and decorated with crystallized cherries and figs.

Where to Eat

$$ ✕ **A Taberna do Valeco.** In a converted mill with exposed stone walls, this tavern on the outskirts of town has been family-run since 1956. Pepe Bouso serves free crispy empanadas, sometimes made from wild boar, with each drink; the small restaurant upstairs serves game (in winter), fresh fish, and excellent meat. There's a good wine list. ✉ *Rúa Os Muiños de Arriba 6* ☎ *982/521861* ▭ *AE, DC, MC, V.*

en route

What were, until the November 2002 oil spill, Spain's cleanest and least-crowded beaches are north of here. Massive cleanup efforts will have restored them fully by spring of 2004. The winding N634 leads to the coast and then east to Asturias.

4

Viveiro

★ 27 *184 km (114 mi) northeast of A Coruña, 81 km (50 mi) northeast of Vilalba.*

At the crux of its own ría, this town is a popular summer resort. The once-turreted city walls are still partially intact. Two festivals are noteworthy: the Semana Santa processions, in which penitents follow religious processions on their knees, and the Rapa das Bestas, a colorful roundup of wild horses the first Sunday in July (on nearby Mt. Buyo).

Where to Stay & Eat

$$ ✕▣ **Hotel Ego.** The view of the ría from this hilltop hotel outside Viveiro is unbeatable—tiny islets and all—and every room enjoys it. Rooms are carpeted and have enormous mirrors and vanity tables. The glassed-in breakfast room faces the ría and a cascade of trees; on a rainy day, you'd much rather be cooped up here than in town. Adjoining the hotel is the elegant Nito restaurant, which serves excellent Galician cuisine. ✉ *Playa de Area, off N642, 27850* ☎ *982/560987* ⎙ *982/561762* ⇄ *29 rooms* ♖ *Restaurant, bar* ▭ *AE, MC, V.*

off the beaten path

CERVO – Distinctive blue and white–glazed contemporary ceramics are made at **Cerámica de Sargadelos** (✉ Ctra. Paraño s/n ☎ 982/557841), 21 km (13 mi) east of Viveiro. Tour the factory and watch artisans work weekdays 8:30–12:30 and 2:30–5:30. Shop hours are 11–2 and 4–7 on weekends and holidays.

Ribadeo

28 *50 km (31 mi) southeast of Viveiro, 40 km (25 mi) northeast of Mondoñedo.*

Perched on the broad ría of the same name, Ribadeo is the last coastal town before Asturias. The views up and across the estuary are marvelous—depending on the wind, the waves appear to roll *across* the ría rather than straight inland. Salmon and trout fishermen congregate upriver. Take the scenic walk or drive north of town to the **Illa de la Pancha** lighthouse (a 5-km [3-mi] round-trip), connected to the coastal cliffs by a small bridge. If the bridge is closed, you can still savor the briny air around the grassy cliff top.

Where to Stay & Eat

$$ ✕▣ **Parador de Ribadeo.** Most rooms here have glassed-in sitting areas with views (208 is best) across the ría to Asturias. Parquet floors and harvest-yellow walls are accented by watercolors and etchings of the surrounding area. In the dining room a cornucopia of local shellfish is served,

much of it swimming around in a holding tank. Try the *sopa de mariscos,* seafood soup with a light pastry top, and don't leave without tasting the tetilla cheese–flavor ice cream, drizzled with honey. Fishing, horseback riding, and boating are easily arranged. ✉ *Amador Fernández 7, 27700* ☎ *982/128825* 📠 *982/128346* 🌐 *www.parador.es* *47 rooms, 2 suites* *Restaurant, bar* 💳 *AE, DC, MC, V.*

WESTERN ASTURIAS

As you cross into the Principality of Asturias, Galicia's intensely green countryside continues, belying the fact that this is a major mining region once exploited by the Romans for its iron- and gold-rich earth. More mountainous than Galicia, Asturias is bordered to the southeast by the imposing, snowcapped Picos de Europa.

Luarca

29 *75 km (47 mi) east of Ribadeo, 92 km (57 mi) northeast of Oviedo.*

The A-8 autopista wanders along the entire Asturian coast through western Asturias toward Oviedo. The village of Luarca is tucked into a cove at the end of a final twist of the Río Negro, with a fishing port and, to the west, a sparkling bay. The town is a maze of cobblestone streets, stone stairways, and whitewashed houses with a harborside decorated with painted flowerpots. The aromas wafting from the port's many bars and restaurants may tempt you to stop for some freshly caught seafood.

Where to Stay & Eat

$$–$$$ ✕ **Sport.** Large windows with river views lead in to a kitchen adept at *fabada* (bean-and-sausage stew) as well as locally caught fish or *pulpo a la gallega,* (octopus on boiled potatoes sprinkled with olive oil, paprika, and garlic). ✉ *Rivero 9* ☎ *985/641078* 💳 *AE, DC, MC, V* ⏲ *Closed last 2 wks in Oct. No dinner Thurs. Sept.–June.*

★ **$$** ✕ **Casa Consuelo.** Opened in 1935, Casa Consuelo, a relaxed, tavern-style dining room, is usually packed. The most celebrated dish is the *merluza* (hake) stuffed with the northern Spanish delicacy *angulitas* (baby eels) and blue cheese. ✉ *Ctra. N634, Km 317 (6 km [4 mi] west of Luarca), Otur* ☎ *985/641809* *Reservations essential* 💳 *AE, DC, MC, V* ⏲ *Closed Mon. and first 3 wks in Nov.*

$–$$ ✕ **El Barómetro.** This small, family-run seafood restaurant in the middle of the harbor front has an inexpensive *menú del día* and a good choice of local fresh fish. For a bit more money, you can dig into *bogavante,* a large-claw lobster. ✉ *Paseo del Muelle 5* ☎ *985/470662* 💳 *MC, V* ⏲ *Closed late Sept.–mid-Oct. No dinner Wed. Sept.–June.*

$$ **Torre de Villademoros.** An artistically restored 18th-century manor house with an elevated *panera* (grain storage structure) and a medieval tower, this lovely retreat 14 km (8½ mi) east of Luarca is a find. Rooms and both sea and meadow views are superb, as is the cuisine. ✉ *Villademoros, Valdés s/n 33788* ☎ *985/645264* 📠 *985/645265* *10 rooms* *Restaurant, breakfast room* 💳 *AE, DC, MC, V.*

$$ **Villa La Argentina.** Beautifully restored by the González family, this charming Asturian mansion on the hill above Luarca was built in 1899 by a wealthy *indiano* (Spaniard who made his fortune in South America). There's a small antiques museum on site. The restaurant is in the old coach house in the garden, surrounded by palm trees and imported shrubs. ✉ *Villar de Luarca s/n, 33700* ☎ *985/640102* 📠 *985/640973* *9 rooms, 3 suites* *Restaurant (summer only), tennis court, pool, billiards, bar, library* 💳 *AE, DC, MC, V.*

Shopping

Aguapaste (✉ Paseo del Muelle 3 ☎ 630/727317) sells the crafts of 60 Asturian artists. Best is the silvery jewelry with azabache (jet).

en route

The coastal road leads to the picturesque town of **Cudillero** (35 km [22 mi] east of Luarca), clustered around its tiny port. The emerald green of the surrounding hills, the bright blue of the water, and the white of the houses make this village one of the prettiest in Asturias. The town of **Pravia** and the river Narcea, one of Spain's best salmon streams, are just inland.

Oviedo

30 *92 km (57 mi) southeast of Luarca, 50 km (31 mi) southeast of Cudillero, 30 km (19 mi) south of Gijón.*

Inland, the Asturian countryside starts to look a bit more prosperous. Wooden, thatch-roof horreos strung with golden bundles of drying corn replace the stark granite sheds of Galicia. A drive through the hills and valleys brings you to the capital city, Oviedo. Though primarily industrial, Oviedo has three of the most famous Pre-Romanesque churches in Spain and a large university, giving it both ancient charm and youthful zest. Start your explorations with the two exquisite 9th-century chapels ★ outside the city, on the slopes of Mt. Naranco. The church of **Santa María del Naranco,** with superb views, and its plainer sister, **San Miguel de Lillo,** 300 yards uphill, are the jewels of an early architectural style called Asturian Pre-Romanesque, a more primitive, hulking, defensive line that preceded Romanesque architecture by nearly three centuries. Commissioned as part of a summer palace by King Ramiro I when Oviedo was the capital of Christian Spain, these masterpieces have survived for more than 1,000 years. ✉ *Ctra. de los Monumentos, 2 km (1 mi) north of Oviedo* ☎ *No phone* 🎫 *€1.20, free Mon.* ⏲ *Apr.–Sept., Mon.–Sat. 10–1 and 3–7, Sun. 10–1; Oct.–Mar., Mon.–Sat. 10–1 and 3–5, Sun. 10–1.*

Oviedo's Gothic **cathedral** was built between the 14th and the 16th centuries around the city's most cherished monument, the **Cámara Santa** (Holy Chamber). King Ramiro's predecessor, Alfonso the Chaste (792–842), built this chamber to hide the treasures of Christian Spain during the long struggle with the Moors. Heavily damaged during the Spanish Civil War, it has since been rebuilt. Inside is the gold-leaf **Cross of the Angels,** commissioned by Alfonso the Chaste in 808 and encrusted with pearls and jewels. On the left is the more elegant **Victory Cross,** actually a jeweled sheath crafted in 908 to cover the oak cross used by Pelayo in the battle of Covadonga. The crosses and other treasures were stolen from the cathedral in 1977 but were recovered relatively intact as thieves tried to spirit them out of Europe through Portugal. ✉ *Pl. Alfonso II El Casto* ☎ *985/221033* 🎫 *€3* ⏲ *Mon.–Sat. 10–1 and 4–7 (8 in summer), Sun. for mass only.*

From the cathedral, look directly across the Plaza Alfonso for the still-inhabited 15th-century **Palacio de la Rúa,** the oldest palace in town. Near the Palacio de la Rúa, on Calle San Francisco, is the beautifully clean 16th-century **Antigua Universidad de Oviedo.** Behind the cathedral, the **Museo Arqueológico,** housed in the splendid Monastery of San Vicente, contains fragments of pre-Romanesque buildings. ✉ *San Vicente 5* ☎ *985/215405* 🎫 *Free* ⏲ *Tues.–Sat. 10–1:30 and 4–6, Sun. 11–1.*

To see some Asturian painting, visit the 9th-century church of **Santullano.** ✉ *Pl. Santullano* 🎫 *Free* ⏲ *May–Oct., Tues.–Sun. 11–1 and 4:30–6; Nov.–Apr., Tues.–Sun. noon–1 and 4–5.*

You might want to have a look at the exquisite **Hotel Occidental de la Reconquista,** a former 18th-century hospice. The Spanish crown prince, who carries the title Prince of Asturias, presents international achievement awards each year in the hotel's ornate chapel. ✉ *Gil de Jaz 16* ☎ *985/241100.*

Where to Stay & Eat

★ $$$ ✕ **Casa Fermín.** Skylights, plants, and an air of modernity belie the age of this sophisticated pink-and-granite restaurant, which opened in 1924. Founder Luis Gil introduced traditional Asturian cuisine to seminars around the world. Specialties include fabada, wild game in season, hake in cider, and *tortilla de angulas* (omelet with spaghetti-thin baby eels), a pricey winter delicacy. The wine cellar is extensive. ✉ *San Francisco 8* ☎ *985/216452* ▭ *AE, DC, MC, V* ⊗ *Closed Sun.*

$$–$$$ ✕ **El Raitán y el Chigre.** This place is styled like an old-fashioned kitchen, with an antique stove in the entrance. There's no lunch menu; at midday everyone is served the same ample portions of Asturian specialties: seafood soup, crab bisque, vegetable-and-bean stew, fabada, potatoes stuffed with meat, onions filled with tomatoes, rice pudding, crepes, and nut pastries. ✉ *Pl. Trascorrales 6* ☎ *985/214218* ▭ *AE, DC, MC, V* ⊗ *No dinner Sun.*

★ $$–$$$ ✕ **La Máquina.** For the best fabada in Asturias, head 6 km (4 mi) outside Oviedo toward Avilés and stop at the farmhouse with the miniature locomotive out front at Lugones. This L-shape, whitewashed dining room has attracted diners from across Spain for decades, some of who think nothing of making a weekend trip solely for the purpose of eating here. Try the rice pudding, topped with a crisp layer of hot caramel. ✉ *Avda. Conde de Santa Bárbara 59, Lugones* ☎ *985/260019* ▭ *DC, MC, V* ⊗ *Closed Sun. and mid-June–mid-July. No dinner.*

★ $$$$ **Hotel de la Reconquista.** In an 18th-century hospice emblazoned with a huge, stone coat of arms, the ultraluxurious Reconquista costs almost twice as much as any other hotel in Asturias. The wide lobby, encircled by a balcony, is decked out with velvet upholstery and 18th-century paintings. A pianist entertains nightly. Guest rooms are large and modern, with comfortable beds and large armchairs. ✉ *Gil de Jaz 16, 33004* ☎ *985/241100* 🖷 *985/241166* 🌐 *www.hoteldelareconquista.com* *142 rooms, 4 suites, 1 apartment* *Restaurant, coffee shop, hair salon, bar* ▭ *AE, DC, MC, V.*

$$$ **NH Principado.** Try this hotel if you prize friendliness over flash. The NH chain is modern and functional, but this branch feels more distinguished than most. The hotel is between the cathedral and the Plaza de la Escandalera; you enter from a pedestrian street, and the hotel takes care of luggage collection and parking. ✉ *San Francisco 6, 33003* ☎ *985/217792* 🖷 *985/213946* 🌐 *www.nh-hoteles.com* *97 rooms* *Restaurant, bar* ▭ *AE, DC, MC, V.*

Nightlife & the Arts

The **Teatro Municipal** presents plays and concerts; check newspapers for schedules. The old town's main strip of dance clubs is on **Calle Canóniga.** A rather rowdy town after dark, Oviedo has plenty in the way of loud live music. **Calle Carta Puebla** is packed with pubs, many of which are Irish—owing to the region's Celtic heritage. If you're still awake when the old town goes to sleep, try **Sir Lawrence** (✉ Eugenio Tamayo 3); you might dance out into daylight here. You can get a nightcap at the plant-filled **Sidrería Venicia** (✉ Doctor Casal 13).

Shopping

You'll find a cluster of antiques shops on a few blocks of **Calle de Mon.** On Sunday mornings an outdoor market, **El Rastrillo,** which has all sorts of stuff, is held in El Fontan. Shops throughout the city carry **azabache jewelry** made of jet, black stone-like compact black coal. For handcrafted leather bags and belts, check out **Artesania Escanda** (✉ Jovellanos 5 ☎ 985/210467). Vacuum-packed fabada is sold at **Casa Veneranda** (✉ Melquiades Alvarez 23 ☎ 985/212454).

Gijón

31 *30 km (19 mi) north of Oviedo, 95 km (59 mi) east of Luarca, 50 km (31 mi) east of Cudillero.*

Gijón (pronounced hee-*hone*) can seem overwhelming at first, with its factories and warehouses. Full of hidden hot spots and friendly people, Gijón is part fishing port, part summer resort, and part university town, packed with inviting cafés and excellent restaurants. The promenade along **Praia San Lorenzo** extends from one end of town to the other. Across the narrow peninsula and the Plaza Mayor is the harbor, where the fishing fleet comes in with the day's catch. The steep peninsula is the old fishermen's quarter, **Cimadevilla,** now the hub of Gijón's nightlife. From the park at the highest point on the headland, beside Basque sculptor Eduardo Chillida's massive sculpture *Elogio del Horizonte* (In Praise of the Horizon), there's a panoramic view of the coast and city. Gijón's **Termas Romanas** (Roman baths), dating back to the time of Augustus, are under the plaza at the end of the beach. ✉ *Campo Valdés* ☎ *985/345147* *€2.50* *Tues.–Sat. 10–1 and 5–8, Sun. 11–2.*

The **Museo de la Gaita** (Bagpipe Museum) is across the river on the eastern edge of town, past Parque Isabel la Católica. A collection of bagpipes from all over the world is augmented by workshops where you can see the instruments crafted. ✉ *La Güelga s/n* ☎ *985/332244* *Free* *Tues.–Sat. 10–1 and 5–8, Sun. 11–2.*

Where to Stay & Eat

$$$ ✕ **El Puerto.** This glass-surrounded, wood-ceiling dining room at the end of a quay overlooks the harbor, and serves fine, imaginative shellfish, seafood, and meats. A specialty is *merluza con bogavante en salsa verde* (hake and lobster with a parsley sauce). Feast on a four-plate menu or a *parillada de mariscos* (mixed platter of grilled shellfish). Game is served in season, and the wine list is substantial. ✉ *Claudio Alvargonzález* ☎ *985/349096* *Reservations essential* *AE, DC, MC, V* *No dinner Sun.*

$$–$$$ ✕ **La Pondala.** This friendly, folksy, and romantic one-time chalet was founded in 1891. When the weather cooperates, the terrace is a perfect spot for grilled meat with rice or one of many sweet and savory crepes, such as the crepe *de centolla* (crab). The restaurant is 3 km (2 mi) east of town. ✉ *Avda. de Dionisio Cifuentes 58, Somió* ☎ *985/361160* *AE, DC, MC, V* *Closed Thurs., last 2 wks in June, and last 2 wks in Nov.*

$$–$$$ ✕ **Parador de Gijón.** In an old water mill in a leafy park not far from the San Lorenzo beach, this parador is one of the simplest and friendliest in Spain. Rooms in the newer wing are small, with bleached-wood floors and thick pine shutters, but most have wonderful views over the adjacent lake or the park. In the restaurant, try the *tigres* (spicy stuffed mussels), *pimientos de piquillo rellenos* (green peppers stuffed with squid, mushrooms, and rice), or *oricios* (sea urchins), served raw or steamed with lemon juice or a spicy sauce. For dessert, try fresh figs (in season) with Cabrales cheese. ✉ *Torcuato Fernández Miranda 15, 33203* ☎ *985/370511* *985/370233* *www.parador.es* *40 rooms* *Restaurant, cafeteria* *AE, DC, MC, V.*

en route

East of Gijón is apple orchard country, the source of the famous hard cider of Asturias. Green rolling hills against a highland backdrop, grazing cows, and white chalets add up to a remarkably Alpine landscape.

Villaviciosa

32 *32 km (20 mi) east of Gijón, 45 km (28 mi) northeast of Oviedo.*

Cider capital Villaviciosa has a big dairy and several bottling plants as well as a picturesque old quarter. Emperor Charles V first set foot in Spain just down the road from here. The town's annual five-day Fiesta de la Manzana (Apple Festival) begins the first Friday after September 8. To taste the regional hard cider, stop into **El Congreso** (☒ Pl. Generalísimo 25), a popular *sidrería* (cider house) that also serves tasty tapas and shellfish straight from the tank. If time allows, check out Villaviciosa's restored 15th-century **castle** (✥ 3 km [2 mi] west of town on the N632). The beautiful sandstone walls, turrets, and archways now enclose a modern hotel and restaurant.

Where to Stay

$ **Carlos I.** From the common-area wood floors, antique furniture, potted plants, and oil paintings to the quaint bar-cafeteria, this late-17th-century mansion is loaded with character. Guest rooms are spotless and relatively large. ☒ *Pl. Carlos I, 4, 33300* ☎ *985/890121* 🖷 *985/890051* *16 rooms* *Bar* *AE, DC, MC, V.*

Ribadesella

33 *67 km (40 mi) east of Gijón, 84 km (50 mi) northeast of Oviedo.*

The N632 twists around green hills dappled with eucalyptus groves and allows you glimpses of the sea and sandy beaches down plunging valleys. The snowcapped Picos de Europa loom inland. This fishing village and beach resort is famous for the international canoe races held on the Sella River the first Saturday of August; for copious fresh seafood; and for its cave. Discovered in 1968 by Señor Bustillo, the **Cueva Tito Bustillo** has 20,000-year-old paintings on par with those in Lascaux, France, and Altamira. Giant horses and deer prance about the walls. To protect the paintings, no more than 375 visitors are allowed inside each day. But for those turned away, there is a museum of Asturian cave finds open all year round. The guided tour is in Spanish. ☎ *985/861120* *€2.50* *Cave Wed.–Sun. 10–5; museum Wed.–Sun. 10–5.*

Where to Stay & Eat

$–$$ ✕ **El Repollu.** A block inland from the port and market, this small, homey grill specializes, sure enough, in fish. Try the fresh-grilled turbot; some sweet, grilled *gambas* (shrimp); and perhaps the house Cabrales cheese. ☒ *Santa Marina 2* ☎ *985/860734* *Reservations not accepted* *AE, DC, MC, V* *Closed Thurs. Oct.–June. No dinner Oct.–June.*

$$ ✕ **Ribadesella Playa.** Passing a peaceful night in this quirky, restored turn-of-the-20th-century mansion on the beach is an unusually pleasant experience. It's family-run, and has a timeless, stately charm that will remind you of black-and-white European art films. ☒ *Ricardo Cangas 3, 33560* ☎ *985/860715* 🖷 *985/860220* *www.ribadesellaplayahotel.com* *17 rooms* *Bar* *AE, DC, MC, V.*

Llanes

34 *40 km (25 mi) east of Ribadesella.*

The sprightly beach town of Llanes is on a pristine stretch of the Costa Verde (Green Coast). Hug the shore in either direction outside town for vistas of vertical cliffs looming over white-sand beaches and isolated caves. The peaceful, well-conserved **Plaza Cristo Rey** marks the center of the old town, partially surrounded by the remains of its medieval walls. The 13th-century church of **Santa María** rises over the square. Nearby, off Calle Alfonso IX, a medieval tower houses the tourist office. A long canal, connected to a small harbor, cuts through the heart of Llanes, and along its banks rise yellow- and salmon-painted houses with glass galleries against a backdrop of the Picos de Europa. At the daily portside fish market, usually held around 1 PM, vendors display heaping mounds of freshly caught seafood. Steps from the old town is **Playa del Sablón**, a pretty little swath of sand that gets predictably crowded on summer weekends. On the eastern edge of town is the larger **Playa de Toró.** Just 1 km ([1//2] mi) east of Llanes is one of the area's most secluded beaches, the immaculate **Playa Ballota,** with private coves for picnicking and one of the few stretches of nudist sand in Asturias. West of Llanes, the most pleasant beaches lie between the towns of Barro and Celorio. Farther west (8 km [5 mi] from Llanes) is **Playa de Torimbia,** a wild, virgin, partially nudist beach yet untouched by development. You can only reach it via footpath, roughly a 15-minute walk.

Dotting the Asturian coast east and west of Llanes are *bufones* (blowholes), which occur nowhere else in Spain. Active blowholes shoot streams of water as high as 100 ft into the air; unfortunately, it's hard to predict when this will happen, as it depends on the tide and the size of the surf. There's a blowhole east of Playa Ballota; try to watch it in action from the **Mirador Panorámico La Boriza,** near the entrance to the golf course. If you miss it, the view is still worth a stop—on a clear day you can see the coastline all the way east to Santander.

Where to Stay & Eat

$–$$ ✕ **Mirentxu.** Minutes from the fish market, near the small harbor bobbing with colorful fishing boats, this friendly Basque-influenced restaurant serves heaping portions of grilled and fried fish. ✉ *Marinero 14* ☎ *985/402236* ▭ *DC, MC, V* ⊙ *Closed Oct.–June.*

$$ 🏨 **La Posada de Babel.** This exquisite family-run inn just outside Llanes has roaring fires in its public rooms. Expect plenty of personal attention here. One guest room is in a converted granary. ✉ *La Pereda, 33509* ☎ *985/402525* 📠 *985/402622* 🌐 *www.laposadadebabel.com* *11 rooms* *Restaurant, bicycles, horseback riding, bar, library* ▭ *AE, DC, MC, V* ⊙ *Closed Jan.–Feb.*

Sports & the Outdoors

Three kilometers (2 mi) east of Llanes, near the village of Cué, is the 18-hole **Club de Golf La Cuesta** (☎ 985/417084). You could hardly ask for a more privileged location: the course sprawls atop a plateau 300 ft above sea level, on the site of a former flying school (during the Spanish Civil War, there was a Falangist airport here). Nine holes offer views of the Asturian coastline, with all its misty coves and crashing waves; the other nine face the towering Picos de Europa.

THE PICOS DE EUROPA

With craggy peaks soaring up to the 8,688-ft Torre Cerredo, the northern skyline of the Picos de Europa has helped seafarers and fishermen navigate the Bay of Biscay for ages. To the south, pilgrims on their way to Santiago enjoy distant but inspiring views of the snowcapped range from the plains of Castile between Burgos and León. Some 300 million years ago, this area was a sea; over a period of 60 million years it collected a layer of calceous deposits more than a mile thick, and a massive shift of the earth's crust threw up the Picos (Peaks). Later, the fractured peaks acquired glaciers, which then left two lakes in their wake. Regular, very heavy rain and snow have created canyons plunging 3,000 ft, natural arches, caves, and sinkholes (one of which is 5,213 ft deep). The Picos de Europa National Park, covering 257 square mi, is perfect for climbers and trekkers. Explore the main trails, hang glide, ride horses, cycle, or canoe. There are two adventure-sport centers in Cangas de Onís, near the Roman Bridge.

Scenic Routes

The best-known road trip in the Picos connects Riaño and Cangas de Onís along the twisting Sella Gorge, a route known as the **Desfiladero de los Beyos,** between Riaño and Cangas de Onís. Another drive takes you up past Covadonga to Lakes Enol and Ercina. The most spectacular walk is the Ruta de Cares, which starts between Cangas de Onís and Panes. There's another gorge road, Desfiladero de la Hermida, between Panes and Potes. It takes two hours (longer with side trips) to drive the Desfiladero de los Beyos. Starting from León, head east on the N601, and then turn right for the N625 to Riaño: the N625 skirts a large dam, crosses a bridge to Riaño, then goes left. For a side trip just before the **Puerto de Pontón** (Pontón Pass; 4,232 ft), follow the signs and turn right to the **Puerto de Panderruedas** (4,757 ft) for a panoramic view of the peaks, especially in the early evening sun. For the **Ruta de Cares,** drive east on the C6312 from Cangas de Onís toward Panes, stopping just before Arenas de Cabrales: here the road descends a wide valley and reaches a *mirador* (lookout) onto the **Naranjo de Bulnes,** a huge tooth of rock way up in the peaks. The mountain was named for its occasional tendency to glow orange, *naranja,* at sunrise and sunset. Turn right in Arenas de Cabrales to reach Poncebos, and leave the car near here for the four-hour Ruta de Cares walk to Caín through the **Garganta de Cares** gorge. The canyon presents itself fairly soon, so you can turn back without pangs if you don't want to make the full hike. This route is popular, so arrive in Poncebos early in the day to avoid parking problems. You can also enter the Ruta at the other end—from **Puerto de Pontón,** a road leads to Puerto de Panderruedas, Posada de Valdeón, and Caín. Groups of friends with two cars sometimes leave them at Poncebos and Caín, then exchange keys when they meet to save the return walk.

If you have another day, leave Cangas and drive via Panes and Potes around the entire park. Consider relocating to the southern side and staying at the Parador de Fuente Dé. Ten kilometers (6 mi) south of Potes, turn right at Urdón's hydroelectric power station to **Tresviso** for unforgettable views and a chance to buy some local cheese. Just west of Potes on the C621 is the left turn for the **Monasterio de Santo Toribio,** with a 13th-century Gothic church and 17th-century cloisters. The C621 ends at Fuente Dé; from Potes the N621 continues south to Riaño, a two-hour drive. About halfway there, turn right at Puerta de San Gloria and head up the rough track to the **Monumento al Oso,** where a white stone bear marks another splendid view.

need a break?

Nestled in the gorge, the simple **Hostal Poncebos** (☎ 985/846447) is good for a quick bar lunch in winter and more substantial dishes like fabada and *cabrito* (kid) in summer. Serious trekkers and mountaineers stay in the 18 rooms upstairs, 8 of which have private bath. A funicular offers 10-minute rides up the mountain between Poncebos and Bulnes for €16 round-trip.

4

Cangas de Onís

35 *25 km (16 mi) south of Ribadesella, 70 km (43 mi) east of Oviedo.*

Partly in the narrow valley carved by the Sella River, Cangas de Onís is the unofficial capital of the Picos de Europa National Park and has the feel of a mountain village. To help plan your rambles, consult the scale model of the park outside the **Picos de Europa visitor center** (✉ Casa Dago, Avda. Covadonga ☎ 985/848614). The store opposite (at No. 22), El Llagar, sells maps and guidebooks, a few in English. Cangas was the first capital of Christian Spain. A high, humpback **medieval bridge** (also known as the Puente Romano, or Roman Bridge, because of its style) spans the Sella River gorge with a reproduction of Pelayo's Victory Cross, or the Cruz de la Victoria, dangling underneath.

Where to Stay & Eat

$$ ✕ **Sidrería Los Arcos.** This busy tavern with lots of polished wood serves local cider, various wines, and sizzling T-bone steaks. *Revuelto de morcilla* (scrambled eggs with dark sausage) is served on *totu* (a maize pastry base). ✉ *Pl. del Ayuntamiento (enter on Avda. Covadonga)* ☎ *985/849277* ▭ *AE, MC, V* ⊗ *Closed 2 wks in Jan., and Mon. Nov.–May.*

★ $$–$$$ ✕▣ **Parador de Cangas de Onís.** On the banks of the River Sella, just west of Cangas, this friendly parador is part 12th-century Benedictine monastery and part modern wing. The older building, connected to the newer one by a glass tunnel, has 11 period-style rooms, some with four-poster beds. Excellent local dishes, such as *merluza del Cantabrica a la sidra* (hake cooked in cider) garnished with asparagus, are served in the bright dining room. ✉ *Monasterio de San Pedro de Villanueva, Ctra. N624 (from N634, take right turn for Villanueva), 33550* ☎ *985/849402* 🖷 *985/849520* 🌐 *www.parador.es* ⇆ *64 rooms* ♁ *Restaurant, bar, meeting room* ▭ *AE, DC, MC, V.*

¢–$ ✕▣ **La Tiendona.** Conveniently situated halfway between the mountains of Cangas de Onís and the beaches of Ribadesella, this restored roadhouse has country-style rooms. The dining room serves regional fare such as smoked salmon, fabada, and cider. ✉ *N634, Km 335, Margolles, Cangas de Onís 33550* ☎ *985/840474* 🖷 *985/841316* ⇆ *28 rooms* ♁ *Restaurant, bar* ▭ *DC, MC, V.*

$$ ▣ **Aultre Naray.** This 19th-century mansion overlooking the Escapa mountain range is a rare find. It's perfectly placed for (and the staff can help organize) hiking, camping, canoeing, and swimming. It's not rustic, though—guest rooms have modern furniture, plenty of light, and, in some cases, pleasant sitting rooms. The hotel is 15 km (9 mi) east of town. ✉ *N634, Km 335, Los Campos, Pereyes, Cangas de Onís 33547* ☎ *985/840808* 🖷 *985/840848* 🌐 *www.aultrenaray.com* ⇆ *10 rooms* ♁ *Restaurant, bar* ▭ *AE, DC, MC, V.*

$–$$ ▣ **Hospedería del Peregrino.** This simple but adequate hostelry looks out at a magnificent church perch. Rooms are small but cozy and decorated with abundant fresh wood and checked curtains. ✉ *Crtra. AS 262 s/n,*

Covadonga 33589 ☎ 985/846047 🖷 985/846051 24 rooms ♨ Restaurant, bar ▭ AE, DC, MC, V ⊗ Closed Jan.

$–$$ **Los Lagos.** This bustling modern hotel has an excellent restaurant and cider bar. Each of the four floors has a different color scheme, ranging from cream to blue. Rooms have modern furniture and white-tile bathrooms. The hotel is right in the center of town, near the tourist office. ✉ *Jardines del Ayuntamiento 3, 33550 ☎ 985/849421 🖷 985/848405 45 rooms ♨ Restaurant, bar, meeting room ▭ AE, MC, V ⊗ Closed Nov.–Mar.*

$ **Hotel La Plaza.** Expect clean, newly remodeled, and airy double rooms at bargain prices. Heading away from the Roman bridge, take the second right after the church on Avenida Covadonga. ✉ *La Plaza 7, Cangas de Onís 33550 ☎🖷 985/848308 10 rooms ♨ Breakfast room; no a/c ▭ MC, V ⊗ Closed Jan.–Mar.*

$ **La Casa del Torrejón.** Built as a stone fortress in 1542, Torrejón has four charming little doubles in the Torrejón proper. It's the only peach-color house around; you'll find it at the back of town, a few blocks off the main road. The price (they accept cash only) includes use of the kitchen. ✉ *Calle Mayor s/n, Arenas de Cabrales 33554 ☎🖷 985/846411 4 rooms ♨ Breakfast room ▭ No credit cards.*

$ **La Naturaleza.** Poised at the foot of the Ruta del Cares, this place has views of Arenas de Cabrales and the Sella River. Four comfy rooms come with large, clean bathrooms. In winter you can take bargain, home-cooked meals in the large living room; in winter you can thaw by the fire. Technically this is a pension, but it has the cozy feel of a bed-and-breakfast. ✉ *La Segada, 33554 ☎ 985/846487 🖷 985/846101 4 rooms ♨ Restaurant, bar ▭ No credit cards ⊗ Closed Dec.–Jan.*

Covadonga

36 *14 km (9 mi) south of Cangas de Onís.*

To see high alpine meadowland, some rare Spanish lakes, and views over the peaks and out to sea (if ever the mist disperses), take the narrow road up past Covadonga to **Lake Enol,** stopping for the view en route. Starting to the right of the lake, a three-hour walk takes in views from the **Mirador del Rey,** where you'll find the grave of pioneering climber Pedro Pidal. Farther up the road from Lake Enol are a summer-only tourist office and **Lake Ercina,** where Pope John Paul II picnicked during his 1989 tour of Asturias and Galicia.

need a break? Near Lake Enol is the **Restaurante el Casín,** with a small terrace bar overlooking the mountains and the lake. The set menu is a mere €9; à la carte options include roasts and restorative fabadas. It's closed January–February.

★ Covadonga's **shrine** is considered the birthplace of Spain. Here, in 718, a handful of sturdy Asturian Christians led by Don Pelayo took refuge in the Cave of St. Mary, about halfway up a cliff, where they prayed to the Virgin Mary to give them strength to turn back the Moors. Pelayo and his followers resisted the superior Moorish forces and set up a Christian kingdom that eventually led to the Reconquest. The cave has an 18th-century statue of the Virgin and Don Pelayo's grave. Covadonga itself has a **basilica,** and the **museum** has the treasures donated to the Virgin of the Cave, including a crown studded with more than 1,000 diamonds. ☎ *985/846039 €1.50 ⊗ Daily 10–2 and 4–7 ⊗ Closed mid-Jan.–mid-Feb.*

Where to Stay & Eat

$$ ✕🏨 **Parador de Fuente Dé.** You'll find this modern parador in a valley beside a cable car that ascends a soaring rock face to 2,705 ft in about four minutes. Somewhat spartan, it's a fine no-frills base for serious climbers and walkers and has a good restaurant with *cocido lebaniego* (a filling local stew) and steaks topped with the local blue cheese. The parador is east of the Cantabrian border, 23 km (14 mi) west of Potes. ✉ *Fuente Dé, 39588* ☎ *942/736651* 📠 *942/736654* 🌐 *www.parador.es* 🛏 *78 rooms* 🍴 *Restaurant, bar, meeting room* 💳 *AE, DC, MC, V* ⏲ *Closed Dec.–Feb.*

4

GALICIA & ASTURIAS A TO Z

To research prices, get advice from other travelers, and book travel arrangements, visit www.fodors.com.

AIR TRAVEL

Carriers **Air Europa** ✉ Aeropuerto de Alvedro, A Coruña ☎ 981/187308 ✉ Aeropuerto de Ranon, Oviedo ☎ 985/127564 ✉ Aeropuerto de Labacolla, Santiago de Compostela ☎ 981/594950. **Iberia** ✉ Aeropuerto de Alvedro, A Coruña ☎ 981/187259 ✉ Aeropuerto de Ranon, Oviedo ☎ 985/127607 ✉ Aeropuerto de Labacolla, Santiago de Compostela ☎ 981/596158 ✉ Aeropuerto de Peinador, Vigo ☎ 096/268220. **Spanair** ✉ Aeropuerto de Ranon, Oviedo ☎ 985/127614 ✉ Aeropuerto de Labacolla, Santiago de Compostela ☎ 981/547770 ✉ Aeropuerto de Peinador, Vigo ☎ 986/268330.

AIRPORTS & TRANSFERS

Galicia's international airport is in Labacolla, 12 km (7 mi) east of Santiago de Compostela. Iberia flies daily from here to London, Paris, Zurich, Geneva, and Frankfurt, and domestic flights connect Santiago with the rest of Spain, including daily service to Madrid and Barcelona. Other Spanish airlines serving this area are Air Europa and Spanair. The region's other domestic airports are in A Coruña, Vigo, and near San Estéban de Pravia, 47 km (29 mi) north of Oviedo, Asturias. Airport shuttles usually take the form of ALSA buses from the city bus station. Occasionally, Iberia runs a private shuttle from its office out to the airport; inquire when you book your ticket.

Airport Information **A Coruña** ✉ Aeropuerto de Alvedro ☎ 981/187200. **Oviedo** ✉ Aeropuerto de Ranon ☎ 985/127500. **Santiago de Compostela** ✉ Aeropuerto de Labacolla ☎ 981/547500. **Vigo** ✉ Aeropuerto de Peinador ☎ 986/268200.

BIKE TRAVEL

The main Camino de Santiago (the St. James pilgrimage route) runs 800 km (525 mi) from St-Jean-Pied-de-Port on the Navarra-France border to Santiago. The official *El Camino de Santiago en Bicicleta* leaflet available from **Información Xacobeo** or from the Santiago tourist office warns that this is a very tough bike trip—bridal paths, tracks, rough stones, and mountain passes. The best time of year is late spring or early autumn. For about €1.20, tourist offices in Asturias sell the booklet *Rutas de Montaña, Senderismo, Montañismo y Bicicleta de Montaña,* which outlines different routes. Some hotels and campsites rent out bicycles, as do some adventure-sports organizations.

Bike Routes **Información Xacobeo** ✉ Pabellón de Galicia, San Lázaro s/n, Santiago de Compostela, 🌐 www.xacobeo.es. **Santiago bike route information** 🌐 www.caminhodesantiago.com, in English.

Bike Rentals **Bici Total** ✉ Avda. de Lugo 221, Santiago de Compostela ☎ 981/564562.

BUS TRAVEL

ALSA runs daily buses from Madrid to Galicia and Asturias. Several other companies connect the region with other parts of Spain.

Bus Company **ALSA** ✉ Pl. Camilo Díaz Valiño s/n, Santiago de Compostela ☎ 981/586133, 981/586453, 902/422242 National 🌐 www.alsa.es.

Bus Stations **A Coruña** ✉ Caballeros 21 ☎ 981/184335. **Lugo** ✉ Pl. de la Constitución s/n ☎ 982/223985. **Oviedo** ✉ Pl. Primo de Rivera 1 ☎ 985/281212. **Pontevedra** ✉ Calvo Sotelo s/n ☎ 986/852408. **Santiago** ✉ Rúa de San Caetano s/n ☎ 981/587700. **Vigo** ✉ Avda. de Madrid s/n ☎ 986/373411.

CAR RENTAL

If you're coming from the United States, remember that rental rates in Spain are as much as double those you can arrange in advance back home. Plan ahead—reserve a car through Hertz, Budget, or National, all of which have offices in Santiago de Compostela, A Coruña, Vigo, Oviedo, and/or Gijón. Several airport branches are listed below.

Agencies **Alamo** ✉ Aeropuerto de Coruña, A Coruña ☎ 981/662365 🌐 www.alamo.com ✉ Aeropuerto de Labacolla, Santiago ☎ 981/599877. **Avis** ✉ Aeropuerto de Ranon, Oviedo ☎ 985/562111 🌐 www.avis.com ✉ Aeropuerto de Labacolla, Santiago ☎ 981/596101 ✉ Aeropuerto de Peinador, Vigo ☎ 986/486863. **Europcar** ✉ Aeropuerto de Alvedro, A Coruña ☎ 981/187285 🌐 www.europcar.es ✉ Aeropuerto de Labacolla, Santiago ☎ 981/547740. **Hertz** ✉ Aeropuerto de Alvedro, A Coruña ☎ 981/663990 🌐 www.hertz.es ✉ Aeropuerto de Labacolla, Santiago ☎ 981/598893. **National/Atesa** ✉ Aeropuerto de Ranon, Oviedo ☎ 985/551217 🌐 www.atesa.com ✉ Aeropuerto de Peinador, Vigo ☎ 986/486561

CAR TRAVEL

The four-lane N-VI expressway links northwestern Spain with Madrid in five hours (650 km [403 mi] to Santiago). Approaching by car is the best way to appreciate the arid Castilian steppe—which gives way to the northwest's stunning green countryside. The expressway north from León to Oviedo and Gijón is the fastest way to cross the Cantabrian Mountains. A north–south Galician ("Atlantic") expressway links A Coruña, Santiago, Pontevedra, and Vigo while another along the coast of Asturias links Santander to Ribadeo. Local roads along the coast or through the hills are more scenic but two or three times as slow.

DISCOUNTS & DEALS

Seniors and children get discounted or free tickets to museums and sights through the Galician tourist board, **Turgalicia** (✉ Rúa do Vilar 43, Santiago de Compostela ☎ 981/542527 🌐 www.turgalicia.es). Discounts for weekend visits to Galicia including a 40%–50% reduction for round-trip transport within Spain or a book of tickets discounting hotels, restaurants, shops, museums, and tours is available through a scheme called *La Escapada Gallega*; call ☎ 981/542511 or check the tourist board's Web site. **Compostela 48 Horas** (✉ Rúa do Vilar 43, Santiago de Compostela ☎ 981/555129 🌐 www.santiagoturismo.com) is a visitor's card that costs €15 that entitles you to discounts or free entry to all key Santiago sites.

EMERGENCIES

Fire, Police or Ambulance ☎ 112. **Policía Local** ☎ 092. **Policía Nacional** ☎ 091. **Servicio Marítimo** (air-sea rescue) ☎ 902/202202. **Guardia Civil** ☎ 062. **Cruz Roja** (Red Cross) ☎ 913/354545. **Insalud** (public health service) ☎ 061. **Información Toxicológica** (poison control) ☎ 915/620420.

ENGLISH-LANGUAGE MEDIA

While there are no local English-language publications or broadcast outlets, English-language print media are on sale daily. Many British papers are also printed in Spain.

Bookstores **Librería Abraxas** ✉ Montero Rios 50, Santiago de Compostela ☎ 981/580377. **Librería Follas Novas** ✉ Montero Rios 37, Santiago de Compostela ☎ 981/594406. **Librería Ojanguren** ✉ Pl. de Riego 1, Oviedo ☎ 985/218824.

LANGUAGE

Personnel in tourist offices, hotels, and the better restaurants in the major cities usually speak some English. Policemen rarely do. In the rural areas, the main language is Gallego, which sounds like Portuguese; little English is spoken. All tourist literature is available in English.

LODGING

APARTMENT & VILLA RENTALS

There are some lovely roadside inns (*albergues*), old farmhouses, country manors, and village homes offering accommodations in both Galicia and Asturias. Advance reservations are essential. Tourist offices have brochures with details of rural tourism, *turismo rural* or *agroturismo,* with pictures of country hotels, B&Bs, and their facilities and prices. Tourist offices can also make reservations for you. In Galicia, contact **Agatur.** In Asturias, you can get brochures from tourist offices. Some areas also have their own regional lists, so contact the nearest tourist office or town hall. Tourist offices also have details of campsites, some of which also offer bungalows for rent.

Local Agents **Agatur** ☎ 986/580050 🌐 www.turismo-rural.com. **Asturias brochures** ☎ 902/300202.

SPORTS & THE OUTDOORS

BALLOONING

Globoastur (✉ Gijón, Asturias, ☎ 985/362368 or 608/474635 🌐 www.globoastur.com).

GOLF

Asturias has golf courses in Llanes, Gijón, and Siero. Galician courses include Monte la Zapateira, near A Coruña; Domaio, in Pontevedra province; La Toja, on the island of the same name near O Grove; and Padrón. Santiago's links are near the airport, at Labacolla. Call the club a day in advance to reserve equipment.

Campo de Golf del Aero Club Labacolla ✉ Lugar de Mourena, Santiago de Compostela ☎ 981/888276. **Club de Golf La Cuesta** ✉ 3 km [2 mi] east of Llanes, near Cué ☎ 985/417084. **Club de Golf de Castiello** ✉ Ctra. N-632, 5 km [3 mi] from Gijón towards Santander ☎ 985/366313. **Campo Municipal la Llorea** ✉ Ctra. N-632 km.62, La Llorea, Gijón ☎ 985/333191. **Campo Municipal de Golf de las Caldas** ✉ La Premaña s/n, Las Caldas, Oviedo ☎ 985/798132. **Domaio** ✉ Pontevedra ☎ 986/330386. **La Barganiza** ✉ San Martí de Anes-Siero, 12 km [7 mi] from Oviedo and 14 km [9 mi] from Gijón ☎ 985/742468. **La Toja** ✉ Isla de la Toja ☎ 986/730158. **Monte la Zapateira** ✉ C. Zapateira s/n, A Coruña ☎ 981/285200. **Padrón** ☎ 981/598891.

HIKING

The tourist offices in Oviedo and Cangas de Onís can help you organize a Picos de Europa trek. The Picos visitor center in Cangas provides general information, route maps, and a useful scale model of the range. In summer, another reception center opens between Lakes Enol and Ercina, on the mountain road from Covadonga. For advice on technical climbing, contact Servicio de Guías de Montaña. The Centro de Aventuro Monteverde can organize canoeing, canyon rappelling, bungee-jumping, spelunking, horseback riding, and jeep trips. Turismo y Aventura Viesca offers rafting, canoeing, jet skiing, climbing, trekking, bungee-jumping, and archery. In A Coruña, Nortrek is a one-stop source for information and equipment pertaining to hiking, rock climbing, skiing, and bungee-jumping. For trekking in the Ourense area, contact the active folks at Galiciaventura.

Centro de Aventuro Monteverde ✉ Sargento Provisional 5, Cangas de Onís ☎ 985/848079, closed November–March. **Nortrek** ✉ Inés de Castro 7, bajo, Apdo. 626, A Coruña ☎ 981/151674. **Picos de Europa visitor center** ✉ Casa Dago, Avda. Covadonga 43, Cangas de Onís ☎ 985/848614.

HORSEBACK RIDING Trastur leads wilderness trips on horseback through the remote valleys of western Asturias. The 5- to 10-day outings are designed for both beginners and experienced cowboys; mountain cabins provide shelter along the trail. Tours begin and end in Oviedo and cost about €108 a day, all-inclusive. The Centro Hípico de Turismo Ecuestre y de Aventuras/"Granjo O Castelo" conducts horseback rides along the pilgrimage routes to Santiago from O Cebreiro and Braga (Portugal). **Federación Hípica Gallega** has a list of all riding facilities in Galicia.

Federación Hípica Gallega ✉ Principe 43, 6th floor, Vigo ☎ 986/224349 📠 986/224387. **Centro Hípico de Turismo Ecuestre y de Aventuras/"Granjo O Castelo"** ✉ Rúa Urzaiz 91–5A, Vigo ☎ 986/425937 🌐 www.galicianet.com/castelo. **Trastur** ✉ Muñalen-Cal Teso, Tineo, Asturias ☎ 985/806036 or 985/806310.

SKIING The region's three small ski areas cater mostly to local families. The largest is San Isidro, in the Cantabrian Mountains, with one chairlift and 12 slopes. Just east of here is Valgrande Pajares, with two chairlifts, eight slopes, and cross-country trails. West of Ourense, in Galicia, Mazaneda has one chairlift, seven slopes, and cross-country trails.

Mazaneda ☎ 988/309747. **San Isidro** ☎ 987/731115 or 987/731116. **Valgrande Pajares** ☎ 985/496123 or 985/957123.

WATER SPORTS In Santiago, contact diving experts Turisnorte for information on scuba lessons, equipment rental, guided dives, windsurfing, and parasailing. Courageous and experienced sailors might find yachting a spectacular way to discover hidden coastal sights; Yatesport Coruña (also in Santiago) rents private yachts and can arrange sailing lessons.

Turisnorte ✉ Raxoeira 14, Milladoiro, A Coruña ☎ 981/530009 or 902/162172. **Yatesport Coruña** ✉ Puerto Deportivo, Marina Sada, Sada, A Coruña ☎ 981/620624. **Profundidad (Diving)** ✉ Garcilaso de Vega 35, Gijón, ☎ 985/362368 or 608/474635. **Club Mirafondos Mundo Azul (Diving)** ✉ Hotel Ciudad de la Coruña, Poligono de Andormideras s/n, A Coruña ☎ 981/211100.

TOURS

Call Santiago's association of well-informed **guides** (✉ La Rosa 22, 3rd floor, Santiago de Compostela ☎ 981/569890) to arrange a private walking tour of the city. If there's enough interest from English-speakers, you may be able to join a group tour.

TRAIN TRAVEL

RENFE runs several trains a day from Madrid to Oviedo (7 hrs) and Gijón (8 hrs), while a separate line serves Santiago (11 hrs). Daytime first- and second-class cars are available, as is an overnight train with sleeping compartments. RENFE has ticket windows at the stations in Santiago, A Coruña, Oviedo, and Gijón. Local RENFE trains connect the major cities of Galicia and Asturias with most of the surrounding small towns, but prepare for dozens of stops. Narrow-gauge FEVE trains clatter slowly across northern Spain, connecting Galicia and Asturias with Santander, Bilbao, and Irún, on the French border. Buy tickets at local travel agencies, any FEVE train station, or the FEVE office in Oviedo or Madrid. FEVE's Transcantábrico narrow-gauge train tour is an eight-day, 1,000-km (600-mi) journey through the Basque country, Asturias, and Galicia. English-speaking guides narrate, and a private bus takes the group from train stations to artistic and natural attractions. Passengers sleep on the train in suites and dine on local specialties. Trains run from May through October, and the all-inclusive cost is €4,000 for two persons in a suite.

Train Information **FEVE** ✉ C. Monte Gamonal s/n, near FEVE-Asturias train station, Oviedo, ☎ 985/297656 or 985/981700 ✉ C. General Rodrígo 6, 2nd floor, Madrid ☎ 91/453-3828. **RENFE** ☎ 902/240202 🌐 www.renfe.es.

Transcantábrico Information **Conference Travel International** ✉ 157 Glen Head Rd., Glen Head, NY 11545, USA ☎ 516/671-5298 or 800/527-4852. **E.C. Tours** ✉ 10153½ Riverside Dr., Toluca Lake, CA 91602 ☎ 818/755-9333 or 800/388-0877. **Marsans** ✉ 66 Whitmore St., London W1H 9LG, UK ☎ 0207/224-0504. **Transcantábrico** ✉ General Rodrígo 6, 3rd floor, 28003 Madrid ☎ 91/453-3806.

VISITOR INFORMATION

The tourist office in Santiago de Compostela has information on all of Galicia; the office in Oviedo covers all of Asturias.

Regional Tourist Offices **A Coruña** ✉ Dársena de la Marina s/n ☎ 981/221822. **Gijón** ✉ Marqués de San Estéban 1 ☎ 985/346046. **Pontevedra** ✉ General Gutierrez Mellado 1 ☎ 986/850814. **Santiago de Compostela** ✉ Rúa do Vilar 43 ☎ 981/584081. **Oviedo** ✉ Uria 64 ☎ 985/213385. **Vigo** ✉ Canovas del Castillo 22 ☎ 986/430577. **Ourense** ✉ Caseta do Legoeiro s/n, 32003 ☎ 988/372020.

Local Tourist Offices **A Coruña** ✉ Edificio Atalaya, Jardines de Méndez Nuñez ☎ 981/184344. **Cangas de Onís** ✉ Jardines del Ayuntamiento 2 ☎ 985/848005. **Covadonga** ✉ Avda. Covadonga s/n, Pl. del Ayuntamiento ☎ 985/846035. **Gijón** ✉ Maternidad 2 ☎ 985/341771, 985/345561. **Llanes** ✉ La Torre, Alfonso IX s/n ☎ 985/400164. **Luarca** ✉ Pl. de Alfonso X el Sabio ☎ 985/640083. **Lugo** ✉ Praza Maior 27, galerías, ☎ 982/231361. **O Grove** ✉ Pl. de Corgo 1 ☎ 986/731415 ⏲ July–October. **Oviedo** ✉ Marqués de Santa Cruz 1 ☎ 985/227586. **Ourense** ✉ Burgas 12 bajo, Puente Romano, 32005 ☎ 988/366064. **Pontevedra** ✉ Pl. de España ☎ 986/804300 ✉ La Herreria ⏲ July–Sept., outdoor kiosks. **Ribadeo** ✉ Pl. de España ☎ 982/128689. **Ribadesella** ✉ Paseo de Muelle ☎ 985/860038, January–February, weekends only. **Santiago de Compostela** ✉ Rúa do Vilar 63 ☎ 981/555129. **Tui** ✉ Colón s/n ☎ 986/601789. **Vigo** ✉ Mercado, Pl. de la Piedra ☎ 986/810216. **Villaviciosa** ✉ Parque Vallina ☎ 985/891759.

THE PYRENEES

FODOR'S CHOICE

Ca la Irene restaurant in Arties

El Fuelle, Aragonese restaurant in Zaragoza

La Torre del Remei Belle Epoque hotel in Bolvir de Cerdanya

Melia Royal Tanau ski resort, Salardú

Mountain hub and preserved medieval village of Benasque

The mysterious ancient town of La Seu d'Urgell

Ordesa and Monte Perdido National Park

HIGHLY RECOMMENDED

RESTAURANTS
Can Ventura, Llívia
Casa Lac, Zaragoza
El Fau, Jaca
Era Mola, Vielha
Galarza, Elizondo
La Formatgeria de Llívia, Gorguja
Los Victorinos, Zaragoza

HOTELS
Casa la Plaza, San Juan de Plan
El Castell, La Seu d'Urgell
Fonda Etxeberria, Arizcun
Valle de Pineta, Bielsa

SIGHTS
Beget, a once-isolated village
Bellver de Cerdanya, typical of mountain-village design
Catedral de Santa Maria, La Seu d'Urgell
Monasterio de San Juan de la Peña
Parc Nacional d'Aigüestortes i Estany de Sant Maurici
Sant Climent, a Romanesque church in Taüll
Sort, a center for skiing, fishing, and white-water kayaking

By George Semler

THE SNOWCAPPED PYRENEES separating the Iberian Peninsula from the rest of the European continent have always been a special realm, a source of legend and superstition, a breeder of myth and mystical religious significance for nearly three millennia of civilization. Along with the magic comes a surprising number of ancient cultures and languages, all Pyrenean and yet each one profoundly different from the next. On a purely physical level, there are soft green valleys along the bright rivers beneath granite and limestone heights of more than 12,000 ft. To explore any of these valleys fully—the flora and fauna, the local gastronomy, the peaks and upper meadows, the remote glacial lakes and streams, the Romanesque art in a thousand hermitages—could take a lifetime.

5

Where to begin? The grassy crest of the Alberes range sweeping from Le Perthus to the Mediterranean; the broad and sunny expanse of the Cerdanya Valley under the sheer rock walls of the Cadí; the Romanesque churches of the Noguera de Tor valley and the lake country above at Sant Mauricio; the towering heights of the Maladeta massif; Ordesa and Monte Perdido National Park's Grand Canyon–like spaces; Hemingway's beloved Irati beech forest and river above Pamplona, and the rolling moist green hills of the Baztán Valley in Pyrenean Navarra are just a few of the most memorable points in this rich anthology of wilderness and civilization.

Each Pyrenean mountain system is drained by one or more rivers, forming some three dozen valleys between the Mediterranean and the Atlantic; these valleys were all but completely isolated until around the 10th century. Local languages still range from Castilian Spanish to Euskera (Basque), in upper Navarra; to dialects such as Grausín, Belsetán, Chistavino, Ansotano, Cheso, or Patués (Benasqués), in Aragón; to Aranés, a dialect of Gascon French, in the Vall d'Aran; to Catalan at the eastern end of the chain from Ribagorça to the Mediterranean.

The earliest inhabitants of the prehistoric Pyrenees—originally cave dwellers, later shepherds and farmers—saw their first invaders when the Greeks landed at Empúries, in Northern Catalonia, in the 6th century BC. The seagoing Carthaginians colonized Spain in the 3rd century BC, and their great general Hannibal surprised Rome by crossing the eastern Pyrenees in 218 BC. After defeating the Carthaginians, the Romans built roads through the mountains: Vía Augusta, from Le Perthus to Barcelona and Tarragona; Strata Ceretana, through the Cerdanya Valley and La Seu d'Urgell to Lleida; Summus Pyrenaecus (or, as the Latin reflects, *Summus Portus,* or highest pass), at Somport, to Jaca and Zaragoza; and the Via Lemovicensis from Bordeaux through Roncesvalles to Pamplona, in the western, or Atlantic, Pyrenees.

After the fall of Rome, the Iberian Peninsula was the last of the empire to be overtaken by the Visigoths, who crossed the Pyrenees in AD 409. In the 8th century, the northern tribes then faced Moorish invaders from the south. Although Moorish influence was weaker in the Pyrenees than in southern Spain, this region at the end of the first millennium became a meeting point for Arabic and European cultures. Toulouse, in France, was the nerve center and melting pot for these influences, the medieval artistic and literary center. The Moorish occupation sent Christianity fleeing to the hills, thus dotting the Pyrenees with Romanesque art and architecture. When Christian crusaders reconquered Spain, the Pyrenees were divided among three feudal kingdoms: Catalonia, Aragón, and Navarra, proud and independent entities with their respective spiritual "cradles" in the Romanesque mountain monasteries of Ripoll, San Juan de la Peña, and San Salvador de Leyre.

Throughout the centuries, the Pyrenees have remained a strategic factor to be reckoned with. Charlemagne, probing south, lost Roland and his rear guard at Roncesvalles in 778, and his heirs lost all of Catalonia in 988. Napoléon never completed his conquest of the Iberian Peninsula largely because the Pyrenees presented insurmountable communication and supply problems. And Hitler was dissuaded by Franco from trying to use post–civil war Spain as a base camp for his African campaign, a decision that rendered the Pyrenees a path to freedom for Jews and *résistants* fleeing the Nazis.

The routes suggested in this chapter combine some of Spain's richest and most remote mountain culture and natural splendor. The cities across the flatlands south of the Pyrenees—Barcelona, Huesca, Zaragoza, and Pamplona—make reliable gateways to and from the highland wilderness; a surprise snowfall in these mountains can bring a hiking or a road trip to an abrupt halt, sending motorists scurrying to lower and warmer climes.

About the Restaurants

Pyrenean cuisine is characterized by thick soups, stews, roasts, and the use of local ingredients prepared differently in every valley, village, and kitchen from the Mediterranean to the Atlantic. The three main culinary schools are those corresponding to the Pyrenees' three main regional and cultural identities—Catalan, Aragonese, and Basque—but within these are further subdivisions such as La Cerdanya, Vall d'Aran, Benasque, Roncal, and Baztán. Game is common throughout. Trout (now often raised in lakes and ponds fed by mountain streams), wild goat, deer, boar, partridge, rabbit, duck, and quail are roasted over coals or cooked in aromatic stews called *civets* in Catalonia and *estofadas* in Aragón and Navarra. Fish and meat are often seared on slabs of slate (*a la llosa* in Catalan, *a la piedra* in Castilian Spanish). Wild mushrooms are a local specialty in season, as are wild asparagus, leeks, and herbs such as marjoram, sage, thyme, and rosemary.

WHAT IT COSTS In Euros

	$$$$	$$$	$$	$	¢
AT DINNER	over €20	€15–€20	€10–€15	€6–€10	under €6

Prices are per person for a main course at dinner.

About the Hotels

Most hotels in the Pyrenees are informal and outdoorsy, with a large fireplace in one of the public rooms. Usually built of wood and slate under a steep roof, they blend with the surrounding mountains. Comfortable and protected, they reflect the tastes of the travelers, who are mostly skiers and hikers. Options include friendly family-owned establishments, grand-luxe places, rural accommodations in Basque *caseríos* (farmhouses), and town houses.

WHAT IT COSTS In Euros

	$$$$	$$$	$$	$	¢
FOR 2 PEOPLE	over €180	€100–€180	€60–€100	€40–€60	under €40

Prices are for two people in a standard double room in high season, excluding tax.

Barcelona is the largest pre-Pyrenean base camp. A three-day trip through the eastern Pyrenees covers an important third of the chain. Five days is enough time to reach the Vall d'Aran and the Noguera de Tor Valley and its Romanesque churches before heading back to Barcelona or farther west or south; such a trip is probably the most cost-effective in terms of time, terrain, art, and architecture. A 10-day trip grants the satisfaction of a sea-to-sea crossing, but you'll spend the bulk of this time in your car.

If you have **3 days**

Starting from Barcelona, head north on the A7 freeway. Take the C150 north of Girona and then the trans-Pyrenean N260 at Besalú to the Capsacosta tunnel and **Camprodón** 1 for your first night. The next day, explore **Ripoll** 6, **Puigcerdà** 7, and **Llívia** 8; then drive west to **La Seu d'Urgell** 12 on your third day. Head back to Barcelona through the Cadí Tunnel on the E9. Alternatively, if you aim to cross the Pyrenees in a few days en route from Barcelona to the Basque Country, stay in **La Seu d'Urgell** 12, **Benasque** 26, and **Jaca** 32 before driving out to Hondarribia (Fuenterrabía).

If you have **5 days**

Starting from Barcelona or the Costa Brava, devote your first afternoon and night to **Camprodón** 1. Explore the Cerdanya Valley and **Llívia** 8 the next day; then head to **La Seu d'Urgell** 12—climbing to **Prat d'Aguiló** 11 on the way—for your third day and night. Spend your fourth day and night in the **Vall d'Aran** 17, your fifth day absorbing **Taüll** 22 and the Noguera de Tor Valley and its Romanesque churches. If you have time, go through lake-dotted **Parc Nacional d'Aigüestortes i Estany de Sant Maurici** 15. Stop in **Huesca** 24 and/or **Zaragoza** 25, the capital of Aragón, on your way out of the mountains.

If you have **10 days**

From Barcelona or the Costa Brava, the classic sea-to-sea crossing begins with a symbolic wade in the Mediterranean at Cap de Creus, peninsular Spain's easternmost point, just north of Cadaqués. From Cap de Creus cross westward to Hondarribia to do likewise at the Cabo Higuer lighthouse on the Bay of Biscay. On the westbound trip, a day's drive up through Figueres and Olot will bring you to **Camprodón** 1 and the surrounding unspoiled mountain towns, skiing, and wildlife. Stop next in **Llívia** 8, moving on to the Cerdanya, the widest, sunniest valley in the Pyrenees. From there move westward through **La Seu d'Urgell** 12 to **Parc Nacional d'Aigüestortes i Estany de Sant Maurici** 15, the **Vall d'Aran** 17, and the winter-sports center Baqueira-Beret. Stop at **Taüll** 22 and the Noguera de Tor Valley's Romanesque churches. Farther west, spend the next few days in **Benasque** 26, **San Juan de Plan and the Gistaín Valley** 28, **Bielsa** 29, the remote valleys of Upper Aragón, **Parque Nacional de Ordesa y Monte Perdido** 30, and **Jaca** 32, the region's most important town. Finally, move through western Aragón into the Basque Pyrenees to visit the Irati Forest; go through the tunnel under the Velate Pass (or, more spectacularly, over the pass itself) to explore the **Baztán Valley** 39; and then follow the Bidasoa River down to Hondarribia and the Bay of Biscay.

Exploring the Pyrenees

Traversing the Pyrenees from the Mediterranean to the Atlantic (or vice versa) is for mountain worshipers a pilgrimage of deep cultural and telluric significance. It's a seven-week hike, but you can drive the route in anywhere from 2 to 14 days. Point to point, the Pyrenees stretch 435 km (270 mi) along Spain's border with France, though the sinuous borderline exceeds 600 km (370 mi). A drive across the N260 trans-Pyrenean axis connecting the destinations in this chapter would exceed 800 km (495 mi) in all. There are three main divisions: the Catalan Pyrenees from the Mediterranean to the Noguera Ribagorçana River, the central Pyrenees of Aragón extending west to the Roncal Valley, and the Basque Pyrenees falling gently westward through the Basque Country to the Bay of Biscay and the Atlantic Ocean. The highest peaks are in Aragón—Aneto, in the Maladeta massif; Posets; and Monte Perdido, all of which are about 11,000 ft above sea level. Pica d'Estats (10,372 ft) is Catalonia's highest peak, while Pic d'Orhi (6,656 ft) is the highest in the Basque Pyrenees.

Numbers in the text correspond to numbers in the margin and on the Catalan Pyrenees and the Central & Western Pyrenees maps.

Timing

If you're a hiker, stick to the summer (June through September, especially July), when the weather is better and there's less chance of a blizzard or lightning storm at high altitudes. October is ideal for the still-green Pyrenean valleys and a hunt for wild mushrooms. November brings colorful leaves, the last mushrooms, and the first frosts. The green springtime thaw, during which you can still ski on the snowcaps, is also spectacular. For skiing, come between December and April.

EASTERN CATALAN PYRENEES

Catalonia's easternmost Pyrenean valley, the Vall de Camprodón, is still out of the way and hard enough to reach to have retained much of its original character. It has several exquisite towns and churches and, above all, mountains, such as the Sierra de Catllar, thick with boar, mountain goat, wild trout, snow partridge, and romantic majesty. Vallter 2000 and Núria are ski resorts at the eastern and western ends of the Pyrenees heights on the north side of the valley, but the middle reaches and main body of the valley have remained pasturage for sheep, cattle, and horses and de facto natural parks. To reach the Vall de Camprodón from Barcelona you can take the N152 through Vic and Ripoll; from the Costa Brava go by way of either Figueres or Girona, Besalú, and the Capsacosta tunnel. From France drive southwest through the Col (Pass) d'Ares, which enters the head of the valley at an altitude of 5,280 ft from Prats de Molló.

Camprodón

❶ *127 km (80 mi) northwest of Barcelona.*

Camprodón, the capital of its *comarca* (county), lies at the junction of the Rivers Ter and Ritort—both excellent trout streams. The rivers flow by, through, and under much of the town, giving it a highland waterfront character as well as a long history of flooding. The town owes much of its opulence to the summer folks from Barcelona who have built important mansions along the leafy promenade, **Passeig Maristany,** at its northern edge. It's also known for its sausages of every imaginable size, shape, and consistency and for its two cookie factories, Birbas and Pujol, locked in the embrace of eternal competition. (Birbas is better—look for the image of the bridge on the box.) Camprodón's best-known

Fishing

Well populated with trout, the Pyrenees' cold-water streams provide excellent angling from the third Sunday in March to the end of August. Notable places to cast a line are the Segre, Aragón, Gállego, Noguera Pallaresa, Arga, Esera, and Esca rivers. Local ponds and lakes also tend to be rich in trout, providing a good way to combine hiking and angling.

Hiking

Hiking and mountain climbing are fundamental Pyrenean activities in summer. Local and trans-Pyrenean trails crisscross the region, most with truly unforgettable views. Walking the often grassy crest of the range, with one foot in France and the other in Spain, is an exhilarating experience and well within the reach of the moderately fit. Try walking from Coll de Núria to Ulldeter over the Sierra Catllar, above Setcases; scaling the Cadí over the Cerdanya; hiking over the Maladeta glacier to Aneto, the Pyrenees' highest peak; or, in autumn, hiking through the Irati beech forest, in upper Navarra. The Iparla Ridge walk, along the Navarra–France border crest, and the Alberes walk from Le Perthus out to the Mediterranean are two more favorite day hikes. In Ordesa and Monte Perdido National Park you can take a magnificent day's walk around Spain's Grand Canyon. Local *excursionista* (outing) clubs can help you get started; local tourist offices may also have brochures and rudimentary trail maps. You can also join equestrian trips, jeep excursions to the upper Pyrenees, and horseback fly-fishing tours of the high streams and lakes from Llívia, in the Cerdanya.

Romanesque Art & Architecture

You could organize many a trip around the treasury of Romanesque chapels, monasteries, hermitages, and cathedrals in these mountains. Sites to seek out include the tiny chapel at Beget, above Camprodón; the superb rose window and 50 carved capitals of the cathedral of Santa Maria, in La Seu d'Urgell; the matched set of churches and bell towers in the Noguera de Tor Valley south of Vall d'Aran; the San Juan de la Peña and Siresa monasteries, west of Jaca; and the village churches of Navarra's Baztán Valley.

Winter Sports

Skiing is the main winter sport in the Pyrenees, and Baqueira-Beret, in the Vall d'Aran, is the leading resort. Thanks to artificial-snow machines, there is usually fine skiing from December through March at more than 20 resorts—from Vallter 2000 at Setcases, in the Camprodón Valley, west to Isaba and Burguete, in Navarra. Although weekend skiing can be crowded in the eastern valleys, Catalonia's western Pyrenees tend to have more breathing room. Cerler-Benasque, Panticosa, Formigal, Astún, and Candanchú are the major ski areas in Huesca. Numerous resorts offer helicopter skiing and Nordic skiing. Leading Nordic areas include Lles, in the Cerdanya; Salardú and Beret, in the Vall d'Aran; and Panticosa, Benasque, and Candanchú, in Aragón. Jaca, Puigcerdà, and Vielha have public skating sessions, figure-skating classes, and ice-hockey programs. The newspapers *El País, El Periódico de Catalunya,* and *La Vanguardia Española* print complete ski information every Friday in winter.

symbol is the elegant **12th-century stone bridge** that broadly spans the River Ter in the center of town, its wide arch descending at a graceful angle from a central peak.

Where to Stay

$ **Güell.** Owned and managed by the pleasant Güell family, this elegant glass, wood, and stone structure welcomes skiers and general enthusiasts to the Camprodón Valley. Rooms are simple but tasteful, with heavy, Pyrenean wood furniture. *Plaça d'Espanya 8, 17867* *972/740011* *972/741112* *www.hotelguell.com* *38 rooms* *Bar, lounge; no a/c* *AE, DC, MC, V* *Closed mid-June and most of Nov.*

Shopping

Cal Xec (C. Isaac Albèniz 1 972/740084), the sausage store at the end of the emblematic Camprodón Bridge, also sells the much-prized Birbas and Pujol cookies.

Golf

Club de Golf de Camprodón (972/130125) has a 9-hole course.

en route

From Camprodón, take C151 north toward the French border at Col d'Ares and turn east toward **Rocabruna**, a village of crisp, clean Pyrenean stone at the source of the crystalline River Beget.

Beget

★ 2 *17 km (11 mi) east of Camprodón.*

The village of Beget, considered Catalonia's *més bufó* (cutest), was completely cut off from motorized vehicles until the mid-1960s and was only connected to the rest of the world by asphalt roadway in 1980. Beget's 30 houses are eccentric stone structures with heavy wooden doors and a golden tone peculiar to the Camprodón Valley. Graceful stone bridges span the stream while protected trout feast confidently below. The 11th-century Romanesque church of **Sant Cristófol** has a diminutive bell tower and a rare 6-ft Majestat, a polychrome wood carving of Christ in a head-to-foot tunic, dating from the 12th or 13th century. The church is usually closed, but townsfolk can direct you to the keeper of the key.

Where to Eat

$–$$ **Can Po.** First-rate cuisine is the draw at this ancient, ivy-covered, stone-and-mortar farmhouse perched over a deep gully in nearby Rocabruna. Specialties are *entrecot amb crema de ceps* (veal in wild mushroom sauce) and *anec amb peras* (duck prepared with stewed pears). *Ctra. de Beget s/n, Rocabruna* *972/741045* *AE, DC, MC, V* *Closed Mon.–Thurs. mid-Sept.–mid-July.*

Molló

3 *25 km (16 mi) northwest of Beget, 24 km (15 mi) south of Prats de Molló.*

Molló lies on route C151 on the Ritort stream toward Col d'Ares. The 12th-century Romanesque church of **Santa Cecilia** is a work of exceptional balance and simplicity. Its delicate Romanesque bell tower seems as naturally set into the building and the surrounding countryside as a Pyrenean mushroom.

Where to Stay

$ **Calitxó.** The rooms are small but comfortable at this friendly, family-run inn, and the views over the mountains in all directions are spectacular. It's a good base for hiking excursions to Beget and other points in the valley. A rustic chalet-type town house, the restaurant serves

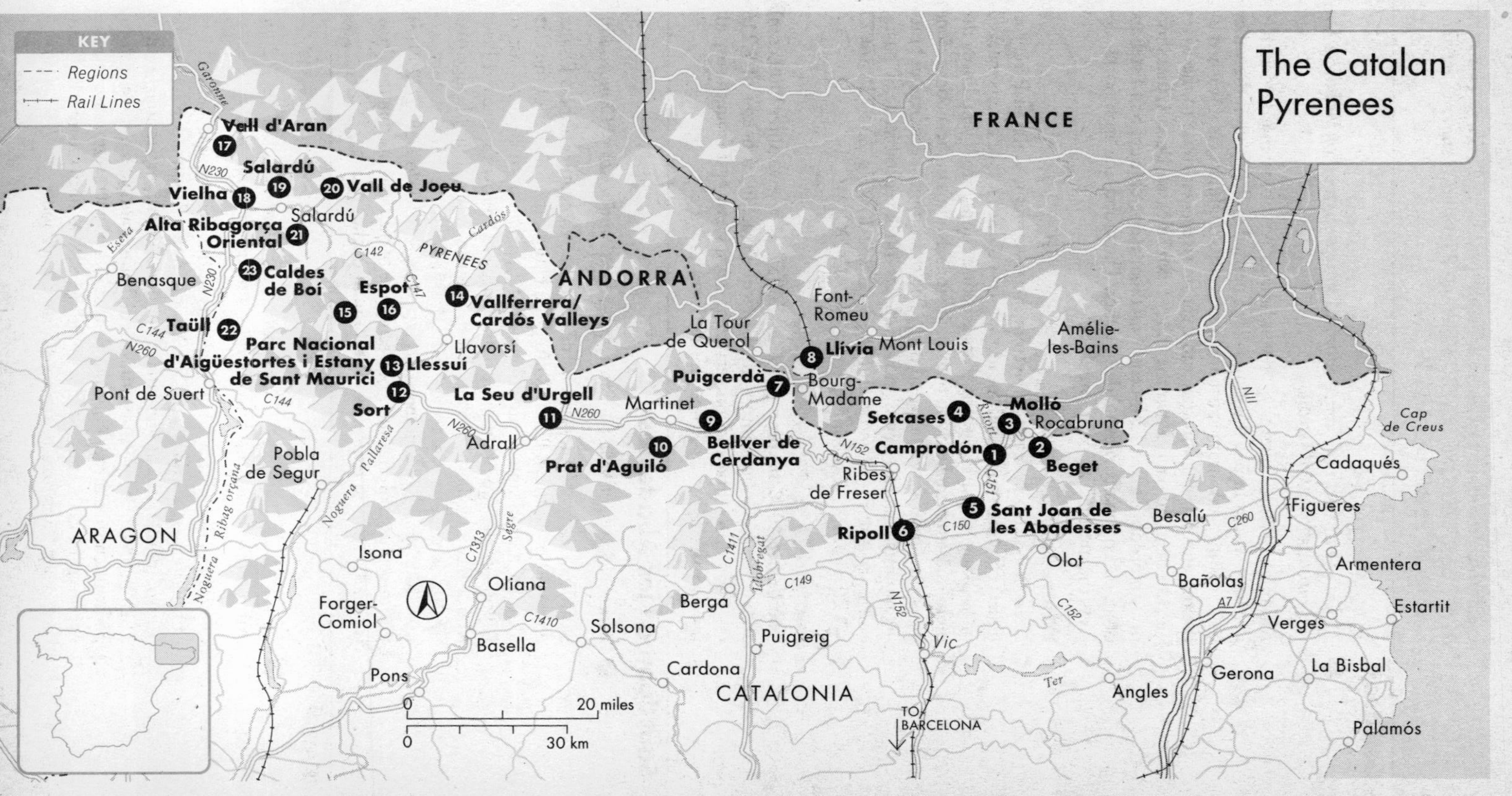
The Catalan Pyrenees
KEY
Regions
Rail Lines
FRANCE
ANDORRA
CATALONIA
ARAGON
PYRENEES
1 Camprodón
2 Beget
3 Molló
4 Setcases
5 Sant Joan de les Abadesses
6 Ripoll
7 Puigcerdà
8 Llívia
9 Bellver de Cerdanya
10 Prat d'Aguiló
11 La Seu d'Urgell
12 Sort
13 Llessuí
14 Vallferrera/ Cardós Valleys
15
16 Espot
17 Vall d'Aran
18 Vielha
19 Salardú
20 Vall de Joeu
21 Alta Ribagorça Oriental
22 Taüll
23 Caldes de Boí
Parc Nacional d'Aigüestortes i Estany de Sant Maurici
Cap de Creus
Cadaqués
Figueres
Armentera
Estartit
Verges
La Bisbal
Palamós
Gerona
Bañolas
Besalú
Angles
Olot
Rocabruna
Amélie-les-Bains
Mont Louis
Font-Romeu
Bourg-Madame
La Tour de Querol
Ribes de Freser
Vic
TO BARCELONA
Puigreig
Berga
Cardona
Martinet
Solsona
Oliana
Basella
Adrall
Llavorsí
Isona
Pons
Forger-Comiol
Pobla de Segur
Pont de Suert
Benasque
Salardú
Garonne
Ritort
Ter
Llobregat
Sagre
Cardós
Noguera Pallaresa
Noguera Ribag orçana
Esera
NII
A7
C260
C152
C151
C150
N152
C149
C1411
N260
C1410
C1313
C147
C142
C144
N230
20 miles
30 km
0

creditable mountain fare at reasonable prices. ✉ *Passatge el Serrat, 17868* ☎ *972/740386* 📠 *972/740746* *23 rooms, 3 suites* *Restaurant; no a/c* 💳 *AE, DC, MC, V.*

Setcases

❹ *11 km (7 mi) north of Camprodón, 15 km (9 mi) west of Molló, 91 km (56 mi) northwest of Girona.*

Although Setcases (literally, "seven houses") is somewhat larger than its name would imply, this tiny village nestled at the head of the valley has a distinct mountain spirit and a gravelly roughness, as if washed by the torrents flowing through and over its streets en route to the River Ter. On the road back down the valley from Setcases, **Llanars,** just short of Camprodón, has a 12th-century Romanesque church, **San Esteban,** of an exceptionally rich shade of ocher. The wood-and-iron portal depicts the martyrdom of St. Stephen.

Where to Stay

¢ **La Coma.** Don't fear oversleeping here—*coma* is Catalan Pyrenean dialect for "high and fertile meadow," so you'll see lots of comas marked on walking maps. The proprietors are kind country folk who know the mountains and can help you plan excursions. Rooms in the modern stone house are done in bright wood trim. The restaurant specializes in bracing mountain *civets* (stews) and *escudellas* (thick vegetable, bean, pasta, and pork soup). ✉ *Setcases 17869* ☎ *972/136074* 📠 *972/136073* *20 rooms* *Restaurant; no a/c* 💳 *AE, DC, MC, V.*

Sports & the Outdoors

The **Vallter 2000 ski area** (☎ 972/136057 🌐 www.vallter2000.com) above Setcases—built into a glacial cirque reaching a height of 8,216 ft—has a dozen lifts and, on very clear days, views east from the top all the way to the Bay of Roses on the Costa Brava.

Sant Joan de les Abadesses

❺ *21 km (13 mi) southeast of Setcases, 14 km (9 mi) south of Camprodón.*

Sant Joan de les Abadesses—named for the 9th-century abbess Emma, daughter of Guifré el Pilós (Wilfred the Hairy), the founder of the Catalonian nation and medieval hero of the Christian Reconquest of Ripoll—is the site of an important church. The town's arcaded Plaça Major has a medieval look and feel, and the 12th-century bridge over the Ter is wide and graceful. The altarpiece in the 12th-century Romanesque church of **Sant Joan** (✉ Plaça de la Abadía s/n ☎ 972/720013), a 13th-century polychrome wood sculpture of the Descent from the Cross, is one of the most expressive and human of that epoch.

Ripoll

❻ *10 km (6 mi) southwest of Sant Joan de les Abadesses, 105 km (62 mi) north of Barcelona, 65 km (40 mi) southeast of Puigcerdà.*

One of the first Christian strongholds of the Reconquest and a center of religious erudition during the Middle Ages, Ripoll is known as the *bressol* (cradle) of Catalonian nationhood. A dark, mysterious country town built around a **9th-century Benedictine monastery,** it was a focal point of culture throughout the Roussillon (French Catalonia and the Pyrenees) from the monastery's founding, in 888, until the mid-19th century, when Barcelona began to eclipse it for good.

The 12th-century doorway to the church of **Santa Maria** is one of Catalonia's great works of Romanesque art, designed as a triumphal arch. Its sculptures portray the glory of God and of all his creatures from the Creation onward. You can pick up a guide to the figures on the portal (crafted by stone masons and sculptors of the Roussillon school) in the church or at the information kiosk nearby. *Cloister €2, museum €6* *Tues.–Sun. 10–2 and 3–7.*

Fourteen kilometers (9 mi) north of Ripoll, the **cogwheel train** (972/ 732–2020) from Ribes de Freser up to Núria offers one of Catalonia's most unusual excursions. Known as the *cremallera* (zipper), the line was built in 1917 to connect Ribes with the Santuari de la Mare de Deu de Núria (Mother of God of Núria) and with mountain hiking and skiing. The ride takes 45 minutes and costs €14 round-trip. **Núria,** at an altitude of 6,562 ft at the foot of Puigmal, is a ski area, and in the 1950s it was the site of some of Spain's earliest ice-hockey activity.

The legend of the **Santuari de la Mare de Deu de Núria,** a Marian religious retreat, is based on the story of Sant Gil of Nîmes, who did penance in the Núria Valley during the 7th century. The saint left behind a wooden statue of the Virgin Mary, a bell he used to summon shepherds to prayer, and a cooking pot; 300 years later, a pilgrim found these treasures in this sanctuary. The bell and the pot came to have special importance to barren women, who were believed to be blessed with as many children as they wished by placing their heads in the pot and ringing the bell, each peal of the bell meaning another child. *Núria* *Free* *Daily except during mass.*

en route

From Ripoll, it's a 65-km (40-mi) drive on the N152 through Ribes de Freser and over the Collada de Toses (Tosses Pass) to Puigcerdà. Above Ribes, the road winds to the top of the pass over a sheer drop down to the Freser stream. Here, even during the driest months, emerald-green pastures remain moist in shaded corners—a sharp contrast to the shale and brown peaks above the timber line. In early spring the climate can range from showers down in Ribes to a blizzard up on the Tosses Pass. This traditional approach to the Cerdanya has been all but replaced by the road through Manresa, Berga, and the Túnel del Cadí (Cadí Tunnel). Tosses was a major barrier for centuries, until the railroad connected Puigcerdà to Barcelona in 1924. The 32 km (20 mi) of switchback curves between Ribes and La Molina kept many would-be travelers in Barcelona until the tunnel cut the driving time from three hours to two and all but eliminated the hazardous-driving factor.

LA CERDANYA

The Pyrenees' widest, sunniest valley is said to be in the shape of the handprint of God. High pastureland bordered north and south by snow-covered peaks, La Cerdanya starts in France, at Col de la Perche (near Mont Louis), and ends in the Spanish province of Lleida, at Martinet. Split into two countries and subdivided into two more provinces on each side, the valley nonetheless has an identity all its own. Cerdanya straddles the border, which meanders through the rich valley floor no more purposefully than the River Segre itself. Residents on both sides of the border speak Catalan, a Romance language derived from early Provençal French, and regard the valley's political border with undisguised hilarity. Unlike any other valley in the upper Pyrenees, this one runs east–west and thus has a record annual number of hours of sunlight. On the French side, two solar stations collect and store energy near Font Romeu, and a solar oven bakes ceramics in Mont Louis.

Puigcerdà

7 *170 km (105 mi) north of Barcelona, 65 km (40 mi) northwest of Ripoll.*

Puigcerdà (*puig* means "hill"; *cerdà* derives from "Cerdanya") is the largest town in the valley. From the small piece of high ground upon which it stands, the views down across the meadows and up into the Pyrenees give a dizzying sense of simultaneous height and humility. The 12th-century Romanesque bell tower (all that remains of the town church destroyed in 1936 at the outset of the Spanish civil war) and the sunny sidewalk cafés facing it are among Puigcerdà's prettiest spots, along with the Gothic church of Santa Maria and its long square, the **Plaça del Cuartel.** On Sunday, markets sell clothes, cheeses, fruits, vegetables, and wild mushrooms to shoppers from both sides of the border.

Plaça Cabrinetty, with its porticoes and covered walks, has a sunny northeastern corner where farmers in for the Sunday market gather. The square is protected from the wind and ringed by two- and three-story houses of various pastel colors, some with engraved decorative designs and all with balconies. From the lower end of Plaça Cabrinetty, Carrer Font d'en Llanas winds down to the *font* (spring), where **"Voldria . . . "** ("I wish . . . "), a haunting verse by the Cerdanya's greatest poet, Magdalena Masip (1890–1970), is inscribed on a plaque over the fountain. Translated from the Catalan, the poem reads: . . . *and I wish that I could have / my house beneath a fir tree / with all the woods for a garden / and all the sky for a roof. / And flee from the world around me / it overwhelms me and confuses me / and stay quietly just there / drinking the forest in great gulps / with clods of earth for a pillow / and a bed of golden leaves . . .*

From the balcony next to the **town hall** (✉ Carrer Querol 1), you get an ample view of the Cerdanya Valley that stretches all the way past Bellver de Cerdanya down to the sheer granite walls of the Sierra del Cadí, at the end of the valley. A 300-yard walk west from the fountain near Carrer Font d'en Llanas around the edge of town will bring you to the stairs leading up from the train station to the balcony. The verse on the corner of the town hall to your left as you look out is by the great Catalan poet Joan Maragall (1860–1910). In English translation, the fragment would read: . . . *I love the balcony over the walls / When the townsfolk stroll there / and with nearly immobile eyes / follow the progress of the distant storm. . . .*

Le petit train jaune (the little yellow train) leaves daily from Bourg-Madame and from La Tour de Querol, both simple walks into France from Puigcerdà. The border at La Tour, a longer but prettier walk, is marked only by a stone painted with the Spanish and French flags. This *carrilet* (narrow-gauge railway) is the last in the Pyrenees and is used for tours as well as transportation; it winds through the Cerdanya to the walled town of Villefranche de Conflent. The 63-km (39-mi) tour can take most of the day, especially if you stop to browse in Mont Louis or Villefranche. ✉ *Boarding at SNCF stations at Bourg-Madame or La Tour de Querol, France* 🎫 *€24 per person, €18 per person in groups of 10 or more* ⏲ *Schedule at Touring travel agency or Turismo office, Puigcerdà; or at RENFE station below Puigcerdà.*

Where to Stay & Eat

$–$$ ✕ **La Tieta.** A 500-year-old town house built into the remains of the ancient walls of Puigcerdà, this is one of the town's top restaurants. Its garden is ideal for a late-night drink in summer. The menu lists Cerdanya specialties such as *trinxat de Cerdanya* (a rib-sticking puree of cabbage and potatoes with bits of fried salt pork or bacon) as well as roasts cooked over coals. ✉ *Carrer Ferrers 20* ☎ *972/880156* ▭ *AE, DC, MC, V.*

$–$$ ✕ **Tapanyam.** Pere Compte's bar and restaurant overlooking the valley is thriving. With live music every Saturday in summer, panoramic views of the Pyrenees, excellent mountain cuisine, and fresh seafood, this friendly spot has become a hub of Puigcerdà life, day and night. Bay windows overlook Puigmal on the south side of the valley. ✉ *Plaça del Alguer 46* ☎ *972/882360* ▭ *AE, DC, MC, V.*

5

¢–$ ✕ **Madrigal.** The original establishment of Pere Compte, this popular restaurant-bar is near the town hall. The low-ceiling, wood-trim dining room is filled with tables and benches. Selections include tapas and meals of assorted specialties, such as *codorniz* (quail), *caracoles* (snails), *calamares a la romana* (calamari dipped in batter), *albóndigas* (meatballs), *esqueixada* (raw codfish with peppers and onion), and wild mushrooms in season. ✉ *Carrer Alfons I 3* ☎ *972/880860* ▭ *AE, DC, MC, V.*

$$$$ FodorsChoice ★ ✕🏨 **La Torre del Remei.** About 3 km (2 mi) west of Puigcerdà is this splendid mansion, built in 1910 and brilliantly restored by José María and Loles Boix of Boix in Martinet. Everything is superb, from the Belle Epoque luxury of the manor house to the plush, tasteful rooms, heated bathroom floors, huge bathtubs, and bottle of Moët & Chandon on your arrival. The restaurant serves fine international cuisine with an emphasis on local products such as lamb, trout, and game; reserve well in advance. ✉ *Camí Reial s/n, Bolvir de Cerdanya 17463* ☎ *972/140182* 🖷 *972/140449* 🌐 *www.torredelremei.com* *10 rooms, 1 suite* *Restaurant, 18-hole golf course, putting green, pool* ▭ *AE, DC, MC, V.*

$$ 🏨 **Hotel del Lago.** This comfortable old favorite near Puigcerdà's emblematic lake is a graceful, tastefully appointed, and renovated series of buildings built around a central garden. A two-minute walk from the bell tower or the town market, it feels bucolic but is virtually in the center of town. ✉ *Av. Doctor Piguillem 7, 17520* ☎ *972/881000* 🖷 *972/141511* *13 rooms, 3 suites* *Pool; no a/c* ▭ *AE, MC, V.*

$–$$ 🏨 **Fontanals Golf.** This modern chalet-style ranch on the floor of the Cerdanya valley places you within striking distance of ski slopes, trout streams and a challenging 18-hole golf course. Lavishly constructed with fresh wood and glass, views into the Pyrenees on both sides of the valley are panoramic and outdoor possibilities are infinite. ✉ *C/Fontanals 2, Soriguerola, 17538* ☎ *972/891818* 🖷 *972/891740* *60 rooms* *Restaurant, golf course, tennis court, pool, bar* ▭ *AE, MC, DC, V.*

$–$$ 🏨 **Hotel del Prado.** Below town on the road to Llívia, a five-minute walk from France (Bourg-Madame), this relaxed and friendly spot is a good clubhouse and base for skiing, hiking, fishing, collecting wild mushrooms, or whatever else you're doing in the Cerdanya Valley. The modernized rooms are chalet-style and trimmed with wood. ✉ *Ctra. de Llívia, Km 1, 17520* ☎ *972/880400* 🖷 *972/141158* *54 rooms* *Restaurant, tennis court, pool, bar* ▭ *AE, MC, V.*

Nightlife

Young Spanish and French night owls fill the town's many clubs until dawn. **N'Ho Sé** (✉ Ctra. 152, Km 170 ☎ 972/882248) is the favored disco on weekend and holiday nights. The **Raig d'Or Claude** (✉ Plaça Cabrinetty 21 ☎ 972/881615) is a cozy tavern with tables under the arcades.

Sports & the Outdoors

Pick up your **fishing license** (✉ Sabino Arana 24, Barcelona ☎ 93/304–6700) for Catalonia in Barcelona. With your Catalonia fishing license, you can buy a day pass (€9) for the Coto del Querol (reserved trout fishing beat) on the Querol River at **Tota Teca** (✉ Ctra. N152, Km 169.5 ☎ 972/141027); there's also good takeout food. The town's **ice rink** (☎ 972/880243) is worth checking out if you skate. The **Reial Club de Golf de la Cerdanya** (☎ 972/141408) near Puigcerdà has 18 holes. Near Puigcerdà, the challenging **Club de Golf de Fontanals** (☎ 972/144374), so called for its myriad water hazards, has 18 holes.

Shopping

Puigcerdà is one big shopping mall, and long a contraband nexus. **Carrer Major** is an uninterrupted series of stores selling everything from books to jewelry to sports equipment. The annual **equine fair,** in early November, is a nonpareil opportunity to study both horses and horse traders. The **Sunday market,** like those in most other Cerdanya towns, is a great place to look for local specialties such as herbs, goat cheese, wild mushrooms, honey, and basketry. It's as social as it is commercial; the Plaça del Cuartel fills with people and produce. In autumn, it's a great chance to learn about wild mushrooms of all kinds.

For the best *margaritas* (no, not those; crunchy-edged madeleines made with almonds) in town, look for **Pasteleria Cosp** (✉ Carrer Major 20 ☎ 972/880103), founded in 1806 and the oldest pastry shop in the province of Girona.

Llívia

❽ *6 km (4 mi) northeast of Puigcerdà.*

A Spanish enclave in French territory, Llívia was marooned by the 1659 Peace of the Pyrenees treaty, which ceded 33 villages to France. Incorporated as a *vila* (town) by royal decree of Carlos V—who spent a night here in 1528 and was impressed by the town's beauty and hospitality—it managed to remain Spanish. The **fortified church** is an acoustic gem; see if anything sonorous is going on. The **ancient pharmacy,** now a museum, was founded in 1415 and is thought to be the oldest in Europe.

Look for the **mosaic** in the middle of town commemorating *Lampègia, princesa de la pau i de l'amor*—princess of peace and of love, erected in memory of the red-haired Lampègia, daughter of the duke of Aquitania and lover of Munuza, a Moorish warlord who governed the Cerdanya during the Arab domination.

Where to Stay & Eat

★ $$$–$$$$ ✕ **Can Ventura.** Built into a 17th-century farmhouse, this superb restaurant is the best around Puigcerdà for decor, cuisine, and value. Trout and beef *a la llosa* are house specialties, and the *entretenimientos* (a wide selection of hors d'oeuvres) are delicious. ✉ *Plaça Major 1* ☎ *972/896178* ✍ *Reservations essential* ▭ *MC, V* ⊙ *Closed Mon.–Tues.*

★ $$$–$$$$ ✕ **La Formatgeria de Llívia.** This restaurant on the eastern edge of Llívia (en route to Saillagousse, France) is built into a former cheese factory, part of which still functions while you watch. Owners Marta Pous and Juanjo Meya have had great success with their fine local specialties, panoramic views south to Puigmal, and general charm and good cheer. ✉ *Pla de Ro, Gorguja* ☎ *972/146279* ✍ *Reservations essential* ▭ *MC, V* ⊙ *Closed Thurs.*

$$ 🏨 **Hotel de Llívia.** Here's an ideal no-frills base of operations for anyone skiing or hiking in France, Andorra, *or* Spain. It's a spacious place with large fireplaces and a glass-walled dining room that's nearly as scenic

as a picnic in a Pyrenean meadow. The hotel runs shuttles to nearby ski resorts and can organize excursions as well as riding, hunting, or trout fishing. ✉ *Avda. de Catalunya s/n, 17527* ☎ *972/896000* 📠 *972/146000* *68 rooms, 10 apartments* *Restaurant, tennis court, pool; no a/c* ▭ *DC, MC, V.*

Bellver de Cerdanya

★ ❾ *31 km (19 mi) southwest of Llívia, 25 km (16 mi) west of Puigcerdà.*

Bellver de Cerdanya has conserved its slate-roof and fieldstone Pyrenean architecture more successfully than many of the Cerdanya's larger towns. Perched on a promontory over the **River Segre,** which folds neatly around the town, Bellver is a mountain version of a fishing village—trout fishing, of course. The river is the town's main event; how much water is coming down—and whether it's low or high, muddy or clear, warm or cold—supplants the weather as a topic of conversation. Bellver's Gothic church of **Sant Jaume** and the arcaded **Plaça Major,** in the upper part of town, are lovely examples of traditional Pyrenean mountain-village design.

Where to Stay & Eat

$ ✕ **Fonda Biayna.** This rustic little retreat with woodsy furnishings seems happily stuck in an early Pyrenean time warp. Guest rooms are simple, old-fashioned, and cozy. The Catalan fare includes such gamey dishes as roast rabbit *allioli* (with a beaten sauce of garlic and olive oil), *galtas de porc amb bolets* (pork cheeks with wild mushrooms), and *tiró amb naps i trumfes* (duck with turnips and potatoes). ✉ *Carrer Sant Roc 11, 25720* ☎ *973/510475* 📠 *973/510853* *16 rooms* *No a/c, no room phones* ▭ *AE, DC, MC, V.*

Sports & the Outdoors

The **Coto de Bellver** (reserved trout fishing beat) on the River Segre is historically one of Spain's finest. **Bar Blanch** (✉ Carrer San Roc 13 ☎ 973/510208) is the town's de facto angling clubhouse, where, along with hearty mountain fare or a beer at the bar, you can buy licenses and day passes to the coto from mid-March through August.

Martinet

❿ *10 km (6 mi) west of Bellver de Cerdanya.*

The town of Martinet hasn't much to offer except a few cozy watering spots that are hard to pass up in the heat of summer. For a course in trout economy and ecology, have a close look over the railing along the River Segre just upstream from its junction with the River Llosa. Martinet's protected trout are famous in these parts: the fish dine from 1 to 4, when the sun slants in, cooks off aquatic-insect hatches, and illuminates every speckle and spot on these sleek leviathans.

For a spectacular excursion, drive or walk up the valley of the Riu Llosa into Andorra, or take the short but stunning walk from the village of **Aransa** to Lles: as you pull away from Aransa and onto an alpine meadow, the Cerdanya's palette changes with every twist of the trail. You'll even pass the ruins of a 10th-century hilltop hermitage. (The tourist office in La Seu d'Urgell has simple trail maps.) The village of **Lles,** north of Martinet, is a famous Nordic-skiing resort with miles of cross-country tracks.

Where to Eat

$$$$ ✕ **Boix.** The modern, Lego-block building doesn't look like much from the outside, but this hotel restaurant is something of an institution for fine Pyrenean cooking. José María Boix and his wife, Loles—of La Torre del Remei near Puigcerdà—are known for innovations on local, Catalan, and French cuisine, featuring *setas* (wild mushrooms) in season and such surprises as *magret de canard amb mel* (duck breast with honey). ✉ *Ctra. N260, Km 204* ☎ *973/515050* ▭ *AE, DC, MC, V.*

Prat d'Aguiló

⓫ *20 km (12 mi) south of Martinet.*

The spectacular Prat d'Aguiló, or Eagle's Meadow, is one of the highest points in the Cerdanya that you can access without either a four-wheel-drive vehicle or a hike. The winding, bumpy drive up the mountain takes about an hour and a half (start with ample fuel) and opens onto some excellent vistas of its own. From the meadow, a roughly three-hour climb to the top of the sheer rock wall of the Sierra del Cadí, directly above, reaches an altitude of nearly 8,000 ft. On a clear day you can see Puigcerdà and beyond; the River Segre seems no more than a thin, silver ribbon on the valley floor. To get here from Martinet, take a dirt road that is rough but navigable by the average car. Follow signs for "Refugio Prat d'Aguiló."

La Seu d'Urgell

⓬ *24 km (15 mi) west of Matinet, 20 km (12 mi) south of Andorra la Vella*
Fodor'sChoice *(in Andorra), 50 km (31 mi) west of Puigcerdà.*
★

La Seu d'Urgell is an ancient town facing the snowy rock wall of the Sierra del Cadí. As the seat (*seu*) of the regional archbishopric since the 6th century, it has a rich legacy of art and architecture. The Pyrenean feel of the streets, with their dark balconies and porticoes, overhanging galleries, and colonnaded porches—particularly **Carrer dels Canonges**—makes Seu mysterious and memorable. Look for the medieval **grain measures** at the corner of Carrer Major and Carrer Capdevila. The tiny food shops on the arcaded Carrer Major are intriguing places to assemble lunch for a hike.

★ The 12th-century **Catedral de Santa Maria** is the finest cathedral in the Pyrenees. One of the most moving sights in northern Spain is a show of sunlight casting the rich reds and blues of Santa Maria's southeastern rose window into the deep gloom of the transept. The 13th-century cloister is known for the individually carved, sometimes whimsical capitals on its 50 columns. (They were crafted by the same Roussillon school of masons who carved the doorway on the church of Santa Maria in Ripoll.) Don't miss either the haunting, 11th-century chapel of **Sant Miquel** or the **Diocesan Museum,** which has a striking collection of medieval murals from various Pyrenean churches and a colorfully illuminated 10th-century Mozarabic manuscript of the monk Beatus de Liébana's commentary on the Apocalypse, along with a short film explaining the manuscript. Ask for the attractive and well-organized book detailing every local church on the medieval Vía Románica (an itinerary covering the area's Romanesque churches)—it makes a lovely souvenir. ✉ *Plaça dels Oms* ☎ *973/350981* 🎫 *Cathedral, cloister, and museum €3* ⏲ *Daily 9–1 and 4–8.*

Where to Stay & Eat

$–$$ ✕ **Cal Pacho.** Sample traditional local specialties at very reasonable prices in this dark, rustic spot, built in the typical Pyrenean style with stone and wood beams. Count on powerful *escudella* (mountain soup of vegetables, pork or veal, and noodles) in winter, and meat cooked over coals or on slate year-round. ✉ *Carrer Lafont 11* ☎ *973/352719* ▭ *AE, DC, MC, V.*

★ $$$ **El Castell.** Just outside Seu, this high, wood-and-slate structure is one of the finest places around. Rooms on the second floor have balconies overlooking the river; those on the third have slanted ceilings and dormer windows. Suites add a salon. The restaurant specializes in mountain cuisine, such as *civet de jabalí* (wild-boar stew) and *llom de cordet amb trinxat* (lamb cooked over coals and served with puree of potatoes and cabbage). Reserve rooms in advance during summer or Semana Santa. *Ctra. de Lleida (N260), Km 129 Apdo. 53, 25700 973/350704 973/351574 www.hotelelcastell.com 38 rooms, 4 suites Restaurant, pool, hair salon, sauna AE, DC, MC, V.*

$$ **Parador de la Seu d'Urgell.** These comfortable quarters right in town are built into the 12th-century church and convent of Sant Domènec. The interior patio—the cloister of the former convent—is a lush and tranquil hideaway. Rooms are simple but warm, and some look past the edge of town to the mountains. The small pool and the dining room have glass ceilings. *Carrer Sant Domènec 6, 25700 973/352000 973/352309 www.parador.es 77 rooms, 1 suite Restaurant, indoor pool AE, DC, MC, V.*

WESTERN CATALAN PYRENEES

"The farther from Barcelona, the wilder" is the rule of thumb, and this is true of the western part of Catalonia. Three of the greatest destinations in the Pyrenees are here: the Garonne-drained, Atlantic-oriented Vall d'Aran; the Noguera de Tor valley with its matching set of gemlike Romanesque churches; and Parc Nacional d'Aigüestortes i Estany de Sant Maurici with its network of pristine lakes and streams. The main geographical units in this section are the valley of the Noguera Pallaresa River, the Vall d'Aran headwaters of the Atlantic-bound Garonne, and the Noguera Ribagorçana River valley, Catalonia's western limit.

Sort

★ 13 *59 km (37 mi) west of La Seu d'Urgell.*

The capital of the Pallars Sobirà (Upper Pallars Valley) is a center for skiing, fishing, and white-water kayaking. Don't be content with the Sort you see from the main road: one block back, the town is honeycombed with tiny streets and protected corners built against heavy winter weather. To get here from La Seu d'Urgell, take N260 toward Lleida, head west at Adrall, and drive 53 km (33 mi) over the Cantó Pass to Sort. Sort is the origin of the road into the unspoiled **Assua Valley**, a hidden pocket of untouched mountain villages, such as Saurí and Olp.

Where to Eat

¢–$ **Fogony.** If you hit Sort at lunchtime, come here for some bracing escudella or some roast lamb or goat before heading into the high country. *Av. Generalitat 45 973/621225 MC, V Closed Mon. except Christmas wk, Easter wk, and Aug.; and 2 wks in Jan.*

Llessuí

14 *15 km (9 mi) north of Sort.*

Llessuí is at the head of the Upper Pallars Valley. The local **ski area** presides over the valley from the slopes of the Altars peak. The Romanesque church of **Sant Pere** is topped with a typical conical bell tower resembling a pointed witch's hat, characteristic of the Vall d'Aran and its environs.

Where to Stay & Eat

¢ ✕🏨 **Vall d'Assua.** A cozy refuge, this little family-run, family-oriented place is a sure bet for simple Pyrenean home cooking, strong on roasts and thick stews and soups. The guest rooms are small but impeccably clean and comfortable. The family also rents several apartments in country houses in the nearby village of Llagunes. ✉ *Ctra. de Llessuí, Altrón 25567* ☎🖷 *973/621738* ⇨ *9 rooms* ♨ *No a/c* ▭ *No credit cards* ⊙ *Closed Nov.*

Parc Nacional d'Aigüestortes i Estany de Sant Maurici

★ ⓯ *After Escaló, 12 km (7 mi) northwest of Llavorsí, the road to Espot and the park veers west.*

Running water and the hydraulic cornucopia of high mountain terrain are the true protagonists in this wild domain of flower-filled meadows and woods in the shadow of the twin peaks of Els Encantats. More than 300 glacial lakes and lagoons (the beautiful Estany de Sant Maurici among them) as well as streams, waterfalls, and marshes make this rocky highland arcadia an aquatic symphony of everything from rills to rivers, tarns, pools, and brooks draining out to the two Noguera watercourses, the Pallaresa and the Ribagorçana, to the east and west. The abundance of water is even more surprising surrounded by the bare rock walls carved out by the quaternary glacier that left these jagged peaks and moist pockets. The twin Encantats measure 9,065 ft and 9,035 ft, respectively; the Beciberri peak reaches 9,950 ft, the Peguera 9,709 ft, the Montarto 9,339 ft, and the Amitges 8,745 ft. The fauna and flora run a wide gamut from the soft lower meadows below 5,000 ft to the highest crags at nearly double that height. Forested by pines, firs, beech, and silver birches, Aigüestortes (which means "twisted waters") also has ample pastureland inhabited by Pyrenean chamois, capercaillie, golden eagle, and ptarmigan.

The dozen Aigüestortes mountain refuges are the stars of the Pyrenees, ranging from the 12-bunk Beciberri, the highest refuge or bivouac in the Pyrenees, at 9,174 ft, to the 80-bunk 7,326-ft Ventosa i Calvell refuge at the foot of Punta Alta. All of these mountain lodging places turn into hearty meeting points for tired and hungry hikers sharing trail tips and mountain lore between June and September.

Accessible from either the Noguera Pallaresa and Espot valleys to the east or the Noguera Ribagorçana and Bohí valleys to the west, the park has strict rules: no camping, no fires, no vehicles beyond certain points, no unleashed pets. Access to the park is free. For information and refuge reservations, contact the **park administration offices** (☎ 973/694000 Barruera, 973/696189 Boí, 973/624036 Espot).

Where to Stay

The 66-bunk **Refugi d'Amitges** (☎ 973/250109) is near the Amitges lakes, at 7,920 ft. The 24-bunk **Refugi Ernest Mallafré** (☎ 973/250118) is at the foot of Els Encantats, near Lake Sant Maurici. **Refugi Josep Maria Blanc** (☎ 973/250108), at 7,755 ft, offers 40 bunks at the base of a peninsula reaching out into the Tort de Peguera lake.

Espot

⓰ *15 km (9 mi) northwest of Llavorsí, 166 km (100 mi) north of Lleida.*

Espot nestles at the valley floor along a clear, aquamarine stream, next to the eastern entrance to Aigüestortes–Sant Maurici National Park. **Super-Espot** is the local ski area. The **Pont de la Capella** (Chapel Bridge), a perfect, mossy arch over the flow, looks as though it might have grown directly from the Pyrenean slate.

HIKING IN THE PYRENEES

THE PYRENEES OFFERS hiking for all seasons. In fall and winter, the Alberes mountains between Cap de Creus, the Iberian Peninsula's easternmost point, and the border with France at Le Perthus is a sky-glide between the Côte Vermeille's curving strand and the green patchwork Empordá.

The walk from Núria to Ulldeter is a grassy corridor in good weather from April to October. La Cerdanya, a luminous valley, is a hiker's paradise year-round. The summertime round-Andorra hike is a 360-degree tour of this independent Pyrenean Principality.

The Parque Nacional de Aigüestortes y Lago San Mauricio offers late spring through fall landscapes.

Year-round, in Parque Nacional de Ordesa y Monte Perdido you can take day trips up to the Cola de Caballo waterfall and back around the southern rim of the canyon or longer hikes via the Refugio de Góriz to La Brèche de Roland and Gavarnie or to Monte Perdido, the Parador at La Pineta, and the village of Bielsa.

Farther west, the Irati Forest and the Basque hills between the 6,617-foot Pic D'Orhi and the Bay of Biscay at Hondarribia are snow-free for nine months of the year, while the Camino de Santiago walk from Saint-Jean-Pied-de-Port to Roncesvalles is a classic segment of the pilgrimage manageable any time of year.

For the full six-week trans-Pyrenean crossing follow the French GR-10 (Gran Recorrido 10), the Spanish GR-11, or the international HRP (Haute Randonnée Pyrenéenne) from the Atlantic to the Mediterranean. Only attempt it in midsummer—from July to mid-August.

5

en route

From Esterri d'Aneu, C142 reaches the sanctuary of Mare de Deu de Ares, a hermitage and shelter, at 4,600 ft, and the Bonaigua Pass, at 6,798 ft. The latter offers a dizzying look back at the Pallars Mountains and ahead to the Vall d'Aran and the Maladeta massif beyond, shimmering white in the distance.

Vall d'Aran & Environs

17 *From Esterri d'Aneu, the valley runs 46 km (27 mi) east to Vielha over the Bonaigua Pass.*

The Vall d'Aran is at the western edge of the Catalan Pyrenees and the northwestern corner of Catalonia. North of the main Pyrenean axis, it is the Catalan Pyrenees' only Atlantic valley, opening northward into the plains of Aquitania and drained by the Garonne, which flows into the Atlantic Ocean above Bordeaux. The 48-km (30-mi) drive from the Bonaigua Pass to the Pont del Rei border with France follows the riverbed faithfully.

The valley's Atlantic personality shows in its climate—wetter and colder—and its language: the 6,000 inhabitants speak Aranés, a dialect of Gascon French derived from the Occitanian language group. With some difficulty, Aranés can be understood by speakers of Catalan and French. Originally part of the Aquitanian county of Comminges, the Vall d'Aran maintained feudal ties to the Pyrenees of Spanish Aragón and became part of Catalonia-Aragón in the 12th century. In 1389 the valley was assigned to Catalonia.

Neither as wide as the Cerdanya nor as oppressively narrow and vertical as Andorra, the Vall d'Aran has a sense of well-being and order, an architectural consonance unique in Catalonia. The clusters of iron-gray slate roofs, the lush vegetation, the dormer windows (a clear sign of French influence)—all make the Vall d'Aran a distinct geographic and cultural pocket that happens to have washed up on the Spanish side of the border. Hiking and climbing are popular here. Guides are available year-round and can be arranged through the **tourist office** (☎ 973/640110) in Vielha.

Vielha

⓲ *79 km (49 mi) northwest of Sort.*

Vielha (Viella, in Spanish), capital of the Vall d'Aran, is a lively crossroads vitally involved in the Aranese movement to defend and reconstruct the valley's architectural, institutional, and linguistic heritage. The octagonal, 14th-century bell tower on the Romanesque parish church of **Sant Miquel** is one of the town's trademarks, as is the 15th-century Gothic altar. The partly damaged 12th-century polychrome wood carving *Cristo de Mig Aran,* displayed under glass, evokes a sense of mortality and humanity with a power unusual in medieval sculpture. The town also has an **ice rink** (☎ 973/642864) that you may want to check out if you enjoy skating.

North of Vielha, the tiny villages over the River Garonne hold intriguing little secrets, such as the sculpted Gallo-Roman heads (funeral steles rehabilitated in the 12th century) carved into the village portal at **Gausac.** The bell tower in **Vilac** has an eccentric charm. The church in **Vilamós,** the oldest in the valley, is known for the three curious carved figures, thought to be Gallo-Roman funeral steles, on its facade. The porticoed square in the border village of **Bossòst** has beautifully carved capitals. East of Vielha is the village of **Escunhau,** with steep alley-stairways. **Arties** makes a good stop, with its famous Casa Irene restaurant and historic parador.

Where to Stay & Eat

$$$–$$$$ Fodor'sChoice ★ ✕ **Ca la Irene.** A rustic little haven, this restaurant 6 km (4 mi) east of Vielha is known for fine mountain cuisine with a French flair. Three tasting menus and gastronomic gems like poached foie gras in black truffles and roast wild pigeon in nuts and mint make this place a must. ✉ *Hotel Valartiés, Carrer Major 3, Arties* ☎ *973/644364* 🖷 *973/642174* *Reservations essential* 💳 *MC, V* ⏲ *Closed mid-Oct.–mid-Nov. and Mon. mid-Nov.–Apr.*

★ $–$$ ✕ **Era Mola.** Also known as Restaurante Gustavo y María José, this former stable with wood beams and whitewash walls serves French-tinged Aranese cuisine. The *confite de pato* (duck stewed with apple) and *magret de pato* (breast of duck served rare with *carradetas,* wild mushrooms from the valley) are favorites. ✉ *Carrer Marrech 14* ☎ *973/642419* *Reservations essential* 💳 *AE, DC, MC, V* ⏲ *No lunch weekdays Dec.–Apr.*

$$–$$$ ✕🏨 **Parador de Arties.** Built around the Casa de Don Gaspar de Portolà, once home to the founder of the colony of California, this modern parador has panoramic views of the Pyrenees. Just 7 km (4 mi) from the Baqueira ski slopes and 2½ km (1½ mi) south of Vielha, it's big enough to seem festive and yet small enough for intimacy. ✉ *Ctra. Baqueira-Beret s/n, Arties 25599* ☎ *973/640801* 🖷 *973/641001* 🌐 *www.parador.es* *54 rooms, 3 suites* *Restaurant, pool, gym* 💳 *AE, MC, V.*

$$ ✕🏨 **Parador de Vielha.** This modern granite parador has a semicircular salon with huge windows and spectacular views over the Maladeta peaks of the Vall d'Aran. Rooms are furnished with traditional carved-wood furniture and floor-to-ceiling curtains. The restaurant serves mainly Catalan cuisine, such as *espinacas a la catalana* (spinach cooked in olive oil with pine nuts, raisins, and garlic). ✉ *Carretera del Túnel s/n, 25530* ☎ *973/640100* 📠 *973/641100* 🌐 *www.parador.es* *126 rooms* *Restaurant; no a/c* 💳 *AE, MC, V.*

$–$$ **Pirene.** This modern hotel, with some of the best views in town, has rooms that are bright and simply furnished. The cozy sitting room and the charming family in charge make a stay here memorable. Book ahead during ski season: you're 15 minutes from the slopes. It's on the left side of the N320 into Vielha. ✉ *Ctra. del Túnel s/n, 25530* ☎ *973/640075* 📠 *973/642295* *32 rooms* *Restaurant, cable TV, bar; no a/c* 💳 *AE, DC, MC, V.*

Nightlife

Elurra (☎ 973/640332), a commercial center in Vielha, is filled with a dozen music bars, pubs, and discos. **Bar Era Crin** (✉ Escunhau ☎ 973/642061) offers live performances and pop rock to dance to, as well as billiards and table football. **Bar la Lluna** (✉ Arties ☎ 973/641115), a local favorite, occupies a typical Aranese house and has live performances on Wednesday.

Salardú

19 *9 km (6 mi) east of Vielha.*

Convenient to Tredós, the Montarto peak, the lakes and Circ de Colomers, the Aigüestortes national park, and the villages of Unha and Mongarri, Salardú is a pivotal point in the Vall d'Aran. The town itself, with just over 700 inhabitants, is known for its steep streets and its octagonal fortified bell tower. The 12th-century **Sant Andreu** church's Romanesque wood sculpture of Christ is said to have miraculously floated up the Garonne River.

The tiny village of **Unha** perches on a promontory 3 km (2 mi) above Salardú, with the elegant Ço de Brastet (Brastet House) at its entrance. Unha's 12th-century church of Santa Eulalia has a curiously bulging 17th-century bell tower. East of Salardú is the village of **Tredós,** home of the Romanesque church of Santa Maria de Cap d'Aran—symbol of the Aranese independence movement and meeting place of the valley's governing body, the Conselh Generau, until 1827.

off the beaten path

SANTA MARIA DE MONTGARRI – This partly ruined 11th-century structure, a chapel, was once an important way station on the route into the Vall d'Aran from France. The beveled, hexagonal bell tower and the rounded stones, which look as if they came from a brook bottom, give the structure a stippled appearance not unlike that of a Pyrenean trout. Try to be there for the Romería de Nuestra Señora de Montgarri (Feast of Our Lady of Montgarri) on July 2, a country fair with dancing, game playing, and general carrying-on. The sanctuary is 12 km (7 mi) northeast of the town of Bagergue, which is just north of Salardú.

Where to Stay & Eat

$ ✕ **Casa Rufus.** Pine and check tablecloths cozily furnish this restaurant nestled in the tiny, gray-stone village of Gessa, between Vielha and Salardú. Rufus himself, who also runs the ski school at Baqueira, specializes in local country cooking; try the *conejo relleno de ternera* (rabbit stuffed with veal). ✉ *Sant Jaume 8, Gessa* ☎ *973/645246 or 973/645872* 💳 *MC, V* ⊗ *Closed May–mid-July, Nov., and weekdays in Oct. No Sun. dinner or weekday lunch mid-Sept.–Apr.*

$$$–$$$$ **Fodor'sChoice** ★ **Melia Royal Tanau.** This luxurious hotel 7 km (4 mi) east of Salardú has lifts directly up to the slopes and every possible comfort and amenity, with prices to match. Undoubtedly the top skiing hotel in the Pyrenees, it's the obvious place to be pampered between assaults on the snowy heights. ✉ *Ctra. Baqueira-Beret, km 7, 25598* ☎ *973/644446* 📠 *973/644344* 🌐 *www.meliaroyaltanau.solmelia.com* *30 rooms, 15 apartments* *Restaurant, pool, indoor and outdoor hot tub; no a/c* 💳 *AE, MC, V.*

$$$ **Val de Ruda.** For rustic surroundings, light on luxury but long on comfort and an outdoorsy, alpine feeling, this modern-traditional construction is a good choice. It was one of the first skiing hotels to go up here in the early '80s. Just 660 ft from the slopes, this glass, wood, and stone refuge has a friendly staff and pine- and oak-beam warmth for après-ski wining and dining. ✉ *Ctra. Baqueira-Beret, 25598* ☎ *973/645258* 📠 *973/644344* 🌐 *www.valderuda-bassibe.com* *35 rooms* *Restaurant, bar; no a/c* 💳 *AE, DC, MC, V.*

Nightlife

Tiffany's (✉ Baqueira ☎ 973/644444) is a longtime favorite in Baqueira.

Sports & the Outdoors

Skiing, white-water rafting, hiking, climbing, horseback riding, and fly-fishing are available throughout the Vall d'Aran. Consult the Vielha **tourist office** (☎ 973/640110) for information.

DOGSLEDDING **La Pirena** (☎ 974/360098 tourist office in Jaca), the Pyrenean version of the Iditarod, rages through the Vall d'Aran in early February. The race runs from Panticosa, above Jaca, to La Molina, near Puigcerdà, February 1–15.

SKIING The **Baqueira-Beret Estación de Esquí** (Baqueira-Beret Ski Station), visited annually by King Juan Carlos I and the royal family, offers Catalonia's most varied and reliable skiing. The station's 87 km (57 mi) of pistas, spread over 53 runs, range from the gentle Beret slopes to the vertical chutes of Baqueira. The Bonaigua area is a mixture of steep and gently undulating trails with some of the longest, most varied runs in the Pyrenees, from forest tracks to open hillsides to jagged drops through tight ravines. The internationally FIS-classified super-giant slalom run in Beret is Baqueira-Beret's star attraction, although the Hotel Pirene runs carefully guided helicopter outings to the surrounding peaks of Pincela, Areño, Parros, Mall de Boulard, Pedescals, and Bassibe, among others. A dozen restaurants and four children's areas are scattered about the facilities, and the thermal baths at Tredós are 4 km (2½ mi) away. ✉ *Salardú* ☎ *973/639000* 📠 *973/644488* ✉ *Barcelona office: Passeig de Gràcia 2, Barcelona* ☎ *93/318–2776* 📠 *93/412–2942* 🌐 *www.baqueira.es.*

Vall de Joeu

20 *9 km (6 mi) northwest of Vielha.*

The Joeu Valley, above the town of Les Bordes, was for centuries the unsolved mystery of Vall d'Aran hydraulics. The Joeu River, one of the two main sources of the Garonne, appears to rise at Artiga de Lin, where it then cascades down in the Barrancs waterfalls. On July 19, 1931, speleologist Norbert Casteret proved, by dumping 132 lbs. of colorant into a cavern in neighboring Aragón, that this "spring" was actually glacier runoff from the Maladeta massif in the next valley to the southwest. The glacier melt flows into a massive crater, Els Aïgualluts, and reappears 4 km (3 mi) northeast at the so-called Uelhs deth Joeu (Eyes of Jupiter in Aranés, so named for the Roman deity's association with the heavens, weather, rainfall, and agriculture), where it flows north toward the Garonne and eventually the Atlantic.

Alta Ribagorça Oriental

21 *From Vall d'Aran take the 6-km (4-mi) Vielha tunnel to the Alta Ribagorça Oriental.*

This valley includes the east bank of the Noguera Ribagorçana River and the Llevata and Noguera de Tor valleys. The latter has the Pyrenees' richest concentration of medieval art and architecture. The quality and unity of design apparent in the Romanesque churches along the Noguera de Tor River, in towns such as Durro, Boí, Erill la Vall, and Taüll, are the result of the sponsorship—and wives—of the counts of Erill. The Erill knights, away fighting Moors in distant theaters of the Reconquest, left their spouses behind to supervise the creation of local houses of worship. The women then brought in Europe's leading masters of architecture, masonry, sculpture, and painting to build and decorate the churches. To what extent a single eye and sensibility was responsible for this extraordinarily harmonious and coherent set of churches may never be known, but it's clear that they all share certain distinguishing characteristics: a miniaturistic tightness combined with eccentric or irregular design, and slender rectangular bell towers at once light and forceful, perfectly balanced against the rocky background.

From Vielha, route N230 runs south 33 km (20 mi) to the intersection with N260 (sometimes marked C144), which goes west over the Fadas Pass to Castejón de Sos. Four kilometers (2½ mi) past this intersection, the road up the Noguera de Tor Valley turns to the northeast, 2 km (1 mi) short of Pont de Suert.

Taüll

22 *58 km (36 mi) south of Vielha.*

Taüll is a town of narrow streets and tight mountain design—wooden balconies, steep slate roofs. The churches of Sant Climent and Santa Maria are lovely, and important churches near Taüll include Sant Feliu, at Barruera; Sant Joan Baptista, at Boí; Santa Maria, at Cardet; Santa Maria, at Col; Santa Eulàlia, at Erill-la-vall; La Nativitat de la Mare de Deu and Sant Quirze, at Durro; Sant Llorenç, at Sarais; and Sant Nicolau, in the Sant Nicolau Valley, at the entrance to Aigüestortes–Sant Maurici National Park. Taüll has a ski resort, **Bohí Taüll,** at the head of the Sant Nicolau Valley.

★ The notable three-nave Romanesque church of **Sant Climent,** at the edge of town, was built in 1123 and has a six-story belfry. The proportions, the Pyrenean stone, the changing hues because of the light, and the general intimacy of the place create an exceptional balance and harmony. The church's murals, including the famous *Pantocrator,* the work of the "Master of Taüll," were moved to Barcelona's Museu Nacional d'Art de Catalunya in 1922; you can see reproductions here. €4 *Daily 10–2 and 4–8.*

Where to Eat

$–$$ ✕ **La Cabana.** Lamb and goat cooked over coals are the specialties of this rustic place, which also serves a fine *escudella* (sausage, vegetable, and potato stew) and an excellent *crema de carrerres* (cream of meadow mushroom) soup. *Ctra. de Taüll 973/696213 AE, DC, MC, V Closed May–late June, Oct.–Nov., and Mon. Dec.–Apr.*

Caldes de Boí

23 *6 km (4 mi) north of Taüll.*

The thermal baths in the town of Caldes de Boí include, between hot and cold sources, 40 springs. The caves inside the bath area are a singular natural phenomenon, with thermal steam seeping through the cracks in the rock. Take advantage of the baths' therapeutic qualities at either Hotel Caldes or Hotel Manantial—services range from a bath, at €6–€9, to an underwater body massage for €18. Arthritic patients are frequent takers. ✉ *Hotel Caldes* ☎ *973/696230* ✉ *Hotel Manantial* ☎ *973/696210* 🌐 *www.caldesdeboi.com* ⊗ *Hotels and baths closed Oct.–late June.*

Where to Stay & Eat

¢–$ ✕🏨 **Fondevila.** Wooden trim and simple country furnishings warm the interior of this stone structure 3 km (2 mi) north of Taüll. The rooms are generously proportioned and cozy. The country cuisine includes game in season and various Catalan specialties. ✉ *Carrer Única, 25528 Boí* ☎ *973/696011* *46 rooms* *No a/c* *AE, DC, MC, V* ⊗ *Closed Oct.–Nov.*

ARAGÓN & THE CENTRAL PYRENEES

The highest, most rugged, wildest, and most spectacular range of the Pyrenees, the uppermost hump of "the dragon's back" is, perhaps unsurprisingly, the part in the middle farthest from sea level at either end. From Benasque on Aragón's eastern side to Jaca at the western edge are the great heights and most dynamic landscapes of Alto Aragón (Upper Aragón), the northern part of the province of Huesca, including the Maladeta (11,165 ft), Posets (11,070 ft), and Monte Perdido (11,004 ft) peaks, the three highest points in the Pyrenean chain.

Communications between the high valleys of the Pyrenees were all but nonexistent until the 19th century. Four-fifths of the region had never seen a motor vehicle of any kind until the early part of the 20th century, and the 150 km (93 mi) of border with France between Portalet de Aneu and Vall d'Aran had never had an international crossing. This combination of high peaks, deep defiles, and lack of communication has produced what were historically some of the Iberian Peninsula's most isolated towns and valleys. Today, numerous ethnological museums preserve evidence of a way of life that has nearly disappeared over the last 50 years. Residents of Upper Aragón speak neither Basque nor Catalan, but local dialects, such as Grausín, Chistavino, Belsetá, and Benasqués, that have more in common with each other and with Occitanian Langue d'Oc than with modern Spanish or French. Furthermore, each valley has its own variations on everything from the typical Aragonese folk dance, the *jota* (such as Bielsa's Chinchecle), to cuisine, to folkloric costumes. Pyrenean wildlife here includes several strains of mountain goat, deer, and, above Jaca between Somport and the French Vall d'Aspe, the reintroduced Pyrenean brown bear.

The largely undiscovered cities of Huesca and Zaragoza are at once useful Pyrenean gateways and destinations in themselves; Zaragoza is off the main highway between Barcelona and Bilbao, too. Both retain an authentic provincial character that is refreshingly original in postmodern Spain. Huesca's lovely old quarter and Zaragoza's immense basilica, La Pilarica, are memorable additions to a mountain trip.

Huesca

24 *75 km (46 mi) southwest of Aínsa, 72 km (45 mi) northeast of Zaragoza, 123 km (74 mi) northwest of Lleida.*

Capital of Aragón until the royal court moved to Zaragoza in 1118, Huesca was founded by the Romans a millennium earlier. The city became an independent state with a senate and an excellent school system organized by the Roman general Sertorius in 77 BC. Much later, after centuries of Moorish rule, Pedro I of Aragón liberated Huesca in 1096. The town's university was founded in 1354 and now specializes in Aragonese studies. Huesca's fiestas for patron saint Lorenzo, held August 2–8, are nearly as riotous as Pamplona's San Fermín. *Albahaca* (basil) is Huesca's great crop and symbol; thus, basil and green neckerchiefs are everywhere in Huesca that week.

An intricately carved gallery tops the eroded facade of Huesca's 13th-century Gothic **cathedral.** Damián Forment, a disciple of the 15th-century Italian master sculptor Donatello, created the alabaster altarpiece with scenes from the Crucifixion. ✉ *Plaza de la Catedral s/n* ☎ *974/292172* 🎫 *Free* ⏲ *Mon.–Sat. 8–1 and 4–6:30.*

Three times daily, the Renaissance ***ayuntamiento*** (town hall) shows a 19th-century painting of the 12th-century beheading of a group of uncooperative nobles, ordered by Ramiro II. Having called a meeting for the purported pouring of a giant bell that would be audible throughout Aragón, Ramiro proceeded to massacre the leading troublemakers; the expression *como la campana de Huesca* ("like the bell of Huesca") is still sometimes used to describe an event of surprising resonance. ✉ *Plaza de la Catedral 1* ☎ *974/292170* 🎫 *Free* ⏲ *Mon.–Sat. at 11:30, 1:30, and 5:30.*

The **Museo Arqueológico Provincial,** in the former university buildings, is an octagonal patio ringed by eight chambers, including the **Sala de la Campana** (Hall of the Bell), where the beheadings of 12th-century nobles took place. The museum is in parts of what was once the royal palace of the kings of Aragón and holds paintings by Aragonese primitives, including *La Virgen del Rosario* by Miguel Jiménez, and several works by the 16th-century Maestro de Sigena. ✉ *Pl. de la Universidad* ☎ *974/220586* 🎫 *Free* ⏲ *Tues.–Sat. 10–2 and 5–8, Sun. 10–2.*

The church of **San Pedro el Viejo** has an 11th-century cloister with sculpted capitals. Ramiro II and his father, Alfonso I, the only Aragonese kings not entombed at San Juan de la Peña, rest in a side chapel. ✉ *Plaza de San Pedro s/n* ☎ *974/292164* 🎫 *Free* ⏲ *Mon.–Sat. 10–2 and 6–8.*

Where to Stay

$$–$$$ 🏨 **Pedro I de Aragón.** Huesca's best hotel by a wide margin, this modern structure over the leafy Parque Miguel Servet is lush with mirrors and marble in the lobby, and furnished with fresh and fragrant pine in the rooms. Comfort is guaranteed, and service is excellent. ✉ *Parque 34, 22003* ☎ *974/220300* 📠 *974/220094* 🌐 *www.gargallo-hotels.com* *125 rooms* *Restaurant, minibars, pool, bar, meeting rooms; no a/c, no pets* 💳 *AE, DC, MC, V.*

¢ 🏨 **San Marcos.** The building dates from 1890, and the rooms, though updated for comfort, remain tastefully decorated with traditional touches. Centrally located just outside the 1st-century Roman walls, the hotel is a five-minute walk from Huesca's cathedral. ✉ *San Orencio 10, 22001* ☎📠 *974/222931* *29 rooms* *No a/c, no pets* 💳 *AE, DC, MC, V.*

Zaragoza

25 *72 km (43 mi) southwest of Huesca, 138 km (86 mi) west of Lleida, 307 km (184 mi) west of Barcelona, 164 km (98 mi) southeast of Pamplona, 322 km (193 mi) northeast of Madrid.*

With the AVE, Spain's high speed railroad, now connecting Zaragoza with Barcelona and Madrid in a little over an hour, this provincial city is on the threshold of its greatest boom since the Romans established a thriving riverine port here in 25 BC. Rated one of Spain's most desirable places to live for reasons such as air quality, cost of living, and population density, Zaragoza seems to breathe a quiet sense of self-contained well-being. Despite its hefty size (pop. 610,976), this sprawling provincial capital midway between Barcelona, Madrid, Bilbao, and Valencia is an oasis of authenticity, a detour from the tourist track.

Straddling Spain's greatest river, the mighty Ebro, 2,000-year-old Zaragoza (named Caesaraugusta for Roman emperor Augustus) offers an eclectic legacy of everything from Roman ruins and Jewish baths to Arab, Romanesque, Gothic-Mudéjar, Renaissance, baroque, neoclassical, and Art Nouveau architecture. Parts of the **Roman walls** are visible near the city's landmark Basílica de Nuestra Señora del Pilar, while, nearby, the medieval **Puente de Piedra** (Stone Bridge) spans the Ebro. Check out the **Lonja** (stock exchange), the Moorish **Aljafería** (jewel treasury), the **Mercado de Lanuza** (produce market), and the various **churches** in the old town—San Pablo, San Miguel, San Gil, Santa Engracia, San Carlos, San Ildefonso, San Felipe, Santa Cruz, and San Fernando—it's a good way to navigate Zaragoza's jumble of backstreets.

Hulking on the banks of the Ebro, the **Basílica de Nuestra Señora del Pilar** (Basilica of Our Lady of the Pillar), affectionately known as "La Pilarica," is Zaragoza's symbol and pride. An immense baroque and eclectic structure with no fewer than 11 tile cupolas, La Pilarica is the home of the Virgen del Pilar, the patron saint not only of peninsular Spain but of the entire Hispanic world. The fiestas honoring this most Spanish of saints, the week of October 12, are events of extraordinary pomp and fervor, with processions, street concerts, bullfights, and traditional *jota* dancing. The cathedral was built in the 18th century to commemorate the appearance of the Virgin on a pillar (*pilar*), or pedestal, to St. James, Spain's other patron saint, during his legendary incarnation as Santiago Matamoros (St. James the Moorslayer) in the 9th century. La Pilarica herself resides in a side chapel that dates from 1754. The frescoes in the cupolas, some of which are attributed to the young Goya, are among the basilica's treasures. The **Museo Pilarista** holds drawings and some of the Virgin's jewelry. The bombs displayed to the right of the altar of La Pilarica fell through the roof of the church in 1936 and miraculously failed to explode. You can still see one of the holes overhead to the left. Behind La Pilarica's altar is the tiny opening where the devout line up to kiss the rough marble pillar where La Pilarica was allegedly discovered. ✉ *Plaza del Pilar s/n* 🎫 *Basilica free; museum €1* ⏲ *Basilica daily 5:45 AM–9:30 PM, museum daily 9–2 and 4–6.*

Zaragoza's cathedral, **La Seo** (Catedral de San Salvador), at the eastern end of the Plaza del Pilar, is the city's bishopric, or diocesan *seo* (seat). An amalgam of architectural styles, ranging from the Mudéjar brick-and-tile exterior to the Gothic altarpiece to exuberant, Churrigueresque doorways, the Seo nonetheless has an 18th-century baroque facade that seems to echo those of La Pilarica. The **Museo de Tapices** within contains medieval tapestries. The nearby quaint, medieval **Casa and Arco del Deán** form one of the city's favorite corners. ✉ *Plaza del Pilar*

Cathedral € 3, museum €3 Cathedral Mon.–Sat. 10–2 and 4–8, Sun. 5–8; museum Tues.–Sat. 10–2 and 4–6, Sun. 10–2.

The **Iglesia de la Magdalena** (Plaza de la Magdalena s/n 976/299598), next to the remains of the Roman forum, has an ancient, brick Mudéjar bell tower. The church is usually open in the mornings.

The **Museo del Foro** displays remains of the Roman forum and the Roman sewage system, though the presentation is in Spanish only. Two more Roman sites, the **thermal baths** at Calle de San Juan y San Pedro and the **river port** at Plaza San Bruno, are also open to the public. *Plaza de la Seo s/n 976/399752 €2 Tues.–Sat. 10–2 and 5–8.*

The **Museo Camón Aznar** has a fine collection of Goya's works, particularly engravings. *Carrer Espoz y Mina 23 976/397328 €1 Tues.–Fri. 9–2 and 6–9, Sat. 10–2 and 6–9, Sun. 11–2.*

The **Museo Provincial de Bellas Artes** (Provincial Museum of Fine Arts) is rich in Goyas. *Plaza de los Sitios 5 976/222181 Free Tues.–Sat. 10–2 and 5–8, Sun. 10–2.*

The **Museo Pablo Gargallo** is one of Zarargoza's most treasured and admired gems, both for the palace as well as for the collection—Gargallo, born near Zaragoza in 1881, was one of Spain's greatest modern sculptors. *Plaza de San Felipe 3 976/392058 Free Tues.–Sat. 9–2 and 5–9, Sun. 9–2.*

Palacio de La Aljafería, Zaragoza's own surprising Alhambra north is somewhat over-restored, but what remains of the original helps explain the singular power and extent of the nearly eight-century Moorish empire on the Iberian Peninsula. Built in the 11th-century fortress, major restoration work and redesign was carried out by the Catholic Monarchs Fernando and Isabel after 1492. Important as a seat of the Spanish Inquisition, the palace, which occupies several acres, is now the home of the Cortes (Parliament) de Aragón. Part of the palace, the 9th-century Torre del Trovador (Tower of the Troubadour) was used by Verdi in his opera *Il Trovatore. Diputados s/n 976/289683 €3 Mon.–Sat. 10–2 and 4–8:30, closed Thurs., Fri. morning.*

Where to Stay & Eat

$–$$ **Casa Emilio.** One of the city's most popular restaurants among artists, journalists, and writers, this haven of straightforward cooking and conversation near the Aljafería and the train station offers excellent value and a friendly environment. *Avda. Madrid 3–5 976/435839 AE, DC, MC, V.*

★ **$–$$** **Casa Lac.** Just off Plaza España, this traditional haunt has creaky wooden floors and well-worn stairs that add to the character of the ancient upstairs dining room. Try the *solomillo al oporto con trufas y setas* (filet mignon in port wine sauce with truffles and wild mushrooms) for a deep, dark taste treat. *Mártires 12 976/299025 AE, DC, MC, V.*

$–$$ **La Venta del Cachirulo.** Just outside Zaragoza, this roadhouse is worth a trip for authentic Aragonese cooking and folklore, including occasional *jota* dancing, singing, and a generally rough-and-tumble approach to delicious food. *Borrajas con almejas* (kale with clams) and *pato con cerezas* (duck with cherries) are among the local dishes served. *Ctra. Logroño (N232), Km 1 976/460146 AE, DC, MC, V Closed Sun., Mon., and first 2 wks in Aug.*

★ **$** **Los Victorinos.** Zaragoza's finest tapas emporium, which opens at 7:30, is a cozy tavern heavily adorned with taurine paraphernalia. It's close behind La Seo. The morsels displayed on the bar are guaranteed to jumpstart your appetite. ✉ *José de la Hera 6* ☎ *976/394213* 💳 *AE, DC, MC, V* ⊗ *No lunch.*

¢–$ Fodor'sChoice ★ ✕ **El Fuelle.** Fine Aragonese fare distinguishes this rustic old-town favorite decorated with giant *fuelles* (bellows), farming tools, and random artifacts of every description. Specialties include *judias estofadas* (white beans stewed in sausage), *migas* (a traditional dish of chorizo, garlic, peppers, and bread crumbs soaked in olive oil and garlic), and a signature dish, *patatas asadas* (roast potatoes). ✉ *Calle Mayor 59* ☎ *976/398033* 💳 *AE, DC, MC, V.*

$$–$$$ **Goya.** Smack in the city center, this hotel provides a balanced combination of comfort and proximity to the historic sights. It's only a five-minute walk from the Basílica del Pilar and the Ebro River; here you'll get the sense that you're part of the city's life. Rooms are modern, but not luxurious. ✉ *Cinco de Marzo, 50004* ☎ *976/229331* 📠 *976/232154* *148 rooms* *Restaurant, café, minibars, cable TV, bar, meeting rooms, parking (fee)* 💳 *AE, DC, MC, V.*

¢–$ **Las Torres.** The rooms are small here but you may be able to admire the domes of La Pilarica from your pillow. You may also need earplugs to muffle the bonging of the bells, but the scenery is nonpareil. ✉ *Plaza del Pilar 11, 50003* ☎ *976/394250* 📠 *976/394254* *54 rooms* *Breakfast room, parking (fee)* 💳 *AE, DC, MC, V.*

Benasque

26 Fodor'sChoice ★ *79 km (49 mi) southwest of Vielha.*

Benasque, Aragón's easternmost town, has always been an important link between Catalonia and Aragón. This elegant mountain hub of just over 1,500 people packs a number of notable buildings, including the 13th-century Romanesque church of **Santa Maria Mayor** and the ancient, dignified manor houses of the town's old families, such as the **palace of the counts of Ribagorza,** on Calle Mayor, and the **Torre Juste.** Take a walk around and peer into the entryways and patios of these palatial facades, left open just for this purpose.

Anciles, 2 km (1 mi) south of Benasque, is one of Spain's best-preserved and -restored medieval villages, an excellent collection of farmhouses and *palacetes* (town houses). The summer classical-music series is a superb collision of music and architecture, and the village restaurant, Ansils, combines modern and medieval motifs in both cuisine and design.

off the beaten path

PICO DE ANETO – Benasque is the traditional base camp for excursions to Aneto, at 11,168 ft the highest peak in the Pyrenees. You can rent crampons and a *piolet* (ice axe) for the two- to three-hour crossing of the Aneto glacier at any sports store in town or at the Refugio de la Renclusa, a way station for mountaineers; it's an hour's walk above the parking area, which is 17 km (11 mi) north of Benasque, off A-139. The trek to the summit and back is not difficult, just long—some 20 km (12 mi) round-trip, with a 1,500-yard vertical ascent. Allow a full 12 hours.

Where to Stay & Eat

$$–$$$ ✕ **Asador Ixarso.** Roast goat or lamb cooked over a raised fireplace in the corner of the dining room is why this place is a fine refuge in chilly weather. The *revuelto de setas* (eggs scrambled with wild mushrooms) is superb, as are the salads. ✉ *Calle San Pedro 9* ☎ *974/552057* 💳 *AE, DC, MC, V* ⊗ *Closed weekdays mid-Sept.–1st wk in Dec. and Easter–last wk in June.*

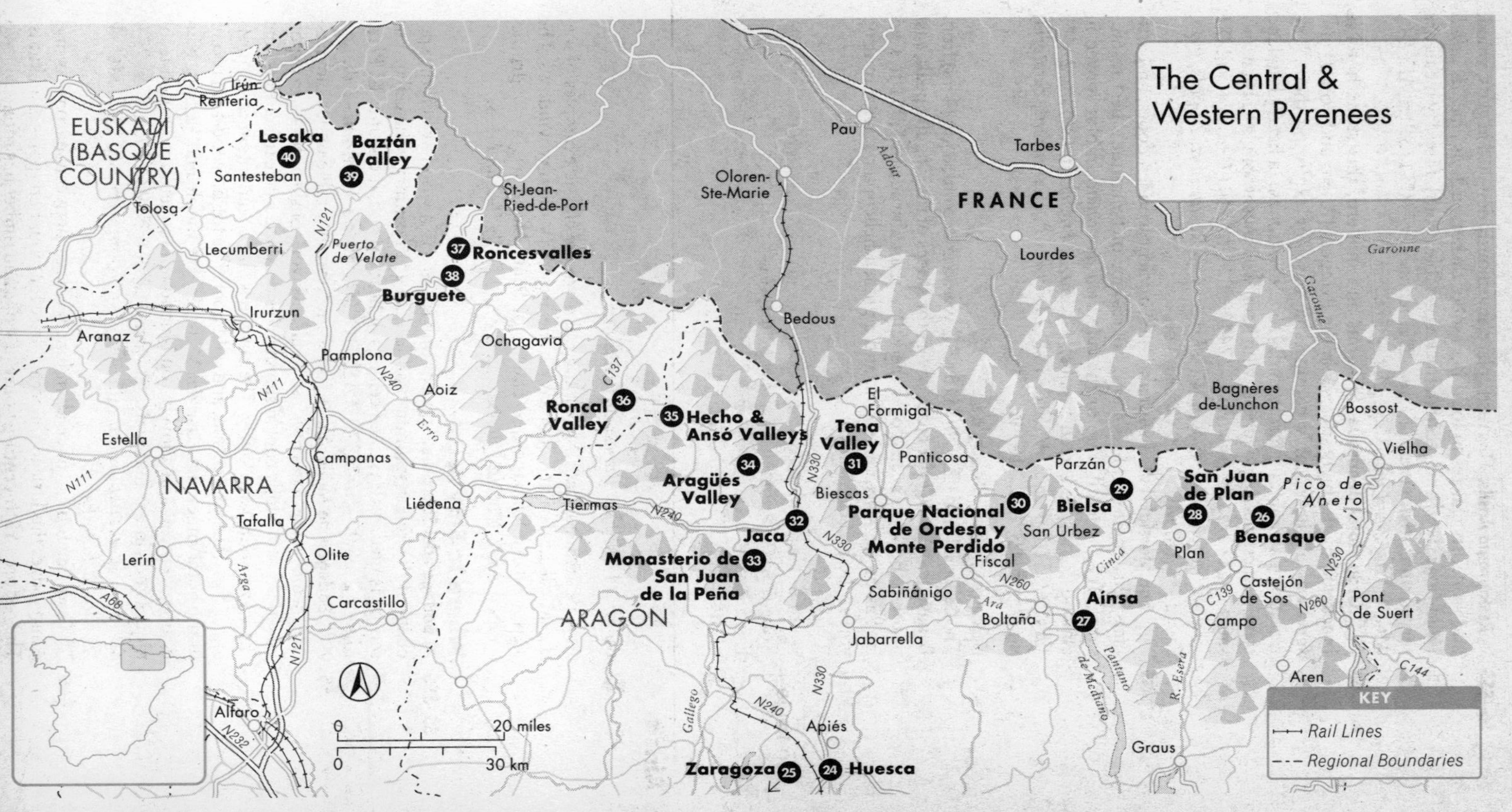

The Central & Western Pyrenees
FRANCE
Pau
Tarbes
Adour
Lourdes
Garonne
Oloren-Ste-Marie
Bedous
St-Jean-Pied-de-Port
Bagnères de-Lunchon
Bossost
Vielha
Pico de Aneto
Pont de Suert
Aren
C144
N230
N260
San Juan de Plan 28
Benasque 26
Castejón de Sos
Campo
C139
Plan
R. Esera
Graus
Pantano de Mediano
Aínsa 27
Bielsa 29
Parzán
San Urbez
Cinca
Parque Nacional de Ordesa y Monte Perdido 30
Fiscal
Boltaña
Ara
El Formigal
Panticosa
Sabiñánigo
Jabarrella
Tena Valley 31
Biescas
N330
Jaca 32
Monasterio de San Juan de la Peña 33
Aragüés Valley 34
Hecho & Ansó Valleys 35
Roncal Valley 36
C137
N240
Tiermas
ARAGÓN
Gallego
Huesca 24
Apiés
Zaragoza 25
Roncesvalles 37
Burguete 38
Baztán Valley 39
Lesaka 40
Ochagavia
Aoiz
Erro
Liédena
Pamplona
Puerto de Velate
N121
Irún
Renteria
Santesteban
Lecumberri
Irurzun
Campanas
Carcastillo
Olite
Tafalla
N111
NAVARRA
Arga
Alfaro
N232
EUSKADI (BASQUE COUNTRY)
Tolosa
Aranaz
Estella
Lerín
A68
0
20 miles
30 km
KEY
Rail Lines
Regional Boundaries

$$–$$$ ✕ **Restaurante Ansils.** This rustic place, ingeniously designed in glass, wood, and stone, specializes in local Benasqués dishes, such as *civet de jabalí* (wild-boar stew) and *recau* (a thick vegetable broth). Holiday meals are served on Christmas and Easter. ✉ *Anciles* ☎ *974/551150* ▭ *AE, DC, MC, V* ⊗ *Closed weekdays Oct.–June.*

$$ ✕🏨 **Gran Hotel Benasque.** Spacious and modern, this stone hotel is bracketed by the highest crests in the Pyrenees (Aneto and Posets) and serves as an impeccably comfortable base for exploring them. The restaurant's mountain fare includes *sopa Benasquesa* (a hearty highland stew) and *crepas Aneto* (crepes with ham, wild mushroom, and béchamel sauce). ✉ *Ctra. de Anciles 3, 22440* ☎ *974/551011* 📠 *974/552821* 🌐 *www.hoteles-valero.com* *69 rooms* *Restaurant, 2 pools, gym, sauna* ▭ *AE, MC, V* ⊗ *Closed Nov.*

$$ ✕🏨 **San Marsial.** Filled with antiques, ancient wooden doors, and artifacts, this comfortable inn also houses one of Benasque's best restaurants. Try the lentil soup or the *caldereta de conejo* (rabbit stewed in almonds, olives, and bread crumbs). ✉ *Ctra. de Francia (C139) s/n, 22440* ☎ *974/551616* 📠 *974/551623* *24 rooms* *Restaurant, cafeteria; no a/c* ▭ *AE, DC, MC, V.*

Sports & the Outdoors

The **Cerler ski area** (☎ 974/551012 🌐 www.cerler.com), 6 km (4 mi) from Benasque on the Cerler road, covers the slopes of the Cogulla peak, east of town. Built on a shelf over the valley at an altitude of 5,051 ft, Cerler has 26 ski runs, three lifts, and a guided helicopter service to drop you at the highest peaks.

en route South of Castejón de Sos, down the Esera Valley through the Congosto de Ventamillo—a sheer slice through the rock made by the Esera River—a turn west on N260 cuts over to Aínsa, at the junction of the Rivers Cinca and Ara.

Aínsa

27 *66 km (41 mi) southwest of Benasque.*

Aínsa's arcaded Plaça Major and old town are classic examples of medieval village design, with heavy stone archways and tiny windows. The 12th-century Romanesque church of **Santa María** has a quadruple-vaulted door. ✉ *Old Quarter* *Free* ⊗ *Daily 9–2 and 4–8.*

Where to Stay & Eat

$$–$$$ ✕ **Bodegas del Sobrarbe.** Superb lamb roasted in a wood oven is the specialty of this fine restaurant built into an 11th-century wine cellar. The setting is medieval: vaulted ceilings of heavy wood and stone. ✉ *Plaza Mayor 2* ☎ *974/500237* ▭ *AE, DC, MC, V* ⊗ *Closed Jan.–Feb.*

$$ ✕🏨 **Bodegón de Mallacán.** If you want to sit at a table under the massive medieval porticoes of Aínsa's Plaza Mayor, consider this breezy spot, which is wonderfully cool in summer. Inside, the ceramic tile murals (and the views south) are lovely. The cuisine is classic mountain fare: roasts and stews of lamb, venison, and wild boar. The fresh, wood-trim rooms in the hotel annex, La Casa del Marqués, are simple and elegant, with beams overhead and a lovely combination of modern restoration techniques and vintage materials. ✉ *Plaza Mayor 6* ☎ *974/500977* 📠 *974/500953* 🌐 *www.posadareal.com* *6 rooms* ▭ *AE, DC, MC, V* ⊗ *Closed Jan.–Feb.*

¢–$ 🏨 **Casa Cambra.** A once-abandoned village between Barbastro and Aínsa lodges this little inn, a perfect base for mountain sports of all kinds. The restored 18th-century house of stone and timber has rooms for two to four people and is part of a tourist complex that includes a restaurant. ✉ *Ctra. Barbastro–Aínsa (C138), Morillo de Tou 22395* ☎📠 *974/500793* *17 rooms* *No a/c* *MC, V.*

off the beaten path

AÑISCLO GORGES – On the road north from Aínsa, the Añisclo Canyon is 5 km (3 mi) north of the town of Escalona. A road to the west runs 14 km (9 mi) along the edge of the sheer rock divide to Urbez. As you drive into Urbez, you'll see the ancient stone bridge. On the far bank of the river is the cave chapel named for St. Urbez, a hermit monk from Bordeaux who lived there in the 8th century.

5

San Juan de Plan & the Gistaín Valley

28 *14 km (8½ mi) east of Salinas.*

San Juan de Plan has become a treasury of local folklore. This detour begins with a well-marked road heading east of Salinas, 25 km (15 mi) north of Aínsa. The Cinqueta River drains the Gistaín Valley, flowing by or through the mountain villages of Sin, Señes, Saravillo, Serveta, and Salinas; the town of San Juan de Plan presides at the head of the valley, where an ethnographic museum, a weaving workshop, and an early music and dance ensemble are the pride of the region. Don't miss a tour of the weaving industry, restored by Amanda Tyson, the town's resident American. The mid-February carnival is among the most original and traditional celebrations in the Pyrenees. The **Museo Etnográfico** is a fascinating glimpse into the valley's way of life until as recently as 1975. ✉ *Plaza Mayor s/n* ☎ *974/506052* *€3* *Daily 9–2 and 4–8.*

Where to Stay & Eat

★ $ **Casa la Plaza.** Josefina Loste's pleasant inn has cozy rooms with antique furniture. Each room tucked into the eaves is different. The restaurant serves excellent local dishes using the freshest ingredients in inventive yet traditional ways. ✉ *Plaza Mayor s/n, 22367* ☎ *974/506052* *13 rooms* *No a/c* *AE, DC, MC, V* *Closed sporadically Oct.–May; call to confirm.*

$ **Hotel Anita.** This modern stone building has become San Juan de Plan's hub and nerve center. Rooms are bright and well equipped, and the restaurant is known as the best in town; its Pyrenean fare includes seasonal game, from partridge to wild boar. For a taste of pure lunacy, try to be here when the Pirene, the 200-husky dogsled race, comes through in late January. ✉ *Calle Alta s/n, 22367* ☎ *974/506211* 📠 *974/506196* *www.elvalledechistau.com* *18 rooms* *Restaurant, cable TV, bar; no a/c* *AE, DC, MC, V* *Closed Nov.*

Bielsa

29 *34 km (21 mi) northeast of Aínsa.*

Bielsa, at the confluence of the Cinca and Barrosa rivers, is a busy summer resort with some lovely mountain architecture and an ancient, porticoed town hall. Northwest of Bielsa the **Monte Perdido glacier** and the icy **Marboré Lake** drain into the **Pineta Valley** and the Pineta Reservoir. You can take three- or four-hour walks from the parador up to Larri, Munia, or Marboré Lake among remote peaks.

Where to Stay & Eat

$$–$$$ **Parador de Bielsa.** Glass, steel, and stone define this modern structure overlooking the national park, the peak of Monte Perdido, and the source of the Cinca River. Rooms are done in bright wood, but the best part is your proximity to the park and the views. The restaurant spe-

cializes in Aragonese mountain dishes, such as *pucherete de Parzán* (a stew with beans, sausage, and vegetables). ✉ *Valle de Pineta s/n, 22350* ☎ *974/501011* 📠 *974/501188* 🌐 *www.parador.es* *26 rooms* *Restaurant, cable TV, bar; no a/c* ▭ *AE, DC, MC, V.*

★ ¢–$ **Valle de Pineta.** This corner castle overlooking the river junction is the most spectacular refuge in town. The restaurant is excellent, the views without compare. Try for the top corner room, which looks up and down both valleys. ✉ *Baja s/n, 22350* ☎ *974/501010* 📠 *974/501191* 🌐 *www.monteperdido.com* *26 rooms* *Restaurant, cable TV, pool, bar; no a/c* ▭ *AE, DC, MC, V* *Closed Nov. and Jan.–Feb.*

en route

You can explore the **Valle del Cinca** from the river's source at the head of the valley above Bielsa. From Bielsa, drive back down to Aínsa and turn west on N260 (alternately marked C138) for Broto.

Parque Nacional de Ordesa y Monte Perdido

30 *108 km (67 mi) west of Bielsa; from Aínsa, turn west on N260 for the 53-km (33-mi) drive to Torla.*

Fodor's Choice ★

Ordesa and Monte Perdido National Park is one of Spain's great underrated wonders, a domain many consider comparable, if on a somewhat smaller scale, to North America's Grand Canyon. The entrance lies under the vertical walls of Monte Mondarruego, source of the Ara River and its tributary, the Arazas, which forms the famous Ordesa Valley. The park was founded by royal decree in 1918 to protect the natural integrity of the Central Pyrenees, and it has expanded from 4,940 to 56,810 acres as provincial and national authorities have added the Monte Perdido massif, the head of the Pineta Valley, and the Escuain and Añisclo canyons. Defined by the Ara and Arazas rivers, the Ordesa Valley is endowed with pine, fir, larch, beech, and poplar forests; lakes, waterfalls, and high mountain meadows; and protected wildlife, including trout, boar, chamois, and the *Capra Pyrenaica* mountain goat.

Hikes through the park (on well-marked and -maintained mountain trails) lead to waterfalls, caves, and spectacular observation points. The standard tour, a full day's hike (eight hours), leads from the parking area in the Pradera de Ordesa, 8 km (5 mi) northeast of Torla, up the Arazas River, past the *gradas de Soaso* (Soaso risers; a natural stairway of waterfalls) to the *cola de caballo* (horse's tail), a lovely fan of falling water at the head of the Cirque de Cotatuero, a sort of natural amphitheater. A return walk on the south side of the valley, past the Refugio de los Cazadores (hunters' hut), offers a breathtaking view followed by a two-hour descent back to the parking area. A few spots, while not technically difficult, may seem precarious. Information and guidebooks are available at the booth on your way into the park at Pradera de Ordesa. The best time to come is from the beginning of May to the middle of November, but check conditions with regional tourist offices before driving into a blizzard in May or missing out on *el veranillo de San Martín* (Indian summer) in the fall. *Pradera de Ordesa information office* ☎ *974/243361* 🌐 *www.mma.es* *Free.*

En route to the park, **Broto** is a prototypical Aragonese mountain town with an excellent 16th-century Gothic church. Nearby villages such as Oto have stately manor houses with classic local features: baronial entryways, conical chimneys, and wooden galleries. **Torla** is noteworthy for its mountain architecture and as the park's entry point; it's a popular base camp for hikers.

Where to Eat

$–$$ **El Rebeco.** In this graceful and rustic building in the upper part of town, the dining rooms are lined with historic photographs of Torla. The black marble stone floor and the *chimenea-hogar,* a traditional open fireplace-room with an overhead smoke vent, are extraordinary. In late fall, *civets* (stews) of deer, boar, and mountain goat are the order of the day. *Calle Lafuente 55 Torla 22376 974/486068 AE, DC, MC, V Closed Dec.–Easter.*

en route

Follow N260 (sometimes marked C140) west over the Cotefablo Pass from Torla to Biescas. This route winds interminably through the pine forest leading up to and down from the pass; expect it to take five times longer than it looks like it should.

5

Tena Valley

31 *40 km (25 mi) west of Ordesa.*

The Valle de Tena, a north–south hexagon of 400 square km (154 square mi), is formed by the Gállego River and its two tributaries, the Aguaslimpias and the Caldares. A glacial valley surrounded by peaks rising to more than 10,000 ft (such as the 10,900-ft Vignemale), Tena is a busy hiking and winter-sports center. **Sallent de Gállego,** at the head of the valley, has long been a jumping-off point for excursions to **Aguaslimpias, Piedrafita,** and the meadows of the Gállego headwaters at **El Formigal** (a major ski area) and **Portalet.** The Pyrenean *ibon* (glacial lake) of **Respumoso,** accessible by a 2½-hour walk above the old road from Sallent to Formigal, is a peaceful and perfectly horizontal expanse amid all the vertical landscape.

Where to Stay & Eat

$ **Morlans.** Rooms here are warm and inviting and look south over the town to Panticosa's ski area and the mountains beyond. The lower restaurant specializes in roast lamb, goat, and suckling pig; the upper restaurant serves *civets* of deer, boar, and mountain goat, as well as such Upper Aragonese favorites as *pochas* (bean soup with sausage). *Calle de San Miguel, Panticosa 22661 974/487057 974/487386 25 rooms 2 restaurants; no a/c AE, DC, MC, V.*

Jaca

32 *24 km (15 mi) southwest of Biescas; down the Tena Valley through Biescas, a westward turn at Sabiñánigo onto N330 leaves a 14-km (9-mi) drive to Jaca.*

Jaca, the most important municipal center in Alto Aragón (with a population of more than 15,000), is anything but sleepy. Bursting with ambition and blessed with the natural resources and first-rate facilities to express their relentless drive, Jacetanos are determined to host a Winter Olympics someday. The town is already Spain's winter-sports capital, playing frequent host to major competitions, such as the World Figure Skating Championships and the national King's Cup in ice hockey.

Founded in 1035 as the kingdom of Jacetania, Jaca was an important stronghold during the Christian Reconquest of the Iberian Peninsula and proudly claims never to have bowed to the Moorish invaders. Indeed, the town still commemorates, on the first Friday of May, the decisive battle in which the appearance of a battalion of women, their hair and jewelry flashing in the sun, so intimidated the Moorish cavalry that they beat a headlong retreat.

need a break?

One of Jaca's most emblematic restaurants is **La Campanilla** (Escuelas Pías 8), behind the ayuntamiento, or town hall. The baked potatoes with garlic and olive oil are an institution, unchanged for as long as anyone can remember.

An important stop on the pilgrimage to Santiago de Compostela, Jaca has the 11th-century **Catedral de Santa María,** one of the oldest in Spain. The **Museo Diocesano,** near the cloisters, is filled with excellent Romanesque and Gothic murals and artifacts. *Museo* ☎ *974/356378* €2 *June–Sept., Tues.–Sun. 10–2 and 4–8; Oct.–May, Tues.–Sun. 11–1:30 and 4–7.*

The door to Jaca's **ayuntamiento** (town hall) has a notable Renaissance design. The massive **Ciudadella** (Citadel) is a good example of 17th-century military architecture. It has a display of thousands of military miniatures. ✉ *Av. Primer Viernes de Mayo s/n* ☎ *974/363018* *€4* *Daily 11–noon and 4–6.*

In summer, a free guided **tour** departs the local RENFE station, covering the valley and the mammoth, semi-derelict Belle Epoque railroad station at Canfranc, surely the largest and most ornate building in the Pyrenees. The train ticket costs €3; ask the tourist office for schedules.

Where to Stay & Eat

$$$–$$$$ ✕ **La Cocina Aragonesa.** This Jaca mainstay in the Hotel Conde Aznar is known far and wide for fresh and innovative cuisine, especially game in season: venison, wild boar, partridge, duck. Try the partridge stuffed with foie gras. ✉ *Cervantes 5* ☎ *974/361050* *AE, DC, MC, V* *Closed Wed. June–Sept.*

★ ¢–$ ✕ **El Fau.** Tucked under cool arcades next to the cathedral, El Fau overlooks Jaca's finest carved capitals and serves excellent *cazuelitas,* small earthenware casseroles containing anything from piping-hot garlic shrimp to wild mushrooms. In summer, the cold beer here is legendary. ✉ *Plaza de la Catedral* ☎ *974/361719* *AE, DC, MC, V* *Closed Mon.*

¢–$ ✕ **La Tasca de Ana.** Ana's tasca (tavern) is one of Jaca's simplest and best. Nearly anyone in town will send you here for superbly interpreted tapas of every kind. Invent your own meal by starting with a round of olives and working through, say, cured *jamó ibérico* (Iberian ham), *sepia* (cuttlefish), *albóndigas* (meatballs), and *civet de jabalí* (wild-boar stew), concluding with cheese from the neighboring Roncal Valley. ✉ *Plaza Ramiro I 3* ☎ *974/363621* *AE, DC, MC, V* *Closed Mon.*

$$ **Gran Hotel.** This rambling hotel, which serves as Jaca's official clubhouse, is central to both life and tourism in Jaca. Done up in wood, stone, and glass, it has a garden and a separate dining wing. The comfortable rooms have rich colors and practical wood furniture. ✉ *Paseo de la Constitución 1, 22700* ☎ *974/360900* *974/364061* *www.inturmark.es* *165 rooms* *Restaurant, pool, meeting rooms* *AE, DC, MC, V.*

$ **Hostal Somport.** A good budget option, this tidy little spot in the center of town is halfway between the cathedral and the town hall. The rooms, beds, and baths are all well kept, and the location is an ideal crawling distance from the nearby taverns and music bars on Calle Gil Bergés. ✉ *Calle Echegaray 11, 22700* *974/363410* *17 rooms* *Restaurant; no a/c* *AE, DC, MC, V.*

¢–$ **Hotel Mur.** This simple place is enclosed by part of the medieval Moorish walls on the northern edge of the Barrio de la Macarena. Rooms are small but decorated in bright colors with fresh wood trim.

The best overlook the walls and the leafy courtyard behind the Iglesia de San Hermendgildo. Prices double during Holy Week and the April Fair but remain rock bottom the rest of the year. ✉ *Santa Orosia 1, 22700* ☎ *974/360100* 📠 *974/356162* *68 rooms* *Restaurant; no a/c* 💳 *AE, DC, MC, V.*

Nightlife

Discos such as Dimensión and Oroel are thronged with skiers and hockey players in season (October–April), but the main nocturnal attractions are Jaca's so-called *bares musicales* (music bars), usually less loud and smoky than the discos. Most of these are in the old town, around Plaza Ramiro I and along Calle Gil Bergés and Calle Bellido.

Sports & the Outdoors

The **ski areas** of Candanchú and Astún are 32 km (20 mi) north of Jaca, on the road to Somport and the French border.

Check out the town's **ice rink** (☎ 974/361032) if you like to skate.

5

THE WESTERN & BASQUE PYRENEES

The Aragüés, Hecho and Ansó valleys, drained by the Estarrún, Osia, Veral and Aragón Subordán rivers, are the westernmost valleys in Aragón and rank among the most pristine parts of the Pyrenees. Today these sleepy hollows are struggling to generate an economy that will save this endangered species of Pyrenean life. Less frequented by tourists, offering Nordic (cross-country) skiing only, the mountain towns here retain ways and means of life more firmly entrenched here than in, say, Jaca and the Tena Valley. As you move west into the Roncal Valley and the Basque Country, you will note smoother hills and softer meadows as the rocky central Pyrenees of Aragón fade into the past. These wet and fertile uplands and verdant beech forests seem reflected in the wide lines and flat profiles of the Basque *caseríos* (farmhouses) hulking firmly into the landscape. The Basque highlands of Navarra, from Roncal through the Irati Forest to Roncesvalles, and along the Bidasoa River leading down to the Bay of Biscay, all seem like some Arcadian paradise with progressively less stone and more vegetation as the Pyrenean heights give way to sheep-filled pasture lands.

Monasterio de San Juan de la Peña

★ 33 *22 km (14 mi) southwest of Jaca.*

South of the Aragonese valleys of Hecho and Ansó is the Monastery of San Juan de la Peña, a site connected to the legend of the Holy Grail and another "cradle" of Christian resistance during the 700-year Moorish occupation of Spain. Its origins can be traced to the 9th century, when a hermit monk named Juan settled here on the *peña* (cliff). A monastery was founded on the spot in 920, and in 1071 Sancho Ramirez, son of King Ramiro I, made use of this structure, which was built into the mountain's rock wall, to found the Benedictine Monasterio de San Juan de la Peña. The **cloister,** tucked under the cliff, dates from the 12th century and contains intricately carved capitals depicting biblical scenes. From Jaca, drive 11 km (7 mi) west on N240 toward Pamplona to a left turn clearly signposted for San Juan de la Peña. From there it's another 11 km to the monastery. ✉ *Off N240* ☎ *974/361476* *€4* ⏲ *Oct.–mid-Mar., Tues.–Sun. 11–1:30 and 4–5:30; mid-Mar.–May, Tues.–Sun. 10–1:30 and 4–7; June–Sept., daily 10–noon and 4–8.*

en route

To get to the westernmost Pyrenean valleys in Aragón from Jaca, head west on N240 and take a hard right at Puente de la Reina (after turning right to cross the bridge) and continue north along the Aragón-Subordán River. The first right after 15 km (9 mi) leads into the Aragüés Valley along the Osia River to Aisa and then Jasa.

Aragüés Valley

34 *Aragüés del Puerto is 2 km (1 mi) from Jasa.*

Aragüés del Puerto is a tidy mountain village with stone houses and lovely little corners, doorways, and porticoes. The distinctive folk dance in Aragüés is the *palotiau*, a special variation of the *jota* performed only in this village. The **Museo Etnográfico** (Ethnographic Museum), in an ancient chapel in Aragüés del Puerto (ask for the caretaker at the town hall), offers a look into the past, from the document witnessing the 878 election of Iñigo Arista as king of Pamplona to the quirky manual wheat grinder. Above Aragüés del Puerto is the **Pico de Bisaurín,** one of the highest peaks in the area (8,638 ft). At the source of the River Osia, the Lizara **cross-country ski area** is in a flat expanse between the Aragüés and Jasa valleys. Look for 3,000-year-old megalithic dolmens sprinkled across the flat.

Where to Stay & Eat

¢ ✕ **Albergue Lizara.** This simple place on the outskirts of Aragüés del Puerto is the only game in town, but it works well for dinner and shelter if you decide on impulse to explore the upper reaches. Rooms are small but pleasantly cozy, and the Pyrenean cuisine is no-frills highland stick-to-your-ribs. ✉ *Calle Lizara s/n* ☎ *974/371519* *12 rooms, plus 60 beds in dormitory* *Restaurant; no a/c* *MC, V.*

Hecho & Ansó Valleys

35 *The Hecho Valley is 49 km (30 mi) northwest of Jaca. The Ansó Valley is 25 km (15 mi) west of Hecho.*

You can reach the Valle de Hecho from the Aragüés Valley by returning to the valley of the Aragón-Subordan and turning north again on the A-176. The **Monasterio de San Pedro de Siresa,** above the town of Hecho, is the area's most important monument, a 9th-century retreat of which only the 11th-century church remains. *Cheso,* a medieval Aragonese dialect descended from the Latin spoken by the Siresa monks, is thought to be the closest to Latin of all Romance languages and dialects. Cheso has been kept alive in the Hecho Valley, especially in the works of the poet Veremundo Mendez Coarasa. ✉ *Calle San Pedro, Siresa* *Free* *July–Aug. 11–1 and 5–8; other months, call the Ayuntamiento de Siresa (☎ 974/375002) for key.*

The **Selva de Oza** (Oza Forest), at the head of the Hecho Valley, is above the **Boca del Infierno** (Mouth of Hell), a tight draw where road and river barely squeeze through. Beyond the Oza Forest is a **Roman road** used before the 4th century to reach France through the Puerto del Palo—one of the oldest routes across the border on the pilgrimage to Santiago de Compostela.

The **Valle de Ansó** is Aragón's western limit. Rich in fauna (mountain goats, wild boar, and even a bear or two), the Ansó Valley follows the Veral River up to Zuriza. The three **cross-country ski areas** above Zuriza are known as the Pistas de Linza. Near Fago is the sanctuary of the **Virgen de Puyeta,** patron saint of the valley. Towering over the head of the valley is Navarra's highest point, the 7,989-ft **Mesa de los Tres Reyes**

(Plateau of the Three Kings), named not for the Magi but for the kings of Aragón, Navarra, and Castile, whose 11th-century kingdoms all came to a corner here—allowing them to meet without leaving their respective realms. Try to be in the town of **Ansó** on the last Sunday in August, when residents dress in their traditional medieval costumes and perform ancestral dances of great grace and dignity.

Where to Stay & Eat

$ **Gaby-Casa Blasquico.** This cozy inn, better known as Hecho's top restaurant, is famous for its Aragonese mountain cuisine. Especially strong on game recipes from wild boar to venison to partridge or migratory pigeon, the menu also lists lamb and vegetable dishes. Make sure you call ahead: Gaby often opens for anyone who reserves in advance, even if the place is theoretically closed. ✉ *Plaza Palacio 1, Hecho* ☎ *974/375007* *Reservations essential* *MC, V* *6 rooms* *No a/c* *Closed 1st 2 wks in Sept.; restaurant closed weekdays Sept.–Holy Week.*

¢–$ **Usón.** For a base to explore the upper Hecho Valley or the Oza Forest, look no further. This friendly little Pyrenean inn will rent you a bike, get you a trout-fishing permit, or send you off in the right direction for a climb or hike. ✉ *Ctra. Selva de Oza (HU2131), Km 7, Usón 22720* ☎ *974/375358* *14 rooms* *Restaurant, bicycles; no a/c* *MC, V* *Closed mid-Oct.–mid-Mar.*

en route

From Ansó, head west to Roncal on the difficult (narrow and winding) but panoramic 17½-km (11-mi) road through the Sierra de San Miguel. To enjoy this route fully, count on taking a good 45 minutes to reach the river Esca and the Valle de Roncal.

Roncal Valley

36 *17½ km (11 mi) west of Ansó Valley.*

The Roncal Valley, the eastern edge of the Basque Pyrenees, is famous for its sheep's-milk cheese, Ronkari, and as the birthplace of Julián Gayarre (1844–90), the leading tenor of his time. The 34-km (21-mi) drive through the towns of **Burgui** and **Roncal** to **Isaba** winds through green hillsides and Basque *caseríos* housing farmers and their livestock. Burgui's red-tile roofs backed by rolling pastures contrast with the vertical rock and steep slate roofs of the Aragonese and Catalan Pyrenees; Isaba's wide-arched bridge across the Esca is a graceful reminder of Roman aesthetics and engineering techniques. To get to the valley from Jaca, take N240 from Jaca west along the Aragón River; a right turn north on NA137 follows the Esca River from the head of the Yesa Reservoir up the Roncal Valley.

Try to be in the Roncal Valley for **El Tributo de las Tres Vacas** (the Tribute of the Three Cows), celebrated every July 13 since 1375. The mayors of the valley's villages, dressed in traditional gowns, gather near the summit of San Martín to receive the symbolic payment of three cows from their French counterparts, in memory of the settlement of ancient border disputes. Feasting and celebrating follow.

The road west (NA140) to **Ochagavia** through the Puerto de Lazar (Lazar Pass) has views of the Anie and Orhi peaks, towering over the French border. Two kilometers (1 mi) south of Ochagavia, at Escároz, a small secondary roadway winds 22 km (14 mi) over the Abaurrea heights to **Aribe,** known for its triple-arched medieval bridge and ancient *horreo* (granary). A 15-km (9-mi) detour north through the town of Orbaiceta up to the headwaters of the Irati River, at the Irabia Reservoir, gets you a good look at the **Selva de Irati** (Irati Forest), one of Europe's major beech forests and the source of much of the timber for the fleet Spain commanded during her 15th-century golden age.

Roncesvalles

★ 37 *2½ km (1½ mi) north of Burguete, 48 km (30 mi) north of Pamplona, 64 km (40 mi) northwest of Isaba in the Roncal Valley.*

Roncesvalles (Orreaga, in Euskera) is the site of the Colegiata, cloister, hospital, and 12th-century **chapel of Santiago,** the first Navarran church on the Santiago pilgrimage route. The **Colegiata** (Collegiate Church), built at the orders of King Sancho VII el Fuerte (the Strong), houses the king's tomb, which measures more than 7 ft long. The 3,468-ft **Ibañeta Pass,** above Roncesvalles, is one of the most beautiful routes into France. A stone **menhir** marks the traditional site of the legendary battle in *The Song of Roland* in which Roland fell after calling for help on his ivory battle horn. The well-marked eight-hour walk to or from St-Jean-Pied-de-Port is one of the most beautiful and dramatic sections of the entire pilgrimage.

Where to Stay & Eat

¢–$ **La Posada.** This 17th-century building with a heavy stone entry is an ancient way station for pilgrims bound for Santiago de Compostela. The accommodations are simple but far more comfortable than the pilgrims' quarters in the neighboring Colegiata. *Ctra. Pamplona–Francia (C135), Km 48, 31650 948/760225 948/760266 18 rooms Restaurant; no a/c AE, DC, MC, V Closed Nov.*

Burguete

38 *2½ km (1½ mi) south of Roncesvalles, 120 km (75 mi) northwest of Jaca.*

Burguete (Auritz in Euskera) lies between two mountain streams forming the headwaters of the Urobi River. The town was immortalized in Ernest Hemingway's *The Sun Also Rises* (1926), with its evocative description of trout fishing in an ice-cold stream above a moist Navarran village. Travelers to Burguete and Roncesvalles can feel securely bracketed between 11th-century French and 20th-century American literary classics.

Where to Stay & Eat

¢ **Hostal Burguete.** Hemingway's character Jake Barnes spent a few days here clearing his head in the cool streams of Navarra before plunging back into the psychodrama of the San Fermín festival and his impossible love for Lady Brett Ashley. The inn still works for this sort of thing, though there don't seem to be as many trout around these days. Good value and simple Navarran cooking make it a good place to stop for a meal or a night. *Calle Única 51, 31640 948/760005 948/790488 22 rooms Restaurant; no a/c MC, V Closed Feb.–Mar.*

en route

To skip Pamplona and stay on the trans-Pyrenean route, continue 21 km (13 mi) southwest of Burguete on NA135 until you reach NA138, just before Zubiri. A right turn takes you to Urtasun, where the small NA252 leads left to the town of Iragui and over the pass at Col d'Egozkue (from which there are superb views over the Arga and Ultzana River valleys) to Olagüe, where it connects with NA121 some 20 km (12 mi) north of Pamplona. Turn right onto N121A and climb over the Puerto de Velate (Velate Pass)—or, in bad weather or a hurry, through the tunnel—to the turn for Elizondo and the Baztán Valley, N121B.

Baztán Valley

39 *80 km (50 mi) north of Pamplona.*

Tucked neatly over the headwaters of the Bidasoa River and under the peak of the 3,545-ft Garramendi mountain, which looms over the border with France, the rounded green hills of the Valle de Baztán make an ideal halfway stop between the central Pyrenees and the Atlantic. Each village in this enchanted Basque valley seems smaller and simpler than the next: tiny clusters of whitewashed, stone-and-mortar houses with red-tile roofs grouped around a central *frontón* (handball court).

Where to Stay & Eat

★ $$ ✕ **Galarza.** The kitchen in this stone town house overlooking the Baztán River turns out excellent Basque fare, with a Navarran emphasis on vegetables. Try the *txuritabel* in season (roast lamb with a special stuffing of egg and vegetables) or *txuleta de ternera* (veal raised in the valley). ✉ *Calle Santiago 1, Elizondo* ☎ *948/580101* ▭ *MC, V* ⊙ *Closed late Sept.–early Oct.*

★ ¢–$ ✕🏨 **Fonda Etxeberria.** This tiny inn is an old farmhouse with creaky floorboards and oak doors. The rooms are small but handsome, and although they share baths, the bathrooms are palatial. The restaurant prepares simple country dishes such as *alubias de Navarra estofadas* (Navarran white beans stewed with chorizo) and roast lamb. ✉ *Next to frontón, Arizcun* ☎ *948/453013* 📠 *948/453433* *16 rooms without bath* *Restaurant; no a/c* ▭ *MC, V.*

Lesaka

40 *21 km (13 mi) west of Elizondo in the Baztán Valley, 71 km (43 mi) northwest of Pamplona.*

If you're around for Pamplona's festival of San Fermín (July 6–14), stop at Lesaka, just 2 km (1 mi) off the N121. Lesaka's patron saint is also San Fermín, and its *sanfermines txikos* (miniature San Fermín fests) may more closely resemble the one described in *The Sun Also Rises* than Pamplona's modern-day international beer brawl does.

off the beaten path

CABO HIGUER – Follow the Bidasoa River down through Vera de Bidasoa to Irún, Hondarribia (Fuenterrabía), and, for its symbolic value as well as the view out into the Atlantic, Cabo Higuer. This is the end of the road, one of two geographical bookends—Cap Creus, on the Mediterranean, is the other—of a complete trans-Pyrenean trek.

THE PYRENEES A TO Z

To research prices, get advice from other travelers, and book travel arrangements, visit www.fodors.com.

AIR TRAVEL

Barcelona's international airport, El Prat de Llobregat, is the largest gateway to the Catalan Pyrenees. Farther west, the airports at Zaragoza, Pamplona, and Hondarribia (Fuenterrabía) serve the Pyrenees of Aragón, Navarra, and the Basque Country. From Madrid, fly to Barcelona on Iberia's shuttle, or fly any of several airlines to Hondarribia or Pamplona.

CAR TRAVEL

Short of hiking, the only practical way to tour the Pyrenees is by car. The Collada de Toses (Tosses Pass) to Puigcerdà is the most difficult route into the Catalan Pyrenees, but it's free and the scenery is spectacular. Safer and faster, if more expensive and somewhat less scenic, is the E9 through the Tuñel del Cadí (Cadí Tunnel). Once you're there, most of the Cerdanya Valley's two-lane roads are wide and well paved. As you move west, roads can be more difficult to navigate, but the Eje Pirenaico (Pyrenean Axis), or N260, is a carefully engineered, safe trans-Pyrenean route. Many Pyrenean roads wind dramatically through mountain passes, so allow extra driving time no matter how well the road is paved. You can rent cars at airports at both ends of the Pyrenees.

EMERGENCIES

General emergency ☎ 091. **Red Cross** ☎ 972/216400 in Girona, 974/221186 in Huesca, 973/267011 in Lleida, 948/203540 in Navarra. **Police** ☎ 972/201381 in Girona, 974/244711 in Huesca, 973/245012 in Lleida, 948/237000 in Navarra.

SPORTS & THE OUTDOORS

Spain's daily newspaper, *El País,* prints complete ski information every Friday in season. For an up-to-the-minute ski report in Spanish or Catalan, call the ski-report hot line in Barcelona. For general information, contact the Catalan Winter Sports Federation. Jaca, Puigcerdà, and Vielha have excellent ice rinks with public skating sessions.

Federació Catalana Esports d'Hivern (Catalan Winter Sports Federation) ✉ Carrer Casp 38, Barcelona ☎ 93/415-5544. **Ski report** ☎ 93/416-0194.

FISHING Ramón Cosiallf and Danica can take you fly-fishing anywhere in the world by horse or helicopter, but the Pyrenees are their home turf. For about €85 a day (depending on equipment), you'll be whisked to high Pyrenean lakes and ponds, streams, and rivers and armed with equipment and expertise. You can buy a fishing license for each autonomous region (Catalonia, Aragón, Navarra) at local rod-and-gun clubs, known as Asociaciones de Pesca and/or Caza. You can pick up a license (€10) in Barcelona at ICONA on a weekday between 9 and 2. In Puigcerdà, licenses are available weekdays 9–2 at the office of Agricultura, Ramadería i Pesca.

Agricultura, Ramadería i Pesca ✉ Calle de la Percha 17, Puigcerdà ☎ 972/880515. **Danica** ☎ 659/735376 or 974/551378. **Agricultura, Ramadería i Pesca** ✉ Carrer Sabino de Arana 24, Barcelona ☎ 93/409-2090. **Departamento de Medio Ambiente** ✉ Travessera de Gràcia 56, Barcelona ☎ 93/444-5000.

HIKING *Excursionista* (outing) clubs, especially the regional club in Barcelona, can advise climbers and hikers.

Centro Excursionista de Catalunya ✉ Carrer Paradís 10, Barcelona ☎ 93/315-2311. **Guies de Muntanya** ☎ 973/626470 🌐 www.guiesdemuntanya.com. **Guies de Meranges** ☎ 93/825-7104. **Giroguies** ☎ 636/490830 🌐 www.giroguies.com. **Cercle d'Aventura** ☎ 972/881017.

TRAIN TRAVEL

There are three small train stations deep in the Pyrenees: Puigcerdà, in the Cerdanya Valley; Pobla de Segur, in the Noguera Pallaresa Valley; and Canfranc, north of Jaca, below the Candanchú and Astún ski resorts. The larger gateways are Huesca and Lleida. From Madrid, connect through Barcelona for the eastern Pyrenees, Zaragoza and Huesca for the central Pyrenees, and Pamplona or San Sebastián for the western Pyrenees.

RENFE ☎ 902/240202 🌐 www.renfe.es/ingles.

VISITOR INFORMATION

Regional Tourist Offices **Barcelona** ✉ Palau Robert, Passeig de Gràcia 107, at Av. Diagonal ☎ 93/238-4000. **Girona** ✉ Rambla de la Llibertat 1 ☎ 972/202679. **Huesca** ✉ Coso Alto 23 ☎ 974/225778. **Lleida** ✉ Plaça de la Paeria 11 ☎ 973/248120. **Navarra** ✉ Duque de Ahumada 3, Pamplona ☎ 948/211287. **Zaragoza (Aragón)** ✉ Torreon de la Zuda, Glorieta de Pío XII ☎ 976/393537.

Local Tourist Offices **Aínsa** ✉ Av. Pirenaica 1 ☎ 974/500767. **Benasque** ✉ Plaça Mayor 5 ☎ 974/551289. **Bielsa** ✉ Plaza del Ayuntamiento ☎ 974/501000. **Camprodón** ✉ Plaça Espanya 1 ☎ 972/740010. **Jaca** ✉ Avda. Rgto. Galicia ☎ 974/360098. **La Seu d'Urgell** ✉ Av. Valira s/n ☎ 973/351511. **Puigcerdà** ✉ Carrer Querol 1 ☎ 972/880542. **San Joan de les Abadesses** ✉ Plaça de la Abadía 9 ☎ 972/720599. **Taüll** ✉ Av. Valira s/n ☎ 973/694000. **Vielha** ✉ Av. Castiero 15 ☎ 973/641196.

BARCELONA & NORTHERN CATALONIA

6

FODOR'S CHOICE

Celler de Can Roca, restaurant in Girona
Claris, one of the top hotels in town, in Eixample
Colón, hotel overlooking cathedral in Barri Gòtic
Condes de Barcelona, popular hotel in Eixample
El Bullí, seaside restaurant in Girona
El Racó, one of Spain's best restaurants, in Sant Celoni
Jardí, chic budget hotel in Barri Gòtic
Majestic, stylish town house hotel in Eixample
Sagrada Família, Gaudí's landmark church in Eixample

HIGHLY RECOMMENDED

RESTAURANTS
Cal Pep, La Ribera
Cal Ros, Girona
Can Gaig, Eixample
Can Majó, Barceloneta
Casa Leopoldo, El Raval
Drolma, Eixample
Empordà, Figures
Sant Pau, Sant Pol de Mar
Tram-Tram, Sarrià

HOTELS
Rey Juan Carlos I, Diagonal
Ritz, Eixample

SIGHTS
Boqueria food market, Rambla
Casa Milà, Gaudí's undulating villa in Eixample
Catalonian National Museum of Art, Montjuïc
Miró Foundation art showcase in Montjuïc
Santa Maria del Mar, Gothic church in La Ribera

By George Semler

CAPITAL OF CATALONIA, 2,000-year-old Barcelona commanded a vast Mediterranean empire when Madrid was still a dusty Moorish outpost on the Spanish steppe. Relegated to second-city status only after Madrid became the seat of the royal court in 1561, Barcelona has long rivaled and often surpassed Madrid's supremacy. One of Europe's most visually stunning cities, Barcelona balances the medieval intimacy of its Gothic Quarter with the grace and distinction of the wide boulevards in the Moderniste Eixample—just as the Mediterranean Gothic elegance of the church of Santa Maria del Mar provides a perfect counterpoint to Gaudí's riotous Sagrada Família. Mies van der Rohe's pavilion seems even more minimalist after a look at the Art Nouveau Palau de la Música Catalana, while such exciting contemporary creations as Bofill's neoclassical, Parthenon-under-glass Teatre Nacional de Catalunya, Frank Gehry's waterfront goldfish, and Norman Foster's Torre de Collserola add spice to Barcelona's visual soup.

Barcelona has long had a frenetically active cultural life. Perhaps most famously, it was the home of architect Antoni Gaudí (1852–1926), whose buildings are the most startling statements of Modernisme. Other leading Moderniste architects include Lluís Domènech i Montaner and Josep Puig i Cadafalch. The painters Joan Miró (1893–1983), Salvador Dalí (1904–89), and Antoni Tàpies (born 1923) are also strongly identified with Catalonia. Pablo Picasso spent his formative years in Barcelona, and one of the city's treasures is a museum devoted to his works. Barcelona's opera house, the Liceu, is the finest in Spain; and the city claims native Catalan musicians such as cellist Pablo (Pau, in Catalan) Casals (1876–1973) and opera singers Montserrat Caballé and José (Josep) Carreras. Barcelona's fashion industry is hard on the heels of those of Paris and Milan, and FC (Futbol Club) Barcelona is arguably the world's most glamorous soccer club.

In 133 BC the Roman Empire annexed the city—even then a crossroads and trading hub—built by the Iberian tribe known as the Laietans, and founded a colony called Colonia Favencia Julia Augusta Paterna Barcino. The Visigoths roared down from the north in the 5th century; the Moors invaded in the 8th; and in 801 the Franks under Charlemagne captured the city and made it their buffer zone at the edge of the Moors' Iberian empire. By 988, the autonomous Catalonian counties had gained independence from the Franks. Not until 1137 was Catalonia united through marriage with the House of Aragón, while yet another marriage, that of Ferdinand II of Aragón and Isabella of Castile (who was also queen of León) in 1474, brought Aragón and Catalonia into a united Spain. As the capital of Aragón's Mediterranean empire, Barcelona grew powerful between the 12th and the 14th centuries and only began to falter when maritime emphasis shifted to the Atlantic after 1492. Despite the establishment of Madrid as the seat of Spain's Royal Court in 1561, Catalonia enjoyed autonomous rights and privileges until 1714, when, in reprisal for having backed the Austrian Habsburg pretender to the Spanish throne, all institutions and expressions of Catalan identity were suppressed by Felipe V of the French Bourbon dynasty. Not until the mid-19th century would Barcelona's industrial growth bring about a *Renaixença* (renaissance) of nationalism and a cultural flowering that recalled Catalonia's former opulence.

Catalan nationalism continued to gain strength in the early 20th century. After the abdication of Alfonso XIII and the establishment of the Spanish Republic in 1931, Catalonia enjoyed a high degree of autonomy and cultural freedom. Once again backing a losing cause, Barcelona was a Republican stronghold and a hotbed of anti-fascist sentiment during the 1936–39 Civil War, with the result that Catalan language and identity were suppressed under the 1939–1975 Franco regime by such means as book burning, the renaming of streets and towns, and the banning of the Catalan language in schools and in the media. This repression had little lasting effect, as the Catalans have jealously guarded their language and culture and generally think of themselves as Catalans first, Spaniards second.

Catalonian home rule was granted after Franco's death in 1975, and Catalonia's governing body, the ancient Generalitat, was reinstated in 1980. Catalan is now Barcelona's co-official language, along with Castilian Spanish, and is eagerly promoted through free classes funded by the Generalitat. Street names are signposted in Catalan, and newspapers, radio stations, and a TV channel publish and broadcast in Catalan. The triumphant culmination of this rebirth was, of course, the staging of the Olympics in 1992—stadiums and pools were renovated, new harborside promenades were created, and an entire set of train tracks was moved to make way for the Olympic Village. The Diagonal Mar community and the new skyscrapers going up at Plaça de les Glories and at the base of the breakwater on the far side of the port are part of the city's relentless drive for novelty and progress. The city is also once again poised to star on the world stage, as the host of the world's first Universal Forum of Cultures, in cooperation with UNESCO, in 2004. With the slogan "all the colors of the world," the forum is being planned as an intercultural meeting with discussion and debate and a World Arts festival. The main events will take place around Poble Nou and the Riu Besòs (Besòs River), an area which is currently being redeveloped into an "eco-park," a model of urban sustainability, with new conference centers, offices, and hotels.

EXPLORING BARCELONA

Barcelona is made up of four distinct areas. Between Plaça Catalunya and the port lies the Old City, or Ciutat Vella, including El Barri Gòtic (the Gothic Quarter), La Ribera (the waterfront), and El Raval, the slums or outskirts southwest of the Rambla. Above Plaça Catalunya is the grid-pattern expansion built after the city's third series of defensive walls were torn down in 1860. Known as the Eixample ("Widening"), this area contains most of Barcelona's Moderniste architecture. Farther north and west are the former outlying towns of Gràcia and Sarrià, the Pedralbes area, and, rising up behind the city to the northwest, the green hills of the Collserola nature reserve. Diagonal Mar, from Torre Agbar and Plaça de les Glòries east, is the new Barcelona built for the 2004 Forum de les Cultures.

Numbers in the margin correspond to points of interest on the neighborhood maps.

El Barri Gòtic & La Ribera

This walk explores Barcelona's Gothic Quarter and spills across Via Laietana into the Barri de la Ribera, where the Picasso Museum, Santa Maria del Mar, and El Born are the main visits. Parts of the Barri Gòtic and the Barri Xinès (or Barrio Chino), Barcelona's notorious red-light district, have been much improved over the last decade; you'll happen on squares freshly begotten by the demolition of whole blocks and the planting of palm trees. Nonetheless, bag-snatching is common in this part of town, so carry, if at all possible, nothing, while keeping your belongings secure and your wits about you. The Barri de la Ribera, once the

If you have **3 days**

Stroll the Rambla and the Boqueria; then cut over to the Catedral de la Seu. Detour through the Plaça del Rei before heading back to the Plaça Sant Jaume, where the Catalonian government, the Palau de la Generalitat, stands across the square from the *ajuntament* (city hall). From there it's a 10-minute walk to the Museu Picasso, from which another, even shorter stroll leads past the church of Santa Maria del Mar to Cal Pep, in Plaça de les Olles, for the best tapas in Barcelona. Try to catch an evening concert at the Palau de la Música Catalana. Day two might be a Gaudí day: spend the morning at the Temple Expiatori de la Sagrada Família, midday at Parc Güell, and the afternoon touring the Casa Milà, Casa Batlló, and Casa Lleó Morera, on Passeig de Gràcia, and the Palau Güell, off the lower Rambla. On day three, climb Montjuïc and take in the Museu Nacional d'Art de Catalunya, in the Palau Nacional. Investigate the Fundació Miró, Poble Espanyol, and Olympic facilities. Take the cable car across the port for a late paella at Can Manel la Puda in Barceloneta.

If you have **5 days**

Walk the Rambla, the Boqueria market, the Plaça del Pi, and the Barri Gòtic, including the Catedral de la Seu, on the first day. The next day, take a few hours to see the Museu Picasso and the church of Santa Maria del Mar. Walk through Barceloneta and down to Port Olímpic or out onto the *rompeolas* (breakwaters) and back. On the third morning you can explore the Raval, to the west of the Rambla, and visit the Museu d'Art Contemporani de Barcelona (MACBA) and the Centre de Cultura Contemporànea de Barcelona (CCCB) as well as the medieval Hospital de Sant Pau and Barcelona's oldest church, Sant Pau del Camp. If you have time, have a look at the Museu Marítim in the Drassanes Reials. In the afternoon you can take a guided tour of the Palau de la Música Catalana and pick up tickets to a concert. Devote your fourth day to Gaudí, the Temple Expiatori de la Sagrada Família in the morning and Parc Güell at midday. In the afternoon, walk down the Passeig de Gràcia to see the Casa Milà, Casa Batlló, and Casa Lleó Morera, in the heart of the city's grid-pattern Eixample, and the Palau Güell, off the Rambla. On day five, explore Montjuïc: visit the Museu Nacional d'Art de Catalunya, in the Palau Nacional; the Fundació Miró; the Poble Espanyol; and the Olympic facilities. In the afternoon, take the cable car across the port and have a paella outdoors at Can Manel la Puda in Barceloneta.

---

waterfront district, surrounds the basilica of Santa Maria del Mar and includes Carrer Montcada, Barcelona's poshest street in the 14th and 15th centuries. Much of the Barri de la Ribera was torn down in 1714 by the victorious Spanish and French army of Felipe V to create fields of fire for La Ciutadella fortress.

a good walk

A good walk through the Barri Gòtic could begin at **Catedral de la Seu** ❶ ⚑ and move through and around the cathedral to the **Museu Frederic Marès** ❷ (and its little terrace café, surrounded by Roman walls). Next, pass the patio of the Arxiu de la Corona d'Aragó (Archives of the House of Aragón); then turn left again and down into **Plaça del Rei** ❸. As you leave Plaça del Rei, the **Museu d'Història de la Ciutat** ❹ is on your left. Crossing Via Laietana, pass through the Plaça del Angel and walk down Carrer Princesa; this will take you to Carrer

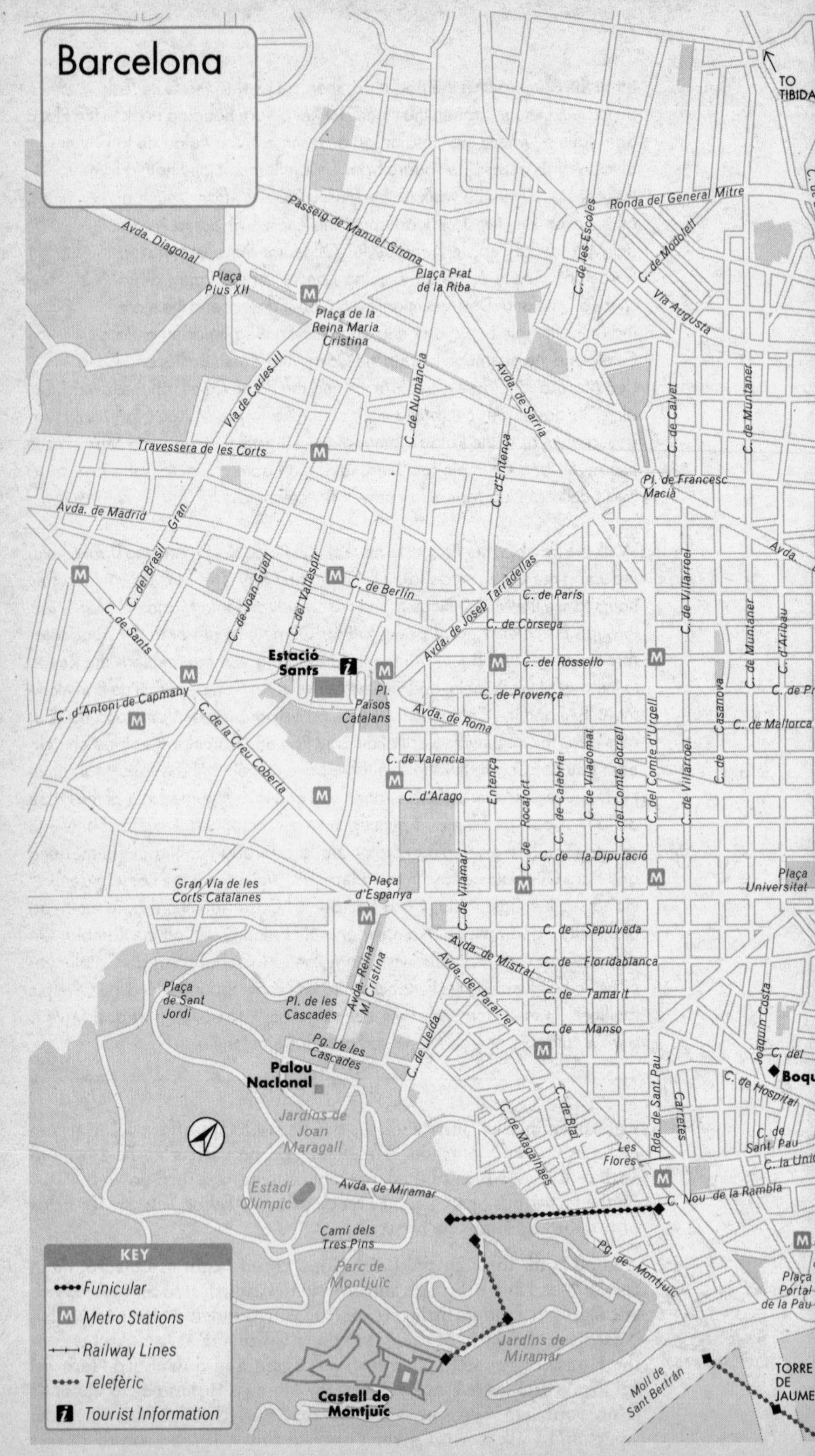
Barcelona
TO TIBIDA
Ronda del General Mitre
Passeig de Manuel Girona
Avda. Diagonal
Plaça Pius XII
Plaça Prat de la Riba
Plaça de la Reina Maria Cristina
C. de les Escoles
C. de Modolell
Via Augusta
Via de Carles III
C. de Numància
Avda. de Sarrià
C. de Calvet
C. de Muntaner
Travessera de les Corts
C. d'Entença
Pl. de Francesc Macià
Avda. de Madrid
Gran
C. del Brasil
C. de Joan Güell
C. del Vallespir
C. de Berlín
Avda. de Josep Tarradellas
C. de París
C. de Còrsega
C. de Villarroel
C. d'Aribau
C. de Sants
Estació Sants
C. del Rosselló
C. de Provença
C. d'Antoni de Capmany
Pl. Països Catalans
Avda. de Roma
C. de Mallorca
C. de la Creu Coberta
C. de Valencia
C. d'Arago
Entença
C. de Rocafort
C. de Calabria
C. de Viladomat
C. del Comte Borrell
C. del Comte d'Urgell
C. de Casanova
C. de la Diputació
Gran Vía de les Corts Catalanes
Plaça d'Espanya
C. de Vilamarí
Plaça Universitat
C. de Sepulveda
Avda. de Mistral
C. de Floridablanca
Avda. del Paral·lel
C. de Tamarit
Plaça de Sant Jordi
Pl. de les Cascades
Avda. Reina M. Cristina
C. de Manso
Pg. de les Cascades
C. de Lleida
Joaquín Costa
C. del
Palou Nacional
Boqu
C. de Hospital
C. de Blai
Rda. de Sant Pau
Carretes
C. de Magalhaes
C. de Sant Pau
Jardins de Joan Maragall
Les Flores
C. la Unió
Estadi Olímpic
Avda. de Miramar
C. Nou de la Rambla
Camí dels Tres Pins
Pg. de Montjuïc
Parc de Montjuïc
Plaça Portal de la Pau
Jardins de Miramar
Moll de Sant Bertrán
TORRE DE JAUME
Castell de Montjuïc
KEY
Funicular
Metro Stations
Railway Lines
Telefèric
Tourist Information

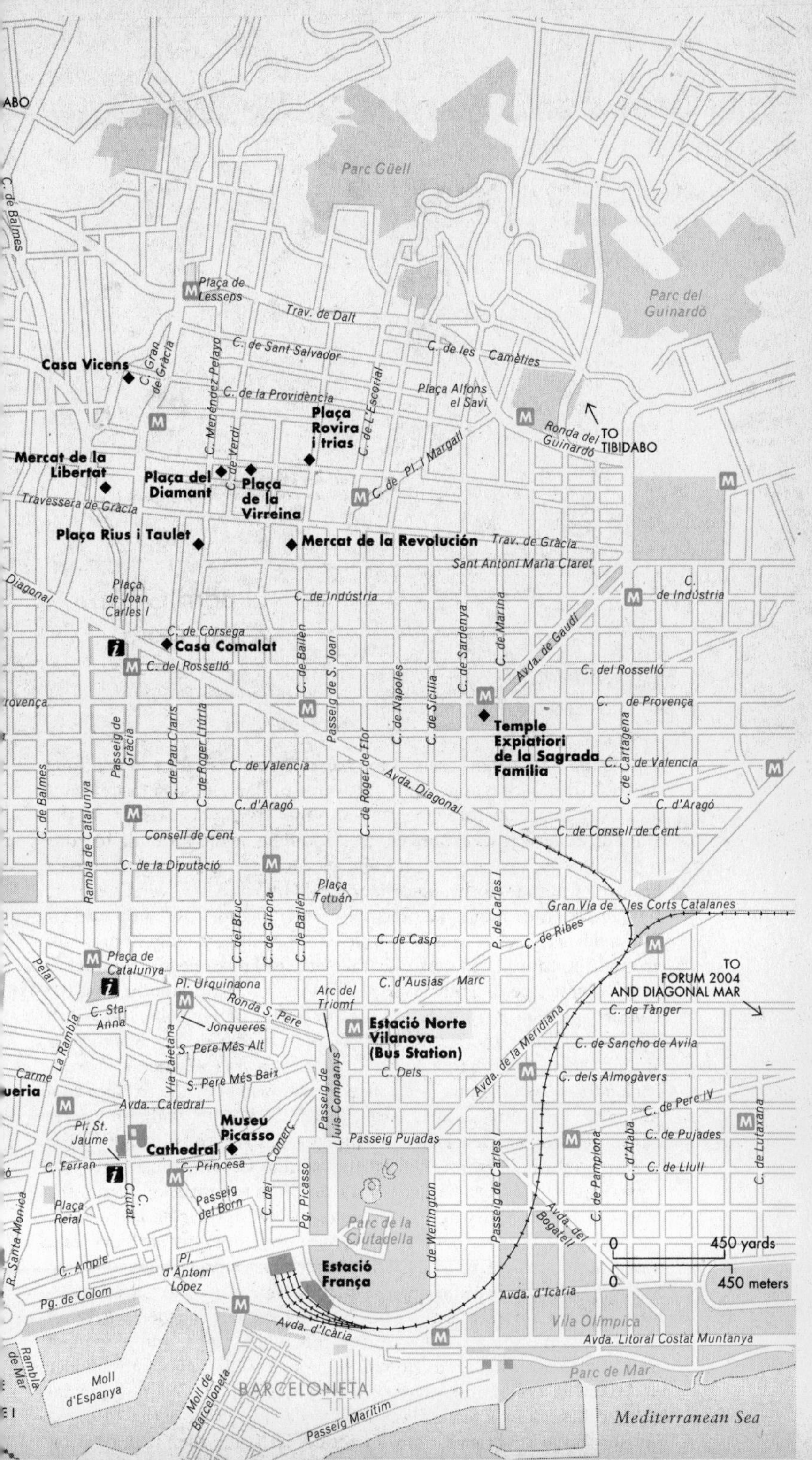
Parc Güell
Parc del Guinardó
Plaça de Lesseps
Trav. de Dalt
C. de Sant Salvador
C. de les Camèlies
Casa Vicens
C. Gran de Gràcia
C. Menéndez Pelayo
C. de la Providència
Plaça Alfons el Savi
Plaça Rovira i trias
C. de L'Escorial
Ronda del Guinardó
TO TIBIDABO
Mercat de la Libertat
Plaça del Diamant
Plaça de la Virreina
C. de Verdi
C. de Pl. i Margall
Travessera de Gràcia
Plaça Rius i Taulet
Mercat de la Revolución
Trav. de Gràcia
Sant Antoni Maria Claret
Diagonal
Plaça de Joan Carles I
C. de Indústria
C. de Còrsega
Casa Comalat
C. del Rosselló
C. de Bailén
Passeig de S. Joan
C. de Sardenya
C. de Marina
Avda. de Gaudí
C. de Napoles
C. de Sicilia
Temple Expiatiori de la Sagrada Família
C. de Provença
C. de Cartagena
C. de Valencia
Passeig de Gràcia
C. de Pau Claris
C. de Roger Llúria
C. de Roger de Flor
Avda. Diagonal
C. de Balmes
Rambla de Catalunya
C. d'Aragó
Consell de Cent
C. de Consell de Cent
C. de la Diputació
Plaça Tetuán
C. del Bruc
C. de Girona
P. de Carles I
Gran Via de les Corts Catalanes
C. de Ribes
C. de Casp
Plaça de Catalunya
Pelai
Pl. Urquinaona
C. d'Ausias Marc
TO FORUM 2004 AND DIAGONAL MAR
Arc del Triomf
C. de Tànger
Ronda S. Pere
C. Sta. Anna
Jonqueres
Estació Norte Vilanova (Bus Station)
La Rambla
Via Laietana
S. Pere Més Alt
C. de Sancho de Avila
Avda. de la Meridiana
S. Pere Més Baix
C. Dels
C. dels Almogàvers
Carme
Avda. Catedral
Passeig de Lluís Companys
C. de Pere IV
Museu Picasso
Pl. St. Jaume
Cathedral
C. Princesa
C. del Comerç
Passeig Pujadas
C. de Pujades
C. de Lutaxana
C. Ferran
C. Ciutat
C. d'Alaba
C. de Llull
C. de Pampiona
Plaça Reial
Passeig del Born
C. del
Pg. Picasso
Parc de la Ciutadella
C. de Wellington
Passeig de Carles I
Avda. del Bogatell
R. Santa Mònica
C. Ample
Pl. d'Antoni López
Estació França
0 450 yards
0 450 meters
Pg. de Colom
Avda. d'Icària
Vila Olímpica
Avda. Litoral Costat Muntanya
Rambla de Mar
Moll d'Espanya
Moll de Barceloneta
BARCELONETA
Parc de Mar
Passeig Marítim
Mediterranean Sea

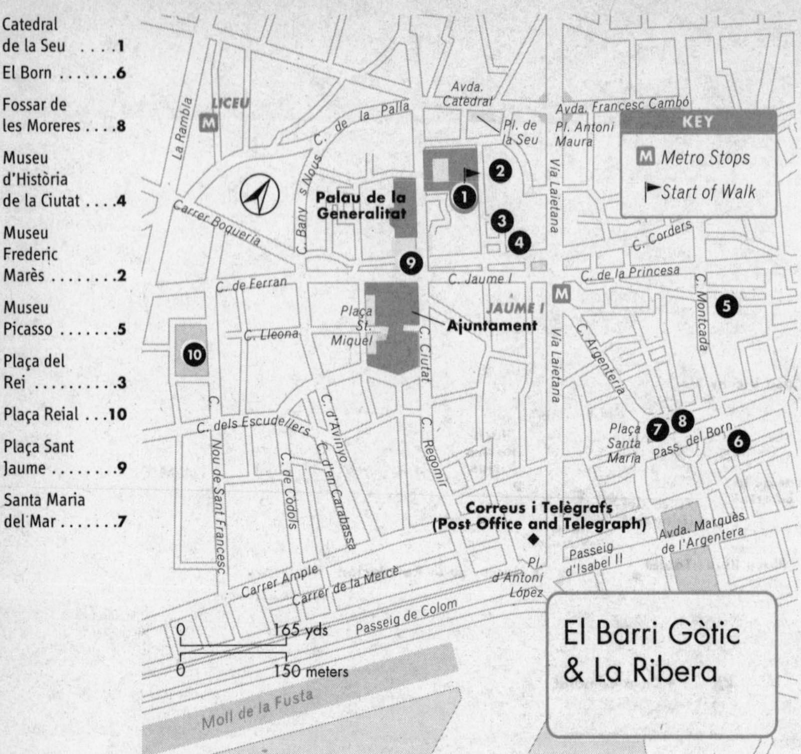

Montcada and a right turn to the **Museu Picasso** 5. As you continue down Carrer Montcada you'll pass some of Barcelona's most elegant medieval palaces before emerging into the Passeig del Born, with the giant steel hangar of **El Born** 6 itself looming at the far end. To your right is the back entrance of the church widely considered Barcelona's best, the Catalan Gothic **Santa Maria del Mar** 7. After spending some time inside (note that it's closed between 1:30 and 4:30), stop into La Vinya del Senyor, the excellent wine bar opposite the main door. Walk around the church's eastern side through the **Fossar de les Moreres** 8. On the west side of Santa Maria del Mar are Carrer Sombrerers, the Gispert spice shop, and the entrance to Carrer Banys Vells, lined with interesting shops and restaurants. Walk to the far end of Banys Vells and go left through Barra de Ferro and Cotoners to Princesa. A walk back across Via Laietana into Carrer Ferran will take you to **Plaça Sant Jaume** 9. From this square, once the Roman Forum, walk up Carrer Paradís (facing La Generalitat it's the second street to your right), take a sharp right and have a look at the **Roman Columns** inside the entryway at Carrer Paradís 10. For a tour of Barcelona's *call* (from the Hebrew *qahal,* "meeting"), the medieval Jewish quarter, leave Plaça Sant Jaume on Carrer del Call, turn right on Sant Domènech del Call, and proceed to the next corner. Early Barcelona's **Sinagoga Major** (Main Synagogue), restored and opened in 2002, opens up into Carrer Marlet across the intersection to your left. On the next corner, where on the right you'll see a stone with Hebrew inscriptions, and a Spanish translation on a plaque, Arc de Sant Ramón del Call is another reminder of the Jewish community that prospered here until a 1391 pogrom destroyed Barcelona's Jewish community a century before the 1492 expulsion. Take a left here, onto Carrer del Call, and then turn right on Carrer Ferran to reach the neoclassical **Plaça Reial** 10.

TIMING This walk covers some 3 km (2 mi) and should take about three hours, depending on stops. Allow another hour for the Picasso Museum.

What to See

1 **Catedral de la Seu.** On Saturday afternoons, Sunday mornings, and occasional evenings, Barcelona folk gather in the Plaça de la Seu to dance the *sardana,* a somewhat demure circular dance and a great symbol of Catalan identity. The Gothic cathedral was built between 1298 and 1450, with the spire and neo-Gothic facade added in 1892. Architects of Catalan Gothic churches strove to make the high altar visible to the entire congregation, hence the unusually wide central nave and slender side columns. The first thing you see upon entering are the high relief sculptures on the choir stalls, telling the story of **Santa Eulàlia** (Barcelona's co-patron along with La Mercé, Our Lady of Mercy). The first scene, on the left, shows St. Eulàlia in front of Roman Consul Decius with her left hand on her heart and her right hand pointing at a cross in the distance. In the next scene, Eulàlia is tied to a column and flagellated by Decius's thugs. To the right of the choir entrance, the senseless Eulàlia is hauled away, and in the final scene she is lashed to the X-shape cross upon which she was crucified in the year 303. To the right of this high relief is a sculpture of St. Eulàlia, standing with her emblematic cross, resurrected as a living saint. Other highlights are the beautifully carved choir stalls; St. Eulàlia's tomb in the crypt; and the battle-scarred crucifix (used as a bowsprit in the famous 1571 naval showdown between the Christian and Turkish fleets at Lepanto) in the Lepanto Chapel. The tall cloisters surround a tropical garden, and outside, at the building's front right corner, is the intimate Santa Llúcia chapel. The cathedral is floodlit in striking yellows at night, and the stained-glass windows are backlit. ✉ *Pl. de la Seu, Barri Gòtic* ☎ *93/315–2213* ⏲ *Daily 7:45–1:30 and 4–7:45.*

6 **El Born.** Once the site of medieval jousts, the Passeig del Born is at the end of Carrer Montcada behind the church of Santa Maria del Mar. The numbered cannon balls under the benches are by the late Joan Brossa "poet of space" in memory of the 1714 siege of Barcelona that concluded the 14-year War of the Spanish Succession. The Bourbon forces obliged local residents to tear down over 900 of their own houses, some 20% of the city, to create fields of fire for the army of Felipe V. Walk down to the Born itself—a great iron hangar, once the city's main produce market designed by Josep Fontseré. Construction of a public library in the Born uncovered the perfectly preserved lost city of 1714, complete with blackened fireplaces, taverns, wells, and the canal that brought water into the city. The area is set to become an archaeological museum, part of the Museu de Història de la Ciutat, in 2004. You'll be able to stroll along a walkway over the ruins of the 14th- to 18th-century Barri de la Ribera. ✉ *Carrer Montcada, La Ribera.*

8 **Fossar de les Moreres** (Cemetery of the Mulberry Trees). This low marble monument is on the eastern side of the church of Santa Maria del Mar, honoring the defenders of Barcelona who gave their lives in the 1714 siege that ended the War of the Spanish Succession and established Felipe V on the Spanish throne. The inscription (EN EL FOSSAR DE LES MORERES NO S'HI ENTERRA CAP TRAIDOR, or IN THE CEMETERY OF THE MULBERRY TREES NO TRAITOR LIES) refers to the story of the graveyard keeper who refused to bury those who had fought on the invading side, even when one of them turned out to be his son. The torch-sculpture over the marble monument, often referred to as a *pebetero* (Bunson burner), was erected in 2002. ✉ *Fossar de les Moreres, La Ribera.*

4 **Museu d'Història de la Ciutat** (City History Museum). Just off the Plaça del Rei, this fascinating museum traces the evolution of Barcelona from its first Iberian settlement to its founding by the Carthaginian Hamilcar Barca in about 230 BC to Roman and Visigothic times and beyond. Antiquity is the focus here: Romans took the city during the Punic Wars, and the striking underground remains of their Colonia Iulia Favencia Paterna Barcino, through which you can roam on metal walkways, are the museum's main treasure. Archaeological finds include parts of walls, fluted columns, and recovered busts and vases. Above ground, off the Plaça del Rei, the **Palau Reial Major,** the splendid **Saló del Tinell,** the chapel of **Santa Àgata,** and the **Torre del Rei Martí,** a lookout tower with views over the Barri Gòtic, complete the self-guided tour. ✉ *Palau Padellàs, Carrer del Veguer 2, Barri Gòtic* ☎ *93/315–1111* 🎫 *€4* ⏲ *Tues.–Sat. 10–2 and 4–8, Sun. 10–2.*

off the beaten path

MUSEU DEL CALÇAT – Hunt down the tiny Shoe Museum, between the cathedral and Carrer Banys Nous. The collection includes a pair of clown's shoes and a pair worn by Pablo Casals. The tiny square, originally a graveyard, is just as interesting as the museum, with its bullet- and shrapnel-pocked walls and quiet fountain. ✉ *Pl. de Sant Felip Neri, Barri Gòtic* ☎ *93/301–4533* 🎫 *€2* ⏲ *Tues.–Sun. 11–2.*

2 **Museu Frederic Marès** (Frederic Marès Museum). Off the left (north) side of the Catedral de la Seu, you can browse for hours among the miscellany assembled by the early 20th-century sculptor-collector Frederic Marès. Everything from paintings and polychrome wood carvings, such as Juan de Juní's 1537 masterpiece *Pietà* and the Master of Cabestany's late-12th-century *Apparition of Christ to his Disciples at Sea,* to Marès's collection of pipes and walking sticks is stuffed into this rich potpourri. ✉ *Pl. Sant Iu 5, Barri Gòtic* ☎ *93/310–5800* 🎫 *€3* ⏲ *Tues.–Wed. and Fri.–Sat. 10–7, Thurs. 10–5, Sun. 10–3.*

5 **Museu Picasso.** The Picasso Museum is across Via Laietana, down Carrer de la Princesa, and right on Carrer Montcada—a street known for Barcelona's most elegant medieval palaces, of which the museum occupies two. Picasso spent several of his formative years in Barcelona (1901–06), and this collection, while not one of the world's best, is particularly strong on his early work. Displays include childhood sketches, pictures from the beautiful Rose and Blue periods, and the famous 1950s Cubist variations on Velázquez's *Las Meninas.* ✉ *Carrer Montcada 15–19, La Ribera* ☎ *93/319–6310* 🎫 *€5, free 1st Sun. of month* ⏲ *Tues.–Sat. 10–8, Sun. 10–3.*

3 **Plaça del Rei.** Long held to be the scene of Columbus's triumphal return from his first voyage to the New World—Ferdinand and Isabella purportedly received him on the stairs fanning out from the corner, though the whole story may be apocryphal—the **Palau Reial Major** was the Catholic Monarchs' official residence in Barcelona. Its main room is the **Saló del Tinell,** a banquet hall built in 1362. Also around the square: the dark 15th-century **Torre Mirador del Rei Martí** (King Martin's Watchtower), above the Saló del Tinell; to the left, the **Palau del Lloctinent** (Lieutenant's Palace); the 14th-century **Capilla Reial de Santa Àgueda** (Royal Chapel of Saint Agatha), to the right of the stairway; and the **Palau Clariana-Padellàs** (Clariana-Padellàs Palace), moved here stone by stone from Carrer Mercaders in the early 20th century and now the entrance to the Museu d'Història de la Ciutat. The hulking bronze sculpture by Eduardo Chillida, the tiny shrine to St. Agatha behind glass above a 1638 shield emblazoned with the Barcelona coat of arms, and,

PICASSO'S BARCELONA

BARCELONA'S CLAIM to Pablo Picasso (1881–1973) has been contested by Málaga, the painter's birthplace, as well as by Madrid, where La Guernica hangs, and even by the town of Guernica itself, victim of the 1937 Luftwaffe saturation bombing that inspired the famous canvas. Picasso, a staunch anti-Franco opponent after the war, refused to return to Franco's Spain. In turn, the Franco regime allowed no public Picasso work until 1961, when the artist's Sardana frieze at Barcelona's Architects' Guild was unveiled. Picasso never set foot on Spanish soil for the last 39 years of his life.

Picasso spent a sporadic but formative period of his youth in Barcelona between 1895 and 1904, when he moved to Paris to join the fertile art scene in the French capital. Picasso's father had been appointed art professor at the Reial Acadèmia de les Belles Arts in La Llotja. Picasso, a precocious draftsman, began advanced classes in the academy at the age of 15. Working in different studios between academic stints in Madrid, the 19-year-old Picasso first exhibited at Els Quatre Gats, a tavern still thriving on Carrer Montsió. Much intrigued with the Bohemian life of Barcelona's popular neighborhoods, Picasso's early Cubist painting, Les Demoiselles d'Avignon, *was inspired not by the French town but by the Barcelona street Carrer d'Avinyó, then known for its brothel. After his move to Paris, Picasso returned occasionally to Barcelona until his last visit in summer of 1934.*

Considering Picasso's off-and-on tenure in Barcelona, followed by a 36- year residence in Paris and a 39-year self-imposed exile, it is remarkable that Barcelona and Picasso should be so intertwined in the world's perception of the city. The Picasso Museum, while an excellent visit, is only the fourth most important art venue on any art connoisseur's list of Barcelona galleries. The Museum was the brainchild of the artist's longtime friend Jaume Sabartés, who believed that his vast private collection of Picasso works should be made public. After much wrangling with the Franco regime, loathe to publically recognize such a prominent anti-Franco figure, author of a work entitled The Dream and the Lie of Franco *(1937), the Picasso Museum finally opened in 1963. Spread through three Renaissance palaces, the collection's best works are Picasso's childhood drawings made in La Coruña between the ages of 10 and 14, his early portraits such as the 1897* Science and Charity, *his 1901–1904 Blue Period paintings including* Terrats de Barcelona *(1902), and his 44 cubist Las Meninas studies.*

***Iconoserveis Culturals** (✉ C. Muntaner 185 Eixample ☎ 93/410–1405 🌐 www.iconoserveis.com) gives walking tours through the key spots in Picasso's Barcelona life, covering studios, galleries, taverns, Picasso family apartments, and the painter's favorite haunts and hangouts.*

if you're lucky, classical guitar on a quiet afternoon, can all add up to a freeze-frame Barcelona moment.

⑩ **Plaça Reial.** A symmetrical 19th-century arcaded square, the Plaça Reial is bordered by elegant ocher facades with balconies overlooking the wrought-iron **Fountain of the Three Graces** and some lampposts designed by Gaudí in 1879. Restaurants and sidewalk cafés, identifiable as tourist traps by the photo-menus (the only good ones are the Taxidermista and Club 13), line the square. On Sunday morning crowds gather to sell and trade stamps and coins; after dark the square is a center of downtown student nightlife.

⑨ **Plaça Sant Jaume.** This central square behind the Catedral de la Seu houses both Catalonia's and Barcelona's governments and was the site of the Roman forum 2,000 years ago. The Plaça was cleared in the 1840s, but the two imposing buildings facing each other across it are much older. The 15th-century ***ajuntament*** (city hall) has an impressive black-and-burnished-gold mural (1928) by Josep Maria Sert and the famous Saló de Cent, from which the Council of One Hundred ruled Barcelona between 1372 and 1714. Filled with art, the ajuntament is open to the public on Sunday mornings and on special holidays. During the week, check listings for free concerts or events here. The **Palau de la Generalitat,** seat of the Catalan government, is a majestic 15th-century palace—through the front windows you can see the gilded ceiling of the Saló de Sant Jordi (St. George), named for Catalonia's dragon-slaying patron saint. Normally you can visit the Generalitat only on certain holidays, such as the Día de Sant Jordi (St. George's Day), April 23; check with the *protocolo* (protocol office). The Generalitat hosts carillon concerts on occasional Sundays at noon. ⏲ *Ajuntament: Sun. 10–1:30.*

★ 7 **Santa Maria del Mar.** The most elegant of all Barcelona's churches is on the Carrer Montcada end of Passeig del Born. Simple and spacious, it's something of an oddity in ornate and complex Moderniste Barcelona. The church was built from 1329 to 1383 in fulfillment of a vow made a century earlier by Jaume I to build a church for the Virgin of the Sailors. Its stark beauty is enhanced by a lovely rose window, soaring columns, and unusually wide vaulting. It's considered the finest existing example of Catalan (or Mediterranean) Gothic architecture. ✉ *Pl. de Santa Maria, La Ribera* ⏲ *Weekdays 9–1:30 and 4:30–8.*

The Rambla & the Raval

Barcelona's best-known promenade is a constant and colorful flood of humanity past flower stalls, bird vendors, mimes, musicians, newspaper kiosks, and outdoor cafés. Federico García Lorca called this street the only one in the world that he wished would never end; traffic plays second fiddle to the endless *paseo* (stroll) of locals and travelers alike. The whole avenue is referred to as Las Ramblas (Les Rambles, in Catalan) or La Rambla, but each section has its own name: Rambla Santa Monica is at the southeastern, or port, end; Rambla de les Flors in the middle; and Rambla dels Estudis at the top, near Plaça de Catalunya. El Raval is the area to the west of the Rambla, originally a slum outside Barcelona's second set of walls which ran down the left side of the Rambla. Alas, Rambla-happy tourists are tempting prey for pickpockets, scam artists, and thieves. Do NOT play the notorious shell game, dress conservatively, keep maps and guidebooks hidden, conceal cameras, and leave wallets and passports in your hotel safe. A credit card and a little cash are all you need.

a good walk

Start on the Rambla opposite the Plaça Reial and wander down toward the sea, to the **Monument a Colom** 11 and the Rambla de Mar. From here you might make a brief probe into the unprepossessing modern **Port** 12. As you move back to the Columbus monument, investigate the **Museu Marítim** 13 and its medieval Drassanes Reials shipyards. Gaudí's **Palau Güell** 14 on Carrer Nou de la Rambla is the next stop before the **Gran Teatre del Liceu** 15, and along the way take a peek at Barcelona's red-light district, the **Barri Xinès** 16. At the Miró mosaic at Pla de la Boqueria, cut right to the Plaça del Pi and the church of **Santa Maria del Pi** 17. Back on the Rambla, take in the facade and perhaps some savories at **Antigua Casa Figueres** 18, stroll through the **Boqueria** 19 food market and the **Palau de la Virreina** 20 exhibition center next door, and then cut around to the courtyards of the medieval **Antic Hospital de la Santa Creu** 21. Next, visit the **Museu d'Art Contemporani de Barcelona**

CATALONIA'S NATIONAL DANCE

AS THE POPULAR JIBE GOES, Catalans are such penny pinchers they count even while they dance. True enough, but the real reason for the serious expressions and the counting is the mathematical intricacy and precision of a dance that comes in four sets of nineteen steps, each of which needs to be carefully accounted for. Dainty, subdued, and magical, the Sardana is everything the athletic Aragonese jota is not.

Said to be an allegorical reference to the passing of time, a metaphor for the revolutions of the moon and stars, the Sardana is a circular dance chronicled by Greek historian Strabo (63 BC–21 AD), who recorded Iberian peoples of northwestern Spain paying homage to the full moon with dances in the round. The Llibre Vermell (Red Book), Catalonia's medieval songbook, recorded pilgrims on the way to Montserrat performing "the round dance" in the 14th century. The name of the dance may come from the 14th-century Catalan colony on the Mediterranean island of Sardinia, though the long-used alternate spelling Cerdana suggests that it may have originated in the Pyrenean Cerdanya valley.

Popularized by the legendary tenora *(oboe) master and composer Pep Ventura after his debut in 1837, the sardana is danced in small or large circles of dancers young and old, hand in hand, arms upraised. The* cobla *(Sardana combo) is composed of five wind instruments, five brass, and the director, who plays a three-holed flute called the* flabiol *and a small drum, the* tabal*. Whether in local fiestas, village squares, or in Barcelona in front of the cathedral Sunday midday or in Plaça Sant Jaume Sunday evenings, the Sardana, for the observant spectator, creates strong emotion, the dancers rapt in concentration, lost in tradition.*

(MACBA) 22 and the **Centre de Cultura Contemporànea de Barcelona** (CCCB) 23, on Carrer Montalegre, before returning to the Rambla. Finish your walk along Carrer Tallers, ending up in **Plaça de Catalunya** 24.

TIMING This walk covers 3 km (2 mi). With stops, allow three hours.

What to See

21 **Antic Hospital de la Santa Creu.** Surrounded by a cluster of other 15th-century buildings, this medieval hospital now has several libraries and cultural and educational institutions. Approach it from the back door of the Boqueria or from either Carrer del Carme or Carrer Hospital. Particularly lovely is the courtyard of the Casa de Convalescència, with its Renaissance columns and, in the entryway, the scenes of the life of St. Paul portrayed in *azulejos* (painted ceramic tiles). Check out the second-floor garden behind the clock dedicated to Catalan novelist Mercé Rodoreda. In the Carrer Hospital side, on the corner nearest the Rambla, is **La Capella,** once the hospital chapel and now a gallery of contemporary art. ✉ *Carrer Hospital 54 and Carrer del Carme 45, Rambla* ⏲ *Casa de Convalescència bookstore weekdays 9–2 and 3–6.*

18 **Antigua Casa Figueres.** This Moderniste café, grocery, and pastry store on the corner of Petxina has a splendid mosaic facade and exquisite Art Nouveau fittings. ✉ *Rambla 83, Rambla* ☎ *93/301–6027* ⏲ *Daily 8:30 AM–9 PM.*

16 **Barri Xinès.** As you walk from Plaça Reial toward the sea, Barcelona's red-light district, the Barri Xinès (traditionally called the Barrio Chino in Castilian Spanish), is on your right. China had nothing to do with this; the name is a generic reference to foreigners of all kinds. The area is ill famed for prostitutes, drug pushers, and street thieves, but it's not

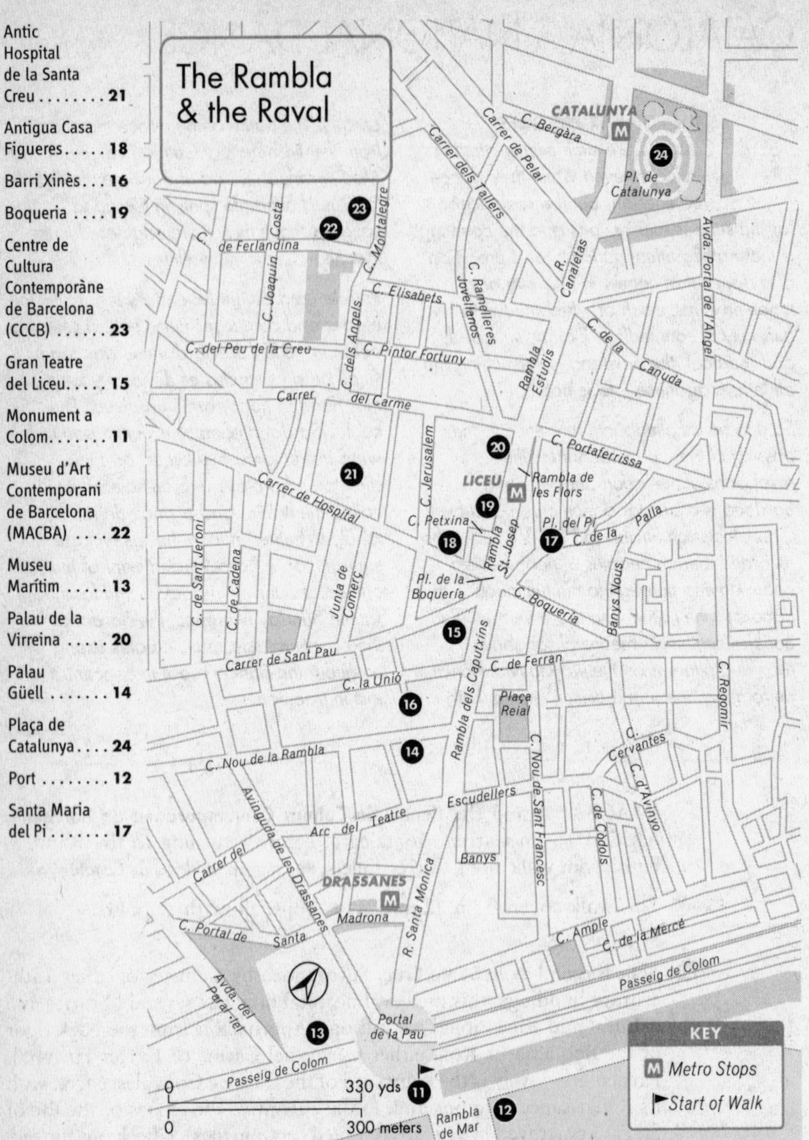

as dangerous as it looks; the reinforced police presence here may make it safer than other parts of the Gothic Quarter.

★ 19 **Boqueria.** Barcelona's most spectacular food market, also known as the Mercat de Sant Josep, is an explosion of life and color sprinkled with delicious little bar-restaurants. **Pinotxo** has long been a sanctuary for food lovers; **El Kiosco Universal** and **Quim de la Boqueria** are hot on its heels. Don't miss mushroom supplier, expert, and author Petràs and his mad display of wild 'shrooms, herbs, nuts, and berries (*Fruits del Bosc*—Fruits of the Forest) at the very back. The Doric columns around the market's perimeter were part of the original square completed in 1840 by Francesc Daniel i Molina, architect of the also neoclassical Plaça Reial. ✉ *Rambla 91, Rambla.*

23 **Centre de Cultura Contemporània de Barcelona** (CCCB). In the renovated Casa de la Caritat, a former medieval convent and hospital, the CCCB, a combination museum, lecture hall, and concert hall, now has a reflecting wall, in which you can see over the rooftops to Montjuïc and beyond. ⊠ *Montalegre 5, Rambla* ☎ *93/412–0781* 🎫 *€4* ⏲ *Tues.–Fri. 11–2 and 4–8, Wed. and Sat. 11–8, Sun. 10–3.*

15 **Gran Teatre del Liceu.** Along with Milan's La Scala, Barcelona's opera house has long been considered one of the most beautiful in Europe. First built in 1848, this cherished landmark was torched in 1861, bombed in 1893, and once again gutted by a blaze of mysterious origins in early 1994. Barcelona's soprano Montserrat Caballé stood on the Rambla in tears as her beloved venue was consumed. Five years later, a restored and renewed Liceu, equipped for modern productions, opened anew. Even if you don't see an opera, don't miss a tour of the building; some of the Liceu's oldest and most spectacular rooms were untouched by the fire, including those of Spain's oldest social club, El Círculo del Liceu. The downstairs Espai Liceu provides the city with daily cultural and commercial interaction with its opera house. With a cafeteria; a shop specializing in opera-related gifts, books, and recordings; an intimate 50-person-capacity circular concert hall; and a Mediateca with recordings and films of past opera productions, Espai Liceu is the final step in the Barcelona opera's Phoenix-like resurrection. ⊠ *La Rambla 51–59, Rambla* ☎ *93/485–9900* ⊕ *www.liceubarcelona.com* 🎫 *Guided tours €4* ⏲ *Daily at 10 AM.*

11 **Monument a Colom** (Columbus Monument). At the foot of the Rambla, take an elevator to the top of this monument for a bird's-eye view over the city. (The entrance is on the harbor side.) ⊠ *Portal de la Pau s/n, Rambla* ☎ *93/302–5224* 🎫 *€3* ⏲ *Weekdays 10–1:30 and 3–6:30, weekends 10–6:30.*

22 **Museu d'Art Contemporani de Barcelona** (Barcelona Museum of Contemporary Art; MACBA). Designed by American architect Richard Meier, this 1992 building's 20th-century masters include Calder, Rauschenberg, Oteiza, Chillida, and Tàpies. The optional guided tour is excellent. ⊠ *Pl. dels Àngels, Rambla* ☎ *93/412–0810* ⊕ *www.macba.es* 🎫 *€6* ⏲ *Weekdays 11–7, Sat. 10–8, Sun. 10–3.*

13 **Museu Marítim.** The superb Maritime Museum is in the 13th-century **Drassanes Reials** (Royal Shipyards), to the right at the foot of the Rambla. This vast medieval space seems more like a cathedral than a boatyard and is filled with ships, including a life-size reconstructed galley, figureheads, and early navigational charts. Take the self-guided tour. ⊠ *Pl. Portal de la Pau 1, Rambla* ☎ *93/342–9920* 🎫 *€5.50, free 1st Sat. of month after 3 PM* ⏲ *Daily 10–7.*

20 **Palau de la Virreina.** The neoclassical Virreina Palace, built by a viceroy to Peru in 1778, is now an exhibition center for paintings, photography, and historical items. The building also has a bookstore and a municipal tourist office. ⊠ *Rambla de les Flors 99, Rambla* ☎ *93/301–7775* ⏲ *Tues.–Sat. 10–2 and 4:30–9, Sun. 10–2, Mon. 4:30–9.*

14 **Palau Güell.** Antoni Gaudí built this mansion during the years 1886–89 for his patron, a textile baron named Count Eusebi de Güell, and soon found himself in the international limelight. The prominent Catalan emblem between the parabolic entrance gates attests to the nationalist leanings that Gaudí shared with Güell. The dark facade is a dramatic foil for the treasure house inside, where spear-shape Art Nouveau columns frame the windows and prop up a series of minutely detailed wood ceilings. Gaudí is most himself on the roof, where his playful, poly-

chrome ceramic chimneys fit right in with later works such as Parc Güell and La Pedrera. Tours are guided. ✉ *Nou de la Rambla 3–5, Rambla* ☎ *93/317–3974* 🎫 *€3* ⏲ *Weekdays 10–2 and 4–7:30.*

24 **Plaça de Catalunya.** Barcelona's main transport hub, the Plaça de Catalunya is the frontier between the old city and the post-1860 Eixample. Café Zurich, at the head of the Rambla and the mouth of the Metro, is a classic rendezvous point. The block behind the Zurich, known as El Triangle, is a strip of megastores.

12 **Port.** Beyond the Columbus Monument—behind the Duana, or former customs building, now site of the Barcelona Port Authority—is the **Rambla de Mar,** a boardwalk with a drawbridge. The Rambla de Mar extends out to the **Moll d'Espanya,** with its Maremagnum shopping center, IMAX theater, and aquarium. Next to the Duana, you can board a Golondrina boat for a tour of the port or, from the Moll de Barcelona on the right, take a cable car to Montjuïc or Barceloneta. Take a boat to the end of the *rompeolas,* 3 km (2 mi) out to sea, and walk back into Barceloneta. Trasmediterránea ferries leave for Italy and the Balearic Islands from the Moll de Barcelona, down to the right. At the end of the quay is Barcelona's World Trade Center.

17 **Santa Maria del Pi** (St. Mary of the Pine). Like Santa Maria del Mar, the church of Santa Maria del Pi is a fine example of Mediterranean Gothic architecture. Its gigantic rose window is the best in Barcelona. The adjoining squares, **Plaça del Pi** and **Plaça de Sant Josep Oriol,** are two of the liveliest, most appealing spaces in the Gothic Quarter. ✉ *Pl. del Pi s/n, Rambla* ☎ *93/318–4743* ⏲ *Daily 9–1:30 and 4:30–8.*

The Moderniste Eixample

North of Plaça de Catalunya is the checkerboard known as the Eixample. With the dismantling of the city walls in 1860, Barcelona embarked upon an expansion scheme fueled by the return of rich colonials, by an influx of provincial aristocrats who had sold their country estates after the debilitating second Carlist War (1847–49), and by the city's growing industrial power. The street grid was the work of urban planner Ildefons Cerdà; much of the building here was done at the height of modernisme. The Eixample's principal thoroughfares are Rambla de Catalunya and Passeig de Gràcia, where the city's most elegant shops vie for space among its best Art Nouveau buildings.

A Good Tour

Starting in the Plaça de Catalunya, walk up Passeig de Gràcia until you reach the corner of Consell de Cent. Enter the Bermuda Triangle of Moderniste architecture, the **Manzana de la Discòrdia** 25 ⚑. The **Casa Montaner i Simó–Fundació Tàpies** 26 is around the corner on Carrer Aragó. Gaudí's **Casa Milà** 27, known as La Pedrera, is three blocks farther up Passeig de Gràcia; after touring the interior and rooftop, walk up Passeig de Gràcia to Vinçon for a look through one of Barcelona's top design stores, with views into the back of Casa Milà. Just around the corner, at Diagonal 373, is Puig i Cadafalch's intricately sculpted **Casa Quadras** 28, and two minutes farther is his Nordic castlelike **Casa de les Punxes** 29 at No. 416–420. From here it's a 10-minute hike to yet another Puig i Cadafalch masterpiece, **Casa Macaia** 30, home of the culturally hyperactive Fundació la Caixa. Finally, take a taxi to Gaudí's emblematic **Temple Expiatori de la Sagrada Família** 31. If you've energy to burn, stroll over to Domènech i Montaner's **Hospital de Sant Pau** 32.

TIMING Depending on how many taxis you take, this is a four- to five-hour tour.

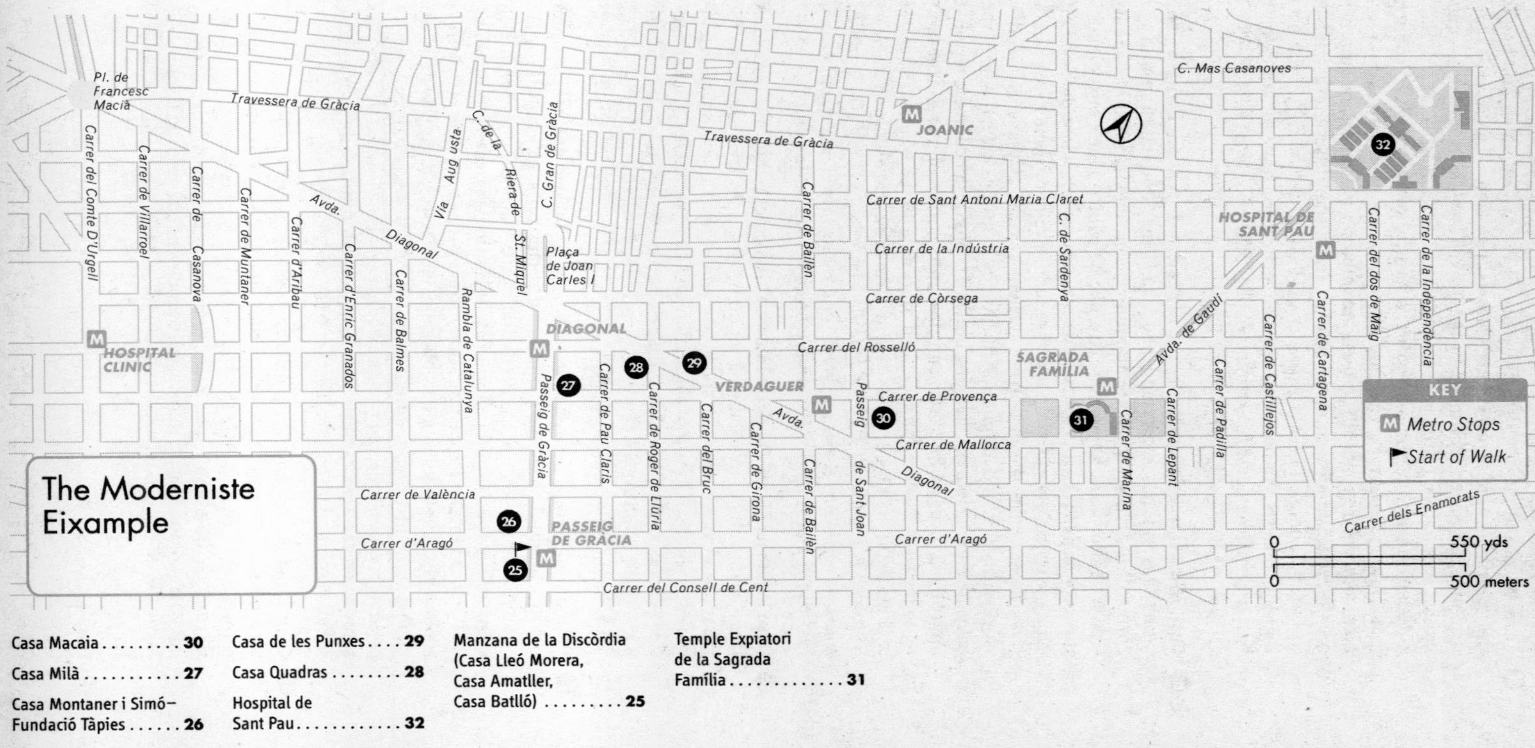
The Moderniste Eixample
KEY
Metro Stops
Start of Walk
0 550 yds
0 500 meters
Pl. de Francesc Macià
Travessera de Gràcia
C. Mas Casanoves
JOANIC
HOSPITAL DE SANT PAU
HOSPITAL CLINIC
DIAGONAL
VERDAGUER
SAGRADA FAMÍLIA
PASSEIG DE GRÀCIA
Carrer del Comte D'Urgell
Carrer de Villarroel
Carrer de Casanova
Carrer de Muntaner
Carrer d'Aribau
Carrer d'Enric Granados
Carrer de Balmes
Rambla de Catalunya
Passeig de Gràcia
Carrer de Pau Claris
Carrer de Roger de Llúria
Carrer del Bruc
Carrer de Girona
Carrer de Bailèn
Passeig de Sant Joan
Carrer de Marina
Carrer de Lepant
Carrer de Padilla
Carrer de Castillejos
Carrer de Cartagena
Carrer del dos de Maig
Carrer de la Independència
Avda. Diagonal
Via Augusta
C. de la Riera de St. Miquel
C. Gran de Gràcia
Plaça de Joan Carles I
Carrer de Sant Antoni Maria Claret
Carrer de la Indústria
C. de Sardenya
Carrer de Còrsega
Carrer del Rosselló
Carrer de Provença
Carrer de Mallorca
Avda. de Gaudí
Carrer de València
Carrer d'Aragó
Carrer del Consell de Cent
Carrer dels Enamorats
Casa Macaia 30
Casa Milà 27
Casa Montaner i Simó–Fundació Tàpies 26
Casa de les Punxes 29
Casa Quadras 28
Hospital de Sant Pau 32
Manzana de la Discòrdia (Casa Lleó Morera, Casa Amatller, Casa Batlló) 25
Temple Expiatori de la Sagrada Família 31

What to See

30 **Casa Macaia.** Built in 1901, this graceful Puig i Cadafalch building is the seat of the ubiquitous Centre Cultural Fundació "La Caixa," a far-reaching cultural entity funded by the Caixa Catalana (Catalan Savings Bank). In addition to the two downstairs exhibition halls there is also a design and architecture bookstore, a library, and a UNESCO-funded music and video library. The Eusebi Arnau sculptures over the door depict, somewhat cryptically, a man mounted on a donkey and another on a bicycle, reminiscent of the similar Arnau sculptures on the facade of Puig i Cadafalch's Casa Amatller on Passeig de Gràcia. Check listings for concerts, lectures, and art exhibits here for some of Barcelona's best cultural events. ✉ *Passeig Sant Joan 108, Eixample* ☎ *93/458–8907* ⏲ *Tues.–Sat. 11–2 and 4–8, Sun. 10–3.*

★ 27 **Casa Milà.** Gaudí's Casa Milà, usually referred to as **La Pedrera** (The Stone Quarry), has a curving stone facade that undulates around the corner of the block. When the building was unveiled, in 1905, residents weren't enthusiastic about these cavelike balconies. Don't miss Gaudí's rooftop chimney park, especially in late afternoon, when the sunlight slants over the city into the Mediterranean. The handsome **Espai Gaudí** (Gaudí Space) in the attic has excellent critical displays of Gaudí's works, theories, and techniques, including an upside-down model of the Sagrada Família made of hanging beads. The **Pis de la Pedrera,** a restored apartment, gives an interesting glimpse into the life of its resident family in the early 20th century. Guided tours are offered weekdays at 6 PM and weekends at 11 AM. ✉ *Passeig de Gràcia 92, Eixample* ☎ *93/484–5995* 🎫 *Espai Gaudí €3, Pis de la Pedrera €3* ⏲ *Daily 10–8; guided tours weekdays at 6 PM, weekends at 11 AM; July–Sept., Espai Gaudí and rooftop also open 9 PM–midnight with bar and live music.*

26 **Casa Montaner i Simó–Fundació Tàpies.** This former publishing house has been beautifully converted to a modern, airy, split-level showcase for the work of contemporary Catalan painter Antoni Tàpies, as well as temporary exhibits. On top of the building is Tàpies' tangle of metal entitled *Núvol i cadira* (*Cloud and Chair*). The bookstore is strong on both Tàpies and Asian art. ✉ *Carrer d'Aragó 255, Eixample* ☎ *93/487–0315* 🎫 *€4.50* ⏲ *Tues.–Sun. 10–8.*

29 **Casa de les Punxes** (House of the Spikes). Also known as Casa Terrades for the family that commissioned it, this cluster of six conical towers ending in impossibly sharp needles is one of several Puig i Cadafalch inspirations rooted in the Gothic architecture of northern Europe, an ur-Bavarian or Danish castle in downtown Barcelona. One of few freestanding Eixample buildings visible from 360 degrees, it has private apartments, some of which are built into the conical towers: three levels of circular rooms connected by spiral stairways. Puig i Cadafalch also designed the Terrades family mausoleum on Montjuïc, albeit in a more sober, respectful style. ✉ *Diagonal 416–420, Eixample.*

28 **Casa Quadras.** Built in 1904 for Baron Quadras, this neo-Gothic and plateresque (intricately carved, as though the stone were silver) facade is by Eusebi Arnau (1864–1934). Look down the facade for St. George slaying the dragon in a spectacularly vertiginous rush of movement. An intimate-looking row of Alpine-chalet windows marks the top floor. ✉ *Av. Diagonal 373, Eixample* ☎ *93/416–1157* 🎫 *€3, free 1st Sun. of month* ⏲ *Tues.–Sat. 10–2 and 5–8, Sun. 10–2.*

32 **Hospital de Sant Pau.** Notable for their Mudéjar motifs and vegetation, these hospital wards are among lush gardens, their exposed-brick facades decorated with mosaics and polychrome ceramic tile. Begun in 1900,

GAUDÍ: EVANGELIST IN STONE

*P**ERHAPS NO SINGLE ARCHITECT** has ever marked a major city as comprehensively and spectacularly as Antoni Gaudí (1852–1926) imprinted Barcelona. The great Moderniste (or Art Nouveau) master's still unfinished Temple Expiatori de la Sagrada Família (Expiatory Temple of the Holy Family) has become Barcelona's most emblematic structure, while another dozen-odd mansions, parks, schools, gateways, lampposts, and other works in and around Barcelona provide a constant Gaudí presence throughout the Catalonian capital.*

***Cátedra Gaudí** (✉ Av. Pedralbes 7 Pedralbes ☎ 93/204–5250), a Gaudí library and study center open to the public, is directed by Joan Bassegoda i Nonell, Barcelona's top Gaudí expert. In one of his many articles, Bassegoda described Gaudí's unique approach to architecture with his legendary "originality is a return to origins." Bassegoda explains the master's conviction that, throughout the history of architecture, architects had become prisoners of the forms they were able to create with the tools of their trade: the compass and the T-square. Buildings had been composed of shapes these instruments could draw: circles, triangles, squares, and rectangles that in three dimensions became prisms, pyramids, cylinders, and spheres used for the construction of pillars, planes, columns, and cupolas.*

Gaudí observed that in nature these shapes are unknown. Admiring the structural efficiency of trees, mammals, and the human form, he noted that ". . . neither are trees prismatic, nor are bones cylindrical, nor are leaves triangular." A closer study of natural forms revealed that bones, branches, muscles, and tendons are all composed of and supported by fibers. Thus, though a surface curves, it is supported from within by a fibrous network that Gaudí translated into what he called "ruled geometry," a system of inner reinforcement he designed to construct hyperboloids, conoids, helicoids, or parabolic hyerboloids, all complicated terms for simple forms and familiar shapes: the femur is hyperboloid; the way shoots grow off a branch is helicoidal; the web between your fingers is a hyperbolic paraboloid.

Gaudí, then, was more than a sculptor playing with form—he was an engineer experimenting with construction. His parabolic (naturally looping) arches were functional techniques first and formal exercises on a second level. His catenary (from cadena, for chain) arches were inverted from chains hanging from stress points over mirrors. Gaudí's evolution away from the T-square and the compass can be traced from his first project onward. Casa Vicens (1883–85) was colorful and daring though angular and rectilinear; in the Palau Güell (1885–89), only his rooftop chimneys hint at what's to come; then in Casa Calvet (1898–1900) the vestibule, elevator, and stairwell are beginning to warp and heave into organic suggestions. Just a few years later arrive the undulating stone face of Casa Milà (La Pedrera, 1905). Casa Batlló (1907), done shortly after, incorporates a scaly dragon back of a roof and its tibias, femurs, and skulls. Finally, the project that consumed the last 20 years of his life, the phantasmagorical Sagrada Família, was a virtual midtown massif and forest.

In the end, though, as Bassegoda recounts, Gaudí's innocent and playful nature, that of the student Gaudí who sculpted the rocks in Josep Fontseré's 1878 La Cascada (Waterfall) in the Parc de la Ciutadella, prevailed. The great master's finest accolade, as reported by Bassegoda, came from the mother of a childhood friend from Reus who, upon seeing Barcelona and Gaudí's architecture for the first time, commented that the famous Moderniste was, after all, "just doing the same things he always did as a kid."

this production won Lluís Domènech i Montaner his third Barcelona "Best Building" award in 1912, following prizes for the Palau de la Música and Casa Lleó Morera. The architect was convinced that patients recovered sooner surrounded by trees and flowers than in sterile hospital wards, and as the mosaics and Pau Gargallo sculptures attest, he also believed in the therapeutic properties of form and color. You'll be able to peruse the art, architecture, and hallways, though not the wards themselves. ✉ *Carrer Sant Antoni Maria Claret 167, Eixample* ☎ *93/291–9000, 93/488–2078 for tour reservation* 🎫 *Free; guided tours €4* ⏲ *Daily 9–2 and 4–7, tours weekends 10–2.*

25 **Manzana de la Discòrdia.** The name is a pun on the word *manzana,* which means both "city block" and "apple," alluding to the architectural counterpoint on this block and to the classical myth of the Apple of Discord. The houses here are spectacular. The ornate **Casa Lleó Morera** (No. 35) was extensively rebuilt (1902–06) by Palau de la Música architect Domènech i Montaner. The pseudo-Gothic, pseudo-Flemish **Casa Amatller** (No. 41) is by Puig i Cadafalch. Next door is Gaudí's **Casa Batlló,** with a mottled facade that resembles nearly anything you want it to. Nationalist symbolism is at work here: the scaly roofline represents the dragon of evil impaled on St. George's cross, and the skulls and bones on the balconies are the dragon's victims. Sadly, all three houses are closed to the public. ✉ *Passeig de Gràcia 35, 41, and 43 (between Consell de Cent and d'Aragó), Eixample.*

31 **Temple Expiatori de la Sagrada Família.** Barcelona's most unforgettable landmark, Antoni Gaudí's Sagrada Família was conceived as nothing short of a Bible in stone. This landmark is one of the most important architectural creations of the 19th–21st centuries. No building in Barcelona, and few in the world, is more deserving of half a day's scrutiny.

Fodor's Choice ★

"My client is not in a hurry," Gaudí was fond of replying to anyone curious about the timetable for his mammoth project . . . and it's a good thing, because the Sagrada Família was begun in 1882 under architect Francesc Villar, passed on to Gaudí in 1891, and is still thought to be half a century from completion, despite today's computerized construction techniques. The scale alone is staggering: the current lateral towers will one day be dwarfed by the main Glory facade and central spire—the Torre del Salvador (Tower of the Savior), which will be crowned by an illuminated polychrome ceramic cross soaring to a final height of 568 ft, one yard shorter than the Montjuïc hill (Gaudí felt it improper for the work of man to surpass that of God). Gaudí's plans called for three immense facades, the present-day Passion (southwest) and Nativity (northeast) facades and the even larger Glory facade above the main entrance, which will be on Carrer de Mallorca. The bell towers will symbolize the 12 apostles (8 are now standing), and the four larger towers around the central Tower of the Savior will represent the evangelists Mark, Matthew, John, and Luke. Between the central tower and the altar will rise the 18th and second-highest tower, in honor of the Virgin Mary. From a height of 148 ft on his respective tower above the Passion facade, Thomas, the apostle who demanded proof of Christ's resurrection ("doubting Thomas"), points to the palm of his hand, asking to inspect Christ's wounds. Bartholomew, to the left, turns his face up toward the culminating element in the Passion facade, not yet in place—a 26-ft, partially gold representation of the resurrected Christ that will rest on a bridge between the four bell towers at a height of almost 200 ft.

After starting in a neo-Gothic style, Gaudí added Art Nouveau touches (floral capitals) to the crypt, supported the naves not with buttresses but with treelike spiral columns, and in 1893 began the north-facing Nativity facade. Soaring spikily skyward in intricate levels of towers, caverns, and spires, the Nativity facade is in fact made partly of stone from Montserrat, Barcelona's cherished mountain sanctuary and home of Catalonia's patron saint, the Black Virgin of Montserrat. Gaudí was fond of comparing the Sagrada Família to the stone flutes and pipes of that saw-toothed massif 50 km (31 mi) west of town.

Walk past the contemporary Passion facade and through the museum to start at the **Nativity facade,** where Gaudí addresses nothing less than the fundamental mystery of Christianity: Why does God the Creator become, through Jesus Christ, a creature? Gaudí's answer-in-stone is that God wanted to free man from the slavery of selfishness, symbolized here by the iron fence around the serpent (complete with apple in mouth) at the base of the central column. The column depicts the genealogy of Christ. Overhead are the constellations in the Christmas sky at Bethlehem: look carefully (consider bringing binoculars) and you'll see two babies representing the Gemini and the horns of a bull for Taurus. Higher up is the Crowning of the Virgin under an overhang, atop which is a pelican feeding its young with its blood, an unusual symbol of the eucharistic sacrifice. Below, two angels adore the initials of Christ (JHS) under the symbols of the cross, the Alpha and Omega. The cypress at the top is the evergreen symbol of eternity pointing to heaven; the white doves, souls seeking eternity.

To the right, the Portal of Faith, above Palestinian flora and fauna, shows scenes from the youth of Jesus, including his preaching at the age of 13. Higher up are grapes and wheat, symbols of the eucharist, and a sculpture of a hand and eye, symbols of divine providence. The left-hand Portal of Hope begins at the bottom with flora and fauna from the Nile; the Slaughter of the Innocents; the flight of the Holy Family into Egypt; Joseph, surrounded by his carpenter's tools, contemplating his son; and the marriage of Joseph and Mary. Above this is a sculpted boat with anchor (representing the Church), piloted by St. Joseph assisted by the Holy Spirit. Overhead is a typical spire from the Montserrat massif. Gaudí intended these towers to house a system of tubular bells capable of playing more complex music than standard bell systems. The towers' peaks represent the apostles' successors in the form of miters, the official headdress of bishops of the western Church.

The **Passion facade** on the southwestern side, at the entrance to the grounds, is a dramatic contrast to the Nativity facade. Josep Maria Subirachs, the sculptor chosen in 1986 to execute Gaudí's plans—initially an atheist, and author of statements such as "God is one of Man's greatest creations"—now confesses to a respectful agnosticism. Known for his distinctly angular, geometrical interpretations of the human form, Subirachs boasted that his work "has nothing to do with Gaudí." When in 1990 artists, architects, and religious leaders called for his resignation after he sculpted an anatomically complete naked Christ on the cross, Subirachs defended the piece as part of the stark realism of the scene he intended to portray. Subirachs pays double homage to Gaudí in the Passion facade: over the left side of the main entry is the blocky figure of Gaudí making notes or drawings, and the Roman soldiers are modeled on Gaudí's helmeted chimneys on the roof of La Pedrera.

Framed by leaning tibialike columns, the bones of the dead, the scenes begin at the left with the Last Supper. The faces of the disciples are contorted in confusion and dismay, especially that of Judas, who clutches a bag of money behind his back over the figure of a reclining hound (symbol of fidelity and foil to the perfidy of Judas). The next sculptural group represents the prayer in the Garden of Gethsemane and Peter awakening, followed by the kiss of Judas. The numerical cryptogram behind this contains 16 numbers that can be added 310 different ways for a total of 33, the age of Christ at his death.

In the center, Jesus is lashed to a pillar during his flagellation, a tear track carved into his expressive countenance. The column's top stone is akilter, a reminder of the stone to be removed from Christ's sepulcher. The knot and broken reed at the base of the pillar symbolize Jesus' physical and psychological suffering. To the right of the door is a rooster, with Peter lamenting his third denial of Christ "before the cock crows." Farther to the right are Pilate and Jesus with a crown of thorns, while just above, back on the left, is Simon of Cyrene helping Jesus with the cross after his first fall. Over the center, where Jesus consoles the women of Jerusalem ("Don't cry for me; cry for your children"), is a faceless Veronica—faceless because her story is considered apocryphal. As Christ was straining toward Calvary, Veronica gave him a veil with which to wipe his face, and when he returned the cloth it was miraculously imprinted with his likeness. Here, the veil is torn in two overhead. To the left is the likeness of Gaudí making notes, and farther left the equestrian figure of a centurion piercing the side of the church with his spear, the church representing the body of Christ. Above are the soldiers rolling dice for Christ's clothing and the naked, crucified Christ. The moon to the right of the Crucifixion refers to the darkness at the moment of Christ's death and to the full moon of Easter; to the right are Peter and Mary at the sepulcher, the egg above Mary symbolizing the Resurrection. At Christ's feet is a figure with a furrowed brow, perhaps suggesting the agnostic's anguished search for certainty, thought to be a self-portrait of Subirachs characterized by the sculptor's giant hand and an "S" on his right arm.

Within 10 years, predicts presiding architect Jordi Bonet, the apse will be covered and thus able to seat an astonishing 15,000 people. In another 50 years, the great central dome, resting on four immense columns of Iranian porphyry (the hardest of all stones), will soar to 568 ft, the culmination of more than 170 years of construction in the tradition of the great medieval and Renaissance cathedrals of Europe. The line from John (13:27) carved into a corner of the Passion facade will no doubt sound even more ponderous once the church is complete: "El que estás fent, fes-ho de pessa" ("Whatever you are doing, do it quickly")—because Judgment Day is at hand.

Gaudí took up residence on the church grounds for the last 15 years of his life. After one tower was finished, he was run over by a tram and, unrecognized for several days, died in a pauper's ward in 1926, short of his 74th birthday. The Sagrada Família **museum** displays the architect's models, construction photos, and photos of Gaudí's multitudinous funeral. Gaudí is buried to the left of the altar in the **crypt**, which has its own entrance on Carrer Provença. For €1.2, you can take an elevator to the top of the **bell towers** for spectacular views; walk slowly back down for a closer look at decorative details ranging from broken-bottle designs to colorful fruit by the Japanese sculptor Etsuro Sotoo. ✉ *Pl. de la Sagrada Família, Eixample* ☎ *93/207–3031* ▣ *€6* ⏲ *Sept.–Mar., daily 9–6; Apr.–Aug., daily 9–8.*

Upper Barcelona: Pedralbes & Sarrià, Parc Güell & Gràcia

Gràcia is a state of mind. More than a neighborhood, it's a sort of village republic that has periodically risen in armed rebellion against city, state, and country. The street names (Llibertat, Fraternitat, Progrès, Venus) reveal the ideological history of this fierce little nucleus of working-class sentiment. Barcelona's first collectivized manufacturing operations (i.e., factories) were clustered here—a dangerous precedent, as workers organized into radical groups ranging from anarchists to feminists to esperantists. Once an outlying town, Gràcia joined Barcelona only under duress and attempted to secede from the Spanish state in 1856, 1870, 1873, and 1909. Lying above the Diagonal from Carrer de Córsega up to Parc Güell, this jumble of streets is filled with appealing bars and restaurants, movie theaters, and outdoor cafés, always alive and usually thronged by young and hip couples. Mercé Rodoreda's novel *La Plaça del Diamant* (translated by David Rosenthal as *The Time of the Doves*) begins and ends in Gràcia's square of the same name during the August Festa Major, a festival that still fills the streets with the rank-and-file residents of this lively yet intimate little pocket of resistance to Organized Life.

a good walk

These sights are spread across Barcelona's upper reaches. Because the Monestir de Pedralbes closes at 2, the best way to attack this part of town is to start with Sarrià and Pedralbes, then visit Parc Güell, Gràcia, and possibly Tibidabo after lunch. From **Sarrià** 33 it's a 20-minute walk or a 5-minute cab ride to the **Monestir de Pedralbes** 34. It's a 20-minute walk downhill from the monastery to the **Palau Reial de Pedralbes** 35. **Tibidabo** 36 has wonderful vistas on clear days, and the restaurant La Venta is a fine place for lunch in the sun. A truly fantastic photo op awaits at **Torre de Collserola** 37. Free transportation is provided to the tower from Plaza Tibidabo. Gaudí's **Parc Güell** 38 is most easily reached by taxi. While there, don't miss the **Casa-Museu Gaudí** 39. After the park, walk down through **Gràcia** 40 to **Casa Vicens** 41. Parc Güell and Tibidabo are best seen in mid- to late afternoon, when the sun backs around to the west and illuminates the Mediterranean.

TIMING If you do it all at once, this is a five- to six-hour outing. Add another two hours if you want to go up to the Collserola Tower.

What to See

41 **Casa Vicens.** Gaudí's first important commission as a young architect was built between 1883 and 1885, at which time Gaudí had not yet thrown away his architect's tools, particularly the T-square. The historical eclecticism of the early Art Nouveau movement is evident in the Orientalist themes and Mudéjar details lavished on the facade. The house was commissioned by a ceramics merchant, which may explain the eye-catching color ceramic tiles that render most of the facade a striking checkerboard—Barcelona's first example of this now-omnipresent technique. The palm leaves on the gate and surrounding fence have been attributed to Gaudí assistant Francesc Berenguer, while the comic iron lizards and bats oozing off the facade are Gaudí's playful nod to the Gothic gargoyle. ✉ *Carrer de les Carolines 24–26, Gràcia.*

39 The **Casa-Museu Gaudí,** within Parc Güell, is in a pink, Alice-in-Wonderland house designed by Gaudí's assistant and, as Gaudí himself put it, "right hand" Francesc Berenguer (1866–1914), in which Gaudí lived with his niece from 1906 to 1926. Exhibits include Gaudí-designed furniture, decorations, drawings, portraits, and a bust of the architect. ✉ *Parc Güell (up hill to right of main entrance), Gràcia* ☎ *93/219–3811* *€3* *May–Sept., daily 10–8; Oct.–Feb., daily 10–6; Mar.–Apr., daily 10–7.*

40 **Gràcia.** Starting in Parc Güell, dig out your city map and follow Carrer Larrard, Travessera de Dalt, and Carrer Torrent de les Flors through upper Gràcia to **Plaça Rovira i Trias,** where a bronze effigy of architect Antoni Rovira i Trias sits elegantly on a bench. Continue downhill and

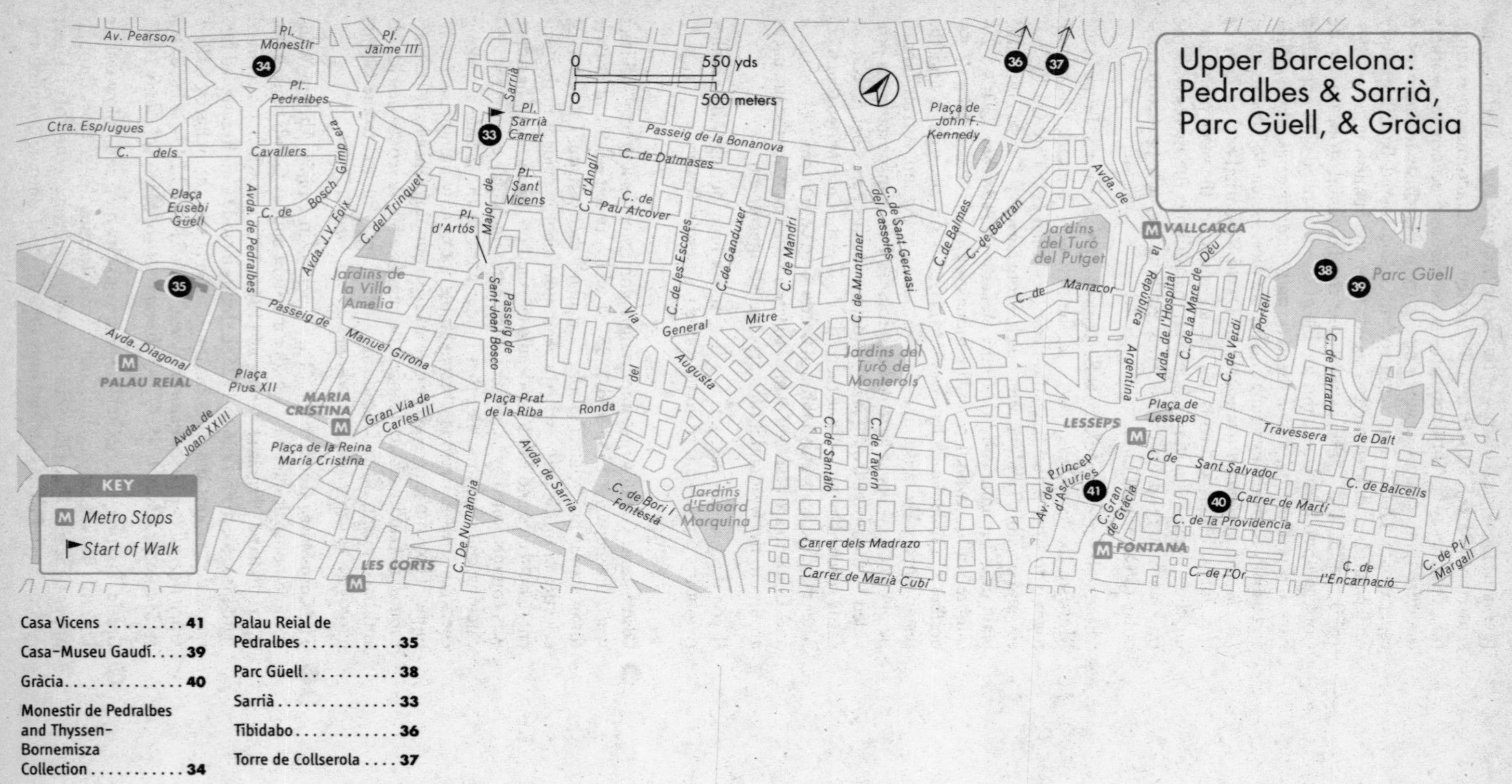

Casa Vicens **41**
Casa-Museu Gaudí. . . . **39**
Gràcia. **40**
Monestir de Pedralbes and Thyssen-Bornemisza Collection **34**
Palau Reial de Pedralbes **35**
Parc Güell. **38**
Sarrià **33**
Tibidabo **36**
Torre de Collserola **37**

west to **Plaça de la Virreina** to see the work of Francesc Berenguer at Carrer del Or 44. (If Barcelona was Gaudí's sandbox, Gràcia was Berenguer's—nearly every major building in this neighborhood is his creation.) Cut over to **Plaça del Diamant** to see in bronze the heroine of Mercé Rodoreda's famous 1962 novel *La Plaça del Diamant*. Moving through Plaça Trilla, cross Gran de Gràcia to Carrer de les Carolines to see Gaudí's very first house, **Casa Vicens.** Your next stop is the produce market **Mercat de la Llibertat,** a sort of uptown Boqueria. Cut east along Cisne, cross Gran de Gràcia, and pass another Berenguer creation on Ros de Olano, the Mudéjar-style **Centre Moral Instructiu de Gràcia. Plaça del Sol,** one of Gràcia's most popular squares, is downhill. From here, continue east to Gràcia's other market, the **Mercat de la Revolució.** Walk three blocks back over to Grácia's main square, **Plaça Rius i Taulet,** with its emblematic clock tower. From Plaça Rius i Taulet, cut out to **Gran de Gracia** for a look at some more Art Nouveau buildings by Berenguer (Nos. 15, 23, 35, 49, 51, 61, and 77). For lunch, consider Galician seafood at Botafumeiro or, near the bottom of Gràcia above Carrer Còrsega, the exquisite Jean Luc Figueras—a few steps from the Gaudí-esque facade of another Art Nouveau gem, **Casa Comalat,** at Carrer de Córsega 316.

34 **Monestir de Pedralbes.** Even without its Thyssen-Bornemisza Collection of Italian and Spanish masters, this is one of Barcelona's hidden treasures. Founded by Reina Elisenda for Clarist nuns in 1326, the convent has an unusual, three-story Gothic cloister, arguably the finest in Barcelona. The chapel has a beautiful stained-glass rose window and famous murals painted in 1346 by Ferrer Bassa, a Catalan much influenced by the Italian Renaissance. You can also visit the medieval living quarters. The monastery alone is a treat, but the **Thyssen-Bornemisza Collection,** installed in 1989 in what was once the dormitory of the nuns of the Order of St. Clare, sends it over the top. Surrounded by 14th-century windows and pointy arches, these canvases by Tiepolo, Canaletto, Tintoretto, Rubens, and Velázquez will restore any weary traveler's soul. ✉ *Baixada Monestir 9, Pedralbes* ☎ *93/203–9282* 🎫 *Monastery and cloister €5, Thyssen-Bornemisza Collection €5, combined ticket €8, free 1st Sun. of month* ⏲ *Tues.–Sun. 10–2.*

off the beaten path

MUSEU DE LA CIÈNCIA – Young minds work overtime in the Science Museum, below Tibidabo—many displays and activities are for children ages seven and up. ✉ *Teodor Roviralta 55, La Bonanova* ☎ *93/212–6050* 🎫 *€3, plus €1.50 for interactive options* ⏲ *Tues.–Sun. 10–8* Ⓜ *Avinguda de Tibidabo and Tramvía Blau halfway.*

35 **Palau Reial de Pedralbes** (Royal Palace of Pedralbes). Built in the 1920s for King Alfonso XII, this palace has a **Ceramics Museum,** which makes a wide sweep of Spanish ceramic art from the 14th to the 18th century. The influence of Moorish design techniques is carefully documented. ✉ *Av. Diagonal 686, Pedralbes* ☎ *93/280–5024* 🎫 *€4, free 1st Sun. of month* ⏲ *Daily 10–3.*

38 **Parc Güell.** Güell Park is one of Gaudí's, and Barcelona's, most pleasant and stimulating places to spend a few hours; it's light and playful, alternately shady, green, floral, and sunny. Named for and commissioned by Gaudí's main patron, Count Eusebio Güell, the park was intended as a hillside garden suburb on the English model. Since Barcelona's bourgeoisie seemed happier living closer to "town," however, so only two of the houses were ever built. The Güell family eventually turned the land over to the city as a public park. Gaudí highlights include an Art Nouveau extravaganza with gingerbread gatehouses topped with, re-

spectively, the hallucinogenic red-and-white fly ammanite wild mushroom (rumored to have been a Gaudí favorite) on the right and the *phallus impudicus* (no translation necessary) on the left. Also notable is the Room of a Hundred Columns—a covered market supported by tilted Doric-style columns, buttresses encrusted with multicolor mosaic, and a patchwork lizard standing guard—as well as the polychrome bench that snakes along the main terrace. Inspired partly by the profile of Gaudí's assistants lying in a pool of plaster, the bench is an icon of the Moderniste movement, the most memorable creation of Gaudí assistant Josep Maria Jujol, who outdid himself here in the art of inlaid broken mosaic. ✉ *Carrer d'Olot 3 (take Metro to Lesseps; then walk 15 steep uphill mins or catch Bus 24 to park entrance), Gràcia* ⏲ *Oct.–Mar., daily 10–6; Apr.–June, daily 10–7; July–Sept., daily 10–9.*

🏳 33 **Sarrià.** This 1,000-year-old village was once a cluster of farms and country houses overlooking Barcelona from the hills. Start your exploration at the main square, Plaça Sarrià, which hosts an antiques and crafts market on Tuesday morning, *sardana* dances on Sunday morning, and Christmas fairs in season. The Romanesque church tower, lighted a bright ocher at night, looms overhead. Across Passeig Reina Elisenda from the church, wander through the brick-and-steel **produce market** and the tiny, flower-choked **Plaça Sant Gaietà** behind it. Back in front of the church, cut through the Placeta del Roser to the left of the main door and you'll come to the elegant **town hall** in the Plaça de la Vila; note the buxom bronze sculpture of Pomona, goddess of fruit, by famed Sarrià sculptor Josep Clarà (1878–1958). After peeking in to see the massive ceiling beams (and tempting set lunch menu) in the restaurant Vell Sarrià, at the corner of Major de Sarrià, go back to the Pomona bronze and turn left into tiny Carrer dels Paletes (with its tiny saint-filled niche on the corner overhead to the right), which leads back to Major de Sarrià. Continue down this pedestrian-only street and turn left onto **Carrer Canet,** with its cottagelike artisans' quarters.

Turn right on Carrer Cornet i Mas and walk two blocks down to Carrer Jaume Piquet. A quick probe to the left will take you to No. 30, Barcelona's most perfect small-format **Moderniste house,** complete with faux-medieval upper windows, wrought-iron grillwork, floral and fruit ornamentation, and organically curved and carved wooden doors. The next stop down Cornet i Mas is Sarrià's prettiest square, **Plaça Sant Vicens,** a leafy space ringed by old Sarrià houses and centered on a statue of the village's patron saint. Note the other renditions of the saint over the square's upper right corner. The café Can Pau is the local hangout, once a haven for such authors as Gabriel García Marquez and Mario Vargas Llosa, who lived in Sarrià in the early 1970s, on the cusp of their fame. To get to the Monestir de Pedralbes from Plaça Sant Vicens, walk back up Mayor de Sarrià and through the market to the corner of Sagrat Cor and Ramon Miquel Planas; then turn left and walk straight west for 15 minutes, past the splendid upper-city mansions of Pedralbes. Other Sarrià landmarks include the two **Foix** pastry stores, one at Plaça Sarrià 9–10 and the other on Major de Sarrià 57, above Bar Tomás. Both have excellent pastries, artisanal breads, and cold cava. The late J. V. Foix, son of the store's founders, was one of the great Catalan poets of the 20th century, a key player in keeping the Catalan language alive during the 40-year Franco regime. Plaça Sarrià, a good place for homemade ice cream, has a bronze bust of the poet, and the Major de Sarrià shop has a plaque identifying the house as the poet's birthplace with memorable verses: *Tota amor és latent en l'altra amor / tot llenguatge és saó d'una parla comuna / tota terra barega a la pàtria de tots / tota fe serà suc d'una mes alta fe.* (Every love is latent in the other love / every language is part of a common tongue / every country contributes to the fatherland of all / every faith will be the lifeblood of a higher faith). ✉ *Pl. Sarrià, Sarrià, take Bus 22 from bottom of Av. de Tibidabo, or U-6 train on FFCC subway to Reina Elisenda.*

need a break?

Bar Tomás, on Major de Sarrià on the corner of Jaume Piquet, is home of the finest potatoes in town. Order the famous *doble mixta* of potatoes with *allioli* and hot sauce and a draft beer (ask for a *caña*).

36 **Tibidabo.** Tibidabo is one of Barcelona's two promontories, along with Montjuïc, and when the wind blows the smog out to sea, the views from this hill are legendary. The shapes that distinguish Tibidabo from below turn out to be a commercialized church, a vast radio mast, and the 850-ft communications tower, the Torre de Collserola. There's not much to see here except the vista, particularly from the tower. Clear days are few and far between in 21st-century Barcelona, but if (and only if) you hit one, this excursion is worth considering. The restaurant **La Venta,** at the base of the funicular, is excellent, a fine place to sit in the sun in cool weather (the establishment provides straw sun hats). The bar **Mirablau** is a popular hangout for evening drinks. ✉ *Tibidabo, Take Tibidabo branch off Sarrià subway; Buses 24 and 22 to Plaza Kennedy; or a taxi. At Av. Tibidabo, catch Tramvía Blau, which connects with funicular to summit.*

37 **Torre de Collserola.** The Collserola Tower, which dwarfs Tibidabo, is a creation of Norman Foster, erected for the 1992 Olympics amid controversy over defacement of the traditional mountain skyline. The tower has a splendid panorama of the city when conditions allow. Take the funicular up to Tibidabo; from Plaza Tibidabo there is free transport to the tower. ✉ *Av. de Vallvidrera, Tibidabo* ☎ *93/406–9354* €4 ⊙ *Wed.–Sun. 11–2:30 and 3:30–8.*

Sant Pere, La Ciutadella & Barceloneta

Barcelona's old textile neighborhood, around the church of Sant Pere, includes the flagship of the city's Moderniste architecture, the Palau de la Música Catalana. Barceloneta, once the open sea, silted in and became a salt marsh until 1753, when French military engineer Prosper de Verboom designed a housing project for families who had lost their homes in La Ribera. Together, the four areas form a good walk within and around what were once Barcelona's 13th-century walls.

a good walk

These neighborhoods northeast of the Gothic Quarter begin with the **Palau de la Música Catalana** 42, just a 10-minute walk from Plaça Catalunya. After the Palau, continue along Carrer Sant Pere Més Alt past the church of **Sant Pere de les Puelles** 43 and out to the **Arc del Triomf** 44, on Passeig de Sant Joan. From there, walk through the **Parc de la Ciutadella** 45, past the **Castell dels Tres Dragons** 46 and the **Museu de la Geologia** 47. Veer to the left past **La Cascada** 48 (a waterfall with rocks, by a young architecture student named Antoni Gaudí) and continue to the **Museu d'Art Modern** 49. The Barcelona **Zoo** 50 next to the Parliament has dolphins, rhinos, and an albino gorilla. Leaving the zoo, pass the **Estació de França** 51, and continue on to the edge of **Port Vell** 52 next to the Palau de Mar. For a look at Catalonia's version (for once) of its own history, check out the interactive **Museu d'Història de Catalunya** 53. Then walk around the port to the **El Transbordador Aeri del Port** 54 for a ride over the harbor, or walk through **Barceloneta** 55, and along the beach to the **Port Olímpic** 56.

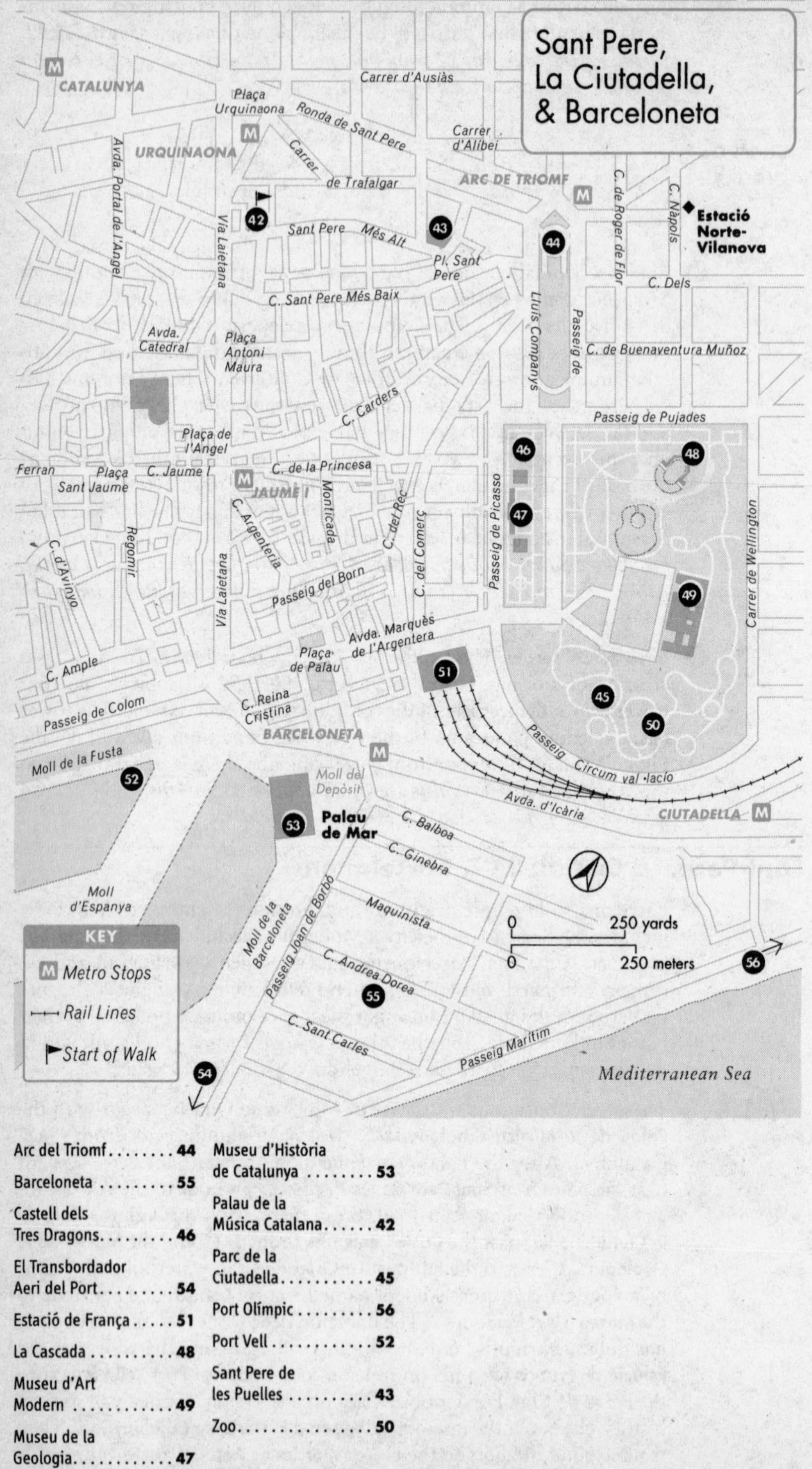

Arc del Triomf........44
Barceloneta.........55
Castell dels Tres Dragons.........46
El Transbordador Aeri del Port.........54
Estació de França.....51
La Cascada..........48
Museu d'Art Modern............49
Museu de la Geologia............47
Museu d'Història de Catalunya........53
Palau de la Música Catalana......42
Parc de la Ciutadella..........45
Port Olímpic.........56
Port Vell............52
Sant Pere de les Puelles..........43
Zoo................50

TIMING Depending on the number of stops, this walk can take a full day. Count on at least four hours of actual walking time.

What to See

44 **Arc del Triomf.** This imposing, exposed-redbrick arch on Passeig de Sant Joan was built by Josep Vilaseca as the grand entrance for the Universal Exposition of 1888. Similar in size and sense to the triumphal arches of ancient Rome, this one refers to Jaume I El Conqueridor's 1229 conquest of the Moors in Mallorca—as suggested by the bats, always part of Jaume I's coat of arms, on either side of the arch.

55 **Barceloneta.** Once Barcelona's pungent fishing port, Barceloneta retains much of its maritime flavor. It's a pretty walk through narrow streets with lines of laundry snapping in the breeze. Stop in Plaça de la Barceloneta to see the baroque church of **Sant Miquel del Port,** with its oversize sculpture of the winged archangel himself. Look for the Barceloneta market and the restaurant Can Ramonet on Carrer de la Maquinista, and for the original two-story houses and the restaurant Can Solé on Carrer Sant Carles. Barceloneta's **beach,** though often overcrowded, offers swimming, surfing, and a lively social scene from late May through September. In summer, the clubs and terraces in the sand off the end of Passeig de Joan de Borbó rage until the sun pushes up over the rim of the Mediterranean.

need a break?

Friendly **Can Manel la Puda,** at Passeig de Joan de Borbó 60–61 in Barceloneta (☎ 93/221–5013), is always good for an inexpensive feast in the sun. Serving lunch until 4 and starting dinner at 7, it's a popular place for *suquets* (fish stew), paella, and *arròs a banda* (rice with shelled seafood). It's closed Monday, and they accept AE, DC, MC, and V.

46 **Castell dels Tres Dragons** (Castle of the Three Dragons). Built by Domènech i Montaner as a restaurant for the Universal Exposition of 1888, this arresting structure was named in honor of a popular mid-19th-century comedy by the father of the Catalan theater, Serafí Pitarra. Greeting you on the right as you enter the Ciutadella from Passeig Lluí Companys, the building has exposed brickwork and visible iron supports, both radical innovations of their time. Moderniste architects later met here to exchange ideas and experiment with traditional crafts; the castle now holds Barcelona's **Museum of Zoology.** ✉ *Passeig Picasso 5, La Ciutadella* ☎ *93/319–6912* 🎫 *€3* ⏲ *Tues.–Sun. 10–2.*

54 **El Transbordador Aeri del Port** (cable car). The cable car leaving from the tower at the end of Passeig Joan de Borbócan connects the Torre de San Sebastián on the Moll de Barceloneta, the tower of Jaime I in the boat terminal, and the Torre de Miramar on Montjuïc. ☎ *93/225–2718* 🎫 *€10 round-trip, €7 one-way* ⏲ *Oct.–mid-June, weekends 10:30–5:30; mid-June–Sept., daily 10:30–8:30.*

51 **Estació de Françia.** Once Barcelona's main train station, the gracefully restored Estació de França is outside the west gate of the Ciutadella. Wander in for a rush of European railroad nostalgia. ✉ *Marquès de l'Argentera s/n, La Ribera.*

48 **La Cascada.** Take a break by this lake, and, behind it, the monumental *Cascada,* by Josep Fontseré, designed for the Universal Exposition of 1888. The waterfall's rocks were the work of a young architecture student named Antoni Gaudí—his first public works, appropriately natural and organic, a hint of things to come. ✉ *Parc de la Ciutadella.*

49 **Museu d'Art Modern.** (Museum of Modern Art). Once the arsenal for the Ciutadella—as evidenced by the thickness of the building's walls—this is the only surviving remnant of Felipe V's fortress and is presently shared by the Catalan Parliament and the Museum of Modern Art. The collection of late-19th- and early 20th-century Catalan paintings and sculptures by such artists as Isidro Nonell, Ramon Casas, Marià Fortuny, Josep Clarà, and Pau Gargallo forms one of Catalonia's most important artistic treasures. Often overlooked in favor of other Barcelona standouts such as the Picasso Museum or the Romanesque collection in the Palau Nacional, the museum is a reminder that Catalonia's most emblematic and universal artists—Picasso, Dalí, Miró—emerged from an exceptionally rich artistic tradition. ✉ *Plaça d'Armes, La Ciutadella* ☎ *93/319–5728* 🎟 *€4* ⏲ *Tues.–Sat. 10–7, Sun. 10–2.*

47 **Museu de la Geologia.** The Museum of Geology is next to the Castell dels Tres Dragons and the Umbracle, the black slats of which help create jungle lighting for a valuable collection of tropical plants. Barcelona's first public museum, it has rocks, minerals, and fossils from Catalonia and the rest of Spain. ✉ *Parc de la Ciutadella, La Ciutadella* ☎ *93/319–6895* 🎟 *€3, free 1st Sun. of month* ⏲ *Tues.–Sun. 10–2.*

53 **Museu d'Història de Catalunya.** Built into what used to be a port warehouse, this state-of-the-art interactive museum makes you part of Catalonian history from prehistoric times through more than 3,000 years and into the contemporary democratic era. Explanations of the exhibits appear in Catalan, Castilian, and English. Guided tours are available on Sundays at noon and 1 PM. The cafeteria has excellent views over the harbor. ✉ *Plaça Pau Vila 1, Barceloneta* ☎ *93/225–4700* 🎟 *€4; free 1st Sun. of month* ⏲ *Tues.–Sat. 10–7, Sun. 10–2:30.*

⚑ 42 **Palau de la Música Catalana.** A riot of color and form, Barcelona's Music Palace is the flagship of the city's Moderniste architecture. Designed by Lluís Domènech i Montaner in 1908, it was originally conceived by the Orfeó Català musical society as a vindication of the importance of music at a popular level—as opposed to the Liceu opera house's identification with the Catalan (often Castilian-speaking monarchist) aristocracy. For decades the Palau and the Liceu were opposing crosstown forces in Barcelona's musical-philosophical discourse. The Palau's exterior is remarkable in itself, albeit hard to see, as there's no room to back up and behold it. Above the main entrance are busts of Palestrina, Bach, Beethoven, and (around the corner on Carrer Amadeu Vives) Wagner. Look for the colorful mosaic pillars on the second upper level, a preview of what's inside. The Miquel Blay sculptural group over the corner of Sant Pere Més Alt and Amadeu Vives depicts everyone from St. George the dragon slayer (at the top) to fishermen with oars over their shoulders—every strain and stratum of Catalan popular life. The removal of a parish church in late 1999 opened up the Palau's southwest corner over Plaça Lluís Millet, while the glass facade over the box-office entrance is a paradigmatic modern reform added to a traditional structure.

The interior is an uproar before the first note of music is ever heard. Wagnerian cavalry explodes from the right side of the stage over a heavy-browed bust of Beethoven, while Catalonia's popular music is represented by the flowing maidens of Lluís Millet's song *Flors de Maig* (*Flowers of May*) on the left. Overhead, an inverted stained-glass cupola seems to offer the divine manna of music; painted rosettes and giant peacock feathers explode from the tops of the walls. Even the stage is populated with muselike Art Nouveau musicians, each half bust, half mosaic. The visuals alone make music sound different in here, and at any important concert the excitement is palpably thick. If you can't attend one,

MODERNISTE BARCELONA

*A**RT NOUVEAU,** Modernisme in Catalan, is the architectural and artistic style that has become Barcelona's aesthetic trademark. Characterized by intense ornamentation and the use of natural or organic lines and forms, Modernisme swept Europe between 1880 and 1914, though nowhere did it proliferate as it did in Barcelona beginning with the Universal Exposition of 1888. Modernisme is everywhere in Barcelona because it tapped into the playful Catalan artistic impulse (as evidenced in the works of Gaudí; because it coincided with Barcelona's late-19th-century industrial prosperity and the resultant surge of nationalistic ebullience; and because the post-1860 Eixample neighborhood was in the process of being built by a rich bourgeoisie eager to outshine each other with opulent mansions.*

A cultural movement that went beyond architecture, Barcelona's Modernisme had repercussions in the design of everything from clothes to hair styles to tombstones. Painters such as Ramón Casas and Santiago Russinyol, sculptors such as Miquel Blay and Eusebi Arnau, stained-glass artisans, ceramicists, acid engravers and woodcarvers all played a part in the explosion of artistic exuberance.

Partly as a protest against the social, economic, and spiritual disappointments of the Industrial Revolution, the curved line replaced the straight line; natural elements such as flowers and fruits were sculpted into facades as a rejection of the "advances" of technology; and the classical and pragmatic gave way to decorative excess. Barcelona's Palau de la Música Catalana by Lluís Domènech i Montaner, widely considered the flagship of the movement, is a stunning compendium of Art Nouveau decorative techniques, including acid-etched glass and stained glass, polychrome ceramic ornamentation, carved wooden arches, and sculptures. Antoni Gaudí has become the most famous of the Moderniste architects. Josep Puig i Cadafalch's Casa Amatller and Casa de les Punxes are examples of Modernisme's eclectic, historical tendencies. Josep Graner i Prat's Casa de la Papallona, Joan Rubió Bellver's Casa Golferichs, Gaudí's Casa Batlló, and Salvador Valeri i Pupurull's Casa Comalat are Moderniste mansions that make Barcelona's Eixample a living architecture museum.

*The **Centre del Modernisme,** Casa Amatller, (✉ Passeig de Gràcia 41 Eixample ☎ 93/488–0139 ⏲ Mon.–Sat. 10–7, Sun. 10–2 Ⓜ Passeig de Gràcia) has a map of the Modernist Route, a guide to the city's noteworthy Art Nouveau (Moderniste) sights. For €3 your ticket gets you 50% off every stop on the map.*

take a tour of the hall. *Box office ✉ Sant Francesc de Paula 2 (off Via Laietana, around a corner from the hall itself), Sant Pere ☎ 93/295–7200 🎫 Guided tour in English €5 ⏲ Tours daily at 10:30, 2, and 3.*

45 **Parc de la Ciutadella** (Citadel Park). Once a fortress designed to consolidate Madrid's military occupation of Barcelona, the Ciutadella is now the city's main downtown park. The clearing dates from shortly after the War of the Spanish Succession, when Felipe V demolished some 2,000 houses in what was then the Barri de la Ribera (waterfront neighborhood) to build a fortress and barracks for his soldiers and fields of fire for his artillery. The fortress walls were pulled down in 1868 and replaced by gardens laid out by Josep Fontserè. Within the park are a cluster of museums, the Catalan parliament, and the city zoo.

56 **Port Olímpic.** Choked with yachts, restaurants, and tapas bars of all kinds, the Olympic Port is 2 km (1 mi) up the beach, marked by the mammoth Frank Gehry goldfish sculpture in front of Barcelona's first real skyscraper, the Hotel Arts. The port rages on Friday and Saturday night, especially in summer, with hundreds of young people of all nationalities circling and grazing until daybreak.

52 **Port Vell** (Old Port). From Pla del Palau, cross to the edge of the port, where the Moll d'Espanya, the Moll de la Fusta, and the Moll de Barceloneta meet. Just beyond the Lichtenstein sculpture *Barcelona Head,* in front of the post office, the modern Port Vell complex—the IMAX theater, aquarium, and Maremagnum shopping mall—looms seaward on the Moll d'Espanya. The Palau de Mar, with its five (somewhat pricey and impersonal) quayside terrace restaurants, stretches along the Moll de Barceloneta. (Try Llevataps or, on the far corner, the Merendero de la Mari.) Stroll through the Museu de Història de Catalunya (MHC) in the Palau de Mar for a lesson in Catalan history. Along the Passeig Joan de Borbó are a dozen more Barceloneta paella and seafood specialists.

43 **Sant Pere de les Puelles** (St. Peter of the Novices). One of the oldest medieval churches in Barcelona, this one has been destroyed and restored so many times that there is little left to see except the beautiful stained-glass window, which illuminates the stark interior. *Puelles* comes from the Latin *puella* (girl)—the convent here was known for the beauty and nobility of its young women and was the scene of some of medieval Barcelona's most tragic love stories. ✉ *Lluís El Piadós 1, Sant Pere* ☎ *93/268–0742* ⊙ *Open for mass only.*

50 **Zoo.** Barcelona's first-rate zoo—home of Snowflake, the world's only captive albino gorilla—occupies the whole bottom section of the Parc de la Ciutadella. Dolphins, reptiles, and a full complement of African animals reside in this animal colony squeezed in between the Catalan Parliament and the Universidad Pompeu Fabra. Look for the statue of *La Senyoreta del Paraigua*(Lady with Umbrella) near the dolphin show. The Barcelona zoo will be moved out of town, possibly as early as 2004, though no firm dates have been set. ✉ *Parc de la Ciutadella, La Ciutadella* ☎ *93/225–6780* *Adults €11, children under 13 €7* ⊙ *Oct.–Apr., daily 10–6; May–Sept., daily 9:30–7:30.*

Montjuïc

This hill to the south of town may have been named for the Jewish cemetery once on its slopes, though an alternate explanation has it named for the Roman deity Jove, or Jupiter. The most dramatic approach is by way of the cross-harbor cable car from Barceloneta or from the mid-station in the port; but Montjuïc is normally accessed by taxi or Bus 61 (or on foot) from Plaça Espanya, or by the funicular that operates from the Paral.lel (Paral.lel Metro stop on the green line).

a good walk

Walking from sight to sight on Montjuïc is possible but not recommended. You'll want fresh feet to see the sights here, especially the Romanesque art in the Palau Nacional and the Miró Foundation.

The *El Transbordador Aeri del Port* cable car drops you at the Jardins de Miramar, a 10-minute walk from the Plaça de Dante. From here, another small cable car takes you up to the **Castell de Montjuïc** 57. From the bottom station, the **Fundació Miró** 58 is a few minutes' walk, and beyond it is the **Estadi Olímpic** 59. From the stadium, walk straight down to the Palau Nacional and its **Museu Nacional d'Art de Catalunya** 60. From

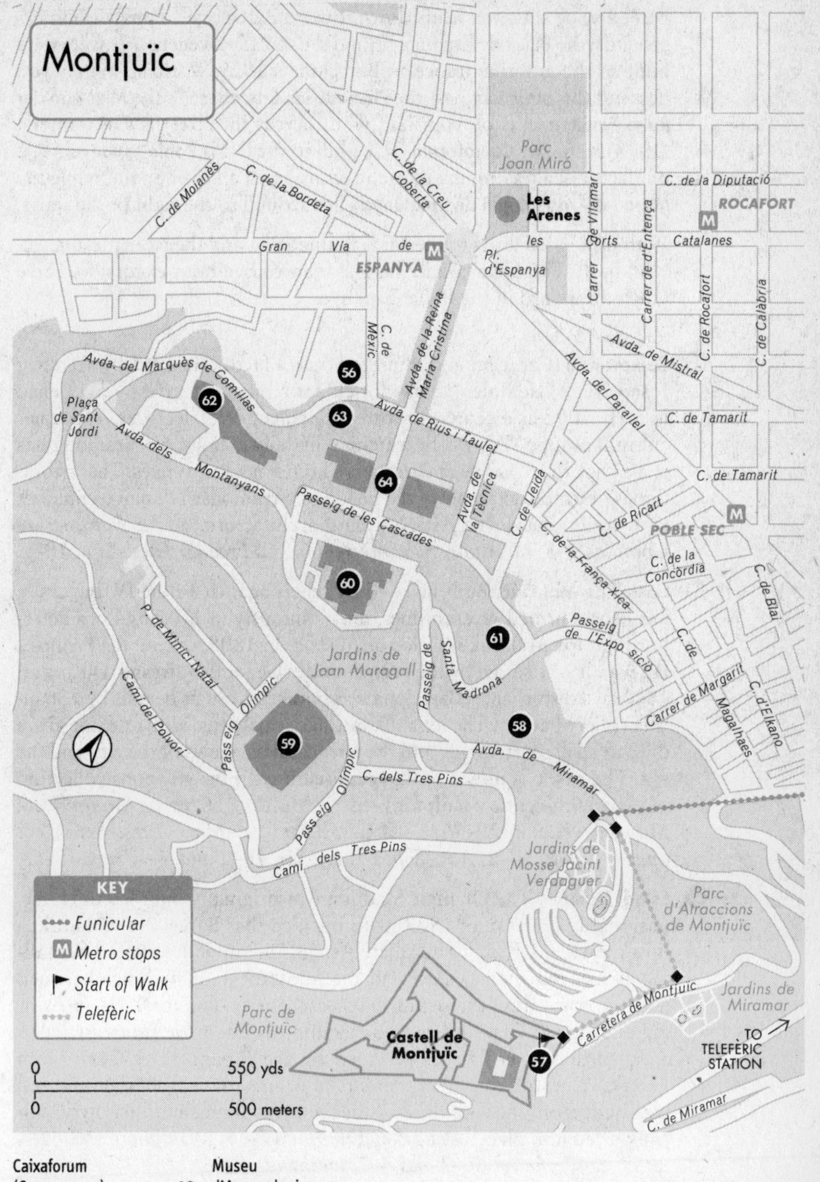

Caixaforum (Casaramona) 63

Castell de Montjuïc. 57

Estadi Olímpic 59

Fundació Miró 58

Mies van der Rohe Pavilion 62

Museu d'Arqueologia de Catalunya 65

Museu Nacional d'Art de Catalunya 60

Plaça de les Cascades 61

Poble Espanyol. 64

here, a wide stairway leads down toward Barcelona's convention fairgrounds; the Plaça de Espanya behind the so-called Venetian Towers were built as the grand entrance to Barcelona's 1929 World's Fair. As you descend this stairway past the **Plaça de les Cascades** 61, the **Mies van der Rohe Pavilion** 62 is on your left, while across the street is Casaramona (1913), now the **Caixaforum** 63. Uphill to the left is **Poble Espanyol** 64, a miniature-scale sampling of architecture from all over Spain, while the **Museu d'Arqueologia de Catalunya** 65 is around to the right of the stairs.

TIMING With unhurried visits to the Miró Foundation and the Romanesque exhibit in the Palau Nacional, this is a four- to five-hour excursion. Have lunch afterward in the Poble Espanyol.

What to See

63 **Caixaforum** (Casaramona). Built to house a factory in 1911 by architect Josep Puig i Cadafalch, this redbrick Art Nouveau fortress was opened in early 2002 as a center for art exhibits, concerts, lectures, and other cultural events. Well worth watching in daily listings, Casaramona has come back to life as one of Barcelona's hottest new art venues. The restoration is one more example of the fusion of ultramodern design techniques with traditional (even Art Nouveau) architecture. ✉ *Av. Marquès de Comillas 6–8, Montjuïc* ☎ *93/476–8600* *Free* ⏲ *Tues.–Sun. 10–8.*

57 **Castell de Montjuïc.** Built in 1640 by rebels against Felipe IV, the castle has been stormed several times, most famously in 1705 by Lord Peterborough for Archduke Carlos of Austria. In 1808, during the Peninsular War, it was seized by the French under General Dufresne. During an 1842 civil disturbance, Barcelona was bombed from its heights by a Spanish artillery battery. The moat has attractive gardens, with one side given over to an archery range, and the terraces have views of the city and the sea. The castle is now a **military museum** with the weapons collection of early 20th-century sculptor Frederic Marès. ✉ *Ctra. de Montjuïc 66, Montjuïc* ☎ *93/329–8613* *€2.50* ⏲ *Oct.–Mar., Tues.–Sat. 10–2 and 4–7, Sun. 10–2; Apr.–Sept., Tues.–Sat. 10–2 and 4–7, Sun. 10–8.*

59 **Estadi Olímpic.** The Olympic Stadium was originally built for the International Exposition of 1929, with the idea that Barcelona would then host the 1936 Olympics (ultimately staged in Hitler's Berlin). After failing twice, Barcelona celebrated the attainment of its long-cherished goal by renovating the semiderelict stadium in time for 1992, providing seating for 70,000. Next door and downhill is the futuristic Palau Sant Jordi Sports Palace, designed by the Japanese architect Arata Isozaki. The structure has no pillars or beams to obstruct the view and was built from the roof down—the roof was built first, then hydraulically lifted into place. ✉ *Passeig Olímpic 17–19, Montjuïc* ☎ *93/426–2089* ⏲ *Weekdays 10–2 and 4–7, weekends 10–6.*

★ 58 **Fundació Miró.** The Miró Foundation was a gift from the artist Joan Miró to his native city and is one of Barcelona's most exciting showcases of contemporary art. The airy, white building was designed by Josep Lluís Sert and opened in 1975; an extension was added by Sert's pupil Jaume Freixa in 1988. Miró's unmistakably playful and colorful style, filled with Mediterranean light and humor, seems a perfect match for its surroundings, and the exhibits and retrospectives that open here tend to be progressive and provocative, from Moore to Mapplethorpe. Look for Alexander Calder's mercury fountain. Miró himself rests in the cemetery on Montjuïc's southern slopes. During the Franco regime, which he strongly opposed, Miró first lived in self-imposed exile in Paris, then moved to Majorca in 1956. When he died in 1983, the Catalans gave him a send-off amounting to a state funeral. ✉ *Av. Miramar 71,*

Montjuïc ☎ *93/329–1908* 🎟 *€7.50* ⏲ *Tues.–Wed. and Fri.–Sat. 10–7, Thurs. 10–9:30, Sun. 10–2:30.*

62 **Mies van der Rohe Pavilion.** The reconstructed Mies van der Rohe Pavilion—the German contribution to the International Exposition of 1929, reassembled between 1983 and 1986—is a "less is more" study in interlocking planes of white marble, green onyx, and glass: Barcelona's aesthetic antonym for the Moderniste Palau de la Música. ⊠ *Av. Marquès de Comillas s/n, Montjuïc* ☎ *93/423–4016* 🎟 *€3* ⏲ *Daily 10–8.*

65 **Museu d'Arqueologia de Catalunya.** Just downhill to the right of the Palau Nacional, the Museum of Archaeology holds important finds from the Greek ruins at Empúries, on the Costa Brava. These are shown alongside fascinating objects from, and explanations of, Megalithic Spain. ⊠ *Passeig Santa Madrona 39–41, Montjuïc* ☎ *93/423–2149* 🎟 *€3* ⏲ *Tues.–Sat. 9:30–1 and 4–7, Sun. 9:30–1.*

★ 60 **Museu Nacional d'Art de Catalunya** (Catalonian National Museum of Art). In the imposing **Palau Nacional,** this museum was built in 1929 and renovated by Gae Aulenti, architect of the Musée d'Orsay, in Paris. Comprising the world's finest collection of Romanesque and Gothic frescoes, altarpieces, and wood carvings, most of the art here was removed from small churches in the Pyrenees during the 1920s to save it from deterioration and theft. Most of the works, such as the *Pantocrator* fresco (a copy of which is now back in the church of Sant Climent de Taüll), have been reproduced and replaced in their original homes. The museum also has works by El Greco, Velázquez, and Zurbarán. ⊠ *Mirador del Palau 6, Montjuïc* ☎ *93/423–7199* 🎟 *€6* ⏲ *Tues.–Wed. and Fri.–Sat. 10–7, Thurs. 10–9, Sun. 10–2:30.*

61 **Plaça de les Cascades.** Upon leaving the Mies van der Rohe Pavilion, you'll see the (at night) multicolor fountain in the Plaça de les Cascades. Stroll down the wide esplanade past the exhibition halls, used for Barcelona fairs and conventions, to the large and frenetic **Plaça d'Espanya.** Across the square is Les Arenes bullring, now used for theater and political rallies rather than bullfights. From here, you can take the Metro or Bus 38 back to the Plaça de Catalunya.

64 **Poble Espanyol.** The Spanish Village was created for the International Exposition of 1929. A sort of artificial Spain-in-a-bottle, with reproductions of Spain's architectural styles, it takes you from the walls of Ávila to the wine cellars of Jerez de la Frontera amid shops, houses, and crafts workshops en route. The liveliest time to come is at night, and a reservation at one of the half dozen restaurants gets you in free, as does the purchase of a ticket for the two discos or the Tablao del Carmen flamenco club. ⊠ *Av. Marquès de Comillas s/n, Montjuïc* ☎ *93/325–7866* 🎟 *€7* ⏲ *Mon. 9–8, Tues.–Thurs. 9–2, weekends 9–4.*

BEACHES

Since Barcelona revamped its beaches for the 1992 Olympics the summer beach scene has been multitudinous. The south end of the Barceloneta beach is the Platja (beach) de Sant Sebastià, a nudist enclave, followed northward by the *platjas* Barceloneta, Passeig Marítim, Port Olímpic, Nova Icaria, Bogatell, and Mar Bella. Topless bathing is common.

The beaches immediately north of Barcelona include Montgat, Ocata, Vilasar de Mar, Arenys de Mar, Canet, and Sant Pol de Mar, all accessible by train from the RENFE station in Plaça de Catalunya. Especially worthy is **Sant Pol,** with clean sand, a lovely old town, and the **Sant Pau** (popularly called La Ruscalleda after its chef, Carme Ruscalleda), one of the best restaurants in Catalonia. The farther north you go, toward the Costa Brava, the better the beaches. Ten kilometers (6 miles) south is the resort **Castelldefels,** with a long, sandy beach and happening bars and restaurants. A 15-minute train ride from Passeig de Gràcia's (or Plaça de Catalunya's) RENFE station to Gavà or Castelldefels deposits you on a 10-km-long (6-mi-long) beach for a superlative walk: from October 25 to February 11 the sun sets into the Mediterranean, thanks to the westward slant of the coastline. There are several good places for lamb chops, *calçots* (spring onions), and paella; the best, **Can Patricio,** has lunch until 4:30. **Sitges,** another 25 minutes south, has better sand and clearer water.

BARS & CAFÉS

Barcelona may have more bars and cafés per capita than any other place in the world. Here you'll find a wide selection of colorful tapas places, sunny outdoor cafés, tearooms, chocolaterias, and, of course, *coctelerías* (cocktail bars), *whiskerias* (often singles bars filled with professional escorts), *xampanyerias* (serving champagne and cava, Catalan sparkling wine), and beer halls. Most stay open until about 2:30 AM.

Cafés

Café de l'Opera. Opposite the Liceu opera house, this high-ceiling Art Nouveau space has welcomed opera goers and performers for more than 100 years. For locals, it's a central point on the Rambla traffic pattern. ✉ *Rambla 74, Rambla* ☎ *93/317–7585.*

Cafe Paris. This café is a lively place to kill time. Everyone from Prince Felipe, heir to the Spanish throne, to poet and pundit James Townsend Pi Sunyer can be spotted here in season. The tapas are excellent, the beer is cold, and the place is open 365 days a year. ✉ *C. Aribau 184, at Carrer Paris, Eixample* ☎ *93/209–8530.*

Cafe Viena. The rectangular perimeter of this inside bar is always packed with travelers in a party mood. The pianist upstairs lends a cabaret touch. ✉ *Rambla dels Estudis 115, Rambla* ☎ *93/349–9800.*

Cafe Zurich. Ever of key importance to Barcelona society, this classic spot at the top of the Rambla is the city's prime meeting place. The outdoor tables offer peerless people-watching; the elegant interior has a high ceiling. ✉ *Pl. de Catalunya 1, Rambla* ☎ *93/317–9153.*

Els Quatre Gats. Picasso staged his first exhibition here, in 1899, and Gaudí and the Catalan Impressionist painters Ramón Casas and Santiago Russinyol held meetings of their Centre Artistic de Sant Lluc in the early 20th century. The restaurant is undistinguished, but the café is a good place to read and people-watch. ✉ *Montsió 3, Barri Gòtic* ☎ *93/302–4140.*

Espai Barroc. Filled with baroque embellishments and music, this unusual "space" (*espai*) is on Carrer Montcada's most beautiful patio, the 15th-century Palau Dalmases. The stairway, with a bas-relief of the rape of Europa, leads up to the Omnium Cultural, a center for the study and diffusion of Catalan history and culture. The patio merits a look even if you find the café too lugubrious. ✉ *Carrer Montcada 20, La Ribera* ☎ *93/310–0673* ⏲ *Closed Mon.*

La Bodegueta. If you can find this dive (literally: it's a short drop below the level of the sidewalk), you'll also find a cluttered space with a dozen small tables, a few places at the marble counter, and happy couples having coffee or beer, and maybe some ham or *tortilla española de patatas* (a typically Spanish, omelet-like potato-and-onion delicacy). ✉ *Rambla de Catalunya 100, Eixample* ☎ *93/215–4894.*

Schilling. Near Plaça Reial, Schilling is always packed. Have coffee by day, drinks and tapas by night. ✉ *Ferran 23, Barri Gòtic* ☎ *93/317–6787.*

Travel Bar. With entrances on Carrer de la Boqueria and Placeta del Pi, and tables in the shady square behind Sant Maria del Pi, this hot spot offers everything from Internet access to walking tours. ✉ *Boqueria 27, Barri Gòtic* ☎ *93/342–5252.*

Coctelerías

Almirall. This Moderniste bar in the Raval is quiet, dimly lit, and dominated by an Art Nouveau mirror and frame behind the marble bar. It's an evocative spot, romantic and mischievous. ✉ *Joaquín Costa 33, Raval* ☎ *93/302–4126* ⏲ *Daily noon–2 AM.*

Boadas. A small, rather formal saloon near the top of the Rambla, Boadas is emblematic of the Barcelona *coctelería* concept, which usually entails a mixture of decorum and expensive mixed drinks amid wood and leather. ✉ *Tallers 1, Rambla* ☎ *93/318–9592* ⏲ *Closed Sun.*

Dry Martini Bar. The eponymous specialty is the best bet at this spot, which exudes a kind of genteel wickedness. This seems to be a popular hangout for mature romantics, husbands, and wives, though not necessarily each other's. ✉ *Aribau 162, Eixample* ☎ *93/217–5072.*

El Born. This former codfish emporium is now a charming and intimate haven for drinks, raclettes, and fondues. The marble cod basins in the entry and the spiral staircase to the second floor are the quirkiest details. ✉ *Passeig del Born 26, La Ribera* ☎ *93/319–5333.*

El Copetín. Right on Barcelona's best-known cocktail avenue, this bar has good cocktails and Irish coffee. Dimly lit, it has a romantic South Seas motif. ✉ *Passeig del Born 19, La Ribera* ☎ *93/317–7585.*

El Paraigua. Behind the *ajuntament,* this rather pricey but stylish bar serves up cocktails and classical music recordings. ✉ *Pl. Sant Miquel, Barri Gòtic* ☎ *93/217–3028.*

Miramelindo. The bar has a large selection of herbal liquors, fruit cocktails, pâtés, and cheeses as well as recorded music, usually jazz. ✉ *Passeig del Born 15, La Ribera* ☎ *93/319–5376.*

Tapas Bars

★ **Cal Pep.** More than tapas, light dinners are served at this lively counter, just east of Santa Maria del Mar. Try the *gambitas* (baby shrimp), *pulpo gallego* (octopus), *garbanzos con espinacas* (garbanzos with spinach), and *pan de coca* (toast with olive oil and fresh tomato paste). A seat at the counter is worth the wait. It's open Tuesday–Saturday 1–4 and 8–midnight, Monday 8–midnight only. ✉ *Pl. de les Olles 8, La Ribera* ☎ *93/319–6183.*

El Irati. Between Plaça del Pi and the Rambla, this boisterous Basque bar has only one drawback: it's hard to squeeze into. Try coming around 1 PM or 7:30 PM. The standard beverage here is *txakolí,* a white Basque wine. The restaurant in back is excellent. ✉ *Cardenal Casañas 17, Barri Gòtic* ☎ *93/302–3084* ⏲ *Closed Mon.*

La Estrella de Plata. This highly respected tapas bar is across the Plaça de les Olles from Cal Pep—a good alternative if the mob there is too daunting. ✉ *Pla del Palau 6, La Ribera* ☎ *93/319–7851.*

Mantequeria Can Ravell. For lovers of exquisite wines, hams, cheeses, oils, whiskies, cigars, caviars, baby eels, and any other delicacy you can think of, this is your spot. The backroom table, where strangers share tastes, is open from mid-morning to 8 PM; it's first come, first served. ✉ *Aragó 313, Eixample* ☎ *93/457–5114* ⏲ *Closed Sun.–Mon.*

Sagardi. This attractive, wood-and-stone cider house comes close to re-creating its Basque prototype, with cider shooting from mammoth barrels, piping-hot tapas, and *txuletas de buey* (beefsteaks) prepared over coals. ✉ *Carrer Argenteria 62, La Ribera* ☎ *93/319–9993.*

Taller de Tapas. Next to Plaça del Pi, facing the eastern lateral facade of Santa Maria del Pi, this fine tapas specialist has it all: cheery young staff, traditional Catalan dishes in bite-size format, and service from midday to midnight. ✉ *Pl. de Sant Josep Oriol 9, Barri Gòtic* ☎ *93/302–6243.*

Xampanyerias & Wine Bars

El Xampanyet. Just down the street from the Picasso Museum, hanging *botas* (leather wineskins) mark one of Barcelona's liveliest *xampanyerias,* usually stuffed to the gills. ✉ *Montcada 22, La Ribera* ☎ *93/319–7003* ⊗ *Closed Mon.*

La Cava del Palau. Handy to the Palau de la Música, this champagne bar has cavas and cocktails, cheeses, pâtés, smoked fish, and caviar. ✉ *Verdaguer i Callis 10, Eixample* ☎ *93/310–0938* ⊗ *Closed Sun.*

La Vinya del Senyor. Ambitiously named "The Lord's Vineyard," this excellent wine bar across from the entrance to Santa Maria del Mar changes its international wine list every fortnight. ✉ *Pl. de Santa Maria 5, La Ribera* ☎ *93/310–3379* ⊗ *Closed Mon.*

Xampú Xampany. Hot and always packed, this cava-tasting emporium on Gran Via is a good way to try Catalan sparkling wines. ✉ *Gran Via 702, Eixample* ☎ *93/265–0483* ⊗ *Closed Sun.*

WHERE TO EAT

Barcelona's restaurant scene is an ongoing surprise. Between the cutting edge of experimental cuisine and the classical roasts and rice dishes of bygone times is a fleet of inventive restaurateurs producing some of Europe's finest Mediterranean cooking.

Catalans are legendary lovers of fish, vegetables, rabbit, duck, lamb, game, and natural ingredients from the Pyrenees or the Mediterranean. The *mar i muntanya* (sea and mountain—that is, surf and turf), a recipe combining seafood with upland products, is a standard. Rabbit and prawns, cuttlefish and meatballs, chickpeas and clams are just a few examples. Combining salty and sweet tastes—a Moorish legacy—is another common theme, as in duck with pears, rabbit with figs, or lamb with olives.

The Mediterranean diet, which is based on virgin olive oil, seafood, fibrous vegetables, onions, garlic, and red wine, is at home in Barcelona, and food tends to be seasoned with Catalonia's four basic sauces —*allioli* (pure garlic and virgin olive oil), romescu (almonds, hazelnuts, tomato, garlic and olive oil), sofregit, (fried onion, tomato, and herbs), and samfaina (a ratatouille-like vegetable mixture).

Typical entrées include *habas a la catalana* (a spicy broad-bean stew), *bullabesa* (fish soup-stew similar to the French bouillabaisse), and *espinacas a la catalana* (spinach cooked with oil, garlic, pine nuts, raisins, and bits of bacon). Bread is often doused with olive oil and spread with tomato to make *pa amb tomaquet,* delicious on its own or as a side order.

Menús del día (menus of the day), served only at lunchtime, are good values. Lunch is served from 1–4, dinner 9–11. Certain restaurants serve continuously from 1 PM to 1 AM. Beware of the advice of hotel concierges and taxi drivers, who have been known to "recommend" places where they get kickbacks.

Catalan wines from the nearby Penedès region, especially the local *méthode champenoise* (sparkling white wine known in Catalonia as *cava*), adequately accompany regional cuisine. Meanwhile, winemakers from the Priorat, Ampurdan, and Costers del Segre regions are producing some of Spain's most exciting new wines.

WHAT IT COSTS In Euros					
	$$$$	$$$	$$	$	¢
	BARCELONA				
AT DINNER	over €25	€18–€25	€12–€18	€8–€12	under €8
	SIDE TRIPS FROM BARCELONA				
AT DINNER	over €20	€15–€20	€10–€15	€6–€10	under €6

Restaurant prices are per person for a main course at dinner.

Ciutat Vella (Old City)

Ciutat Vella comprises the Rambla, Barri Gòtic, Ribera, and Raval districts between Plaça de Catalunya and the port. Chic new restaurants and cafés seem to open daily in Barcelona's Old City.

$$$$ ✕ **Àbac.** In the tradition of Catalonia's finest restaurants, Chef Xavier Pellicer leaves nothing to chance here. With carefully selected ingredients and innovative recipes, this Catalan cuisine with international tendencies is all, in the end, "cuisine d'auteur"—original Pellicer from soup to nuts. ✉ *Rec 79–89, La Ribera* ☎ *93/319–6600* ✍ *Reservations essential* ▭ *AE, DC, MC, V* ⊙ *Closed Sun. and Aug. No lunch Mon.*

$$$$ ✕ **Can Isidre.** Just inside the Raval from Avinguda del Paral.lel,this is a favorite with Barcelona's art mob. Pictures and engravings, some original, by Dalí and other stars line the walls. The traditional Catalan cooking draws on fresh produce from the nearby Boqueria and has a slight French accent. Isidre's wines are invariably novelties from all over the Iberian Peninsula; ask for his advice and you'll get a great wine as well as an oenology, geography, and history course delivered with charm, brevity, and wit. The homemade foie gras is superb. Come and go by cab at night; the area gets sketchy. ✉ *Les Flors 12, El Raval* ☎ *93/441–1139* ✍ *Reservations essential* ▭ *AE, MC, V* ⊙ *Closed Sun., Holy Week, and mid-July–mid-Aug.*

$$$$ ✕ **Comerç 24.** Artist, aesthete, and chef Carles Abellan playfully reinterprets traditional Catalan favorites at this minimalist treasure. Try the *arròs a banda* (paella without the morsels), *tortilla de patatas* (potato omelet), and, for dessert, a postmodern version of the traditional after-school snack of chocolate, olive oil, salt, and bread. The menu is far out, but always hits the mark. ✉ *Carrer Comerç 24, La Ribera* ☎ *93/319–2102* ✍ *Reservations essential* ▭ *AE, DC, MC, V* ⊙ *Closed Sun.*

$$$$ ✕ **Passadis del Pep.** Hidden away through a tiny passageway off the Pla del Palau near the Santa Maria del Mar church, this lively bistro serves a rapid-fire succession of delicious seafood tapas and wine as soon as you appear. Sometime late in the proceedings you may be asked to make a decision about your main course, usually fish of one kind or another. You are free to stop at this point. Avoid *bogavante* (lobster) unless you're on an expense account. ✉ *Pla del Palau 2, La Ribera* ☎ *93/310–1021* ▭ *AE, DC, MC, V* ⊙ *Closed Sun. and last 2 wks of Aug.*

$$$$ ✕ **Valentí.** Chef Enrique Valentí combines original touches with classical Mediterranean and international influences in this rising star tucked in behind Barcelona's town hall. Trained by Fermí Puig at Drolma, this is a refuge for fine palates and adventurous diners and tasters. ✉ *Ciutat 13, Barri Gòtic* ☎ *93/310–7034* ✍ *Reservations essential* ▭ *AE, DC, MC, V* ⊙ *Closed Sat. lunch and Sun.*

KEY
Funicular
Metro Stations
Railway Lines
Telefèric
Tourist Information
Passeig de Manuel Girona
Avda. de Pedralbes
Plaça Pius XII
Plaça Prat de la Riba
Ronda del General Mitre
C. de les Escoles
C. de Modolell
Via Augusta
Calle de Sant Elíes
C. de Ganduxer
C. de Numància
C. Deu i Mata
Travessera de les Corts
C. de Calvet
C. Santaló
C. de Muntaner
Pl. de Francesc Macià
C. de Tuset
Travessera
Augusta
Via
Avda. Diagonal
C. d'Entença
C. de Loreto
C. de Joan Güell
C. del Vallespir
C. de Berlín
Avda. de J. Tarradellas
C. de París
C. de Còrsega
C. del Rosselló
C. de Villarroel
C. d'Aribau
Estació Central-Sants
Pl. Països Catalans
C. de Provença
Avda. de Roma
C. de Mallorca
C. de la Creu Coberta
C. de Valencia
C. d'Aragó
Entença
C. de Rocafort
C. de Calabria
C. de Viladomat
C. del Comte Borrell
C. del Comte d'Urgell
C. de Casanova
C. de Balmes
Rambla de Catalunya
C. de la Diputacio
Plaça Universitat
Plaça d'Espanya
C. de Vilamarí
Gran Via de les Corts Catalanes
Ronda Universitat
C. dels Tallers
Pelai
C. de Sepulveda
Avda. de Mistral
C. de Floridablanca
Avda. del Paral·lel
Avda. Reina M. Cristina
Ronda Sant Antoni
Plaça de Sant Jordi
Pl. de les Cascades
C. de Tamarit
C. de Manso
Joaquín Costa
Pg. de les Cascades
C. de Lleida
Palou Nacional
C. de Hospital
C. del Carme
Rda. de Sant Pau
Carretes
C. de Blai
C. de Magalhaes
Jardins de Joan Maragall
Boquería Market
Pl. St Jaume
C. de Sant Pau
C. la Unió
C. Nou de la Rambla
Les Flors
Estadi Olímpic
Avda. de Miramar
Camí dels Tres Pins
Plaça Reial
Parc de Montjuïc
Pg. de Montjuïc
Portal de la Pau
C. dels Mondials
Jardins de Miramar
Moll de Sant Bertrán
TORRE DE JAUME I
Castell de Montjuïc
1
2
3
4
5
6
7
8
9
15
16
21
22
23
24
40

Àbac 31
Acontraluz 5
Agut 25
Antiga Casa Solé 36
Botafumeiro 10
Ca l'Estevet 16
Café de l'Acadèmia 28
Can Gaig 38
Can Isidre 40
Can Majó 37
Can Manel la Puda 35
Casa Calvet 17
Casa Leopoldo 21
Comerç 24 33
Cometacinc 27
Drolma 13
El Asador de Aranda 9
El Convent 22
El Foro 32
El Leopoldo Petit 23
El Mató de Pedralbes 2
El Racó de Can Fabes 19
El Racó d'en Freixa 8
El Tragaluz 11
Folquer 14
Gorría 18
Jean Luc Figueras 12
La Taxidermista 24
Le Quattro Stagione 6
L'Olivé 15
Mey Hoffman 29
Neichel 1
Passadis del Pep 30
Reial Club Marítim 34
Sant Pau 20
Silvestre 7
Talaia Mar 39
Tram-Tram 3
Valentí 25
Vivanda 4

★ **$$$–$$$$** ✕ **Casa Leopoldo.** Hidden in the dark Raval west of the Rambla, Rosa Gil's fine restaurant serves stellar seafood and Catalan fare. Approach either by taxi or along Carrer Hospital, take a left through the Passatge Bernardí Martorell, and go 50 ft right on Sant Rafael. Try the *revuelto de ajos tiernos y gambas* (eggs scrambled with young garlic and shrimp) or the famous *cap-i-pota,* stewed head and hoof of pork. ✉ *Sant Rafael 24, El Raval* ☎ *93/441–3014* 💳 *AE, DC, MC, V* ⊗ *Closed Mon. No dinner Sun.*

$$$–$$$$ ✕ **Mey Hofmann.** This thickly vegetated dining room just up Argenteria from Santa Maria del Mar is a cooking academy and first-rate restaurant specializing in Mediterranean cuisine *"de creación"* (meaning original recipes). The young waiters and waitresses are chefs-in-training, and are usually encyclopedic about ingredients and preparations from aperitif wines to cheeses and desserts. ✉ *Argenteria 74–78, La Ribera* ☎ *93/319–5889* 💳 *AE, DC, MC, V* ⊗ *Closed weekends.*

$$–$$$ ✕ **Café de l'Acadèmia.** With wicker chairs, stone walls, and background classical music, this place is sophisticated-rustic, and the excellent Catalan cuisine makes it more than a mere café. It's frequented by politicians and functionaries from the nearby Generalitat and is always boiling with life. Be sure to reserve at lunchtime. ✉ *Lledó 1, Barri Gòtic* ☎ *93/319–8253* 💳 *AE, DC, MC, V.*

$$–$$$ ✕ **El Leopoldo Petit.** Rosa Gil's second restaurant offers the market hustle and bustle of the Boqueria with an emphasis on Portuguese recipes of cod, rice dishes, duck, and fish and pork combinations. From the fish market in the entryway to the intimate nooks and crannies inside, this is another Gil family success story. ✉ *Petxina 7, El Raval* ☎ *93/317–9509* 💳 *AE, MC, V* ⊗ *Closed Mon. and July. No dinner Sun.*

$$–$$$ ✕ **La Taxidermista.** Don't worry: no road kill is served here. Once a natural-science museum and taxidermy shop (from which Dalí once purchased 200,000 ants and a stuffed rhinoceros), this is the only recommendable restaurant in the sunny Plaça Reial. Interior decorator Beth Gali designed the interior around original beams and steel columns. Delicacies such as *bonito con escalivada y queso de cabra* (white tuna with braised aubergines, peppers, and goat cheese) are served at outside tables best enjoyed in the winter sun. ✉ *Plaça Reial 8, La Rambla* ☎ *93/412–4536* 💳 *AE, DC, MC, V* ⊗ *Closed Mon.*

$$ ✕ **Cometacinc.** This stylish place in the Barri Gòtic, an increasingly chic neighborhood of artisans and antiquers, is a fine example of Barcelona's new-over-old architecture and interior design panache. Although the 30-ft floor-to-ceiling wooden shutters are already a visual feast, the carefully prepared interpretations of old standards, such as the *carpaccio de toro de lidia* (carpaccio of fighting bull) with basil sauce and pine nuts, address the palate brilliantly. ✉ *Carrer Cometa 5, Barri Gòtic* ☎ *93/310–1558* 💳 *AE, DC, MC, V* ⊗ *Closed Tues.*

$–$$ ✕ **Agut.** Wood paneling surmounted by white walls, on which hang 1950s canvases, create a comfortable setting for the mostly Catalan crowd in this homey restaurant in the lower reaches of the Gothic Quarter. Agut was founded in 1924, and its popularity has never waned—not least because the hearty Catalan fare is a fantastic value. In season (September–May) try the *pato silvestre agridulce* (sweet-and-sour wild duck). There's a good selection of wine, but no frills such as coffee or liqueur. ✉ *Gignàs 16, Barri Gòtic* ☎ *93/315–1709* 💳 *AE, MC, V* ⊗ *Closed Mon. and July. No dinner Sun.*

$–$$ ✕ **Ca l'Estevet.** Facing the journalism school and around the block from Barcelona's *La Vanguardia* daily, this romantic little spot near the MACBA (contemporary art museum) is popular with journalists, students, and artists. Estevet and family are charming, and the carefully elaborated Catalan cuisine sparkles, especially at these prices. Try the asparagus cooked over coals, the *chopitos gaditanos* (deep-fried baby octopus), or the *magret de pato* (duck breast). The house wine is inexpensive and perfectly drinkable. ✉ *Valdoncella 46, El Raval* ☎ *93/302–4186* ▭ *AE, DC, MC, V* ⊗ *Closed Sun.*

$–$$ ✕ **El Convent.** Hidden away behind the Boqueria market, this traditional restaurant is good value. The Catalan home cooking, with such favorites as *faves a la catalana* (broad beans stewed with sausage), comes straight from the Boqueria. The intimate balconies and dining rooms have marble-top tables and can accommodate groups of 2 or 20. A bargain *menú del día* makes lunch the best time to come. ✉ *Jerusalem 3, El Raval* ☎ *93/317–1052* ▭ *AE, DC, MC, V.*

$–$$ ✕ **El Foro.** This hot spot near the Born is always full to the rafters with lively young and not-so-young people. Painting and photographic exhibits line the walls, and the menu is dominated by pizzas, salads, and meat cooked over coals. Flamenco and jazz performances downstairs are a good post-dinner option. ✉ *Princesa 53, La Ribera* ☎ *93/310–1020* ▭ *AE, DC, MC, V* ⊗ *Closed Mon.*

Barceloneta & the Port Olímpic

Barceloneta and the Port Olímpic (Olympic Port) have little in common beyond their seaside location, the former a traditional fishermen's quarter and the latter a crazed disco strip with thousand-seat restaurants.

$$$$ ✕ **Antiga Casa Solé.** Two blocks from the sea side of Plaça de Sant Miquel, Barceloneta's prettiest square, you'll find this traditional midday-Sunday pilgrimage site, which occupies a characteristic waterfront house and serves fresh, well-prepared, piping hot seafood. Whether it's *lenguado a la plancha* (grilled sole) or the exquisite *arroç negre amb sepia en su tinta* (black rice with squid in its ink), everything here comes loaded with flavor. In winter try to sit near the open kitchen for the aromas, sights, sounds, and warmth. ✉ *Sant Carles 4, Barceloneta* ☎ *93/221–5012* ▭ *AE, DC, MC, V* ⊗ *Closed Mon. and last 2 wks of Aug. No dinner Sun.*

$$$$ ✕ **Talaia Mar.** Generally recognized as the finest restaurant in the Olympic Port, this bright spot has wonderful Mediterranean views and fresh seafood. The taster's menu is a bargain; it's a good way to sample the chef's best work for little more than a regular meal would cost. ✉ *Marina 16, Port Olímpic* ☎ *93/221–9090* ▭ *AE, MC, V.*

★ $$$–$$$$ ✕ **Can Majó.** On the beach in Barceloneta is one of Barcelona's premier seafood restaurants. House specialties include *caldero de bogavante* (a cross between paella and lobster bouillabaisse) and *suquet* (fish stewed in its own juices), but whatever you choose will be excellent. In summer, the terrace overlooking the Mediterranean is the closest you can come to beachside dining. ✉ *Almirall Aixada 23, Barceloneta* ☎ *93/221–5455* ▭ *AE, DC, MC, V* ⊗ *Closed Sun.–Mon.*

$$$ ✕ **Reial Club Marítim.** For sunset or harbor views, excellent maritime fare, and a sense of remove from the city, try Barcelona's yacht club, just around the harbor through Barceloneta. Highlights are *paella marinera* (seafood paella), *rodaballo* (turbot), *lubina* (sea bass), and *dorado* (sea bream). Ask for the freshest fish they have and you won't be disappointed. ✉ *Moll d'Espanya, Barceloneta* ☎ *93/221–7143* ▭ *AE, DC, MC, V* ⊗ *No dinner Sun.*

¢–$ ✕ **Can Manel la Puda.** The first choice for paella in the sun, year-round, Can Manel is near the end of the main road out to the Barceloneta beach. Any time before 4 o'clock will do; it then reopens at 7. *Arròs a banda* (rice with peeled shellfish) and paella *marinera* (with seafood) or *fideuà* (with noodles instead of rice) are all delicious. ✉ *Passeig Joan de Borbó 60, Barceloneta* ☎ *93/221–5013* ▭ *AE, DC, MC, V* ⊙ *Closed Mon.*

Eixample

Eixample dining, invariably upscale and elegant, ranges from traditional cuisine in Moderniste houses to designer fare in sleek minimalist-experimental spaces.

★ $$$$ ✕ **Can Gaig.** This exquisite Barcelona favorite is famous for superb design *and* cuisine. Market-fresh ingredients and experimental cooking are based on ancient recipes from Catalan home cooking, while the menu balances seafood and upland specialties, game, and domestic raw materials. Try the *perdiz asada con jamón ibérico* (roast partridge with Iberian ham). ✉ *Passeig de Maragall 402, Eixample* ☎ *93/429–1017* 📠 *93/429–7002* ✍ *Reservations essential* ▭ *AE, DC, MC, V* ⊙ *Closed Mon., Holy Week, and Aug.*

$$$$ ✕ **Casa Calvet.** This Art Nouveau space in Antoni Gaudí's 1898–1900 Casa Calvet just a block down from the Ritz is an opportunity to break bread in one of the great Moderniste's creations. The dining room is a graceful and spectacular design display featuring signature Gaudí ornamentation from looping parabolic door handles to polychrome stained glass, acid engravings, and wood carved in floral and organic motifs. The menu is Mediterranean, with an emphasis on light, contemporary fare. ✉ *Casp 48, Eixample* ☎ *93/412–4012* ▭ *AE, DC, MC, V* ⊙ *Closed Sun. and last 2 wks of Aug.*

★ $$$$ ✕ **Drolma.** Named (in Sanskrit) for Buddha's female side, Fermin Puig's intimate refuge in the Hotel Majestic was an instant success. The *menú de degustaciò* (taster's menu) might have pheasant cannelloni in foie-gras sauce with fresh black truffles or giant prawn tails with *trompettes de la mort* (black wild mushrooms) with *sôt-l'y-laisse* (free-range chicken nuggets). Fermin's foie gras *a la ceniza con ceps* (cooked over wood coals with wild mushrooms)—a recipe rescued from Fermin's boyhood farmhouse feasts—is typical of Drolma's blend of tradition and inspiration. ✉ *Passeig de Gràcia 70, Eixample* ☎ *93/496–7710* ✍ *Reservations essential* ▭ *AE, DC, MC, V* ⊙ *Closed Sun. and Aug.*

$$$$ ✕ **L'Olivé.** Specializing in Catalan home cooking, this busy, attractive Eixample spot is always filled with trendy diners having a great time. You soon see why: excellent hearty food, smart service, and some of the best *pa amb tomaquet* (toasted bread with olive oil and squeezed tomato) in town. ✉ *Balmes 47, Eixample* ☎ *93/452–1990* ▭ *AE, DC, MC, V* ⊙ *No dinner Sun.*

$$$–$$$$ ✕ **El Tragaluz.** *Tragaluz* means skylight—literally, "light-swallower"—and this is an excellent choice if you're still on a design high from Gaudí's Pedrera. The sliding roof opens to the stars in good weather, while the chairs, lamps, and fittings by Javier Mariscal (creator of 1992 Olympic mascot Cobi) reflect Barcelona's passion for whimsy and playful design. The Mediterranean cuisine is light and innovative. ✉ *Passatge de la Concepció 5, Eixample* ☎ *93/487–0196* ▭ *AE, DC, MC, V* ⊙ *No lunch Mon.*

$$$–$$$$ ✕ **Gorría.** One of the two best Basque restaurants in Barcelona, everything from the stewed *pochas* (white beans) to the heroic *chuletón* (steak) is as pure as the Navarran Pyrenees. The Castillo de Sajazarra reserva '95, a semi-secret brick-red Rioja, provides perfect accompaniment at this delicious pocket of Navarra in the Catalan capital. ✉ *Diputació 421, Eixample* ☎ *93/245–1164* ▭ *AE, DC, MC, V* ⊙ *Closed Sun.*

Gràcia

This exciting yet intimate neighborhood has everything from the most sophisticated cuisine in town to Basque taverns and eastern cuisine in a lively, young context.

$$$$ ✕ **Botafumeiro.** Fleets of waiters in white outfits move at the speed of light in Barcelona's best Galician restaurant, a seafood medley from shellfish to fin-fish to cuttlefish to caviar. An assortment of *media ración* (half-ration) selections is available at the bar, where *pulpo a feira* (squid on potato) and *jamón bellota de Guijuelo* (acorn-fed ham) make peerless late-night fare. People-watching is tops, and the waiters are stand-up comics. ✉ *Gran de Gràcia 81, Gràcia* ☎ *93/218–4230* ▭ *AE, DC, MC, V.*

$$$$ ✕ **Jean-Luc Figueras.** A Gràcia town house that was once Cristóbal Balenciaga's studio houses this perennial favorite on everyone's short list of Barcelona restaurants. The berry-pink walls, polished dark-wood floors, and brass sconces make a rich backdrop for unforgettable Catalan cuisine with a French accent. The *menú de degustaciò* is, for value and variety, the best choice for innovative interpretations such as the fried prawn with ginger pasta and mustard and mango sauce. ✉ *Carrer Santa Teresa 10, Gràcia* ☎ *93/415–2877* ✍ *Reservations essential* ▭ *AE, DC, MC, V* ⊙ *Closed Sun. No lunch Sat.*

$–$$ ✕ **Folquer.** This little hideaway in the bottom of Gràcia is a good way to end a tour of this village within a city. With one of the best-value taster's menus in Barcelona, Folquer serves creatively prepared traditional Catalan specialties that use first-rate ingredients. ✉ *Torrent de l'Olla 3, Gràcia* ☎ *93/217–4395* ▭ *AE, DC, MC, V* ⊙ *Closed Sun. and last 2 wks of Aug. No lunch Sat.*

Sarrià-Pedralbes & Sant Gervasi

Take an excursion to the upper reaches of town for an excellent selection of restaurants, along with cool summer evening breezes and a sense of village life in Sarrià.

$$$$ ✕ **El Racò d'en Freixa.** Chef Ramó Freixa, one of Barcelona's established culinary lights, is taking founding father José María's work to another level. His clever reinterpretations of traditional recipes, all made with high-quality raw ingredients, have qualified the younger Freixa's work as *cuina d'autor* (designer cuisine). One specialty is *peus de porc en escabetx de guatlle* (pig's feet with quail in a garlic-and-parsley gratin). ✉ *Sant Elíes 22, Sant Gervasi* ☎ *93/209–7559* ▭ *AE, DC, MC, V* ⊙ *Closed Mon., Holy Week, and Aug. No dinner Sun.*

$$$$ ✕ **Le Quattro Stagioni.** For excellent, streamlined Italian cuisine that will remind you more of postmodern Catalan cooking than of *The Godfather,* this chic spot just down from the Bonanova metro stop on the Sarrià line is a winner. It's always filled with intriguing-looking bons vivants (evenly balanced between hip locals and clued-in tourists), and the garden is cool and fragrant on summer nights. ✉ *Dr. Roux 37, Sant Gervasi* ☎ *93/205–2279* ▭ *AE, DC, MC, V.*

$$$$ ✕ **Neichel.** Alsatian chef Jean-Louis Neichel is universally respected for such French delicacies as *ensalada de gambas al sésamo con puerros* (shrimp in sesame-seed sauce with leeks). The restaurant is on the ground floor of a Pedralbes apartment block. ✉ *Carrer Bertran i Rozpide 16 bis (off Av. Pedralbes), Pedralbes* ☎ *93/203–8408* ✍ *Reservations essential* ▭ *AE, DC, MC, V* ⊙ *Closed Sun., Mon., and Aug.*

$$$$ ✕ **Silvestre.** This sleek youngster in Barcelona's culinary firmament serves modern cuisine to some of Barcelona's most distinguished diners. Just below Via Augusta in upper Barcelona, a series of intimate dining rooms and cozy corners are carefully tended by chef Guillermo Casañé and Marta Cabot, his charming (and perfect-English-speaking) partner and maître d'. Look for fresh market produce lovingly prepared and dishes such as tuna tartare or noodles and shrimp. ✉ *Santaló 101, Sant Gervasi* ☎ *93/241–4031* ▭ *AE, DC, MC, V* ⊙ *Closed Sun. and 3 wks in Aug. No lunch Sat.*

★ $$$$ ✕ **Tram-Tram.** At the end of the old tram line above the village of Sarrià, Isidre Soler and his stunning wife, Reyes, have put together one of Barcelona's finest culinary offerings. Try the *menú de degustaciò* (taster's menu) and you might score marinated tuna salad, cod medallions, and venison filet mignons. Perfect portions and a streamlined reinterpretation of space within this traditional Sarrià house—especially in or near the garden out back—make this a memorable dining experience. Reservations are a good idea, but Reyes can almost always invent a table. ✉ *Major de Sarrià 121, Sarrià* ☎ *93/204–8518* ▭ *AE, DC, MC, V* ⊙ *Closed Sun. and late Dec.–early Jan. No lunch Sat.*

$$–$$$ ✕ **Vivanda.** Just above the Plaça de Sarrià, this leafy garden is especially wonderful between May and mid-October, when outside dining is a delight. The menu has Catalan specialties such as *espinacas a la catalana* (spinach with raisins, pine nuts, and garlic) and inventive combinations of seafood and inland products. ✉ *Major de Sarrià 134, Sarrià* ☎ *93/203–1918* ▭ *AE, DC, MC, V* ⊙ *Closed Sun.*

$$ ✕ **Acontraluz.** This stylish covered terrace in the leafy upper-Barcelona neighborhood of Tres Torres has a strenuously varied menu ranging from game in season, such as *rable de liebre* (stewed hare) with chutney, to the more northern *pochas con almejas* (beans with clams). All dishes are prepared with care and flair, and the lunch menu is a bargain. ✉ *Milanesat 19, Tres Torres* ☎ *93/203–0658* ▭ *AE, DC, MC, V.*

$–$$ ✕ **El Mató de Pedralbes.** Named for the *mató* (cottage cheese) traditionally prepared by the Clarist nuns across the street in the Monestir de Pedralbes, this is a fine stop after touring the monastery, which closes at 2. The restaurant has one of the most typically Catalan, best-value menus in town. Look for *sopa de ceba gratinée* (onion soup), *trinxat* (chopped cabbage with bacon bits), and *truite de patata i ceba* (potato and onion omelet). ✉ *Obispo Català, Pedralbes* ☎ *93/204–7962* ▭ *AE, DC, MC, V* ⊙ *Closed Sun.*

Tibidabo

$$$ ✕ **El Asador de Aranda.** Designed by Art Nouveau architect Rubió i Bellver, this immense palace 1,600 ft above the Avenida Tibidabo metro station is a hike—but worth remembering if you're in upper Barcelona. The kitchen specializes in *cordero lechal* (roast lamb); try *pimientos de piquillo* (hot, spicy peppers) on the side. The dining room has a terracotta floor and a full complement of Art Nouveau ornamentation ranging from intricately carved wood trimmings to stained-glass partitions, acid-engraved glass, and Moorish archways. ✉ *Av. del Tibidabo 31, Tibidabo* ☎ *93/417–0115* ▭ *AE, DC, MC, V* ⊙ *Closed Holy Week and Sun. in Aug. No dinner Sun.*

Outskirts of Barcelona

With the many fine in-town dining options available in Barcelona, any out-of-town recommendations must logically rank somewhere in the uppermost stratosphere of gastronomic excellence. These two, both rated among the top five or six establishments below the Pyrenees—one at the foot of Montseny, the other on the coast—undoubtedly do.

$$$$ Fodor's Choice ★ ✕ **El Racó de Can Fabes.** Santi Santamaria's master class in Mediterranean cuisine merits the 45-minute train ride (or 30-minute drive) north of Barcelona to Sant Celoni. One of the four best restaurants in Spain (along with El Bullí in Roses and Arzak and Berasategui in San Sebastián), this is a must for anyone interested in fine dining. Every detail from the six flavors of freshly baked bread to the cheese selection is superb. The taster's menu is the wisest solution. The RENFE stations are at Passeig de Gràcia or Sants (the last train back is at 9:30, so this is a lunchtime-only transport solution). ✉ *Sant Joan 6, Sant Celoni* ☎ *93/867–2851* ▭ *AE, DC, MC, V* ⊗ *Closed Mon., 1st 2 wks of Feb., and late June–early July. No dinner Sun.*

★ $$$$ ✕ **Sant Pau.** Carme Ruscalleda's Sant Pol de Mar treasure is a scenic 40-minute train ride along the beach from Plaça Catalunya's RENFE station: the Calella train stops at the door. (The last evening train is too early for dinner, so this a lunchtime-only operation.) Star dishes include *vieiras* (scallops) with crisped artichoke flakes on roast potato, and *lubina* (sea bass) on baby leeks and chard in *garnatxa* (sweet Catalan wine) sauce. The *misiva de amor* (love letter) is a pastry envelope with slivers of raspberries, wild strawberries, blueberries, and julienned peaches. ✉ *Nou 10, Sant Pol de Mar* ☎ *93/760–0662* ▭ *AE, DC, MC, V* ⊗ *Closed Mon., 2 wks in Mar., and 2 wks in Nov. No dinner Sun.*

WHERE TO STAY

Barcelona's hotels offer clear distinctions. Hotels in the Ciutat Vella (Old City)—the Gothic Quarter and along the Rambla—are charming and convenient for sightseeing but, with notable exceptions, weaker on creature comforts. Eixample hotels (including most of the best) are often in late-19th- or early 20th-century town houses restored and converted into exciting modern hubs. Downtown hotels, including the Ritz, the Claris, the Majestic, the Condes de Barcelona, and the Colón, probably best combine style and luxury with a sense of where you are, while the sybaritic peripheral palaces (the Hotel Arts and the Rey Juan Carlos I) are less about Barcelona and more about generic luxury. Sarrià and Sant Gervasi upper city hotels get you up out of the the urban crush, and Olympic Port and Diagonal Mar hotels are in highrise towers (requiring taxis to and from the real Barcelona). Smaller hotels, of course, are less than half as expensive and more a part of city life.

Hotels will negotiate room rates if they're not full. Ask about weekend rates, which are often half; faxing for reservations may also get you a good deal. Business travelers may get a 40% break.

WHAT IT COSTS In Euros

	$$$$	$$$	$$	$	¢
	BARCELONA				
FOR 2 PEOPLE	over €225	€150–€225	€80–€150	€50–€80	under €50
	SIDE TRIPS FROM BARCELONA				
FOR 2 PEOPLE	over €180	€100–€180	€60–€100	€40–€60	under €40

Hotel prices are for two people in a standard double room in high season, excluding tax.

Ciutat Vella (Old City)

$$$$ **Eurostar Grand Marina Hotel.** A cylindrical tower built around a central patio, the Grand Marina offers maximum luxury just two minutes

from the Rambla over Barcelona's port. With stunning views of the city or the Mediterranean, this ultracontemporary monolith is in the middle of, though well above, Barcelona's best sites. ✉ *Moll de Barcelona (World Trade Center), Port Olímpic, 08039* ☎ *93/603-9000* 🖷 *93/603-9090* 🌐 *www.grandmarinahotel.com* 258 rooms, 15 suites 3 restaurants, minibars, cable TV, pool, fitness club, hair salon, bar, parking (fee) ▭ *AE, DC, MC, V.*

$$$$ **Le Meridien.** English-owned and -managed despite its name, Le Meridien vies with the Rivoli Ramblas as the premier hotel in the Rambla area. Guest rooms are light, spacious, and decorated in pastels. The hotel has hosted its share of celebrities and is very popular with businesspeople. Fax machines and computers for your room are available on request. A room overlooking the Rambla is worth the extra noise. ✉ *Rambla 111, Rambla, 08002* ☎ *93/318-6200* 🖷 *93/301-7776* 🌐 *www.meridienbarcelona.com* *206 rooms* *Restaurant, bar, baby-sitting, business services, car rental, parking (fee)* ▭ *AE, DC, MC, V.*

$$$–$$$$ **Colón.** Surprisingly charming and intimate for such a sizable hotel,
Fodor'sChoice ★ this Barcelona standby is directly across the plaza from the cathedral, overlooking weekend *sardana* dancing, Thursday antiques markets, and, of course, the floodlit cathedral by night. Rooms are comfortable and tasteful; try to get one with a view of the cathedral. The Colón was a favorite of Joan Miró. Considering its combination of comfort, style, and location it may be the best hotel in Barcelona. ✉ *Av. Catedral 7, Barri Gòtic, 08002* ☎ *93/301-1404* 🖷 *93/317-2915* 🌐 *www.hotelcolon.es* *147 rooms* *Restaurant, in-room data ports, minibars, cable TV, bar, baby-sitting, meeting room, car rental, travel services* ▭ *AE, DC, MC, V.*

$$$–$$$$ **Montecarlo.** The ornate, illuminated entrance takes you from the Rambla through an enticing marble hall; upstairs, you enter a sumptuous reception room with a dark-wood Art Nouveau ceiling. Guest rooms are modern, bright, and functional, and many overlook the Rambla. ✉ *Rambla 124, Rambla, 08002* ☎ *93/412-0404* 🖷 *93/318-7323* 🌐 *www.montecarlobcn.com* *55 rooms* *Cafeteria, minibars, cable TV, bar, parking (fee)* ▭ *AE, DC, MC, V.*

$$–$$$ **Nouvel.** Centrally located below Plaça de Catalunya, this hotel blends white marble, etched glass, elaborate plasterwork, and carved, dark woodwork in its handsome Art Nouveau interior. The rooms have marble floors, firm beds, and smart bathrooms. The narrow street is pedestrian-only and therefore quiet, but views are nonexistent. ✉ *Santa Anna 18–20, Rambla, 08002* ☎ *93/301-8274* 🖷 *93/301-8370* 🌐 *www.hotelnouvel.com* *71 rooms* *Restaurant, cable TV, bar* ▭ *AE, DC, MC, V.*

$$–$$$ **Racó del Pi.** This sleek, modern space on a bustling Gothic Quarter street offers first-rate service and flawless if somewhat characterless accommodations. Equidistant from the cathedral, the Boqueria market, Plaça Catalunya, and the Palau de la Musica, this cozy *racó* (corner) is as practical as it is spotless. ✉ *Carrer del Pi 7, Rambla, 08002* ☎ *93/342-6190* 🖷 *93/342-6191* 🌐 *www.h10.es* *37 rooms* *Bar, breakfast room, minibars, cable TV* ▭ *AE, DC, MC, V.*

$$ **Citadines.** This Rambla hotel is impeccably bright and modern, soundproof, and generally well equipped. All rooms have kitchenettes and small dining areas. The rooftop solarium has views of Montjuïc and the Mediterranean. ✉ *Rambla 122, Rambla, 08002* ☎ *93/270-1111* 🖷 *93/412-7421* 🌐 *www.citadines.com* *115 studios, 16 apartments* *Kitchenettes, minibars, bar, meeting rooms* ▭ *AE, DC, MC, V.*

$$ **Rialto.** This hotel seems to have taken a leaf from the paradors' book, with pine floors, white walls, and walnut doors. The rooms (ask for an interior one if street noise bothers you) echo this look, with heavy furniture set against light walls. There's a bar in the basement and a modern *salón* off the lobby. ✉ *Ferran 42, Barri Gòtic, 08002* ☎ *93/318–5212* 📠 *93/318–5312* 🌐 *www.gargallo-hoteles.com* *199 rooms* *Restaurant, bar, meeting rooms* 💳 *AE, DC, MC, V.*

$$ **Rivoli Ramblas.** Behind this upper-Rambla facade lies an imaginative, state-of-the-art interior, complete with marble floors. The rooms are pastel in hue and contemporary in design. The roof-terrace bar has panoramic views. ✉ *Rambla 128, Rambla, 08002* ☎ *93/481–7676* 📠 *93/317–2038* 🌐 *www.rivolihotels.com* *81 rooms* *Restaurant, health club, bar, meeting rooms, parking (fee)* 💳 *AE, DC, MC, V.*

$$ **San Agustí.** Just off the Rambla in the leafy square of the same name, the San Agustí has long been popular with musicians performing at the Liceu opera house. Rooms are small but pleasantly modern, with plenty of fresh wood and clean lines. ✉ *Pl. de San Agustí 3, Raval, 08001* ☎ *93/318–1658* 📠 *93/317–2928* 🌐 *www.hotelsa.com* *77 rooms* *Cafeteria, bar* 💳 *AE, DC, MC, V.*

$$ **Suizo.** The public rooms have elegant, modern seating and good views over the noisy square east of Plaça del Rei. The guest rooms have bright walls and wood or tile floors. ✉ *Pl. del Àngel 12, Barri Gòtic, 08002* ☎ *93/310–6108* 📠 *93/315–0461* 🌐 *www.gargallo-hotels.com* *59 rooms* *Bar* 💳 *AE, DC, MC, V.*

$–$$ **Continental.** This modest hotel stands at the top of the Rambla, below Plaça de Catalunya. Space is tight, but rooms manage to accommodate large, firm beds. It's high enough over the Rambla to escape street noise, so ask for a room overlooking Barcelona's most emblematic street. This is a good place to read *Homage to Catalonia,* as George Orwell stayed here with his wife in 1937 after recovering from a bullet wound. ✉ *Rambla 138, Rambla, 08002* ☎ *93/301–2570* 📠 *93/302–7360* 🌐 *www.hotelcontinental.com* *35 rooms* 💳 *AE, DC, MC, V.*

$ **Jardí.** Perched over the traffic-free and charming Plaça del Pi and Plaça Sant Josep Oriol, this chic budget hotel has rooms with views of the Gothic church of Santa Maria del Pi. All rooms have pine furniture and small bathrooms. The in-house breakfast is excellent, and the alfresco tables at the Bar del Pi, downstairs, are ideal in summer. With five floors and an elevator, this is not the Ritz, and it can be noisy in summer, but it's still a great value. ✉ *Pl. Sant Josep Oriol 1, Barri Gòtic, 08002* ☎ *93/301–5900* 📠 *93/342–5733* 🌐 *www.hoteljardi.com* *40 rooms* 💳 *AE, DC, MC, V.*

Fodor's Choice ★

Barceloneta & the Port Olímpic

$$$$ **Hotel Arts.** This luxurious Ritz-Carlton monolith overlooks Barcelona from the Olympic Port, providing views of the Mediterranean, the city, and the mountains behind. A short taxi ride from the center of the city, the hotel is virtually a world of its own, with three restaurants (one specializing in California cuisine), an outdoor pool, and the beach. ✉ *C. de la Marina 19–21, Port Olímpic, 08005* ☎ *93/221–1000* 📠 *93/221–1070* 🌐 *www.harts.es* *397 rooms, 59 suites, 27 apartments* *3 restaurants, minibars, cable TV, pool, hair salon, beach, bar, parking (fee)* 💳 *AE, DC, MC, V.*

¢–$ **Marina Folch.** This little Barceloneta hideaway is crisp, clean, and contemporary. Five minutes from the beach, with views over the port, an excellent restaurant, and a generous and caring family at the helm, it's a winner. ✉ *Carrer Mar 16 pral., Barceloneta, 08003* ☎ *93/310–3709* 📠 *93/310–5327* *7 rooms* *Restaurant* 💳 *AE, DC, MC, V.*

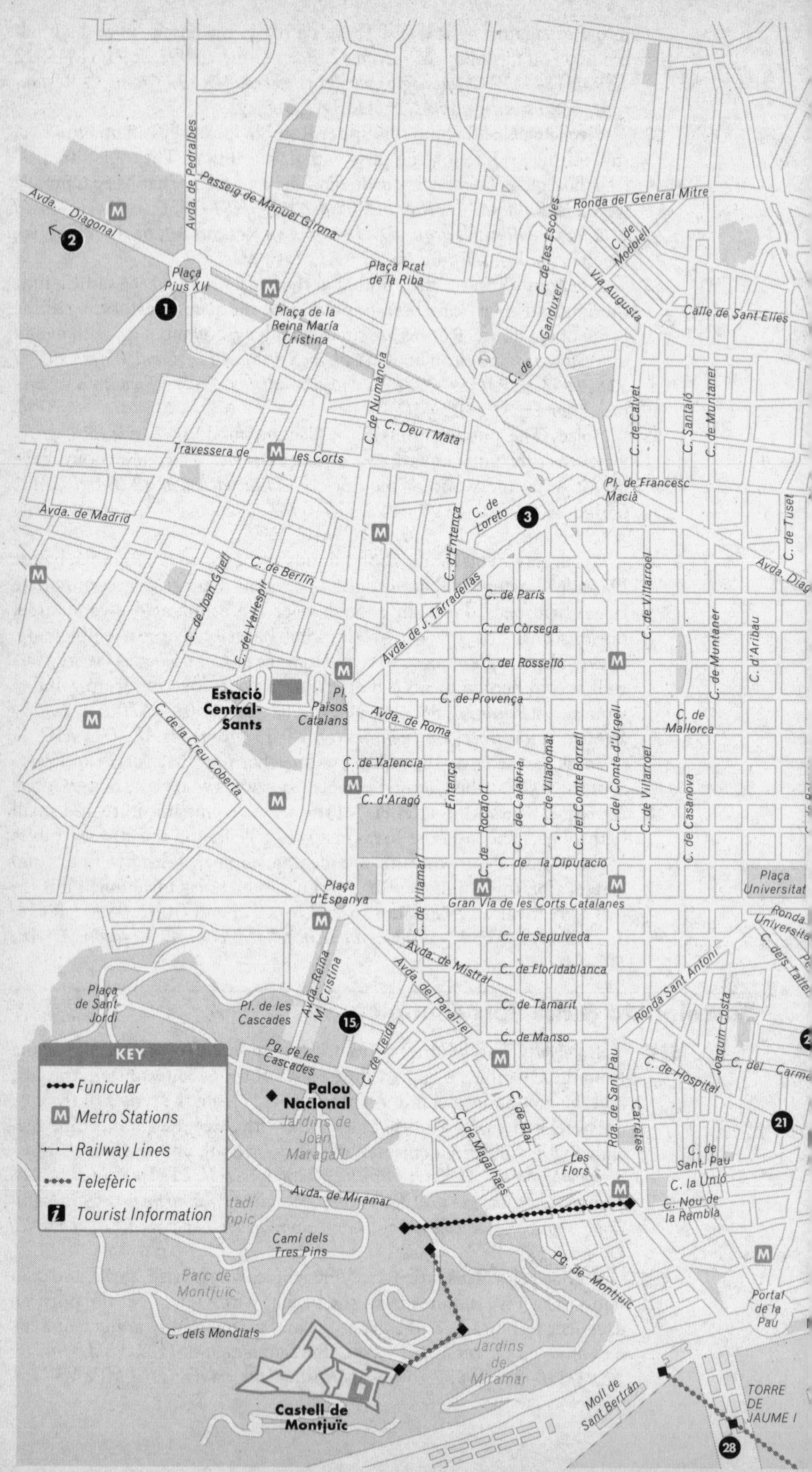

Avda. Diagonal
2
Passeig de Manuel Girona
Avda. de Pedralbes
Plaça Pius XII
1
Plaça Prat de la Riba
Plaça de la Reina María Cristina
Ronda del General Mitre
C. de les Escoles
C. de Modolell
Via Augusta
C. de Ganduxer
Calle de Sant Elies
C. de Numància
C. Deu i Mata
C. de Calvet
C. Santaló
C. de Muntaner
Travessera de les Corts
Pl. de Francesc Macià
Avda. de Madrid
C. de Loreto
3
C. d'Entença
C. de Tuset
Avda. Diag
C. de Berlín
C. de Joan Güell
C. del Vallespir
Avda. de J. Tarradellas
C. de París
C. de Còrsega
C. del Rosselló
C. de Villarroel
C. de Muntaner
C. d'Aribau
Estació Central-Sants
Pl. Països Catalans
C. de Provença
Avda. de Roma
C. de Mallorca
C. de la Creu Coberta
C. de Valencia
C. d'Aragó
Entença
C. de Rocafort
C. de Calabria
C. de Viladomat
C. del Comte Borrell
C. del Comte d'Urgell
C. de Villarroel
C. de Casanova
C. de la Diputacio
Plaça Universitat
Plaça d'Espanya
C. de Vilamarí
Gran Via de les Corts Catalanes
Ronda Universitat
C. dels Tallers
C. de Sepulveda
Avda. de Mistral
C. de Floridablanca
Avda. Reina M. Cristina
Plaça de Sant Jordi
Pl. de les Cascades
15
Avda. del Paral·lel
C. de Tamarit
Ronda Sant Antoni
Joaquín Costa
C. de Manso
Pg. de les Cascades
C. de Lleida
C. de Hospital
C. del Carme
Palau Nacional
Jardins de Joan Maragall
C. de Blai
C. de Magalhaes
Rda. de Sant Pau
Carretes
21
Les Flors
C. de Sant Pau
C. la Unió
C. Nou de la Rambla
Avda. de Miramar
Camí dels Tres Pins
Parc de Montjuïc
Pg. de Montjuïc
Portal de la Pau
C. dels Mondials
Jardins de Miramar
Castell de Montjuïc
Moll de Sant Bertrán
TORRE DE JAUME I
28
KEY
Funicular
Metro Stations
Railway Lines
Telefèric
Tourist Information

Alexandra 6
Avenida Palace 12
Calderón 11
Citadines. 20
Claris. 10
Colón 24
Condes de Barcelona. 7
Continental 16
Eurostar Grand Marina Hotel. 28
Fira Palace 27
Gallery 4
Gran Derby 3
Gran Vía 13
Hotel Arts 30
Jardí 23
Le Meridien. 22
Majestic. 9
Marina Folch. 29
Montecarlo 19
Nouvel 18
Paseo de Gràcia. 5
Princesa Sofía 1
Racó del Pi 25
Regente. 8
Rey Juan Carlos I. 2
Rialto 15
Ritz 14
Rivoli Ramblas 17
San Agustí. 21
Suizo. 26

Eixample

$$$$ Fodor'sChoice ★ **Claris.** Widely considered Barcelona's best hotel, this wonderful place is a fascinating mélange of design and tradition. The rooms come in 60 different modern layouts, some with restored 18th-century English furniture and some with contemporary furnishings from Barcelona's endlessly playful legion of lamp and chair designers. Lavishly endowed with wood and marble, the hotel also has a Japanese water garden. The restaurant East 47 is stellar. *Carrer Pau Claris 150, Eixample, 08009 93/487–6262 93/215–7970 www.derbyhotels.es 80 rooms, 40 suites 2 restaurants, rooftop pool, gym, sauna, bar, meeting rooms, parking (fee) AE, DC, MC, V.*

$$$$ Fodor'sChoice ★ **Majestic.** On Barcelona's most stylish boulevard, surrounded by fashion emporiums, you'll find this near-perfect place to stay. The building is part Eixample town house and part modern extension, but each room is stylishly decorated. The superb restaurant, Drolma, is a destination in itself. *Passeig de Gràcia 70, Eixample, 08008 93/488–1717 93/488–1880 www.hotelmajestic.es 273 rooms, 30 suites 2 restaurants, in-room data ports, minibars, cable TV, pool, health club, bar, parking (fee) AE, DC, MC, V.*

★ $$$$ **Ritz.** Founded in 1919 by Caesar Ritz, this grande dame of Barcelona hotels has been restored to the splendor of its earlier years. The imperial lobby is at once loose and elegant; guest rooms contain Regency furniture, and some have Roman baths and mosaics. Service is generally excellent. *Gran Via 668, Eixample, 08010 93/318–5200 93/318–0148 www.ritzbcn.com 122 rooms Restaurant, coffee shop, gym, sauna, bar, baby-sitting, business services, meeting rooms AE, DC, MC, V.*

$$$–$$$$ **Alexandra.** Behind the reconstructed Eixample facade, everything is slick and contemporary. The rooms are spacious and attractively furnished with dark-wood chairs; those that face inward have thatch screens on the balconies for privacy. From the airy, marble hall on up, the Alexandra is perfectly suited to modern martini sippers. *Mallorca 251, Eixample, 08008 93/467–7166 93/488–0258 www.hotel-alexandra.com 99 rooms Restaurant, minibars, bar, meeting rooms, parking (fee) AE, DC, MC, V.*

$$$–$$$$ **Avenida Palace.** At the bottom of the Eixample, between the Rambla de Catalunya and Passeig de Gràcia, this hotel conveys elegance and antiquated style despite dating from only 1952. The lobby has curving staircases leading off in many directions. Everything is patterned, from the carpets to the plasterwork, a style largely echoed in the bedrooms, though some have been modernized and the wallpaper tamed. If you want contemporary minimalism, stay elsewhere. *Gran Via 605–607, Eixample, 08007 93/301–9600 93/318–1234 www.avenidapalace.com 160 rooms Restaurant, minibars, cable TV, bar, baby-sitting, business services, meeting room AE, DC, MC, V.*

$$$–$$$$ Fodor'sChoice ★ **Condes de Barcelona.** Reserve well in advance—this is one of Barcelona's most popular hotels. The pentagonal lobby has a marble floor and the original columns and courtyard from the 1891 building. The newest rooms have hot tubs and terraces overlooking interior gardens. An affiliated fitness club nearby has golf, squash, and swimming. The restaurant, Thalassa, is excellent. *Passeig de Gràcia 75, Eixample, 08008 93/467–4780 93/467–4785 www.condesdebarcelona.com 183 rooms Restaurant, pool, gym, hot tub, piano bar, business services, meeting room, parking (fee) AE, DC, MC, V.*

$$$–$$$$ **Fira Palace.** Built in the early '90s, this hotel has established itself among Barcelona's finest business and convention havens. Close to the Convention Palace, it offers easy access to Montjuïc and its attractions. Im-

peccably modern, it's also a solid choice for generic creature comfort rather than local color. ✉ *Av. Rius i Taulet 1, Eixample, 08004* ☎ *93/426–2223* 📠 *93/424–8679* 🌐 *www.fira-palace.com* *220 rooms, 40 suites* *Restaurant, in-room data ports, minibars, cable TV, pool, gym, hair salon, massage, squash, bar, meeting room, car rental, parking (fee)* 💳 *AE, DC, MC, V.*

$$$–$$$$ **Gallery.** In the upper part of the Eixample, just below the Diagonal, this modern hotel offers impeccable comfort and service and a central location for middle and upper Barcelona. (In the other direction, you're only half an hour's walk from the waterfront.) It's named for its proximity to the city's prime art-gallery district, a few blocks away on Rambla de Catalunya and Consell de Cent. ✉ *Roselló 249, Eixample, 08008* ☎ *93/415–9911* 📠 *93/415–9184* 🌐 *www.galleryhotel.com* *110 rooms, 5 suites* *Restaurant, cafeteria, in-room data ports, minibars, cable TV, health club, bar, meeting rooms, parking (fee)* 💳 *AE, DC, MC, V.*

$$$–$$$$ **Gran Derby.** Contemporary, sleek, and slick, this Eixample hotel is ideal for families, composed entirely of suites, junior suites, and duplexes with sitting rooms. Only the location is less than ideal; for sightseeing purposes, it's a bit out of the way, below Plaça Francesc Macià, but a 20-minute march down the Diagonal puts you on Passeig de Gràcia. ✉ *Loreto 28, Eixample, 08029* ☎ *93/322–2062* 📠 *93/419–6820* 🌐 *www.derbyhotels.es* *40 suites* *Café, minibars, cable TV, pool, bar, meeting rooms, parking (fee)* 💳 *AE, DC, MC, V.*

$$$–$$$$ **Regente.** Moderniste furnishings and copious stained glass lend style and charm to this smallish hotel. The public rooms are carpeted in a mix of patterns; guest rooms, fortunately, are restrained. The verdant roof terrace and the prime position on the Rambla de Catalunya seal the positive verdict. ✉ *Rambla de Catalunya 76, Eixample, 08008* ☎ *93/487–5989* 📠 *93/487–3227* 🌐 *www.hcchotels.com* *79 rooms* *Cable TV, pool, bar, meeting rooms* 💳 *AE, DC, MC, V.*

$$–$$$ **Calderón.** On leafy Rambla de Catalunya, this modern high-rise has facilities normally found in hotels farther out of town. Public rooms are huge, with cool, white-marble floors, and the bedrooms follow suit. For stunning views, ask for one of the higher rooms. ✉ *Rambla de Catalunya 26, Eixample, 08007* ☎ *93/301–0000* 📠 *93/412–0120* 🌐 *www.nh-hoteles.com* *224 rooms* *Restaurant, minibars, cable TV, 2 pools (1 indoor), health club, bar, piano bar, parking (fee)* 💳 *AE, DC, MC, V.*

$$ **Gran Vía.** This 19th-century town house is a Moderniste enclave, with an original chapel, hall-of-mirrors breakfast room, ornate Moderniste staircase, and Belle Epoque phone booths. Guest rooms have plain alcoved walls, bottle-green carpets, and Regency-style furniture; those overlooking Gran Via itself have better views but are quite noisy. ✉ *Gran Via 642, Eixample, 08007* ☎ *93/318–1900* 📠 *93/318–9997* 🌐 *www.nnhotels.es* *53 rooms* *Minibars, parking (fee)* 💳 *AE, DC, MC, V.*

$ **Paseo de Gràcia.** Formerly a hostel, the Paseo has soft-color bedrooms with plain, good-quality carpets and sturdy wooden furniture. Add the location, on a handsome Eixample boulevard, and you have a good budget option. Some rooms, though not necessarily the newest, have balconies with views west over the city and the Collserola hills beyond. ✉ *Passeig de Gràcia 102, Eixample, 08008* ☎ *93/215–5828* 📠 *93/215–3724* *33 rooms* *Bar* 💳 *AE, DC, MC, V.*

Sarrià-Pedralbes & Sant Gervasi

$$$$ **Princesa Sofía.** This modern high-rise has numerous facilities and everything from shops to three different restaurants. The rooms, decorated in soft colors, are ultracomfortable. ✉ *Plaça Pius XII 4, at Av.*

Diagonal, Diagonal, 08028 ☎ *93/508–1000* 🖷 *93/508–1001* 🌐 *www.interconti.com* *475 rooms, 25 suites* *3 restaurants, 2 pools (1 indoor), hair salon, health club, bar, parking (fee)* ▭ *AE, DC, MC, V.*

★ $$$$ **Rey Juan Carlos I.** Towering over the western end of Barcelona's Avinguda Diagonal, this luxury hotel is also an exciting commercial complex where you can even buy or rent a fur or limousine. The lush garden, which includes a pond with swans, has an Olympic-size swimming pool, and the green expanses of Barcelona's finest in-town country club, El Polo, are beyond. The restaurant Chez Vous serves French cuisine, and Café Polo has a sumptuous buffet. ✉ *Av. Diagonal 661–671, Diagonal, 08028* ☎ *93/364–4040* 🖷 *93/364–4232* 🌐 *www.hrjuancarlos.com* *375 rooms, 37 suites* *2 restaurants (3 in summer), in-room data ports, minibars, cable TV, tennis court, pool, hair salon, health club, spa, paddle tennis, 2 bars, shops, meeting rooms* ▭ *AE, DC, MC, V.*

NIGHTLIFE & THE ARTS

Barcelona's art and nightlife scenes start early and never quite stop. To find out what's on, look in newspapers or the weekly *Guía Del Ocio*, available at newsstands all over town. *Activitats* is a monthly list of cultural events, published by the *ajuntament* and available from its information office in Palau de la Virreina (Rambla 99).

The Arts

Classical Music

The basilica of Santa Maria del Mar, the church of Santa Maria del Pi, the Monestir de Pedralbes, Drassanes Reials, and the Saló del Tinell, among other ancient and intimate spaces, host concerts. Barcelona's music festival brings a long series of concerts in June and July. In late September, the **International Music Festival** is part of the feast of Nostra Senyora de la Mercè (Our Lady of Mercy), Barcelona's patron saint. Pop concerts are held in the Palau Sant Jordi on Montjuïc.

Barcelona's most famous concert hall is the Moderniste **Palau de la Música Catalana** (✉ Sant Francesc de Paula 2, Sant Pere ☎ 93/295–7200), with performances September–June. Tickets go from €6 to €100 and are best purchased well in advance. The contemporary **Auditori de Barcelona** (✉ Lepant 150, near Plaça de les Glòries, Eixample ☎ 93/317–1096) has classical music, with occasional jazz and pop thrown in. Barcelona's **Gran Teatre del Liceu** (box office ✉ Rambla de Capuchinos 63, Rambla ☎ 93/317–4142) stages operas and recitals.

Dance

L'Espai de Dansa i Música de la Generalitat de Catalunya (✉ Travessera de Gràcia 63, Eixample ☎ 93/414–3133)—generally listed as L'Espai, or "The Space" —is the prime venue for ballet and modern dance, as well as some musical offerings. **El Mercat de les Flors** (✉ Lleida 59, Eixample ☎ 93/426–1875), near Plaça de Espanya, is a traditional venue for seeing modern dance and theater.

Film

Though many foreign films are dubbed, Barcelona has a full complement of original-language cinema; look for listings marked "v.o." (*versión original*). **Verdi** (✉ Carrer Verdi 32, Gràcia) screens current releases with original-version sound tracks in a fun neighborhood for pre- and post-movie eating and drinking. The **Icaria Yelmo** (✉ Salvador Espriu 61, near Carles I Metro stop, Port Olímpic) complex in the Olympic Port has the city's largest selection of English-language films. **Renoir Les Corts** (✉ Eugeni d'Ors 12, behind Diagonal's El Corte Inglés, Diagonal) is a good choice for recently released English-language features of all kinds. **Casablanca** (✉ Passeig de Gràcia 115, Eixample) plays (generally art-flick) original-language movies.

Flamenco

Barcelona is not richly endowed with flamenco haunts, as Catalans consider flamenco—like bullfighting—a foreign import from Andalusia. On the Plaça Reial, **Los Tarantos** (✉ Pl. Reial 17, Barri Gòtic ☎ 93/318–3067) spotlights Andalusia's best flamenco. **El Patio Andaluz** (✉ Aribau 242, Eixample ☎ 93/209–3378) has rather touristy flamenco shows twice nightly (10 and midnight) and a karaoke section upstairs. Tour groups in search of flamenco gravitate to **El Cordobés** (✉ Rambla 35, Rambla ☎ 93/317–6653). **El Tablao de Carmen** (✉ Poble Espanyol, Montjuïc ☎ 93/325–6895) hosts touring flamenco troupes up on Montjuïc. **La Taberna Flamenca** (✉ Art 12, Horta-Guinardó ☎ 93/351–8757) is a *sala rociera,* meaning they sing a salve to La Virgen del Rocío every night and welcome amateur flamencos.

Theater

Most plays are performed in Catalan, though some are in Spanish. Barcelona is known for avant-garde theater and troupes that specialize in mime, large-scale performance art, and special effects (La Fura dels Baus, Els Joglars, Els Comediants). Several theaters along Avinguda Parallel specialize in musicals. In April, there's a **Festival de Títeres** (Puppet Festival). The **Teatre Nacional de Catalunya** (✉ Pl. de les Arts 1 ☎ 93/306–5700), near Plaça de les Glories at the eastern end of the Diagonal, is a glass-enclosed classical temple designed by Ricardo Bofill, architect of Barcelona's airport. Programs cover everything from Shakespeare to ballet to avant-garde theater. The **Teatre Poliorama** (✉ Rambla Estudios 115, Rambla ☎ 93/317–7599) is below Plaça de Catalunya. The **Teatre Romea** (✉ Hospital 51, Raval ☎ 93/301–5504) is behind the Boqueria. The **Teatre Tívoli** (✉ Casp 8, Eixample ☎ 93/412–2063), above Plaça de Catalunya, has theater and dance performances. Gràcia's **Teatre Lliure** (✉ Montseny 47, Gràcia ☎ 93/218–9251) stages theater, dance, and musical events. The **Mercat de les Flors** (✉ Lleida 59, Montjuïc ☎ 93/426–1875), near Plaça de Espanya, is the city's most traditional dance and theater venue. Musicals run at the **Apolo** (✉ Paral.lel 56, Eixample ☎ 93/241–9007). An old chestnut among the Avinguda Parallel's musical venues is **Teatre Arnau** (✉ Paral.lel 60, Eixample ☎ 93/441–4881). **Victòria** (✉ Paral.lel 67–69, Eixample ☎ 93/441–3979) is a historic venue for musicals and reviews. In July and August, an open-air summer theater festival brings plays, music, and dance to the **Teatre Grec** (Greek Theater; ✉ Rambla 99, Montjuïc ☎ 93/316–2700) on Montjuïc, as well as to Plaça del Rei, Mercat de les Flors, and other sites.

Nightlife

Cabaret

Near the bottom of the Rambla, the minuscule **Bar Pastis** (✉ Santa Mònica 4, Rambla ☎ 93/318–7980) has both live performances and LPs of every Edith Piaf song ever recorded. **Arnau** (✉ Paral.lel 60, Eixample ☎ 93/242–2804) is an old-time music hall that's still going strong. **Starlets** (✉ Av. Sarrià 44, Eixample ☎ 93/430–9156) has a combination cabaret and disco program. **Joy's** (✉ Rocafort 231, Eixample ☎ 93/430–9156) offers a floor show, cabaret, and dancing.

Casino

The **Gran Casino de Barcelona** (✉ Carrer de la Marina, Port Olímpic ☎ 93/225–7878), under the Hotel Arts, is open daily from 1 PM to 5 AM with everything from slots to roulette, a disco, and floor shows.

Jazz & Blues

The Palau de la Música Catalana hosts an **international jazz festival** in November. **La Cova del Drac** (⊠ Vallmajor 33, La Bonanova ☎ 93/200–7032), above Via Augusta in lower San Gervasi, is Barcelona's perennial jazz venue. The Gothic Quarter's **Harlem Jazz Club** (⊠ Comtessa Sobradiel 8, Barri Gòtic ☎ 93/310–0755) is small but atmospheric, with good jazz and country bands. **Jamboree-Jazz & Dance-Club** (⊠ Pl. Reial 17, Rambla ☎ 93/301–7564) is a center for jazz, rock, and flamenco. **La Boîte** (⊠ Av. Diagonal 477, Eixample ☎ 93/419–5950) has an eclectic musical menu. **Luz de Gas** (⊠ Muntaner 246, Eixample ☎ 93/209–7711) hosts every genre from Irish fusion to Cuban *son.* **Luna Mora** (⊠ Port Olímpic, next to Hotel Arts, Port Olímpic ☎ 93/221–6161) stages everything from country blues to salsa and soul. The bustling **Blue Note** (☎ 93/225–8003), in Port Vell's Maremagnum shopping complex, draws a mixture of young and not-so-young nocturnals.

Late-Night Bars

Bar musical is Spanish for any bar with music loud enough to drown out conversation. Wildly active but, on balance, better to avoid, are the **Port Olímpic** and the Port Vell's **Maremagnum.** Raging until dawn in summer and on weekends, these two nocturnal lowlifes are far from Barcelona's best nightlife options.

Universal (⊠ Marià Cubí 182–184, Eixample ☎ 93/200–7470) has been the hottest bar in town for 30 years. **Mas i Mas** (⊠ Marià Cubí 199, Eixample ☎ 93/209–4502), across the street from Universal, is so crowded that social intimacy is guaranteed. **Nick Havanna** (⊠ Roselló 208, Eixample ☎ 93/215–6591) has, along with a consistently hot program of live music, Barcelona's most entertaining urinals. **L'Ovella Negra** (⊠ Sitjàs 5, Raval ☎ 93/317–1087) is the top student tavern. **Glaciar** (⊠ Pl. Reial 13, Rambla ☎ 93/302–1163) is *the* spot for young out-of-towners. For a more laid-back scene, with high ceilings, billiards, tapas, and hundreds of students, visit the popular **Velodrom** (⊠ Muntaner 211–213, Eixample ☎ 93/230–6022), below the Diagonal. Two blocks from Velodrom is the intriguing *barmuseo* (bar-cum-museum) **La Fira** (⊠ Provença 171, Eixample ☎ 93/323–7271). Downtown, deep in the Barrio Chino, try the **London Bar** (⊠ Nou de la Rambla 34, Raval ☎ 93/302–3102), an Art Nouveau circus haunt with a trapeze suspended above the bar. **Bar Almirall** (⊠ Joaquin Costa 33, Raval ☎ 93/412–1535) has Art Nouveau chic. **Bar Muy Buenas** (⊠ Carme 63, Raval ☎ 93/442–5053) is an Art Nouveau gem. Over by the Sagrada Família, the **Michael Collins Irish Pub** (⊠ Pl. Sagrada Família 4, Eixample ☎ 93/459–1964) has a strong Anglo following. Above Via Augusta in upper Barcelona, the **Sherlock Holmes** (⊠ Copernic 42–44, Eixample ☎ 93/414–2184) is an ongoing Brit-fest with live musical performances and darkly intimate corners. Above Via Augusta, **Opiniao** (⊠ Ciutat de Balaguer 67, La Bonanova, below Bonanova ☎ 93/418–3399) is another upper-Barcelona dive, a hot local club. **Carrer del Rec,** near the Born, is a street that's solid heat from stem to stern—that is, from the bar/art gallery La Rosa de Foc to the fine restaurant Abac. Café-restaurant-bar **Salero** (⊠ Carrer del Rec 60, La Ribera ☎ 93/318–4399) is always packed with young miscreants.

Nightclubs & Discos

Most clubs have a discretionary cover charge and like to inflict it on foreigners, so dress up and be prepared to talk your way past the bouncer. Any story can work; for example, you own a chain of nightclubs and are on a world tour. Don't expect much to happen until 1:30 or 2. Tops for some time now is the prisonesque nightclub **Otto Zutz** (⊠ Lincoln 15, Eixample ☎ 93/238–0722), off Via Augusta. The nearly classic **Up and Down** (✉ Numancia 179, Eixample ☎ 93/280–2922), pronounced "Pen-*dow,*" is a good choice for elegant carousers. A line forms at **Bikini** (✉ Deu i Mata 105, at Entença, Eixample ☎ 93/322–0005) on festive Saturday nights. **Torres de Avila** (✉ Marquès de Comillas 25, Montjuïc ☎ 93/424–9309), in Pueblo Espanyol, is wild and woolly until broad daylight on weekends. **Danzatoria** (✉ Avda. Tibidabo 61, Tibidabo ☎ 93/211–6261), a fusion of Salsitas and Partycular is a "multi-space" with five venues (disco, hall, dance, chill-out, garden) and fills with models and hopeful guys. **Sala Razzmatazz** (✉ Almogavers 122, Poble Nou ☎ 93/320–8200) offers Friday and Saturday disco madness 'til dawn. Weeknight concerts have international stars such as Ani DiFranco and Enya. **La Boîte Mas i Mas** (✉ Av. Diagonal 477, Eixample ☎ 93/419–5950) has live music and a nice balance of civilization and insanity. **Bucaro** (✉ Aribau 195, Eixample ☎ 93/209–6562) rocks until dawn, albeit largely for the almost criminally young. **It Café** (✉ Joaquin Costa 4, Raval ☎ 93/443–0341) is a design oasis not far from the MACBA in the Raval. The **Loft** (✉ Pamplona 88, Poble Nou ☎ 93/272–0910), an offshoot of Sala Razzmatazz, is dedicated to electronic music. **Row Club** (✉ Roselló 208, Eixample ☎ 93/237–5405) is big on techno. **Sala Cibeles** (✉ Córsega 363, Eixample ☎ 93/272–0910) has big sound and singing DJs. Salsa sizzles at the exuberantly Caribbean **Antilla BCN Latin Club** (✉ C. Aragó 141, Eixample ☎ 93/451–4564). **Luz de Luna** (✉ C. Comerç 21, La Ribera ☎ 93/310–7542) lays down wall-to-wall salsa; oxygen masks are advised. **Agua de Luna** (✉ Viladomat 211, Eixample ☎ 93/410–0440) is a torrid salsa scene in the western Eixample. **Pachá** (✉ Dr. Marañon 17, Pedralbes-Les Corts ☎ 93/204–0412) offers two raging discos and a restaurant.

Oliver y Hardy (✉ Av. Diagonal 593, Eixample ☎ 93/419–3181), next to the Barcelona Hilton, is popular with grownups. **Costa Breve** (✉ Aribau 230, Eixample ☎ 93/200–7346) accepts postgraduates with open arms. **El Otro** (✉ Valencia 166, Eixample ☎ 93/323–6759) is kind to aging (over 30) miscreants. For big-band tango in an old-fashioned *sala de baile* (dance hall), head to **La Paloma** (✉ Tigre 27, Raval ☎ 93/301–6897). The kitschy 1950s furnishings are wonderfully peculiar.

SPORTS & THE OUTDOORS

Golf

Call ahead to reserve tee times. Weekday greens fees range from about €36 at most courses to €72 on weekends and holidays. San Cugat's **Club de Golf de San Cugat** (✉ Calle Villa s/n ☎ 93/674–3908) has 18 hilly holes. Greens fees are €65 on weekdays and €130 on weekends. Sitges' **Club de Golf Terramar** (☎ 93/894–0580) offers 18 along the beach.

Health Clubs

For specifics, look in the *Páginas Amarillas/Pàgines Grogues* (*Yellow Pages*) under "Gimnasios/Gimnasis." The **DiR** (☎ 901/304030 general information ✉ main branch ✉ DiR Diagonal, Ganduxer 25–27, Eixample ☎ 93/202–2202) network of fitness centers is worthy, with addresses all over Barcelona. A day membership, €11, includes aerobics classes and the use of a sauna, a steam room, a swimming pool, squash courts, and MTV. **Crack** (✉ Pasaje Domingo 7, Eixample ☎ 93/215–2755), off Passeig de Gràcia near the Hotel Condes de Barcelona, has a gym, a sauna, pool (summer only), squash courts, and paddle tennis; day membership here costs €12, with a small supplement for courts. **O2 Centre Wellness** (✉ Eduardo Conde 1–3, Sarrià–Sant Gervasi ☎ 93/

205–3976) offers day passes for €50 with access to state of the art gym, sauna, pool, hydromassage, sundeck, and aesthetic treatments.

Hiking

The **Collserola** hills behind the city offer well-marked trails, fresh air, and lovely views. Take the San Cugat, Sabadell, or Terrassa FFCC train from Plaça de Catalunya and get off at Baixador de Vallvidrera; the information center, 10 minutes uphill next to **Vil.la Joana** (now the Jacint Verdaguer Museum), has maps of this mountain woodland 20 minutes from downtown. The walk back into town can take from two to five hours depending on your speed and the trails you pick. **Club Excursionista de Catalunya** (✉ Paradis 10, Barri Gòtic ☎ 93/315–2311) has information on hiking in Barcelona's outskirts. Ask the **Asociació Excursionista, Etnográfica i Folklorica** (✉ Avinyó 19, Barri Gòtic ☎ 93/302–2730) about hikes, including treks in the Pyrenees.

Soccer

If you're in Barcelona between September and June, go see FC Barcelona ("El Barça") play, preferably against Real Madrid. Games are generally played Saturday night or Sunday afternoon at 5, but there may be cup or international games during the week as well, usually on Wednesday. Ask your hotel concierge how to get tickets, or call the club in advance. The massive Camp Nou stadium seats 110,000 and fills almost to capacity. **Museu FC Barcelona** has trophies and a five-screen video showing memorable goals in the history of one of Europe's most colorful soccer clubs. *✉ Arístides Maillol, Diagonal ☎ 93/330–9411 Museum €5 ⊙ Oct.–Mar., Tues.–Fri. 10–1 and 4–6, weekends 10–1 and 3–6; Apr.–Sept., Mon.–Sat. 10–1 and 3–6.*

Swimming

Piscines Bernat Picornell (✉ Av. del Estadi 30–40, Montjuïc ☎ 93/423–4041) comprises indoor and outdoor pools plus a sauna, gymnasium, and fitness equipment. Overlooking the beach from Barceloneta, the **Club Natació de Barceloneta** (✉ Passeig Joan de Borbó, Barceloneta ☎ 93/221–0010), also known as Complex Esportiu Municipal Banys Sant Sebastiá, has an indoor pool.

Tennis

The Olympic tennis facilities at **Vall d'Hebron** (✉ Passeig Vall d'Hebron 178–196, Vall d'Hebron ☎ 93/427–6500) are open from 8 AM until 11 PM; clay costs €15 per hour, hard courts €17. **Complejo Deportivo Can Caralleu** (Can Caralleu Sports Complex; ✉ Calle Esports 2–8 ☎ 93/203–7874), above Pedralbes, a 30-minute walk uphill from the Reina Elisenda subway stop (FFCC de la Generalitat), has hard courts and clean air. It's open daily 8 AM–11 PM and costs €8 per hour by day, €10 by night. The upscale **Club Vall Parc** (✉ Ctra. de la Rabassada 79, Tibidabo ☎ 93/212–6789) is open daily 8 AM–midnight and charges €15 per hour by day, €19 by night.

SHOPPING

Between fashions, designer home furnishings, foodstuffs, and art and antiques, Barcelona is the best place in Spain to unload extra ballast from your wallet. True, bargains are few outside saffron and rope-sole shoes, but quality and selection are excellent. Most stores are open Monday–Saturday 9–1:30 and 5–8, but some close in the afternoon. Virtually all close on Sunday.

Shopping Districts

For high fashion, browse along Passeig de Gràcia and the Diagonal between Plaça Joan Carles I and Plaça Francesc Macià. There are two dozen antiques shops in the Gothic Quarter, another 70 shops off Passeig de Gràcia on Bulevard dels Antiquaris, and still more in Gràcia and Sarrià. Barcelona's prime shopping districts are the Passeig de Gràcia, Rambla de Catalunya, Plaça de Catalunya, Porta de l'Àngel, and Avinguda Diagonal up to Carrer Ganduxer. For old-fashioned Spanish shops, prowl the Gothic Quarter, especially **Carrer Ferran.** The area surrounding **Plaça del Pi,** from the Boqueria to Carrer Portaferrissa and Carrer de la Canuda, is thick with boutiques, jewelry, and design shops. The **Barri de la Ribera,** around Santa Maria del Mar, has design and food shops. Design, jewelry, and knickknack shops cluster on Carrer Banys Vells and Carrer Flassaders, near Carrer Montcada. The shopping colossus **L'Illa,** on the Diagonal beyond Carrer Ganduxer, includes the department store FNAC and other temptations. **Carrer Tuset,** north of the Diagonal, has lots of small boutiques. The **Maremagnum** mall, in Port Vell, is convenient to downtown. **Diagonal Mar,** at the eastern end of the diagonal, along with the **Fòrum 2004** complex offer many shopping options in a mega-shopping-mall environment.

Specialty Stores

Antiques

Antiques shopping is headquartered in the Gothic Quarter, where **Carrer de la Palla** and **Carrer Banys Nous** are lined with shops full of prints, maps, books, paintings, and furniture. An antiques market is held in front of the **cathedral** every Thursday from 10 to 8. In upper Barcelona, the entire village of **Sarrià** is becoming an antiquer's destination, with shops along Cornet i Mas, Pedró de la Creu, and Major de Sarrià. The Eixample's **Centre d'Antiquaris** (⊠ Passeig de Gràcia 55, Eixample) contains 75 antiques stores. Moderniste aficionados should check out **Gothsland** (⊠ Consell de Cent 331, Eixample). **La Maison Coloniale** (⊠ Sant Antoni Abat 61, Raval) has 15th-century stone vaulting and colonial treasures. **Novecento** (⊠ Passeig de Gràcia 75, Eixample) has antique art and jewelry. **Alcanto** (⊠ Passeig de Gràcia 55–57, Eixample) is a clearinghouse for buying and selling. **Antiguedades J. Pla** (⊠ C. Aragó 517, Eixample) buys and sells antiques.

Art

There is a cluster of art galleries on Carrer Consell de Cent between Passeig de Gràcia and Carrer Balmes, and around the corner on Rambla de Catalunya. The Born–Santa Maria del Mar quarter is another art destination, along Carrer Montcada and the parallel Carrer Bany Vells. **Galeria Joan Prats** (⊠Rambla de Catalunya 54, Eixample) is a veteran, known for the quality of its artists' works. **Eude** (⊠ Consell de Cent 278, Eixample) showcases young artists. **Sala Dalmau** (⊠ Consell de Cent 347, Eixample) is an established art outlet. **Sala Rovira** (⊠ Rambla de Catalunya 62, Eixample) has shown top artists Tom Carr and Blanca Vernis. The **Joan Gaspar** (⊠ Pl. Letamendi 1, Eixample) started with Picasso and Miró. Carrer Petritxol, which leads down into Plaça del Pi, is lined with galleries, notably **Sala Parès** (⊠ Petritxol 5, Barri Gòtic).The ticking **Metrònom** (⊠ Carrer Fussina 4, La Ribera) at the north end of the Born has a weakness for performance art and edgy erotic photography.

The three locations of **Fundació La Caixa** (✉ La Pedrera ✉ Provença 261–265, Eixample ✉ Centre Cultural ✉ Passeig Sant Joan 108, Eixample ✉ Sala Montcada ✉ Carrer Montcada 14, La Ribera) are important spaces for seeing (not buying) local contemporary art. **La Capella de l'Antic Hospital de la Santa Creu** (✉ Hospital 56, Raval) exhibits installations and new art. The **Espai Xavier Miserachs** (✉ Rambla 99, Rambla) in the Palau de la Virreina has eclectic temporary exhibits of painting, photography, design, and illustration.

Books

La Central (✉ C. Mallorca 237, Eixample ☎ 93/487–5018) is Barcelona's best bookstore. **Altair** (✉ Gran Via 616, Eixample ☎ 93/342–7171) is Barcelona's premier travel and adventure bookstore, with many titles in English. **BCN Books** (✉ Roger de Llúria 118, Eixample ☎ 93/476–3343) is a top store for books in English. **Casa del Llibre** (✉ Passeig de Gràcia 62, Eixample ☎ 93/272–3480) is a book feast with English titles. **Laie** (✉ Pau Claris 85, Eixample ☎ 93/318–1357) is a book lover's sanctuary, with cultural events as well as stacks. The bookstore in the **Palau de la Virreina** (✉ Rambla 99, Rambla ☎ 93/301–7775) has books on art, design, and Barcelona in general. **El Corte Inglés**, especially the branch in Porta del Àngel, sells English guidebooks and novels.

Boutiques & Jewelry

Chanel, Armani, Loewe, and the other big names have stores on Passeig de Gràcia. **El Bulevard Rosa** (✉ Passeig de Gràcia 53–55, Eixample) is a collection of boutiques with the latest outfits. The stretch of Avinguda Diagonal between Passeig de Gràcia and Carrer Ganduxer is lined with high-end shops. **Adolfo Domínguez** (✉ Passeig de Gràcia 35, Av. Diagonal 570, Eixample) is one of Spain's leading designers. **Groc** (✉ C. Muntaner 382, Eixample ✉ Rambla de Catalunya 100, Eixample), Toni Miró's two shops, have the latest looks for men, women, and children. **David Valls** (✉ C. Valencia 235, Eixample) represents new, young Barcelona fashion design. **May Day** (✉ C. Portaferrissa 16, Barri Gòtic) carries cutting-edge clothing, footwear, and accessories. **Joaquim Berao** (✉ C. Roselló 277, Eixample) is a top jewelry designer. Beatriz Würsch displays her unusual jewelry designs in **Forum Ferlandina** (✉ Ferlandina 31, Raval), next to the MACBA. Young designers show their work in New Yorker Annie George's **Candela** (✉ Santa Maria 6, La Ribera) next to Santa Maria del Mar in a superb 17th-century house.

Ceramics

Art Escudellers (✉ C. Escudellers 23–25, Barri Gòtic) has ceramics from all over Spain, with more than 200 different artisans represented and maps showing where the work is from. In addition, the art gallery and the wine, Iberian ham, and cheese-tasting bar downstairs makes this Barcelona's hands-down ceramics non-plus-ultra. **Itaca** (✉ C. Ferrán 26, Barri Gòtic) has ceramic plates, bowls, and pottery from Talavera de la Reina and La Bisbal. For Lladró, try **Pla de l'Os** (✉ Boqueria 3, Barri Gòtic), off the Rambla. In Sarrià, behind the market on your way into bougainvillea-choked Plaça Sant Gaietà, check out the ceramics store **Nica & Bet** (✉ Pare Miquel de Sarrià 10, Sarrià); don't miss the beautifully restored wooden doors. While perusing smaller establishments is always worthwhile, one of Barcelona's big department stores, El Corte Inglés, at Plaça Catalunya or Diagonal, is a good bet for ceramics shoppers.

Department Stores

Among other emporiums, Plaça de Catalunya now includes **FNAC** and **Habitat.** The ubiquitous **El Corte Inglés** has four locations: Plaça de Catalunya 14, Porta de l'Angel 19–21, Avinguda Francesc Macià 58, and Avinguda Diagonal 617.

Design & Interiors

The area around the church of Santa Maria del Mar, an artisans' quarter since medieval times, is now full of cheerful design stores and art galleries. Habitat has stores on Tuset at the Diagonal and in the Plaça de Catalunya Triangle complex behind Bar Zurich.

Vinçon (✉ Passeig de Gràcia 96, Eixample) occupies a rambling Moderniste house and carries everything from Filofaxes to handsome kitchenware. You'll also find one of Barcelona's most spectacular Art Nouveau fireplaces, complete with a stylized face for a hearth. Upscale **Gimeno** (✉ Passeig de Gràcia 102, Eixample) has everything from clever suitcases to the latest in furniture design. **bd** (barcelona design; ✉ Carrer Mallorca 291–293, Eixample) is a spare, cutting-edge home-furnishing store in another Moderniste gem, Domènech i Montaner's Casa Thomas. **Vientos del Sur** (✉ C. Argenteria 78, La Ribera), part of the Natura chain, has a good selection of crafts. **Ici et Là** (✉ Pl. Santa Maria del Mar 2, La Ribera) is across the square and has an eclectic selection of clothing, gifts, and knickknacks. **Fem** (✉ Palau 6, Barri Gòtic, behind the ajuntament) has interesting artifacts and artisanship. **Papers Coma** (✉ Montcada 20, La Ribera) has inventive gewgaws. **Estudi Pam2** (✉ Sabateret 1–3, La Ribera), behind Carrer Montcada, sells ingenious design items. **Suspect** (✉ Comerç 29, La Ribera), north of the Born, specializes in clothes and furniture made by Spastor, a group of Barcelona designers. **Gotham** (✉ Cervantes 7, Barri Gòtic), behind Town Hall, restores furniture from the '50s and '60s. It is a perennial set for Almodóvar movies. Amid mouthwatering interior design, **La Comercial** (✉ Rec 52 and 73, La Ribera) off Passeig del Born has clothes by Paul & Joe, Paul Smith, and Isabel Marant. **Sita Murt** (✉ Avinyó 18, Barri Gòtic)is a stunning subterranean space with a clever play of mirrors and collections from Antik Batik, Save the Queen, and Esteve Sita Murt.

Fine Foods

Casa Gispert (✉ Sombrerers 23, La Ribera), on the inland side of Santa Maria del Mar, is one of the most aromatic and picturesque shops in Barcelona, bursting with spices, saffron, chocolates, and nuts. **Jobal** (✉ C. Princesa 38, La Ribera) is a charming and fragrant saffron and spice shop. **La Barcelonesa** (✉ C. Comerç 27, La Ribera) specializes in dry goods, spices, tea, and saffron. **Tot Formatge** (✉ Passeig del Born 13, La Ribera) has cheeses from all over Spain and the world. **Vila Viniteca** (✉ C. Agullers 7, La Ribera), near Santa Maria del Mar, is one of the best wine shops in Barcelona, and the produce store across the way sells some of the prettiest cheeses around. **La Botifarreria de Santa Maria** (✉ Carrer Santa Maria 4, La Ribera), next to the church of Santa Maria, has excellent cheeses, hams, pâtés, and homemade *sobrassadas* (pork pâté with paprika). **El Magnífico** (✉ C. Argenteria 64, La Ribera) is famous for its coffees. **La Casa del Bacalao** (✉ Condal 8, off Portal del Angel, Barri Gòtic) specializes in salt cod and books of codfish recipes. **La Palmera** (✉ C. Enric Granados 57, Eixample) has a superb collection of wines, hams, cheeses, and olive oils. **Caelum** (✉ C. de la Palla 8, Barri Gòtic) sells crafts and such foods as honey and preserves, made in convents and monasteries all over Spain. **Vilaplana** (✉ Francesc Perez Cabrero, Eixample) is famous for its pastries, cheeses, hams, pâtés, caviars, and fine deli items. **Tutusaus** (✉ C. Francesc Perez Cabrero 5, Sant Gervasi) specializes in the finest Iberian hams and cheeses from all over Europe.

Food & Flea Markets

Spectacular food markets include the Mercat de la Llibertat, near Plaça Gal.la Placidia, and Mercat de la Revolució, on Travessera de Gràcia, both in Gràcia. On Thursday, a natural-produce market (honeys, cheeses) fills Plaça del Pi with interesting tastes and aromas; on Sunday morning, a stamp and coin market fills Plaça Reial; also on Sunday, the Plaça Sant Josep Oriol holds a painter's market, along with another general crafts and flea market near the Columbus monument at the port end of the Rambla. The **Boqueria** (✉ Rambla 91, Rambla) is Barcelona's most colorful food market and the oldest of its kind in Europe. Open Monday–Saturday 8–8, it's most active before 3 PM. Barcelona's biggest flea market, **Els Encants** (✉ Dos de Maig, on the Plaça de les Glòries, Eixample Ⓜ Glòries) is held Monday, Wednesday, Friday, and Saturday 8–7. The **Mercat Gòtic** (✉ Pl. de la Seu, Barri Gòtic) fills the area in front of the Catedral de la Seu on Thursday. The **Mercat de Sant Antoni** (✉ Ronda Sant Antoni, Eixample) is an old-fashioned food, clothing, and used-book (many in English) market that's best on Sunday.

Gifts & Miscellany

Lovers of fine stationery will linger in the Gothic Quarter's **Papirum** (✉ Baixada de la Llibreteria 2, Barri Gòtic), a tiny, medieval-tone shop with exquisite hand-printed papers, marbleized blank books, and writing implements. **La Manual Alpargartera** (✉ Avinyó 7, Barri Gòtic), off Carrer Ferran, specializes in handmade rope-sole sandals and espadrilles. **Solé** (✉ C. Ample 7, Barri Gòtic) makes shoes by hand and sells others from all over the world. La Lionesa (✉ C. Ample 21, Barri Gòtic) is an old-time grocery store. The best music store in Barcelona is **Discos Castelló** (✉ C. Tallers 3, Raval). For textiles, **Teranyina** (✉ C. Notariat 10, Raval), an elegant weaving workshop near the MACBA, is a lucky find. **Baclava** (✉ C. Notariat 10, Raval) shares an address with Teranyina and sells artisanal products and gifts. **Otman** (✉ Banys Vells 21 bis, La Ribera), with a branch in Asilah, Morocco, has light and racy frocks, belts, blouses, and skirts. Cutlery flourishes at the stately **Ganiveteria Roca** (✉ Pl. del Pi 3, Barri Gòtic), opposite the giant rose window of the Santa Maria del Pi church.

SIDE TRIPS

Numbers in the margin correspond to points of interest on the Side Trips from Barcelona map.

Montserrat

64 *50 km (30 mi) northwest of Barcelona.*

A nearly obligatory side trip from Barcelona is the shrine of La Moreneta, the Black Virgin of Montserrat, high in the mountains of the Serra de Montserrat. These weird, saw-tooth peaks have given rise to countless legends: here St. Peter left a statue of the Virgin Mary carved by St. Luke, Parsifal found the Holy Grail, and Wagner sought inspiration for his opera. Montserrat is as memorable for its strange, pink hills as it is for its religious treasures, so be sure to explore the area. The vast monastic complex is dwarfed by the grandeur of the jagged peaks, and the crests are dotted with hermitages. The hermitage of **Sant Joan** can be reached by funicular. The views over the mountains to the Mediterranean and, on a clear day, to the Pyrenees are breathtaking, and the rugged, boulder-strewn terrain makes for dramatic walks and hikes.

A monastery has stood on the same site in Montserrat since the early Middle Ages, though the present 19th-century building replaced the rubble left by Napoléon's troops in 1812. The shrine is world-famous, and one of Catalonia's spiritual sanctuaries: honeymooning couples flock here by the thousands seeking La Moreneta's blessing on their marriages,

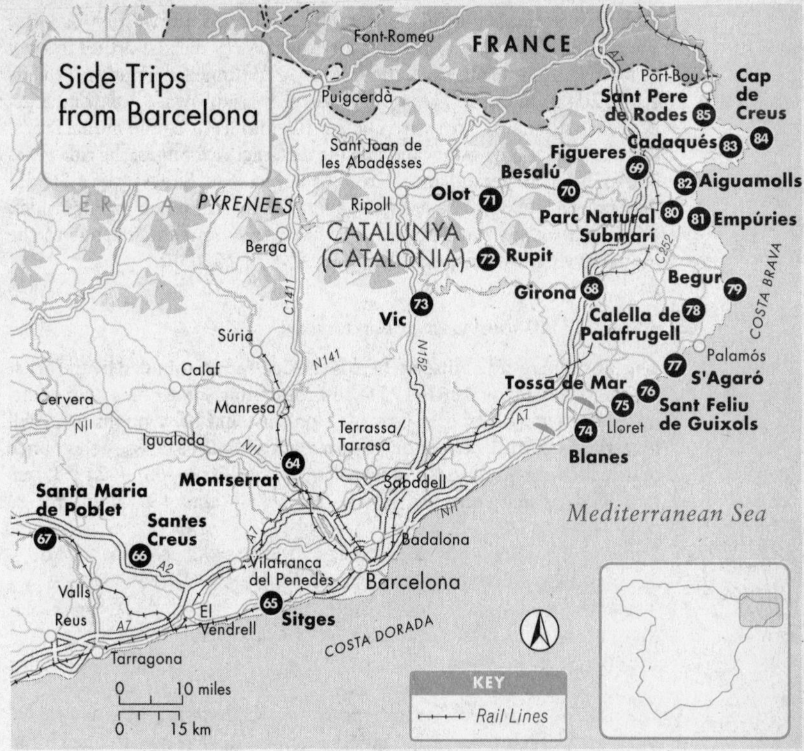

and twice a year, on April 27 and September 8, the diminutive statue of Montserrat's Black Virgin becomes the object of one of Spain's greatest pilgrimages. To get here, follow the A2/A7 *autopista* on the upper ring road (Ronda de Dalt), or from the western end of the Diagonal as far as Salida (Exit) 25 to Martorell. Bypass this industrial center and follow signs to Montserrat. You can also take a train from the Plaça Espanya Metro station (hourly from 8:36 to 6:36, connecting with the funicular leaving every 15 minutes) or a guided tour with Pullmantur or Julià.

Only the basilica and museum are regularly open to the public. The **basilica** is dark and ornate, its blackness pierced by the glow of hundreds of votive lamps. Above the high altar stands the famous polychrome statue of the Virgin and Child, to which the faithful can pay their respects by way of a separate door. ☎ *93/877–7777* ⏲ *Daily 6–10:30 and noon–6:30.*

The monastery's **museum** has two sections: the Secció Antiga has old masters, among them works by El Greco, Correggio, and Caravaggio, and the amassed gifts to the Virgin; the Secció Moderna concentrates on recent modern Catalan painters. ☎ *93/877–7766 abbey and museum* ⏲ *Secció Antiga Tue.–Sat. 10:30–2, Secció Moderna Tue.–Sat. 3–6.*

Sitges, Santes Creus & Poblet

This trio of attractions south and west of Barcelona can be seen comfortably in a day. Sitges is the prettiest and most popular resort in Barcelona's immediate environs, flaunting an excellent beach, a picturesque old quarter, and some interesting Moderniste bits. It's also one of Europe's premier gay resorts. The Cistercian monasteries west of here, at Santes Creus and Poblet, are characterized by monolithic Romanesque architecture and beautiful cloisters. By car, head southwest along Gran Via or Passeig Colom to the freeway that passes the airport on its way to Castelldefels. From here, the freeway and tunnels will get you to Sitges in 20–30 minutes. From Sitges, drive inland toward Vilafranca del Penedès and the A7 freeway. The A2 (Lleida) leads to the monasteries. Regular trains leave Sants and Passeig de Gràcia for Sitges; the ride takes half an hour. To get to Santes Creus or Poblet from Sitges, take a Lleida-line train to L'Espluga de Francolí, 4 km (2½ mi) from Poblet. For Poblet, you can also stay with the train to Tarragona and catch a bus to the monastery (Autotransports Perelada, ☎ 973/202058).

Sitges

65 *43 km (27 mi) southwest of Barcelona.*

The most interesting museum here is the **Cau-Ferrat,** founded by the artist Santiago Russinyol (1861–1931) and containing some of his own paintings together with two El Grecos. Connoisseurs of wrought iron will love the beautiful collection of *cruces terminales,* crosses that once marked town boundaries. ✉ *Fonollar s/n* ☎ *93/894–0364* *€3, free first Wed. of every month* ⏲ *Tues.–Sat. 9:30–2 and 4–6, Sun. 9:30–2.*

need a break?

Linger over excellent Mediterranean products and cooking with a nonpareil sea view at **Vivero** (Passeig Balmins, ☎ 93/894–2149). The clean-lined contemporary style enhances both the seascapes and the seafood. The restaurant is closed Tuesday from February through April.

en route

Upon leaving Sitges, make straight for the A2 *autopista* by way of Vilafranca del Penedès. Wine buffs may want to stop here to taste some excellent Penedès wines; you can tour and sip at the **Bodega Miguel Torres** (✉ C. Comerç 22 ☎ 93/890–0100). There's an interesting **Museu del Vi** (Wine Museum) in the Royal Palace, with descriptions of wine-making history. *€4* ⏲ *Tues.–Sun. 10–2 and 4–7.*

Santes Creus

66 *95 km (59 mi) west of Barcelona.*

Founded in 1157, Santes Creus is the first of the monasteries you'll come upon as A2 branches west toward Lleida. Three austere aisles and an unusual 14th-century apse combine with the newly restored cloisters and the courtyard of the royal palace. ☎ *977/638329* *€4* ⏲ *Oct.–Mar., daily 10–1 and 3–6; Apr.–Sept., daily 10–1 and 3–7.*

Montblanc is off A2 at Salida (Exit) 9, its ancient gates too narrow for cars. A walk through its tiny streets reveals Gothic churches with stained-glass windows, a 16th-century hospital, and medieval mansions.

Santa Maria de Poblet

67 *8 km (5 mi) west of Santes Creus.*

This splendid Cistercian foundation at the foot of the Prades Mountains is one of the great masterpieces of Spanish monastic architecture. The cloister is a stunning combination of lightness and size; on sunny days the shadows on the yellow sandstone are extraordinary. Founded in 1150 by Ramón Berenguer IV in gratitude for the Christian Reconquest, the monastery first housed a dozen Cistercians from Narbonne. Later, the Crown of Aragón used Santa Maria de Poblet for religious retreats and burials. The building was damaged in an 1836 anticlerical revolt, and monks of the reformed Cistercian Order have managed the difficult task of restoration since 1940. Today, monks and novices again pray before the splendid retable over the tombs of Aragonese rulers, restored to their former glory by sculptor Frederic Marès; sleep in the cold, barren dormitory; and eat frugal meals in the stark refectory. You can join them if you'd like—18 very comfortable rooms are available (for men only). Call **Padre Benito** (☎ 977/870089) to arrange a stay of up to 15 days within the stones and silence of one of Catalonia's gems. *Tour €5* *Guided tour Apr.–Sept., daily 10–12:30 and 3–6; Oct.–Mar., daily 10–12:30 and 3–5:30.*

off the beaten path

VALLS – The town of Valls, famous for its early spring *calçotada* (long-stemmed onion roast) held on the last Sunday of January, is 10 km (6 mi) from Santes Creus and 15 km (9 mi) from Poblet. Even if you miss the big day, *calçots* are served up from November to April at rustic and rambling farmhouses such as **Cal Ganxo** (☎ 977/605960) in nearby Masmolets, and the Xiquets de Valls, Catalonia's most famous *castellers* (human castlers), might be putting up a human skyscraper.

6

Girona & Northern Catalonia

Often ignored by travelers who bolt from its airport to the resorts of the Costa Brava, Girona is an easy and worthy day trip from Barcelona. Much of the city's charm comes from its narrow medieval streets—with frequent stairways, as required by the steep terrain. Historic sites include the cathedral, which dominates the city from the top of 90 steps; Arab baths; and a charming Jewish quarter. Northern Catalonia is memorable for the soft, green hills of the Ampurdan farm country, the Alberes mountain range at the eastern tip of the Pyrenees, and the rugged Costa Brava. Sprinkled across the landscape are charming *masías* (farmhouses) with austere, grayish or pinkish staggered-stone rooftops and ubiquitous square towers that make them look like fortresses. Even the tiniest village has its church, arcaded square, and *rambla,* where villagers take their evening *paseo.*

Girona

68 *97 km (60 mi) northeast of Barcelona.*

If you drive here, park in the free lot next to the River Onyar, under the train trestle. Walk along the river to Plaça de la Independencia, admiring Girona's best-known view as you go: the town's pastel yellow, pink, and orange waterfront facades, their windows draped with a colorful mix of drying laundry reflected in the shimmering Onyar. Cross the bridge from under the arcades in the corner of the Plaça and find your way to the tourist office, to the right at Rambla Llibertat 1. Then work your way up through the labyrinth of steep streets, using the cathedral's huge baroque facade as a guide.

At the base of the Girona cathedral's 90 steps and left through the Sobreportes gate are the **Banys Arabs**, or Arab Baths. Built by Morisco craftsmen in the late 12th century, long after Girona's Islamic occupation (795–1015) had ended, the baths are both Romanesque and Moorish in design. *€1.50* *May–Sept., Tues.–Sat. 10–2 and 4–7, Sun. 10–2; Oct.–Apr., Tues.–Sun. 10–1.*

Across the River Galligants is the church of **Sant Pere** (Holy Father), finished in 1131 and notable for its octagonal Romanesque belfry and the finely detailed capitals atop the columns in the cloister. Next door is the **Museu Arqueològic,** which documents the region's archaeological history since Paleolithic times. *€2* *Church and museum daily 10–1 and 4:30–7.*

A five-minute walk uphill behind the Girona cathedral leads to the **Torre de Gironella,** the highest point in the Jewish quarter. It was here that Girona's Jewish community took refuge in early August of 1391, emerging 17 weeks later to find their houses in ruins. Even though Spain's expulsion decree didn't take effect until 1492, this attack ended the Girona Jewish community. On December 20, 1998, the first Hanukkah celebration in 607 years was held in the gardens, with representatives of the Jewish communities of Spain, France, Portugal, Germany, and the United States present and Jerusalem's chief Sephardic rabbi, Rishon Letzion, presiding.

To see the inside of Girona's **cathedral,** designed by Guillem Bofill in 1416, complete the loop around it. The cathedral is known for its immense, uncluttered Gothic nave, which at 75 ft is the widest in the world and the epitome of the spatial ideal of Catalan Gothic architects. The **museum** contains the famous *Tapis de la Creació* (*Tapestry of the Creation*) and a 10th-century copy of Beatus's manuscript *Commentary on the Apocalypse.* The stepped Passeig Arquaeològic runs below the walls of the Old City; climb through the Jardins de la Francesa to the highest ramparts for a view of the 11th-century Romanesque **Torre de Carlomagno** (Charlemagne Tower), the oldest part of the cathedral. *€3 Oct.–June, daily 9:30–1:15 and 3:30–7; July–Sept., daily 9:30–7.*

Next door to Girona's cathedral is **Palau Episcopal** (Bishop's Palace), which houses the **Museu d'Art,** a good mix of Romanesque, Catalan Gothic, and modern art. *€2, free with ticket for Arab Baths Tues.–Sat. 10–7, Sun. 10–1.*

What was once the cramped and squalid center of the 13th-century *Call,* or Jewish quarter, is the sight of the **Centre Bonastruc ça Porta,** the lifeblood of the activities that refer to the recuperation of the Jewish heritage of Girona. Its **Museu de Història dels Jueus** (Museum of Jewish History) has 21 stone tablets, one of the finest collections in the world of medieval Jewish funerary slabs. *Carrer de la Força 8 972/216761 €2 Tues.–Sat. 10–2 and 4–7, Sun. 10–2.*

WHERE TO STAY & EAT

$$$–$$$$ **Albereda.** Excellent Ampurdan cuisine is served in a bright but soothing dining room. Try the *galleta con langostinos glaceada,* a zucchini bisque with prawns. *C. Albereda 7 bis 972/226002 AE, DC, MC, V Closed Sun.*

$$$–$$$$ Fodor's Choice ★ **Celler de Can Roca.** Girona's best restaurant and one of Catalonia's top six, this unusual spot west of town might serve anything from steak tartare with mustard ice cream to simple *vieiras* (scallops) with peas or a surf 'n turf of *pies de porc amb espardenyes* (trotters with sea slugs). *Ctra. Taialà 40, 2 km (1½ mi) west of Girona, Sant Gregori first roundabout to Taialà 972/222157 AE, DC, MC, V Closed Dec. 23–Jan. 15, 1st 2 wks in July, and Sun. and Mon.*

★ $–$$ **Cal Ros.** Tucked under the arcades just behind the north end of Plaça de la Llibertat, this historic place combines ancient stone arches with a crisp, contemporary interior and cheerful lighting. The cuisine is gamey and delicious: hot goat-cheese salad with pine nuts and *garum* (black-olive and anchovy paste dating back to Roman times), *oca amb naps* (goose with turnips), and a blackberry sorbet not to miss. *C. Cort Reial 9 972/217379 AE, DC, MC, V Closed Mon. No dinner Sun.*

$–$$ **Penyora.** Here you'll find both good local fare and, if you order from the prix-fixe menu, a bargain. *C. Nou del Teatre 3 972/218948 AE, DC, MC Closed Tues.*

$$ **Ultonia.** Traditionally furnished with antique corner cabinets and sturdy tables, the rooms here are a good-size and comfortable. *Gran*

Via Jaume I 22, 17001 ☎ 972/203850 🖷 972/203334 45 rooms ♿ Coffee shop, bar, meeting rooms ▭ AE, DC, MC, V.

$ **Bellmirall.** A charming little hostel across the Onyar in the Jewish quarter, Bellmirall offers top value in the heart of Girona's historic section. ✉ *Carrer Bellmirall 3, 17001* ☎ *972/204009* *7 rooms* ▭ *AE, DC, MC, V* ⊙ *Closed Jan.*

Figueres

69 *37 km (23 mi) north of Girona on the A7.*

This bustling country town is the capital of the Alt Empordà (Upper Ampurdan). Take a walk along the Figueres Rambla, scene of the *passeig* (*paseo* in Castilian; the constitutional midday or evening stroll), and have a coffee in one of several traditional cafés. The **Teatre-Museu Dalí** pays spectacular homage to a unique artist. The museum is installed in a former theater next to the bizarre, ocher-color Torre Galatea, where Dalí lived until his death in 1989. The remarkable Dalí collection includes a vintage Cadillac with ivy-cloaked passengers whom you can water for less than a euro. Dalí himself is entombed beneath the museum. ✉ *Pl. Gala–Salvado Dalí 5* ☎ *972/677970* *€7* ⊙ *Oct.–May, Tues.–Sun. 10:30–5:15; June–Sept., Tues.–Sun. 9–7:15.*

WHERE TO STAY & EAT

★ $$–$$$ **Empordà.** Hailed as the birthplace of modern Catalan cuisine, this hotel and restaurant 1½ km (1 mi) north of Figueres on the N-II is better known for its cooking than for its lodging. The restaurant serves hearty portions of superb French, Catalan, and Spanish cooking. Try one of the fish mousses. ✉ *N-II, 17600* ☎ *972/500562* 🖷 *972/509358* *39 rooms* ♿ *Restaurant, bar, parking (fee)* ▭ *AE, DC, MC, V.*

$–$$ **Hotel Duràn.** Once a stagecoach relay station, the Duran is now a hotel and restaurant open every day of the year. Salvador Dalí had his own private dining room here, and you can take a meal amid pictures of the great surrealist. Try the *mandonguilles amb sepia al estil Anna* (meatballs and cuttlefish), a *mar i muntanya* (surf-and-turf) specialty of the house. ✉ *C. Lasauca 5, 17600* ☎ *972/501250* 🖷 *972/502609* 🌐 *www.hotelduran.com* *65 rooms* ♿ *Restaurant, bar, meeting rooms, parking* ▭ *AE, MC, V.*

off the beaten path

AMPURDAN UPLANDS – To explore the Alt Empordà (Upper Ampurdan), take the N-II 10 km (6 mi) north of Figueres and turn west on Gi502. Work your way 13 km (8 mi) west to the village of Maçanet de Cabrenys. Continue to the Santuari de les Salines, where you'll find a chapel and a tiny restaurant open in summer. Above Salines is one of the greatest beech forests in the Pyrenees. Follow signs from Le Perthus to Puig Neulós, at 4,148 ft the highest point in the Alberes range and the easternmost major Pyrenean peak. One of the greatest walks in the Pyrenees is the six-hour hike from Puig Neulós to Banyuls-sur-Mer, on the Mediterranean: the grassy border crest has views south over the Ampurdan and north over the yellow curving strand of the Côte Vermeille.

Besalú

70 *34 km (21 mi) north of Girona.*

Once the capital of a feudal county as part of Charlemagne's 8th- and 9th-century Spanish March, Besalú is 25 km (15 mi) west of Figueres on C260. This ancient town's most emblematic sight is its **fortified bridge,** complete with crenellated battlements. **Sant Vicenç** (✉ Carrer de Sant Vicenç s/n) is Besalú's best Romanesque church. The church of **Sant Pere** (✉ Pl. de Sant Pere s/n) is all that remains of the 10th-century Benedictine monastery torn down in 1835. The ruins of the convent of **Santa**

Maria on the hill above town are a panoramic vantage point over Besalú. The **tourist office** (☎ 972/591240) in the arcaded Plaça de la Llibertat can provide opening hours for Sant Pere as well as keys to the *miqwe,* the rare **Jewish baths** discovered in the 1960s. A **Tren Turistic** leaves from the bridge every 45 minutes and visits the baths and the two churches for a cost of €3. The extraordinary town of **Castellfollit de la Roca** perches on its prowlike basalt cliff over the Fluvià River 16 km (10 mi) west of Besalú.

Olot

71 *21 km (13 mi) west of Besalú, 55 km (34 mi) northwest of Girona.*

Capital of the Garrotxa area, Olot is famous for its 19th-century school of landscape painters and has several excellent Art Nouveau buildings, including one with a facade by Moderniste master Lluís Domènech i Montaner. The **Museu Comarcal de la Garrotxa** (County Museum of La Garrotxa) has an assemblage of Moderniste art and design as well as sculptures by Miquel Blai, creator of the long-tressed maidens who support the balconies along Olot's main boulevard. ✉ *Carrer Hospici 8* ☎ *972/279130* *€3* ⏲ *Mon. and Wed.–Sat. 10–1 and 4–7, Sun. 10–1:30.*

The villages of **Vall d'En Bas** lie south of Olot off Route A153. The twisting old road goes past farmhouses whose dark wooden balconies are bedecked with bright flowers. Turn off for **Sant Privat d'En Bas** for a step back in time. The village of **Els Hostalets d'En Bas** eloquently defines rustic. A modern freeway cuts across this countryside to Vic, but you'll miss a lot by taking it.

WHERE TO STAY & EAT

$$–$$$ ✕ **Restaurante Ramón.** Ramon's eponymous restaurant is the opposite of rustic: sleek, modern, refined, and international. Samples of the *cuina de la terra* (home cooking of regional specialties) include *patata de Olot* (potato stuffed with veal) and *cassoleta de judias amb xoriç* (white haricot with sausage). ✉ *Pl. Clarà 10* ☎ *972/261001* *Reservations essential* *AE, DC, MC, V* ⏲ *Closed Thurs.*

¢–$ **La Perla d'Olot.** Known for its family friendliness, this hotel is always Olot's first to fill up. On the edge of town toward the Vic road, it is within walking distance of two parks. ✉ *Av. Santa Coloma 97, 17800* ☎ *972/262326* *972/270774* *30 rooms, 30 apartments* *Restaurant, bar* *MC, V.*

Rupit

72 *33 km (20 mi) south of Olot, 97 km (60 mi) north of Barcelona.*

Rupit is a spectacular stop for its medieval houses and its food, the highlight of which is beef-stuffed potatoes. Built into a rocky promontory over a stream in the rugged Collsacabra region (about halfway from Olot to Vic), the town has some of the most aesthetically perfect **stone houses** in Catalonia, some of which were reproduced for Barcelona's "Spain-in-a-bottle" architectural sampler, Poble Espanyol.

WHERE TO EAT

$–$$ ✕ **El Repòs.** Hanging over the river that runs through Rupit, this restaurant serves the best meat-stuffed potatoes around. Ordering a meal is easy: just learn the word *patata.* Other specialties include duck and lamb. ✉ *C. Barbacana 1* ☎ *93/856–5000* *MC, V.*

Vic

73 *66 km (41 mi) north of Barcelona.*

Known for its conservatism and Catalan nationalism, Vic rests on a 1,600-ft plateau at the confluence of two rivers and serves as the area's commercial, industrial, and agricultural hub. The wide **Plaça Major,** surrounded by Gothic arcades and well supplied with bars and cafés, perfectly expresses the city's personality. Vic's religiosity is demonstrated by its 35 churches, of which the largely neoclassical **cathedral** (☒ Pl. de la Catedral s/n ☎ 93/886–4449 €2 ⊙ Mon.–Sat. 10–1 and 4–7, Sun. 10–1:30) is the foremost. The 11th-century Romanesque tower, El Cloquer, built by the Abbot Oliva, and the powerful modern murals painted twice by Josep Maria Sert (first in 1930 and again after fire damage in 1945) are the cathedral's high points. The **Museu Episcopal** (Bishop's Museum; ☒ Pl. de la Catedral s/n ☎ 93/886–4449 €2 ⊙ Mon.–Sat. 10–1 and 4–7, Sun. 10–1:30) has a fine collection of religious art and relics.

6

WHERE TO STAY & EAT

$$$–$$$$ ✕ **Jordi Parramon.** The brightest star in the Vic culinary firmament these days defines his experimental tendencies with radical and playful combinations, such as his *pato con peras y regaliz* (duck with pears and licorice). *☒ Cardona 7 ☎ 93/886–3815 AE, DC, MC, V ⊙ Closed Mon., last 2 wks in Feb., and 1st 2 wks in Sept. No dinner Sun.*

$–$$ ✕ **Ca l'U.** Translated as "The One," Ca l'U is in fact *the* place in Vic for hearty local cuisine with a minimum of pretense and expense. Try the *llangostinos i llenguado* (prawns and sole) or the regional standard, *botifarra i mongetas* (sausage and beans). *☒ Pl. Santa Teresa 4–5 ☎ 93/886–3504 MC, V ⊙ Closed Mon. No dinner Sun.*

$–$$ **Parador de Vic.** This quietly charming parador is 14 km (9 mi) northeast of town off the Roda de Ter road past the village of Tavernoles. The views take in a stunning mountain and nearly lunar landscape over the Sau Reservoir. *☒ Ctra. Vic Roda de Ter, 08500 ☎ 93/888–7311 36 rooms Coffee shop, tennis court, pool MC, V.*

Girona & Northern Catalonia Essentials

ARRIVING & DEPARTING

By Bus: Sarfa (☒ Estació Norte–Vilanova C. Alí Bei 80 ☎ 93/265–1158) has buses every 1½ hours to Girona, Figueres, and Cadaqués. If you want to go to Vic contact **Segalés** (☎ 93/889–2577). For Ripoll call **Teisa** (☒ Pau Claris 118 ☎ 93/488–2837).

By Car: Barcelona is surrounded by a network of *rondas,* or ring roads, with quick access from every corner of the city. Look for signs for these rondas; then follow signs to France (Francia), Girona, and the A7 *autopista,* which goes all the way to France. For Girona, roughly a one-hour drive from Barcelona, leave the autopista at Salida (Exit) 7.

By Train: RENFE (☎ 902/24–0202) operates trains, which leave Sants and Passeig de Gràcia every 1½ hours for Girona, Figueres, and Port Bou (France). Some trains for northern Catalonia and France also leave from the França Station. For Vic and Ripoll, catch a Puigcerdà train (every hour or two) from Sants or Plaça de Catalunya.

GUIDED TOURS

Trenes Turísticos de RENFE (☎ 902/24–0202) operates guided tours to Girona by train May through September, leaving Sants at 10 AM and returning at 7:30 PM. The company also runs train tours to Vic and Ripoll, leaving Sants at 9 AM and returning at 8:40 PM. The cost for each is €10. Call RENFE to confirm.

The Costa Brava

The Costa Brava (Wild Coast) is a rocky stretch of shoreline that begins at Blanes and continues north through 135 km (84 mi) of coves and beaches to the French border at Port Bou. This tour concentrates on selected pockets—Tossa, Cap de Begur, Cadaqués—where the rocky terrain has discouraged the worst excesses of real-estate speculation. Here, on a good day, the luminous blue of the sea still contrasts with red-brown headlands and cliffs; the distant lights of fishing boats reflect on wine-color waters at dusk; and umbrella pines escort you to the fringes of secluded *calas* (coves) and sandy white beaches.

Exploring the Costa Brava

74 The beaches closest to Barcelona are at **Blanes,** where **launches** (✉ Crucetours ☎ 972/314–969) can take you to Cala de Sant Francesc or the double beach at Santa Cristina between May and October.

75 The next stop north from Blanes on the coast road is **Tossa de Mar,** christened "Blue Paradise" by painter Marc Chagall, who summered here in 1934. The only Chagall painting in Spain is in Tossa's **Museu Municipal** (Municipal Museum; ☎ 972/340–709), open Tuesday–Sunday 10–1 and 5–8. Admission is €2.50. Tossa's walled **medieval town** and pristine beaches are among Catalonia's best.

76 **Sant Feliu de Guixols** follows Tossa de Mar, after 23 km (15 mi) of hairpin curves over hidden inlets. Tiny turnouts or parking spots on this route nearly always lead to intimate coves with stone stairways winding down from the road. Visit Sant Feliu's two fine beaches, church and monastery, Sunday market, and lovely **Passeig del Mar.**

77 **S'Agaró,** one of the Costa Brava's most elegant clusters of seaside mansions, is 3 km (2 mi) north of Sant Feliu. The 30-minute walk along the **sea wall** from Hostal de La Gavina to Sa Conca beach is a delight.

Up the coast from S'Agaró, a road leads east to **Llafranc,** a small port
78 with quiet waterfront hotels and restaurants, and forks right to **Calella de Palafrugell,** a pretty fishing village known for its July Habaneras (Catalan-Cuban sea chanties inspired by the Spanish-American War) festival. Just south is the panoramic promontory **Cap Roig,** with views of the barren Formigues (Ants) Isles and a fine botanical garden that you can tour with a guide March–December, daily 9–9, for €4. The left fork drops down to **Tamariu,** one of the Costa's prettiest inlet towns. A climb over the bluff leads down to the parador at **Aiguablava,** a modern eyesore overlooking magnificent cliffs and crags.

79 From **Begur,** north of Aiguablava, you can go east through the *calas* or take the inland route past the rose-color stone houses and ramparts of the restored medieval town of **Pals.** Nearby **Peratallada** is another medieval town with fortress, castle, tower, palace, and well-preserved walls. North of Pals there are signs for **Ullastret,** an Iberian village dating from the 5th century BC. **L'Estartit** is the jumping-off point for the
80 spectacular **Parc Natural Submarí** (Underwater Natural Park) by the Medes Isles, famous for diving and for underwater photography.

81 The Greco-Roman ruins at **Empúries** are Catalonia's most important archaeological site. This port, complete with breakwater, is one of the most monumental ancient engineering feats on the Iberian Peninsula. As the Greeks' original point of arrival in Spain, Empúries was also where the Olympic Flame entered Spain for Barcelona's 1992 Olympic Games.

82 The **Aiguamolls** (Marshlands), a nature reserve with migratory waterfowl from all over Europe, lies mainly around **Castelló d'Empúries,** but the main information center is at El Cortalet, on the road in from Sant Pere Pescador. Follow the road from Empúries, crossing the Fluvià River at Sant Pere Pescador, and proceed north through the wetlands to Castelló. From Castelló d'Empúries, a series of roadways and footpaths traverses the marshes, the latter well marked on the information center's maps.

83 **Cadaqués,** Spain's easternmost town, still has the whitewashed charm that made this fishing village into an international artists' haunt in the

early 20th century. The Marítim is the central hangout both day and night; after dark, you might also enjoy the Jardí, across the square. Salvador Dalí's house, now a museum, still stands at Portlligat, a 30-minute walk north of town.

The **Casa Museu Salvador Dalí,** Dalí's summer house and a site long associated with the artist's notorious frolics with everyone from poets such as Federico García Lorca and Paul Eluard (whose wife, Gala, became Dalí's muse and spouse) to filmmaker Luis Buñuel. Filled with bits and pieces of the surrealist's daily life, it's an important point in the "Dalí triangle," completed by the castle at Pubol and the Museu Dalí, in Figueres. ✉ *Cala de Portlligat, 3-km (2-mi) walk from town center, along beach* ☎ *972/677–500* 🎫 *€9* ⏲ *Sept. 30–June, Tues.–Sun. 10:30–5:15; July and Sept., daily 9–7:15; Aug., daily 10 PM–1 AM (limited access).*

6

The **Castillo Pubol,** Dalí's former castle-home, is now the resting place of Gala, his perennial model and mate. It's a chance to wander through yet more Dalí-esque landscape: lush gardens, fountains decorated with masks of Wagner (the couple's favorite composer), and distinctive elephants with giraffe's legs and clawed feet. Two lions and a giraffe stand guard near Gala's tomb. ✉ *Rte. 255 toward La Bisbal, 15 km (9 mi) east of A7* ☎ *972/488–655* 🎫 *€8* ⏲ *Mar. 15–June 14, Tues.–Sun. 10:30–5:15; June 15–Sept. 15, daily 10:30–8; Sept. 16–Jan. 6, Tues.–Sun. 10:30–5:15.*

84 **Cap de Creus,** north of Cadaqués, Spain's easternmost point, is a fundamental pilgrimage, if only for the symbolic geographical rush. The hike out to the lighthouse—through rosemary, thyme, and the salt air of the Mediterranean—is unforgettable. The Pyrenees officially end (or rise) here. New Year's Day finds mobs of revelers awaiting the first emergence of the "new" sun from the Mediterranean.

85 The monastery of **Sant Pere de Rodes,** 7 km (4½ mi) by car (plus a 20-minute walk) above the pretty fishing village El Port de la Selva, is the last site, and one of the most spectacular, on the Costa Brava. Built in the 10th and early 11th centuries by Benedictine monks—and sacked and plundered repeatedly since—this Romanesque monolith, now being restored, commands a breathtaking panorama of the Pyrenees, the Empordà plain, the sweeping curve of the Bay of Roses, and Cap de Creus. (Topping off the grand trek across the Pyrenees, Cap de Creus is a spectacular six-hour walk from here on the well-marked GR11 trail.)

Where to Stay & Eat

$$$$ Fodor'sChoice ★ ✕ **El Bullí.** This seaside hideaway has become such a global phenomenon that getting a table here involves reserving months in advance and probably planning your trip around whatever you get. Open for dinner only and only from April through October, Ferran Adrià makes your palate his playground with a 12-course taster's menu that includes concepts like *espuma de humo* (foam of smoke)—no joke. It's near Roses in Cala Montjoi, 7 km (4½ mi) from Cadaqués by boat or footpath and 22 km (14 mi) by car. ✉ *Cala Montjoi, Roses, Girona* ☎ *972/150457* 📠 *972/150717* 🌐 *www.elbulli.com* ✍ *Reservations essential* 💳 *AE, DC, MC, V* ⏲ *Closed Nov.– Mar., Mon.–Tues. except Jul.–Sept. No lunch.*

$$–$$$ ✕ **La Xicra.** The local fare here includes *es niu,* an explosive combination of game fowl, fish tripe, pork meatballs, and cuttlefish, stewed in a rich sauce. ✉ *C. Estret 17, Palafrugell* ☎ *972/305630* 💳 *AE, DC, MC, V* ⏲ *Closed Wed. and Nov. No dinner Tues.*

$–$$ ✕ **Can Pelayo.** This tiny, family-run restaurant serves the best fish in Cadaqués. It's hidden behind Plaça Port Alguer, a few minutes' walk south of the town center. ✉ *Carrer Nou 11, Cadaqués* ☎ *972/258356* 💳 *MC, V* ⏲ *Closed weekdays Oct.–May.*

$–$$ ✕ **Royal.** This sunny, beachside spot serves fisherman-style creations of creditable freshness and quality. The suquet (fish cooked slowly to create its own juice, or *suc*) is especially commendable. ✉ *Passeig de Mar 9, Tamariu* ☎ *972/620041* ▭ *MC, V.*

$$$$ ✕🏨 **El Hostal de la Gavina.** At the eastern corner of Sant Pol beach in S'Agaró, La Gavina is a superb display of design and food founded in 1932 by Josep Ensesa, who invented S'Agaró itself. Fine comforts and dining are augmented by tennis, golf, and horseback riding. ✉ *Pl. de la Rosaleda s/n, 17248* ☎ *972/321100* 📠 *972/321573* 🌐 *www.lagavina.com* *58 rooms, 16 suites* *Restaurant, café, minibars, cable TV, tennis courts, pool, health club, bar, meeting rooms* ▭ *AE, DC, MC, V* ⏲ *Closed Nov.1–Easter except Dec. 30–Jan. 2.*

$$–$$$ ✕🏨 **Bar Cap de Creus.** Right next to the Cap de Creus lighthouse, this restaurant has spectacular views. The food is simple and good, and the proprietor rents three apartments (four beds each) upstairs. ✉ *Cadaqués, 17488 Girona* ☎ *972/199005* ▭ *MC, V* ⏲ *Closed Mon.–Thurs. Oct.–June.*

$$–$$$ ✕🏨 **Rocamar.** Rocamar has modern rooms with splendid views over Cadaqués or out to sea. Service is excellent, and the food is first-rate. ✉ *C. Doctor Bartomeus s/n, 17488 Cadaqués, Girona* ☎ *972/258150* 📠 *972/258650* 🌐 *www.rocamar.com* *70 rooms* *Restaurant, tennis court, indoor pool, bar* ▭ *AE, DC, MC, V.*

$–$$ ✕🏨 **La Riera.** Built into a medieval house, this rustic hotel-restaurant is a quiet hideaway in lovely Peratallada, near Begur. The dining room is in the former wine cellar and the rooms have ceiling beams over painted ceramic tiles. Food includes such local specialties as *anec amb naps* (duck with turnips) and *peu de porc amb cargols* (pig's feet with snails). ✉ *Pl. de les Voltes 3, Peratallada* ☎ *972/634142* 📠 *972/635040* *8 rooms* *Restaurant, bar* ▭ *AE, DC, MC, V.*

$$$ 🏨 **Mar Menuda.** This modern Costa Brava hideaway offers as much peace and quiet—*and* as many varieties of water sports—as you can possibly handle. Equipment and instruction are available for windsurfing, sailing, swimming, and scuba diving. The hotel terrace overlooks the coast and the town of Tossa de Mar, with a medieval castle and an old quarter full of cobble streets. ✉ *Playa Mar Menuda s/n, 17320 Tossa de Mar, Girona* ☎ *972/341000* 📠 *972/340087* 🌐 *www.marmenuda.com* *48 rooms, 10 suites* *Restaurant, minibars, tennis court, pool, bar, meeting rooms* ▭ *AE, DC, MC, V* ⏲ *Closed Nov.–late Dec.*

$$$ 🏨 **Parador de Aiguablava.** The service is impeccable at this modern parador on a promontory overlooking sheer cliffs and surging seas. ✉ *17255 Begur, Girona* ☎ *972/622162* 📠 *972/622166* 🌐 *www.parador.es* *87 rooms* *Restaurant, minibars, cable TV, pool, gym, sauna, bar* ▭ *AE, DC, MC, V.*

$$–$$$ 🏨 **Llané Petit.** This charming Cadaqués inn is below Hotel Rocamar, at beach level, though slightly less expensive. It has a very Mediterranean air. ✉ *C. Doctor Bartomeus 37, 17488 Cadaqués, Girona* ☎ *972/258050* 📠 *972/258778* 🌐 *www.llanepetit.com* *37 rooms* *Minibars, bar, parking* ▭ *AE, DC, MC, V.*

Costa Brava Essentials

ARRIVING & DEPARTING

By Bus: Sarfa (✉ Estació Norte–Vilanova C. Alí Bei 80 ☎ 93/265–1158 Ⓜ Arc de Triomf) operates buses to Blanes, Lloret, Sant Feliu de Guixols, Platja d'Aro, Palamos, Begur, Roses, and Cadaqués.

By Car: For the fastest trip from Barcelona, start up the A7 *autopista* as if to Girona and take Salida (Exit) 10 for Blanes. Coastal traffic can be slow and frustrating, and the roads tortuous.

By Train: The local train to the Costa Brava pokes along the coast to Blanes every 30 minutes, departing Sants at 13 and 43 minutes after every hour and Plaça de Catalunya 5 minutes later.

GUIDED TOURS From June to September, bus and boat tours from Barcelona to Empúries, L'Estartit, the Medes Isles underwater park, and the medieval town of Pals are run by **Julià Tours** (✉ Ronda Universitat 5 ☎ 93/317–6454). Buses leave Barcelona at 9 and return at 6. The price is €65 per person with lunch, €48 without. **Pullmantur** (✉ Gran Via 635 ☎ 93/318–5195) runs tours to several main points on the Costa Brava.

6

BARCELONA & NORTHERN CATALONIA A TO Z

To research prices, get advice from other travelers, and book travel arrangements, visit www.fodors.com.

AIR TRAVEL

All international and domestic flights arrive at the spectacular glass, steel, and marble El Prat de Llobregat airport, 14 km (9 mi) south of Barcelona. For flight-status information, call Iberia.

Airport Information **Aeroport del Prat** ☎ 93/298-3838. **Airport Lost and Found** ☎ 93/298-3349.

CARRIERS Most flights from the United States connect in Madrid or at other European points such as London, Amsterdam, Paris, or Frankfurt; only Continental, Delta, and Iberia fly nonstop to Barcelona.

Iberia ☎ 902/400-500. **Continental Airlines** ☎ 901/101-522. **Delta Airlines** ☎ 901/116-946.

AIRPORT TRANSFERS The Aerobus leaves the airport for Plaça de Catalunya every 15 minutes (6 AM–11 PM) on weekdays and every 30 minutes (6:30 AM–10:30 PM) on weekends. From Plaça de Catalunya, it leaves for the airport every 15 minutes (5:30 AM–10 PM) on weekdays and every 30 minutes (6:30 AM–10:30 PM) on weekends. The fare is €3.25.

Cab fare from the airport into town is about €20. If you're driving your own car, follow signs to the Centre Ciutat and you'll enter the city along Gran Via. For the port area, follow signs for the Ronda Litoral. The journey to the center of town can take anywhere from 15 to 45 minutes depending on traffic. Peak rush hours are between 7:30 and 9:30 in the morning, 1:30–2:30 in the afternoon, and 7–9 in the evening.

The train's only drawback is that it's a 10- or 15-minute walk (with moving walkway) from your gate through the terminal and over the bridge. Trains leave the airport every 30 minutes between 6:12 AM and 10:13 PM, stopping at the Estació de Sants, then at the Plaça de Catalunya, later at the Arc de Triomf, and finally at Clot. Trains going to the airport begin at 6 AM from the Clot station, stopping at the Arc de Triomf at 6:05 AM, Plaça de Catalunya at 6:08 AM, and Sants at 6:13 AM. The fare is €2.25.

BIKE TRAVEL

Bicitram is a bike-rental outfit that stays open on weekends and holidays. Los Filicletos rents bikes, skates, and scooters. Un Menys—"One Less," in Catalan, meaning one less car on the streets of Barcelona—organizes increasingly popular outings that tack drinks, dinner, and dancing on to a gentle bike ride for a total price of about €30.

Bike Rentals **Bicitram** ✉ Marquès de l'Argentera 15 ☎ 636/401997. **Los Filicletos** ✉ Passeig de Picasso 38 ☎ 93/319-7811. **Un Menys** ✉ Esparteria 3 ☎ 93/268-2105 📠 93/319-4298.

BOAT & FERRY TRAVEL

Ferries to and from the Balearic Islands (Majorca, Menorca, Ibiza) arrive and leave from the Estació Marítim in the port south of the Columbus Monument. Trasmediterránea transports passengers and vehicles to the Balearics. Golondrina harbor boats make short trips from the Portal de la Pau, near the Columbus Monument. The fare is €7 for a 90-minute ride out past the beaches, half that for a 30-minute harbor ride. There is also a longer excursion in a glass-bottom catamaran that parallels the coast up to the Platja del Bogatell east of Barcelona's Olympic Port. Depending on the weather, the catamarans (€9 per person) leave every hour on the half hour from 11:30 to 5:30 (6:30 from Holy Week through September). Regular Golondrina departures are spring and summer (Holy Week through September), daily 11–7; fall and winter, weekends and holidays only, 11–5. It's closed mid-December–early January. For information call ☎ 93/442–3106.

Estació Marítim ☎ 93/295-9100. Trasmediterránea ☎ 902/454-645.

BUS TRAVEL TO & FROM BARCELONA

Barcelona's main bus station is Estació del Nord, east of the Arc de Triomf. Buses also depart from the Estació de Sants as well as from the depots of Barcelona's various private bus companies. Rather than pound the pavement (or the telephone, usually futile because of overloaded lines) trying to sort out Barcelona's complex and confusing bus system, go through a travel agent, who can quickly book you the best bus passage to your destination.

BUS TRAVEL WITHIN BARCELONA

City buses run daily from 5:30 AM to 11:30 PM. The fare is €1. For multiple journeys purchase a Targeta T1 (valid for bus or Metro), which buys you 10 rides for €5.75. Route maps are displayed at bus stops. Note that those with a red band always stop at a central square—Catalunya, Universitat, or Urquinaona—and blue indicates a night bus. Barcelona's 30 night buses generally run until about 4:30 AM, though some stop as early as 3:30 AM and others continue until as late as 5:20 AM. Schedules are available at bus and Metro stations or at 🌐 www.bcn.es/guia/welcomea.htm

CABLE-CAR TRAVEL

The Montjuïc Funicular is a cog railroad that runs from the junction of Avinguda Paral.lel and Nou de la Rambla to the Miramar station on Montjuïc (Paral.lel). It operates weekends and holidays 11 AM–8 PM in winter, daily 11 AM–9:30 PM in summer; the fare is €1.75. A *telefèric* then takes you up to Montjuïc Castle. In winter the telefèric runs weekends and holidays 11–2:45 and 4–7:30; in summer, daily 11:30–9. The fare is €3. A Transbordador Aeri Harbor Cable Car runs between Miramar and Montjuïc across the harbor to Torre de Jaume I, on Barcelona's *moll* (quay), and on to Torre de Sant Sebastià, at the end of Passeig Joan de Borbó in Barceloneta. You can board at either stage. The fare is €7 round-trip, and the car runs October–June, weekdays noon–5:45, weekends noon–6:15, and July–September, daily 11–9. To reach the summit of Tibidabo, take the Metro to Avinguda de Tibidabo, then the Tramvía Blau (€2 one-way) to Peu del Funicular, and finally the Tibidabo Funicular (€3 one-way) from there to the Tibidabo fairground. It runs every 30 minutes, 7:05 AM–9:35 PM ascending, 7:25 AM–9:55 PM descending.

CAR RENTAL

Note that National Car Rental is affiliated with the Spanish agency Atesa, or Avis. Europcar has good weekend deals. Vanguard rents motorcycles as well as cars.

Major Agencies **Avis** ✉ Casanova 209, Eixample ☎ 93/209-9533 ✉ Aragó 235, Eixample ☎ 93/487-8754. **Europcar** ✉ Viladomat 214, Eixample ☎ 93/439-8403 ✉ Estació de Sants ☎ 93/491-4822. **Hertz** ✉ Estació de Sants, Eixample ☎ 93/490-8662 ✉ Tuset 10, Eixample ☎ 93/217-3248.

Local Agencies **Atesa** ✉ El Prat Airport, El Prat ☎ 93/298-3433 ✉ Muntaner 45, Eixample ☎ 93/323-0266. **Vanguard** ✉ Londres 31, Eixample ☎ 93/439-3880.

CAR TRAVEL

Getting around Barcelona by car is generally more trouble than it's worth. The *Rondas* (ring roads) make entering and exiting the city easy, unless it's rush hour, in which case traffic comes to a halt. Between parking, navigating, alcoholemia patrols, and the general wear and tear of driving in the city, the subway, taxis, buses and walking are your best bets in Barcelona.

For travel outside of Barcelona, the freeways to Girona, Figueres, Sitges, Tarragona, and Lleida are surprisingly fast. Routine cruising speed on Spanish freeways is 140 km (84 mph) or more. If you drive at the official speed limit of 120 (72 mph) you seriously risk high-speed rear-ending. The distance to Girona, 97 km (58 mi), is a 45-minute shot. The French border is an hour away. Perpignan is, at 188 km (113 mi), an hour and twenty minutes.

On freeways (possibly because official driving-school manuals date before the invention of Spain's excellent network of freeways), do not expect motorists coming down the inside lane to move left and give way. The "merging" concept does not exist in Spain. Expect to come to a full stop at the red yield triangle at the end of the on-ramp and wait for a break in traffic.

Spanish highway engineers have discovered the British roundabout. Remember that the motorist *in the roundabout* has the right of way, even if you are the vehicle to the right (which is the normal rule of thumb elsewhere: vehicles coming from your right have right of way).

PARKING You can often find a legal and safe parking place on the street, and underground public parking is plentiful, easy, and cheap.

TRAFFIC Barcelona's rush hours take place from 8:30 to 9:30AM, from 2 to 3 PM, and, intermittently, from 5 to 9 PM.

CHILDREN IN BARCELONA

Check listings in daily newspapers for children's activities on Saturday and Sunday mornings. The **Fundació Miró** is one of Barcelona's most child-friendly venues, with clowns, storytellers, and events of all kinds from 10–2 on weekends. The **Barcelona zoo** and especially the dolphin show are great favorites with small *barcelonins*. The **Museu de la Ciència** offers excellent interactive scientific games and virtual experiences. Drassanes Reials and the **Museu Marítimo** have superb maritime displays designed for children. Last of all is the amusement park up on **Tibidabo,** a once-popular children's event that has simply been eclipsed by superior activities.

BABY-SITTING For baby-sitters in Barcelona, the hotel desk offers an added guarantee of reliability, although there are also a dozen baby-sitting agencies offering *cangurs* (kangaroos), carriers with a pouch for the little one.

CONSULATES

Canada **Barcelona** ✉ Elisenda de Pinos, Pedralbes ☎ 93/204-2700.
United Kingdom **Barcelona** ✉ Av. Diagonal 477, Eixample ☎ 93/366-6200.
United States **Barcelona** ✉ Passeig Reina Elisenda 23, Pedralbes ☎ 93/280-2227.

DISCOUNTS & DEALS

Obtainable in Turisme de Barcelona offices in Plaça de Catalunya and Plaça Sant Jaume (both open Mon.–Sat. 9–9 and Sun. 10–2), as well as in the Sants train station (open daily 8–8) and the El Prat airport, the Barcelona card offers discounts in nearly all of Barcelona's major museums, in stores, access to public transport gratis, and discounts on theater and music events.

Discounts **Plaça de Catalunya** ✉ Pl. de Catalunya 17 bis, Eixample ☎ 906/301282 🌐 www.barcelonaturisme.com. **Plaça Sant Jaume** ✉ Pl. Sant Jaume 1, Barri Gòtic ☎ 906/301282. **Estació de Sants** ✉ Pl. dels Països Catalans s/n, Eixample.

EMERGENCIES

Tourist Attention, a service provided by the local police department, can help if you're the victim of a crime or need medical or psychological assistance. English interpreters are on hand. To find out which pharmacies are open late at night or 24 hours on a given day, look on the door of any pharmacy or in any local newspaper under "*Farmacias de Guardia.*" Alternatively, dial ☎ 010.

Tourist Attention ✉ Guardia Urbana, Ramblas 43, Rambla ☎ 93/290-3440. **Ambulance** Creu Roja ☎ 93/300-2020. **Medical assistance** ☎ 061. **Police** ☎ 091 or 092 ✉ main police station ✉ Via Laietana 43, Barri Gòtic ☎ 93/301-6666.

Hospital **Hospital Clinic** ✉ Villarroel 170, Eixample ☎ 93/454-6000 or 93/454-7000 Ⓜ blue line to Hospital Clinic.

24-Hour Pharmacies **24-Hour Pharmacies** ☎ 010.

INTERNET ACCESS

Surrounded by medieval stone, the art gallery–cum–Internet café bcnet offers everything from e-mail checking to video conferences until 1 AM. Idea, which also has a bookstore, is perfect for drafting e-mail alone *or* together.

Internet Cafés **Bar Travel** ✉ Boqueria 27, Barri Gòtic ☎ 93/410-8592. **bcnet** ✉ Barra de Ferro 3, La Ribera ☎ 93/268-1507. **Cafe Internet Navego** ✉ Provença 546, Eixample ☎ 93/436-8459. **Idea** ✉ Pl. Comercial 2, El Born ☎ 93/268-8787.

SIGHTSEEING TOURS

BUS TOURS

From mid-June to mid-October, the Bus Turistic (9:30–7:30 every 30 minutes) runs on a circuit that passes all the important sights. A day's ticket, which you can buy on the bus, costs €9 (€6 half day) and also covers the fare for the Tramvía Blau, funicular, and Montjuïc cable car across the port. The ride starts at the Plaça de Catalunya. Julià Tours and Pullmantur run day and half-day excursions outside the city. The most popular trips are those to Montserrat and the Costa Brava resorts, the latter including a cruise to the Medes Isles.

Julià Tours ✉ Ronda Universitat 5, Eixample ☎ 93/317-6454. **Pullmantur** ✉ Gran Via 635, Eixample ☎ 93/318-5195.

Asociación Profesional de Informadores Turísticos ☎ 93/319-8416. **Barcelona Guide Bureau** ☎ 93/268-2422. **City Guides Barcelona** ☎ 93/412-0674.

WALKING TOURS

Julià Tours and Pullmantur both lead walks around Barcelona. Tours leave from their offices, but you may be able to arrange a pickup at your hotel. Prices are €30 for half a day and €65 for a full day, including lunch. Turisme de Barcelona offers weekend walking tours of the Gothic Quarter (at 10 AM) for €6. Tours depart from the office. Urbancultours has English-language walking tours covering Gaudí's Sagrada Família, the medieval Jewish quarter, and other sights.

Julià Tours ✉ Ronda Universitat 5, Eixample ☎ 93/317-6454. **Palau de la Virreina** ✉ La Rambla 99, Rambla. **Pullmantur** ✉ Gran Via 635, Eixample ☎ 93/318-5195. **Turisme de Barcelona** ✉ Pl. de Catalunya 17 bis, Eixample ☎ 906/301282. **Urbancultours** ☎ 93/417-1191.

Barcelona Metro
KEY
L1 Metro Terminals
Metro Stations
Transfer Stations
Railway Lines
Funicular
Telefèric
Tramvia Blau
FF.CC. Generalitat
Mediterranean Sea
Sta. Coloma de Gramenet
Besòs
A19
AVDA. MERIDIANA
GRAN VIA
AVDA. DIAGONAL
G. VIADE CARLES III
TO AIRPORT
Cornellà
L5
Gavarra
Sant Ildefons
Can Boixeres
Can Vidalet
Pubilla Cases
Collblanc
Badal
Plaça de Sants
Hostafrancs
Espanya
Zona Universitària
L3
Palau Reial
María Cristina
Les Corts
Plaça del Centre
Sants-Estació
Tarragona
Rocafort
Urgell
Universitat
Entença
Hospital Clínic
Diagonal
Provença
Feixa Llarga
L1
Bellvitge
L'Hospitalet Sant Josep
Rambla Just Oliveras
Can Serra
Florida
Torrassa
Sta. Eulàlia
Mercat Nou
Cornellà
Almeda
Gornal
Ildefons Cerdà
a Sant Cugat a Sabadell Rbla. i a Terrassa
Vallvidrera Superior
Peu del Funicular
Reina Elisenda
Sarrià
Les Tres Torres
La Bonanova
Muntaner
St. Gervasi
Tibidabo
Peu del Funicular
Avda. del Tibidabo
El Putget
Pl. Molina
Gràcia
Montbau
L3
Vall d'Hebron
Penitents
Vallcarca
Lesseps
Fontana
Joanic
Verdaguer
Girona
Passeig de Gràcia
Urquinaona
Catalunya
Liceu
Drassanes
Paral.lel
L2
Sant Antoni
Poble Sec
Parc de Montjuïc
Miramar
Castell
Barceloneta
Jaume I
Arc de Triomf
Ciutadella
Horta
L5
Vilapicina
Virrei Amat
Maragall
Guinardó
Alfons X
Hospital de Sant Pau
Camp de l'Arpa
Congrés
Sagrada Família
Monumental
Tetuan
Encants
Clot
Navas
Sagrera
Roquetes
L4
Llucmajor
Fabra i Puig
Sant Andreu
Torras i Bages
Trinitat Vella
Baró de Viver
Sta. Coloma
Fondo
L1
La Pau
Verneda
Joan XXIII
Sant Roc
Gorg
Pep Ventura
L4
Bac de Roda
L2
Glòries
Marina
Bogatell
Llacuna
Poblenou
Selva de Mar
Besòs
Besòs-Mar

SUBWAY TRAVEL

The subway is the fastest, cheapest, and easiest way to get around Barcelona. You pay a flat fare of €1 no matter how far you travel, but it's more economical to buy a Targeta T10 (valid for Metro and FFCC Generalitat trains, Tramvía Blau [blue tram], and the Montjuïc Funicular), which costs €6 for 10 rides. Lines 2, 3, and 5 run weekdays 5 AM–midnight. Lines 1 and 4 close at 11. On Friday, Saturday, and holiday evenings all trains run until 2 AM. The FFCC Generalitat trains run until 12:30 on weekdays and 2:15 AM on weekends and eves of holidays. Sunday trains run on weekday schedules.

TAXIS

Taxis (☎ 93/387–1000, 93/490–2222, or 93/357–7755 24 hours a day) are black and yellow and show a green rooftop light when available for hire. The meter starts at €1.10, and rises in increments of centimos. There are supplements for luggage, night travel, Sundays and holidays, rides from a station or to the airport, and for trips to or from the bullring or a football match. There are cab stands all over town, and you can also hail cabs on the street.

TRAIN TRAVEL

Almost all long-distance trains arrive and depart from Estació de Sants. En route to or from Sants, some trains stop at another station on Passeig de Gràcia at Carrer Aragó; this can be a good way to avoid the long lines that form at Sants during holidays. The Estació de França, near the port, handles certain long-distance trains within Spain and some international trains. For schedules and fares, call RENFE. While overnight train travel is convenient, time-efficient, and easy if you like to sleep on trains, beware: unless you have a fairly pricey compartment for two (or four), you will be packed in with strangers in a four-person compartment with windows that do not open and often suffocating heat. The air shuttle (or a scheduled flight) between Madrid and Barcelona can, if all goes well, get you door to door in under three hours for only about €40 more.

Train Information & Stations **RENFE** ☎ 902/240202. **Estació de França** ✉ Av. Marquès de l'Argentera s/n, La Ribera. **Estació de Sants** ✉ Pl. dels Països Catalans s/n, Eixample.

TRANSPORTATION WITHIN BARCELONA

Modern Barcelona, above the Plaça de Catalunya, is built on a grid system. The old town, however, from the Plaça de Catalunya to the port, is a labyrinth of narrow streets, so you'll need a good street map. Most sightseeing can be done on foot—you won't have any choice in the Barri Gòtic—but you'll have to use the Metro, buses, or taxis to link sightseeing areas. The Dia T1 pass is valid for one day of unlimited travel on all subway, bus, and FFCC lines. Maps showing bus and Metro routes are available free from booths in the Plaça de Catalunya; for general information on public transport, call ☎ 93/412–0000. Turisme de Barcelona sells 24-, 48-, and 72-hour versions of the very worthwhile Barcelona Card. For €14, €20, €23, you get unlimited travel on all public transport as well as discounts at 27 museums, 10 restaurants, 14 leisure sites, and 20 stores. Other services include walking tours of the Gothic Quarter, an airport shuttle, a bus to Tibidabo, and the Tombbus, which connects key shopping areas.

By early 2004 Barcelona will have tramways connecting Plaça Francesc Macià with the city's western suburbs via Av. Diagonal. Barcelona's eastern peripheral developments will also be served by tramways originating in Plaça de les Glories. Tramway lines will also connect Barceloneta

and Badalona, and Estació del Nord with Sant Adrià and Poble Nou.
Turisme de Barcelona ✉ Pl. de Catalunya 17 bis, Eixample ☎ 906/301-282.
American Express ✉ Roselló 257, at Passeig de Gràcia, Eixample ☎ 93/217-0070. **Bestours** ✉ Diputació 241, Eixample ☎ 93/487-8580. **Iberia** ✉ Diputació 258, at Passeig de Gràcia, Eixample ☎ 93/401-3381 ✉ Pl. de Espanya, Eixample ☎ 93/325-7358. **WagonsLits Cook** ✉ Passeig de Gràcia 8, Eixample ☎ 93/317-5500.

VISITOR INFORMATION

Turisme de Barcelona has two main locations, both open Monday through Saturday 9–9 and Sunday 10–2: Plaça de Catalunya, in the center of town, and Plaça Sant Jaume, in the Gothic Quarter. There are smaller facilities at the Sants train station, open daily 8–8; the Institut de Cultura, open Monday–Saturday 9–9 and Sunday 10–2, has cultural information only. The Palau de Congressos is open daily 10–8 during trade fairs and conventions only. For general information in English, dial ☎ 010 between 8 AM and 10 PM any day but Sunday. El Prat Airport has an office with information on Catalonia and the rest of Spain, open Monday–Saturday 9:30–8 and Sunday 9:30–3. The tourist office in Palau Robert, open Monday–Saturday 10–7, specializes in provincial Catalonia. From June to mid-September, tourist information aides patrol the Gothic Quarter and Ramblas area 9 AM–9 PM. They travel in pairs and are recognizable by their uniforms of red shirts, white trousers or skirts, and badges.

City Tourist Offices **Plaça de Catalunya** ✉ Pl. de Catalunya 17 bis, Eixample ☎ 906/301282 🌐 www.barcelonaturisme.com. **Plaça Sant Jaume** ✉ Pl. Sant Jaume 1, Barri Gòtic ☎ 906/301282. **Palau de Congressos** ✉ Av. María Cristina s/n, Eixample ☎ 902/23-3200. **Institut de Cultura** ✉ Rambla 99, Rambla ☎ 93/316-1000. **Estació de Sants** ✉ Pl. Països Catalans s/n, Eixample ☎ 93/491-4431.

Regional Tourist Offices **Palau Robert** ✉ Passeig de Gràcia 107, at Diagonal, Eixample ☎ 93/238-4000. **El Prat Airport** ☎ 93/478-4704.

SOUTHERN CATALONIA & THE LEVANTE

7

HIGHLY RECOMMENDED

RESTAURANTS	El Timonel seafood restaurant in Valencia
	Gargantua restaurant in Valencia
	Joan Gatell restaurant in Cambrils
	La Matandeta restaurant in Albufera Nature Park, Valencia
	Les Voltes restaurant in Tarragona
	Mesón del Pastor restaurant in Morella
HOTELS	Cardenal Ram, Morella
	Excelsior, Valencia
	Monte Picayo, Puzol
	Parador de Alcañiz
	Parador de Tortosa
	Reina Victoria, Valencia
SIGHTS	Archaeology Museum, Tarragona
	Lonja de la Seda silk exchange, Valencia
	Museum of Fine Arts, Valencia
	Palacio del Marqués de Dos Aguas, Valencia
	Peñíscola's old town
	Tarragona's Roman amphitheater
	The walled city of Morella

By Philip Eade

Updated by AnneLise Sorensen

THIS REGION STRADDLES CATALONIA (Catalunya) and Valencia, allowing you to sample the differences and similarities between these two feuding Mediterranean cousins. Valencia was part of the House of Aragón, Catalonia's medieval Mediterranean empire, after Jaume I conquered it in the 13th century. Valencia was incorporated, along with Catalonia, into a united Spanish state in the 15th century, but the most energetic cultivators of Valencia's separate cultural and linguistic identity still resent their centuries of Catalan domination. The Catalan language prevails in Tarragona, a city and province of Catalonia, but Valenciano, widely considered a dialect of Catalan (many Valencianos consider it a language proper), is spoken and written on street signs in the Valencian provinces. You may notice the subtle difference in dialect as you move south.

The *huerta* (fertile, irrigated coastal plain) is devoted mainly to citrus and vegetable farming, which lends color to the landscape and fragrance to the air. Grayish, arid mountains form a stark backdrop to the lush coast. Over the years these shores have entertained Phoenician, Greek, Carthaginian, and Roman visitors—the Romans stayed several centuries and left archaeological reminders all the way down the coast, particularly in Tarragona, the capital of Rome's Spanish empire by 218 BC. Rome's dominion did not go uncontested, however; the most serious challenge came from the Carthaginians of North Africa. The three Punic Wars, fought over this territory between 264 BC and 146 BC, led to the immortalization of the Carthaginian general Hannibal.

The same coastal farmland and beaches that attracted the ancients call to modern-day tourists, and unfortunately a chain of ugly developments has marred much of this shore. Venture inland, though, and you'll find a world where local culture has survived intact. This rugged and often beautiful territory is dotted with small, fortified towns, several of which bear the name of Spain's 11th-century national hero, El Cid, as proof of the battles he fought here against the Moors 900 years ago. Each town has a porticoed Plaza Mayor, a warren of whitewashed houses, and countless coats of arms. Founded by the Greeks, the city of Valencia was in Moorish hands from 712 to 1238, apart from a brief interlude from 1094 to 1102, when El Cid reconquered it. Colorful *azulejos* (glazed, patterned tiles) and bright-blue church cupolas reflect Moorish traditions here. Spain's golden age left striking souvenirs of the 15th century as well: the Gothic Lonja (Silk Exchange) and mansions, and the primitive paintings of Jacomart and Juan Reixach in the Museum of Fine Arts. The flamboyant, 18th-century Palacio de las Dos Aguas embodies the vitality of Churrigueresque, the early Spanish baroque.

About the Restaurants

In and around Valencia, indeed all along the Mediterranean coast, you're in the homeland of *paella valenciana*—a hearty rice dish flavored with saffron and embellished with seafood, poultry, meat, peas, and peppers. Prepared to order in a *caldero* (shallow pan), paella takes a full 20 minutes to cook, so it's not for when you're in a hurry. Good paella is fabulous, but it's often overpriced due to tourist demand, and you should never choose paella from a *menú del día,* where it's usually tasteless and disappointing. A variant is *arroz a la banda,* in which the fish and rice are cooked separately; the fish is fried in garlic, onion, and tomato, and the rice is boiled in the resulting stock. *Romesco,* a spicy blend of almonds, peppers, and olive oil, is used as a fish and seafood sauce in Tarragona, especially during the *calçotada* (spring onion) feasts of February. If you're here for September's Santa Tecla festival, look for *espineta amb cargolins* (tuna with snails), perhaps accompanied by some excellent wine from the nearby Penedés or Priorato vineyard. The Ebro Delta is renowned for its fresh fish and eels, as well as specialties like *rossejat* (fried rice in a fish broth, dressed with garlic sauce). *Jamones* (hams), *cecinas* (smoked meats), and *carnes a la brasa* (meats cooked over coals) are all staples of Maestrazgan (mountain) cooking, together with good *trucha* (trout), *conejo* (rabbit), and local *trufas* (truffles).

WHAT IT COSTS In Euros

	$$$$	$$$	$$	$	¢
AT DINNER	over €20	€15–€20	€10–€15	€6–€10	under €6

Prices are per person for a main course at dinner.

About the Hotels

Antique, one-of-a-kind lodgings are in gratifying abundance on the Ebro Delta and in the Maestrazgo mountains. On the shore, hotels are more mundane, with modern high-rises predominating. Tarragona has several standard hotels. Just north and south of Valencia, the towns of Puzol and El Saler have some famous luxury properties; the city itself offers a reasonable mix of historic and modern hotels. If you plan to be in Valencia for Las Fallas, in mid-March, book your room months in advance; prices rise as the festivities approach.

WHAT IT COSTS In Euros

	$$$$	$$$	$$	$	¢
FOR 2 PEOPLE	over €180	€100–€180	€60–€100	€40–€60	under €40

Prices are for two people in a standard double room in high season, excluding tax.

Exploring Tarragona to Valencia

The ancient city of Tarragona—with a Roman amphitheater and aqueduct—infuses the northern wedge of Southern Catalonia with a medieval flavor. Southwest of Tarragona are the wetlands of the Ebro Delta, rich in birdlife. Inland lie the rugged Sierra de Beceite mountains and the walled town of Morella. The Ebro River snakes its way through the interior, passing through the historical town of Tortosa. Southern Catalonia's interior is best accessed by car, as the bus and trains have limited routes. South of Tortosa, lively resort towns—including Benicarlo, Peñíscola, and Benicassim—dot the Costa del Azahar. The region's crown jewel is Valencia, a thriving, artistic city perched on the southern end of the Costa del Azahar.

Numbers in the text correspond to numbers in the margin and on the Southern Catalonia & the Levante and the Valencia maps.

Timing

Try to avoid this region in summer. The weather is hot and arid, and the beaches are crowded. Fall and spring are probably the best times to come, though anyone who has seen slanting December light in the delta or the dramatic shadows that winter sun casts on medieval stone facades might recommend a winter visit just as heartily. Hours for most sights change with the seasons; many close as early as 5:30 in winter.

TARRAGONA

1 *98 km (60 mi) southwest of Barcelona, 251 km (155 mi) northeast of Valencia.*

Less than an hour from Barcelona, Tarragona offers a bracing mélange of activities in a fresh provincial capital. An ancient outpost of the

If you have 3 days Spend one day exploring the Roman, Visigothic, medieval, and modern wonders of **Tarragona** ①, stopping occasionally to savor its sweeping sea views. Have lunch in the Serallo fishing quarter, dine within the Roman walls, and spend the night in the heart of town. Set out the next morning for the **Delta de l'Ebre** ⑥ and explore its world-famous nature preserve before having lunch at the restaurant-museum Estany, near Villafranca del Delta. Head south to **Peñíscola** ⑰ for your second night, and devote your third day to **Valencia** ⑳–㉝.

If you have 5 days Begin with **Tarragona** ①. After a night there, move on to explore the **Delta de l'Ebre** ⑥, taking a late lunch at the restaurant-museum Estany. Drive up to **Tortosa** ⑦ for a night in the Castillo de la Zuda parador. Devote day three to the Sierra de Beceite, with visits to Miravet, **Gandesa** ⑧, Calaceite, Valderrobres, Beceite, and Fredes before an overnight in **Morella** ⑪. On day four, drive through the Maestrazgo mountains to see some of the least-visited valleys and villages on the entire Iberian Peninsula. Take the slow but scenic CS802 up through Iglesuela del Cid and around to Villafranca del Cid before driving through **Ares del Maestre** ⑫, Albocácer, and **San Mateu** ⑮ on your way to **Peñíscola** ⑰, where you can spend the night. Finally, travel down the Costa del Azahar to **Valencia** ⑳–㉝.

Roman Empire, it remains a pungent fishing port, busy shipping harbor, and vibrant cultural center. As capital of the Roman province of Tarraconensis (from 218 BC), Tarraco, as it was then called, formed the empire's principal stronghold in Spain, and by the 1st century BC the city was regarded as one of the empire's finest urban creations. Its wine was already famous, and its people were the first in Spain to become Roman citizens. The apostle Paul preached here in AD 58, and Tarragona became the seat of the Christian Church in Spain until it was superseded by Toledo in the 11th century. Approaching the city from Barcelona, you'll pass the **triumphal arch of Berà,** dating from the 3rd century BC, 19 km (12 mi) north of Tarragona. From the Lleida (Lérida) road, or *autopista,* you can see the 1st-century **Roman aqueduct** that helped carry fresh water 32 km (19 mi) from the River Gayo. Tarragona is divided clearly into old and new by the Rambla Vella—the old town and most of the Roman remains are to the north, while modern Tarragona spreads out to the south.

Start your tour at the acacia-lined Rambla Nova, at the end of which is a balcony overlooking the sea, the Balcó del Mediterràni. Walking uphill along Passeig de les Palmeres, you'll arrive at the remains of Tarragona's ★ **amphitheater,** sitting in the shadow of the modern, semicircular Hotel Imperial Tarraco, artfully echoing the amphitheater's curve. Walk down the steps to the amphitheater to see just how well preserved it is—you're free to wander through the access tunnels and along the seating rows. In the center of the theater are the remains of two superimposed churches, the earlier of which was a Visigothic basilica built to mark the bloody martyrdom of St. Fructuós and his deacons in AD 259. ✉ *Passeig de les Palmeres* €1.87 ⏲ *June–Sept., Tues.–Sat. 9–9, Sun. 9–3; Oct.–May, Tues.–Sat. 9–5, Sun. 10–3.*

Explore the excavated vaults from the 1st-century Roman **Circus Maximus.** The plans just inside the gate show that these formed only a small corner of a vast arena (350 yards long), where 23,000 spectators gathered to watch chariot races. As medieval Tarragona grew, the city gradually swamped the Circus. The Circus is across the Rambla Vella from the Tarragona amphitheater. *€1.87 (joint entry with the Praetorium) June–Sept., Tues.–Sat. 9–9, Sun. 9–3; Oct.–May, Tues.–Sat. 9–7, Sun. 10–3.*

The former **Praetorium** once served as Augustus's town house and is reputed to be the birthplace of Pontius Pilate. Its Gothic appearance is the result of extensive alterations during the Middle Ages, when it housed the kings of Catalonia and Aragón during their visits to Tarragona. The Praetorium now has a **Museu d'Història** (History Museum), with plans showing the evolution of the city; the highlight is the **Hippolytus sarcophagus,** which has a bas-relief depicting the legend of Hippolytus and Fraeda. The Preatorium is around the corner from the Circus Maximus. *Passeig Sant Antoni €1.87 (joint entry with the Circus Maximus) June–Sept., Tues.–Sat. 9–9, Sun. 9–3; Oct.–May, Tues.–Sat. 9–7, Sun. 10–3.*

★ Inside a 1960s neoclassical building is Tarragona's **Museu Arqueològic,** which includes Roman statuary, keys, bells, and belt buckles. The beautiful mosaics include the Head of Medusa, famous for its piercing stare. There's an excellent video on Tarragona's history. The museum is next door to Tarragona's Praetorium. *Passeig Sant Antoni 977/236209 €2.40, free Tues. June–Sept., Tues.–Sat. 10–8, Sun. 10–2; Oct.–May, Tues.–Sat. 10–1:30 and 4–7, Sun. 10–2.*

Under the arcade on the Carrer de la Merceria you'll find a stairway leading to Tarragona's **cathedral.** The initial rounded placidity of the Romanesque apse, begun in the 12th century, later gave way to the spiky restlessness of the Gothic; the result is confused. If no mass is in progress, enter the cathedral through the cloister. The main attraction is the **altarpiece** of St. Tecla, a richly detailed depiction of the life of Tarragona's patron saint. *Pla de la Seu €2.40 June–mid-Sept., Mon.–Sat. 10–7; mid-Sept.–mid-Nov., Mon.–Sat. 10–5; mid-Nov.–mid-Mar., Mon.–Sat. 10–2; mid-Mar.–May, Mon.–Sat. 10–1 and 4–7.*

Built by Tarragona nobility in the 18th century, **Casa Castellarnau,** a Gothic *palacete,* or town house, is now a museum with furnishings from the 18th and 19th centuries. The last member of the Castellarnau family vacated the house in 1954. *Carrer Cavallers, 977/242220 €1.87 June–Sept., Tues.–Sat. 9–9, Sun. 9–3; Oct.–May, Tues.–Sat. 9–7, Sun. 10–3.*

Les Voltes (end of Carrer Cavallers at Plaça Pallol), is a Roman forum with a Gothic upper story and also one of the prettiest corners in Tarragona. The **Passeig Arqueològic** (through the Portal del Rose) is a path that skirts the 3rd-century BC Ibero-Roman ramparts and is built on even earlier walls of giant rocks. The glacis was added by English military engineers in 1707, during the War of the Spanish Succession. Look for the rusted bronze of Romulus and Remus. At the **Serallo** fishing quarter, boats unload their catch at the quayside. Sneak a look inside the market, where fish are swiftly auctioned off to fishmongers and restaurateurs. The market is accessible by Bus 2 if you happen to be traveling from the Portal del Rose. Near the fish market is the **Necròpolis i Museu Paleocristià** (Tomb and Paleochristian Museum). Both Christian and pagan tombs have been unearthed here. *Passeig de la Independencia Combined ticket with Museu Arqueològic €2.40, free Tues. June–Sept., Tues.–Sat. 10–1 and 4:30–8, Sun. 10–2; Oct.–May, Tues.–Sat. 10–1:30 and 3–5:30, Sun. 10–2.*

Beaches

Beaches here are endless swaths of fine-grain sand. At the northern end of the region, Salou has the best beaches, along with a lively, palm-lined promenade. More tranquil are the beaches of the Ebro Delta, the best of which is Playa de los Eucaliptos, reached by a pretty road from Amposta via Montells. Peñíscola's beach seems to go on forever—the sand is soft, and the old city rises scenically out of the sea at one end. Alcocéber has a series of small, uncrowded sandy crescents, and just to its north is the sophisticated marina at Las Fuentes. Benicàssim's long, crescent-shape beach is the most dramatic, with mountains rising steeply in the background. Valencia itself has a long beach that's wonderful for sunning and has numerous restaurants, but it's not the best place to swim; for cleaner water, head south to El Saler.

Fiestas

In Valencia, **Las Fallas** fill an entire week in March, reaching their climax on March 19, El Día de San José (St. Joseph's Day), when families throughout Spain celebrate Father's Day. The time-honored feast of Las Fallas grew from the fact that St. Joseph is the patron saint of carpenters; in medieval times, carpenters' guilds celebrated his feast day by making huge bonfires with their wood shavings. Today Valencia explodes into a weeklong celebration of fireworks, flower-strewn floats, carnival processions, bullfights, and uncontrolled merrymaking. On March 19, huge and often grotesque effigies of popular and not-so-popular figures are ceremoniously burned, inspiring a surprising sense of nostalgia and the ephemerality of life itself. If you're allergic to firecrackers or large crowds, stay away from this one. Tarragona's most important fiestas are those of **St. Magí** (August 19) and **St. Tecla** (September 23), both marked by colorful processions.

Where to Stay & Eat

$$$ ✕ **La Puda.** The prime quayside location, opposite the fish auction house, guarantees fresh seafood. Locals love this place, even though the menu is written in several languages. The restaurant is simply decorated: a tile floor, salmon-color walls, and white tablecloths. ✉ *Muelle Pescadores 25* ☎ *977/211511* ▭ *AE, DC, MC, V* ⊙ *No dinner Sun. Oct.–Mar.*

$$–$$$ ✕ **Les Coques.** If you have time for only one meal in Tarragona, take it at this elegant little restaurant in the heart of the old town. Both mountain and Mediterranean food are served. Meat lovers will appreciate the *costillas de cordero* (lamb chops in a dark burgundy sauce); seafood fans should consider the *calamarsets* (baby calamari sautéed in olive oil, garlic, and secret seasonings). ✉ *Bajada Nueva del Patriarca 2 lower level* ☎ *977/228300* ✍ *Reservations essential* ▭ *AE, DC, MC, V* ⊙ *Closed Sun. and first half of Feb.*

★ **$$–$$$** ✕ **Les Voltes.** Built into the vaults of the Roman Circus Maximus, this out-of-the-way spot is a tasteful combination of 2,000-year-old chiseled stone, contemporary polished steel, and thick plate glass. The hearty food includes international recipes and Tarragona fish dishes, including the specialty of the house, *rap al all cremat* (monkfish in fried garlic). In winter, they serve calçotadas; it's best to order the calçotadas a day in advance. ✉ *Carrer Trinquet Vell 12* ☎ *977/230651* ▭ *MC, V* ⊙ *Closed Mon. No dinner Sun.*

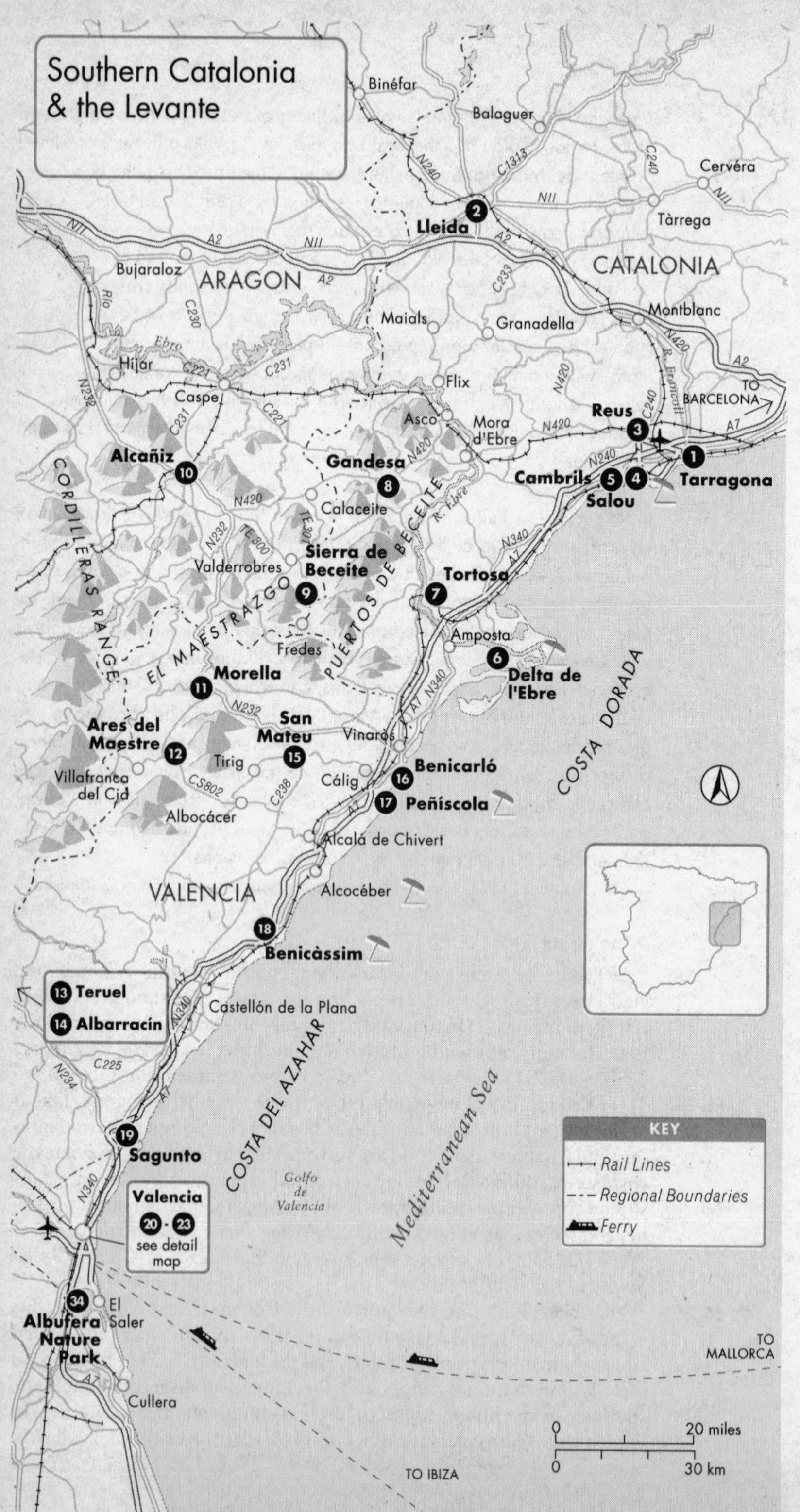
Southern Catalonia & the Levante
Binéfar
Balaguer
Cervéra
Lleida
Tàrrega
CATALONIA
ARAGON
Bujaraloz
Montblanc
Maials
Granadella
Hijar
Caspe
Flix
TO BARCELONA
Reus
Asco
Mora d'Ebre
Alcañiz
Gandesa
Tarragona
Cambrils
Salou
Calaceite
CORDILLERAS RANGE
Valderrobres
Sierra de Beceite
PUERTOS DE BECEITE
Tortosa
EL MAESTRAZGO
Amposta
Fredes
Morella
Delta de l'Ebre
Ares del Maestre
San Mateu
Vinaròs
Tirig
Benicarló
Villafranca del Cid
Càlig
Peñíscola
Albocácer
COSTA DORADA
Alcalá de Chivert
VALENCIA
Alcocéber
Benicàssim
Teruel
Albarracín
Castellón de la Plana
COSTA DEL AZAHAR
Mediterranean Sea
Sagunto
Golfo de Valencia
Valencia
see detail map
El Saler
Albufera Nature Park
Cullera
TO MALLORCA
TO IBIZA
KEY
Rail Lines
Regional Boundaries
Ferry
20 miles
30 km

¢–$ ✕ **La Teula.** On a narrow, shop-studded street in Tarragona's medieval quarter, this pint-size restaurant with green-and-white check tablecloths serves simple but tasty Catalan food. Dishes include *llom a la brasa* (grilled pork loin), *pit de pollastre* (chicken breast), and toasted bread topped with tuna and *salsa Romesco,* a spicy blend of almonds, peppers, and olive oil. ✉ *Carrer Mercería 16* ☎ *977/239989* 💳 *MC, V* ⏲ *Closed Mon.*

$$$ **Hotel Ciutat de Tarragona.** This gleaming addition to Tarragona looms over Plaça Imperial Tarraco, a plaza-cum-traffic circle at one of the principal entrances into the city. Pale-wood furnishings in the comfortable rooms are a pleasant contrast to the dark-blue curtains and bedspreads. Retire to the light-flooded café-bar, the *Punt de Trobada* (Catalan for "meeting point"), for nibbles, cocktails, and bustling street views. ✉ *Pl. Imperial Tarraco 5, 43005* ☎ *977/250999* 📠 *977/250699* 🌐 *www.sbhotels.es* *156 rooms, 12 suites* *Restaurant, bar, pool, sauna, gym, meeting rooms* 💳 *AE, DC, MC, V.*

$$$ **Imperial Tarraco.** Overlooking the Mediterranean, this large, white, half-moon-shape hotel has plain but comfortable guest rooms, and each has a private balcony. Insist on a sea view. The large public rooms have cool marble floors and black leather furniture. ✉ *Passeig Palmeres, 43003* ☎ *977/233040* 📠 *977/216566* *170 rooms* *Restaurant, tennis court, pool, hair salon, bar, meeting room* 💳 *AE, DC, MC, V.*

$–$$ **Lauria.** Guest rooms are spacious and comfortable, and their terraces overlook the serene pool and patio area, the Rambla Nova, or the sea. This is the most pleasant place to stay downtown. ✉ *Rambla Nova 20, 43004* ☎ *977/236712* 📠 *977/236700* 🌐 *www.hlauria.es* *72 rooms* *Bar* 💳 *AE, DC, MC, V.*

¢ **Pensión La Noria.** Rising above the spirited Plaça de la Font, this small place sports a cheery yellow façade with wrought-iron balconies. The interior, unfortunately, is drab and institutional, but the basic, functional rooms (linoleum floors, simple furnishings) are clean and fresh-smelling, and some have small balconies, making this the best of Tarragona's budget digs. The entrance is through the bar-cafeteria on the ground floor. ✉ *Pl. de la Font 53, 43003* ☎ *977/238717* *25 rooms* *Bar.*

Nightlife & the Arts

Nightlife in Tarragona takes two forms: older and quieter in the upper city, younger and more raucous down below. There are some lovely, rustic bars in the Casco Viejo, the upper section of old Tarragona. There's a row of restaurants and dance spots in the Puerto Deportivo, a pleasure-boat harbor separate from the working port; young people flock here on weekends and summer nights. **Poetes** (✉ Sant Llorenç 15), near Tarragona's cathedral, is a *bar musical* (bar with loud music, usually rock or blues) in a bodega-like cellar. For a dose of culture to go with your cocktail, try **Antiquari** (✉ Santa Anna 3), a laid-back bar that hosts readings, art exhibits, and occasional film screenings. For quiet talking and tippling, **El Cándil** (✉ Pl. del Forum) is a serene spot.

The **Teatro Metropol** (✉ Rambla Nova 46 ☎ 977/244795) is Tarragona's center for music, dance, theater, and cultural events ranging from *castellers* (human-castle formations), usually performed in August and September, to folk dances.

Shopping

Expect to haggle for bargains; **Carrer Major** has some exciting antiques stores. Rummage thoroughly, as the gems are often hidden away. You might also try the shops in front of the cathedral. **Poblet** (✉ Carrer Major 27–29, ☎ 977/23492) has antique furniture, lamps, fans, watches, porcelain, and bronze busts. Tarragona's **Mercat d'Antiguitats** (antiques market) fills the Pla de la Seu on Sundays 9–3. For Tarragona crafts—handmade by regional artisans—browse the tiny **D'Aquí** ("From Here,")

(✉ Carrer Mercería 6, ☎ 977/226063), which has ceramics, blown-glass olive oil and vinegar servers, and wine jugs (and a fine selection of regional wines).

Lleida

❷ *150 km (90 mi) south of Taüll, 150 km (90 mi) east of Zaragoza.*

With more than 2,000 years of history, it's not surprising that Lleida contains some distinguished architectural gems.

The landmark **La Seu Vella,** the old cathedral, was built between the 13th and 15th centuries in a transitional Romanesque-Gothic style and was converted to a military barracks after the 1707 siege of Felipe V. That explains why it looks, with its Vauban-style walls and esplanades, more like a fortress than a cathedral. A visit to the cathedral (open daily 10–1:30 and 4–7:30), by escalator and elevator from Plaça Sant Joan or on foot up Carrer Cavallers, is especially panoramic in late afternoon, when the low light spotlights the city, the Segre river, and the countryside beyond.

One block inside the old town, the most vital pedestrian artery, Carrer Major, runs parallel to the river. After 8 o'clock the newer area around Plaça Ricard Viñas is the hub of café, terrace, and restaurant life. Carrer Major's two principal architectural sights are **La Paeria,** a noble 13th-century Gothic mansion, and the **Antic Hospital de Santa Maria.** Both are distinguished by massive stone archways and a strong sense of past elegance. These doors, especially the immense arched entrance to the old hospital, now the city's Cultural Center, are Lleida's most impressive sights.

Worth checking out while you're here is the **Arc del Pont,** opposite the Pont Vell (Old Bridge), the bridge leading across the Segre just upstream from La Paeria. This arch was the ancient gateway into the walled city; the bronze figures depict the two fallen heroes of the local Ilergetes tribe, Indíbil and Mandoni. The 14th-century church of **Sant Llorenç,** with its slender bell tower and porticoed doorway, is worth a visit. The chapel of **Sant Jaume Peu de Romeu** is on Carrer Major between La Paeria and the Hospital.

SOUTH TO THE MAESTRAZGO

This segment ranges from the ridiculous, such as the Port Aventura theme park, to the sublime, encompassing the extraordinary natural resources from the Ebro Delta to the Sierra de Beceite. This wildly varied route takes you from below sea level (in parts of the delta) to high stone villages in the hills; from wetlands to the arid hinterlands of Tarragona.

Reus

❸ *13 km (8 mi) northwest of Tarragona.*

Reus is an industrial town with the distinction of having been the birthplace of Antoni Gaudí, as well as the longtime home of his fellow Moderniste architect Lluís Domènech i Montaner. If you're into Moderniste buildings, Lluís Domènech's **Casa Navàs** is well worth the short detour. Following signs to the center of Reus, you'll arrive in the Plaça del Mercadal; the Casa Navàs is beside the *ajuntament* (town hall). The rich interior decoration includes mosaics, stained glass, tiles with characteristic Moderniste floral motifs, and oddly shaped leather chairs. There are no formal visiting hours, but the house is usually open Thursday–Saturday, 10–1. (It's generally closed December–February.) Stop by the **tourist** office (✉ San Juan s/n ☎ 977/778149) to arrange a visit; they only allow groups with a minimum of six people to tour the house. Admission is €5. **Teatre Fortuny** (✉ Plaça Prim 4 ☎ 977/318307) is the Reus's primary theater and opera showcase.

Salou

❹ *11 km (7 mi) south of Reus.*

If you're starting to crave a sunny afternoon on the beach, stop in Salou, a modern resort with a long esplanade of young palms. The town itself is long on glitz and short on culture and charm, but history buffs can note that the conquerors of Mallorca set out from the old port here in 1229. On the edge of Salou, the theme park **Port Aventura** (✉ Autovéia Salou/Vila-Seca, Km 2, Apartat 90/43480 Vila-Seca, Tarragona ☎ 902/202220 or 977/779000 🌐 www.portaventura.es) boldly offers "the adventure of your life" to anyone brave enough to shell out €32 (€25 per child under 12) for rides, water slides, steam engines, and boat rides through Mexico, China, Polynesia, the American West, and the Mediterranean. Port Aventura is closed from early January to late March.

Cambrils

❺ *7 km (4½ mi) west of Salou, 18 km (11 mi) southwest of Tarragona.*

Food lovers come to coastal Cambrils to dine in Fanny Gatell's restaurant. Less built-up than Salou, the town also has a pretty marina.

Where to Eat

★ $$$$ ✕ **Joan Gatell.** Fanny Gatell and her sister used to run two restaurants side by side; Fanny now carries on the tradition of exquisite local meals by herself. Try the *fideos negros amb sepionets* (paella in baby-squid ink) or *lubina al horno con cebolla y patata* (roast sea bass with onion and potato). ✉ *Miramar 26* ☎ *977/360057* 💳 *AE, DC, MC, V* ⊗ *Closed Mon., Oct., and late Dec.–Jan. No dinner Sun.*

Delta de l'Ebre

❻ *77 km (48 mi) southwest of Tarragona, 60 km (37 mi) south of Cambrils.*

The Ebro Delta, a flat piece of wetland à la the Netherlands, juts into and embraces the Mediterranean. The **Parc Natural del Delta de l'Ebre** (Ebro Delta Natural Park) is a major stopping and breeding place for more than 200,000 birds of more than 300 species—an impressive 60% of Europe's bird species can be seen here during the year. To get to the park, take N230 and follow signs to Sant Jaume d'Enveja; at Sant Jaume, take a ferry to the town of Deltebre. The **Park Information Office** (✉ Carrer Doctor Martí Buera 22 ☎ 977/489679) can tell you how to visit the reserve proper—which occupies the delta's northern, eastern, and southern tips—and give you the required permit. The information office is open weekdays 10–2 and 3–6, Saturday 10–1 and 3:30–6, and Sunday 10–1.

Where to Stay & Eat

$–$$ ✕ **L' Estany.** At this restaurant (also known as Casa de la Fusta) smack in the middle of wetlands and rice paddies, Chef-owner Luis Garcia is committed to serving the best fish and game, caught just off the doorstep—and to the cultural heritage of the area. During the lunch hour (2:30–4:30) a merry band of musicians perform Ebro Delta folk music for diners. In a separate building, groups of 20 or more can arrange for a meal surrounded by traditional dress, recipes, and live ducks. ✉ *Partida La En-*

canyissada s/n (en route from Amposta to Sant Jaume) ☎ *977/261026* ▭ *MC, V* ⏲ *No dinner Mon.–Thurs. Oct.–June.*

$ **Lo Molí de Rosquilles.** Once an olive-oil mill, this old stone building with original furnishings functions as a charming and cozy hotel. A library about the region invites you to delve into the history, geography, and ecology of the Ebro Delta. Food is served for guests only; don't miss the excellent bread, cooked in a wood-burning oven. ✉ *C. Catalunya 6, 43878 Masdenverge* ☎ *977/718052 or 629/358929* 🌐 *www.teleline.terra.es/personal/lomoli* *8 rooms* *Dining room, library* ▭ *MC, V.*

Tortosa

❼ *80 km (50 mi) southwest of Tarragona.*

Tortosa, straddling the Ebro River 10 km (6 mi) inland, was successively Roman, Visigothic, Moorish, and Christian. The town was the scene of one of the Spanish Civil War's bloodiest battles. The Republicans, loyal to the democratically elected government and already in control of Catalonia, crossed the Ebro here in July 1936 to attack the rebel Nationalists' rear guard. They got no farther than Tortosa, however, and were pinned down in trenches until they were forced to retreat with the loss of 150,000 lives. You can cover Tortosa's sights in a few hours. Tortosa's local parador, in the ruined hilltop **Castillo de la Zuda,** is worth visiting even if you don't stay the night. Originally a Templar fortress, the castle (and town) passed, around 713, into the hands of the Moors, who kept it until its reconquest by Ramón Berenguer IV, count of Barcelona, in 1153. Moors, Christians, and Jews then lived peacefully together in the town for more than 300 years. From the castle walls are views across the fertile Ebro Valley to the Sierra de Beceite. ✉ *Parador Castillo de la Zuda, 43500 Tortosa* ☎ *977/444450.*

The Renaissance **Colegio Sant Lluís** has a pretty arcaded patio, embellished with a frieze depicting the kings of Aragón. It houses an impressive archive collection, evidence of Tortosa's formidable history. A population map of Tortosa is dated 1149 and is signed by Ramón Berenguer IV. The 13th-century *El Llibre de les Costums de Tortosa* is the first judicial text written in Catalan. ✉ *Sant Domènec s/n, Tortosa.*

The main facade of Tortosa's **cathedral** is baroque, but if you enter through the cloister you'll see that the building itself is purely Gothic. It was common in 18th-century Spain to tack these exuberant stuccos on to Gothic structures; the style is called Churrigueresque, after its first practitioner, José Churriguera. ✉ *Croera s/n, Tortosa* ⏲ *Cloister daily, cathedral for mass only.*

Where to Stay & Eat

$$ ✕ **Rosa Pinyol.** Following in his mother's illustrious footsteps, chef and owner Joan Pinyol concocts regional dishes based on the Ebro Delta's teeming underwater population, from sea bass to sole. His careful preparation of each dish can sometimes delay your food—but it's worth the wait. Try the *rape asado con calcots* (grilled monkfish with calcots, a springtime green onion native to this region). The small restaurant is just west of the old town, across the Pont de l'Estat (Estat Bridge). ✉ *Hernan Cortés 17* ☎ *977/502001* ▭ *AE, DC, MC, V* ⏲ *Closed Sun. No dinner Mon.*

$$ ✕ **Sant Carles.** Joan Ros, chef-owner of this long-running small restaurant on the northern edge of the old town, excels in seafood and freshwater fish from the Ebro Delta. *Almejas a la marinera* (marinated clams) and *lubina a la plancha* (grilled sea bass) are specialties. ✉ *Rambla Felip Pedrell 13* ☎ *977/441048* ▭ *AE, DC, MC, V* ⏲ *Closed Sun.*

★ $$ **Parador de Tortosa.** Few sights around Tortosa can equal the superb view from the old Arab Castillo de la Zuda across the Ebro Valley to the Sierra de Beceite. Dark shades of mahogany and copious tapestries evoke the past. Guest rooms have heavy wood furniture, terra-cotta floors, rugs, and plain walls. The wood-beam restaurant serves a wide selection of Catalan fare, including *bacalao con espinacas y allioli* (cod with spinach and garlic mayonnaise) and *pato del Delta con mandarinas* (Delta duck with mandarins). *Parador Castillo de la Zuda, 43500 Tortosa 977/444450 977/444458 www.parador.es 72 rooms Restaurant, pool, bar, playground, meeting room, free parking AE, DC, MC, V.*

Nightlife & the Arts

October marks the **Felip Pedrell Musical Festival,** named after the Tortosa-born composer and musician, when classical and chamber music concerts are showcased at the **Teatre Auditori Felip Pedrell** (Pl. Salvador Videllet 977/510144).

Gandesa

8 *87 km (54 mi) west of Tarragona.*

Renowned for its strong wine (up to 16% alcohol), Gandesa also has two architectural landmarks. The extraordinary **Cooperativa Agrícola** (Wine Cooperative) was designed by the Moderniste architect Cèsar Martinell in 1919. The white, Islamic-looking facade does little to prepare you for the remarkable vaulting inside, constructed entirely of small bricks ingeniously arranged to allow for expansion and contraction. This is a working building (open weekdays 9–1 and 3–7, Saturday 9–1, Sunday 10–2), and you can buy some local wine here for a sleepy picnic on the way to Alcañiz or Beceite. *Avga. Catalunya 28, Gandesa 977/420017.*

Gandesa's parish church, **L'Assumpció,** has a Romanesque doorway with some unusual geometric patterns, attributed to Moorish influence. *Town center, Gandesa Daily.*

Where to Stay & Eat

¢ **Hostal Piqué.** Though uninviting from the outside, this modern roadhouse has a large, smart dining room with white tablecloths and professional service. The restaurant menu mixes everyday local options with rarer, pricier delicacies; try the *gambas al ajillo* (garlic shrimp). Rooms are comfortable. *Via Catalunya 68, 43780 977/420068 977/420329 48 rooms Restaurant; no a/c in some rooms AE, MC, V.*

Sierra de Beceite

9 *15 km (9 mi) southwest of Gandesa on N420.*

The mountains of the Sierra de Beceite offer a beautiful excursion near Gandesa, as long as you and your car can handle some bumpy roads. Just after you enter the Aragonese province of Teruel, you'll come to **Calaceite** on your right: explore its ancient, labyrinthine streets, which converge at the arcaded Plaza Porticada. For a closer inspection of the Beceite massif, turn left at the Calaceite crossroads and drive along TE301. Turn right after 18 km (11 mi) at a T junction to reach **Valderrobres,** with a fortified palace and a Renaissance town hall that served as the model for Barcelona's Poble Espanyol. Continue to **Beceite** and follow signs to a *panorama* for a bumpy drive culminating in an impressive vista. Depending on the condition of these forest roads, you can drive all the way to **Fredes,** due south of Beceite: the kings of Catalonia, Aragón, and Valencia are said to have met near here, on the Tossal dels Tres Reis (4,450 ft), to iron out disputes. The best way to explore these hills is on foot (or on horseback); a sign on the way into Beceite points you toward the tourist office, which has trail maps and can arrange horseback rides. From Valderrobres, you can cut back to the Alcañiz road via TE300, which follows the River Matarraña.

Alcañiz

10 *62 km (38 mi) west of Gandesa, 74 km (46 mi) north of Morella.*

Alcañiz lies on a plain, encircled by the River Guadalope and surrounded by ugly, modern apartment blocks, the result of a population explosion following the success of the nearby olive and almond orchards. The highway (N420) enters the town along a street that bustles with ongoing construction. For the old town, turn left at the end of this street to the Plaza Mayor. The **Lonja** (Exchange; ⊠ Pl. Mayor) has pointed arches defining its Gothic origin. The galleries and overhanging eaves on both buildings of the Renaissance ***ayuntamiento*** (town hall; ⊠ Pl. Mayor, adjoining the Lonja) mark them as Aragonese. The **Colegiata** (⊠ Pl. Mayor) church has a rhythmic baroque facade and an impressively ornate portal, but its painted interior is disappointing. Alcañiz's hilltop **castle** (⊠ Castillo de Calatrava ☎ 978/830400) was the seat of the Calatrava Knights in the 14th century and is now a parador.

Where to Stay & Eat

★ $$ **Parador de Alcañiz.** Installed in the sturdy castle of the Calatrava Knights, this hotel grandly surveys the olive-growing plain and the foothills of the Maestrazgo. Guest rooms have terra-cotta tile floors, patterned rugs, dark furniture, generous beds, and good views. The restaurant serves Aragonese fare, such as *cordero chilindrón* (lamb in a sauce of tomato, garlic, and pepper). ⊠ *Castillo de Calatrava, 44600* ☎ *978/830400* *978/830366* *www.parador.es* *37 rooms* *Restaurant, sauna, bar, meeting room* *AE, DC, MC, V.*

Morella

★ 11 *74 km (46 mi) south of Alcañiz, 64 km (40 mi) northwest of Benicarló.*

The walled town of Morella stands on a towering crag in Castellón, the northernmost Valencian province. It's not immediately evident if you approach from the north, but from the south and east the land drops away sharply, creating a natural fortress—the scene of several bloody battles. Morella's main thoroughfare is the arcaded **Calle Don Blasco de Alagón.** The numerous bars here are packed on weekends. Morella's **castle** is accessible through the gate on the Plaza de San Francisco, on the uppermost of the town's contoured streets. Just inside the gate is the ruined cloister of an old Franciscan monastery. The walk up to the castle takes a good 15 minutes. In 1088 El Cid scaled these walls and wrought havoc among the occupying Moors. During the Carlist Wars of the 16th century, the castle became a stronghold for General Cabrera, who captured Morella in 1838 for Don Carlos, pretender to the Spanish throne. ☎ *964/173128* *€1.20* *Oct.–Mar., daily 10:30–6:30; Apr.–Sept., daily 10:30–7:30.*

The blue-tile dome on the beautiful church of **Santa María la Mayor** lends an exotic note to this otherwise Gothic structure. The larger of the church's two doorways, depicting the Apostles, dates from the 14th century. A spiral marble staircase leads to the raised, flat-vaulted choir. The sanctuary got the full baroque treatment, as did the high altar. The **museum** has a painting by Francisco Ribalta and some 15th-century Gothic panels. The church is near Morella's castle on Calle Hospital. €1.50 *June–Sept., daily 11–2 and 4–7; Oct.–May, daily noon–2 and 4–6.*

Where to Stay & Eat

★ $$$ **Mesón del Pastor.** In a restored 14th-century stone mansion on a side street off Calle Don Blasco de Alagón, chef José Ferrer specializes in Maestrazgan fare like *conejo relleno trufado* (rabbit and truffles enveloped in ham) and dishes with wild and farmed mushrooms. Desserts include *buñuelos con miel* (fried dumplings with honey) or *mousse de trufa blanca* (white truffle mousse). There's a simple 12-room inn next door. *Cuesta Jovaní 5 and 7 964/160249 AE, DC, MC, V Closed Wed. Sept.–July. No dinner weekdays and no lunch Sat. Sept.–July.*

★ $ **Cardenal Ram.** In what was originally the 14th-century ancestral home of the famous Spanish prelate Cardinal Ram, this hotel oozes history from its bare, stone walls and ubiquitous coats of arms. The lobby has a huge tapestry depicting the 1414 visit of Antipope Papa Luna, named Pope Benedict XIII during the Great Schism of 1378–1417. (Cardinal Ram was named by the antipope, whom he then served.) Rooms have pine floors, bare white walls, high beamed ceilings, and magnificent heavy furniture. The wide beds are covered with Morellan striped bedspreads. *Cuesta Suñer 1, 12300 964/173085 964/173218 19 rooms Restaurant; no a/c MC, V.*

¢ **Hostal La Muralla.** Right on the street that delineates Morella's city walls, this hostelry is comfortable and clean. A small living and dining area offers relaxation and breakfast. *Muralla 12, 12300 964/160243 20 rooms Cafeteria; no a/c MC, V.*

Shopping

The Maestrazgo region produces brightly colored handwoven woolens. The best buys are striped *mantas morellanas* (Morellan bedspreads), available along Calle Blasco de Alagón and around Plaza Arciprestal.

Ares del Maestre

12 *50 km (31 mi) southwest of Morella on N232, the main road to Villafranca del Cid, and CS802 toward Albocácer.*

Ares del Maestre is on the most dramatic site of any village in this area—like Morella, it rests on a crag, but here the drop is more severe and the vistas more rewarding. A very steep climb, windy in winter and scorching in summer, takes you to a ruined **castle.**

Teruel

13 *110 km (68 mi) southwest of Ares del Maestre (backtrack on CS802 toward Morella, then get on TE811 at Villafranca del Cid), 148 km (92 mi) northwest of Valencia.*

This provincial Aragonese capital is famous for its Mudéjar architecture, its medieval lovers of lore, and its cured ham, haunches of which are displayed proudly in shops and grocery stores throughout town. Once part of the city walls, Teruel's **Mudéjar towers** were built between the 12th and 16th centuries in a style more reminiscent of Muslim minarets than Christian belfries. The highlight of the **cathedral** is its coffered ceiling with 13th-century court and hunting scenes, visible from the upper gallery.

The church of **San Pedro** has a Mudéjar tower but is best known for its adjoining **Mausoleo de los Amantes** (Lovers' Mausoleum). Here lie the tombs of Diego and Isabel, two 13th-century Teruel lovers who died, it is said, of broken hearts. A wealthy merchant's daughter named Isabel de Segura fell in love with a young man named Diego de Marcilla, who had no means to marry a woman of Isabel's status. Her father naturally forbade the match. Determined to marry his true love and prove himself worthy in her father's eyes, Diego set out to seek his fortune. He returned five years later in triumph to ask for Isabel's hand—only to find that she was being married that very day to the son of a wealthy merchant from the nearby town of Albarracín. Overcome with grief, Diego died on the spot; the next day, at his funeral, Isabel, overcome with grief, also died. Their story—Spain's version of Romeo and Juliet—captured the imagination of 16th-century European artists, including Tirso de Molina and Hartzenbusch. ✉ *North of Pl. Bretón.*

Where to Stay & Eat

$$ ✕🏨 **Parador de Teruel.** Teruel's parador was built in 1956 to match the town's famous Mudéjar-style architecture. The spacious rooms have parquet floors and floral wallpaper befitting an Aragonese palacete. The flower and herb gardens are beautifully maintained, as are the pool and tennis courts. The restaurant serves both regional and national cuisine—everything from paella valenciana to *cochinillo asado al horno* (roast suckling pig). ✉ *Ctra. Sagunto–Burgos (N234), Km 124, 44080* ☎ *978/601800* 📠 *978/608612* 🌐 *www.parador.es* *56 rooms, 2 suites* *Restaurant, 2 tennis courts, pool* 💳 *AE, DC, MC, V.*

Albarracín

⓮ *37 km (23 mi) west of Teruel, 185 km (116 mi) northwest of Valencia.*

West of Teruel are the grand Sierras de Albarracín, a vast massif carved into spectacular ravines by the powerful Guadalaviar and Curvo rivers. Rocky mountain plateaus loom above fertile valleys rich with wild vegetation, hulking pine and fir trees, and a population of deer and wild boar—which often end up as succulent dishes on the menus of mountain restaurants. Trekking trails cross the region, much of which remains refreshingly untamed, and there are 30-odd delightful villages, with ancient stone and wood houses and cobble streets. The area's natural and cultural riches all seem to come together in the small town of Albarracín. Perched at 3,840 ft above a luxuriant gorge with the Guadalaviar rushing below, the village makes an eye-catching picture of ancient stone houses and crenellated walls, against a gorgeous backdrop of evergreen hills and craggy cliffs. Climb the steep cobble streets past tiny old-fashioned carnicerías (butcher shops) and groups of old men leaning on their canes, and you really start feeling like you're in deep Spain. Rising above the Plaza Mayor is the **cathedral** with a beautiful 16th-century retablo (altarpiece) featuring St. Peter.

Where to Stay & Eat

$ ✕🏨 **Casa Santiago.** At the top of an ancient staircase near the Plaza Mayor is this family-run hotel in a beautifully restored country house. The fresh-smelling rooms are all individually decorated, and you'll find ample sitting rooms on every floor. A cozy common room is outfitted with oversize brown-leather sofas that you can sink into, a rope-woven rocking chair, and big baskets of magazines. One flight up is a sunlit attic suite with a wrought-iron writing desk and splendid views of the valley and the red-tile roofs of town. ✉ *Subida a las Torres 11, 44100* ☎ *978/700316* *8 rooms, 1 suite* *Restaurant* 💳 *MC, V.*

San Mateu

⓯ *26 km (16 mi) west of Benicarló; take CS802 southeast from Ares del Maestre to Albocácer, and then turn left.*

The small town of San Mateu proudly bears the subtitle Capital del Maestrazgo because it was from here that King Jaume I set out on his decisive reconquering raids in the 13th century, freeing the region finally from Moorish control. Sturdy Gothic mansions near the Plaza Mayor attest to San Mateu's regal past. Visit the Iglesia Arciprestal (Archpriest's Church) on the corner of the plaza—its nave is a fine example of the Catalan Gothic style, and the vault covers a wide expanse, dispensing with the need for columns.

THE COSTA DEL AZAHAR

Named for the orange blossom and its all-pervading fragrance along this sweet coastal plain, the Costa del Azahar was hit hard by the tourist-inspired building boom of the 1960s and '70s. Benicarló and Peñíscola are, with Vinaròs, the northernmost towns on the Costa del Azahar (province: Castellón de la Plana), while Sagunto marks the start of the Costa de Valencia.

Benicarló

16 *55 km (34 mi) south of Tortosa.*

Benicarló has become a major tourist center. The harbor is a lively confusion of fishing and pleasure craft, and the beaches are jammed with locals and northern European sunseekers most of the year.

Where to Stay & Eat

$$$–$$$$ ✕ **Casa Pocho.** Named after its owner, Paco Puchal—also known as El Pocho, or "the Tubby One"—the restaurant has wood paneling and maritime motifs. The style sets the scene for the restaurant's famously good seafood. *Langostinos* (prawns) are the best choice. ✉ *San Gregorio 49, Vinaròs* ☎ *964/451095* ▭ *DC, MC, V* ⊙ *Closed Mon. No dinner Sun.*

$$–$$$ ✕ **Parador de Benicarló.** The main attraction here is its large, semiformal garden, which runs down to the sea—a perfect place to rest, away from the crowded beaches. The public rooms are huge, bright, and tasteful, with white-wicker furniture and white walls. Guest rooms have shiny tile floors, white walls, and functional furniture; ask for a sea view. Travelers with disabilities are well accommodated. ✉ *Avda. Papa Luna 5, 12580* ☎ *964/470100* 🖷 *964/470934* 🌐 *www.parador.es* *108 rooms* *Restaurant, tennis court, pool, bar, meeting rooms* ▭ *AE, DC, MC, V.*

Peñíscola

17 *7 km (4½ mi) south of Benicarló, 60 km (37 mi) northeast of Benicàssim.*

Peñíscola owes its foundation to the Phoenicians. It later became the bridgehead by which the Carthaginian Hamilcar (father of Hannibal) imported his elephants and munitions to wage the first of the three Punic Wars. Carthaginian influence in Iberia reached its zenith some 20 years later, in 230 BC, but was eventually eroded by that of Rome. Peñíscola's ★ **old town** is a cluster of white houses and tiny, narrow streets leading up to the castle on a promontory, which affords perfect surveillance of the coast. You can drive up to the **castle,** but in summer the traffic makes it smarter to leave your car by the town walls and walk. Of chief interest are the chapel and study of the antipope Papa Luna, to whom the 14th-century castle passed in the 15th century. Hardly any of Papa Luna's effects remain, but while you're in his drafty quarters, try to imagine this 90-year-old Frenchman (formerly Pope Benedict XIII) passing the last six years of his life attending mass and composing schismatic bulls while surrounded by hostile Moorish townsfolk. ☎ *964/480021*

€2 ⊙ Apr.–mid-June and mid-Sept.–mid-Oct., daily 9–8:30; mid-June–mid-Sept. 9:30–2:30 and 4:30–9:30; mid-Oct.–Mar., daily 9:30–1 and 3:15–6.

Where to Stay

$$$ **Hostería del Mar.** Officially a "semi-parador," this modern, white hotel next to Peñíscola's long beach meets the paradors' high standards. Most guest rooms have balconies; some overlook the old town, and others the beach. Inside, they have white walls, striped bedspreads, tile floors, and Castilian-style dark wood and leather furniture. The rustic, beamed public rooms surround a leafy pool terrace. ✉ *Avda. Papa Luna 18, 12598* ☎ *964/480600* 🖷 *964/481363* 🌐 *www.hosteriadelmar.net* *86 rooms* *Restaurant, tennis court, pool, bar, some pets allowed (fee)* 💳 *AE, DC, MC, V.*

en route

A trip down the Costa del Azahar south of Peñíscola takes you through carob and orange plantations. The autopista is the fastest road south, but the N340 shares the same scenery and grants easier access to places en route. The town of **Alcalá de Chivert** can claim the tallest belfry in the Valencian provinces. This stretch of the road is separated from the sea by the Sierra de Hirta, whose rugged outlines contain some ruined castles easily visible from the road. **Alcocéber** is an expanding but still quiet holiday town with two good beaches. Although Castellón de la Plana, the provincial capital, has little to warrant the struggle through its suburbs, **Convento de las Religiosas Capuchinas** has 10 works by Spanish baroque painter Zurbarán. ✉ C. *Nuñez de Arce* ⊙ *Open for mass.*

Benicàssim

18 *60 km (37 mi) southwest of Peñíscola, 13 km (8 mi) northeast of Castellón de la Plana.*

Geographically blessed, the coastal town of Benicàssim is backed by the dramatic shapes of the Desierto de las Palmas mountain range, and the Mediterranean laps the town's long, sandy bathing beaches. Early vacationers—mostly wealthy Valencians—were suitably charmed, and the first vacation villa was built here in 1887. By the turn of the century Benicàssim was a genteel getaway, prompting its nickname the Biarritz of the Costa de Azahar. This all changed during Spain's tourist boom in the early 1960s, when package tours arrived en masse along the coast; resort replaced rusticity, and the local flavor of many coastal towns faded in the face of high-rise concrete jungles and quadrilingual menus. Although Benicàssim has its share of tasteless apartment blocks, it was spared the worst resort-style excesses. Pleasant pedestrian promenades run alongside its clean, sandy beaches, and today most summer visitors are vacationing Spanish families. The well-preserved 16th-century **Torre de San Vicente,** a watchtower (not open to the public) once guarded against marauding pirates and looms over a popular beach of the same name.

Since 1995 Benicàssim has made a name for itself on the indie-music circuit. Thousands descend for the annual **music festival** held in August, which has headlined everyone from Suede and Sonic Youth to Björk and Primal Scream. On a more traditional note, late July brings on the **Festival de Habaneras,** featuring typical 19th-century sorrowful sailor songs on the guitar, often with a Cuban rhythm.

Seven kilometers (4 mi) inland from Benicàssim and set against the soothing backdrop of silent mountain peaks is the **Monasterio del De-**

sierto de las Palmas, a Carmelite monastery founded in 1694. The small museum houses Carmelite religious figurines and clothing from centuries past. ✉ *Carretera Desierto de las Palmas s/n* ☎ *964/300950* 🎫 *Free* ⏲ *Monastery daily 10:30–1 and 4:30–7; museum Sun. noon–2.*

Where to Stay & Eat

$–$$ ✕ **Villa del Mar.** Elegant and secluded, this old country manor house has a dining terrace ringed by palms and pines. Inside, the look is modern and the food international and regional; look for *arroces valencianos* (Valencian rice dishes). On summer evenings a barbecue is held in the garden. ✉ *Paseo Marítimo Pilar Coloma 24, Benicàssim* ☎ *964/302852* ▭ *AE, MC, V* ⏲ *Closed late Oct.–late Nov.*

$$ 🏨 **Orange.** If it's facilities you're after, look no farther: this huge, modern, chalet-style hotel has them. It's central, only 150 yards from the beach, and surrounded by trees and a garden. Loud patterns in brown and orange set the tone in the public rooms, and the plain guest rooms are no more than functional. Ask for a sea view, and note that rooms over the pool can be noisy. The price includes breakfast. ✉ *Avda. Gimeno Tomás 9, 12560 Benicàssim* ☎ *964/394400* 📠 *964/301541* 🌐 *www.intur.com* *415 rooms* *Restaurant, cafeteria, miniature golf, tennis court, 2 pools, bar, dance club, meeting rooms* ▭ *AE, DC, MC, V* ⏲ *Closed early Nov.–Feb.*

$–$$ 🏨 **Voramar.** On the beach at the north end of Benicàssim, this small white hotel is encircled by classic balconies. Ask for a room overlooking the sea, and you'll have a large balcony to yourself. Rooms are plain and functional, with tile floors, white walls, and 1970s furniture. ✉ *Paseo Pilar Coloma 1, 12560 Benicàssim* ☎ *964/300150* 📠 *964/300526* 🌐 *www.voramar.net* *59 rooms* *Restaurant, tennis court, some pets allowed* ▭ *AE, DC, MC, V* ⏲ *Closed early Jan.–early Feb.*

Sagunto

19 *65 km (40 mi) southwest of Benicàssim, 23 km (14 mi) northeast of Valencia.*

Sagunto will ring a bell if you've read Caesar's history: Saguntum, as the Romans called it, was the sparking point for the Second Punic War. When Hannibal laid siege to the town (at that time a port, from which the sea has since receded), the people heroically held out, faithfully expecting a Roman relief force, and eventually burned the town rather than surrender to the Carthaginians. Rambling Moorish fortifications dominate Sagunto from the hilltops, and within this citadel earlier **Roman remains** are now being excavated. In the citadel (on Plaza de San Fernando) you'll also find the **Antiquarium Epigráfico,** a rich collection of inscriptions on marble and epigraphs dedicated to various Roman emperors, and Roman funeral stones. Visit the well-restored **amphitheater** (signposted from the town center). More complete than Tarragona's, it went up during the Roman rebuilding five years after Hannibal's siege. 🎫 *Free* ⏲ *Amphitheater and citadel: May–Sept., Tues.–Sat. 10–8, Sun. 10–2; Oct.–Apr., Tues.–Sat. 10–6, Sun. 10–2. Epigraph collection: May–Sept., Tues.–Sat. 10–2 and 5–8, Sun. 10–2; Oct.–Apr., Tues.–Sat. 10–2 and 4–6, Sun. 10–2.*

Nightlife & the Arts

The month of August brings **Sagunto a Escena,** a festival of classical Mediterranean drama for which theater groups perform ancient plays in Sagunto's Roman amphitheater. Contact the **tourist office** (✉ Pl. Cronista Chabret ☎ 962/662213) for information.

VALENCIA & ENVIRONS

Spain's third-largest city and the capital of the Levante, Valencia is nearly equidistant from Barcelona and Madrid. If you have time for a day trip (or you decide to stay in the coastal town of El Saler), make your way to the Albufera, a scenic coastal wetland teeming with native wildlife.

Valencia

362 km (224 mi) south of Barcelona, 351 km (218 mi) southeast of Madrid.

Despite its proximity to the Mediterranean, Valencia's history and geography have been defined most significantly by the River Turia and the fertile flood plain, or huerta, that surrounds it. The city has been fiercely contested ever since it was founded by the Greeks. El Cid captured Valencia from the Moors in 1094 and won his strangest victory here in 1099: his corpse was strapped to his saddle and so frightened the waiting Moors as to cause a complete rout. In 1102, his widow, Jimena, was forced to return the city to Moorish rule; Jaume I finally drove them out in 1238. Modern Valencia was best known for its flooding disasters until the River Turia was diverted to the south in the late 1950s. Since then the city has been on a steady course of urban beautification. The lovely *puentes* (bridges) that once spanned the Turia look equally graceful spanning a wandering municipal park, and the spectacular Ciudad de las Artes y de las Sciencias (City of Arts and Sciences) has at long last created an exciting architectural link between this river town and the Mediterranean.

a good walk

Begin your stroll through Valencia's historic center at the **cathedral** 20 ⚑, in the Plaza de la Reina; inside you can visit the museum and climb the Miguelete Tower for good views of the city. Cross the **Plaza de la Virgen** and you'll see the Gothic **Palau de la Generalitat** 21. Continuing down Calle Caballeros, you'll pass Valencia's oldest church, **San Nicolás** 22. After spending some time inside, walk to the Plaza del Mercado and the 15th-century **Lonja de la Seda** 23. Opposite are the Iglesia de los Santos Juanes, whose interior was destroyed during the civil war, and the Mercado Central. Travel down Avenida María Cristina to the **Plaza del Ayuntamiento** 24, home of the town hall and one of the city's liveliest areas. After a five-minute walk down Avenida Marqués de Soto, you'll find the Moderniste **Estación del Tren** 25. Next to the train station is the **Plaza de Toros** 26. Back in the city center, go to Plaza Patriarca and enter the **Real Colegio del Patriarca** 27. Cross Calle Poeta Querol to the wedding-cake facade of the **Palacio del Marqués de Dos Aguas** 28. Leave the city center and cross the riverbed by Puente de la Trinidad to see the **Museo de Bellas Artes** 29. The **Jardines del Real** (Royal Gardens) adjoin the museum. Walk up Calle San Pio V to the Puente de Serranos and cross back to the 14th-century **Torre de Serranos**, which once guarded the entrance to this Mediterranean city. Turn right for the **Casa Museo José Benlliure** 30, and continue west to the fabulous **Institut Valencià d'Art Modern (IVAM)** 31. On a separate outing, cross the riverbed and stroll south to the modern **Palau de la Música** 32 and the landmark-in-progress **Ciutat de les Arts i les Ciències** 33.

TIMING Allow a full day for a tour of the old quarter, the Museo de Bellas Artes, and the IVAM. Tack on a few hours the next day for the Palau de la Música and Ciutat de les Arts i les Ciències.

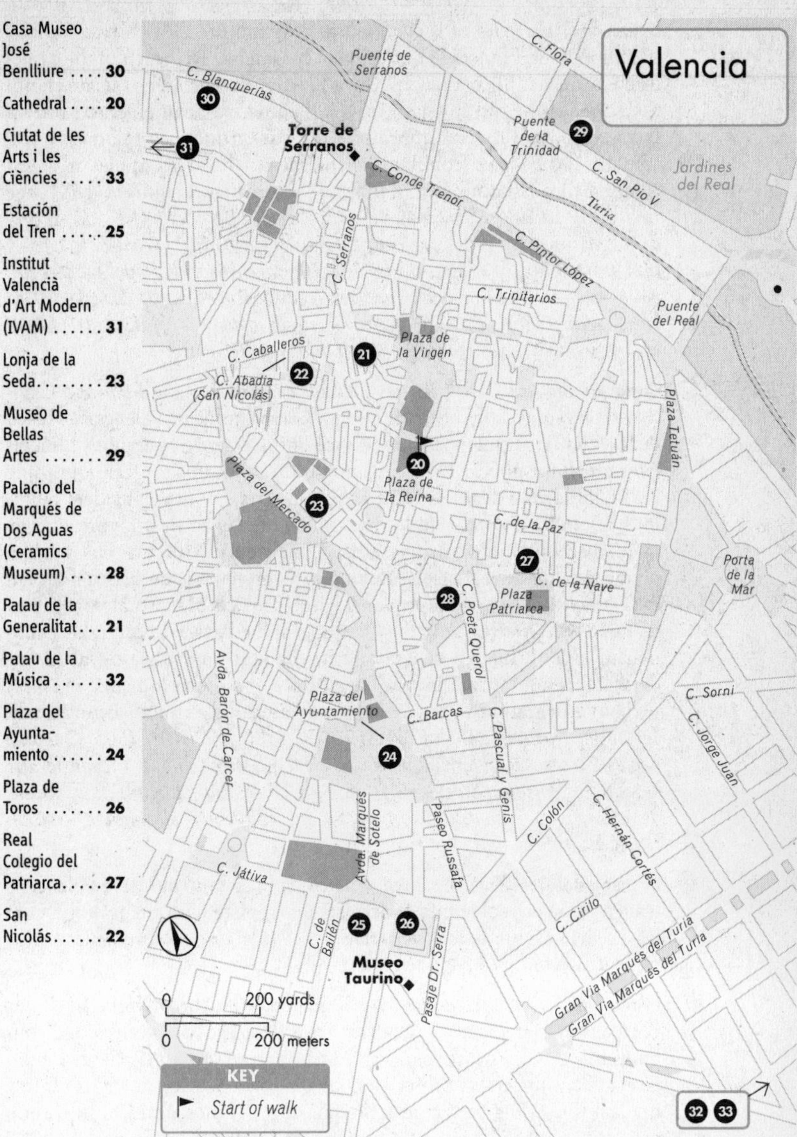

What to See

30 **Casa Museo José Benlliure.** Cross the Puente de Serranos, turn right down Calle Blanquerías, and stop at No. 23. The elegant house of this modern Valencian painter-sculptor contains many of his works. *Free* *Tues.–Sat. 9:15–2 and 5:30–9, Sun. 9:30–2.*

20 **Cathedral.** Valencia's 13th- to 15th-century cathedral is the heart of the city. The building has three portals, respectively Romanesque, Gothic, and rococo, the last leading off Plaza de Zaragoza. Inside, Renaissance and baroque marble were removed in a successful restoration of the original Gothic style, as is now the trend in Spanish churches. The Capilla del Santo Cáliz (Chapel of the Holy Chalice) displays a purple agate vessel said to be the **Holy Grail** (Christ's cup at the Last Supper) and thought to have been brought to Spain in the 4th century. Behind the altar you can see the left arm of **St. Vincent,** who was martyred in Va-

lencia in 304. Stars of the cathedral **museum** are Goya's two famous paintings of St. Francis de Borja, Duke of Gandia. To the left of the cathedral entrance is the octagonal tower **El Miguelete,** which you can climb: the roofs of the old town create a kaleidoscope of orange and brown terra-cotta, and the sea appears in the background. It's said that you can see 300 belfries from here, including bright-blue cupolas made of ceramic tiles from nearby Manises. The tower was built in 1381, the final spire added in 1736. ✉ *Pl. de la Reina,* ☎ *963/918127* 🎫 *Cathedral free, museum €1.20, tower €1.20* ⏲ *Cathedral Mon.–Sat. 7:15–1 and 4:30–8:30, Sun. 7:30–1 and 5–8:30; museum and chapel Dec.–Feb., Mon.–Sat. 10–1; Mar.–May and Oct.–Nov., Mon.–Sat. 10–1 and 4:30–6; June–Sept., Mon.–Sat. 10–1 and 4:30–7; tower weekdays 10–12:30 and 4:30–6:30, weekends 10–1:30 and 5–6:30.*

33 **Ciutat de les Arts i les Ciències.** Designed by native son Santiago Calatrava, this sprawling futuristic complex is the home of Valencia's **Museu de les Ciències Príncipe Felipe** (Prince Philip Science Museum), **L'Hemisfèric** (Hemispheric Planetarium), **L'Oceanogràfic** (Oceanographic Park), and **Palau de les Arts** (Palace of the Arts). With resplendent buildings resembling combs and crustaceans, the Ciutat is a favorite of architecture buffs and curious kids. The Science Museum has soaring platforms filled with lasers, holograms, simulators, and hands-on lab experiments. The eye-shape planetarium projects 3D virtual voyages on its huge IMAX screen. At the Oceanographic Park you can take a submarine ride through a coastal marine habitat (and a glass-walled underwater restaurant). The space-age Palace of the Arts (opening in 2004) will have an amphitheater, an indoor theater, and a chamber-music hall. ✉ *Avda. Autovía del Saler 7* ☎ *961/974500* 📠 *961/974505* 🌐 *www.cac.es* 🎫 *Museu de les Ciències €6, L'Hemisfèric €6.6, L'Oceanogràfic €19.8* ⏲ *Museum Sun.–Fri. 10–8, Sat. 10–9; Planetarium daily shows at noon, 1, 2, 5, 6, and 8 (on weekdays, additional show at 11 AM; on Fri.–Sat., additional show at 9 PM).*

25 **Estación del Tren.** Designed by Demetrio Ribes Mano in 1917, Valencia's train station is a splendid Moderniste pile replete with citrus motifs that lets passengers know they've arrived. ✉ *Down Avda. Marqués de Sotelo from ayuntamiento.*

31 **Institut Valencià d'Art Modern (IVAM).** Out near the Turia riverbed's elbow, the Valencian Institute of Modern Art is dedicated to modern and contemporary art. The permanent collection, in the 1989 Centro Julio González, comprises 20th-century avant-garde works, European Informalism (including the Spanish artists Saura, Tàpies, and Chillida), pop art, and photography. ✉ *Guillem de Castro 118* ☎ *963/863000* 🎫 *€2.10, free Sun.* ⏲ *June–Aug., Tues.–Sun. 10–10; Sept.–May, Tues.–Sun. 10–8.*

★ 23 **Lonja de la Seda** (Silk Exchange). Downhill from San Nicolás, on the Plaza del Mercado, the 15th-century Lonja is a product of Valencia's golden age, when the arts came under the patronage of Ferdinand I. Widely regarded as one of Spain's finest Gothic buildings, it has a perfect Gothic facade dotted with ghoulish gargoyles, complemented inside by high vaulting and twisted columns. Opposite the Lonja stands the **Iglesia de los Santos Juanes** (Church of the Sts. John), whose interior was destroyed during the civil war, and, next door, the Moderniste **Mercado Central** (Central Market), built entirely of iron and glass. 🎫 *Free* ⏲ *Tues.–Fri. 9:15–2 and 4:30–8, weekends 9:15–1:30.*

★ 29 **Museo de Bellas Artes** (Museum of Fine Arts). Valencia was a thriving center of artistic activity in the 15th century, and the city's Museum of

Fine Arts is one of the best in Spain. To get here, walk behind the cathedral and cross the Puente de la Trinidad (Trinity Bridge) to the river's north bank; the museum is at the edge of the **Jardines del Real** (Royal Gardens), with fountains, rose gardens, tree-lined avenues, and a small zoo. It's open daily 8–dusk. Many of the best paintings by Jacomart and Juan Reixach, two of several artists known as the Valencian Primitives are here, as is work by Hieronymus Bosch—or El Bosco, as they call him here. The ground floor has the murky, 17th-century Tenebrist masterpieces of Francisco Ribalta and his pupil José Ribera, together with a Velázquez self-portrait and a room devoted to Goya. Upstairs, look for Joaquín Sorolla (Gallery 66), the luminous Valencian painter of everyday Spanish life in the 19th century. ✉ *C. San Pío V s/n* ☎ *963/932046* 💳 *Free* ⏲ *Tues.–Sun. 10–8.*

★ 28 **Palacio del Marqués de Dos Aguas.** Soon after leaving the Plaza Patriarca and crossing Calle Poeta Querol, you'll come face-to-face with this building's fascinating baroque alabaster facade. The famous Churrigueresque facade around the corner, embellished with fruits and vegetables, centers on the figures of the *Dos Aguas* (*Two Waters*), carved by Ignacio Vergara in the 18th century. The palace contains the **Museo Nacional de Cerámica,** with a magnificent collection of mostly local ceramics. Look for the Valencian kitchen on the second floor. ☎ *963/516392* 🌐 *www.mcu.es/nmuseos/ceramica* 💳 *Palace and museum €2.40, free Sat. afternoon and Sun. morning* ⏲ *Tues.–Sat. 10–2 and 4–8, Sun. 10–2.*

21 **Palau de la Generalitat.** On the left side of the Plaza de la Virgen, fronted by orange trees and box hedges, is the elegant eastern facade of what was the Gothic home of the Valencia Cortés (Parliament), until it was suppressed by Felipe V for supporting the wrong (losing) side during the War of the Spanish Succession in the 18th century. The two *salones* (reception rooms) in the older of the two towers have superb woodwork on the ceilings. Call in advance for permission to enter. ☎ *963/863461* ⏲ *Weekdays 9–2.*

32 **Palau de la Música** (Concert Hall). On one of the nicest stretches of the Turia riverbed, a pond is backed by a huge glass vault: Valencia's Palace of Music. Supported by 10 porticoed pillars, the dome gives the illusion of a greenhouse, both from the street and from within its sun-filled, tree-landscaped interior. Home of the Orquesta de Valencia, the main hall also hosts world-class performers on tour. For concert schedules, pick up a *Turia* guide at any newsstand. To see the building without concert tickets, pop into the **art gallery,** which hosts free changing exhibits. ✉ *Paseo de la Alameda 30* ☎ *963/375020* 🌐 *www.palauvalencia.com* ⏲ *Gallery daily 10:30–1:30 and 5:30–8:30.*

24 **Plaza del Ayuntamiento.** Down Avenida María Cristina from the market, this plaza is the hub of city life, a fact well conveyed by the massiveness of its baroque facades. The **ayuntamiento** itself contains the city tourist office and a museum on the history of Valencia. ⏲ *Ayuntamiento weekdays 8:30–2:30.*

Plaza de la Virgen. Leaving the cathedral by the Gothic Puerta de los Apóstoles (Apostle Door), you'll emerge on this pedestrian plaza, a lovely place for a refreshing *horchata* (tiger-nut milk) in the late afternoon. Next to its portal, market gardeners from the huerta bring their irrigation disputes before the Water Tribunal, which has met every Thursday at noon since 1350. Verdicts are given on the spot, and sentences range from fines to deprivation of water.

26 **Plaza de Toros.** Adjacent to the train station is the bullring, one of the oldest in Spain. The best bullfighters are featured on and around July

25 and during the Fallas in March. Just beyond, down Pasaje Dr. Serra, the **Museo Taurino** (Bullfighting Museum) has bullfighting memorabilia, including bulls' heads and matadors' swords from Valencian bullfights. *Free Bullring and museum Mon. 10–2, Tues.–Sun. 10–8.*

27 **Real Colegio del Patriarca** (Royal College of the Patriarch). The colegio stands on the far side of Plaza Patriarca, toward the center of town. Founded by San Juan de Ribera in the 16th century, it has a lovely Renaissance patio and an ornate church, and its museum holds works by Juan de Juanes, Francisco Ribalta, and El Greco. *Entrance off C. de la Nave €1.20 Daily 11–1:30.*

22 **San Nicolás.** A small plaza contains Valencia's oldest church, once the parish of the Borgia Pope Calixtus III. The first portal you come to, with a tacked-on, rococo bas-relief of the Virgin Mary with cherubs, hints well at what's inside: every inch of the originally Gothic church is covered with Churrigueresque embellishments. *C. Abadía San Nicolás Free Open for mass daily 8–9 AM and 7–8 PM; Sat. 6:30–8:30 PM; Sun. various masses 8–1.*

Where to Stay & Eat

$$$–$$$$ **Civera.** This restaurant enjoys local renown for its fresh fish and seafood, cooked *a la plancha* (grilled), *hervidos* (boiled), or *a la sal* (baked in salt). The marine theme is underscored by white walls, beams, and sumptuous displays of fish, fruit, and vegetables. The restaurant is three blocks northwest of the Museo de Bellas Artes. *C. Lérida 11 963/475917 AE, DC, MC, V Closed Mon., Easter wk, and Aug. No dinner Sun.*

$$$–$$$$ **Eladio.** Some way out of town, this welcoming restaurant is decorated with oak and marble. The many Galician fish dishes here are prepared with a mixture of tradition and invention by chef Eladio Rodríguez; try the *mero a la brasa* (char-grilled grouper) or the *rodaballo a la Gallega* (turbot with sweet paprika oil) and finish up with a mouthwatering Swiss pastry. *Chiva 40 963/842244 AE, DC, MC, V Closed Sun. and Aug.*

★ $$$–$$$$ **El Timonel.** Decorated like the inside of a yacht, this central restaurant (two blocks east of the bullring) serves outstanding shellfish. The cooking is simple yet benefits from the freshest ingredients; try the *pescado de roca* (rockfish) or *lubina a la plancha* (grilled sea bass). Lunch attracts businesspeople, dinner a fashionable crowd. *Félix Pizcueta 13 963/526300 AE, DC, MC, V Closed Mon.*

★ $$–$$$ **Gargantua.** Intimate and chic, this 1910 town house has apricot-color rooms crowded with pictures. The cooking is nouvelle and imaginative; *Esgarrat* (grilled cod with green peppers) is a good regional dish. *Navarro Reverter 18 963/346849 AE, DC, MC, V Closed Sun., Easter wk, and last two weeks of Aug. No lunch Sat.*

$$–$$$ **La Pepica.** For the best in Valencia's seafood paella, head for the waterfront. Dig into *arroz marinero* (seafood paella) topped with shrimp and mussels at this long-time bustling family restaurant. *Paseo Neptuno 6 963/710366 MC, V Closed Nov.*

$–$$ **La Riuà.** This local secret, which serves Valencian food, is decorated with beautiful ceramic tiles. Order a rice dish, fresh fish prepared with *all i pebre* (garlic and pepper), or *pulpitos guisados* (stewed baby octopus). Wash it all down with a cold bottle of *Llanos de Titaguas,* a dry yet snappy white Valencian table wine. *C. del Mar 27 963/914571 AE, DC, MC, V Closed Sun., Easter wk, and Aug. No dinner Mon.*

$ **Patos.** Small, cozy, and very popular with locals, this restored 18th-century town house has an earthy look, thanks to the terra-cotta tiles, wood-panel walls, and overhead beams. On weekdays, the set menu is a real bargain at €9.50 and often includes *pato* (duck); on the weekends, the price goes up to €16. Get here by 9:30 PM to snag a table; you can also dine outside in summer. The restaurant is just north of Calle de la Paz, in the old quarter. ✉ *C. del Mar 28* ☎ *963/921522* ▭ *MC, V* ⊙ *No dinner Mon.*

★ **$$$$** **Monte Picayo.** If you want a casino nearby and don't mind looking at the sea from a distance, consider this place. Set into a hill and draped in greenery, its modern, tiered structure overlooks the huerta north of Valencia. The public areas and guest rooms are spacious and cheerful, and service is impeccable. Each room has a terrace, and nine have private pools. ✉ *Urbanización Monte Picayo, Autopista Valencia–Barcelona, 46530 Puzol, Valencia* ☎ *961/420100* 🖷 *961/422168* ⊕ *www.hvsl.es* *83 rooms* *Restaurant, miniature golf, 2 tennis courts, 2 pools, hair salon, 2 bars, casino, free parking* ▭ *AE, DC, MC, V.*

$$$–$$$$ **Sidi Saler.** The stretch of coastline just south of Valencia suffers from ongoing construction, but this hotel's contemporary khaki facade rings an oasis of luxury. The guest rooms are modern, bright, and unremarkable, though they help convey the impression that the beach belongs only to you. ✉ *Playa del Saler, 46012 Valencia* ☎ *961/610411* 🖷 *961/610838* ⊕ *www.hotelessidi.es* *276 rooms* *Restaurant, cable TV with movies, 2 pools (1 indoor), hair salon, massage, sauna, 2 bars, meeting rooms, some pets allowed (fee)* ▭ *AE, DC, MC, V.*

$$$ **Parador de El Saler.** Definitely for golf enthusiasts, this modern parador 18 km (11 mi) south of Valencia has a famous course, with the first tee just outside the front door. The building has an exposed position on the edge of a pine forest, fronted by sand dunes. The bright, spacious reception rooms have cool marble floors, white walls, and baronial furniture, and guest rooms echo this style. Insist on a sea view. ✉ *El Saler, 46012 Valencia* ☎ *961/611186* 🖷 *961/627016* ⊕ *www.parador.es* *58 rooms* *Restaurant, 18-hole golf course, pool, gym, sauna, soccer, bar* ▭ *AE, DC, MC, V.*

$$–$$$ **Ad Hoc.** Small and beautifully designed, this 19th-century town house offers immediate access to the old quarter and the Turia gardens. Owner Luis García Alarcón is an antiquarian, and the hotel reflects his eye for ancient design and general architectural elegance. Weekend rates (a third less than weekday prices) are an excellent value. ✉ *Boix 4, 46003* ☎ *963/919140* 🖷 *963/913667* ⊕ *www.sercotel.es* *28 rooms* *Restaurant, some pets allowed* ▭ *AE, DC, MC, V.*

★ **$$–$$$** **Excelsior.** For its price category, this hotel in an 1930s building offers the best value. From the art deco restaurant-cum-bar, a spiral marble staircase leads to a dark, wood-paneled salon with a terrace. Rooms have olive-green carpets and beds with brass headboards. The general vibe is very friendly, and the hotel is central ✉ *Barcelonina 5, 46002* ☎ *963/514612* 🖷 *963/523478* ⊕ *www.hoteles-catalonia.es* *81 rooms* *Bar* ▭ *AE, DC, MC, V.*

$$–$$$ **Meliá Confort Inglés.** Once the palace of the dukes of Cardona, this hotel is convenient to the old town. Rooms are plush and ultramodern; ask for one overlooking the alabaster doorway of the neighboring Palacio del Marqués de Dos Aguas, with the brawny twin atlantes pouring water from two amphorae in illustration of the marqués's name. Ask about weekend rates—prices dip considerably. ✉ *Marqués de Dos Aguas 6, 46002* ☎ *963/516426* 🖷 *963/940251* ⊕ *www.solmelia.com* *63 rooms* *Restaurant, cable TV with movies, bar* ▭ *AE, DC, MC, V.*

$$–$$$ **Meliá Plaza.** The doors of this beauty open onto the bustling Plaza del Ayuntamiento, in the heart of Valencia. You're a short walk from all major downtown sights and cultural activities. The hotel mixes elegance with modern convenience. ✉ *Pl. del Ayuntamiento 4, 46002*

963/520612 *963/520426* *www.solmelia.com* *101 rooms* *Restaurant, cable TV with movies, gym, sauna, bar, meeting rooms* *AE, DC, MC, V.*

★ $$–$$$ **Reina Victoria.** Valencia's grande dame is an excellent choice if you want time-worn charm and a good location. The spacious reception rooms have cool marble floors (with rugs to take the chill off), as does the smart, classy restaurant. The smallish guest rooms are clothed in green or burgundy chintz and deep-pile carpets with a subdued pattern. *Barcas 4, 46002* *963/520487* *963/522721* *www.husa.es* *97 rooms* *Restaurant, bar* *AE, DC, MC, V.*

$$–$$$ **Villarreal.** Rustic on the outside, modern on the inside, this little, family-friendly hotel is between the Mercado Central and Plaza del Ayuntamiento. In a neighborhood where a moderately priced room is a scarce commodity, this is your very best bet. The neutral-hue rooms are spotless. *Ángel Guimerá 58, 46008* *963/824633* *963/840247* *28 rooms* *AE, DC, MC, V.*

Nightlife & the Arts

Sleep seems to be anathema here. You can experience Valencia's nocturnal way of life at any time except summer, when locals disappear on vacation and the international set moves to the beach. Nightlife in the old town centers on Calle Caballeros, leading off Plaza de la Virgen; the Plaza del Tossal has some popular cafés, as does Calle Alta, leading off Plaza San Jaime. Across the river in the new town, look for appealing hangouts along Avenida Blasco Ibáñez and on Plaza de Cánovas del Castillo and Plaza Zuquer. Out by the sea, Calle de Eugenia Viñes is lined with loud clubs and bars. Castellón and Valencia jointly publish *Que y Donde,* the major listings magazine; *Turia* focuses on Valencia. If you read a little Spanish, get ideas from the fabulous Web site, www.valencia.hoy.

The **Feria de Julio** is July's monthlong festival of theater, film, dance, and classical, jazz, and pop music. Contact the **ayuntamiento** (963/520694). In case you're homesick, the **Instituto Shakespeare** (Avda. Blasco Ibáñez 28 963/601950) performs in both Spanish and English. The **Filmoteca** (Pl. del Ayuntamiento 17 963/539300) has changing monthly programs of films in their original language (look for *v.o.—versión original*) and an artsy haunt of a café. An 11th-century Arab wall is incorporated into the 18th-century palace that is **Carmen** (C. Caballeros 38 963/925273), a sleek bar-club whose many floors are connected by ramps. There are 12 art installations, and the music is always sharp; pick up a monthly program inside. For quiet after-dinner drinks, try the jazzy, lighthearted bar **Café de la Seu** (Santo Cáliz 7 963/915715), with pop art and animal-print chairs. For a taste of *el ambiente andaluz* (Andalusian atmosphere) tuck into tapas and cocktails at **El Albero** (Ciscar 12 963/337428) at 11 PM Thursday–Saturday; there is Andalusian singing. In the new town, southeast of Calle Colón, **Albahaca** (Almirante Cadarso 30 963/341484) offers *sevillanas* (flamenco) and Andalusian music. **Xuquer Palace** (Pl. Xuquer 8 963/615811) has Barcelona-style Moderniste furnishings. **Casablanca** (Eugenia Viñes 152 963/713366) has an elegant postwar look; it's open Thursday–Sunday and has everything from waltz to swing music. The aptly named **Vivir Sin Dormir** (Living Without Sleeping; Paseo Neptuno 42, Playa de las Arenas 963/727777) is a hot-wired music club.

Shopping

A flea market is held every Sunday morning in the streets around the cathedral. Another crafts and flea market takes place on Sunday morning in Plaza Luis Casanova, near the *campo de fútbol* (soccer stadium). The town of **Manises,** 9 km (5½ mi) west of Valencia, is another center for Valencian ceramics, known particularly for its azulejos. **Salvador Ribes** (✉ Vilaragut 7) has top-quality antiques with correspondingly daunting price tags. For better deals, try the stores on Calle Avellanas near the cathedral.

Albufera Nature Park

34 *11 km (7 mi) south of Valencia.*

This beautiful freshwater lagoon was named by Moorish poets—*albufera* means "the sun's mirror." Dappled with rice paddies, the Parque Natural de la Albufera is a nesting site for more than 250 bird species and hosts many indigenous fish and marine species. Admission is free, and there are miles of lovely walking trails. Fishermen offer boat rides through the lagoon's innumerable canals; from Valencia, Herca buses depart from the corner of Sueca and Gran Vía de Germanías on the hour (every half hour in summer) daily 7 AM–9 PM. To learn more, stop into the **Information and Learning Centre** (✉ Ctra. del Palmar ☎ 961/627345) on the highway in El Palmar.

Where to Eat

★ **$$$–$$$$** ✕ **La Matandeta.** With its white garden walls, this engaging restaurant appears from a distance to be a shining island in a sea of rice paddies. Thanks to the local bird life—snowy egrets, gray herons—a lunchtime drive to La Matandeta can be almost as eye-opening as the culinary creations of its proprietors, Maria Dolores Baixauli and Rafael Galvez. Delicious appetizers include *higado de rape con alcaparras y piñones* (monkfish liver in a caper and pine-nut vinaigrette). Don't forget to specify which of the 55 types of olive oil you'd like on your whole-wheat bread or salad. *✉ Ctra. Alfafar, Km 4 ☎ 962/112184 ▭ MC, V ⊗ Closed Mon. and first half of Sept. and second half of Jan.*

SOUTHERN CATALONIA & THE LEVANTE A TO Z

To research prices, get advice from other travelers, and book travel arrangements, visit www.fodors.com.

AIR TRAVEL

The international airport closest to the northern end of this terrain—100 km (62 mi) north of Tarragona—is in Barcelona. Valencia has an international airport with direct flights to London, Paris, Brussels, Lisbon, Zurich, and Milan.

Airport Information Aeropuerto de Valencia ☎ 961/598500.

CARRIERS **Airline** Iberia ☎ 902/400500.

BOAT & FERRY TRAVEL

Trasmediterránea ferries leave Valencia for Majorca and Ibiza Monday–Saturday. They go from Tarragona daily in July and August only.

Ferry Information Trasmediterránea ✉ Estación Marítima, Valencia ☎ 902/454645, 977/225506 Tarragona shuttle 🌐 www.trasmediterranea.es.

BUS TRAVEL

The trip from Barcelona to Tarragona is easy; nine buses leave Barcelona's Estación Vilanova-Norte every day. Connections between Tarragona and Valencia are frequent, and from Valencia buses continue down the coast and on to Madrid. Valencia's bus station is across the river from the old town; take Bus 8 from the Plaza del Ayuntamiento. Transport inland to Morella and Alcañiz can be arranged from Vinaròs, while Castellón and Sagunto have bus lines west to Teruel. Within Valencia, buses are the main mode of public transport; central lines begin at the Plaza del Ayuntamiento. Buses to the beaches and suburbs leave from the Plaza Puerta del Mar. The tourist office has details.

Bus Information **Bacoma SA bus line** ✉ Plaça Imperial Tarraco s/n, Tarragona ☎ 977/222072. **Valencia bus station** ✉ Avda. Menendez Pidal 13 ☎ 963/497222.

CAR RENTAL

In Tarragona, Avis works out of the travel agency Viajes Vibus. In Valencia you have a choice of Avis, Hertz, or Europcar.

Major Agencies **Avis** ✉ Pin Soler 10, Tarragona ☎ 977/219156 🌐 www.avis.com ✉ Isabel la Católica 17, Valencia ☎ 963/510734. **Europcar** ✉ Antiguo Reino de Valencia 7, Valencia ☎ 963/741512 🌐 www.europa-rentacar.es ✉ airport, Valencia ☎ 961/521872 ✉ Estación RENFE, Játiva 24, Valencia ☎ 963/3519055. **Hertz** ✉ Segorbe 7, Valencia ☎ 963/415036 🌐 www.hertz.es ✉ airport, Valencia ☎ 961/523791.

CAR TRAVEL

The A7 autopista leads into this region at both ends. The coastal N340 can get clogged, so you're often better off paying to use the autopista. A car is extremely valuable, even necessary, if you want to explore the inland Maestrazgo mountains, where much of the driving is smooth, uncrowded, and scenic.

CONSULATES

The U.S. Consulate in Valencia is open weekdays 10–1 only.

United States **Valencia** ✉ C. de la Paz 6 ☎ 963/516973.

EMERGENCIES

Pharmacies (*farmacias de guardia*) stay open late on a rotating basis: one stays open 24 hours in every sizable town or city. To find out whose turn it is, look on the door of any pharmacy or check the local press.

Ambulance ☎ 964/211253 in Castellón, 977/244728 in Gandesa, 964/160962 in Morella, 977/252525 in Tarragona, 963/677375 in Valencia. **Police** ☎ 091 national toll-free.

Hospitals **Hospital Clínico** ✉ Valencia ☎ 963/862600. **Hospital Joan XXIII** ✉ Tarragona, ☎ 977/295800. **Hospital Provincial** ✉ Castellón ☎ 964/210522.

LODGING

APARTMENT & VILLA RENTALS

Throughout Catalonia are farmhouses (called a *casa rural* in Spanish and a *casa de pagès* in Catalan), where you can spend a weekend, a week, or more. Accommodations vary widely, from small, rustic homes with a few rooms to spacious farmhouses with wood-beam ceilings, fireplaces, and outdoor pools. The high-end farmhouses are called Gîtes. Most tourist offices have a pamphlet, called *Gîtes de Catalunya,* with color photos, and also sell a book on the *Cases de Pagès de Catalunya* for €4.80. You can also peruse listings of farmhouses on 🌐 www.gencat.es/probert, the Catalunya Tourist Office Web site. Another helpful source is Agroturisme, which has Spanish and English listings of Catalonia's farmhouses. Rental apartments, available for short- and long-term stays, are available throughout Southern Catalonia, both along the coast and in the interior.

Local Agents **Torrecorinto Apartamentos Turisticos** ✉ Avda. de Corinto 1, Playa de Canet, Sagunto ☎ 96/2608911. **Federació d'Agroturisme i Turisme Rural Comarques de Tarragona** ✉ Sant Francesc 1, 43360 Cornudella de Montsant ☎ 977/821082 🌐 www.agroturisme.org.

SPORTS & THE OUTDOORS

GOLF All golf courses are near or on the coast. They are listed from north to south; call in advance to reserve tee times.

Club de Golf Costa Dorada ✉ Apdo. 43, Calafells, Tarragona ☎ 977/168032, 9 holes. **Club de Golf Costa de Azahar** ✉ Ctra. Grao-Benicàssim, Grao de Castellón ☎ 964/280979, 9 holes. **Club de Campo del Mediterráneo** ✉ Urbanización La Coma, Borriol ☎ 964/321227, 18 holes. **Club de Campo El Bosque** ✉ Chiva, 31 km [19 mi] west of Valencia ☎ 963/263800, 18 holes. **Club de Golf Escorpión** ✉ Apdo. 1, Betera, Valencia ☎ 961/601211, 18 holes. **Campo de Golf de Manises** ✉ Apdo. 22029, Valencia ☎ 961/523804, 9 holes. **Campo de Golf El Saler** ✉ Apdo. 9034, Valencia ☎ 961/611186, 18 holes.

SAILING The safe waters off Spain's eastern coast make for good sailing conditions. Ask the local tourist office about procuring a boat, contact one of the clubs below, or just chance upon rental outfits.

Real Club Náutico Tarragona ✉ Puerto Deportivo ☎ 977/240360. **Club Náutico Salou** ✉ Port Salou ☎ 977/382166. **Club Náutico Castellón** ✉ Escollera de Poniente ☎ 964/280354. **Club Náutico Valencia** ✉ Camino del Canal 91 ☎ 963/679011.

TOURS

In Tarragona, the city tourist office (just below the cathedral) leads a tour of the cathedral and archaeological sites. From Amposta, Servei Turistic Parc runs guided tours through the Ebro Delta, Amposta, and Tarragona province in general—covering vineyards, Templar castles, Cistercian monasteries, and gondola-like *perxar* excursions through the delta. Pop in and talk it over with official Tarragona Diputació guide Josep Valldeperas. Throughout the year, the double-decker Valencia Bus Turistic (daily 10:30–7:30, until 9:30 in summer; departing every hour) travels on a circuit throughout the city that passes all the main sights. A 24-hour ticket (€10) allows you to get on and off when you wish at four main boarding points: Plaza de la Reina, Institut Valencià d'Art Modern (IVAM), Museo de Bellas Artes, and Ciutat de les Arts i les Ciències. In summer (and during the rest of the year depending on demand) Valencia's regional tourist office organizes tours of the Albufera Nature Park. You tour the port area before continuing south to the lagoon itself, where you can visit a traditional *barraca* (thatch farmhouse). You'll end up in the Devesa Gardens, where you can hire a boat to explore the rice paddies.

Servei Turistic Parc ✉ Rambla Nova 118, Amposta ☎ 977/702324. **Valencia Bus Turistic** 🌐 www.valenciabusturistic.com.

TRAIN TRAVEL

Trains bound for Tarragona (via Zaragoza) leave Barcelona's Passeig de Gràcia and Sants stations every half hour or so. Tarragona's RENFE station is downhill from the Mediterranean Balcony, south toward the port. Leaving Valencia, you have a choice of train connections to Madrid (via Cuenca) or Alicante (via Játiva). The main station, Estación del Norte, is on Calle Játiva next to the bullring, a short walk or cab ride from most hotels. Within the region, trains run more or less down the coast: Tarragona–Salou/Cambrils–Tortosa–Vinaròs–Peñíscola–Benicàssim–Castellón–Sagunto–Valencia. A line also goes from Valencia to Zaragoza by way of Sagunto and Teruel, and local lines go around Valencia from the station on Cronista Rivelles.

Train Information **RENFE** ☎ 902/240202 🌐 www.renfe.es.

Train Stations **Valencia-Cronista Rivelles** ☎ 902/240202. **Valencia-Estación del Norte** ☎ 902/240202.

VISITOR INFORMATION

Regional tourist offices—in Castellón, Tarragona, and Valencia—have area-wide information. There are local tourist offices in Albarracín, Benicàssim, Morella, Peñíscola, Reus, Sagunto, Tarragona, Teruel, Tortosa, and Valencia. There are information phone lines in Castellón and Valencia. In Valencia, a 24-hour machine in front of the regional tourist office dispenses information in exchange for €1.20.

Regional Tourist Offices **Castellón** ✉ Pl. María Agustina 5 ☎ 964/358688 🌐 www.castellon-costaazahar.com. **Tarragona** ✉ Rambla Nova 118 ☎ 977/238033. **Valencia** ✉ Paz 48 ☎ 963/986422 🌐 www.comunidad-valenciana.com.

Local Tourist Offices **Albarracín** ✉ Diputación 4 ☎ 978/710251. **Benicàssim** ✉ Médico Segarra 4 ☎ 964/300962 🌐 www.benicassim.org. **Morella** ✉ Pl. San Miguel ☎ 964/173032 🌐 www.morella.net. **Peñíscola** ✉ Paseo Marítimo ☎ 964/480208. **Reus** ✉ San Juan s/n ☎ 977/778149 🌐 www.reus.net. **Sagunto** ✉ Pl. Cronista Chabret ☎ 962/662213 🌐 www.sagunt.com/turismo. **Tarragona** ✉ Carrer Major 39 ☎ 977/245203. **Teruel** ✉ Tomás Nogués 1 ☎ 978/602279 🌐 www.teruel.net. **Tortosa** ✉ Pl. España ☎ 977/442567. **Valencia** ✉ Pl. Ayuntamiento 1 ☎ 963/510417 ✉ Estación RENFE, Játiva 24 ☎ 963/528573.â

THE SOUTHEAST

FODOR'S CHOICE

El Girasol restaurant, Moraira

Moors and Christians festival, Alcoy

HIGHLY RECOMMENDED

RESTAURANTS
- Cándido, Lorca
- Les Mouettes, Cullera

HOTELS
- Cortijo El Sotillo, San José
- Huerto del Cura, Elche
- Parador de Albacete
- Parador de Mojácar
- Rincón de Pepe, Murcia

SIGHTS
- Calpe's scalable monolithic outcrop in the sea
- Castillo de Santa Bárbara, an ancient fortress in Alicante
- Lorca, scene of colorful Holy Week celebrations
- Murcia's eclectic cathedral (". . . like a drawn out telescope")

By Philip Eade

Updated by Annelise Sorensen

SPAIN'S SOUTHEASTERN CORNER is a land of natural contrasts. To the north, the *huerta* (fertile, irrigated coastal plain) generates an orange harvest from late November through April; in spring, fragrant flowers adorn the same trees. The rice paddies stretching south from the Albufera lagoon to Gandía give rise to Valencia's culinary specialty, paella. The farther south you go, the drier and more mountainous the land, until you reach the desert-lunar landscape of Almería—backdrop for spaghetti-western films in the 1960s. The inland province of Albacete, historically part of Murcia, was the scene of Don Quijote's exploits in the Castilian expanse of La Mancha. The striking architecture in most southeastern towns attests to the area's long Moorish occupation. Alicante was in Moorish hands from 718 to 1249; Murcia, from 825 to 1243; and Almería, from 712 to 1489, when it was finally reconquered by Ferdinand and Isabella.

Most people come here for the beaches, from the crowded Costa Blanca to the nearly deserted stretches of Almería's Cabo de Gata, renowned for its scuba diving. Mild temperatures in spring and fall allow you to vacation before and after the thickest crowds.

South of Valencia, you can drive along a thin strip between the sea and the Albufera before following the coast around the Cabo de la Nao to the Costa Blanca. Just south of Cullera, detour inland through the historic towns of Xátiva and Alcoy en route to the exotic Mediterranean port city of Alicante. Heading back inland toward Murcia, you'll pass the palm forest at Elche and the ancient town of Orihuela. (In the opposite direction, a trip to Murcia from Madrid takes you through *Don Quijote* country, the province of Albacete.) Stop at Murcia, with its superb cathedral, before you approach the Africanesque Almería by way of Lorca, Mojácar, and the coast around Cabo de Gata.

About the Restaurants

Rice grows better in the Valencian provinces than anywhere else in Spain, which explains why paella was born here. Another rice dish to try is *arroz a la banda* (rice and vegetables with meat or fish, cooked over a wood fire). Remember that paella should be eaten immediately after it's cooked—don't order it from a *menú del día* (menu of the day) unless you can be sure it's fresh. Alicante and Jijona are known for their *turrón,* nougat made with almonds and flavored with honey. In Elche you can savor fresh dates. Murcian cooking uses products of the huerta and the sea, with a marked Arab influence in preparation. *Caldero de Mar Menor,* a traditional fisherman's rice dish, is cooked in huge iron pots and has a distinctly oily consistency, flavored by fish cooked in its own juices. Delicious as tapas or a first course are *muchirones* (broad beans in a spicy sauce, similar to the Catalan *habas a la catalana*) and *cocas* (meat pies akin to empanadas). In Almería, the menu has gazpacho *andaluz* (sometimes described as a spicy, liquid salad; characterized here by the addition of croutons) and *pescaditos fritos* (small fried fish), and grapes make a frequent appearance.

WHAT IT COSTS In Euros

	$$$$	$$$	$$	$	¢
AT DINNER	over €20	€15–€20	€10–€15	€6–€10	under €6

Prices are per person for a main course at dinner.

About the Hotels

Many hotels on this coast are modern high-rises. If you prefer to avoid these, you'll probably have to choose between comfort and character.

Wanderers can choose from three different coastal experiences (the lagoon, the populous beaches of the Costa Blanca, and the deserted strands south of Mojácar), two distinct inland programs (the steppe around Albacete and the mountains near Murcia), and four major cities (Alicante, Albacete, Murcia, and Almería). In seven days you can see nearly everything—unless, of course, you find the beach or the golf course of your dreams and decide to stay put. Five days will allow a sampling of beaches, inland villages, and the three coastal cities. Three days is enough for a beach or two, an inland village, and a short peek at Alicante, Murcia, and Almería.

If you have **3 days**

Start with **El Palmar** 1 and the Albufera, and continue through **Cullera** 2 and **Denia** 4 to the **Cabo de la Nao** 6. Overnight at the parador in **Jávea** 5 *or* in the village of **Moraira** 7. Begin the next day in the fishing village of **Altea** 9, then head to **Alicante** 17 for lunch and move on through **Elche** 18 and **Orihuela** 19 to **Murcia** 22 for the night. On your third day, visit **Lorca** 25, **Mojácar** 26, and the **Cabo de Gata Nature Reserve** 27 on the way to **Almería** 28 for the night.

If you have **5 days**

Explore **El Palmar** 1 and the Albufera before moving through **Cullera** 2 and **Denia** 4 to the **Cabo de la Nao** 6. Stay at the parador in **Jávea** 5 or in the village of **Moraira** 7. The next day, visit the fishing village of **Altea** 9; then hook inland to **Polop** 10 and **Alcoy** 13 for lunch at the Venta del Pilar. Spend the night in **Alicante** 17. On day three, see **Elche** 18 and **Orihuela** 19 before stopping in **Murcia** 22 for the night. On day four, explore **Cartagena** 23 and **La Manga del Mar Menor** 24 before heading inland to **Lorca** 25 for the night. On your last day, explore the coast from **Mojácar** 26 to the **Cabo de Gata Nature Reserve** 27 before settling into **Almería** 28 for the night.

Spain's paradors have traditionally solved this conundrum, and there are four in this territory: Jávea, Puerto Lumbreras (Lorca), Mojácar, and Albacete. The last, though likely to be off most people's itineraries, best represents the rustic parador style; the others are tasteful but modern. Calpe, Alicante, San José, and Almería have older, one-of-a-kind hotels for which you'll need to reserve in advance. Note that some coastal hotels close for the winter.

WHAT IT COSTS In Euros

	$$$$	$$$	$$	$	¢
FOR 2 PEOPLE	over €180	€100–€180	€60–€100	€40–€60	under €40

Prices are for two people in a standard double room in high season, excluding tax.

Exploring the Southeast

From Valencia's Albufera, inland to Xátiva and Albacete, and down the coast through Alicante and on to Murcia, Cartagena, and Almería, this part of Spain is rich in beaches, salt lagoons, steppes, mountain villages, and Mediterranean port cities. The Costa Blanca coastline of coves and white-sand beaches stretches from Cabo de la Nao to Cabo de Palos. It's peppered with resorts—Denia and Benidorm are two of the splashiest and most crowded—and the resulting onslaught of summer tourists. The parched inland expanse of Albacete and Murcia are true Don Quijote country, a flat, unpopulated landscape dotted only sparingly with traditional villages. Farther south unfolds the grape-scented province of Almeria, one of the least developed, and refreshingly least touristed, parts of Spain.

Numbers in the text correspond to numbers in the margin and on the Southeast map.

Timing

Try to visit this region between mid-autumn and April, as summer gets oppressively hot. Easter is interesting for its often-bizarre pageants and processions, especially in remote towns and villages.

FROM VALENCIA TO THE COSTA BLANCA

This short drive takes you through the Albuferas wetlands and into the northern end of the Costa Blanca, known as La Marina Alta (the High Shore). Compared to the sunbathers' strip south of Denia, these lonely marshlands and deserted beaches are wonderfully undiscovered.

El Palmar

❶ *16 km (10 mi) south of Valencia.*

South of Valencia, the coastal road follows a thin strip of land (La Dehesa) that barely separates the sea from the **Albufera** wetland, rimmed with rice fields and shady pine woods. There are large-scale duck shoots here in fall and winter. For a closer look at the Albufera's unique aura, turn right toward El Palmar—a one-lane road hugs the edge of the lagoon, passing thatched *barracas* (shacks). In town, you can hire a boat to explore the lagoon up close.

Cullera

❷ *39 km (24 mi) south of Valencia, 27 km (17 mi) north of Gandía.*

Past the lighthouse and around the rocky point is modern Cullera, a resort with futuristic high-rises. The climb up to the **Ermita de Nuestra Señora del Castillo** (Hermitage of Our Lady of the Castle) and **castle ruins** culminates in views of the sea, the huerta, and the mountains.

Where to Eat

★ $$–$$$ ✕ **Les Mouettes.** On the road up to the castle, this tiny restaurant has a lovely terrace with stunning sea views. French owner and manager Jean Lagarce speaks perfect English, while chef Jacqueline Lagarce prepares secret recipes from home; try the *lenguado con salsa de nata y champiñones* (sole with mushroom and cream sauce), the *escalope de foie caliente con uvas* (breaded duck liver with grapes), or the *hojaldre de higado de conejo con puerros* (rabbit liver in puff pastry with leeks). ✉ *Ctra. Subida al Castillo* ☎ *961/720010* ✍ *Reservations essential* 💳 *AE, MC, V* ⏲ *Closed mid-Dec.–mid-Feb. No lunch Mon.–Sat.*

Gandía

❸ *30 km (19 mi) northwest of Denia.*

Gandía's old town lies 4 km (2½ mi) inland from its modern beach development. This became the Borgia (Borja, in Spanish) fief after King Ferdinand granted the duchy to the family in 1485. The canny Borgia

Beaches

Like the region as a whole, the southeastern coastline is abundantly varied, from the long stretches of sand dunes north of Denia and south of Alicante to the coves and crescents of the Costa Blanca. The benign climate permits lounging on the beach almost year-round. Major beaches have Cruz Roja (Red Cross) stations with helicopters and flags to warn swimmers of conditions: green for safety, red for danger.

Altea, popular with families, is busy and pebbly, but the old town is pretty. Benidorm's two white, crescent-shape beaches, packed in summer, extend for more than 5 km (3 mi) and are widely considered the best in Spain. Benidorm takes all prizes for après-beach entertainment. Calblanque is on the road between Los Belones and Cabo de Palos, which takes you down a longish, rough track to a succession of nearly deserted sands frequented mainly by young Murcians. Calpe's beaches have the scenic advantage of the sheer outcrop Peñón de Ifach (Cliff of Ifach), which stands guard over stretches of sand to either side. Denia and Jávea both have family beaches where children paddle in relatively safe waters. Gandía's sandy beach is well kept, its promenade lined with bars and restaurants.

The narrow La Manga del Mar Menor (*manga* refers to a thin "sleeve" of land) has some stunning views, but it has been ruined by a tasteless sprawl of hotels and condos. Mojácar has a pebbly beach backed by bars and good sports facilities, but if you have a car, try some of the deserted beaches to the south. There are no facilities save the odd water tap for campers, and nudity, though illegal, seems generally accepted here, at Calblanque, and just north of Cullera. In Moraira, the best beach is Playa Castillo, just outside the center. Santa Pola and Guardamar del Segura are other good options, with fine, clean sand and pine trees behind the dunes.

Fiestas

Almería's lively **Festival Internacional de Títeres** (Puppet Theater Festival) is held in January. Denia throws a **mini Fallas** March 16–19. Alcoy's spectacular **Moros y Cristianos** (Moors and Christians) festival, held April 21–24, includes a reenactment of clashes from the Christian Reconquest, the battle to dislodge the Moors at the end of the 15th century. Murcia's **Semana Santa** (Holy Week) processions are among the most illustrious in Spain; those in Lorca are known for the opulent costumes of both Christian and Roman participants and for the penitents' solemn robes. Altea's **Moros y Cristianos** spectacle, staged the third Sunday in May, is a combination of battle reenactment and pageant, complete with elaborate costumes and the town's youngsters dressed up as knights in shining armor. Alicante's main festival is **Hogueras de San Juan** (St. John's Day Bonfires), June 21–24. **El Misteri** (the Mystery Play) is performed in Elche in two parts, August 14–15, preceded by a public dress rehearsal (August 13).

Golf

Spain is one of Europe's top golf destinations. The mild southeastern climate makes this region a fine choice for winter golfing.

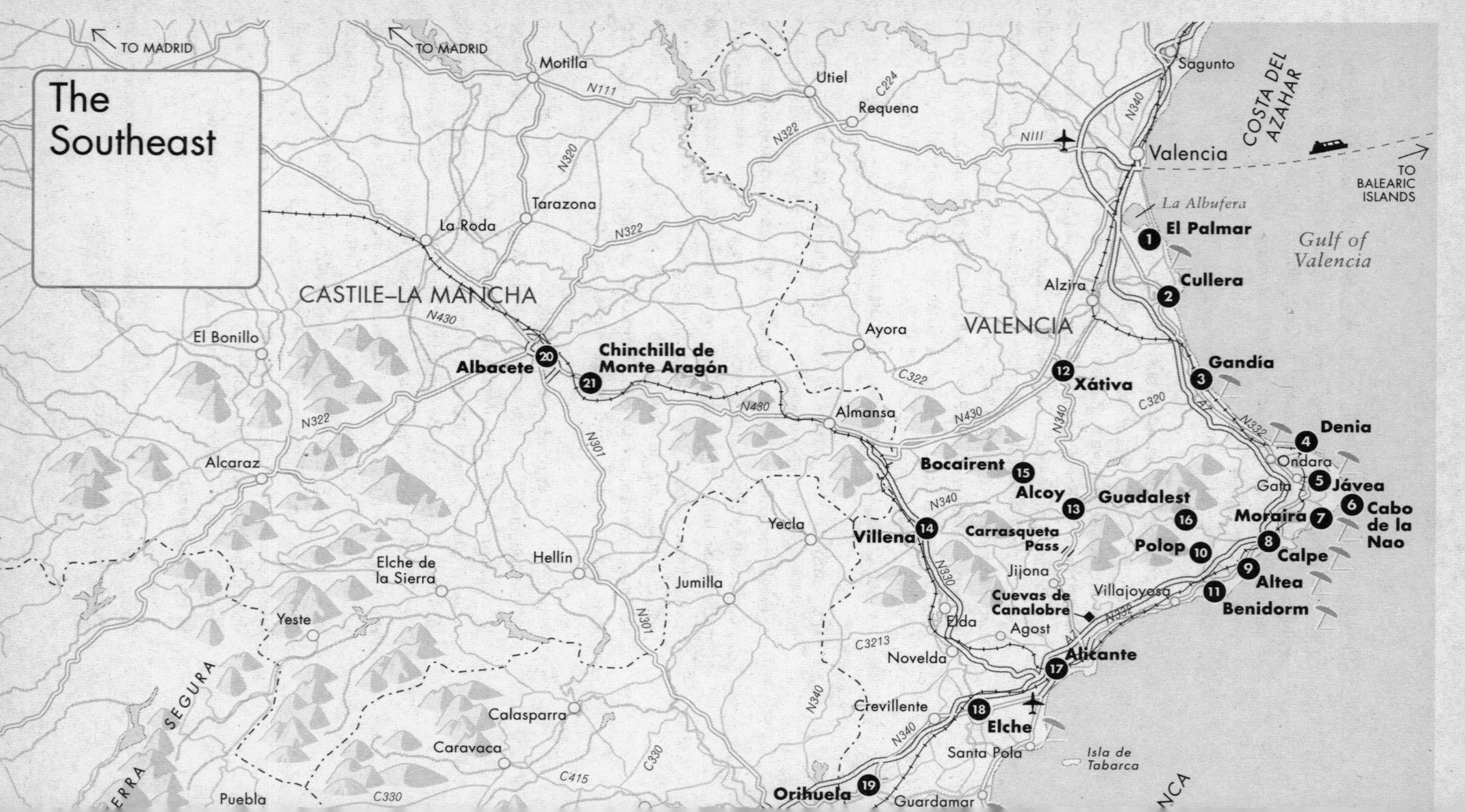

The Southeast
TO MADRID
TO MADRID
Motilla
Utiel
Requena
Sagunto
COSTA DEL AZAHAR
Valencia
TO BALEARIC ISLANDS
La Albufera
1 El Palmar
Gulf of Valencia
2 Cullera
Alzira
Tarazona
La Roda
CASTILE–LA MANCHA
VALENCIA
Ayora
El Bonillo
20 Albacete
21 Chinchilla de Monte Aragón
12 Xátiva
3 Gandía
Almansa
4 Denia
Ondara
Gata
5 Jávea
6 Cabo de la Nao
7 Moraira
15 Bocairent
13 Alcoy
16 Guadalest
Alcaraz
14 Villena
Yecla
Carrasqueta Pass
10 Polop
8 Calpe
9 Altea
11 Benidorm
Jijona
Villajoyosa
Cuevas de Canalobre
Elda
Agost
Hellín
Elche de la Sierra
Jumilla
Yeste
Novelda
17 Alicante
Crevillente
18 Elche
Santa Pola
Isla de Tabarca
Calasparra
Caravaca
SEGURA
Puebla
19 Orihuela
Guardamar
N111
C224
N322
N320
N340
N430
C322
C320
N332
A7
N301
N330
C3213
C330
C415

MURCIA
ANDALUSIA
Orihuela
Guardamar del Segura
Torrevieja
Mar Menor
Murcia
Mula
Puebla
Castril
Totana
San Javier
Río Segura
La Manga del Mar Menor
Vélez Rubio
Lorca
Puerto Lumbreras
Cúllar
Baza
Cartagena
Cabo de Palos
Huércal-Overa
Aguilas
Albox
Purchena
Cuevas
Vera
Guadix
Mojácar
Sorbas
Níjar
SIERRA NEVADA
Almería
San José
Cabo de Gata
Cabo de Gata Nature Reserve
COSTA BLANCA
COSTA CALIDA
COSTA DE ALMERIA
Mediterranean Sea
TO MOROCCO
C330
C321
C323
N301
N332
N340
N342
N324
KEY
Ferry
Rail Lines
Regional Boundaries
0
20 miles
0
30 km

pope Alexander VI was one of the most notorious of all Renaissance prelates, but the family's reputation was later redeemed by the Jesuit St. Francis Borgia (1510–72), born in Gandía and canonized in 1671. The **Palacio de los Duques** (Ducal Palace), signposted from the city center, was founded by St. Francis in 1546 and still serves as a Jesuit college. Elaborate ceilings and brightly colored *azulejos* (glazed tiles) adorn the 17th-century state rooms. ☎ *962/871465* 🌐 *www.palauducal.com* 🎫 *€3* ⏲ *Guided tours June–Aug., Tues.–Sat. hourly 10:30–1:30 and 5–9, Sun. 10:30–12:30; Sept.–May, Tues.–Sat. hourly 10:30–12:30 and 5–7, Sun. 10:30–12:30.*

Where to Eat

$–$$ ✕ **Mesón Gallego.** This Galician restaurant is a lucky discovery in the port area. The rough, simple surroundings complement such hearty Galician dishes as *pulpo* (octopus) or the fish and meat specialties cooked over coals. Ask for Galician *culcas,* shallow ceramic bowls for drinking the young Ribeiro wines. ✉ *Levante 37, Grao de Gandía* ☎ *962/841892* 💳 *AE, MC, V* ⏲ *Closed Wed. No dinner Tues. Sept.–June.*

en route

As you head south, parchment-color hills mark the beginning of the province of Alicante. Past Ondara, which has an unusual stone bullring, you can detour to the **Cueva de las Calaveras** (Skull Cave), near Benidoleig, inhabited by prehistoric humans some 40,000 years ago. ☎ *966/404235* 🎫 *€3* ⏲ *Daily 10–6 in winter, 10–8:30 in summer.*

THE COSTA BLANCA

The popular name for the stretch of coast between Cabo de la Nao and Cabo de Palos is the Costa Blanca, or White Coast. Carnations grow in such abundance here that they faintly perfume the local wine. The Costa Blanca includes the cities of Alicante and Cartagena as well as numerous beach resorts, which have expanded uncontrollably since the 1960s and early '70s. A drive down this shore grants some quiet and picturesque stops, especially off-season. One especially scenic segment is the road that branches off N332 at Gata de Gorgos (also known as Gata) to the coastal towns of Denia and Jávea.

Denia

❹ *100 km (62 mi) south of Valencia, 8 km (5 mi) north of Jávea and east of Ondara.*

The northernmost beach resort on the Costa Blanca, Denia is a busy tourist town known for its fishing boats, fiestas, and celebrations, culminating in the midsummer St. John's Day bonfires (June 23). Backed by the Montgó massif, rising to more than 2,100 ft to the west, Denia's beaches to the north—Les Marines, Les Bovetes, and Les Deveses—are smooth and sandy, while the coast to the south is rocky, forming *calas* (tiny secluded inlets that recall the Costa Brava, north of Barcelona).

Known as the gastronomic capital of the Costa Blanca, Denia is a good place to sample fresh Mediterranean seafood—try a plate of *picaetes de sepia y calamar* (squid and cuttlefish) or *suquet de rape* (stewed monkfish) at any of the town's fine restaurants.

Denia's most interesting architectural attraction is the **Palau del Governador** (Governor's Palace; ✉ Castillo de Denia), overlooking the town, with its 12th-century tower and Renaissance bastion. The latter has a Moorish portal with a lovely horseshoe arch. One notable church is **Igle-**

sia de la Asunción (Church of the Assumption). Denia also has the closest ferry connection to the **Balearic Islands.** The company **Balearia** (☎ 966/428600 🌐 www.balearia.com) makes the 80-km (50-mi) crossing to Ibiza (3½ hours) and Palma de Mallorca (5 hours) daily, more frequently in summer.

Where to Eat

$–$$ ✕ **Drassanes.** Built into Denia's original medieval shipyards (for which it's named), Drassanes is a well-known place for fresh local seafood. The food is authentic and good. Arroz a la banda is the house specialty. ✉ *C. Puerto 15* ☎ *965/781118* 💳 *AE, MC, V* ⊗ *Closed Mon. and Nov.*

Jávea

5 *108 km (67 mi) southeast of Valencia, 92 km (57 mi) northeast of Alicante, 8 km (5 mi) south of Denia.*

A labyrinth of tiny streets and houses with arched portals and Gothic windows, Jávea has an antique aspect contrasted only (ironically) by its modern church, **Santa María de Loreto.** The church-fortress of **San Bartolomé** is the town's architectural gem. The **Soler Blasco** ethnological and archaeological museum is another interesting visit. Around the port, the **Aduanas del Mar** area is well sprinkled with restaurants serving *arroz a la marinera* (seafood paella) and other local dishes.

Where to Stay

$$–$$$ 🏨 **Parador de Jávea.** Ensconced in a lush palm grove, with terrific views of the bay and white-sand beach below, this modern parador is a low structure—only four stories—and is far more tasteful than the high-rise hotels elsewhere on the Costa Blanca. The oak-trim, ceramic-tile guest rooms are airy and pleasant. ✉ *Av. del Mediterráneo 7, 03730* ☎ *965/790200* 📠 *965/790308* 🌐 *www.parador.es* *70 rooms* *Restaurant, pool, gym, sauna, bar* 💳 *AE, DC, MC, V.*

Cabo de la Nao

6 *10 km (6 mi) southeast of Jávea.*

Cabo de la Nao (Cape Nao) is a great spur of land jutting into the Mediterranean toward Ibiza, barely 100 km (62 mi) away. As you round the point, you'll turn from a coast that looks toward Italy to one that mirrors Africa. In the same few miles, you'll pass from an agriculture of oranges and rice to one of olives and palms, from a benign (if variable) climate to one of tawny aridity.

Moraira

7 *12 km (7 mi) northeast of Calpe, 20 km (12 mi) southeast of Jávea.*

The narrow streets leading down to Moraira's harbor preserve an air of seclusion. The ***casco viejo*** (old town) has a good selection of bars and restaurants, while the outskirts have been edified with chalets and private homes. The **castle** and watchtower overlooking the port were built in the Middle Ages to ward off Mediterranean pirates.

Where to Stay & Eat

$$$$ Fodor's Choice ★ ✕ **El Girasol.** An elegant, ivy-cloaked villa on the Calpe road houses one of the finest restaurants in southeastern Spain. Owners Joachim and Victoria Koerper preside over the small dining room and terrace. Their cooking is imaginative, with an emphasis on French fare; highlights include *ensalada de salmonetes a la vinagretta de naranja* (red-mullet salad with orange vinegar) and *solomillo de lechal a la ficele* (veal poached

in sherry). ✉ *Ctra. Moraira a Calpe* ☎ *965/744373* 🌐 *www.relaischateaux.fr/girasol* 💳 *AE, DC, MC, V* ⏲ *Closed Mon. No dinner Sun. Nov.–Mar.*

$$–$$$ **Swiss Moraira.** Secluded in a pine forest above Moraira (off the road to Calpe) with smart, modern rooms arranged around a creatively shaped swimming pool, this low-rise luxury hotel is ideal if you're looking for peace and comfort. The beach and marina are 3 km (2 mi) away. ✉ *C. Haya 175, Club Moraira, 03724* ☎ *965/747104* 📠 *965/747074* *25 rooms* *Tennis court, pool, bar* 💳 *AE, DC, MC, V.*

Calpe

★ 8 *15 km (9 mi) southwest of Jávea, 8 km (5 mi) north of Altea.*

South of Moraira are Calpe and the incredible outcrop known as the **Peñón de Ifach.** Calpe was deserted for nearly 100 years after Barbary pirates killed or enslaved the entire population in the 17th century. The Peñón rises from the sea as a 1,000-ft monolith; the summit is accessible by a man-made underground tunnel that goes part of the way up—you can climb up the rest of the way. It is said that those who scale these heights at full moon will be hurled to their deaths by goatlike spirits.

Where to Stay & Eat

$$$ ✕ **Al-Zaraq.** Just down the road from the Venta la Chata, Al-Zaraq offers a tasty break from traditional Spanish fare. The Lebanese menu includes such lamb dishes as *cordero en salsa de dátiles* (lamb with date sauce) and *lubina con costra de piñones* (sea bass with a pine-nut crust). For a bit of everything, order the *menú de degustación,* the taster's menu (of which there are several to choose). ✉ *Ctra. de Valencia (N332, Km 172)* ☎ *965/731615* 💳 *AE, MC, V* ⏲ *No lunch. Closed Sun.–Thurs. Oct.–Mar.*

$ **Venta la Chata.** This pretty hotel was an 18th-century horse-changing post on the Valencia–Alicante road. The lower floor is rustic, as are the wood furnishings and azulejo floors in the rooms. Ask for a room with a balcony or terrace. The terrace gardens have sea views. ✉ *Ctra. de Valencia (N332, Km 172), 03710* ☎📠 *965/830308* *17 rooms* *Tennis court, Ping-Pong, bar* 💳 *AE, DC, MC, V.*

Altea

9 *10 km (6 mi) south of Calpe, 11 km (7 mi) north of Benidorm.*

Altea is an old fishing village with white houses and blue, ceramic-tile domes. One of the best-conserved towns on the Costa Blanca, it serves as a foil to the skyscraping tourist towers of Benidorm.

Where to Eat

$$$–$$$$ ✕ **La Costera.** This extremely popular restaurant mixes excellent Swiss cooking with bizarre furnishings and a nightly show. Specialties include the delicious, typically Swiss dish *rostit con carne troceada y champiñon* (chopped meat with mushrooms and potatoes). ✉ *Costera del Mestre la Música 8* ☎ *965/840230* *Reservations essential* 💳 *MC, V* ⏲ *No lunch Mon.–Wed. Closed Nov.–Feb.*

Polop

10 *10 km (6 mi) northwest of Altea.*

This whitewashed hilltop town has an interesting feature: the aptly named Plaza Fuente de la Provincia (*fuente* means "fountain") holds a collection of more than 200 taps, each donated by a different town in the province. Villagers armed with jugs enjoy free, constant mountain water from three sides of the unique square.

Benidorm

11 *11 km (7 mi) south of Altea on C3318, 42 km (26 mi) northeast of Alicante.*

Benidorm is a hugely overdeveloped resort with a seemingly bottomless capacity for tourists. Its twin, white crescent-shape beaches are enhanced by a continual accumulation of sand from other local beaches. For a fantastic view, follow signs to Club Sierra Dorada at the eastern edge of town and climb up to the **Rincón de Loix** (Loix Corner). Hidden among the concrete blocks, the old village still survives.

Where to Stay & Eat

$$–$$$ ✕ **Tiffany's.** The red and white tones of Tiffany's draw Benidorm's jet set for intimacy and fine food. You can eat delicacies, such as *salmón con langostinos* (salmon with shrimp), *entrecôte al roquefort* (steak with Roquefort cheese), and *lubina a la sal* (sea bass cooked in its own juices), accompanied by piano music. ✉ *Av. Mediterráneo, Edifício Coblanca 3* ☎ *965/854468* ▭ *AE, DC, MC, V* ⊙ *Closed Jan. No lunch.*

$ ✕ **I Fratelli.** The cooking here is Italian, with contemporary French and international accents. Neapolitan music complements the stylish Moderniste touches: sleek black chairs, white tablecloths, and exotic potted plants. Best bets are pasta and *pescados a la sal* (fish baked in salt). ✉ *Doctor Orts Llorca* ☎ *965/853979* ▭ *AE, DC, MC, V* ⊙ *Closed Nov.*

$$–$$$ **Gran Hotel Delfín.** The Gran Delfín is the most quietly situated hotel in Benidorm—no mean feat, especially in summer. The salon downstairs is filled with amusingly motley '70s-style furniture. The bedrooms are Castilian-style, with a smattering of bric-a-brac on the walls. Ask for a room at the front, overlooking the beach. ✉ *Playa de Poniente, 03500* ☎ *965/853400* *965/857154* *www.webic.com/granhoteldelfin* *92 rooms, 1 suite* *Restaurant, tennis court, pool, bar* ▭ *AE, DC, MC, V* ⊙ *Closed early Jan.–early Mar.*

Nightlife & the Arts

Countless bars and discos with names like Jockey's and Harrods (reflecting Benidorm's popularity with Brits and Germans) line Avenida de Europa and the Ensanche de la Playa de Levante. The **Benidorm Palace** (✉ Av. Severo Ochoa ☎ 965/851661) offers a cabaret with Spanish dance and an international musical show. Dinner starts at 8:30, the show at 10 (both one hour later in summer). Don a crown at the **Nuevo Gran Castillo Conde de Alfaz** (✉ Camino Viejo del Albir ☎ 966/865265) and dine in front of jousting medieval knights. Dinner, drinks, and the show (Friday and Saturday only) cost €21 per person.

INLAND: XÁTIVA & ALCOY

For a break from sea and sand, cut inland to Xátiva, Alcoy, Villena, and Bocairent, which have some of the most rustic villages in the Southeast. People here live far more traditional, small-town lives than most of their compatriots.

Xátiva

12 *42 km (26 mi) southwest of Cullera, 50 km (31 mi) north of Alcoy.*

Resting on the dry, vine- and cypress-covered slopes of the Sierra de Alcoy, Xátiva (pronounced *cha*-ti-va; also spelled and pronounced Játiva) retains a pink **casco antiguo** (old town) dotted with fountains. Under the Moors, Xátiva was famous for paper production; centuries later it became the birthplace of two of the Borgia popes—Calixtus III and his nephew Alexander VI. The latter issued the famous 1493 Papal Bull granting the Indies to Ferdinand and Isabella, though he's more often remembered for his scandalous private life, including his role as the father of Caesar and Lucrezia.

To reach the **castle,** on the slopes of Mt. Bernisa, follow signs up a steep path from the Plaza del Españoleto. Halfway up Mt. Bernisa, the 13th-century **Ermita de San Feliú** (Hermitage of St. Felix) has a beautiful group of Valencian primitive paintings. Felipe V destroyed the fortress as part of his retribution for Xátiva's opposition in the War of the Spanish Succession. You can see a partial restoration of the castle. ☎ *962/274274* *Castle €1.90, Ermita free* ⏲ *Castle Mar.–Oct., Tues.–Sun. 10–8; Nov.–Feb., Tues.–Sun. 10–6. Ermita Tues.–Sun. 10–1 and 3–6.*

On the Plaza del Seo stands Xátiva's enormous **Colegiata** (collegiate church), which houses some Borgia Renaissance marble. Opposite the Colegiata is the 16th-century plateresque facade of the **hospital.** Down Calle Corretgeria, the **Museo Municipal** has a small collection of archaeological finds and paintings by Xátiva's other famous son, José de Ribera. *€2* ⏲ *Mid-June–mid-Sept., Tues.–Sun. 10–2; mid-Sept.–mid-June, Tues.–Fri. 10–2 and 4–6, weekends 10–2.*

Alcoy

13 *55 km (34 mi) north of Alicante, 50 km (31 mi) south of Xátiva.*

Fodor's Choice ★

Alcoy sits at the confluence of three rivers and is famous for the bridges spanning its deep gorges. The town owes its size (population 67,000) to its textile, paper, and fruit-canning industries. Alcoy's annual **Moros y Cristianos** (Moors and Christians festival), around the time of Sant Jordi (St. George's Day, April 23), is the most spectacular fiesta of its kind in Spain—colorful processions and mock battles commemorate the Battle of Alcoy, in 1275, when St. George's intervention helped liberate the city from the besieging forces of Al Azraq, ensuring victory for the Christians. If you miss Moros y Cristianos, walk down Calle Sant Miquel, which leads off the Plaza de España, to **Casal de Sant Jordi** (St. George Civic Center), which has fiesta paraphernalia, including costumes worn by the combatants. ✉ *C. Sant Miquel 60* ☎ *965/540580* *€1* ⏲ *Tues.–Fri. 10–1 and 5:30–7:30, weekends 10–1.*

Where to Stay & Eat

$ ✕ **Venta Saltera.** A few minutes' drive south of Alcoy, this restaurant serves typical local fare, of which the staff is extremely proud. Try the *olleta alcoyana* (Alcoy-style stew, made with white beans and pork). ✉ *Ctra. N340* ☎ *965/544330* ▭ *AE, DC, MC, V* ⏲ *Closed Wed. and last 2 wks in Aug.*

$$ **Reconquista.** There's nothing memorable about this modern high-rise, but it's the most comfortable hotel for miles around. Compensate for the plain, dated guest rooms by requesting a view over the river gorge to old Alcoy. Public rooms are institutional, with gray-tile floors and functional plastic furniture. ✉ *Puente San Jorge 1, 03803 Alcoy* ☎ *965/330900* *965/330955* 🌐 *www.hotelodon.com* *72 rooms* *Restaurant, bar, meeting room, some pets allowed (fee)* ▭ *AE, DC, MC, V.*

Villena

14 *40 km (25 mi) west of Alcoy.*

In 1963, a collection of priceless Bronze Age rings, bracelets, coronets, and bowls of gold was discovered in a dry Villena riverbed. Peruse the collection in the *ayuntamiento* (town hall).

Bocairent

15 *27 km (17 mi) northeast of Villena.*

Heading up the N340 from Villena, find time to stop in Bocairent: the **Museo Parroquial** (Parish Museum; ✉ Abadía, 38 ☎ 962/350062) has paintings by Juan de Juanes, who died here in 1579, along with works by Francisco Ribalta and Joaquín Sorolla.

Guadalest

16 *36 km (22 mi) east of Alcoy.*

Guadalest is an old, originally Moorish town. Perched atop a crag within the walls of a ruined castle, it conquers the steep terrain with tiny, stepped streets. Continue as far as Callosa, turn left toward Tarbena, and brave a dip at the foot of the icy **Cascada de El Algar** (El Algar Falls). The nearby village of **Tarbena,** known for its sausages, has spectacular rocky-mountain scenery.

ALICANTE, ELCHE & ORIHUELA

Alicante seems to shimmer with the kind of light for which the Mediterranean is famous, while inland Elche's palm forest shades its ancient treasures from the summer heat. Orihuela's twisting back streets tunnel through old Moorish neighborhoods.

Alicante

17 *82 km (51 mi) northeast of Murcia, 183 km (113 mi) south of Valencia by the coast road, 42 km (26 mi) south of Benidorm, 55 km (34 mi) south of Alcoy.*

A crossroads for inland and coastal routes, Alicante has always been known for its luminous skies. The Greeks called it Akra Leuka (White Summit); the Romans named it Lucentum (City of Light). The city is dominated by the Castillo de Santa Bárbara, set on a rocky peak, but its immediate pride is its grand **Explanada,** lined with date palms. Begin your walk at the tourist office on the arcaded **Plaza de Ayuntamiento.** Look inside the baroque town hall and ask gate officials for permission to explore the ornate halls and rococo chapel on the first floor. Follow the arched passage through the ayuntamiento to Plaza Santísima Faz, a pedestrian square packed with cafés and restaurants.

From Plaza Santísima Faz, walk down the busy, pedestrian Calle Mayor and take your first right to reach the **Cathedral of San Nicolás de Bari,** built on the site of a former mosque. The cathedral has both an austere Renaissance facade in the style of Herrera (of Escorial fame) and a lavish baroque side chapel. ✉ *Pl. del Abad Penalva 1* ☎ *965/212662* ⏲ *Open for mass only.*

The **Museo de la Asegurada** is the oldest civil edifice in Alicante. Built as a town granary in 1685, it has works by Picasso, Miró, Braque, Tàpies, Hockney, and Rauschenberg. ✉ *C. Mayor at C. Villavieja* ☎ *965/*

140768 🎫 *Free* ⏲ *Oct.–Apr., Tues.–Sat. 10–2 and 4–8; May–Sept., Tues.–Sat. 10–2 and 5–9, Sun. 10:30–2:30.*

The church of **Santa María** (✉ Place de Santa Maria), across from the Museo de la Asegurada, has a rich baroque facade. From here, it's a short walk down steps, then left along the back of Playa Postiguet, to the foot of Mt. Benacantil (700 ft) and the elevator to the castle.

★ Originally built as a Carthaginian fortress around 3 BC, the **Castillo de Santa Bárbara** was modified for numerous wars. From here you have a spectacular bird's-eye view of the city. Within the castle walls, a small museum displays objects associated with the annual St. John's Day bonfires on midsummer's eve. Note that you'll have to traverse a boardwalk to reach the elevator. ✉ *Playa del Postiguet* ☎ *965/263131* 🎫 *Castle €2.40, museum free* ⏲ *Castle and elevator Sun.–Fri. 10–7 (last elevator ride 6:30); museum, spring–fall Sun.–Fri. 9–7:30.*

Where to Stay & Eat

$$–$$$ ✕ **Dársena.** This old Alicante standard is in the Marina Deportiva, a stretch of harbor front lined with restaurants and cafés. Mediterranean rice dishes (more than 140 options) are the house specialty, but pay close attention to the outstanding fish specials, which vary depending on the season and the luck of the local fishermen. Highlights include paella *con bogavante* (with lobster) and *arroz de caracoles y calamares* (short-grain rice with escargots and calamari). ✉ *Marina Deportiva–Muelle 6* ☎ *965/207589* 💳 *AE, DC, MC, V.*

$$ ✕🏨 **Eurhotel Abba.** This modern hotel 300 yards from Alicante's port can satisfy all your practical needs. Its proximity to the train and bus stations makes it fairly handy. Rates are often reduced by as much as half on weekends. The on-site restaurant, open weekdays, does a thriving business in Mediterranean fish and meat dishes. Try the *merluza con langostinos a la sidra* (hake and crayfish cooked in cider) or the *menestra de verdura a la bilbaína* (Basque-style vegetable soup). ✉ *C. Pintor Lorenzo Casanova 33, 03003* ☎ *965/130440* 📠 *965/928323* 🌐 *www.abbahoteles.com* 🛏 *117 rooms* 👍 *Restaurant, cafeteria, bar, meeting rooms, parking (fee)* 💳 *AE, DC, MC, V.*

$$$ 🏨 **Meliá Alicante.** Stay here if you want both comfort and proximity to the sea—this behemoth stands on a reclaimed peninsula that juts into the sea right near the city center. Guest rooms are bright and modern, with sweeping views of the beaches and marina. Downstairs, the lobby is a shrine to postmodernism, with cool marble floors and low black tables. ✉ *Playa del Postiguet, 03001* ☎ *965/205000* 📠 *965/204756* 🌐 *www.meliaalicante.solmelia.com* 🛏 *545 rooms* 👍 *Restaurant, cable TV with movies, pool, piano bar, meeting rooms, car rental* 💳 *AE, DC, MC, V.*

¢–$ 🏨 **Hostal Les Monges Palace.** In a restored 18th-century building behind the ayuntamiento, this family-run pension has an ideal location in Alicante's central old quarter. Rooms are basic but comfortable, with cable TV and data ports. Pleasure seekers should go for the special Japanese Suite (*suite japonés*), equipped with hot tub and sauna. ✉ *C. San Agustín 4, 03002* ☎ *965/215046* 📠 *965/140120* 🌐 *www.lesmonges.net* 🛏 *18 rooms* 👍 *In-room data ports, some in-room hot tubs, parking (fee)* 💳 *MC, V.*

Nightlife & the Arts

Roughish bars populate the streets behind the ayuntamiento. In summer, the liveliest places are along the water, on the Ruta del Puerto and Ruta de la Madera. Among the slicker pubs and discos is **Z-Club** (✉ Calle San Fernando s/n), where Alicante twentysomethings groove to house and techno. Thirtysomething couples gather at **Paseíto** (✉ C. Jorge Juan 18).

Shopping

Local **crafts** include basketwork, embroidery, leatherwork, and weaving, each specific to a single town or village. You'll find these in the major resorts, though their prices may be inflated. The most satisfying places to shop are often neighborhood markets, so inquire about market days. For **ceramics** travel to the town of Agost, 20 km (12 mi) inland from Alicante. Potters here make jugs and pitchers from the local white clay, whose porosity is ideal for keeping liquids cool. You're bound to see a few potters at work in Agost, and you can learn more about their craft, and, more to the point, shop for ceramics at the **Museo de Alfarería** (Pottery Museum). ✉ *Teuleria 11* ☎ *965/691199* 🎫 *€1.50* ⏲ *Sept.–May, Tues.–Sat. 10–2 and 5–8; June–Aug., Tues.–Sun. 11–2 and 5–9.*

Elche

18 *24 km (15 mi) southwest of Alicante, 34 km (21 mi) northeast of Orihuela, 58 km (36 mi) northeast of Murcia.*

If Alicante is torrid in summer, Elche is even hotter. Fortunately, the latter is surrounded by the largest palm forest in Europe, granting occasional escape from the worst of the heat. The Moors first planted the palms for dates, Europe's most reliable crop, and the trees still produce these as well as yellow fronds. (Throughout Spain, the fronds are blessed on Palm Sunday and hung on balconies to ward off evil during the coming year.) Colonized by ancient Rome, Elche was later ruled by the Moors for 500 years. The remarkable stone bust known as *La Dama de Elche,* one of the earliest examples of Iberian sculpture (now in Madrid's Museum of Archaeology), was discovered here in 1897.

In the **Jardín del Huerto del Cura,** a lush botanical garden and palm grove across from the Hotel Huerto del Cura, vibrantly colored flowers grow beneath magnificent palms. ✉ *Porta de la Morera* ☎ *965/451936* 🎫 *€4* ⏲ *Apr.–Sept., daily 9–8:30; Oct.–Mar., daily 9–6.*

The traditional Misteri (Mystery Play), performed on the Feast of the Assumption, August 14 and 15, draws crowds to the **Basilica de Santa María**; performances are spectacular, with a platform bearing the Virgin Mary and guitar-playing angels winched 150 ft up into the church's dome. ⏲ *Daily 7–1:30 and 5:30–9.*

Where to Stay & Eat

★ $$ ✕🏨 **Huerto del Cura.** A subtropical location and a large, private garden in Elche's palm grove make this modern hotel-in-the-spirit-of-a-parador perfect for relaxation. The bedrooms are in bungalow huts—gloomy, due to their shady location, but tastefully decorated. The palm-ringed swimming pool looks like something you'd hope to find in the Seychelles. The main building has the excellent restaurant Els Capellans, which serves regional rice and fish dishes. ✉ *Porta de la Morera 14, 03203* ☎ *966/610011* 📠 *965/421910* 🌐 *www.huertodelcura.com* *81 rooms, 4 suites* *Restaurant, cafeteria, cable TV with movies, putting green, tennis court, pool, gym, sauna, bar* 💳 *AE, DC, MC, V.*

Orihuela

19 *24 km (15 mi) northeast of Murcia, 34 km (21 mi) southwest of Elche, 29 km (18 mi) inland from Guardamar del Segura.*

Palm and orange groves dominate the southeastern countryside as far as Orihuela, on the banks of the Segura—another excuse to linger on the N340 south. The town's air of fading grandeur stems from its past life as the capital of Murcia (until the Reconquest). Stroll through Orihuela's winding streets and visit the Gothic cathedral of **El Salvador** to see its rare, spiral vaulting. The adjoining **museum** has paintings by Velázquez and Ribera. ✉ *C. Ballesteros Villanueva* ☎ *966/744089.*

FROM MADRID TO MURCIA

To get the feel of Don Quijote country, drive to Murcia through Albacete and the flat, arid La Mancha region. During this three- to four-hour drive, take in the paradors at Alarcón and Albacete, the village promontory of Chinchilla de Monte Aragón, and the Roman town of Cieza.

Albacete

20 *172 km (107 mi) northwest of Alicante, 146 km (91 mi) northwest of Murcia, 183 km (114 mi) southwest of Valencia.*

In the Spanish version of Trivial Pursuit, Albacete is the answer to the question "Which town is known as the New York City of La Mancha?" Apart from being the largest town in the province, with a population of 160,000, Albacete bears no resemblance to Gotham whatsoever and is better characterized as an agricultural center for wine and saffron. The **Museo Arqueológico** has Roman mosaics, ivory dolls, and Paleolithic objects. ✉ *Parque Abelardo Sánchez,* ☎ *967/228307* *€1.30* *Tues.–Sat. 10–2 and 4:30–7, Sun. 9–2.*

Where to Stay & Eat

★ $$ **Parador de Albacete.** Set back from the highway, this whitewashed, ranchlike *manchego*-style parador has a rustic, wood-beam interior and cozy, comfortable bedrooms. The restaurant serves local cuisine; you can never go wrong with the *chuletas de cordero* (lamb chops grilled with garlic). ✉ *N301, Km 251, Apdo. 384, 02000* ☎ *967/245321* *967/243271* *www.parador.es* *70 rooms* *Restaurant, cafeteria, 2 tennis courts, pool, bar* *AE, DC, MC, V.*

Chinchilla de Monte Aragón

21 *12 km (7 mi) east of Albacete.*

If you detour slightly en route to Alicante, you'll soon see the imposing 15th-century castle of Chinchilla de Monte Aragón to your left and, if the day is clear, the distant Sierra de Alcaraz rising to nearly 6,000 ft to the south. Chinchilla is a fine old pottery town.

en route

Once you're back on the N301 (assuming you take the Alicante detour), most of the 146 km (91 mi) to Murcia runs adjacent to the uplands of La Mancha, where Don Quijote adventured in Cervantes's famous novel. Across the border into Murcia and through the Roman town of Cieza, dominated by its feudal castle, the road drops some 2,700 ft to farmland before reaching the provincial capital.

MURCIA TO ALMERÍA

Soon after Orihuela, you'll enter the province of Murcia, where the N340 follows the course of the Segura, though the foothills of the Sierra de Carrascoy often intervene. This is the driest part of Spain, and the least visited. Tawny hills are punctuated by stretches of fertile huerta, moistened by life-giving rivers whose waters irrigate three crops in succession a year. Rich metal deposits supply a busy mining industry. Valenciano gives way to the Andalusian accent.

Murcia

22 *82 km (51 mi) southwest of Alicante, 146 km (91 mi) southeast of Albacete, 219 km (136 mi) northeast of Almería.*

A provincial capital and university town of more than 300,000, Murcia was first settled by Romans; later, in the 8th century, the conquering Moors used Roman bricks to build the city proper. The result was reconquered and annexed to the crown of Castile in 1243. The Murcian dialect contains many Arabic words, and many Murcians clearly reveal Moorish ancestry.

★ Murcia's **cathedral** is a masterpiece of eclectic architecture. Begun in the 14th century, it received its magnificent facade—considered one of Spain's fullest expressions of the Churrigueresque style—as late as 1737; the 19th-century English traveler Richard Ford described it as "rising in compartments, like a drawn out telescope." The 15th century brought the Gothic **Door of the Apostles** and, inside, the splendid chapel of **Los Vélez,** with a beautiful, star-shape stone vault. Carvings by the 18th-century Murcian sculptor Francisco Salzillo were added later. Pop into the **museum,** off the north transept, to see Salzillo's polychrome-wood sculpture of the penitent St. Jerome. The 312-ft **bell tower,** built between 1521 and 1792, is undergoing repairs and is sometimes closed to the public. ☎ *968/216344* 🎫 *€1.20* ⏲ *Daily 10–1 and 5–8 (4–7 in winter).*

Wander north on the pedestrian shopping street Calle Trapería and you'll soon reach the 19th-century **Casino,** which retains the aura of a British gentleman's club. The facade is a mixture of classical and modern styles; the inside, inspired by the Alhambra in Granada, has a *patio arabe* (Moorish courtyard). Despite the name, this has never been a gambling center—Murcians (that is, Murcian men) come to read the newspaper and play billiards. ✉ *C. Trapería.*

The **Museo Salzillo,** out by the bus station, has the main collection of Francisco Salzillo's disturbingly realistic polychrome *pasos* (carvings), carried in processions every Easter. ✉ *Plaza San Agustín* ☎ *968/291893* 🎫 *€3* ⏲ *Tues.–Sat. 9:30–1 and 4–7, Sun. 11–1.*

Where to Stay & Eat

$$–$$$ ✕ **Hispano.** For a typically Spanish brand of rusticity, look no further. A well-known Murcian family of restaurateurs-hoteliers named Abellán opened the Hispano back in 1979, and it remains extremely popular for Murcian and nouvelle cuisine, and traditional fare such as paella and *solomillo* (veal). ✉ *Arquitecto Cerdá 3* ☎ *968/216152* 💳 *AE, DC, MC, V* ⏲ *Closed Sun. July–Aug.*

★ $$$ ✕🏨 **Rincón de Pepe.** In the center of the old town, 50 yards from the cathedral's apse, this hotel combines comfort and hospitality. Guest rooms are bright and modern, and the lobby and reception rooms have cool marble floors. The very fine restaurant serves a good selection of *tapeo murciano,* samples of favorite Murcian dishes. Chef Francisco Gonzáles uses produce from the hotel's own organic farm, plus fish from the nearby Mar Menor and lamb from Segura. Highlights on the extensive menu include *cordero segureño asado a la murciana* (local lamb roasted Murcian-style). ✉ *Apóstoles 34, 30002* ☎ *968/212239* 📠 *968/221744* 🌐 *www.nh-hoteles.com* *148 rooms* *Restaurant, cable TV with movies, parking (fee)* 💳 *AE, DC, MC, V* ⏲ *No dinner Sun.*

¢–$ 🏨 **Hispano 1.** Rooms at this centrally located budget hotel are bright and airy, and the public sitting area is large and tasteful. Ask for an exterior room, with a view of the pedestrian street below. ✉ *Trapería 8–10,*

30001 ☎ 968/216152 📠 968/216859 ⇐ 45 rooms, 35 with bath ♁ Parking (fee); no a/c, no room TVs ▭ AE, DC, MC, V.

Nightlife

Murcia is a university town, which in Spain guarantees a good time, but this place has some creative energy that many other cities lack. Bars come and go, but you'll always find action on both edges of the university, especially **Calle Doctor Fleming.** West of campus, a well-dressed young set gathers on the streets in front of the Teatro Romea; **Los Claveles** (✉ C. Alfaro 10) is the center of action in this zone. It's closed Sunday–Tuesday. When the university bars close, there's always the main disco in the city center, **Dance Club** (✉ Centrofama, C. Puerta Nueva s/n).

Cartagena

23 *48 km (29 mi) south of Murcia.*

Founded in the 3rd century BC by the Carthaginians, this is Spain's principal naval base. From Cartagena you have easy access to the resort La Manga del Mar Menor and the twisty, scenic 100-km (62-mi) drive along the N332 to the start of the Costa de Almería.

La Manga del Mar Menor

24 *45 km (28 mi) southeast of Murcia.*

Because it's warmer, saltier, and higher in iodine than the Mediterranean, La Manga del Mar Menor—which forms Europe's largest saltwater lake (170 square km [105 square mi])—is well known as a therapeutic health resort for rheumatism patients. The Manga ("sleeve") itself is a 21-km (13-mi) spit of sand averaging some 990 ft wide and enclosing the Mar Menor (Smaller Sea), a famously flat, calm expanse of shallow water about 20 ft deep. Four canals, called *golas,* connect the Mar Menor with the Mediterranean. The Manga has 42 km (26 mi) of immense, sandy beaches on both the Mediterranean and the Mar Menor sides, allowing bathers to choose more or less exposed locations and warmer or colder water according to season and weather. La Manga Club-Hotel claims to be Europe's most complete sports hotel.

Where to Stay

$$$$ ▣ **Hyatt Regency La Manga.** Golf pervades this superbly situated luxury clubhouse-hotel, just above the Mar Menor. For nongolfers, the resort has no fewer than 22 tennis courts and a regulation cricket pitch, the latter of which may account for the surfeit of British-registered Range Rovers in the parking lot. You can also rent apartments or villas. ✉ *Los Belones, 30385 Murcia ☎ 968/331234 📠 968/331235 🌐 www.lamanga.hyatt.com ⇐ 192 rooms ♁ 3 restaurants, cable TV with movies, 3 golf courses, 22 tennis courts, pool, hot tub, sauna, horseback riding, squash, 2 bars ▭ AE, DC, MC, V.*

Sports & the Outdoors

Notable for its absence of waves of any kind, the Mar Menor is a serious sailing destination. Various schools offer windsurfing, waterskiing, catamaran sailing, and other marine diversions.

Lorca

★ 25 *62 km (39 mi) southwest of Murcia, 158 km (98 mi) northeast of Almería, 37 km (23 mi) inland from the Mediterranean at Águilas.*

Leave the highway for a glimpse of Lorca, an old market town and the scene of some of Spain's most colorful Holy Week celebrations. The Casa de los Guevara, on Lope Gisbert, houses the tourist office; from here head down Alamo to the elegant **Plaza de España,** ringed by rich baroque buildings, including the ayuntamiento, law courts, and Colegiata (collegiate church). Follow signs from the plaza up to the **castle.**

Where to Eat

★ $ ✕ **Cándido.** Just outside the town center, this rustic, relaxed, old-fashioned restaurant has been going strong on home cooking for more than half a century. A happy mix of Lorcans and travelers partake of the food, which is locally inspired; try the classic *trigo con conejo y caracoles* (wheat with rabbit and snails). ✉ *Santo Domingo 13* ☎ *968/466907* ▭ *MC, V* ⊙ *No dinner Sun.*

Mojácar

㉖ *93 km (58 mi) northeast of Almería, 73 km (45 mi) southeast of Puerto Lumbreras, 135 km (83 mi) southwest of Murcia.*

A few miles inland, on a hillside overlooking the sea, Mojácar is a cluster of whitewashed cubist houses attesting to the town's Moorish past. In the 1960s, painters and writers gravitated to Mojácar's cliff-dwelling simplicity in search of inspiration, creating a movement that became known as the *Movimiento Indaliano,* named for the *Indalo,* an anthropomorphic protective deity associated with Almería (and especially with Mojácar) since prehistoric times. The nearby beaches and the town's reflective charm make Mojácar a prime destination in this refreshingly undeveloped corner of Spain. The most attractive part of the Almerían coast lies south of here.

Where to Stay & Eat

$–$$ ✕ **El Palacio de Mojácar.** In an old, white Mojácar house with exposed beams and fireplace, this restaurant specializes in, well, good food. The friendly chef-owner doesn't have a large menu, but whatever he serves tends to be inventive and generally has an international twist. ✉ *Pl. del Cano* ☎ *950/472846* ▭ *AE, MC, V* ⊙ *Closed Thurs. and Nov.–Feb.*

★ $$ 🏨 **Parador de Mojácar.** If you'd rather sleep by the sea than in the old town, this rambling, modern parador is the best option in Mojácar. The public rooms are some of the most spacious and tasteful in Spain. Large, open-plan fireplaces add a rustic element. Guest rooms are bright, with Castilian furniture. ✉ *Ctra. de Garrucha Carboneras, 04638* ☎ *950/478250* 📠 *950/478183* 🌐 *www.parador.es* *98 rooms* *Restaurant, tennis court, pool, bar, meeting room* ▭ *AE, DC, MC, V.*

$–$$ 🏨 **El Moresco.** Up in the village itself, El Moresco has a stunning position and tasteful country feel, but it's often beset by large tour groups. ✉ *Av. D'encamp 15, 04638* ☎ *950/478025* 📠 *950/478262* 🌐 *www.arturocantoblanco.com* *147 rooms* *Restaurant, pool, bar, meeting room; no a/c in some rooms* ▭ *AE, DC, MC, V.*

San José & the Cabo de Gata Nature Reserve

㉗ *40 km (25 mi) east of Almería, 86 km (53 mi) south of Mojácar.*

San José is a small, relaxed village perched over its eponymous bay. As yet out of developers' clutches—it has one tiny hotel, a handful of cheap *hostales,* and a campground—the town is well placed to take advantage of the all-but-deserted beaches nearby. Just south of San Jose is the **Parque Natural Marítimo y Terrestre Cabo de Gata–Níjar** (nature reserve; ✉ road from Almería to Cabo de Gata, Km 6 ☎📠 950/160435). Birds are the main attraction; the park is home to several species proper to Africa, including the *camachuelo trompetero,* which is not found anywhere else outside Africa. The **Centro Las Amuladeras visitor center,** at the park entrance, has an exhibit and information on the region. For beach action, follow signs south to the **Playa Los Genoveses** and **Playa Monsul.** A dirt track follows the coast around the spectacular cape, eventually linking up with the N332 to Almería.

Where to Stay

★ $$ **Cortijo El Sotillo.** For access to the beautifully rugged coast toward Cabo de Gata, establish temporary headquarters in this restored 18th-century country estate at the very entrance to San José. Many people come here just to take advantage of modern equestrian facilities and the myriad riding trails that run through the Cabo de Gata Nature Reserve. *Entrada de San José, 04118 950/611100 950/611105 www.hotelsotillo.com 17 rooms, 3 suites Restaurant, tennis court, pool, archery, billiards, horseback riding, Ping-Pong AE, MC, V.*

Almería

28 *219 km (136 mi) southwest of Murcia, 183 km (114 mi) east of Málaga.*

Warmed by the sunniest climate in Andalusia, Almería is a youthful Mediterranean city, basking in sweeping views of the sea from its coastal perch. Almería is also a capital of the grape industry, thanks to its wonderfully mild climate in spring and fall. Rimmed by tree-lined boulevards dotted with landscaped squares, the city's core is still a maze of narrow, winding alleys formed by flat-roof, distinctly Mudéjar houses. Though now surrounded by modern apartment blocks, these dazzling-white older homes give Almería an Andalusian flavor. Dominating the city is its **Alcazaba** (fortress), built by Caliph Abd ar-Rahman I and provided with a bell tower by Carlos III. From here you have sweeping views of the port and city. Among the ruins of the fortress, damaged by earthquakes in 1522 and 1560, are landscaped gardens of rock flowers and cacti. *C. Almanzor 950/271617 €1.50; free for EU citizens Apr.–Oct., Tues.–Sun. 10–8; Nov.–Mar., Tues.–Sun. 9–6:30.*

Below the Alcazaba stands the **cathedral,** whose buttressed towers make it look like a castle. The overall design is Gothic, with some classical touches around the doors; the defenses were built to fend off frequent raids by Barbary pirates in the 16th century. *€2 Weekdays 10:30–4:30, Sat. 10–1.*

If you're a film devotee and want to see where spaghetti westerns have long been shot, drive 24 km (15 mi) north on the N340 to **Mini Hollywood,** a film set open to the public when filming is not in progress. *950/365236 €16 Tues.–Sun. 10–7.*

Where to Stay & Eat

$$ **Veracruz.** In Almería's beach barrio, El Zapillo, this justly popular seafood restaurant has its own storage tank for oysters, clams, prawns, and lobsters. The specialty is *parillada de pescado*, a mixed grill of everything that swims in the Mediterranean. *Av. Cabo de Gata 119 950/251220 AE, MC, V.*

$–$$ **Valentin.** This central spot serves fine regional specialties. *Cazuela de rape* (monkfish baked in a sauce of almonds and pine nuts) is a typical entrée. The surroundings are Andalusian: white walls, wood, and glass. Valentin is popular, so come on the early side (around 9) to get a table. *Tenor Iribarne 7 950/264475 AE, MC, V Closed Mon.*

$$ **Torreluz III.** Value is the overriding attraction of this comfortable yet elegant modern hotel. Guest rooms are slick and bright, with the kind of installations for which you'd expect to pay more. Its restaurant, Torreluz Mediterráneo, is famous among locals for its robust portions and brisk lunchtime service. It serves an excellent cross section of south-

eastern fare—try the *zarzuela de marisco a la marinera* (mixed seafood in a zesty red marinade). ✉ *Plaza Flores 1, 04001* ☎ *950/234399* 📠 *950/281428* 🌐 *www.torreluz.com* *94 rooms* *2 restaurants, cafeteria, bar* *AE, DC, MC, V.*

$$–$$$ **Gran Hotel Almería.** These guest rooms frame their fine views over Almería's harbor with brightly painted walls and chintz fabrics. The huge, marble reception rooms evoke the hotel's golden age, when it hosted spaghetti-western film directors. ✉ *Av. Reina Regente 8, 04001* ☎ *950/238011* 📠 *950/270691* 🌐 *www.granhotelalmeria.com* *108 rooms* *Restaurant, pool, bar* *AE, DC, MC, V.*

¢ **Hostal Bristol.** One block east of the Puerta de Purchena, this centrally located, family-friendly hostal has inexpensive, basic rooms. Half of them overlook the bustling Plaza San Sebastián. ✉ *Plaza San Sebastián, 8, 04003* ☎📠 *950/231595* *30 rooms* *Some pets allowed* *MC, V.*

¢ **Hostal Sevilla.** If you want inexpensive comfort, look no further. In the labyrinth of the old town, you'll find healthy doses of Andalusian style and charm. The rooms vary; those on the street side have small terraces, while those on the quiet interior look over the courtyards and rooftops of the old town. All have ceramic-tile floors. ✉ *Granada 25, 04001* ☎📠 *950/230009* *37 rooms* *MC, V.*

Nightlife & the Arts

Nocturnal action centers on **Plaza Flores,** moving down to the beach in summer. In town, try the small **Cajón de Sastre** (✉ Plaza Marques de Heredia 8) for typical *copas* (libations). For an ancient Greek experience minus the toga, look into **Pub Minerva** (✉ C. Marchales 44). **El Café del Irlandés** (✉ C. General Segura 15) offers darts and hearty beers in an Irish environment. **Alabama** (✉ C. Pablo Picasso 22) plays a blend of country and classic rock.

Shopping

The towns of Biar, Chinchilla, and Níjar, all north of Almería, are known for ceramics. Among the best buys in antiques, if you can find them at about €6 each, are azulejos. Look for copper and brass, too, especially in the form of art deco oil lamps. For quality, more-expensive antiques, visit **Galeria Real** (✉ C. Real 73 ☎ 950/233566).

THE SOUTHEAST A TO Z

To research prices, get advice from other travelers, and book travel arrangements, visit www.fodors.com.

AIR TRAVEL

There are four airports: Valencia, Alicante, San Javier (for Mar Menor and Murcia), and Almería.

Airport Information **Aeropuerto de Valencia** ☎ 961/598500. **Alicante** ✉ El Altet, 12 km [7 mi] south of town ☎ 96/691–9000. **Almería** ✉ Carretera de Níjar, Km 9, 8 km [5 mi] east of town ☎ 950/213700. **San Javier** ✉ Mar Menor north shore, off N332 ☎ 968/570073.

CARRIERS Iberia has the most flights to this part of Spain.

Iberia ☎ 902/400500.

BOAT & FERRY TRAVEL

From Denia, Balearia offers two ferry services to Ibiza and Palma de Mallorca; the fast ferry departs at 5 PM Monday through Saturday, arriving in Ibiza town at 7 PM and in Palma at 10 PM. The overnight ferry departs at 9 PM daily, arriving on Ibiza's west coast, in the town of Sant Antoni, at around 12:30 PM and reaching Palma at around 6 PM. Note that the fast ferry usually doesn't sail when the weather is inclement, so in the winter it's best to call ahead. From Almería, Trasmediterránea sails to Melilla, a Spanish outpost on the Moroccan coast, at 11 PM Monday–Saturday. In summer you can cross from either Alicante or Santa Pola to the tiny island of Tabarca. Boats leave Benidorm hourly for the outcrop Isla de Benidorm; the round-trip fare is €9.

Boat & Ferry Information **Alicante** ☎ 96/521-6396. **Balearia** ✉ Puerto de Denia ☎ 96/642-8600 🌐 www.balearia.com. **Santa Pola** ☎ 96/541-1113. **Trasmediterránea** ☎ 902/454645 🌐 www.trasmediterranea.es.

BUS TRAVEL

Private companies run buses down the coast and from Madrid to Valencia, Benidorm, Alicante, Murcia, Mar Menor, and Almería.

Bus Stations **Almería** ✉ Plaza Barcelona ☎ 950/210029. **Alicante** ✉ Av. Portugal ☎ 96/513-0700. **Murcia** ✉ Plaza San Andrés, west of town ☎ 968/292211.

CAR RENTALS

You'll find numerous car-rental companies, from all the major firms to local operations, along the coast, particularly in the larger cities such as Denia, Benidorm, and Alicante. Always shop around for the best price. Note, however, that you'll pay less if you reserve a rental car before you leave home. Reservations are generally only necessary during the Christmas and Easter holidays.

Agencies **Europa Rent-a-Car** ✉ Av. de la Comunidad Valenciana 10, Benidorm ☎ 96/6802902 🌐 www.europa-rentacar.es ✉ Aeropuerto de Alicante ☎ 96/5683362. **Primercars** ✉ Av. Aguilera 40, Alicante ☎ 96/5982194.

CAR TRAVEL

The *autopista* (toll highway) A7 from Barcelona runs through Valencia and Alicante as far as Murcia. Tolls, though quite high, are often worth it for the time saved, as well as the safe driving conditions. The other main links with the region are the N111 from Madrid to Valencia and the N301 from Madrid to Murcia via Albacete.

Avoid coastal roads in summer, as the crowds will slow you down. An exception is the road that hugs the Almerían coast—the varied beach landscapes and the views straight down to the water from sheer rocky cliffs are worth the extra time.

CONSULATES

The U.K. and U.S. consulates are open weekday mornings only.

United Kingdom **Alicante** ✉ Pl. Calvo Sotelo ☎ 96/521-6022.

United States **Valencia** ✉ C. de la Paz 6, 3rd floor ☎ 96/351-6973.

EMERGENCIES

In case of an emergency, dial 091 for the police, or call an ambulance or local hospital.

Pharmacies in each town take turns staying open 24 hours. All pharmacies display the address of the *farmacia de guardia,* the one on duty that night.

Ambulance ☎ 96/511-4676 in Alicante, 968/218893 in Murcia. **General emergencies** ☎ 091. **Cruz Roja** (Red Cross) ☎ 96/5252525 in Alicante. **Hospital del SVS** ☎ 965/938300 in Alicante. **Hospital La Arrixaca** ☎ 112 in Murcia. **Hospital Torrecárdenas** ☎ 950/212100 in Almería.

LODGING

APARTMENT & VILLA OR HOUSE RENTALS

The Southeast is liberally sprinkled with apartments, villas, and farmhouses (called *casas rurales*) that you can rent for a weekend, a week, or longer. Accommodations range from roomy farmhouses with wood-beam ceilings to basic, self-catering apartments with beach views.

Local Agents **Albir Confort Holidays** ✉ Av. Albir 36, Albir ☎ 96/6865202. **Fincas de Arena** ✉ Av. Europa 23, Benidorm ☎ 96/5852512 🌐 www.fincasarena.com.

SPORTS & THE OUTDOORS

GOLF Be sure to reserve tee times in advance. Expect to pay €48–€90 for 18 holes, €24–€60 for 9. Club de Golf Don Cayo has 9 holes. Villa Martín and Almerimar have 18 holes, and La Manga Club packs two 18-hole courses.

Club de Golf Don Cayo ✉ Conde de Altea 49, Altea ☎ 96/584-8046. **Campo de Golf Villa Martín** ✉ Plaza Comercial de Villa Martín, Torrevieja ☎ 96/676-5160. **Golf Almerimar** ✉ Almerimar, El Ejido ☎ 950/497454. **La Manga Club** ✉ Los Belones ☎ 968/331234 🌐 www.lamanga.hyatt.com.

TAXIS

In the main towns, taxis can be hailed on the street. Alternately, ask for the nearest taxi stand (*parada de taxi*). Taxis use meters to calculate the fare. Drivers may charge separate fees for luggage.

Taxi Companies **Radio Taxi** ☎ 96/5252511 in Benidorm. **Cooperativa de Taxis** ☎ 965/786565 in Denia.

TOURS

Alicante's ayuntamiento and travel agencies arrange tours of the city and bus and train tours to Guadalest, the Algar waterfalls, Benidorm, the Peñón de Ifach (Calpe), and Elche. In Benidorm, large hotels arrange similar excursions. Elche's town hall organizes tours of the city and environs. From Almería, Viajes Alborán runs tours of the city and region. In Murcia, contact Alquibla for city and regional tours. Alicante's town hall also runs tours to Jijona, where you can visit one of the famous turrón factories before seeing the amazing stalactites and stalagmites at the Cuevas de Canalobre (Canalobre Caves).

Alicante ayuntamiento ✉ Plaza del Ayuntamiento ☎ 96/514-9280 🌐 www.comunitat-valenciana.com. **Alquibla** ✉ González Adalid 13, Murcia ☎ 968/221219. **Elche ayuntamiento** ✉ Plaça de Baix ☎ 96/665-8000 🌐 www.ayto-elche.es. **Viajes Alborán** ✉ Reina Regente 1, Almería ☎ 950/237477.

TRAIN TRAVEL

RENFE trains connect the region's chief cities. The local FGV line runs along the Costa Blanca from Denia to Alicante. Alicante has a RENFE station and a separate RENFE booking office; the FGV station is at the far end of Playa Postiguet, plied by buses C1 and C2 from downtown. Murcia's RENFE station is some way out, but there's a RENFE office in town. Almería's train station is on Plaza de la Estación.

Train Information **RENFE** ☎ 902/240202 🌐 www.renfe.es/ingles. **RENFE booking office** Alicante ✉ Explanada de España 1 ☎ 96/521-1303 ✉ Murcia ✉ Barrionuevo ☎ 968/212842.

Train Stations **Alicante-FGV** ✉ Av. Villajoyosa ☎ 96/526-2731. **Alicante-RENFE** ✉ Av. Salamanca ☎ 96/522-6840. **Almería** ☎ 950/251135. **Murcia** ✉ Industria ☎ 968/252154.

TRAVEL AGENCIES

Viajes Barceló ✉ San Telmo 9, Alicante ☎ 971/771700 🌐 www.barcelo.com ✉ Gerona, Edificio Pinos, Benidorm ☎ 971/771700 🌐 www.barcelo.com. **Viajes Hispania** ✉ Urbanización Las Sirenas 3, La Manga del Mar Menor ☎ 968/564161.

VISITOR INFORMATION

Regional Tourist Offices **Alicante** ✉ Rambla de Mendez Nuñez 23 ☎ 96/520-0000 🌐 www.comunitat-valenciana.com. **Almería** ✉ Parque Nicolás Salmerón ☎ 950/274355 🌐 www.andalucia.org. **Murcia** ✉ Plaza Julian Romea 4 ☎ 902/101070 🌐 www.

murcia-tourismo.com. **Valencia** ✉ Plaza Ayuntamiento 1 ☎ 963/510417 ✉ Estación RENFE, Játiva 24 ☎ no phone.

Local Tourist Offices **Albacete** ✉ Virrey Morcillo 1 ☎ 967/580522 🌐 www.jccm.es. **Alcoy** ✉ C. San Lorenzo 2 ☎ 965/537155. **Alicante** ✉ Av. Portugal 17 ☎ 96/592-9802 🌐 www.costablanca.org. **Benidorm** ✉ Av. Martínez Alejos 166 ☎ 96/585-3224 🌐 www.benidorm.org. **Calpe** ✉ Av. Ejércitos Españoles s/n ☎ 96/583-1250. **Cartagena** ✉ Plaza Almirante Bastarreche ☎ 968/506483. **Denia** ✉ Plaza Oculista Builges 9 ☎ 96/642-2367 🌐 www.denia.net. **Elche** ✉ Parque Municipal ☎ 96/545-3831 or 96/545-2747 🌐 www.ayto-elche.es. **Gandía** ✉ Marqués de Campo s/n ☎ 96/287-7788 🌐 www.gandia.org. **Jávea** ✉ Plaza Almirante Bastarreche 24 ☎ 96/646-0605 🌐 www.comunitat-valenciana.com. **Lorca** ✉ López Gisbert ☎ 968/466157. **Orihuela** ✉ Francisco Díez 25 ☎ 96/530-2747. **Santa Pola** ✉ Plaza Diputación ☎ 96/669-2276 🌐 www.costablanca.org. **Torrevieja** ✉ Costera del Mar s/n ☎ 96/570-3433. **Xátiva** ✉ Alameda Jaume I 50 ☎ 96/227-3346.

THE BALEARIC ISLANDS

FODOR'S CHOICE

La Residencia manor house, Deià, Majorca
Palma de Mallorca's Cathedral, Majorca

HIGHLY RECOMMENDED

RESTAURANTS

Ca Na Joana, Ibiza Town
C'as Pagès, Santa Eulàlia des Riu, Ibiza
Gregal, Mahón, Minorca
Koldo Royo, Palma de Mallorca, Majorca
Molí d'es Reco, Monte Toro, Minorca

HOTELS

Born, Palma de Mallorca, Majorca
Cas Gasí, Santa Gertrudis, Ibiza
Cas Pla, Ibiza Town
El Guía, Sóller, Majorca
Gran Hotel Son Net, Puigpunyent, Majorca
Hacienda Na Xamena, San Miguel, Ibiza
Los Molinos, Figueretas, Ibiza
Mar i Vent, Banyalbufar, Majorca
Palau Sa Font, Palma de Mallorca, Majorca
San Lorenzo, Palma de Mallorca, Majorca
Villa Italia, Port D'Andratx, Majorca

Updated by AnneLise Sorensen

PART OF THE PHOENICIAN, Roman, and Byzantine empires before the Moors invaded them in 902, the Balearic Islands—Majorca (Mallorca), Minorca (Menorca), Ibiza, and Formentera—have long been an important maritime trading and staging post. Lying between 80 and 242 km (50 and 150 mi) from Spain's Mediterranean coast, they are halfway between France and Africa. Beaches, of course, are a major attraction here, even if some of them are far from peaceful. (Note that *cala* is the local word for "cove" or "inlet.")

The Moors remained until ousted by Jaume I of the House of Aragón between 1229 and 1235. The islands were part of the independent kingdom of Majorca (which included Roussillon and the Cerdanya Valley on the mainland) from 1276 until 1343, when they returned to the Crown of Aragón under Pedro IV. Upon the marriage of Isabella of Castile to Ferdinand of Aragón in 1469, the Balearics became part of a united Spain. During the War of the Spanish Succession, Great Britain occupied Minorca in 1704 to secure the superb natural harbor of Mahón as a naval base. The British stayed for almost a century, interrupted only by an invasion in 1756, which gave the French control for 12 years, and a shorter reoccupation by the Spanish 20 years later. Under the Treaty of Amiens, Britain finally returned Minorca to Spain in 1802.

Minorca diverged once more during the Spanish Civil War, remaining loyal to Spain's democratically elected Republican government while Majorca and Ibiza sided with Franco's insurgents. Majorca became a home base for the Italian fleet supporting the fascist cause. This topic is still broached delicately on the islands; they remain fiercely independent of one another in many ways. Even Mahón and Ciutadella, at opposite ends of Minorca—all of 44 km (27 mi) apart—remain locked in bitter opposition over differences dating from the war with Britain. The tourist boom, which began during Franco's regime (1939–75), turned great stretches of Majorca's and Ibiza's coastlines into unplanned strips of high-rise hotels, fast-food restaurants, and discos. Only recently have ecology-minded residents begun to make headway in lobbying for restrictions on shoreline development.

In 1983 the Balearics became an Autonomous Community. One result has been the replacement of Castilian Spanish by the Catalan language (banned for official use by Franco) in its Mallorquín, Menorquín, and Ibizencan dialects. This can be confusing, because outside the islands you'll still hear island locations named in Spanish. Within the islands, the problem is compounded by road signs that have not been officially altered and are often obliterated by spray paint. This guide uses Catalan or Spanish according to whichever is used locally. *Avinguda* (avenue), *carrer* (street), and *plaça* (square) are Catalan; *avenida, calle,* and *plaza* are Spanish.

About the Restaurants

MAJORCA Seafood forms the basis of many local specialties, such as *espinigada* (a pie topped with tiny eels and spinach) and *panades de peix* (fish pies). Lamb, chicken, pork, and their derivatives are also traditional. *Sobrasada,* the bright-red Majorcan sausage paste, is basically pork and red pepper, and even the fluffy, super-sweet *ensaimada*—a powdery spiral pastry that ranges in size from a breakfast snack to a gift-box party special a foot in diameter—is based on *saim* (pork fat). Other specialties are *butifarra* and *llonganissa* sausages, *coques amb verdura* and *trampó* (pizzalike pastries covered with vegetables or finely chopped salad), and *cocarrois* (pastries filled with meat or a mixture of vegetables). *Sopa mallorquina* is a meal of fried vegetables in meat stock, usually served over pieces of thinly sliced bread. *Escaldum* is a stew of chicken legs

If you have 3 days

Fly to **Palma de Mallorca** 1 and spend that day and the next morning exploring the historic city center. The next day, head for the hills—specifically the Sierra de Tramuntana, on the island's north coast—and see the **Raixa palace** 2 on your way to the **Jardins d'Alfàbia** 3, **Sóller** 4, **Deià** 5 (where the English writer and poet Robert Graves lived during much of the 20th century), **Son Marroig** 6, and Sa Foradada. Spend the night in **Valldemossa** 7, and visit the church, pharmacy, and museum at the Royal Carthusian Monastery the next morning. Then, for the remainder of your third day, finish exploring the Tramuntana mountains: see Sa Granja, and hike down into the Torrent de Pareis ravine and beach if you have time. Visit the monastery at **Lluc** 14 before exploring the town and the port of **Pollença** 13. Make Alcúdia your last stop before the 40-minute drive back to Palma for your last night.

If you have 5 days

You can either do the Majorca loop from Palma (along the north coast and back through the center), with more time to settle in and explore, *or* devote your trip to Minorca, a good fit for a five-day visit. Spend your first day exploring **Mahón** 23. The next day, settle into a secluded beach on the southern coast, and perhaps tour the cave dwellings at Cales Coves. Spend the night at **Son Bou** or **Sant Lluís.** On day three, visit the megalithic ruins at Torre d'en Gaumés, Torralba, on your way to Es Mercadal and Minorca's highest point, **Monte Toro** 25. Have dinner and spend the night in **Fornells.** On day four, take in the beaches at Fornells and Cap de Cavalleria before returning through Es Mercadal and Ferreries to **Cala Santa Galdana.** Dedicate your fifth day to the ruins at Naveta des Tudons, Cala Morell, and **Ciutadella** 24.

---

with potatoes and ground almonds; *tumbet* is a stew of meat or fish with peppers, tomatoes, potatoes, and eggplant.

Artà, Benissalem, Felanitx, and Inca are all wine-making areas, and some excellent vintages are now produced. Majorca also makes sweet or dry herb liquors.

MINORCA Minorcan restaurant fare used to consist almost entirely of seafood and was served mainly along the harbors in Mahón, Ciutadella, and the fishing village of Fornells, famous for its very expensive *llagosta* (lobster), sold by weight and grilled or served as *caldereta* (soup). A country influence has also developed, based on inland and upland products such as rabbit, pork, and other meats often made into stews and roasts. Mayonnaise—which was invented in Minorca during the French occupation and named after Mahón—is usually freshly prepared. Local tapas include *tornellas*—sheep's intestines stuffed with bread crumbs, garlic, and meat, then braided and cooked. Mahón cows' cheese on Minorca has been made since 3,000 BC, and the best handcrafted Mahón cheeses have a *Denominación de Origen* label. The *curado,* fully cured, is the best. The British occupation left a tradition for making excellent, aromatic *ginebra* (gin).

IBIZA & FORMENTERA Because much produce comes to Ibiza and Formentera from mainland Spain via Palma, the cost of dining may seem high, especially in such simple surroundings. Many local products, however, such as potatoes and the native sea bass and bream, are prized for their distinctive taste. You can find authentic Balearic specialties inland, off the tourist track; look for *sofrit pagès* (potatoes and red peppers stewed in olive oil and garlic) and *ratjada eivissenca* (grilled, semi-poached ray).

WHAT IT COSTS In Euros					
	$$$$	**$$$**	**$$**	**$**	**¢**
AT DINNER	over €20	€15–€20	€10–€15	€6–€10	under €6

Prices are per person for a main course at dinner.

About the Hotels

MAJORCA Majorca's newer resorts, concentrated mainly on the southern coast, amount to more than 1,500 hotels, many of which serve the package-tour industry. There are plenty of charming, low-cost spots, however, on the northwest coast and in the central countryside.

MINORCA Apart from a few hotels and hostels in Mahón and Ciutadella, almost all of Minorca's tourist lodgings are in beach resorts. As on the other islands, many of these are fully reserved by travel operators in the high season, so it's generally most economical to book a package that combines airfare and accommodations. But ask at the tourist office for details of boutique and country hotels, *agroturismo*.

IBIZA Ibiza's hotels are mainly in coastal Sant Antoni and Playa d'en Bossa. Many of these are excellent, but unless you're eager to be part of a mob, Sant Antoni has little to recommend it. Playa d'en Bossa, close to the town of Ibiza, is less brash, but it lies under the flight path to the airport. To get off the track and into the island's largely pristine interior, look for *agroturismo* lodgings in Els Amunts (The Uplands) and in villages such as Santa Gertrudis or Sant Miquel de Balanzat.

FORMENTERA If July and August are the only months you can visit, reserve well in advance. To get the true feel of this smallest major member of the archipelago, look for the most out-of-the-way calas and fishing villages.

WHAT IT COSTS In Euros					
	$$$$	**$$$**	**$$**	**$**	**¢**
FOR 2 PEOPLE	over €180	€100–€180	€60–€100	€40–€60	under €40

Prices are for two people in a standard double room in high season, excluding tax.

Exploring the Balearic Islands

Of the four main islands, Majorca and Ibiza are the most heavily developed. Minorca and Formentera remain less populated and wilder. The north coast of Majorca and parts of Ibiza still have as much rocky coastline and diaphanous water as anyone can use at once, but—on balance—go to Formentera for solitude and intimacy; Ibiza for wilderness with heavy concentrations of humanity; Majorca for the mixture of Palma's urban cosmopolitanism with the wild north coast and interior; and Minorca for what may be the best blend of all of the above.

MAJORCA The closer a beach is to Palma, the more crowded it's likely to be. West of the city, the lovely, narrow beach of Palma Nova/Magalluf is backed by one of the noisiest resorts on the Mediterranean. Paguera, with several small beaches, is the only sizable local resort not overshadowed by high-rises. A little farther along, Camp de Mar, with a good beach of fine white sand, is small and relatively undeveloped but is sometimes

Majorca

Sant Antoni d'Abat (January 17) is the annual blessing of animals. **Sant Joan Pelós** is celebrated June 23–24 in Felanitx; a man dressed in sheepskins represents John the Baptist. The **Romería de Sant Marçal** (Pilgrimage of St. Mark), held June 30 in Sa Cabaneta, involves primitive ceramic whistles.

Minorca

Ciutadella's feast of **Sant Joan** (June 23–24) has townspeople dancing on horseback, trying to keep the horses up on their hind legs while the crowd gathers beneath. **Sant Lluís**, at the end of August, spotlights equestrian activities; Mahón's **Fiestas de Gràcia** (September 7–8) are the season's final celebrations.

Ibiza

Ibiza's patron saint, **Mare de Déu dels Neus** (Our Lady of the Snows), is honored on August 8 in memory of the conquest of Ibiza. **Sant Antoni d'Abat** (January 17) has processions of pets, cavalry, and livestock. On February 12 the **Festes de Santa Eulalia** is a virtual winter carnival. **Sant Josep** (March 19) is known for folk dancing, which you can also see in Sant Joan every Thursday evening. On June 23–24, witness the island-wide **Festa Major de Sant Joan** (Feast of St. John the Baptist). The **Festa del Mar**, honoring the Mare de Déu del Carme (Our Lady of Carmen), is held July 15–16 in Eivissa, Santa Eulalia, Sant Antoni, and Sant Josep, and on Formentera. The August 28 feast of **Sant Agustí** is a tiny fiesta with folk dancing.

Formentera

On July 15–16 islanders honor the **Virgen del Carmen**, patron saint of sailors, with processions of boats and anything else that floats. On July 25, Sant Francesc dances in honor of **Sant Jaume** (St. James), Spain's male patron saint.

---

overrun with day-trippers from other resorts. Sant Telm, at the end of this coast, has a pretty little bay and a tree-shaded parking lot. East of Palma, a 5-km (3-mi) stretch of sand runs along the main coastal road from C'an Pastilla to Arenal, forming a package-tour nexus also known collectively as Playa de Palma. The beach is nice, but crowded.

The only *real* beach on the northwest coast is at Port de Sóller, a scenic bay nearly enclosed by its headlands. Cala St. Vicenç, at the top end of this coast, has fine, soft sand in two narrow bays and is only moderately developed. At Port de Pollença, on the north coast, the sand is imported, but the resort is attractive and has good water sports. There is frequent water-taxi service from Port de Pollença to Formentor, one of the finest beaches on Majorca. The north coast also has the island's longest sand beach; gently shelved, and backed in part by pines, it stretches 8 km (5 mi) from Port de Alcúdia to C'an Picafort and beyond. Ses Casetes, near Port des Pins, is the best stretch.

Majorca's Levante, or southeast coast, is peppered with beaches and coves, though few are easily accessed by car. Canyamel, near the Caves of Artà, is a large, undeveloped strand. Farther south, Costa d'es Pins is an extensive, expensive urbanization, but it has a good sandy stretch backed by a thin line of pines. Tourist buses, decorated to look like train engines, run from here to Cala Millor, which has a long, narrow, sloping beach of soft sand. Much of Cala Millor's beach is accessible only on foot. Farther south still, Cala d'Or is a pleasant resort, and Cala Gran, a short walk away, is even more attractive. Cala Mondrajó is a tiny, sandy bay with little development; it's most easily reached by boat from Portopetre or Cala Figuera. On the south coast, the dune-back beach at Es Trenc, near Colònia de Sant Jordi, is a quiet seaside patch. The 10-km (6-mi) walk along the beach from Colònia de Sant Jordi to the Cap Salines lighthouse is one of Majorca's treasures.

MINORCA Cala Mesquida, north of Mahón, is popular with the Mahonese; you'll see few tourists here. Another small beach, also development-free, lies on a headland beyond one of Minorca's many watchtowers. Farther west, Es Grau, a sandy stretch with dunes behind it, is a bit littered. Behind Es Grau is the S'Albufera nature reserve. Before the lighthouse at the end of Cap Favàritx are the nudist beaches Cala Presili and Playa Tortuga. Arenal d'en Castell, a sheltered circular bay, and Arenal de Son Saura (Son Parc) are the north's biggest sandy beaches. At the junction of the Mahón–Fornells and Mercadal–Fornells roads, take the small lane leading west and follow signs to Binimel.là, an excellent sandy beach. It's often deserted, and the caves in the tiny coves to the west provide welcome shade in the summer.

The only reasonable and generally accessible beach north of Ciutadella is Cala Morell. Minorcans claim that the inlets and beaches at Cala Algaiarens are the nicest on the island. Son Saura, Cala en Turqueta, and Macarella, at the west end of the south coast, are all reached by driving southeast from Ciutadella toward Son Saura. You'll be halted by a gate and a sign prohibiting entry, but no one will bother you if you close the gate behind you. All three are classic Minorcan beaches with trees down to the water's edge, horseshoe coves, and white sand. To the east, Cala Mitjana, Cala Trebaluger, Cala Fustam, and Cala Escorxada are accessible on land only by foot, but you can rent boats with outboard engines to reach them or Son Saura. You can get to the long, straight, sandy stretches of Binigaus, Sant Adeodato, and Santo Tomas from Mercadal, and to Son Bou, the island's longest beach (with a nudist section), from Alaior. Cala'n Porter is a British enclave; the rectangular cove has a sandy beach sheltered by cliffs.

IBIZA Immediately south of Ibiza Town is a long, sandy beach, the nearly 3-km (2-mi) Playa d'en Bossa, almost entirely developed. Farther on, a left turn at Sant Jordi on the way to the airport leads across the salt pans to Cavallet and Ses Salines, two of the most natural beaches on the island. Topless bathing is accepted all over Ibiza, but Es Cavallet is the official nudist beach, the first in Spain. All the remaining beaches on this part of the island are accessible from the Ibiza–Sant Josep–Sant Antoni highway, down side roads that often end in rough tracks. North of Sant Antoni, there are no easily accessible beaches until you reach Puerto San Miguel, an almost rectangular cove with relatively restrained development. Next along the north coast, accessible via San Juan, is Portinatx, a series of small coves with sandy beaches, of which the first and last, Cala Xarraca and Caló d'Es Porcs, are the best. The beaches on the east coast have been developed, but Santa Eulalia remains attractive. The resort has a narrow, sloping beach in front of a pedestrian promenade that, despite being lined by hotels and apartment blocks, is not frenetic, like Sant Antoni.

FORMENTERA If you like wild and lonely beaches, you'll love it here. The undeveloped Playa de Mitjorn stretches for 7 km (4 mi) along the south of the island. Trucadors, a long, thin spit at the north, has 2 km (1 mi) of sand on each side, and in summer you can wade to Es Palmador, where you'll find more sandy beaches and preponderantly nudist bathers.

Timing

Summer is hot and crowded. May and October are ideal, with June and September just behind. Winter (November–March) is quiet, sometimes too cold for the beach, but fine for hiking, golfing, and exploring.

MAJORCA

More than five times the size of either Minorca or Ibiza, Majorca is shaped roughly like a saddle. The Sierra de Tramuntana, a tough mountain range soaring to nearly 5,000 ft, runs the length of its northwest coast, and a ridge of hills borders the southeast shores; between the two lies a great, flat plain that in early spring becomes a sea of almond blossoms, "the snow of Majorca." Having acquired a reputation as a cheap getaway, especially among Britons and Germans, Majorca gets more than 10 million visitors per year, but the package-tour industry is confined to a narrow coastal strip. Elsewhere, Majorca has relatively undiscovered charms, particularly in the mountains of the northwest and in the interior: caves, bird sanctuaries, abandoned monasteries, tiny museums, and village markets form a good mixture of natural and man-made sights.

Numbers in the text correspond to numbers in the margin and on the Majorca, the Minorca, and the Ibiza & Formentera maps.

Palma de Mallorca

❶ *40-min flight from Barcelona.*

If you look north of the cathedral (La Seu, or the "seat" of the Bishopric, to Majorcans) on a map of the city of Palma, you'll see around the Plaça Santa Eulalia the jumble of tiny streets that made up the early town. Farther out, a ring of wide boulevards, known as the Avenues, zigzags around—these follow the path of the walls built by the Moors to defend the larger city that had grown up by the 12th century. The zigzags mark the bastions that jutted out at regular intervals. By the end of the 19th century the walls were largely torn down; the only place where you can still see the massive defenses is Ses Voltes, along the seafront west of the cathedral.

A streambed (*torrent*) used to run through the middle of the old city, dry for most of the year but often a raging flood in the rainy season, causing destruction and drowning. In the 17th century it was diverted to the east, along the moat that ran outside the city walls. The stream's natural course is now followed by La Rambla and the Passeig d'Es Born, two of Palma's main arteries. The traditional evening *paseo* (promenade) takes place on the Born.

If you come to Palma by car, park in the garage beneath the Parc de la Mar and stroll along the park. Beside it run the huge bastions guarding the Almudaina Palace; the cathedral, golden and massive, rises beyond. The park has several **ceramic murals** by the late Catalan artist and Majorca resident Joan Miró, as well as various modern **sculptures.**

If you begin early enough, a walk along the ramparts at Ses Voltes from the ***mirador*** (lookout) beside the Palma cathedral is spectacular. The first rays of the sun turn the upper pinnacles of La Seu bright gold and begin to work their way down the sandstone walls. From the Parc de la Mar, follow Avinguda Antoni Maura past the steps to the palace. At the Plaça de la Reina, the **Passeig des Born** begins, an avenue with a pedestrian promenade down its center, lined with towering plane trees and fashionable shops. For an even more spectacular and intimate walk up to the Born, retrace your steps to the beginning of Avinguda Antoni Maura

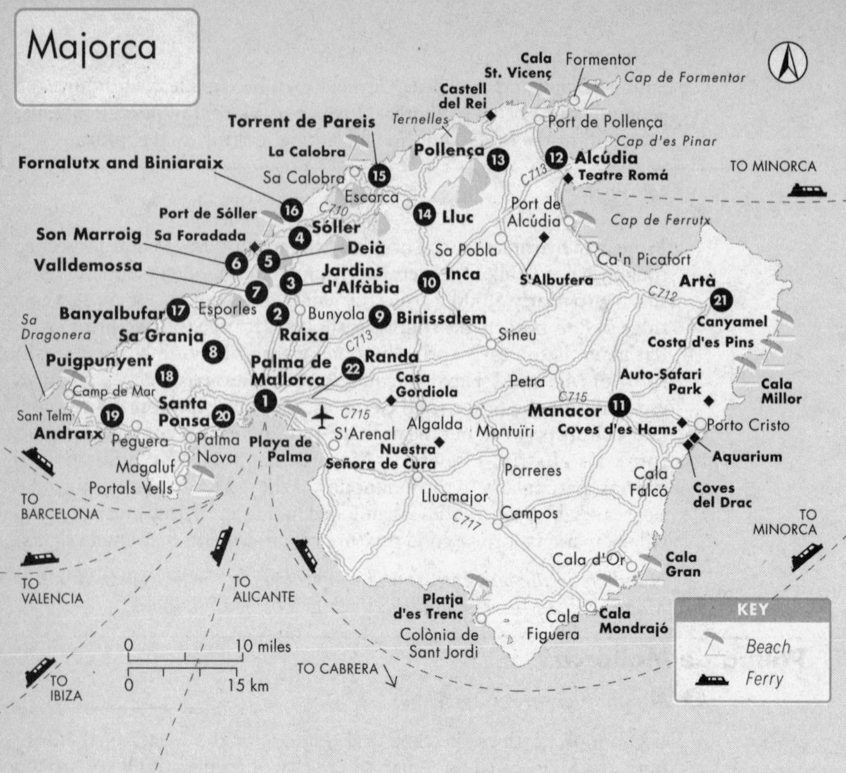

and walk left through the Plaça de la Llotja (don't miss a chance to visit the Mediterranean's finest civic Gothic building if it's open), then up Carrer de Sant Joan. The stately town house at No. 1 is the well-known nightspot Abaco. The **Des Puig** (⊠ Carrer Montenegro) house and entryway, at No. 2, is under an impressive coat of arms and is worth admiring during your walk around Palma. Check out the Renaissance facade of No. 8, the 16th-century **Can Salas** (⊠ corner of Carrer Sant Feliu). Take note of the sculpted masks on the doorway at No. 10, known as **Casa de Ses Carasses** (⊠ Carrer Sant Feliu).

The 14th-century church of **San Nicolau** (⊠ Plaça del Mercat) is notable for its hexagonal bell tower. The ornate facades of the **Casas Casasayas** (⊠ Carrer Santacilia), now a bank and a boutique, were designed by Moderniste (Art Nouveau) architect Francesc Roca Simó in 1908. The ornate **Gran Hotel** (⊠ Carrer Santacilia), in its blinding alabaster splendor, was built between 1901 and 1903 by Moderniste master Luis Domènech i Montaner, author of Barcelona's Palau de la Música Catalana. Don't miss the permanent exhibit of the famous Majorcan impressionist Anglada Camarassa.

The **Forn des Teatre** (Theater Bakery; ⊠ Plaça Weyler 12) is a unique shop known for its ensaimadas (a typically Spanish fluffy pastry) and *cocas* (meat pies). It's near the steps leading up to the right of the Teatre Principal. Take time to appreciate the neoclassical symmetry of the **Teatre Principal** (⊠ top of the Plaça Weyler). From here, you can stroll up the **Rambla**, around the corner and up to the left. It's a 15-minute walk to the top and back, through flower and book stalls. From the Forn des Teatre, you can climb the steps to the Plaça Marqués Palmer, where an archway on the left leads to the greater expanse of the **Plaça Major.** A crafts market fills this elegant neoclassical square on Monday, Friday, and Saturday mornings between 10 and 2.

Worth a look is the **El Aguila** (✉ Carrer Colom), a department store in an Art Nouveau building. Above a corner bookstore you'll find an interesting Art Nouveau specimen: the **Can Forteza Rei** (✉ Carrer Colom), which its owner, Luis Forteza Rei, designed in 1909. You'll find the 17th-century ***ajuntament*** (town hall; ✉ Plaça Cort) down the Carrer Colom. The olive tree on the right side of the square is one of Majorca's so-called *olivos milenarios*—thousand-year-old olives—and may be even older. The bank **Caja de Baleares Sa Nostra** (✉ corner of Carrer Jaume II and the Plaça Cort) is in a superb Art Nouveau building.

need a break?

When you're ready to sink your teeth into an ensaimada, head for the soothing **Ca'n Joan de S'aigo** (C. de C'an Sanç 10, ☎ 971/710759) in Barrio Antiguo. Founded in 1700, this café-confectionery has been serving sweets longer than anyone on the island, and is known for its ensaimadas. Immense green-glass chandeliers, antique candelabra, and marble-top tables give the room a stately elegance.

The beautiful 13th-century monastery church of **Sant Francesc** was founded by Jaume II when his eldest son took monastic orders and gave up rights to the throne. Fray Junípero Serra, the missionary who founded San Francisco, California, was later educated here; his effigy stands to the left of the main entrance. Enter the church and cloisters through the collegiate buildings on the east side. ✉ *Plaça Sant Francesc* ⏲ *Mon.–Sat. 9:30–1 and 3:30–7.*

The eminent 13th-century scholar Ramón Llull allegedly rode his horse into the church of **Santa Eulalia** in pursuit of a married noblewoman of whom he was enamored in his wild youth. In 1435, 200 Jews were converted to Christianity in this church after their rabbis were threatened with being burned at the stake. ✉ *Plaça Santa Eulalia.*

Just south of the Plaça Santa Eulalia, off Carrer d'en Morey, is Carrer Almudaina. The **archway** over the narrow street was one of the gates to the early Moorish citadel and is now one of the few relics of Moorish occupation on Majorca, along with the Arab Baths. At Carrer d'en Morey 9, peek into the Can Oleza patio, one of Palma's best. At No. 5 is the graceful Renaissance facade of the **Museu de Mallorca,** which displays Moorish art and some prehistoric bronze objects culled from local archaeological digs. ✉ *Portella 5* ☎ *971/717540* 🎫 *€2.40, free Sat. afternoon and Sun.* ⏲ *Apr.–Sept., Tues.–Sat. 10–2 and 5–7 (Thurs. 6–9), Sun. 10–2; Oct.–Mar., Tues.–Sat. 9:30–1:30 and 4–6, Sun. 10–2.*

One of Palma's oldest monuments, the 10th-century **Banys Arabs** (Arab Baths) are in a quiet lemon grove. ✉ *Serra 7,* ☎ *971/721549* 🎫 *€1.50* ⏲ *Daily 9–7.*

Fodor'sChoice ★

Palma's **cathedral** is an architectural wonder that took almost 400 years to build (1230–1601). It can be approached from the top of Carrer de Can Serra, where you turn left and follow the meandering streets west to the Plaça Almoina, with a cluster of antiques shops and restorers. The extraordinarily wide (63 ft) expanse of the nave is supported on 14 extraordinarily slender 70-ft-tall columns, which fan out like palm trees at the top. The nave is dominated by an immense rose window, 40 ft in diameter, from 1370. Look up into the nave: suspended above the Royal Chapel is the curious **asymmetrical canopy** built by Antoni Gaudí, who remodeled the chapel at the beginning of the 20th century. Lights within the canopy come on at regular intervals. The **bell tower** above the cathedral's Plaça Almoina door holds nine bells, the largest of which is known as N'Eloi, meaning "praise." N'Eloi was cast in 1389, weighs 5½ tons, needs six men to ring it, and has shattered stained-glass windows with its sound. Continue around the cathedral to see the **west facade**, whose blocked windows are the result of alterations following earthquake damage in 1851. ✉ *Pl. Almoina s/n* ☎ *971/723130* 🎫 *€3.50* ⏲ *Apr.–Oct., weekdays 10–6:30, Sat. 10–2:30; Nov.–Mar., weekdays 10–3, Sat. 10–2:30.*

Opposite Palma's cathedral is the **Palau de l'Almudaina** (Almudaina Palace), residence of the royal house of Majorca during the Middle Ages and originally an Arab citadel. Now a military headquarters, it can be toured only with a guide. Reservations are recommended. ✉ *Pl. Almoina* ☎ *971/727145* 🎫 *€3.30, EU citizens free Wed.* ⏲ *Weekdays 10–2 and 4–6, Sat. 10–2. Guided tours at 11, noon, 1, 4, and 5.*

The **Llotja** (Exchange), on the seafront a little west of the Born, was built in the 15th century and soon became the most important maritime commodities exchange on the Mediterranean. It's also the Mediterranean's finest example of civic Gothic architecture, with decorative turrets, battlements, and buttresses surrounding tracery-trim Gothic windows and perfectly balanced and fluted pillars. ✉ *Pl. de la Llotja, La Llotja* ⏲ *During exhibits, Tues.–Sat. 11–2 and 5–9, Sun. 11–2.*

The **Castell de Bellver** (Bellver Castle) overlooks the city and the bay from a hillside above the Terreno nightlife area. Built in the 14th century on a circular design, it's a sturdy fortress complete with dry moat and drawbridge. Within the walls is a fascinating historical **museum.** ✉ *Camilo José Cela s/n* ☎ *971/730657* 🎫 *€1.68* ⏲ *Oct.–Mar., Mon.–Sat. 8–7; Apr.–Sept., Mon.–Sat. 8–8:30.*

The **Museu Fundació Pilar y Joan Miró** (Pilar and Joan Miró Foundation Museum) has many works by the Catalan artist, who spent his last years on Majorca (1979–83). ✉ *Carrer Joan de Saridakis 29, Cala Major Marivent* ☎ *971/701420* 🌐 *www.a-palma.es/fpjmiro* 🎫 *€4.30* ⏲ *Oct.–mid-May, Tues.–Sat. 10–6, Sun. 10–3; mid-May–Sept., Tues.–Sat. 10–7, Sun. 10–3.*

The **Poble Espanyol** (Spanish Village), in Palmas's western suburbs, is a reproduction of Spanish buildings, complete with shops and studios. ✉ *Carrer Poble Espanyol s/n, Poble Espanyol* ☎ *971/737075* 🎫 *€5* ⏲ *Village daily 9–6, crafts shops daily 9–6 (some closed Sun.).*

Where to Stay & Eat

★ $$–$$$ ✕ **Koldo Royo.** Crowded with modern art, this chic yellow dining room overlooks the marina through glass walls. Chef-owner Koldo Royo conjures up Basque specialties like lamprey, salt cod, baked hake, tripe, and stuffed quail; try the *cochinillo confitado con salsa de miel* (roast suckling pig with honey sauce) or the *merluza con risotto del calamar* (grilled hake with risotto in black squid ink). ✉ *Av. Gabriel Roca 3, Paseo Marítimo* ☎ *971/732435* 💳 *AE, MC, V* ⏲ *Closed Mon. Sept.–May. No dinner Sun.*

$$–$$$ ✕ **Porto Pi.** Dining in this old Majorcan villa in the Terreno area, 1 km (½ mi) west of Plaza Gomila, is like eating in a private home. The elegant central hall–cum–drawing room opens onto several high-ceiling dining rooms with round tables and oil paintings, and you can dine on the terrace in summer. Foie gras specialties include *foie con emulsion de miel y aceite de oliva al azafran* (foie gras seared with honey and saffron olive oil) and *foie con ensalada al aceite de avellanas* (foie served with salad seasoned by hazelnut oil). ✉ *Carrer Garita 25, at Av. Joan Miró 174, Terreno* ☎ *971/400087* 💳 *AE, MC, V* ⏲ *No lunch Sat. and Sun.*

$–$$ ✕ **Caballito de Mar.** Across from the Llotja at the very center of Palma's port, this handy place focuses on thick caldereta *de pescado* (fish stew) and fish concoctions of all kinds. Try the *rodaballo en vino blanco* (turbot cooked in white wine). The place is much frequented by locals and tourists alike; the only drawback is the noisy traffic nearby. ✉ *Passeig de Sagrera 5, La Llotja* ☎ *971/721074* 💳 *AE, DC, MC, V* ⊙ *Closed Mon.*

$–$$ ✕ **La Bóveda.** On a backstreet next to the Llotja, this shaded place is excellent for light or heavy tapas and full meals. Seafood, such as grilled tuna topped with tomato sauce, and light dishes (salads, vegetables) are available. ✉ *Carrer de la Botería 3, La Llotja* ☎ *971/714863* 💳 *AE, DC, MC, V* ⊙ *Closed Sun.*

¢–$ ✕ **Café la Lonja.** Both the sunny terrace in front of the Llotja—a privileged dining spot—and the *Orient Express*–style train wagon inside are excellent places for a drink, a tapa, a baguette, a sandwich, or a salad. It's a good rendezvous point and watering hole. ✉ *Carrer Marina 2, La Llotja* ☎ *971/722799* 💳 *AE, MC, V* ⊙ *Closed Sun.*

$$$$ ✕🏨 **Read's Hotel.** Occupying part of an 18th-century house in the countryside, on a 10-acre *finca* (farm), is this exclusive rural retreat. It has excellent amenities, spacious rooms, large gardens, and a superb restaurant—with an English chef, Marc Fosh, who is considered one of the best in Spain. The soaring dining room has 17th-century-style murals. The hotel is a 15-min drive from Palma. ✉ *Ctra. Santa María–Alaró s/n, 07320* ☎ *971/140261* 📠 *971/140762* 🌐 *www.readshotel.com* 🛏 *12 rooms, 9 suites* 👍 *Restaurant, tennis court, 2 pools (1 indoor), hot tub, sauna, bicycles, horseback riding, bar, library, meeting rooms* 💳 *AE, DC, MC, V.*

$$$–$$$$ ✕🏨 **Son Vida.** On a hillside outside Palma, this hotel still contains sections of the 13th-century castle it was built around. The antique furniture of the public rooms is typical of the old-style decoration here. Most rooms have panoramic views of Palma Bay, to the south; a few overlook the service area and hillside but, to compensate, are double the size of the others. A few rooms accommodate people with disabilities. ✉ *Castillo Son Vida, Son Vida, 07015* ☎ *971/790000* 📠 *971/790017* 🌐 *www.hotelsonvida.com* 🛏 *171 rooms* 👍 *2 restaurants, 18-hole golf course, 4 tennis courts, 3 pools (1 indoor), hair salon, health club, 2 bars, library, playground, some pets allowed* 💳 *AE, DC, MC, V.*

$$–$$$ ✕🏨 **Son Caliu.** Its grande-dame comfort, service, and style, and its location on a quiet, private beach makes this hotel a fine spot to unwind. It has a sleek, modern exterior and applies, believe it or not, NASA technology to ensure a virtually chlorine-free swimming environment in the pools. Golfers love it, as there are five courses within a half-hour drive. The hotel is 15 km (9 mi) west of Palma, and ideally placed for touring northwestern Majorca. ✉ *Urb. Son Caliu, 07184 Costa de Calvia* ☎ *971/682200* 📠 *971/683720* 🌐 *www.soncaliu.com* 🛏 *215 rooms, 8 suites* 👍 *Restaurant, tennis court, 2 pools (1 indoor), hair salon, sauna, bar, some pets allowed, no-smoking rooms* 💳 *AE, DC, MC, V.*

★ **$$$–$$$$** 🏨 **San Lorenzo.** This tiny place is a gem, and you're lucky if you can get a room. It's built into an aristocratic Majorcan town house, but the rooms are completely modern: exposed wood beams; watermarked silks in pastel blues, greens, and yellows; and traditional furniture. The suites have terraces and working fireplaces. Book a month in advance for summer stays. ✉ *Carrer San Lorenzo 14, Barrio Antiguo, 07012* ☎ *971/728200* 📠 *971/711901* 🌐 *www.hotelsanlorenzo.com* 🛏 *4 rooms, 2 suites* 👍 *Café, minibars, pool, bar, some pets allowed* 💳 *AE, DC, MC, V.*

★ **$$$** 🏨 **Palau Sa Font.** Warm Mediterranean tones and crisp and clean lines imbue this boutique hotel with an avant-garde sensibility unmatched in Palma. In this former 16th-century Episcopal palace are ample rooms with linen curtains and plump comforters. A hearty complimentary breakfast is served in a small dining room. From the tower, complete with terrace, you'll get 360-degree views of Palma's old quarter. ✉ *Carrer Apuntadores 38, Barrio Antiguo, 07012* ☎ *971/712277* 🖷 *971/712618* 🌐 *www.palausafont.com* *19 rooms* *Dining room, minibars, bar, some pets allowed* 💳 *AE, DC, MC, V.*

★ $$ **Born.** Romanesque arches and a giant palm tree spectacularly cover the central courtyard and reception area of the hotel, which occupies the former mansion of a noble Majorcan family. Guest rooms are modest, but the price, after all, is more than reasonable. You'll find the hotel on a quiet street off the busy Plaça Rei Juan Carlos. ✉ *Carrer Sant Jaume 3, Centro 07012* ☎ *971/712942* 🖷 *971/718618* 🌐 *www.hotelborn.com* *30 rooms* 💳 *AE, DC, MC, V.*

Nightlife & the Arts

NIGHTLIFE With some 200 discos and music bars scattered throughout the city and across the island, Majorca's nightlife is never hard to find. The cobble streets of the old town are jammed with restaurants and bars. The section of the Passeig Marítim known as **Avinguda Gabriel Roca** is a nucleus of taverns and pubs, the most popular of which are Pachá, Tito's, and Ib's. The most incandescent hot spots are concentrated 6 km (4 mi) west of Palma at **Punta Portals,** in Portals Nous, where King Juan Carlos I moors his yacht along with many of Europe's most beautiful people. Try Flannigan's, Tristan (the best and most expensive), and Diablito, a pizza emporium. In Palma, the **Plaça de la Llotja** and surrounding streets are the place to go for *copas* (drinking, tapas sampling, and general carousing).

Darsena (✉ Roca s/n ☎ 971/18054) is beside the water with great harbor views. **Carrer Apuntadores,** on the Born's west side, is always lively at night. Some of Palma's best jazz acts play the small, smoky jazz club **Barcelona** (✉ Carrer Apuntadores s/n, La Llotja) on weekends. **Abaco** (✉ Carrer de Sant Joan 1, La Llotja ☎ 971/714939) offers baroque music amid flowers and fruit. **Bluesville** (✉ Carrer Ma de Morro 3) is a laidback, grunge-style bar popular with both locals and foreigners. Groove to live funk on Thursday, rock and blues on Saturday. The elegant **Wellies Pub** (✉ Portals Nous ☎ 971/676444) has a great view of the marina and does great fish-and-chips. Magalluf's gargantuan **BCM Planet Dance** (✉ Av. S'Olivera s/n) is the top disco, with a pan-European crowd. Palma's **casino** is on the harbor promenade. There's a nominal entry charge, and you'll need your passport (and a shirt and tie) to enter. ✉ *Av. Gabriel Roca 4* ☎ *971/454012 or 971/450563* 🌐 *www.casinodemallorca.com* *Mon.–Thurs. 3 PM–4 AM; Fri.–Sun. 3 PM–5 AM.*

THE ARTS Outside in summer, the City of Palma Symphony Orchestra performs about twice a month at the **Auditorium** (✉ Passeig Marítim 18, Paseo Marítimo ☎ 971/734735), which also hosts ballet, opera, and plays throughout the year. The neoclassical **Teatre Principal** (✉ near Pl. Major, Barrio Antiguo ☎ 971/713346 🌐 www.teatreprincipal.com) normally presents plays, concerts, and operas, but is closed for renovations.

Sports & the Outdoors

Turisme Actiu, a leaflet that details all sports clubs, describes everything from sea diving to skydiving; the leaflet is available at tourist offices.

BALLOONING If up, up, and away is what you're after, try **Mallorca Balloons** (✉ Ca'n Melis 22, Cala Rajada ☎ 971/818182).

BICYCLING The Mallorca tourist board has an excellent series of leaflets on cycle routes with maps, details of terrain, sights, and distances. The tourist office of Cala Ratjada, northeast of the island, has a 12-page brochure on cycle routes, complete with maps and photographs.

FISHING For deep-sea fishing, contact **Asociación Balear de Chárters, de Pesca y de Recreo** (✉ Antoni Riera Xamena 6, 1st floor, Palma ☎ 670/356530).

GOLF Majorca is well stocked with golf courses. For more information contact the Federación Balear de Golf (Balearic Golf Federation) on Avenida Jaime III 17 in Palma (☎ 971/722753 🌐 www.fbgolf.com).

HANG GLIDING Find ultralights at **Escuela de Ultrligeros "Es Cruce"** (✉ Ctra. Palma–Manacor, Km 42, Petra ☎ 629/392776). For hang gliding, contact **Parapente Alfabia** (✉ Camino d'es Puig, Finca Es Puxet, Alcúdia ☎ 971/891366). **Club de Vuelo Libre Mallorca** (✉ Baluard del Princep 10C, 3rd Floor B, Palma ☎ 971/754316 🌐 www.cvlmallorca.com) offers hang gliding.

HIKING/WALKING Majorca is an excellent destination for hiking. In the Sierra de Tramuntana, you can easily arrange a combination of walking out and taking a boat, bus, or train back. Ask the tourist office for the free booklet "20 Hiking Excursions on the Island of Majorca," with detailed maps and itineraries. For excellent drawings and maps, track down *12 Classic Hikes Through Majorca*, by the German author Herbert Heinrich, available in the bookstores at key sights. For more hiking information contact the **Grup Excursionista de Mallorca** (Majorcan Hiking Association; ✉ Can Cavalleria 17 ☎ 971/711314). A useful outfit for foreign trekkers is **Explorador** (✉ Pueblo Espanyol, Despacho 7, 07014 Palma ☎ 600/557770 🌐 www.exploradors-mallorca.com).

HORSEBACK RIDING The **Federación Hipica Territorial Balear** (Balearic Equestrian Federation; ✉ Garita 21, Palma ☎ 971/404073) has details of horseback riding on the islands. Children can ride ponies and camels at **Pueblo Árabe** (✉ Ctra. Palma a Alcúdia, Km 25, El Foro de Mallorca, Benissalem, ☎ 971/886198).

SAILING For information on sailing, call the **Federación Balear de Vela** (Balearic Sailing Federation; ✉ Av. Joan Miró 327, Palma ☎ 971/402412 🌐 www.oninet.es/fbv). The **Escuela Nacional de Vela de Calanova** (National Sailing School; ✉ Av. Joan Miró 327, Palma ☎ 971/402512) can clue you in about sailing in the Balearics. The **Club de Mar** (✉ Muelle de Pelaires, south end of Passeig Marítim, La Llotja, Palma ☎ 971/403611 🌐 www.clubdemar-mallorca.com) is famous among yachties. It has its own hotel, bar, disco, and restaurant. Charter a yacht at **Cruesa Mallorca Yacht Charter** (✉ Paseo Marítimo 16, Edificio Tròpic, Paseo Marítimo, Palma ☎ 971/282821).

SCUBA DIVING Inquire about scuba diving at **Escuba Palma** (✉ Via Rey Jaume l, 84, Santa Ponsa ☎ 971/694968). **Big Blue** (✉ Marti Ros García 6, Edificio Ski Club, Palma Nova, Calvìa ☎ 971/681686) is a resource for scuba divers.

TENNIS Tennis is very popular here; you'll find courts at many hotels and private clubs, and tennis schools as well. For information about playing in the area, call the **Federación Balear de Tenis** (Balearic Tennis Federation; ✉ Costa de Sa Pols 6, Local 16 ☎ 971/720956 🌐 www.sportw.com).

WATER SPORTS You can rent Windsurfers and dinghies at most beach resorts; both skin- and scuba diving are excellent; and the island has a whopping 30 yacht marinas. On the northwest coast at Port de Sóller, canoes, Windsurfers, dinghies, motor launches, and waterskiing gear are available for rent from Easter to October at **Escola d'Esports Nàutics** (✉ Paseo Playa d'en Repic s/n, Port de Sóller ☎ 971/633001 🌐 www.nauticsoller.com).

Shopping

Majorca's specialties are leather shoes and clothing, porcelain, souvenirs carved from olive wood, and artificial pearls. Top-name fashion boutiques line **Avinguda Jaume III.** Less-expensive shopping strips are **Car-**

rer Sindicat and **Carrer Sant Miquel**—both pedestrian streets running north from the Plaça Major—and the small streets south of the Plaça Major. The **Plaça Major** itself has an excellent crafts market Monday, Friday, and Saturday mornings 10–2. Another crafts market is held May 15–October 15, 8 PM–midnight in **Plaça de les Meravelles.** You'll also find several antiques shops on Plaça Almoina.

Find Majorcan crafts at Spain's major department store chain, **El Corte Inglés** (✉ Av. Jaume lll 15 or Av. Rossell 12–16, Centro, Palma ☎ 971/770177), open Monday–Saturday 10–10. Leather is best in the high-end **Loewe** (✉ Av. Jaime III 1, Centro ☎ 971/715275), a branch of the famed Spanish firm founded in 1846. Bags, jackets, and the like are artfully displayed in classy, perfumed surroundings; the expert staff provides personal attention. The family-owned **Pink** (✉ Av. Jaime III 3, Centro ☎ 971/722333), one of Palma's oldest leather stores, sells leather goods in summer. Off season, it caters to locals with sweaters and knitwear as well as leather. If you find the leather jacket of your dreams, Pink can alter it within 48 hours. The small Pink shop next door, known as Pink Pequeña (Little Pink), specializes in leather bags. The coolest local footwear is rope-sole espadrilles, which come in different colors and are very cheap at **Alpargatería La Concepción** (✉ Concepción 17, Palma ☎ 971/710709).

Perlas Majorica (✉ Av. Jaume III 11, Centro ☎ 971/712159) sells artificial pearls. **Persépolis** (✉ Av. Jaume III 23, Centro ☎ 971/724539) has quality antiques. **Las Columnas** (✉ C. Sant Domingo 24, opposite tourist office, Barrio Antiguo) has ceramics from all over the Balearic Islands. For gift-wrapped ensaimadas, pop into **Forn Teatro** (✉ Pl. Weyler, at foot of steps leading to Pl. Major, Barrio Antiguo ☎ 971/715254). The much-photographed shop front of **Colmado Sto. Domingo** (✉ Santo Domingo 1, Barrio Antiguo, Palma ☎ 971/714887) explains why this is a popular place for *sobrasada* (sausage paste) as well as liqueurs and other local produce. Local, national, and foreign wines are on sale at **La Vinoteca** (✉ Plaza Virgen de la Salud 3, Plaza de España, Palma ☎ 971/728829).

Raixa

❷ *13 km (8 mi) north of Palma.*

Heading north from Palma, look to the left to see Raixa, an 18th-century palace set in landscaped gardens. You'll see it above a great flight of steps, flanked by statues and fountains.

Jardins d'Alfàbia

❸ *4 km (2½ mi) north of Raixa on right side.*

As you walk up the flight of steps leading to the Raixa palace you'll see a huge, vaulted cistern, built by a Moorish overlord to irrigate the gardens here. A path leads around to a café, then winds through a small, thick wood. What's most remarkable about the Alfàbia Gardens is that they're here at all; water is not abundant in this climate. The house is furnished with antiques and lined with painted panels. ✉ *Ctra. Palma–Sóller, Km 17* ☎ *971/613123* *€4.50* ⊙ *Weekdays 9:30–6:30, Sat. 9:30–1.*

Where to Eat

$–$$ ✕ **Ses Porxeres.** Former stables at the gardens' edge have been converted into a fine, airy restaurant with a high ceiling and a charming outside garden. Catalan and Majorcan specialties include pheasant stuffed with tiny plums and rabbit prepared with snails. The wine racks lining the walls are well stocked with excellent selections from the Penedès and La Rioja. ✉ *Ctra. Palma–Sóller, Km 17* ☎ *971/613762* ▭ *AE, MC, V* ⊙ *Closed Aug. and Mon. No dinner Sun.*

Sóller

❹ *17 km (11 mi) north of Raixa, 30 km (19 mi) north of Palma.*

Sóller is a rough but cozy gray-stone town with both a maritime and a mountain sensibility. Find your way to the Plaça Constitució, dominated by the cathedral; arm yourself with a map at the tourist office, in the ajuntament; and hop a tram down to the Port de Sóller.

Where to Stay & Eat

★ $$ **El Guía.** Typical of the houses built by Sóller's merchants on the rich rewards of the citrus trade, this hotel is furnished in keeping with that fin-de-siècle style. It's in the center of town, next to the train station. The excellent restaurant serves Majorcan specialties. ✉ *Carrer Castanyer 2, 07100* ☎ *971/630227* 🖷 *971/632634* *18 rooms* *Restaurant* ▭ *MC, V* ⊙ *Closed Nov.–Mar.*

$–$$ **Hotel Es Port.** This 17th-century manor house is the spectacular ancestral home of the Montis family, who added a modern extension. Try to get a room in the old section, which has more character. The restaurant is in an old mill with endless beams, where the olive press makes a striking centerpiece. For a fee, the hotel provides guides who lead walking excursions. A hearty breakfast is included in the price. ✉ *Carrer Antoni Montis s/n, 07108 Port de Sóller* ☎ *971/631650* 🖷 *971/631662* 🌐 *www.hotelesport.com* *156 rooms.* *Restaurant, 3 tennis courts, pool, sauna, bar, playground, some pets allowed* ▭ *AE, MC, V.*

Deià

❺ *9 km ($5\frac{1}{2}$ mi) southwest of Sóller.*

Laid-back Deià (Deyá in Castilian Spanish) was made famous by the English poet and writer Robert Graves, who lived here from 1929 until his death in 1985. The village café—on Deià's main drag, up some steps on the left as you enter town—is still a favorite haunt of writers and artists, such as Graves's son, Tomás Graves, author of *P'amb oli* (*Bread and Olive Oil*), a guide to Majorcan cooking. Relaxing on the café's terrace, shaded by a roof of vines and branches, is one of the nicest ways to soak up Deià. In the distance, you can see Deià's green-shutter stone houses against the backdrop of the Sierra de Tramuntana. There's live jazz on summer evenings. On warm afternoons, literati gather at the beach bar in the rocky cove 2 km (1 mi) downhill from the village. From here, walk up the narrow street, lined with the stations of the cross, to the village church; the small **cemetery** behind it affords views of mountains terraced with olive trees and of the coves below. It's a fitting spot for Graves's final resting place, which is in a quiet corner beneath a simple slab.

Where to Stay & Eat

$$$$ Fodor'sChoice ★ **La Residencia.** This former 16th-century manor house amidst olive and citrus groves, above the village, is superbly furnished with antiques, modern canvases, and four-poster beds. Britain's late Princess Diana was a regular guest. The arched dining room of the restaurant, El Olivo, was once an olive mill. The inventive menu includes *consomme de bogavante con ravioli de azafrán* (lobster consommé with saffron-flavored ravioli) and sweetbread with white truffles and green asparagus. Breakfast is included. ✉ *Finca Son Canals, 07179* ☎ *971/639011* 🖷 *971/639370* 🌐 *www.hotel-laresidencia.com* *64 rooms* *2 restaurants, 2 tennis*

courts, 3 pools (1 indoor), hair salon, bar, Internet, no-smoking rooms ▭ *AE, DC, MC, V.*

$$ **Costa d'Or.** This attractive villa, north of Deià, is on the terraced cliff side and has a footpath down to the cove. Rooms are small and spare. ✉ *Llucalcari, 07179* ☎ *971/639025* 📠 *971/639347* *40 rooms* *Restaurant, pool* ▭ *MC, V* ⊙ *Closed Nov.–Apr.*

Son Marroig

❻ *4 km (2½ mi) west of Deià.*

West of Deià is Son Marroig, one of the estates of Austrian archduke Luis Salvador (1847–1915), who arrived in Majorca as a young man and fell in love with the place. Speaker of 14 languages and a prolific writer, the archduke acquired estates and built great houses, mostly along the northwest coast, which he then furnished with miradors at each spectacular viewpoint. Now a museum, Son Marroig contains the archduke's collections of Mediterranean pottery and ceramics, old Majorcan furniture, and paintings. From late July through early October, the Deià International Festival holds classical concerts here. ✉ *Ctra. Deià–Valldemossa s/n* ☎ *971/639158* *€3* ⊙ *Apr.–Sept., Mon.–Sat. 10–7:30; Oct.–Mar., Mon.–Sat. 10–5:30.*

From the mirador you can see, nearly 1,000 ft below, **Sa Foradada,** a spectacular rock peninsula pierced by a huge archway, beneath which the archduke moored his yacht. A pathway, beginning near the café in the parking area, leads down to Sa Foradada (1 hour down, 1½ hours up). Four kilometers (2½ mi) farther, behind the restaurant C'an Costa, on the right, is another of the archduke's miradors, **Ses Pites,** named for the spiky cactus plants that surround it.

Valldemossa

❼ *18 km (11 mi) north of Palma.*

The **Reial Cartuja** (Royal Carthusian Monastery) was founded in 1339, but when the monks were expelled in 1835, it was privatized, and the cells became lodgings for travelers. Later they were leased as summer apartments, which they largely remain today. The most famous lodgers were Frédéric Chopin and the French novelist George Sand, who spent three difficult months here (both the weather and their affair have always been described as tempestuous) in the winter of 1838–39. The tourist office, in the plaza next to the church, sells a ticket good for the monastery's various attractions.

The guided tour begins in the **church.** Note the frescoes above the nave—the monk who painted them was Goya's brother-in-law. The next stop, in the cloisters, is perhaps the most interesting: a **pharmacy,** equipped by the monks in 1723 and almost completely preserved. Up a long, wide corridor are the apartments occupied by Chopin and Sand, furnished in period style. Only the piano is original, and transporting it here from France was a monumental effort. Nearby, another set of apartments houses the local **museum,** with mementos of Archduke Luis Salvador and a collection of old printing blocks. From here you return to the ornately furnished **King Sancho's palace,** a group of rooms originally built by King Jaume II for his son Sancho. A short piano recital of works by Chopin concludes the optional guided tour, except on Monday and Thursday morning, when Majorcan folk dancers perform. ✉ *Pl. de la Cartuja* ☎ *971/612106* *€6* ⊙ *Nov.–Feb., Mon.–Sat. 9:30–4:30, Sun. 10–1; Mar.–Oct., Mon.–Sat. 9:30–6.*

Costa Nord, opened in 2000 by actor Michael Douglas, is a cultural center dedicated to Majorca's northwest Sierra de Tramuntana and to Archduke Luis Salvador. A 15-minute film on the natural wonders of the Sierra de Tramuntana (produced and narrated by Douglas) and a life-size reproduction of the interior of the archduke's yacht make this a fascinating visit. Classical music is performed in the small amphitheater on summer Friday nights, and tickets cost about €30. ✉ *Av. Palma 6, 07170* ☎ *971/612425* 🖷 *971/612410* 🎫 *€7.50* 🕑 *Nov.–Mar., Mon. 9–3, Tues.–Sun. 9–5; Apr.–Oct., Mon. 9–3, Tues.–Sun 9–7.*

Where to Stay & Eat

$$$–$$$$ ✕🏨 **Vistamar.** Search out this charming small hotel amid 250 acres of olive groves overlooking the sea. The manor house has been faithfully restored to its original, early 19th-century appearance, and the sitting rooms and bedrooms have exposed beams, heavy furniture, and modern art. The restaurant is popular for its excellent Mediterranean cooking. Breakfast is included. ✉ *Ctra. Valldemossa–Andratx, Km 2, 07170* ☎ *971/612300* 🖷 *971/612583* 🌐 *www.vistamarhotel.es* ⇆ *19 rooms* ♨ *Restaurant, pool, bar* 💳 *AE, DC, MC, V* 🕑 *Hotel closed Nov.–mid-Feb. No lunch Mon.*

Sa Granja

❽ *21 km (13 mi) northwest of Palma.*

Sa Granja (The Farm) was built by a noble family in the 17th century on what was once a farm. Once settled, they created pools and gardens. Now an open-air museum of the Majorcan countryside, the house has an olive mill and many ethnographic artifacts. If you come on Wednesday or Friday afternoon, you might catch some folk dancing; on Thursday at 4 PM and Sunday at noon you can watch a horse show. Admission fee includes a sampling of local wines, *Sobrasada,* (typical Majorcan sausage paste), cheeses, and pastries. ☎ *971/610032* 🌐 *www.lagranja.net* 🎫 *€8 Sat.–Tues. and Thurs., €10 Wed. and Fri.* 🕑 *May–Oct., daily 10–7; Nov.–Apr., daily 10–6. Folk dancing Wed. and Fri. 3–5.*

Binissalem

❾ *18 km (11 mi) northeast of Palma.*

Drive east along the Passeig Marítim from Palma and take the bypass north. Follow it for about 3 km (2 mi) to the Inca turnoff; this becomes a fast *autopista* (toll highway), which takes you to the outskirts of Binissalem, the home of Majorca's main **vineyards** and its only D. O. (Denominación de Orígen, i.e., guaranteed-vintage) label.

Where to Stay

$$$–$$$$ 🏨 **Scott's.** American George Scott and Englishwoman Judy Brabner have converted this 18th-century Majorcan *palacete* (elegant town house) into a graceful and tranquil hideaway, an ideal base for forays around the island. The couple serve a memorable breakfast, included in the room price, until high noon, and give extraordinarily helpful suggestions about what to see and do. They also run a bistro 300 yards away. ✉ *Pl. Iglesia 12, 07350* ☎ *971/870100* 🖷 *971/870267* 🌐 *www.scottshotel.com* ⇆ *18 rooms* ♨ *Some pets allowed, no-smoking rooms* 💳 *MC, V.*

Inca

❿ *28 km (17 mi) northeast of Palma.*

Inca is known for its leather factories and its Thursday market, the largest on Majorca.

Where to Eat

$$–$$$ **Celler C'an Amer.** A *celler* is a peculiarly Majorcan combination of wine cellar and restaurant, and Inca has no fewer than six. C'an Amer is the best, with tables tucked under huge wine vats and heavy oak beams. There's a very pretty garden for warm evenings. Antonia, the dynamic chef-owner, serves some of the best *lechona* (suckling pig) and tumbet (vegetables baked in layers) on the island. *Carrer Pau 39 971/501261 AE, DC, MC, V No dinner Sun. Closed Sat. and Sun. in summer.*

Shopping

Along the old Palma–Inca Road you'll find brightly colored ***siurells*** (primitive ceramic whistles) in Cabaneta, **pottery** in Marratxi, and ***ilengos*** (a peasant fabric) in Santa María, where the amusingly named shop Mas Vieja que mi Abuela (Older Than My Grandmother) sells **antiques.** Inca has **leather** goods and ***galletas*** (local biscuits). If you don't find what you want in Inca, hunt for crafts, leather, and pottery at the emporium outside town, on the left side of the road to Alcúdia.

Manacor

11 *50 km (30 mi) east of Palma.*

Majorca's second-largest town, Manacor is known primarily for its pearl-manufacturing process and is an ideal center from which to storm the island's southeastern holiday coast. The Romans first settled this site, followed by the Moors, who built a mosque where the Gothic parish church of **Nostra Senyora de les Dolores** (Our Lady of Sorrows) now stands.

Where to Stay & Eat

$$$$ **La Reserva Rotana.** This luxury hotel is in a beautifully restored manor house 3 km (2 mi) north of Manacor. Most of the original coffered ceilings, ancient woodwork, and Venetian stucco are still in place. The 500-acre Rotana estate has its own 9-hole golf course, orchards, and kitchen gardens, which supply the excellent restaurant with fresh produce. Price includes breakfast and greens fee. *Camí de Savai s/n, Apdo. de Correos 69, 07500 971/845685 971/555258 www.reservarotana.com 21 rooms Restaurant, 9-hole golf course, putting green, tennis court, pool, gym, sauna, Internet AE, DC, MC, V.*

Shopping

The weekly market in Manacor is held on Monday morning. To see Majorca's famous artificial pearls being made, go to **Fábrica de Perlas Majórica** (Vía Majórica 971/550200).

Alcúdia

12 *54 km (34 mi) northeast of Palma.*

Circle the restored remains of Alcúdia's Moorish city walls—on Sunday and Tuesday (morning), there's a market outside. Inside, in a maze of narrow streets, are some fine 17th-century houses.

The **Museu Monogràfic de Pollentia** has an excellent collection of Roman items. *Carrer Sant Jaume 30 971/547004 Museum €1.50, museum and Roman ruins €2.42 Tues.–Fri. 10–1:30 and 3.30–5:30, weekends 10:30–1.*

Just outside Alcúdia, off the port road, a signposted lane leads to the small, 1st-century BC **Teatre Romá** (Roman Amphitheater), carved from the hillside rock—facing south, so the audience could enjoy the evening sun. Excavated in the 1950s, the haunting site never closes. From the

Teatre Romá, turn back toward Alcúdia, but at the Inca junction keep right for **Port de Pollença,** less hectic than many of Majorca's coastal resorts. Its waterfront is lined with cafés and bars.

Sports & the Outdoors

BICYCLING You'll find excellent bicycling in the flatlands around Port de Pollença, and Alcúdia and C'an Picafort—on the north coast—are ideal. The roads have special bike lanes, and there are rental outlets on every block.

Pollença

13 *5 km (3 mi) inland of the port.*

This pretty little port town has lovely views of the water and old-world charm, plus a weekly market on Sunday morning. Climb the **Calvari,** a stone staircase with 365 steps. At the top is a tiny **chapel** with a Gothic wooden crucifix and a view of the bays: Alcúdia and Pollença, and Capes Formentor and Pinar. Almost opposite the turnoff to Ternelles is Pollença's **Roman bridge.**

off the beaten path

CAP DE FORMENTOR – If you enjoy twisty, scenic roads to nowhere, pack a picnic and drive to Cap de Formentor, north of Puerto de Pollença. The road threads its way among huge teeth of rock before reaching a lighthouse at the extreme tip, where the view is spectacular.

Where to Stay

$$$$ **Formentor.** Founded in 1929, this famous hotel is perched on a cliff at Majorca's northern tip. Terrace gardens descend to an attractive private beach, where a barbecue is fired up at lunchtime. The building is long and white, and the rooms comfortable; despite the remote site, the place lacks intimacy because it's so large. Former guests include the Duke of Windsor, Winston Churchill, Charlie Chaplin, Aristotle Onassis, and the Spanish royal family. ✉ *Playa de Formentor, 07470* ☎ *971/899100* 📠 *971/865155* 🌐 *www.hotelformentor.net* *127 rooms* *Restaurant, grill, miniature golf, 5 tennis courts, hair salon, beach, windsurfing, boating, waterskiing, horseback riding, 3 bars, playground, airport shuttle* 💳 *AE, DC, MC, V* ⊗ *Closed Nov.–Mar.*

The Arts

Pollença hosts an international **music festival** in August and early September, during which concerts are performed in the cloisters of the former monastery of Santo Domingo. For information, contact Pollença's **ajuntament** (✉ Calvari 2 ☎ 971/534012 or 971/534016).

Lluc

14 *20 km (12 mi) southwest of Port de Pollença.*

The **monastery** in the remote mountain village of Lluc is widely considered Majorca's spiritual sanctuary. La Moreneta, also known as La Virgen Negra de Lluc (the Black Virgin of Lluc), is here in the 17th-century **church.** The **museum** has an eclectic collection of ceramics, paintings, clothing, folk costumes, and religious items. A boys' choir sings psalms in the chapel every day at 11:15 AM and 7:30 PM (except mid-June–July). The Christmas Eve performance of the pre-Christian Cant de la Sibila (Song of the Sybil) is an annual choral highlight. ☎ *971/871525* €2 ⊗ *Daily 11–1:30 and 2.30–5:30.*

Where to Stay & Eat

¢ **Santuari de Lluc.** The Lluc monastery offers simple, clean, and cheap accommodation, mostly in cells once occupied by priests. Although the vast building has one bar and three Majorcan restaurants, nightlife is restricted, and guests are asked to be silent after 11 PM. *Santuari de Lluc, Plaça Pelegrins s/n 07315 971/871525 971/517096 113 rooms 3 restaurants, cafeteria, bar, shop V.*

Torrent de Pareis

15 *2 km (1 mi) east of Sa Calobra.*

From Escorca's church of Sant Pere, you can hike down the Torrent de Pareis, a ravine that drops dramatically to the sea. Use proper footwear, don't go alone, and don't go at all if rain is forecast. The "torrent" becomes just that after a downpour and has been known to cause drownings.

en route

It's worth taking the turn to Sa Calobra to see the bottom of the torrent without climbing down. The road descends in a series of sharp loops to the Mediterranean, where the touristy town and beach at its end are a letdown. For solitude, take the left turn before Sa Calobra and continue to Cala Tuent, where the only beach development is a fisherman's hut. Beyond the Sa Calobra junction, C710 passes through tunnels and beside reservoirs, with terrific views. Try to detour left through Fornalutx and Biniaraix before you reach Sóller.

Fornalutx & Biniaraix

16 *3 km (2 mi) northeast of Sóller.*

Both Fornalutx and Biniaraix have been spruced up by tourist cash, but their cobbled, honey-color plazas and stepped streets are still undeniably charming. Each village has a resident artists' colony.

Banyalbufar

17 *23 km (14 mi) northwest of Palma.*

Originally terraced by the Romans, this tiny town overlooks its tiny harbor from high on a cliff. A 1½-km (1-mi) walk southwest leads to the **Mirador Ses Animes** observation point.

Where to Stay

★ $$–$$$ **Mar i Vent.** This small, modern, family-run hotel is at the north end of Banyalbufar. Paths lead down to two small, rocky coves for sea bathing. All guest rooms are furnished in traditional style and have mountain and/or ocean views. *Carrer Major 49, 07191 971/618000 971/618201 www.hotelmarivent.com 29 rooms Restaurant, 2 tennis courts, pool, bar, no-smoking rooms MC, V Closed Dec.–Jan.*

Puigpunyent

18 *25 km (15 mi) northwest of Palma.*

This village and the little roadways leading to and from it in all directions are a welcome relief from some of Majorca's more heavily traveled routes and routines. Visit the parish church, look through the Son Bru historical center, and hike up the nearby Puig de Galatzó (3,368 ft).

Where to Stay & Eat

★ $$$$ Gran Hotel Son Net. The creation of American David Stein, this restored mansion is one of Majorca's most luxurious hotels. Sweeping interior spaces of glass and stone overlook the village of Puigpunyent and the surrounding countryside. The restaurant, Sa Tafona, set in an ancient olive press, is an ideal showcase for the culinary skills (French, Majorcan, Mediterranean) of chef Borja Ochoa. *Carrer Castillo de Son Net Puigpunyent, 07194 971/147000 971/147001 www.sonnet.es 24 rooms Restaurant, grill, tennis court, pool, gym, sauna, bar, some pets allowed AE, DC, MC, V.*

9

Andratx

19 *23 km (14 mi) southwest of Banyalbufar.*

Andratx is a charming cluster of white and ocher hillside houses, rather like cliff dwellings, watched over by the 3,363-ft Mt. Galatzó. You can take a pleasant walk or drive from here through S'Arracó to the Castell Sant Elmo (St. Elmo's Castle) and on to the rocky shore opposite the Isla Sa Dragonera (Dragon Cave Isle). The weekly market in Andratx is held on Wednesday morning.

Where to Stay

★ $$$–$$$$ **Villa Italia.** This ornate, rose-color hideaway was built in a Florentine style, with marble floors and faux-classical columns. It has splendid views over the port and, to the west, the Mediterranean. *Camino San Carlos 13, 07157 Port D'Andratx 971/674011 971/673350 www.hotelvillaitalia.com 10 rooms, 6 suites Restaurant, pool, bar, some pets allowed AE, MC, V.*

Santa Ponsa

20 *15 km (9 mi) west of Palma.*

Santa Ponsa has a sandy beach on its north side and a small fishing port to the south. A spell on the beach and lunch in the port may beckon before you return to Palma by way of the C719 and the autopista.

Side Trips

Artà

21 *78 km (48 mi) northeast of Palma.*

The hills of Majorca's northeast, beyond Artà, are nearly roadless, thus keeping Artà somewhat off the beaten path. The north side of town is notable for its castle and the church of San Salvador. Just below the church, a sign points, somewhat ambiguously, to the Ermita de Betlem (Bethlehem Hermitage), some 9 km (5 mi) farther on. The road soon degenerates into a rocky track that twists hair-raisingly up between dwarf palms and sea holly and then circles down to the isolated hermitage, the home of a few hermetic monks. Behind it, a path leads up the hillside to a fine mirador. The weekly market in Artà is held on Tuesday morning.

Randa

22 *26 km (16 mi) southeast of Palma.*

For a quick jaunt from Palma, take C715 east from the city to PM501, turn right, and follow signs to Llucmajor until, after about 3 km (2 mi), a left turn leads to Randa. At the center of this tiny village, turn right and follow a twisting road up the Puig de Randa, with three separate hermitages. Take in the views from the terrace of the Franciscan monastery of **Nuestra Señora de Cura** (known as El Santuari de Cura), on the summit. Long a pilgrimage destination for the sick, it was founded in the 13th century by philosopher Ramón Llull; its library has valuable books that you may be able to see during quiet times. Next to the terrace are a bar and restaurant; the monastery also rents rooms (doubles €18–€20 per person) and apartments. ✉ *Puig de Randa,* ☎ *971/120260* 💰 *Donation suggested* ⏲ *Daily 10–1:30 and 4–6:30.*

MINORCA

Minorca, the northernmost Balearic island, is a knobby, cliff-bound plateau with a single central hill—Monte Toro—from whose 1,100-ft summit you can see the whole island. Prehistoric monuments—*taulas* (huge stone T-shapes), *talayots* (spiral stone cones), and *navetes* (stone structures shaped like overturned boats)—left by the first Neolithic settlers are scattered thickly around the countryside. The British controlled Minorca for much of the 18th century; their legacy is Georgian architecture (especially in Mahón); a landscape of small, tidy fields bounded by hedgerows and drystone walls and grazed by Holsteins; and language—Minorcan speech is sprinkled with English words. Tourism came late to Minorca, as it was traditionally more prosperous than its neighbors and Franco punished the Republican island by restricting development here. Having sat out the early Balearic boom, Minorca has avoided many of the other islands' industrialization troubles: there are no high-rise hotels, and the herringbone road system, with a single central highway, means that each resort is small and separate. A lively ecological movement succeeded in having Minorca designated a World Reserve of the Biosphere by UNESCO in 1993.

Mahón (Maó)

23 *Overnight boat or 40-min flight from Barcelona; six-hour ferry from Palma.*

Begin your tour at the northwest corner of the Plaça de S'Esplanada and turn right onto Carrer Comte de Cifuentes. Stop in at No. 25, the **Ateneo,** a cultural and literary society with wildlife, seashells, seaweed, minerals, and stuffed birds. On the staircase are ceramics and old tiles; side rooms include paintings and mementos of Minorcan writers, poets, and musicians. ✉ *Rovellada de Dalt 25* ☎ *971/360553* 💰 *Free* ⏲ *Mon.–Sat. 10–2 and 4–10.*

The **Teatre Principal** (✉ C. Costa d'en Ga s/n ☞ currently undergoing renovations), was built in 1824 as an opera house and is now a cinema and theater. If the construction has abated, try to peek inside at the semicircular auditorium, its columns supporting tiers of boxes and a gilded ceiling. The church of **La Verge del Carme** (✉ Plaça del Carme) has a fine painted and gilded altarpiece. Adjoining the church are the cloisters, now used, surprisingly, as a **public market.** As you wander through the colorful piles of fruit and vegetables, notice the carvings on the church's west and north walls. You can approach the church from Carrer S'Arravaleta, a pedestrian street with attractive shops. The church of **Santa María** (✉ Pl. de la Constitució) was originally from the 13th century but was rebuilt during the British occupation. It was restored after being sacked during the civil war. The church's pride is its 3,200-pipe baroque organ, imported from Austria in 1810. Behind the church of Santa María is the **Plaça de la Conquesta,** with a statue of Alfons III of Aragón. At the end of the tiny Carrer Alfons III, which leads off the square, is the best view of Mahón's harbor. The **ajuntament** (✉ Pl. de la Constitució) will be on your right side if you're walking from the port to the Plaça de la Con-

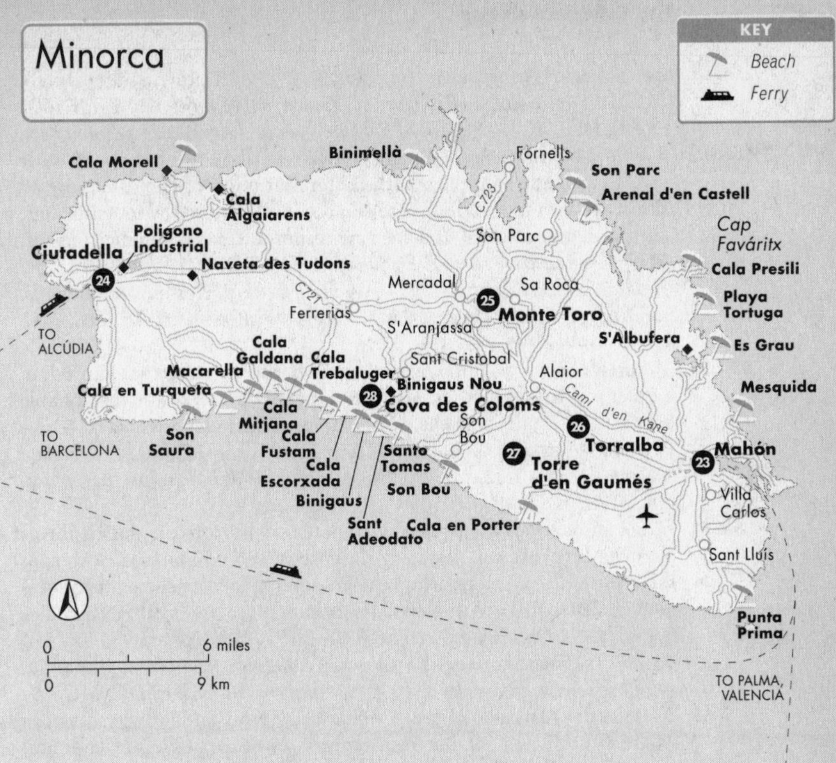

stitució. Stroll up Carrer Isabel II, a pleasant street of fine houses. Take note of the statue of the Virgin up on the wall and the **Palau del Governador** (Governor's Palace; ✉ Carrer de Rosari), as well as the courtyard. If you're walking from Carrer de Rosari, return to the ajuntament and follow Carrer Port de Sant Roc, immediately opposite. Ahead is the 16th-century gate **Puerta de San Roque,** the only remnant of the city walls built to protect Mahón from the pirate Barbarossa (Redbeard).

Where to Stay & Eat

$$–$$$ ✕ **Es Moli de Foc.** Enjoy fine Mediterranean cooking, with the freshest of ingredients, in a charming old house 3 km (2 mi) outside Mahón. Book a table in summer on the interior patio. ✉ *Sant Llorenç 65, Sant Climent* ☎ *971/153222* ▭ *AE, DC, MC, V* ⊙ *Closed Jan. and Mon. Sept.–June. No dinner Sun. Oct.–June.*

★ **$$–$$$** ✕ **Gregal.** This waterside spot in Mahón's port excels in fresh fish. The *pescado a la sal* (fish baked in salt) is a specialty. Whether you sit inside or on the airy terrace, you'll have a fine view of the harbor and its yachts, berthed on the seaward side of the palm-fringed esplanade. ✉ *Moll de Llevant 306* ☎ *971/366606* ▭ *AE, DC, MC, V.*

$$–$$$ ✕ **La Minerva.** This spectacular quayside restaurant has a floating terrace and a boat, the *Anita,* which serves as an adjoining bar and dining room in summer. Not surprisingly, fish reigns supreme here (try the lobster stew), but meat roasted over charcoal makes a good showing. ✉ *Moll de Llevant 87* ☎ *971/351995* ▭ *AE, DC, MC, V* ⊙ *Closed Mon. Oct.–Mar.*

$$–$$$ ✕ **Rocamar.** At the extreme end of the twisting, quayside road toward Villacarlos, this restaurant is a favorite for its fresh, simply prepared seafood. You dine four floors up, overlooking the port of Mahón and surrounded by dark-wood paneling and maritime lights. The *pimien-*

tos rellenos de langostinos (peppers stuffed with prawns) are superb. ✉ *Cala Fonduco 32, Villacarlos, Puerto de Mahón* ☎ *971/365601* ▭ *AE, DC, MC, V* ⊗ *Closed Nov. and Mon. in winter. No dinner Sun.*

$$$–$$$$ **Hotel Biniarroca.** Near Mahón, an English artist and a fashion designer have charmingly restored a 15th-century farmhouse. The rooms are all different, with tile floors, pastel shades, and exposed wooden beams. The garden is colorful and the fine restaurant has a summer terrace. ✉ *Ctra. Villacarlos s/n, 07780 San Luis* ☎ *971/150059* 🖷 *971/151250* 🌐 *www.biniarroca.com* *11 rooms, 1 suite* *Restaurant, 2 pools, bar, lounge, library, free parking, some pets allowed* ▭ *AE, DC, MC, V* ⊗ *Closed Nov.–Feb.*

$$–$$$ **Port Mahón.** This hotel overlooks the harbor from terrace gardens in a quiet residential district. Steps lead directly down to the fashionable bars and restaurants in the port. The price includes breakfast. ✉ *Av. Fort de l'Eau 13, 07701* ☎ *971/362600* 🖷 *971/351050* 🌐 *www.sethotels.com* *82 rooms* *Restaurant, pool, hair salon, bar, piano bar* ▭ *AE, DC, MC, V.*

$$–$$$ **Sol Mirador des Port.** Just five minutes' walk from the docks, this is a convenient base for exploring the eastern end of Minorca. Although the furnishings are modern and chic, rooms range from adequate to spectacular, depending on the views. The restaurant serves breakfast and dinner only. ✉ *Dalt Vilanova 1, 07701* ☎ *971/360016* 🖷 *971/367346* 🌐 *www.solmelia.com* *67 rooms, 3 suites* *Restaurant, cafeteria, minibars, pool, bar, baby-sitting, meeting rooms* ▭ *AE, DC, MC, V.*

$–$$ **Hotel del Almirante** (a.k.a. Collingwood House). Halfway between Mahón and Es Castell, the 18th-century residence of Nelson's admiral friend Lord Collingwood has spectacular views of the port. The main Georgian house became a hotel in 1964 but retains its originality *and* Collingwood's ghost, said to favor Room 7. Newer, ghost-free cottages are arranged around the secluded pool. ✉ *Ctra. Villacarlos s/n, 07780 Es Castell* ☎ *971/362700* 🖷 *971/362704* 🌐 *www.menorca.net* *40 rooms* *Restaurant, tennis court, pool, bar, recreation room* ▭ *AE, DC, MC, V* ⊗ *Closed Nov.–Apr.*

Nightlife & the Arts

The bars opposite the ferry terminal in Mahón's harbor fill with locals late at night. **Cova d'en Xoroi** (✉ C. Cova s/n, Mahón ☎ 971/377236) hides in a series of cliff-side caves high above the sea and is reached by a path. By day it is a tourist attraction and by night a wild disco. **Mambo** (✉ Moll de Llevant 209, Mahón ☎ 971/351852) is run by a pair of former celebrity DJs. The music is good, as are the cocktails. **Latitude 40** (✉ Moll de Llevant 314, Mahón ☎ 971/364176) is where yachtsmen and their chic companions enjoy evening cocktails and tapas. **Akelarre** (✉ Anden de Poniente 41–43, Mahón, ☎ 971/368520) is a smart drinking venue near the port, often with loud music. Catch live jazz Tuesday (April–September) at the **Casino** (✉ Sant Jaume 4, Sant Climent ☎ 971/153418) bar and restaurant.

Sports & the Outdoors

BIRD-WATCHING **S'Albufera,** a wetland nature reserve north of Mahón, attracts many species of migratory birds.

DIVING Equipment and lessons are available at Cala En Bosc, Son Parc, Fornells, and Cala Tirant. The island's only decompression chamber is at S'Algar. Compressed air is available at **Club Marítimo** (✉ Moll de Llevant, 287, Mahón, ☎ 971/365022). **Club Náutico** (✉ Camí del Baix s/n, Ciutadella, ☎ 971/383918) is a source for compressed air.

GOLF Minorca's sole golf course is the 9-hole **Golf Son Parc** (✉ Urb. Son Parc ☎ 971/188875 🌐 www.clubsonparc.com), 9 km (6 mi) east of Mercadal.

HORSEBACK RIDING There are stables on the left side of the main road between Alayor and Mercadal, after the Son Bou turn, as well as between Sant Climent and Cala 'n Porter. Elsewhere on the island, look for the sign *picadero* (riding school). **Picadera Menorca** (✉ Ctra. Marcadal a Son Bou, Km 5, before bridge, Alaior ☎ 608/323566) organizes horseback tours and has a school for dressage and jumping.

WALKING In the south, each cove is approached by a *barranca* (ravine or gully), often from several miles inland. These make pleasant, reasonably easy excursions. The head of **Barranca Algendar** is down a small, unmarked road immediately on the right of the Ferreries–Cala Galdana Road; the barranca ends in the beach resort Cala Galdana.

WINDSURFING & SAILING Knowledgeable windsurfers and dinghy sailors head for Fornells Bay. Several miles long and a mile wide, but with a narrow entrance to the sea, it gives the beginner a feeling of security and the expert plenty of excitement. **Windsurfing Fornells** (✉ Nou 33, Es Mercadal ☎ 971/188150 or 659/577760) rents boards in Bahia Fornells and gives lessons in English or Spanish.

A little south of Fornells, at Ses Salines in Bahia Fornells, Tim Morris of **Minorca Sailing Holidays** (☎ 971/376589 ✉ 58 Kew Rd., Richmond, Surrey, England TW9 2PQ ☎ 0181/948–2100) sells a package that includes airfare and accommodations along with various activities. Charter a yacht from **Nautica Matias** (✉ Pl. Quintana de Mar 2, Ciutadella ☎ 971/380538 🌐 www.nauticamatias.com). For charters and trips around the island, contact **Blue Mediterraneum–Rago** (✉ Moll de Llevant s/n, Mahón ☎ 971/154677 or 609/305314).

Shopping

Minorca is known for gin and shoes. Look for leatherwear along **S'Arravaleta.** Up on the Esplanade, an **open-air market** on Tuesday and Saturday offers cheap clothing and souvenirs. The **Xoriguer distillery** (✉ Anden de Poniente 91 ☎ 971/362197), on Mahón's quayside, near the ferry terminal, offers a guided tour, free samples, and, of course, bottles for sale. Buy leather goods at **Marks** (✉ S'Arravaleta 18 ☎ 971/322660). **Musupta** (✉ S'Arravaleta 26 ☎ 971/364131) is a source for leatherwear. Costume jewelry is best at **Bali** (✉ Carrer de Lluna at Carrer de Ses Moreres).

Ciutadella

24 *44 km (27 mi) west of Mahón.*

Ciutadella was Minorca's capital before the British settled in Mahón, and its history is richer than Mahón's. As you arrive via the C721 across the island, turn left at the traffic light and circle the old part of the city to the north end of the coniferous **Plaça de s'Esplanada.** Turn left here, down Camí de Sant Nicolau. At the end, near an old watchtower and two rusty cannons, is a **monument to David Glasgow Farragut,** the first admiral of the U.S. Navy, whose father emigrated from Ciutadella to the United States. From the Farragut monument, return up Sant Nicolau and park near the Plaça d'es Born. From Ciutadella's **ajuntament** (✉ Pl. d'es Born), on the west side of the Born, steps lead up to the **Mirador d'es Port,** a lookout from which you can survey Ciutadella's harbor. The town hall has an interesting collection of ancie[illegible] artifacts and pictures. The local **museum** has old street signs, keys, even a record of land grants made by Alfons III after [illegible] Moors. It's in an ancient defense tower at the east [illegible] the Bastió de Sa Font (Bastion of the Fountain). ☎ [illegible] *museuciutadella.cjb.net* €1.20 ⏲ *Tues.–Sat* [illegible]

The monument in the middle of the Plaça d'es Born commemorates the citizens' resistance of a Moorish invasion in 1588. South from the plaza along the east side of the Born is the block-long 19th-century **Palau Torresaura** (✉ Carrer Major 8), built by the Baron of Torresaura, one of the many noble families from Aragón and Catalonia that repopulated Minorca after it was captured from the Moors in the 13th century. Take note of the strange carving of a veiled female face over the palace's doorway, and visit one of the shops on the street to look at the complex pattern of archways and stairwells. The **Palau Salort** has door knockers carved to resemble entwined serpents. This is the only noble home regularly open to the public. The coats of arms on the ceiling are those of the families Salort (a salt pit and a garden: *sal* and *ort*, or *huerta*) and Martorell (a marten). ✉ *Carrer Major des Born,* 🎫 *€2.40* ⏲ *May–Oct., Mon.–Sat. 10–2.*

The Gothic **cathedral** (✉ Pl. de la Catedral at Plaça Píus XII) has some beautifully carved, intricate choir stalls. The side chapel has round Moorish arches, remnants of the mosque that once stood on this site. The ground floor of **Can Saura** (✉ Carrer Santíssim) has one of the best antiques shops in the Balearic Islands. Don't miss the coat of arms dated 1718, the primitive naval paintings at the end of the entrance hall, or the carved ceiling dome. The **Seminari** (✉ Carrer del Seminari at Carrer Obispo Vila) hosts Ciutadella's summer festival of classical music. Ciutadella's **port** (✉ Carrer Sant Sebastià) is accessible from steps that lead down from Carrer Sant Sebastià. The waterfront here is lined with seafood restaurants, some of which burrow into caverns far under the Born.

off the beaten path

CIUTADELLA – This town is near many of the archaeological curiosities for which Minorca is famous. Returning around the Avenidas, continue straight at the traffic lights, take the next right (Carrer de Pere Martorell), and follow the signs for Cala Morell. Soon you'll be in open countryside, where numerous **talayots** dot the fields. Returning to Ciutadella from Cala Morell, take a shortcut through the Polígono Industrial (Industrial Estate) on the left, to the Ciutadella–Mahón Road. Turn left toward Mahón, and 2 km (1 mi) or so farther on the right are a parking lot and a path leading to the **Naveta des Tudons,** one of the best preserved of Minorca's prehistoric remains.

Where to Stay & Eat

$$$–$$$$ ✕ **Cafe Balear.** Seafood doesn't get much fresher than this. The owners' boat docks nearby with its catch each day—except Sunday—and the restaurant fish tank is seldom empty. The house special, *arroz caldoso de langosta* (lobster and rice stew), is a masterpiece (€45). ✉ *Paseo San Juan 15* ☎ *971/380005* 💳 *AE, DC, MC, V* ⏲ *Closed Nov., Sun. July–Sept., and Mon. Oct.–June. No dinner Sun.*

$$–$$$ ✕ **Casa Manolo.** On the east side of Ciutadella's narrow port, this well-established paella and seafood restaurant has a summer terrace. The dining room's walls and exposed beams extend back into the rock face of the steep cliffs rising above. ✉ *Marina 117–121* ☎ *971/380003* 💳 *AE, DC, MC, V* ⏲ *Closed Dec.–Feb.*

$$$ 🏨 **Patricia Hesperia.** This hotel on a quiet boulevard south of the main plaza is close to Ciutadella Creek. The marble hall is light and modern, and the bedrooms have pale carpets, pastel wallpaper, and watercolor paintings. ✉ *Camí Sant Nicolau 90–92, 07760* ☎ *971/385511* 📠 *971/481120* 🌐 *www.hoteles-hesperia.es* *35 rooms, 4 suites* *Restaurant, minibars, bar, meeting rooms* 💳 *AE, DC, MC, V.*

$–$$ **Hostal Residencia Ciutadella.** This pleasant modern bar with guest rooms upstairs is in the center of town, a block southwest of the Plaça Alfonso III. The rooms have white walls, shutters, shiny tile floors, and comfortable beds. ✉ *Carrer Sant Eloi 10 07760* ☎ *971/383462* *17 rooms* *Cafeteria, bar; no a/c* *AE, MC, V.*

Shopping

Gin, shoes, leather, costume jewelry, and cheese are the items to shop for here; try the Ses Voltes area, the Es Rodol zone near Plaça Artrutx and Ses Voltes, and along the Camí de Maó between Plaça Palmeras and Plaça d'es Born. The industrial complex (*polígono industrial*) on the right as you enter Ciutadella has shoe factories, each with shops. Prices may be the same as in stores, but the selections are greater. In Plaza del Borne, a market is held on Friday and Saturday. For Mahón cheeses and sausages, go to **Ca Na Riera** (✉ Hospital de Santa Magdalena 7, ☎ 971/380748). The town's only ***alferería*** (pottery maker; ✉ Carrer Curniola s/n) has a studio store.

Side Trips

Monte Toro

25 *24 km (15 mi) northwest of Mahón.*

Follow signs in Es Mercadal (the crossroads at the island's center) to the peak of Monte Toro, Minorca's highest point, at all of 1,555 ft. From the monastery on top you can see the whole island and across the sea to Majorca. Stop in the village for a late lunch or an early dinner on the way back to Ciutadella.

WHERE TO EAT

$$$–$$$$ ✕ **Ca N' Aguedet.** This rustic spot is open every day of the year, serves a good homegrown wine, and has such Menorquín dishes as *conejo con higos* (rabbit with figs), *arrò de terra* (rough, whole-grain rice with meat sauce), *sepia con gambas* (cuttlefish with shrimp), and *cranc* (crab). Also on the menu are *peix a la plancha* (grilled fish) from *mero* (grouper) to *merluza* (hake). ✉ *Lepanto 30* ☎ *971/375391* *AE, DC, MC, V.*

$$$–$$$$ ✕ **Es Pla.** The modest wooden exterior of this waterside restaurant in Fornells' harbor, on the north coast, is misleading. Es Pla is reputedly King Juan Carlos's favorite Minorcan restaurant; the king is said to make regular detours here during Balearic jaunts to indulge in the *Es Pla caldereta de langosta* (a rich lobster stew). ✉ *Pasaje Es Pla, Puerto de Fornells* ☎ *971/376655* *AE, DC, MC, V.*

$$$ ✕ **Ca N' Olga.** It's hard to find, but the inventive country cuisine served here—local snails, quail in sherry—is definitely worth it. Off the Camino de Tramuntana, in central Mercadal, Olga's is under an archway to the left (ask for directions if you don't see it). Make for the small patio. ✉ *Pont Na Macarrana s/n, Es Mercadal* ☎ *971/375459* *AE, DC, MC, V* *Closed mid-Dec.–mid–Mar., and Tues. Nov.–Dec. and Mar.–May. No lunch June–Oct., or Mon. or Wed. Nov.–Dec. and Mar.–May.*

★ $$–$$$ ✕ **Molí d'es Reco.** The hotel is an old mill that sits high above the main Mahón–Ciutadella highway, outside Mercadal. In winter or on cold evenings, the ground floor offers snug dining, while the rustic, airy terrace is ideal on warm summer days. Rabbit dishes are the specialty, but the fish offerings are excellent, too. ✉ *Carrer Major 53* ☎ *971/375392* *AE, DC, MC, V.*

Torralba

26 *14 km (8½ mi) west of Mahón.*

Coming from Mahón, turn south immediately upon entering Alaior toward Cala en Porter. Torralba, a megalithic site with a number of stone constructions, is 2 km (1 mi) ahead at a bend in the road, marked by an information kiosk on the left. (As is so often the case in Minorca, you'll be lucky if you find it open.) The massive, T-shape stone **taula** is through an opening to the right. Behind it, from the top of a stone wall, you can see, in a nearby field, the monolith **Fus de Sa Geganta.**

Torre d'en Gaumés

27 *16 km (9½ mi) west of Mahón.*

Turn south toward Son Bou on the west side of Alayor. In about 1 km (½ mi), the first fork left will lead you to Torre d'en Gaumés, a far more complex set of stone constructions with fortifications, monuments, deep pits of ruined dwellings, huge vertical slabs, and taulas.

Cova des Coloms

28 *40 km (24 mi) west of Mahón.*

The Cave of Pigeons is the most spectacular cave on Minorca. To reach it, take the Ferreries road at San Cristobal and turn up to the primary school; beyond the school the paved road continues for about 3 km (2 mi) toward Binigaus Nou. You'll see wheel marks and possibly cars at the designated parking area; leave the car. Climb a stile and take the path that follows the right-hand side of the barranca toward the sea—you'll come to a well-trodden path bearing down into the bottom of the barranca and up the other side. The entrance to the cave is around an elbow, camouflaged by a tree. A flashlight helps.

IBIZA & FORMENTERA

Ibiza has a reputation as a hedonistic Mediterranean party spot. Yet only on Ibiza and on tiny Formentera, off Ibiza's southern tip, will you still see locals in the fields gathering almonds or herding errant goats.

Ibiza

29 *40-min flight from Barcelona.*

Settled by the Carthaginians in the 5th century BC, Ibiza (Eivissa, in Majorcan and Catalan) remained largely untouched by mass tourism until the 1960s, when it emerged as a wild, anything-goes gathering place for hippies and the international jet set. By the 1990s, its principal resort, Sant Antoni, had become an overdeveloped Balearic version of Torremolinos. Now the island is invaded during the summer by European clubbers packing mega-discos.

Running along the quay in Ibiza Town (Eivissa) is the area known as **Sa Penya** (the Crag, or the Cliff). Once a quiet fisherman's quarter, this neighborhood has been a tourist haunt since the 1960s, springing into life each evening with lively bars, restaurants, and flea markets.

Enter Sa Penya via Carrer Rimbau, which you'll find at the end of Passeig Vara de Rey opposite Hotel Montesol, whose fashionable pavement café is a favorite place for people-watching. **Carrer Rimbau** has some of the exotic boutiques for which Ibiza is renowned, and the alleys off it are crammed with stalls, more boutiques, and restaurants. Continue on Carrer Major to the **Plaça de la Constitució,** north of the church of San Telmo, where a pretty little building that looks something like a miniature Parthenon houses the local market. Beyond it, a ramp leads up to Las Tablas, the main gate of **Dalt Vila,** the walled upper town. On each side stands a statue, Roman in origin and now headless: Juno on the right, an armless male on the left.

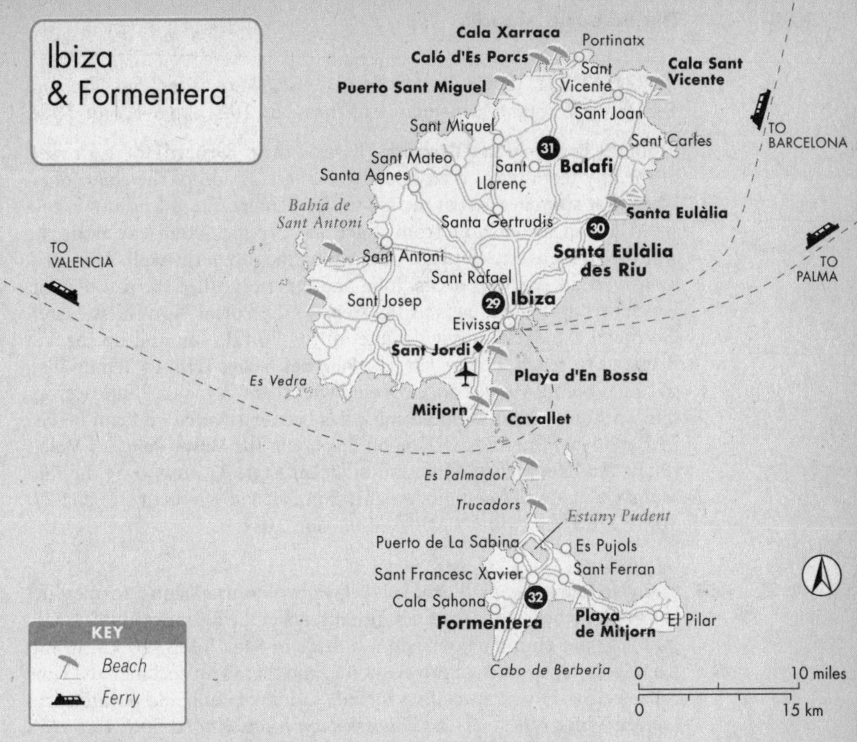

Inside Dalt Vila, the ramp continues to the right between the outer and inner walls and opens into a long, narrow plaza lined with stalls and pavement cafés. Don't worry about losing your way: aim uphill for the cathedral, downhill for the gate. A little way up Sa Carroza, a sign on the left points back toward the **Museu d'Art Contemporani,** housed in the gateway arch. Uphill from the museum is a sculpture of a priest sitting on one of the stone seats in the gardens. On the left, the wide **Bastió de Santa Llúcia** (Bastion of St. Lucia) has a panoramic view. ✉ *Ronda Pintor Narcis Putget s/n* ☎ *971/302723* 🎫 *€1.20* ⏲ *Oct.–Apr., Tues.–Fri. 10–1:30 and 4–6, weekends 10–1:30; May–Sept., Tues.–Fri. 10–1:30 and 5–8, weekends 10–1:30.*

Wind your way up past the 16th-century church of **Sant Domingo** (✉ Carrer de Balanzat), its roof an irregular landscape of tile domes, and turn right in front of the ajuntament housed in the church's former monastery. From the church of San Domingo, follow any of the streets or steps leading uphill to Carrer Obispo Torres (Carrer Major). The **cathedral** is on the site of religious structures from each of the cultures that have ruled Ibiza since the Phoenicians. Built in the 13th and 14th centuries and renovated in the 18th century, the cathedral has a Gothic tower and a baroque nave. The painted panels above the small vault adjoining the sacristy depict souls in purgatory being consumed by flames and tortured by devils while angels ascend to heaven. The **museum,** which you enter through the nave, was closed for building work at press time. It has religious art, relics, and ecclesiastical treasures. ✉ *Carrer Major,* ☎ *971/312774* 🎫 *Museum €.60* ⏲ *Cathedral and museum Sun.–Fri. 10–1 and 4–6:30, Sat. 10–1.*

The **Museu Arqueològic** has Phoenician, Punic (Carthaginian), and Roman artifacts. It's across the plaza from the cathedral. ✉ *Plaça Catedral 3*

☎ 971/301231 €2.40 ⏲ *Mid-Oct.–mid-Mar., Tues.–Sat. 9–3 and 4–6, Sun. 10–2; mid-Mar.–mid-Oct., Tues.–Sat. 10–2 and 6–8, Sun. 10–2.*

From the **Bastió de Sant Bernardo** (Bastion of St. Bernard) there's a view of the bay from Playa d'en Bossa to Figueretas and of the chain of islands that stretches across the sea to Formentera. Steps lead down to a small gate in the bastion, from which you can pick your way along the cliff top to Figueretas and continue along the top of the wall. This trail, by way of the bastions of Sts. John and James, is called the Route of St. John the Baptist and ends at the steps to the **Portal Nou** (New Gate). Go down the dark, curving tunnel of the Portal Nou and up the Vía Romana to reach, on the left, the **Puig des Molins** (Hill of Windmills), so called because it was once covered with them. A major Punic necropolis, with more than 3,000 tombs, has been excavated and can be visited; many of the finds will be on display in the **Museu Puig des Molins** (Punic Archaeological Museum) adjacent to it. At press time the museum was closed for major restoration. ✉ *Vía Romana 31* ☎ *971/301771* *Museum €1.80* ⏲ *Mon.–Sat. 10–1.*

Where to Stay & Eat

★ **$$$–$$$$** ✕ **Ca Na Joana.** Joana Biarnés, a well-known journalist in a former life, has put together one of the finest restaurants in the Balearics in this small, 200-year-old country house on a hillside in Sant Josep (10 km [6 mi] from Ibiza). It feels like a private home, and there's an acclimatized wine cellar below. House specialties include saddle of lamb and potato slices layered with truffles. ✉ *Ctra. Eivissa–Sant Josep, Km 10* ☎ *971/800158* ▭ *AE, MC, V* ⏲ *Closed Mon. and Nov.–Jan. No dinner Sun. Jan.–May, no lunch June–Oct.*

$$–$$$ ✕ **El Portalón.** Just inside and left of the main gate into Dalt Vila, this intimate French restaurant has two dining rooms; one medieval, with heavy beams, antiques, oils, and coats of arms; another, modern, with dark-orange walls and sleek black furniture. Try the *pato con salsa de frambuesa* (duck with raspberry sauce). ✉ *Pl. Desamparados 12, Dalt Vila* ☎ *971/300852* ▭ *AE, DC, MC, V* ⏲ *Closed Oct.–Apr. No lunch Sun.*

$$–$$$ ✕ **S'Oficina.** You'll find some of the best Basque cuisine on Ibiza just 2 km (1 mi) outside town at this attractive restaurant with a small patio. Marine prints hang on the white walls and ships' lanterns from the ceiling, and the bar is adorned with ships' wheels. *Lomo de merluza con almejas* (hake with clams) and *kokotxas* (cod cheeks) are the specialties. ✉ *C. Begonias 17 (from Ibiza Town, take Carretera toward airport and turn off for Playa d'en Bossa)* ☎ *971/390081* ▭ *AE, DC, MC, V* ⏲ *Closed Mon. No dinner Sun.*

$$$$ **Apartamentos Torre del Canónigo.** Built into a 16th-century tower at the top of the Dalt Vila, 55 yards from the cathedral, these modern apartments have open fireplaces. Three apartments have a view of the port and sea. Vehicle access is limited. ✉ *Carrer Major 8, Dalt Vila, 07800* ☎ *971/303884* 📠 *971/307843* 🌐 *www.elcanonigo.com* *6 apartments* *Snack bar, kitchenettes, minibars, Internet, some pets allowed* ▭ *AE, DC, MC, V* ⏲ *Closed Nov.–Mar.*

★ **$$$$** **Cas Gasí.** With splendid views of Ibiza's one and only mountain, the 1,567-ft Sa Talaiassa, this lovely late-19th-century manor house is surrounded by hills of olive trees, redolent of Tuscany. Airy rooms with wood-beam ceilings and walls in soft orange hues are sparsely and gracefully furnished with brass beds and contemporary designer chairs. Dinner is served on request, breakfast daily on a terrace. ✉ *Camino Viejo de Sant Mateu s/n, 07814 Santa Gertrudis* ☎ *971/197700* 📠 *971/197899* 🌐 *www.casgasi.com* *10 rooms* *Restaurant* ▭ *AE, DC, MC, V.*

★ $$$$ **Hacienda Na Xamena.** Ibiza's most exclusive hotel is also its most isolated: it's on a rocky headland in Sant Miquel, toward the north end of the island. Access to the sea is difficult, involving a long hike down steep steps; but the rooms, arranged around a pretty little patio with a fountain and trees, are spare—classical Ibizan with clean lines—and nearly half have hot tubs. Reserve well in advance. *Apdo. 423, 07815 San Miguel 971/334500 971/334514 www.hotelhacienda-ibiza.com 56 rooms, 9 suites 3 restaurants, café, tennis court, 3 pools (1 indoor), gym, hair salon, massage, sauna, steam room, bicycles, some pets allowed AE, MC, V Closed Nov.–Apr.*

★ $$$–$$$$ **Cas Pla.** Surrounded by thousand-year-old olive trees and blessed with views over the sea and the fortified church in the village of Sant Miquel, this rural hotel is tastefully decorated and well managed. A cozy retreat from the Ibiza "scene," it's still minutes from the beach. *Apdo. 777, Cam Putel, 07800 San Miguel de Balanzat, San Juan 971/334587 971/334604 16 rooms Tennis court, pool, some pets allowed AE, DC, MC, V Closed mid-Nov.–Mar.*

★ $$$ **Los Molinos.** This is the best hotel in Ibiza Town, although technically it's in Figueretas (it's only a five-minute walk from the center of Ibiza). The hotel is at the end of a relatively quiet street. Guest rooms are standard modern; the more expensive ones have balconies facing the bay. *Carrer Ramón Muntaner 60, Apdo. 504, 07800 Figueretas 971/302250 or 971/302254 971/302504 www.thbhotels.com 154 rooms Restaurant, pool, gym, hair salon, sauna, bar AE, DC, MC, V.*

Nightlife

If the arts are relatively neglected on Ibiza, nightlife certainly is not. Ibiza's discos are famous throughout Europe. Keep your eyes open during the day for free invitations to discos, handed out on the street. This will save you on a sometimes expensive (€12 to €40) entry fee. Also note that a handy, all night "Discobus" service (971/192456) runs between Ibiza, Sant Antoni, Santa Eulalia, and the major discos. Some discos—such as Amnesia, Privilege, and Space—are only open from June to September, plus New Year's Eve.

On summer nights, gays and lesbians gather in the top part of Ibiza Town, **Dalt Vila.** Down in the town, the trendy place to start the evening is **Keeper** (Paseo Don Juan Carlos 1), where you can sip your drink sitting on a carousel horse. There's also a lively, very young scene at **El Divino Cafe** (C. Vara De Ray), with boats leaving between 1 AM and 4 AM in summer in front for **El Divino Disco** (Puerto de Ibiza Nueva, 971/190176 www.eldivino-ibiza.com), which is a typical Ibiza disco with throbbing dance music. The "in" place for older nighthawks is the foyer of the former **Teatre Pereira** (Carrer Comte Roselló 3 971/191468). A young, stylish crowd dances to techno at **Pachá** (Av. 8 de Agosto s/n 971/313612 www.pacha.com). The popular **Amnesia San Rafael** (Sant Antoni road, opposite Km 5 marker, 971/198041) has several ample dance floors that throb to house and funk. **Privilege** (Ctra. Ibiza–Sant Antoni, Km 7, San Rafael 971/198477 www.privilege-ibiza.com) is the grande dame of Ibiza's nightlife, with a giant dance floor, a swimming pool, and more than a dozen bars. Hardened discomaniacs end the night at **Kiss.** Neighboring **Space** (far end of Playa d'en Bossa, 971/396793 www.space-ibiza.com), which doesn't even open until 5 AM, is where the serious clubbers come to dance away their night—or morning. Ibiza's **casino** is in a cubist building that resembles an Ibizan church, albeit with a pizzeria and piano bar in the side chapels. *Paseo Juan Carlos 1 971/313312 www.casinoibiza.com Weekdays 10 AM–4 AM, weekends 10 AM–5 AM.*

Sports & the Outdoors

For information on sports on Ibiza and Formentera, obtain a free copy of **Touribisport** (🌐 www.touribisport.com), a multilingual magazine available locally.

BICYCLING **Mr. Bike** (✉ Av. Isidoro Nacabich 63, Ibiza Town ☎ 971/392300) rents bicycles in Ibiza Town.

BOATING Explore Ibiza by sea with **Coral Yachting** (✉ Marina Botafoc, Ibiza Town ☎ 971/313524). **Cruiser Ibiza** (✉ Marina Botafoc, Ibiza Town ☎ 971/316170 🌐 www.cruiser-ibiza.com) runs charters. Charters are available from **Keywest** (✉ Marina Botafoc, Ibiza Town ☎ 971/316070). Procure a boat from **Marbella Charter** (✉ Marina Botafoc, Ibiza Town ☎ 971/314010).

GOLF Ibiza's only 18-hole course is **Golf de Ibiza** (✉ Ctra. Jesús–Cala Llonga, Km 6, Santa Eulalia ☎ 971/196118 🌐 www.golfysol.com). **Club Roca Lisa** (✉ Ctra. Jesús–Cala Llonga, Km 8, Santa Eulalia, ☎ 971/313718) has 9 holes.

HORSEBACK RIDING **Centro Ecuestre Easy Rider** (Easy Rider Equestrian Center; ✉ Camí del Sol d'en Serra, Cala Llonga, Santa Eulària des Riu ☎ 971/339192) offers a two-hour ride along the coast and inland.

SCUBA DIVING Year-round a team with a decompression chamber is on standby at the **Policlnica de Nuestra Señora del Rosario** (✉ Via Romana s/n, Ibiza Town ☎ 971/301916). **Anfibios** (✉ Playa d'en Bossa, Sant Jordi ☎ 971/303915) can see to your scuba needs. Scuba in Sant Antoni with **Centro de Buceo Sirena** (✉ Balanzat 21 bajo, Sant Antoni ☎ 971/342966). Dive in Sant Joan with **Centro Subfari** (✉ Portinatx, San Joan ☎ 971/333067). **Diving Centre San Miguel** (✉Puerto de San Miguel ☎971/334539 🌐 www.divingcenter-sanmiguel.com) offers diving. **Ibiza Best Dive** (✉Cantabra s/n, Bahíia de San Antonio ☎971/804125) is a scuba source in Sant Antoni. Dive in Santa Josep with **Orca Sub** (✉ Club Hotel Tarida Beach, Santa Josep ☎ 971/806307). **Punta Dive** (✉ Cala Martina, Santa Eularia ☎ 971/336726) offers diving in Santa Eularia. Rent scuba gear in Ibiza Town at **Vellmari** (✉ Marina Botafoc, Ibiza Town ☎ 971/192884 🌐 www.vellmari.com).

TENNIS **Ibiza Club de Campo** (✉Ctra. Sant Josep, Km 2, Ibiza Town ☎971/391458 🌐 www.ibiza-spotlight.com/clubdecampo) offers tennis. A good place to volley is **Aqualandia** (✉ Urb. Punta Martinet, Playa Talamanca ☎ 971/314060). **Port Sant Miquel** (☎ 971/333019) has tennis facilities.

WALKING **Ecoibiza** (✉ C. Abad y Lasierra 35, 07800 Ibiza Ciutat ☎ 971/302347 🌐 www.ecoibiza.com) has lots of ecologically friendly countryside walks, and can also arrange horseback riding, sailing, and sea fishing.

Shopping

In the late 1960s and '70s, Ibiza built a reputation for extremes of fashion. Little of this phenomenon survives, though the softer designs of Smilja Mihailovich (under the Ad Lib label) still prosper. Along Carrer d'Enmig are an eclectic collection of shops and stalls selling fashion and crafts. While the Sa Penya area of Ibiza Town still has a few designer boutiques, much of the area is now a "hippie market" (literally—locals call it the Mercat dels Hippies) with more than 80 stalls of overpriced tourist ephemera. For trendy casual gear, sandals, belts, and bags, try **Ibiza Republic** (✉ Antoni Mar 15, Ibiza Town ☎ 971/314175). For leather wear, belts, bags, and shoes, go to **Heltor** (✉Madrid 12, Ibiza Town ☎971/391225). For wines and spirits, visit **Enotecum** (✉ Av. d'Isidoro Macabich 43, Ibiza Town ☎ 971/399167).

Side Trips

Santa Eulalia des Riu

30 *15 km (9 mi) northeast of Ibiza.*

At the edge of this town (a.k.a. Santa Eulària des Riu), to the right below the road, a Roman bridge crosses what is claimed to be the only permanent river in the Balearics (hence "des Riu," or "of the river"). Ahead, on the hilltop, are the cubes and domes of the church—to reach it, look for a narrow lane to the left, signed PUIG DE MISSA, itself so named for the hill where Mass was once held. A stoutly arched, cryptlike covered area guards the entrance; inside are a fine gold reredos and blue-tile stations of the cross.

WHERE TO EAT

$$–$$$ ✕ **Doña Margarita.** This immaculately whitewashed waterfront restaurant is famous for its seafood. Dine at pine tables, overlooked by Ibizan landscapes on the alabaster walls. The terrace, next to the crescent beach, is especially pleasant in the evening. ✉ *Passeig Marítim s/n* ☎ *971/332200* ▭ *AE, DC, MC, V* ⊙ *Closed Mon. and Nov.*

★ $$ ✕ **C'as Pagès.** Meateaters will love this restaurant in an old farmhouse with bare stone walls, wood beams, and columns made of giant olive-press screws. Try the leg of *cordero asado* (roast lamb with baked potato), *pimientos rellenos* (roast peppers), or *sofrit pagès* (lamb and chicken stew), and finish with *graixonera,* a mixture of sugar, milk, eggs, and cinnamon. ✉ *Ctra. de San Carlos, Km 10 (Pont de S'Argentara)* ☎ *no phone* ▭ *No credit cards* ⊙ *Closed Tues. and Feb.–Mar.*

$$ ✕ **Sa Capella.** It's a 20-minute, 15-km (9-mi) drive west of Ibiza, but this enchanting restaurant in the resort of Sant Antoni is well worth seeking out. A former chapel, it was converted with flair and style into a splendid restaurant. Try the roast suckling pig—you won't find better. ✉ *Puig d'en Basora, Sant Antoni* ☎ *971/340057* ▭ *MC, V* ⊙ *Closed Nov.–Mar.*

SPORTS & THE OUTDOORS

Charter yachts from **Tagomago Yachting** (✉ Puerto Deportivo, Santa Eulalia ☎ 971/338101 ⊕ www.ibizanautica.com/tagomago).

Club Terra Nova (✉ Ctra. Cala Llonga, Km 10, Santa Eulalia ☎ 971/338135 ⊕ www.clubterranova.com) has six tennis courts plus archery, badminton, table tennis, bowling, a swimming pool, and a Jacuzzi.

Balafi

31 *10 km (6 mi) northwest of Santa Eulalia.*

To reach the fortified village of Balafi, take the Sant Joan road from Ibiza and, passing the left turn to Sant Llorenç, look for a bar on the right next to a ceramics workshop. Turn right onto Sant Carles: almost opposite, on the left, a rough, narrow track leads to Balafi. You'll see some towers in the distance. These have no entrance on the ground floor; in times of peril, residents climbed a ladder to the second floor and pulled the ladder up after them.

Formentera

32 *90 mins (30–40 mins by fast boat) by ferry from Ibiza.*

You can begin this tour from Ibiza, Sant Antoni, or Santa Eulalia, as all have ferries to La Sabina. Because Formentera is mostly beach and countryside, you may be inspired to picnic; buy supplies in Ibiza. It's worth standing on deck during the short passage, for the excellent views of Ibiza's Dalt Vila and the smaller islands en route. Look for Trucadors, the stretch of sand that almost links Formentera with Es Palmador.

La Sabina has several car, bicycle, and moped rental agencies, and most people rent bikes to explore this flat little island. From La Sabina, it's only 3 km (2 mi) to Formentera's tiny capital, **Sant Francesc Xavier,** a few yards off the main road. There's an active hippie market in the small plaza before the church. The interior of the whitewash church is quite simple, its rough, old wooden door encased in iron and studded with nails. Down a short street directly opposite the church, on the left, an antiques and junk shop has a small art gallery with paintings and olive-wood carvings. At the main road, turn right toward **Sant Ferran,** 2 km (1 mi) away. Beyond Sant Ferran the road travels for 7 km (4 mi) along a narrow isthmus, keeping slightly closer to the rougher, northern side, where waves come crashing over the rocks when a wind is blowing. Just beyond El Pilar you'll see a windmill on the right.

The plateau on the island's east side ends at the lighthouse **Faro de la Mola.** Nearby is a **monument to Jules Verne,** who set part of his novel *Journey Through the Solar System* in Formentera. Despite being trampled by tourists, the bare rock around the lighthouse is carpeted with flowers, purple thyme, and sea holly in spring and fall, while hundreds of swallows soar below. At the edge of the cliff you may see one of the turquoise-viridian lizards endemic to Ibiza and Formentera.

Back on the main road, turn right at Sant Ferran toward Es Pujols. The few hotels here are the closest Formentera comes to beach resorts, even if the beach is not the best. Beyond Es Pujols the road skirts **Estany Pudent,** one of two lagoons that almost enclose La Sabina. Salt was once extracted from Pudent, hence its name, which means "stinking pond," although the pond now smells fine. The other lagoon, **Estany de Peix** (Fish Pond), was once a fish farm. At the northern tip of Pudent, a road to the right leads to a footpath that runs the length of **Trucadors,** the narrow sand spit that leads to Es Palmador. The beaches here are excellent.

Where to Stay & Eat

$$–$$$ ✕ **Le Cyrano.** This family-run restaurant on the Es Pujols waterfront is one of the best on Formentera. Foie gras, snails, and pastries are favorites, as is the simple fresh fish. ✉ *Passeig Marítim* ☎ *971/328386* 💳 *AE, DC, MC, V* ⊙ *Closed mid-Nov.–Mar.*

$$ ✕ **Sa Palmera.** On the beachfront in Es Pujols, Sa Palmera is known for paella and extremely fresh fish. ✉ *Playa Es Pujols* ☎ *971/328356* 💳 *MC, V* ⊙ *Closed Nov.–Feb.*

$$–$$$ ✕🏨 **Cala Saona.** On a charming fisherman's cala and a sleepy little beach, this friendly hotel will be difficult to leave behind. Rooms are simple, comfortable, and breezy, and the restaurant—serving dinner only—prepares the daily catch with skill and care. ✉ *Apdo. de Correos 88, 07860 San Francisco* ☎ *971/322030* 📠 *971/322509* 🌐 *www.guiaformentera.com/calasaona* *116 rooms* *Restaurant, tennis court, pool, bar* 💳 *AE, DC, MC, V* ⊙ *Closed mid-Oct.–Apr.*

$–$$ ✕🏨 **Fonda C'an Rafalet.** Yards from the water at the tiny fishing port of Es Caló is this simple inn, which is known for its seafood and rustic surroundings. The sound of inboard engines is the most distressing noise you'll hear, but the thought that they'll return with raw materials for your lunch is bound to make up for any lost sleep. The hotel is 12 km (7 mi) from La Sabina. ✉ *Ctra. La Mola, Km 12, Apdo. de Correos 225, 07860 Es Caló de Sant Agustí, Sant Francesc Xavier* ☎📠 *971/327016* *15 rooms* *Restaurant, bar* 💳 *MC, V* ⊙ *Closed Nov.–early Apr.*

$$–$$$ 🏨 **Club La Mola.** At Playa de Migjorn, this whitewashed waterfront spa has a certain cliff-dwelling Aztec look and as many comforts as you can possibly consume. The *playa,* while not as wild as it once was, is still one of the least-spoiled beaches on the Mediterranean. ✉ *Apdo. de*

Correos 23, 07860 Playa de Migjorn ☎ 971/327069 📠 971/328069 326 rooms Restaurant, miniature golf, tennis court, bar, meeting room, car rental ▭ AE, DC, MC, V.

$$–$$$ **Sa Volta.** Near the beach in Es Pujols, one of the island's busiest villages, this is a small and, if you choose one of the more modest rooms, economical lodging choice. ✉ *Miramar 94, 07860 San Francisco* ☎ *971/328125* 📠 *971/328228* 🌐 *www.guiaformentera.com/savolta* *25 rooms* *Cafeteria, pool* ▭ *AE, DC, MC, V* ⊙ *Closed Jan.–Feb.*

Shopping

Crafts are sold at Formentera's various markets: mornings in San Francesc, evenings until late in Es Pujols, and Sunday afternoon in El Pilar, which also has live music.

Sports & the Outdoors

BICYCLING La Sabina has numerous rental outlets. Plan routes and rent mountain bikes at **Asociación de la BTT de Formentera** (✉ Espalmador s/n, Es Pujols ☎ 971/328315 🌐 www.formentera.net/btt). Rent bicycles or motorcycles at **Moto Rent Pujols** (✉ Es Pujols ☎ 971/322138 🌐 www.guiaformentera.com/rentpujols). **Moto Rent Mitjorn** (✉ Playa de Migjorn ☎ 971/328611 🌐 www.guiaformentera.com/mitjorn) has both bikes and motorcycles for rent.

BOATING The graceful sloop ***Princesa de Mar*** (☎ 608/830827 or 610/421431) circumnavigates Formentera twice daily 9–1 and 4–8. Xicu Castelló and his merry crew provide plenty of laughs, and lovely views await aboard the sunset cruise. The boat departs from the port in La Sabina and costs €24 per person. Boats are for hire at **Náutica Pins** (✉ Av. Mediterráneo 15–19, La Savina ☎ 971/322651 🌐 www.formenteraonline.com/comercial/nauticapins). For fun or fishing, board the ***Barça Yaya II*** (✉ La Savina ☎ 609/847186).

DIVING You can take diving courses at **Vell Marí** (✉ Av. Mediterráneo 90, La Savina ☎ 971/322105 🌐 www.vellmari.com). There is diving, and canoes and boats for hire, at **Formentera Diving** (✉ Almadrava, Puerto de la Savina, ☎ 971/323323 🌐 www.formenteradiving.com).

HORSEBACK RIDING Ride with **Formentera Saona Horses** (✉ Cala Saona, Sant Francesc Xavier ☎ 971/323001).

TENNIS Get ready to serve at **Formentera** (✉ Av. Port Saler, Sant Francesc ☎ no phone).

THE BALEARIC ISLANDS A TO Z

To research prices, get advice from other travelers, and book travel arrangements, visit www.fodors.com.

AIR TRAVEL

CARRIERS Iberia, Spanair, and Air Europa have direct daily flights between Palma and Barcelona, Madrid, Alicante, Valencia, Minorca, and Ibiza, as well as direct flights two or three times a week to Bilbao and Vitoria. Inter-island flights should be booked well in advance for summer travel. Iberia and a large number of charter operators also serve other European cities. Iberia flies direct to Mahón from Barcelona and Palma three or four times daily, and most of these flights start and end in Madrid. Air Europa and Spanair also fly to Mahón, and in summer several European cities send charter flights to Minorca. Iberia has direct daily flights to Ibiza from Barcelona, Madrid, Valencia, and Palma.

Air Europa ☎ 902/401501. **Air Nostrum** ☎ 902/200222. **British Airways** ☎ 971/787737. **British Midland** ☎ 971/789269. **Easyjet** ☎ 902/299992. **Iberia** ☎ 902/400500. **Spanair** ☎ 902/131415.

AIRPORTS & TRANSFERS

Bus 17 runs between Palma's airport and the bus station on Plaça d'Espanya, next to the Inca train station. The last bus from town is at 1:30 AM; the last bus from the airport leaves at 2:10 AM. The fare is €1.80, and the trip takes 30 minutes. A taxi is about €16.50. A meter taxi to Mahón from the airport costs about €7. An hourly bus service runs between Ibiza's airport and Ibiza Town from 7 AM to 10:30 PM (on the hour from town, on the half hour from the airport; fare €2.70, journey time 15 minutes). By taxi, the same trip costs about €15.

Airport Information **Aeropuerto de Ibiza** ☎ 971/157000. **Aeropuerto de Palma de Mallorca** ☎ 971/262600 or 971/789000.

BIKE TRAVEL

The Balearic Islands—especially Formentera and Ibiza—are ideal for exploration by bicycle, although Majorca is quite large and fairly mountainous. Bicycles are easy to rent, and tourist offices have details for either touring or country routes for adventurous mountain bikers.

BOAT & FERRY TRAVEL

BARCELONA For travelers with a strong sense of romance, the only way to get to the Balearic Islands is the overnight Trasmediterránea ferry from Barcelona. The boat sails at 11, leaving time for a proper dinner before embarking, and the view of the lights of the Mediterranean's greatest city sinking into the horizon lasts more than three hours when visibility is good. The Christopher Columbus statue at the foot of the Rambla points directly at the Trasmediterránea station. Umafisa sails to Ibiza six days a week. For a speedier service, passengers only, 43-knot Turbocat catamarans operate between Barcelona and Alcúdia (three hours) and Barcelona and Ciutadella, Minorca (five hours).

DENIA Balearia runs a daily two-hour "Super Fast Ferry" service for passengers and cars between Denia and Ibiza (town or Sant Antoni) and a similar three-hour service between Denia and Palma on weekends. Pitiusa de Transportes (Pitra) runs a slower car-and-truck ferry service between Denia and Sant Antoni, Ibiza.

VALENCIA Every day but Sunday, Trasmediterránea leaves Valencia for Palma at 10:30 PM, arriving 7 AM. Service is faster and more frequent in summer. Ferries return from Palma weekdays at 11:30 AM, Saturday at 10 AM, and Sunday at 11:30 PM. Ferries from Valencia to Ibiza leave only on Thursday from October to May.

MAJORCA Trasmediterránea sails daily (and twice on Sunday) from Palma to Barcelona, daily from Palma to Valencia, and weekly (Sunday) from Palma to Mahón and Ibiza. From May to October, a daily hydrofoil (Hidrojet) service connects Palma and Ibiza; call Naviera Mallorquina. Balearia has a daily "Super Fast Ferry" car ferry service between Palma and Denia, direct on weekends but via Ibiza on weekdays. From June to September, a twice-weekly service connects Palma with Sète, France.

MINORCA Trasmediterránea sails between Mahón and Barcelona six days a week in summer (mid-June to mid-September) and to Palma and Valencia every Sunday.

IBIZA Trasmediterránea sails at least twice a week from Barcelona and Valencia to Ibiza and once a week (Sunday) to Palma. Umafisa sails to Barcelona six days a week. From May to October there is also a daily hydrofoil (Hidrojet) service from Palma and Denia, in the province of Alicante, as well as less frequent service from Valencia and Barcelona. Balearia runs a "Super Fast Ferry" to Denia daily, which takes two hours. A service operates between Sète (France) and Ibiza twice a week, June to September, calling at Palma on the way.

INTER-ISLAND Boats from Palma, Majorca, to neighboring beach resorts leave from the jetty opposite the Auditorium, on the Passeig Marítim. The tourist office has a schedule. In summer, excursions to Minorca's remotest beaches leave daily from the jetty next to the Nuevo Muelle Comercial, in Mahón's harbor. Flebasa, represented by all travel agencies on Majorca, ferries people and cars daily from Alcúdia (Majorca) to Ciutadella (Minorca) in three to four hours, depending on the weather. Turbocat runs services between Ciutadella and Alcúdia, taking one hour. Frequent ferry, catamaran, and hydrofoil services between Ibiza and Formentera are run by Transmapi, Umafisa, Flebasa, Mediterránea Pitiusa, and Inserco. In summer, Flebasa runs a daily 2½-hour hovercraft between Sant Antoni (Ibiza) and mainland Benidorm; contact Coral Travel. Flebasa also runs a car ferry and a fast hydrofoil between Sant Antoni (Ibiza) and mainland Denia, with bus connections from Denia to Madrid and Valencia.

Boat & Ferry Information **Balearia** ☎ 902/160180 www.balearia.com. **Coral Travel** ✉ Carrer Mar 11, Sant Antoni, Ibiza ☎ 971/343711 or 971/343752 ✉ Carrer Isadoro Macabich 14, Santa Eulalia, Ibiza ☎ 971/330512 or 971/330561. **Flebasa** ✉ Estación Marítim, Ibiza ☎ 971/310711 ✉ Edificio Faro, Sant Antoni, Ibiza ☎ 971/342871 ✉ Madrid ☎ 91/473-2055 ✉ Denia ☎ 96/784011. **Formentera port information** ☎ 971/320157. **Inserco** ☎ 971/322210. **Iscomar** Alcúdia-Ciutadella ☎ 902/119128 www.iscomar.com. **Mediterránea Pitiusa** ☎ 971/32244. **Naviera Mallorquina** ☎ 971/710153. **Pitra** ☎ 971/191068. **Transmapi** Formentera ☎ 971/322930 or 971/322703. **Trasmediterránea** ✉ Estación Marítima, Barcelona ☎ 902/454645 www.trasmediterranea.es ✉ Estación Marítima, Valencia ☎ 963/676512 ✉ Estación Marítima 2, Muelle de Paraires, Palma de Mallorca ☎ 971/707377 ✉ Nuevo Muelle Comercial, Mahón, Minorca ☎ 971/366050 ✉ Ibiza, Estación Marítima ☎ 971/315050. **Turbocat** ☎ 902/181888 www.turbocat.com. **Umafisa Lines** ☎ 902/191068.

BUS TRAVEL

A good network of bus service fans out from Palma to towns throughout Majorca. Most buses leave from the city station, next to the Inca railway terminus on the Plaça d'Espanya; a few terminate at other points in Palma. The tourist office on the Plaça d'Espanya has schedules. Several buses a day run the length of Minorca between Mahón and Ciutadella, stopping at Alayor, Mercadal, and Ferreries en route. From smaller towns there are daily buses to Mahón and connections, though often indirect, to Ciutadella. A regular bus service from the west end of Ciutadella's Plaça Explanada shuttles beachgoers between town and the resorts to the south and west. On Ibiza, buses run every half hour from Ibiza Town (Avinguda Isidoro Macabich) to Sant Antoni and Playa d'en Bossa, roughly hourly to Santa Eulalia. Buses from Ibiza to other parts of the island are less frequent, as is the cross-island bus between Sant Antoni and Santa Eulalia. The schedule is published in newspapers. A very limited bus service connects Formentera's villages, shrinking to one bus each way between San Francisco and Pilar on Saturday and disappearing altogether on Sunday and holidays.

Bus Stations **Ibiza Town** ✉ corner of Av. Isidoro Macabich and Extremadura www.ibizabus.com. **Palma de Mallorca** ✉ Estación Central ☎ 971/752224.

CAR RENTAL

While reserving a car from home through a major agency can often lead to savings, don't count out the local companies, whose rates are often inexpensive. Many of these local vendors also rent out *motos* (motorscooters) and bicycles.

National Agencies **Avis** ☎ 902/135531 🌐 www.avis.com. **Europcar** ☎ 902/105030 🌐 www.europcar.es. **Hertz** ☎ 902/402405 🌐 www.hertz.es. **National/Atesa** ☎ 902/100101 🌐 www.atesa.com.

Majorca **Arash** ✉ Ctra. de Andratx, Km 10, Portals Nous ☎ 971/675490. **Avance Rent a Car** ✉ Benito Feijoo 9, Puerto Portals ☎ 971/675539. **Avis** ✉ Aeropuerto de Palma ☎ 971/789187 🌐 www.avis.com. **Betacar** ✉ Juan XXlll 95–97, Puerto Pollensa ☎ 971/864418 🌐 www.betacar.es. **Centauro** ✉ Aeropuerto de Palma ☎ 971/789360 🌐 www.centauro.net. **Europcar** ☎ 971/789135 🌐 www.europcar.es. **Hertz** ✉ Aeropuerto de Palma ☎ 971/789670 🌐 www.hertz.es. **National/Atesa** ✉ Aeropuerto de Palma ☎ 971/789896 🌐 www.atesa.com. **Recar Touristic** ✉ Gremio Tejedores 35, Palma ☎ 971/919494. **Topcar Car Hire** ✉ Ctra. Porto Cristo–Son Severa, Sa Coma ☎ 902/496969.

Minorca **Autos 21** ✉ S'Espero s/n, Poima, Mahón ☎ 971/353439. **Autos Amigo** ✉ Local 12, Centro Comercial Cala n'Porter, Cala n'Porter ☎ 971/377290 🌐 www.menorcacarhire.com. **Avis** ✉ Aeropuerto de Menorca ☎ 971/361576. **Europcar** ☎ 971/366400 🌐 www.europcar.es. **Hertz** ✉ Aeropuerto de Menorca ☎ 971/353967 🌐 www.hertz.es. **Doncars** ✉ Camí de Ses Vinyes 13, Mahón ☎ 971/360467 🌐 www.doncars.com. **Maó Cars** ✉ Bayolí 73, Mahón, ☎ 971/366629 🌐 www.mao-cars.com. **National/Atesa** ✉ Aeropuerto de Menorca ☎ 971/366213 🌐 www.atesa.com. **Rent a Car S'Algar** ✉ Paseo Marítimo s/n, San Luis ☎ 971/150919.

Ibiza **Avis** ✉ Aeropuerto de Ibiza ☎ 971/809177 🌐 www.avis.com. **Europcar** ✉ Aeropuerto de Ibiza ☎ 971/395384 🌐 www.europcar.es. **Hertz** ✉ Aeropuerto de Ibiza ☎ 971/809178 🌐 www.hertz.es. **Motoluis** ✉ Av. Portmany 5, Sant Antoni ☎ 971/340521. **Motosud** ✉ Av. Sant Jordi 1, Figueretas ☎ 971/302442. **National/Atesa** ✉ Aeropuerto de Ibiza ☎ 971/395393 🌐 www.atesa.com.

Formentera **Avis** ☎ 971/322123 🌐 www.avis.com. **Europcar** ✉ Sabina ☎ 971/322031 or 971/322073 🌐 www.europcar.es. **Hertz** ☎ 971/395384 or 971395385 🌐 www.hertz.es. **Motorent Mirada** ✉ Apts. Porto Soler, Es Pujols ☎ 971/328888. **Moto Rent Mitjorn** ✉ Ctra. La Sabina, Km 2.5 ☎ 971/322787 🌐 www.guiaformentera.com/mitjorn. **Moto Rent Pujols** ☎ 971/322138 🌐 www.guiaformentera.com/rentpujols.

CAR TRAVEL

Majorca's main highways are well surfaced, and a fast, 25-km (15-mi) motorway penetrates deep into the island between Palma and Inca. Palma is ringed by an efficient beltway, the Vía Cintura. For destinations in the north and west, follow the ANDRATX and OESTE signs on the beltway; for the south and east, follow the ESTE signs. Driving in the mountains that parallel the northwest coast and descend to a cliff-side corniche is a different matter; you'll be slowed not only by winding roads but by tremendous views and tourist traffic. The tunnel through the mountains to Sóller obviates the spectacular but tiring serpentine mountain route, making the island's northwest coast a safe, simple, 20-minute drive from downtown Palma. A car is essential if you want to beach-hop on Minorca, as few of the beaches and calas are served by public transport. However, most historic sights are in Mahón or Ciutadella, both of which have reasonable bus service from other parts of the island; and once you're in town, everything is within walking distance. You can see the island's archaeological remains in a day's drive, so you may just want to rent a car for part of your visit. Ibiza is best explored by car or motor scooter, as many of the beaches lie at the end of rough, unpaved roads.

CONSULATES

Ireland **Palma de Mallorca** ✉ Sant Miquel 68A ☎ 971/719244.

United Kingdom **Palma de Mallorca** ✉ Plaça Major 3D ☎ 971/718501. **Ibiza** ✉ Isidoro Macabich 45 ☎ 971/301818.

United States **Palma de Mallorca** ✉ Av. Jaume III 26, Palma de Mallorca ☎ 971/725051.

EMERGENCIES

Emergency Services **Fire, Police or Ambulance** ☎ 112. **Guardia Civil** ☎ 062. **Insalud** (public health service) ☎ 061. **Policía Local** (local police) ☎ 092. **Policía Nacional** (national police) ☎ 091. **Servicio Marítimo** (Air-Sea Rescue) ☎ 902/202202. **Información Toxicológica** (poisoning) ☎ 915/620420.

24-Hour Pharmacies **24-Hour Pharmacy Emergency Line** ☎ 112 in four languages.

ENGLISH-LANGUAGE MEDIA

Majorca's daily English-language newspaper, the *Majorca Daily Bulletin*, also has a useful Web site; the city's weekly English-language paper is the *Reader*. Ibiza's sole English-language publication is the *Ibiza Sun*; the Ibiza Spotlight Web page is also worth a look.

Newspapers **Majorca Daily Bulletin** ✉ Paseo Mallorca 9A, 07011 Palma de Mallorca ☎ 971/788400 🌐 www.majorcadailybulletin.es. **Ibiza Sun** ✉ Edificio Igloo, Cala de Bou, 07839 San Agustí ☎ 971/342815 🌐 www.theibizasun.ibiza-show.com. **Ibiza Spotlight** 🌐 www.ibiza-spotlight.com.

LANGUAGE

The regional language is a version of Catalan, but everyone speaks Castilian Spanish. English and German are widely understood at most tourist venues.

LODGING

Villas, apartments, and rural houses are rented out to tourists throughout the Balearic Islands. There are hundreds of estate agents offering properties for short-term rentals. Contact the tourist offices or check the local papers for listings, but also consider booking through a travel agent, who can usually put together an attractive lodging package that includes transportation. Kuhn and Partner is a major Majorca real estate agency with numerous branches. For information on more than 100 charming, small country hotels away from the crowds contact Associació Agroturisme Balear.

Local Agents **Associació Agroturisme Balear** ✉ Av. Gabriel Alomar i Villalonga 8A. 2A, 07002 Palma de Mallorca ☎ 971/721508 📠 971/717317. **Kuhn and Partner** ✉ Paseo Marítimo 26, 07014 Palma ☎ 971/228020 🌐 www.atlas-iap.es/kuhn.

TAXIS

Taxis in Palma are metered. For trips beyond the city, charges are posted at the taxi ranks. On Minorca, you can pick up a taxi at the airport or in Mahón and Ciutadella; on Ibiza, taxis are available at the airport and in Ibiza Town, Figueretas, Santa Eulalia, and Sant Antoni. On Formentera, there are taxis in La Sabina and Es Pujols.

Taxi Companies **Formentera** ✉ La Sabina ☎ 971/322002 ✉ Sant Francesc ☎ 971/322016 ✉ Es Pujols ☎ 971/328016. **Ibiza** ✉ Aeropuerto de Ibiza, ☎ 971/305230 ✉ Passeig Vara de Rey, Ibiza Town ☎ 971/301794, 971/307000, or 971/306602 ✉ Figueretas ☎ 971/301676 ✉ Santa Eulalia ☎ 971/333033 ✉ Sant Antoni ☎ 971/340074 or 971/341721. **Majorca** ✉ Palma ☎ 971/755440, 971/401414, or 971/728081. **Minorca** ✉ Explanada, Mahón ☎ 971/367111 ✉ Carrer Josep Antoni, Ciutadella ☎ 971/381896.

TOURS

Most Majorca hotels offer guided tours. Typical itineraries are the Caves of Artà or Drac, on the east coast, including the nearby Auto Safari Park and an artificial-pearl factory in Manacor; the Chopin museum in the old monastery at Valldemossa, returning through the writers' and artists' village of Deià; the port of Sóller and the Arab gardens at Alfàbia; the Thursday market and leather factories in Inca; Port de Pollença; Cape Formentor; and northern beaches. Nearly every Majorcan resort runs excursions to neighboring beaches and coves—many inaccessible by road—and to the islands of Cabrera and Dragonera. You can also take a morning shopping trip by boat from Magalluf or Palma Nova to Palma; the tourist office has details. Various sightseeing trips leave Mahón's harbor from the quayside near the Xoriguer gin factory; several boats have glass bottoms. Fares average around €6. Every Ibiza resort runs trips to neighboring beaches and to smaller islands off the coast. Trips from Ibiza to Formentera include an escorted bus tour. In Sant Antoni, which has little to offer in the way of beaches, a whole flotilla advertises trips.

TRAIN TRAVEL

The Palma–Inca line travels to Inca, with stops at about half a dozen villages en route, from the Palma terminus. A journey on the privately owned Palma–Sóller railway is a must: built by the citrus-fruit magnates of Sóller in 1912, it still uses the carriages of that era. The line trundles across the plain to Bunyola, then winds through tremendous mountain scenery to emerge high above Sóller. An ancient tram connects the Sóller terminus to Port de Sóller, leaving every hour on the hour, 9–7; the Palma terminal is near the corner of the Plaça d'Espanya, on Calle Eusebio Estada next to the Inca rail station.

Train Information **Palma train station** ✉ Ferrocarriles de Majorca, Plaça d'Espanya ☎ 971/752245. **Sóller tram** ✉ Eusebi Estada 1 ☎ 971/752051.

VISITOR INFORMATION

The regional tourist office for the Balearic Islands is the Consellaria de Turismo de Balear in Palma de Mallorca. Several tourist offices in Palma's airport have information on Majorca and towns nearby. The offices in Mahón and Ciutadella have local information.

Regional Tourist Office **Consellaria de Turismo de Balear** ✉ Av. Jaume III 10, 07012 Palma de Mallorca ☎ 971/712216 🌐 www.visitbalears.com.

Local Tourist Offices–Majorca **Oficina de Turismo de Mallorca** ✉ Aeropuerto de Palma ☎ 971/789556. **Alcúdia** ✉ Passeig Marítim s/n ☎ 971/547257. **Arenal** ✉ Pça Reina M Cristina s/n ☎ 971/440414. **Cala d'Or** ✉ Perico Pomar 10 ☎ 971/657463. **Cala Millor** ✉ Badia de Llevant 2 ☎ 971/585409 ✉ Passeig Marítim ☎ 971/585864. **Cala Rajada** ✉ Plaça dels Pins ☎ 971/563033. **Cala Sant Vicenç** ✉ Plaça Cala Vicenç s/n ☎ 971/533264. **Cales de Mallorca** ✉ Passeig Manacor s/n ☎ 971/834144. **Ca'n Picafort** ✉ Plaça Gabriel Roca 6 ☎ 971/850310. **Colònia de Sant Jordi** ✉ Doctor Barraquer 5 ☎ 971/656073. **Illetes** ✉ Ctra. Andratx 33 ☎ 971/405444. **Illot** ✉ Llevant 7 ☎ 971/810699. **Magalluf** ✉ Av. Magaluf 22 ☎ 971/131126. **Manacor** ✉ Plaça Ramon Llull s/n ☎ 971/847241. **Palma** ✉ Plaça de la Reina 2 ☎ 971/712216 ✉ kiosk on northeast side of Plaça d'Espanya, facing train station ☎ 971/754329 ✉ Sant Domingo 11 ☎ 971/724090. **Palmanova** ✉ Passeig de la Mar 13 ☎ 971/682365. **Peguera** ✉ Sebel.li 5 ☎ 971/687083. **Playa de Muro** ✉ Av. s'Albufera 33 ☎ 971/891013. **Pollença** ✉ Sant Domingo 2 ☎ 971/535077. **Port de Pollença** ✉ Monges 9 ☎ 971/865467. **Portocristo** ✉ Bordils 53-B ☎ 971/815103. **Santa Ponça** ✉ Puig de Galatzó s/n ☎ 971/691712. **Sóller** ✉ Plaça de Sa Constitució 1 ☎ 971/630200 ✉ Carrer Canónigo Oliver ☎ 971/630101. **Valldemossa** ✉ Cartuja de Valldemossa ☎ 971/612106.

Local Tourist Offices–Minorca **Ciutadella** ✉ Plaça de la Catedral 5 ☎ 971/382693. **Mahón** ✉ Sa Rovellada de Dalt 24 ☎ 971/363790. **Minorca** ✉ Aeropuerto de Menorca ☎ 971/157115.

Local Tourist Offices–Ibiza (Eivissa) & Formentera **Aeropuerto de Ibiza** ☎ 971/809118. **Formentera** ✉ Port de La Sabina ☎ 971/322057 🌐 www.visitformentera.com. **Ibiza Town** ✉ Carrer Antonio Riquer 2 ☎ 971/301900. **Santa Eulalia** ✉ Carrer Mariano Riquer Wallis s/n ☎ 971/330728. **Sant Antoni** ✉ Passeig de Ses Fonts s/n ☎ 971/343363. **Sant Joan** ✉ Ajuntament ☎ 971/333003.

THE COSTA DEL SOL

FODOR'S CHOICE

Café de París, Málaga

Marbella Club hotel, Marbella

Parador de Málaga–Gibralfaro, Málaga

Town of Ronda

HIGHLY RECOMMENDED

HOTELS
Byblos Andaluz, Mijas-Costa
Las Dunas, Estepona
Puente Romano, Marbella

RESTAURANTS
Tragabuches, Ronda

SIGHTS
Cable Car, Gibraltar
Town of Mijas
Town of Nerja

By Hilary Bunce

Updated by Mary Mclean

TECHNICALLY, THE STRETCH OF ANDALUSIAN SHORE known as the Costa del Sol runs west from the Costa Tropical, near Granada, to the tip of Tarifa, the southernmost tip of Europe, just beyond Gibraltar. For most of the Europeans who have flocked here over the past 40 years, though, the Sun Coast has been largely restricted to the 70 km (43 mi) sprawl of hotels, holiday villas, golf courses, marinas, and nightclubs between Torremolinos, just west of Málaga, and Estepona, down toward Gibraltar. Since the late 1950s this area has mushroomed from a group of impoverished fishing villages into an overdeveloped seaside playground and retirement haven.

Construction continued unabated along the Coast until the early '90s, which saw a brief economic slump due, in part, to a drop in international airfares. Travelers became more adventurous and Spain's favorite bucket-and-spade Costa was now competing with seemingly more sophisticated locations. Local municipalities poured money into elaborate landscaping, better roads, and infrastructure. It paid off. In 1997 the prestigious Ryder Cup was held in Sotogrande, seeming to mark the Costa del Sol's return to the world stage. The result was still more golf courses, luxury marinas, villa developments, and upscale hotels. The Costa averages some 320 days of sunshine a year, and balmy days are not unknown even in January or February. Despite the hubbub, you *can* unwind here, basking or strolling on mile after mile of sandy beach. Choose your base carefully. Málaga is a vibrant Spanish city, virtually untainted by tourism. Ronda is similarly intrinsically Andalusian, with the added perk of a stunning inland setting. Back on the coast, Torremolinos is a budget destination catering almost exclusively to the mass market; it appeals to singles and to those who come purely to soak up the sun and dance the night away. Fuengirola is quieter and geared more toward families; farther west, the Marbella–San Pedro de Alcántara area is more exclusive.

About the Restaurants

Spain's southern coast is known for fresh seafood, breaded with fine flour and exquisitely fried. Sardines roasted on skewers at beachside restaurants are another popular and unforgettable treat. Gazpacho shows up in the Andalusian culinary canon as both complement and antidote. Málaga is best for traditional Spanish cooking, with a wealth of bars and seafood restaurants serving *fritura malagueña,* the city's famous fried fish. Torremolinos' Carihuela district is also a locus for lovers of Spanish seafood. The resorts serve every conceivable foreign cuisine as well, from Thai to the Scandinavian smorgasbord; Marbella has internationally renowned restaurants. At the other end of the scale, and perhaps even more enjoyable, are the Costa's traditional *chiringuitos*; strung out along the beaches, these rough-and-ready, summer-only restaurants serve seafood fresh off the boats. Because there are so many foreigners, meals on the coast are served earlier than elsewhere in Andalusia, with restaurants opening at 1 or 1:30 for lunch and 7 or 8 for dinner. Reservations are advisable for all Marbella restaurants listed as $$$–$$$$ and for the better restaurants in Málaga; elsewhere, they're rarely necessary. Expect beach restaurants, such as Málaga's Casa Pedro and all those on the Carihuela seafront in Torremolinos, to be packed after 3 PM on Sunday.

WHAT IT COSTS In Euros

	$$$$	$$$	$$	$	¢
AT DINNER	over €20	€15–€20	€10–€15	€6–€10	under €6

Prices are for per person for a main course at dinner.

If you have **3 days**

Explore Granada's Costa Tropical, the eastern end of Sol. See the villages of **Salobreña** 1 and **Almuñecar** 2 and the town of **Nerja** 3. Have lunch at one of the sea-view restaurants. Visit the village of **Frigiliana** 4 before proceeding to **Málaga** 6 for the night. The next morning, explore Málaga before heading into the hills for lunch in **Antequera** 7. Make the 100-km (62-mi) drive to **Ronda** 17 for your second night. Explore Ronda in the morning and drive to coastal **Marbella** 15 for lunch at the beach. Then move west to Sotogrande, **San Roque** 24, and **Gibraltar** 25–37 or head back east to **Torremolinos** 11 for a night on the town.

If you have **5 days**

Follow the itinerary above for your first day, settling down in **Málaga** 6 for the night. On your second day explore Málaga before driving into the hills for sunset and a night in the parador in **Antequera** 7. On day three, drive to the village of Archidona, and follow a small road north to the **Garganta del Chorro** 8. Continue on to **Torremolinos** 11. On your fourth day, explore the **Mijas** 14 before continuing to **Marbella** 15 to check out the glitterati. Alternately, escape to the village of **Ojén** 16. In early evening, drive to **Ronda** 17. On day five check out Ronda before touring **Setenil de las Bodegas** 18 and **Olvera** 19, the Roman settlement of Acinipo, **Zahara de la Sierra** 20, and the **Sierra de Grazalema** 21. Finish this ambitious day with a look at Sotogrande and **San Roque** 24 on your way into **Gibraltar** 25–37.

About the Hotels

Most hotels on the developed stretch, between Torremolinos and Fuengirola, offer large, functional rooms near the sea at competitive rates. The area's popularity as a budget destination means that most such hotels are booked in high season by package-tour operators. Finding a room at Easter, in July and August, or around the October 12 holiday weekend can be difficult if you haven't reserved in advance. Málaga is poorly endowed with hotels for a city of its size; it has an excellent but small parador that can be hard to book and few other hotels of note. Marbella, conversely, packs more than its fair share of grand hotels, including some of Spain's most expensive accommodations. Rooms in Gibraltar's handful of hotels tend to be more expensive than most comparable lodgings in Spain.

WHAT IT COSTS In Euros

	$$$$	$$$	$$	$	¢
FOR 2 PEOPLE	over €180	€100–€180	€60–€100	€40–€60	under €40

Prices are for two people in a standard double room in high season, excluding tax.

Exploring the Costa del Sol

The towns and resorts along the Costa del Sol vary considerably according to whether they lie to the west or to the east of Málaga. The coastal strip between Torremolinos and Marbella is the most densely populated—one resort merges into the next, separating the mountains from the sea. Seamless though it may appear, each town has a distinctive character, with associated infrastructure and amenities. To the east of Málaga, the coast is more rugged and far less developed. Towns like Nerja also act as a gateway to the mountainous region of La Axarquía. The Costa del Sol is also ideal if you want to explore the rest of Andalusia. Many of the province's most charming pueblos blancos (white villages) lie just inland, and Granada, Córdoba, and Seville are only a few hours away by road.

Numbers in the text correspond to numbers in the margin and on the Costa del Sol and Gibraltar maps.

Timing

Winter is a good time to be on this coast; the temperatures are moderate, and there are fewer tourists. Fall and spring are also good. Avoid July and August; it's too hot and crowded. May and June bring the longest days and the fewest travelers. Holy Week offers memorable ceremonies and processions.

THE COSTA TROPICAL

East of Málaga and west of Almería, the so-called Costa Tropical has escaped the worst excesses of the property developers, and its tourist onslaught has been mild. A flourishing farming center, this area earns its keep not from tourism but from tropical fruit, including avocados, mangoes, papaws, and custard apples. Housing developments are generally inspired by Andalusian village architecture rather than concrete towers. You may find packed beaches and traffic-choked roads at the height of the season, but for most of the year the Costa Tropical is relatively free of tourists, if not devoid of expatriates.

Salobreña

❶ *102 km (63 mi) east of Málaga.*

You can reach Salobreña by descending through the mountains from Granada or by continuing west from Almería on the N340. A detour to the left from the highway brings you to this unspoiled village of near-perpendicular streets and old white houses, slapped onto a steep hill beneath a Moorish fortress. It's a true Andalusian pueblo, separated from the beachfront restaurants and bars in the newer part of town.

Almuñecar

❷ *85 km (53 mi) east of Málaga.*

Almuñecar has been a fishing village since Phoenician times, 3,000 years ago, when it was called Sexi. Later, the Moors built a castle here for the treasures of Granada's kings. Today Almuñecar is a small-time resort with a shingle beach, popular with Spanish and northern-European vacationers. The road west from Motril passes through the former empire of the sugar barons who brought prosperity to Málaga's province in the 19th century. The cane fields are now giving way to litchis, limes, mangoes, papaws, and olives; avocado groves line your route as you descend into Almuñecar. The village is actually two, separated by the dramatic rocky headland of Punta de la Mona. To the east is Almuñecar proper, and to the west is **La Herradura**, a quiet fishing community. Between the two is the pretty Marina del Este yacht harbor, a popular diving center along with La Herradura.

Crowning Almuñecar is the **Castillo de San Miguel** (St. Michael's Castle). A Roman fortress once stood here, later enlarged by the Moors, but the castle's present aspect owes more to 16th-century additions. The building was bombarded during the Peninsular War at the beginning of

Beaches

Beaches range from shingle and pebbles (Almuñecar, Nerja, Málaga) to a fine, gray, gritty sand (from Torremolinos westward). All beaches are free, and are packed July–August and on Sunday May–October. It's acceptable for women to go topless; if you want to take it *all* off, go to beaches designated *playa naturista*. The most popular nude beaches are in Maro (near Nerja) and near Tarifa. The best—and most crowded—beaches are El Bajondillo and La Carihuela, in Torremolinos; the stretch between Carvajal, Los Boliches, and Fuengirola; and those around Marbella. You may find a secluded beach west of Estepona. For wide beaches of fine sand, head west past Gibraltar, to Tarifa and the Cádiz coast, though winds are quite strong.

Fiestas

Málaga has a parade on January 5, the eve of the **Día de los Tres Reyes** (Feast of the Three Kings); the city's **Semana Santa** (Holy Week) processions are dramatic. Nerja and Estepona celebrate **San Isidro** (May 15) with typically Andalusian ferias. Midsummer, or the feast of **San Juan** (June 23–24), is marked by midnight bonfires on beaches along the coast. The **Virgen del Carmen** is the patron saint of fishermen, so coastal communities honor her feast day (July 16) with processions. The annual ferias in Málaga (early August) and Fuengirola (early October) are among the best on the Coast.

Golf

There are nearly 40 golf courses between Rincón de la Victoria (east of Málaga) and Gibraltar. The best season is October to June; greens fees are lower during the summer. Pick up *Sun Golf,* a free magazine, at hotels and golf clubs. The *Andalucía Golf Guide,* published by Andalusia's tourist office details all the courses on the Costa del Sol.

---

the 19th century, and what was left became initially a cemetery until the 1990s, when excavation and restoration began. You can wander the ramparts and peer into the dungeon; the skeleton at the bottom is a replica of human remains discovered on the spot. *€2 (includes admission to Cueva de Siete Palacios) July–Aug., Tues.–Sat. 10:30–1:30 and 6–9, Sun. 10–2; Sept.–June, Tues.–Sat. 10:30–1:30 and 4–6:30, Sun. 10:30–2.*

Beneath the Castillo de San Miguel is a large, vaulted stone cellar of Roman origin, the **Cueva de Siete Palacios** (Cave of Seven Palaces), now Almuñecar's archaeological museum. The collection is small but interesting, with Phoenician, Roman, and Moorish artifacts. *€2 (includes admission to Castillo de San Miguel) July–Aug., Tues.–Sat. 10:30–1:30 and 6–9, Sun. 10–2; Sept.–June, Tues.–Sat. 10:30–1:30 and 4–6:30, Sun. 10:30–2.*

Where to Stay & Eat

$$–$$$ ✕ **Jacqui-Cotobro.** One of the finest French restaurants on Spain's southern coast is at the foot of the Punta de la Mona. The dining area is cozy, with bare brick walls and green wicker chairs; a beachfront terrace is open in summer. Try the *menú de degustación,* with three courses plus dessert; it might include breast of duck in sweet-and-sour sauce followed by *hojaldre de langostinos con puerros* (shrimp pastry with leeks) and *suprema de rodaballo* (turbot). ✉ *Edificio Río, Playa Cotobro* ☎ *958/631802* *MC, V* *Closed Nov.–Mar.*

The Costa del Sol
Olvera 19
Algodonales
Zahara de la Sierra 20
Grazalema 21
El Bosque
El Saucejo
Campillos
Bobadilla
Archidona
Loja
Granada
Fuente de Piedra
Parque Natural del Torcal de Antequera
7 Antequera
Setenil de las Bodegas 18
Carratraca 9
8 Garganta del Chorro
Ardales
Alora
Casabermeja
Comares
ANDALUSIA
Alhama
Padul
Orgiva
CUEVAS DE NERJA
17 Ronda
CUEVA DE LA PILETA
10 Pizarra
Vélez-Málaga
The Axarquía 5
Frigiliana 4
Málaga 6
3 Nerja
2 Almuñecar
1 Salobreña
Motril
Rincón de la Vieja
Torre del Mar
Torrox Costa
Cortes de la Frontera
Coín
Churriana
Alhaurín el Grande
Alhaurín de la Torre
Mijas 14
11 Torremolinos
12 Benalmádena-Costa
13 Fuengirola
16 Ojén
Marbella 15
Gaucín
Puerto Banús
Casares 23
San Pedro de Alcántara
Estepona 22
Jimena de la Frontera
COSTA DEL SOL ORIENTAL
COSTA DEL SOL OCCIDENTAL
Mediterranean Sea
San Roque 24
Gibraltar 25 - 37 see detail map
Tarifa 38
La Linea
Algeciras
Punta Grande de Europa
A473
N342
N334
C337
N331
N321
C340
N323
C341
C344
C335
N340
E15
C3331
KEY
Rail Lines
Beach
0 10 miles
0 15 km

$$$ **Los Fenicios.** Near the beach in La Herradura, this modern, Andalusian-style hotel has views of the bay and the cliffs of Punta de Mona to the east and the rocky headland of Cerro Gordo to the west. Each room has a terrace and a sitting area with wicker chairs; ask for a room with a sea view. *Paseo de Andrés Segovia, La Herradura 18697 958/827900 958/827910 www.sollosfenicios.solmelia.com 42 rooms Restaurant, cafeteria, in-room data ports, minibars, pool, meeting room AE, DC, MC, V.*

$-$$ **Casablanca.** There's something quaint about this family-run hotel with a neo-Moorish facade. Rooms have modern fittings and antiques. Rooms on the top two floors are the newest. The building is next to the beach in the center of town; some rooms have balconies. *Pl. San Cristóbal 4, 18690 958/635575 www.almunecar.info/casablanca 25 rooms Restaurant, bar D, MC, V.*

Nerja

★ 3 *52 km (32 mi) east of Málaga, 22 km (14 mi) west of Almuñecar.*

Nerja—the name comes from the Moorish word *narixa,* meaning "abundant springs"—is a developing resort. Much of its growth has been confined to *urbanizaciones* ("village" developments) outside town. The old village is on a headland above small beaches and rocky coves, which offer reasonable bathing despite the gray, gritty sand. In high season, Nerja's beaches are packed with northern Europeans, but the rest of the year it's a pleasure to wander the old town's narrow streets. Nerja's highlight is the **Balcón de Europa,** a lookout high above the sea, on a promontory just off the central square. The **Cuevas de Nerja** (Nerja Caves) lie between Almuñecar and Nerja on a road surrounded by giant cliffs and dramatic seascapes. Signs point to the cave entrance above the village of Maro, 4 km (2½ mi) east of Nerja. The caves were discovered in 1959 by children playing on the hillside; they're now floodlit for better views of the spires and turrets created by millennia of dripping water. One suspended pinnacle, 200 ft long, is in fact the world's largest known stalactite. The awesome subterranean chambers are perfect for concerts and ballets during July's Nerja Caves Festival. *952/529520 €5 Daily 10–2 and 4–6:30 (4–8 in summer).*

Where to Stay & Eat

$$-$$$ **Udo Heimer.** Your eponymous host, a genial German, welcomes you warmly to this stylish art deco villa in a development to the east of Nerja. The visual flair extends to the food, which mixes German and Spanish flavors. Try the warm salad of prawns and avocado mousse or the stuffed quail with Armagnac sauce and sauerkraut. The excellent wine list has rarities from all over Spain. *Pueblo Andaluz 27 952/520032 MC, V Closed Wed. No lunch in summer.*

$$ **Casa Luque.** One of Nerja's most authentic Spanish restaurants, Casa Luque is in an old Andalusian house behind the Balcón de Europa church. The menu has dishes from northern Spain, often of Basque or Navarrese origin, with an emphasis on meat and game; good fresh fish is also on offer. Ask to sit on the patio during the summer. *Pl. Cavana 2 952/521004 AE, DC, MC, V Closed Wed.*

$$-$$$ **Parador de Nerja.** On a cliff's edge is this modern parador, with rooms that have balconies overlooking a garden and the sea. Rooms in the newer, single-story wing open onto their own patios; some have whirlpool baths. An elevator descends to the rocky beach. The restaurant is known for its fish; offerings might include *pez espada a la naranja* (swordfish in orange sauce) or giant *langostino* (shrimp). *Almuñecar 8, 29780*

☎ *952/520050* 🖷 *952/521997* 🌐 *www.parador.es* 🛏 *73 rooms* ♿ *Restaurant, pool* 💳 *AE, DC, MC, V.*

$$ 🏨 **Paraiso del Mar.** An erstwhile private villa was expanded to form this small hotel, on the edge of a cliff overlooking the sea east of the Balcón de Europa. Light-blue and yellow fabrics, potted plants, and sunlight streaming through picture windows lend lots of cheer. Some rooms have terraces, four have hot tubs, and most have sea views. ✉ *Prolongación del Carabeo 22, 29780* ☎ *952/521621* 🖷 *952/522309* 🛏 *7 rooms, 9 suites* ♿ *Minibars, in-room hot tubs, pool, sauna, bar* 💳 *AE, DC, MC, V* ⏲ *Closed mid-Nov.–mid-Dec.*

Nightlife & the Arts

El Colono (✉ Granada 6, Nerja ☎ 952/521826) is a flamenco club in the town center. Dinner shows begin at 9 PM on Wednesday and Friday from Easter week until the end of October. You can choose from three prix-fixe menus.

Frigiliana

❹ *58 km (36 mi) east of Málaga.*

The village of Frigiliana sits on a mountain ridge overlooking the sea. One of the last battles between the Christians and the Moors was waged here in 1567. The short drive off the highway rewards you with spectacular views and an old quarter full of cobble streets and ancient houses. (If you don't have a car, take a bus here from Nerja.)

The Axarquía

❺ *Vélez-Málaga: 36 km (22 mi) east of Málaga.*

The Axarquía region is in the eastern third of Málaga's province, stretching from Nerja to the city of Málaga. Its coast consists of narrow, pebbly beaches and drab fishing villages on either side of the high-rise resort town of Torre del Mar. The region's charm lies in its mountainous interior, peppered with pueblos, vineyards, and tiny farms. The four-lane E-15 highway speeds across the region a few miles in from the coast; traffic on the old coastal road (N340) is slower. **Vélez-Málaga** is the capital of the Axarquía. A pleasant agricultural town of white houses, Vélez-Málaga is a center for strawberry fields and vineyards. Worth quick visits are the **Thursday market,** the ruins of a **Moorish castle,** and the church of **Santa María la Mayor,** built in Mudéjar style on the site of a mosque that was destroyed when the town fell to the Christians in 1487.

If you have a car and an up-to-date road map, explore the Axarquía's inland villages. You can follow the **Ruta del Vino** (Wine Route) 22 km (14 mi) from the coast, stopping at villages that produce the sweet, earthy local wine, particularly **Competa.** Alternatively, you can take the **Ruta de la Pasa** (Raisin Route) through Moclinejo, El Borge, and Comares. The latter perches like an eagle's nest atop one of the highest mountains and dates back to Moorish times. This area is especially spectacular during the late-summer grape-harvest season or in late autumn, when the leaves of the vines turn gold. A short detour to **Macharaviaya** (7 km [4 mi] north of Rincón de la Victoria) might lead you to ponder the past glory of this now sleepy village: in 1776 one of its sons, Bernardo de Gálvez, became Spanish governor of Louisiana and later fought in the American Revolution (Galveston, Texas, takes its name from the governor). Macharaviaya prospered under his heirs and for many years enjoyed a lucrative monopoly on the manufacture of playing cards for South America.

Where to Stay & Eat

$–$$ ✕ **Museo del Vino.** Barrels and bottles of muscatel wine line the bodega of this rustic restaurant with brick walls and a wood-beam ceiling. Start out the evening sampling wines and tasty tapas, including pungent Manchego cheese, cured hams, and olives. If you're still hungry, settle in for a full meal featuring grilled meats, the house specialty. ✉ *Calle Constitución s/n* ☎ *952/553314* ▭ *MC, V* ⊙ *Closed Mon.*

$$ **Molino de Santillán.** This small country hotel is on a farm at the end of a 1-km (½-mi) dirt road just north of the main highway. Rooms have clay-tile floors and antiques; those upstairs have balconies and views of the countryside; downstairs rooms have direct access to the garden. The Añoreta golf club and course is a short drive away. ✉ *Ctra. de Macharaviaya, Km 3, Rincón de la Victoria 29730* ☎ *952/115780* 🖷 *952/115782* *10 rooms* *Restaurant, pool* ▭ *AE, DC, MC, V.*

¢–$ **El Molino de los Abuelos.** Under a canopy of jasmine and bougainvillea is this splendidly renovated former olive mill with a cobbled courtyard. The rooms are all different, ranging from small and simple with shared bath, to a sumptuous suite with hot tub. The restaurant serves solidly traditional fare, with an emphasis on fish—despite the fact that this pueblo blanco sits some three thousand feet above sea level. ✉ *Plaza 2, Comares 29195* ☎ *952/509309* 🖷 *952/214220* *6* *Restaurant; no TV in some rooms* ▭ *AE, MC, V.*

MÁLAGA & INLAND

The city of Málaga and the towns of the upland hills and valleys to the north create the kind of contrast that makes travel in Spain exciting. The region's Moorish legacy is a unifying visual theme, connecting the tiny streets honeycombing the steamy depths of Málaga, the rocky cliffs and gorges between Alora and Archidona, the layout of the farms, and the crops themselves, including oranges and lemons.

Málaga

6 *175 km (109 mi) southeast of Córdoba.*

With about 550,000 residents, the city of Málaga is technically the capital of the Costa del Sol, though most travelers use the airport and bypass the city itself. Approaching the city from the airport, you'll be greeted by huge 1970s high-rises that march determinedly toward Torremolinos. But don't despair: in its center and its eastern suburbs, Málaga is a pleasant port city, with ancient streets and lovely villas amid exotic foliage. Blessed with a subtropical climate, it's covered in lush vegetation and averages some 324 days of sunshine a year.

Málaga has had a good cleaning up; many of the older buildings have been tastefully restored. Although tourism is nothing like on a scale of that in Granada or Seville, it's on the rise. Most hotels organize sightseeing tours and there's an inexpensive (€1.15) open-top tourist bus, which you can hop on and off of at leisure at any of the major sights. The long-awaited Picasso Museum, slated to open in fall 2003, is sure to boost the number of visitors to the Costa capital. On the down side, more tourists usually means more pickpockets, so be careful, particularly around the historic city center.

Arriving from Nerja, you'll enter Málaga through the suburbs of El Palo and Pedregalejo, once traditional fishing villages in their own right. Here you can eat fresh fish in the numerous crusty chiringuitos on the beach and stroll Pedregalejos's seafront promenade or the tree-lined streets of El Limonar. At sunset, walk along the **Paseo Marítimo** and watch the lighthouse start its nightly vigil. A few blocks inland from here is Málaga's bullring, **La Malagueta,** built in 1874. In the city center, the **Plaza de la Marina,** with cafés and an illuminated fountain overlooking the port, is a pleasant place for a drink. From here, stroll through the shady, palm-lined gardens of the **Paseo del Parque** or browse on **Calle Marqués de Larios,** the main shopping street.

The narrow streets and alleys on each side of Calle Marqués de Larios have charms of their own. Wander the warren of passageways around **Pasaje Chinitas,** off Plaza de la Constitución, and peep into the dark, vaulted bodegas where old men down glasses of *seco añejo* or *Málaga Virgen,* local wines made from Málaga's muscatel grapes. Silversmiths and vendors of religious books and statues ply their trades in shops that have changed little since the turn of the last century. Across Larios, in the streets leading to Calle Nueva, you'll see shoe-shine boys, lottery-ticket vendors, carnation-sporting Gypsies, beggars, and tapas bars dispensing wine from huge barrels. From the Plaza Felix Saenz, at the southern end of Calle Nueva, turn onto Sagasta to reach the **Mercado de Atarazanas,** the most colorful market in all of Andalusia. Stalls sell fresh fish, spices, and vegetables. The typical 19th-century iron structure incorporates the original **Puerta de Atarazanas,** the attractive 14th-century Moorish gate that once connected the city with the port.

Málaga's **cathedral,** built between 1528 and 1782, is not one of the greatest in Spain, having been left unfinished when funds ran out. Because it lacks one of its two towers, the building has been called *La Manquita* (The One-Armed Lady). The enclosed choir, which miraculously survived the burnings of the civil war, is the work of 17th-century artist Pedro de Mena, who carved the wood wafer-thin in some places to express the fold of a robe or shape of a finger. The choir also has a pair of massive 18th-century pipe organs, one of which is still used for the occasional concert. Adjoining the cathedral is a small museum of religious art and artifacts, and a walk around the cathedral on Calle Cister will take you to the Late Gothic Puerta del Sagrario. ✉ *C. de Molina Larios* ☎ *952/215917* 🎫 *€2* ⏲ *Mon.–Sat. 10–6:45.*

Palacio Episcopa (Bishop's Palace) is used for art exhibits. The palace faces the main entrance of the cathedral. ✉ *Pl. Obispo 6* ☎ *952/602722* 🎫 *Free* ⏲ *Tues.–Sun. 10–2 and 6–9.*

Palacio de Buenavista. The home of the future Museo Picasso will have a core collection donated by Picasso's daughter-in-law Christine and grandson Bernard. Restoration work has been fraught with delays caused, in part, by a fire and the discovery of archaeological remains. The museum is slated to open on October 25, 2003 (Picasso's birthday). Even though Picasso's family moved to the north of Spain when he was 10, and he spent the last three decades of his life in exile following the Spanish Civil War, he always considered himself first and foremost an Andalusian. ✉ *C. de San Agustín.*

Fundación Picasso. On the Plaza de la Merced, No. 15 was the childhood home of Málaga's most famous native son, Pablo Picasso, born here in 1881. It now houses the foundation and a library for art historians. The interior has been remodeled, with no trace of its original furnishings. The second floor, where Picasso's family lived, now has a permanent exhibit with engravings, sculpture and ceramics; temporary exhibits of art or memorabilia fill the ground floor. ✉ *Pl. de la Merced 15* ☎ *952/600215* 🎫 *Free* ⏲ *Mon.–Sat. 11–2 and 5–8, Sun. 11–2.*

Just beyond the ruins of a Roman theater on Calle Alcazabilla, the Moorish **Alcazaba** is Málaga's greatest monument. This fortress was begun in the 8th century, when Málaga was the principal port of the Moorish kingdom, though most of the present structure dates from the 11th century. The inner palace was built between 1057 and 1063, when the Moorish emirs took up residence; and Ferdinand and Isabella lived here for a while after conquering Málaga in 1487. The ruins are dappled with orange trees and bougainvillea, and from their heights you can see over the park and port. ✉ *Entrance on Alcazabilla* 🎫 *€1.80* ⏲ *Oct.–Mar., Tues.–Sun. 9–8; Apr.–Sept., Tues.–Sun. 9:30–8.*

Magnificent vistas beckon at **Gibralfaro,** which is floodlit at night. The fortifications were built for Yusuf I in the 14th century; the Moors called them Jebelfaro, from the Arab word for "mount" and the Greek word for "lighthouse," after a beacon that stood here to guide ships into the harbor and warn of pirates. The beacon has been succeeded by a small parador. You can drive here by way of Calle Victoria or take a minibus that leaves 10 times a day between 11 and 7, or roughly every hour, from the bus stop in the park near the Plaza de la Marina. ✉ *Gibralfaro Mountain* ☎ *952/220043* 🎫 *€1.80* ⏲ *Castle daily 9–6.*

In the old Mesón de la Victoria, a 17th-century inn, is the **Museo de Artes Populares** (Arts and Crafts Museum). On display are horse-drawn carriages and carts, old agricultural implements, folk costumes, a forge, a bakery, an ancient grape press, and Malagueño ceramics and sculptures. ✉ *Pasillo de Santa Isabel 10* ☎ *952/217137* 🎫 *€1.20* ⏲ *Weekdays 10–1:30 and 4–7 (5–8 in summer), Sat. 10–1:30.*

A 150-year-old botanical garden, **La Concepción** was created by the daughter of the British consul, who married a Spanish shipping magnate—the captains of the Spaniard's fleet had standing orders to bring back seedlings and cuttings from every "exotic" port of call. The garden was abandoned for years, but La Concepción has been restored. The garden is just off the exit road to Granada—too far to walk, but well worth the cab fare from the city center. ✉ *Ctra. de las Pedrizas, Km 166* ☎ *952/252148* 🎫 *€2.80* ⏲ *Tues.–Sun. 10 AM–sundown.*

need a break?

The **Antigua Casa de la Guardia** (Alameda 18), around the corner from the Mercado de Atarazanas, is Málaga's oldest bar, founded in 1840. Andalusian wines flow straight from the barrel, and the floor is ankle-deep in discarded shrimp shells.

Where to Stay & Eat

$$–$$$ ✕ **Adolfo.** On Málaga's Paseo Marítimo, this small restaurant has a solid reputation for Spanish food with a contemporary touch. The dining room has a wood floor and exposed-brick walls; service is smooth and professional; and there's a good wine list. Entrées include *vieiras con setas* (scallops with wild mushrooms) and *cabrito lechal a la miel de romero* (roast baby kid in rosemary-honey sauce). ✉ *Paseo Marítimo Pablo Ruíz Picasso 12* ☎ *952/601914* 💳 *AE, D, MC, V* ⏲ *Closed Sun.*

$$–$$$ ✕ **Antonio Martín.** Once a humble snack shack, this sprawling beachfront restaurant has a large sea-view terrace that's covered with glass in winter. Favored by matadors from the nearby bullring, popular local dishes include *zarzuela de pescado y mariscos de la Bahía* (seafood stew) and *solomillo de cerdo estilo Montes de Málaga* (Málaga-style pork fillet). ✉ *Pl. de la Malagueta* ☎ *952/227382* 💳 *AE, D, MC, V* ⏲ *No dinner Sun. Oct.–Mar.*

$$–$$$ Fodor's Choice ★ ✕ **Café de París.** This is one of Málaga's time-tested, top restaurants. The owner was once a chef at Madrid's Horcher, so the cuisine has a city-slick sophistication that's rare on the coast. The red-and-mahogany interior is warm and intimate—ideal for a romantic dinner. There's always an excellent selection of appetizers, meat, and fish. Rodaballo and *lubina* (sea bass) are usually present in one form or another, as is *solomillo de buy café de París* (beef fillet with herb-butter sauce). The menú de degustación lets you try a bit of everything. ✉ *C. Vélez Málaga 8* ☎ *952/225043* *Reservations essential* ▭ *AE, DC, MC, V* ⊙ *Closed Sun. No dinner Mon.*

$$–$$$ ✕ **El Chinitas.** Decorated with tiles, this place sits at one end of Pasaje Chinitas, Málaga's most *típico* street. The tapas bar is popular, especially for its cured ham. The second floor has two private dining rooms—groups of 12–20 can and do reserve the Sala Antequera, with a Camelot-style round table—and the third a banquet hall. Try the *sopa viña AB,* a fish soup flavored with sherry and thickened with mayonnaise, and consider *solomillo al vino de Málaga,* fillet steak in Málaga wine sauce. ✉ *Moreno Monroy 4* ☎ *952/210972* ▭ *DC, MC, V.*

$–$$ ✕ **La Cancela.** In an alley off Calle Granada, at the top of Molina Larios (one block from the Palacio Episcopal), this pretty bistro serves standard Spanish fare, such as *riñones al jerez* (kidneys sautéed with sherry) and *cerdo al vino de Málaga* (pork with Málaga wine sauce), and is ideal for lunch after a morning of shopping. The two dining rooms (one upstairs, one down) are crowded with iron grilles, birdcages, potted plants, and plastic flowers. In summer, tables appear on the sidewalk for outdoor lunches on what amounts to a sheltered patio. ✉ *Denís Belgrano 5* ☎ *952/223125* ▭ *AE, DC, MC, V* ⊙ *Closed Wed. No dinner Mon.*

¢–$ ✕ **Logueno.** Shoehorned into a deceptively small space, this well-loved traditional tapas bar is on a side street near Calle Larios. The L-shape wooden bar is crammed with a choice of more than 75 tantalizing tapas, including many Logueno originals, like grilled oyster mushrooms with garlic, parsley, and goat cheese. There's an excellent selection of Rioja wines, and the service is fast and good, despite the lack of elbow room. ✉ *Marin Garcia s/n* ☎ *No phone* ▭ *No credit cards* ⊙ *Closed Sun.*

¢–$ ✕ **Pitta Bar.** Populated with shoppers and students, this no-frills place serves Middle Eastern fast food, such as *falafel, kebabs, hummus,* and *tabbouleh* salad, as well as more mainstream food, such as French fries. The location is ideal if you're sightseeing—it's between the Cathedral and Picasso Museum, in the old part of town. ✉ *Echegaray 8* ☎ *952/608675* ▭ *No credit cards* ⊙ *Closed Sun.*

$$$ ✕ **Parador de Málaga–Gibralfaro.** Surrounded by pine trees on top of Gibralfaro, 3 km (2 mi) above the city, this cozy, gray-stone parador has spectacular views of Málaga and the bay. Rooms are attractive—with blue curtains and bedspreads, and woven rugs on bare tile floors—and are considered the best in Málaga. Reserve well in advance. The restaurant has regional and international food. ✉ *Monte de Gibralfaro, 29016* ☎ *952/221902* *952/221904* *www.parador.es* *38 rooms* *Restaurant, cafeteria, minibars, pool, bar, meeting room* ▭ *AE, DC, MC, V.*

Fodor'sChoice ★

$$$ **Larios.** On the central Plaza de la Constitución is this elegantly restored 19th-century building. Black-and-white tile floors lend subdued elegance to the second-floor lobby; the rooms are furnished with light wood and cream-color fabrics and polished off with artsy black-and-white photographs. ✉ *Marqués de Larios 2, 29005* ☎ *952/222200* *952/222407* *www.hotel-larios.com* *34 rooms, 6 suites* *Restaurant, in-room data ports, cable TV with movies, meeting room* ▭ *AE, DC, MC, V.*

$$ **Don Curro.** Just around the corner from the cathedral, this family classic is going through continual renovations, but an old-fashioned air permeates the wood-paneled common rooms, the fireplace lounge, and the somewhat stodgy wood-floor guest rooms. The best rooms are in the new wing, at the back of the building. ✉ *Sancha de Lara 7, 29015* ☎ *952/227200* *952/215946* *www.hoteldoncurro.com* *112 rooms, 6* *suites* ♨ *Restaurant, cafeteria, minibars, cable TV, some pets allowed* ▭ *AE, DC, MC, V.*

$$ **Las Vegas.** In a pleasant, if somewhat tumultuous, part of Málaga just east of the center, Las Vegas has a dining room with a fine sea view over the Paseo Marítimo. Guest rooms are bright; most have sunny balconies. For the best water view, ask for a room in the modern extension or on one of the top two floors of the old wing. ✉ *Paseo de Sancha 22, 29016* ☎ *952/217712* 🖷 *952/224889* *107 rooms* ♨ *Restaurant, pool, bar* ▭ *AE, DC, MC, V.*

$$ **Venecia.** This four-story hotel has a central location on the Alameda Principal, next to the Plaza de la Marina. The rooms are simply furnished but spacious. ✉ *Alameda Principal 9, 29001* ☎ *952/213636* 🖷 *952/213637* *40 rooms* ▭ *AE, DC, MC, V.*

$ **Carlos V.** There's a slightly shabby, old-fashioned charm about this long-standing hotel. The carpets may need replacing, but the rooms are large and homey. Ask for a balcony overlooking the quiet side street. The location is excellent: it's around the corner from the cathedral, and close to some of the best tapas bars and cafés in town. ✉ *Cister 10, 29015* ☎ *952/215120* 🖷 *952/215129* *50* ▭ *MC, V.*

Nightlife & the Arts

Málaga's main nightlife districts are Maestranza, between the bullring and the Paseo Marítimo, and the beachfront in the suburb of Pedregalejos. Central Málaga also has a lively bar scene. The region's main theater is the **Teatro Cervantes** (✉ Ramos Marín ☎ 952/224109 or 952/220237 🌐 www.teatrocervantes.com), whose programs include Spanish-language plays, concerts, and flamenco. The **Málaga Symphony Orchestra** has a winter season of orchestral concerts and chamber music, with most performances held at the**Teatro Cervantes** (✉ Ramos Marín ☎ 952/224109 or 952/220237 🌐 www.teatrocervantes.com). In summer, larger concerts are staged in the bullring or the newer **Palacio Municipal de Deportes,** where recent big name billings have included The Rolling Stones and Tom Jones.

Shopping

The **Corte Inglés** department store offers English interpreters, shipping, VAT refunds, and currency exchange. ✉ *Avda. de Andalucía 4–6* ☎ *952/300000* ⏲ *Mon.–Sat. 10–10.*

Antequera

❼ *64 km (40 mi) northwest of Málaga, 43 km (27 mi) northeast of Pizarra, 108 km (67 mi) northeast of Ronda (via Pizarra).*

Antequera became a stronghold of the Moors following their defeat at Córdoba and Seville in the 13th century. Its fall to the Christians in 1410 paved the way for the reconquest of Granada—the Moors retreated, leaving a **fortress** on the town heights. Next door is the former church of **Santa María la Mayor,** one of 27 churches, convents, and monasteries in Antequera. Built of sandstone in the 16th century, it has a fine ribbed vault and is now a concert hall. The church of **San Sebastián** has a brick baroque Mudéjar tower topped by a winged figure called the Angelote ("big angel"), the symbol of Antequera. The church of **Nuestra Señora del Carmen** (Our Lady of Carmen) has an extraordinary baroque altarpiece that towers to the ceiling. East of Antequera, along N342, is the dramatic silhouette of the **Peña de los Enamorados** (Lovers' Rock), an Andalusian landmark. Legend has it that a Moorish princess and a Christian shepherd boy eloped here one night and cast themselves to their deaths from the peak the next morning. The rock's outline is often likened to the profile of the Córdoban bullfighter Manolete. Antequera's pride and joy is Efebo, a beautiful bronze statue of a boy that dates back to Roman times. Standing almost 5 ft high, it's on display in the **Museo Municipal.** ✉ *Palacio de Nájera, Coso Viejo* ☎ *952/704051* 🎫 *€3* ⏲ *Tues.–Fri. 10–1:30 and 4.30–6.30, Sat. 10–1:30, Sun. 11–1:30.*

The mysterious prehistoric **Dolmens** are megalithic burial chambers, built some 4,000 years ago out of massive slabs of stone weighing more than 100 tons each. The best-preserved dolmen is La Menga. They're just outside Antequera. ✉ *Off Málaga exit road, Antequera* 🎫 *Free* ⏲ *Tues. 9–3:30, Wed.–Sat. 9–6, Sun. 9:30–2:30.*

Europe's major nesting area for the greater flamingo is **Fuente de Piedra,** a shallow saltwater lagoon. In February and March, these birds arrive from Africa by the thousands to spend the summer. The visitor center has information on wildlife. ✉ *10 km (6 mi) northwest of Antequera, off the A92 highway to Seville* ☎ *952/111715* 🎫 *Free* ⏲ *Wed.–Sun. 10–2 and 4–6 in summer, Wed.–Sun. 10–2 and 6–8 in winter.*

About 8 km (5 mi) from Antequera's Lovers' Rock, the village of **Archidona** winds its way up a steep mountain slope beneath the ruins of a Moorish castle. This picturesque white cluster is worth a detour for its **Plaza Ochavada,** a magnificent 17th-century square resplendent with contrasting red and ocher stone. ✉ *8 km (5 mi) beyond Peña de los Enamorados, along N342, Antequera.*

Well-marked walking trails guide you at the **Parque Natural del Torcal de Antequera** (El Torcal Nature Park). You'll walk among eerie pillars of pink limestone sculpted by aeons of wind and rain. Wear sturdy shoes and be careful not to wander from the marked paths, as it's easy to get lost in the maze of rock formations. ✉ *10 km (6 mi) south of Antequera on C3310, Antequera.*

Where to Stay & Eat

$$ ✕ **El Angelote.** Across the square from the Museo Municipal, these two wood-beam dining rooms are usually packed. Try the *porrilla de setas* (wild mushrooms seasoned with thyme and rosemary) or *perdiz hortelana* (stewed partridge). Antequera's typical dessert is *bienmesabe,* a sponge cake with almonds dusted with sugar and cinnamon. ✉ *Pl. Coso Viejo* ☎ *952/703465* 💳 *DC, MC, V* ⏲ *Closed Mon. No dinner Sun.*

$ ✕ **Caserío San Benito.** If it weren't for the cell-phone transmission tower looming next to this country restaurant 11 km (7 mi) north of Antequera, you might think you've stumbled into an 18th-century scene. In fact, the building was constructed by its current owner, a history buff and collector of old items and documents. Popular local dishes include *porra antequerana* (a thick version of gazpacho) and *migas* (fried bread with sausage). ✉ *Ctra. Málaga–Córdoba, Km 108* ☎ *952/111103* 💳 *MC, V* ⏲ *Closed Mon. and 1st 2 wks in July. No dinner Tues.–Thurs.*

$$ ✕🏨 **Parador de Antequera.** Overlooking the *vega,* Antequera's fertile valley is this modern white parador on a hill. Common rooms are simple but tasteful, with antique carpets on tile floors and taurine prints on the walls. The comfortable guest rooms have twin beds, covered with woven rugs, and spacious tile bathrooms. The large dining room, with a lofty wood ceiling, serves good local dishes, such as *pío antequerano* (a salad of orange, cod, and olives) or oxtail in a sauce made with the sweet wine from nearby Mollina. ✉ *García del Olmo, 29200* ☎ *952/840261* 📠 *952/841312* 🌐 *www.parador.es* 🛏 *55 rooms* 🛎 *Restaurant, pool, cable TV with movies, bar* 💳 *AE, DC, MC, V.*

$$$–$$$$ 🏨 **La Posada del Torcal.** Surrounded by the lunar landscape of El Torcal, this small hotel is just the place to chill out and relax after a long day on the trail. There are king-size and four-poster beds (shipped from England) and a fireplace in each room. You'll find skillful copies of Spanish paintings throughout. The Posada's restaurant specializes in local Spanish food. ✉ *Carretera La Hoya-La Higuera, 29230* ☎ *952/031177* 📠 *952/031006* 🌐 *www.eltorcal.com/posadatorcal* ⇨ *8* ♁ *Restaurant, cable TV, tennis court, pool, gym, sauna, bar* ▭ *AE, MC, V* ⏲ *Closed Jan.*

The Guadalhorce Valley

Leave Antequera via the El Torcal exit and turn right onto the A343 to reach the village of Alora. From here, follow a small road north to the
8 awe-inspiring **Garganta del Chorro** (Gorge of the Stream), a deep limestone chasm where the Guadalhorce River churns and snakes its way some 600 ft below the road. The railroad track that worms in and out of tunnels in the cleft is, amazingly, the main line heading north from Málaga for Bobadilla junction and, eventually, Madrid. Clinging to the cliff side is the **Caminito del Rey** (King's Walk), a suspended catwalk built for a visit by King Alfonso XIII at the beginning of the 19th century. At press time, the catwalk was closed for major construction and renovations intended to make it passable for walkers.

North of the gorge, the Guadalhorce has been dammed to form a series of scenic reservoirs surrounded by pine-clad hills, which constitute the **Parque de Ardales** nature area. Informal, open-air restaurants overlook the lakes and a number of picnic spots. Driving along the southern shore of the lake, you reach Ardales and, turning onto the A357 road,
9 the old spa town of **Carratraca.** Once a favorite watering hole for both Spanish and foreign aristocracy, it has a Moorish-style *ayuntamiento* (town hall) and an unusual **polygonal bullring.** Carratraca's old hotel, the **Hostal del Príncipe,** once sheltered Empress Eugénie, wife of Napoléon III; Lord Byron also came seeking the cure. The splendid Roman-style marble-and-tile **bathhouse** re-opened during the summer of 2003 after extensive restoration. From Carratraca, head south along the A357
10 toward Málaga until you reach the turnoff to **Pizarra.**

The **Museo Municipal de Pizarra** is in a renovated farmhouse just south of the village. Over their two decades in Pizarra, American artist Gino Hollander and his wife, Barbara, built up this collection of paintings and objets d'art, furniture, and archaeological finds. One section has the archaeological displays, including Moorish and Roman objects; the other is devoted to rustic Andalusian furniture and farm implements. ✉ *Cortijo Casablanca 29* ☎ *952/483237* 🎟 *€2* ⏲ *Tues.–Sun. 10–2 and 4–7.*

THE COSTA DEL SOL OCCIDENTAL

After you rejoin N340 11 km (7 mi) west of Málaga, the sprawling outskirts of Torremolinos signal that you're leaving the "real" Spain and entering, well, the "real" Costa del Sol, with its beaches, high-rise hotels, and serious tourist activity.

Torremolinos

11 *11 km (7 mi) west of Málaga, 16 km (10 mi) northeast of Fuengirola, 43 km (27 mi) east of Marbella.*

Torremolinos is all about fun in the sun. It may be more subdued than it was in the roaring '60s and '70s, but northern Europeans of all ages still jam its streets in season. Scantily attired and fair in hue, they shop for bargains on Calle San Miguel, down sangría in the bars of La Nogalera, and dance the night away in discotheques. By day, the sunseekers flock to the beaches El Bajondillo and La Carihuela, whose sand is a fine, gray grit; in high summer it's hard to find a patch of your own.

Torremolinos has two sections. The first, **Torremolinos,** known to ex-pats as Central T-town, is built around the Plaza Costa del Sol; Calle San Miguel, the main shopping street; and the brash Nogalera Plaza, which is full of overpriced bars and international restaurants. The Pueblo Blanco area, off Calle Casablanca, is more pleasant; and the Cuesta del Tajo, at the far end of San Miguel, winds down a steep slope to the Bajondillo beach. Here, crumbling walls, bougainvillea-clad patios, and old cottages hint at the quiet fishing village this once was. The second, much nicer, section is **La Carihuela.** (To find it, head west out of town on Avenida Carlota Alessandri and turn left by the Hotel La Paloma.) Far more authentically Spanish, the Carihuela has many old fishermen's cottages and excellent fish restaurants. The traffic-free esplanade makes for a pleasurable stroll, especially on a summer evening or Sunday at lunchtime, when it's packed with Spanish families.

The **Aquapark,** off the bypass near the Palacio de Congresos convention center, has water chutes, artificial waves, water mountains, and pools. ☎ *952/388888* ✉ *€14.50* ⊙ *May–June and Sept., daily 10–6; July–Aug., daily 10–7.*

Where to Stay & Eat

$$$ ✕ **Juan.** With a sunny outdoor patio facing the sea, this Carihuela hot spot is a good place for seafood in summer. House specialties include the great Costa del Sol standbys—*sopa de mariscos* (shellfish soup), *dorada al horno* (oven-roasted sea bream), and fritura malagueña. ✉ *Paseo Marítimo 29, La Carihuela* ☎ *952/385656* ▭ *AE, DC, MC, V.*

$$–$$$ ✕ **Casa Guaquin.** On a seaside patio in La Carihuela, Casa Guaquin is known as the best seafood restaurant in the area. Daily catches are served alongside such stalwarts as *coquinas* (wedge-shell clams) and *boquerones fritos* (fried anchovies). ✉ *Paseo Marítimo 63* ☎ *952/384530* ▭ *AE, MC, V* ⊙ *Closed Mon. and mid-Dec.–mid-Jan.*

¢ ✕ **Albahaca.** It's rare that you'll find a vegetarian restaurant on the carnivorous Costa, and this one—worth seeking out, even if you're not a vegetarian—deserves to do well. Its daily four-course menu is a bargain. Starters always include a choice of home-made soup or salad and a main course is usually something like lentil and spinach patties with brown rice. The restaurant is around the corner from the tourist office on Plaza de la Independencia. ✉ *Doña Maria Barrabino 11* ☎ *95/2375182* ▭ *No credit cards* ⊙ *Closed Sun. No dinner Mon.–Thurs.*

$$$ ⊞ **Meliá Costa del Sol.** In the Bajondillo (eastern beach) section of town, the Meliá looks somewhat boxy from the outside, with the assembly-line architecture typical of 1970s Torremolinos. Inside, however, it's modern and well run. Every room has a sea-view balcony and gets lots of sun; before you book a room, decide whether you prefer morning or evening sunlight. ✉ *Paseo Marítimo 11, Playa del Bajondillo, 29620* ☎ *952/386677* 🖷 *952/386417* ⊕ *www.meliacostadelsol.solmelia.com* ⇆ *517 rooms, 18 suites* ♁ *Restaurant, cable TV, pool, health club, bar, meeting rooms* ▭ *AE, DC, MC, V.*

$$$ ⊞ **Tropicana.** On the beach at the far end of the Carihuela, in one of the most pleasant parts of Torremolinos, you'll find this resort hotel—with its own beach club. A tropical theme runs throughout, from the leafy gardens and kidney-shape pool to the common areas, with exotic plants, raffia floor mats, and bamboo furniture, to the rooms, with ceiling fans and marble floors. Here you're only a five-minute walk from several good restaurants. ✉ *Trópico 6, 29620* ☎ *952/386600* 📠 *952/380568* *84 rooms* *Restaurant, cable TV, pool, beach* 💳 *AE, DC, MC, V.*

$$ **Sidi Lago Rojo.** In the heart of old Carihuela, this modern, four-story apartment building is just two blocks from the seafront. The rooms are well maintained, and all have balconies; some overlook the pool and small, tree-filled garden. There's no great sea view, but prices are moderate, and you're close to the town's best bars and restaurants. ✉ *C. Miami 5, 29620* ☎ *952/387666* 📠 *952/380891* *144 rooms* *Restaurant, in-room data ports, cable TV with movies, pool, bar* 💳 *AE, DC, MC, V.*

$ **Hotel El Pozo.** A pretty, flower-filled patio and traditional whitewashed exterior are why this hotel is a pleasant change from the surrounding Lego-style holiday blocks. It's right in town but is within (downhill) walking distance of the beach. Rooms are painted white and are decorated with colorful fabrics. Some have balconies. There is a lively bar downstairs, plus a sitting room with a good-size collection of mainly English books. ✉ *Casablanca 2, 29620* ☎ *952/380622* 📠 *952/384717* *28* *Cable TV, bar, library* 💳 *AE, MC, V.*

$ **Miami.** In an old Andalusian villa in a shady garden west of the Carihuela, this hotel is something of a find amid the ocean of concrete towers. Staying here is like visiting a private Spanish home; the rooms are individually furnished and bathrooms are modern. There is also a sitting room with a cozy fireplace. It's very popular, so reserve ahead. ✉ *Aladino 14, at C. Miami, 29620* ☎ *952/385255* *26 rooms* *Pool, bar, some pets allowed; no a/c, no room TVs* 💳 *No credit cards.*

Nightlife & the Arts

Most nocturnal action is in the center of town and along the Montemar strip heading west. Some bars have live music, but Torremolinos is best known for its discos. As the gay capital of the Costa del Sol, Torremolinos also has numerous bars and clubs catering to an almost exclusively gay clientele. The trends are in constant flux, but one of the most enduring clubs is **Paladium** (✉ Avda. Palma de Mallorca 36 ☎ 952/384289), with two floors and a covered swimming pool. For flamenco, your best bet is **Taberna Flamenca Pepe López** (✉ Pl. de la Gamba Alegre ☎ 952/381284). There are nightly shows at 10 PM from April to October and on weekends only during the rest of the year.

Benalmádena

12 *9 km (5½ mi) west of Torremolinos, 9 km (5½ mi) east of Mijas.*

Benalmádena-Costa is practically an extension of Torremolinos, run almost exclusively by package-tour operators. It has little for the independent traveler, but there's a pleasant-enough marina, which draws Málaga's youth at night. **Benalmádena-Pueblo,** the village proper, is on the mountainside 7 km (4 mi) from the coast and is surprisingly unspoiled, offering a glimpse of the old, pretourist Andalusia.

In Benalmádena-Costa's marina, **Sea Life Benalmádena** is a better-than-average aquarium with fish from local waters, including rays, sharks, and sunfish. ✉ *Puerto Marina Benalmádena* ☎ *952/560150* 🌐 *www.sealife.es* *€8* *Daily 10 AM–midnight in summer, 10–6 in winter.*

The Costa del Sol's leading amusement park is **Tivoli World,** with a 4,000-seat, open-air auditorium that showcases international stars alongside cancan, flamenco, or Spanish ballet performances. The park has roller coasters, a Ferris wheel, illuminated fountains, a Chinese pagoda, Wild West shows, and 40-odd restaurants and snack bars. Check out the flea market here on Sunday. ✉ *Arroyo de la Miel* ☎ *952/*

442848 €4, €1 Sun. 11–2 *Daily 1 PM–1 AM in summer. Weekends noon–8 in winter.*

Where to Stay & Eat

$$ **Mar de Alborán.** Next to the Benalmádena yacht harbor, this restaurant has a touch more class than most of its peers. Fish dishes, such as the Basque-inspired *lomo de merluza con kokotxas y almejas* (hake stew with clams), can be a welcome switch from standard Costa fare. Choices include *pechuguitas de pichón asadas con setas* (roast breast of dove with wild mushrooms). *Avda. de Alay 5* *952/446427* *AE, MC, V* *Closed Mon. No dinner Sun.*

$–$$ **Casa Fidel.** This Benalmádena-Pueblo restaurant is rustic, with heavy beams, a large fireplace, and a small leafy patio. For a starter, try *carlota de calabacin con queso de cabra* (zucchini stuffed with goat cheese) or *sopa de pimientos rojos con crema y cebollino* (red pepper soup with fresh cream and spring onions). Main courses include *langostinos con shalotas y puré de garbonzos* (king prawns with shallots and garbanzos) and T-bone steak for two. *Maestra Ayala 1* *952/449165* *AE, DC, MC, V* *Closed Tues. and Aug. No lunch Wed.*

$–$$ **Ventorillo de la Perra.** If you've been scouring the coast for something typically Spanish, you may find it at this old inn, which dates from 1785. Outside, there's a leafy patio; inside is a cozy dining room and bar with hams hanging from the ceiling. Choose between local Malagueño cooking, including *gazpacuelo malagueño* (a warm gazpacho of potatoes, rice, and shrimp), and typical Spanish food, such as *conejo en salsa de almendras* (rabbit in almond sauce). The *ajo blanco* (a cold, garlicky almond-based soup) is particularly good. *Avda. Constitución 115, Km 13, Arroyo de la Miel* *952/441966* *AE, DC, MC, V* *Closed Mon. and Nov.*

$$ **La Fonda.** You'll find a true taste of Andalusia at this small hotel on one of the prettiest streets in the village. Rooms have white walls, marble floors, and floral fabrics. Some rooms have peerless views of the coast and the Mediterranean; others look onto the cool interior patio. The pool is heated in winter. In the same building, under different management, is a restaurant run by Málaga's official hotel school; it's open for lunch on weekdays. *Santo Domingo 7, 29639* *952/568273* *27 rooms* *Cable TV, minibars, pool, bar* *AE, DC, MC, V.*

Nightlife

For discos, piano bars, and karaoke, head for the port. The **Fortuna Nightclub** in the **Casino Torrequebrada** (Km 220 on N340, Benalmádena Costa 952/446000) has flamenco and an international dance show with a live orchestra, starting at 10:30 PM. A passport, jacket, and tie are required in the casino, open daily 9 PM–4 AM.

Fuengirola

13 *16 km (10 mi) west of Torremolinos, 27 km (17 mi) east of Marbella.*

Fuengirola is less frenetic than Torremolinos. Many of its waterfront high-rises are holiday apartments that cater to budget-minded sunseekers from northern Europe and, in summer, a large contingent from Córdoba and other parts of Spain. The town is also a haven for British retirees (with plenty of English and Irish pubs to serve them) and a shopping and business center for the rest of the Costa del Sol. Its Tuesday market is the largest on the coast, and a major tourist attraction.

The most prominent landmark in Fuengirola is **Castillo de Sohail,** whose partly Arabic name means Castle of the Star. The original structure dates from the 12th century, but the castle served as a military fortress until the early 19th century, and there were many intervening additions. Just west of town, the castle makes an emblematic performance venue for the annual summer season of music and dance. €1.30 *Tues.–Sun. 10–3.*

Where to Stay & Eat

$$–$$$ **La Langosta.** Two blocks from the water on a side street in Los Boliches, this tiny restaurant has been a favorite for 40 years. Needless to say, the specialty is *langosta* (lobster), which you can get prepared several ways, including *al champán* (in champagne sauce). The *mejillones a la crema de azafrán* (mussels in saffron sauce) are a savory alternative. *Francisco Cano 1 952/475049 AE, MC, V Closed Sun. No lunch.*

$$–$$$ **Patrick Bausier.** Patrick was a student of Paul Bocuse, the grand-père of nouvelle-cuisine in Paris. And it shows. Don't worry, the food is predictably pretty to look at, but you won't go hungry. Dishes include exquisitely prepared fowl and fish, like pot-au-feu of crayfish and a coulis of Norwegian smoked salmon blinis and vodka. The desserts are fabulous and the service impeccable. There's complimentary champagne and hors d'oeuvres. *Rotondade la Luna 1, Pueblo López 952/585120 Reservations essential AE, MC, V Closed Sun. No lunch.*

$–$$ **Moochers Jazz Café and Restaurant.** It's one of the most popular on a street of restaurants, and is a pebble's throw from the beach. There's live music nightly during the summer, ranging from blues to lightweight rock (don't expect true jazz here), and former Londoners Andy and Yvonne are super-friendly hosts. The menu is international; particularly good are the giant pancakes with every imaginable filling. There are vegetarian choices, plus a 10% discount before 7:30 PM. *Calle de la Cruz 17 952/477154 Reservations essential AE, DC, MC, V No lunch.*

$$ **Villa de Laredo.** This is the place to stay if you want to be near Fuengirola's nightlife and restaurants, although you may need earplugs on a Saturday night. It has a prime location on the seaside promenade, one block east of the port. It's also one of the town's newest mid-range hotels, and it shows. Rooms are cream and navy blue; all have terraces and sea views. *Paseo Marítimo 42, 29640 952/477689 952/477950 50 rooms Restaurant, cable TV, minibars, pool AE, DC, MC, V.*

$ **Hostal Italia.** Cheery and bright, right off the main plaza and near the beach, this small, family-run hotel is deservedly popular. People come here year after year, particularly during the October *feria*.The rooms are small yet comfy and nearly all have balconies. There is a larger sun terrace for catching the rays. C. *de la Cruz 1, 29640 952/474193 952/461909 40 MC, V.*

Nightlife & the Arts

Amateur local troupes regularly stage plays and musicals in English at the **Salón de Variétés Theater** (Emancipación 30 952/474542). For concerts—from classical to rock to jazz—check out the modern **Palacio de la Paz** (Recinto Ferial, Avda. Jesús Santo Rein 952/589349) between Los Boliches and the town center.

Mijas

★ 14 *8 km (5 mi) north of Fuengirola, 18 km (11 mi) west of Torremolinos.*

Mijas is in the foothills of the sierra just north of the coast. Buses leave Fuengirola every half hour for the 20-minute drive through hills peppered with villas. If you have a car and don't mind a mildly hair-raising drive, take the more dramatic approach from Benalmádena-Pueblo, a winding mountain road with splendid views. Mijas was discovered long ago by foreign retirees, and the large, touristy square where you arrive may look like an extension of the Costa, yet beyond this are hilly streets of whitewashed houses. Try to arrive late in the afternoon, when the tour buses have left. Park in the Plaza Virgen de la Peña, where you should take a quick look at the chapel of Mijas's patron, the **Virgen de la Peña,** and hire a *burro taxi* (guided donkey) to explore the village. Mijas extends down to the coast, and the coastal strip between Fuengirola and Marbella is officially called **Mijas-Costa.** This area has several hotels, restaurants, and golf courses.

If miniature curiosities are your thing, explore **Carromato de Max,** a museum that has a rendition of the Last Supper on a grain of rice, Abraham Lincoln painted on a pinhead, and fleas wearing clothes. ✉ *Avda. del Compás* 🎫 *€3* ⏲ *Daily 10–7.*

Bullfights take place throughout the year, usually on Sunday at 4:30 PM, at Mijas's tiny **bullring.** It's one of the few square bullrings in Spain. It's off the Plaza Constitución—Mijas's old village square—and up the slope beside the Mirlo Blanco restaurant. ✉ *Pl. Constitución* ☎ *952/485248* 🎫 *€3* ⏲ *June–Sept. 10–10; Oct.–Feb. 9:30–6:30; Mar. 10–7:30; Apr.–May 10–8:30.*

Worth a visit is the delightful village church **Iglesia Parroquial de la Inmaculada Concepción** (The Immaculate Conception). It's impeccably decorated, especially at Easter, and its terrace and spacious gardens afford a splendid panorama. The church is just up the hill from the Mijas bullring. ✉ *Pl. Constitución.*

need a break?

The **Bar Menguiñez** (or Casa de los Jamones), at Calle San Sebastián 4, has a ceiling strung with row after row of hams. Inexpensive meals are served on a handful of tables here.

Where to Stay & Eat

$$$–$$$$ ✕ **El Padrastro.** Perched on a cliff above the Plaza Virgen de la Peña, "The Stepfather" is accessible by an elevator from the square or, if you're energetic, by stairs. Views over Fuengirola and the coast are the restaurant's main drawing card. Dishes might include *solomillo de cerdo asado con salsa de jerez y puré de patatas al aceite de oliva* (roast pork fillet with sherry sauce and mashed potatoes with olive oil), and *magret de pato ahumado al té con frutas flameadas* (duck magret smoked in tea with flambé fruit). When the weather's right, dine alfresco on the large terrace. ✉ *Paseo del Compás* ☎ *952/485000* 💳 *AE, DC, MC, V.*

$$$ ✕ **Mirlo Blanco.** In an old house on the pleasant Plaza de la Constitución, with a terrace for outdoor dining, this place is run by the second generation of a Basque family that has been in the Costa del Sol restaurant business for decades. Try such Basque specialties as *txangurro* (crab) and *merluza a la vasca* (hake with asparagus, eggs, and clam sauce). ✉ *Pl. de la Constitución 2* ☎ *952/485700* 💳 *AE, MC, V* ⏲ *Closed Jan.*

$$–$$$ ✕ **Valparaíso.** Halfway up the road from Fuengirola to Mijas, this sprawling villa stands in its own garden, complete with swimming pool. In summer, you can dine outdoors on the terrace and dance to live music. Valparaíso is a favorite among local (mainly British) expatriates, some of whom come in full evening dress to celebrate their birthdays. In winter, logs burn in a cozy fireplace. Try the *pato a la naranja* (duck in orange sauce). ✉ *Ctra. de Mijas–Fuengirola, Km 4* ☎ *952/485996* 💳 *AE, DC, MC, V* ⏲ *Closed Sun. Oct.–June.*

★ $$$$ ✕🏨 **Byblos Andaluz.** On the edge of Mijas's golf course (closer to Fuengirola than to Mijas), this luxury hotel is the most expensive on the entire Costa del Sol. In a huge garden of palms, cypresses, and fountains, it is primarily a spa known for its thalassotherapy, a skin treatment that uses seawater and seaweed—applied here in a Roman temple of cool, white marble and blue tiles. Both outstanding restaurants serve savory regional and international dishes. ✉ *Urbanización Mijas-Golf, Mijas-Costa 29640* ☎ *952/473050* 🖷 *952/476783* 🌐 *www.byblos-andaluz.com* *109 rooms, 35 suites* *2 restaurants, in-room data ports, minibars, cable TV with movies, 2 18-hole golf courses, 5 tennis courts, 2 pools (1 indoor), hair salon, health club, spa, bar, some pets allowed* 💳 *AE, DC, MC, V.*

10

$$$$ **La Cala Resort.** Set within its own two golf courses a few miles inland, this stylish modern resort is a world unto itself. All rooms have large balconies with unspoiled views over the fairways and greens and the countryside beyond. La Cala's appeal extends to non-golfers as well. ✉ *La Cala de Mijas, Mijas-Costa 29649* ☎ *952/669000* 🖷 *952/669039* 🌐 *www.lacala.com* *96 rooms, 5 suites* *2 restaurants, cafeteria, cable TV, minibars, 2 18-hole golf courses, 2 tennis courts, 2 pools (1 indoor), sauna, squash, bar, meeting rooms* 💳 *AE, DC, MC, V.*

$$–$$$ **Mijas.** It's easy to unwind here, thanks to the poolside restaurant and bar, and the gardens with views of the hillsides stretching down to Fuengirola and the sea. The hotel has marble floors throughout, wrought-iron window grilles, and Moorish shutters. The lobby is large and airy, and there's a delightful glass-roof terrace. All rooms are well furnished, with wood fittings and marble floors, but only some enjoy the sweeping view of the coast. The hotel is right at the entrance to Mijas village. ✉ *Urbanización Tamisa, 29650* ☎ *952/485800* 🖷 *952/485825* 🌐 *www.hotasa.es* *101 rooms, 2 suites* *Restaurant, coffee shop, tennis court, pool, hair salon, health club* 💳 *AE, DC, MC, V.*

Marbella

15 *27 km (17 mi) west of Fuengirola, 28 km (17 mi) east of Estepona, 50 km (31 mi) southeast of Ronda.*

Playground of the rich and home of movie stars, rock musicians, and dispossessed royal families, Marbella has attained the top rung on Europe's social ladder. Dip into any Spanish gossip magazine, and chances are the glittering parties that fill its pages are set in Marbella. Much of this action takes place on the fringes, for grand hotels and luxury restaurants line the waterfront for 20 km (12 mi) on each side of the town center. In the town itself, you may well wonder how Marbella became so famous. The main thoroughfare, Avenida Ricardo Soriano, is distinctly lacking in charm; and the Paseo Marítimo, though pleasant enough, with a mix of seafood restaurants and pizzerias overlooking an ordinary beach, is far from spectacular.

Marbella's appeal lies in the heart of the **old village**, which remains miraculously intact. Here, a block or two back from the main highway, narrow alleys of whitewashed houses cluster around the central **Plaza de los Naranjos** (Orange Square), where colorful restaurants vie for space under the orange trees. Climb onto what remains of the old fortifications, and stroll along the quaint Calle Virgen de los Dolores to the Plaza de Santo Cristo. Wander the maze of lanes and enjoy the geranium-speckled windows and splashing fountains. Punctuating the opulence of this city is the road to **Puerto Banús,** which has been called the Golden Mile. Here, a mosque, Arab banks, and the onetime residence of Saudi Arabia's King Fahd betray the influence of petro-dollars in this wealthy enclave. About 7 km (4½ mi) west of central Marbella (between Km 175 and Km 174), a sign indicates the turnoff leading down to Puerto Banús. Though now hemmed in by a belt of high-rises, Marbella's plush marina, with 915 berths, is a gem of ostentatious wealth, a Spanish answer to St. Tropez. Huge and flashy yachts, beautiful people, and countless expensive stores and restaurants make up the glittering parade that marches long into the night. The backdrop is an Andalusian pueblo—built in the 1970s to resemble the fishing villages that once lined this coast.

The **Museo del Grabado Español Contemporáneo** (Museum of Contemporary Spanish Engraving), in a restored 16th-century building, has modern Spanish etchings. The museum is in the old village. ✉ *Hospital Bazán* ☎ *952/825035* 🌐 *www.museodelgrabado.com* 🎫 *€2.50* ⏲ *Tues.–Sat. 10–2 and 5:30–8:30.*

In a modern building just east of Marbella's old quarter, the **Museo de Bonsai** has a collection of miniature trees. ✉ *Parque Arroyo de la Repesa, Avda. Dr. Maiz Viñal* ☎ *952/862926* 🎫 *€3* ⏲ *Daily 10:30–1:30 and 5–8:30 in summer; daily 10:30–1:30 and 4–7 in winter.*

need a break?

Stop for a glass of wine and some fried fish at **La Pesquera** (Pl. de la Victoria, ☎ 952/765170). This is one of Marbella's most typical old-fashioned tapas bars, located at the western entrance to the old town.

Where to Stay & Eat

$$$–$$$$ ✕ **La Hacienda.** In a large, pleasant villa 12 km (7 mi) east of Marbella, the Hacienda was founded in the early '70s by the late Belgian chef Paul Schiff, who helped transform the Costa del Sol culinary scene with his modern approach and judicious use of local ingredients. His legacy lives on here through his family. Schiff's signature dish, *pintada con pasas al vino de Málaga* (guinea fowl with raisins in Málaga wine sauce), is often available. The four-course menú de degustación gives you the chef's choices. ✉ *Urbanización Las Chapas, N340, Km 193* ☎ *952/831267* 💳 *AE, MC, V* ⏲ *Closed Mon. and Tues. mid-Nov.–mid-Dec. No lunch July–Aug.*

$$$–$$$$ ✕ **La Meridiana.** The local jet set favors this spot, 100 yards inland from the mosque west of town. The modern architecture has a Moorish flavor, and the enclosed terrace allows "outdoor" dining year-round. Try either the menú de degustación or such à la carte items as *lubina grillé al tomillo fresco* (sea bass grilled with fresh thyme). In summer, sample the restaurant's upmarket version of ajo blanco, a garlicky gazpacho based on almonds instead of tomatoes. ✉ *Camino de la Cruz* ☎ *952/776190* 💳 *AE, DC, MC, V* ⏲ *Closed Jan. No lunch.*

$$$–$$$$ ✕ **Santiago.** Facing the seafront promenade, this busy place has long been considered the best fish restaurant in Marbella. Try the *ensalada de langosta* (lobster salad), followed by *besugo al horno* (baked red bream). The menu also has roasts, such as *cochinillo* (pig) and *cordero* (lamb) of the owner's native Castile. Around the corner from the original restaurant (and sharing the same phone number) is Santiago's popular tapas bar. ✉ *Paseo Marítimo 5* ☎ *952/770078* 💳 *AE, DC, MC, V* ⏲ *Closed Nov.*

$$–$$$ ✕ **Antonio.** Perched on the front line in the Puerto Banús, Antonio is one of the oldest of the many restaurants in Marbella's famous yacht harbor. Specialties include *brocheta de rape* (monkfish kebab) and large fish such as bream and sea bass baked in salt. Several rice dishes are also available. Dine on the terrace to observe the port's parade of Rolls-Royces, luxury yachts, and beautiful people. ✉ *Muella de Ribera, Puerto Banús* ☎ *952/813536* 💳 *AE, D, MC, V.*

$–$$ ✕ **Aquavit.** Cream and yellow paintwork, titanium cutlery, and hand-crafted illuminated tables provide just the right sunny, snazzy look at one of the port's latest talk-of-the-town eateries. Fusion starters include sushi nori rolls, Thai fishcakes, and fresh rocket salad while the signature dish just has to be the potato and anchovy gratin with a shot of (what else?) chilled Aquavit vodka. There are over 45 different vodkas on offer, as well as some unusual wines and liquors. ✉ *Plaza del Puerto, Puerto Banús* ☎ *952/819127* ▭ *AE, MC, V* ⊗ *No lunch.*

$$$$ Fodor'sChoice ★ **Marbella Club.** The grande dame of Marbella hotels was a creation of Alfonso von Hohenlohe, the man who "founded" Marbella. The Club attracts both international clientele and local patricians. The bungalow-style rooms, some with private pools, come in various sizes and are truly luxurious. The grounds are similarly exquisite, with lofty palm trees and dazzling flower beds. The pool area has a tropical feel and is just a pebble's throw from the beach. Breakfast is served on a patio where songbirds weave through the vegetation. ✉ *Blvd. Alfonso von Hohenlohe at Ctra. de Cádiz, Km 178 (3 km [2 mi] west of Marbella), 29600* ☎ *952/822211* 📠 *952/829884* 🌐 *www.marbellaclub.com* *84 rooms, 37 suites, 16 bungalows* *3 restaurants, in-room data ports, minibars, cable TV with movies, 2 pools, gym, sauna* ▭ *AE, DC, MC, V.*

★ **$$$$** **Puente Romano.** West of Marbella, between the Marbella Club and Puerto Banús, is this deluxe modern hotel and apartment complex of low, white stucco buildings. As the name suggests, there's a genuine Roman bridge on the landscaped grounds, which run right down to the beach. There are four restaurants, including El Puente, and Roberto; the latter serves Italian food in the hotel's beach club, a popular summer nightlife venue. During the summer there's a beachfront chiringuito (seafood restaurant) where you can sample fresh fish. ✉ *Ctra. Cádiz, Km 177, 29600* ☎ *952/820900* 📠 *952/775766* 🌐 *www.puenteromano.com* *149 rooms, 77 suites* *4 restaurants, in-room data ports, minibars, cable TV with movies, 10 tennis courts, 2 pools, nightclub, meeting room* ▭ *AE, DC, MC, V.*

$$$ **El Fuerte.** The building is vintage 1950s, and the furnishings—lots of dark wood—are a bit gloomy for the sunny South, but everything is well maintained. El Fuerte is still the best choice if you want a central hotel near the old town. Most rooms have balconies overlooking the sea. The hotel is at the end of the Paseo Marítimo, separated from the beach by a palm-filled garden with a pool. ✉ *Avda. El Fuerte, 29600* ☎ *952/861500* 📠 *952/824411* 🌐 *www.fuertehoteles.com* *261 rooms, 2 suites* *2 restaurants, minibars, cable TV, 2 pools (1 indoor), health club, meeting room* ▭ *AE, DC, MC, V.*

$$ **Artola.** Pretty and traditional—with green shutters and painted with yellow trim—this hotel has lush, expansive gardens and direct access to the beach. The rooms are pleasant, if a little on the small side; some have balconies. Golfers will enjoy perfecting their game within putting distance of the Med. The location is between Fuengirola and Marbella, so you should plan on renting a car. ✉ *Ctra. de Cádiz, km 194, 29600* ☎ *952/831390* 📠 *952/830450* 🌐 *www.hotelartola.com* *35* *Restaurant, cable TV, 9-hole golf course, pool, bar* ▭ *AE, DC, MC, V.*

$–$$ **Lima.** Here's a good mid-range option in downtown Marbella, two blocks from the beach. Simple rooms have dark-wood furniture and small balconies. The corner rooms are the largest. ✉ *Avda. Belón 2, 29600* ☎ *952/770500* 📠 *952/863091* *64 rooms* *Cable TV* ▭ *AE, DC, MC, V.*

Nightlife & the Arts

Much of the nighttime action revolves around the Puerto Banús, in such bars as Sinatra's, Joy's Bar, and La Comedia. Art exhibits are held in private galleries and in several of Marbella's leading hotels, notably the Puente Romano. The **tourist office** (✉ Glorieta de la Fontanilla ☎ 952/822818) publishes a free monthly calendar of exhibits and other events.

Marbella's most famous nightspot is the **Olivia Valére disco** (✉ Ctra. de Istán, Km 0.8 ☎ 952/828861), decorated to resemble a Moorish palace; you'll find it near the mosque. The trendy **La Notte** (✉ Camino de la Cruz ☎ 952/866996) is an art deco bar with live music, next to La Meridiana. The **Casino Nueva Andalucía** (✉ Bajos Hotel Andalucía Pl., N340 ☎ 952/814000), open 8 PM to 6 AM in summer (until 5 AM in winter), is a chic gambling spot in the Bajos Hotel Andalucía Pl., just east of Puerto Banús. Jacket and tie are required for men, and passports for all. In the center of Marbella, **Ana María** (✉ Pl. de Santo Cristo 5 ☎ 952/775646) is a popular flamenco venue during the summer months.

Ojén

16 *10 km (6 mi) north of Marbella.*

For a contrast to the glamour of the coast, drive up to Ojén, in the hills above Marbella. Take note of the beautiful **pottery** sold here. Four kilometers (2½ mi) from Ojén is the **Refugio del Juanar,** a former hunting lodge in the heart of the Sierra Blanca, at the southern edge of the Serranía de Ronda, a mountainous wilderness. Not far from the Refugio, you might spot the **wild ibex** that dwell among the rocky crags; the best times to watch are dawn and dusk, when they descend from their hiding places. A bumpy trail takes you a mile from the Refugio to the **Mirador** (lookout), with a sweeping view of the Costa del Sol and the coast of northern Africa.

Where to Stay & Eat

$$ ✕🏨 **Refugio del Juanar.** Once an aristocratic hunting lodge (King Alfonso XIII came here), this secluded hotel and restaurant is now part of the parador chain. In 1984 it was sold to its staff for the symbolic sum of 1 peseta. The hunting theme prevails, both in the common areas—where a log fire roars in winter—and on the restaurant menu, where game is emphasized. The rooms are simply decorated in a rustic style, and six (including the three suites) have their own fireplace. ✉ *Sierra Blanca, 29610* ☎ *952/881000* 📠 *952/881001* 🌐 *www.juanar.com* *23 rooms, 3 suites* *Restaurant, cafeteria, cable TV, tennis court, pool, meeting room* 💳 *AE, DC, MC, V.*

$$$ 🏨 **Castillo de Monda.** Designed to resemble a castle, this parador-like hotel incorporates the ruins of Monda's Moorish fortress, some of which date back to the 8th century. Rooms are decorated with authentic Andalusian tiles and antique fittings. The bar, which has walls covered with Alhambra-style carvings, and the light-flooded restaurant are on the top floor of the seven-story building; from here you get terrific views of the surrounding countryside. ✉ *Monda 29110* ☎ *952/457142* 📠 *952/457336* 🌐 *www.costadelsol.spa.es/hotel/monda* *17 rooms, 6 suites* *Restaurant, cable TV, pool, bar* 💳 *AE, MC, V.*

RONDA & THE PUEBLOS BLANCOS

Ronda and the whitewashed villages of the mountains behind the Costa del Sol form one of Spain's most scenic and emblematic driving routes. The contrast with Torremolinos could not be more complete.

Ronda

17 *61 km (38 mi) northwest of Marbella, 108 km (67 mi) southwest of Antequera (via Pizarra).*

Fodor'sChoice ★

Ronda, one of the oldest towns in Spain, is accordingly picturesque and dramatic. To get here, take the winding but well-maintained A473 from

San Pedro de Alcántara north up through the mountains of the Serranía de Ronda. Secure in its mountain fastness on a rock high over the River Guadalevín, the town is 49 km (30 mi) inland. Once a stronghold for the legendary Andalusian bandits who held court here from the 18th to early 20th centuries, Ronda is now known for its spectacular position and views. The town's most dramatic element is its ravine (360 ft deep and 210 ft across)—known as **El Tajo**—which divides La Ciudad, the old Moorish town, from El Mercadillo, the "new town," which sprang up after the Christian Reconquest of 1485. Tour buses roll in daily with sightseers from the coast, and on weekends affluent Sevillanos flock to their second homes here. Stay overnight midweek to see this noble town's true colors.

The most attractive approach is from the south. Take the first turnoff to Ronda on the road from San Pedro (A473). Entering the lowest part of Ronda, known as El Barrio, you'll see parts of the old walls, including the 13th-century **Puerta de Almocobar** and the 16th-century **Puerta de Carlos V** gates. The road climbs past the Iglesia del Espíritu Santo (Church of the Holy Spirit) and up into the heart of town. Begin in the Plaza de España, where the tourist office can supply you with a map. Immediately south is Ronda's most famous bridge, the **Puente Nuevo** (New Bridge), an architectural marvel built between 1755 and 1793. The bridge's lantern-lit parapet offers dizzying views of the river far below. Just how many people have met their ends in this gorge nobody knows, but the architect of the Puente Nuevo fell to his death here while inspecting work on the bridge. During the civil war, hundreds of victims on both sides were hurled from it. Cross the Puente Nuevo into **La Ciudad**, the old Moorish town, and wander the twisting streets of white houses with birdcage balconies.

The so-called House of the Moorish King, **Casa del Rey Moro,** was actually built in 1709 on the site of an earlier Moorish residence. Despite the name and the *azulejo* (painted tile) plaque depicting a Moor on the facade, it's unlikely that Moorish rulers ever lived here. The garden has a great view of the gorge, and from here a stairway of some 365 steps (known as La Mina) descends to the river. The house, across the Puente Nuevo on Santo Domingo, being converted into a luxury hotel due for completion in early 2004, is closed to the public until then, though you can visit the gardens and La Mina. ✉ *Cuesta de Santo Domingo 9* ☎ *952/187200* 🎫 *€4* ⏲ *Daily 10–8 in summer, 10–7 in winter.*

The excavated remains of the **Baños Arabes** (Arab Baths) date from Ronda's tenure as capital of a Moorish *taifa* (kingdom). The star-shape vents in the roof are an inferior imitation of the ceiling of the beautiful bathhouse in Granada's Alhambra. Gangs of youths have been known to threaten tourists for money here, so be on guard. The baths are beneath the Puente Arabe (Arab Bridge) in a ravine below the Palacio del Marqués de Salvatierra. 🎫 *Free* ⏲ *Tues. 9–1:30 and 4–6, Wed.–Sat. 9:30–3:30.*

The collegiate church of **Santa María la Mayor,** which serves as Ronda's cathedral, has roots in Moorish times: originally the Great Mosque of Moorish Ronda, it was rebuilt as a Christian church and dedicated to the Virgen de la Encarnación after the Reconquest. Its mixture of styles reflects Ronda's heterogeneous past: the naves are Late Gothic, and the main altar is heavy with baroque gold leaf. The church is around the corner from the remains of a mosque, Minarete Árabe (Moorish Minaret), at the end of the Marqués de Salvatierra. ✉ *Pl. Duquesa de Parcent* 🎫 *€2* ⏲ *Daily 10–8 in summer, 10–6 in winter.*

A stone palace with twin Mudéjar towers is known as the **Casa de Mondragón** (Plaza de Mondragón). Appropriated by Ferdinand and Isabella after their victory in 1485, it had probably been the residence of Ronda's Moorish kings. Today you can wander through the patios, with their brick arches and delicate, Mudéjar stucco tracery, and admire the mosaics and *artesonado* (coffered) ceiling. The second floor holds a small museum with archaeological items found near Ronda, plus the reproduction of a dolmen. ✉ *Ronda de Gameros* ☎ *952/878450* 💴 *€2* ⊙ *Weekdays 10–6 (10–8 in summer), weekends 10–3.*

The main sight in Ronda's commercial center, El Mercadillo, is the **Plaza de Toros.** Pedro Romero (1754–1839), the father of modern bullfighting and Ronda's most famous native son, is said to have killed 5,600 bulls here during his long career. In the museum beneath the plaza you can see posters for Ronda's very first fights, held here in 1785. The plaza is owned by the famous, now-retired bullfighter Antonio Ordóñez, on whose nearby ranch Orson Welles's ashes were scattered (as directed in his will)—indeed, the ring has become a favorite of filmmakers. Every September, the bullring is the scene of Ronda's *corridas goyescas,* named after Goya, whose bullfight sketches (*tauromaquias*) were inspired by the skill and art of Pedro Romero. Both participants and the dignitaries in the audience don the costumes of Goya's time for the occasion. Seats for these fights cost a small fortune and are booked far in advance. Other than that, the plaza is rarely used for fights except during Ronda's May festival and sometimes in September. ☎ *952/874132* 💴 *€4* ⊙ *Daily 10–6, 10–8 in summer.*

need a break?

Beyond the bullring in El Mercadillo, you can relax in the shady **Alameda del Tajo** gardens, one of the loveliest spots in Ronda. At the end of the garden, a balcony protrudes from the face of the cliff, offering a vertigo-inducing view of the valley below. Stroll along the cliff-top walk to the Reina Victoria hotel, built by British settlers from Gibraltar at the turn of the 20th century as a fashionable rest stop on their Algeciras–Bobadilla railroad line.

Where to Stay & Eat

★ $$$–$$$$ ✕ **Tragabuches.** This restaurant has taken the Spanish culinary scene by storm. The food has earned the Ronda-born cook, Sergio López, a national award as Best Young Chef in Spain; there's now a cookbook containing some of its best-loved dishes. The menú de degustación, a taster's menu of five courses and two desserts, includes imaginative choices: *rabo de toro* (oxtail stew) accompanied by a sweet chestnut puree, and thyme ice cream. Traditional and modern furnishings blend in the two dining rooms (one with a picture window). The restaurant is around the corner from Ronda's parador and the tourist office. ✉ *José Aparicio 1* ☎ *952/190291* ▭ *AE, DC, MC, V* ⊙ *Closed Mon. No dinner Sun.*

$$ ✕ **Mesón Santiago.** Eating at this tavern is like dining in with your extended Spanish family. The several dining rooms are decorated with Sevillian tiles and ceramic plates. In summer, you can lunch outdoors on the patio. The simple Spanish fare includes tongue, partridge, quail, and the rib-sticking *cocido de la casa* (a savory stew of chard, potatoes, and chickpeas). ✉ *Marina 3* ☎ *952/871559* ▭ *AE, DC, MC, V* ⊙ *Closed Dec.–Feb. No dinner.*

$–$$ ✕ **Pedro Romero.** Named after the father of modern bullfighting, this restaurant opposite the bullring is packed with colorful taurine objects. Bulls peer down at you as you tuck into the *sopa del mesón* (house soup), rabo de toro, or *perdiz estofada con salsa de vino blanco y hierbas* (stewed partridge with white wine and herb sauce), and, for dessert, *tocinillo* *del cielo al coco* (a sweet caramel custard flavored with coconut). ✉ *Virgen de la Paz 18* ☎ *952/871110* 💳 *AE, DC, MC, V.*

$$$ ✕🏨 **Parador de Ronda.** The exterior of this parador is the old town hall, perched at the very edge of the Tajo gorge, but only the shell of the building remains—inside, the design is daringly modern, beginning with the glass-enclosed courtyard. The large guest rooms, in cream tones, are comfortable, with enormous bathrooms. The restaurant is famous in its own right: try the gazpacho based on green peppers, a regional specialty; for dessert, get the *helado de aceite de oliva* (olive oil ice cream), the chef's invention. ✉ *Pl. de España, 29400* ☎ *952/877500* 📠 *952/878188* 🌐 *www.parador.es* *70 rooms, 8 suites* *Restaurant, minibars, cable TV, pool, meeting room* 💳 *AE, DC, MC, V.*

$$ ✕🏨 **Don Miguel.** Perched on the edge of the Tajo next to the Puente Nuevo, this long-standing Ronda establishment has undergone a complete face-lift, and its rooms now have a comfortable and modern, if rather plain, style. Some rooms have views of the gorge and bridge. In the popular restaurant, which has spacious terraces with equally attractive views, you might find *codornices a la serrana* (mountain-style quail) or *trucha almendrada* (trout with almonds). ✉ *Villanueva 4, 29400* ☎ *952/877722* 📠 *952/878377* 🌐 *www.dmiguel.com* *30 rooms* *Restaurant, cafeteria* 💳 *AE, D, MC, V.*

$$ ✕🏨 **El Molino del Santo.** In a converted mill ("The Saint's Mill") next to a rushing stream near Benaoján, 10 km (7 mi) from Ronda, this British-run establishment was one of Andalusia's first country hotels and has served as a model for the rest. Guest rooms are arranged around a pleasant patio and come in various sizes, some with a terrace. This is a good base for walks in the mountains, and the hotel rents mountain bikes as well. The restaurant is justifiably popular. ✉ *Estación de Benaoján, Benaoján 29370* ☎ *952/167151* 📠 *952/167327* 🌐 *www.andalucia.com/molino* *15 rooms* *Restaurant, pool* 💳 *AE, DC, MC, V* ⏲ *Closed mid-Nov. to mid-Feb.*

$$$ 🏨 **Maestranza.** This bright and modern hotel, across the street from the Ronda bullring, occupies the site of the house where the legendary bullfighter Pedro Romero once lived (only one facade remains of the original). The carpeted rooms are large, with dark-wood furniture that contrasts nicely with cream-color walls and light, pastel fabrics. Some rooms have views of the *plaza de toros*. The large Sol y Sombra restaurant serves regional dishes, such as *conejo a la rondeña* (braised rabbit with vegetables and herbs). ✉ *Virgen de la Paz, 29400* ☎ *952/187072* 📠 *952/190170* 🌐 *www.hotelmaestranza.com* *52 rooms, 2 suites* *Restaurant, cafeteria, cable TV, minibars, meeting rooms, parking (fee)* 💳 *AE, D, MC, V.*

$$$ 🏨 **Reina Victoria.** Built in 1906 by the Gibraltar British as a weekend stop for passengers on the rail line between Algeciras and Bobadilla, this classic Spanish hotel rose to fame in 1912, when the ailing German poet Rainer Maria Rilke came here to convalesce. (His room has been preserved as a museum.) Although the Queen Victoria has had more than a lick of paint to ensure that it is in line with the *pueblo's* top hotels, it still exudes old-fashioned charm—despite the predominance of tour groups. The views from the clifftop gardens, hanging over an approximately 500-foot precipice, are particularly dramatic. ✉ *Jerez 25, 29400* ☎ *952/871240* 📠 *952/871075* 🌐 *www.ronda.net/usuar/reinavictoria/* *89 rooms* *Restaurant, cable TV, minibars, pool, parking (fee), some pets allowed* 💳 *AE, DC, MC, V.*

$$ 🏨 **Alavera de los Baños.** This small, German-run hotel featured as a backdrop for the film classic *Carmen*. Fittingly, given its location next to the Moorish baths, there's an Arab–influenced theme throughout with ocher and pastel tones. The two rooms on the first floor have their own terraces, opening up onto the garden. The restaurant uses predominantly organically grown foods; breakfast is included in the price. ✉ *San Miguel, 29400* ☎📠 *952/879143* 🌐 *www.andalucia.com/alavera* 🛏 *10 rooms* 🛎 *Restaurant, pool, lounge, library; no a/c* 💳 *MC, V.*

$$ **Polo.** Family owned, cozy, and convenient, this hotel is decorated in a style that's classically Spanish: wrought-iron headboards, Mallorca-weave curtains, and a cool and elegant hall with marble columns offset by black and white tiles. Bedrooms are spacious and light, and several have views across the rooftops to the mountains beyond. One of the best rooms even has a bathroom with a view. There is a good, reasonably priced restaurant and bar. ✉ *Mariano Souvirón 8, 29400* ☎ *952/872447* 📠 *952/872449* 🛏 *36 rooms* 🛎 *Restaurant, cafeteria* 💳 *AE, DC, MC, V.*

$$ **San Gabriel.** In the oldest part of Ronda, this hotel is run by a family who converted their 18th-century home into an elegant yet informal hostelry (part of the building is still the family residence). The common areas, furnished with antiques, are warm and cozy, and include a video screening room with autographed photos of actors. (John Lithgow, Isabella Rossellini, and Bob Hoskins, in town to film *Don Quixote,* were among the first to stay at the hotel.) Some rooms have small sitting rooms; all are stylishly furnished with antiques. ✉ *Marqués de Moctezuma, 19, 29400* ☎ *952/190392* 📠 *952/190117* 🛏 *15 rooms, 1 suite* 🛎 *Cafeteria, minibars, parking (fee)* 💳 *AE, MC, V.*

Around Ronda: Caves, Romans, & Pueblos Blancos

About 20 km (12 mi) west of Ronda is the prehistoric **Cueva de la Pileta** (Pileta Cave). To see it, head west out of Ronda, toward Seville, and exit left for the village of Benaoján—from here the caves are well signposted. There are Spanish speaking guides to lead you on a roughly 90-minute walk that reveals prehistoric wall paintings of bison, deer, and horses outlined in black, red, and ocher. One highlight is the Cámara del Pescado (Chamber of the Fish), whose drawing of a huge fish is thought to be 15,000 years old. ☎ *952/167343* 🎫 *€6* ⏲ *Daily 10–1 and 4–5 (4–6 in summer).*

Ronda la Vieja (Old Ronda), 20 km (12 mi) west of Ronda, is the site of the old Roman settlement of **Acinipo.** A thriving town in the 1st century AD, Acinipo was abandoned for reasons that still baffle historians. Today it's a windswept hillside with piles of stones, the foundations of a few Roman houses, and what remains of a theater. Excavations are often under way at the site, in which case it will be closed to the public. Call the tourist office in Setenil before visiting to get an update. ☎ *956/134261* ✣ *Take A473 toward Algodonales; turnoff for ruins is 9 km (5 mi) from Ronda.* 🎫 *Free* ⏲ *Wed.–Sat. 9–3:30, Sun. 10–4:30.*

18 **Setenil de las Bodegas,** 8 km (5 mi) north of Acinipo, is in a cleft in the rock cut by the River Guadalporcín. The village seems to have been sculpted out of the rock itself: the streets resemble long, narrow caves, and on many houses the roof is formed by a projecting ledge of heavy rock.

Thirteen kilometers (8 mi) north of Setenil is the picturesque profile of
19 **Olvera.** Two imposing silhouettes dominate the crest of its hill: the 11th-century castle Vallehermoso, a legacy of the Moors, and the neoclassical church of La Encarnación, reconstructed in the 19th century on the foundations of the old Moorish mosque.

20 A solitary watchtower dominates a crag above the village of **Zahara de la Sierra,** its outline visible for miles around. The tower is all that remains of a Moorish castle where King Alfonso X once fought the emir of Morocco; the building remained a Moorish stronghold until it fell to

the Christians in 1470. Along the streets you can see door knockers fashioned like the hand of Fatima: the fingers represent the five laws of the Koran and serve to ward off evil. ✣ *From Olvera, drive 21 km (13 mi) southwest to the village of Algodonales.*

Sierra de Grazalema

Village of Grazalema: 28 km (17 mi) northwest of Ronda, 23 km (14 mi) northeast of Ubrique.

The 323-square-km (125-square-mi) Sierra de Grazalema straddles the provinces of Málaga and Cádiz. These mountains trap the rain clouds that roll in from the Atlantic and thus have the distinction of being the wettest place in Spain, with an average annual rainfall of 88 inches. Thanks to the park's altitude and prevailing humidity, it's one of the last habitats for the rare fir tree *Abies pinsapo*; you'll also find ibex, vultures, and birds of prey. Parts of the park are restricted, accessible only on foot and accompanied by an official guide. Standing dramatically at the en-
21 trance to the park, the village of **Grazalema** is the prettiest of the pueblos blancos. Its cobble streets of houses with pink-and-ocher roofs wind up the hillside, red geraniums splash white walls, and black, wrought-iron lanterns and grilles cling to the house fronts.

From Grazalema, C3331 takes you to **Ubrique,** on the slopes of the Saltadero Mountains, and known for its leather tanning and embossing industry. Look for the **Convento de los Capuchinos** (Capuchin Convent) and the churches of **San Pedro** and **Nuestra Señora de la O.** Another excursion from Grazalema takes you through the heart of the nature park: follow the A344 west through dramatic mountain scenery, past the village of Benamahoma, to **El Bosque,** home of the main park-information center and a trout stream.

Where to Stay

$ **Villa Turística de Grazalema.** Across the valley from the village of Grazalema, this complex consists of a hotel proper and 38 semidetached apartments sleeping two to six. Most have splendid views of the village and the mountains beyond. It's popular with families, so the noise level can rise during school holidays. ✉ *El Olivar (exit just before village), Grazalema 11610* ☎ *956/132136* 🖷 *956/132213* 🌐 *www.tugasa.com* *24 rooms, 38 apartments* *Restaurant, pool, meeting room* 💳 *MC, V.*

ESTEPONA TO GIBRALTAR

You can still see Estepona's fishing village and Moorish old quarter amid its booming coastal development. Just inland, Casares piles whitewashed houses over the bright-blue Mediterranean below. Sotogrande, with its golf courses and long beach, and old San Roque are the last stops before the British colony at Gibraltar, a bizarre anomaly of Moorish, Spanish, and British influences. Finally, the windy town of Tarifa marks the southernmost tip of mainland Europe.

Estepona

22 *17 km (11 mi) west of San Pedro de Alcántara.*

Estepona used to mark the tail end of the Costa del Sol's urban sprawl, but today—thanks largely to the increasing importance of Gibraltar's airport—it's fast becoming the biggest boomtown on the coast. Still, the old fishing village hangs on. The beach, more than 1 km (½ mi) long, is lined with fishing boats, and the promenade passes well-kept, aromatic flower gardens. The gleaming white **Puerto Deportivo** is lively and packed with restaurants, serving everything from fresh fish to pizzas and Chinese food. Back from the main Avenida de España, the old Moorish village is surprisingly unspoiled.

Where to Stay & Eat

$$–$$$ ✕ **Alcaría de Ramos.** José Ramos, a winner of Spain's National Gastronomy Prize, opened this restaurant in the El Paraíso complex, between Estepona and San Pedro de Alcántara, and has watched it garner a large and enthusiastic following. Try the ensalada *de lentejas con salmón ahumado* (with lentils and smoked salmon), followed by *cordero asado* (roast lamb) and Ramos's deservedly famous fried ice cream. ✉ *Urbanización El Paraíso, Ctra. N340, Km 167* ☎ *952/886178* ▭ *MC, V* ⊙ *Closed Sun. No lunch.*

$–$$ ✕ **La Rada.** Locals flock to this bright, busy establishment for inexpensive, freshly caught fish and shellfish. Service is brisk—waiters dash among the tables in the two dining rooms. Ask about the daily specials or dig into the house specialty, *arroz a la marinera* (seafood rice). ✉ *Avda. España 16* ☎ *952/791036* ▭ *AE, MC, V* ⊙ *Closed Tues.*

$$$$ **Atalaya Park.** Closer to San Pedro de Alcántara than to Estepona, this resort hotel is set in subtropical gardens beside the sea and has extensive sports facilities—often used by Olympic teams. The hotel allows you to try up to 58 sports and activities without charge. Rooms overlook either the Mediterranean or the mountains; some have nice touches like exposed brick, dark carpets, and picture windows. ✉ *N340, Km 168, 29688* ☎ *952/889000* 🖷 *952/889022* 🌐 *www.atalaya-park.es* *454 rooms, 33 suites, 14 bungalows* *7 restaurants, minibars, cable TV with movies, 2 18-hole golf courses, 9 tennis courts, 6 pools (2 indoor), gym, hair salon, massage, sauna, beach, windsurfing, canoeing, kayaking, scuba, jet skiing, parasailing, mountain bikes, archery, basketball, hiking, horseback riding, volleyball, 3 bars* ▭ *AE, DC, MC, V.*

$$$$ **Kempinski.** From the outside, this luxury resort between the coastal highway and the beach looks like a cross between a Moroccan Casbah and the hanging gardens of Babylon. Tropical gardens, with a succession of large swimming pools, meander down to the beach. The rooms are spacious, modern, and luxurious, with faux–North African furnishings and balconies overlooking the Mediterranean. The Sunday-afternoon jazz brunch, with a live band and lavish buffet, is something of a social occasion for locals. ✉ *Playa El Padrón, Ctra. N340, Km 159, 29680* ☎ *952/809500* 🖷 *952/809550* 🌐 *www.kempinski-spain.com* *133 rooms, 16 suites* *Restaurant, in-room data ports, minibars, cable TV with movies, 4 pools (1 indoor), gym, hair salon, shop, some pets allowed* ▭ *AE, DC, MC, V.*

★ $$$$ **Las Dunas.** Rising like a multicolor apparition next to the beach, this spectacular hotel is halfway between Estepona and Marbella. Trickling fountains and copious exotic plants help create a sense of the palatial, and the large guest rooms are bright and airy, with large easy chairs, hemp carpets, and light-green furniture. Sea views command a premium. The restaurant serves first-class international food, and the health center offers several alternative therapies. ✉ *La Boladilla Baja, Ctra. de Cádiz, Km 163, 29689* ☎ *952/794345* 🖷 *952/794825* 🌐 *www.las-dunas.com* *33 rooms, 39 suites, 33 apartments* *2 restaurants, minibars, cable TV with movies, pool, health club, massage* ▭ *AE, DC, MC, V.*

Casares

㉓ *20 km (12 mi) northwest of Estepona.*

The mountain village of Casares lies high above Estepona in the Sierra Bermeja. Streets of ancient white houses piled one on top of the other perch on the slopes beneath a ruined but impressive Moorish castle. The heights afford stunning views over orchards, olive groves, and cork woods to the Mediterranean, sparkling in the distance.

San Roque

24 *92 km (57 mi) southwest of Ronda, 64 km (40 mi) west of Marbella.*

The town of San Roque was founded within sight of Gibraltar by Spaniards who fled the Rock when the British captured it in 1704. Almost 300 years of British occupation have done little to diminish the chauvinism of San Roque's inhabitants, who still see themselves as the only genuine Gibraltarians. Fourteen kilometers (10 mi) east of San Roque is the luxury **Sotogrande** complex, a gated community with sprawling millionaires' villas, a yacht marina, and four golf courses, including the legendary Valderrama, which once hosted the Ryder Cup.

Where to Stay & Eat

$$–$$$ ✕ **Los Remos.** The dining room in this gracious colonial villa has peach-color walls with quasi-baroque adornments: gilt rococo mirrors, swirling cherubs, friezes of grapes, and crystal lamps. It overlooks a formal, leafy garden full of palms, cedars, and trailing ivy. Entrées include *urta del estrecho en salsa de erizos marinos* (perch from the Straits of Gibraltar in sea-urchin sauce). All seafood comes from the Bay of Algeciras area—the restaurant's name means "The Oars"—and the wine cellar contains some 20,000 bottles. ✉ *Villa Victoria, Campomento de San Roque* ☎ *956/698412* ▭ *AE, DC, MC, V* ⏲ *Closed Sun.*

$$$$ **Almenara.** This deluxe resort is a complex of semidetached Andalusian-style houses clustered around a main building on the edge of an 18-hole golf course, 6 km (4 mi) from the coast, in the Sotogrande development. Gardens surround each house, accessible via golf cart. Each house also has a private terrace or patio. The best views—over the golf course with the Mediterranean in the distance—are from rooms in the 600s. ✉ *Avda. Almenara, Sotogrande 11310* ☎ *956/582000* 📠 *956/582001* 🌐 *www.sotogrande.com* *136 rooms, 12 suites* *Restaurant, snack bar, in-room data ports, minibars, cable TV with movies, 18-hole and 9-hole golf course, pool, spa, bar* ▭ *AE, DC, MC, V.*

$$$$ **The Suites.** In this Moorish-Andalusian–style pueblo, the main building houses the reception area, golf clubhouse, and two restaurants, one specializing in Japanese food. The rooms and suites are in white houses scattered around a garden with fountains and exotic plants; each room has a little garden patio, and each suite has an enclosed courtyard as well. The houses are connected by paved paths, on which the cleaning staff tool around on golf carts. The hotel is next to the San Roque golf course, halfway between the village and Sotogrande. ✉ *San Roque Club, Ctra. N340, Km 127, San Roque 11360* ☎ *956/613030* 📠 *956/613013* 🌐 *www.sanroqueclub.com* *50 rooms, 50 suites* *2 restaurants, minibars, cable TV with movies, 18-hole golf course, 4 tennis courts, pool, horseback riding, some pets allowed* ▭ *AE, DC, MC, V.*

Nightlife

The **Casino de San Roque** (✉ Ctra. N340, Km 124 ☎ 956/780100 ⏲ Daily 8 PM–5 AM, 9 PM–5 AM in winter) has a gaming room with roulette and blackjack tables and a less formal slot-machine area. A passport and jacket and tie for men are required in the casino.

Gibraltar

20 km (12 mi) east of Algeciras, 77 km (48 mi) southwest of Marbella.

The tiny British colony of Gibraltar—nicknamed Gib, or simply "the Rock"—whose impressive silhouette dominates the strait between Spain and Morocco, was one of the two Pillars of Hercules in ancient times, marking the western limits of the known world. Gibraltar's ace position, commanding the narrow entrance to the Mediterranean, inspired the Moors to seize it in 711 as a preliminary to the conquest of Spain.

After the Moors had ruled for 750 years, the Spaniards recaptured Tariq's Rock in 1462. The English, heading an Anglo-Dutch fleet in the War of the Spanish Succession, seized the Rock in 1704 and following several years of local skirmishes, Gibraltar was finally ceded to Great Britain in 1713 by the Treaty of Utrecht. Spain has been trying to get it back ever since. In 1779 a combined French and Spanish force laid siege to the Rock for three years, to no avail. During the Napoleonic Wars, Gibraltar served as Admiral Nelson's base for the decisive naval Battle of Trafalgar, and during the two World Wars, it served the Allies well as a naval and air base. In 1967, Franco closed the land border with Spain to strengthen his claims over the colony, and it remained closed until 1985.

Britain and Spain have been talking about joint Anglo-Spanish sovereignty, much to the ire of the majority of Gibraltarians, who remain fiercely patriotic to the crown. The Rock is like Britain with a suntan. There are double-decker buses, policemen in helmets, and bright red mailboxes. Millions of dollars have been spent in developing the Rock's tourist potential, while a steady flow of expatriate Britons come here daily from Spain to shop at Safeway and their favorite High Street shops. Gibraltar's economy is further boosted by its important status as an offshore financial center.

There must be few places in the world that you enter by walking or driving across an airport runway, but that's what happens in Gibraltar. First, show your passport; then make your way out onto the narrow strip of land linking Spain's La Linea with Britain's Rock. Unless you have a good reason to take your car—like loading up on cheap gas or duty-free goodies—you're best off leaving it in a guarded parking area in La Linea, the Spanish border town, and relying on buses and taxis in Gibraltar, whose streets are narrow and congested. The Official Rock Tour—conducted either by minibus or, at a greater cost, taxi—takes about 90 minutes and includes all the major sights, allowing you to choose which places to come back to and linger at later. When you call Gibraltar from Spain, the area code is 9567; when you call from another country, the code is 350. Prices in this section are given in British pounds; Gibraltar permits the use of U.K. currency and its own sterling government notes and coins. Euros can also be used in most of the shops, but the exchange rate may be high.

25 **Catalan Bay,** a fishing village founded by Genoese settlers, is now a picturesque resort on the eastern shores. You'll see the massive water catchments that once supplied the colony's drinking water. ✣ *From the Rock's eastern side, go left down Devil's Tower Road as you enter Gibraltar.*

26 From **Europa Point,** have a look across the straits to Morocco, 23 km (14 mi) away. You are now standing on one of the two ancient Pillars of Hercules. In front of you, the lighthouse has dominated the meeting place of the Atlantic and the Mediterranean since 1841; sailors can see its light from a distance of 27 km (17 mi). ✣ *Continue along the coast road to the Rock's southern tip.*

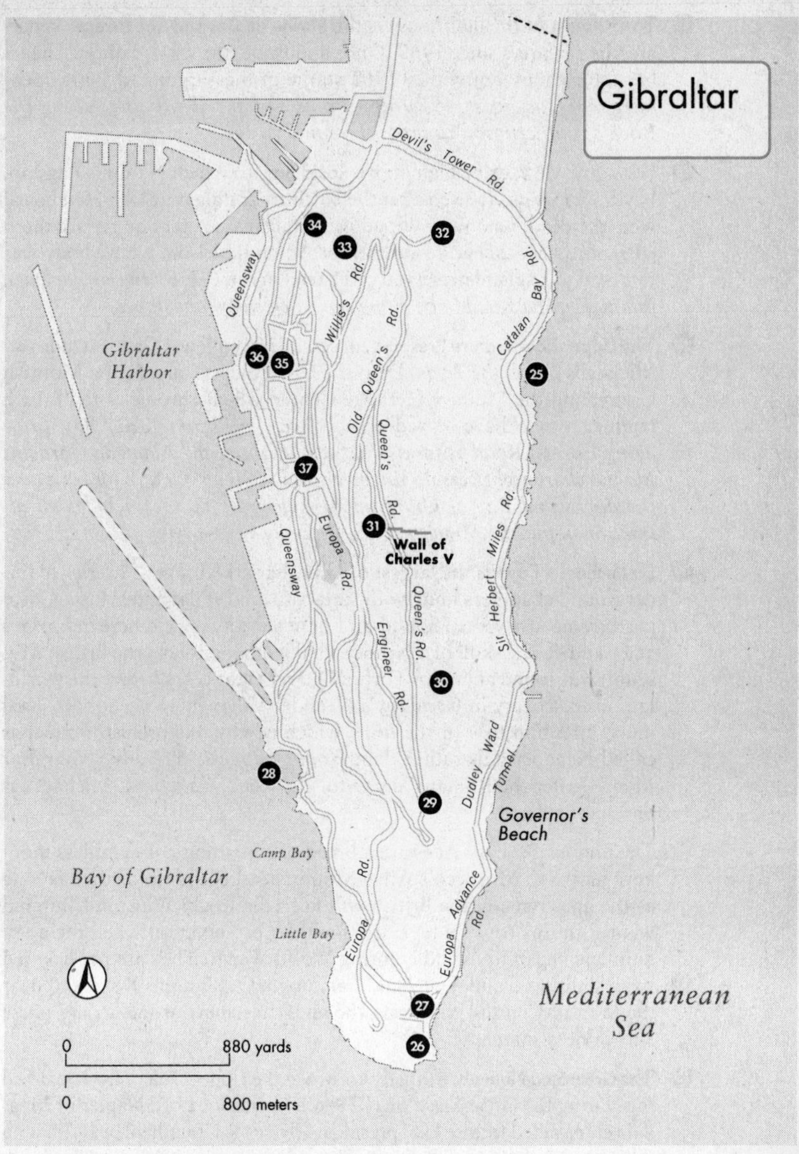

Apes' Den **31**
Casemates Square **34**
Catalan Bay **25**
Europa Point. **26**
Gibraltar Museum **36**
Great Siege Tunnel **32**
Moorish Castle **33**
Nefusot Yehudada Synagogue **37**
Rosia Bay **28**
Shrine of Our Lady of Europe **27**
St. Michael's Cave. **30**
Town of Gibraltar **35**
Upper Rock Nature Reserve. **29**

27 To the west of the lighthouse is the **Shrine of Our Lady of Europe,** venerated by seafarers since 1462. Once a mosque, the small catholic chapel has a little museum with a 1462 statue of the Virgin and some documents. *Just west of Europa Point and the lighthouse, along the Rock's southern tip.* *Free* *Mon.–Fri. 10–7.*

28 For a fine view, drive high above **Rosia Bay,** to which Nelson's flagship, HMS *Victory,* was towed after the Battle of Trafalgar in 1805. On board were the dead, who were buried in Trafalgar Cemetery on the southern edge of town—except, of course, for Admiral Nelson, whose body was returned to England preserved in a barrel of rum. *From Europa Flats, follow Europa Road back along the Rock's western slopes.*

29 The **Upper Rock Nature Preserve,** accessible from Jews' Gate, includes St. Michael's Cave, the Apes' Den, the Great Siege Tunnels, the Moorish Castle, and the Military Heritage Center, which chronicles the British regiments who have served on the Rock. *From Rosia Bay, drive along Europa Road as far as the Casino, above the Alameda Gardens. Make a sharp right here up Engineer Road to Jews' Gate, a lookout over the docks and Bay of Gibraltar to Algeciras.* *£7 (includes all attractions), plus £1.50 per vehicle* *Daily 9:30–6:30.*

30 **St. Michael's Cave** is the largest of Gibraltar's 150 caves. A series of underground chambers hung with stalactites and stalagmites, it's an ideal performing arts venue. Sound-and-light shows are held here most days at 11 and 4. The skull of a Neanderthal woman (now in the British Museum) was found at nearby Forbes Quarry eight years *before* the world-famous discovery in Germany's Neander Valley in 1856; nobody paid much attention to it at the time, which is why this prehistoric race is called Neanderthals rather than *Homo calpensis* (literally, "Gibraltar Man"—after the Romans' name for the Rock, *Calpe*). St. Michael's is on Queens Road.

The famous Barbary Apes are a breed of cinnamon-color, tailless monkeys native to Morocco's Atlas Mountains. Legend holds that as long as the apes remain, the British will keep the Rock; Winston Churchill went so far as to issue an order for their preservation when the apes' numbers began to dwindle during World War II. They are publicly fed
31 twice daily, at 8 and 4, at **Apes' Den,** down Old Queens Road and near the Wall of Charles V. Among the apes' mischievous talents are purse and camera snatching.

32 The **Great Siege Tunnels,** formerly known as the Upper Galleries, were carved out during the Great Siege of 1779–82. Governor Lord Napier of Magdala entertained former U.S. president Ulysses S. Grant here in 1878, with a banquet in St. George's Hall. These tunnels form part of what is arguably the most impressive defense system anywhere in the world.

33 The **Moorish Castle** was built by the descendants of Tariq, who conquered the Rock in 711. The present Tower of Homage dates from 1333, and its besieged walls bear the scars of stones from medieval catapults (and, later, cannonballs). Admiral Rooke hoisted the British flag from its summit when he captured the Rock in 1704, and it has flown here ever since. The castle is on Willis's Road.

34 **Casemates Square,** in the northern part of town, is Gibraltar's social hub, and pedestrianized. There are now plenty of places to sit out with a drink and watch the world go by.

35 The colorful, congested **town of Gibraltar** is where the dignified Regency architecture of Great Britain blends well with the shutters, balconies,

and patios of southern Spain. The main tourist office is on Cathedral Square; there's a smaller branch on Casemates Square. Apart from the shops, restaurants, and pubs that beckon on busy Main Street, you'll want to see the **Governor's Residence,** where the ceremonial Changing of the Guard takes place six times a year and the Ceremony of the Keys takes place twice a year. Also make sure you see the **Law Courts,** where the famous case of the sailing ship *Mary Celeste* was heard in 1872; the Anglican **Cathedral of the Holy Trinity;** and the Catholic **Cathedral of St. Mary the Crowned.**

10

36 Don't miss the **Gibraltar Museum,** which houses a beautiful 14th-century Moorish bathhouse, an 1865 model of the Rock, and which has displays that evoke the Great Siege and the Battle of Trafalgar. There's also a reproduction of the "Gibraltar Woman," the Neanderthal skull discovered here in 1848. ✉ *Bomb House La.* ☎ *9567/74289* 🌐 *www.gibraltar.gi/museum* 🎫 *£2* ⏲ *Weekdays 10–6, Sat. 10–2.*

37 The 18th-century **Nefusot Yehudada Synagogue,** on Line Wall Road, is worth a look for its inspired architecture. For weapons aficionados, **Koehler Gun,** in Casemates Square at the northern end of Main Street, is an example of the type of gun developed during the Great Siege. You can ride ★ to the top of Gibraltar on a **cable car.** Reminiscent of a ski gondola, the car doesn't go high off the ground, but the views of Spain and Africa from the Rock's pinnacle are superb. It leaves every day from a station on Grand Parade, at the southern end of Main Street. 🎫 *Cable car £5 round-trip* ⏲ *June–Sept., daily 9:30–5:15; Oct.–May, Mon.–Sat. 9:30–5:15.*

WHAT IT COSTS In £					
	$$$$	$$$	$$	$	¢
AT DINNER	over £25	£18–£25	£12–£18	£5–£12	under £5

Prices are for per person for a main course at dinner.

WHAT IT COSTS In £					
	$$$$	$$$	$$	$	¢
FOR 2 PEOPLE	over £165	£120–£165	£80–£120	£30–£80	under £30

Prices are for two people in a standard double room in high season, excluding tax.

Where to Stay & Eat

$$–$$$ ✕ **Terrace Restaurant.** Upstairs from the casino, this is one of the best restaurants for sea views. Tarifa's colorful kite-surfers and Africa's Atlas mountains are visible on a clear day. The menu here is comfortably traditional and good as the black bow-tie service. Dishes include beef Wellington, chicken Roquefort, and lobster thermidor. Afterwards, choose from the diet-defying dessert trolley with classic English desserts, like trifle, and glistening fresh fruit tarts. ✉ *7 Europa Rd.* ☎ *9567/76666* *Reservations essential* 💳 *AE, DC, MC, V* ⏲ *No lunch.*

¢–$ ✕ **Maharaja.** Curry is the national dish in the United Kingdom these days, and this restaurant won't disappoint a discerning Brit. Curries are good and spicy, and are made as hot (or mild) as you like. The *mattar paneer* (cheese and pea curry) is delicious. Tucked into a side street, this is one of the best Indian restaurants in town. ✉ *5 Tuckey's Lane* ☎ *9567/75233* 💳 *AE, MC, V.*

$$$$ **The Eliott.** If you want to stay at the most slick and modern of the Rock's hotels, try this place right In the center of the town, in what used to be the Gibraltar Holiday Inn. Rooms have been revamped, so you

can expect all the extras. Ask for a room at the top of the hotel, with a view over the Bay of Gibraltar. ✉ *2 Governor's Parade* ☎ *9567/70500* 🖷 *9567/70243* 🌐 *www.gibraltar.gi/eliotthotel* *106 rooms, 8 suites* *Internet, 2 restaurants, cable TV with movies, pool, sauna, 2 bars, meeting room; no smoking* ▭ *AE, DC, MC, V.*

$$$–$$$$ **The Rock.** Overlooking Gibraltar, this hotel first opened in 1932. Furnishings in the rooms and restaurant can compete with those in good international hotels anywhere, yet they manage to preserve something of the English colonial style—bamboo, ceiling fans, and a fine terrace bar with a wisteria-covered terrace. ✉ *3 Europa Rd.* ☎ *9567/73000* 🖷 *9567/73513* 🌐 *www.blandgroup.gi* *101 rooms, 2 suites* *Restaurant, pool, hair salon, bar* ▭ *AE, DC, MC, V.*

$ **Bristol.** This colonial-style hotel in the heart of town has splendid views of the bay and the cathedral. Rooms are spacious and comfortable, and the downstairs lounge exudes a faded elegance with sink-into sofas and chandeliers. The tropical garden is a haven. ✉ *10 Cathedral Sq.* ☎ *9567/76800* 🖷 *9567/77613* 🌐 *www.gibraltar.gi/bristolhotel* *60 rooms* *Cable TV, pool, bar, free parking* ▭ *AE, DC, MC, V.*

Nightlife

At the **Ladbrokes Casino** (✉ 7 Europa Rd. ☎ 9567/76666 🌐 www.ladbrokescasino.com) the gaming room is open 9 PM–4 AM, the cocktail bar 7:30 PM–4 AM. Dress in the gaming room is smart casual.

Tarifa

38 *35 km (21 mi) west of San Roque.*

On the Straits of Gibraltar at the southernmost tip of mainland Europe—where the Mediterranean and the Atlantic meet—Tarifa was one of the earliest Moorish settlements in Spain. Strong winds kept Tarifa off the tourist maps for years, but they have ultimately proven a source of wealth; aeolic power is generated on the vast wind farm on the surrounding hills, and the wide, white-sand beaches stretching north of the town have become Europe's biggest wind- and kitesurfing center.

As a result, the town has continued to grow and prosper. Downtown cafés which, a couple of years ago, were filled with men in flat caps playing dominoes and drinking *anís,* now serve croissants with their *café con leche* and make fancier tapas for a more cosmopolitan crowd. Tarifa's 10th-century **castle** is famous for its siege of 1292, when the defender Guzmán el Bueno refused to surrender even though the attacking Moors threatened to kill his captive son. In defiance, he flung his own dagger down to them, shouting "Here, use this"—or something to that effect. The Spanish military turned the castle over to the town in the mid-1990s, and it now has a **museum** on Guzmán and the sacrifice of his son. *€1.20* ⏲ *Tues.–Sun. 10–2 and 4–6.*

Ten kilometers (6 mi) north of Tarifa on the Atlantic coast are the Roman ruins of **Baelo Claudia.** This settlement was a thriving production center of *garum,* a salty fish paste appreciated in Rome. ☎ *956/688530* *Free* ⏲ *July–mid-Sept., Tues.–Sat. 10–6, Sun. 10–2; mid-Sept.–June, Tues.–Sat. 10–5, Sun. 10–2.*

Where to Stay

$$$ **Hurricane Hotel.** A laid-back, palm-kissed hotel next to the beach, this is a favorite hangout of the windsurfing set. It's fun and informal, and the rooms simple but adequate. The staff can organize horseback-riding trips along the beach or inland. Their restaurant is excellent. ✉ *Ctra. Cádiz–Málaga, Km 77, 11380* ☎ *956/684919* 🖷 *956/684329* *28* *rooms, 5 suites* ♨ *Restaurant, pool, horseback riding, some pets allowed* ▭ *AE, MC, V.*

$ 🏨 **La Calzada.** This delightful small hotel has a handful of rooms and is right off the main square. Recently refurbished with colorful tiles and dazzling white paintwork, it's an excellent choice if you want to be in town rather than part of the surfer set on the beach. ✉ *Justino Pertinez 7, 11380* ☎ *956/680366* ⇨ *8* ▭ *MC, V* ⊙ *Closed Nov.*

THE COSTA DEL SOL A TO Z

10

To research prices, get advice from other travelers, and book travel arrangements, visit www.fodors.com.

AIR TRAVEL

Air Plus Comet operates a direct flight from New York to Málaga every Thursday. Otherwise you will have to connect in Madrid. Iberia and British Airways fly once daily from London, and numerous British charter companies link London with Málaga. Most major European cities have direct flights to Málaga on Iberia or their own national airlines. Iberia has up to eight flights daily from Madrid (flying time one hour), three flights a day from Barcelona (1½ hours), and regular flights from other Spanish cities.

Air Plus Comet ✉ 420 Lexington Ave., Ste. 2633, New York ☎ 212/983-1277 **Iberia** ✉ Molina Lario 13, Málaga ☎ 952/121902/, 952/136166 at airport, 902/400500 inquiries.

AIRPORTS & TRANSFERS

Málaga's airport is 10 km (6 mi) west of town. If you're coming from Britain and heading for the coast west of Marbella, fly into Gibraltar instead: the airport is right next to the frontier, and once you've crossed into Spain you can get buses in La Linea for all coastal resorts. Trains connect Málaga's airport with several nearby cities, and an Iberia bus leaves every 20 minutes for downtown Málaga (6:30 AM–midnight) at a fare of €1. Taxis are plentiful, and official fares to Málaga, Torremolinos, and other resorts are posted inside the terminal. The trip from the airport to Torremolinos costs about €12.

Airports **Gibraltar Airport** ☎ 9567/73026. **Aeropuerto de Málaga** ☎ 952/048804.

BIKE TRAVEL

The Costa del Sol is famous for its sun and sand, but increasingly people are supplementing their beach time with mountain-bike forays into the hilly interior, particular around Ojén, near Marbella, and also along the mountain roads around Ronda. A popular route, which affords sweeping vistas, is via the mountain road from Ojén west to Istán. The Costa del Sol's temperate climate is ideal for biking, though it's best not to exert yourself on the trails in July and August, when temperatures soar. There are numerous bike rental shops around the Costa del Sol, particularly in Marbella, Ronda, and Ojén; many shops can also arrange bike excursions. The cost to rent a mountain bike for the day ranges between €15 and €20. Guided bike excursions, which include the bikes and support staff and cars, generally start at about €62 a day.

Bike Rentals **Monte Aventura** ✉ Pl. de Andalucía 1, Ojén ☎ 952/881519. **Antonio Ortiz Bicicletas** ✉ Avda. Arias de Velasco 28, Marbella ☎ 952/770490. **Spanish Cycling Federation** ✉ Ferraz 16, 28008 Madrid ☎ 91/2429-4334.

BUS TRAVEL

Buses are the best way to reach the Costa del Sol from Seville or Granada, and the best way to get around once you're here. Long-distance buses connect Málaga with Madrid, Cartagena, Almería, Granada, Úbeda, Córdoba, Seville, and Badajoz. You can also reach Marbella and Algeciras directly from Madrid or Seville; other useful routes are Seville–Fuengirola and Cádiz–Algeciras. (In Fuengirola you can also catch buses for Mijas, Marbella, Estepona, and Algeciras.) The Portillo bus company serves most of the Costa del Sol; Alsina Gräells serves Granada, Córdoba, Seville, and Nerja. Málaga's tourist office has details on other bus lines.

Bus Companies **Alsina Gräells** ☎ 952/318295. **Portillo** ✉ Málaga bus station ☎ 952/360191.

Bus Stations **Málaga** ✉ Paseo de los Tilos ☎ 952/350061. **Marbella** ✉ Avda. Trapiche ☎ 952/764400.

CAR TRAVEL

Málaga is 580 km (360 mi) from Madrid via the N-IV to Córdoba, then the N331 to Antequera and N321; 182 km (114 mi) from Córdoba via Antequera; 214 km (134 mi) from Seville; and 129 km (81 mi) from Granada by the shortest route of N342 to Loja, then N321 to Málaga. A car allows you to explore some of Andalusia's famous mountain villages. Mountain driving can be an adventure—hair-raising curves, precipices, and mediocre road services are common—but it's getting more manageable as highways are resurfaced, widened, and in some cases completely rebuilt. To take a car into Gibraltar you need, in theory, an international driver's license, an insurance certificate, and a logbook. In practice, all you need is your passport. Prepare for parking problems—space is scarce—and beware of phony offers of help from "parking-insurance agents" on the frontier approach.

Car Rental Agencies **Hertz** ✉ Málaga airport ☎ 952/233086 🌐 www.hertz.com. **Autopro** ✉ Carril de Montañez 49, Málaga ☎ 952/176030 🌐 www.autopro.es. **Caramba Car** ✉ Ramal Hoyo 7, Torremolinos ☎ 952/376517 🌐 www.carambacar.com.

CONSULATES

Canada **Málaga** ✉ Pl. de la Malagueta 3 ☎ 952/223346.

United Kingdom **Málaga** ✉ Mauricio Moro 2 ☎ 952/352300.

United States **Fuengirola** ✉ Avenida Juan Gomez 8 ☎ 952/474891.

EMERGENCIES

In an emergency, call one of the Spain-wide emergency numbers, for police, ambulance, or fire services. The local Red Cross (Cruz Roja) can also dispatch an ambulance in case of an emergency. Also, there are numerous private ambulance services, which are listed under *ambulancias* (ambulances) in the *Paginas Amarillas* (Yellow Pages). For nonemergencies, you'll find private medical clinics throughout the Costa del Sol, where the staff can often speak some English. Every town has at least one pharmacy that is on-duty for 24 hours; the address of the on-duty pharmacy is generally posted on the front door of all pharmacies. You can also dial Spain's general information number for the location of a doctor's office or pharmacy that's open nearest you.

National police ☎ 091. **Local police** ☎ 092. **Fire department** ☎ 080. **Emergencies** ☎ 112. **Medical service** ☎ 061. **Red Cross** ☎ 952/443545. **National Information Line** ☎ 1003.

ENGLISH-LANGUAGE MEDIA

Many newspaper stands sell international periodicals (such as the *International Herald Tribune* and *Time*) and beach paperbacks in English. The glossy, monthly magazines *Essential* and *Absolute Marbella* have chatty articles on entertainment, culture, travel, and restaurants around the Costa del Sol. The monthly magazine *The Reporter* covers news and entertainment along the Costa del Sol. All these magazines are free and can be picked up at various stores, restaurants, and, occasionally tourist offices in the larger towns, including Málaga and Marbella. The weekly newspaper *Costa del Sol News* reports local and international news and has TV and entertainment listings. Once a week there's an English version of the Spanish daily *Sur,* with local news and a large classifieds section.

RADIO & TELEVISION There are a number of English-language radio stations on the dial in the Costa del Sol, all of which offer a mix of tunes and talk. Many also broadcast the BBC news at various times of the day, usually in the evenings and on weekends. Central FM (98.6 FM), Spectrum FM (107.9 and 105.5 FM), and Onda Cero (101.6 FM) are the three main English-language stations.

LODGING

APARTMENT & VILLA RENTALS The Costa del Sol caters to those in search of some uninterrupted R&R and, accordingly, there is no shortage of apartments and villas—from basic to luxury—for both short- and long-term stays. The coast and rural interior are peppered with accommodations tailored to fit all tastes and styles, from traditional Andalusian farmhouses to self-catering rustic cottages to luxury villas. An excellent source for apartment and villa rentals is www.andalucia.com. For those with an eye to buy, you'll find a host of magazines, in English, that cover the Costa del Sol's real estate market, including *Real(i)ty News*.

Local Agents **Golden Mile Residences** Centro Comercial, Oficina 1, Guadelmina Alta, Marbella 29670 952/880086 www.goldenmile.es. **La Posada del Torcal's Rural Retreats** Partido de Jeva, Villanueva de la Concepción 29230 952/031177.

TOURS

Many one- and two-day excursions from Costa del Sol resorts are run by the national company Pullmantur and various smaller firms. All local travel agents and most hotels have leaflets on hand and can book you a tour; excursions leave from Málaga, Torremolinos, Fuengirola, Marbella, and Estepona, with prices varying by departure point. Most tours last half a day, and in most cases you can be picked up at your hotel. Popular tours include Málaga, the Cuevas de Nerja, Mijas, Marbella, and Puerto Banús; a burro safari in Coín; and a countryside tour of Alhaurín de la Torre, Alhaurín el Grande, Coín, Ojén, and Ronda. Night tours include a barbecue evening, a bullfighting evening with dinner, and a night at the Casino Torrequebrada.

If you plan to visit Málaga independently, but are on a tight schedule, the colorful, open-topped Málaga Tour City Sightseeing Bus is a good way to view the city's attractions within a day. The bus stops at all the major sights in town, including the Gibralfaro and the Cathedral.

Málaga Tour City Sightseeing Bus Málaga 952/363133 www.citysightseeing-spain.com. **Pullmantur** Avda. Imperial, Torremolinos 952/384400.

TRAIN TRAVEL

Málaga is the main rail terminus, with eight trains a day from Madrid and one from Barcelona and Valencia. Most Madrid–Málaga trains leave from Atocha station, though some leave from Chamartín. Travel time varies between 4½ and 10 hours; the best and fastest train is the daytime *Talgo 200* from Atocha. All Madrid–Málaga trains stop at Córdoba. From both Seville (4 hours) and Granada (3–3½ hours) to Málaga, you have to change at Bobadilla, making buses a more efficient mode of travel from those cities. In fact, aside from the direct Madrid–Córdoba–Málaga line, trains in Andalusia can be slow due to the hilly terrain. Málaga's train station is a 15-minute walk from the city center, across the river. Call RENFE for schedules and fares.

A useful suburban train service connects Málaga, Torremolinos, and Fuengirola, stopping at the airport and all resorts along the way. The train leaves Málaga every half hour between 6 AM and 10:30 PM and Fuengirola every half hour from 6:35 AM to 11:35 PM. For the city center get off at the last stop—Centro-Alameda—not the previous stop, which will land you at Málaga's RENFE station. A daily train connects Málaga and Ronda via the dramatic Chorro gorge, with a change at Bobadilla. Travel time is about three hours. Three trains a day make the direct two-hour trip between Ronda and Algeciras on a spectacular mountain track.
Train Information **Málaga train station** ✉ Explanada de la Estación ☎ 952/360202. **RENFE** ☎ 902/240202.

TRAVEL AGENCIES

American Express ✉ Avda. Duque de Ahumada, Marbella ☎ 952/821494.

VISITOR INFORMATION

Regional Tourist Office **Málaga** ✉ Pasaje de Chinitas 4 ☎ 952/213445.
Local Tourist Offices **Almuñecar** ✉ Palacete de La Najarra, Avda. Europa ☎ 958/631125. **Antequera** ✉ Palacio de Najera, Coso Viejo ☎ 952/702505. **Benalmádena Costa** ✉ Avda. Antonio Machado 14 ☎ 952/442494. **Estepona** ✉ Avenida San Lorenzo 1 ☎ 952/802002. **Fuengirola** ✉ Avda. Jesús Santos Rein 6 ☎ 952/467625. **Gibraltar** ✉ 6 Kent House, Cathedral Sq. ☎ 9567/74950. **Málaga** ✉ Avda. Cervantes 1, Paseo del Parque ☎ 952/604410. **Marbella** ✉ Glorieta de la Fontanilla ☎ 952/822818. **Nerja** ✉ Puerta del Mar 2 ☎ 952/521531. **Ronda** ✉ Pl. de España 1 ☎ 952/871272. **Torremolinos** ✉ Pl. Blas Infante 1 ☎ 952/379512.

GRANADA, CÓRDOBA & EASTERN ANDALUSIA

11

FODOR'S CHOICE

Albaicín, Moorish neighborhood in Granada
Alhambra, Granada
Alhambra Palace, hotel in Granada
Amistad Córdoba, hotel in Córdoba
City of Granada
El Caballo Rojo, restaurant in Córdoba
Judería, Córdoba
La Bobadilla, Loja
Mezquita, Córdoba
Parador de Granada, Granada
Parador de Jaén, Jaén
Parador de Úbeda, Úbeda
Town of Baeza
Town of Úbeda

HIGHLY RECOMMENDED

RESTAURANTS
Bodegas Campos, Córdoba
Carmen de San Miguel, Granada
El Churrasco, Córdoba
Las Camachas, Montilla
Ruta del Veleta, Cenes de la Vega
Sevilla, Granada

HOTELS
Reina Cristina, Granada

SIGHTS
Castillo de Santa Catalina, Jaén

Updated by Mary Mclean

FROM THE DARK MOUNTAINS of the Sierra Morena down to the mighty, snowcapped peaks of the Sierra Nevada, Andalusia (Andalucía) rings with echoes of the Moors. These North African Muslims dwelled in southern Spain for almost 800 years, from their first conquest of Spanish soil (Gibraltar) from the Visigoths in AD 711 to their final expulsion from Granada in 1492. The name Andalucía comes from the Moors' own name for their new acquisition: Al-Andalus. Two of Spain's most famous monuments, Córdoba's mosque and Granada's Alhambra palace, were the inspired creations of Moorish architects and craftsmen. Typical Andalusian architecture—brilliant-white villages with narrow, shady streets; thick-walled houses clustered around cool, private patios; whitewashed facades with modest, grilled windows—comes from centuries of Moorish occupation. The Guadalquivir, the Moors' "Great River," runs through the entire region; town names like Úbeda and Jaén are derivations of old Arabic names; ruined *alcázares* (fortresses) dot the landscape; and *azahar* (orange blossom) perfumes the patios.

The Moors left their mark here, but so did the Christian conquerors and their descendants: Andalusia today has Gothic chapels, Renaissance cathedrals, and baroque monasteries and churches. The sturdy sandstone mansions of Úbeda and Baeza contrast intriguingly with the humble, whitewashed villages elsewhere in the province.

The landscape, too, is varied and powerful. Granada's plain (known as *la vega*), covered with lush orchards and tobacco and poplar groves, stretches up to the mountains of the majestic Sierra Nevada. Snow-clad for half the year, this range has the highest peaks on mainland Spain, Mulhacén (11,407 ft) and Veleta (11,125 ft). Farther north, the Guadalquivir flows west toward Córdoba from the heights of the Sierra de Cazorla, bounded by the rugged, shrub-covered Sierra Morena to the north and by the olive groves of Jaén to the south. Fruit and almond trees line the river's banks in Córdoba's orchards. Vineyards cover the Córdoban *campiña* (fertile plain south of the Guadalquivir), and villages cling to hillsides beneath ruined castles.

About the Restaurants

Lunch is the main meal in this part of the country. Restaurants start serving around 2, but they don't fill up until at least 3, and most people are still at the table at 5. After such a long, late lunch, few Andalusians dine out in the evening; instead, they make the rounds of the bars, dipping into tapas and plates of ham or cheese. (Hams from the Pedroches valley, in Córdoba province, and from the Alpujarran village of Trevélez are famous throughout Spain.) You shouldn't have trouble getting a table if you show up early—around 2 for lunch, 9 or 10 for dinner. Córdoba has numerous high-quality restaurants; in Granada the selection is more limited. Córdoba's specialties are *salmorejo* (a thick version of gazpacho) and *rabo de toro* (bull's-tail or oxtail stew), and many Córdoban restaurants are now inventing new dishes based on old Arab recipes. Here, *fino de Montilla,* a dry, sherrylike wine from the local Montilla-Moriles district, makes a good aperitif or bar drink. Granada's typical dishes are *tortilla al Sacromonte* (an omelet traditionally made of calves' brains, sweetbreads, diced ham, potatoes, and peas), *habas con jamón* (ham stewed with broad beans), *sopa sevillana* (fish and seafood soup made with mayonnaise), and *choto al ajillo* (braised kid with garlic). Local taverns serve the earthy *vino de la costa,* from the Alpujarras region. And thanks to its Moorish heritage, Granada serves some of the best mint tea in Spain.

If you have 3 days

Begin in Granada 1–17. On day one, visit the Alhambra and wander the Albaicín, Granada's ancient Moorish quarter. Have lunch along the Caldería. Spend the afternoon in the alleyways of the Alcaicería, visiting the cathedral and the Capilla Real; then take an evening tour of the Alhambra (only the Palacios Nazaríes). The morning of the second day, leave Granada for Baena, north of the **Subbética** 48 region, and part of the Route of the Caliphs, a cultural itinerary that extends along a cluster of history-packed towns and villages on the way from Córdoba to Granada. Take in the scenery before heading to **Córdoba** 29–45 for the night. Spend the morning of the third day touring Córdoba's Mezquita and wandering the Judería. Walk out to the River Guadalquivir and cross the Puente Romano to the Torre de la Calahorra.

If you have 5 days

Explore **Córdoba** 29–45 on day one, lingering in the Mezquita and Judería. Stay the night; then head the next morning toward Granada, stopping in the wine-growing town of **Montilla** 47 and the villages of the **Subbética** 48 region along the way. Spend the night in **Granada** 1–17, and devote day three to the Alhambra, the Albaicín, and the alleys of the Alcaiçería. After a second night in Granada, rise early to hit the mountain roads toward the **Alpujarras** 22; spend your fourth night there, take a morning walk, and return to Granada.

WHAT IT COSTS In Euros					
	$$$$	**$$$**	**$$**	**$**	**¢**
AT DINNER	over €20	€15–€20	€10–€15	€6–€10	under €6

Prices are for per person for a main course at dinner.

About the Hotels

Andalusia has lodging for all budgets, from simple inns to luxurious paradors. At the high end, the Parador de Granada, beside Granada's Alhambra, is a magnificent way to enjoy both Granada and the storied past of southern Spain. Bed-and-breakfast and rural lodgings, close to or in many villages, give you better access to the countryside and its rich folk traditions. In Córdoba, several pleasant hotels are set in houses in the old quarter, close to the mosque. It's easy to find a room in Córdoba, even if you haven't reserved one; just watch out for Holy Week and the May Patio Festival. Granada can be very difficult, as the Alhambra is the most popular tourist attraction in Spain. The city has plenty of hotels, but the high season runs long, from Easter to late October. Hotels on the Alhambra hill—especially the Parador—must be reserved long in advance, and those in the city center, around the Puerta Real and Acera del Darro, are unbelievably noisy—ask for rooms at the back. Beware of Holy Week and the International Festival of Music and Dance (mid-June–mid-July). Also, if you're driving, inquire with hotels in both cities about parking, especially in Córdoba.

WHAT IT COSTS In Euros					
	$$$$	$$$	$$	$	¢
FOR 2 PEOPLE	over €180	€100–€180	€60–€100	€40–€60	under €40

Prices are for per two people in a standard double room in high season, excluding tax.

Exploring Eastern Andalusia

Eastern Andalusia includes the magnificent city of Córdoba surrounded by countryside in the fertile valley of the Rio Guadalquivir. To the east of here is fabled Granada, in a province that spans the Sierra Nevada mountains and the beautifully rugged Alpujarras. This is where you'll find some of the prettiest, most ancient villages; it has become one of the foremost destinations for Andalusia's increasingly popular rural tourism. The coastline of Eastern Andalusia is similarly stunning, with towering cliffs, coves, and unspoiled seaside resorts.

Numbers in the text correspond to numbers in the margin and on the Andalusia: Granada to Córdoba; Granada; and Córdoba maps.

Timing

Spring and autumn are the best seasons to visit. Summer can be stifling, especially in Córdoba; in winter, temperatures can drop to the 30s, and the wind off the Guadalquivir in Córdoba can be as stiff as any in New England. Note that most monuments close for lunch, anywhere between 1:30 and 4, and most museums are closed on Monday.

GRANADA & ENVIRONS, THE SIERRA NEVADA & THE ALPUJARRAS

Granada yields the Alhambra, the gardens of the Generalife, the tomb of Ferdinand and Isabella, and the streets of the ancient Albaicín. Outside the city rise the craggy peaks of the Sierra Nevada; the picturesque and crafts-rich Alpujarra region; the cave communities of Guadix and Purullena; and the fantasy hotel La Bobadilla, near Loja.

Granada

Fodor'sChoice ★

430 km (265 mi) south of Madrid, 261 km (162 mi) east of Córdoba.

Granada rises majestically from a plain onto three hills, dwarfed—on a clear day—by the mighty snowcapped peaks of the Sierra Nevada. Atop one of these hills perches the pink-gold Alhambra palace. The stunning view from its mount takes in the sprawling medieval Moorish quarter, the caves of the Sacromonte, and, in the distance, the fertile vega, rich in orchards, tobacco fields, and poplar groves. Split by internal squabbles, Granada's Moorish Nasrid dynasty gave Ferdinand of Aragón an opportunity in 1491; spurred by Isabella's religious fanaticism, he laid siege to the city for seven months, and on January 2, 1492, Boabdil, the "Rey Chico" (Boy King), was forced to surrender the keys of the city to the Catholic Monarchs. As Boabdil fled the Alhambra by the Puerta de los Siete Suelos (Gate of the Seven Floors), he asked that the gate be sealed forever.

a good walk

Save a full day for the **Alhambra** 1 and the neighboring sites on the Alhambra hill: the Alcazaba, Generalife, Alhambra Museum, **Casa-Museo de Manuel de Falla** 2, and **Carmen de los Mártires** 3. The following walk deserves a day of its own and covers the other major spots in Granada's nucleus.

Southern Cooking

As with all things Granadan, the Moorish culinary influence is stronger here than anywhere else in Andalusia. The use of almonds and the combinations of sweet and salt are strongly redolent of North African cuisine, as are the bitter oranges and the widespread use of Granada's emblematic fig. Sugar mills were one of the chief sources of Granada's wealth until well into the 19th century, and as a result pastries made of syrups, almonds, and flour became specialties, particularly in convents, all over the province.

Habas con jamón de Trevélez (broad beans with ham from the Alpujarran village of Trevélez) is Granada's most famous regional dish, with *tortilla de Sacromonte* (an omelet made of calf's brains, sweetbreads, diced ham, potatoes, and peas) just behind. *Sopa sevillana* (tasty fish and seafood soup), surprisingly named for Granada's most direct rival city, is another staple, and *choto albaicinero* (braised kid with garlic, also known as *choto al ajillo*) is also a specialty. Moorish dishes such as *bstella* (from the Moorish *bastilla,* a salty-sweet puff pastry with pigeon or other meat, pine nuts, and almonds) and spicy *crema de almendras* (almond cream soup) are not uncommon on Granada menus.

Hiking & Walking

Thanks to outdoor clubs and an interest in preserving the wilderness, Andalusia has many parks for recreation and camping. The village of Cazorla, in the province of Jaén, leads to the pine-clad slopes of the Cazorla Nature Park. South of Granada, the Sierra Nevada and the Alpujarras have some of the most impressive vistas in all of Spain, plus terrific skiing in winter and many outdoor sports in summer.

Skiing

Andalusia's Sierra Nevada is the site of the 1996 World Alpine Ski Championships; at the Pradollano and Borreguiles stations there's good skiing from December through May. Both stations have a special snowboarding circuit, floodlit night slopes, a children's ski school, and après-ski sun and swimming in the Mediterranean less than an hour (33 km/20 mi) away.

Fiestas

Granada observes **La Toma** (the Capture), the 1492 surrender to the Catholic Monarchs, on January 2. On January 5, the eve of the **Día de los Reyes Magos** (Feast of the Three Magic Kings), every city and village holds processions of the three Wise Men. On February 1, Granada organizes a ***romería*** (pilgrimage) to the Monastery of San Cecilio, on Sacromonte. Both Granada and Córdoba party hard during **Carnival,** on the days leading up to Ash Wednesday; and both celebrate **Semana Santa** (Holy Week) with dramatic religious processions. The shrine of the **Virgen de la Cabeza,** near Andújar in the province of Jaén, is the scene of one of Spain's biggest romerías on the last weekend in April. May brings to Córdoba **Las Cruces de Mayo** (May Days of the Cross), the **Fiesta de los Patios** (Patio Festival), and the Feria de **Nuestra Señora de la Salud** (Feast of Our Lady of Health). In Granada **Día de la Cruz** (Day of the Cross) is observed the first Sunday in May, **San Isidro** on May 15, and **Mariana Pineda** (a 19th-century political heroine) on May 26. In mid-June, Granada celebrates **Corpus Christi** and **San Pedro** (June 29); the **Festival Internacional de Música y Danza** (International Festival of Music and Dance), with some events in the Alhambra, begins in late June and runs into July. The **International Guitar Festival** brings major artists to Córdoba in early July. Córdoba celebrates **Nuestra Señora de Fuensanta,** and Granada honors **Nuestra Señora de las Angustias** (Our Lady of Distress) on the last Sunday in September and holds the **Romería de San Miguel** (Procession of St. Michael) on the closest Sunday to September 29.

Begin at the Plaza Isabel la Católica (at the junction of the Gran Vía and Calle Reyes Católicos), with its statue of Columbus presenting Queen Isabella with his maps of the New World. Walk down Calle Reyes Católicos and turn left into the **Corral del Carbón** 4—the tourist office here has maps and brochures. Cross back over Calle Reyes Católicos: directly ahead is the Alcaicería, once the Arabs' silk market and now a maze of alleys packed with souvenir shops and restaurants. Turn left from the Alcaicería to reach the relaxed Plaza Bib-Rambla, with its flower stalls and colorful Gran Café Bib-Rambla, the latter a perfect place for an ice cream. From the northeast corner of the square, Calle Oficios takes you to the **Palacio Madraza** 5, the old Arab University, and the **Capilla Real** 6, next to which is the **cathedral** 7. Just outside the cathedral's west front is the 16th-century Escuela de las Niñas Nobles, with a plateresque facade. Next to the cathedral, along the Plaza de Alonzo Cano, are the impressive Curia Eclesiástica, used as an Imperial College until 1769; the Palacio del Arzobispo; and the 18th-century Iglesia de Sagrario, with Corinthian columns. Behind the cathedral is the Gran Vía de Colón, named after Columbus, one of Granada's main thoroughfares. Cross the Gran Vía and head right, back to Plaza de Isabel la Católica. If it's after 2:30, make a short detour to the **Casa de los Tiros** 8. Make your way back to Plaza Isabel la Católica and turn right to reach the Plaza Nueva, overlooked by the 16th-century Real Cancillería (Royal Chancery), which now houses the Tribunal Superior de Justicia (High Court). Artisans have set up shops in the surrounding area. At the north end of the plaza is the adjacent Plaza Santa Ana, where you'll find the church of Santa Ana, designed by Diego de Siloé. Walk north through the Plaza Santa Ana onto Carrera del Darro and you'll reach the 11th-century Arab bathhouse, **El Bañuelo** 9. Just up Carrera del Darro is the 16th-century **Casa de Castril** 10, site of Granada's Archaeological Museum. Follow the river along the Paseo del Padre Manjón—also known as the Paseo de los Tristes—to the end, to see the **Palacio de los Córdoba** 11. Head north up the Cuesta del Chapíz to the Morisco **Casa del Chapíz** 12. East of here are the caves of the **Sacromonte** 13, which require a special expedition by minibus. For now, turn west and plunge into the streets of the **Albaicín** 14. Granada's other major sights are just outside town and best reached by car or taxi: 2 km (1 mi) north of the city center, off Calle Real de Cartuja, is the 16th-century baroque **Monasterio de La Cartuja** 15. To the south are the **Parque de las Ciencias** 16, an interactive science museum, and **Casa-Museo Federico García Lorca** 17.

TIMING This walk takes the better part of a day; remember that it does not include the Alhambra hill.

What to See

14 **Albaicín.** Covering a hill of its own, across the Darro ravine from the Alhambra, this ancient Moorish neighborhood is a mix of dilapidated white houses and immaculate *carmenes* (private villas in gardens enclosed by high walls). It was founded in 1228 by Moors who fled Baeza after Ferdinand captured the city. Full of cobble alleyways and secret corners, the Albaicín guards its old Moorish roots jealously, though its 30

Fodor'sChoice ★

mosques were converted to baroque churches long ago. A stretch of the Moors' original city wall runs beside the Cuesta de la Alhacaba. If you're walking—the best way to explore—you can enter the Albaicín from either the Cuesta de Elvira or the Plaza Nueva. Alternatively, on foot or by taxi (parking is impossible), begin in the Plaza Santa Ana and follow the Carrera del Darro, Paseo Padre Manjón, and Cuesta del Chapíz. One of the highest points in the quarter, the plaza in front of the church of San Nicolás—called the **Mirador de San Nicolás**—has one of the finest views in all of Granada: on the hill opposite, the turrets and towers of the Alhambra form a dramatic silhouette against the snowy peaks of the Sierra Nevada. The sight is most magical at dawn, dusk, and on nights when the Alhambra is floodlit.

Fodor's Choice ★ 1 **Alhambra.** With nearly 2 million visitors a year, the Alhambra is Spain's most popular attraction. Walking *to* the Alhambra can be as inspiring as walking *around* it. If you're up to a long, scenic approach, start in the Plaza Nueva and climb the Cuesta de Gomérez—through the slopes of green elms planted by the Duke of Wellington—to reach the **Puerta de las Granadas** (Pomegranate Gate), a Renaissance gateway built by Charles V and topped by three pomegranates, symbols of Granada. Just past the gate, take the path branching off to the left to the **Puerta de la Justicia** (Gate of Justice), one of the Alhambra's entrances. Yusuf I built the gate in 1348; its two arches are carved with a key and a hand, its five fingers representing the five laws of the Koran. Unless you've already bought a ticket, continue up the hill along the Alhambra's outer walls to the parking lot and the adjacent ticket office. If you're driving, you'll approach the Alhambra from the opposite direction. There is a large parking lot. Don't be tempted to park on the surrounding streets, which may leave your car vulnerable to a break-in. Alternatively, you can park in the underground car park on Calle San Agustín, just north of the cathedral, and take a taxi or the minibus that runs from the Plaza Nueva every 15 minutes. The complex has three main parts: the Alcazaba, the Palacios Nazaríes, and the Generalife. Access to the second, the Palacios Nazaríes, is restricted to 350 people every half hour. The other two sections can be visited at will during the morning or afternoon schedule.

The Alhambra was begun in the 1240s by Ibn el-Ahmar, or Alhamar, the first king of the Nasrids. The great citadel once comprised a complex of houses, schools, baths, barracks, and gardens surrounded by defense towers and seemingly impregnable walls. Today, only the Alcazaba and the Nasrid Royal Palace, built chiefly by Yusuf I (1334–54) and his son Mohammed V (1354–91), remain. The palace is an endless, intricate fantasy of patios, arches, and cupolas fashioned from wood, plaster, and tile; lavishly colored and adorned with marquetry and ceramics in geometric patterns; and surmounted by delicate, frothy profusions of lacelike stucco and *mocárabes* (ornamental stalactites). Built of perishable materials, it was never intended to last but to be forever replenished and replaced by succeeding generations. By the early 17th century, ruin and decay had set in, and the Alhambra was abandoned by all but tramps and stray dogs. Napoléon's troops commandeered it in 1812, but their attempts to destroy it were, happily, foiled. In 1814, the Alhambra's fortunes rose with the arrival of the Duke of Wellington, who came here to escape the pressures of the Peninsular War. Soon afterward, in 1829, Washington Irving arrived to live on the premises and helped revive interest in the crumbling palace, in part through his 1832 book *Tales of the Alhambra*. In 1862, Granada finally launched a complete restoration program that has been carried on ever since.

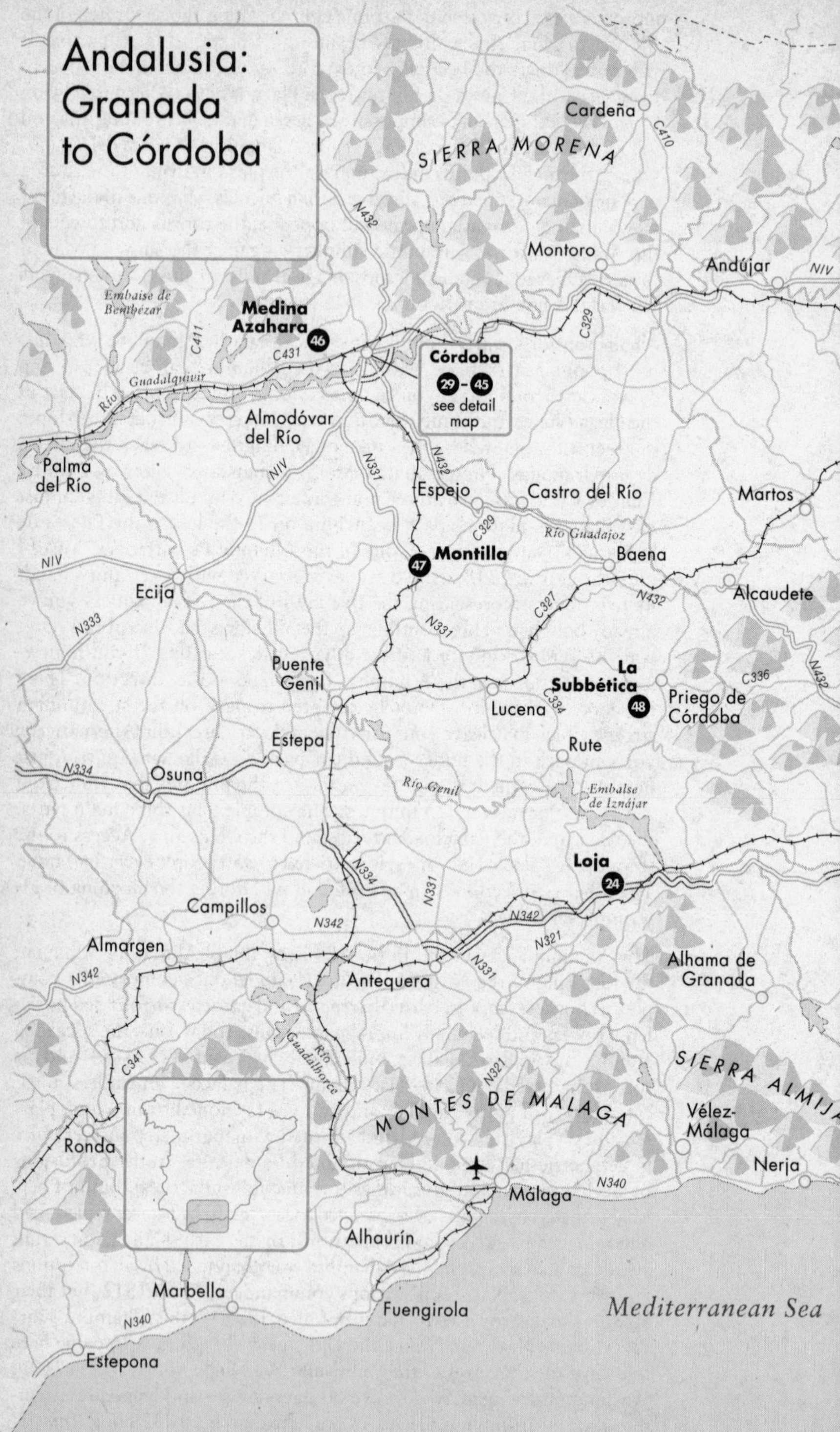
Andalusia: Granada to Córdoba
Cardeña
C410
SIERRA MORENA
N432
Montoro
Andújar
NIV
Embaise de Bembézar
Medina Azahara
46
C411
C431
C329
Córdoba
29 - 45
see detail map
Río Guadalquivir
Almodóvar del Río
Palma del Río
NIV
N331
N432
Espejo
Castro del Río
Martos
C329
Río Guadajoz
Montilla
47
Baena
NIV
Ecija
Alcaudete
N432
C327
N333
N331
Puente Genil
La Subbética
48
Priego de Córdoba
C336
N432
Lucena
C334
Estepa
Rute
N334
Osuna
Río Genil
Embalse de Iznájar
Loja
24
N334
N331
Campillos
N342
N342
N321
Almargen
N331
Alhama de Granada
N342
Antequera
Río Guadalhorce
C341
N321
SIERRA ALMIJA
MONTES DE MALAGA
Vélez-Málaga
Ronda
Nerja
N340
Málaga
Alhaurín
Marbella
Fuengirola
Mediterranean Sea
N340
Estepona

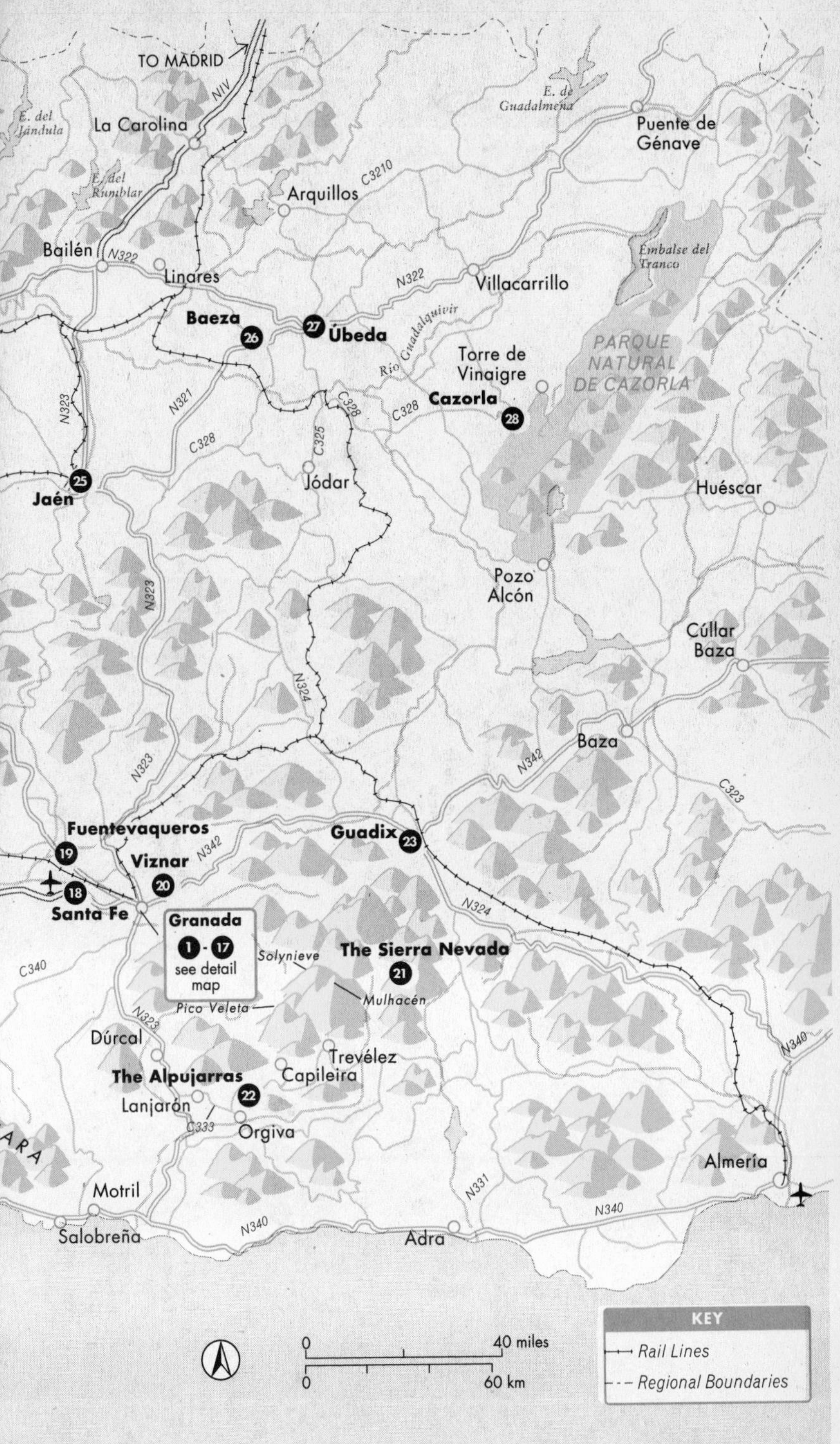

TO MADRID
NIV
E. del Jándula
La Carolina
E. del Rumblar
Arquillos
C3210
E. de Guadalmena
Puente de Génave
Bailén
N322
Linares
N322
Villacarrillo
Embalse del Tranco
Baeza
26
27
Úbeda
Río Guadalquivir
Torre de Vinaigre
PARQUE NATURAL DE CAZORLA
Cazorla
28
C328
C328
C325
N321
N323
C328
25
Jaén
Jódar
Huéscar
Pozo Alcón
N323
Cúllar Baza
N324
Baza
N342
N323
C323
Fuentevaqueros
19
Guadix
23
Viznar
20
N342
18
Santa Fe
Granada
1 - 17
see detail map
N324
Solynieve
The Sierra Nevada
21
C340
Mulhacén
Pico Veleta
N323
Dúrcal
Trevélez
The Alpujarras
Capileira
22
N340
Lanjarón
C333
Orgiva
Almería
Motril
N331
N340
Salobreña
N340
Adra
0
40 miles
0
60 km
KEY
Rail Lines
Regional Boundaries

Albaicín 14
Alhambra 1
Capilla Real 6
Carmen de los Mártires 3
Casa de Castril 10
Casa de los Tiros. 8
Casa del Chapíz 12
Casa-Museo de Manuel de Falla 2
Casa-Museo Federico García Lorca 17
Cathedral 7
Corral del Carbón 4
El Bañuelo 9
Monasterio de la Cartuja. 15
Palacio de los Córdoba 11
Palacio Madraza 5
Parque de las Ciencias 16
Sacramonte 13

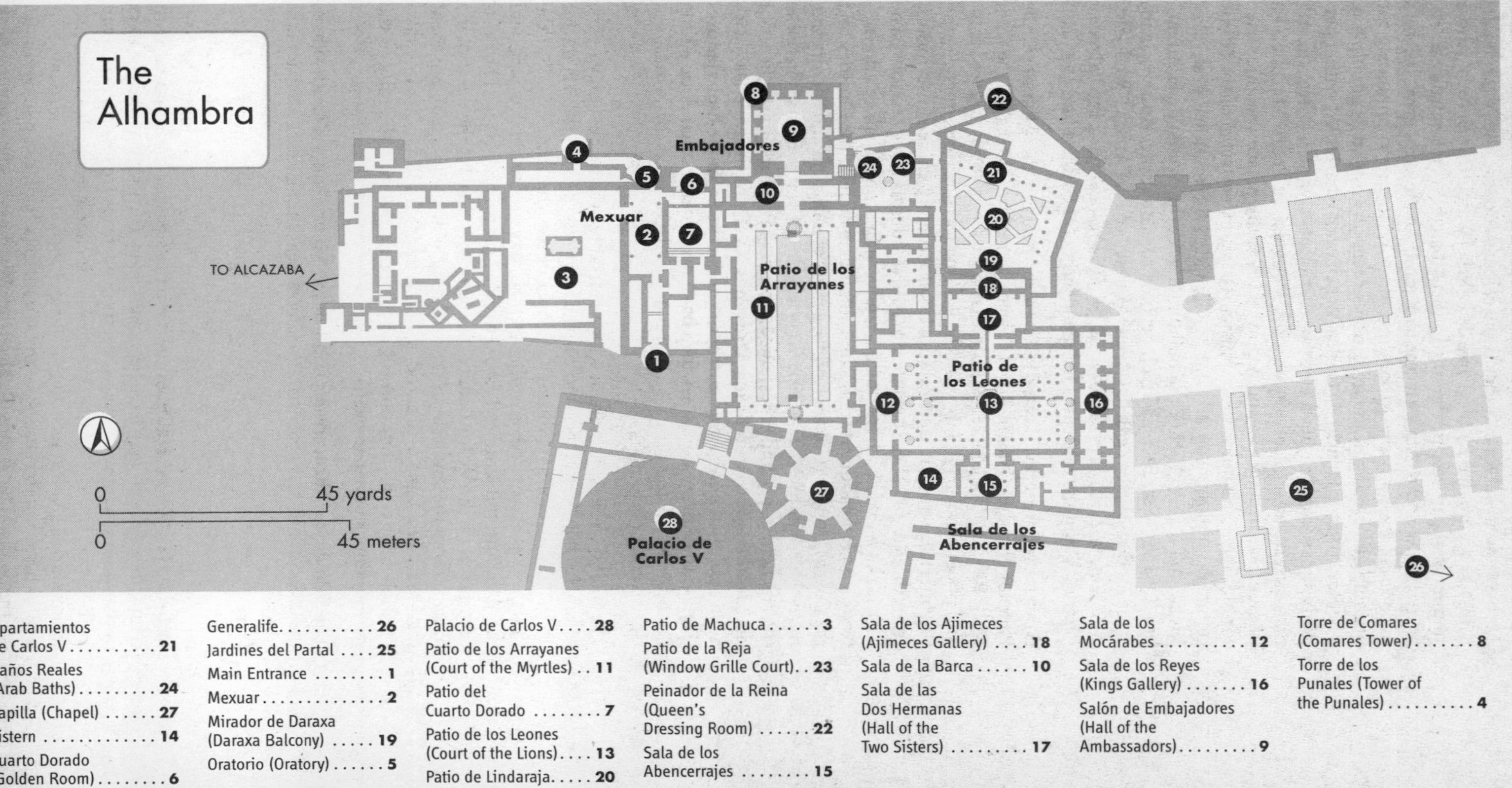

Apartamientos de Carlos V 21
Baños Reales (Arab Baths) 24
Capilla (Chapel) 27
Cistern 14
Cuarto Dorado (Golden Room) 6
Generalife. 26
Jardines del Partal 25
Main Entrance 1
Mexuar 2
Mirador de Daraxa (Daraxa Balcony) 19
Oratorio (Oratory) 5
Palacio de Carlos V 28
Patio de los Arrayanes (Court of the Myrtles) . . 11
Patio del Cuarto Dorado 7
Patio de los Leones (Court of the Lions) 13
Patio de Lindaraja. 20
Patio de Machuca 3
Patio de la Reja (Window Grille Court). . 23
Peinador de la Reina (Queen's Dressing Room) 22
Sala de los Abencerrajes 15
Sala de los Ajimeces (Ajimeces Gallery) 18
Sala de la Barca 10
Sala de las Dos Hermanas (Hall of the Two Sisters) 17
Sala de los Mocárabes 12
Sala de los Reyes (Kings Gallery) 16
Salón de Embajadores (Hall of the Ambassadors). 9
Torre de Comares (Comares Tower) 8
Torre de los Punales (Tower of the Punales) 4

Across from the main entrance is the original fortress, the **Alcazaba.** Its ruins are dominated by the **Torre de la Vela** (Watchtower), from whose summit you can see, to the north, the Albaicín; to the northeast, the Sacromonte; and to the west, the cathedral. The tower's great bell was once used, by both the Moors and the Christians, to announce the opening and closing of the irrigation system on Granada's great plain. The Renaissance **Palacio de Carlos V** (Palace of Charles V), with a perfectly square exterior but a circular interior courtyard, is where the sultans' private apartments once stood. Designed by Pedro Machuca—a pupil of Michelangelo—and begun in 1526, the palace was once used for bullfights and mock tournaments. Today, its perfect acoustics draw summer symphony concerts during Granada's International Festival of Music and Dance. Part of the building houses the **Museo de la Alhambra** (⏲ Tues.–Sat. 9–2 🎫 Free), devoted to Islamic art. Upstairs is the more modest **Museo de Bellas Artes** (Museum of Fine Arts; ⏲ Wed.–Sat. 9–6, Sun. 9–2:30, Tues. 2:30–6 🎫 €1.50). You can visit the Palace of Charles V and the museums independently of the Alhambra.

A wisteria-covered walkway leads to the heart of the Alhambra, the **Palacios Nazaríes** (Nasrid Royal Palace), sometimes also called the Casa Real (Royal Palace). Here, delicate apartments, lazy fountains, and tranquil pools contrast vividly with the hulking fortifications outside, and the interior walls are decorated with elaborately carved inscriptions from the Koran. The Royal Palace is divided into three sections. The first is the *mexuar,* where business, government, and palace administration were headquartered. These chambers include the Oratory and the Cuarto Dorado (Golden Room); gaze at the Albaicín and Sacromonte from their windows. The *serrallo* is a series of state rooms where the sultans held court and entertained their ambassadors. In the heart of the *serrallo* is the **Patio de los Arrayanes** (Court of the Myrtles), with a long goldfish pool. At its northern end, in the **Salón de Embajadores** (Hall of the Ambassadors)—which has a magnificent cedar door—King Boabdil signed the terms of surrender and Queen Isabella received Christopher Columbus.

The final section is the **harem,** which in its time was entered only by the sultan, his family, and their most trusted servants, most of them eunuchs. To reach it, you'll pass through the **Sala de los Mocárabes** (Hall of the Ornamental Stalactites): note the splendid, though damaged, ceiling, and the elaborate stalactite-style stonework in the arches above. The postcard-perfect **Patio de los Leones** (Court of the Lions) is the heart of the harem. From the fountain in the center, 12 lions, which may represent the months or signs of the zodiac, leer out at you. Four streams flow symbolically to the four corners of the earth and more literally to the surrounding state apartments.

The **Sala de los Abencerrajes** (Hall of the Moors), on the south side of the palace, may be the Alhambra's most beautiful gallery, with its fabulous, ornate ceiling and a star-shape cupola reflected in the pool below. Here Boabdil's father is alleged to have massacred 16 members of the Abencerrajes family—whose chief was the lover of his favorite daughter, Zoraya—and piled their bloodstained heads in this font. The **Sala de los Reyes** (Kings' Hall) lies on the patio's east side, decorated with ceiling frescoes that may have been painted by Christians in the last days of the Moors' tenure. To the north, the **Sala de las Dos Hermanas** (Hall of the Two Sisters) was Zoraya's abode. Its name comes from the two white-marble slabs in its floor, and its ceiling is stucco, an intricate pattern of honeycomb cells. Note the symmetrically placed pomegranates on the walls. The **Baños Reales,** the Alhambra's semi-subterranean bathhouse, is where the sultan's favorites luxuriated in baths of brightly tiled mosaic and performed their ablutions lit by star-shape pinpoints of light from the ceiling above. The baths are only open to visitors on specific days, which change throughout the year. An up-to-date timetable can be obtained from the tourist office. Over on the Cerro del Sol (Hill of the Sun) is the **Generalife,** ancient summer palace of the Nasrid kings. Its name comes from the Arabic *gennat alarif*—garden of the architect—and its terraces and promenades grant incomparable views of the city, stretching to the distant vega. During the summer's International Festival of Music and Dance, these stately cypresses are the backdrop for evening ballets in the Generalife amphitheater. Between the Alhambra and Generalife is the 16th-century convent of San Francisco, one of Spain's most luxurious paradors.

It is a good idea to visit the Alhambra Web site for the latest booking arrangements and prices before leaving for Spain. Be advised that there is a limited number of tickets on sale at the gate each day, so whatever the time of year, it is always prudent to reserve in advance. This may be done through any Banco Bilbao Vizcaya (BBV) for a €1 surcharge. Same-day tickets are sold at the BBV branch on Plaza Isabel la Católica 1, or you can reserve by phone, Internet, or at any BBV branch up to a year in advance. By phone or Internet, you pay by credit card, then pick up your tickets at the Alhambra's ticket office the day of your visit. Your ticket will show the half-hour time slot for your entry to the Palacios Nazaríes; once inside, you can stay as long as you like. On busy days, you may have several hours to spare before your visit to the interior palaces; take the time to explore the Generalife, the Alcazaba, the Alhambra Museum, and the Fine Arts Museum. There might even be enough time to walk to the charming Casa-Museo de Manuel de Falla and the Carmen de los Mártires and have lunch at one of the restaurants on the Alhambra hill. For a different (and calmer) perspective, come back for a floodlit tour of the Palacios Nazaríes at night. ✉ *Cuesta de Goméréz, Alhambra* ☎ *902/224460 within Spain for advance ticket sales (BBV), 91/3465936 from outside Spain* 🌐 *www.alhambra-patronato.es (booking information and prices), www.alhambratickets.com (tickets)* 🎫 *Alhambra and Generalife €7* ⏲ *Mar.–Oct., daily 8:30–2 (morning ticket); Mon.–Sun. 2–8 (afternoon ticket); floodlit visits Tues.–Sat. 10 PM–11:30 PM. Nov.–Feb., daily 8:30–2 (morning ticket); daily 2–6 (afternoon ticket); floodlit visits Fri. and Sat. 8 PM–9:30 PM. Ticket office opens 30 mins before opening time and closes ½ hr before closing time.*

❻ **Capilla Real** (Royal Chapel). Catholic Monarchs Isabella of Castile and Ferdinand of Aragón are buried at this shrine. The couple originally planned to be buried in Toledo's San Juan de los Reyes, but Isabella changed her mind when the pair conquered Granada in 1492. When she died, in 1504, her body was first laid to rest in the Convent of San Francisco (now the parador), on the Alhambra hill. The architect Enrique Egas began work on the Royal Chapel in 1506 and completed it 15 years later, creating a masterpiece of the ornate Gothic style now known in Spain as Isabelline. In 1521 Isabella's body was brought to a simple lead coffin in the Royal Chapel crypt, where it was joined by that of her husband, Ferdinand, and later her unfortunate daughter, Juana la Loca (Joanna the Mad), and son-in-law, Felipe el Hermoso (Philip the Handsome). Felipe died young, and Juana had his casket borne about the peninsula with her for years, opening the lid each night to kiss her embalmed spouse good night. A small coffin to the right contains the remains of Prince Felipe of Asturias, a grandson of the Catholic Monarchs and nephew of Juana la Loca who died in his infancy. The underground **crypt** containing the five lead coffins is quite simple, but it's topped by elaborate marble **tombs** showing Ferdinand and Isabella lying side-by-side (commissioned by their grandson Charles V and sculpted by Domenico Fancelli). The **altarpiece,** by Felipe Vigarini (1522), comprises 34 carved panels depicting religious and historical scenes; the bottom row shows Boabdil surrendering the keys of the city to its conquerors and the forced baptism of the defeated Moors. The **sacristy** holds Ferdinand's sword, Isabella's crown and scepter, and a fine collection of Flemish paintings once owned by Isabella. ✉ *Oficios, Centro* ☎ *958/229239* 💶 *€2.10* ⏲ *Mar.–Sept., daily 10:30–1 and 4–7; Oct.–Feb., Mon.–Sat. 10:30–1 and 3:30–6:30, Sun. 11–1 and 3:30–6:30.*

❾ **Carmen de los Mártires.** Just up the hill from the Hotel Alhambra Palace, this turn-of-the-20th-century Granada carmen, or private villa, and its gardens—the only area open to tourists—are like a Generalife in miniature. ✉ *Paseo de los Mártires, Alhambra* ☎ *958/227953* 💶 *Free* ⏲ *Apr.–Oct., weekdays 10–2 and 5–7; Nov.–Mar., weekdays 10–2 and 4–6.*

❿ **Casa de Castril.** This richly decorated 16th-century palace once belonged to Bernardo Zafra, secretary to Queen Isabella. Before you enter, notice the exquisite portal, and the facade carved with scallop shells and a phoenix. Inside is the **Museo Arqueológico** (Archaeological Museum), where you'll find artifacts from provincial caves and from Moorish times, Phoenician burial urns from the coastal town of Almuñécar, and a copy of the *Dama de Baza,* a large Iberian sculpture discovered in northern Granada province in 1971 (the original is in Madrid). ✉ *Carrera del Darro 41, Albaicín* ☎ *958/225640* 💶 *€1.50, EU citizens free* ⏲ *Wed.–Sat. 9–8, Sun. 9–2:30; Tues. tour groups only.*

need a break?

The park at **Paseo Padre Manjón,** along the Darro River—also known as the Paseo de los Tristes (Promenade of the Sad) because funeral processions once passed this way—is a terrific place for a coffee break. Dappled with fountains and stone walkways, the park has a stunning view of the Alhambra's northern side.

❽ **Casa de los Tiros.** This 16th-century palace was named House of the Shots for the musket barrels that protrude from its facade. The stairs to the upper-floor displays are flanked by portraits of Spanish royals from Ferdinand and Isabella to Philip IV, none of whom look very happy. The highlight is the carved wooden ceiling in the Cuadra Dorada (Hall of Gold), adorned with gilded lettering and portraits of royals and knights. Old lithographs, engravings, and photographs show life in Granada in the 19th and early 20th centuries. ✉ *Pl. Padres Suarez, Realejo* ☎ *958/221072* 💶 *Free* ⏲ *Weekdays 2:30–8.*

⓬ **Casa del Chapíz.** The fine 16th-century Morisco house (built by Moorish craftsmen under Christian rule) has a delightful garden. It houses the School of Arabic Studies and is not generally open to the public, but if you knock, the caretaker might show you around. ✉ *Cuesta del Chapíz at Camino del Sacromonte, Albaicín.*

❷ **Casa-Museo de Manuel de Falla.** The composer Manuel de Falla (1876–1946) lived and worked for many years in this rustic house, tucked into a charming little hillside lane with lovely views of the Alpujarra mountains. The house is currently closed for repairs, but the exterior is worth a peek. In 1986 Granada finally paid homage to Spain's classical champion by naming its new concert hall (down the street from the Carmen de los Mártires) the Auditorio Manuel de Falla—and from this institution, fittingly, you have a nice view of the little white house from above. Note the bust in the small garden: it stands where the composer once sat to enjoy the sweeping view. ✉ *C. Antequeruela Alta 11, Alhambra* ☎ *958/229421* ⏲ *By appointment only.*

⑰ **Casa-Museo Federico García Lorca.** Granada's most famous native son, the poet Federico García Lorca, gets his due here, in the middle of a park on the southern fringe of the city. The poet's onetime summer home, **La Huerta de San Vicente,** is now a museum—run by the poet's niece, Laura García Lorca—with such artifacts as the poet's beloved piano and temporary exhibits on specific aspects of Lorca's life. ✉ *Parque García Lorca, C. Arabial, Arabial* ☎ *958/258466* 🌐 *www.huertadesanvicente.com* 🎫 *€1.80, free Wed.* ⏲ *Oct.–Apr., Tues.–Sun. 10–1 and 4–7; May–Sept., Tues.–Sun. 10–1 and 5–8. Guided tours every ½ hr until 30 mins before closing.*

⑦ **Cathedral.** Granada's cathedral was commissioned in 1521 by Charles V, who considered the Royal Chapel "too small for so much glory" and wanted to house his illustrious late grandparents someplace more worthy. Charles undoubtedly had great designs, as the cathedral was created by some of the finest architects of its time: Enrique Egas, Diego de Siloé, Alonso Cano, and sculptor Juan de Mena. Alas, his ambitions came to little, for the cathedral is a grand and gloomy monument, not completed until 1714 and never used as the crypt of his parents *or* grandparents. You enter through a small door at the back, off the Gran Vía. Old hymnals are displayed throughout, and there's a museum, which includes a 14th-century gold and silver monstrance given to the city by Queen Isabella. ✉ *Gran Vía s/n, Centro* ☎ *958/222959* 🎫 *€2.10* ⏲ *Mon.–Sat. 10:30–1 and 4–7, Sun. 4–7.*

④ **Corral del Carbón** (Coal House). This building was used to store coal in the 19th century, but it's actually one of the oldest Moorish buildings in the city. Dating from the 14th century, when Moorish merchants used it as a lodging house, it's the only Arab inn of its kind in Spain. It was later used by Christians as a theater, but it has been restored and is the site of the **regional tourist office.** ✉ *C. Mariana Pineda, Centro* ☎ *958/225990* 🎫 *Free* ⏲ *Mon.–Sat. 9–8, Sun. 10–2.*

⑨ **El Bañuelo** (Little Bath House). These 11th-century Arab steam baths might be a little dark and dank now, but try to imagine them filled, some 900 years ago, with Moorish beauties, backed by bright ceramic tiles, tapestries, and rugs on the dull brick walls. Light comes in through star-shape vents in the ceiling, à la the bathhouse in the Alhambra. ✉ *Carrera del Darro 31, Albaicín* ☎ *958/027800* 🎫 *€1.50, EU citizens free* ⏲ *Tues.–Sat. 10–2.*

⑮ **Monasterio de La Cartuja.** This Carthusian monastery in northern Granada (2 km [1 mi] from the center) was begun in 1506 and moved to its present site in 1516, though construction continued for the next 300 years. The exterior is sober and monolithic, but when you enter and see twisted, multicolor marble columns; a profusion of gold, silver, tortoiseshell, and ivory; intricate stucco; and an extravagant Churrigueresque sacristy, you'll see why Cartuja has been called the Christian answer to the Alhambra. ✉ *Camino de Alfacar, Cartuja* ☎ *958/161932* 🎫 *€2.50* ⏲ *Mon.–Sat. 10–1 and 4–7, Sun. 10–noon.*

⑪ **Palacio de los Córdoba.** At the end of the Paseo Padre Manjón, this palace was a noble house in the 17th century. Today it keeps Granada's municipal archives and is used for municipal functions and art exhibits. You're free to wander around the large garden.

⑤ **Palacio Madraza.** This building conceals the old Moorish university, built in 1349 by Yusuf I. The baroque facade is dark and intriguing; inside, across from the entrance, an octagonal room is crowned by a Moorish dome. There are occasional free art and cultural exhibitions. ✉ *Oficios, Centro* ☎ *958/223447.*

16 **Parque de las Ciencias** (Science Park). Across from Granada's convention center, this museum has interactive exhibits, scientific experiments, and a planetarium. The 165-ft observation tower has views to the south and west. ✉ *Avda. del Mediterráneo, Zaidín* ☎ *958/131900* *www.parqueciencias.com* *Park €3.60, planetarium €1.60* *Tues.–Sat. 10–7, Sun. 10–3.*

13 **Sacromonte.** The third of Granada's three hills, the Sacromonte rises behind the Albaicín, dotted with prickly pear cacti and riddled with caverns. These caves may have sheltered early Christians; 15th-century treasure hunters found bones inside and assumed they belonged to San Cecilio, the city's patron saint. Thus the hill was sanctified—*sacro monte* (holy mountain)—and an abbey built on its summit, the **Abadía de Sacromonte** (✉ Camino del Sacromonte, Sacromonte ☎ 958/221445). The abbey is open Tuesday–Saturday 11–1 and 4–6, Sunday noon–1 and 4–6, with guided tours every half hour. Admission is €1.80. The Sacromonte has long been notorious as a domain of Granada's Roma (Gypsies) and a den of pickpockets, but its reputation is largely undeserved. The quarter is more like a quiet Andalusian *pueblo* (village) than a rough neighborhood. Many of the quarter's colorful *cuevas* (caves) have been restored as middle-class homes, and some of the old spirit lives on in a handful of *zambras*—flamenco performances in caves garishly decorated with brass plates and cooking utensils. These differ from formal flamenco shows in that the performers mingle with you, usually dragging one or two onlookers onto the floor for an improvised dance lesson. Ask your hotel to book you a spot on a cueva tour, which usually includes a walk through the neighboring Albaicín and a drink at a tapas bar in addition to the zambra.

Tapas Bars

Poke around the Plaza del Carmen–Calle Navas, Campo del Príncipe, Plaza Nueva–Calle Elvira, and Albaicín–Sacromonte for Granada's most colorful twilight hangouts. Also try the bars and restaurants in the arches underneath the Plaza de Toros (Bullfighting Ring), on the west of the city and a bit farther from the city center. For a change, check out some Moroccan-style tea shops, known as Teteírs—these first emerged in Granada and are now equally popular in Seville and Málaga, particularly among students. The only catch is that they can be expensive, so do check the price of your brew before you order. The highest concentration is in the Albaicín, particularly around Calle Caldereria Nueva where, within a few doors from each other, you find Teteria Kasbah, Teteria, Oriental and Le Renez Vous, which also sells delicious crepes.

El Almirez (✉ C. Navas 8, Puerta Real) serves local tapas like *calabaza frita* (fried pumpkin). **La Tana** (✉ Placeta del Agua, Centro) has great wine to accompany its savory tapas (ask the staff for recommendations). The food is simple, fresh and filling. Off Calle Navas in Plaza Campillo is **Chikito** (✉ Plaza del Campillo 9, Puerta Real ☎ 958/223364), best known for its tasty sit-down meals, but the bar is an excellent place for tapas. The place is usually packed, so additional tables are set up on the square in summer. Moroccan-run **Al-Andalus** (✉ Elvira, Centro) serves tasty tapas, including bite-size *falafel* and other veggie options. **La Taberna de Baco** (✉ Campo del Príncipe, Realejo) fuses Ecuadoran and Andalusian flavors. **El Pilar del Toro** (✉ C. Hospital de Santa Ana s/n, Albaicín) is a bar and restaurant with a beautiful patio. The popular **Bodegas Castañeda** (✉ Elvira 6, Centro ☎ 958/226362) serves classic tapas, as well as baked potatoes with a choice of fillings. **Bodega Peso La Harina** (✉ Placeta del Peso de la Harina, Sacromonte), on a square right at the entrance of Camino de Sacromonte, prepares tapas not to be missed. Southeast of Granada's cathedral, **Café Botánico** (✉ Málaga 3, Centro ☎ 958/271598) is a modern hot spot with a diverse menu that includes an interesting twist on traditional cuisine for a young, trendy crowd.

Where to Stay & Eat

★ $$$ ✕ **Ruta del Veleta.** It's worth the short drive 5 km (3 mi) out of town to this Spanish restaurant, which serves some of the best food in Granada. House specialties include *carnes a la brasa* (succulent grilled meats) and fish dishes cooked in rock salt, as well as regional dishes like *jabalí estilo mozárabe* (wild boar cooked with apples). Dessert might be *cuajada de leche de oveja y helado de miel* (sheep's-milk curd with honey ice cream). ✉ *Cenes de la Vega, Ctra. Sierra Nevada, Km 5.4, on road to Sierra Nevada* ☎ *958/486134* ▭ *AE, DC, MC, V* ⊙ *No dinner Sun. in summer.*

★ $$–$$$ ✕ **Carmen de San Miguel.** Hidden down a lane near the Alhambra Palace hotel, this hillside villa with a spacious dining room and classic Andalusian summer terrace would be worth a stop just for its view over the city. Happily, the food also gets high marks. Look for *habas a la granadina* (broad beans with mint and prawns) and *pichón asado con anís estellado y puré de castañas* (roast squab with aniseed and chestnut sauce) or, better yet, order the sampler menu. ✉ *Plaza de Torres Bermejas 3, Alhambra* ☎ *958/226723* ▭ *AE, MC, V* ⊙ *No dinner Sun.*

$$–$$$ ✕ **Cunini.** Around the corner from the cathedral is Granada's best fish house, where seafood is displayed in the window at the front of the tapas bar. Both the *pescaditos fritos* (fried) and the *parrillada* (grilled) fish are good choices, and if it's chilly you can warm up with *caldereta de arroz, pescado y marisco* (rice, fish, and seafood stew). There are tables outdoors in warm weather. ✉ *Pescadería 14, Centro* ☎ *958/250777* ▭ *AE, DC, MC, V* ⊙ *Closed Mon. No dinner Sun.*

★ $$–$$$ ✕ **Sevilla.** Since 1930 this colorful, central two-story restaurant has fed the likes of de Falla and García Lorca. There are four picturesque dining rooms and an outdoor terrace overlooking the Royal Chapel. There's a small but superb tapas bar; the dinner menu includes Granadino favorites like *sopa sevillana* and *tortilla Sacromonte,* as well as more elaborate dishes. ✉ *Oficios 12, Centro* ☎ *958/221223* ▭ *AE, DC, MC, V* ⊙ *No dinner Sun.*

$$ ✕ **Velázquez.** Tucked into a side street one block west of the Puerta de Elvira and Plaza del Triunfo, this cozy, very Spanish restaurant has long been popular with locals. At street level, the brick-wall bar is hung with hams; the intimate, wood-beam dining room is upstairs. House specialties include *zancarrón cordero a la miel* (lamb with honey) and *lomitos de rape* (braised monkfish medallions). ✉ *Emilio Orozco 1, Triunfo* ☎ *958/280109* ▭ *MC, V* ⊙ *Closed Sun.*

$–$$ ✕ **La Colina de Almanzora.** At the foot of the Alhambra hill, in a restored carmen, is a multistory restaurant with wood and stucco carved ceilings and furniture. The food is a combination of traditional Andalusian and Granadian dishes and condiments such as sweet spices, nuts, and sweet and sour sauces. Specialties include *berenjenas a la miel* (honeyed eggplant) and *alcachofas alhamar* (steamed artichokes with salmorejo). The owners run a traditional Arab-style bath house next door, where you can pamper yourself with aromatherapy, massage, and a session in the hot tub. ✉ *Santa Ana 16, Albaicín* ☎ *958/229516* ▭ *MC, V.*

$–$$ ✕ **La Mimbre.** Location, location, location: this small, slightly cramped lunch spot is tucked right under the walls of the Alhambra, next to the

Generalife. Inside, you sit on chairs upholstered with typical Alpujarran fabric; outside, the spacious patio is shady, romantic, and delightful in warm weather. The food is classically Granadino: habas con jamón and *choto al ajillo* (braised kid with garlic). ✉ *Avda. del Generalife, Alhambra* ☎ *958/222276* ▭ *AE, MC, V* ⊗ *Closed Sat. Nov–Feb. No dinner Oct.–Apr.*

$–$$ ✕ **Mirador de Morayma.** Buried in the Albaicín, this place is hard to find and might appear to be closed (ring the doorbell). Once inside, you'll have unbeatable views across the gorge to the Alhambra, particularly from the outside wisteria-covered terrace. The adequate menu has some surprises, such as smoked *esturión* (sturgeon) from Riofrío, served cold with cured ham and a vegetable dip, and the *ensalada de remojón granadino,* a salad of cod, orange, and olives. ✉ *Pianista García Carrillo 2, Albaicín* ☎ *958/228290* ▭ *AE, MC, V* ⊗ *Closed Sun.*

$ ✕ **Mesón Blas Casa.** In the choicest square in the Albaicín, cuisine here is solidly traditional including *rabo de toro* oxtail and habas con jamón. There's a cheap and belly-filling menú del dí and a fireplace for warming the toes when there's snow on the Sierras. ✉ *Plaza San Miguel Bajo 15 Albaicín* ☎ *958/273111* ▭ *MC, V* ⊗ *Closed Mon.*

$ ✕ **Rabo de Nube.** This is the best-value snack bar and restaurant of several on this scenic stretch with Alhambra views. Popular with students and strollers, the tapas are complimentary and you can choose from an extensive *bocadillo* (sandwich roll) menu. Best value of all are the heaping plates of pasta with various sauces, including creamy Roquefort. ✉ *Paseo de Los Tristes Albaicín* ☎ *958/220421* ▭ *No credit cards.*

$$$$ **Parador de Granada.** This is Spain's most expensive and popular parador, and it's right on the Alhambra precinct. The building is soul-stirring and gorgeous; a former Franciscan monastery built by the Catholic Monarchs after they captured Granada. If possible, go for a room in the old section where there are beautiful antiques, woven curtains, and bedspreads. The rooms in the newer wing are simpler, although still very charming. Reserve four to six months in advance. ✉ *Alhambra, 18009* ☎ *958/221440* 📠 *958/222264* 🌐 *www.parador.es* *36 rooms, 2 suites* *Restaurant, minibars, bar* ▭ *AE, DC, MC, V.*

Fodor'sChoice ★

$$$ **Alhambra Palace.** Built by a local duke in 1910, this neo-Moorish hotel is on leafy grounds at the back of the Alhambra hill. The interior is very Arabian Nights, with orange and brown overtones, multicolor tiles, and Moorish arches and pillars. Even the bar is incongruously decorated as a mosque. Rooms overlooking the city have incredible views, as does the terrace, a perfect place to watch the sun set on Granada and its fertile vega. ✉ *Peña Partida 2, Alhambra, 18009* ☎ *958/221468* 📠 *958/226404* 🌐 *www.h-alhambrapalace.es* *122 rooms, 13 suites* *Restaurant, in-room data ports, minibars, cable TV with movies, 2 bars* ▭ *AE, DC, MC, V.*

Fodor'sChoice ★

$$$ **Casa Morisca Hotel.** This 15th-century building was transformed into a hotel by its architect owner, who was given the 2001 National Restoration Award for this project. The brick building has many original architectural elements. It has three floors and a central courtyard with a small pond and well. All rooms have Andalusian and Moroccan wood furniture and some have views of the Alhambra. ✉ *Cuesta de la Victoria 9, Albaicín, 18010* ☎ *958/221100* 📠 *958/215796* 🌐 *www.hotelcasamorisca.com* *12 rooms, 2 suites* *Dining room, minibars, cable TV* ▭ *AE, DC, MC, V.*

$$$ **Inglaterra.** This hotel in a 19th-century house has a comfortable, modern interior. Guest rooms are painted in pastel tones and have functional furniture and polished wood floors. The hotel is just two blocks east of the Gran Vía de Colón, in the heart of town. ✉ *Cetti Meriem 4, Centro, 18010* ☎ *958/221558* 📠 *958/227100* 🌐 *www.nh-hoteles.com*

36 rooms Restaurant, meeting room, parking (fee) AE, DC, MC, V.

$$–$$$ **Casa del Capitel Nazarí.** East of the River Darro in a palace built in 1503, this cozy two-story hotel has been refurbished to preserve some of its palatial elements, including the nazarí capital (the top structure of a column) carved in alabaster, which gives the name to the hotel. The rooms are sober and elegant with dark wooden beams and furniture. Prices vary according to room size. *Cuesta Aceituneros 6, Albaicín, 18010 958/215260 958/215260 17 rooms Dining room, in-room data ports, cable TV, lounge AE, DC, MC, V.*

$$–$$$ **Palacio de Santa Inés.** It's not often you stay in a 16th-century palace, and this one in particular has a stunning location in the heart of the Albaicín. Rooms on the two upper floors are centered on a courtyard with frescoes painted by a disciple of Raphael. Each room is magnificently decorated with antiques and modern art; some have balconies with Alhambra views. *Cuesta de Santa Inés 9, Albaicín, 18010 958/222362 958/222465 www.palaciosantaines.com 15 rooms, 4 suites Dining room, minibars, cable TV, parking (fee) AE, DC, MC, V.*

$$ **Alojamientos con Encanto.** A bargain for groups and families, these elegant, comfortable, and large apartments are on the pictorial hills of the Albaicín. Tiles, wrought-iron headboards, and other local crafts accent the apartments; quarters at the top of the neighborhood share a pebble patio crowded with plants and a terrace with magnificent views of the Alhambra. *C. Cuesta del Chapíz 54, Albaicín, 18010 958/222428 958/222810 www.granada-in.com Cable TV, Internet, free parking AE, DC, MC, V.*

$$ **América.** This simple but charming hotel within the Alhambra precincts is popular, especially for its location. The place feels like a private home, with simple bedrooms, a sitting room decorated with local crafts, and a shady patio where home-cooked meals are served in summer. Reserve three to four months in advance. *Real de la Alhambra 53, Alhambra, 18009 958/227471 958/227470 13 rooms Restaurant MC, V Closed Nov.–Feb.*

$$ **Casa del Alijarife.** This 17th-century house—in a tiny square with an Alhambra view—has been sensitively restored into an exclusive four-room hotel. Rooms surround a shady central courtyard and have plenty of character, with interesting angles and use of space. There is also a rooftop terrace you can use. *Placeta de la Cruz Verde 2, Albaícin, 18010 958/222425 4 rooms MC, V.*

★ $$ **Reina Cristina.** In the former Rosales family residence, where the poet Lorca was arrested after taking refuge here when the Spanish Civil War broke out, the Reina Cristina is near the lively and central Plaza de la Trinidad. Plants trail from the windowsills of the reception area, a covered patio with a small marble fountain and a marble stairway leads to the guest rooms, which are simply but cheerfully furnished with red fabrics on a white background. *Tablas 4, Centro, 18002 958/253211 958/255728 www.hotelreinacristina.com 43 rooms Restaurant, cafeteria, bar, parking (fee) AE, DC, MC, V.*

$ **Hotel Los Tilos.** With a comfortable, modern interior and a central location overlooking a pleasant square with a daily flower market, this good-value no-frills hotel is worth a try. Best of all is the fourth-floor terrace where you can sip a drink, read a book, or just enjoy the fabulous panoramic view of the skyline. *Plaza Bib-Rambla 4 Centro, 18010 958/266712 958/266801 30 rooms MC, V.*

$ **La Ninfa.** Rooms are clean and decorated with charm at this small and friendly hostelry in a corner of a small square—one of Granada's most popular tavern areas. The noise is far enough away that it won't bother you. ✉ *Campo del Príncipe s/n, Realejo, 18009* ☎ *958/222661* ☎🖷 *958/227985* *11 rooms* ▭ *MC, V.*

¢ **Britz.** If you plan on spending a lot of time at the Alhambra and don't have wads of cash, consider this hostel within walking distance of the Alhambra. Rooms are more than adequate, and some have terraces and brightly tiled en-suite bathrooms. Its location on the bustling Plaza Nueva means noise can be a problem, but on the other hand you'll also have a wide choice of pavement cafés just a short stroll away. ✉ *Cuesta de Gomérez 1, Centro, 18010* ☎ *958/223652* *22* *No room TVs* ▭ *MC, V.*

Nightlife & the Arts

Granada's ample student population makes for a lively bar scene. Some of the trendiest bars are in converted houses in the Albaicín and Sacromonte and in the area between Plaza Nueva and Paseo de los Tristes. Calle Elvira and Caldería Vieja and Nueva are crowded with laid-back coffee and pastry shops. In the modern part of town, Pedro Antonio de Alarcón and Martinez de la Rosa have larger but less glamorous offerings. Another nighttime gathering place is the Campo del Príncipe, a large plaza surrounded by typical Andalusian taverns.

Gustave Klimt (✉ Imprenta 3, Albaicín) is a large and nicely decorated nighttime hangout. **Rincón de San Pedro** (✉ Carrera del Darro 12, Albaicín) is a café in the afternoon and a dance club in the evening. **Fondo Reservado** (✉ Santa Inés 4, Albaín) is a hip hang-out for a mainly student crowd, and has late-night dance music. **Granada 10** (✉ Carcel Baja 10, Centro ☎ 958/224001), with an upscale crowd, is a a discotheque in a former theater. **La Industrial Copera** (✉ Paz 7, Ctra. de la Armilla) is a popular disco, especially on Friday nights. **Zoo** (✉ Mora, Puerta Real) is one of the more popular discos in town. Get the latest on arts events at the **Diputacíon de Cultura** (Department of Culture), in the **Palacio de los Condes de Gabia** (✉ Pl. de los Girones 1, Centro ☎ 958/247383); the palace hosts art and photography exhibitions as well. Free magazines at the tourist offices also have schedules of cultural events. Granada's orchestra performs in the **Auditorio Manuel de Falla** (✉ Paseo de los Mártires, Realejo ☎ 958/222188). Plays are staged at the **Teatro Alhambra** (✉ Molinos 56, Realejo ☎ 958/220447). Granada's **Festival Internacional de Teatro** fills 10 days with drama each May; contact the *ayuntamiento* (city hall; ✉ Pl. del Carmen, Centro) for details. The **Festival Internacional de Música y Danza** (☎ 958/276200, 958/221844 tickets) is held annually from mid-June to mid-July, with some events in the Alhambra; tickets are available at the Corral del Carbón on Mariana Pineda, one block from Reyes Católicos. Contact the tourist office or visit the Web site for information on November's **Festival Internacional de Jazz** (🌐 www.jazzgranada.com).

FLAMENCO Flamenco is played throughout the city, especially in the *cuevas* (caves) of the Albaicín and Sacromonte, where *zambra* shows—informal performances by Gypsies—take place almost daily. The most popular cuevas are along the Camino de Sacromonte, the major street in the neighborhood of the same name. For any Sacromonte show prepare to part with lots of money. In August, open shows are held at El Corral del Carbón, an old and beautiful small square off Reyes Católicos. The annual *Encuentro Flamenco* festival held during the first days of December typically attracts some of the country's best performers. If you do not want to show up randomly at the flamenco clubs, join a tour through a travel agent or your hotel, or contact **El Museo de María la Canastera** (✉ Camino del Sacromonte 89, Sacromonte ☎ 958/121183), which doubles as a flamenco museum, to confirm performance times. **Sala Alhambra** (✉ Parque Empresarial Olinda, Edif. 12 ☎ 958/412269 or 958/412287) runs well-organized, scheduled performances. **Sala Albayzin** (✉ Mirador de San Cristóbal, Albaicín ☎ 958/804646) is a good spot for authentic flamenco shows. **Cueva de la Bulería** (✉ Camino de Sacromonte 51, Sacromonte) is one of several cuevas on Camino de Sacromonte with unscheduled zambra shows.

Shopping

A Moorish aesthetic pervades Granada's silver-, brass- and copperware, ceramics, marquetry (especially the *taraceas,* wooden boxes with inlaid tiles on their lid), and woven textiles. The main shopping streets, centering on the Puerta Real, are the Gran Vía de Colón, Reyes Católicos, Zacatín, Ángel Ganivet, and Recogidas. Most antiques stores are on Cuesta de Elvira, and Alcaicería—off Reyes Católicos—and Cuesta de Gomérez, on the way up to the Alhambra, also has many handicraft shops. **Cerámica Fabre** (✉ Pl. Pescadería 10, Centro), near the cathedral, has typical Granada ceramics: blue and green patterns on white, with a pomegranate in the center. For wicker baskets and esparto-grass mats and rugs, head off the Plaza Pescadería to **Espartería San José** (✉ C. Jaudenes 22, Centro).

en route

A few miles south of Granada on N323, the road reaches a spot known as the **Suspiro del Moro** (Moor's Sigh). Pause here a moment and look back at the city, just as Granada's departing "Boy King," Boabdil, did 500 years ago. As he wept over the city he'd surrendered to the Catholic Monarchs, his scornful mother pronounced her now legendary rebuke: "You weep like a boy for the city you could not defend as a man."

Santa Fe

18 *8 km (5 mi) west of Granada just south of N342.*

Santa Fe was founded in winter 1491 as a campground for Ferdinand and Isabella's 150,000 troops as they prepared for the siege of Granada. It was here, in April 1492, that Isabella and Columbus signed the agreements that financed his historic voyage, and thus the town has been called the Cradle of America. Santa Fe was originally laid out in the shape of a cross, with a gate at each of its four ends, inscribed with Ferdinand and Isabella's initials. The town has long since transcended those boundaries, but the gates remain—to see them all at once, stand in the square next to the church at the center of the old town.

Fuentevaqueros

19 *10 km (6 mi) northwest of Santa Fe.*

Federico García Lorca was born in this village on June 5, 1898, and lived here until the age of six. The **Casa Museo Federico García Lorca,** the poet's childhood home, opened as a museum in 1986, when Spain commemorated the 50th anniversary of Lorca's assassination and celebrated his reinstatement as a national figure after 40 years of nonrecognition during the Franco regime. The house has been restored with original furnishings, while the former granary, barn, and stables have been converted into exhibition spaces, with temporary art shows and a permanent display of photographs, clippings, and other memorabilia. A two-minute video shows the only existing footage of Lorca. ✉ *Poeta García Lorca 4* ☎ *958/516453* *€1.20* ⊙ *July–Sept., Tues.–Sun. 10–1 and 6–8; Oct.–Mar., Tues.–Sun. 10–1 and 4–6; Apr.–June, daily 10–1 and 5–7; guided tours hourly.*

Viznar

20 *9 km (5½ mi) northeast of Granada (head northeast on N342, then turn left, then left again when you see signs for Viznar).*

If you're a Lorca devotee, make the short trip to Viznar. The **Federico García Lorca Memorial Park,** 3 km (2 mi) from Viznar up a narrow winding road, marks the spot where Lorca was shot without trial by Nationalists at the start of the civil war in August 1936 and where he is probably buried. Lorca, who's now venerated by most Spaniards, was hated by Fascists for his liberal ideas and his homosexuality.

The Sierra Nevada

21 *The drive southeast from Granada to Pradollano along C420, by way of Cenes de la Vega, takes about 45 mins. It's wise to carry snow chains even as late as April or May.*

The mountains of the Sierra Nevada make for an easy and worthwhile excursion, especially for those keen on trekking. The **Pico de Veleta,** Spain's third-highest mountain, is 11,125 ft, and the view from its summit across the Alpujarra range to the sea, at distant Motril, is stunning; on a very clear day you can even see the coast of North Africa. In July and August you can drive or take a microbus to within hundreds of yards of the summit—a trail takes you to the top—on Europe's highest road. It's cold up here, so bring a warm jacket and scarf, even if Granada is sizzling hot. Away to your left, the mighty **Mulhacén,** the highest peak in mainland Spain, soars to 11,407 ft. For more information on trails to the two summits call the Natural Park's Service office at Pampaneira (☎ 958/763127). The Sierra Nevada ski resort's two stations—Pradollano and the higher Borreguiles—draw crowds from December to May. In the winter, buses to Pradollano (✉ Autocar Bonal ☎ 958/465022) leave Granada daily at 8 AM, returning at 6:30 PM; in the summer they leave at 9 AM at return at 5 PM. They depart from Granada's bus station, where can you also buy tickets for €5.40 round-trip. As for Borreguiles, you can only get there on skis.

Skiing

The **Estación de Esquí Sierra Nevada** is one of the best-equipped ski centers in Europe, with 21 lifts, 45 runs, and about 60 km (37 mi) of marked trails; a snowboarding circuit; and two floodlit slopes for night skiing on weekends. A **children's ski school** and rental shop round out the facilities. There's an **information center** (☎ 958/249111) at Plaza de Andalucía 4; you can also dial for **snow, weather, and road conditions** (☎ 958/249119 🌐 www.sierranevadaski.com).

Where to Stay

$$$$ **El Lodge.** A fantastic slope-side location and friendly, professional service adds up to the best hotel in the Sierra Nevada. It's built of Finnish wood—unusual for southern Spain, yet perfectly appropriate in this alpine area—and has a warm, cozy quality. Know, however, that accommodations are not particularly large. Rooms are entirely wood, from the ceiling to the walls and floors. ✉ *C. Maribel 8, 18196* ☎ *958/480600* 📠 *958/481314* *16 rooms, 4 suites* *Restaurant, cable TV, health club, bar, meeting rooms* 💳 *AE, DC, MC, V* ⏲ *Closed May–Oct.*

The Alpujarras

22 *Village of Lanjarón: 46 km (29 mi) south of Granada.*

A trip to the Alpujarras, on the southern slopes of the Sierra Nevada, takes you to one of Andalusia's highest, most remote, and most picturesque areas, home for decades to hippies, painters, writers, and a great foreign population. Attractive villages hide handsome crafts shops where you can buy handwoven textiles and handmade basketware, pottery, and other goods. If you're driving, the road as far as Lanjarón and Orgiva is smooth sailing; after that come steep, twisting mountain roads with few gas stations. Buses run from Granada to Orgiva seven to nine times a day, from Granada to Capileira three times a day. Beyond sightseeing, the area is a haven for outdoor activities such as trekking or horseback riding. Inquire at the **Information Point** at Plaza de la Libertad, s/n, at Pampaneira. The Alpujarras region was originally populated by Moors fleeing the Christian Reconquest (from Seville after its fall in 1248, then from Granada after 1492). It was also the final fiefdom of the unfortunate Boabdil, conceded to him by the Catholic Monarchs after he surrendered Granada. In 1568, rebellious Moors made their last stand against the Christian overlords, a revolt ruthlessly suppressed by Philip II and followed by the forced conversion of all Moors to Christianity and their resettlement farther inland and up Spain's eastern coast. The villages were then repopulated with Christian soldiers from Galicia, who were granted land in return for their service against the Moors. To this day, the Galicians' descendants continue the Moorish custom of weaving rugs and blankets in the traditional Alpujarran colors of red, green, black, and white, and they sell their crafts in many of the villages. Houses here are squat and square; they spill down the southern slopes of the Sierra Nevada, bearing a strong resemblance to the Berber homes in the Rif Mountains, just across the sea in Morocco.

en route

Marking one of the entrances to the Alpujarras, **Lanjarón,** some 46 km (29 mi) from Granada, is a spa town famous for its mineral water, gathered from the melting snows of the Sierra Nevada and drunk throughout Spain. Lanjarón's many hostales can be grim during the spa season (May–November) when most people are seeking cures for various ailments. Press on to **Orgiva,** the main town in the western Alpujarras, where you can leave the C333 and follow signs for Pampaneira and Capileira, in the Alpujarra Alta (High Alpujarra). The villages of the **Barranco del Poqueira** (Poqueira Ravine)—Pampaneira, Bubión, and Capileira—are the best known in the Alpujarras. The looms in **Pampaneira**'s workshops produce many of the textiles sold nearby. **Capileira** (☎ 958/763051 town hall), at the end of the road, is one of the prettiest villages, and its Museo Alpujarreño, in the Plaza Mayor, has a colorful display of local crafts. The museum is open Tuesday–Sunday 11:30–2. Continue along C332, passing a succession of pictorial villages: Pitre—south of which you will find Mecina, Mecinilla, Fondales, and Ferreirola, a cluster of small and remarkable villages whose origin dates back to the Romans—Pórtugos, and Busquístar. If you make it as far as **Trevélez,** which lies on the slopes of the Mulhacén at 4,840 ft above sea level, you will have driven one of the highest roads in Europe. Reward yourself with a plate of the locally produced *jamón serrano*. Trevélez has three levels, the Barrio Alto, Barrio Medio, and Barrio Bajo; the butchers are concentrated in the lowest section (Bajo). Try the higher levels with narrow cobblestone streets, whitewashed houses, and fewer shops. From Trevélez you can return to Granada the way you came, or continue until Juviles, then to Torvizcón and back to the Granada–Motril highway through A348; alternatively, if you continue eastward on C332, you'll eventually reach Almería.

Where to Stay & Eat

If you're looking for the unusual—or a slightly longer stay—rural houses scattered throughout the region are an affordable alternative. For information, contact the tourist office of Granada or **Rustic Blue** (✉ Barrio de la Ermita, Bubión ☎ 958/763381 🌐 www.rusticblue.com).

$ **Hotel Albergue de Mecina.** In a peaceful and tiny village, the two-story hotel's entrance leads onto an enclosed small patio with a glass-dome ceiling. The whitewashed rooms, some with balcony and some with terrace, are simple and comfortable. Nearby is a good vegetarian restaurant, L'Atelier, with Mediterranean specialties. ✉ *C. La Fuente s/n, Mecina Fondales 18416 ☎ 958/766241 📠 958/766255 21 rooms Restaurant, cafeteria, refrigerators, cable TV, pool AE, DC, MC, V.*

¢ **La Fragua.** Spotless rooms with baths (and some with balconies), fresh air, and views over the rooftops of Trevélez to the valley beyond are the rewards of this small, friendly hostelry in a typical village house behind the town hall. The restaurant is in a separate house up the street, serving regional dishes like *arroz liberal* (hunter's rice), *lomo a los aromas de la sierra* (herb-scented pork loin), and *choto al ajillo* (meat of a piglet in garlic sauce). ✉ *San Antonio 4, Barrio Medio, Trevélez 18417 ☎ 958/858626 📠 958/858614 14 rooms Restaurant MC, V.*

$–$$ **Taray.** This hotel has its own farm and makes a perfect base for exploring the Alpujarras. Public areas and guest rooms are in a low whitewashed building. The sunny quarters are decorated with Alpujarran handwoven bedspreads and curtains; three rooms have rooftop terraces, and there's a pleasant common terrace. Most of the restaurant's food comes from the estate, including trout and lamb; in season, you can even pick your own raspberries or oranges for breakfast. ✉ *Ctra. Tablate–Albuñol, Km 18, Órgiva 18400 ☎ 958/784525 📠 958/784531 15 rooms Restaurant, cafeteria, cable TV, pool AE, DC, MC, V.*

Guadix

23 *47 km (30 mi) east of Granada on A92.*

Guadix was an important mining town as far back as 2,000 years ago and has its fair share of monuments, including a cathedral (built between 1594 and 1706) and a 9th-century Moorish alcazaba. But Guadix and the neighboring village of Purullena are best known for their cave communities. Around 2,000 caves were carved out of the soft, sandstone mountains at various times, and most are still inhabited. Far from being troglodytic holes in the wall, they are well furnished and comfortable, with a pleasant year-round temperature; a few serve as hotels. Follow signs to the **Cueva Museo**, a small cave museum, in Guadix's cave district. Toward the town center, the **Cueva la Alcazaba** has a ceramics workshop. A number of private caves have signs welcoming you to inspect the premises; a tip is expected if you do. Purullena, 6 km (4 mi) from Guadix, is also known for ceramics.

Where to Stay & Eat

$ **Comercio.** In the historic center of Guadix, this 1905 building is an enchanting little family-run hotel. Rooms have dark wooden classic furniture, modern bathrooms, and, except for a few carpeted ones, marble floors. The public areas include an art gallery, a jazz concert room, and the best restaurant in Guadix, serving such local specialties as roast lamb with raisins and pine nuts. ✉ *C. Mira de Amezcua 3, 18500 ☎ 958/660500 📠 958/665072 🌐 www.hotelcomercio.com 23 rooms Restaurant, cafeteria AE, DC, MC, V.*

$ **Cuevas Pedro Antonio de Alarcón.** If you're looking for a so-called authentic experience, consider staying in a cave. Located not in Guadix's main cave district but in a cave "suburb" outside town, this unique lodging is installed in 19 adjoining caves and one suite. Each cave sleeps two to five and has a kitchenette; the honeymoon cave has a whirlpool bath. The whitewashed walls and polished clay-tile floors are decorated with charming Granadino crafts and colorful rugs; handwoven Alpujarran tapestries serve as doors between the rooms. The restaurant, also subterranean, serves regional dishes. ✉ *Barriada San Torcuato, 18500* ☎ *958/664986* 🖷 *958/661721* 🌐 *www.andalucia.com/cavehotel* 🛏 *19 rooms, 1 suite* 🛎 *Restaurant, cable TV, some in-room hot tubs, kitchenettes, pool* 💳 *AE, MC, V.*

Loja

24 *55 km (34 mi) west of Granada, 40 km (25 mi) northeast of Málaga.*

Standing guard at the entrance to Granada's plain (halfway between Granada and Málaga on the A92), and suitably connected by bus to the capital of the region, Loja is a traditional pit stop for travelers, who like to pay a visit to its alcazaba, as well as to munch on the famous *roscos de Loja,* a hard, sugar-coated, doughnut-shape pastry. The town's name comes from the Lascivis of Roman times—"place of water and delight"—and the town still has numerous fountains, including the 25-spout Fuente de los Veinticinco Caños. Eight kilometers (5 mi) west of Loja on A92 is the hamlet of **Riofrío,** next to a rushing trout stream. Trout and sturgeon raised at Riofrío's fish farm are enjoyed throughout Andalusia. Several restaurants, all inexpensive, serve fresh trout several ways: *a la plancha* (grilled), *a la romana* (batter-fried), *a la navarra* (with ham), and *ahumado* (smoked).

Where to Stay & Eat

★ $$$$ ✕🏨 **La Bobadilla.** Standing on its own 860-acre estate amid olive and holm-oak trees, this complex 14 km (9 mi) west of Loja resembles a Moorish village, or a rambling *cortijo* (ranch). It has white walls, tile roofs, patios, fountains, and an artificial lake. Guest buildings center around a 16th-century-style chapel that houses a 1,595-pipe organ. Each room has a balcony, a terrace, or a garden. One restaurant serves highly creative international cuisine, and the other more down-to-earth regional items. Inquire about special deals. ✉ *Finca La Bobadilla (north of A92 between Salinas and Rute; exit north onto 334, toward Iznájar), 18300* ☎ *958/321861* 🖷 *958/321810* 🌐 *www.la-bobadilla.com* 🛏 *62 rooms, 8 suites* 🛎 *2 restaurants, minibars, cable TV with movies, 2 tennis courts, 2 pools (1 indoor), gym, hot tub, sauna, mountain bikes, horseback riding, convention center* 💳 *AE, DC, MC, V.*

JAÉN, BAEZA, ÚBEDA & CAZORLA

Jaén, north of Granada, has a rich Moorish legacy—Arab baths and a former alcázar—and an ornately decorated cathedral. From Jaén, head northeast along the N321 to the olive-producing towns of Baeza and Úbeda. The typical Andalusian town of Cazorla is the gateway to the Cazorla Nature Park, where you might spot wild boar.

Jaén

25 *93 km (58 mi) north of Granada.*

Nestled in the foothills of the Sierra de Jabalcuz, Jaén is surrounded by towering peaks and olive-clad hills. The Arabs called it Geen (Route of the Caravans) because it formed a crossroad between Castile and Andalusia. Captured from the Moors by the Saint King Ferdinand in 1246,

Jaén became a frontier province, the site of many a skirmish and battle over the next 200 years between the Moors of Granada and Christians from the north and west. Today the province earns a living from its lead and silver mines and endless olive groves.

★ The **Castillo de Santa Catalina,** perched on a rocky crag 5 km (3 mi) from the center of town, is Jaén's star monument. The castle may have originated as a tower built by Hannibal; the site was fortified continuously over the centuries. The Nasrid king Alhamar, builder of Granada's Alhambra, constructed an alcázar here, but King Ferdinand III captured it from him in 1246 on the feast day of Santa Catalina (St. Catherine). Catalina consequently became Jaén's patron saint, so when the Christians built a castle and chapel here, they dedicated both to her. ✉ *Castillo de Santa Catalina* 🎫 *Free* ⏲ *Thurs.–Tues. 10–2 and 4:30–7 in summer; Thurs.–Tues. 10–2 and 3:30–6 in winter.*

Jaén's **cathedral** is a hulk that looms above the modest buildings around it. Begun in 1500 on the site of a former mosque, it took almost 300 years to build; its chief architect was Andrés de Vandelvira (1509–75), many more of whose buildings can be seen in Úbeda and Baeza. The ornate facade was sculpted by Pedro Roldán, and the figures on top of the columns include San Fernando (King Ferdinand III) surrounded by the four evangelists. The cathedral's most treasured relic is the **Santo Rostro** (Holy Face), the cloth with which, according to tradition, St. Veronica cleansed Christ's face on the way to Calvary, leaving his image imprinted on the fabric. The rostro is displayed every Friday. In the underground **museum,** look for the *Immaculate Conception,* by Alonso Cano; *San Lorenzo,* by Martínez Montañés; and a Calvary scene by Jácobo Florentino. ✉ *Pl. Santa María* 🎫 *Cathedral free, museum €1.80* ⏲ *Cathedral Mon.–Sat. 8:30–1 and 4–7, Sun. 9–1:30 and 5–7; museum Mon.–Sat. 10–1 and 5–7, Sun. 10–1:30 and 6–7.*

Explore the narrow alleys of old Jaén as you walk from the cathedral to the **Baños Árabes** (Arab Baths), which once belonged to Ali, a Moorish king of Jaén, and probably date from the 11th century. Four hundred years later, a viceroy of Peru built himself a mansion, the **Palacio de Villardompardo,** right over the baths, so it took years of painstaking excavation to restore them to their original form. The palace contains a small museum of folk crafts and a larger museum devoted to native art. ✉ *Palacio de Villardompardo, Pl. Luisa de Marillac* ☎ *953/236292* 🎫 *Free* ⏲ *Tues.–Fri. 9–8, weekends 9:30–2:30.*

Jaén's **Museo Provincial** has one of the best collections of Iberian (pre-Roman) artifacts in Spain. The newest wing has 20 life-size Iberian sculptures discovered by chance near the village of Porcuna in 1975. The museum proper is in a 1547 mansion, on a patio with the facade of the erstwhile Church of San Miguel. The fine-arts section has a roomful of Goya lithographs. ✉ *Paseo de la Estación 29* ☎ *953/250600* 🎫 *€1.50, free for EU citizens* ⏲ *Tues. 3–8, Wed.–Sat. 9–8, Sun. 9–3* ⏲ *Closed summer afternoons.*

Where to Stay & Eat

$$$ ✕ **Casa Antonio.** Exquisite Andalusian food is served at this sober and elegant restaurant with three small dining rooms—all with cherrywood-panel walls, dark plywood floors, and a few modern art paintings on display. Try the *foie y queso en milhojas de manzana verde caramelizada en aceite de pistacho* (foie and cheese with green apples caramelized in pistachio oil in a pastry puff) or *salmonetes de roca en caldo tibio de molusco y aceite de vainilla* (red mullet in a warm mollusk broth and

vanilla oil). ✉ *Fermín Palma, 3* ☎ *953/270262* ▭ *AE, MC, V* ⏲ *No dinner Sun. Closed Mon.*

$$ ✕ **Casa Vicente.** Locals typically pack this popular family-run restaurant around the corner from the cathedral square. You can have drinks and tapas in the colorful tavern, then move on to the cozy courtyard dining room. The traditional Jaén dishes—game casseroles, Jaén-style spinach, and *cordero Mozárabe* (Mozarab-style roast lamb with a sweet-and-sour sauce)—are especially good. ✉ *Francisco Martín Mora 1* ☎ *953/232222 or 953/232816* ▭ *AE, MC, V* ⏲ *No dinner Sun.*

$$$ Fodor'sChoice ★ **Parador de Jaén.** Built amid the mountaintop towers of the Castillo de Santa Catalina, this is one of the showpieces of the parador chain and a reason in itself to visit Jaén. Lofty ceilings, tapestries, baronial shields, and suits of armor underscore the castle motif. The comfortable bedrooms, with canopy beds, have balconies overlooking the mountains. ✉ *Castillo de Santa Catalina, 23001* ☎ *953/230000* 📠 *953/230930* *45 rooms* *Restaurant, minibars, cable TV, pool* ▭ *AE, DC, MC, V.*

Baeza

26 *48 km (30 mi) northeast of Jaén on the N321.*

Fodor'sChoice ★ The historic town of Baeza snuggles between hills and olive groves. Founded by the Romans, it later housed the Visigoths and became the capital of a *taifa* (kingdom) under the Moors. The Saint King Ferdinand captured Baeza in 1227, and for the next 200 years it stood on the frontier of the Moorish kingdom of Granada. In the 16th and 17th centuries, local nobles gave the city a wealth of Renaissance palaces. The **Casa del Pópulo,** in the central paseo—where the Plaza del Pópulo (or Plaza de los Leones) and Plaza de la Constitución (or Plaza del Mercado Viejo) merge to form a delightful cobble square—is a beautiful structure from around 1530. The first mass of the Reconquest was reputedly celebrated on its curved balcony. It now houses Baeza's tourist office, which is unfortunately closed on weekends. In the center of the town square is an ancient Iberian-Roman statue thought to depict Imilce, wife of Hannibal; at the foot of her column is the **Fuente de los Leones** (Fountain of the Lions). To find Baeza's **university,** follow the steps on the plaza's south side. The college opened in 1542, closed in 1824, and later became a high school, where the poet Antonio Machado taught French from 1912 to 1919. The building still functions as a school, but you can visit Machado's classroom—request the key—and the patio. ✉ *Beato Juan de Ávila s/n* ☎ *953/740150* ⏲ *Oct.–Mar., Thurs.–Tues. 10–1 and 4–6; Apr.–Sept., Thurs.–Tues. 10–1 and 5–7.*

Baeza's **cathedral** was originally begun by Ferdinand III on the site of a former mosque. The structure was largely rebuilt by Andrés de Vandelvira, architect of Jaén's cathedral, between 1570 and 1593, though the west front has architectural influences from an earlier period. A fine 14th-century rose window crowns the 13th-century Puerta de la Luna (Moon Door). Don't miss the baroque silver monstrance, which is carried in Baeza's Corpus Christi processions—the piece is kept in a concealed niche behind a painting, but you can see it in all its splendor by putting a coin in a slot to reveal the hiding place and shed light on it (money well spent). Next to the monstrance is the entrance to the clock tower, where a small donation and a narrow spiral staircase take you to one of the best views of Baeza. The remains of the original mosque are in the cathedral's Gothic cloisters. You can take a guided visit for €2.50. ✉ *Pl. de Santa María* ⏲ *Mon.–Sat. 10:30–1 and 4–6 (10–1 and 5–7 in summer), Sun. noon–2.*

The ancient student custom of inscribing names and graduation dates in bull's blood (as in Salamanca) is still evident on the walls of the seminary of **San Felipe Neri** (⊠ Cuesta de San Felipe), built in 1660. It's opposite Baeza's cathedral. Baeza's **ayuntamiento** (⊠ Pl. Cardenal Benavides, just north of the Pl. del Pópulo) was designed by cathedral master Andrés de Vandelvira. The facade is ornately plateresque; look between the balconies and you'll see the coats of arms of Felipe II, the city of Baeza, and the magistrate Juan de Borja. Arrange for a visit to the *salón de plenos,* a major hall with painted, carved woodwork. The 16th-century **Convento de San Francisco** (⊠ C. de San Francisco) is one of Vandelvira's architectural religious masterpieces. You can see its restored remains—the building was spoiled by the French army and partially destroyed by a light earthquake in the beginning of the 19th century. It's a few blocks west of the ayuntamiento.

Where to Stay & Eat

$$–$$$ ✕ **Vandelvira.** Seldom does one have the chance to eat in a 16th-century convent. The restaurant, within two galleries on the first floor of the Convento de San Francisco, has lots of character and magnificent antiques. Specialties include the *pâté de perdiz con aceite de oliva virgen* (partridge pâté with olive oil) or the *manitas de cerdo rellenas de perdiz y espinacas* (pig's knuckles filled with partridge and spinach). It has a summer terrace that doubles as a tavern and night bar. ⊠ *C. de San Francisco 14, 23440* ☎ *953/748172* ▭ *MC, V* ⊗ *Closed Mon. No dinner Sun.*

¢ ✕▣ **Juanito.** Rooms in this small, unpretentious hotel are simple and comfortable. The restaurant's proprietor is a champion of Andalusian food, and the chef has revived such regional specialties as *alcachofas Luisa* (braised artichokes), *ensalada de perdiz* (partridge salad), and *cordero con habas* (lamb and broad beans); desserts are based on old Moorish recipes. The hotel is next to a gas station on the edge of town, toward Úbeda. ⊠ *Paseo Arca del Agua, 23440* ☎ *953/740040* 🖷 *953/742324* ⇆ *36 rooms, 1 suite* ♁ *Restaurant* ▭ *MC, V* ⊗ *No dinner Sun.–Mon.*

$$ ▣ **Hospedería Fuentenueva.** It's hard to believe, but this small, charming hotel was once a women's prison. The interior has undergone a sophisticated overhaul: colors are harmonious and warm, and there's stencilling on salmon-color walls. Floors are marble, furnishings modern, and there's a bubbling fountain in the interior patio. The result is an upbeat, contemporary look. There are also regular art exhibitions. ⊠ *Paseo Arca del Agua, 23440* ☎ *953/743100* 🖷 *953/743200* 🌐 *www.rgo.net/fuentenueva* ⇆ *12 rooms* ♁ *Restaurant, cafeteria, pool* ▭ *AE, MC, V.*

¢ ▣ **El Patio.** Considering the setting—the former 16th-century palace of the Marqués Cuentacilla—you're getting a pretty good deal here. The place is comfortable and homey, and several generations of the owner's family are often around. Rooms are set around a vast central patio interspersed with original columns and filled with overstuffed, heavily brocaded furniture. Rooms are basic but comfortable. The location—on a cobble side street leading to an old church—is wonderfully quiet and reasonably central to shops and restaurants. ⊠ C. *Conde Romanones 13, 23440* ☎ *953/740200* ⇆ *12* ▭ *MC, V.*

Úbeda

27 *9 km (5½ mi) northeast of Baeza on the N321.*

Fodor's Choice ★

Úbeda is in the heart of Jaén's olive groves, and olive oil is indeed the main concern here. Although this modern town of 30,000 is relatively dull, the *casco antiguo* (old town) is one of the most outstanding enclaves of 16th-century architecture in Spain. Follow signs to the Zona Monumental, where you'll pass countless Renaissance palaces and stately mansions, most closed to the public. The Plaza del Ayuntamiento is crowned by the privately owned **Palacio de Vela de los Cobos,** designed by Andrés de Vandelvira for Úbeda's magistrate, Francisco de Vela de los Cobos, in the mid-16th century. The corner balcony has a central white-marble column that's echoed in the gallery above.

Vandelvira's Palacio Juan Vázquez de Molina is better known by its nickname, the **Palacio de las Cadenas** (House of Chains), because decorative iron chains were once affixed to the columns of its main doorway. With entrances on both Plaza Vázquez de Molina and Plaza Ayuntamiento, it is now the town hall. An entrance around the corner, on Callejón de Jesús, leads to the building's vaulted stone cellars and the **Museo de Alfarería** (€1.83), where you can learn about Spanish ceramics. The large, well-displayed collection hails mainly from Úbeda's own workshops. The museum is open May–September, Tuesday–Saturday 10:30–2 and 5:30–8; October–April, Tuesday–Saturday 4:30–7.

The Plaza Vázquez de Molina, in the heart of the old town, is the site of the **Sacra Capilla del Salvador.** This building is photographed so often that it has become the city's unofficial symbol. Sacra Capilla was built by Vandelvira, but he based his design on some 1536 plans by Diego de Siloé, architect of Granada's cathedral. Sacked in the frenzy of church burnings at the outbreak of the civil war, it retains its ornate west front and altarpiece, which has a rare Berruguete sculpture. ✉ *Pl. Vázquez de Molina* *€2.25* *Daily 10:30–2 and 4:30–6.*

The **Ayuntamiento Antiguo** (Old Town Hall), begun in the early 16th century but restored as a beautiful arcaded baroque palace in 1680, is now a conservatory of music. From the hall's upper balcony, the town council watched celebrations and autos-da-fé ("acts of faith"—executions of heretics sentenced by the Inquisition) in the square below. On the north side is the 13th-century church of San Pablo, with an Isabelline south portal. ✉ *Pl. Primero de Mayo, off C. María de Molina* *Guided visits 7–8 PM.*

The **Hospital de Santiago,** now a cultural center in the modern section, sometimes jokingly called the Escorial of Andalusia, is a huge, angular building. It holds some of the events at the annual International Spring Dance and Music Festival that takes place in May and June. The plain facade is adorned with ceramic medallions and, over the main entrance, is a carving of Santiago Matamoros (St. James the Moorslayer) in his traditional horseback pose. Inside are an arcaded patio and a grand staircase. ✉ *Avda. Cristo Rey* ☎ *953/750842* *8–3 and 3:30–10.*

Where to Stay & Eat

$$$ Fodor'sChoice ★ **Parador de Úbeda.** This splendid parador is in a 16th-century ducal palace on the Plaza Vázquez de Molina, next to the Capilla del Salvador. A grand stairway, decked with tapestries and suits of armor, leads up to the guest rooms, which have tile floors, lofty wood ceilings, dark Castilian-style furniture, and large bathtubs. The dining room serves perhaps the best food in Úbeda, specializing in regional dishes; try one of the *perdiz* (partridge) entrées. There's a bar in the vaulted basement. ✉ *Pl. Vázquez de Molina 1, 23400* ☎ *953/750345* *953/751259* *www.parador.es* *35 rooms, 1 suite* *Restaurant, bar, minibars, cable TV with movies* *AE, DC, MC, V.*

$$ **María de Molina.** In the heart of the Zona Monumental, this hotel is in a large town house formerly known as La Casa de los Curas (The Priests' House), as it once housed two priests who were twins. Each room

is different, but all are dressed in warm pastels and elegant Andalusian furnishings, and some have balconies. Rooms 204–207 have the best views over the town's rooftops. Note that rates go up on weekends and holidays. The restaurant is a good place for a light lunch or get serious with the three-course menú del día dishing up a nouvelle twist to local cuisine. ✉ *Pl. del Ayuntamiento, 23400* ☎ *953/795356* 📠 *953/793694* 🌐 *www.hotel-maria-de-molina.com* *18 rooms, 2 suites* *Restaurant, bar, cable TV, meeting room* ▭ *AE, DC, MC, V.*

$$ **Palacio de la Rambla.** In old Úbeda, this wonderful 16th-century mansion has been in the same family since it was built, and part of it still hosts the Marquesa de la Rambla when she's in town. Eight of the rooms are open to overnighters; each is unique, but all are large and furnished with original antiques, tapestries, and works of art, and some have chandeliers. The palace is arranged on two levels, around a cool, ivy-covered patio. ✉ *Pl. del Marqués 1, 23400* ☎ *953/750196* 📠 *953/750267* *7 rooms, 1 suite* ▭ *AE, MC, V.*

$ **La Paz.** On a busy street in modern Úbeda, this homey hostel has simply furnished rooms with plain white walls and traditional dark-wood furniture. ✉ *Andalucía 1, 23400* ☎ *953/750848* 📠 *953/752140* *40 rooms* *Parking (fee)* ▭ *AE, MC, V.*

Shopping

Little Úbeda is the crafts capital of Andalusia, with workshops devoted to carpentry, basket weaving, stone carving, wrought iron, stained glass, and, above all, pottery. Calle Valencia is the traditional potters' row, running from the bottom of town to Úbeda's general crafts center, northwest of the old quarter (follow signs to Calle Valencia or Barrio de Alfareros). Úbeda's most famous potter was Pablo Tito, whose craft is carried on at three different workshops run by two of Tito's sons (Paco and Juan) and a son-in-law, Melchor, each of whom claims to be the sole true heir to the art. The extrovert **Juan Tito** (✉ Pl. del Ayuntamiento 12 ☎ 953/751302) can often be found at the potter's wheel in his rambling shop, packed with ceramics of every size and shape. **Paco Tito** (✉ C. Valencia 22 ☎ 953/751496) devotes himself to clay sculptures of characters from *Don Quijote,* which he fires in an old Moorish-style kiln. His shop has a small museum as well as a studio. **Melchor Tito** (✉ C. Valencia 44 ☎ 953/753365) focuses on classic green-glaze items. **Antonio Almazara** (✉ C. Valencia 34 ☎ 953/751200) is one of several shops specializing in Úbeda's green-glaze pottery. All kinds of ceramics are sold at **Alfarería Góngora** (✉ Cuesta de la Merced 32 ☎ 953/754605). For handmade esparto-grass ware, such as rugs, mats, and baskets, go to **Artesanía Blanco** (✉ Real 47 ☎ 953/750456), supplied by its own local factory.

Cazorla

28 *48 km (35 mi) southeast of Úbeda.*

The remote, unspoiled Andalusian village of Cazorla, at the east end of the province of Jaén, is a treat for both young and old. The pine-clad slopes and towering peaks of the Cazorla and Segura sierras rise above the village, and below it stretch endless miles of olive groves. In spring, purple Judas trees blossom in picturesque plazas. For a break from man-made sights, drink in the scenery or watch for wildlife in the **Parque Natural de Cazorla** (Cazorla Nature Park). Try to avoid the summer and late spring months, when the park teems with tourists and locals. For information on hiking, camping, canoeing, horseback riding, or going on guided excursions, contact Agencia de Medio Ambiente (AMA; ✉ Tejares Altos ☎ 953/720125) in Cazorla or in Jaén (✉ Avda. de Andalucía 79 ☎ 953/

215000), or the park visitor center. For hunting or fishing permits, apply to the Jaén office well in advance. Deer, wild boar, and mountain goats roam the slopes of this carefully protected patch of mountain wilderness 80 km (50 mi) long and 30 km (19 mi) wide, and hawks, eagles, and vultures soar over the 6,000-ft peaks. Within the park, at **Cañada de las Fuentes** (Fountains' Ravine), is the source of Andalusia's great river, the Guadalquivir. The road through the park follows the river to the shores of **Lago Tranco de Beas.** Alpine meadows, pine forests, springs, waterfalls, and gorges make Cazorla a perfect place to hike. A short film shown in the **visitor center,** in Torre de Vinagre, introduces the park's main sights; displays explain the park's plants and geology; and the staff can advise you on camping, fishing, and hiking trails. There's also a **hunting museum,** with such cheerful attractions as the interlocked antlers of bucks who clashed during the autumn rutting season, became helplessly trapped, and died of starvation. Nearby are a **botanical garden** and a **game reserve.** Between June and October the park maintains seven well-equipped **campsites.** Past Lago Tranco and the village of Hornos, a road goes to the **Sierra de Segura** mountain range, the park's least crowded area. At 3,600 ft, the spectacular village of **Segura de la Sierra,** on top of the mountain, is crowned by an almost perfect castle with impressive defense walls, a Moorish bath, and a square bullring.

en route

Leave Cazorla Nature Park by an alternative route—the spectacular **gorge** carved by the river Guadalquivir, a rushing torrent beloved of kayak enthusiasts. At the El Tranco dam, follow signs to Villanueva del Arzobispo, where the N322 takes you back to Úbeda, Baeza, and Jaén.

Where to Stay & Eat

$ ✕ **Juan Carlos.** As you might expect from the row of wild boar heads baring their teeth from the wall, the menu includes a predominance of game dishes. There are some surprisingly innovative starters, however, including cream of melon soup with mint. The homemade fig ice cream makes a refreshing finale to your meal, especially during steamy summer days. ✉ *Plaza Consuelo Mendieta 2* ☎ *953/721201* ▭ *No credit cards.*

$$ ✕ **Parador de Cazorla.** Isolated in a valley at the edge of the nature park, 26 km (16 mi) above Cazorla village, you'll find this modern, whitewashed parador with a red-tile roof. It's a quiet place, popular with hunters and anglers. The restaurant serves regional dishes such as *pipirrana* (a salad of finely diced peppers, onions, and tomatoes) and, in season, game. ✉ *Sierra de Cazorla, 23470* ☎ *953/727075* 🖷 *953/727077* 🌐 *www.parador.es* *33 rooms* *Restaurant, cable TV, pool* ▭ *AE, DC, MC, V* ⊙ *Closed Dec.*

$$ ✕ **Villa Turística de Cazorla.** On a hill with superb views of the village of Cazorla, this leisure complex rents semi-detached apartments sleeping one to six. Each has a balcony or terrace as well as a kitchenette—some have a full kitchen—and fireplace. The restaurant, done in cheerful yellows, specializes in trout, lamb, and game. ✉ *Ladera de San Isicio, Cazorla 23470* ☎ *953/710100* 🖷 *953/710152* 🌐 *www.villacazorla.com* *32 units* *Restaurant, cafeteria, kitchenettes, pool, bar, meeting rooms* ▭ *MC, V.*

$ ✕ **La Hortizuela.** Deep in the heart of Cazorla Nature Park in what was once a game warden's house is a small hotel that's the perfect base for exploring the wilderness. Guest rooms are in the back, beyond the central courtyard, and most have unhindered views of the forest-clad mountainside (a few look onto the patio). Wild boar, game, deer, and fresh trout are usually on offer in the restaurant. ✉ *Ctra. del Tranco,*

Km 50.5 (2 km [1 mi] east of visitor center up a dirt track), Coto Ríos 23478 ☎/fax *953/713150* *23 rooms* *Restaurant, pool* *MC, V.*

$–$$ **Sierra de Cazorla.** Nestled in a bend of the road leading up into the mountains 2 km (1 mi) above Cazorla village, at La Iruela, is this low, white hotel. Rooms have clay-tile floors and are functional and comfortable. Those in the two-story modern section are larger than those in the older building. Most rooms in both sections have nice views of the olive groves in the valley below and of the ruins of La Iruela's castle, teetering on its rocky outcrop. ✉ *Ctra. Sierra de Cazorla, Km 2, La Iruela 23476* ☎ *953/720015* fax *953/720017* *www.hotelsierradecazorla.com* *53 rooms, 2 suites* *Restaurant, pool* *AE, DC, MC, V.*

CÓRDOBA & ENVIRONS

In Córdoba is one of Spain's most spectacular monuments, the Moorish Mezquita (mosque), which dates from the 8th through the 10th centuries. The city's old quarters, particularly the old Jewish Quarter, invite quiet exploration: you wander through narrow, whitewashed alleys past private tile patios and effusions of jewel-tone flowers, and visit the only synagogue in Andalusia to survive the expulsion of the Jews in 1492. If you have time to go beyond Córdoba, head west to the ruins of Medina Azahara, site of a once-magnificent palace complex, or south to the wine country around Montilla and the Subbética region, a cluster of small towns virtually unknown to travelers.

Córdoba

166 km (103 mi) northwest of Granada, 407 km (250 mi) southwest of Madrid.

On the south bank of the Guadalquivir, Córdoba is integral to the cultural history of the Iberian Peninsula. It was both the Roman and Moorish capital of Spain, and its old quarter, clustered around its famous mosque (Mezquita), remains one of the country's grandest and yet most intimate examples of its Moorish heritage. The Moorish emirs and caliphs of the West held court here from the 8th to the 11th century, when Córdoba became one of the greatest centers of art, culture, and learning in the Western world; one of its libraries had more than 400,000 volumes, a staggering number at the time. Moors, Christians, and Jews lived together in harmony within its walls. Chroniclers of the day put the city's population at around a million, making it the largest city in Europe, though historians believe the real figure was closer to half a million (there are fewer than 300,000 today).

Córdoba remained in Moorish hands until it was conquered by King Ferdinand in 1236, after which the Catholic Monarchs used the city as a base from which to plan the conquest of Granada. In Columbus's time, the Guadalquivir was navigable as far upstream as Córdoba, and great galleons sailed its waters. Today, the river's muddy water and marshy banks evoke little of Córdoba's glorious past, but the city's bridge—of Roman origin, though much restored by the Arabs and successive generations—and an old Arab waterwheel recall a far grander era.

a good walk

Allow a full day for this walk. Begin on Cardenal Herrero, at the **Mezquita** 29. Facing the western side of the mosque, in the sacristy of a former hospital on Calle Torrijos, is the regional tourist office. Walk up Calle Velázquez Bosco to a tiny alleyway known as **Calleja de las Flores** 30. Come back to Cardenal Herrero and enter the **Judería** 31. Go up Calle Judería and continue along Calle Albucasis past the Plaza Juda Levi, site of the municipal tourist office. Just around the corner, in the

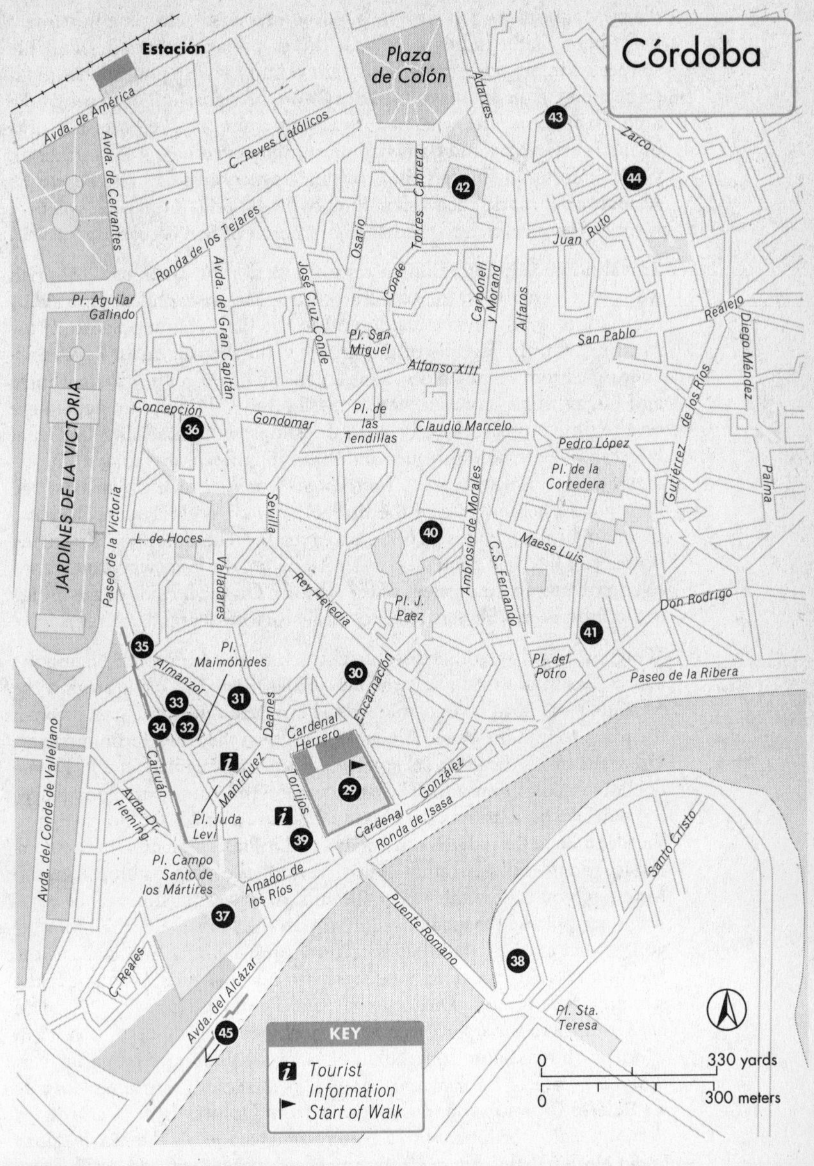
Córdoba
Estación
Plaza de Colón
Avda. de América
Avda. de Cervantes
C. Reyes Católicos
Adarves
Zarco
Torres Cabrera
Ronda de los Tejares
Osario
Juan Rufo
José Cruz Conde
Conde
Avda. del Gran Capitán
Carbonell y Morand
Alfaros
Pl. Aguilar Galindo
Pl. San Miguel
San Pablo
Realejo
Diego Méndez
Alfonso XIII
de los Ríos
Concepción
Gondomar
Pl. de las Tendillas
Claudio Marcelo
Pedro López
Pl. de la Corredera
Gutiérrez
Palma
JARDINES DE LA VICTORIA
Paseo de la Victoria
Sevilla
L. de Hoces
Ambrosio de Morales
C.S. Fernando
Maese Luis
Valladares
Rey Heredia
Pl. J. Paez
Don Rodrigo
Pl. Maimónides
Almanzor
Encarnación
Pl. del Potro
Paseo de la Ribera
Deanes
Cardenal Herrero
Avda. del Conde de Vallellano
Cairuán
Manríquez
Torrijos
González
Avda. Dr. Fleming
Pl. Juda Levi
Cardenal
Ronda de Isasa
Pl. Campo Santo de los Mártires
Amador de los Ríos
Santo Cristo
Puente Romano
C. Reales
Avda. del Alcázar
Pl. Sta. Teresa
KEY
Tourist Information
Start of Walk
0
330 yards
0
300 meters

Plaza Maimónides, is Córdoba's **Museo Taurino** 32. Leading northwest from here, Calle Judíos goes past the tiny Plaza Tiberiades and the statue of Maimónides, the famous 12th-century Jewish philosopher. Continue along Calle Judíos to the **Zoco** 33 on the right, and go through the arch to the courtyard, where a former Arab *souk* (market) houses working artisans by day and flamenco on summer evenings. A bit farther up Calle Judíos, on the left, is Córdoba's **synagogue** 34. The **Puerta de Almodóvar** 35 marks the western limit of the Judería. From here, you may want to detour north to the Mudéjar church of **San Nicolás de Villa** 36.

Travel down Cairuán, along a restored section of Córdoba's Moorish walls and past the statue of 12th-century Moorish philosopher Averröes (another prominent Córdoban) to the Plaza Campo Santo de los Mártires. On the far side of the square is the **Alcázar de los Reyes Cristianos** 37. From Plaza Campo Santo, you can hire a *coche caballo* (horse and buggy) for a city tour, between €24 and €36 an hour, depending on the time of year; head back to the shops on Deanes and Cardenal Herrero by way of Manríquez and Plaza Juda Levi; or walk back along Amador de los Ríos to the bottom of Torrijos, turn down past the Puerta del Puente (Gate of the Bridge), and cross the Puente Romano (Roman Bridge), whose 16 arches span the Guadalquivir. From the bridge you'll have a good view of La Albolafia, the huge wheel once used to carry water to the gardens of the Alcázar. On the far side of the bridge is the **Torre de la Calahorra** 38, now a history museum.

Whichever option you choose, backtrack to the Mezquita. Facing the south side of the mosque is the **Museo Diocesano** 39. Walk around the Mezquita and head up Encarnación to Plaza Jerónimo Paez; pass through the plaza to find the **Museo Arqueológico** 40, on the Plaza Jerónimo Paez. Off to the east is the Plaza del Potro (Colt Square)—named after its Fuente del Potro (Colt Fountain). The cafés around this square are good places for a drink; here, too, is the **Museo de Bellas Artes** 41. Go northwest to the **Plaza de la Corredera** (some maps call it Plaza Constitución), an arcaded square built around 1690. West of the plaza, along Claudio Marcelo, you'll pass the town hall and the towering columns of what was once a **Roman temple** on your way to the Plaza de las Tendillas. If you've had enough walking, head down Jesús María and back to the Mezquita, saving the remaining sights for another time. If you have the strength, follow Calle Diego León from the north side of the Plaza de las Tendillas to the small **Plaza San Miguel,** whose 13th-century Gothic-Mudéjar church dates from the time of Córdoba's conquest by King Ferdinand. North of the Plaza San Miguel is the small, charming **Plaza de los Dolores** 42, and around the corner from Dolores is the Casa de los Fernández de Córdoba, with a plateresque facade. At the nearby **Plaza Santa Marina de las Aguas** 43, on the edge of the Barrio de los Toreros, is a statue of the bullfighter Manolete. Southeast of here stands the **Palacio de los Marqueses de Viana** 44. Córdoba's **Jardín Botánico** 45, across from the zoo by the river south of the city center, is best visited by car (there's plenty of parking) or taxi.

What to See

Córdoba's council authorities and private institutions frequently change the hours of the city's sights; confirm hours with the tourist office or the sight itself.

37 **Alcázar de los Reyes Cristianos** (Fortress of the Christian Monarchs). Built by Alfonso XI in 1328, the Alcázar is a Mudéjar-style palace with splendid gardens. (The original Moorish Alcázar stood beside the Mezquita, on the site of the present Bishop's Palace.) This is where, in the 15th century, the Catholic Monarchs held court and launched their conquest

of Granada. Boabdil was imprisoned here in 1483, and for nearly 300 years the Alcázar served as the Inquisition's base. ✉ *Pl. Campo Santo de los Mártires, San Basilio* ☎ *957/421015* 💶 *€1.90, free Fri.* ⏲ *Apr.–Sept., Tues.–Sat. 10–2 and 6–8, Sun. 9:30–3; Oct.–Mar., Tues.–Sat. 10–2 and 4:30–6:30, Sun. 9:30–2:30.*

30 **Calleja de las Flores.** You'd be hard pressed to find prettier patios than those along this tiny street, just a few yards off the northeastern corner of the Mezquita. Patios, many with ceramics, foliage, and iron grilles, are key to Córdoba's architecture, at least in the old quarter, where life is lived behind sturdy white walls—a legacy of the Moors, who honored both the sanctity of the home and the need to shut out the fierce summer sun. Between the second and the third week of May, right after the **Crosses Competition,** Córdoba throws a **Patio Festival,** during which private patios are filled with flowers, opened to the public and judged in a municipal competition. Córdoba's council publishes a map with an itinerary of the best patios in town. Note that most of the patios are only open in the late afternoon during the week and all day on weekends.

45 **Jardín Botánico** (Botanical Garden). Across from Córdoba's modest zoo is its modern botanical garden, with both outdoor spaces—including a section devoted to aromatic herbs—and greenhouses full of interesting plants from South America and the Canary Islands. The **Museo de Etnobotánica** explores humans' relationships with the plant world. ✉ *Avda. del Zoológico, Parque Zoológico* ☎ *957/200018* 💶 *€1.80* ⏲ *Tues.–Sun. 10:30–2:30 and 4:30–6:30 (5:30–7:30 in summer).*

31 **Judería.** Córdoba's medieval Jewish Quarter is its most photogenic warren, a fascinating labyrinth of narrow streets and alleyways lined with ancient white houses. Alas, the streets around the Mezquita leading up to the Judería have a few too many tourist shops selling the same souvenirs.

Fodor's Choice ★

need a break?

The lively **Plaza Juda Levi** at the heart of the Judería is great for indulging in a little people watching. Sit outside here with a drink or, better still, an ice cream from Helados Juda Levi.

29 **Mezquita** (Mosque). Built between the 8th and 10th centuries, Córdoba's mosque is one of the earliest and most transportingly beautiful examples of Spanish Muslim architecture. The plain, crenulated walls of the outside do little to prepare you for the sublime beauty of the interior. As you enter through the **Puerta de las Palmas** (Door of the Palms), some 850 columns rise before you in a forest of jasper, marble, granite, and onyx. The pillars are topped by ornate capitals taken from the Visigothic church that was razed to make way for the mosque. Crowning these, red-and-white-stripe arches curve away into the dimness. The ceiling is carved of delicately tinted cedar. The Mezquita has served as a cathedral since 1236, but its origins as a mosque are clear. Built in four stages, it was founded in 785 by Abd ar-Rahman I (756–88) on a site he bought from the Visigoth Christians. He pulled down their church and replaced it with a mosque, one-third the size of the present one, into which he incorporated marble pillars from earlier Roman and Visigothic shrines. Under Abd ar-Rahman II (822–52), the Mezquita held an original copy of the Koran and a bone from the arm of the prophet Mohammed and became a Muslim pilgrimage site second only to Mecca in importance.

Fodor's Choice ★

Al Hakam II (961–76) built the beautiful **Mihrab,** the Mezquita's greatest jewel. Make your way over to the **Qiblah,** the south-facing wall in which this sacred prayer niche was hollowed out. (Muslim law decrees that a Mihrab face east, toward Mecca, and that worshipers do likewise when they pray. Here, because of an error in calculation, the Mihrab faces more south than east. Al Hakam II spent hours agonizing over a means of correcting such a serious mistake, but he was persuaded by wise architects to let it be.) In front of the Mihrab is the **Maksoureh,** a kind of anteroom for the caliph and his court; its mosaics and plasterwork make it a masterpiece of Islamic art. The last addition to the mosque as such was completed around 987 by Al Mansur, who more than doubled its size.

After the Reconquest, the Christians left the Mezquita largely undisturbed, dedicating it to the Virgin Mary and using it as a place of Christian worship. The clerics did erect a wall closing off the mosque from its courtyard, which helped dim the interior and thus separate the house of worship from the world outside. In the 13th century, Christians had the **Capilla de Villaviciosa** built by Moorish craftsmen, its Mudéjar architecture blending with the lines of the mosque. Not so the heavy, incongruous baroque structure of the **cathedral,** sanctioned in the very heart of the mosque by Charles V in the 1520s. To the emperor's credit, he was supposedly horrified when he came to inspect the new construction, exclaiming to the architects, "To build something ordinary, you have destroyed something that was unique in the world" (not that this sentiment stopped him from tampering with the Alhambra, to build the Palacio Carlos V, or with Seville's Alcázar). Rest up and reflect in the **Patio de los Naranjos** (Orange Court), perfumed in springtime by orange blossoms. The **Puerta del Perdón** (Gate of Forgiveness), on the north wall, is the formal entrance to the mosque. The **Virgen de los Faroles** (Virgin of the Lanterns), a small statue in a niche along the north wall of the mosque, on Cardenal Herrero, is behind a lantern-hung grille, rather like a lady awaiting a serenade. The painting of the Virgin is by Julio Romero de Torres, an early 20th-century Córdoban artist. The **Torre del Alminar,** the minaret once used to summon the faithful to prayer, has a baroque belfry. ✉ *Torrijos and Cardenal Herrero, Judería* ☎ *957/470512* 🎫 *€6.50* ⏲ *Mon.–Sat. 10–5 (10–7 in summer), Sun. for morning mass and 2–5 (2–7 in summer).*

40 **Museo Arqueológico.** In the heart of the old quarter, the Museum of Archaeology has finds from Córdoba's varied cultural past. The ground floor has Roman statues, mosaics and artifacts, and ancient Iberian statues; the upper floor is devoted to Moorish art. By chance, the ruins of a Roman theater were discovered right next to the museum in 2000—have a look from the window just inside the entrance. Avoid exploring this area in the deserted siesta hours, when it's prime territory for muggers. Otherwise, the alleys and steps along Altos de Santa Ana make for great wandering. ✉ *Pl. Jerónimo Paez, Judería* ☎ *957/474011* 🎫 *€1.50, EU citizens free* ⏲ *Tues. 3–8, Wed.–Sat. 9–8, Sun. 9–3.*

41 **Museo de Bellas Artes.** Faced in deep pink, in a courtyard just off the Plaza del Potro, Córdoba's Museum of Fine Arts belongs to a former Hospital de la Caridad (Charity Hospice). It was founded by Ferdinand and Isabella, who twice received Columbus here. The collection includes paintings by Murillo, Valdés Leal, Zurbarán, Goya, and Sorolla. Across the courtyard from the entrance is a museum devoted to the early 20th-century Córdoban artist **Julio Romero de Torres** (admission €2.95; free Fri.; closed at lunchtime), who specialized in portraits of demure Andalusian temptresses and is regarded locally as something of a hero. ✉ *Off Pl. del Potro, San Francisco* ☎ *957/473345* 🎫 *€1.50, EU citizens free* ⏲ *Tues. 3–8, Wed.–Sat. 9–8, Sun. 9–3.*

39 **Museo Diocesano.** Housed in the former Bishop's Palace, facing the mosque, the Diocesan Museum is devoted to religious art, with illustrated prayer books, tapestries, paintings (including some of Julio Romero de Torres's tamer works), and sculpture. The medieval wood sculptures are especially interesting. ✉ *Torrijos 12, Judería* ☎ *957/496085* 🎫 *€1.20* ⏲ *Weekdays 9:30–1:30 and 3:30–5:30, Sat. 9:30–1:30 in winter; weekdays 9:30–3, Sat. 9:30–1:30 in summer.*

need a break?

Wander over to the **Plaza de las Tendillas,** which you'll find halfway between the Mezquita and Plaza Colón. The terraces of the Café Boston and Café Siena are both nice places to relax with a coffee when the weather is warm.

32 **Museo Taurino** (Museum of Bullfighting). This museum on the Plaza Maimónides (or Plaza de las Bulas) is in two adjoining mansions. Whatever your thoughts on bullfighting, it's worth a visit, as much for the chance to see a restored mansion as for the posters, Art Nouveau paintings, and memorabilia of famous Córdoban bullfighters. ✉ *Pl. Maimónides, Judería* ☎ *957/201056* 🎫 *€2.95, free Fri.* ⏲ *Tues.–Sat. 10–2 and 4:30–6:30 (6–8 in summer), Sun. 9:30–2:30.*

44 **Palacio de los Marqueses de Viana.** This 17th-century palace is one of Córdoba's most splendid aristocratic homes. Also known as the **Museo de los Patios,** it contains 12 interior patios, each one different; the patios and gardens are planted with cypresses, orange trees, and myrtles. Inside the building are a carriage museum, a library, embossed leather wall hangings, filigree silver, and grand galleries and staircases. ✉ *Pl. Don Gomé, Barrio de los Toreros* ☎ *957/496741* 🎫 *€3, tour of patios and interior €6* ⏲ *June–Sept., Thurs.–Tues. 9–2; Oct.–May, weekdays 10–1 and 4–6, Sat. 10–1.*

42 **Plaza de los Dolores.** This small square north of Plaza San Miguel is surrounded by the 17th-century Convento de Capuchinos. The square is where you feel most deeply the city's languid pace. In its center, a statue of **Cristo de los Faroles** (Christ of the Lanterns) stands amid eight lanterns hanging from twisted, wrought-iron brackets. ✉ *Centro.*

43 **Plaza Santa Marina de las Aguas.** At the edge of the **Barrio de los Toreros,** a quarter where many of Córdoba's famous bullfighters were born and raised, stands a statue of the famous bullfighter Manolete. Not far from here, on the Plaza de la Lagunilla, is a bust of Manolete. ✉ *Barrio de los Toreros.*

35 **Puerta de Almodóvar.** Outside this old Moorish gate is a statue of **Seneca,** the Córdoban-born philosopher who rose to prominence in Nero's court in Rome and who committed suicide on his emperor's command. It lies at the top of the narrow and colorful Calle San Felipe. ✉ *Judería.*

36 **San Nicolás de Villa.** This classically dark Spanish church displays the Mudéjar style of Islamic decoration and art forms. Córdoba's well-kept city park, the **Jardínes de la Victoria,** with tile benches and manicured bushes, is just a block west of here. ✉ *C. San Felipe, Centro.*

34 **Synagogue.** This synagogue is the only Jewish temple in Andalusia to survive the expulsion and inquisition of the Jews in 1492 and one of only three ancient synagogues left in all of Spain (the other two are in Toledo). Though it's no longer in use as a place of worship, it is a treasured symbol for Spain's modern Jewish communities. The outside is plain, but inside is some exquisite Mudéjar stucco tracery—look for the fine plant motifs and the Hebrew inscription stating that the synagogue

was built in 1315. The women's gallery, not open for visits, still stands, and in the east wall is the arch where the sacred scrolls of the Torah were kept. ✉ *C. Judíos, Judería* ☎ *957/202928* 🎟 *€.50, EU citizens free* ⏲ *Tues.–Sat. 10–1:30 and 3:30–5:30, Sun. 10–1:30.*

38 **Torre de la Calahorra.** The tower on the far side of the Puente Romano (Roman Bridge) was built in 1369 to guard the entrance to Córdoba. It now houses the **Museo Vivo de Al-Andalus** (Museum of Al-Andalus), with films and audiovisual guides (in English) on Córdoba's history. Climb the narrow staircase to the top of the tower for the view of the Roman bridge and city on the other side of the Guadalquivir. ✉ *Avda. de la Confederación, Sector Sur* ☎ *957/293929* 🎟 *€3.60, €4.80 with audiovisual show* ⏲ *May–Sept., daily 10–2 and 4:30–8:30; Oct.–Apr., daily 10–6. Last tour 1 hr before closing.*

33 **Zoco.** *Zoco* is the Spanish word for the Arab souk, the one-time function of this courtyard near the synagogue. It now hosts a daily crafts market, where you can see artisans at work, and evening flamenco in summer. ✉ *Judíos 5, Judería* ☎ *957/204033* 🎟 *Free.*

Where to Stay & Eat

$$$–$$$$ Fodor's Choice ★ ✕ **El Caballo Rojo.** This is one of the most famous traditional restaurants in Andalusia, frequented by royalty and society folk. The interior resembles a cool, leafy Andalusian patio and the elegant dining room is furnished with stained glass, dark wood, and gleaming marble. The menu mixes traditional specialties, such as *rabo de toro* (oxtail stew) and *salmorejo* (a thicker version of gazpacho), with dishes inspired by Córdoba's Moorish and Jewish heritage, such as *alboronia* (a cold salad of stewed vegetables flavored with honey, saffron, and aniseed), *cordero a la miel* (lamb roasted with honey), and *rape mozárabe* (grilled monkfish with Arab spices). ✉ *Cardenal Herrero 28, Judería* ☎ *957/478001* 💳 *AE, DC, MC, V.*

★ $$$ ✕ **Bodegas Campos.** A block east of the Plaza del Potro, this restaurant is the epitome of all that is great about Andalusian cuisine and service, in the unbeatable surroundings of a traditional old wine cellar. The dining rooms are in a warren of barrel-heavy dining rooms and leafy courtyards. Regional dishes include *ensalada de bacalao y naranja* (salad of salt cod and orange with olive oil) and *solomillo al oloroso con foie y setas* (sirloin with Jerez's wine, foie, and mushroom). ✉ *Los Lineros 32, San Pedro* ☎ *957/497643* 💳 *AE, MC, V* ⏲ *No dinner Sun.*

★ $$$ ✕ **El Churrasco.** The name suggests grilled meat, but this restaurant in the heart of the Judería serves much more than that. The colorful bar is an ideal place for tapas, the grilled fish is supremely fresh, *and* the steak is the best in town. There's alfresco dining on the inner patio, and a staff that functions with pinpoint precision. In a separate house two doors away is the restaurant's wine cellar, which is also a small museum; if you're interested, ask your waiter to take you there before or after your meal. ✉ *Romero 16, Judería* ☎ *957/290819* 💳 *AE, DC, MC, V* ⏲ *Closed Aug.*

$$$ ✕ **La Almudaina.** This attractive restaurant is in a 16th-century house across the square from the Alcázar gardens, at the entrance to the Judería. The cellar hides both an Andalusian patio topped with a stained-glass cupola and a *mesón bodega* (wine cellar). The menu might include *calabacín con salsa de carabineros* (squash with prawn sauce), *lubina con salteado de verduritas* (sea bass with sautéed vegetables), or *lomo de venado en salsa de setas* (venison in wild-mushroom sauce). ✉ *Campo Santo de los Mártires 1, Judería* ☎ *957/474342* 💳 *AE, DC, MC, V* ⏲ *No dinner Sun.*

$$–$$$ ✕ **El Blasón.** In an old inn one block west of Avenida Gran Capitán, the Moorish-style entrance bar leads onto a patio enclosed by ivy-covered walls. Downstairs there is a lounge with a red tile ceiling and old polished clay plates on the walls. Upstairs are two elegant dining rooms where blue walls, white silk curtains, and candelabras evoke early 19th-century luxury. The menu includes *salmón fresco al cava* (fresh salmon in cava) and *muslos de pato al vino dulce* (leg of duck in sweet wine). ✉ *José Zorrilla 11, Centro* ☎ *957/480625* 💳 *AE, DC, MC, V.*

$$ ✕ **Casa Pepe de la Judería.** This three-floor labyrinth of neat rooms is just around the corner from the mosque, toward the Judería. In summer (May–October) the rooftop opens for barbecues, and there is live Spanish guitar music most nights; in winter the tables on the patio are individually heated with coal. There is a full selection of tapas and house specialties, such as *presa de paletilla ibérica* (pork shoulder fillet). The restaurant also has a fixed-price menu. ✉ *Romero 1, off Deanes, Judería* ☎ *957/200744* 🌐 *www.casapepedelajuderia.com* 💳 *AE, DC, MC, V.*

$–$$ ✕ **Federación de Peñas Cordobesas.** You'll find this popular restaurant on one of the old quarter's main thoroughfares, halfway between the mosque and the Plaza Tendillas. You can eat inside or at one of several tables around the fountain in the spacious courtyard, surrounded by horseshoe arches. The food is traditional Spanish fare, and there are several set menus at attractive prices. ✉ *Conde y Luque 8, Judería* ☎ *957/475427* 💳 *MC, V* ⊙ *Closed Wed.*

$–$$ ✕ **Posada de Vallina.** The innovative young chef here turns out such specialties as *berenjenas al vermouth y arroz griego* (eggplant with vermouth and Greek rice) and the *perol de almejas con espinacas* (pot of clams with spinach). Facing the south wall of the Mezquita, the restaurant is in the airy inner patio of a small and comfortable hotel, underneath the balconies and gallery of the first floor. The building dates back an awesome 1,600 years, with Roman columns and an ancient well to prove it. ✉ *Corregidor Luis de la Cerda 83, Judería* ☎ *957/498750* 💳 *AE, DC, MC, V.*

$ ✕ **Paseo la Ribera.** With plenty of choices and a self-service buffet, this is just the place for fussy families. There's even a kiddie menu with either Spanish or international food (including spaghetti or pizza). You can dine in the brick-and-beam interior or alfresco on the *tipico* patio outside. Other dishes include paella, *cuscus de cordero* (lamb couscous), and *lomo con champiñon* (pork loin with mushrooms). ✉ *Plaza Cruz del Rastro 3 Judería* ☎ *957/471530* 💳 *MC, V* ⊙ *Closed Wed.*

¢–$ ✕ **Taberna Plateros.** This place dates from the 17th century. A large patio restaurant leads to more rooms and the traditional marble bar, where blue-collar types and businessmen meet. Photographs of late local bullfighter Manolete line the walls, and the patio is decorated with giddily patterned tiles and bricks. The food is solid homestyle cooking, and the starters are meals in themselves. ✉ *San Francisco 6, San Pedro* ☎ *957/470042* 💳 *No credit cards* ⊙ *Closed Sun. and Mon.*

$$$ Fodor's Choice ★ 🏨 **Amistad Córdoba.** This stylish hotel is built around two former 18th-century mansions that look out on the Plaza de Maimónides in the heart of the Judería. (You can also enter through the old Moorish walls on Calle Cairuán.) It has a cobblestone Mudéjar courtyard, carved-wood ceilings, and a plush lounge area; the newer wing is done in blues and grays and Norwegian wood. Guest rooms are large and comfortable. ✉ *Pl. de Maimónides 3, Judería, 14004* ☎ *957/420335* 📠 *957/420365* 🌐 *www.nh-hoteles.com* 🛏 *84 rooms* 👍 *Restaurant, room service, bar, in-room data ports, minibars, cable TV, laundry service, parking (fee)* 💳 *AE, DC, MC, V.*

$$$ **Conquistador.** This contemporary, Andalusian-Moorish style hotel next to the Mezquita makes good use of ceramic tiles and inlaid marquetry in the bar and public rooms. The reception area overlooks a colonnaded patio, fountain, and small enclosed garden. Rooms are comfortable, elegant, and classically Andalusian; those at the front have small balconies overlooking the mosque, which is floodlit at night. ✉ *Magistral González Francés 17, Judería, 14003* ☎ *957/481102 or 957/481411* 📠 *957/474677* 🌐 *www.hotel-conquistador.com* *99 rooms, 3 suites* *Room service, bar, minibars, cable TV with movies, parking (fee)* 💳 *AE, DC, MC, V.*

$$$ **Maimónides.** The hotel's entrance opens into a colonnaded sand-color hall with tile floors and a remarkable *mocárabe* (ornamental wood sculpture) overlooking the front desk. Outside there's a small patio with wrought-iron tables and chairs. Rooms and bathrooms have marble floors and are decorated in light tones. Some of the rooms make you feel like you're so close to the Mezquita that you can touch it. ✉ *Torrijos 4, Judería, 14003* ☎📠 *957/471500* 🌐 *www.hotel-maimonides.com* *82 rooms* *Restaurant, minibars, cable TV* 💳 *MC, V.*

$$$ **Parador de Córdoba.** This modern parador is set in a peaceful, leafy garden on the slopes of the Sierra de Córdoba, 5 km (3 mi) north of town. Rooms are sunny, with wood or wicker furnishings, and the pricier ones have balconies overlooking the garden or facing Córdoba. ✉ *Avda. de la Arruzafa, El Brillante, 14012* ☎ *957/275900* 📠 *957/280409* 🌐 *www.parador.es* *89 rooms, 5 suites* *Restaurant, room service, minibars, cable TV, tennis court, pool* 💳 *AE, DC, MC, V.*

$$ **Albucasis.** Tucked away in the heart of the old quarter is the friendly, family-run Albucasis. The air-conditioned rooms are spotless, with marble floors and green-tile bathrooms. Doubles overlook the pretty patio and have a limited view of the Torre del Alminar. Breakfast and drinks are served in the attractive reception area. ✉ *Buen Pastor 11, Judería, 14003* ☎📠 *957/478625* *15 rooms* *Bar* 💳 *MC, V* *Closed Jan.*

$$ **Mezquita.** Situated next to the mosque, this hotel is in a restored 16th-century home. Dappled with bronze sculptures on Andalusian themes, the public areas are filled with antiques collected by the owner. The best rooms face the interior patio, and one of them is what used to be the house's old chapel. Rooms have elegant dark wooden headboards and matching pink curtains and bedspreads. The only real drawback is the lack of parking. ✉ *Pl. Santa Catalina 1, Judería, 41003* ☎ *957/475585* 📠 *957/476219* *21 rooms* *Cable TV* 💳 *MC, V.*

$ **Maestre.** Rooms here overlook a gracious inner courtyard framed by arches. The Castilian-style furniture, gleaming marble, and quality oil paintings add a touch of elegance to a place that's an excellent value. The hotel is around the corner from the Plaza del Potro. Management also runs an even cheaper lodging, the Hostal Maestre, and two types of self-catered apartments down the street; the top of the lot, Apartamentos el Potro, are large and clean and offer one of the best deals in town. ✉ *Romero Barros 4–6, San Pedro, 14003* ☎ *957/472410* 📠 *957/475395* 🌐 *www.hotelmaestre.com* *26 rooms* *Parking (fee)* 💳 *AE, MC, V.*

¢–$ **Los Arcos.** Tucked into a quiet side street, this hotel has rooms that are basic, cool, and comfortable. There is a traditional tile patio with plenty of sit-down space, surrounded by colorful plants and greenery. All the rooms have en-suite bathrooms and there are two lounges with TV (Spanish only) in the unlikely event of free time. ✉ *Romero Barros 14, San Pedro, 14003* ☎ *957/485643* 📠 *957/486011* *17* 💳 *No credit cards.*

¢ **Hostal Deanes.** This typical Córdoban private residence turned hostel has plenty of old-fashioned charm. A narrow tapas bar in front has impressive (if indigestible) sounding specials, like thistles in almond sauce, while photos of local bullfighters adorn the walls. The large central patio has lived-in appeal and the rooms are simple and far enough from the street to be quiet, despite the location in the center of town. ✉ *Deanes 6, Judería, 14003* ☎ *957/293744* *5 rooms* *No room TVs* *No credit cards.*

Nightlife & the Arts

During the **Patio Festival**, on the second and third weeks of May, the city is invaded by flamenco dancers and singers. The **Festival de Córdoba-Guitarra** attracts Spanish and international guitarists for more than two weeks of great music in July, and orchestras perform in the Alcázar's garden on Sunday throughout the summer. The **Feria de Mayo** (the last week of May) draws popular performers to the city. Córdoba locals hang out mostly in the areas of Ciudad Jardín—the old university area—Plaza de las Tendillas, and the top section of the Avenida Gran Capitán. **Café Málaga** (✉ Málaga 3, Centro), a block away from Plaza de las Tendillas, is a laid-back hangout. **Tetería** (✉ Buen Pastor 13, Judería) is a beautiful place for tea with a courtyard, side rooms filled with cushions, and a shop selling Moroccan clothing, just a few blocks away from the Mezquita. It closes at midnight. **Sojo** (✉ Benito Pérez Galdós 3, off Avenida del Gran Capitán, Centro ☎ 957/487211 ✉ José Martorell 12, Judería) has a trendy crowd. The branch in the Judería has DJs on weekends. **O'Donoghue's** (✉ Gran Capitán 38, Centro ☎ 957/481678) is an Irish pub favored by locals. For some of the best views of Córdoba, drop by **Hotel Hesperia** (✉ Avda. de la Confederación 1, Sector Sur), across the River Guadalquivir, almost facing the mezquita. The hotel has a rooftop bar, open only in summer. Córdoba's most popular flamenco club, the year-round **Tablao Cardenal** (✉ Torrijos 10, Judería ☎ 957/483320), facing the Mezquita, is worth the trip just to see the courtyard of the 16th-century building that was Córdoba's first hospital. Admission is €18. **Mesón la Bulería** (✉ Pedro López 3 Judería ☎ 957/483839) stages flamenco shows between Easter and September. Flamenco is performed in the **Zoco** (✉ off C. Judíos, Judería ☎ 957/483839) on summer evenings. See concerts, ballets, and plays year-round in the **Gran Teatro** (✉ Gran Capitán 3, Centro ☎ 957/480237).

Shopping

Córdoba's main shopping district is around Avenida Gran Capitán, Ronda de los Tejares, and the streets leading away from Plaza Tendillas. **Artesanía Andaluza** (✉ Tomás Conde 3), near the Museo Taurino, sells Córdoban crafts, including fine embossed leather (a legacy of the Moors) and jewelry made of filigree silver from the mines of the Sierra Morena. Córdoba's artisans sell their crafts in the **Zoco** (✉ C. Judíos, opposite synagogue); note that many stalls are open May–September only. **Meryam** (✉ Calleja de las Flores 2 ☎ 957/475902) is one of Córdoba's best workshops for embossed leather.

Medina Azahara

46 *8 km (5 mi) west of Córdoba on the C431.*

The ruins and partial reconstruction of the Muslim palace Medina Azahara (sometimes spelled Madinat Al-Zahra) are well worth a detour. Begun in 936, Medina Azahara was built by Abd ar-Rahman III for his favorite concubine, az-Zahra. Historians say it took 10,000 men, 2,600 mules, and 400 camels 25 years to erect this fantasy of 4,300 columns in dazzling pink, green, and white marble and jasper brought from Carthage. Here, on three terraces, stood a palace, a mosque, luxurious baths, fragrant gardens, fishponds, an aviary, and a zoo. In 1013 the place was sacked and destroyed by Berber mercenaries. In 1944 the Royal Apartments were rediscovered, and the Throne Room was carefully reconstructed. The outline of the mosque has also been excavated. The only covered part of the site is the Salon de Abd Al Rahman III; the rest is a sprawl of foundations, defense walls, and arches that hint at the splendor of the original city-palace. ✉ *Off C431; follow signs en route to Almodóvar del Río* ☎ *957/329130* *€1.50, EU citizens free* ⏲ *May–Sept., Tues.–Sat. 10–2 and 6–8:30, Sun. 10–2; Oct.–Apr., Tues.–Sat. 10–2 and 4–6:30, Sun. 10–2.*

off the beaten path

ALMODÓVAR DEL RÍO – If you're driving, continue to Almodóvar del Río, a busy and attractive agricultural town 18 km (11 mi) farther along C431. Just beyond the town a restored castle towers dramatically over the countryside, dominating the view for miles in all directions. You can drive to the castle or, alternatively, simply walk here from the town center.

Montilla

47 *46 km (28 mi) south of Córdoba.*

Heading south from Córdoba to Málaga through hills ablaze with sunflowers in early summer, you reach the Montilla-Morilés vineyards of the Córdoban campiña. Every fall, 47,000 acres' worth of Pedro Ximénez grapes are crushed here to produce the region's rich Montilla wines, not unlike sherry except that, because the local grapes contain so much sugar (transformed into alcohol during fermentation), they are not fortified with the addition of extra alcohol. For this reason—or so the locals claim—Montilla wines do not give you a hangover. On the outskirts of town, coopers' shops produce barrels of various sizes, some small enough to serve as creative souvenirs. The oldest winery, in the town of Montilla itself, is **Alvear** (✉ Avda. María Auxiliadora 1 ☎ 957/664014), founded in 1729.

Where to Stay & Eat

★ $–$$ ✕ **Las Camachas.** The best-known restaurant in southern Córdoba province is in an Andalusian-style hacienda outside Montilla—near the main road toward Málaga. Start with tapas in the attractive, tile bar, and then move to one of six dining rooms. Regional specialties include alcachofas *al Montilla* (braised in Montilla wine), salmorejo, perdiz *campiña* (country-style), and cordero a la miel *de Jara* (from Jara). You can also buy local wines here. ✉ *Antigua Carretera Córdoba–Málaga* ☎ *957/650004* ▭ *AE, DC, MC, V.*

$$ **Don Gonzalo.** Just 2 km (1 mi) south of Montilla is one of Andalusia's better roadside hostelries. The wood-beam common areas have a mixture of decorative elements; note the elephant tusks flanking the TV in the lounge. The clay-tile rooms are large and comfortable; some look onto the road, others onto the garden and pool. Ask to see the wine cellar. ✉ *Ctra. Córdoba–Málaga, Km 47, 14550* ☎ *957/650658* 🖷 *957/650666* 🌐 *www.hoteldongonzalo.com* *35 rooms, 1 suite* *Restaurant, cable TV, tennis court, pool, bar, dance club, meeting rooms* ▭ *AE, MC, V.*

La Subbética

48 *Priego de Córdoba: 103 km (64 mi) southeast of Córdoba.*

In the southeastern corner of Córdoba's province lies a largely undiscovered cluster of villages and small towns known to locals as the Subbética and protected as a nature park. You'll need a car to explore this area, and in some places you'll find the roads rather rough. For general information or hiking advice, contact the **Mancomunidad de la Subbética** (✉ Ctra. Carcabuey–Zagrilla, Km 5.75, Carcabuey ☎ 957/704106 🌐 www.subbetica.org). You will find an exit to the small road on the right side of the road from Lucena to Priego, once you pass the detour to Carcabuey. At the southern tip of the province, southeast of Lucena, C334 crosses the **Embalse de Iznájar** (Iznájar Reservoir) amid spectacular scenery. On C334 halfway between Lucena and the reservoir, in **Rute,** you can sample the potent *anís* (anise) liqueur for which this small, whitewashed town is famous. In **Lucena,** called the city of the three cultures (Christian, Arab, and Jewish), is the Torre del Moral, where Boabdil was imprisoned in 1483 after launching an unsuccessful attack on the Christians, and the Parroquia de San Mateo, a remarkable Renaissance-Gothic small cathedral. Today the town makes furniture and brass and copper pots.

The jewel of this area is **Priego de Córdoba,** a town of 14,000 at the foot of Mt. Tinosa. (From Lucena, head north 5 km [3 mi] on C334 to Cabra, and turn right, or east, on C340; after 32 km [20 mi], you'll reach Priego.) Wander down Calle del Río opposite the town hall to see 18th-century mansions, once the homes of silk merchants. At the end of the street is the Fuente del Rey (King's Fountain), with some 130 water jets, built in 1803. Don't miss the lavish baroque churches of La Asunción and La Aurora or the Barrio de la Villa, an old Moorish quarter with a maze of narrow streets of white-wall buildings. **Zuheros,** at the northern edge of the Subbética, is a jewel of a mountain village. Within the rocky mountain face that towers over the town is the **Cueva de los Murciélagos** (Cave of the Bats; ☎ 957/694545), which you can explore by appointment. **Baena,** outside the boundaries of Subbética and surrounded by chalk fields producing top-quality olives, is an old town of narrow streets, whitewashed houses, ancient mansions, and churches clustered beneath Moorish battlements. The family behind one of Spain's best-known olive-oil brands, **Nuñez del Prado** (✉ Avda. de Cervantes 14 ☎ 957/670141), offers free tours of its mill, particularly interesting during harvest season (November–December). It's open weekdays 9–1:30 and 4–7. The walk reveals a cellar containing old clay storage jars, each dating from 1795 and holding 525 gallons.

Where to Stay

$$ **Santo Domingo.** This dignified, stone-face 17th-century convent makes for a pleasant stay in Lucena. The lobby opens onto a large interior courtyard with a fountain. Rooms are stylishly dressed in different colors. Exterior rooms can be noisy. ✉ *El Agua 12, Lucena 14900* ☎ *957/511100* 🖷 *957/516295* 🌐 *www.husa.es* *28 rooms, 2 suites* *Restaurant, cable TV, parking (fee)* 💳 *AE, DC, MC, V.*

$$ **Villa Turística de Priego.** You'll find this gleaming-white complex right in the heart of the Subbética nature park—near Zagrilla, 6 km (4 mi) from Priego de Córdoba. Clustered to form an Andalusian pueblo, the semidetached units sleep between two and six people each. Some have a terrace or balcony. ✉ *Aldea de Zagrilla, 14816* ☎ *957/703503* 🖷 *957/703573* 🌐 *www.villaturisticadepriego.com* *52 units* *Restaurant, some kitchenettes, pool, bar* 💳 *AE, DC, MC, V* ⏲ *Closed Jan.*

$ **Zuhayra.** On a narrow street in Zuheros, this delightful small hotel has comfortable large rooms with views over the village rooftops to the valley below. ✉ *C. Mirador 10, Zuheros 14870* ☎ *957/694693* 🖷 *957/694702* *18 rooms* *Restaurant, bar* 💳 *AE, DC, MC, V.*

EASTERN ANDALUSIA A TO Z

To research prices, get advice from other travelers, and book travel arrangements, visit www.fodors.com.

AIR TRAVEL

CARRIERS Aviaco has three daily flights to Granada from Madrid and Barcelona. Malaga's International airport is the best alternative for people flying from abroad.

AIRPORTS

TRANSFERS Granada's airport is 18 km (11 mi) west of the city. J. González buses (€3) run between the city center and the airport, leaving from the Palacio de Congresos, and making a few other stops along the way to the city. Times are listed at the bus stop; service is reduced in winter. By taxi, which go by the meter and are more convenient as well as more expensive: expect to pay around €18 to the city center and €21 to the Alhambra. Córdoba has no airport; the closest is in Seville.

Airport Information **Aeropuerto de Granada** ☎ 958/245200.

Shuttle Buses **J. González** ☎ 958/131309.

BIKE TRAVEL

Córdoba La Llana rents bikes and leads rides around Córdoba and out to Medina Azahara. For information on bike routes check with the tourist office (which also has information on tours around the city) at Corral del Carbón.

Córdoba La Llana en Bici ✉ C. Lucano 20, Córdoba ☎ 639/425884 🌐 www.cordobaenbici.com.

BUS TRAVEL

If you're not driving, buses are the best way to get around this region. They serve most small towns and villages, and their trips between major cities are generally faster and more frequent than those of trains. If you're headed for the Alpujarras, check bus schedules carefully with Granada's tourist office and the Alsina Gräells bus line before you set off. Buses serve Córdoba as well, but the various routes are covered by myriad companies. For schedules and details, go to Córdoba's bus station—next to the AVE (high-speed train) station—and inquire with the appropriate company. Only Ramírez has an office in town. Alsina Gräells connects Córdoba with Granada, Seville, Cádiz, Badajoz, and Málaga; Ureña goes to Seville and Jaén; Secorbus runs north to Madrid. Ramírez serves small towns near Córdoba. From Granada, Alsina Gräells serves Córdoba, Jaén, Seville, Cádiz, Marbella, Motril, Algeciras, Almería, Guadix, and Madrid. Granada's bus station is on the highway to Jaén.

Córdoba Bus Information **Bus station** ✉ Glorieta de las Tres Culturas ☎ 957/404040. **Alsina Gräells** ☎ 957/278100. **Ramírez** ✉ Avda. Torrecilla s/n ☎ 957/422106. **Secorbus** ☎ 902/229292. **Ureña** ☎ 957/404558.

Granada Bus Information **Bus station** ✉ Ctra. Jaén ☎ 958/185010. **Alsina Gräells** ☎ 958/185480.

BUS TRAVEL WITHIN GRANADA & CÓRDOBA

Córdoba and Granada have extensive public bus networks. The average waiting time usually does not exceed 15 minutes.

FARES & SCHEDULES Normally, buses in both cities start running at around 6:30–7 AM and stop around 11 PM in Granada, midnight in Córdoba. However, schedules can be slightly reduced for some lines. In Granada, you can buy 6- and 21-trip discount passes on the buses and 10-trip passes at the newsstands. In Córdoba, newsstands and the bus office at Plaza de Colón sell 10-trip discount tickets. The single-trip fares are €.85 in Granada and €.80 in Córdoba. Rober and Aucorsa manage the bus networks in Granada and Córdoba, respectively.

Rober ☎ 900/710900. **Aucorsa** ☎ 957/764676.

CAR RENTAL

Avis, Europcar, and Hertz have offices at Granada Aeropuerto.

Major Agencies Avis ✉ Aeropuerto de Granada ☎ 958/446455. **Europcar** ✉ Aeropuerto de Granada ☎ 958/245275. **Hertz** ✉ Aeropuerto de Granada ☎ 958/204454.

Local Agency Autos Fortuna ✉ Infanta Beatriz 2, Camino de Ronda, Granada ☎ 958/260254 📠 958/2602564.

CAR TRAVEL

Most roads in this region are smooth, and driving is one of the most enjoyable ways to see the countryside. Be prepared, however, for serious parking problems. Most of Córdoba's hotels are ensconced in a labyrinth of narrow streets that can be a nightmare to negotiate, even with a small car. A good bet for Córdoba parking is in the underground lot near the Campo Santo de los Mártires, west of the Judería; or try to park in that general area or across the river, on Avenida de la Confederación and its nearby streets. In both cities, Córdoba and Granada (particularly the latter), parking problems are exacerbated by the substantial threat of break-ins. It's best to park in an underground lot. In Córdoba, all the sights are within walking distance of one another; in Granada, you can take a cab or shuttle-bus from the center to the Alhambra or Albaicín. Small towns, too, date from Moorish times and are ill suited to present-day traffic; park on the outskirts and walk.

DISABILITIES & ACCESSIBILITY

Although four- and five-star hotels throughout the province are equipped to handle people with disabilities, those with disabilities may still have difficulty finding budget accommodation and navigating some of the sights in Andalusia.

In Granada, the palacios and most of the gardens of the Alhambra are wheelchair accessible. At the ticket office there are wheelchairs available upon request. The cathedral and the Royal Chapel do not meet disability standards. In Córdoba, the Mosque and the Museo Arqueológico are accessible to people with disabilities, whereas the Alcázar and the Sinagogue—where just one step needs to be overcome—may pose more difficulties. Medina Azahara, the archaeological site outside of Córdoba, has a special route for people with disabilities—but it nonetheless requires accompaniment. In Jaén, those with disabilities will have to steer clear of the castle—only the Patio de Armas is accessible—and the Palacio of Villardompardo. Head instead to the cathedral and the Museo Provincial. In Úbeda, most of the churches allow wheelchair entry, including the Sacra Capilla del Salvador. In Baeza, the cathedral does not have a wheelchair ramp.

DISCOUNTS & DEALS

To ease the flow of people to some of the featured monuments (Alhambra, Generalife, cathedral, Capilla Real, Monasterio de San Jerónimo, and the interactive Science Park Museum) of the town, the Granada Council has introduced a City Pass. This gives you direct access (one visit only) to all those monuments without having to stop at the ticket office—and you save 30%. Moreover, the €18 pass includes 10 free trips on any of Granada's minibuses or city buses. The pass can be acquired at the Alhambra, Generalife, and Capilla Real ticket offices and must be used within a 7-day period. There is a 12% surcharge for advance booking.

Córdoba offers a more limited pass for €7.05 that grants access to the Alcázar, Museo Taurino, and the Museo Julio de Torres; it can be purchased at the ticket offices of any of the three sights.

EMERGENCIES

The **national emergency number** is ☎ 112; it does not yet directly cover all of Spain, but operators can redirect you if you provide them with additional information. Otherwise, you may call the **police** at ☎ 092 (local) or 091 (national). For an **ambulance,** dial ☎ 061. Córdoba's main hospitals, both with 24-hour emergency rooms, are the Reina Sofía and the private Cruz Roja. In Granada, two of the more prominent hospitals are the Hospital Clínico Universitario and the Hospital de Traumatología San Rafael, which specializes in trauma cases.

Hospitals **Reina Sofía** ✉ Ramón Menéndez Pidal, s/n ☎ 957/010903. **Cruz Roja** ✉ Paseo de la Victoria s/n ☎ 957/420666. **Hospital Clínico Universitario** ✉ Avda. de Doctor Oloriz, 16 ☎ 958/270200. **Hospital de Traumatología San Rafael** ✉ San Juan de Dios 19–29 ☎ 958/275700.

ENGLISH-LANGUAGE MEDIA

Bookstore **Librería Metro** ✉ C. Gracia 31, Granada ☎ 958/261565.

HOLIDAYS

Aside from national holidays and February 28 (the Day of Andalusia), all cities and villages have some local holidays. In Granada these are January 2 and Corpus Christi, which changes every year but is always around the middle of June; in Córdoba, September 8 (Nuestra Señora de Fuensanta) and October 24 (San Rafael); in Jaén, October 18 (San Lucas) and, alternating annually, June 11 (Virgen de la Capilla) or November 25 (Santa Catalina de Alejandría); in Úbeda, December 14 (San Juan de la Cruz); in Baeza, August 15 (Virgen de Santa María), September 7 (Fiesta de la Hiedra), November 30 (San Andrés) and, some years, May 15 (San Isidro). Local authorities may occasionally change these days.

LODGING

APARTMENT & VILLA RENTALS

The best bet for apartment housing outside the cities is rural housing, which is growing in popularity. Unfortunately, rural lodging in Andalusia, especially in the Alpujarras, isn't always up to the same standards as other regions of Spain. On the other hand, the Subbética region has some good rural properties. While you might find some rural housing bargains on your own, it's advisable to make reservations through an authorized agent to avoid unpleasant surprises.

Local Agents **Apartamentos Santa Ana** ✉ Puente Espinosa 2 Centro Granada ☎ 958/228130 or 647/774173 mobile. **Apartamentos Mariola** ✉ Camino de Ronda 193, Vellarejo, Granada ☎ 958/281111.

Local Agents, Rural Housing **Cegestur** ✉ Juan Jiménez Cuenca 33, Lucena ☎ 902/113480 🌐 www.cegestur.com. **Red Andaluza de Alojamiento Rural** ☎ 902/442233 🌐 www.raar.es. **Rustic Blue** ☎ 958/763381 🌐 www.rusticblue.com. **Ruralia** ☎ 902/107070 🌐 www.ruralia.com.

MAIL & SHIPPING

Córdoba's main post office—the only one open in the afternoons—is north of the mosque near the Plaza de las Tendillas, whereas the one in Granada is in the Plaza Real. Internet cafés with competitive prices are plentiful in both cities, especially Granada, which has a large student population.

SAFETY

In Córdoba, watch out for small groups of three teenage boys, known as jumpers. They are known to sneak up behind you, place an arm against your windpipe until you lose consciousness, and steal your money.

SPORTS & THE OUTDOORS

Based in the Alpujarras, Nevadensis leads guided tours of the region on foot, horseback, and mountain bike. In Granada, Sólo Aventura offers one- to seven-day outdoor sports—trekking, mountaineering, climbing, mountain biking, and other activities—around the Alpujarras, Sierra Nevada, and the rest of the province. Kayak Sur organizes kayaking and canoeing trips to the River Guadalfeo. Granada Romántica takes up to five people in balloon trips above the city and its surroundings. Quercus arranges jeep and horseback trips and special-interest nature tours. Excursiones Bujarkay leads guided hikes as well as horseback and four-wheel-drive tours.

Excursiones Bujarkay ☎ 953/721111 ⊕ www.guiasnativos.com. **Nevadensis** ✉ Pl. de la Libertad, Pampaneira ☎ 958/763127. **Quercus** ☎ 953/720115 ⊕ www.excursionesquercus.com. **Sólo Aventura** ✉ Pl. de la Romanilla 1 Centro, Granada ☎ 958/804937 ⊕ www.soloaventuragranada.com. **Kayak Sur** ✉ Arabial, Urbanizació Parque del Genil, Edificio Topacio, Sur, Granada ☎ 958/523118 ⊕ www.kayaksur.com. **Granada Romántica** ✉ Santa Ana 6 Albaicín, Granada ☎ 958/210127 ⊕ www.grupoalandalus.com/granadaromantica.html.

HORSEBACK RIDING

Horseback-riding tours, some with English-speaking guides, are offered in the villages of the Alpujarras, Sierra Nevada, and in the Sierra de Cazorla; Cabalgar Rutas Alternativas is one established Alpujarras agency. Contact the nearest tourist offices for more choices.

Cabalgar Rutas Alternativas ✉ Bubión, Alpujarras ☎ 958/763135. **Dallas Love** ✉ Ctra. de la Sierra Bubión, Alpujarras ☎ 958/763058.

TAXIS

Taxis can be hailed on the street in both Córdoba and Granada. In Córdoba you'll find taxi stations, or *paradas de taxis,* at Avenida de América near the Hotel Gran Capitán, at the corner of El Corte Inglés, and near the hotel Meliá, among other locations. In Granada there's a station in almost every major area. You can also phone Radio Taxi in Córdoba, Tele Radio Taxi or Asociación de Radio Taxi in Granada.

In both cities you will be charged by the meter; the minimum fare is about €3. Fares are based on the time of the day, and are higher at night and on public holidays. In Córdoba you will be charged an additional amount when taking a taxi at the train station, as well as for every piece of luggage you carry (this last is also applicable to Granada). At press time, those extra fares didn't exceed €.50. When in doubt, check the sticker of official fares found in taxi back windows. If you're dissatisfied with either the fare or the driver, remember to record the taxi's licence number.

Taxi Companies **Radio Taxi** ☎ 957/764444. **Tele Radio Taxi** ☎ 958/280654. **Asociació de Radio Taxi** ☎ 958/132323.

TOURS

Pullmantur and Julià Tours run numerous excursions to this region, which you can book through most travel agents, many hotels, or through the companies' Madrid and Costa del Sol offices. GranaVisión and Córdoba Visión offer both day- and nighttime tours, including an excursion to Medina Azahara. In Córdoba, you can hire an English-speaking guide for the mosque and synagogue through the Asociación Profesional de Informadores Turísticos. In Granada and Jaén—where they will also help you find local guides for Baeza and Úbeda—contact a multilingual guide through the Asociación Provincial de Guías. Artificis leads tours of Úbeda and Baeza. Pópulo is also a good company for touring Baeza.

Pullmantur ✉ Avda. Imperial, Torremolinos ☎ 952/384400. **Julià Tours** ✉ Gran Vía 68, Centro ☎ 91/559-9605 ⊕ www.juliatours.es. **Artificis** ✉ Juan Ruíz González 19, next to parador, Úbeda ☎ 953/758150. **Asociación Profesional de Informadores**

Turísticos ✉ Museo Diocesano, Torrijos 12, Judería, Córdoba ☎ 957/486997. **Asociación Provincial de Guías** ✉ Pl. Nueva 2, Albaicín, Granada ☎ 958/229936 ✉ Jaén ☎ 957/254442. **Córdoba Visión** ✉ Avda. de Doctor Fleming, Centro ☎ 957/231734. **GranaVisión** ✉ Reyes Católicos 47–49, Centro ☎ 958/535872, 902/330002 reservations. **Pópulo** ✉ Pl. de los Leones 1, Baeza ☎ 953/744370.

TRAIN TRAVEL

The wonderful, high-speed AVE connects Madrid with Córdoba in less than two hours. Train service from Córdoba to Granada and Jaén, however, is poor, and there is no service at all between Granada and Jaén. Both Córdoba and Jaén have trains to Linares-Baeza, but from there you must take a bus to Úbeda.

Train Information RENFE ☎ 902/240202.

VISITOR INFORMATION

The regional tourist offices in Granada and Córdoba will supply you with information, including free periodicals and city guides, some for a nominal free. The monthly magazines, *Welcome to Granada* and *What's On in Andalusia,* will clue you in about goings-on in the region. You may also want to ask Córdoba's and Granada's municipal tourist offices for maps of the *Ruta de Tabernas* or *Ruta de Tapas*, pointing out bars and tapas bars, respectively.

Regional Tourist Offices Córdoba ✉ Palacio de Exposiciones, Torrijos 10, Judería, next to mosque ☎ 957/471235. **Granada** ✉ Corral del Carbón, C. Mariana Pineda, Centro ☎ 958/225990.

Local Tourist Offices Baeza ✉ Pl. del Pópulo ☎ 953/740444. **Córdoba** ✉ Pl. Juda Levi, Judería ☎ 957/200522 ☎ 957/200277. **Granada** ✉ Pl. Mariana Pineda 10, Centro ☎ 958/247128. **Jaén** ✉ C. Maestra 13 ☎ 953/242624. **Úbeda** ✉ Palacio Marqués del Contadero, C. Baja del Marqués 4 ☎ 953/750897.

SEVILLE & WESTERN ANDALUSIA

12

FODOR'S CHOICE

Alfonso XIII, Mudéjar palace and hotel in Sevilla
Convento de Santa Paula, Sevilla
Doñana National Park
El Faro fishing-quarter restaurant, Cádiz
La Casa Grande town house hotel in Arcos de la Frontera
Museum of Fine Arts, Sevilla
Poncio restaurant in Sevilla
Royal Andalusian School of Equestrian Art, Jerez

HIGHLY RECOMMENDED

World headquarters for sherry: Jerez de la Frontera

RESTAURANTS
Egaña-Oriza, Sevilla
El Ventorrillo del Chato, Cádiz
Enrique Becerra, Sevilla
La Mesa Redonda, Jerez de la Frontera

HOTELS
Finca de la Silladilla, Jabugo
Hacienda Benazuza, Sanlúcar la Mayor
Hotel Amadeus, Sevilla
Los Seises, Sevilla
Monasterio de San Miguel, Puerto de Santa María
Parador Alcázar del Rey Don Pedro, Carmona
Parador Casa del Corregidor, Arcos de la Frontera
Royal Sherry Park, Jerez de la Frontera

SIGHTS
Arcos de la Frontera, a dramatic village overlooking a gorge
Barrio de Santa Cruz, Seville's ancient Jewish Quarter
Seville's Moorish Alcázar (fortress)

By Mark Little and Hilary Bunce

Updated by George Semler

ALL THE ROMANTIC IMAGES of Andalusia—and Spain in general—spring vividly to life in Seville, Spain's fourth-largest city. Fiestas, flamenco, bullfights, and colorfully painted houses are so tempting that many travelers spend their entire Andalusian time here—but don't; Western Andalusia holds many surprises, from the aristocratic towns and Roman ruins of Seville's *campiña* (fertile plains) to the farmlands, sandy coastline, and tree-clad sierras of the neighboring provinces of Cádiz and Huelva.

Predating Seville by a millennium, the ancient city of Cádiz sits like a worn but still-shining jewel at the tip of a sandy isthmus in an Atlantic bay. Stretching north from here is the gently sloping Marco de Jerez area, bordered by the towns of Jerez de la Frontera, Sanlúcar de Barrameda, and Puerto de Santa María—a land of bull ranches, prancing Andalusian horses, and one of the world's best-known wines, sherry, aged in cobweb-filled cellars that have barely changed in centuries. In the province of Huelva, across the Guadalquivir River from the sherry region, stretches Doñana National Park, where marshy wetlands alternate with pine forests and shifting sand dunes. Beyond the park are coastal towns that played key roles in modern Western history: Christopher Columbus set sail from these shores in 1492. To the north is the Sierra de Aracena where free-range Iberian pigs fatten in one of Andalusia's prettiest highland oak forests.

Today's Andalusian scenery is of fairly recent vintage. Flowing west at a sluggish pace from Jaén's Sierra Morena to the Atlantic Ocean, the mighty Guadalquivir River has shaped the landscape and history of southwestern Spain. Two thousand years ago, as the capricious river shifted course, it left the thriving Roman city of Itálica high and dry. As Itálica slid gradually into oblivion, nearby Hispalis—today's Seville—rose on the river's banks 11 km (7 mi) away. Seville's fortunes would continue to climb under the Moors, and again after its conquest by the Castilian Christians under King Ferdinand "the Saint" in the 13th century. During their reign the city acquired its cathedral—the largest Gothic building in the world—and its Moorish-inspired palace, the Alcázar.

With the discovery of the New World, Seville reached even dizzier heights of splendor, outshining Madrid in riches and culture as Spanish ships loaded with booty from the Americas sailed upriver past the Torre de Oro (Tower of Gold) and into Seville's port. Much of this treasure was siphoned off to pay for the Spanish throne's increasingly expensive foreign entanglements and bankers' debts, but enough was left over to fuel a cultural flowering and building bonanza that can still be seen today in Seville's lovely houses, courtyards, palaces, and monuments.

About the Restaurants

Spaniards drive for miles to sample the succulent seafood of Puerto de Santa María and Sanlúcar de Barrameda and to enjoy *fino* (a dry and light sherry from Jerez) and *manzanilla* (a dry and delicate Sanlúcar sherry with a hint of saltiness). Others come just to feast on tapas in Seville or Cádiz. The village of Jabugo, in Huelva, is famous for its cured ham from the free-ranging Ibérian pig. Note that many restaurants are closed on Sunday evenings, and several close for a month's vacation in August. Most restaurants and bars in this region offer a *menú del día,* mainly at lunchtime, which will include a starter, main course, sweet or coffee, bread, and wine or beer for between €8 and €12.

If time is short, two days will cover Seville. From there, you can wander Doñana National Park and visit coastal villages, or head south to sip sherry in Jerez de la Frontera, relax in the village of Arcos de la Frontera, and feast on seafood in Cádiz.

If you have **3 days**

Base yourself in **Seville** 1–32. On day one, visit the cathedral, the Giralda, and the nearby Alcázar, and walk through the Barrio de Santa Cruz. On day two, explore the Barrio de Macarena in the morning, starting at the Mercado de Feria and ending at the Museo de Bellas Artes. In the afternoon stroll in the Parque de María Luisa, the Plaza de América, and the Plaza de España. In the evening cross the Guadalquivir and visit the Barrio de Triana and the tapas bars of Calle Betis. Devote the next day to the ancient town of **Carmona** 33, with its Roman necropolis, and then the Roman ruins at **Itálica** 34 before returning to Seville.

If you have **5 days**

Follow the itinerary above for the first day and a half. On the afternoon of the second day, walk the Paseo de Colón by the river—to see the Maestranza Bullring and visit the Torre de Oro. On day three, wander the Parque de María Luisa, stopping at the Plaza de América and Plaza de España. When returning to the city center, look for the University of Seville, the former tobacco factory of *Carmen* fame. In the afternoon cross the Guadalquivir to explore the Barrio de Triana. On day four, head south to **Jerez de la Frontera** 43. If it's a Thursday, catch the spectacular horse show at the Royal Andalusian School of Equestrian Art. Spend your last night in **Puerto de Santa María** 46, and on your final day visit **Cádiz** 47 before heading back.

WHAT IT COSTS In Euros

	$$$$	$$$	$$	$	¢
AT DINNER	over €20	€15–€20	€10–€15	€6–€10	under €6

Prices are per person for a main course at dinner.

About the Hotels

Western Andalusia has four paradors, including converted palaces at Carmona and Arcos de la Frontera, both worth a special visit. The parador at Mazagón and the parador Hotel Atlántico, in Cádiz, are comfortable modern hotels. You can also stay at a converted monastery, in Puerto de Santa María, or on a private luxury ranch, near Arcos de la Frontera. Seville has grand old hotels, such as the Alfonso XIII and a number of former palaces converted into sumptuous hostelries. For top hotels during Seville's Holy Week or April Fair or Jerez's Horse Fair or Harvest Festival, book early—four to eight months in advance, though taking just-show-up potluck works fine for the lower end of the lodging food chain. To see Cádiz during Carnival, reserve months in advance. Prices in Seville's top hotels rise by at least half during Holy Week and the April Fair; the same applies in Jerez during the May and September ferias. Hotel prices fluctuate dramatically with the seasons—much more so than in most other parts of Spain—so inquire in advance and ask about discounts.

	WHAT IT COSTS In Euros				
	$$$$	$$$	$$	$	¢
FOR 2 PEOPLE	over €180	€100–€180	€60–€100	€40–€60	under €40

Prices are for two people in a standard double room in high season, excluding tax.

Exploring Seville & Western Andalusia

Although exploring the city of Seville is the main event here, there is also nearby Itálica, with its Roman ruins, as well as the farmland south of the Guadalquivir river known as La Campiña, along the *vega* (fertile river basin) of the Upper Guadalquivir. Huelva's Sierra de Aracena is an hour to the southwest, while the Doñana wetlands at the mouth of Guadalquivir offer a chance to explore some of the Iberian Peninsula's wildest country. Cádiz and the triangle formed by Jerez de la Frontera, El Puerto de Santa María, and Sanlucar de Barrameda offer culinary delights, beaches, Andalusian equestrian art, and flamenco dance and music, while Arcos de la Frontera is the gateway to the Sierra de Grazalema and the highlands.

Numbers in the text correspond to numbers in the margin and on the Andalusia: Seville & Western Andalusia and on the Seville maps.

Timing

Aside from timing your visit with a fiesta, spring and late fall are particularly nice, when the weather is warm but not unpleasantly hot. Winters are mild and uncrowded. Bear in mind that many museums and monuments are closed on Monday.

SEVILLE & ENVIRONS

Seville's whitewashed houses bright with bougainvillea, its ocher-color palaces, and its baroque facades have long enchanted both Sevillanos and travelers. This bustling city of almost 800,000 has a downside, however: traffic-choked streets, high unemployment, a notorious petty-crime rate, and at times the kind of impersonal treatment you won't find in smaller cities like Granada and Córdoba. But Seville's artistic heritage and its citizens' zest for life more than compensate for its disadvantages. If you want to venture out of Seville on a day trip, head to Carmona—the parador is perfect for a leisurely lunch—or Itálica.

Seville

1–32 *550 km (340 mi) southwest of Madrid, 220 km (140 mi) northwest of Málaga.*

Seville has a long and noble history. Conquered by the Romans in 205 BC, it gave the world two great emperors, Trajan and Hadrian. The Moors held Seville for more than 500 years and left it one of their greatest works of architecture, the much-loved Giralda tower. Saint King Ferdinand (Ferdinand III) lies enshrined in the glorious cathedral; and his rather less saintly descendant, Pedro the Cruel, builder of the Alcázar, is buried here as well. Seville is justly proud of its literary and artistic associations. The painters Diego Rodríguez de Silva Velázquez (1599–1660) and Bartolomé Estéban Murillo (1617–82) were sons of Seville, as were the poets Gustavo Adolfo Bécquer (1836–70), Antonio Machado (1875–1939), and Nobel prize winner Vicente Aleixandre (1898–1984). The tale of the ingenious knight of La Mancha was begun in a Seville jail—Don Quijote's creator, Miguel de Cervantes,

Bullfighting

In Seville is one of Spain's most celebrated bullrings: the Maestranza. Few *toreros* (bullfighters) gain nationwide recognition until they have fought in this "cathedral of bullfighting." The season runs from Easter until late October, but it peaks early on, when Seville's April Fair draws Spain's leading toreros for a string of daily fights.

Fiestas

Seville's Holy Week processions and April fair draw visitors worldwide. Many Seville attractions are closed during this time, especially on Holy Thursday and Good Friday. The Carnival in Cádiz is one of the best in the land. Folks also flock to the revelries of Jerez's May Horse Fair and September Harvest Festival. Cádiz celebrates the weeklong Carnival in February, just before Lent begins. Seville's dramatic **Semana Santa** (Holy Week) processions (in mid-April) are the most famous in Spain. Jerez and Cádiz also have Semana Santa processions. The **Feria de Abril** (two weeks from the day after Holy Week) Seville's annual city fair, is celebrated with top bullfights, horse parades, flamenco costumes, and singing, dancing, and fireworks nightly in the fairground across the river. In May, Jerez de la Frontera shows off its Andalusian horses in the **Feria del Caballo** (Horse Fair). In early June, worshipers make a Whitsuntide pilgrimage to the shrine of the **Virgen del Rocío** (Virgin of the Dew) in the village of El Rocío (Huelva). **Corpus Christi** (the second Thursday after Whitsunday; June 19 in 2003) is celebrated with processions in Cádiz, Jerez, and Seville. The Assumption of the Virgin Mary is acknowledged throughout Spain on August 15, but especially in Seville, where it's the day of the city's patron, **Nuestra Señora de los Reyes** (Our Lady of the Kings). In September, all wine-producing towns in the province of Cádiz celebrate the **Fiesta de la Vendimia** (Grape Harvest Festival). Jerez's **Fiesta de Otoño** (Autumn Festival) is spectacular. Cádiz commemorates its patron, the **Virgen del Rosario** (Virgin of the Rosary), in October.

Flamenco

Seville and Jerez de la Frontera are headquarters for this quintessentially Andalusian art form combining dance, song, guitar, and percussion. Seville offers flamenco opportunities ranging from professional clubs to the grassroots amateur *cante jondo* (literally, "deep song") heard in little taverns, *tablaos*(clubs), and *peñas* (societies) all over town. What the commercial clubs lack in spontaneity they make up for in skill and polish, though the true emotion, the *duende* (witchcraft) of authentic flamenco is best found in performances that break out off the beaten tourist track in the *tascas* (bars) of popular barrios, such as Triana and La Macarena, or in the great flamenco factory of Las Tres Mil Viviendas, Seville's outlying, largely Gypsy, community. Ask around—at the tourism office, your hotel, or just about any bar—for the *peñas* (societies), semiprivate clubs. If you blend in, improvised flamenco, the real thing, may materialize.

Horses

Jerez's purebred Carthusian horses are featured in the annual Feria del Caballo, in May, though these handsome animals perform every Thursday throughout the year at Jerez's Royal Andalusian School of Equestrian Art. Horse races are held on the beach in Sanlúcar de Barrameda on two weekends in August, a tradition dating back to 1845.

Andalusia:
Seville & Western
Andalusia
PORTUGAL
Gulf of Cádiz
COSTA DE LA LUZ
ANDALUCIA
42 Aracena
41 Ríotinto
Puebla de Guzmán
Valverde del Camino
Alosno
Gibraleón
Huelva
Ajaraque
Ayamonte
La Palma
Bollullos par del Condado
40 Moguer
39 Palos de la Frontera
38 La Rábida
37 Mazagón
36 Matalascañas
El Rocío
Doñana National Park 35
Seville
1 - 32 see detail map
34 Itálica
Santiponce
Cantillana
33 Carmona
Lora
Palma
Posadas
Almodóvar
Córdoba
TO MADRID
La Carlota
Ecija
Marchena
El Arahal
Utrera
El Rubio
Estepa
Osuna
La Roda de Andalucia
Morón de La Frontera
Las Cabezas
Sanlúcar de Barrameda 45
Chipiona
Jerez de la Frontera
43
Rota
Cádiz 47
46 Puerto de Santa María
44 Arcos de la Frontera
Algodonales
Olvera
Ubrique
Ronda
Ardales
Campillos
Bobadilla
TO GRANADA
Antequera
Guadalquivir
Guadalete
N433
N630
N435
N431
A49
C445
C432
N334
NIV
N333
C430
A4
C441
N342
0 10 miles
0 15 km
KEY
Rail Lines

twice languished in a debtors' prison here. Tirso de Molina's Don Juan seduced in Seville's mansions, and Rossini's barber, Figaro, was married in the Barrio de Santa Cruz. And it was at the old tobacco factory where Bizet's sultry Carmen first met Don José.

Seville's color and vivacity are most intense during Semana Santa (Holy Week), when lacerated Christs and bejeweled, weeping Virgins from the city's 24 parishes are paraded through the streets on floats borne by penitents, who often walk barefoot. A week later, and this time in flamenco costume, Sevillanos throw their April Fair. This celebration began as a horse-trading fair in 1847 and still honors its equine origins: midday horse parades include men in broad-brim hats and Andalusian riding gear astride prancing steeds, with their women in ruffled dresses riding sidesaddle behind them. Bullfights, fireworks, and all-night singing and dancing in the fairground's *casetas* (tents) complete the spectacle.

a good walk

Start with the **cathedral** 1, in the Plaza Virgen de los Reyes. Then climb the Giralda, the minaret of the former Moorish mosque. Walk down Avenida de la Constitución for a look at the **Archivo de Indias** 2. Behind the archives is the **Alcázar** 3, surrounded by high walls. Backtrack to the Giralda and the Plaza Virgen de los Reyes and plunge into the **Barrio de Santa Cruz** 4, home of Seville's Jews in the Middle Ages. While you're in the neighborhood, don't miss the **Hospital de los Venerables** 5. On Calle Santa Teresa is the **Casa de Murillo** 6; from there you can stroll through the **Jardines de Murillo** 7. At the far end of the gardens is the **University of Seville** 8, once the tobacco factory where the mythical Carmen worked as a cigar roller. Across the Glorieta de San Diego is the **Parque de María Luisa** 9, which encompasses the **Plaza de España** 10 at its east end as well as the **Plaza de América** 11 at its south end. In the Plaza de América you'll find the **Museo Arqueológico** 12, with marble statues and mosaics from the Roman era. Opposite is the **Museo de Artes y Costumbres Populares** 13. Head back north along the Paseo de las Delicias toward the city center. Near downtown Seville, on Avenida de Roma, is the baroque **Palacio de San Telmo** 14, home of the Andalusian regional government. Behind the Palacio is the Mudéjar-style **Hotel Alfonso XIII** 15. On the north side of Puerta de Jerez is **Palacio de Yanduri** 16, birthplace of the Nobel prize winner Vicente Aleixandre.

Walking toward the Guadalquivir River along Calle Almirante Lobo, you'll come to the riverside **Torre de Oro** 17, which stands opposite the **Teatro de la Maestranza** 18. Behind the theater is the **Hospital de la Caridad** 19, with a collection of works by Seville's leading painters. Continuing north along the river, you'll reach the **Plaza de Toros Real Maestranza** 20. Finally, head away from the river toward the Plaza Nueva, in the heart of Seville, and have a look at the **ayuntamiento** 21. If you have energy and two more hours, walk north from the town hall along the pedestrian **Calle Sierpes** 22, Seville's most famous shopping street. Backtrack down Calle Cuna, parallel to Sierpes, stopping at No. 8 to see the **Palacio de la Condesa de Lebrija** 23. Continue down Calle Cuna to Plaza del Salvador and the **Iglesia del Salvador** 24, a former mosque. Walk up Alcaicería to Plaza de la Alfalfa and along Sales Ferre toward Plaza Cristo del Burgos—in a small alley off the square is the **Casa Natal de Velázquez** 25, where the painter was born in 1599. From Plaza Cristo de Burgos follow the narrow streets Descalzos and Caballerizas to the **Casa de Pilatos** 26, believed to be modeled on Pilate's house in Jerusalem.

A number of other sights are scattered throughout northern Seville and require separate trips. If you're an art lover, set aside half a day for the **Museo de Bellas Artes** 27. From here, head down to the river and across the Pasarela de la Cartuja bridge to the island of **La Cartuja** 28. Another

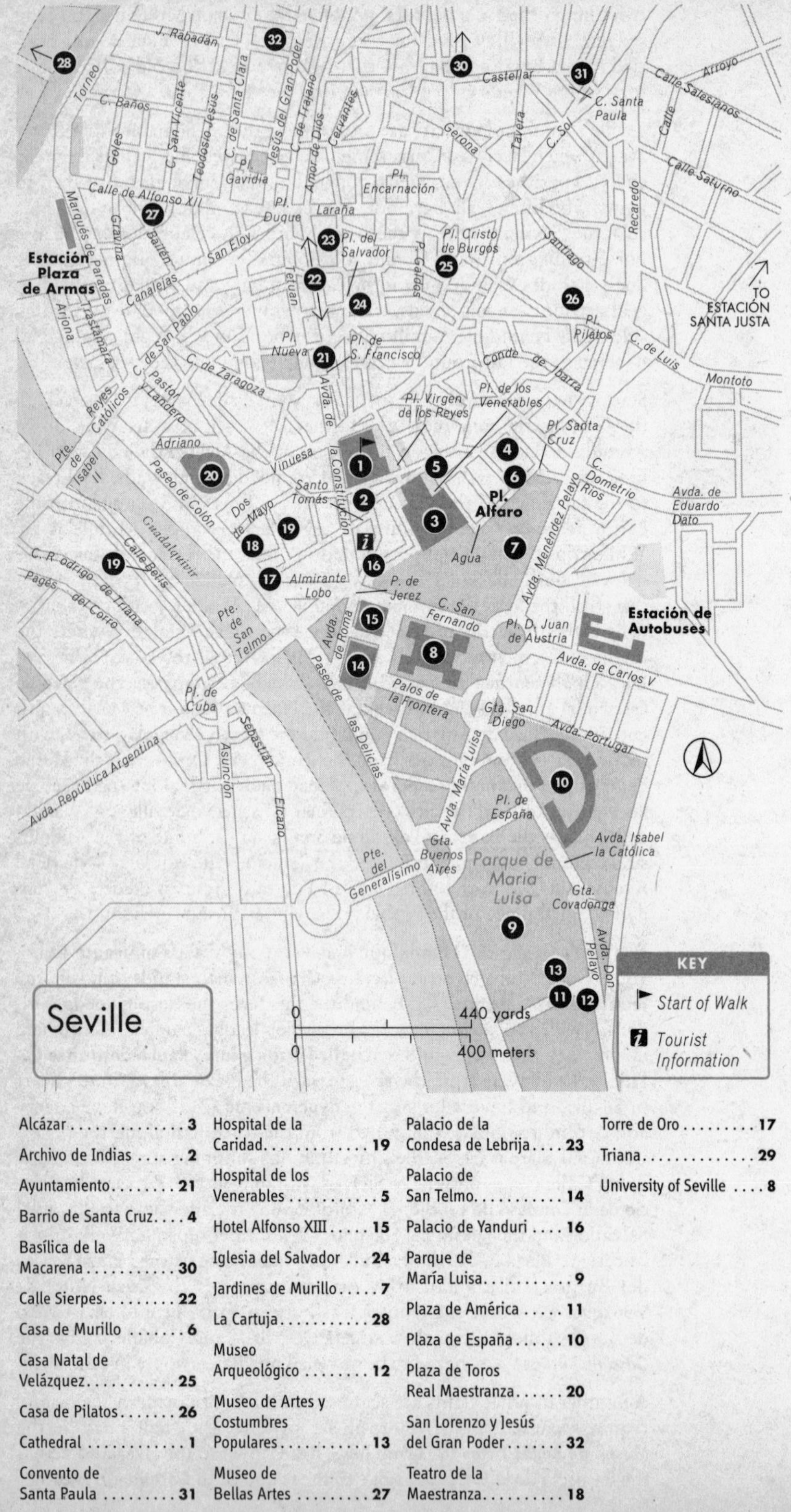

Alcázar 3
Archivo de Indias 2
Ayuntamiento. 21
Barrio de Santa Cruz. . . . 4
Basílica de la Macarena 30
Calle Sierpes. 22
Casa de Murillo 6
Casa Natal de Velázquez. 25
Casa de Pilatos 26
Cathedral 1
Convento de Santa Paula 31
Hospital de la Caridad. 19
Hospital de los Venerables 5
Hotel Alfonso XIII 15
Iglesia del Salvador . . . 24
Jardines de Murillo 7
La Cartuja. 28
Museo Arqueológico 12
Museo de Artes y Costumbres Populares. 13
Museo de Bellas Artes 27
Palacio de la Condesa de Lebrija. . . . 23
Palacio de San Telmo. 14
Palacio de Yanduri 16
Parque de María Luisa. 9
Plaza de América 11
Plaza de España. 10
Plaza de Toros Real Maestranza. 20
San Lorenzo y Jesús del Gran Poder 32
Teatro de la Maestranza. 18
Torre de Oro 17
Triana. 29
University of Seville 8

half day should be set aside to explore the **Triana** (29) neighborhood, on the river's western bank. To visit the **Basílica de la Macarena** (30), site of the Virgen de la Macarena, it's best to take a taxi from the city center. Other religious sites in the Macarena area are the Gothic **Convento de Santa Paula** (31) and the church of **San Lorenzo y Jesús del Gran Poder** (32), where colorful floats used in Seville's Holy Week processions are on display. If you just feel like a leisurely trip, hire a horse-drawn carriage. Fees vary according to the route, so negotiate first, but you can find carriages by the cathedral, the Parque Maria Luisa, Plaza de España, Plaza del Triunfo, Plaza de los Reyes, and the Torre del Oro.

TIMING Allow a full day for the grand Seville tour. A trip to the Museo de Bellas Artes and the monastery at La Cartuja takes half a day (allow more time if you're visiting the island's theme park), and Triana and La Macarena each take two to three hours. Note that hours for the city's monuments and other sights may change monthly.

What to See

★ (3) **Alcázar.** The Plaza Triunfo forms the entrance to the Mudéjar palace built by Pedro I (1350–69) on the site of Seville's former Moorish *alcázar* (fortress). Don't mistake the Alcázar for a genuine Moorish palace, like Granada's Alhambra—it may look like one, and it was indeed designed and built by Moorish workers brought in from Granada, but it was commissioned and paid for by a Christian king more than 100 years after the reconquest of Seville. In its construction, Pedro the Cruel incorporated stones and capitals he pillaged from Valencia, from Córdoba's Medina Azahara, and from Seville itself. The palace serves as the official Seville residence of the king and queen.

You enter the Alcázar through the Puerta del León (Lion's Gate) and the high, fortified walls. You'll first find yourself in a garden courtyard, the **Patio del León.** Off to the left are the oldest parts of the building, the 14th-century **Sala de Justicia** (Hall of Justice) and, next to it, the intimate **Patio del Yeso** (Courtyard of Plaster), part of the original 12th-century Almohad Alcázar. Cross the **Patio de la Montería** to Pedro's Mudéjar palace, arranged around the beautiful **Patio de las Doncellas** (Court of the Damsels), resplendent with delicately carved stucco. Its name probably refers to the annual gift of 100 virgins to the Moorish sultans. Opening off this patio, the **Salón de Embajadores** (Hall of the Ambassadors), with its cedar cupola of green, red, and gold, is the most sumptuous hall in the palace. It was here that Carlos V married Isabel of Portugal in 1526, for which occasion he added the wooden balconies.

Other royal rooms include Felipe II's dining hall and the three baths of Pedro's wily mistress, María de Padilla. María's hold over her royal lover—and apparently over his courtiers, too—was so great that they supposedly lined up to drink her bathwater. The **Patio de las Muñecas** (Court of the Dolls) takes its name from two tiny faces carved on the inside of one of its arches, no doubt as a joke on the part of its Moorish creators. Here Pedro reputedly had his half brother, Don Fadrique, slain in 1358, and here, too, he murdered guest Abu Said of Granada for his jewels. Pedro presented one of these, a huge, uncut ruby, to the Black Prince (Edward, Prince of Wales [1330–76], eldest son of England's Edward III) in 1367. It now sits among other priceless gems in the Crown of England.

You come next to the Renaissance **Palacio de Carlos V,** built by the emperor at the time of his marriage and endowed with a rich collection of Flemish tapestries depicting Carlos's victories at Tunis. Look for the map of Spain: it shows the Iberian Peninsula upside-down, as was the custom in Arab mapmaking. There are more goodies—rare clocks, antique furniture, paintings, and more tapestries—on the Alcázar's upper floor, in the **Estancias Reales** (Royal Chambers). These are the apartments used by King Juan Carlos I and his family when in town. The required guided tour leads you through the dining room, other protocol rooms, and the king's office. Tours depart in the morning only, every half hour in summer and every hour in winter.

At the end of your visit, pause in the **gardens** to inhale jasmine and myrtle, wander among terraces and ornamental baths, and peer into the well-stocked goldfish pond. In the midst of this green oasis is an orange tree said to have been planted in the time of Pedro the Cruel. From the gardens, a passageway leads to the **Patio de las Banderas** (Court of the Flags), which has a classic view of the Giralda. ✉ *Pl. del Triunfo, Santa Cruz* ☎ *95/450–2324* 🌐 *www.patronato-alcazarsevilla.es* 🎫 *€5, tour of Royal Chambers €3* ⏲ *Apr.–Sept., Tues.–Sat. 9:30–8, Sun. 9:30–6; Oct.–Mar., Tues.–Sat. 9:30–6, Sun. 9:30–2:30.*

❷ **Archivo de Indias** (Archives of the Indies). Opened in 1785 in the former Lonja (Merchants' Exchange), this dignified Renaissance building was designed by Juan de Herrera, architect of El Escorial, in 1572. The archives include drawings, trade documents, plans of South American towns, even the autographs of Columbus, Magellan, and Cortés. Many of the 38,000 documents have yet to be properly cataloged. Presently closed for renovations, the building is open only for research purposes. ✉ *Av. de la Constitución, Santa Cruz* ☎ *95/421–1234* 🎫 *Free* ⏲ *Weekdays 10–1 (8–3 for researchers).*

㉑ **Ayuntamiento** (City Hall). This Diego de Riaño original, built between 1527 and 1564, is in the heart of Seville's commercial center, the Plaza Nueva. The facade, which overlooks the plaza, dates from the 19th century, but if you walk around to the other side, on the Plaza de San Francisco, you'll see Riaño's work. ✉ *Pl. Nueva 1, Centro* ☎ *95/459–0101* 🌐 *www.sevilla.org* 🎫 *Free* ⏲ *Tours mid-Sept.–mid-July, if enough visitors, Tues.–Thurs. at 5:30 and 6:30, Sat. at 12:30.*

★ ❹ **Barrio de Santa Cruz.** The twisting alleyways and cobble squares of Seville's old Jewish quarter were much favored by the city's nobles in the 17th century. Some of the white and ocher houses still rank among Seville's most expensive properties. Wrought-iron lanterns cast shadows on the whitewashed walls, and ocher-frame windows hide behind rectangular grilles. On some streets, bars alternate with antiques stores and souvenir shops, but most of the quarter is quiet and residential. The Callejón del Agua, beside the wall of the Alcázar's gardens, has some of the quarter's finest mansions and patios. Pause to enjoy the antiques shops and outdoor café on the **Plaza Alianza.** A simple crucifix hangs on the dazzling-white wall shrouded in bougainvillea. In the **Plaza de Doña Elvira,** with its fountain and *azulejo* (painted tile) benches, young Sevillanos gather to play guitars. Here you'll see one side of the **Hospital de los Venerables.** Just around the corner from the hospital, at Callejón del Agua and Jope de Rueda, Rossini's Figaro serenaded Rosina on her **Plaza Alfaro** balcony. Adjoining the Plaza Alfaro, in the **Plaza Santa Cruz,** a 17th-century filigree iron cross marks the site of the erstwhile church of Santa Cruz, destroyed by Napoléon's General Soult. The painter Murillo was buried here in 1682, though his current resting place is unknown.

㉚ **Basílica de la Macarena.** This church holds Seville's most revered image, the Virgin of Hope—more familiarly known as La Macarena because her church adjoins the Puerta de la Macarena, a remnant of the old Roman wall. Bedecked with candles and carnations, her cheeks streaming with glass tears, the Macarena is the focus of the procession on Holy Thursday, the highlight of Seville's Holy Week pageant. She is the patron of Gypsies and the protector of the matador. So great are her charms that the Sevillian bullfighter Joselito spent half his personal fortune buying her four emeralds. When he was killed in the ring at the tender age of 25, in 1920, the Macarena was dressed in widow's weeds for a month. *Puerta de la Macarena, La Macarena* *95/490–1800* *Basilica free, treasury €2.70* *Basilica daily 9–1 and 5–8, treasury daily 9:30–1 and 5–8.*

22 **Calle Sierpes.** This is Seville's main shopping street. Near the southern end, at No. 85, a plaque marks the spot where the Cárcel Real (Royal Prison) once stood. Miguel de Cervantes began writing *Don Quijote* in one of its cells. A bank is now on the prison site.

6 **Casa de Murillo.** Bartolomé Estéban Murillo (1617–82) lived here for a time. The street is named for St. Teresa of Ávila (1515–82), who once stayed here and was so enchanted by Seville that she decreed that anyone who stayed free from sin in this city was indeed on the path to God. The building now houses the Andalusian Department of Culture, but you can wander the courtyard and lower floor. One room has panels showing the locations of all of Murillo's works on display in Seville; another room illustrates the history of the building. *C. Santa Teresa 8, Alfalfa* *95/422–9415* *Free* *Weekdays 10–2 and 4–7.*

25 **Casa Natal de Velázquez.** One of Spain's greatest painters, Diego de Velázquez was born in this *casa de vecinos* (town house shared by several families) in 1599. The house fell into ruin, but was bought in the 1970s by the well-known fashion designers Victorio y Lucchino, who restored it for use as their studio. It is not open to the public. *Padre Luis María Llop 4, Centro.*

26 **Casa de Pilatos.** This palace was built in the first half of the 16th century by the dukes of Tarifa, ancestors of the present owner, the Duke of Medinaceli. It's known as Pilate's House because Don Fadrique, first marquis of Tarifa, allegedly modeled it on Pontius Pilate's house in Jerusalem, where he had gone on a pilgrimage in 1518. With its fine patio and superb azulejo decorations, the palace is a beautiful blend of Spanish Mudéjar and Renaissance architecture. The upstairs apartments, which you can see on a guided tour, have frescoes, paintings, and antique furniture. *Pl. Pilatos 1, Santa Cruz* *95/422–5298* *Apartments €8; lower floor only, €5* *Daily 9–6; apartments sometimes closed.*

1 **Cathedral.** After Ferdinand III captured Seville from the Moors in 1248, the great mosque begun by Yusuf II in 1171 was reconsecrated to the Virgin Mary and used as a Christian cathedral. But in 1401 the people of Seville decided to erect a new cathedral, one that would equal the glory of their great city. They promptly pulled down the old mosque, leaving only its minaret and outer court, and set about constructing the existing building in just over a century—a remarkable feat for the time. The clergy renounced their incomes for the cause, and a member of the chapter is said to have proclaimed, "Let us build a church so large that we shall be held to be insane." This they proceeded to do, for today Seville's cathedral can be described only in superlatives: it is the largest and highest cathedral in Spain, the largest Gothic building in the world, and the world's third-largest church, after St. Peter's in Rome and St. Paul's in London.

Enter the cathedral grounds via the **Patio de los Naranjos** (Courtyard of Orange Trees), part of the original mosque. The fountain in the center was used for ablutions before people entered the mosque. Near the Puerta del Lagarto (Lizard's Gate), in the corner near the Giralda, try to find the wooden crocodile—thought to have been a gift from the emir of Egypt in 1260 as he sought the hand of the daughter of Alfonso the Wise—and the elephant tusk, found in the ruins of Itálica. The cathedral's exterior, with its rose windows and flying buttresses, is a monument to pure Gothic beauty. Aside from the well-lighted high altar, the dimly illuminated interior can be disappointing, its five naves and numerous side chapels shrouded in gloom; Gothic purity has been largely submerged in ornate baroque decoration. Enter the cathedral through the Puerta de la Granada or the Puerta Colorada. In the central nave rises the **Capilla Mayor** (Main Chapel) and its intricately carved altarpiece, begun by a Flemish carver in 1482. This magnificent *retablo* (altarpiece) is the largest in Christendom (65 ft by 43 ft). It depicts some 36 scenes from the life of Christ, with pillars carved with more than 200 figures. The whole work is lavishly adorned with gold leaf.

Make your way to the opposite (southern) side of the cathedral to see the **monument to Christopher Columbus.** The great explorer knew both triumph and disgrace but found no repose—he died, bitterly disillusioned, in Valladolid in 1506. No one knows for certain where he is buried: he was reportedly laid to rest for the first time in the Dominican Republic and then moved over the years to other locations. Still, his remains are thought to be here. Columbus's coffin is borne aloft by the four kings representing the medieval kingdoms of Spain: Castile, León, Aragón, and Navarra. Columbus's son, Hernando Colón (1488–1539), is also interred here; his tombstone, inscribed with the words A CASTILLA Y A LEÓN, MUNDO NUEVO DIO COLÓN (to Castile and León, Columbus gave a new world), lies between the great west door, the Puerta Mayor, and the central choir. Between the elder Columbus's tomb and the Capilla Real, at the eastern end of the central nave, the cathedral's treasuries include gold and silver (much of it from the New World), relics, and other works of art. In the **Sacristía de los Cálices** (Sacristy of the Chalices) look for Martínez Montañés's wood carving, *Crucifixion, Merciful Christ*; Valdés Leal's *St. Peter Freed by an Angel*; Zurbarán's *Virgin and Child*; and Goya's *St. Justa and St. Rufina.* The **Sacristía Mayor** (Main Sacristy) holds the keys to the city, which Seville's Moors and Jews presented to their conqueror, Ferdinand III. Finally, in the dome of the **Sala Capitular** (Chapter House), in the cathedral's southeastern corner, is Murillo's *Immaculate Conception,* painted in 1668.

One of the cathedral's highlights, the **Capilla Real** (Royal Chapel), is reserved for prayer and concealed behind a ponderous curtain, but you can duck in if you're quick, quiet, and properly dressed. To do so, explore the rest of the cathedral and the Giralda and enter again from a separate door, the Puerta de los Palos, on Plaza Virgen de los Reyes (signposted ENTRADA PARA CULTO—entrance for worship). Along the sides of the chapel are the tombs of the wife of Ferdinand III, Beatrix of Swabia, and his son, Alfonso X, called The Wise (died 1284); in a silver urn before the high altar rest the precious relics of Ferdinand III himself, Seville's liberator (canonized 1671), who was said to have died from excessive fasting. In the (rarely open) vault below lie the tombs of Ferdinand's descendant Pedro the Cruel and Ferdinand's mistress, María de Padilla. Above the entrance grille, you can see a Jerónino Roldán sculpture of Ferdinand III receiving the keys to Seville.

Before you duck into the Capilla Real, climb to the top of the **Giralda,** which dominates Seville's skyline. Once the minaret of Seville's great mosque, from which the faithful were summoned to prayer, it was built between 1184 and 1196, just 50 years before the reconquest of Seville. The Christians could not bring themselves to destroy this tower when they tore down the mosque, so they incorporated it into their new cathedral. In 1565–68 they added a lantern and belfry to the old minaret and installed 24 bells, one for each of Seville's 24 parishes and the 24 Christian knights who fought with Ferdinand III in the Reconquest. They also added the bronze statue of Faith, which turned as a weather vane—*el giraldillo,* or "something that turns," thus the name Giralda. To give it a rest after 400 years of wear and tear, the original statue was replaced with a copy in 1997. With its baroque additions, the slender Giralda rises 322 ft. Inside, instead of steps, 35 sloping ramps—wide enough for two horsemen to pass abreast—climb to a viewing platform 230 ft up. It is said that Ferdinand III rode his horse to the top to admire the city he had conquered. If you follow in his (horse's) footsteps, you'll be rewarded with a view of tile roofs and the Guadalquivir shimmering beneath palm-lined banks. ✉ *Pl. Virgen de los Reyes, Santa Cruz* ☎ *95/421–4971* 🎫 *Cathedral, museum, Giralda, and Patio de los Naranjos €7* ⏲ *Cathedral Mon.–Sat. 11–5, Sun. 2–6, and for Mass.*

31 **Convento de Santa Paula.** This 15th-century Gothic convent has a fine facade and portico, with ceramic decoration by Nicolaso Pisano. The chapel has some beautiful azulejos and sculptures by Martínez Montañés. There is also a small museum packed with religious objects. ✉ *C. Santa Paula, La Macarena* ☎ *95/453–6330* 🎫 *€2* ⏲ *Tues.–Sun. 10:30–1 and 4:30–6:30.*

Fodor'sChoice ★

19 **Hospital de la Caridad.** Behind the Maestranza Theater is this almshouse for the sick and elderly, where six paintings by Murillo (1617–82) and two gruesome works by Valdés Leal (1622–90) depicting the Triumph of Death are displayed. The baroque hospital was founded in 1674 by Seville's original Don Juan, Miguel de Mañara (1626–79). A nobleman of licentious character, Mañara was returning one night from a riotous orgy when he had a vision of a funeral procession in which the partly decomposed corpse in the coffin was his own. Accepting the apparition as a sign from God, Mañara renounced his worldly goods and joined the Brotherhood of Charity, whose unsavory task it was to collect the bodies of executed criminals and bury them. He devoted his fortune to building this hospital and is buried before the high altar in the chapel. Artist Murillo was a personal friend of Mañara's, thus La Caridad's chief attractions. ✉ *C. Temprado 3, Arenal* ☎ *95/422–3232* 🎫 *€4* ⏲ *Mon.–Sat. 9–1:30 and 3:30–7, Sun. 9–1.*

5 **Hospital de los Venerables.** Once a retirement home for priests, this baroque building now has a cultural foundation that organizes concerts and exhibitions here. The required 20-minute guided tour takes in a splendid azulejo patio with an interesting sunken fountain (designed to cope with low water pressure) and upstairs gallery, but the hospital's highlight is its chapel, with frescoes by Juan Valdés Leal. The pews face not the altar but the imposing pipe organ, built in 1991 using a 17th-century design and pieces cannibalized from original instruments. ✉ *Pl. de los Venerables 8, Santa Cruz* ☎ *95/456–2696* 🎫 *€3.61 with guide* ⏲ *Daily 10–2 and 4–8.*

15 **Hotel Alfonso XIII.** Seville's most emblematic hotel, this grand, Mudéjar-style building next to the university was built—and named—for the king's visit to the 1929 fair. Nonguests are welcome to admire the inner courtyard or sip a cool martini in the bar, which has an ornate Moorish interior. ✉ *San Fernando 2, El Arenal* ☎ *95/491–7000.*

Fodor'sChoice ★

24 **Iglesia del Salvador.** Built between 1671 and 1712, the Church of the Savior stands on the site of Seville's first great mosque. Inside, look especially for the image of *Jesús de la Pasión,* carved by Martínez Montañés: this statue is borne through the streets on Holy Thursday in one of Holy Week's most moving processions. ✉ *Pl. del Salvador, Centro* ☎ *95/421–1679* 🎫 *Free* ⏲ *Mon.–Sat. 9–1 and 6:30–8:30.*

7 **Jardines de Murillo** (Murillo Gardens). From the Plaza Santa Cruz you can embark on a stroll through these shady gardens, where you'll find a statue of Christopher Columbus.

28 **La Cartuja.** Named after its 14th-century Carthusian monastery, the island of La Cartuja, across the river from northern Seville, was the site of the decennial Universal Exposition (Expo) in 1992. Five bridges were built across the river for this event. The island has the Teatro Central, used for concerts and plays; Parque del Alamillo, Seville's largest and least-known park; and the Estadio Olímpico, a 60,000-seat covered stadium. The eastern shore holds the largest theme park in Andalusia, **Isla Mágica,** with 14 different attractions around a lake, including the hair-raising Jaguar roller coaster. ☎ *95/448–7000* 🌐 *www.islamagica.es* 🎫 *Apr. and May €19, June–Oct. €21* ⏲ *Apr. and May, weekends 11 AM–midnight; June–Oct., daily 11AM–midnight.*

The 14th century **Monasterio de Santa María de las Cuevas,** or the Monasterio de La Cartuja, was regularly visited by Christopher Columbus, who was buried here for a few years. From 1841 to 1980 the building had a ceramics factory, where Seville's famous Cartuja china was made. The monastery was restored for use as the Royal Pavilion during the 1992 Expo and is now open to the public; part of the building houses the Centro Andaluz de Arte Contemporáneo, which has art exhibits. ✉ *Isla de la Cartuja* ☎ *955/037070* 🎫 *€1.80, free Tues. for EU citizens* ⏲ *Tues.–Fri. 10–8, Sat. 11–8, Sun. 10–3.*

12 **Museo Arqueológico.** In a fine Renaissance-style building, Seville's Museum of Archaeology has artifacts from Phoenician, Tartessian, Greek, Carthaginian, Iberian, Roman, and medieval times. Displays include marble statues and mosaics from the Roman excavations at Itálica and a faithful replica of the fabulous Carambolo treasure found on a hillside outside Seville in 1958: 21 pieces of jewelry, all of 24-karat gold, dating from the 7th and 6th centuries BC. ✉ *Pl. de América, El Porvenir* ☎ *95/423–2401* 🎫 *€1.50, free for EU citizens* ⏲ *Tues. 3–8, Wed.–Sat. 9–8, Sun. 9–2.*

13 **Museo de Artes y Costumbres Populares** (Museum of Folklore). The Mudéjar pavilion opposite the Museum of Archaeology is the site of this museum of mainly 19th- and 20th-century Spanish folklore. The first floor has re-creations of a forge, a bakery, a wine press, a tanner's shop, and a pottery studio. Upstairs, exhibits include 18th- and 19th-century court dress, regional folk costumes, carriages, and musical instruments. ✉ *Pl. de América 3, El Porvenir* ☎ *95/423–2576* 🎫 *€1.50, free for EU citizens* ⏲ *Wed.–Sun. 9–8.*

27 Fodor's Choice ★ **Museo de Bellas Artes** (Museum of Fine Arts). Along with its counterpart in Bilbao, this museum is second only to Madrid's Prado in Spanish art. It's in the former convent of La Merced Calzada, most of which dates from the 17th century. The collection includes Murillo, Zurbarán, Valdés Leal, and El Greco; outstanding examples of Seville Gothic art; and baroque religious sculptures in wood (a quintessentially Andalusian art form). In the rooms dedicated to Sevillian art of the 19th and 20th centuries, look for Gonzalo Bilbao's *Las Cigarreras,* a group portrait of Seville's famous cigar makers. ✉ *Pl. del Museo 9, El Porvenir*

95/422–0790 €1.50, free for EU citizens Tues. 3–8, Wed.–Sat. 9–8, Sun. 9–2.

23 **Palacio de la Condesa de Lebrija.** Until a few years ago this 16th-century palace was the private residence of its aristocratic owner, the late Countess of Lebrija. Her heirs have opened the ground floor to the public, including a spectacular courtyard graced by a Roman mosaic purloined from the ruins in Itálica and surrounded by Moorish arches and fine azulejos. The side rooms house an eclectic collection of archaeological goodies. *Cuna 8, Centro 95/422–7802 €3.60 Weekdays 10:30–1 and 4:30–7, Sat. 10–1.*

14 **Palacio de San Telmo.** This splendid baroque palace is largely the work of architect Leonardo de Figueroa. Built between 1682 and 1796, it was first a naval academy and then the residence of the Bourbon dukes of Montpensier, during which time it outshone Madrid's royal court for sheer brilliance. The palace gardens are now the Parque de María Luisa, and the building itself is the seat of the Andalusian government. The main portal, vintage 1734, is a superb example of the fanciful Churrigueresque style. You can tour the interior with a guide on Monday or Wednesday by contacting the Departamento de Protocolo. *Av. de Roma, El Arenal 955/035558 Protocolo, 955/035505 Free Guided tours Mon. and Wed. by appointment.*

16 **Palacio de Yanduri.** Nobel prize–winning poet Vicente Aleixandre was born here. *North side of Puerta de Jerez, Santa Cruz.*

9 **Parque de María Luisa.** Formerly the garden of the Palacio de San Telmo, the park is a blend of formal design and wild vegetation. In the burst of development that gripped Seville in the 1920s, it was redesigned for the 1929 Exhibition, and the impressive villas you see now are the fair's remaining pavilions, many of them consulates or schools. Note the **statue of El Cid** by Rodrigo Díaz de Vivar (1043–99), who fought both for and against the Muslim rulers during the Reconquest, and the old **Casino** building from the 1929 Hispanic-American Exhibition, now the Teatro Lope de Vega. *Main entrance: Glorieta San Diego, El Arenal.*

11 **Plaza de América.** Walk to the south end of the Parque de María Luisa, past the Isla de los Patos (Island of Ducks), to find this plaza, designed by Aníbal González. It's a blaze of color, with deep-orange sand, flowers, shrubs, ornamental stairways, and fountains tiled in yellow, blue, and ocher. The three impressive buildings surrounding the square—in neo-Mudéjar, Gothic, and Renaissance styles—were built by González for the 1929 fair. Two of them now house Seville's museums of archaeology and folklore.

10 **Plaza de España.** Designed by architect Aníbal González, the grandiose half-moon on the eastern edge of the Parque de María Luisa was Spain's centerpiece pavilion at the 1929 Exhibition. The brightly colored azulejo pictures in its arches represent the 50 provinces of Spain, and the four bridges over its ornamental lake symbolize the medieval kingdoms of the Iberian Peninsula.

20 **Plaza de Toros Real Maestranza** (Royal Maestranza Bullring). Sevillanos have spent many a thrilling Sunday afternoon in this bullring, built between 1760 and 1763. Painted a deep ocher, the stadium is the one of the oldest and loveliest plazas de toros in Spain. An adjoining museum has prints and photos. *Paseo de Colón 12, El Arenal 95/422–4577 Plaza and bullfighting museum €4 with English-speaking guide Daily 9:30–2 and 3–7 (9:30–3 only on bullfight days).*

32 **San Lorenzo y Jesús del Gran Poder.** This church has many fine works by such artists as Montañés and Pacheco, but its outstanding piece is Juan de Mesa's *Jesús del Gran Poder* (*Christ Omnipotent*). The *paso* (float), used in the Good Friday morning procession of El Gran Poder, is the work of Ruíz Gijón (1690). ✉ *C. Jesús del Gran Poder, Alameda* ☎ *95/438–4558* 🎫 *Free* ⏲ *Daily 8–1:30 and 6–9.*

18 **Teatro de la Maestranza** (Maestranza Theater). Opposite the Torre de Oro is Seville's opera house, opened in 1991. Now one of Europe's leading halls, the Maestranza presents opera, classical music, *zarzuela* (Spanish light opera), and jazz. ✉ *Paseo de Colón 22, El Arenal* ☎ *95/422–6573 or 95/422–3344.*

17 **Torre de Oro.** The Tower of Gold stands on the banks of the Guadalquivir near the Puerta de Jerez. A 12-sided tower built by the Moors in 1220 to complete the city's ramparts, it served to close off the harbor when a chain was stretched across the river from its base to another tower on the opposite bank. In 1248 Admiral Ramón de Bonifaz broke through this barrier, and thus did Ferdinand III capture Seville. The tower now houses a small naval museum. ☎ *95/422–2419* 🎫 *€1, free Tues.* ⏲ *Tues.–Fri. 10–2, Sat 11–2.*

29 **Triana.** Across the Guadalquivir from central Seville, Triana used to be the city's Gypsy quarter. Today it has a tranquil, neighborly feel by day, while its trendy clubs and flamenco bars throb at night. Enter Triana by the **Puente Isabel II** (better known as the Puente de Triana), built in 1852, the first bridge to connect the city's two sections. Walk across Plaza Altozano up Calle Jacinto and turn right at **Calle Alfarería** (Pottery Street) to see a slew of pottery stores and workshops. Return to Plaza Altozano and walk down Calle Pureza as far as the small **Capilla de los Marineros** (Seamen's Chapel), home to a venerated Virgin Mary called the Esperanza de Triana, which native-born Trianeros claim is prettier than the rival Virgen de la Macarena, across the river. Head back toward the river and **Calle Betis** for some of the city's most colorful bars, clubs, and restaurants.

8 **University of Seville.** At the far end of the Jardines de Murillo, opposite Calle San Fernando, stands what used to be the **Real Fábrica de Tabacos** (Royal Tobacco Factory). Built between 1750 and 1766, the factory employed some 3,000 *cigarreras* (female cigar makers) less than a century later, including, of course, the heroine of Bizet's opera *Carmen*, who rolled her cigars on her thigh. You're free to wander around the lower floors and courtyards, usually teeming with students. The enormous building has been the university's home only since the 1950s; today's factory is across the river. ✉ *C. San Fernando, Santa Cruz* ☎ *95/455–1000* 🎫 *Free* ⏲ *Weekdays 9–8:30.*

Where to Eat

★ $$$$ ✕ **Egaña-Oriza.** Owner José Mari Egaña is Basque, but he is today considered one of the fathers of modern Andalusian cooking. The restaurant, which is on the edge of the Murillo Gardens, has a modern interior with deep peach walls. The menu might include *lomos de lubina con salsa de erizos de mar* (sea bass with sea-urchin sauce) or *solomillo con foie natural y salsa de ciruelas* (fillet steak with foie gras and plum sauce). The adjoining Bar España is a good place for refined tapas. ✉ *San Fernando 41, Jardines de Murillo* ☎ *95/422–7211* 💳 *AE, DC, MC, V* ⏲ *Closed Sun. and Aug. No lunch Sat.*

$$$ ✕ **La Albahaca.** Ensconced in one of Seville's prettiest neighborhoods, the Barrio de Santa Cruz, this typical Andalusian house was built by the celebrated architect Juan Talavera as a home for his own family; in-

EASTER WEEK IN SEVILLE

Holy Week in Seville combines religious emotion, Gypsy passion, and pagan joy. From Palm Sunday to Good Friday some 65 cofradías *(brotherhoods) parade over 120* pasos *(floats) with vivid representations of Christ on the cross followed by the grieving Virgin Mary. More than 50,000 pointy-hooded penitents, known as* Nazarenos *(20,000 of them lugging wooden crosses), accompany processions through the streets, while central Seville becomes a vast wine and tapas fest. Throughout Holy Week, and the Feria de Abril a week later, Seville is officially "de fiesta," partying, with the whole town slicked up as if headed for weddings, possibly their own.*

The week builds to a crescendo with La Madrugá *(dawn), from midnight Thursday into the early hours of Good Friday.* El Llamador, *the official program, has timetables and information about the* cofradías, *the icons, the music, and the number of* Nazarenos.

side, three dining rooms are colorfully decorated with ceramic tiles and leafy potted plants. Service is friendly and professional. Consider the *lubina al horno* (baked sea bass) and the restaurant's star dish, *foie de oca salteado* (lightly sautéed goose liver perfumed with honey vinegar). ✉ *Pl. Santa Cruz 12, Santa Cruz* ☎ *95/422–0714* ▭ *AE, DC, MC, V* ⊗ *Closed Sun.*

$$$ Fodor'sChoice ★ ✕ **Poncio.** Named for the seaman who first sighted the New World, this happy place combines Andalusian tradition with a French flair. Chef Willy Moya trained in Paris and blends local and cosmopolitan cuisine flawlessly. Try the *salmorejo encapotado* (thick, roughly chopped gazpacho topped with diced egg and chunks of acorn-fed ham), or the *besugo con gambitas* (sea bream with shrimp). The restaurant is around the corner from Calle de Rodrigo de Triana. While you're here, don't miss the nearby Iglesia de Santa Ana, Seville's oldest church. ✉ *C. Victoria 8, Triana* ☎ *95/434–0010* ▭ *AE, DC, MC, V.*

$$$ ✕ **Taberna del Alabardero.** Installed in a 19th-century mansion near the Plaza Nueva, this restaurant is also a hotel with seven guest rooms. Preceded by a courtyard and a bar, the dining area is decorated in Sevillian tiles. Modern dishes include *bacalao fritado con manitas guisadas con Pedro Ximénez* (fried cod with pig's trotters stewed in Pedro Ximénez wine) or *ensalada de espárragos verdes naturales con bogavante* (fresh green asparagus with lobster). The pricey but worthy *menú de degustación* (tasting menu) includes the chef's own choices. ✉ *Zaragoza 20, Arenal* ☎ *95/456–0637* ▭ *AE, DC, MC, V* ⊗ *Closed Aug.*

$$–$$$ ✕ **La Isla.** Using fresh fish from Cádiz and Huelva, La Isla serves up wonderful *parrillada de mariscos y pescados,* a fish and seafood grill for two people. *Zarzuela,* the Catalan seafood stew, is another favorite; and simple meat dishes are also served. The two attractive dining rooms have blue-and-white tile designs and cream-color stucco walls. ✉ *Arfe 25, Arenal* ☎ *95/421–5376* ▭ *AE, DC, MC, V* ⊗ *Closed Aug.*

$$–$$$ ✕ **Manolo León.** This elegant town house has an enticing selection of excellent offerings from savory black olives to acorn-fed Iberian ham. The service is abundant, professional, and friendly, and the upstairs terrace offers a breath of river-cooled air in hot weather. The restaurant is not far from the Puente de la Barqueta, in the northwestern corner of the Barrio de la Macarena. Manolo León's other location at Calle Juan Pablos 8 is equally impressive. Try the gazpacho in summer, or the *ajo blanco,* a white gazpacho made primarily of almonds instead of tomato. ✉ *C. Guadalquivir 12, Barrio de la Macarena* ☎ *95/437–3735* ▭ *AE, DC, MC, V.*

$$ ✕ **Becerrita.** Favored by Sevillanos and found by few tourists, this small establishment—cozy verging on cramped—has diligent service and tasty modern treatments of such classic Spanish dishes as *carrillada de ibérico estofado* (Ibérian pork stew)—order it in advance—and *dados de merluza frita* (fried hake medallions). Inquire about the fresh dish of the day. ✉ *Recaredo 9, Santa Catalina* ☎ *95/441–2057* 🌐 *www.becerrita.com* ▭ *AE, MC, V* ⏲ *No dinner Sun.*

★ $$ ✕ **Enrique Becerra.** Excellent tapas await at this cozy restaurant, in a whitewashed house with wrought-iron window grilles. The lively, crowded bar, decorated with ceramic tiles, is a meeting place for locals. The menu focuses on traditional, home-cooked Andalusian dishes, such as *pez espada al amontillado* (swordfish cooked in dark sherry), *rape al azafrán* (monkfish in saffron sauce), and cordero *a la miel* (honey-glazed). Don't miss the cumin seed–laced *espinacas con garbanzos* (spinach with chickpeas). ✉ *Gamazo 2, Arenal* ☎ *95/421–3049* ▭ *AE, DC, MC, V* ⏲ *Closed Sun.*

$–$$ ✕ **El Corral del Agua.** Abutting the outer walls of the Alcázar on one of the prettiest streets in the Barrio Santa Cruz is a restored 18th-century house, centered on a patio with a profusion of potted plants and a central fountain. Here's where Andalusian specialties, such as *cola de toro al estilo de Sevilla* (Seville-style bull's tail), are prepared with contemporary flair. ✉ *Callejón del Agua 6, Santa Cruz* ☎ *95/422–4841 or 95/422–0714* ▭ *AE, DC, MC, V* ⏲ *Closed Sun. and Jan.–Feb.*

$–$$ ✕ **Hostería del Laurel.** This restaurant—also a small hotel—has a large tapas selection and is geared toward tourists, capitalizing on its location in the Barrio de Santa Cruz. In summer you can dine outdoors on the plaza, surrounded by beautiful white and ocher houses. Inside, the dining room ceilings are festooned with hanging hams, garlic, dried herbs, peppers, squash, and corn cobs. ✉ *Pl. de los Venerables 5, Santa Cruz* ☎ *95/422–0295* ▭ *AE, DC, MC, V.*

$ ✕ **San Marco.** In an old neoclassical house in the shopping district, this Italian restaurant has a leafy patio, and a menu that combines Italian, French, and Andalusian cuisine. Pasta dishes, such as ravioli stuffed with shrimp and pesto sauce, are notable. The restaurant now has four satellites, but this one, the original, is the most charming. ✉ *Cuna 6, Centro* ☎ *95/421–2440* ✍ *Reservations essential* ▭ *AE, DC, MC, V.*

¢–$ ✕ **La Raza.** The main attraction here is an unbeatable location on the edge of Parque María Luisa. In fair weather you can dine outside, under the shade of enormous rubber trees and palms. The house specialties are rice dishes, such as *arroz con langostinos y puntillas* (rice with prawns and baby squid) and the classic paella, cooked for two. ✉ *Av. Isabel la Católica 2, Pl. de España* ☎ *95/423–2024* ▭ *AE, MC, V.*

¢–$ ✕ **Mesón Don Raimundo.** Although this place is tucked into an alleyway off Calle Argote de Molina (which leads up from the cathedral's Plaza Virgen de los Reyes), it's nonetheless often packed with tour groups. Still, it's worth the trip for its generous portions of traditional fare, including Mozarab-style wild duck (braised in sherry) and solomillo *a la castellana* (Castilian-style). Open with the crunchy *tortillitas de camarones* (batter-fried shrimp pancakes) or stuffed peppers. ✉ *Argote de Molina 26, Santa Cruz* ☎ *95/422–3355* ▭ *AE, DC, MC, V.*

¢–$ ✕ **Modesto.** The downstairs is a lively, crowded tapas bar; upstairs is the dining room, which has stucco walls decorated with blue-and-white tiles. The house specialty is a crisp *fritura Modesto* (a selection of small fish fried in top-quality olive oil); another excellent choice is the *cazuela al Tío Diego* ("Uncle Jim's Casserole"—ham, mushrooms, and shrimp). You can dine cheaply here, but beware: *mariscos* (shellfish) take the bill to another level. ✉ *Cano y Cueto 5, Santa Cruz* ☎ *95/441–6811* ▭ *AE, DC, MC, V.*

Where to Stay

★ $$$$ **Hacienda Benazuza.** This five-star luxury hotel is in a rambling country palace near Sanlúcar la Mayor, 15 km (9 mi) outside Seville off the main road to Huelva. Surrounded by olive and orange trees and in a courtyard with towering palms, the building incorporates an 18th-century church. The interior has clay-tile floors and ocher walls. The acclaimed restaurant, La Alquería, serves Spanish and international dishes, creative variations on the recipes of acclaimed Catalan chef Ferran Adria. *C. Virgen de las Nieves, 41800 Sanlúcar la Mayor 955/703344 955/703410 www.hbenazuza.com 41 rooms, 3 suites 2 restaurants, tennis court, pool, paddle tennis, Internet, some pets allowed AE, DC, MC, V.*

★ $$$$ **Alfonso XIII.** Inaugurated by King Alfonso XIII on April 28, 1929, this grand hotel is a splendid, historical Mudéjar Revival palace, built around a huge central patio surrounded by ornate brick arches. The public rooms have marble floors, wood-panel ceilings, heavy Moorish lamps, stained glass, and ceramic tiles in the typical Sevillian colors. The two restaurants serve Spanish and Japanese food. *San Fernando 2, El Arenal, 41004 95/491–7000 95/491–7099 www.westin.com/hotelalfonso 127 rooms, 19 suites 2 restaurants, pool, hair salon, bar, Internet, meeting room AE, DC, MC, V.*

$$$$ **Casa Imperial.** Adjoining the Casa de Pilatos, and once connected to it via underground tunnel, this restored 16th-century palace is the former residence of the marquis of Tarifa's majordomo. Public areas surround four different courtyards. The 24 suites are approached by a stairway adorned with trompe l'oeil tiles. Each suite is different—one has a private courtyard with a trickling fountain—but all have kitchenettes. The bathroom fixtures are stylishly old-fashioned. *Imperial 29, Santa Catalina, 41003 95/450–0300 95/4500330 www.casaimperial.com 25 suites Kitchenettes, Internet AE, DC, MC, V.*

$$$$ **Meliá Colón.** Built for the 1929 Exhibition, the grand old Colón has a white-marble staircase that leads up to the central lobby—which has a magnificent stained-glass dome and crystal candelabra. Downstairs is the El Burladero restaurant, with a bullfight theme, and La Tasca tavern. The old-fashioned rooms are elegantly furnished with silk drapes and bedspreads and wood fittings. *Canalejas 1, San Vicente, 41001 95/450–5599 95/422–0938 www.solmelia.com 204 rooms, 14 suites Restaurant, bar, Internet, meeting room AE, DC, MC, V.*

$$$$ **Meliá Sevilla.** Behind the Plaza de España, this vast, modern hotel resembles the best American business hotels. Ask for a room at the front, facing the pool and the Plaza de España, which is illuminated on weekends. The best rooms and suites are on the ninth floor. Travelers with disabilities are well accommodated here. *Doctor Pedro de Castro 1, Pl. de España, 41004 95/442–2611 95/442–1608 364 rooms, 5 suites Restaurant, coffee shop, pool, hair salon, bar, Internet, meeting room, parking (fee) AE, DC, MC, V.*

$$$–$$$$ **Giralda.** Why stay at this modern hotel that caters largely to the tour-bus crowd and is far from the sights in a cul-de-sac off Recaredo? Service is friendly and professional, and rates are reasonable. The rooms, comfortable, spacious, and light, have relaxing, contemporary beige tones. Older rooms are carpeted; the newer ones have wooden floors. *Sierra Nevada 3, Puerta Carmona, 41003 95/441–6661 95/441–9352 111 rooms Restaurant, bar, meeting room AE, DC, MC, V.*

★ $$$–$$$$ **Los Seises.** This hotel is in a section of Seville's 16th-century Palacio Episcopal (Bishop's Palace), and the combination of modern and Renaissance architecture is striking: Room 219, for instance, is divided by a 16th-century brick archway, and breakfast is served in the old chapel. A pit in the center of the basement restaurant reveals the building's foundations and some archaeological finds, including a Roman mosaic. The rooftop pool and summer restaurant are in full view of the Giralda. ✉ *Segovia 6, Santa Cruz, 41004* ☎ *95/422–9495* 📠 *95/422–4334* 🌐 *www.hotellosseises.com* *40 rooms, 2 suites* *Restaurant, pool, Internet, parking (fee), some pets allowed* 💳 *AE, DC, MC, V.*

$$$–$$$$ **Pasarela.** Cozier than its giant neighbor, the Meliá Sevilla, this hotel has several ground-floor sitting rooms, some with oil paintings and table lamps, that give the place a homey feel. Guest rooms are large and fully carpeted, done in predominantly green and beige tones. ✉ *Av. de la Borbolla 11, Pl. de España, 41004* ☎ *95/441–5511* 📠 *95/442–0727* *77 rooms, 5 suites* *Gym, sauna, bar, Internet, meeting room* 💳 *AE, DC, MC, V.*

$$$–$$$$ **Zenit Sevilla.** Hidden behind Triana's main police station is this comfortable, modern property. A spacious courtyard leads to the bright, airy reception area. Rooms are carpeted and handsomely dressed in blue-on-white fabrics. Room price includes breakfast. ✉ *Pagés de Corro 90, Triana, 41010* ☎ *95/434–7434* 📠 *95/434–2797* 🌐 *www.zenithoteles.com* *128 rooms* *Restaurant, cafeteria, minibars, in-room data ports, in-room safes, bar, meeting rooms, parking (fee)* 💳 *AE, D, MC, V.*

$$$ **Bécquer.** Near the main shopping district, Bécquer has marble floors, dark wood, and leather furniture in its public areas, which include a small sitting room dedicated to the poet Gustavo Adolfo Bécquer. The guest rooms have peach-color walls, floral prints, matching woven bedspreads, and carved-wood headboards. ✉ *Reyes Católicos 4, Centro, 41001* ☎ *95/422–8900* 📠 *95/421–4400* 🌐 *www.hotelbecquer.com* *137 rooms, 2 suites* *Cafeteria, bar, Internet, parking (fee), some pets allowed* 💳 *AE, DC, MC, V.*

$$$ **Doña María.** This is one of Seville's most charmingly old-fashioned hotels, and it's not far from the cathedral. Some rooms are small and plain; others are tastefully furnished with antiques. Room 310 has a four-poster double bed, and 305 has two single four-posters; both have spacious bathrooms. There's also a rooftop pool with a good view of the Giralda, just a stone's throw away. ✉ *Don Remondo 19, Santa Cruz, 41004* ☎ *95/422–4990* 📠 *95/421–9546* 🌐 *www.hdmaria.com* *67 rooms* *Pool* 💳 *AE, DC, MC, V.*

$$$ **Inglaterra.** This classic hotel has long been known for excellent service. Next door to the British Consulate, it's something of a historic British outpost in Spain (even the courtesy car is an old London taxi). The rooms might be said to reflect this—furnishings are traditional, understated, and relaxing. Rooms on the fifth floor have large balconies. The spacious lobby lounge is a genteel meeting place, and the on-site Trinity Irish Pub lends a literary twist to this family-run enterprise. The second-floor dining room overlooks orange trees and the busy Plaza Nueva, as does La Galería, which serves some of Seville's finest Andalusian and Mediterranean cuisine. ✉ *Pl. Nueva 7, Centro, 41001* ☎ *95/422–4970* 📠 *95/456–1336* 🌐 *www.hotelinglaterra.es* *109 rooms* *Restaurant, bar, lobby lounge, pub, Internet, some pets allowed* 💳 *AE, DC, MC, V.*

$$$ **Las Casas de la Judería.** This labyrinthine hotel occupies three of the barrio's old palaces, each arranged around inner courtyards. Ocher predominates in the palatial common areas; the spacious guest rooms are dressed in tasteful pastels and decorated with prints of Seville. The hotel is tucked into a passageway off the Plaza Santa María. ✉ *Callejón de Dos Hermanas 7, Santa Cruz, 41004* ☎ *95/441–5150* 📠 *95/442–2170* *103 rooms, 3 suites* *Restaurant* 💳 *AE, DC, MC, V.*

★ **$$** **Hotel Amadeus.** You'll find here a musical haven in the heart of Seville. With pianos in the soundproof rooms and a music room off the central patio and lobby, this acoustical oasis is ideal for touring professional musicians and music fans in general. The breakfast terrace on the roof overlooks the Judería and the Giralda. The 18th-century palace has been charmingly restored and equipped with such modern amenities as in-room Internet, satellite TV, and a small glass-wall elevator whipping quietly up and down a corner of the central patio. ✉ *Calle Farnesio 6, Barrio de Santa Cruz, 41004* ☎ *95/450–1443* 📠 *95/450–0019* 🌐 *www.hotelamadeussevilla.com* *14 rooms* *Dining room, minibars, cable TV, Internet* 💳 *AE, DC, MC, V.*

$$ **Patio de la Alameda.** This charming small hotel in what was once a hospital is not especially convenient to the major Seville sights, but it's a good choice for exploring the Barrio de la Macarena, and you'll discover much that's attractive about Seville as you walk across Calle Sierpes to the cathedral or down Calle Feria to the Convento de Santa Paula. Convenient to the Alameda de Hércules, the pristine hotel, filled with plants and fountains, is a surprise after the dusty hubbub outside. Rooms, centered around small courtyards painted an attractive ocher, are modern and have kitchenettes and sitting rooms. ✉ *Alameda de Hércules 56, Barrio de la Macarena, 41002* ☎ *95/490–4999* 📠 *95/490–0226* 🌐 *www.patiosdesevilla.com* *22 apartments* *Kitchenettes, cable TV, bar, parking (fee)* 💳 *AE, D, MC, V.*

$$ **Simón.** In a rambling turn-of-the-19th-century town house, this hotel is a good choice for inexpensive, basic accommodation near the cathedral. The spacious, fern-filled, azulejo-tile patio makes a fine initial impression; the elegant marble stairway and high-ceilinged and pillared dining room are cool and stately spaces. The rooms are less grand, but the mansion's old-world style permeates throughout the house. ✉ *García de Vinuesa 19, El Arenal, 41001* ☎ *95/422–6660* 📠 *95/456–2241* 🌐 *www.hotelsimonsevilla.com* *29 rooms* *Dining room, some pets allowed* 💳 *AE, DC, MC, V.*

$ **Hostal Londres.** This simple but comfortable place near the Museo de Bellas Artes is a good value. Rooms are plain but clean, and some have balconies. Between the nearby art treasures, the lively nightlife around the Barrio de San Lorenzo, and the good vibrations emanating from the plaque to Manuel Machado (fellow poet and brother of the more famous Antonio) across from the door of the hotel, this is a find. ✉ *San Pedro Mártir 1, El Arenal, 41001* ☎ *95/421–2896* 📠 *95/450–3830* *23 rooms* *Dining room* 💳 *MC, V.*

$ **Hostal Sierpes.** This pleasant hostelry near the cathedral, with covered courtyard graced with arches, Seville tiles, and easy chairs, is in one of the quieter parts of the Barrio de Santa Cruz. The best rooms are upstairs, around a smaller, glass-roof patio. ✉ *Corral del Rey 22, Barrio de Santa Cruz, 41004* ☎ *95/422–4948* 📠 *95/421–2107* 🌐 *www.hsierpes.com* *36 rooms* *Restaurant, bar, some pets allowed* 💳 *AE, MC, V.*

Nightlife & the Arts

Seville has a lively nightlife and plenty of cultural activity. The monthly magazine *El Giraldillo* lists classical and jazz concerts, plays, dance performances, art exhibits, and films in Seville and all major Andalusian cities. (For films in English, look for the designation *v.o.*, for *versión original.*) The magazine is free at tourist offices and sold for a small fee at newsstands.

TAPAS BARS **Bar Estrella.** This prizewinning tapas emporium does excellent renditions of everything from *paté de esparragos trigueros* (wild asparagus paté) to *fabas con pringá* (stewed broad beans). ✉ *C. Estrella 3, Barrio de Santa Cruz* ☎ *95/422–7535.*

Bar Gran Tino. Named for the giant wooden wine cask that once (but no longer) dominated the bar, this busy spot on the funky Plaza Alfalfa is always alive and serves a representative range of Andalusian tapas, from *chocos* (cuttlefish) to chacina. ✉ *Plaza Alfalfa 2, Centro* ☎ *95/421–0883.*

Bodega Amarillo Albero. One of a cluster of good bars on the northwestern corner of Plaza de la Gavidia, this handy saloon serves delicious chacinas and a wide selection of cazuelitas. ✉ *Plaza de la Gavidia 5, Barrio de San Lorenzo* ☎ *95/421–1346* ⏲ *Daily 10 AM–2 AM.*

Bodeguita Entrecarceles. Literally meaning "between jails," this rustic spot just around the corner from Plaza del Salvador is roughly where Miguel de Cervantes, serving time for squandering the king's taxes, started *Don Quijote.* Try the montaditos and cazuelitas, some of the best in Seville. ✉ *C. Manuel Cortina 3, Centro* ☎ *95/422–1365* ⏲ *Closed Sun.*

Casablanca. This little slot is easy to overlook on busy Calle de Zaragoza, but everything they serve here is carefully selected, well presented, and delicious, from *crianzas* (aged wines) to finos, cheese to chacina. The small dining room in the back serves the same excellent food. ✉ *C. Zaragoza 50, El Arenal* ☎ *95/422–2498* ⏲ *Closed Sun.*

El Rinconcillo. Founded in 1670, just too late for Migúel de Cervantes to have hoisted a libation here, this lovely spot continues to chalk your tally on the wooden counters and serve a classic selection of dishes such as the fabas con pringá, *caldereta de venao* (venison stew), a superb *salmorejo* (cold vegetable soup), and espinacas con garbanzos. The views of the Iglesia de Santa Catalina out the front window are unbeatable. ✉ *C. Gerona 40, Barrio de la Macarena* ☎ *95/422–3183* ⏲ *Closed Wed.*

FLAMENCO

Seville has a handful of regular flamenco clubs, patronized more by tourists than by locals. Tickets are sold in most hotels; otherwise, make your own reservations (essential for groups, advisable for everyone in high season) by calling the club in the evening. For details of the huge Biannual Flamenco Festival in Sevilla, coming next in 2004, see 🌐 www.bienalflamenco.org.

El Arenal is in the back room of the picturesque Mesón Dos de Mayo. Here you get your own table, rather than having to sit in rows. ✉ *Rodo 7, Arenal* ☎ *95/421–6492* 🎫 *Dinner and show €69; show only, €27.65* ⏲ *Shows nightly at 9 and 11.*

El Patio Sevillano caters mainly to tour groups. The show is a mixture of regional Spanish dances (often performed to taped music) and pure flamenco by some outstanding guitarists, singers, and dancers. ✉ *Paseo de Colón 11, Arenal* ☎ *95/421–4120* 🎫 *Dinner and show €69 dinner; show only, €27.65* ⏲ *Shows nightly at 7:30 and 10.*

El Tamboril is a late-night bar in the heart of the Barrio de Santa Cruz noted for its great glass case in which the Virgin of Rocío sits in splendor. At 11 each night, locals pack in to sing the *Salve Rociera,* an emotive prayer to her (learn the words at 🌐 www.rocio.com/salve.htm). Afterward everything from flamenco to salsa continues until the early hours. ✉ *Pl. Santa Cruz, Santa Cruz* 🎫 *Free admission.*

La Anselma has both spontaneous announced performances, for which payment is required. In the heart of the Triana district, it is much less touristy than the posh *tablaos.* ✉ *Pagé de Corro, corner of Antillano Campos, Triana.*

Los Gallos is an intimate club in the heart of the Barrio de Santa Cruz. Performances are good and reasonably pure. ✉ *Pl. Santa Cruz 11, Santa Cruz* ☎ *95/421–6981* 🎫 *€27 with 1 drink* ⏲ *Shows nightly at 9 and 11:30* ⏲ *Closed 3 wks in Jan.*

MUSIC Concerts are performed at various venues, including the cathedral and the church of San Salvador; check *El Giraldillo* for details. Long prominent in the opera world, Seville is particularly proud of its opera house, the **Teatro de la Maestranza** (✉ Paseo de Colón 22, Arenal ☎ 95/422–3344). Classical music and ballet are performed at the **Teatro Lope de Vega** (✉ Av. María Luisa s/n, Parque de María Luisa ☎ 95/459–0853). The modern **Teatro Central** (✉ José de Gálvez s/n, Isla de la Cartuja ☎ 955/037200 🌐 www.teatrocentral.com) stages theater, dance, and classical and contemporary music. Seville's music college, the **Conservatorio Superior de Música** (✉ Baños 48, San Vicente ☎ 95/491–5630), offers its own performances. Built for outdoor shows at Expo'92, the **Auditorio de Sevilla** (✉ Camino de los Descubrimientos s/n, Isla de la Cartuja ☎ 915/186229) stages concerts. The **Teatro Alameda** (✉ Crédito 13, Alameda ☎ 95/438–8312) stages plays in Spanish, including some for children.

Sports & the Outdoors

BOATING The Guadalquivir is prime territory for boating enthusiasts. Paddleboats, canoes, and river cruises are great ways to see Seville and the surrounding countryside from the water. Inquire about rentals at the tourist office or on the riverbank near the Torre del Oro. **Cruceros Turísticos Torre del Oro** (✉ Paseo Alcalde Marqués de Contadero, beside Torre del Oro, Arenal ☎ 95/421–1396) runs river cruises daily every half hour, April–October 11 AM–midnight, November–March 11–7 and at 8 PM and 9 PM, for €12 per person.

BULLFIGHTING Bullfighting season is from Easter through Columbus Day, with most *corridas* (bullfights) held on Sundays. The season highlight is the April Fair, with Spain's leading toreros; other key dates are Corpus Christi, Assumption (August 15), and the last weekend in September. Fights take place at the **Maestranza Bullring,** on the Paseo de Colón 12 (☎ 95/422–4577). Bullfighting tickets are expensive; buy them in advance from the official ***despacho de entradas*** (ticket office) on Calle Adriano 37 (☎ 95/450–1382), alongside the bullring. Other legitimate despachos sell tickets on Calle Sierpes, but these are unofficial and charge a 20% commission.

Shopping

Seville is the region's main shopping area and the place for archetypal Andalusian souvenirs; most souvenirs are sold in the Barrio de Santa Cruz and around the cathedral and Giralda, especially Calle Alemanes. The main shopping street for Sevillanos themselves is Calle Sierpes, along with its neighboring streets Tetuan, Velázquez, Plaza Magdalena, and Plaza Duque—boutiques abound here. Near the Puente del Cachorro bridge, the old Estación de Córdoba train station has been converted into a stylish shopping center, the **Centro Comercial Plaza de Armas** (✉ enter on Pl. de la Legión, Almas), with boutiques, bars, fast-food joints, a microbrewery, and a cinema complex. The pan-Spanish department store **El Corte Inglés** stays open all day; check out Seville's main branch (✉ Pl. Duque de la Victoria 8, Centro ☎ 95/422–0931).

ANTIQUES For antiques, look along Mateos Gago, opposite the Giralda, and in the Barrio de Santa Cruz on Jamerdana and on Rodrigo Caro, between Plazas Alianza and Doña Elvira.

BOOKS A large assortment of books in English, Spanish, French, and Italian is sold at the American-owned **Librería Vértice** (✉ San Fernando 33–35, Santa Cruz ☎ 95/421–1654), near the gates of the university.

CERAMICS In the Barrio de Santa Cruz, browse along Mateos Gago; Romero Murube, between Plaza Triunfo and Plaza Alianza, on the edge of the Barrio; and between Plaza Doña Elvira and Plaza de los Venerables. Look for traditional azulejo tiles and other ceramics in the Triana **potters' district,** on Calle Alfarería and Calle Antillano Campos. **Cerámica Santa Isabel** is one of a string of Triana ceramics shops (✉ Alfarería 12, El Zurraque ☎ 95/434–4608). In central Seville, **Martian Ceramics** (✉ Sierpes 74, Centro ☎ 95/421–3413) has high-quality dishes, especially the flowers-on-white patterns native to Seville. It's a bit touristy but fairly priced. A permanent arts-and-crafts market near the cathedral is **El Postigo** (✉ Arfe s/n, Arenal ☎ 95/456–0013).

FANS **Casa Rubio** (✉ Sierpes 56, Centro ☎ 95/422–6872) is Seville's premier fan store, no mean distinction, with both traditional and contemporary designs.

FLAMENCO CULTURE & DRESSES Beware: flamenco paraphernalia is prohibitively expensive—a *mantón de Manila,* a typical Andalusian silk shawl, can range from €200 to €800, although cheaper versions can be found. One of the best flamenco shops, with a wide range of prices, is **María Rosa** (✉ Cuna 13, Centro ☎ 95/422–2143). For privately fitted and custom-made flamenco dresses, try **Delia and Maria del Mar Nuñez Pol** (✉ Cardenal Ilundain 3, Centro ☎ 95/423–6028), which are among the best. For music, books, and everything related to flamenco art, **Quejío** (✉ Huelva 34, Centro ☎ 95/456–2491) is the place to go.

GUITARS **Cayuela** (✉ Zaragoza 4, Arenal ☎ 95/422–4557) is run by the second generation of a family of guitar makers from Andújar, near Jaén. They carry unique, handcrafted guitars and quality factory-made instruments.

INTERNET In Seville there are various places that, apart from a terminal, may offer anything from body piercing to coffee. Surf at **Downtown New York** (✉ Pérez Galdós 1, La Alfalfa ☎ 95/450–1046). Check your mail at **Internet Pumarejo** (✉ San Luis 91, Alameda ☎ 95/490–8175 ⊕ www.sol.com/internet/pumarejo).

PASTRIES Seville's most celebrated pastry outlet is **La Campana,** founded in 1885 (✉ Sierpes 1, Centro ☎ 95/422–3570). Andalusia's convents are known for their homemade pastries—sample sweets from several convents at **El Torno** (✉ Pl. del Cabildo s/n, Santa Cruz ☎ 95/421–9190).

PORCELAIN La Cartuja china, originally crafted at La Cartuja Monastery but now made outside Seville, is sold at **La Alacena** (✉ Alfonso XII 25, San Vicente ☎ 95/422–8021). **El Corte Inglés** department stores are a good second choice.

STREET MARKETS The **Plaza del Duque** has a crafts market on Friday and Saturday. The flea market **El Jueves** is held on Calle Feria on Thursday morning. Sunday morning brings the **Alameda de Hercules** crafts market and, in the **Plaza del Cabildo,** a coin and stamp market.

TEXTILES You'll find all kinds of blankets, shawls, and embroidered tablecloths woven by local artisans at the three shops of **Artesanía Textil** (✉ García de Vinuesa 33, Arenal ☎ 95/456–2840 ✉ Sierpes 70, Centro ☎ 95/422–0125 ✉ Pl. de Doña Elvira 4, Santa Cruz ☎ 95/421–4748).

Carmona

33 *32 km (20 mi) east of Seville off N-IV.*

Claiming to be one of the oldest inhabited places in Spain (the Phoenicians and Carthaginians had settlements here), Carmona, on a steep, fortified hill, later became an important town under both the Romans and the Moors. Its Roman necropolis contains about 900 tombs dating from the 2nd century BC. As you wander its ancient, narrow streets, you'll see many Mudéjar and Renaissance churches, medieval gateways, and simple whitewashed houses of clear Moorish influence, punctuated here and there by a baroque palace. Local fiestas are held September 8–16. Park your car near the Puerta de Sevilla in the imposing **Alcázar de Abajo** (Lower Fortress), a Moorish fortification built on Roman foundations at the edge of the old town. In the tower beside the gate is the tourist office, where you can grab a map.

On the edge of the "new town," across the road from the Alcázar de Abajo, is the church of **San Pedro** (✉ Calle San Pedro), begun in 1466. Its interior is an unbroken mass of sculptures and gilded surfaces, and its baroque tower, erected in 1704, is an unabashed imitation of Seville's Giralda. Up Calle Prim is the **Plaza San Fernando,** in the heart of the old town, whose 17th-century houses have Moorish overtones. The Gothic church of **Santa María** (✉ Calle Martín) was built between 1424 and 1518 on the site of Carmona's former Great Mosque. Santa María is a contemporary of Seville's cathedral, and it, too, retains its Moorish courtyard, once used for ritual ablutions. Behind Santa María is the 18th-century **Palacio del Marqués de las Torres,** which has been restored to house a small museum on the history of Carmona. ☎ *95/414–0128* €2 *Oct.–May, Wed.–Mon. 11–7, Tues. 11–2; June–Sept., Wed.–Mon. 10–2 and 6:30–9:30, Tues. 10–2.*

Stroll down to the **Puerta de Córdoba** (Córdoba Gate) on the eastern edge of town. This old gateway was first built by the Romans around AD 175, then altered by Moorish and Renaissance additions. The Moorish **Alcázar de Arriba** (Upper Fortress) was built on Roman foundations and later converted by King Pedro the Cruel into a fine Mudéjar palace. Pedro's summer residence was destroyed by a 1504 earthquake, but the parador amid its ruins has a breathtaking view.

At the western end of town lies the splendid **Roman necropolis.** Here, in huge underground chambers, some 900 family tombs were chiseled out of the rock between the 2nd and 4th centuries BC. The walls, decorated with leaf and bird motifs, have niches for burial urns. The most spectacular tombs are the **Elephant Vault** and the **Servilia Tomb,** which resembles a complete Roman villa with its colonnaded arches and vaulted side galleries. Its lone occupant, a young woman, was embalmed, unlike the rest of the dead in the necropolis, who were cremated. ✉ *C. Enmedio* ☎ *95/414–0811* *Free* *Mid-Sept.–mid-June, Tues.–Fri. 9–4:45, weekends 10–1:45; mid-June–mid-Sept., Tues.–Fri. 8:30–1:45, Sat. 10–2.*

off the beaten path

ECIJA – This town 48 km (30 mi) from Carmona on the N-IV to Córdoba has 11 baroque church towers. It is known as "the frying pan of Andalusia," as midsummer temperatures often reach 37°C (100°F). From Ecija, take C430 south to **Osuna.** In the 16th century, the dukes of Osuna were among the wealthiest people in Spain, which accounts for the town's Renaissance palaces, Colegiata de Santa María church, and old university. From Osuna, take the A92 (N334) back to Seville (64 km [40 mi]).

Where to Stay & Eat

$–$$ ✕ **San Fernando.** You enter from a side street, but this second-floor restaurant looks out onto the Plaza de San Fernando. The beige dining room is pleasant in its simplicity, with nothing to distract from the view of daily life below. The kitchen serves Spanish dishes with flair—as in thin, fried potato slivers shaped as a bird's nest. Kid and partridge are perennial favorites, and there's a fine dessert selection. ✉ *Sacramento 3* ☎ *95/414–3556* *AE, DC, MC, V* *Closed Mon. and Aug. No dinner Sun.*

$$–$$$ **Alcázar de la Reina.** Stylish and contemporary, this hotel has public areas that incorporate three bright and airy courtyards, with marble floors and pastel walls. Guest rooms are spacious and comfortable. The elegant Ferrara serves tasty Spanish dishes, served à la carte or on a menú de degustación with four courses and dessert. *Pl. de Lasso 2, 41410* *95/419–6200* *95/414–0113* *66 rooms, 2 suites* *Restaurant, café, pool, bar, Internet, meeting rooms, parking (fee), some pets allowed* *AE, DC, MC, V.*

$$$$ **Casa de Carmona.** Every guest room has a different tone, some with Moorish accents, but all are luxuriously furnished. Rooms vary in size from the tiny, intimate Room 21 to the enormous Suite Azul (Blue Suite). Public rooms are decorated with antiques, rich fabrics, and museum-quality rugs. Relax in the Arabian-style garden, with orange trees and a fountain. *Pl. de Lasso 1 41410* *95/419–1000* *95/419–0189* *www.casadecarmona.com* *30 rooms, 1 suite* *Restaurant, pool, gym, hair salon, health club, massage, sauna, bar, library, laundry service, concierge, Internet, business services, meeting rooms, free parking, some pets allowed* *AE, DC, MC, V.*

★ **$$–$$$** **Parador Alcázar del Rey Don Pedro.** This delightful parador has superb views from its hilltop position among the ruins of Pedro the Cruel's summer palace. The public rooms open off a central, Moorish-style patio, and the vaulted dining hall and adjacent bar open onto an outdoor terrace overlooking the sloping garden. Spacious rooms have rugs and dark furniture. All but six, which face onto the front courtyard, look south over the valley; the best rooms are on the top floor. *Alcázar, 41410* *95/414–1010* *95/414–1712* *63 rooms* *Restaurant, pool, bar* *AE, DC, MC, V.*

Itálica

34 *12 km (7 mi) north of Seville, 1 km (½ mi) beyond Santiponce.*

Founded by Scipio Africanus in 205 BC as a home for veteran soldiers, Itálica had grown into one of Roman Iberia's most important cities by the 2nd century AD and had given the Roman world two great emperors, Trajan (52–117) and Hadrian (76–138). Ten thousand people once lived here, in 1,000 dwellings. About 25% of the site has been excavated, and work is still in progress. You'll find traces of city streets, cisterns, and the floor plans of several villas, some with mosaic floors, though all the best mosaics and statues have been removed to Seville's Museum of Archaeology. Itálica was abandoned and plundered as a quarry by the Visigoths, who preferred Seville. It fell into decay around AD 700. The huge, elliptical **amphitheater** held 40,000 spectators. Other remains, including a **Roman theater** and **Roman baths,** are visible in the small town that has grown up next door, Santiponce. *955/997376 or 95/499–6583* *€1.50, free for EU citizens* *Oct.–Mar., Tues.–Sat. 9–5:30, Sun. 10–4; Apr.–Sept., Tues.–Sat. 9–8, Sun. 9–3.*

PROVINCE OF HUELVA

When you're had enough of Seville's urban bustle, nature awaits in Huelva. From the Parque Nacional de Doñana, the pristine beaches on the Costa de la Luz, or the oak forests of the Sierra de Aracena nothing is much more than an hour's drive from Seville. Columbus's voyage to the New World was sparked here, at the monastery of La Rábida and in Palos de la Frontera. From Seville, turn off the Seville–Huelva highway, drive through Almonte and El Rocío—scene of the Whitsuntide pilgrimage to the Virgin of the Dew—and you'll come to the visitor center at La Rocina.

Doñana National Park

35 *100 km (62 mi) southwest of Seville.*

Fodor'sChoice ★

One of Europe's last swaths of wilderness are these wetlands beside the Guadalquivir estuary. The site was named for Doña Ana, wife of a 16th-century duke: prone to bouts of depression, she crossed the river and wandered into the wetlands one day, never to be seen alive again. Covering 188,000 acres, it's a haven for bird-watchers: the park sits on the migratory route from Africa to Europe and is the winter home and breeding ground for as many as 150 species of rare birds. The park's habitats range from beaches and shifting sand dunes to marshes, dense brushwood, and sandy hillsides of pine and cork oak. Two of Europe's most endangered species, the imperial eagle and the lynx, make their homes here, and kestrels, kites, buzzards, egrets, storks, and spoonbills breed among the cork oaks. A good base of exploration is the hamlet of **El Rocío,** on the park's northern fringe. In spring, during the Romería del Rocío pilgrimage, up to a million people converge on the local *santuario* (shrine) to worship the Virgen del Rocío (May 31 in 2004). The rest of the year, most of El Rocío's pilgrim-brotherhood houses are empty. Most of the streets are unpaved to make them more comfortable for horses.

At the Doñana visitor center at **La Rocina** (☎ 959/442340), less than 2 km (1 mi) from El Rocío, you can peer at the park's many bird species from a 3½-km (2-mi) footpath. It's open daily 9–2 and 3–sunset. Five kilometers (3 miles) away, an exhibit at the **Palacio de Acebrón** (☎ no phone) explains the park's ecosystems. It's open daily 8–3 and 4–sunset; last entrance is one hour before closing. Two kilometers (1 mile) before Matalascañas, you'll find **Acebuche,** the park's main interpretation center and the departure point for jeep tours, which must be reserved in advance (☎ 959/430432 for jeep tours). The center is open June–September, daily 8 AM–9 PM, October–May, daily 9–7. Tours leave daily June–September at 8:30 and 5 and October–May at 8:30 and 3 and last four hours, and they cover a 70-km (43-mi) route across beaches, sand dunes, marshes, and scrub. Cost is €18.20. Off-season (November–February) you can usually book a tour with just a day's notice; at other times, book as far in advance as possible.

Where to Stay

$$$ **Cortijo Los Mimbrales.** On the Rocío–Matalascañas road, this convivial, one-story Andalusian farm-hacienda is perched on the park's edge, a mere 1 km (½ mi) from the visitor center at La Rocina. The large common lounge with comfy chairs and fireplace makes for relaxed evening chitchat with fellow nature lovers. Pick a colorfully decorated room, or a bungalow that sleeps two to four, with kitchenettes and small private gardens. Some rooms and bungalows have fireplaces. There are stables on the premises, and the hotel can arrange horseback rides on the fringes of the park. ✉ *Ctra. del Rocío (A483), Km 30 21750* ☎ *959/442237* 🖷 *959/442443* 🌐 *www.cortijomimbrales.com* *20 rooms, 6 bungalows* *Restaurant, pool, horseback riding, some pets allowed; no a/c* 💳 *AE, DC, MC, V.*

$–$$ **Toruño.** Despite its location behind the famous Rocío shrine, the theme at this simple, friendly hotel is nature: it's run by the same cooperative that leads official park tours and has become a favorite of bird-watchers. Each room is named after a different species of local bird, and some have priceless views over the marshes. ✉ *Pl. del Acebuchal 22 21750* ☎ *959/442323* 🖷 *959/442338* *30 rooms* *Restaurant* 💳 *MC, V.*

Matalascañas

36 *3 km (2 mi) south of Acebuche, 85 km (53 mi) southwest of Seville.*

Its proximity to Acebuche, the main reception center at Doñana, makes Matalascañas a convenient lodging base for park visitors. Otherwise, it's a rather incongruous and ugly sprawl of hotels and vacation homes, very crowded at Easter and in summer and eerily deserted the rest of the year (most hotels are closed from November to March). There are some nice beaches for those who just want to relax, and the local ocean waters draw windsurfers and other water athletes.

Where to Stay

$$–$$$ **Tierra Mar.** Try this large beachfront hotel if you want to combine Doñana with the seashore. The nearby 18-hole Dunes golf course (€35 greens fee) is windy and challenging year round. *Matalascañas Parcela 120, Sector M, 21760 959/440300 959/440720 www.hoteltierramar.com 250 rooms Restaurant, café, pool, sauna AE, DC, MC, V.*

Mazagón

37 *22 km (14 mi) northwest of Matalascañas.*

There isn't much to see or do in this coastal town, but its parador makes a nice base for touring La Rábida, Palos de la Frontera, and Moguer. Mazagón's beautiful beach is among the nicest in the region.

Where to Stay & Eat

$$$ **Parador Cristóbal Colón.** This peaceful modern parador stands on a cliff surrounded by pine groves, overlooking a sandy beach 3 km (2 mi) southeast of Mazagón. Most rooms have balconies overlooking the garden. The restaurant serves Andalusian dishes and local seafood specialties, like stuffed baby squid, and hake medallions. *Ctra. San Juan del Puerto–Matalascañas, Km 30, 21130 959/536300 959/536228 www.parador.es 63 rooms Restaurant, cable TV, 2 tennis courts, outdoor pool, hot tub, sauna, fishing, bicycles, horseback riding, bar, meeting room, free parking AE, DC, MC, V.*

La Rábida

38 *30 km (19 mi) northwest of Doñana, 8 km (5 mi) northwest of Mazagón.*

You may want to extend your Doñana tour to see the monastery of **Santa María de La Rábida,** "the birthplace of America." In 1485 Columbus came from Portugal with his son Diego to stay in this Mudéjar-style Franciscan monastery. Here he discussed his theories with friars Antonio de Marchena and Juan Pérez, who interceded on his behalf with Queen Isabella. The early 15th-century church holds a much-venerated 14th-century statue of the **Virgen de los Milagros** (Virgin of Miracles). The **frescoes** in the gatehouse were painted by Daniel Vázquez Díaz in 1930. *959/350411 €3 with audio guide, €2.50 without Mar.–July and Sept.–Oct., Tues.–Sun. 10–1 and 3–7; Aug., Tues.–Sun. 10–1 and 4:45–8; Nov.–Feb., Tues.–Sun. 10–1 and 4–6:15.*

Two kilometers (1 mile) from the monastery, on the seashore, is the **Muelle de las Carabelas** (Caravels' Wharf), a reproduction of a 15th-century port. The star exhibits here are the full-size replicas of Columbus's flotilla, the *Niña, Pinta,* and *Santa María,* built using the same techniques as in Columbus's day. Board each one and learn more about the discovery of the New World in the adjoining museum. ✉ *Paraje de la Rábida* ☎ *959/530597 or 959/530312* 🎫 *€3* ⏲ *Oct.–Mar., Tues.–Sun. 10–7; Apr.–Sept., Tues.–Fri. 10–2 and 5–9, weekends 11–8.*

Palos de la Frontera

39 *4 km (2½ mi) northwest of La Rábida, 12 km (7 mi) northeast of Mazagón.*

On August 2, 1492, the *Niña,* the *Pinta,* and the *Santa María* set sail from Palos de la Frontera. Most of the crew were men from Palos and neighboring Moguer. At the door of the church of **San Jorge** (1473), the royal letter ordering the levy of the ships' crew and equipment was read aloud, and the voyagers took their water supplies from the Fontanilla (fountain) at the town's entrance.

Moguer

40 *12 km (7 mi) northeast of Palos de la Frontera.*

The inhabitants of this old port town now spend more time growing strawberries than they do seafaring, as you'll see from the surrounding fields. The **Convento de Santa Clara** dates from 1337. ✉ *Pl. de los Monjes s/n* ☎ *959/370107* 🎫 *€2* ⏲ *Tues.–Sat. guided tours at 11, noon, 1, 5, 6, and 7.*

While in Moguer, see the **Casa-Museo Juan Ramón Jiménez,** former home of the Nobel prize–winning poet who penned the much-loved *Platero y Yo.* At press time the Casa-Museo building was undergoing renovations and the exhibition (same price and hours) had been moved to the **house where he was born** (✉ Casa Natal, Ribera 2). ✉ *C. Juan Ramón Jiménez* ☎ *959/372148* 🎫 *€2* ⏲ *Tues.–Sat. 10:15–1:15 and 5:15–7:15, Sun. 10:15–1:15.*

Riotinto

41 *74 km (46 mi) northeast of Huelva.*

Heading north from Palos and Huelva on the N435, you'll reach the turnoff to Minas de Riotinto, the mining town near the source of the Riotinto (literally, "Red River"). The waters are the color of blood due to the minerals leached from the surrounding mountains: this area has some of the richest copper deposits in the world, as well as gold and silver. In 1873 the mines were taken over by the British Rio Tinto Company Ltd., which started to dig an open-pit mine and build a 64-km (40-mi) railway to the port of Huelva to transport mineral ore. The British left in 1954, but mining activity continues today, albeit on a smaller scale. Riotinto's landscape, scarred by centuries of intensive mining, makes for a well-organized **tour** conducted by the Fundación Riotinto. The tour's first stop, the **Museo Minero** (Museum of Mining), has archaeological finds and a collection of historical steam engines and rail coaches. Next comes the **Corta Atalaya,** one of the largest open-pit mines in the world (4,000 ft across and 1,100 ft deep), and **Bellavista,** the elegant English quarter where the British mine managers lived. The tour ends with an optional ride on the **Tren Minero** (Miners' Train), which follows the course of the Riotinto along more than 24 restored km (15 mi) of the old mining railway. You can opt for the full tour as described, or just visit the individual sights. ☎ *959/590025 Fundación Riotinto* 🎫 *Full tour €15 with steam engine 1st Sun. of month Oct.–May, €17 with diesel engine* ⏲ *Museum daily 10:30–3 and 4–7; miners' train mid-July–mid-Sept., daily at 1:30 PM; mid-June–mid-July, weekends at 4 PM; mid-Apr.–mid-*

May and mid-Sept.–mid-Oct., weekends at 5 PM; mid-Oct.–mid-Apr., weekends at 4 PM.

Aracena

42 *105 km (65 mi) northeast of Huelva, 100 km (62 mi) northwest of Seville.*

Stretching north of the Riotinto mines is the 460,000-acre Sierra de Aracena nature park, an expanse of hills cloaked in cork and holm oak. This region is known for its cured hams, which come from the prized free-ranging Iberian pigs that gorge on acorns in the autumn months prior to slaughter; the hams are buried in salt and then hung in cellars to dry-cure for at least two years. The best hams come from the village of **Jabugo.** The capital of the region is Aracena, whose main attraction is the spectacular cave known as the **Gruta de las Maravillas** (Cave of Marvels). The 12 caverns hide long corridors, stalactites and stalagmites arranged in wonderful patterns, and stunning underground lakes. ✉ *Pl. Pozo de Nieves, Pozo de Nieves* ☎ *959/128355* 🎫 *€7* ⏲ *Guided tours, if sufficient numbers, of caverns daily at 10:30, 11:30, 12:30, 1:30, 3, 4, 5, and 6.*

Where to Stay & Eat

$$ ✕ **José Vicente.** Diners come all the way from Seville and beyond for the food at this small restaurant near the Seville exit from Aracena. This is an ideal place to try dishes made with fresh pork (as opposed to the more commonly available cured ham) from the free-ranging Iberian pig. If the main dining room is full, you can dine at one of four tables in the adjoining Despensa de José Vicente, which doubles as a bar and a shop selling local produce. ✉ *Av. de Andalusia 51–3, Aracena* ☎ *959/128455* 💳 *AE, DC, MC, V* ⏲ *Closed Fri.*

$$$ **Finca Buenvino.** This lovely country house nestles in 150 acres of woods and is run like a small, beautifully furnished, stately home by a charming British couple, Sam and Jeannie Chesterton. Jeannie runs Andalusian, Mediterranean, and North African cooking courses. The room price includes a big breakfast and an excellent dinner with tapas beforehand. Barbecues can also be served by the large pool. There are three woodland self-catering cottages to let, each with its own pool. Reservations are essential. The house is 6 km (4 mi) from Aracena. ✉ *Crtra. N433 Km 95, 21293 Los Marines,* ☎ *959/124034* 📠 *959/501029* 🌐 *www.buenvino.com* *5 rooms, 3 cottages* *Restaurant, some kitchens, 3 pools, bar, Internet; no a/c, no room phones, no in-room TVs* 💳 *MC, V.* ⏲ *Closed mid-July–mid-Sept.*

★ $$–$$$ **Finca de la Silladilla.** In a wild Iberian pig–infested live oak and cork oak forest, this ranch offers a chance to see Spain's most prized products priming themselves for your palate. The rooms and small stone houses are impeccably decorated in heavy slabs of beautifully finished wood. The bathroom of one house has an oak tree growing through the roof. The staff can organize tours of the Sierra de Aracena, equestrian outings, or visits to nearby Jabugo, bellota (acorn-fed) ham capital of Spain. ✉ *Ctra. Los Romeros, Los Romeros 21290 Jabugo* ☎ *959/501350* 📠 *959/501184* 🌐 *www.visionrent.com* *2 rooms, 2 suites, 3 houses for 4, 1 house for 6* *Kitchens, horseback riding* 💳 *AE, DC, MC, V.*

$ **Galaroza Sierra.** On the outskirts of the village of Galaroza, 3 km (2 mi) from Jabugo, this hotel has common areas with light wood and woven blankets. Rooms have small balconies and views of the mountains, while the four bungalows face the swimming pool. Noise from the nearby road can be a problem. Ibérico pork is the restaurant's specialty. ✉ *Ctra. Sevilla–Lisboa, Km 69.5, 21291 Galaroza,* ☎ *959/123237*

959/123236 www.hotelgalaroza.com 22 rooms, 7 bungalows Restaurant, pool, some pets allowed; no a/c in some rooms DC, MC, V.

¢–$ **Los Castãnos.** Basic and comfortable, this hotel has small, simple rooms. Some face the street, others an interior patio; upstairs rooms have balconies. *Av. de Huelva 5, 21200 Aracena* *959/126300* *959/126287* *33 rooms* *Restaurant, café, parking (fee), some pets allowed; no a/c in some rooms* *AE, DC, MC, V.*

PROVINCE OF CÁDIZ

12

A trip through Cádiz is a trip back in time. Winding roads take you through scenes ranging from flat and barren plains to seemingly endless vineyards, and the rolling countryside is carpeted with blindingly white soil known as *albariza*—unique to this area, and the secret to the grapes used in sherry. Throughout the province, *los pueblos blancos* (the white villages) provide striking contrasts with the terrain, especially at Arcos de la Frontera, where the village sits dramatically on a crag overlooking the gorge of the Guadalete River. In Jerez, you can savor the town's internationally known sherry or delight in the skills and forms of purebred Carthusian horses. Finally, in the city of Cádiz, absorb about 3,000 years of history: this may be the oldest continuously inhabited city in the Western world.

Jerez de la Frontera

★ 43 *97 km (60 mi) south of Seville.*

Jerez, world headquarters for sherry, is surrounded by vineyards of chalky soil, whose Palomino grapes have funded a host of churches and noble mansions. Names such as González Byass, Domecq, Harvey, and Sandeman are inextricably linked with Jerez. The word *sherry,* first used in Great Britain in 1608, is an English corruption of the town's old Moorish name, Xeres. Both sherry and horses are very much the domain of Jerez's Anglo-Spanish aristocracy, whose Catholic ancestors came here from England centuries ago.

At any given time, more than half a million barrels of sherry are maturing in Jerez's vast aboveground wine cellars. If you visit a **bodega** (winery), your guide will explain the *solera* method of blending old wine with new, and the importance of the *flor* (a sort of yeast that forms on the surface of the wine as it ages) in determining the kind of sherry. Most bodegas welcome visitors, but it's advisable to phone ahead for an appointment, if only to make sure you join a group that speaks your language. Cellars usually charge an admission fee of €3–€6, and some close in August. Tours, about an hour, go through the aging cellars, with their endless rows of casks. (You won't see the actual fermenting and bottling, which take place in more modern, less romantic plants outside town.) Finally, you'll be invited to sample generous amounts of pale, dry fino; nutty *amontillado*; or rich, deep *oloroso,* and, of course, to purchase a few robustly priced bottles in the winery shop. For the other attractions, an hour's stroll around the city center is all you'll need. May and September are the most exciting times to visit Jerez, as their spectacular fiestas transform the town. For the Feria del Caballo (Horse Fair), in early May, carriages and riders fill the streets, and purebreds from the School of Equestrian Art compete in races and dressage displays. September brings the Fiesta de Otoño (Autumn Festival), when the first of the grape harvest is blessed on the steps of the cathedral.

If you only have time for one bodega, tour the **González Byass** (☎ 956/357000), home of the famous Tío Pepe. This tour is well organized and includes La Concha, an open-air aging cellar designed by Gustave Eiffel. Jerez's oldest bodega is **Domecq** (☎ 956/151500), founded in 1730. Aside from sherry, Domecq makes the world's best-selling brandy, Fundador. **John Harvey** (☎ 956/346004) is the source of Harvey's Bristol Cream. **Sandeman** (☎ 956/151700) is known for its man-in-a-cape logo.

Museo de Vino (✉ Cervantes 3, La Atalaya, Jerez de la Frontera ☎ 956/182100), a sherry museum, offers a multimedia show, exhibits, a bar, restaurant, and shop. Admission prices and opening hours were not known at press time.

The 12th-century **Alcázar** was once the residence of the caliph of Seville. Its small, octagonal **mosque** and **baths** were built for the Moorish governor's private use. The baths have three sections: the *sala fria* (cold room), the larger *sala templada* (warm room), and the *sala caliente* (hot room), for steam baths. In the midst of it all is the 17th-century **Palacio de Villavicencio,** built on the site of the original Moorish palace. A camera obscura, a lens-and-mirrors device that projects the outdoors onto a large indoor screen, offers a 360-degree view of Jerez and its principal monuments from the palace's highest tower. If you have a mobile phone, dial 650/800100 and you can access an English-language audio guide to the Alcázar that costs about €.30 per minute. ✉ *Alameda Vieja* ☎ *956/319798* 🎫 *€1.50, €3.25 including camera obscura* ⏲ *Mid-Sept.–Apr., daily 10–6; May–mid-Sept., daily 10–8.*

need a break?

Bar Juanito (Pescadería Vieja 8 and 10, ☎ 956/334838) has a pretty patio and is a past winner of the national Best Tapas Bar in Spain award. Jolly Faustino Rodríguez and his family serve 50 different stews and other fare. It's closed Monday and during El Rocó pilgrimage.

Across from the Alcázar and around the corner from the González Byass winery, the **cathedral** (✉ Pl. del Arroyo ⏲ open for Mass only) has an octagonal cupola and a separate bell tower. One block from the Plaza del Arenal, near the Alcázar, **San Miguel** is the only church in Jerez that opens during the day for sightseers. Built over the 15th and 16th centuries, the interior is an interesting illustration of the evolution of Gothic architecture, with various styles mixed into the design. ✉ *Pl. de San Miguel* ☎ *956/343347* 🎫 *€1.80* ⏲ *Tues.–Fri. 10:30–1:30, weekends for Mass only.*

On the **Plaza de la Asunción,** one of Jerez's most intimate squares, you'll find the Mudéjar church of **San Dionisio** and the ornate **cabildo municipal** (city hall), whose lovely plateresque facade dates from 1575. The unusual **Museo de los Relojes** is a museum devoted entirely to clocks, with 300 timepieces. ✉ *C. Cervantes 3* ☎ *956/182100* 🎫 *€4.50* ⏲ *Feb.–mid-Jan., Tues.–Sat. 10–2 and 5–7, Sun. 10–2.*

The **Centro Andaluz de Flamenco** is a modern flamenco museum, complete with an audio and visual library, and a multimedia show. ✉ *Palacio Pemartín, Pl. San Juan 1* ☎ *956/321127* 🌐 *www.caf.cica.es* 🎫 *Free* ⏲ *Weekdays 9–2.*

Diving into the maze of streets that form the scruffy San Mateo neighborhood east of the town center, you'll come to the **Museo Arqueológico,** one of Andalusia's best archaeological museums. The collection is strongest on the pre-Roman period. The star item, found near Jerez, is a Greek helmet dating from the 7th century BC. ✉ *Pl. del Mercado s/n*

☎ *956/341350* 🎫 *€21.66* ⏲ *Sept.–mid-June, Tues.–Fri. 10–2 and 4–7, weekends 10–2:30; mid-June–Aug., Tues.–Sun. 10–2:30.*

Fodor'sChoice ★ The **Real Escuela Andaluza del Arte Ecuestre** (Royal Andalusian School of Equestrian Art) operates on the grounds of the Recreo de las Cadenas, a 19th-century palace. This prestigious school was masterminded by Alvaro Domecq in the 1970s. Every Thursday the Cartujana horses—a cross between the native Andalusian workhorse and the Arabian—and skilled riders in 18th-century riding costume demonstrate intricate dressage techniques and jumping in the spectacular show "Cómo Bailan los Caballos Andaluces" (roughly, "The Dancing Horses of Andalusia"). Reservations are essential. Admission price depends on how close to the arena you sit; the first two rows are the priciest. ✉ *Av. Duque de Abrantes s/n* ☎ *956/319635* 🌐 *www.realescuela.org* 🎫 *€18, €15, or €12* ⏲ *Nov.–Feb., Thurs. at noon; Mar.–July 14, Tues. and Thurs. at noon; July 15–Oct., Fri. at midday; during Mar. fair nightly at 10:30.* The rest of the week, you can visit the stables and tack room, watch the horses being schooled, and see **rehearsals** for the show. 🎫 *€6* ⏲ *Mon.–Wed., Thurs. 10–1.*

Just outside Jerez de la Frontera is **Yeguada de la Cartuja,** the largest state-run stud farm in Spain for Carthusian horses. In the 15th century, a Carthusian monastery on this site started the breed for which Jerez and the rest of Spain are now famous. Every Saturday at 11 AM a full tour and show begin. ✉ *Finca Fuente El Suero, Ctra. Medina–El Portal, Km 6.5, Jerez de la Frontera* ☎ *956/162809* 🌐 *www.yeguadacartuja.com* 🎫 *€9.02* ⏲ *Sat. at 11 AM.*

Bullfighting

Jerez's bullring is on Calle Circo, northeast of the city center. Tickets are sold at the official ticket office on Calle Porvera, though only about five bullfights are held each year, in May and October. Six blocks from the bullring is the **Museo Restaurante Taurino,** a bullfighting museum where admission includes a drink. ✉ *Pozo del Olivar 6, Jerez de la Frontera* ☎ *956/323000* 🎫 *€2.40* ⏲ *Weekdays 9–1.*

Where to Stay & Eat

$–$$ ✕ **El Bosque.** Housed in a modern villa with contemporary paintings of bullfighting themes, this is one of the most stylish dining spots in town. Most tables are round and seat four; the smaller of the two dining rooms has picture windows overlooking a park. The food is contemporary Spanish. *Sopa de galeras* (soup of mantis shrimp) makes a rich appetizer; follow up with *confit de pato de laguna* (leg of wild duck) or *perdiz estofado con castañas* (stewed partridge with chestnuts). ✉ *Av. Alcalde Alvaro Domecq 26* ☎ *956/307030* 💳 *AE, DC, MC, V* ⏲ *Closed Sun. No dinner Aug.*

$–$$ ✕ **Gaitán.** Within walking distance of the riding school, this restaurant has white walls and brick arches decorated with colorful ceramic plates and photos of famous guests. It's crowded with businesspeople at lunchtime. The menu is Andalusian, with a few Basque dishes thrown in. *Setas* (wild mushrooms) make a delicious starter in season; follow them with cordero asado in a sauce of honey and Jerez brandy. ✉ *Gaitán 3* ☎ *956/345859* 💳 *AE, DC, MC, V* ⏲ *No dinner Sun.*

$–$$ ✕ **La Posada.** This place is strange in that its two small dining rooms, both enlivened by bullfight-red tablecloths, are on opposite sides of the street. Waiters dash back and forth to attend to their customers. The menu offers only grilled meat and grilled fish, according to what's best at the market, plus salad. Each course can be ordered in a full or half portion. ✉ *Arboledilla 1–2* ☎ *956/348165 or 607/515797* 💳 *AE, MC, V* ⏲ *Closed Sun. and Aug. No dinner Sat.*

$–$$ ✕ **Venta Antonio.** Crowds come to this roadside inn for superb, fresh seafood cooked in top-quality olive oil. You enter through the busy bar, where lobsters await their fate in a tank. Try the specialties of the Bay of Cádiz, such as *sopa de mariscos* (shellfish soup) followed by *bogavantes de Sanlúcar* (succulent local lobster). ✉ *Ctra. de Jerez–Sanlúcar, Km 5* ☎ *956/140535* 💳 *AE, DC, MC, V.*

★ ¢–$ ✕ **La Mesa Redonda.** Owner José Antonio Valdespino spent years researching the classic recipes once served in aristocratic Jerez homes, and now his son, José, presents them in this small, friendly restaurant off Avenida Alcalde Alvaro Domecq, around the corner from the Hotel Avenida Jerez. The eight tables are surrounded by shelves lined with cookbooks. (The round table at one end of the room gives the restaurant its name.) Ask the chef's mother, Margarita—who has an encyclopedic knowledge of Spanish wines—what to eat. ✉ *Manuel de la Quintana 3* ☎ *956/340069* 💳 *AE, DC, MC, V* ⊗ *Closed Sun. and mid-July–mid-Aug.*

¢–$ ✕ **Tendido 6.** The name gives you this restaurant's location: near the bullring, opposite Gate 6. The two dining rooms, the larger on a covered patio, are enlivened with bright-red tablecloths and bullfight posters. Dishes include *jamón serrano* (cured ham), *gambas al ajillo* (garlic shrimp), and *tarta de almendra* (almond tart). ✉ *Circo 10* ☎ *956/344835* 🌐 *www.tendido6.com* 💳 *AE, DC, MC, V* ⊗ *Closed Sun.*

$$$$ 🏨 **Montecastillo Hotel and Golf Resort.** Outside Jerez near the racetrack, the sprawling, modern Montecastillo adjoins a golf course designed by Jack Nicklaus. The spacious common areas have marble floors. Rooms are cheerfully decorated, with off-white walls, bright floral bedspreads, and rustic clay tiles. Ask for a room with a terrace overlooking the golf course. ✉ *Ctra. de Arcos, Km 9, 11406* ☎ *956/151200* 📠 *956/151209* 🌐 *www.montecastillo.com* *119 rooms, 2 suites, 20 villas* *Restaurant, 18-hole golf course, 3 pools (1 indoor), health club, sauna, spa, soccer, Internet* 💳 *AE, DC, MC, V.*

$$$ 🏨 **Jerez.** This luxury hotel is in a low, white, three-story building in a residential neighborhood north of town. The bar and the elegant restaurant, El Cartujano, overlook the sun terrace, large pool, and big, leafy garden. Public rooms get lots of natural light through picture windows. The best guest rooms overlook the pool and garden; those in back face the tennis courts and parking lot. ✉ *Av. Alcalde Alvaro Domecq 35, 11405* ☎ *956/300600* 📠 *956/305001* 🌐 *www.jerezhotel.com* *116 rooms, 4 suites* *Restaurant, 2 tennis courts, 2 pools (1 indoor), gym, hair salon, hot tubs, massage, sauna, bar, Internet, free parking* 💳 *AE, DC, MC, V.*

★ $$$ 🏨 **Royal Sherry Park.** Set back from the road in an unusually large, tree-filled garden, this modern hotel is designed around several patios filled with exotic foliage. The sunny hallways are hung with contemporary paintings. Rooms are bright and airy, and most have balconies overlooking the garden. ✉ *Avda. Alvaro Domecq 11 Bis, 11405* ☎ *956/317614* 📠 *956/311300* 🌐 *www.sherryparkhotel.com* *173 rooms* *Restaurant, coffee shop, 2 pools (1 indoor), gym, sauna, hair salon, bar, meeting room* 💳 *AE, DC, MC, V.*

$$–$$$ 🏨 **NH Avenida Jerez.** This modern hotel opposite the Royal Sherry Park has bright, sunny beige-and-blue rooms with hardwood floors. All rooms have VCRs. Ask for one at the back; rooms in front are close to the road and can be noisy, despite double glazing. Weekends bring discounts: inquire when you book. ✉ *Avda. Alvaro Domecq 10, 11405* ☎ *956/347411* 📠 *956/337296* 🌐 *www.nh-hoteles.es* *95 rooms* *Restaurant, coffee shop, bar* 💳 *AE, DC, MC, V.*

$–$$ 🏨 **Ávila.** This friendly hostelry on a side street off Calle Arcos offers affordable central lodgings. The rooms have basic furnishings and tile floors; beds are European twin-size. A TV lounge and a small bar and breakfast room adjoin the lobby. ✉ *Ávila 3, 11401* ☎ *956/334808* 📠 *956/336807* *32 rooms* *Bar, parking (fee)* *AE, DC, MC, V.*

Racing

Formula One Grand Prix races—including the Spanish motorcycle Gran Prix on the first weekend in May—are held at Jerez's racetrack, the **Circuito Permanente de Velocidad.** Call the track (✉ Ctra. Arcos, Km 10 ☎ 956/151100 🌐 www.circuitodejerez.com) or check with the tourist office for more information.

Shopping

Browse for wicker and ceramics along **Calle Corredera** and **Calle Bodegas. Duarte** (✉ Lancería 15 ☎ 956/342751) is the best-known saddle shop in town, sending its beautifully wrought leather all over the world (it sells to the British royal family). You can also buy other splendidly worked leather items.

12

Arcos de la Frontera

★ 44 *31 km (19 mi) east of Jerez.*

Its narrow and steep cobblestone streets, whitewashed houses, and finely crafted wrought-iron window grilles make Arcos the quintessential Andalusian pueblo blanco. Make your way to the main square, the Plaza de España, the highest point in the village: one side of the square is open, and a balcony at the edge of the cliff offers views of the Guadalete valley. On the opposite end is the church of **Santa María de la Asunción,** a fascinating blend of architectural styles: Romanesque, Gothic, and Mudéjar, with a plateresque doorway, a Renaissance retablo, and a 17th-century baroque choir. The *ayuntamiento* (Town Hall) stands at the foot of the old castle walls on the northern side of the square; across from here is the Casa del Corregidor, onetime residence of the governor and now a parador. Arcos is the most western of the 19 pueblos blancos, whitewashed towns dotted around the Sierra de Cádiz.

Where to Stay & Eat

$$ ✕ **El Convento.** With tables set around a graceful Andalusian patio, this cozy restaurant (owned by but separate from the hotel) is known for its fine regional cooking. The *sopa de tagarninas* (wild asparagus soup) is one of the town treasures, as are the *garbanzos con tomillo* (chickpeas with thyme) and the *abajado* (wild rabbit or lamb stew). ✉ *Marqués de Torresoto 7* ☎ *956/703222* *AE, DC, MC, V.*

★ $$–$$$ ✕ **Parador Casa del Corregidor.** Expect a spectacular view from the terrace—this parador clings to the cliff side overlooking the rolling valley of the Guadalete River. Public rooms include a popular bar and a restaurant that opens onto the terrace, and an enclosed patio. Spacious rooms are furnished with dark Castilian furniture, *esparto* (grass) rugs, and abundant tiles. The best rooms are Nos. 15–18, which overlook the valley. The restaurant's local dishes include *berenjenas arcenses* (spicy eggplant with ham and chorizo); or you can ask for the *menú gastronómico,* with 10 different regional specialties. ✉ *Pl. del Cabildo, 11630* ☎ *956/700500* 📠 *956/701116* 🌐 *www.parador.es* *24 rooms* *Restaurant, café, bar* *AE, DC, MC, V.*

$$ **Cortijo Faín.** This intimate resort hotel is in a 17th-century farmhouse on a ranch 3 km (2 mi) southeast of Arcos. The old *cortijo* (farm estate) is surrounded by olive groves and enclosed in high, white walls covered in bougainvillea. Try to get one of the two suites that have their own fireplaces. Reservations are essential. ✉ *Ctra. de Algar, Km 3, 11630* ☎ *956/231396* 📠 *956/231961* 🌐 *http://cortijofain.en.eresmas.com*

3 rooms, 5 suites Restaurant, pool, horseback riding, library, meeting room, some pets allowed; no room TVs AE, DC, MC, V Closed Jan.–mid-Feb.

$$ **El Convento.** Perched on top of the cliff behind Parador Casa del Corregidor, this tiny hotel shares the same amazing view, though the rooms are much smaller, more simply furnished, and cheaper (half the price, in fact). The building is a former convent. *Maldonado 2, 11630 956/702333 957/704128 www.webdearcos.com/elconvento 11 rooms Cafeteria AE, DC, MC, V.*

$$ Fodor'sChoice ★ **La Casa Grande.** Built in 1729, this extraordinary town house encircles a lushly vegetated central patio and is perched on the edge of the 400-ft cliff to which Arcos de la Frontera clings. Each room has been restored by owners Elena Posa and Ferran Grau. The artwork, the casually elegant design of the living quarters, and inventive bathrooms are all a delight. The breakfast terrace allows you to look down on falcons circling hundreds of feet above the riverbed below. The rooftop rooms "El Palomar" (the pigeon roost) and "El Soberao" (the attic) are the best. *C. Maldonado 10, 11630 Arcos de la Frontera 956/703930 956/703930 www.lacasagrande.net 4 rooms, 2 suites Library AE, DC, MC, V.*

$$ **Marqués de Torresoto.** This hotel is in a restored 17th-century palace, with a large courtyard, a mesón-style restaurant, and an ornate baroque chapel. Rooms are spacious; those on the uppermost of the three floors are the nicest, and some look over the village rooftops. You'll have to walk up, however, as there's no elevator. Rooms that face the street can be noisy. *Marqués de Torresoto, 11630 956/700717 956/704205 www.tugasa.com 15 rooms Restaurant, bar, some pets allowed AE, DC, MC, V.*

Sanlúcar de Barrameda

45 *24 km (15 mi) northwest of Jerez.*

Columbus sailed from this harbor on his third voyage to the Americas, in 1498. Twenty years later, Magellan began his circumnavigation of the globe from here. Today this unspoiled fishing town is known for its *langostinos* (giant shrimp) and manzanilla, an exceptionally dry sherry. The most popular restaurants are in the **Bajo de Guía** neighborhood, on the banks of the Guadalquivir. Here, too, is the Fábrica de Hielo, which serves as a visitor center for Doñana National Park. Boat trips can take you up the river, stopping at various points in the park; the ***Real Fernando*** makes a four-hour cruise, with bar and café, up the Guadalquivir to the Coto de Doñana. *Bajo de Guía, Sanlúcar de Barrameda 956/363813 €15 Cruise times Oct.–Dec. and Feb. at 10 AM; Mar. at 10 AM and 4 PM; June–Sept. at 10 AM and 5 PM.*

A riverboat service with a three-hour cruise, a café, and binoculars for hire is **Los Cristóbal** (Av. Bajo de Guía, Sanlúcar de Barrameda 956/960766). Call to check the timetable and prices.

From the *puerto pesquero* (fishing port) of **Bonanza,** 4 km (2½ mi) upriver from Sanlúcar, there's a fine view of fishing boats and the pine trees of Doñana on the opposite bank. Sandy beaches extend along Sanlúcar's southern promontory to Chipiona, where the Roman general Scipio Africanus built a beacon tower.

Where to Stay & Eat

$$ **Mirador de Doñana.** This Bajo de Guía landmark serves fresh sole, shrimp, and *puntillas* (baby squid). The dining area overlooks the large, busy bar. *Bajo de Guía 956/364205 MC, V.*

$-$$ ✕ **Bigote.** Colorful and informal, this spot on the beach is known for its fried *acedias* (a type of small sole) and langostinos, which come from these very waters. The seafood paella is also good. Reservations are essential in summer. ✉ *Bajo de Guía* ☎ *956/362696* 💳 *AE, DC, MC, V* ⊗ *Closed Sun.*

$-$$ ✕ **Casa Balbino.** After the sunset at Bajo de Guía beach, the serious tapas and tippling begins in Sanlúcar's local party nerve center in the Plaza del Cabildo. Balbino is the best of these taverns—though the *patatas aliñá* (potatoes dressed in an olive oil vinaigrette) at Bar Barbiana are noteworthy as well. ✉ *Plaza del Cabildo 14* ☎ *956/362647* 💳 *AE, DC, MC, V.*

$$ 🏨 **Posada de Palacio.** Across the street from the luxuriant gardens of the Palacio de los Infantes de Orleans—now the Sanlúcar town hall—this restored 18th-century palace houses a friendly family-run hotel, with rooms grouped around a cool patio. ✉ *Caballeros 11, 11540* ☎ *956/364840* 📠 *956/365060* *24 rooms* *Restaurant, pool, some pets allowed; no a/c, no room TVs* 💳 *AE, DC, MC, V.*

$ 🏨 **Los Helechos.** Named for the ferns *(los helechos)* that dominate the patio and entryway, this breezy place with a lovely rooftop terrace has the distinct advantage of being out of earshot but within crawling distance of the Plaza del Cabildo. ✉ *Plaza Madre de Dios 9, 11540* ☎ *956/361349* 📠 *956/369650* *56 rooms* *Restaurant, cable TV, bar, parking (fee)* 💳 *AE, DC, MC, V.*

Puerto de Santa María

46 *12 km (7 mi) southwest of Jerez, 17 km (11 mi) north of Cádiz.*

This attractive, if somewhat dilapidated, little fishing port on the northern shores of the Bay of Cádiz, with lovely beaches nearby, has white houses with peeling facades and floor-length green grilles covering the doors and windows. The town is dominated by the Terry and Osborne sherry and brandy bodegas. Columbus once lived in a house on the square that bears his name (Cristóbal Colón), and Washington Irving spent the autumn of 1828 at Calle Palacios 57. The marisco bars along the Ribera del Marisco (Seafood Way) are Puerto de Santa María's current claim to fame. Casa Luis, Romerijo, La Guachi, and Paco Ceballos are among the most popular as well as Er Beti, at Misericordia 7. The tourist office has a list of six tapa routes taking in 39 tapas bars, listing their specialties.

The **Castillo de San Marcos** was built in the 13th century on the site of a mosque. Created by Alfonso X, it was later home to the Duke of Medinaceli. Among the guests were Christopher Columbus—who tried unsuccessfully to persuade the duke to finance his voyage west—and Juan de la Cosa, who, within these walls, drew up the first map ever to include the New World. The red lettering on the walls is a 19th-century addition. ✉ *Pl. del Castillo* ☎ *956/851751* *€3, free Tues.* ⊗ *Tues., Thurs., and Sat. 10–2.*

The neo-Mudéjar **Plaza de Toros** was built in 1880 thanks to a donation from the wine maker Thomas Osborne. It originally had seating for exactly 12,816 people, the population of Puerto at that time. ✉ *Los Moros* *Free* ⊗ *Apr.–Oct., Thurs.–Tues. 11–1:30 and 6–7:30; Nov.–Mar., Thurs.–Tues. 11–1:30 and 5:30–7* ⊗ *Closed bullfight days plus 1 day before and after each bullfight.*

Where to Stay & Eat

$$-$$$ ✕ **El Faro de El Puerto.** In a villa outside town, the "Lighthouse in the Port" is run by the same family that established the classic El Faro in

Cádiz. Like its predecessor, it serves excellent fish, but you can also sample such delicacies as veal rolls filled with foie gras in a sweet sherry sauce. ✉ *Ctra. Fuenterabia–Rota, Km 0.5* ☎ *956/858003 or 956/870952* 🌐 *www.elfarodelpuerto.com* ▭ *AE, DC, MC, V* ⊗ *No dinner Sun. except during Aug.*

$–$$ ✕ **Casa Flores.** This place serves the same fresh seafood as the neighboring Ribera del Marisco haunts, but is a bit more upmarket. You approach the two dining rooms, decorated with tiles and wood paneling, through a long bar hung with hams. Specialties include *filete de urta al camarón* (fillet of bream in shrimp sauce) and *fritos de la bahía* (assorted fried fish from the Bay of Cádiz). ✉ *Ribera del Río 9* ☎ *956/543512* 🌐 *www.casaflores.com* ▭ *AE, DC, MC, V.*

$–$$ ✕ **Los Portales.** A Ribera del Marisco favorite, this comfortable dining room has a marine motif. At the popular bar you can sample *ortiguillas* (fried sea anemones, a local favorite) plus more standard seafood, grilled or fried. ✉ *Ribera del Río 13* ☎ *956/542116* ▭ *AE, DC, MC, V.*

★ $$$–$$$$ **Monasterio de San Miguel.** Dating from 1733, this monastery is a few blocks from the harbor. There's nothing spartan about the former cells; they're now air-conditioned rooms with all the trappings. The restaurant is in a large, vaulted hall; the baroque church is now a concert hall; and the cloister's gardens provide a peaceful refuge. Beamed ceilings, polished marble floors, and huge brass lamps enhance the 18th-century feel. ✉ *Larga 27, 11500* ☎ *956/540440* 📠 *956/542604* *139 rooms, 11 suites* *Restaurant, pool, paddle tennis, squash, bar, parking (fee)* ▭ *AE, DC, MC, V.*

Nightlife

The **Casino Bahía de Cádiz,** on the road between Jerez and Puerto de Santa María, is the only casino in this part of Andalusia. You can play the usual games, and there's a restaurant and a disco. You must present your passport to enter. On weekends there is a disco and, in summer, live shows. ✉ *N-IV, Km 649, Puerta de Santa María* ☎ *956/871042* *€3; free for first-time visitors, also free entry vouchers at tourist office* ⊗ *Sun.–Wed. 5 PM–3 AM, Thurs. 5 PM–4 AM, weekends and daily in Aug. 5 PM–6 AM* *Restaurant, café, bar.*

Cádiz

★ 47 *32 km (20 mi) southwest of Jerez, 149 km (93 mi) southwest of Seville.*

Surrounded by the Atlantic Ocean on three sides, Cádiz was founded as Gadir by Phoenician traders in 1100 BC and claims to be the oldest continuously inhabited city in the Western world. Hannibal lived in Cádiz for a time, Julius Caesar first held public office here, and Columbus set out from here on his second voyage, after which the city became the home base of the Spanish fleet. When the Guadalquivir silted up in the 18th century, Cádiz monopolized New World trade and became the wealthiest port in Western Europe. Most of its buildings—including the cathedral, built in part with gold and silver from the New World—date from this period.

The old city is African in appearance and immensely intriguing—a cluster of narrow streets opening onto charming small squares. The golden cupola of the cathedral looms above low white houses, and the whole place has a slightly dilapidated air. Spaniards flock here in February to revel in the famous Carnival celebrations, but few foreigners have yet to discover the city's real charm. You might begin your explorations in the Plaza de Mina, a large, leafy square with palm trees and plenty of benches. On the square's western flank, the ornamental facade of the

Colegio de Arquitectos (College of Architects) is especially beautiful. In the northwestern corner of the square is the tourist office. On the east side of the Plaza de Mina, you'll find the **Museo de Cádiz** (Provincial Museum), well worth visiting for its works by Murillo and Alonso Cano, and the *Four Evangelists* and set of saints by Zurbarán, which have much in common with his masterpieces at Guadalupe, in Extremadura. The archaeological section contains Phoenician sarcophagi from the time of this ancient city's birth. ✉ *Pl. de Mina* ☎ *956/212281* 🎫 *€1.80, free for EU citizens* ⏲ *Tues. 2:30–8, Wed.–Sat. 9–8, Sun. 9–2.*

A few blocks east of the Plaza de Mina, next door to the Iglesia del Rosario, is the **Oratorio de la Santa Cueva,** an oval 18th-century chapel with three frescoes by Goya. ✉ *C. Rosario 10* ☎ *956/222262* 🎫 *€1.50* ⏲ *Tues.–Fri. 10–1 and 4:30–7:30, weekends 10–1.*

Heading up Calle San José from the Plaza de la Mina, you'll see the **Oratorio de San Felipe Neri.** Spain's first liberal constitution was declared at this church in 1812, and here the Cortes (Parliament) of Cádiz met when the rest of Spain was subjected to the rule of Napoléon's brother, Joseph Bonaparte (more popularly known as Pepe Botella, for his love of the bottle). On the main altar is an *Immaculate Conception* by Murillo, the great Sevillian artist who in 1682 fell to his death from a scaffold while working on his *Mystic Marriage of St. Catherine* in Cádiz's Chapel of Santa Catalina. ✉ *Santa Inés 38* ☎ *956/211612* 🎫 *€1.20* ⏲ *Mon.–Sat. 10–1.*

Next door to the Oratorio de San Felipe Neri, the small but pleasant **Museo Histórico Municipal** has a 19th-century mural depicting the establishment of the Constitution of 1812. Its real showpiece, however, is a 1779 ivory and mahogany model of Cádiz, with all of the city's streets and buildings in minute detail, looking much as they do now. ✉ *Santa Inés 9* ☎ *956/221788* 🎫 *Free* ⏲ *Oct.–May, Tues.–Fri. 9–1 and 4–7, weekends 9–1; June–Sept., Tues.–Fri. 9–1 and 5–8, weekends 9–1.*

Four blocks west of Santa Inés is the Plaza Manuel de Falla, overlooked by an amazing neo-Mudéjar redbrick building, the **Gran Teatro Manuel de Falla.** The classic interior is impressive as well; try to attend a performance. ✉ *Pl. Manuel de Falla* ☎ *956/220828.*

Backtrack along Calle Sacramento toward the city center to **Torre Tavira.** At 150 ft, this tower, attached to an 18th-century palace that is now a conservatory of music, is the highest point in the old city. More than a hundred such watchtowers were used by Cádiz ship owners to spot their arriving fleets. A camera obscura gives a good overview of the city and its monuments, last shows half an hour before closing time. ✉ *Marqués del Real Tesoro 10* ☎ *956/212910* 🎫 *€3* ⏲ *Mid-June–mid-Sept., daily 10–8; mid-Sept.–mid-June, daily 10–6.*

Five blocks southeast of the Torre Tavira are the gold dome and baroque facade of Cádiz's **cathedral,** begun in 1722, when the city was at the height of its power. The Cádiz-born composer Manuel de Falla, who died in 1946 at the age of 70, is buried in the **crypt.** The cathedral **museum,** on Calle Acero, displays gold, silver, and jewels from the New World, as well as Enrique de Arfe's processional cross, which is carried in the annual Corpus Christi parades. The cathedral is known as the New Cathedral because it supplanted the original 13th-century structure next door, which was destroyed by the British in 1592, rebuilt, and renamed the church of **Santa Cruz** when the New Cathedral came along. The cathedral is currently being restored, but you can visit the crypt, museum, and church of Santa Cruz. ✉ *Pl. Catedral* ☎ *956/259812 museum*

Museum €3 Mass Sun. at noon; museum Tues.–Fri. 10–2 and 4:30–7:30, Sat. 10–1.

Next door to the church of Santa Cruz are the remains of a 1st-century BC **Roman theater** (Campo del Sur), discovered by chance in 1982. Call Museo de Cádiz (956/212281) to see if it's open, as it has been undergoing repairs. The impressive **ayuntamiento** overlooks the Plaza San Juan de Diós, one of Cádiz's liveliest hubs. Built in two parts, in 1799 and 1861, the building is attractively illuminated at night. The **Plaza San Francisco,** near the ayuntamiento, is a pretty square surrounded by white and yellow houses and filled with orange trees and elegant street lamps. It's especially lively during the evening *paseo* (promenade).

Where to Stay & Eat

$$–$$$ Fodor'sChoice ★ **El Faro.** Gonzalo Córdoba's fishing-quarter restaurant is deservedly known as the best restaurant in the province. Outside, it's one of many low white houses with bright-blue flowerpots; inside it's warm and inviting, with half-tile walls, glass lanterns, oil paintings, and photos of old Cádiz. Fish dominates the menu, but alternatives include *cebón al queso de cabrales* (venison in blue-cheese sauce). *San Felix 15 956/211068 AE, DC, MC, V.*

★ **$$** **El Ventorrillo del Chato.** Standing on its own on the sandy isthmus connecting Cádiz to the mainland, this former inn was founded in 1780 by a man ironically nicknamed "El Chato" (pug-nosed) for his prominent proboscis. Run by a scion of El Faro's Gonzalo Córdoba, the restaurant serves tasty regional specialties in charming Andalusian surroundings. Seafood is a favorite, but meat, stews and rice dishes are also well represented on the menu, and the wine list is very good. *Vía Augusta Julia s/n 956/250025 AE, DC, MC, V Closed Sun.*

$–$$ **Casa Manteca.** Cádiz's most quintessentially Andalusian tavern is just down the street from El Faro restaurant and a little deeper into La Viña barrio (named for the vineyard that once grew here). *Chacina* (Iberian ham or sausage) served on waxed paper and Manzanilla (sherry from Sanlúcar de Barrameda) are standard fare at this low wooden counter that has served bullfighters and flamenco singers, as well as dignitaries from around the world. *Corralón de los Carros 66 956/213603 AE, DC, MC, V No lunch Sun.*

$$–$$$ **Parador Atlántico.** Cádiz's modern parador has a privileged position on the headland overlooking the bay and is the only hotel in its class in the old part of Cádiz. The spacious indoor public rooms have gleaming marble floors, and tables and chairs surround a fountain on the small patio. The cheerful, bright-green bar, decorated with ceramic tiles and bullfighting posters, is a popular meeting place for Cádiz society. Most rooms have small balconies facing the sea. *Duque de Nájera 9, 11002 956/226905 956/214582 www.parador.es 143 rooms, 6 suites Restaurant, pool, gym, sauna, bar, Internet, free parking, some pets allowed AE, DC, MC, V.*

$$ **Francia y Paris.** The advantage here is the central location, on a pretty pedestrian square in the heart of the old town. The dull modern interior includes a vast lobby and sitting room and a small bar and breakfast room. Guest rooms are simple; some have small balconies facing the square. *Pl. San Francisco 2, 11004 956/222348 956/222431 57 rooms Bar, Internet, meeting rooms AE, DC, MC, V.*

Nightlife & the Arts

The cultural hub in Cádiz is the **Gran Teatro Manuel de Falla** (Pl. Manuel de Falla 956/220828). The tourist office has performance schedules.

Shopping

Traditional Andalusian handicrafts, especially ceramics and wicker, are plentiful in Cádiz. Just off the Plaza de la Mina, **Belle Epoque** (✉ Antonio Lopez 2 ☎ 956/226810) is one of the city's better—and more reasonably priced—antiques stores, specializing in furniture.

SEVILLE & WESTERN ANDALUSIA A TO Z

12

To research prices, get advice from other travelers, and book travel arrangements, visit www.fodors.com.

AIR TRAVEL

International flights arrive in Seville from Amsterdam, Brussels, Frankfurt, London, and Paris. Domestic flights connect the Andalusian capital with Madrid, Barcelona, Valencia, and other major cities. Iberia flies from Jerez de la Frontera to Madrid, Barcelona, Valencia–Palma de Mallorca, and Zaragoza.

Iberia ✉ Almirante Lobo 2, Seville, ☎ 95/422-9345, 95/451-0677, 902/400500 at Aeropuerto de Sevilla, 956/150010 at Jerez de la Frontera airport. **Air Europa** ✉ Almirante Lobo 2, Seville, ☎ 95/444-9179. **Air Nostrum** ✉ Aeropuerto de Sevilla ☎ 902/400500 Spain. **Spanair** ✉ Almirante Lobo 2, Seville, ☎ 902/121415 Spain.

AIRPORTS

The region's main airport belongs to Seville, 12 km (7 mi) east of the city on the N-IV to Córdoba. There is a bus from the airport to the center of Seville every half hour on weekdays (between 6:30 AM and 8 PM), less often on weekends. A smaller airport, the Aeropuerto de la Parra, is 7 km (4 mi) north of Jerez on the road to Seville.

Airport Information **Aeropuerto de la Parra** Jerez ☎ 956/150000. **Aeropuerto de Sevilla** ☎ 95/444-9000.

BIKE TRAVEL

If you are thinking of bringing a bicycle with you, Spain has severe restrictions on taking bikes on trains (⇨ Bike Travel *in* Smart Travel Tips). Seville city is perfect for bike travel since it's flat, but make sure you have a good padlock or two handy; for rentals, contact Sevilla Mágica. The route from Seville to Puerto de Santa María, Jerez, and Cádiz is also flat but it is hillier toward Portugal and northward. Many local tourist offices have details of mountain-bike routes.

In Seville or Cádiz, if you want to rent a four-wheel bike—these modern-day rickshaws are good with children or bags—or want to rent a bike with an audio guide, call Cyclotour/Telebike. In Puerto de Santa María, Bigote will rent you a bike.

Bike Rentals **Bigote** ✉ Rodrigo de Bastidas 6 ☎ 956/875418. **Cyclotour/Telebike** ✉ Residencial Virgen de Rocío 3, 4th Floor, A, Mairena del Aljarafe, Seville ☎ 605/2528312 🌐 www.cyclotouristic.com. **Sevilla Mágica** ✉ Miguel de Mañra 11, Santa Cruz ☎ 95/456-3838

BOAT & FERRY TRAVEL

See Sports & the Outdoors *in* Seville and Environs and details on boating services *in* Sanlúcar de Barrameda. Boats cruise along the Guadalquivir river, which links both places. From Cádiz, Trasmediterránea operates truck, car, and passenger ferry services to the Canary Islands. For foot passengers, boats leave every Tuesday and call at Gran Canaria, Tenerife, and La Palma. Fares range from €200–to €429 for this trip, which takes 36–48 hours.

Boat & Ferry Information **Trasmediterránea** ✉ Estación Marítima ☎ 956/227421 or 902/454645 🌐 www.trasmediterranea.es

BUS TRAVEL

Alsa long-distance buses connect Seville with Madrid; with Cáceres, Mérida, and Badajoz in Extremadura; and with Córdoba, Granada, Málaga, Ronda, and Huelva in Andalusia. Regional buses connect all of the towns and villages in this region—indeed, buses within Andalusia (and between Seville and Extremadura) tend to be more frequent and convenient than trains. The coastal route links Granada, Málaga, and Marbella to Cádiz. From Ronda, buses run to Arcos, Jerez, and Cádiz. Seville has two bus stations. The older one is the Estación del Prado de San Sebastián, off Plaza de San Sebastián between Manuel Vázquez Sagastizabal and José María Osborne; buses from here serve points west and northwest. The second station, a modern terminal on the banks of the Guadalquivir River downtown, next to the east end of Cachorro Bridge, is called Estación Plaza de Armas and serves central and eastern Spain. Cádiz also has two bus stations: Comes, which serves most destinations in Andalusia, and Los Amarillos, which serves Jerez, Seville, Córdoba, Puerto de Santa María, Sanlúcar de Barrameda, and Chipiona. The bus station in Jerez, on Plaza Madre de Dios, is served by two companies: La Valenciana and Los Amarillos.

Bus Companies **Alsa/Enatcar** Spain ☎ 902/422242 🌐 www.alsa.es. **Comes** ✉ Pl. Hispanidad, Cádiz ☎ 956/224271. **La Valenciana** ✉ Bus station, Pl. Madre de Dios, Jerez de la Frontera ☎ 956/341063. **Los Amarillos** ✉ Diego Fernández Herreras 34, Cádiz ☎ 956/285852, 956/329347 in Jerez.

Bus Stations **Seville-Estación del Prado de San Sebastián** ✉ Prado de San Sebastián s/n ☎ 95/441-7111 or 95/441-7118. **Seville-Estación Plaza de Armas** ✉ Cristo de la Expiración ☎ 95/490-7737. **Huelva-Estación de Autobuses** ✉ Av. Doctor Rubio s/n ☎ 959/256900. **Jerez de la Frontera-Estación de Autobuses** ✉ Cartuja ☎ 956/345207. **Cádiz-Estación de Autobuses Comes** ✉ Pl. de la Hispanidad 1 ☎ 956/807059.

BUS TRAVEL WITHIN SEVILLE

Seville's urban bus service is efficient and covers the greater city area. Buses do not run within the popular tourist area Moorish Santa Cruz because the streets are too narrow.

FARES & SCHEDULES

Seville's urban bus services cover the city and operate limited night service between midnight and 2 AM, with no service between 2 and 4 AM. Single rides cost 90 centimos, but it is more economical to buy a ticket for 10 rides, which costs €4.50 for use on any bus and €3.80 for use on only the city's urban bus service. There is also a ticket valid for any ride during 30 days, which costs €26 and is transferrable between anyone. Tickets are on sale at newspaper kiosks and at the main bus station, Prado de San Sebastián.

Prado de San Sebastián ✉ Pl. San Sebastián, ☎ 95/455-7200, open weekdays 8-3.

CAR RENTAL

Arranging a rental through a major international firm before leaving home is your best, and least expensive, bet. Spain's leading agency is Atesa, which works in tandem with National. You'll generally find rental prices more competitive in Seville and other cities outside of Madrid.

Major National Agencies **Avis** ☎ 902/135531 🌐 www.avis.com. **Europcar** ☎ 902/105030 🌐 www.europcar.es. **Hertz** ☎ 902/402405 🌐 www.hertz.es. **National/Atesa** ☎ 902/100101 🌐 www.atesa.com.

CAR TRAVEL

The main road from Madrid is the N-IV through Córdoba, a four-lane *autovía* (highway), but it's one of Spain's busiest roads, and trucks can cause delays. From Granada or Málaga, head for Antequera; then take A39 *autovíi* by way of Osuna to Seville. Road trips from Seville to Córdoba, Granada, and the Costa del Sol (by way of Ronda) are reasonably quick and pleasant. From the Costa del Sol, the coastal N340 highway is rarely very busy west of Algeciras. Driving within Western Andalusia is easy—the terrain is mostly flat land or slightly hilly, and the roads are straight. From Seville to Jerez and Cádiz, you can choose between the N-IV and the faster A4 toll road. The only way to access Doñana National Park by road is to take the A49 Seville–Huelva highway, exit for Almonte/Bollullos par del Condado, then follow the signs for El Rocío and Matalascañas. The A49 west of Seville will also lead you to the freeway to Portugal and the Algarve. Getting in and out of Seville is not difficult thanks to the SE30 ring road, but getting around the city by car is still trying. In Seville and Cádiz, avoid the lunchtime rush hour (around 2–3 PM) and the 7:15–8:30 PM rush hour. Don't try to bring a car to Cádiz at Carnival time (pre-Lent) or to Seville during Holy Week or the April Fair—processions close most of the streets to traffic.

CHILDREN IN SEVILLE

A monthly guide from the Seville Provincial Tourist Office, "El Guiraldillo," includes a children's section. For a fee, some hotels offer baby-sitting—usually a friend of one of the staff—but practically all restaurants and bars welcome children and their parents at any hour.

CONSULATES

Australia **Seville** ✉ Federico Rubio 14, Santa Cruz ☎ 95/422-0971 or 95/422-0240.

Canada **Seville** ✉ Av. de los Pinos 34, Casa 4, 41927 Mairena del Aljarafe ☎ 95/422-9413.

United Kingdom **Seville** ✉ Pl. Nueva 8 ☎ 95/422-8874 or 95/422-8875.

United States **Seville** ✉ Paseo de las Delicias 7, Arenal ☎ 95/423-1885.

EMERGENCIES

For a list of pharmacies and their opening hours, consult local newspapers. Pharmacies have a flashing green cross outside their premises. Aspirin and other common medicines are generally not sold over the counter in retail outlets. Many bars, however, have first-aid kits.

Emergencies: Fire, Police or Ambulance ☎ 112. **Guardia Civil** ☎ 062. **Insalud** (public health service) ☎ 061. **Policía Local** (local police) ☎ 092. **Policía Nacional** (national police) ☎ 091. **Servicio Marítimo** (Air-Sea Rescue) ☎ 902/202202. **Información Toxicológica** (poisoning) ☎ 915/620420.

ENGLISH-LANGUAGE MEDIA

There are no local English-language newspapers in Seville and Western Andalusia. U.K. papers and the *International Herald Tribune* are available at main news outlets. English-language books and guides are sold at International House.

English-Speaking Bookstore **International House** ✉ Mendez Nuñez 13, Centro, Seville ☎ 95/450-2792.

HEALTH

In very hot weather, avoid home-made mayonnaise or dishes like Russian salad (*ensalada rusa*) and ensure that shellfish is fresh and kept well refrigerated. Most tap water is drinkable, unless stated otherwise, but mineral water is readily available.

HOLIDAYS

In Seville city, local public holidays are as follows: San Fernando, May 30; Virgen de los Reyes, August 15; plus Easter Week, Semana Santa, and the Feria de Abril, which takes place two weeks after Easter. In Cádiz, holidays are La Festividad del Rosario, October 7; and Carnival week in February. Celebrated in Huelva are San Sebastian, January 20; Virgen de la Cinta, September 8; and Colombinas Fiestas, first week in August. In Jerez, holidays include La Merced, September 24; and San Dionisio, October 9 (with the Fiesta de Otoño in between).

LODGING

APARTMENT & VILLA RENTALS

Rural accommodations are available throughout Western Andalusia.

Local Agents **Viajes Rural Andalus** ✉ Montes de Oca 18, 29007 Málaga ☎ 952/276229 🌐 www.ruralandalus.es. **Asociación de Hoteles Rurales de Andalusia** ✉ Cristo Rey 2, 23400 Úbeda, Jaén ☎ 953/755867 🌐 www.hotelesruralesandaluces.org.

MONEY MATTERS

The main banks are in the city and town centers, and most have ATMs that accept major credit cards. Banks are open weekdays 9–2, except public holidays.

SAFETY

Seville has long been notorious for petty crime. Tourists continue to be thieves' favored victims, so take common-sense precautions at the very least. Drive with your car doors locked; lock all your luggage out of sight in the trunk; *never* leave *anything* in a parked car; and keep a wary eye on scooter riders, who have been known to snatch purses or even smash the windows of moving cars. Take only a small amount of cash and one credit card out with you. Leave your passport, traveler's checks, and other credit cards in the hotel safe, if possible, and avoid carrying purses and expensive cameras or wearing valuable jewelry.

SIGHTSEEING TOURS

In Seville, A.P.I.T., Guidetur, and I.T.A. can hook you up with a qualified English-speaking guide. Sevi-Ruta offers a two-hour walking tour in English, leaving Plaza Nueva (Statue of San Fernando) at 9:30 AM weekdays. The fee is €9.02. The tourist office has information on open-bus city tours run by Servirama, Hispalense de Tranvias, and others; buses leave every half hour from the Torre del Oro, with stops at Parque María Luisa and the Isla Mágica theme park. You can hop on and off at any stop; the complete tour lasts about 90 minutes. For an English-speaking guide in Cádiz or Jerez, contact the local tourist office.

Asociación Provincial de Informadores Turísticos ✉ Glorieta de Palacio de Congresos, Seville ☎ 95/425-5957. **Guidetour** ✉ Lope de Rueda 13 ☎ 95/422-2374 or 95/422-2375. **ITA** ✉ Santa Teresa 1 ☎ 95/422-4641. **Hispalense de Tranvias** ✉ Teniente Coronel Segui 2, Centro ☎ 95/421-4169 or 95/422-9006. **Sevilla Visión** ✉ Pl. Cristo de Burgos 9, Santa Catalina ☎ 95/422-4641. **SevillaTour** ☎ 95/450-2099 🌐 www.citysightseeing-spain.com. **Sevirama** ✉ Paseo de las Delicias, 2nd floor on the right, Edifico Cristina, Arenal ☎ 95/456-0693. **Sevi-Ruta** ☎ 902/158226 or 616/501100 🌐 www.sevi-ruta.com. **Puerta de Santa María-Hesperia tour guides** ☎ 649/535925.

DOÑANA NATIONAL PARK

Jeep tours of the reserve depart twice daily (Tuesday–Sunday 8:30 and 3) from the park's Acebuche reception center, 2 km (1 mi) from Matalascañas. Tours are limited to 125 people and should be booked well in advance. Passengers can often be picked up from hotels in Matalascañas.

Parque Nacional de Doñana ✉ Cooperativa Marisma del Rocío, Centro de Recepción, 21760 Matalascañas ☎ 959/430432 🌐 www.donana.es.

SHERRY BODEGAS

Winery tours can be arranged from Seville and Cádiz. In Jerez, most bodegas are open to visitors year-round. Tours, which include a tasting of brandy and sherry, should be reserved in advance; English-speaking guides are usually available. It is best to call the bodega and ask for Public Relations and book a time and language. To see a bodega in Puerto de Santa María, contact Osborne or Terry. In Sanlúcar de Barrameda, contact Barbadillo.

Barbadillo ✉ Calle Luis de Eguilaz 11, Sanlúcar de Barrameda ☎ 956/385500 or 956/385521 🌐 www.barbadillo.com, visits weekdays 10–2:30 September–mid-June, admission €3. **Pedro Domecq** ✉ San Idelfonso 3, Jerez de la Frontera ☎ 956/151500 🌐 www.vinos-domecq.com, visits weekdays 10–1, admission €3.71. **González Byass** ✉ Manuel María González 12, Jerez de la Frontera ☎ 956/357000 🌐 www.gonzalezbyass.es, visits Monday–Saturday between 11:30 and 1:30, 3:30 and 5:30, in August also at 6:30; Sunday between 11:30 and 1:30; admission €7. **John Harvey** ✉ Arcos 57, Jerez de la Frontera ☎ 956/346004 🌐 www.domecq.es/ie/bodegas/harveys/harveys.htm, visits weekdays at 10 and noon, admission €3. **Osborne** ✉ Los Moros 7, Puerto de Santa María ☎ 956/869000 🌐 www.osborne.es, tour in English weekdays at 10:30, in Spanish 11 and 12; admission €3. **Sandeman-Coprimar** ✉ Pizarro 10, Jerez de la Frontera, ☎ 956/301100 🌐 www.sandeman.com, visits mid-November–mid-March, Monday–Wednesday and Friday hourly between 10:30 and 1:30; Thursday hourly between 10:30 and 2; mid-March–mid-November, Monday, Wednesday, and Friday hourly between 10:30 and 2:30; Tuesday and Thursday, 10:30 and 2:45; Saturday between 11:30 and 1:30; admission weekdays €4, Saturday €5. **Terry** ✉ Santísima Trinidad s/n ☎ 956/857700, tour weekdays at 10 AM in English, 12:30 in Spanish; groups only on weekends; admission €2.70. **Williams and Humbert** ✉ N-IV, Km 641.75, Jerez de la Frontera ☎ 956/353406 🌐 www.williams-humbert.com, visits weekdays 9–3, admission €3.91.

SPORTS & THE OUTDOORS

Golfers, equestrians, sailors, hikers, and other sports enthusiasts will not be disappointed in the resources available in Seville and Western Andalusia. Pastimes might include renting a Vespasur scooter in Seville or sailing from one of the marinas in Huelva or Cádiz. Jerez de la Frontera hosted the World Equestrian Championships in 2002 and is home to one of the world's most famous equestrian schools as well as the superb Spanish Carthusian horse. So naturally there are top-quality riding opportunities around the town.

TAXIS

Taxi Companies **Radio Taxi** ✉ Seville ☎ 95/458-0000 or 95/457-1111. **Tele Taxi** ☎ 95/462-2222 or 95/462-1461. **Radio Teléfono Giralda** ✉ Seville ☎ 95/467-5555. **Tele Taxi** ✉ Jerez de la Frontera ☎ 956/344860. **Unitaxi** ✉ Cádiz ☎ 956/212121. **Tele Taxi** ✉ Huelva ☎ 959/250022.

TRAIN TRAVEL

Seville, Jerez, and Cádiz all lie on the main rail line from Madrid to southwestern Spain. Trains leave from Madrid for Seville (via Córdoba) almost hourly, most of them high-speed AVE trains that reach Seville in 2½ hours. Two of the non-AVE trains continue on to Jerez and Cádiz; travel time from Seville to Cádiz is 1½ to 2 hours. From Granada, Málaga, Ronda, and Algeciras, trains go to Seville by way of Bobadilla, where, more often than not, you have to change. A dozen or more local trains each day connect Cádiz with Seville, Puerto de Santa María, and Jerez. There are no trains to Doñana National Park, Sanlúcar de Barrameda, or Arcos de la Frontera or between Cádiz and the Costa del Sol. In Seville, the sprawling Santa Justa station is on Avenida Kansas City. Cádiz's station is on Plaza de Sevilla near the docks. Jerez's station is on Plaza de la Estación, off Diego Fernández Herrera, in the eastern part of town. *Al Andalus* is a vintage 1920s luxury train that makes a weekly six-day trip in season from Seville to Córdoba, Granada, and Antequera, with side trips to Carmona and Jerez.

Train Information RENFE ☎ 902/240202.

Train Stations **Seville-Estación Santa Justa** ☎ 95/454-0202. **Huelva-Estación** ✉ Av. de Italia ☎ 959/246666. **Cádiz-Estación** ✉ Av. de Gibraltar [Cortadura] ☎ 956/251010. **Jerez de la Frontera-Estación** ✉ Pl. de la Estación s/n ☎ 956/342319.

VISITOR INFORMATION

English is spoken in most hotels, top restaurants, and the main tourist sites but rarely in bars and rural destinations.

Seville has both regional and provincial tourist offices and also has branches at the Seville Airport and Santa Justa railway station. Seville's provincial tourist office publishes a monthly events guide called **"El Giraldillo,"** which is in Spanish but is easy to understand for novice speakers. Also in Seville is the free **"Sevilla Welcome and Olé!,"** published at the beginning of the month. It has both English and Spanish text, a map, and tourist information. **"Seville at Your Fingertips"** is also free, with useful names (no descriptions), addresses, and a street finder.

Andalusian Regional Tourist Offices **Seville** ✉ Av. de la Constitución 21 ☎ 95/422-1404, 95/421-8157, or 95/444-9128 🌐 www.andalucia.org. **Cádiz** ✉ Av. Ramón de Carranza s/n ☎ 956/258646.

EXTREMADURA

FODOR'S CHOICE

Cáceres, the vibrant provincial capital

Mérida's Roman ruins

HIGHLY RECOMMENDED

RESTAURANTS

Atrio, Cáceres

Pizarro, Trujillo

HOTELS

Meliá Cáceres

Meliá Trujillo

Parador de Guadalupe

Parador de Mérida

Parador de Trujillo

Parador de Zafra

Rocamador, Almendral

SIGHTS

The ancient city of Trujillo

Guadalupe's monastery in the mountains

National Museum of Roman Art, Mérida

By Michael Jacobs

Updated by AnneLise Sorensen

THE VERY NAME *EXTREMADURA*—the "land beyond the Duero"—suggests the wild, remote, and isolated character of this haunting region. With its poor soil and minimal industry, Extremadura has not experienced the kind of economic gains typical to other parts of Spain. Although in recent decades a series of dams has brightened the region's agricultural outlook, Extremadura is still among the least developed regions in the country. It was not always isolated and impoverished. No other place in Spain has as many Roman monuments as Mérida, the capital of the vast Roman province of Lusitania (the Iberian Peninsula); the town guarded the Vía de la Plata, the major Roman highway that crossed Extremadura from north to south, connecting Gijón with the port of Seville. Economic and artistic decline set in after the Romans left, but the region revived in the 16th century, when the surviving explorers and conquerors of the New World—from Francisco Pizarro and Hernán Cortés to Nuñez de Balboa and Francisco de Orellana, first navigator of the Amazon—returned to their birthplace. These men built the magnificent palaces that now glorify towns such as Cáceres and Trujillo, and they turned the remote monastery of Guadalupe—whose miraculous Virgin had inspired their exploits overseas—into one of the great artistic repositories of Spain.

Despite its strongly provincial character, Extremadura has long been influenced by its neighbors. Officially, Extremadura comprises two provinces: Cáceres to the north and Badajoz to the south, divided by the Montes de Toledo (Toledo Mountains). The villages and landscapes of Badajoz share much in common with neighboring Andalusia; Cáceres, with its wooded mountain valleys and half-timber, gray-stone houses, recalls both Castile and northern Spain. And Portugal, just over the western border, lends its accent to all of western Spain.

About the Restaurants

Extremaduran food reflects the austerity of the landscape: true peasant fare, with a strong character. Extremadurans rely on fresh produce and especially the pig, of which no part is spared, including the *criadillas* (testicles)—not to be confused with the *criadillas de la tierra* (literally, earth testicles), which are truffles. The dressed meats are outstanding, most notably the sweetish cured hams from Montánchez; chorizo (spiced sausage); and *morcilla* (blood pudding), which is often made here with potatoes. The *caldereta de cordero* (lamb stew) is particularly tasty, as is the beef from the *retinto,* a local breed of long-horned cattle. Game is also common; *perdiz al modo de Alcántara,* partridge cooked with truffles, is a specialty. Local lake tench and river trout are also worth trying. Extremadurans make a gazpacho based on cucumbers, green peppers, and broth rather than tomatoes and water. A common accompaniment is *migas,* bread crumbs soaked in water and fried in olive oil with garlic, peppers, and sausage. Some local dishes disconcert foreigners—such as those involving *ranas* (frogs)—although the local favorite *lagarto* (lizard) is no longer available, as the main ingredient is now a protected species.

Local cheeses generally have a crumbly texture and strong flavors. If you have a chance, savor *tortas,* the round, semisoft cheeses of Cáceres; those from Casar and La Serena are especially prized. Favorite *extremeño* desserts include the *técula mécula* (an almond-flavor marzipan tart), which combines the flavors of Spain and Portugal. Marketed under the generic appellation "Ribera del Guadiana," Extremadura's little-known, light and fruity red wines are good values; try Lar de Lares. Typical digestifs include liqueurs made from cherries or acorns.

Dining out is not much of a tradition in Extremadura; some of the best food is served in modest bars. Reservations are generally unnecessary.

If you have 1 day You can get a lightning impression of Extremadura in a day's drive from Madrid. Enter Extremadura through the Valle del Jerte (the scenic route) by taking the N110. Stay on the same road to **Cáceres** 6, and then head east to **Trujillo** 7 on the N521. From here you can return to Madrid on the N-V. If you're pressed for time and don't mind missing one of the most breathtaking parts of Extremadura, enter the province by the N-V and go straight to Trujillo and Cáceres. For another day drip, enter the province from Valle del Jerte, then head to Cáceres and farther south to **Mérida** 9. Another one-day outing is to the monastery of **Guadalupe** 8. Then head west to Trujillo; either overnight there, or return to Madrid that afternoon.

If you have 3 days From Madrid, take the slow and winding but highly scenic C501 to **Plasencia** 3 and wander through the *casco viejo* (old town). Drive next to the **Monasterio de Yuste** 4 and spend the night nearby. The next day, head south to the provincial capital of **Cáceres** 6 and continue on to **Mérida** 9. On day three, travel back north by way of **Trujillo** 7 and **Guadalupe** 8. Spend the night there *or* return to Madrid that evening on the N-V.

If you have 5 days From Madrid, drive over the Tornavacas Pass on the N110 through the **Valle del Jerte** 1 to **Plasencia** 3. If you can, detour to the ancient Judería (Jewish Quarter) of **Hervás** 2. Spend the night at the parador in Jarandilla de la Vera—the fortified palace where Carlos V lived—before visiting the emperor's final home, the nearby **Monasterio de Yuste** 4. On day two, go south on the C524 to the **Parque Natural de Monfragüe** 5. Spend the night in **Trujillo** 7 and explore the town the next morning. Continue to picturesque **Cáceres** 6 for lunch and afternoon sightseeing. Spend night three in **Mérida** 9 and take in its Roman monuments on day four. Head west to the provincial capital, **Badajoz** 10, with a side trip to the Spanish-Portuguese town of **Olivenza** 11. From here you can move on to Andalusia, stopping to see the castle-parador at **Zafra** 12, *or* drive back north on the N-V and turn off to admire the monastery of **Guadalupe** 8.

WHAT IT COSTS In Euros

	$$$$	$$$	$$	$	¢
AT DINNER	over €20	€15–€20	€10–€15	€6–€10	under €6

Prices are per person for a main course at dinner.

About the Hotels

Extremadura has the most remarkable group of paradors in Spain, occupying buildings of great historic or architectural interest in all major tourist areas. Reserve well in advance for a weekend stay. The Extremaduran government runs a few *hospederías,* a sort of regional version of the parador chain; some have historic quarters in scenic areas. Most other high-end hotels, with a few exceptions, are modern boxes with little character. There are a number of charming bed-and-breakfast inns (*hoteles rurales*) and more than 100 (and growing) guest houses (*casa rurales*) throughout Extremadura's countryside, particularly in the Valle del Jerte and Valle de la Vera. Despite their number, space in popular guest houses is limited, so reservations are a must. Your best base for a series of day trips might be Cáceres—from there it's a just a hop to Trujillo, Mérida, and Plasencia.

WHAT IT COSTS In Euros					
	$$$$	$$$	$$	$	¢
FOR 2 PEOPLE	over €180	€100–€180	€60–€100	€40–€60	under €40

Prices are for two people in a standard double room in high season, excluding tax.

Exploring Extremadura

Rugged Extremadura is a boon for outdoor enthusiasts. The lush Jerte Valley and the craggy peaks of the Sierra de Gredos mark Upper Extremadura's fertile landscape. South of the Jerte Valley is the historical town of Plasencia and the 15th-century Yuste Monastery. In Extremadura's central interior is the provincial capital of Cáceres and the Monfrague Nature Park. Lower Extremadura's main towns—Mérida, Badajoz, Olivenza, and Zafra—lie near the Portuguese border, and have long exuded a Portuguese flavor, bolstered by the sizeable Portuguese population. The best way to explore Extremadura is by car, as bus and train connections are not ideal for roaming such sparsely populated terrain.

Numbers in the text correspond to numbers in the margin and on the Extremadura map.

Timing

Summer is a good time to roam the nature parks or mountains, but note that southern Extremadura can get brutally hot. Spring and fall are ideal, as winter can be cold and rainy. The spectacle of cherry-blossom season in the Jerte Valley and La Vera erupts over two weeks around mid-March. Bird-watchers: visit in late February, after the migrating storks have arrived to nest and before the European cranes have returned to northern Europe.

UPPER EXTREMADURA

Extremadura stretches from Portugal to Ciudad Real and from Salamanca to Seville. Crossed from east to west by the Tajo (Tagus) and the Guadiana rivers, its rugged and fertile landscape has exported food to much of Europe for centuries, including wheat, lamb, and pork. The Serena reservoir (fed by the Zújar River, which is fed by the Guadiana) is one of the largest in Europe.

Valle del Jerte

❶ *34 km (21 mi) northeast of Plasencia, 260 km (160 mi) west of Madrid. For a scenic route, follow N110 from Ávila.*

There is no more striking introduction to Extremadura than the **Puerto de Tornavacas** (Tornavacas Pass)—literally, the "point where the cows turn back." Part of the N110 road northeast of Plasencia, the pass marks the border between Extremadura and the stark plateau of Castile, and at 4,183 ft above sea level it has a breathtaking view of the valley formed by the fast-flowing Jerte River. The valley's lower slopes are covered with a dense mantle of ash, chestnut, and cherry trees, whose richness contrasts with the granite cliffs of the Sierra de Gredos. Cherries, harvested May–July, are the principal crop. Camping is popular in this region, and even the most experienced hikers can find some challeng-

Fiestas

Extremadura is not a land of running bulls, except for the fiestas de **San Juan** in Coria, Cáceres, on the week of June 24, or the **Capeas,** in Segura de León, Badajoz, around September 14, when locals show off their bullfighting skills. The province of Cáceres has its share of colorful festivals commemorating past saints and sinners. January 20, the **Fiesta de San Estéban** (Feast of St. Stephen), inspires interesting folklore in several small towns. In Acehúche (near Garovillas), *carantoñas* ("ugly mugs," men costumed in animal skins and frightening masks) bow before the statue of St. Stephen during his procession through town. In Piornal (near Plasencia), a *jaramplas* (a grotesquely costumed, masked jester) is pursued through the town and pelted with turnips. February 3 is the day to toast **San Blas** (St. Blaise), believed to heal sore throats, with hot cakes bearing his name and various feasts. On Shrove Tuesday, during February's **Carnival,** you can see the **Pero Palo,** a large rag-doll figure—representing a bandit who was sentenced and executed during the Middle Ages—with a deadpan expression, carried throughout the town and burned at the end of the three-day festival of Villanueva de la Vera (near Jarandilla).

Semana Santa (Holy Week) is celebrated with various rituals in Badajoz, Cáceres, Mérida, and Trujillo. One of the most dramatic rituals is the **Empalaos** ("impaled ones"), on Holy Thursday in the smaller Valverde de la Vera, when young men's outstretched arms are tightly bound with rope tied to heavy logs across their backs for a procession recalling Christ's crucifixion. More savory is Trujillo's **Feria del Queso** (Cheese Festival) at the beginning of May. Plasencia welcomes on the first Tuesday of August its **Martes Mayor,** when its famous market offers food products from all over the region. For Cáceres's September **Celebración del Cerdo y Vino** (Pig and Wine Celebration), the area's innumerable sausages and other pork products are prepared in public demonstrations. If watching the process doesn't ruin your appetite, you can sample free wine and pork afterward. For December's medieval **La Encamisá,** in Torrejoncillo (off the highway between Plasencia and Cáceres), white-robed riders brandish torches and thunder through the narrow streets on horseback in honor of the Immaculate Conception. On the same day, December 7, Jarandilla de la Vera fills the city with bonfires to celebrate **Los Escobazos,** when locals play-fight with torches made out of brooms.

In Badajoz the year opens on January 16 and 17 with **La Encamisá,** in Navalvillar de Pela. Horsemen re-create a medieval battle of the town's citizens against the Arab invaders. During the **Carnival** celebration in Badajoz, parades of thousands wear extravagant costumes. Also colorful are the **Holy Week** celebrations at Oliva de la Frontera. Badajoz says *adios* to winter with the fiestas of **La Primavera** and **Los Mayos** (Spring Festival and May Days, respectively), usually at the end of April and beginning of May. A significant date in Badajoz is May 3, **El Día de la Santa Cruz** (the Exaltation of the Holy Cross), celebrated in the villages of Corte de Peleas and Feria, where a local family is selected a month in advance to prepare a processional floral cross in its own home. Some of these crosses become magnificent works of art and patience, tended to the point of depleting hard-earned savings.

The crowd sings as a stone cross, the floral crosses, and a statue of the Virgin Mary are paraded through various neighborhoods.

Fishing

Trout fishing is popular in the Vera and Jerte districts, while tench, carp, royal carp, barbel, and pike abound in the Tajo (Tagus) and Guadiana rivers.

Wildlife

You can keep busy with trails in the Gredos and Tormantos ranges; forests of oak, poplar, and cherry; massive gorges; and the winding waterways of the Jerte River valley, where the blossoming of the cherry trees in March attracts tourists from all over the country. In Monfragüe Nature Park and in the smaller and less touristy Cornalvo Nature Park, bird-watchers might spot eagles, falcons, and vultures. Thousands of European cranes spend the winter around La Serena, in eastern Badajoz. From February to August, white storks nest on every available church tower, battlement, and electricity pylon.

---

ing trails. **Cabezuela del Valle,** full of half-timber stone houses, is one of the best preserved of the valley's many attractive villages. From the Jerte Valley, you can follow the N110 along the river to Plasencia or, if you have a taste for mountain scenery, detour from the village of Jerte to Hervás, traveling a narrow road that winds 35 km (22 mi) through forests of low-growing oak trees and over the Honduras Pass, Extremadura's highest road (4,700 ft).

Where to Stay & Eat

$ **Valle del Jerte.** Service is always cheerful in this family-run inn just off the highway in the village of Jerte. Specialties include Extremaduran-style gazpacho, *cabrito* (kid), and local trout. The homemade, regional desserts are outstanding, and many feature the Jerte Valley's famed cherries; try the *tarta de cerezas* (cherry tart) or the *queso fresco de cabra con miel cerezo* (goat cheese topped with cherry-flavored honey). If your Spanish is up to snuff, opt for one of the verbally delivered suggestions of the day. The family's son is knowledgeable about Spanish wines (ask to see the wine cellar). Upstairs, five, comfortable guest rooms have chestnut-wood furniture, cotton bedspreads, and beamed ceilings. ☒ *Gargantilla 16, 10612 Jerte* ☎ *927/470052* 🖷 *927/470307* 🌐 *www.donbellota.com.* *5 rooms* *MC, V.*

$$$ **El Molino del Sol.** A few miles past the town of Navaconcejo toward Cabezuela del Valle you'll find this rural lodging in an old mill that sits on the bank of the Jerte River. The house is surrounded by cherry and fruit orchards, and rooms are individually decorated. Take a refreshing dip in the Jerte, just a few yards away. The house is only rented in full (it accommodates up to 12 people) for €150 daily. ☒ *N110, Km. 373, 3, 10613 Navaconcejo* ☎ *927/470313 or 927/470045* 🖷 *927/470313* 🌐 *www.alojamientorural.com* *6 rooms* *Restaurant, meeting room* *AE, D, MC, V.*

$$$ **Hospedería Valle del Jerte.** This attractive turn-of-the-20th-century building is at the edge of the village, next to the Jerte River. The interior is modern and functional. Some rooms have river views, while others face the village; those on the top floor have slope ceilings. There's a pleasant Japanese garden out back. ☒ *Ramón Cepeda 118, 10612 Jerte* ☎ *927/470403* 🖷 *927/470131* *25 rooms* *Restaurant, meeting room* *AE, D, MC, V.*

$–$$ **Hotel Rural Finca El Carpintero.** In two adjacent stone buildings, this hotel has three types of rooms, the best of which has a chimney, a salon, and its own entrance. The simpler rooms are elegant and colorful, and have canopy wrought-iron beds. The restaurant has a €20 dinner menu.

✉ *N110, Km 360,5, 10611 Tornavacas* ☎ *927/177089 or 659/7328110* 🌐 *www.valledeljerte.es.org* *9 rooms* *Restaurant, meeting room* *AE, D, MC, V.*

$$ **La Casería.** One of Extremadura's first rural guest houses, this rambling home is on a 120-acre working farm, run by a couple that also raises sheep. You do have to love animals, as the household includes lots of dogs and cats. Aside from the six rooms, there are three cottages, each of which can sleep two to four. The charming country feel compensates for the lack of amenities. It's wise to reserve in advance, and keep your eyes peeled as you approach: the sign is easy to miss. ✉ *N110, Km 378.6, 10613 Navaconcejo* ☎ *927/173141* *927/177384* 🌐 *www.valledeljerte.es.org* *6 rooms, 3 cottages* *Pool* *MC, V.*

Hervás

❷ *63 km (39 mi) northeast of Plasencia, 142 km (88 mi) northeast of Cáceres, 25 km (16 mi) west of Cabezuela del Valle.*

Surrounded by pine and chestnut groves, this picturesque village makes an interesting detour from either the Valle del Jerte or Plasencia. Hervás, it's believed, grew into a predominantly Jewish settlement during the Middle Ages, populated by Jews escaping Christian and Muslim persecution in the larger cities. In 1492, when the Jews were expelled from Spain altogether, their neighborhood was left intact but their possessions were ceded to the local nobility. Stripped of its wealth, the village lost its commercial reputation and was forgotten. Now fully restored, the **Judería** (Jewish Quarter) is among the best-preserved in Spain. In it is the remarkable 18th-century **Convento de los Trinitarios** (☎ 927/474828) part of which has been turned into a hospedería. At the top of the quarter there is a 16th- to 17th-century renaissance church called the **Santa Maria de Aguas Vivas.**

Plasencia

❸ *270 km (169 mi) west of Madrid, 79 km (49 mi) north of Cáceres, 126 km (78 mi) northwest of Trujillo.*

Rising dramatically from the banks of the narrow Jerte River and backed by the peaks of the Sierra de Gredos, this community was founded by Alfonso VIII in 1180, just after he captured the whole area from the Moors. The town's motto, *placeat Deo et hominibus* ("It pleases both God and men"), might well have been a ploy on Alfonso's part to attract settlers to this wild, isolated place on the southern border of the former kingdom of León. Badly damaged during the Peninsular War of 1808, Plasencia retains far less of its medieval quarter than do other Extremaduran towns, but it still has extensive fragments of its medieval walls and a smattering of fine old buildings, and it makes a good base for side trips to Hervás and the Jerte Valley, the Monasterio de Yuste and Monfragüe Nature Park, or, farther northwest, the wild Las Hurdes and Sierra de Gata.

Plasencia's **cathedral** was founded in 1189 and rebuilt after 1320 in an austere Gothic style that looks a bit incongruous looming over the town's red-tile roofs. In 1498, the great architect Enrique Egas designed a new structure, intending to complement or even overshadow the original, but despite the later efforts of other notable architects of the time, such as Juan de Alava and Francisco de Colonia, Egas's plans were never fully realized. The entrance to this incomplete, curious, and not wholly satisfactory complex is through the portal on the cathedral's ornate but somber north facade. The dark interior of the new cathedral is notable for the beauty of its pilasters, which sprout like trees into the ribs of the vaulting. You enter the old cathedral through the Gothic cloister, which has four enormous lemon trees. Off the cloister stands the building's oldest surviving section, the 13th-century chapter house (now the chapel of San Pablo)—a late-Romanesque structure with an idiosyncratic, Moorish-inspired dome. Inside are medieval hymnals and a 13th-century gilded wood sculpture of the Virgen del Perdón. The **museum** in the truncated nave of the old cathedral has ecclesiastical and archaeological objects. ☎ *927/414852* *Old cathedral €2* *Mon.–Sat. 9–12:30 and 4–5:30 (5–6:30 in summer), Sun. 9–1.*

The cloister of the elegant **Palacio Episcopal** (Bishop's Palace; ✉ Pl. de la Catedral) is open weekdays from 9 to 2. The **Casa del Deán** (Dean's House; ✉ Pl. de la Catedral), a Renaissance structure, is now a courthouse. The sober **Hospital de Santa María** serves as a cultural center.

The **Museo Etnográfico-Textil**, at the back of the Hospital de Santa María, has displays of colorful regional costume. ✉ *Enter on C. Plaza Marqués de la Puebla* ☎ *927/421843* *Free* *Sept.–June, Wed.–Sat. 11–2 and 5–8, Sun. 11–2; July–Aug., daily 9:30–2:30.*

Lined with orange trees, the narrow, carefully preserved **Plaza de San Vicente** is at the northwest end of the old quarter. At one end is the 15th-century church of **San Vicente Ferrer**, with an adjoining convent that's now a parador. The north side of the square is dominated by the Renaissance **Palacio de Mirabel** (Palace of the Marquis of Mirabel; ☎ 927/410701)—go through the central arch for a back view. It's usually open daily 10–2 and 4–6; tip the caretaker. East of the Plaza de San Vicente, at the other end of the Rúa Zapatería, is the **Plaza Mayor**, a cheerful, arcaded square where a market has been held every Tuesday morning since the 12th century. The mechanical figure clinging to the town-hall clock tower depicts the clockmaker himself and is called the **Mayorga** in honor of the craftsman's Castilian hometown. East of the Plaza de San Vicente you'll find a large section of the town's medieval wall—on the other side of which is a heavily restored Roman aqueduct. Walk southeast from the Plaza de San Vicente to the **Parque de los Pinos**, with wildlife that includes peacocks, cranes, swans, pheasants, and monkeys.

Where to Stay & Eat

$$–$$$ **Alfonso VIII.** Grand but slightly past its prime, with undistinguished modern rooms, this curious Franco-era relic is strangely agreeable. The restaurant has long been regionally renowned for its food; the typical caldereta de cordero is usually available. There's parking in a garage around the corner. ✉ *Alfonso VIII 32–34, 10600* ☎ *927/410250* *927/418042* *55 rooms, 2 suites* *Restaurant, parking (fee)* *AE, DC, MC, V.*

¢–$ **Rincón Extremeño.** Just off the Plaza Mayor in the heart of the old quarter, this property is basic and well maintained. The ground floor has a popular bar and restaurant, the latter serving regional dishes. You'll have nicer views—though more noise—in a room facing the narrow street. ✉ *Vidrieras 6 10600* ☎ *927/411150* *927/420627* *12 rooms* *Restaurant, bar* *MC, V.*

$$$ **Parador de Plasencia.** In a 15th-century convent, this parador cultivates a medieval environment. The common areas are majestic and sober, and the guest rooms are decorated with monastic motifs and heavy wood furniture. Rooms are spacious and comfortable, most have sitting rooms, and bathrooms are stylishly modern. The high-ceiling, stone-and-wood-beam restaurant—called the "refectory"—is almost intimidating in its magnificence. Parking adds a hefty €12 nightly. ✉ *Pl. de San Vicente Ferrer 10600* ☎ *924/425870* *924/425872*

www.parador.es 66 rooms Restaurant, pool, bar, parking (fee) AE, D, MC, V.

Shopping

If you happen to be in Plasencia on a Tuesday morning, head for the Plaza Mayor and do what the locals have been doing since the 12th century: scout bargains in the weekly market; on the first Tuesday of every August the market is host to a *feria,* which welcomes vendors from all over Extremadura. For local art and crafts, try **Bámbara de Artesanía** (Sancho Polo, 12 927/411766). For pottery, leather, and wooden goods head to **Serete** (C. Blanca 2 no phone). Near the parador is **Artesanías Canillas** (C. San Vicente Ferrer s/n 927/411668), which has regional costumes, pottery, and handmade straw hats. At **Casa del Jamón** (C. Sol 18, east of Pl. Mayor 927/414271 C. Zapatería 17, between Pl. Mayor and parador 927/419328), stock up on sausages, *jamón ibérico* (Iberian ham), cheeses, Extremeño wines, and cherry liqueur from the Jerte Valley.

Monasterio de Yuste & La Vera

4 *17 km (11 mi) southeast of Jarandilla de la Vera, 45 km (28 mi) from Plasencia. Turn left off C501 at Cuacos and follow signs for the monastery (1 km [½ mi]).*

The **Monasterio de Yuste** (Yuste Monastery) was founded by Hieronymite monks in the early 15th century. Badly damaged in the Peninsular War, it was left to decay after the suppression of Spain's monasteries in 1835, but it has since been restored and taken over once more by the Hieronymites. Carlos V spent his last years in the Royal Chambers—the bedroom where he died has a view into the church, which enabled the emperor to hear Mass from his bed. The required guided tour also includes the church, the crypt where Carlos V was buried before being moved to El Escorial (near Madrid), and a glimpse of the monastery's two cloisters. The cloisters and gardens were renovated in 2002, a hospedería within the monastery was opened in 2003, and the Royal Chambers is open to the public. ☎ *927/172130* 🌐 *www.fundacionyuste.org* 🎫 *€2.5* ⏲ *Oct.–May, daily 9:30–12:30 and 3–6; June–Sept., daily 9:30–12:30 and 3:30–6:30.*

The Yuste Monastery is in the heart of **La Vera,** a place of steep ravines (*gargantas*), rushing rivers, and villages. Following the road that climbs from the monastery into the mountains for 6 km (4 mi), you'll come to the village of **Garganta La Olla**—as you approach, the road winds through cherry orchards and eventually dips into the village's narrow, twisting streets. The **Casa de la Muñeca** (Doll's House; also called the Casa de Putas), once a brothel used by soldiers of Carlos V's army, is still painted the traditional "brothel" blue, and the bas-relief figure on the doorway hints at its former purpose. There are barely any hotels in La Vera, so if you're enchanted with the mountainous isolation and want to relax in the company of the villagers, **El Abuelo Marciano** (Grandpa Marciano; ✉ Cruce Jaraiz s/n ☎ 927/460426) provides room and board, preferably to groups, in his sizable house in the countryside.

Where to Stay & Eat

$$$ ✕🏨 **Parador Jarandilla de la Vera.** Nestled in the town of Jarandilla, this parador was built in the early 16th century as a fortified palace. The emperor Carlos V stayed here for three months while he waited for his quarters at Yuste to be completed. The halls have stylish medieval furnishings, and the regal dining room is the perfect place to indulge royal fantasies. Start with *huevos fritos con migas* (fried eggs with bread crumbs); then savor one of the house specialties, perhaps *caldereta de cabrito* (kid stew). ✉ *Av. García Prieto 1 (59 km [36 mi] east of Plasencia, 17 km [11 mi] west of Monasterio de Yuste), 10450* ☎ *927/560117* 📠 *927/560088* 🌐 *www.parador.es* 🛏 *53 rooms* 🛎 *Restaurant, tennis court, pool, bar, playground* 💳 *AE, DC, MC, V.*

$$$ 🏨 **Camino Real.** In a small village in the highest valley of La Vera, this hotel is in a restored mansion. Rooms have exposed stone walls and wooden beam ceilings; most have a hot tub. The rate includes breakfast and dinner. ✉ *C. El Monje 27, 10459 Guijo de Santa Bárbara* ☎ *927/561119* 🌐 *www.casaruralcaminoreal.com* 🛏 *6 rooms* 🛎 *Restaurant* 💳 *MC, V.*

$$ 🏨 **Hotel Peña Alba.** Isolated by a small oak forest is this manorlike lodging, where each room is eclectically done with Indonesian furniture, canopy beds, hardwood floors, wrought-iron basins, and bright-ocher or exposed-stone walls. What was once a brick oven between the lobby and salon is now a chimney. ✉ *Arroyomolinos de la Vera, 10410 Cáceres* ☎ *927/177516* 🌐 *www.pdelalba.com* 🛏 *13 rooms, 5 suites* 🛎 *Restaurant, library* 💳 *MC, V.*

$ 🏨 **Antigua Casa del Heno.** Run by a Spanish-Argentine couple, this 150-year-old stone farmhouse is a wonderfully rustic refuge near a natural spring. With wood floors, stone walls, and sprightly fabrics, the rooms are cozy and cheerful; some have balconies or skylights, and all have unhindered views of the countryside. The inn is a favorite with stressed-out executives from Madrid, so reservations are essential. The restaurant, for guests only, serves Spanish dishes. Beware: the narrow, unpaved road uphill is challenging and remote. ✉ *Finca Valdepimienta, Losar de la Vera (follow signs from village), 10460 Cáceres* ☎📠 *927/198077* 🛏 *7 rooms* 🛎 *Restaurant* 💳 *MC, V* ⏲ *Closed mid-Jan.–mid-Feb.*

Shopping

If you like to cook, pick up a tin or two of *pimentón de la Vera* (paprika), made from the region's prized red peppers, in Jarandilla or another town around La Vera.

Parque Natural de Monfragüe

5 *20 km (12 mi) south of Plasencia, off C524.*

At the junction of the Rivers Tiétar and Tajo is the Monfragüe Nature Park, a rocky-mountain wilderness known for its plant and animal life, including lynx, boar, deer, fox, black storks, imperial eagles, and the world's largest colony of black vultures. Bring binoculars and find the lookout point called **Salto del Gitano** (Gypsy's Leap), on the C524 just south of the Tajo River, where the vultures can often be spotted wheeling in the dozens at close range. The park's visitor center is in the hamlet of Villareal de San Carlos, on the C524 between Plasencia and Trujillo. ☎ *927/199134* ⏲ *Daily 9–2:30 and 5–7 (4–6 in winter); audiovisual show every hour on the ½ hr.*

Where to Stay

$$ **Hospedería Parque de Monfragüe.** On the main road just south of the park, this hotel is in a trio of stark modern buildings. The interior, furnished with contemporary pieces, has been in several Spanish design magazines; in the guest rooms, neutral grays and browns are backed by salmon-color walls. Rooms in the wing farthest from the road have the best mountain views. The light-flooded restaurant has large windows overlooking the park and serves top-notch regional cuisine, including locally produced sausages, cured hams, and cheeses. ✉ *Ctra. Plasencia–Trujillo, Km 39.1, 10694 Torrejón el Rubio* ☎ *927/455245* 📠 *927/455016* 🌐 *www.hotelmonfrague.com* *48 rooms, 12 suites* *Restaurant, pool, meeting room* 💳 *AE, DC, MC, V.*

Cáceres

6 *307 km (190 mi) west of Madrid.*

Fodor'sChoice ★

Cáceres is a provincial capital and prosperous agricultural town whose vibrant nightlife draws villagers from the surrounding pueblos every weekend. The bus and train stations are next to each other on the uninspiring Avenida de España, a good half-hour walk from the old quarter. Once you reach Calle San Antón, the look of the town improves considerably, particularly as you reach the intimate Plaza de San Juan, where you'll find one of Extremadura's greatest restaurants, El Figón de Eustaquio.

Beyond Plaza de San Juan is the long, inclined, arcaded **Plaza Mayor,** where you'll see several outdoor cafés, the tourist office, and—on breezy summer nights—nearly everyone in town. In the middle of the arcade opposite the old quarter is the entrance to the lively Calle General Ezponda, lined with tapas bars, student hangouts, and discos that keep the neighborhood awake and moving until dawn. On high ground on the eastern side of the Plaza Mayor, a portal beckons through the town's intact (though heavily restored) wall, which in turn surrounds one of the best-preserved old quarters in Spain. Literally packed with treasures, Cáceres's **Ciudad Monumental** (old town; also called the *casco antiguo*) is a marvel: small, but without a single modern building to distract from its aura. Crammed with somber, gray medieval and Renaissance palaces but very few shops, restaurants, or bars, the old town is virtually deserted in winter. At night it looks like a stage set for a tragedy, while the warm glow of the sun suggests the mythical city of gold that so moved the conquistadors.

Once you pass through the gate leading to the old quarter, note the **Palacio de los Golfines de Arriba** (✉ C. Adarve de Santa Ana), dominated by a soaring tower dating from 1515. The ground floor is a restaurant. Check out the **Casa de Sanchez de Paredes** (✉ C. Ancha), a 16th-century palace that now serves as a parador. On the Plaza San Mateo is the **San Mateo** church (✉ C. Ancha). Built mainly in the 14th century, but with a 16th-century choir, it has an austere interior, the main decorative notes being the baroque high altar and some heraldic crests. The battlement tower of the **Palacio de Las Cigüeñas** (✉ Pl. San Mateo) is officially named the Palacio del Capitán Diego but is also known as the Palace of the Storks, so called because of the storks' nests that adorned it before its restoration. It's now a military residence, but some rooms are occasionally opened up for exhibitions.

The **Casa de las Veletas** (House of the Weather Vanes) is a 12th-century Moorish mansion that is now the **Museo de Cáceres.** With archaeological finds, some dating as far back as the Neolithic era, this collection is an excellent way to acquaint yourself with the area's many inhabitants. One highlight is the eerie but superb Moorish cistern—the *aljibe*—with arches supported by moldy stone pillars. It's downhill from Plaza San Mateo. ✉ *Pl. de las Veletas s/n,* ☎ *927/247234* 🌐 *www.museosextremadura.com* 🎫 *€1.20, free for EU citizens* ⏲ *Tues.–Sat. 9–2:30 and 4–7:15 (5–8:15 in summer), Sun. 10–2:30.*

The stony severity of the **Palacio de los Golfines de Abajo** (✉ Cuesta de la Companía), with the finest exterior of any palace in Cáceres, is relieved by Mudéjar and Renaissance decorative motifs. The Gothic church of **Santa María,** built mainly in the 16th century, is now Cáceres's cathedral. The elegantly carved high altar, from 1551, is just about visible in the gloom. A small museum displays religious objects. ✉ *Cuesta de la Companía.* ☎ *927/215313* 🎫 *Cathedral free, museum €1.20* ⏲ *Mon.–Sat. 10–2 and 5–8, Sun. 9:30–2 and 5–7:30.*

Near the cathedral of Santa María is the elegant **Palacio de Carvajal,** the only old palace you can tour besides the Casa de las Veletas. The palace has an imposing granite facade and an arched doorway, and the interior has been restored, with period furnishings and art, to look as it did when the Carvajal family lived here in the 16th century. ✉ *Pl. de Santa María* 🎫 *Free* ⏲ *Weekdays 8 AM–9 PM, Sat. 9:30–2 and 5–8, Sun. 10–3.*

From Santa María, a 110-yard walk down Calle Tiendas takes you to the town's northern wall. Don't miss the 16th-century **Palacio de los Moctezuma-Toledo** (now a public-record office), built by Juan Cano de Saavedra with his wife's dowry—his wife being the princess daughter of the Aztec ruler Montezuma. ✉ *Pl. Conde de Canilleros 1* ☎ *927/249294* 🎫 *Free* ⏲ *Weekdays 8:30–2:30.*

The chief building of interest outside the wall of the old town is the church of **Santiago de los Caballeros** (✉ C. Villalobos), rebuilt in the 16th century by Rodrigo Gil de Hontañón, Spain's last great Gothic architect. Exit the old town on its west side, through the Socorro gate, to reach the church.

Just up the hill behind the Ciudad Monumental is the **Santuario de la Virgen de la Montaña** (Sanctuary of the Virgin of the Mountain), which has a golden baroque altar. The statue of the patroness virgin is paraded through the town in May. On a clear day the view of old Cáceres from the front of this building is spectacular, well worth the 15-minute drive. ✣ *Follow C. Cervantes until it becomes Ctra. Miajadas (sanctuary is just off town tourist map)* ☎ *927/220049* 🎫 *Donation suggested* ⏲ *Daily 8:30–2 and 4–8.*

off the beaten path

GAROVILLAS AND MONASTERIO DEL PALANCAR – Garovillas, 10 km (6 mi) off the main road between Cáceres and Plasencia (turn left [northwest] onto the C522, 25 km [15 mi] north of Cáceres), is a perfectly preserved, though partially deserted, village. Its must-see square from the late-15th century has an impressive hospedería. East of Garovillas and near the Portuguese border, you will find the Puente de Alcántara, a 2nd-century AD Roman bridge over the River Tajo and one of Spain's prized architectural marvels. On the same road to Plasencia, and once you pass the Puerto de los Castañeos, you'll find a detour to the **Monasterio del Palancar** (☎ 927/192023). In this Franciscan convent, San Pedro de Alcantára, an ascetic friar and saint, spent most of his life in a cell so tiny that he had to sleep sitting up. It's open Thursday–Tuesday 10–1 and 4:30–7.

13

Where to Stay & Eat

★ $$$$ ✕ **Atrio.** On a side street off the southern end of Cáceres's leafy main boulevard, this elegant restaurant is arguably the best in Extremadura. It specializes in ultrarefined yet adventurous modern cooking. The menu changes often, but you won't be disappointed with any of your selections, especially if they include mushrooms or truffles. ✉ *Signo 18, off Av. de América* ☎ *927/242928* ▭ *DC, MC, V* ⊗ *No dinner Sun.*

$$–$$$ ✕ **El Figón de Eustaquio.** A fixture on the quiet and pleasant Plaza San Juan, Eustaquio is always busy, especially at lunchtime. In its jumble of small, old-fashioned dining rooms you'll be served mainly regional delicacies, including cured ham from Montánchez or *perdiz estofada* (partridge with beans). Fine Spanish wines are also available. ✉ *Pl. San Juan 12* ☎ *927/244362 or 927/248194* ✍ *Reservations essential* ▭ *AE, MC, V.*

$$ ✕ **La Gallofa.** Delicacies from a Dominican chef and live music from African musicians set the eclectic tone at this Galician restaurant in the heart of Extremadura. Specialties include *pulpo* (octopus) and *vieiras con arroz* (Galician mussels with rice). ✉ *C. Maestro Sáchez Garrido 1 (off Gran Vía)* ☎ *927/210237* ▭ *DC, MC, V.*

$$$ ✕ **Parador de Cáceres.** In the 16th-century palace Casa de Sanchez de Paredes, this parador has soft cream and ocher tones. Wood beams warm up the plain interiors, and the rooms are cozy and comfortable. Dine on the terrace in the summer or in the dining room: local game specialties include *lomo de venado al queso del Casar* (venison with Caesar cheese sauce) or *cabrito asado al romero* (young goat roasted with rosemary). From Thursday to Sunday, you can sample wines in the parador's wine cellar, Enoteca Torregaz. ✉ *Ancha 6, 10003* ☎ *927/211759* 🖷 *927/211729* 🌐 *www.parador.es* *30 rooms, 1 suite* *Restaurant, minibars, meeting room* ▭ *AE, DC, MC, V.*

★ $$$ **Meliá Cáceres.** This erstwhile 16th-century palace just outside the walls of the old town on the Plaza San Juan gracefully blends exposed stone, indirect spotlighting, and designer furnishings. Rooms have wall-to-wall carpeting and ample bathrooms. La Cava del Emperador, a street-level bar with a vaulted brick ceiling and charming wine-bottle lighting, is a popular meeting place for the town's well heeled. ✉ *Pl. San Juan 11–13, 10003* ☎ *927/215800* 🖷 *927/214070* 🌐 *www.solmelia.com* *84 rooms, 2 suites* *Restaurant, room service, bar, laundry service, meeting rooms* ▭ *AE, DC, MC, V.*

Nightlife & the Arts

Bars in Cáceres are lively until the wee hours. Nightlife centers on the **Plaza Mayor,** which fills after dinner with families out for a *paseo* (promenade) as well as students swigging *calimocho*, a combination of, believe it or not, red wine and Coca-Cola. To escape the college crowd or sample more modern surroundings, try **Calle de Pizarro,** with plenty of cafés and bars. With the best (and priciest) discos, the new town starts hopping when the old one begins to fizzle; **La Madrila,** on the east side of the city, is packed with bars and discos. If you're content with the relative quiet of the old town, take in some live music at **El Corral de las Cigueñas** (✉ Cuesta de Aldana 6), which is only open Thursday–Sunday evenings in the winter. At the **Sala de Promoción de la Artisania,** (✉ San Antón 15 ☎ 927/220927) artists and craftsmen from around the province display and sell their work.

Trujillo

★ 7 *48 km (30 mi) east of Cáceres, 250 km (155 mi) southwest of Madrid; at the junction of N521 and N-V.*

Trujillo is an extreme example of the Extremaduran look: a lonely, nearly deserted place, built of cold and imposing stone. Nonetheless, it's thrilling to behold. The storks' nests that top several towers in and around the center of the old town—and have become something of a symbol of Trujillo—add to this strange effect. The city dates back at least to Roman times, when its castle was first constructed. The city was captured from the Moors in 1232 and colonized by a number of leading military families. It was only after Spain's discovery of the Americas in 1492, however, that the town's renown spread. Known today as the Cradle of the Conquistadors, Trujillo spawned some of the leading explorers and conquerors of the New World. The most famous of these was Francisco Pizarro, conqueror of Peru, born in Trujillo in 1475. Note that it is only practical to see Trujillo on foot, as the streets are mostly cobbled or crudely paved with stone. The two main roads into Trujillo leave you at the unattractive bottom of town. Things get progressively older the farther you climb, but even on the lower slopes—where most of the shops are concentrated—you need walk only a few yards to step into what seems like the Middle Ages.

Trujillo's large **Plaza Mayor,** one of the finest in Spain, is a superb Renaissance creation and the site of the tourist office. At the foot of the stepped platform on the plaza's north side stands a large, bronze equestrian statue of Francisco Pizarro—the work, curiously, of a U.S. sculptor, Carlos Rumsey. The church behind Pizarro, **San Martín** (✉ Pl. Mayor), is a Gothic structure from the early 16th century, with Renaissance tombs and an old organ. Some of Spain's most prominent kings prayed there, including Carlos V, Felipe II, and Felipe V. If you visit at dusk, you may hear the men's choir rehearsing, adding a magical note to eventide.

The **Palacio de los Duques de San Carlos** (Palace of the Dukes of San Carlos) is next to the church of San Martín. The palace's majestically decorated facade dates from around 1600. The building is now a convent of Hieronymite nuns, who can occasionally be glimpsed on the balconies in full habit, hanging laundry or watering their flowers. To visit, ring the bell by pulling the chain in the foyer. The convent also produces and sells typical pastries, including *perrunillas* (small lard cakes) and *tocinillos del cielo* (custardlike egg-yolk sweets). ✉ *Pl. Mayor,* ☎ *927/320058* 🎫 *€1* ⏲ *Mon.–Sat. 10–1 and 4:30–6, Sun. 10–12:30.*

need a break?

If the intense summer sun leaves you parched and tired, revivify yourself at the **Bar Pillete Cafeteria** (Pl. Mayor 28, ☎ 927/321449), which sells a lot of fresh-squeezed juices, shakes, and other exotic fruit concoctions—this is a rarity in these remote parts.

The **Palacio de la Conquista** (Palace of the Conquest; ✉ Pl. Mayor) is the most dramatic building on the square. Built by Francisco Pizarro's half brother Hernando, the stone palace is immediately recognizable by its rich covering of exquisite Renaissance ornamentation. Flanking its corner balcony, around which most of the decoration is clustered, are lively, imaginative busts of the Pizarro family.

Adjacent to the Palacio de la Conquista is the arcaded former town hall, now a court of law; the alley that runs through its central arch takes you to the **Palacio de Orellana-Pizarro,** now a school with the most elegant Renaissance courtyard in town. Cervantes, on his way to thank the Virgin of Guadalupe for his release from prison, spent some time writing here. *Donation suggested* ⏲ *Weekdays 9–2 and 4:30–7, weekends 11–2 and 4:30–7.*

Trujillo's oldest section, known as **La Villa,** is entirely surrounded by its original (if much restored) walls. Follow the wall along Calle Almenas, which runs west from the Palacio de Orellana-Pizarro, beneath the **Alcázar de Los Chaves,** a castle-fortress that was turned into a guest lodge in the 15th century and hosted visiting dignitaries, including Ferdinand and Isabella. The building has seen better days and is now a college. Passing the Alcázar, continue west along the wall to the **Puerta de San Andrés,** one of La Villa's four surviving gates (there were originally seven). Walk through and you're in a world inhabited by storks, who, in spring and early summer, hunker down in the many crumbling chimneys and towers of Trujillo's palaces and churches.

Attached to a Romanesque bell tower, the Gothic church of **Santa María** is occasionally used for masses, but its interior has been virtually untouched since the 16th century. The upper choir has an exquisitely carved balustrade; the coats of arms at each end indicate the seats Ferdinand and Isabella occupied when they attended Mass here. Note the high altar, circa 1480, adorned with great 15th-century Spanish paintings; to see it properly illuminated, place a coin in the box next to the church entrance. ✉ *Pl. de Santa María.* *€1.25* ⏲ *Daily 10:30–2 and 4:30–7 (4–8 in summer.*

The Pizarro family home has been restored and is now a museum, the **Casa Museo de Pizarro,** is dedicated to the links between Spain and Latin America. ✉ *Pl. de Santa María* *€1.25* ⏲ *Daily 11–2 and 4–6 (4–8 in summer).*

Near the Puerta de la Coria, the former convent of San Francisco el Real has the **Museo de la Coria.** As in the Pizarro Museum, the focus is on the conquest of the Americas, with an emphasis on the troops as well as other (non-Pizarro) conquistadors who led missions over the water. ☎ *927/321898* *Free* ⏲ *Weekends 11:30–2.*

Beyond the Casa Museo de Pizarro is the fortress of Trujillo's large **castle,** built by the Moors on Roman foundations. Climb to the top for spectacular views of the town and its surroundings. From here you can compare modern with medieval: to the south are grain silos, warehouses, and residential neighborhoods. To the north are only green fields and flowers, partitioned by a maze of nearly leveled Roman stone walls. *€1.25* ⏲ *Daily 10–2 and 4–7 (5–8:30 in summer).*

Where to Stay & Eat

★ **$–$$** ✕ **Pizarro.** Traditional Extremaduran home cooking is the draw of this friendly restaurant in a small but quietly elegant upstairs room. A house specialty is *gallina trufada,* an elaborately prepared chicken pâté with truffles. This was once a common Christmas dish, but today few people know how to make it. ✉ *Pl. Mayor 13* ☎ *927/320255* ▭ *MC, V* ⊙ *Closed Tues.*

$ ✕ **Mesón La Troya.** Don't be daunted by the gamblers playing the slots in the front room; once you pass the bar, littered with dirty napkins from the tapas crowd, you'll enter the dining room, a vaulted chamber within a beautiful old building. At the beginning of the (optional) fixed-price meal (€15) you're served a *tortilla de patatas* (potato omelet), *chorizo ibérico* (pork sausage), and a salad, whether you want it or not. One notable main dish is the caldereta de cordero. ✉ *Pl. Mayor 10* ☎ *927/321364* ▭ *MC, V.*

★ $$$ ✕▣ **Meliá Trujillo.** Once a convent, this hotel has an ocher color scheme on its facade, in its cloisters, and in its courtyard, which has a swimming pool surrounded by wrought-iron furniture. The handy restaurant is in what once was the refectory. ✉ *Pl. del Campillo 1, 10200* ☎ *927/458900* 🖷 *927/323046* 🌐 *www.solmelia.com* *79 rooms, 1 suite* *Restaurant, pool, bar, meeting room* ▭ *AE, DC, MC, V.*

★ $$ ✕▣ **Parador de Trujillo.** Originally the Convent of St. Clare, Trujillo's homey parador centers on a harmonious Renaissance courtyard. A living-museum quality is reflected in the furniture, paintings, and engravings, and, in this case, the knickknacks. The back wall of the dining room is lined with shelves of typical regional plates and copperware. Sup on the *embutidos* (a raw pork meat sampler), any of the *revueltos* (scrambled eggs with criadillas, asparagus, or mushrooms), or any of the roasted kid or lamb courses. ✉ *C. Beatriz de Silva 1, 10200* ☎ *927/321350* 🖷 *927/321366* 🌐 *www.parador.es* *45 rooms, 1 suite* *Restaurant, bar, meeting room* ▭ *AE, DC, MC, V.*

$$ ✕▣ **Soterrãa.** Just 10 km (6 mi) away from Trujillo on the road to Guadalupe, this cozy rural hotel is divided between two buildings. The rooms are neat and warm (especially the ones in the newer building) and look out onto the street or the courtyard, where barbecues are held in the summer. Even if you don't stay here, it's worth the trek from Trujillo just for dinner (weekends only); Soterrãa's dark-wood-panel-and-slate stable has been converted into a restaurant, especially pleasurable in winter when you can enjoy the dining room's huge fireplace. ✉ *C. Real 75, 10210* ☎ *927/334262* 🖷 *927/319339* 🌐 *www.soterrana.com* *21 rooms, 2 suites* *Restaurant, pool, bar, meeting room* ▭ *MC, V.*

$$ ▣ **Finca Santa Marta.** Surrounded by 60 acres of olive, cherry, and almond trees, this ancient olive-oil mill and wine farm is run by a retired couple as a country refuge. Fourteen kilometers (9 miles) outside Trujillo on the road to Guadalupe, it's a relaxing alternative to staying in town. The restored living quarters have stone floors (rugs keep your feet warm), wood-beam ceilings, and fresh flowers. Meals are available if requested in advance. Reservations are essential. ✉ *Pago de San Clemente, 10600* ☎🖷 *927/319203* 🌐 *www.fincasantamarta.com* *13 rooms, 1 suite* *Pool, bar, meeting room* ▭ *MC, V.*

Shopping

Trujillo sells more folk arts and crafts than almost any other place in Extremadura, among the most attractive of which are multicolor rugs, blankets, and embroideries. Several shops on the **Plaza Mayor** have enticing selections; the one next door to the tourist office displays a centuries-old loom along with the work of local craftswoman Maribel Vallar, though opening hours are erratic. **Eduardo Pablos Mateos** (✉ Plazuela de San Judas 12 ☎ 927/321066), specializes in local wood carvings, basketwork, and furniture. For other stores selling pottery, glass, or iron crafts, request addresses at the tourist office.

Guadalupe

★ 8 *200 km (125 mi) southwest of Madrid, 143 km (88 mi) east of Cáceres, 96 km (60 mi) east of Trujillo, 200 km (125 mi) northeast of Mérida.*

The **Monastery of Our Lady of Guadalupe** is one of the most inspiring sights in Extremadura. Whether you come from Madrid, Trujillo, or Cáceres, the last stage of the ride takes you through wild, astonishingly beautiful mountain scenery. The monastery itself clings to the slopes, forming a magical profile that echoes the gaunt wall of mountains behind it. Pilgrims have been coming here since the 14th century, but only in recent years have they been joined by a growing number of tourists; even so, the monastery's very isolation—it's a good two-hour drive from the nearest town—has saved it from commercial excess. The story of Guadalupe goes back to around 1300, when a local shepherd uncovered a statue of the Virgin, supposedly carved by St. Luke. King Alfonso XI, who often hunted here, had a church built to house the statue and later vowed to found a monastery should he defeat the Moors at the battle of Salado in 1340. After his victory, he kept his promise. The greatest period in the monastery's history was between the 15th and 18th centuries, when, under the rule of the Hieronymites, it was turned into a pilgrimage center rivaling Santiago de Compostela in importance. Documents authorizing Columbus's first voyage to the New World were signed here. The Virgin of Guadalupe became the patroness of Latin America, honored by the dedication of thousands of churches and towns in the New World. The monastery's decline coincided with Spain's loss of overseas territories in the 19th century. Abandoned for 70 years and left to decay, it was restored after the civil war by Franciscan brothers.

On sale everywhere in Guadalupe is the copperware that has been crafted here since the 16th century. In the middle of the tiny, irregularly shaped **Plaza Mayor** (also known as the Plaza de Santa María de Guadalupe, and transformed during festivals into a bullring) is a 15th-century **fountain,** where Columbus's two Native American servants were baptized in 1496. Looming in the background is the late-Gothic south facade of the **monastery church,** flanked by battlement towers.

The entrance to the monastery is to the left of the church. From the large Mudéjar cloister, the required guided tour progresses to the **chapter house,** with hymnals, vestments, and paintings, including a series of small panels by Zurbarán. The ornate 17th-century **sacristy** has a series of eight Zurbarán paintings of 1638–47. These powerfully austere representations of monks of the Hieronymite order and scenes from the life of St. Jerome are the artist's only significant paintings still in the setting for which they were intended. The tour concludes with the garish, late-baroque **Camarín,** the chapel where the famous Virgen Morena (Black Virgin) is housed. The dark, mysterious wooden figure hides under a heavy veil and mantle of red and gold; painted panels tell the Virgin's life story; on September 8, the Virgin is brought down from its altarpiece and the procession walks the Virgin around the cloister with pilgrims following on their knees. Outside, the monastery's gardens have been relandscaped in their original, geometric Moorish style. ✉ *Entrance on Pl. Mayor* ☎ *927/367000* €3 ⏲ *Daily 9:30–1 and 3:30–6:30; guided tours every ½ hr.*

en route

Four kilometers (2½ miles) outside of Guadalupe toward Navalmoral de la Mata, there is a 15th-century Gothic hermitage, **Humilladero.** On the same road immediately before it is a lookout point with a good view of the monastery and Guadalupe.

Where to Stay & Eat

$–$$ ✕ **Isabel.** Across the square from the monastery, this kitschy, family-run bar and restaurant serves tapas and other inexpensive dishes. The migas and cuchifrito are good bets. The small dining room is accented with copper and ceramic crafts, and often fills up with busloads of tourists. ✉ *Pl. Santa María de Guadalupe 13* ☎ *927/367126.*

$ ✕ **Extremadura.** For a hearty meal, particularly if you like mushrooms, try this restaurant just down the road from the monastery. The menú *de la casa* (of the house) includes migas, *sopa de ajo* (garlic soup), pork chops with green beans, and steak topped with mushrooms. ✉ *Gregorio López 18* ☎ *927/367351.*

★ $$ ✕🏨 **Parador de Guadalupe.** The first autopsy in Spain was performed in this building, a 15th-century hospital and pilgrim's hostel. Thanks to its Mudéjar architecture, Moorish-style rooms, and exotic vegetation, the parador has an unusually luxurious feel. All the rooms are renovated, and the best look out onto the monastery. In keeping with the spirit of the region, the restaurant serves simple local dishes, such as *bacalao monacal* (cod with spinach and potatoes), migas, and *frite de cordero* (lamb stew). ✉ *C. Marqués de la Romana 12, 10140* ☎ *927/367075* 📠 *927/367076* 🌐 *www.parador.es* *41 rooms* *Restaurant, tennis court, pool, bar, meeting room* 💳 *AE, DC, MC, V.*

$ ✕🏨 **Hospedería del Real Monasterio.** An excellent alternative if the Parador de Guadalupe is full, this inn was built around the 16th-century Gothic cloister of the monastery itself. The courtyard of the Gothic cloister is used as an outdoor café open to all during the summer months. The simple, traditional rooms with wood-beam ceilings are exceptionally quiet. Scrumptious local dishes include caldereta de cabrito, *revuelto de cardillos* (scrambled eggs with thistle), and *morcilla de acelga* (blood pudding with beets). ✉ *Pl. Juan Carlos I s/n, 10140* ☎ *927/367000* 📠 *927/367177* *46 rooms, 1 suite* *Restaurant, bar* 💳 *MC, V* ⏲ *Closed mid-Jan.–mid-Feb.*

Shopping

Guadalupe is the place to go for copper and tinware, as the local metalwork industry is 400 years old.

LOWER EXTREMADURA

Extremadura's southern half sometimes seems more Andalusian or even Portuguese than classically Spanish. Long stretches of dusty farmland and a Portuguese-influenced Spanish dialect make it feel light-years away from Castile. Mérida was established in 25 BC as a settlement for Roman soldiers; it soon became the capital of the Roman province of Lusitania, and its many ruins bear witness to its former splendor. Badajoz has also been a settlement since prehistoric times; Paleolithic remains have been found nearby. Minutes from the Portuguese border, it has long served as a gateway to Portugal and is home to many Portuguese as well as Portuguese descendants. Extremadura's links with Portugal come alive in Olivenza, while Zafra, near the southern end of the province, suggests an Andalusian town.

Mérida

9 *70 km (43 mi) south of Cáceres, 66 km (40 mi) east of Badajoz, 250 km (155 mi) north of Seville.*

Strategically situated at the junction of major Roman roads from León to Seville and Toledo to Lisbon, Mérida was founded by the Romans in 25 BC on the banks of the River Guadiana. Then named Augusta

Emerita, it became the capital of the vast Roman province of Lusitania (the Iberian Peninsula) soon after its founding. A bishopric in Visigothic times, Mérida never regained the importance that it had under the Romans, and as the administrative capital of Extremadura, it is now a rather plain large town—with the exception of its Roman monuments; they pop up all over town, surrounded by thoroughly modern buildings. The new, glass-and-steel bus station is in a modern district on the other side of the river from the town center. It commands a good view of the exceptionally long **Roman bridge,** which spans two forks of this sluggish river. On the farther bank is the Alcazaba fortress.

Some other Roman sites require a drive. Across the train tracks in a modern neighborhood is the **circo** (circus), where chariot races were held. Little remains of the grandstands, which seated 30,000, but the outline of the circus is clearly visible and impressive for its size: 1,312 ft long and 377 ft wide. Of the various remains of aqueducts, the most impressive is the **Acueducto de los Milagros** (Aqueduct of Miracles), north of the train station. It carried water from the Roman dam of Proserpina, which still stands, 5 km (3 mi) away. If you're driving around Mérida, follow signs to the MUSEO DE ARTE ROMANO to reach Mérida's best-preserved **Roman monuments,** the **teatro** (theater) and **anfiteatro** (amphitheater), arranged in a verdant park. Parking is usually easy here. Next to the entrance to the Roman ruins is the main tourist office, where you can pick up maps and brochures. You can buy a ticket to see only the Roman ruins or, for a slightly higher fee, an *entrada conjunta* (joint admission), which also grants access to the Basílica de Santa Eulalia and the Alcazaba. ☎ *924/312530* *Theater and amphitheater €5.10; combined admission to Roman sites, basilica, and Alcazaba €7.20* *Daily 9:30–1:45 and 4–6:15 (5–7:15 in summer).*

Fodor's Choice ★

★ Across the street from the entrance to the Roman sites, and connected by an underground passageway, is Mérida's superb, modern **Museo Nacional de Arte Romano** (National Museum of Roman Art), in a monumental building designed by the renowned Spanish architect Rafael Moneo. You walk through a series of passageways to the luminous, cathedral-like main exhibition hall, supported by arches the same proportion and size (50 ft) as the Roman arch in the center of Mérida, the Arco de Trajano (Trajan's Arch). The exhibits include mosaics, frescoes, jewelry, statues, pottery, household utensils, and other Roman works. Before leaving, be sure to visit the **crypt** beneath the museum—it houses the remains of several homes and a necropolis that were uncovered while the museum was built, in 1981, and were incorporated into the project as part of the exhibits. The museum is wheelchair-accessible. ✉ *José Ramón Mélida 2* ☎ *924/311690* *www.mnar.es* *€2.40, free Sat. afternoon and Sun.* *Tues.–Sat. 10–2 and 4–6 (5–7 in summer), Sun. 10–2.*

From the Museo Nacional de Arte Romano, make your way west down Suarez Somontes toward the river and the city center. Turn right at Calle Baños and you'll see the towering columns of the **Templo de Diana,** the oldest of Mérida's Roman buildings. If you continue toward the river along Sagasta and Romera, you'll come to the sturdy, square **Alcazaba** (fortress), built by the Romans and later strengthened by the Visigoths and Moors. To go inside, follow the fortress walls around to the side farthest from the river. Climb up to the battlements for sweeping river views. ☎ *924/317309* *€7.20 (includes Roman theater and amphitheater)* *Daily 9:30–1:45 and 4–6:15 (5–7:15 in summer).*

Mérida's main square, the **Plaza de España,** adjoins the northwestern corner of the fortress and is highly animated both day and night. The plaza's oldest building is a 16th-century palace, now being converted to a Meliá hotel. Behind the palace stretches Mérida's most charming area, with Andalusian-style white houses shaded by palms—in the midst of which stands the **Arco de Trajano,** part of a Roman city gate.

An abandoned 18th-century church contains the dusty **Museo Visigótico,** with fragments of Visigothic stonework. The museum is north of the Plaza de España in the heart of Mérida's casco viejo. ✉ *Pl. de Santa Clara* ☎ *924/300106* 💶 *Free* ⏲ *Oct.–June, Tues.–Sat. 10–2 and 4–6, Sun. 10–2; July–Sept., Tues.–Sat. 10–2 and 5–7.*

The **Basílica de Santa Eulalia,** originally a Visigothic structure, marks both the site of a Roman temple and supposedly where the child martyr Eulalia was roasted alive in AD 304 for spitting in the face of a Roman magistrate. In 1990, excavations surrounding the tomb of the famous saint revealed layer upon layer of Paleolithic, Visigothic, Byzantine, and Roman settlements. ✉ *Rambla Mártir Santa Eulalia* ☎ *924/303407* 💶 *€2.55* ⏲ *Mon.–Sat. 10–1:15 and 4–6:15 (5–7:15 in summer).*

off the beaten path

EXTREMADURAN SIBERIA – For a taste of truly elemental Spain, drive to the "Extremaduran Siberia," between Mérida and the Castilian town of Ciudad Real (leave N430, which links the two towns, by following signs for Casas de Don Pedro, and continue south toward Talarrubias). This poor area of wild, rolling scrubland owes its nickname to the 12th duke of Osuna, who in the late 1800s came here after 10 years as the Spanish ambassador to Russia and was reminded of the Siberian steppes. The oldest village is Puebla de Alcocer, which has an arcaded square. In nearby Peloche, to the north of Talarrubias, women still embroider in the streets. Many people come to this region for water sports at its three reservoirs: Cíjara, García de Sola, and Orellana.

Where to Stay & Eat

$$ ✕ **Nicolás.** Mérida's best-known restaurant, around the corner from the parador and across from the local market, has a tavern serving tapas downstairs and a dining room, decorated in dark wood, upstairs. The regionally inspired food includes *perdiz en escabeche* (marinated partridge), various lamb dishes, and frogs' legs. Desserts might include the traditional técula mécula, or creamy cheese from La Serena. The wine list is extensive, the service professional. ✉ *Felix Valverde Lillo 13,* ☎ *924/319610* 💳 *AE, DC, MC, V* ⏲ *No dinner Sun.*

$$ ✕ **Rufino.** The dining room is above the popular bar, accessed by a separate door and a narrow flight of stairs. Tables are slightly cramped, but the food is authentic and tasty, and might include lamb caldereta, partridge, and *cochinillo frito* (fried suckling pig). It also has a fixed-price menu and an excellent regional wine list. ✉ *Pl. Santa Clara 2,* ☎ *924/312001* 💳 *AE, DC, MC, V* ⏲ *Closed Sun. and Aug.*

$–$$ ✕ **Altair.** Under the same ownership as the renowned Atrio in Cáceres, Altair, on the bank of the river Guadiana, delivers quality regional food with a modern twist. The chef's specialties include *rollitos de pruva de ibérico* (pasta rolls stuffed with pork meat), *bacalo fresco con manitas de cerdo* (fresh cod with pig's hands), and *lechón confitado* (caramelized baby pig). Consider going for the €25 five-course sampler menu. A translucent wall facing the river provides a silhouetted view of the Roman Bridge. ✉ *Av. José Fernández López s/n,* ☎ *924/304512* 💳 *AE, MC, V* ⏲ *Closed Sun.*

$–$$ ✕ **Casa Benito.** It looks like just a tapas place, but this bar-restaurant hidden on a square off Calle Santa Eulalia has a small, informal dining area in the back and serves from a limited but tasty menu. The walls at

Benito's are covered with pictures and memorabilia of matadors and bullfights. ✉ *C. San Francisco 3,* ☎ *924/315502* 💳 *AE, MC, V* ⊙ *Closed Sun.*

★ $$$ ✕🏨 **Parador de Mérida.** Built over the remains of what was first a Roman temple, then a baroque convent, then a prison, this spacious, whitewashed building exudes an Andalusian cheerfulness, with hints at its Roman and Mudéjar past. Guest rooms are bright, with traditional dark-wood furniture. The brilliant-white interior of the convent's former church has been turned into a restful lounge. Try the restaurant's *revuelto* (scrambled eggs) prepared various ways, including *con aroma de pimentón* (in paprika sauce) and *cabrito al ajillo* (baby goat fried with garlic). ✉ *Pl. Constitución 3, 06800* ☎ *924/313800* 📠 *924/319208* 🌐 *www.parador.es* *80 rooms, 2 suites* *Restaurant, pool, health club, sauna, bar, parking (fee)* 💳 *AE, DC, MC, V.*

Nightlife & the Arts

The highlight of the cultural calendar is the annual **Festival de Teatro Clásico,** held in the Roman theater from early July to mid-August. Contact the tourist office in advance for information and tickets. The many cafés, tapas bars, and restaurants surrounding the Plaza España and in Plaza de la Constitución fill with boisterous crowds late into the evening. Calle John Lennon, off the northwest corner of the plaza, is your best bet for late-night dance action, especially in summer. As you walk south on Santa Eulalia, the bars get cheaper, the music louder. Locals pack **Rafael II** (✉ C. Santa Eulalia 13) for ham, cheese, and sausages; there's also a small, cork-lined dining room in the back.

Shopping

On Calle José Ramón Mélida are shops with kitschy tourist souvenirs, replicas of nearby Roman excavations, and regional crafts.

Badajoz

 *66 km (40 mi) west of Mérida, 90 km (59 mi) southwest of Cáceres.*

A sprawling mass of concrete and glass in the midst of desolate terrain, Badajoz looks like an urban oasis on approach and is indeed modern and well stocked relative to the surrounding towns. Hardly an aesthetic haven, however, the city has little to offer the traveler; it tries (not quite successfully) to make up for its lack of architectural interest with nighttime energy and the intellectual punch of its university. A mere 7 km (4 mi) from Portugal, this "border town" serves mainly as a suitable resting point on the way though Extremadura. The newish **Museo Extremeño e Iberoamericano de Arte Contemporáneo** is the main daytime incentive to spend a few hours here. Dedicated to contemporary Spanish and Latin American painting and sculpture, the museum is south of the city center in a striking circular building that was once the Badajoz prison. ✉ *Nuestra Señora de Guadalupe s/n* ☎ *924/013060* 🎫 *Free* ⊙ *Tues.–Sat. 10:30–1:30 and 5–8 (6–9 in summer), Sun. 10:30–1:30.*

Make your way to the older section of town and wander down to the edge of the Guadiana River to admire the **Puerta de Palmas,** the 16th-century gateway to Badajoz and modern-day symbol of the city. Its two circular, crenellated towers are surrounded by decorative guard posts. The **Torre Espantaperros**—literally, Dog-Scarers' Tower; effectively a Christian-scarers' tower—is the watchtower of Badajoz's **Alcazaba.** The practice of building these towers eventually inspired Seville's Giralda. Within the Alcazaba is the city's **Museo Arqueológico,** with lots of artifacts from the region. ✉ *C. de San Juan* ☎ *924/222314* 🎫 *Free* ⊙ *Tues.–Sun. 10–3.*

Where to Stay & Eat

$$$ ✕ **Aldebarán.** This restaurant has a spacious interior and elegant touches like bohemian glassware and embroidered tablecloths. A former head chef of the renowned Arzak in San Sebastián runs the kitchen. Specialties include *merluza al aroma de romero* (hake infused with rosemary) and *manitas de cerdo con judías verdes* (pig's hands with green beans). ✉ *Av. de Elbas s/n, Centro Comercial, 06001 Las Terrazas* ☎ *924/274261* ▭ *AE, DC, MC, V.*

$$–$$$ ✕ **Gran Hotel Zurbarán.** This large, modern building is near the River Guadiana and overlooks the Parque de Castelar. Although the exterior is brash and slightly dated, the service is impeccable, and few hotels in Extremadura have as many amenities. The elegant restaurant, Los Monjes, is one of the best in town. ✉ *Paseo Castelar s/n, 06001* ☎ *924/001400* 📠 *924/220142* 🌐 *www.barcelo.com* *210 rooms, 4 suites* *Restaurant, pool, bar, dance club, meeting room, parking (fee)* ▭ *AE, DC, MC, V.*

Nightlife & the Arts

Many of the bars and tapas places are situated around Plaza España, especially Calle Zurbarán and Muñoz y Torrero.

Olivenza

⓫ *22 km (14 mi) south of Badajoz.*

Olivenza is worth seeing for its curious double personality. Looking at the airy, elongated main square, with its patterned cobblestones and various facades in the Portuguese Manueline style, you might think you've inadvertently crossed the border into Portugal. In fact, this originally Spanish town was occupied by Portugal in 1297, recaptured by the Spanish duke of San Germán in 1657, recovered by Portugal in 1668, and definitively reclaimed for Spain again in 1801. Olivenza's Portuguese influence is most evident in the twisted Manueline columns and tiling in the **Iglesia de la Magdalena** (Church of Mary Magdalene; ✉ Pl. de la Constitución s/n). As befits a long-disputed border town, Olivenza has numerous fortifications, the largest of which is the castle, with its 15th-century **Torre del Homenaje** (Tower of Homage; ✉ Pl. de Santa María). Adjoining the Torre del Homenaje is the **Museo Etnográfico González Santana,** surprisingly ambitious for a town this size. One room is devoted to archaeological finds (including a stone stele from the 8th century BC), but the main thrust is recent history: exhibits cover traditional trades and crafts along with collections of musical instruments, toys, and other paraphernalia of daily rural life in the first half of the 20th century. ✉ *Pl. de Santa María* ☎ *924/490222* *Free* ⏲ *Oct.–May, Tues.–Sun. 11–2 and 4–6; June–Sept., Tues.–Sun. 11–2 and 5–8.*

Zafra

⓬ *62 km (38 mi) south of Mérida, 85 km (53 mi) southeast of Badajoz, 135 km (84 mi) north of Seville.*

During the first week of October, Zafra hosts one of Spain's oldest and largest livestock fairs, the **Feria de Ganado,** which dates back to 1417. Breeders and traders come from all over the country, and hotel rates rise accordingly; reserve well in advance. Worth a stop on your way to or from Seville, Zafra is an attractive and lively town with a **Plaza Mayor** that's actually two contiguous squares, the Plaza Chica (once a marketplace) and the 18th-century Plaza Grande (ringed by mansions flaunting their coats of arms). Connected by a graceful archway, both plazas make for enjoyable tapas crawls. There are several churches here, the finest being **Nuestra Señora de Candelaria** (✉ Conde de la Corte) a block west off the Plaza Mayor and a short walk from the parador—its *retablo* (altarpiece) has nine extraordinary panels by Zurbarán. The main reason travelers stop in Zafra, however, is the parador itself, otherwise known as the 15th-century **Alcázar de los Duques de Feria** (✉ Pl. Corazón de María 7).

Where to Stay & Eat

★ $$$ **Rocamador.** Between Olivenza and Zafra, the hotel is a renovated 16th-century monastery on top of a hill. Tourists can stay in the former library, the kitchen, or the monk's cells, which have cavernous arches and wooden beam ceilings, brick-arch doorways, stone or clay tile floors, and rustic furniture. The monastery's chapel is a renowned restaurant run by two young, imaginative Basque chefs. It includes two fixed-price sampler menus. Reserve well in advance. ✉ *Ctra. Nacional Badajoz–Huelva, Km 41.1, 06160 Almendral* ☎ *924/489000* 📠 *924/489001* 🌐 *www.rocamador.com* *25 rooms, 5 suites* *Restaurant, pool, bar* 💳 *AE, DC, MC, V.*

$$ **Huerta Honda.** Across a small square from the castle-parador, this gleaming-white Andalusian-style hotel has rooms painted in pastel pinks or blues. Ten luxurious ("Gran Clase," and more expensive) rooms have four-poster beds and sumptuous furnishings; those on the ground floor, including one with wheelchair access, have private patios. At Barbacana, savor gazpacho *a la extremeña* (Extremeño-style) or tasty retinto beef. The Huerta's lively cafeteria serves more modest fare. There's also an English-style pub. ✉ *Lopez Asme 30, 06300* ☎ *924/554100* 📠 *924/552504* 🌐 *www.hotelhuertahonda.com* *35 rooms, 9 suites* *Restaurant, cafeteria, pool, pub* 💳 *AE, DC, MC, V.*

★ $$ **Parador de Zafra.** This parador is in the 15th-century castle where Cortés stayed before his voyage to Mexico. The military exterior conceals an elegant, 16th-century courtyard attributed to Juan de Herrera. The suite and the chapel, which together now serve as a conference room, have a superbly elaborate *artesonado* (coffered) ceiling. The rooms here are spacious and elegant, with high ceilings, antique furniture, and decorative ironwork. Try *pierna de cordero asado* (roasted leg of lamb). Local desserts include bishop's hearts (marzipan) and acorn cakes. ✉ *Pl. María Cristina 7, 06300* ☎ *924/554540* 📠 *924/551018* 🌐 *www.parador.es* *44 rooms, 1 suite* *Restaurant, pool, meeting room* 💳 *AE, DC, MC, V.*

EXTREMADURA A TO Z

To research prices, get advice from other travelers, and book travel arrangements, visit www.fodors.com.

AIR TRAVEL

There are no airports in Extremadura. The nearest international airports are in Madrid and Seville.

BIKE TRAVEL

A good way to see Extremadura by bike is to follow the Ruta Vía de la Plata. It runs through Extremadura from north to south along N630, dividing it in two, and passes by such villages as Plasencia, Cáceres, Mérida, and Zafra. This route more or less follows the ancient Roman walkway Via de la Plata. Parts of the road are still preserved and walkable. Note that the region north of the province of Cáceres, including the valley of Jerte, La Vera, and the area surrounding Guadalupe, is mountainous and uneven. Be prepared for a bumpy and exhausting ride. The regional government is preparing to open another path, a Vía Verde, which goes from Logrosán (a couple of miles southwest of Guadalupe) to Villanueva de la Serena (east of Mérida and near Don Benito). This new path is a roughly cleared walkway, more like a nature walkway, and not for vehicles. Other options for bicyclists are the paved areas of the national parks of Monfragüe and Montalvo. Ask the local tourist offices about where to rent bikes. Rural lodgings also often provide bikes for their guests.

BUS TRAVEL

Bus links between Extremadura and the other Spanish provinces are far more plentiful and reliable than train or plane service. Regular buses, some of them express, serve Extremadura's main cities from Madrid, Seville, Lisbon, Valladolid, Salamanca, and Barcelona. The main company involved in trips to and from Madrid is Auto Res. Buses serve nearly every village in Extremadura. Note, however, that on lesser routes, buses tend to set off extremely early in the morning; plan carefully to avoid getting stranded.

Bus Information **Auto Res** ☒ Pl. Conde de Casal 6, Madrid ☎ 91/5517200 ☒ Estación de Autobuses, Av. de la Libertad, Mérida ☎ 924/371955. **Bus Station: Badajoz** ☒ José Rebollo López, s/n, Badajoz ☎ 924/258661. **Bus Station: Cáceres** ☒ Crta. Gijó–Sevilla, Cáceres ☎ 927/232550.

CAR RENTALS

It's best to reserve a car outside Extremadura, either in Madrid or Seville, or before you leave for Spain. Locally, you can rent a car in Badajoz, Cáceres, or Mérida.

Badajoz **Hertz** ☒ Hotel Río ☎ 924/273510. **Avis** ☒ Hotel Zurbarán ☎ 924/224313. **EuropCar** ☒ Juan Sebastián Elcano, 66 ☎ 924/243187.

Cáceres **EuropCar** ☒ Plus Ultra 1 ☎ 927/212988.

Merída **Avis** ☒ Av. de la Libertad s/n, Estación de Autobuses ☎ 924/373311 or 909/923441.

CAR TRAVEL

Traffic moves quickly on the four-lane N-V, the main highway from Madrid to Extremadura. The N630, or Vía de la Plata, which crosses Extremadura from north to south, is also effective. The fastest approach from Portugal is the N-IV from Lisbon to Badajoz. If you're in any kind of hurry, driving is the most feasible way to get around Extremadura. The main roads are well surfaced and not too congested. Side roads—particularly those that cross the wilder mountainous districts, such as the Sierra de Guadalupe—can be poorly paved and badly marked.

DISABILITIES & ACCESSIBILITY

Extremadura abounds with ancient buildings that cannot easily accommodate travelers with disabilities. In Cáceres, visitors with disabilities have access to the old part of the city and, with some help, the Concatedral de Santa María. Plasencia's only accessible site is the Museo Etnográfico-Textil. Trujillo's celebrated main square was renovated in 2002 to provide, among other things, easier access for people with disabilities. From there, tourists can move into the old area and visit, with the help of a ramp, the Iglesia of Santa María. In Mérida, the Roman ruins and the Basílica de Santa Eulalia are accessible with accompaniment, unlike the Alcazaba; the Museo Nacional de Arte Romano, on the contrary, is accessible. In Badajoz, only the Museo Extremeño provides access and facilities for travelers with disabilities.

DISCOUNTS & DEALS

Trujillo has two different types of multisight passes. The first, at €4.50, provides access to Casa Museo Pizarro, the castle, the church of Santiago, and a guidebook (also sold separately). The second, at €6.50, grants access to the above plus Museo del Traje, Aljibe del Altamirano, and a guided tour. In Mérida, aside from the combined ticket for the Roman theater and amphitheater, there is a multisight pass for €7.20 that includes these sights plus Zona Arqueológica de Morerís, excavations of Basílica de Santa Eulalia, and Casa de Mitrea.

EMERGENCIES

Police ☎ 091. **Ambulance** ☎ 061.

FISHING PERMITS

Non-EU residents can apply for one of two possible licenses to fish in public waters. You'll need to pick up a *Modelo 50* form, available from most banks in Extremadura. The licenses are called *especial*; the especial granting permission to fish for trout is €15.60, the nontrout license is €10.40. Note that the licenses are mailed to your home address, so the Modelo form serves as proof of license for up to two months.

Dirección General del Medio Ambiente ✉ Av. de Portugal s/n, Mérida ☎ 924/002211 or 924/002467.

LODGING

Plenty of comfortable and reasonably priced rural housing is available in Extremadura. The terms of the rentals differ significantly: some lodgings require guests to rent the entire house or to bring their own linens. There is no centralized way to make reservations, so you'll have to call the individual proprietor.

Local Agents **Extremadura Rural Accommodation Guide** 🌐 www.turismoextremadura.com/ingles/alojamiento/home.html. **Top Rural** 🌐 www.toprural.com.

SPORTS & THE OUTDOORS

Nat Rural organizes hiking, bird-watching, fishing, botanical, and four-wheel drive tours around Guadalupe and also in the Monfragüe and Cornalvo nature parks. Valle Aventura arranges similar activities in Valle del Jerte; if you want to hike here, ask the tourist office near Cabezuela for its helpful maps, which describe each hike and detail the route. To visit the Cornalvo Nature Park, the second largest park in the region next to Monfragüe, contact (in advance) the nature park's department at the Dirección General del Medio Ambiente, as most of the park is private land and a guide is recommended for visiting. The regional government is in the process of setting up a Centro de Interpretación, an information and permit center, in Trujillanos.

Nat Rural ✉ C. Gregorio López 177, Guadalupe ☎ 927/154224 🌐 www.puebladeguadalupe.com/natural. **Valle Aventura** ✉ Av. de Plasencia, Cabezuela del Valle ☎ 927/472196 🌐 www.valleaventura.com. **Dirección General del Medio Ambiente** ✉ Av. de Portugal s/n, Mérida ☎ 924/002520 or 924/002386.

TAXIS

Taxis are available at train or bus stations, most tourist sights, and on some commercial streets. The fares are detailed on taxi windows, and tipping is optional.

Taxi Companies **Radio Taxi Cáceres** ☎ 927/242424. **Radio Taxi Badajoz** ☎ 924/243101. **Radio Taxi Mérida** ☎ 924/371111. **Tele Taxi Mérida** ☎ 924/315756.

TOURS

Guías Turísticos de Cáceres offers guided tours around the city and provides information on accredited guides throughout Extremadura.

Guías Turísticos de Cáceres ✉ Pl. Mayor 2, Cáceres ☎ 927/217237.

TRAIN TRAVEL

Trains from Madrid stop at Monfragüe, Plasencia, Cáceres, Mérida, Zafra, and Badajoz. They run daily a few times a day except to Zafra and Badajoz, which only have two trains daily. From Seville there are daily trains to Zafra, Mérida, Cáceres, and Plasencia. The journey from Madrid to Cáceres takes about five hours; from Seville to Cáceres, 7½ hours. There is also a direct train from Lisbon to Badajoz, which takes five hours. Call the RENFE information line for details. Note that train stations in Extremadura tend to be some distance from the town centers.

Train Information **RENFE** ☎ 902/240202 www.renfe.es.

VISITOR INFORMATION

Extremadura's regional government is striving to restructure tourism, which until now has been geared toward Spanish-speaking travelers. The local and regional tourist offices have been turning out lots of information in English. Most of the regional tourist offices provide general information not just on the town in which they are based but also on the major sites of Extremadura.

Regional Tourist Offices **Plasencia** ✉ C. del Rey 8 ☎ 927/422159. **Badajoz** ✉ Pl. de la Libertad 3 ☎ 924/222763. **Cáceres** ✉ Pl. Mayor s/n ☎ 927/010834. **Mérida** ✉ Av. José Álvarez Saez de Buruaga s/n, at entrance to Roman theater ☎ 924/009730.

Local Tourist Offices **Badajoz** ✉ Pasaje de San Juan s/n ☎ 924/224981. **Guadalupe** ✉ Pl. Mayor ☎ 927/154128. **Plasencia** ✉ Pl. de la Catedral ☎ 927/423843. **Trujillo** ✉ Pl. Mayor s/n ☎ 927/322677. **Valle del Jerte** ✉ Paraje de Peñas Alba, just off N110 north of Cabezuela, ☎ 927/472122 or 927/472558. **Zafra** ✉ Pl. de España 30 ☎ 924/551036.

THE CANARY ISLANDS

14

FODOR'S CHOICE

Seaside Hotel Palm Beach, Maspalomas
Timanfaya National Park, Yaiza

HIGHLY RECOMMENDED

RESTAURANTS	Chipi Chipi, Santa Cruz de la Palma
	El Coto de Antonio, Santa Cruz
	Masía del Mar, Los Cristianos
	Playa Mont, Tazacorte
	Tenderete II, Maspalomas
HOTELS	Gran Meliá Bahía del Duque, Adeje
	Gran Meliá Salinas, Costa Teguise
	Hacienda San Jorge, Los Cancajos
	Jardines Tecina, Playa de Santiago
	Los Jameos Playa, Puerto del Carmen
	Parador Conde de La Gomera, San Sebastián
	Parador de Santa Cruz de la Palma
	Timanfaya Palace, Yaiza
SIGHTS	Cuevas Verdes, Costa Teguise
	Los Jameos del Agua, Costa Teguise
	Santa Cruz de la Palma
OUTDOORS	Playa del Inglés, Gran Canaria's famous white-sand beach

By Deborah Luhrman

Updated by AnneLise Sorensen

A VOLCANIC CONSTELLATION 1,280 km (800 mi) southwest of mainland Spain and 112 km (70 mi) off the coast of southern Morocco, the seven Canary Islands lie at about the same latitude as central Florida. La Gomera and El Hierro, as well as parts of La Palma and Gran Canaria, are fertile and overgrown with exotic tropical vegetation, while Lanzarote, Fuerteventura, and stretches of Tenerife are as dry as a bone, with lava caves and desert sand dunes. Yet Spain's highest peak, Mt. Teide, on Tenerife, is capped with snow several months of each year.

The Canaries are geographically African, culturally European, and spiritually Latin American. Many islanders have close blood ties to Cuba and Venezuela. The language spoken here is, in both diction and pronunciation, a South American version of Spanish. Salsa music, exotic to peninsular Spain, is the exclusive genre of the Canaries' wild Carnival fiestas.

The best thing about the Canaries is their climate, warm in winter and tempered by cool Atlantic breezes in summer. You can swim year-round. This is no secret to vacationing Europeans: the islands' first modern-day tourists arrived from England at the turn of the 20th century to spend the winter at Puerto de la Cruz, in Tenerife. Today, huge charter flights from Düsseldorf, Stockholm, Zürich, Manchester, and dozens of other northern European cities unload 6 million sun-starved visitors a year. Only a handful of tourists on these islands at any given time are from the United States, in contrast to mainland Spain.

The presence of northern travelers helps create a strange duality of natural beauty and heavy tourism. On Gran Canaria and Tenerife in particular, you'll hear more German than Spanish, and the resort towns' endless international eateries, car-rental agencies, water parks, travel agents, and miniature-golf parks suggest a sort of foreign annexation. Most people congregate, however, on a few unexceptional beaches, leaving the Canaries' purer aspects intact. An excellent system of natural parks and protected zones serves hikers, bikers, and beachcombers.

Before the Spanish arrived, the Canaries were populated by cave-dwelling people called Guanches. In the late 15th century the islands fell one at a time to Spanish conquistadors, then lay on the edge of navigators' maps for centuries. Columbus resupplied his ships here in 1492 before heading west to the New World then went on to help establish the archipelago as an important trading port. The Guanches were decimated by slave traders by the end of the 16th century. Their most significant remains are the Cenobio de Valerón ruins on Gran Canaria.

About the Restaurants

Canarian cuisine is based on the delicious rockfish that abound near the coast, and its specialties are worth searching out. A typical meal begins with a hearty stew, such as *potaje canario* (a stew of vegetables, potatoes, and garbanzo beans), *rancho canario* (vegetables and meat), and *potaje de berros* (watercress soup). Canarians eat *gofio* (similar to mashed potatoes but made by toasting wheat, corn, or barley flour and then adding milk or broth) with their first course, though it's hard to find in restaurants. The next course is fresh native fish, the best of which are *vieja, cherne,* and *sama,* all firm-flesh white rockfish. Accompanying the fish are *papas arrugadas* (literally, "wrinkled potatoes"), tiny new potatoes boiled in seawater so that salt crystals form on them as they dry. Other specialties include *cabrito* (roast baby goat) and *conejo* (rabbit), both served in *salmorejo,* a slightly spicy paprika sauce. Finally, no Canarian meal is complete without a dab of *mojo picón,* a spicy sauce made with *pimientos* (red chili peppers), garlic, and toma-

Go to the Canary Islands to relax, but dig a bit deeper once you're there. Try to combine a visit to the more congested islands (Tenerife, Gran Canaria, or Lanzarote) with side trips to the quieter ones (Fuerteventura, La Palma, La Gomera, or El Hierro).

If you have 3 days

If you're flying in from mainland Spain, pick one resort, go directly there, and unwind. Tenerife is good for first-time visitors—Playa de las Américas in the winter, **Puerto de la Cruz** 2 in the summer. On your second day, rent a car and drive up to **Mt. Teide** 5, stopping at the historic town of Orotava and the Casa de Vino near Los Rodeos Airport. Spend the third day working on your tan. An indulgent alternative is to fly into Reina Sofía Airport and go to **Los Cristianos** 6, where a 35-minute hydrofoil ride can whisk you to tiny La Gomera for three days of swimming and hiking.

If you have 7 days

You can do two islands in a week. Begin your stay in Tenerife with an afternoon at the beach or pool. The next day, rent a car to explore the center of the island, visiting **Mt. Teide** 5 and the town of Orotava. On day three, spend the morning in **Santa Cruz** 1 and perhaps the nearby town of La Laguna. Stop for lunch or wine-tasting at the Casa de Vino, and in the afternoon explore the north-coast villages of **Icod de los Vinos** 3 and **Garachico** 4. A 30-minute flight brings you to Lanzarote, where you can spend the next two days exploring the northern part of this island, with stops at the Jameos del Agua, Cuevas Verdes, Fundación César Manrique, and Mirador del Río lookout. On your sixth day, hit Timanfaya National Park for a tour of the volcanic zone. In the afternoon, detour to Playa Blanca and Playa Papagayo, at the island's southern tip. Save your last day for sunning and swimming.

If you have 14 days

Two weeks permit you to complete the above itinerary, relax, and see a third island. From Tenerife, La Gomera is a one-hour ferry ride; from Lanzarote it's a 45-minute ride to Fuerteventura. Either option allows you to keep the same rental car and take advantage of weekly rates. If you choose La Gomera, make an excursion to the **Parque Nacional de Garajonay** and the island's northern coast. You'll need a second day to explore the southern coast with a drive out to **Valle Gran Rey.** Fuerteventura is a better choice for beachcombers or windsurfers; one day here should be sufficient for exploring the island, leaving the rest of the time for loafing or taking part in sports.

---

toes. Most restaurants serve mojo with each main course, and Canarians heap it liberally on everything from fish to papas arrugadas. The tamer version is *mojo verde*, made with cilantro and parsley. Another island specialty is goat cheese, made best in La Palma. Canarian malmsey wines from Lanzarote, a favorite with Falstaff in Shakespeare's *Henry IV*, are still produced today.

WHAT IT COSTS In Euros

	$$$$	$$$	$$	$	¢
AT DINNER	over €20	€15–€20	€10–€15	€6–€10	under €6

Prices are per person for a main course at dinner.

About the Hotels

There are hundreds of hotels on the Canary Islands, but they tend to fray rapidly under heavy use. With a few exceptions, noted in the individual reviews, it's best to stay in the newer facilities. Through package tours, most vacationers pay reasonable prices for hotel rooms, but rates for independent travelers are often exorbitant and do not reflect the quality of accommodation. Budget-minded independent travelers should look into newly constructed apartment complexes: though simply furnished, these have reception desks, swimming pools, and often restaurants, and each unit has a kitchenette. Note that arriving in the Canary Islands without either a package or independent reservations can lead to a real hassle. Many of the islands' hotels are booked solid by package travelers most of the year, and some properties do no business whatsoever with indie travelers. Bottom line: finding a last-minute room can be extremely difficult. This is particularly true if you want budget lodging, as pensions and hostales are scarce; most are on La Gomera and in the other islands' larger cities, such as Santa Cruz de Tenerife, Las Palmas, and Arrecife.

Tenerife's Gran Meliá Bahía del Duque has been voted Spain's best vacation hotel and is worth a trip in itself. The Canaries also have two of the most romantic paradors in the national chain, the colonial Parador Conde de La Gomera and the seafront Parador Nacional El Hierro, both unbeatable retreats.

WHAT IT COSTS In Euros

	$$$$	$$$	$$	$	¢
FOR 2 PEOPLE	over €180	€100–€180	€60–€100	€40–€60	under €40

Prices are for two people in a standard double room in high season, excluding tax.

Exploring the Canary Islands

Tenerife has suffered most at the hands of developers, but it also has the most attractions. Ride a cable car up the slopes of Mt. Teide, swim in a huge artificial lake, wander botanical gardens, or dance at glittering discos. The beaches are small, with black sand. The verdant (read: rainy) north coast retains unspoiled villages, while the southern Playa de las Américas' skyline is filling with high-rise hotels.

Gran Canaria was the hot spot of the '60s and is seen as rather passé, but its Maspalomas beach is one of the islands' most beautiful, and some sand dunes behind the beach are being turned into a nature reserve. The capital, Las Palmas, is crawling with sailors, soldiers, and tourists. Though the city is a bit seedy, it does have a sparkling stretch of beach right downtown, with a lantern-lit boardwalk lined with restaurants and bars.

Lanzarote is a desert isle kept beautiful through thoughtful development. It has golden beaches, white villages, caves, and a volcanic national park where heat from an eruption in 1730 is still rising through vents in the earth. Vegetation is scarce, but the grapes grown by farmers in volcanic ash produce a distinctive Canarian wine.

Fuerteventura used to be less visited than the other islands, but construction is now racing to keep up with the demands of tourists, who come to windsurf and enjoy the endless white beaches. Luxury hotels now dot the coast, though the barren interior remains largely the domain of goatherds.

Beaches

The sun is what draws most people to the Canaries, and each island has different kinds of beaches on which to soak it up. The longest and most pristine are the white-sand strands of Fuerteventura. Lanzarote and Gran Canaria offer golden-sand beaches with lounge chairs and parasailing. Tenerife has few natural beaches, and makes due with crowded, man-made ones with imported yellow sand. La Palma, La Gomera, and El Hierro have black-sand beaches, usually in rock-flanked coves. Remember that the Atlantic Ocean can be rough and chilly in winter.

Fiestas

There may be no better reason to come to the Canary Islands than to experience **Carnaval.** Although this classic pre-Lenten celebration takes place in most of the Canaries' large towns, it might be argued—Rio de Janeiro notwithstanding—that there are no greater celebrations than the yearly fests at Las Palmas de Gran Canaria and Santa Cruz de Tenerife. These two island capitals whip themselves up into 10 days of all-night partying. Canary *carnavales* are like drunken Halloween nights set to salsa music: of the half million people on the streets in each city, it's hard to spot one person not in costume. Although Las Palmas's Carnival lasts a month, the serious fun begins in sync with the start of Santa Cruz's the weekend before Ash Wednesday and running through the final Sunday. It's possible to experience both cities' mayhem, even on the same night, by jetfoil; don't miss Las Palmas's Drag Queen gala or Santa Cruz's hilarious mock "sardine burial," which marks the end of the fiesta.

Shopping

The Canary Islands are free ports—no value-added tax is charged on luxury goods. The streets are packed with shops, but don't expect significant savings. The islands are also known for lacy, hand-embroidered tablecloths and place mats.

La Palma, called "the Garden Isle," has lush foliage, tropical storms, rainbows, and black crescents of beach. The capital, Santa Cruz, is a beautifully preserved example of Spanish colonial architecture, and its people are some of the most genuine and hospitable in all of Spain.

La Gomera is a gift to backpackers. Ruggedly mountainous, it offers good hiking, and UNESCO protects its forests. Most of the black-sand beaches are fringed by banana plantations.

El Hierro is the smallest and least-visited Canary, ideal for those who really want to be alone. It has a few black-sand beaches and a cool, highland pine forest for walking and picnicking.

Many places on these islands have the same or similar names. Be careful not to confuse the island of La Palma with the city of Las Palmas, which is the capital of Gran Canaria. Equally confusing, the capitals of La Palma and Tenerife are both called Santa Cruz. When writing to an address on one of the islands, note that they comprise two provinces: the province of Santa Cruz de Tenerife, which includes Tenerife, La Palma, La Gomera, and El Hierro, and the province of Las Palmas, which includes Gran Canaria, Lanzarote, and Fuerteventura.

The Canary Islands

Numbers in the margin correspond to points of interest on the Tenerife and Gran Canaria maps.

Timing

The Canaries enjoy warmth in the winter and cool breezes in summer. Winter, especially Christmas, and Easter are peak periods for northern Europeans, while Spaniards and Italians tend to come in the summer, particularly during the August holidays. Reservations are extremely difficult at those times. Spring—when a profusion of wildflowers colors the islands—is the low season and the most beautiful time to be here. Since the Canaries are a year-round destination, prices tend to be roughly the same no matter when you come. You may have some luck negotiating discounts during the slowest months, May and November.

TENERIFE

Tenerife is the largest of the Canary Islands. Triangular in shape, it is towered over by the volcanic peak of Mt. Teide, which at 12,198 ft is Spain's highest mountain. The slopes leading up to Teide are covered with pines in the north and with barren lava fields in the south. Tenerife's capital, Santa Cruz de Tenerife, is a giant urban center. Forget whitewashed villas and sleepy streets, and imagine the traffic, activity, and crowds of an important shipping port. In the rainy north, mixed among the tourist attractions, are banana plantations and vineyards. In the dry south, the resort Playa de las Américas has sprung up at the edge of the desert over the last 15 years. It's especially popular with young couples and singles drawn to the hotels and nightlife.

Santa Cruz

1 *10 km (6 mi) southeast of Los Rodeos Airport, 75 km (45 mi) northeast of Playa de las Américas.*

The heart of Santa Cruz de Tenerife is the **Plaza de España.** The cross is a monument to those who died in the Spanish civil war, which was actually launched from Tenerife by General Franco during his exile here. For two weeks before Lent each year, during Carnival, Santa Cruz throbs to a Latin beat emanating from this plaza.

Primitive ceramics and mummies are on display at the **Museo de la Naturaleza y el Hombre** (Museum of Nature and Man). The ancient Guanches mummified their dead by rubbing the bodies with pine resin and salt and leaving them in the sun to dry for two weeks. ✉ *Fuentes Morales s/n* ☎ *922/535816* 🌐 *www.museosdetenerife.org* 🎫 *€3, free Sun.* ⏲ *Tues.–Sun. 9–7.*

The **Iglesia de la Concepción** (Church of the Conception) has a six-story Moorish bell tower. The church was renovated as part of an urban-renewal project that razed blocks of slums in this area. ✉ *Pl. de la Iglesia* ☎ *922/243847* 🎫 *Free* ⏲ *Open before and after Mass, usually weekdays 9:30–12:30 and 5:30–7, weekends 9:30–12:30.*

The colorful city market **Mercado de Nuestra Señora de Africa** (Market of Our Lady of Africa; ✉ Av. de San Sebastián) is part bazaar and part food emporium. Stalls outside sell household goods; inside, stands displaying everything from flowers to canaries are arranged around a patio. Downstairs, a stroll through the seafood section will acquaint you with the local fish. A flea market with antiques and secondhand goods is held here on Sunday. The market is open daily 8 to 2.

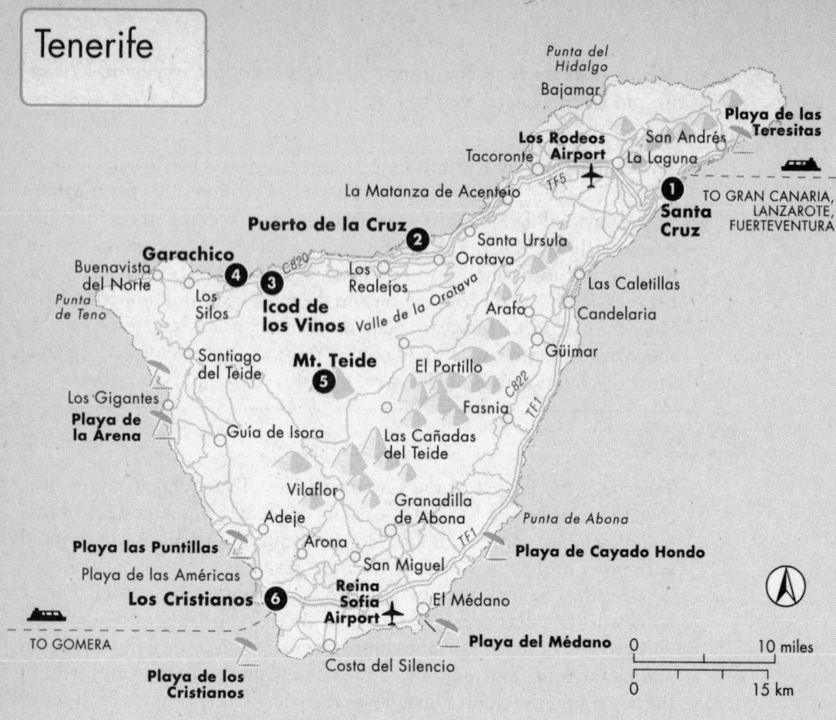

Old masters and modern works are in the two-story **Museo de Bellas Artes** (Museum of Fine Arts), including canvases by Breughel and Ribera. Many works depict local events. The museum is on the Plaza Príncipe de Asturias. ✉ *José Murphy 12* ☎ *922/244358* 🎫 *Free* 🕙 *weekdays 10–8.*

A plaza on the northern outskirts of town preserves 18th-century cannons on the site of what was the **Paso Alto Fortress.** In 1794 these weapons held off an attack led by Britain's Admiral Nelson; the cannon on the right fired the shot that cost Nelson his right arm.

Santa Cruz's beach, **Las Teresitas,** is about 7 km (4½ mi) northeast of the city, near the town of San Andrés, and is especially popular with local families. It was created using white sand imported from the Sahara and planted with palms.

off the beaten path

LA LAGUNA – The university town of La Laguna was the first capital of Tenerife and retains many colonial buildings along Calle San Agustín. One of these buildings, the 400-year-old colonial home of a former slave trader, was reopened as the **Tenerife Museo de Historia** (Tenerife History Museum), with antique navigational maps and other displays. It's 5 km (3 mi) northwest of Santa Cruz. Afterward, soak up the academic buzz from local students at the coffee shops and bars. ✉ *C. San Agustín 22* ☎ *922/825949* 🌐 *www.museosdetenerife.org* 🎫 *€3, free Sun.* 🕙 *Tues.–Sun. 9–7.*

Where to Stay & Eat

★ $$ ✕ **El Coto de Antonio.** In a cozy, tavernlike room, dip into a succulent earthenware pot of seafood stew, enhanced with potatoes, yams, blanched gofio, and cheese; or order one of the house specialties, *ensalada de papas* *negras con bacalao y pimientos* (black-potato salad with cod and red peppers) and *muslo de conejo relleno con hongos y trufa* (rabbit thigh stuffed with mushrooms and truffles). ✉ *C. de General Goded 13* ☎ *922/272105* ▭ *AE, DC, MC, V* ⊙ *No dinner Sun.*

$–$$ ✕ **Los Troncos.** In a middle-class neighborhood near the bullring you'll find one of the few restaurants in Santa Cruz that serves Canarian cuisine. There's a white Andalusian entryway; inside, steak and spareribs are grilled to perfection. ✉ *C. de General Goded 17* ☎ *922/284152* ▭ *AE, DC, MC, V* ⊙ *Closed Wed. and mid-Aug.–mid-Sept. No dinner Sun.*

$$$$ **Mencey.** "Mencey" was the ancient Guanches' name for their kings, and you may well feel like one at this grandiose, beige stucco-and-marble hotel. Crystal chandeliers and gold-leaf columns ornament the lobby, behind which is a placid interior courtyard. The rooms are furnished à la Louis XIV. ✉ *Dr. José Naveiras 38, 38004* ☎ *922/276700* 🖷 *922/280017* 🌐 *www.starwood.com* *286 rooms* *Restaurant, tennis court, pool, bar, casino, meeting rooms* ▭ *AE, DC, MC, V.*

$$ **Taburiente.** Across the street from the city park, this hotel is favored by those with early morning flights at Los Rodeos Airport. The white-marble lobby is luxurious, and the rooms are large and comfortable. Try to get one with a balcony facing the park. Breakfast is included in the price. ✉ *Dr. José Naveiras 24A, 38001* ☎ *922/276000* 🖷 *922/270562* 🌐 *www.canaryweb.es/htabu/* *116 rooms* *Restaurant, pool; no a/c in some rooms* ▭ *AE, DC, MC, V.*

need a break?

After dinner, you may want to kick back in the **Condal & Peñamil House** (Callejón del Combate, ☎ 922/244976), a civilized tea-and-cigar café on a pleasant pedestrian alley. Waitresses dress like the city's early 19th-century *pureras* (cigar rollers). Try an offering called "Copa, Café y Puro," which combines brandy, whiskey, or rum, a specialty coffee, and a select cigar.

Nightlife & the Arts

The core of Santa Cruz nightlife is **Avenida Anaga,** facing the port. For about seven blocks beginning at Plaza España, Anaga crawls with upscale disco-bars. The more traditional bars, where you can have drinks and tapas outdoors, are near **Plaza España.** Farther away from the plaza you'll find the louder bars and dance clubs, dominated by booming electronica and *pop español* (Spanish pop) and populated by a younger crowd; the most prominent venues are BB+, Mastil, and Ñoh.

Sports & the Outdoors

DIVING Call **Real Club Nautico de Tenerife** (✉ Avda. Francisco La Roche s/n ☎ 922/273700 🌐 www.rcnt.es) for information on diving and underwater fishing.

GOLF **Real Club de Golf de Tenerife** (✉ El Peñon ☎ 922/636487 🌐 www.tenerifegolf.es) is open to nonmembers on weekdays from 8 to 12:30 only. Reservations are essential. The club is near the northern airport, between La Laguna and Tacorante at Guamasa, and the course has 18 holes.

HORSEBACK RIDING The **Club Hípica La Atalaya** (✉ La Luna 88, La Laguna ☎ 922/253997), on the outskirts of Santa Cruz, helps arrange riding.

Shopping

By Canary Island standards, Santa Cruz de Tenerife is a major shopping center. Calle Castillo, the main pedestrian street through the center of town, is lined with everything from souvenir shops to trendy boutiques to electronics stores. Calle del Pilar has higher-end fashions and the department stores Marks & Spencer and El Corte Inglés. **Artenerife** (✉ Pl. de España, near tourist office) sells traditional crafts made by local artisans and guaranteed by the island's government as *productos artesanos*. The selection includes Tenerifan *calado*—exquisitely embroidered linen tablecloths and place mats—and clay pottery made using the same methods as those used by the island's aboriginal settlers. (The aborigines didn't use potter's wheels; rather, they rolled the clay into *churros,* or cylindrical strips, and hand-kneaded these into bowls. Pebbles, branches, and shells were used to buff the results.) **La Casa de Los Balcones** (✉ Edificio Olympo, Pl. de la Candelaria), near Plaza España, has colorful Canarian blankets, embroideries, jars of mojo sauce, and hefty bags of gofio. **La Casa del Regalo** (✉ C. Castillo 30) is less authentic than Los Balcones, but its wall-to-wall shelves of souvenir trinkets can be useful in a pinch.

Puerto de la Cruz

❷ *36 km (22 mi) west of Santa Cruz.*

Puerto de la Cruz is the oldest resort in the Canaries. Despite mass tourism, it has retained some of its Spanish charm and island character. The old sections of town have colonial plazas and *paseos* (promenades) for evening strolls. Because Puerto de la Cruz has uninviting black-sand beaches, the town commissioned Lanzarote artist César Manrique in 1965 to build **Lago Martiánez,** a forerunner of today's water parks. It's an immense, immensely fun public pool on the waterfront, with landscaped islands, bridges, and a volcanolike fountain that sprays sky-high. The complex also includes several smaller pools and a restaurant-nightclub. Stroll from Lago Martiánez along the coastal walkway until you reach the **Plaza de la Iglesia,** beautifully landscaped with flowering plants. Here you can stop at the **tourist office** for a copy of a walking tour that details all of Puerto's architecturally important buildings.

Loro Parque is a subtropical garden with 1,300 parrots, many of which are trained to ride bicycles and perform other tricks. The garden also has the world's largest penguin zoo. The dapper Antarctic birds receive round-the-clock care from marine biologists and other veterinary specialists in a climate-controlled environment; more than 50 penguins have been born here. Also here is one of Europe's largest aquariums, with an underwater tunnel and a dolphin show, plus an imitation Thai village. ✉ *Puerto de la Cruz* ☎ *922/373841* 🌐 *www.loroparque.com* 🎫 *€21* 🕙 *Daily 8:30–6:45.*

Filled with thousands of varieties of tropical trees and plants, and sonorous birds, the **Jardín de Aclimatación de La Orotava** (Orotava Botanical Garden) was founded in 1788, on the orders of King Carlos III, to propagate warm-climate species brought back to Spain from the Americas. ✉ *C. Retama 2* ☎ *922/383572* 🎫 *€.60* 🕙 *Oct.–Mar., daily 9–6; Apr.–Sept., daily 9–7.*

Wine lovers should visit the **Casa de Vino La Baranda,** about halfway between Puerto de la Cruz and Los Rodeos Airport, at the El Sauzal exit on the main highway. It was opened by the Canary Islands' government to promote local vintners, and it includes a wine museum, shop, and tasting room, where for a small fee you can sample some of Tenerife's best wines. The complex also has a tapas bar and a restaurant with nouvelle Canarian fare. ✉ *Autopista General del Norte, Km 21* ☎ *922/572535* 🌐 *www.cabtfe.es/casa-vino* 🕙 *Tues.–Sat. 10–10, Sun. 11–6.*

Where to Stay & Eat

$$–$$$ ✕ **La Magnolia.** At this restaurant, named for its proximity to the town's botanical garden, you can dine in the restaurant's cozy garden or a simply decorated dining room. The open kitchen, which specializes in Catalan and international dishes, turns out huge platters of seafood in garlicky sauces. ✉ *Av. Marqués de Villanueva del Prado s/n* ☎ *922/385614* ▭ *AE, DC, MC, V.*

$$ ✕ **Casa de Miranda.** Just off the central square, this restored house can trace its history back to 1730. On the ground floor is an inviting tapas bar, strung with hams, gourds, and garlands of red peppers; farther inside is a plant-filled patio. Upstairs, the high-ceiling dining room serves such favorites as filet mignon in pepper sauce and *merluza* (hake) in *salsa a la cava* (sparkling wine) or *salsa a la sidra* (hard cider). ✉ *Santo Domingo 13* ☎ *922/373871* ▭ *AE, DC, MC, V* ⊗ *Closed June.*

$–$$ ✕ **El Pescador.** This restaurant claims to be inside the oldest house in town, and you'll believe it when you feel the wood floor shake as the waiters walk by. Slatted green shutters, high ceilings, and salsa music create a tropical air. The specialties include avocado stuffed with shrimp. Ask for papas arrugadas or you'll get french fries. ✉ *Puerto Viejo 8* ☎ *922/384088* ▭ *AE, DC, MC, V.*

$–$$ ✕ **Mi Vaca y Yo.** The name, "My Cow and I," hints at the outdoor summer feast you can put together at this friendly, laid-back, plant-filled farmhouse. Most diners, particularly finicky kids, ought to appreciate the tasty barbecued beef and fried and grilled fish, as well as spaghetti, chocolate cake, banana flambé, and various crepes. It's popular with local families. ✉ *Cruz Verde 3* ☎ *922/385247* ▭ *AE, DC, MC, V* ⊗ *Closed Mon. No lunch Tues.*

$$$–$$$$ ✕ **Botánico.** The soothing subtropical garden at this luxury hilltop hotel is famous in its own right. The hotel's plain exterior belies its elegant furnishings, marble baths, and flowery terraces. Owner Wolfgang Kiessling, an honorary consul of Thailand, opened Tenerife's first Thai restaurant, the **Oriental,** on the ground floor, and on some days you can also partake of Japanese and Vietnamese food. A spiral staircase leads to the second-floor restaurant, **La Parilla,** with Spanish dishes and seafood. The adjacent piano bar has live music nightly. ✉ *Av. Richard J. Yeoward 1, 38400 Urb. Botánico* ☎ *922/381400* 🖷 *922/381504* 🌐 *www.hotelbotanico.com* *246 rooms, 6 suites* *4 restaurants, minibars, putting green, 2 tennis courts, 2 pools, hair salon, health club, bar, meeting rooms* ▭ *AE, DC, MC, V.*

$$–$$$ **San Felipe.** Eighteen stories tall, this hotel has the best location in Puerto de la Cruz—steps from the beach, with million-dollar views of the coast and Mt. Teide. The large rooms have balconies and spacious bathrooms. Rates include an excellent breakfast buffet, served with champagne. ✉ *Av. de Colón 22, 38400* ☎ *922/383311* 🖷 *922/373718* 🌐 *www.h10.es* *256 rooms, 5 suites* *Restaurant, miniature golf, 2 tennis courts, 2 pools, health club, 2 bars, meeting rooms* ▭ *AE, DC, MC, V.*

$$ **Monopol.** You're welcomed here by hibiscus scattered across the front steps. The Monopol has had more than a century to perfect its brand of hospitality: built as a private home in 1742, the property opened as a hotel in 1888, and has been run by the same family for more than 70 years. The neatly furnished rooms are arranged on four stories with wooden balconies around a verdant central courtyard. Most overlook the sea or one of the town's main squares, Plaza de la Iglesia. ✉ *Quintana 15, 38400* ☎ *922/384611* 🖷 *922/370310* 🌐 *www.hotelmonopoltenerife.com* *92 rooms* *Restaurant, pool, sauna, Ping-Pong, 2 bars; no a/c* ▭ *AE, DC, MC, V.*

Nightlife & the Arts

Almost all hotels have live music at night. The **Casino Taoro** (✉ Parque Taoro 22 ☎ 922/380550) makes room for gambling in a stately former hotel. For dancing, try **Victoria** (✉ Av. de Colón s/n), at the Hotel Tenerife Playa, a favorite with all age groups. The **Cotton Club** (✉ Av. Litoral 24) is usually jammed with a fast-moving young crowd. The side streets of Avenida Colón are packed with bars and underground clubs, catering mostly to tourists. Many offer imported beer, German or British food, or Irish music. For a more authentic experience, try **Dos Besos** (✉ C. Genovés 12), where you can sip a fruity island drink or sangría to Latin and African rhythms.

Shopping

Find many hand-embroidered tablecloths and place mats at **Casa Iriarte** (✉ San Juan 17), on the patio of a ramshackle Canarian house.

Icod de los Vinos

❸ *26 km (16 mi) west of Puerto de la Cruz.*

Attractive plazas rimmed by unspoiled colonial architecture and pine balconies form the heart of Tenerife's most historic wine district. A 3,000-year-old **dragon tree** towers 57 ft above the coastal highway, C820. The Guanches worshiped these trees as symbols of fertility and knowledge; the sap, which turns red upon contact with air, was used in healing rituals. The **Casa Museo del Vino** (✉ Pl. de la Pila 4) is a tasting room where you can sample the sweet local malmsey and other Canary Island wines and cheeses.

Garachico

❹ *5 km (3 mi) west of Icod de los Vinos.*

Garachico is one of the most idyllic and best-preserved towns on the islands. It was the main port of Tenerife until May 5, 1706, when Mt. Teide blew its top, sending twin rivers of lava downhill. One filled Garachico's harbor, and the other destroyed most of the town. Legend has it that the eruption was unleashed by an evil monk. One of the buildings that withstood the eruption was the **Castillo San Miguel,** a tiny 16th-century fortress on the waterfront. Island crafts, such as embroidery and basket making, are demonstrated inside. From the roof you can see the two rivers of lava, now solidified on the mountainside. You can also visit the **Convento de San Francisco,** also unscathed, and the 18th-century parish church of **Santa Ana.**

Mt. Teide

❺ *60 km (36 mi) southwest of Puerto de la Cruz, 63 km (39 mi) north of Playa de las Américas.*

Four roads lead to Mt. Teide from various parts of Tenerife, each getting you to the park in about an hour, but the most beautiful approach is the road from Orotava. As you head out of town into the higher altitudes, banana plantations give way to fruit and almond orchards that bloom early in the year. Higher up is a fragrant pine forest.

A mile uphill from Puerto de la Cruz, Orotava has a row of stately mansions on Calle San Francisco, north of the baroque church Nuestra Señora de la Concepción. Women in regional dress embroider tablecloths at **Casa de los Balcones** (✉ C. San Francisco 3, Orotava). Craftspeople, including basket makers, cigar rollers, and sand painters, work at the embarrassingly named **Casa del Turista** (✉ C. San Francisco 4).

You enter the **Parque Nacional del Teide** (Teide National Park) at El Portillo. Exhibits at the visitor center explain the region's natural history; a garden outside labels the flora found within the park. The center also offers trail maps, video presentations, guided hikes, and bus tours. The park includes the volcano itself and the **Cañadas del Teide,** a violent jumble of volcanic leftovers from El Teide and the neighboring Pico Viejo. Within this area you can find blue hills (the result of a process called hydrothermal alteration); spiky, knobby rock protrusions; and lava in various colors and textures. The bizarre, photogenic rock formations known as the **Roques de García** are especially memorable; a two-hour trail around these rocks—one of 21 well-marked hikes inside the park—is recommended. A second park information center, near Los Roques de García and next to the Parador Nacional Cañadas del Teide, has details and trail maps.

A **cable car** (☎ 922/533720 €18.50 daily 9–5 (last trip up at 4) carries you close to the top of Mt. Teide, past sulfur steam vents. The difficult final 656 ft to the volcano's rim takes about 40 minutes to climb, and you need a special free pass to do so—bring a photocopy of your passport's information page to the **Patronato del Parque Nacional** (✉ C. Emilio Calzadilla, 4th floor, door 5, Santa Cruz), open weekdays 9–2. It's best to get the pass one morning, then hike the following morning. The Santa Cruz tourist office has more information. The trail to the top is closed when it's snowy, usually about four months of the year. You can still get a good view of southern Tenerife and Gran Canaria from the top of the cable-car line, but you'll be confined to the tiny terrace of a bar. The station also has a restaurant. ☎ *922/290129* *daily 9:15–4.*

Where to Stay & Eat

$$ **Parador Cañadas del Teide.** The rooms in this classic mountain retreat overlook the intriguing rock formations of the Las Cañadas plateau, at the foot of Mt. Teide. It's a privileged position: the only accommodation inside this huge park. The large, inviting rooms have wood floors. In the mountain-view restaurant, friendly waitstaff in folk costume serve tasty Canarian cuisine. Try the papas arrugadas with a dab of spicy mojo sauce. ✉ *38300 La Orotava* ☎ *922/386415* *922/382352* *www.parador.es* *37 rooms* *Restaurant, cafeteria, pool, gym, sauna, bar* *AE, DC, MC, V.*

Shopping

Browse for contemporary island crafts and traditional musical instruments at the government-sponsored shop **Casa Torrehermosa** (✉ Tomás Zerolo 27) in Orotava.

Los Cristianos

6 *74 km (44 mi) southwest of Santa Cruz, 10 km (6 mi) west of Reina Sofía Airport.*

This is the newest and sunniest tourist area on Tenerife, with high-rise hotels built chockablock above the beaches. Sun, beaches, and nightlife constitute the attractions here. Playa de las Américas and Los Cristianos are on the southwestern shore, about 1 km (½ mi) from each other. The town of **Los Cristianos** has two small crescents of gray sand surrounded by apartment houses. **Playa de las Américas,** around the corner, is a series of man-made yellow-sand beaches protected by an artificial reef. **Los Gigantes,** about 12 km (7 mi) north of Playa de las Américas, is a small, gray-sand cove surrounded by rocks and cliffs.

Aquapark, a huge water park, has tall slides, meandering streams for inner tubes, and swimming pools. ✉ *Av. Austria 15, San Eugenio Alto* ☎ *922/715266* *€15* *Daily 10–6.*

Where to Stay & Eat

$$$ **El Patio.** This seaside eatery has a spectacular location on the grounds of the Jardín Tropical hotel. It ranks as the top restaurant on the south coast, serving such treats as cold mussel-cream soup with saffron and duck-liver terrine with pear in Málaga wine. ✉ *Gran Bretaña s/n, San Eugenio, Adeje* ☎ *922/746061* ▭ *AE, DC, MC, V* ⊗ *No lunch.*

★ $–$$ ✕ **Masía del Mar.** There's no menu here; you simply point to what you want from the vast display of fresh fish and shellfish. Add a salad and a bottle of white wine to the order, and find a seat on the wide terrace. ✉ *Caleta de Adeje, 5 km (3 mi) west of Playa de las Américas* ☎ *922/710895* ▭ *AE, DC, MC, V.*

★ $$$$ **Gran Meliá Bahía del Duque.** A cross between a Canarian village and an Italian hill town, this sprawling hotel is a striking jumble of pastel houses and palaces, all presided over by a clocktower replica of the Torre de la Concepción in Santa Cruz. The five-story lobby is a marvel in itself, with tropical birds, palm-filled bars, and two glass elevators. Guest rooms have oversize beds and wicker and pine furnishings. The hotel can arrange sailing and diving trips and run boat rides to see the whales cavorting off the coast. ✉ *Pl. del Duque, 38670 Adeje* ☎ *922/713000* 🖷 *922/712616* 🌐 *www.bahia-duque.com* *362 rooms* *5 restaurants, miniature golf, tennis court, 4 pools, gym, hair salon, sauna, dive shop, boating, squash, 4 bars* ▭ *AE, DC, MC, V.*

$$$$ **Jardín Tropical.** White turrets and archways, Moorish-tile floors, and cascading profusions of bright, flowering plants describe this multi-level hotel spread over several hills. The rooms are furnished with carved-pine and wicker furniture and pastel paisley prints; all have balconies. ✉ *Gran Bretaña s/n, San Eugenio, 38670 Adeje* ☎ *922/746000* 🖷 *922/746060* *433 rooms* *5 restaurants, cable TV with movies, 2 pools, gym, hair salon, sauna, bar* ▭ *AE, DC, MC, V.*

$$$–$$$$ **Marco Antonio Palace.** One of five hotels in the Mare Nostrum Resort complex, this one has the best site on Playa de Los Cristianos. Massive columns and reproduction Greek statues line the entrance and the vast pool, while the six-story lobby is a high-tech synthesis of marble, neon, and chrome. Glass elevators glide up to the rooms, done in black leather and brass. The baths are black marble, and every room has a balcony. ✉ *Av. de las Américas s/n, 38660 Arona* ☎ *922/757509* 🖷 *922/757510* *116 rooms* *3 restaurants (12 within complex), cable TV with movies, tennis court, pool, gym, hair salon, sauna, squash, piano bar* ▭ *AE, DC, MC, V.*

$$–$$$ **Atlantic Playa.** This beachfront hotel near Reina Sofía Airport has a lobby arranged around a rock fountain in an interior atrium; the rooms have separate sleeping and sitting areas, modern furniture, and terraces. A breakfast buffet is included, and kids under 12 stay at half price. ✉ *Av. Europa 2, 38612 El Médano* ☎ *922/176234* 🖷 *922/176114* *152 rooms* *Restaurant, pool, gym, sauna, windsurfing, squash, recreation room* ▭ *AE, DC, MC, V.*

Nightlife & the Arts

Most bars in Playa de las Américas are in a three-building complex called Veronica's. Here, places like the Kangaroo Pub, Busby's, Bobby's, and Sgt. Pepper's draw young, rowdy, mostly foreign crowds. For gambling on the south island, hit **Casino Playa de las Américas** (✉ Av. Marítima s/n ☎ 922/793758), in the Hotel Gran Tenerife. The **Banana Garden** (☎ 922/790365) attracts an older but no less lively crowd with live salsa music. The disco at **Prismas,** in the Hotel Tenerife Sol, has become a perennial favorite.

Sports & the Outdoors

DIVING The PADI-licensed school at **Las Palmeras Hotel** (✉ Av. Marítima ☎ 922/752948), in Playa de las Américas, has information on diving and underwater fishing.

GOLF Southern Tenerife has five of the island's six golf courses, and these five lie within 20 km (12 mi) of each other. Near Reina Sofía Airport, **Campo Golf de Sur** (☎ 922/738170 🌐 www.golfdelsur.net) has 27 holes. In San Miguel, not far from Campo Golf, the **Amarilla Golf Club** (☎ 922/730319 🌐 www.amarillagolf.es) has an 18-hole course. In Arona, near Los Cristianos, **Centro de Golf Los Palos** (☎ 922/169080 🌐 www.golf-tenerife.com) has nine holes. Adjacent to Playa de las Américas is **Golf Las Américas** (☎ 922/752005 🌐 www.golf-tenerife.com) with an 18-hole course. Also near Playa las Américas is **Golf Costa Adeje** (☎ 922/710000 🌐 www.costaadeje.com) with an 18-hole course and views of the sea.

WINDSURFING Windsurfing rentals and lessons can be arranged at the **SunWind Windsurf School** (☎ 922/176174), in Playa del Médano.

GRAN CANARIA

The circular island of Gran Canaria has three distinct identities. Its capital, Las Palmas, population 370,000, is a thriving business center and shipping port, while the white-sand beaches of the south coast are tourist magnets. The interior is rural. Las Palmas, the largest city in the Canary Islands, is overrun by sailors, tourists, traffic jams, diesel-spewing buses, and hordes of shoppers. One side of the city is lined with docks for huge container ships, while the other harbors the 7-km (4½-mi) Canteras beach. The south coast, a boxy 1960s development along wide avenues, is a family resort. At the southern tip of the island, the popular Playa del Inglés gives way to the empty dunes of Maspalomas. The isle's interior is a steep highland that reaches 6,435 ft at Pozo de las Nieves. Although it's green in winter, Gran Canaria does not have the luxurious tropical foliage of the archipelago's western islands.

Las Palmas

7 *35 km (21 mi) north of Gran Canaria Airport, 60 km (36 mi) north of Maspalomas.*

Las Palmas is strung out for 10 km (6 mi) along two waterfronts of a peninsula. Though most of the action centers on the peninsula's northern end, the sights are clustered around the city's southern edge. Begin in the old quarter, La Vegueta, at the **Plaza Santa Ana,** with its bronze dog statues. It's quite a walk from one end of town to the other, so at any point you may want to hop one of the many canary-yellow buses, named *guaguas* (pronounced *wa*-was) in honor of the Guanches. You may be surprised to learn that the Canary Islands were named not for the yellow songbirds but for a breed of dog (*canum* in Latin) found here by ancient explorers. The birds were later named after the islands.

The smog-stained **Catedral Santa Ana** (St. Anne's Cathedral) faces the Plaza Santa Ana. The cathedral took four centuries to complete, so the 19th-century exterior with its neoclassical Roman columns contrasts sharply with the Gothic ceiling vaulting of the interior. Baroque statues are displayed in the cathedral's **Museo de Arte Sacro** (Museum of Religious Art), arranged around a peaceful cloister. Ask the curator to open the *sala capitular* (chapter house) to see the 16th-century Valencian tile floor. The treasury is closed to the public. ✉ *Espíritu Santo 20,* ☎ *928/314989* 🎟 *€3* ⏲ *Weekdays 10–5, Sat. 10–1:30.*

The **Casa Museo Colón** (Columbus Museum) is in a palace where Christopher Columbus may have stayed when he stopped to repair the *Pinta*'s rudder. Nautical instruments, copies of early navigational maps, and models of Columbus's three ships are on display. Two rooms hold pre-

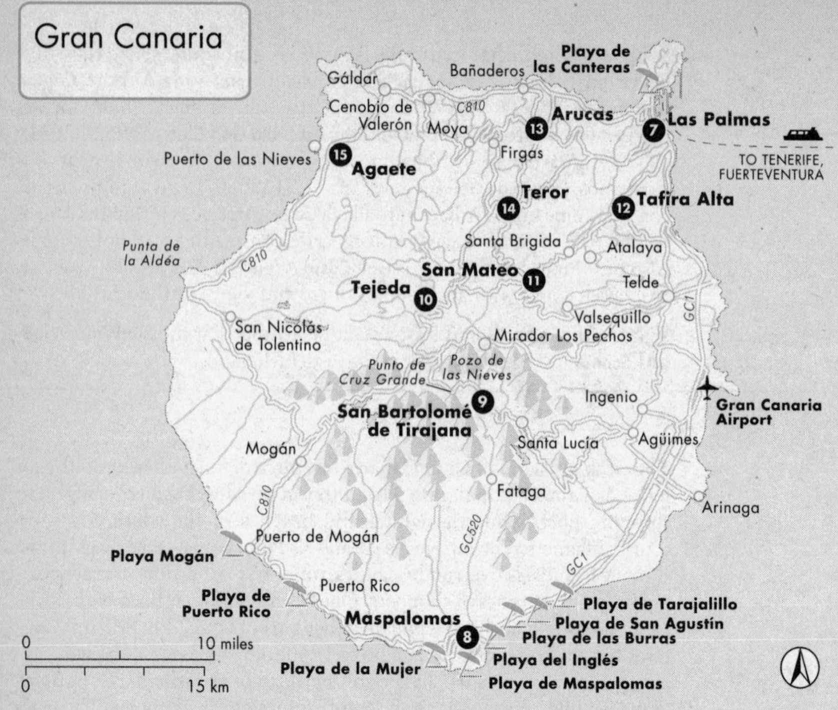

Columbian artifacts. ✉ *C. Colón 1* ☎ *928/311255* 🎫 *Free* ⏱ *Weekdays 9–7, weekends 9–3.*

It's been open just over a decade, but the **Centro Atlántico de Arte Moderno** (Atlantic Center for Modern Art) has already earned a name for curating some of the best avant-garde shows in Spain. The excellent permanent collection includes Canarian art from the 1930s and 1940s and works by well-known Lanzarote artist César Manrique. Reflecting the Canary Islands' proximity to Africa, the center also has a fine collection of contemporary African art. ✉ *Los Balcones 11* ☎ *928/311824* 🌐 *www.caam.net* 🎫 *Free* ⏱ *Tues.–Sat. 10–9, Sun. 10–2.*

Ride a guagua to Parque Santa Catalina or get off at the **Parque Doramas** (stops are listed on big yellow signs; the 2, 3, and 30 generally cover the entire city) to peek at the elegant Santa Catalina Hotel and Casino. Next to the Parque Doramas is the **Pueblo Canario,** a model village with typical Canarian architecture. Regional folk dances are performed here on Sunday from 11 to 1.

need a break?

Escape to the tranquil, air-conditioned quiet of the **Casa Suecia Salon de Té** (Swiss Tea House, 928/271626) on Luis Morote 41—near Playa de las Canteras—for comfortable booths, foreign newspapers, picture windows, delicious pastries and sandwiches, and perhaps the only free coffee refills on the islands.

On a hill north of Parque Santa Catalina, looming over the rather tough port district, is the **Castillo de la Luz,** a fortress built in 1494. Due west of Parque Santa Catalina are the sparkling white sands of **Las Canteras,** a perfect spot for a stroll along the paseo.

Beaches

The beaches along Gran Canaria's eastern and southern coasts are the island's major attraction. **Las Canteras,** in Las Palmas, is made safe for swimming by an artificial reef. It can be extremely crowded in summer, but the sand is swept clean every night.

Where to Stay & Eat

$$–$$$ ✕ **Casa Montesdeoca.** This romantic restaurant occupies a 14th-century mansion in the heart of the historic quarter. The hallways are stone labyrinths—during the Inquisition, the Jewish Montesdeoca family escaped from their pursuers through hidden doors and secret tunnels. The outdoor patio is draped with bougainvillea, the wine list has the best bottles from each island, and fresh fish is prepared on an outdoor grill steps from your table. ✉ *Montesdeoca 10* ☎🖷 *928/333466* ▭ *AE, DC, MC, V* ⊗ *Closed Sun. and Aug.*

$–$$ ✕ **Julio.** In this small dining room, decorated with ropes, portholes, and polished wood, you can try 12 different types of shellfish or local fish, such as *cherne* (sea bass) served in a white-wine clam sauce and *bocinegro* (a fish akin to grouper) in a whiskey sauce. A different Canarian soup or stew is prepared each day. ✉ *La Naval 132* ☎ *928/460139* ▭ *AE, DC, MC, V* ⊗ *Closed Sun.*

$ ✕ **Tapadel.** It's easy to fill up at this classic Spanish tapas bar, with everything from paella to calamari to mussels with garlic. To the delight of hungry night owls, it's open until 2 AM. ✉ *Pl. de España 5* ☎ *928/271640* ▭ *No credit cards.*

$$$ **Imperial Playa.** You'll find this business-oriented hotel at the far end of Las Canteras beach. The bright rooms have Scandinavian furniture and marble baths, and their small terraces have nice beach views. ✉ *Ferreras 1, 35008* ☎ *928/468854* 🖷 *928/469442* 🌐 *www.nh-hotels.com* *142 rooms* *Restaurant, cafeteria, minibars, beach, meeting rooms; no a/c* ▭ *AE, DC, MC, V.*

$$$ **Meliá Las Palmas.** Aimed at business and upscale leisure travelers, the hotel has a superb location at the narrowest point of the isthmus, and has large, bright rooms. The terrace pool overlooks the sea. ✉ *Gomera 6, 35008* ☎ *928/267600* 🖷 *928/268411* 🌐 *www.solmelia.com* *390 rooms, 12 suites* *Restaurant, coffee shop, cable TV with movies, pool, piano bar, dance club, meeting rooms* ▭ *AE, DC, MC, V.*

$–$$ **Apartments Brisamar Canteras.** The best maintained of all the local beach apartments, Brisamar is popular with travelers from Scandinavia. The rooms are merely functional, but they're freshly painted and cheerful. ✉ *Paseo de las Canteras 49, 35010* ☎ *928/269400* 🖷 *928/269404* *52 studio apartments* ▭ *AE, DC, MC, V.*

Nightlife & the Arts

Las Palmas has a lively, if sometimes scruffy, nightlife, with most of the bars and discos clustered between Playa de las Canteras and Parque Santa Catalina. **Calle Tomás Miller** is lined with restaurants featuring foods from every corner of the world. The **Orquesta Filarmonica de Gran Canaria** (✉ Bravo Murillo 2123 ☎ 928/320513), one of Spain's oldest orchestras, offers an ample program between October and May. Its January festival draws leading musicians from around the world. Ticket information is available at the box office at **Teatro Pérez Galdós** (✉ Pl. Mercado ☎ 928/361509).

Gamblers choose the **Gran Casino de Las Palmas** (✉ León y Castillo 227, Parque Doramas ☎ 928/291103) in the Santa Catalina Hotel. The elegant and expensive **Restaurant Doramas** (☎ 928/233908), inside the casino, will make you feel like a high roller. Dance music emanates from **Wilson** (✉ C. Franchy Roca). **Pacha** (✉ C. Simón Bolivar 3) draws beautiful people with cash to burn on the pricey cover and drinks. The discotheque **Coto,** in the Meliá Las Palmas (✉ C. Gomera 6 ☎ 928/268050), is alive with a middle-age international crowd.

Sports & the Outdoors

GOLF Founded in 1891, the **Real Club de Golf de Las Palmas** (☎ 928/350104 🌐 www.golfysol.com), on the rim of the Bandama crater 15 minutes outside Las Palmas, is Spain's oldest course. Redesigned and relocated in 1956, it now has 18 holes, two putting greens, two tennis courts, a restaurant, and a bar.

HORSEBACK RIDING To rent horses, contact the **Real Club de Golf de Las Palmas** (☎ 928/350104 🌐 www.golfysol.com), with 48 stables and five riding rings.

Shopping

Gran Canaria has the best duty-free shops in the islands. Try **Antigüedades Linares** or **La Fataga,** in the Pueblo Canario, which have crafts from all over Spain. If you want to one-stop-shop for souvenirs, try the department store **El Corte Inglés** (✉ Av. Mesa y Lopez 18 ☎ 928/272600) in central Las Palmas. The glittering form at the southern edge of the beach is Las Palmas' glass-and-chrome shopping mall, **Las Arenas** (✉ Ctra. del Rincón s/n ☎ 928/277008), packed with boutiques, restaurants, and cinemas.

Maspalomas

8 *60 km (36 mi) southwest of Las Palmas, 25 km (15 mi) southwest of Gran Canaria Airport.*

Maspalomas is a beach resort with all the trappings, incongruously backed by empty sand dunes that resemble the Sahara. Despite beachfront overdevelopment in the town, it retains appealing stretches of isolated beach on the outskirts, as well as a bird sanctuary. Over the last decade, German tour operators, who bring masses of visitors, have helped place an emphasis on protecting the environment.

Holiday World amusement park has bumper cars and other carnival rides, including a Ferris wheel visible from miles away. ✉ *Ctra. General, Campo Internacional, Lote 18, Maspalomas* ☎ *928/767176* 📠 *928/766355* 🎟 *€12* ⏲ *Daily 6 PM–midnight.*

AquaSur is the largest water park in the Canary Islands. It has wave pools, slides, and everything else splash-related. ✉ *Ctra. Palmitos Park, Km 3* ☎ *928/140525* 🎟 *€13.50* ⏲ *July–Oct., weekdays 10–6, weekends 10–7; Nov.–June, daily 10–5.*

Ocean Park is next to Holiday World, closer to town than AquaSur but not as extensive. There's a branch of this park, called **Aqua Park,** in the south-coast resort town of Puerto Rico. ✉ *Av. Touroperator Tui* ☎ *928/764361* 📠 *928/765331* 🎟 *€10* ⏲ *June–Sept., daily 10–6; Oct.–May, daily 10–5.*

Palmitos Park, part botanical garden, part zoo, has tropical birds, a butterfly sanctuary, and an orchid house. Trained parrots perform. ✉ *Ctra. Palmitos, 6 km (4 mi) inland from Maspalomas* ☎ *928/143050* 🎟 *€15* ⏲ *Daily 10–6.*

Beaches

All of these beaches abut one another, and you can walk them in sequence (hindered only by a pair of rocky dividers) along the shore. A boardwalk links Playa de Tarajalillo to the rest of the beaches until the dunes separate it from the Maspalomas beach and Playa de la Mujer. **Playa de Tarajalillo,** with alternating areas of black sand and gravel, is the first beach of the southern resort area and a popular choice with local families. **Playa de San Agustín** is a 1-km (½-mi) strip of black sand fringed with a palm garden; it has rental areas for sailboards, pedal boats, and lounge chairs. **Playa de las Burras** is a gray-sand beach surrounding a crescent-shape harbor sometimes used by local fishermen.

★ **Playa del Inglés** is Gran Canaria's most famous beach. Its white sands, more than 3 km (2 mi) long, swarm with beach-chair rentals, ice cream vendors, and fast-food restaurants. West of here are sand dunes and a signposted nude beach.

The **Maspalomas** beach, a 1-km (½-mi) stretch of golden sand, is bordered by endless dunes that provide a sense of isolation and refuge. Dozens of varieties of native birds and plants also take refuge in a lagoon alongside the dunes. The western edge of Maspalomas is marked by a lighthouse. Watch the sunset from **Playa de la Mujer,** a rocky beach around the point from Maspalomas.

Where to Stay & Eat

$–$$ ✕ **Loopy's Tavern.** An almost irresistible island tradition, Loopy's is styled as an American steak house, with friendly waiters, imaginative cocktails, and great meat. Try the shish kebabs, served dangling from a hook. ✉ *Las Retamas 7, San Agustín* ☎ *928/762892* ▭ *MC, V.*

★ **$–$$** ✕ **Tenderete II.** Canarian fare is cherished at Tenderete, especially its fresh gofio, made with roasted-corn flour and fish broth. After a first course of soup or stew, the main course is always fish, grilled or baked in rock salt. Pick it out from the display hooks inside. Wines from Lanzarote, El Hierro, and Tenerife are available. ✉ *Av. de Tirajana 5, Edificio Aloe* ☎ *928/761460* ▭ *AE, DC, MC, V.*

$$$$ **Don Gregory.** This modern brown-brick hotel is on Las Burras beach. The large, carpeted rooms have blond-wood furniture, marble baths, and large terraces; all overlook the beach. ✉ *Las Dalias 11, 35100* ☎ *928/773877* 📠 *928/769996* 🌐 *www.hotelesdunas.com* *244 rooms* *Restaurant, tennis court, pool, beach, bar, some pets allowed (fee)* ▭ *AE, DC, MC, V.*

$$$$ **Seaside Hotel Palm Beach.** Not only the most sophisticated and luxurious hotel in the Canary Islands, it's also a stone's throw from the edge of Maspalomas beach. In the backyard is a 1,000-year-old palm oasis, arranged around the pool. The pleasant chirping of birds wafts from the sanctuary and nearby pond. The tastefully decorated rooms have huge closets and large marble baths; terraces overlook the sea or the palms. ✉ *Av. del Oasis s/n, 35106* ☎ *928/140806* 📠 *928/141808* 🌐 *www.seaside-hotels.de* *358 rooms* *Restaurant, tennis court, pool, gym, hair salon, hot tub, sauna, beach, bar* ▭ *AE, DC, MC, V.*

Fodor's Choice ★

$$–$$$ **Buenaventura.** A veritable wonderland of color, music, pool parties, and dancing, this resort has bright canary-yellow rooms, with flowers and big sliding-glass doors opening onto pool-view balconies. With a thatch-roof poolside bar playing thumping music from noon until late, Buenaventura is popular with young couples, singles, and anyone who doesn't mind late-night laughter in the halls. ✉ *Pl. Ansite, C. Ganigo 6, 35100* ☎ *928/763450* 📠 *928/768348* 🌐 *www.creativhotel.com* *724 rooms* *6 restaurants, 4 tennis courts, 2 pools, sauna, billiards, Ping-Pong, 6 bars, dance club, playground; no a/c* ▭ *AE, DC, MC, V.*

Nightlife

Gamblers go to the **Casino Palace Gran Canaria** (✉ Las Retamas 3, Playa de San Agustín ☎ 928/762724) in the Hotel Tamarindos, in San Agustín. On the south coast, an international college crowd dances to Euro-techno at **Spider** (✉ Av. Italia s/n, Playa del Inglés). **San Agustín Beach Club** (✉ Playa Cocoteros s/n) offers dancing to Euro-pop. **La Bamba** (✉ Av. Tirajana s/n, Playa del Inglés) has salsa and merengue.

Sports & the Outdoors

GOLF The 18-hole **Maspalomas Campo de Golf** (☎ 928/762581 ⊕ www.maspalomasgolf.net) is near the dunes.

HORSEBACK RIDING To rent horses, contact the **Palmitos Park** (✉ Ctra. Palmitos, about 6 km [4 mi] inland from Maspalomas ☎ 928/760458).

SAILING The famous **Escuela de Vela de Puerto Rico sailing school** (☎ 928/560772), where Spain's 1984 Olympic gold medalists trained and teach, is at Puerto Rico, about 13 km (8 mi) west of Maspalomas.

WINDSURFING Rent windsurfing gear, kayaks, and boogie boards from **Club Mistral** (✉ Ctra. del Sur, Km 44, Playa del Tarajalillo, 35479 ☎ 928/157158).

Central Highlands

From Maspalomas, take Route GC520 toward Fataga for a good drive through the center of the island. This is sagebrush country, with interesting rock formations and cacti. A ***mirador*** (lookout) about 7 km (4½ mi) uphill offers views of the coast and mountains.

San Bartolomé de Tirajana

9 *23 km (14 mi) north of Maspalomas, 20 km (12 mi) east of Cruz de San Antonio.*

The administrative center of the south coast, San Bartolomé de Tirajana is an attractive town planted with pink geraniums. At its popular Sunday-morning market, in front of the church, you'll find tropical produce and island crafts. Just to the east, the village of **Santa Lucía** has crafts shops and a small museum devoted to Guanche artifacts.

en route

Drive up to the Cruz Grande summit on GC520. To the left are several of the island's reservoirs, known as the lakes of Gran Canaria; they're stocked with trout, and you can fish in them with a permit from the forest service, ICONA (☎ 928/248735). Continue along GC520 in the direction of Tejeda, past rural mountain villages. On the right is the spike-shape Roque Nublo, an eroded volcanic chimney worshiped by the Guanches.

Tejeda

10 *About 7 km (4½ mi) southwest of Las Palmas de Gran Canaria.*

At the village of Tejeda, the road begins to ascend through a pine forest dotted with picnic spots to the **Parador Cruz de Tejeda,** currently not offering rooms. From the parador, continue uphill about 21 km (13 mi) to the **Mirador Pico de las Nieves,** the highest lookout on Gran Canaria. Here, too, is the **Pozo de la Nieve,** a well built by clergymen in 1699 to store snow.

off the beaten path

ARTENARA – From the road leading to the parador, follow signs west to the village of Artenara (about 13 km [8 mi]) for views of the rocky valley and its chimneylike formations. You can see both Roque Nublo and Roque Ventaiga, sitting like a temple on a long ridge in the valley. The entrance to the bargain restaurant **Mirador de la Silla** (☎ 928/666108) takes you through a long tunnel, on the far side of which you can sit in the sun and enjoy a spectacular view—more than worth the trip to Artenara.

WHERE TO STAY $$ **El Refugio.** Ideal for excursions into Roque Nublo National Park, the Refuge does quite nicely while Parador Cruz de Tejeda is closed for renovations. Decorated in American country style, it's small and homey. The restaurant has traditional local fare, including potaje canario. ✉ *Cruz de Tejeda s/n* ☎ *928/666513* 🖷 *928/666520* *10 rooms* *Restaurant, miniature golf, pool, sauna, bicycles* ▭ *AE, DC, MC, V.*

San Mateo

11 *15 km (9 mi) northeast of Parador Cruz de Tejeda.*

From Tejeda, the road winds down to San Mateo, where you'll find the **Casa Cho Zacarias** museum of rural life and a winery. The museum is open Monday–Saturday 9–1. Pass **Santa Brigida** and turn right toward the golf club on the rim of the Bandama crater. Continue to the village of Atalaya, with cave houses and pottery workshops.

Tafira Alta

12 *7 km (4½ mi) west of Las Palmas.*

Along the main road leading into Las Palmas from San Mateo is Tafira Alta, an exclusive enclave of the city's wealthy families. In Tafira Alta is the **Jardín Canario Viero y Clavijo,** with plants from all the Atlantic islands grouped in their natural habitats. ⏲ *Daily 9–6.*

The North Coast

Leaving Las Palmas by the northern road, you pass grim shantytowns before reaching the banana plantations of the coastal route. This is the greenest part of the island. Have a seaside lunch in Agaete.

Arucas

13 *13 km (8 mi) west of Las Palmas.*

An agricultural center, Arucas is the island's third-largest town. Its big stone Gothic church is wildly out of place among the small houses.

Teror

14 *10 km (6 mi) south of Arucas.*

Amid the most verdant vegetation on Gran Canaria is the village of Teror. In the 18th-century church of **Nuestra Señora del Pino** (Our Lady of the Pine Tree), Gran Canaria's patron saint is seated on a silver throne above the altar. The statue, reportedly found in a pine tree in the 15th century, is removed for special fiestas. As you head west, you'll see increasingly tropical foliage in the hillside villages of **Firgas** and **Moya.**

SHOPPING **Parfumes Oceano,** near the church parking lot in the village of Teror, sells perfumes made locally from tropical flowers.

Agaete

15 *8 km (5 mi) southwest of Galdar.*

The quiet, leafy town of Agaete is famous for the annual fiesta of the *rama* (branch), on August 4, in which pine branches from the island's upper slopes are carried to the town by dancing crowds. The ritual is a variation on a pre-Christian rain dance that was used by the Guanches in times of drought. Just beyond Agaete is **Puerto de las Nieves** (Port of the Snows), where painted boats bob in the tiny harbor and larger ferries depart for Tenerife. The short Avenida de las Poetas leads to an old windmill on the point. Look for the rocky point called the **Dedo de Dios** (Finger of God), off the tall cliffs.

LANZAROTE

With mostly solidified lava and dark, disconcerting dunes, Lanzarote's interior is right out of a science-fiction film. There are no springs or lakes, and it rarely rains, so all fresh water comes from desalination plants.

Despite its surreal and sometimes intimidating volcanic landscape, Lanzarote—the fourth-largest Canary—has turned itself into an inviting resort through good planning, an emphasis on outdoor adventure, and conservation of its natural beauty. No buildings taller than two stories are allowed (seven stories in Arrecife), leaving views of the spectacular geology unobstructed.

Lanzarote was named for the Italian explorer Lancelotto Alocello, who arrived in the 14th century. The founder of modern-day Lanzarote, however, was artist and architect César Manrique, the unofficial artistic guru of the Canary Islands. He designed most of the tourist attractions and convinced authorities to require all new buildings to be painted white with green or brown trim (white with blue on the coast), to suggest coolness and fertility. He also led the fight against overdevelopment. All over this island, and especially in Arrecife, Lanzarote feels like North Africa. Like Moroccans, many locals drink *café con leche condensada* (coffee with condensed milk) out of glasses, rather than café con leche out of cups. Try this sweet concoction in any café or bar.

Arrecife

6 km (4 mi) east of the airport.

The island's cinder-block capital, Arrecife (named for its many reefs), is the most unattractive part of Lanzarote. The well-organized **tourist office,** in the municipal park, can guide you toward the highlights. The **Castillo San Gabriel** is a double-wall fortress once used to keep pirates at bay. It now houses an archaeology museum, where you can see copies of some of the Guanche cave drawings found on Lanzarote. *€1.50* *Weekdays 9–1 and 5–8.*

The old, waterfront fortress **Castillo San José** was turned into the stunning **Museo de Arte Contemporáneo** (Museum of Contemporary Art) by Manrique, one of whose paintings is on display along with other modern Spanish works. *Av. de Naos s/n* *928/812321* *Free* *Museum daily 11–9.*

Where to Eat

$–$$ ✕ **Castillo San José.** Black-and-white furniture, glass walls, and modern art give this remodeled fortress an elegant feel. Try the cold avocado soup with caviar or the salmon steak wrapped in cured ham. *C. Puerta de Naos s/n* *928/812321* *AE, MC, V.*

Sports & the Outdoors

Mountain biking is a popular and practical way to tour the island, as Lanzarote is not particularly hilly. Rent wheels at **CicloMania** (Almirante Boado Endeiza 9 928/817535).

Costa Teguise

7 km (4½ mi) northeast of Arrecife.

Costa Teguise is a green-and-white complex of apartments and a few large hotels. Each of the chimneys on the bungalows has a different shape. King Juan Carlos owns a villa here, near the Meliá Salinas hotel. The best of Costa Teguise's several small beaches is **Las Cucharas.**

The **Jardín de Cactus** (Cactus Garden), north of Costa Teguise between Guatiza and Mala, was Manrique's last creation for Lanzarote. The giant metal cactus that marks the entrance comes close to tacky, but the gardens artfully display nearly 10,000 cacti of more than 1,500 varieties from all over the world. *928/529397* *€3* *Daily 10–5:45.*

Playa de la Garita, not far from the Jardín de Cactus, is a wide bay of crystal water favored by surfers in winter and snorkelers in summer.

★ **Los Jameos del Agua** (water caverns), 15 km (9 mi) north of the Costa Teguise, was created when molten lava streamed through an underground tunnel and hissed into the sea. Eerie music plays as you explore, and at 11 PM on Tuesday, Friday, and Saturday, musicians appear for live Canarian folk tunes. Look for the tiny white crabs on the rocks in the underground lake—this species, a blind albino crab, is found nowhere else in the world. The **Casa de los Volcanes** is a good museum of volcanic science. *928/848020 Days €6.60, nights €7.20 Sun.–Mon. and Wed.–Thurs. 9:30–6:45, Tues. and Fri.–Sat. 9:30–6:45 and 7 PM–3 AM.*

★ Across the highway from the Jameos del Agua, the **Cuevas Verdes** (Green Caves) are for more adventurous cave explorers. Guided walks take you through a 1-km (½-mi) section of underground volcanic passageway. This gentle spelunk is one of the best tours on the island. *928/848484 €6.60 Daily 10–5.*

The little fishing village of **Orzola** is 9 km (5½ mi) north of Jameo del Agua. Small boat excursions leave here each day for the neighboring islet of **La Graciosa,** with fewer than 500 residents and plenty of quiet beaches. Spy the islet from **Mirador del Río,** a Manrique-designed lookout. You'll also see smaller protected isles—Montaña Clara, Legranza (the Canary closest to Europe), and Roque del Este. *€2.40 Daily 10–5:45.*

Guinate Tropical Park, in the northern part of the island, has 1,300 species of exotic birds and animals and great views of La Graciosa. *928/835500 €10 Daily 10–5.*

Where to Stay & Eat

$$ **Grill Casa Blanca.** In an octagonal house, this place resembles an English country cottage, with stained-wood floors and wreaths of dried flowers. Watch the chef in the open kitchen of the main dining room. Try the avocado-and-shrimp salad, steak with green peppercorns, or local fish dishes. *Las Olas 4 928/590155 AE, DC, MC, V No lunch.*

$–$$ **La Jordana.** This popular, unpretentious venue, with a beam ceiling and white walls, has international fare with French touches. Try the homemade pâté, veal with apples, or locally caught cherne in orange sauce. *Centro Comercial Lanzarote Bay, Los Geranios 10–11 928/590328 AE, DC, MC, V Closed Sun. and Sept.*

$ **El Pescador.** Cats will lead you here as they prowl neighboring alleys for tasty scraps. With the sounds and smells of the marina so close by, you'll know you're getting the freshest of fish. Carved wooden ceilings, fishnets, and simple benches at long plank tables make this an authentic haunt for local fishermen. *Centro Comercial Pueblo Marino no phone No credit cards Closed Mon.*

★ $$$$ **Gran Meliá Salinas.** Built around an interior tropical garden with hanging vines, palms, waterfalls, and songbirds, the hotel often hosts vacationing European political leaders. The rooms have louvered closets and doors and large, flower-filled, sea-view terraces. The hotel's swanky La Graciosa serves giant prawns, duck breast in plum sauce, or halibut wrapped in chard. The private garden villas pamper utterly, with 24-hour butler service and individual pools. *Urb. Costa Teguise 35509 928/590040 928/590390 www.solmelia.com 310 rooms, 10 villas 5 restaurants, cable TV with movies, golf privileges, putting green, 3 tennis courts, 2 pools, gym, hair salon, sauna, beach, archery, basketball, 2 bars AE, DC, MC, V.*

$$$ **Teguise Playa.** Don't be put off by the cold, glass exterior; the six-story lobby is filled with plants, and the staff is friendly. Rooms have white-tile floors and bamboo furniture, and each has a geranium-filled terrace with a sea view over the beach. ✉ *Av. del Jabillo s/n, 35509 Urb. Costa Teguise* ☎ *928/590654* 📠 *928/590979* 🌐 *www.occidental-hoteles.com* *314 rooms* *Restaurant, 2 tennis courts, 2 pools, gym, hair salon, hot tub, sauna, beach, squash, 2 bars* ▭ *AE, DC, MC, V.*

Sports & the Outdoors

DIVING The island's only official diving center is at Las Cucharas. **Diving Lanzarote** (☎ 928/590407 🌐 www.diving-lanzarote.net) is run by a German who speaks perfect English; he rents equipment, leads dives, and offers a certification course.

GOLF Lanzarote's 18-hole **Campo de Golf Costa Teguise** (☎ 928/590512) is outside the Costa Teguise development and has unusual sand traps filled with black-lava cinders.

SURFING Some of the best surfing in the world is found on Lanzarote's west coast. Ride the waves at **La Santa Surf** (☎ 928/528676).

WINDSURFING You can arrange windsurfing lessons and rent equipment from the **Lanzarote Surf Company** (☎ 928/591974) at Las Cucharas beach.

Shopping

For island crafts, go to the open market in the village of **Teguise** on Sunday between 10 and 2. Some vendors set up stalls in the plaza; others just lay out a blanket in the street and sell embroidered tablecloths, leather goods, costume jewelry, African masks, and other items.

Puerto del Carmen

11 km (7 mi) southwest of Arrecife.

Most beach-bound travelers to Lanzarote head to the sandy strands of the Puerto del Carmen area. **Playa Grande,** the main beach, is a long strip of yellow sand where you can rent sailboards, Jet Skis, skates, and lounge chairs. It's backed by a 3-km (2-mi) stretch of souvenir shops and restaurants. **Playa de los Pocillos** is slightly north of Puerto del Carmen and the site of most of the area's development; hotels and apartments are restricted, however, to the other side of the highway, leaving the 2-km (1-mi) yellow-sand beach surprisingly pristine. **Playa Matagorda,** the northern extension of Playa de los Pocillos, has alternating sections of gravel and gray sand; it's favored by surf fishermen.

Where to Stay & Eat

$–$$ ✕ **La Cascada Puerto.** Plump steaks sizzle on an open grill at the entrance to this wood-beam restaurant in the heart of the old town. For decades, La Cascada Puerto has retained a Spanish authenticity lacking in the area's other restaurants; you sit on comfortable leather chairs amid walls bedecked with baskets and pitchforks. Consider *langostinos al whiskey* (king prawns in a whiskey sauce). At meal's end, you're served a little glass of decadently sweet *ron miel,* Canarian honey rum. ✉ *Roque Nublo 3* ☎ *928/512953* ▭ *MC, V.*

$ ✕ **El Varadero.** This converted fishermen's warehouse on the tiny harbor has an informal style. The Canarian food includes fresh fish and papas arrugadas. The tapas bar at the entrance is littered with toothpicks and napkins dropped by a lively crowd enjoying marinated *calamares* (calamari) and *pulpo en tinto* (octopus in its own ink). ✉ *Varadero 22* ☎ *928/513162* ▭ *MC, V* ⊗ *Closed Sun.*

$ ✕ **La Casa Roja.** A harborside terrace makes this place a favorite; there's also a cozy upstairs dining room with old black-and-white photos of

Puerto del Carmen. The Canarian food centers on fresh fish and seafood. *✉ Varadero s/n ☎ no phone ▭ AE, DC, MC, V.*

★ $$$–$$$$ **Los Jameos Playa.** The huge lobby atrium here has brown wooden balconies overlooking tall palms and a wide wooden staircase leading outside. The central outdoor area has fun pools, lots of shady bars, and white villas with light-blue trim. Most of the stylish rooms have terraces overlooking the garden, pool, or beach. There's a nude zone on the grounds. *✉ Playa de los Pocillos, 35510 Puerto del Carmen ☎ 928/511717 ℻ 928/514219 ⊕ www.seaside-hotels.de 530 rooms Restaurant, 4 tennis courts, pool, gym, hair salon, sauna, piano bar, playground ▭ AE, DC, MC, V.*

$$$ **Los Fariones.** The granddaddy of Lanzarote's resorts has retained an exclusive, elegant feel as its tropical gardens designed by César Manrique have matured. Rooms are small, with rattan furniture and linoleum flooring, but each has a terrace with views of the gardens and sea. You may use the sports center a block away. *✉ Roque del Este 1, 35510 Puerto del Carmen ☎ 928/510175 ℻ 928/510202 242 rooms Restaurant, miniature golf, tennis court, pool, gym, hair salon, hot tub, massage, billiards, squash, bar, meeting room ▭ AE, DC, MC, V.*

Nightlife

Lanzarote's nightlife is headquartered here. The main party strip is Avenida de las Playas. For a more relaxed night out, head to the old town, where most locals spend their time. The crowd is still mostly foreign, but the bars are more intimate and the drinks are cheaper. The **Big Apple** (✉ Av. de las Playas ☎ no phone), in the back of the Centro Comercial Atlántico, is small and dark with a cozy bar and outdoor tables. Late-night dance music draws young Spaniards and foreigners. The **Beach Club Paradise** (✉ Av. de las Playas ☎ no phone), in the Centro Comercial Columbus, is an airy, second-floor club with big windows. The bottle-spinning bartenders enjoy hamming it up with the crowds. The DJs start with crowd-pleasing '80s tunes, moving on to house and disco after midnight. At the quasi-tropical **Ruta 66** (✉ Av. de las Playas 19 ☎ 928/514027), you can sip a frothy mixed drink on a cushioned wicker chair looking toward the ocean. A cluster of bars is packed into the Centro Comercial Roque Nublo, including the pint-size, nautical-theme **Bar El Pescador** (☎ no phone). Guitars hang from the ceiling, and old pictures of Scotland adorn the walls in the **Scotch Corner Bar** (✉ C. Tenerife 14 ☎ no phone). There's live music nightly, usually acoustic and sometimes Scottish. The **Bonkers Variety Cabaret Bar** (✉ Centro Comercial La Hoya ☎ no phone) spotlights the spirited duo of Christine and Gerri, a.k.a. the Femmes Fatales, who perform everything from Abba to the Blues Brothers to Etta James, changing their glittering costumes between sets. Both mothers, they keep their act wholesome so it's "fun for all the family."

Tahíche

5 km (3 mi) south of Teguise.

In Tahíche, the unusual former home of artist Manrique has been opened as the **Fundación César Manrique.** On display are a collection of Manrique's paintings and sculptures, as well as works by other 20th-century artists. But the real attraction is the house itself, designed by Manrique to blend with the volcanic landscape. Built into a series of lower-level caves, with palm trees ascending into the upper floor, are a series of unusual, whitewashed living rooms. The maze of spaces invites you to walk from room to room through indoor tunnels and outdoor courtyards. *✉ Ctra. Tahíche–San Bartolomé, 2 km (1 mi) west of Tahíche ☎ 928/843138 ⊕ www.fcmanrique.org €6.50 ⏲ July–Oct., daily 10–7; Nov.–June, Mon.–Sat. 10–6, Sun. 10–3.*

Yaiza

13 km (8 mi) west of Puerto del Carmen.

Yaiza is a quiet, whitewashed village with good restaurants. Largely destroyed by a river of lava in the 1700s, it's best known as the gateway to the volcanic national park.

Fodor's Choice ★ The **Parque Nacional Timanfaya** (Timanfaya National Park), popularly known as "the Fire Mountains," takes up much of southern Lanzarote. As you enter the park from Yaiza, the first thing you'll see is the staging area for the Canaries' best-known **camel rides.** A bumpy camel trek lasts about 20 minutes. The volcanic landscape inside Timanfaya is a violent jumble of exploded craters, cinder cones, lava formations, and heat fissures. The park is protected, and you can visit only on a bus tour. A taped English commentary explains how the parish priest of Yaiza took notes during the 1730 eruption that buried two villages. He had plenty of time—the eruption lasted six years, making it the longest known eruption in volcanic history. By the time it was over, more than 75% of Lanzarote was covered in lava. Throughout the park, on signs and road markers, you'll see a little devil with a pitchfork; this *diablito* was designed by Manrique. ☎ 928/840057 €6 ⏲ *Daily 9–6 (last trip at 5).*

Where to Eat

$–$$ ✕ **El Diablo.** This must be one of the world's most unusual restaurants. Here, in the middle of Timanfaya National Park, chicken, steaks, and spicy sausages are cooked over a volcanic crater using the earth's natural heat. ✉ *Timanfaya National Park* ☎ *928/173105* ▭ *AE, MC, V.*

¢–$ ✕ **La Era.** One of only three buildings to survive the 1730 eruption of Yaiza's volcano, this farmhouse has simple dining rooms with blue-and-white check tablecloths on tables arranged around a center patio. Try the goat stew, cherne in cilantro sauce, and the Canarian cheeses. ✉ *Barranco 3, Yaiza* ☎ *928/830016* ▭ *AE, DC, MC, V.*

Playa Blanca

15 km (9 mi) south of Yaiza.

Playa Blanca is Lanzarote's newest resort. The ferry for Fuerteventura leaves from here, but there's not much more to the town. Tourists come for the white beaches, reached via hard-packed dirt roads on **Punta de Papagayo.** The most popular beach is **Playa Papagayo.** Bring your own picnic; there's just one bar. Just north of Playa Blanca is Lanzarote's agricultural belt. In **La Geria,** grapes are grown in cinder pits ringed by volcanic rock. The rocks provide protection from the wind, and the cinders allow dew to drip down to the roots.

Where to Stay

★ **$$$–$$$$** **Timanfaya Palace.** At the far end of Playa Blanca rises the graceful sight of whitewashed Arabic towers, backed by the sea and Fuerteventura. Enhanced by the cool Moorish fountain in the lobby, this vision is almost a tourist attraction in itself. It's on the water and a two-minute walk from Playa Flamingo, but Timanfaya Palace has no beach; it compensates with a small, sandy, palm-lined ledge overlooking the sea. Spacious rooms have terraces or balconies, and prices include breakfast and dinner. Twenty rooms are specially equipped for travelers with disabilities, and Internet access is a perk for all. ✉ *Playa Blanca, 35570 Yaiza* ☎ *928/517676* 📠 *928/517011* 🌐 *www.h10.es* *302 rooms, 3 suites* *2 restaurants, cable TV with movies, miniature golf, tennis court, 2 pools, hot tub, sauna, archery, piano bar, dance club, convention center* ▭ *AE, DC, MC, V.*

$$–$$$ Lanzarote Princess. Near the virgin beaches of Lanzarote's south shore, this modern four-story building has an airy, plant-filled lobby. Rooms are small and a bit sterile, but are perked up by bright floral bedspreads. The grounds, on the other hand, are vast and encompass good sports facilities and a huge pool with a bar in the middle. ✉ *Playa Blanca, 35570 Yaiza* ☎ *928/517108* 🖷 *928/517011* 🌐 *www.h10.es* *410 rooms* *Restaurant, miniature golf, tennis court, 2 pools, hair salon, squash, 2 bars, piano bar, dance club, recreation room, playground* *AE, DC, MC, V.*

Sports & the Outdoors

Rent mountain bikes at **Zafari Cycle** (☎ 928/517691).

14

FUERTEVENTURA

Some of Fuerteventura's towering sand dunes have blown across the sea from the Sahara Desert, 96 km (60 mi) away, and indeed it's not hard to imagine Fuerteventura as a detached piece of Africa. Despite being the second-largest Canary Island, Fuerteventura is the least populous, and tourism is relatively new to its 20,000 inhabitants. The two main resort areas are at the island's far north and south ends. Corralejo, across from Lanzarote, is known for its sand dunes, many miles of which are protected and pristine. The Jandia peninsula, with dozens of beaches—including one that's 26 km (16 mi) long—is caught up in a building craze, but there are still miles of virgin coastline left.

Puerto del Rosario

5 km (3 mi) north of the airport.

Fuerteventura's capital, Puerto del Rosario, has long suffered from an image problem. It used to be called Puerto de Cabra (Goat Port), but the new and improved name has not changed the fact that this is a poor city with little of interest to travelers.

Corralejo

38 km (23 mi) north of Puerto Rosario.

This small port town has one street of tourist restaurants and some pedestrian plazas with good seafood. South 19 km (11 mi) on the inland road is the **Casa de los Coroneles,** the island's main historic building. Military governors built the immense house in the 1700s and ruled the island from it until the turn of the 20th century. It is not open to the public.

Beaches

Playa de Corralejo, about 2 km (1 mi) south of the town, is fringed by mountainous sand dunes and faces Los Lobos Island, across the channel. Nude sunbathing is common at the more remote spots. **Playa del Aljibe de la Cueva,** on the northwest side of the island, has a castle once used to repel pirates. It's popular with locals.

Where to Stay

$$$–$$$$ **Tres Islas.** Sitting on an empty white beach near the Corralejo dunes, this resort is built around a swimming-pool complex with green-and-white-striped tents. The bedrooms are more formal, with soft green carpeting, dark-wood furniture, and floral prints. All have terraces. ✉ *Av. Grandes Playas, 35660 Corralejo* ☎ *928/535700* 🖷 *928/535858* 🌐 *www.riu.es* *365 rooms* *Restaurant, 4 tennis courts, 3 pools, gym, hair salon, sauna, beach, piano bar, playground* *AE, DC, MC, V.*

$$–$$$ **Oliva Beach.** Rooms in this boxy, eight-story hotel are fairly small, with linoleum floors and orange drapes, but each has a furnished ter-

race with views of the beach. The hotel needs a paint job, but it's Tres Islas's only neighbor on this side of the dunes—which is to say it has a perfect location. There is an Olympic-size swimming pool, and the friendly staff runs a miniclub to keep youngsters busy all day. ✉ *Av. Grandes Playas, 35660* ☎ *928/535334* 📠 *928/866154* 🌐 *www.riu.es* *410 rooms* *Restaurant, 2 tennis courts, 2 pools, hair salon, bar, children's programs, playground; no a/c* 💳 *AE, DC, MC, V.*

Sports & the Outdoors

DIVING The channel between Corralejo and the tiny Isla de Lobos is rich in undersea life and favored by divers as well as sportfishermen.

WINDSURFING Rent windsurfing boards at most hotels; one of the main schools is **Ventura Surf** (☎ 928/866040).

Betancuria

25 km (15 mi) southwest of Puerto Rosario.

Betancuria was once the capital of Fuerteventura but is now almost a ghost town, with only 150 residents. The weatherworn colonial church of **Santa María de Betancuria** was meant to be the cathedral of the Canary Islands. The **Museo de la Iglesia** (Church Museum) contains a replica of the banner carried by the Norman conqueror Juan de Bethancourt when he seized Fuerteventura in the 15th century. Most of the artwork was salvaged from the nearby convent, now in ruins. The museum is open weekdays 9:30–5, Saturday 9:30–2; admission is €.60.

The **Museo Arqueológico** (Museum of Archaeology; ✉ C. Roberto Roldán) and a crafts workshop are on the other side of the ravine that cuts through the tiny hamlet.

In **Antigua,** 8 km (5 mi) east, you can visit a restored, white Don Quijote–style windmill once used for grinding gofio. The modern metal windmills throughout the island were imported from the United States and are used to pump water.

Pájara

16 km (10 mi) south of Betancuria.

Pájara is the administrative center of the booming southern peninsula of Jandia and sports a two-block strip of boulevard, pretty wrought-iron street lamps, and a brand-new city hall. Fuerteventura was once divided into two kingdoms, and a wall was built across the Jandia peninsula to mark the border. Remnants of that wall are still visible today inland from **Matas Blancas** (White Groves), 42 km (26 mi) south of Pájara on Highway GC640.

Costa Calma

7 km (4½ mi) south of Matas Blancas.

As you continue south along the coast from Matas Blancas, the beaches get longer, the sand gets whiter, and the water gets bluer. The famous **Playas de Sotavento** begin near the Costa Calma developments and extend gloriously for 26 km (16 mi). Nude sunning is favored here, except directly in front of hotels.

Where to Stay & Eat

$ ✕ **Don Quijote.** This hotel does its best to bring Old Castile to the beach. Shields bearing coats of arms hang amid wooden beams, near a suit of armor that would have been too fancy for Don Quijote himself. Though the food is mainly Castilian, you mustn't leave without a taste of the island's famous *majorero* cheese. ✉ *Jandia Beach Center 39* ☎ *no phone* ▭ *V.*

$$$–$$$$ **Fuerteventura Playa.** Built around a large, kidney-shape pool and thatch-roof bar, this sophisticated, low-slung hotel is at the north end of the Sotavento Beaches. Rooms have slate-blue carpets and modern white furnishings, including oversize beds, and a few have sea views. ✉ *Urb. Cañada del Río Poligono C1, 35627* ☎ *928/547344* 📠 *928/547097* 🌐 *www.riu.com* *300 rooms* *Restaurant, 2 tennis courts, pool, gym, hair salon, sauna, bar* ▭ *AE, DC, MC, V.*

14

$$$ **Jandia Princess.** If tour groups haven't booked all the rooms, your stay will be memorable for the pools with island bars, complete amenities, and the best design on Fuerteventura—a graceful white Moorish look. Every room has a balcony facing the sea or the gardens. ✉ *Urb. Esquinzo, 35626* ☎ *928/544089* 📠 *928/544097* 🌐 *www.princess-hotels.com* *528 rooms* *2 restaurants, 6 tennis courts, 6 pools, hair salon, hot tub, sauna, 6 bars, laundry service* ▭ *AE, DC, MC, V.*

$$$ **Robinson Club Playa Jandia.** No cash changes hands, all meals are included, and drinks are paid for with brightly colored chips that make it easy to forget how much you're spending at the flower-strung terrace bar, cozy tavern bar, and romantic cocktail lounge. With nude beaches to the north and south, a thumping nightclub, and lots of tanned yuppies on holiday, this is Fuerteventura's answer to Club Med. ✉ *Playa Jandia, 35625* ☎ *928/541348* 📠 *928/541100* *362 rooms* *Restaurant, cable TV with movies, 10 tennis courts, 2 pools, hair salon, windsurfing, volleyball, 3 bars, dance club* ▭ *AE, DC, MC, V.*

$$–$$$ **Costa Calma Beach.** The building may resemble a convention center, and the lobby may be excessively colorful, but at least you can book a room here—it's one of few hotels on the coast that will deal with individuals as well as tour groups. Besides regular rooms, private apartments with kitchens are available. Prices at this entirely modern hotel include breakfast and dinner; all-inclusive packages are also available. Several rooms are equipped for travelers with disabilities. ✉ *Av. de las Palmeras, 35627* ☎ *928/875046* 📠 *928/875202* 🌐 *www.sunrisebeachhotels.com* *322 rooms, 75 apartments* *2 restaurants, cable TV with movies, 3 tennis courts, 2 pools, gym, hair salon, hot tub, sauna, bar, dance club, playground* ▭ *MC, V.*

Sports & the Outdoors

For windsurfing lessons and board rentals, try **Fun Center** (☎ 928/535999) on Sotavento Beach.

Morro Jable

At the southernmost tip of the island.

At the very southern tip of Fuerteventura is the old fishing port of Morro Jable. Many more miles of virgin coast stretch beyond here—down a dirt road that eventually leads to the lighthouse—and beaches along the entire windward side of the peninsula remain untouched.

Beaches

Beyond the town of Morro Jable, a dirt road leads to the isolated beaches of Juan Gomez and **Playa de las Pillas.** Following the dirt tracks across the narrow strip of land, you can enjoy the equally empty **Playa de Cofete** and **Playa de Barlovento de Jandia.**

Sports & the Outdoors

For **scuba diving** and **snorkeling,** head for the rocky outcrops on the windward side of Jandia.

LA PALMA

La Palma is a green and prosperous island that managed quite successfully in the past without tourism. But now that it has been "discovered," La Palma is handling its newfound tourism with good taste by emphasizing the island's natural beauty, traditional crafts, and cuisine. The residents, called Palmeros, are especially friendly.

Santa Cruz de la Palma

★ *6 km (4 mi) north of the airport.*

Santa Cruz is the capital of La Palma and was an important port and bustling shipbuilding center in the 16th century. Then, in 1533, a band of buccaneers led by French pirate François le Clerc raided the city and burned it to the ground. La Palma was rebuilt with money from the Spanish king, which is why it now has such a unified colonial appearance. Walk up the cobblestone main street, Calle O'Daly, which everyone calls Calle Real. Take a peek inside the elegant patio of the **Palacio Salazar,** which contains the tourist office.

The triangular **Plaza de España,** in front of the church of **El Salvador** (✉ C. O'Daly) is the focus of La Palma's social life and is jammed in the early evening. The church is the only building that survived the pirate fire; it has a handsome carved Moorish ceiling. Bring a flashlight if you want to see the religious art on the walls. Note the stone shields on the **city hall** (✉ C. O'Daly) across the Plaza de España. One is the coat of arms of Spain's Habsburg kings, and the other is the emblem of La Palma. Walk uphill a block to the corner of Calle de la Puente; then look back at one of the most charming streets in the Canaries.

In the restored 16th- and 18th-century cloisters of the church of San Francisco, the **Museo Insular** (Island Museum) traces the navigational and trading history of La Palma and displays Guanche remains. The **Museo de Bellas Artes** (Museum of Fine Arts) upstairs has a good collection of 19th-century Spanish paintings. ✉ *Pl. de San Francisco 3* ☎ *922/420558* 🎫 *€1.80* ⏲ *Oct.–June, weekdays 9:30–2 and 4–6; July–Sept., weekdays 9–2.*

You can't miss the life-size cement replica of Columbus's ship the *Santa María,* at the end of the Plaza de la Alameda. There's a tiny **naval museum** inside; climb up to the deck for a look at a collection of old maps. ☎ *922/416550* 🎫 *€1.20* ⏲ *Oct.–June, Mon.–Thurs. 9:30–2 and 4–7, Fri. 9:30–2:30, Sat. 10–1 and 5–7:30, Sun. 10–1:30; July–Sept., weekdays 9:30–2:30.*

The star-shape **Castillo Real** (Royal Castle; ✉ C. Mendez Cabrezola) is a 16th-century fortress. Along **Avenida Marítima** is a much-photographed row of colorful Canarian houses with typical double balconies, complete with shielded posts looking out to the sea. The balconies are actually on the backs of the houses; they front Calle Pérez de Brito, which is a continuation of O'Daly. Stop in at **Tabacos Vargas** (✉ Av. Marítima 55) to buy some famous *palmero* cigars, or just watch them being hand-rolled at the **factory** (✉ Balthasar Martin 83) a few blocks uphill. The cigar industry is a result of constant migration between the Canary Islands and Cuba. Many with a taste for fine cigars claim that hand-rolled palmeros are better than today's Cubans.

The hilltop village of **Las Nieves** (The Snows), 3 km (2 mi) northwest of Santa Cruz, has a beautifully preserved colonial plaza and the opulent church of **Nuestra Señora de las Nieves,** which houses La Palma's patron saint, the Virgin of the Snows. The Virgin, credited with saving many a ship from disaster, sits on a silver altar wearing vestments studded with pearls and emeralds.

Where to Stay & Eat

$–$$ ✕ **Los Braseros.** From Santa Cruz, follow the signs to the OBSERVATORIO high above the city. The restaurant's outdoor terrace has wonderful views, and the friendly and funny staff serves grilled steaks, pork, and hearty Canarian soups. ✉ *Candelaria Mirca, Ctra. del Roque 54, Los Alamos* ☎ *922/414360* ▭ *DC, MC, V* ⊙ *Closed Tues.*

$–$$ ✕ **Mesón del Mar.** If you venture to the north part of the island, follow the road down from San Andrés to the tiny fishing harbor at Puerto Pesquero Espindola, and you'll end up at this popular seafood house. ✉ *Puerto Pesquero Espindola* ☎ *922/450305* ▭ *AE, MC, V.*

★ $ ✕ **Chipi Chipi.** This unlikely restaurant is tucked away behind dense tropical gardens—complete with chirping parrots—in the hills above Santa Cruz, 3 km (2 mi) beyond the church in Las Nieves. Each party is seated in a private stone hut. The food is strictly local, and portions are huge. You can start with salad or garbanzo-bean soup, followed by grilled meats—from pork to chicken to rabbit—washed down with local red wine. ✉ *Ctra. de las Nieves 42* ☎ *922/411024* ▭ *AE, MC, V* ⊙ *Closed Wed., Sun., and Oct.–mid-Nov.*

$ ✕ **Tamanca.** A sign marks the entrance to this restaurant-in-a-cave, 16 km (10 mi) north of Fuencaliente. The menu centers on traditional meat and fish dishes with an island flair. ✉ *Ctra. General s/n, Montaña Tamanca, Las Manchas* ☎ *922/462155* ▭ *AE, DC, MC, V.*

¢–$ ✕ **El Parral.** Tucked behind the Castillo Real is this informal, family-owned restaurant with wooden tables topped with functional paper tablecloths. Come here for some of the best—and most affordable—Italian food in town. The tasty canneloni hits the spot; try them stuffed with meat and mushrooms or tuna and fresh vegetables. ✉ *C. Castillete 7* ☎ *922/416778* ▭ *AE, DC, MC, V* ⊙ *Closed Mon. and last two weeks of Mar. and Sept.*

★ $$$ 🏨 **Parador de Santa Cruz de la Palma.** The site of the Canaries' parador, 8 km (5 mi) inland from Santa Cruz, was chosen for its sweeping views of both the capital and the sea. Guest rooms have parquet floors and traditional wooden balconies. The parador's wonderful reading room has a high wooden ceiling, tranquil interior patios, and outdoor terraces. The restaurant, with a wood beam ceiling and a traditional Canarian style, serves excellent grilled fish. ✉ *Ctra. de Zumacal s/n, 38712* ☎ *922/435828* 📠 *922/435999* 🌐 *www.parador.es* ⇐ *78 rooms* ♿ *Restaurant, pool, gym, sauna, bar, recreation room, meeting room* ▭ *AE, DC, MC, V.*

$ 🏨 **Castillete Aparthotel.** Right on the ocean but down the street from the heavy traffic, this is the best choice if you want to stay in the city proper. Most of the units are studios with separate sleeping and sitting areas and small kitchens. White wood and natural-pine furniture give the rooms a clean, modern look. ✉ *Av. Marítima 75, 38700* ☎ *922/420054* 📠 *922/420067* ⇐ *42 apartments* ♿ *Restaurant, pool; no a/c* ▭ *AE, DC, MC, V.*

Shopping

La Palma's best crafts and foods are sold at **La Graja Centro de Artesanía,** near the Mirador de la Concepción outside Santa Cruz, where you'll find embroidery, baskets, pottery, cookbooks, bottled mojo sauce, cigars, and more.

Playa de los Cancajos

5 km (3 mi) south of Santa Cruz de la Palma.

La Palma is not known for its beaches, but these black-sand coves are popular with swimmers in the summer. Los Cancajos, 5 km (3 mi) south of the capital, is a small town with a crescent-shape beach and crystalline water.

Where to Stay & Eat

$$ ✕ **Las Tres Chimineas.** An outgoing Palmero and his English wife run this attractive black-stone restaurant in Breña Alta, 6 km (4 mi) west of Santa Cruz. The building is named for its three decorative chimneys; inside, the sunny aesthetic is heightened by fresh flowers. Local fish are the specialty—vieja is the best. ✉ *Ctra. de Los Llanos de Aridane, Km 8* ☎ *922/429470* ▭ *MC, V* ⊗ *Closed Tues. No dinner Mon.*

$$$ **Taburiente Playa.** This crescent-shape resort has fantastic sea views from nearly every room. It's designed so that the guest need never leave the premises, with two swimming pools, a gym, activities for kids, and nighttime entertainment. ✉ *Playa de los Cancajos, 38712* ☎ *922/181277* 🖷 *922/181285* ⊕ *www.h10.es* *283 rooms, 9 suites* *Restaurant, tennis court, 2 pools, wading pool, gym, sauna, nightclub, playground* ▭ *AE, MC, V.*

★ $$ **Hacienda San Jorge.** Built to resemble a Canarian village, the San Jorge groups apartments in pastel bungalows. The apartments have summer-house furniture and separate bedrooms, living rooms, baths, and terraces. The complex is built on several different levels surrounding a lake-size swimming pool steps from the black-sand beach. ✉ *Playa de los Cancajos 22, Breña Baja, 38712* ☎ *922/181066* 🖷 *922/434528* ⊕ *www.hsanjorge.com* *155 apartments* *Restaurant, kitchenettes, pool, gym, hot tub, sauna, beach, bar* ▭ *AE, DC, MC, V.*

Fuencaliente

28 km (17 mi) south of Santa Cruz de la Palma.

Near Fuencaliente, the scenery grows dry as you reach La Palma's volcanic southern tip. Visit the **San Antonio volcano** and the **Teneguía volcano,** the site of the Canaries' most recent eruption. In 1971, Teneguía burst open, sending rivers of lava toward the sea and extending the length of the island by 3 km (2 mi). There are good beaches in the cinders below the volcano, reached via unpaved roads. Fuencaliente is the heart of La Palma's wine region. While there, visit the modern **Llanovid winery,** makers of the islands' best-known label, Teneguía. ✉ *C. Los Canarios 8* ☎ *922/444078.*

Tazacorte

28 km (17 mi) northwest of Fuencaliente.

Drive down through the banana plantations to Tazacorte, the old Guanche capital, or explore Puerto Naos, 5 km (3 mi) south, where a sunny, black-sand bay created by a 1947 volcanic eruption is now a beach resort.

Beaches

The black-sand bay of **Puerto Naos** is the island's biggest beach and the most popular on the west coast.

Where to Stay & Eat

★ $–$$ ✕ **Playa Mont.** Looking like an upscale beach shack, open on one side to the ocean breezes, this place serves some of the best seafood in the islands; the secret is the sauces—including a rich allioli (garlic mayonnaise) and delicious lemon-butter. You can also get traditional mojos. ✉ *Puerto de Tazacorte* ☎ *922/480443* 💳 *MC, V* ⊗ *Closed Thurs.*

$$–$$$ **Sol La Palma.** Perched at the end of La Palma's best beach, this hotel was the island's first real resort and is still the place to be on the west coast. The rooms are huge, with understated beige furnishings, gray-tile floors, sun terraces, and enormous baths. The bountiful restaurant buffet has expensive treats (such as fresh shrimp and papaya) not normally found at moderately priced hotels. ✉ *Puerto Naos, 38760* ☎ *922/408000* 📠 *922/408014* 🌐 *www.solmelia.com* *307 rooms, 164 apartments* *2 restaurants, tennis court, 2 pools, gym, sauna, 4 bars, meeting room; no a/c in some rooms* 💳 *AE, DC, MC, V.*

14

Parque Nacional de La Caldera de Taburiente

10 km (6 mi) east of Tazacorte.

The striking Taburiente Crater National Park fills most of the center of La Palma. The visitor center is 3 km (2 mi) east of El Paso. The park is inside what looks like a huge crater; modern geologists think that the crater was formed by a series of small eruptions that pulled the center of the mountain apart. A narrow paved road leads through pine forests to the **Mirador Cumbrecita,** a lookout at 6,014 ft, on the crater's rim. It's often raining or snowing up here, and bright rainbows span the canyon. The white dome and tower on the opposite side are the **Observatorio Roque de los Muchachos** (Boys' Castle Observatory), home of Europe's largest telescope. Astronomers say the Canary Island peaks have some of the cleanest air and darkest skies in the world. Canarian pine trees are especially adapted to fire and volcanic eruptions, taking only four years to regenerate themselves. The park has lots of interesting hiking trails, and you can camp on the valley floor with a permit, obtainable at the visitor center.

LA GOMERA

One of the least developed of the Canary Islands, tiny La Gomera attracts scores of denim-clad backpackers on shoestring budgets, as well as other travelers who care little for the disco beat of the more touristy islands. The mossy, fern-filled central peaks make up the **Garajonay National Park** and include a rare forest of fragrant laurel trees. The forest, a UNESCO World Heritage Site, preserves Tertiary flora that the Ice Age wiped out everywhere else in the world.

The park's mountains fan out into six steep-sided valleys called *barrancos.* Villages in the barrancos are dedicated mainly to small-scale banana growing, and you'll see three or four stalks of bananas outside each house in the morning awaiting pickup. The serpentine roads leading in and out of the valleys are so filled with switchbacks that traveling is slow, and villages remain isolated. Allow plenty of time—two days if possible—for a drive around La Gomera. The distances are short, but they take a long time to cover, and the roads are not for those afraid of heights.

San Sebastián

La Gomera's scraggly capital makes the most of its historical links with Christopher Columbus—he made his last stop on charted territory at San Sebastián before setting out for the edge of the earth in 1492. The sights east of the capital are all close together.

The **Torre del Conde** (Tower of the Count) was built by the Spanish in 1450 for protection from Guanche tribes. It came in particularly handy in 1487, when the count's wife, Beatriz de Bobadillo, took refuge in the tower after island chieftains killed her husband. The beautiful, black-haired widow is better known for her love affair with Columbus.

The explorer used the **Pozo de la Aguada** (Water Well) at the head of Calle del Medio to resupply his ships with water, which he also used to baptize the New World. *Free ⏲ Mon.–Sat. 9–1:30 and 3:30–6, Sun. 10–1.*

The church of **Nuestra Señora de la Asunción** (Our Lady of the Assumption) was just a tiny chapel when Columbus prayed there. Since then it has been enlarged in several styles. Up the street, visit the **Casa Colón,** the simple Canarian house where the explorer supposedly stayed during his time with Beatriz. It's now devoted to exhibits by local artists. ✉ *C. Real 56* ☎ *no phone* *Free ⏲ Weekdays 4–6.*

The **Degollada de Peraza,** 15 km (9 mi) south of San Sebastián over a winding road, has a lookout with great views. Guanche chiefs pushed Beatriz's cruel husband, Fernan Peraza, to his death from this cliff.

Beaches

A strong current makes La Gomera's northern beaches dangerous for swimming. If you want sun, head for the volcanic sands of the southern shores. **San Sebastián**'s black-sand beach near the ferry dock is clean and popular with local families.

Where to Stay & Eat

$ ✕ **Marqués de Oristano.** This is really two restaurants in one. The Canarian patio in the entryway is a tapas bar; in the back, reserved for special occasions, is an informal, open-air grill where you can select fresh fish or a cut of beef or lamb from a butcher's case. The dining room upstairs serves pricier, more-sophisticated dishes, such as pork tenderloin in palm honey, or bass filet in champagne with saffron and pine nuts. ✉ *C. del Medio 24* ☎ *922/141457* ▭ *AE, V* ⏲ *Closed Tues.*

★ $$$ ✕ **Parador Conde de La Gomera.** Built in 1970 in the style of an old island manor, the parador has breezeways decorated with Spanish antiques. The large rooms combine bare-wood floors with French provincial furniture and have louvered shutters that open onto interior patios. The pool and yard, perched above the city, have sea views. On a clear day, you can see Tenerife's Mt. Teide from the top-floor sitting room. The dining room has a barnlike Canarian ceiling, and the kitchen specializes in such local dishes as rabbit in salmorejo with papas arrugadas. ✉ *38800 San Sebastián* ☎ *922/871100* 🖷 *922/871116* 🌐 *www.parador.es* *58 rooms* *Restaurant, pool, bar* ▭ *AE, DC, MC, V.*

Shopping

La Gomera has refreshingly few shops. For a souvenir, buy a bottle of palm syrup or a bag of macaroons from the little market on the Plaza de América in San Sebastián. Ceramics, made without a potter's wheel, are still made and sold by village women in El Cercado. The Hermigua region has handmade textiles, including colorful blankets made from old dresses. In a 16th-century hermitage, **Artesanía Santa Ana** (✉ C. Real 41 ☎ 922/141864) sells Gomeran crafts from all over the island: baskets made of dried plantain leaves, Gomeran musical instruments such as goatskin tambourines, and Gomeran food, including a pâté of goat cheese, red peppers, and garlic.

Playa de Santiago

34 km (20 mi) southwest of San Sebastián.

Playa de Santiago, complete with fishing port and banana plantations, is at the bottom of a steep canyon. Until recently, the people who lived on the almost vertical slopes of the island's canyons used a mysterious whistling language to communicate across the gorges. The language was en route to oblivion until the Gomeran school board, in a move to keep the island's traditions alive, made *el silbo Gomera* (the Gomeran whistle) compulsory for all elementary and junior-high students. Most older people in rural areas still understand it, and the gardeners at the parador in San Sebastián sometimes give demonstrations. Boat excursions leave several times a week from Playa de Santiago to view **Los Organos**, a cliff made up of hundreds of tall basalt columns that resemble organ pipes.

Beaches

Playa de Santiago is a rocky black-sand beach surrounding a small fishing bay. It has the sunniest weather on the island and is destined to become La Gomera's major resort area.

Where to Stay

★ $$$ **Jardines Tecina.** La Gomera's only real resort sprawls luxuriously over a series of terraces high above the sea and provides an elevator down to the beach. The rooms, grouped in hillside bungalows, all have summery-green pine furniture, with big wooden terraces for sunbathing. Head to the elegant restaurant Club Laurel for grilled lamb, beef, and other meats or dig into a BBQ platter at the informal buffet restaurant. ✉ *Playa de Santiago, 38811* ☎ *922/145850* 🖷 *922/145851* 🌐 *www.jardin-tecina.com* *434 rooms* *4 restaurants, miniature golf, 5 tennis courts, 4 pools, hair salon, health club, squash, 4 bars, dance club, Internet* ▭ *AE, MC, V.*

$ **Apartamentos Tapahuga.** This attractive building is right on the fishing harbor, and the apartments' Canarian, carved-pine balconies overlook it. Kitchens and country-style Spanish furnishings make the apartments homey, and there's a swimming pool on the roof. ✉ *Av. Marítima, 38800* ☎ *922/895159* 🖷 *922/895127* *29 apartments* *Kitchenettes, pool; no a/c* ▭ *MC, V.*

Parque Nacional de Garajonay

20 km (12 mi) west of San Sebastián.

You drive past fantastic geological formations as you enter Garajonay National Park from the central highway. The road heads into dense forest; much of the year this area is in the clouds thanks to the natural mountain barrier that diverts the trade winds, and the mossy trees drip with mist. La Gomera's humidity, mild temperatures, and geographic isolation have proved just the right mixture for the survival of the various evergreens here. The highest point on the island, the peak of Garajonay (4,832 ft), is to your right. To learn more about the park, take the turnoff at Las Rosas for the **Juego de Bolas** visitor center. Exhibits and an excellent 20-minute video, with English translation, explain the laurel forest, and a garden outside labels vegetation from the 150 species exclusive to this park. In nearby crafts shops, you can watch artisans at work. *Visitor center* ☎ *922/800993* *Free* ⏲ *Daily 9:30–4:30.*

Sports & the Outdoors

Garajonay National Park has miles of interesting hikes. Pick up a trail map at the visitor center or the San Sebastián tourist office.

Shopping

At **Artisans Cooperación Los Organos** (✉ Ctra. Las Rosas, Centro de Visitantes del Parque N. Garajonay ☎ 922/800993), local artists make and sell everything from rag rugs and baskets to local white wines and Gomeran drums. It's right next to the visitor center in Garajonay National Park.

Valle Gran Rey

72 km (43 mi) west of San Sebastián.

The terraced farms of Valle Gran Rey, planted with bananas and palms, look like something out of a Gauguin painting. The valley has two black-sand beaches and has become a refuge for a number of German families. In Valle Gran Rey, **Playa del Inglés** is a sandy black crescent of a beach favored by young people in search of a cheap hideaway. **Las Vueltas** beach is popular with residents.

off the beaten path

CASA EFIGENIA – In the hamlet of Las Hayas, about 30 minutes uphill from Valle Gran Rey, this plain, inexpensive spot has walls with a few cobs of dried corn and a dusty case of citations—many handwritten—that Doña Efigenia has received for her efforts in preserving traditional Gomeran cookery. It's simple, authentic food, prepared and served by Doña Efigenia herself. The main course is a vegetable stew; dessert is a heavy, cheese-filled cake that you smother in palm-tree syrup. The Casa is open 9–7 daily for breakfast and lunch.

Where to Stay & Eat

$–$$ ✕ **Charco del Conde.** Sample good fish, steaks, and chicken with papas arrugadas and mojo sauce from a great backyard patio or a people-watching front porch. Across from Playa del Charco, the restaurant is named for the beach inlet that creates a naturally occurring pool (*charco*), refilled at high tide. This is also where the Guanche chiefs hatched their plot to toss the *conde* (count) of La Gomera off the cliff. ✉ *Ctra. Puntilla Vueltas* ☎ *922/805403* ▭ *AE, DC, V* ⊗ *Closed Sun. and July.*

$–$$ ✕ **Mirador de César Manrique.** Take in a powerful view of the entire Gran Rey valley through the angled glass walls of this government-run restaurant school. Service and food are on par with the island's best. The terrace lookout—indeed the entire complex, which merges with its natural surroundings—was built by César Manrique. ✉ *Ctra. de Arure* ☎ *922/805868* ▭ *AE, DC, MC, V* ⊗ *Closed Mon.*

$$–$$$ **Hotel Gran Rey.** The largest hotel in the area is right on the black-sand beach. The best thing about the tidy three-story complex is the rooftop pool overlooking the sea and the valley town. ✉ *La Puntilla s/n, 38870* ☎ *922/805859* 🖷 *922/805651* 🌐 *www.hotel-granrey.com* *99 rooms* *Restaurant, tennis court, pool, meeting room* ▭ *MC, V.*

$ **Apartamentos Charco del Conde.** These low-rise, flower-clad apartments across from Las Vueltas Beach have simple pine furnishings, a kitchen, and a private terrace. Half the rooms have sea views, and the other half overlook the pool. ✉ *Av. Marítima s/n, 38870* ☎ *922/805597* 🖷 *922/805502* 🌐 *www.charcodelconde.com* *50 apartments, 50 studios* *Kitchenettes, 2 pools; no a/c* ▭ *MC, V.*

Alojera

43 km (26 mi) northwest of San Sebastián.

With its beautiful little black-sand beach, Alojera, like other northern Gomeran villages, is becoming a center of bed-and-breakfast tourism. Contact the tourist office in San Sebastián for color brochures of the small homes available. This area is known for its palm syrup (*miel de palma*). At night, the syrup trees, which have metal collars around them, produce up to 3 gallons of sap each, which is boiled down into syrup over wood fires the following day.

EL HIERRO

The smallest Canary Island, El Hierro is strictly for those who enjoy nature and solitude. Most residents live in mountain villages. The few who do find their way to El Hierro come for the hiking, scuba diving, or relaxing.

Valverde

10 km (6 mi) west of the airport.

El Hierro's capital, Valverde, sits on a hillside at 2,000 ft. The town was built inland, in the clouds, to protect it from pirate raids, and its cobblestone streets always seem to be wet with mist. The church, with a balcony bell tower, was once a lookout for pirates. Driving around El Hierro, you'll pass terraced farms still plowed with mules. Note that the rocky coast along El Golfo is safe for swimming only in summer. The **Mirador de la Peña,** 8 km (5 mi) west of Valverde, stands at 2,200 ft and offers a spectacular view of El Golfo, on the island's northeastern corner.

El Golfo (the Bay) was formed by what looks like a half-submerged volcanic crater; the part above water is a fertile, steep-side valley. At the far end is a health spa with salty medicinal waters, called **Pozo de la Salud.** Those who prefer tastier medicine can visit the island's **winery** in the big, beige building near Frontera. The **Hoya del Morcillo** picnic area is in the fragrant pine forest that covers the center of El Hierro. It has barbecue pits, rest rooms, and a playground. Camping is permitted, and this makes a good starting point for forest hikes.

Where to Stay & Eat

$–$$ ✕ **Mirador de la Peña.** One of César Manrique's final works, this is surely El Hierro's most elegant place to dine. Glass walls grant a panoramic view of the bay below. The varied menu includes *vieja* (a type of white rockfish native to the Canaries), smoked salmon, *conejo al salmorejo* (rabbit topped with a mojo sauce), and *pimientos rellenos de cordero* (peppers stuffed with lamb). ✉ *Ctra. General de Guarazoca 40* ☎ *922/550300* 💳 *AE, DC, MC, V* ⊗ *Closed Mon. No dinner Sun.*

$$$ ✕🏨 **Parador Nacional El Hierro.** The road to the parador takes you around a point jutting into the sea and deposits you at the bottom of a 3,500-ft cliff. Guest rooms are large, with Castilian furniture and heavy folk-art bedspreads. In the dining room, try tasty tidbits of island specialties, laid out as appetizers; otherwise, stick to grilled fish and steak. ✉ *Las Playas 15, 38915* ☎ *922/558036* 📠 *922/558086* 🌐 *www.parador.es* 🛏 *47 rooms* 🛎 *Restaurant, miniature golf, pool, health club, bar, playground* 💳 *AE, DC, MC, V.*

$ 🏨 **Boomerang.** Owned by a local islander who once worked in Australia, this hotel is right in the middle of town. Rooms are clean and comfortable, with country pine furniture and tile baths. ✉ *Dr. Gost 1, 38900* ☎ *922/550200* 📠 *922/550253* 🛏 *17 rooms* 🛎 *Restaurant, bar; no a/c* 💳 *AE, DC, V.*

La Restinga

54 km (33 mi) south of Valverde.

At the southern tip of El Hierro, La Restinga is a small, rather ugly fishing port surrounded by lava fields. The few who come here tend to be scuba fanatics; some say the diving is the best in the Canaries.

Where to Stay & Eat

$ ✕ **Casa Juan.** These two plain dining rooms have large tables to accommodate families, who come from all over the island for the seafood soup. The mojo sauces, served with papas arrugadas, are outstanding, as is the grilled *cherne.* ✉ *Juan Gutierrez Monteverde 23* ☎ *922/557102* ▭ *MC, V* ⊗ *Closed Wed.*

$ ✕ **Punta Grande.** Built on an old dock that extends into the sea, the four-room Punta Grande was cited in the *Guinness Book of Records* as the world's smallest hotel. Rooms have exposed rock walls and erstwhile porthole windows as nightstands. An old diving suit and ships' lanterns hang in the dining room, which serves piping-hot shellfish soups and stews with hunks of bread and goat cheese. Call at least a month ahead; this hotel is a must. ✉ *Las Puntas, Frontera, 38911* ☎ *922/559081* *4 rooms* *Restaurant, bar; no a/c, no room phones, no room TVs* ▭ *No credit cards.*

¢ **Apartamentos La Marina.** These tourist apartments occupy a three-story building on the harbor. The furnishings are basic, and balconies have unbeatable sunset views. ✉ *Av. Marítima 10, 38915* ☎ *922/559016* *8 apartments* *Kitchenettes* ▭ *No credit cards.*

Sports & the Outdoors

Club El Submarino (✉ Frontera, 38915 ☎ 922/559706) organizes diving, hiking, spelunking, hang-gliding, windsurfing, mountain biking, and deep-sea fishing in La Restinga and El Golfo.

THE CANARY ISLANDS A TO Z

To research prices, get advice from other travelers, and book travel arrangements, visit www.fodors.com.

AIR TRAVEL

There are no nonstop flights to the Canary Islands from the United States; Americans can transfer in Madrid, in England, or elsewhere in Europe. Iberia and its sister carrier Aviaco have several direct flights daily to Tenerife, Gran Canaria, La Palma, and Lanzarote from most cities in mainland Spain (2½ hours from Madrid). Air Europa and Spanair have flights from Madrid and Barcelona at slightly lower prices. The other three islands are accessible by connecting flights.

Interisland flights are handled by Iberia and its regional subsidiary, Binter, using small turboprop planes with great low-altitude views of the islands. Binter has a fixed-rate coupon that allows you to hop from island to island. Spanair also operates interisland flights, often with slightly lower prices than Binter.

Binter ☎ 928/579561 🌐 www.bintercanarias.com. **Tenerife** ✉ Aeropuerto de los Rodeos ☎ 922/635855. **Gran Canaria** ✉ Alcalde Ramirez de Bethancourt 8, Las Palmas ☎ 928/370877. **Lanzarote** ✉ Av. Rafael Gonzalez 2, Arrecife ☎ 928/810358. **Fuerteventura** ✉ 23 de Mayo 11, Puerto de Rosario ☎ 928/852310. **La Palma** ✉ Apurón 1 ☎ 922/411345. **La Gomera** ✉ Aeropuerto de La Gomera ☎ 922/373094. **El Hierro** ✉ Dr. Quintero 6 ☎ 922/550854.

AIRPORTS

All seven Canary Islands are served by air. Tenerife has two airports: Reina Sofía (TFS), near Playa de las Américas in the south, and Los Rodeos (TFN), in the north near Puerto de la Cruz. As a general rule, long-distance flights arrive at the southern terminal while inter-island flights use the northern one, but there are exceptions. Try to book a flight that gets you to the part of the island where you'll be staying, and allow plenty of time to travel between airports for connecting flights. Driving time from one airport to the other is about 1½ hours; you can hire a taxi for about €45 or rent a car for around €24.

Airports **Tenerife** ☎ 922/759200 Reina Sofía/TFS, 922/635998 Los Rodeos/TFN. **Gran Canaria** ☎ 928/579094 Gando/LPA. **Lanzarote** ☎ 928/823450 Arrecife/ACE. **Fuerteventura** ☎ 928/860600 Puerto Rosario/FVE. **La Palma** ☎ 922/426100 Santa Cruz/SPC. **El Hierro** ☎ 922/553700 VDE. **La Gomera** ☎ 922/873000 QGZ.

BOAT & FERRY TRAVEL

Trasmediterránea runs a slow, comfortable ferry service between Cádiz and the Canary Islands (Tenerife, 42 hours; Gran Canaria, 48 hours). The boat has cabins, a tiny pool, restaurants, a recreation room, and a dance club, but it's not a luxury cruise.

Fred Olsen and Trasmediterránea operate inexpensive ferries between all seven islands. Fred Olsen's fleet is newer, and Olsen is the only company with helpful brochures indicating schedules and fares. Most inter-island trips take one to four hours; the few boats departing near midnight are equipped with sleeping cabins. Note that schedules change frequently, so it's imperative to call ahead to double check. Trasmediterránea runs passenger-only jetfoil service three times a day between Las Palmas and Tenerife (80 minutes). The ultra-sleek Fred Olsen jetfoil, which accommodates vehicles, takes only 55 minutes from Gran Canaria (Agaete) to Santa Cruz de Tenerife. Free bus service is provided between Agaete and Las Palmas in both directions.

From Tenerife you can reach any of the other six islands. Ferries to La Palma, El Hierro, and La Gomera depart Los Cristianos; from Santa Cruz you can sail to both of Gran Canaria's main ports, Agaete in the west and Las Palmas in the north.

From Gran Canaria you can ferry to Lanzarote and Fuerteventura, which are mutually connected. One Trasmediterránea hydrofoil daily links Morro Jable, in southern Fuerteventura, with Las Palmas (90 minutes) and Tenerife (3½ hours). Fred Olsen runs several ferries a week between Las Palmas, Arrecife (Lanzarote), and Puerto Rosario (Fuerteventura). La Gomera can be reached by ferry (55 minutes) from Los Cristianos, in southern Tenerife. Fred Olsen's jetfoil on the same route takes less time. Ferry Gomera takes cars and people between Tenerife and La Gomera three times daily; at night, the same ferry plies between La Gomera and La Palma.

Southern Lanzarote and northern Fuerteventura are linked by two companies. Fred Olsen makes four round-trips a day from Lanzarote. It offers free bus service between Puerto del Carmen and Playa Blanca one hour prior to two of these daily departures. The Fuerteventura office is in Corralejo. Naviera Armas covers the same one-hour route. Armas is also the least expensive way to reach Lanzarote or Fuerteventura from Santa Cruz, Tenerife, or Las Palmas, Gran Canaria.

Ferry Gomera **Tenerife** ✉ Muelle Los Cristianos, Santa Cruz de Tenerife ☎ 922/628231 ✉ Av. Fred Olsen, San Sebastián ☎ 922/871007.

Fred Olsen **General information** 🌐 www.fredolsen.es. **Tenerife** ✉ Muelle Ribera, Santa Cruz ☎ 922/290011, 922/628231 general information ✉ Muelle Los Cristianos, Los Cristianos ☎ 922/790556. **Gran Canaria** ✉ C. Luis Morote 4, Las Palmas ☎ 928/495040 ✉ Puerto de las Nieves, Agaete ☎ 928/554005. **Fuerteventura** ✉ Corralejo ☎ 928/535090. **La Palma** ✉ Muelle Santa Cruz, Santa Cruz de la Palma ☎ 922/417495. **Lanzarote** ✉ Av. de Llegada s/n, Playa Blanca ☎ 928/517266. **La Gomera** ✉ Estación Marítima del Puerto, San Sebastián ☎ 928/850877. **El Hierro** ✉ Puerto de la Estaca.

Naviera Armas **Lanzarote** ✉ Main Pier, Playa Blanca ☎ 928/517912. **Gran Canaria** ☎ 928/267700. **Tenerife** ☎ 922/534052.

Trasmediterránea **Fuerteventura** ✉ León y Castillo 58 ☎ 928/850877. **General information** ☎ 902/454645 🌐 www.trasmediterranea.es. **Gran Canaria** ✉ Muelles de León y Castillo, Las Palmas ☎ 928/474439. **La Gomera** ✉ Estación Marítima del Puerto, San Sebastián ☎ 922/871324. **El Hierro** ✉ Puerto de la Estaca ☎ 922/550129. **La Palma** ✉ Av. Perez de Brito 2, Santa Cruz de la Palma ☎ 922/411121. **Lanzarote** ✉ José Antonio 90, Arrecife ☎ 928/811188. **Madrid** ✉ C. Alcalá 6 ☎ 91/423–8832. **Tenerife** ✉ Marítima Muelle Rivera, Santa Cruz de Tenerife ☎ 922/842246.

BUS TRAVEL

In Tenerife, buses meet all arriving Iberia flights at Reina Sofía Airport and transfer passengers to the bus terminal on the outskirts of Santa Cruz. From there, you can take a taxi or another bus to the northern side of the island. Buses also meet the Gomera hydrofoil and ferry to take passengers on to Santa Cruz. Each island has its own bus service geared toward residents. Buses generally leave each village early in the morning for shopping in the capital, then depart from the main plaza in early afternoon. Tourist offices have details.

CAR RENTAL

Car-rental companies abound on every island, sometimes doubling as bars. Shop around for the best price. Reservations are only necessary during the Christmas and Easter holidays. Hertz and Avis have representatives on all seven islands, but rates are better at the Spanish company Cicar, which has branches in all the airports and major towns.

Local Agencies **Cicar** in Puerto de la Cruz, Tenerife ☎ 922/368591 🌐 www.cicar.com ✉ Aeropuerto de los Rodeos, Tenerife ☎ 922/635926. **Betacar Europcar** in Puerto de la Cruz, Tenerife ☎ 922/372856.

CAR TRAVEL

Most travelers rent a car or jeep for at least part of their stay on the Canaries, as this is by far the best way to explore the countryside. Note that the roads are not always kind to those with vertigo; they often curve over high mountain cliffs with nothing but the sea below.

LANGUAGE

Canarians are much accustomed to dealing with foreign tourists, and the result is that English (and German) is widely spoken throughout the islands, particularly in main towns and tourist establishments, such as hotels and souvenir shops.

LODGING

APARTMENT & VILLA RENTALS

Villas and apartments abound in the Canary Islands, ranging from spacious villas with private pools to basic, self-catering apartments with kitchenettes. The self-catering apartments are competitively priced and you can often find excellent deals, particularly if you stay for a week or more; the downside is that many apartments are often in drab, cement complexes surrounded by throngs of vacationing sun-seekers, usually from England and Germany. For detailed listings and photos of apartment and villas throughout the islands, check out 🌐 www.canary-isles.com.

SPORTS & THE OUTDOORS

The Canaries are blessed with year-round sunny weather, and the region's steady winds and perfect waves attract sailboarders and surfers from all over the world. International windsurfing competitions are held each year on Tenerife. Surfers claim that the best waves in Europe break on the west coast of Lanzarote. Fuerteventura's east coast has strong winds and steady seas, ideal conditions for windsurfing and sailing. You'll also find a slew of snorkeling and scuba diving outfits throughout the islands. The volcanic seabed that surrounds many of the islands makes for spectacular underwater scenery, and the warm waters mean that for much of the year you don't need to wear a wet suit. For surfing info, including listings of surf shops and schools and upcoming surfing events, log on to www.surfcanarias.com.

TAXIS

In major towns, taxis can be hailed on the street. Alternately, ask for the nearest taxi stand (*parada de taxi*). Taxis use meters to calculate the fare, and drivers may charge separate fees for luggage. Taxi Ucanca, in La Laguna, Tenerife, can pick you up from most parts of the island, as can Radio Taxi, in Las Palmas, Gran Canaria.

Taxi Companies **Radio Taxi** 928/579130. **Taxi Ucanca** 922/255555.

TOURS

Viajes Insular, which has branches on every island except La Gomera and El Hierro, can arrange one-day tours of Tenerife, and excursions to other islands with English-speaking guides. Tours generally last all day and include lunch and/or a folklore presentation.

Viajes Insular Av. Generalísimo 20, Puerto de la Cruz 922/380262.

VISITOR INFORMATION

Tourist Offices **El Hierro** Licinardo Bueno 1, Valverde 922/550302. **Fuerteventura** 1 de Mayo 33, Puerto de Rosario 928/851024. **Gran Canaria** Parque de Santa Catalina, Las Palmas 928/220947. **La Gomera** C. del Medio 20, San Sebastián 922/140147. **Lanzarote** Parque Municipal, Arrecife 928/801517. **La Palma** O'Daly 22, Santa Cruz de la Palma 922/412106. **Tenerife** Pl. de España 1, Santa Cruz de Tenerife 922/239592 Pl. Europa, Puerto de la Cruz 922/386000.

UNDERSTANDING SPAIN

A SHORT HISTORY

OVER THE FINAL QUARTER of the 20th century, Spain's transformation from cloistered third-world dictatorship to booming high-tech European democracy must rank as the mother of all metamorphoses. A palpable sense of satisfaction bordering on exhilaration seems to electrify Spain today, from remote mountain villages to the slickest, postmodern boulevards of Barcelona and Madrid. Naturally, there are dark spots in the picture—more homeless, more beggars, overflow immigration, petty larceny, and, most of all, Basque terrorism—yet it's difficult not to be infected by the overall optimism. Spain is undergoing a general sprucing up, which is palpable in the newest designer bars and restaurants. Life is fiercely enjoyed and celebrated here; Spaniards have a huge capacity for living intensely and fully. Perhaps as a result of the ups and downs of a turbulent history and, in the past century, a bloody civil war, the Spanish embrace Horace's *carpe diem* (seize the day) so fervently they often appear to be trying to seize two at a time. Richard Wright, visiting in the 1950s, called it "pagan Spain"—but for 36 years of the 20th century, Spain labored under a repressive, ultraconservative, religious regime that ended only with the death of Francisco Franco in 1975. The renaissance that followed has been not just political but also cultural, artistic, social, and economic.

In imagining the Spanish landscape, you may picture the scorched, ocher plains of La Mancha where Don Quijote fought windmills, or the softly rolling hills of Andalusia, or even the overdeveloped beaches of the Costa del Sol. But, surprisingly, after Switzerland, Spain is the most mountainous country in Europe and has the longest coastline after France. These mountains, serving as barriers that long separated the peoples of the Iberian Peninsula, are largely responsible for Spain's cultural and linguistic diversity. Spain's geography ranges from the green and soggy northwest (wetter than Ireland) to the high and arid steppe of the central *meseta* (plain), from the cascading trout streams of the Pyrenees to the marshes and dunes of Doñana National Park at the mouth of the River Guadalquivir on the Atlantic ocean. There are deep caves, lonely coves, rocky canyons, mountain meadows, coastal rice paddies, volcanic island peaks . . . and, of course, the great ice and granite wall of the Pyrenees, which has always isolated Spain from France and northern Europe far more effectively than the 15 km (9 mi) of Mediterranean sea that separate Spain from North Africa across the Straits of Gibraltar.

Spain's extraordinary heritage of history, art, and architecture begins with the ancient caves at Altamira, in which people wearing skins for warmth painted delicate pictures of animals on a rock ceiling. During the Age of Exploration, robust adventurers left Extremadura, Spain's poorest province, to probe the New World, and some returned to build great stone palaces on this stark, scrubby landscape. Stretched across northern Spain are the Romanesque churches of the Camino de Santiago (Way of St. James), Europe's most famous Christian pilgrimage in the Middle Ages, culminating at the soaring cathedral of Santiago de Compostela. Pre-Romanesque and cave churches built by the Visigoths (who were early Christians) are scattered across the north as a rough stone counterpoint to the opulent Moorish mosques and palaces of Andalusia. More than 10,000 castles are sprinkled across the Iberian Peninsula; some are merely ruins, others are in extraordinarily good shape. Villages of whitewashed buildings, harbors stuffed with brightly painted fishing boats, and majestic towns welded to craggy mountaintops are easy to find. Still washed by that subtle light that inspired Velázquez, the Spanish countryside remains mercifully unchanged.

More than any other country of its size—it's the second largest in Europe, after France—Spain is characterized by the distinctness of its many parts and peoples. The Galicians of the northwest are descended from the same Celtic tribes that colonized the British Isles. Bagpipes are a local instrument, kilts are not unknown, and the local language, Gallego, is closer to Portuguese than to Spanish. The Basque Country, which straddles the western end of Spain's border with France, also has its own language, Euskera, a non-Indoeuropean tongue so mysterious that linguists have never been able to agree on its origin. Local pride is fierce here: the Basque language and culture are purposefully celebrated, and nationalist sentiment is strong. Tragically, the terrorist group ETA (Euskadi Ta Askatasuna/Basque Homeland and Liberty) has killed almost 900 Spaniards over the past three decades. (The violence is extremely unlikely to affect travelers.) The 6 million Catalans who populate northeastern Spain around Barcelona are the speakers of Spain's most widely spoken regional language, Catalan, which is closer to Provençal French than to Castilian Spanish, while residents of the province of Valencia and the Balearic Islands speak and study in their own languages, generally considered dialects of Catalan. All of these areas suffered systematic cultural and linguistic repression under the totalitarian centralist pressure of the Franco regime.

The Iberian Peninsula's early peoples included Basques, Celts, Iberians, Phoenicians, Greeks, Romans, Visigoths, and (for fully 781 years from 711 until 1492) Moors. By the end of the Middle Ages, Christians had intermarried widely with the Moorish and Jewish minorities, so while most Spaniards today see themselves as Christian Catholics, many have Muslim and/or Jewish ancestors.

Most of Spain transformed itself from an agrarian and largely feudal economy to a modern, industrialized one in remarkably little time, over the first half of the 20th century. Now, a lively economy and an optimistic outlook are giving modern Spain an anything-is-possible air, despite a high unemployment rate and the continuing scourge of terrorism. The 1992 Olympic Games, the Guggenheim Museum Bilbao, new freeways, high-speed trains, and state-of-the-art technology have replaced a country that was often described as borderline third-world in the '60s and '70s.

Modernity has come at a price. For generations, Spain was the travel destination of choice for the penniless artist or the adventurer willing to forego comfort for rugged romance. All that has changed. After years of inflation, and a value-added tax imposed as a condition of entry into the European Union, Spain's cost of living compares to that of neighbors like France. The 1992 Summer Olympics in Barcelona and Universal Exposition in Seville further inflated hotel and restaurant prices in those cities. The rate of price increases slowed in the late 1990s, although with the advent of the euro a combination of "rounding up" and rampant inflation has brought about a new surge in the cost of life in Spain.

The Turning & Overturning of Civilizations

The story of this land, a romance-tinged tale of counts, caliphs, crusaders, and kings, begins long before written history. The Basques were among the first here, fiercely defending the green mountain valleys of the Pyrenees. The Iberians came next, apparently crossing the Mediterranean from North Africa around 3,000 BC. The Celts arrived from the north about a thousand years later. The seafaring Phoenicians founded Gadir (now Cádiz) and several coastal cities in the south three millenniums ago. The parade continued with the Greeks, who settled parts of the east coast, and then the Carthaginians, who founded Cartagena around 225 BC—and who dubbed the then-wild, forested and game-rich country Ispania, after their word for rabbit: *span*.

Modern civilization began with the Romans, who expelled the Carthaginians and turned the peninsula into three imperial provinces. It took the Romans 200 years to subdue the fiercely resisting Iberians, but their influence was lasting. Evidence of the Roman epoch is left today in the great ruins at Mérida, Segovia, Tarragona, Barcelona, and other cities; in the peninsula's legal system; and in the Latin base of Spain's Romance languages and dialects. In the early 5th century, invading barbarians crossed the Pyrenees to attack the weakening Roman empire. The Visigoths became the dominant force in northern Spain by 419, establishing their kingdom at Toledo and eventually adopting Christianity.

But the Visigoths, too, were to fall before a wave of invaders. The Moors, an Arabled Berber force, crossed the Strait of Gibraltar from North Africa in 711. The

Moors swept through Spain in an astonishingly short time, meeting only token resistance and launching almost eight centuries of Muslim rule—a period that in many respects was the pinnacle of Spanish civilization. Unlike the semibarbaric Visigoths, the Moors were extremely cultured. Arabs, Jews, and Christians lived together in peace during their reign, although many Christians did convert to Islam. The Moors also brought with them citrus fruits, rice, cotton, sugar, palm trees, glassmaking, and the complex irrigation system still used around Valencia. The influence of Arabic in modern Spanish includes words beginning with "al", such as *albóndiga* (meatball), *alcalde* (mayor), *almohada* (pillow), and *alcázar* (fortress), as well as prominent phonetic characteristics ranging from the fricative "j" to, in all probability, the lisping "c". Moorish culture is most spectacularly evident in Andalusia, derived from the Arabic name for the Moorish reign on the Iberian Peninsula, al-Andalus, which meant "western lands." The fairy-tale Alhambra palace overlooking Granada captures the refinement of the Moorish aesthetic, while the earlier, 9th-century mosque at Córdoba bears witness to the power of Islam in al-Andalus.

The Moors never managed to subdue Spain's northwest corner, and it was in Asturias that a minor Christian king, Pelayo, began the long crusade that came to be known as the *Reconquista* (Reconquest). By 1085, Alfonso VI of Castile had captured Toledo, giving the Christians a firm grip on the north. In the 13th century, Valencia, Seville, and finally Córdoba—the capital of the Muslim caliphate in Spain—fell to Christian forces, leaving only Granada in Moorish hands. Nearly two hundred years later, the so-called Catholic Monarchs—Ferdinand of Aragón and Isabella of Castile—were joined in a marriage that would change the world, and on January 2, 1492, 244 years after the fall of Córdoba (longer than the entire history of the United States), Granada surrendered and the Moorish reign was over.

1492: A Turning Point

The year 1492 is a watershed in Spanish history, the beginning of the nation's political golden age: Christian forces conquered Granada and unified all of current-day Spain as a single kingdom; in what was, at the time, viewed as a peacekeeping measure promoting national unity, Jews and Muslims who did not convert to Christianity were expelled from the country; and Christopher Columbus, under the sponsorship of Isabella, landed in the Americas, initiating the Age of Exploration. Despite all of this, the departure from Spain of educated Muslims and Jews was a blow to the nation's agriculture, science, and economy that would require a bloody civil war and nearly 500 years to expiate. The colonies of the New World greatly enriched Spain at first, but massive shipments of Peruvian and Mexican gold later produced terrible inflation while inhibiting other kinds of economic development and placing most of Spain in the hands of the grandees and the church. The Catholic Monarchs and their centralizing successors maintained Spain's unity, but they sacrificed the spirit of international free trade that was beginning to bring prosperity to other parts of Europe.

Ferdinand and Isabella were succeeded by their grandson Carlos, who became the first Spanish Habsburg and one of the most powerful rulers in history. Cortés reached Mexico, and Pizarro conquered Peru under his rule. Carlos also inherited Austria and the Netherlands and in 1519, three years into his reign, became Holy Roman Emperor (as Charles V), wasting little time in annexing Naples and Milan. He championed the Counter-Reformation and saw the Jesuit order created to help defend Catholicism against European Protestantism. But Carlos V weakened Spain with his penchant for waging war, particularly against the Ottomans and German Lutherans. His son, Felipe II (Phillip II), followed in the same, expensive path, defeating the Turks at the Battle of Lepanto in 1571 but losing the "Invincible Spanish Armada" in the English Channel in 1588. Depressed at what he must have known was the turning of the tide for Spain's golden age, Felipe II dedicated the rest of his life to the construction of the somber Escorial monastery west of Madrid, where he died 10 years after losing the world's greatest fleet while attacking Protestant England.

From Empire to Civil War to Democracy

Under Felipes III and IV, the 17th century saw the full cultural flowering of Spain's golden age, even while the empire was crumbling under the weight of its own sprawling unmanageability. After a century of artistic brilliance and economic erosion, the War of the Spanish Succession was ignited by the death in 1700, without issue, of Charles II, the last Spanish Habsburg. After the 1700–14 War of the Spanish Succession between the Bourbons and Habsburgs, Philip of Anjou was crowned Philip V and inaugurated the Bourbon line in Spain (a representative of which sits on the throne today). The Bourbons of that era, a Frenchified lot, copied many of the attitudes and fashions of their northern neighbors, but the infatuation ended when Napoléon Bonaparte, on the pretext of crossing Spain to fight the English in Portugal, decided to stay after all, invited the Spanish monarchs Carlos IV and his son Fernando VII to abdicate and, in 1808, installed his brother Joseph Bonaparte on the throne. Mocked bitterly as "Pepe Botella" for his fondness for drink (*botella* means "bottle"), Bonaparte was widely despised, and an 1808 uprising against him in Madrid—chronicled harrowingly by the great painter Francisco de Goya y Lucientes (1746–1828)—began the War of Independence, known to foreigners as the Peninsular War. Britain, siding with Spain, sent the Duke of Wellington to the rescue. With the aid of Spanish guerillas, the French were finally expelled, but not before they had looted many of Spain's major churches, museums, and cathedrals. Fernando VII returned to the throne in 1814; in 19 catastrophic years he managed to alienate and embitter progressives with his autocratic regime and enrage reactionaries by overturning the Salic law in order to place his daughter Isabella II on the throne instead of his conservative brother Don Carlos. Meanwhile, many of Spain's American colonies took advantage of the war to claim their independence.

The rest of the 19th century was not a happy one for Spain, as conservative regimes grappled with civil wars and revolts inspired by the currents of European republicanism. The final blow came with the loss of Cuba, Puerto Rico, and the Philippines in 1898, a military disaster that ironically sparked a remarkable literary renaissance—the so-called Generation of '98, whose members included novelists Miguel de Unamuno and Pío Baroja, philosopher and essayist José Ortega y Gasset, and poet Antonio Machado. In 1902 Alfonso XIII, grandson of Isabella II, was restored to the throne, but a popular Republican mandate in the elections of 1931 resulted in his self-imposed exile. The Second Spanish Republic followed, to the delight of most Spaniards, but the 1936 election of a left-wing Popular Front government ignited bitter opposition from the right. In July 1936 the assassination of a monarchist leader gave the Spanish army the long-awaited opportunity to rise in revolt to restore law and order. A young general named Francisco Franco was soon named commander-in-chief of the anti-Republican rebels representing Spain's traditional right wing alliance of church, feudal grandees, and army.

The Spanish Civil War (1936–39) was the single most tragic episode in Spanish history. More than half a million people died in the conflict. Intellectuals and leftists the world over sympathized with the elected government, and the International Brigades with many American, British, and Canadian volunteers, took part in some of the worst fighting, including the storied defense of Madrid. But Franco, backed by the Catholic Church, got far more help from Nazi Germany, whose Condor legions destroyed the Basque town of Guernica (in a horror made infamous by Picasso's monumental painting), and from Fascist Italy. For three years, European governments stood quietly by as Franco's armies ground their way to victory. After the fall of Barcelona in January 1939, the Republican cause became hopeless and Franco's Nationalist forces entered Madrid on March 27, 1939.

Officially neutral during World War II but sympathetic to the Axis powers, Spain was largely shunned by the world until, in a 1953 agreement, the United States provided aid in exchange for land on which to build NATO bases. Gradually, the shattered economy began to pick up, especially with the late-1960s surge of a new sector: tourism. But when Franco announced in 1969 that his successor would be Juan Carlos, the grandson of Alfonso XIII and a prince whose militaristic education had been strictly overseen by the aging general, the hopes of a nation longing for democracy and progress sagged. Imagine the Spaniards' surprise when, six years later, Franco died and the young monarch revealed himself to be a closet democrat. Under his nurturing, a new constitution restoring civil liberties and freedom of expression was adopted in 1978. On February 23, 1981, the king proved his mettle once and for all, when a nostalgic Civil Guard colonel with visions of a return to Franco's authoritarian regime, along with a unit of would-be rebels, held the Spanish parliament—then center-right—captive for some 24 hours. Only the heroism of King Juan Carlos, who personally called military commanders across the country to ensure their loyalty to the Constitution and the elected government, quelled the coup attempt. The Socialists ruled Spain from 1982 until early 1996, when conservative José María Aznar was elected prime minister. Aznar's increasingly authoritarian tenure ends in 2004, when it appears likely that Socialist José Luis Rodríguez Zapatero will continue in the plural and progressive direction of the early post-Franco years.

In the arts, Spain seems to have picked up where it left off when the civil war and the ensuing 40-year cultural silence of the Franco regime intervened. Whereas the first third of the century produced such towering figures as poet Federico García Lorca, filmmaker Luis Buñuel, composer Manuel de Falla, and painters Pablo Picasso, Joan Miró, and Salvador Dalí, the final quarter (since Franco's death in 1975) will be known for novelist Camilo José Cela's 1989 Nobel Prize, Basque sculptor Eduardo Chillida's blocky forms, the conceptually challenging works of Catalan painter Antoni Tapiès, and filmmaker Pedro Almodóvar's postmodern Spanish films.

All in all, to experience the best from this diverse peninsula, take the country as the modern Spanish have learned to do, piece by piece. Spain at the turn of the 21st century is a patchwork of cultures and nationalities: Andalusia and Catalonia are as different as France and England, maybe more so. The miracle is that a common language and a central government have managed to bring these so-called Autonomous Communities as close together as they are. Castilians, Basques, Galicians, Asturians, Catalans, and Andalusians all contribute separately and equally to a Spain that begins the new millennium as one of the most vibrant nations in Europe.

— George Semler

SPANISH FOOD & WINE

SPAIN'S POST-FRANCO cultural Renaissance has encouraged richness and variety in everything from arts and letters to gastronomy. As with all things Iberian, food and wine take a great many forms. This is a country where each village takes pride in its unique way of preparing the simplest dishes, where a Pyrenean valley serves dishes whose very names are incomprehensible to fellow Catalans from the next valley.

Each of modern Spain's 17 Autonomous Communities, from the equatorial Canary Islands to the snowcapped Picos de Europa, has its own cuisine. The only Spanish dishes that might be called universal are the *tortilla española de patatas* (potato and onion omelet), *gazpacho* (a cold Andalusian soup of ground vegetables, garlic, and bread in a tomato base), and *paella* (a Valencian feast of saffron-spiked rice and seafood). Generally speaking, central Spain is known for roasts and stews, eastern Spain for rice and seafood dishes, northern Spain for meat and fish, and southern Spain for deep-fried seafood. Fresh vegetables, onions, olive oil, and garlic are consumed in abundance throughout.

Blessed with a geological diversity unusual for a country its size, Spain has been known since ancient times for rich wheat fields, vineyards, olive groves, and pig and sheep farming. The upper slopes of Andalusia's snowcapped Sierra Nevada, for example, have Alpine gentian, while the lower ones yield tropical produce unique to southern Europe, such as olives.

Nearly surrounded by a combination of the Atlantic and the Mediterranean, Spain is in large part a maritime nation. A statistic surprising to all but the Spanish themselves is that Spain ranks third in the world in per-capita fish and seafood consumption, closely behind Japan and Iceland. Moreover, those two islands have no population more than 200 km (120 mi) from the coast, whereas Spanish villagers in tiny Aranda de Duero, 500 km (300 mi) inland, were cooking fish back in the 14th century. Madrid, at the dead center of the Iberian Peninsula, has long been considered a "first port" for the freshest fish in Spain. And, of course, the Mediterranean diet—high in fresh vegetables, fruit, virgin olive oil, fish, fowl, rabbit, garlic, onions, and wine; low in red meat, dairy products, and carbohydrates—is one of the healthiest of all regimes.

The almost 800-year Moorish presence on the Iberian Peninsula was a major influence on Spanish cuisine. The Moors brought exotic ingredients such as saffron, almonds, and peppers; introduced sweets and pastries; and created refreshing dishes such as cold almond- and vegetable-based soups still popular today. One of the world's culinary pioneers was Ziryab, a 10th-century Moorish chef who worked in Córdoba: he's credited with bringing to Europe the Arab fashion for eating a standard sequence of dishes, beginning with soup and ending with dessert.

Another legacy of the Moorish taste for small and varied delicacies is Spain's best-known culinary innovation, the *tapa* (hors d'oeuvre; derived from the verb *tapar*, meaning "to cover"). Early tapas are said to have been pieces of ham or cheese laid across glasses of wine, both to keep flies out and to keep stagecoach drivers sober. It is said that as far back as the 13th century, ailing Spanish king Alfonso X El Sabio ("The Learned") took small morsels with wine by medical prescription and so enjoyed the cure that he made it a regular practice in his court. Even Cervantes refers to tapas as *llamativos* (attention getters), for their stimulating properties, in *Don Quijote*. Often miniature versions of classic Spanish dishes, tapas originated in Andalusia, where a combination of heat and poverty made nomadic grazing preferable to the formal meal. Today tapas are generally taken as appetizers before lunch or dinner, but in the south they're still often regarded as a meal in themselves. Eating tapas allows you to sample a wide variety of food and wine with minimal alcohol poisoning, especially on a *tapeo*—the Spanish version of a pub crawl but lower in alcohol and higher in protein. You basically walk off your wine and tapas as you move around.

In some of the more old-fashioned bars in Madrid and points south, you may be automatically served a tapa of the barman's choice upon ordering a drink—olives, a piece of cheese, sausages, or even a cup of hot broth. A few standards to watch for: *calamares fritos* (fried squid or cuttlefish, easily mistaken for onion rings), *pulpo feira* (octopus on slices of potato), *chopitos* (baby octopi), *angulas* (baby eels), *chistorra* (fried spicy sausage), chorizo (hard pork sausage), *champiñones* (mushrooms), *gambas al ajillo* (shrimp cooked in oil, garlic, and parsley), *langostinos* (jumbo shrimp or prawns), *patatas bravas* (potatoes in spicy sauce), *pimientos de Padrón* (peppers, some very hot, from the Galician town of Padrón), *sardinas* (fresh sardines cooked in garlic and parsley), *chancletes* (whitebait cooked in oil and parsley), and *salmonetes* (small red mullet).

Just to complicate things, the generic term *tapas* covers various forms of small-scale nibbling. *Tentempiés* are small snacks designed to (literally) "keep you on your feet." *Pinchos* are bite-size offerings impaled on toothpicks, as are *banderillas,* the latter so called because the toothpick is wrapped in colorful paper resembling the barbed batons used in bullfights. *Montaditos* are canapés, innovative combinations of delicacies "mounted" on toast. *Raciones* (rations, or servings) are hot tapas served in small earthenware casseroles. The preference for small quantities of different dishes also shows up in restaurants, where you can often order a series of small dishes *para picar* (to pick at). A selection of *raciones* or *entretenimientos* (a platter of delicacies that might range from olives to nuts to cheese, ham, or sausage) makes a popular starter for those dining in a group. The modern gourmet *menú de degustación* (taster's menu) is essentially a succession of complex tapas.

A standard Spanish soup, especially in and around Madrid, is *sopa de ajo* (garlic soup), made with water, oil, garlic, paprika, bread, and cured ham. *Sopa de pescado* (fish soup) appears on many menus, concocted in many different ways. The classic gazpacho is a cold blend of tomatoes, water, garlic, bread, and vegetables. Though most gazpacho today is made in a blender, it tastes best when prepared by hand in an earthenware mortar. Gazpacho has several variations, including Córdoba's *salmorejo,* which has a denser texture, and *ajo blanco,* based on almonds rather than tomatoes and served with peeled muscatel grapes or slices of honeydew melon—another example of Moorish influence, combining sweet and spicy flavors.

Far more substantial are the heavy soups and bean stews of the central Castilian meseta and northern coast. *Cocido madrileño* is a hearty highland stew or thick soup of garbanzos, black sausage, cabbage, potatoes, carrots, pork, and chicken served in three courses, called *vuelcos* ("overturnings" of the pot): the broth, the vegetables and legumes, and finally the meat. *Escudella* is the Catalan version of cocido, using ground pork and no garbanzos. *Fabada asturiana* is the best-known Asturian dish, a powerful stew of white kidney beans, fatback, ham, black sausage, and hard pork sausage. *Judias estofadas,* made of white kidney beans with chorizo, black sausage, onion, tomato, and bacon, is a close cousin found across the north of Spain. Galicia's *caldo gallego* mixes white beans, turnip greens, chickpeas, cabbage, and potatoes. *Pisto manchego,* from La Mancha, is a stew of sausage and ham with onions, peppers, tomatoes, and squash. *Migas de pastor* (shepherd's crumbs) is a legendary Aragonese and Castilian specialty consisting of bread crumbs and bacon sautéed in garlic and olive oil. Don't miss a chance to try *marmitako,* a hearty tuna and potato stew, during one of the Basque country's frequent Atlantic storms.

Spain is kind to carnivores, who can choose from thick and tender *txuletas de buey* or *solomillos* (beef steaks) in the Basque country and fragrant roasts in Castile. In Segovia, Burgos, and Madrid, the *cochinillo al horno* (roast suckling pig) and *cordero asado* (roast lamb) are cooked in wood ovens until at once crisp and tender enough to portion with the edge of a blunt plate.

Fish and seafood are prepared countless ways in Spain, but the Basques and the Andalusians are particular masters of the art. The Basque country is especially known for *bacalao al pil-pil*—cod cooked in oil and garlic at a low temperature, generating a sauce of juice from the fish itself. (The dish is named for the popping sound that the oil makes as the fish cooks.) *Besugo* (sea bream), either *al horno* (roasted) or *a la brasa* (over coals), is another Basque classic. *Rape* (monkfish) in crayfish sauce; *merluza* (hake) in tomato, pepper, or green (olive oil, garlic, and parsley) sauce; and *dorada a la sal* (gilthead bream baked in salt) are also popular. Common all over Spain is *trucha a la Navarra,* trout wrapped in, or stuffed with, pieces of bacon or ham. In Andalusia most fish is deep-fried in batter, a practice requiring very fresh fish and the right kind of oil to achieve the proper counterpoint of crispness and succulence. *Chancletes* (whitebait) and *sardinas* (sardines) are especially good in Málaga, while the *salmonetes* (red mullet) and *acedías* (miniature sole) of the Cádiz coast are legendary. *Adobo,* also delicious, is fried fish marinated in wine.

Spain's ham and sausage products are renowned, particularly those derived from the *cerdo ibérico,* a remarkable breed of free-range pig that produces *jamón serrano*—roughly translatable as "ham from the sierra, or mountains." This term covers three levels of quality: *bellota* (the finest, from Iberian pigs fed exclusively acorns), *de recebo* (from pigs fed acorns but finished off with corn over the last three months), and simply *serrano* (from pigs fattened on feed pellets). Extremadura and the provinces of Salamanca and Huelva produce Spain's best cured hams; look for those of Guijuelo, Lasa, and Jabugo. The chorizo and *morcilla* (blood sausage) of Pamplona, Granada, and Burgos are known beyond Spain's borders. *Sobrasada* is a delicious pork-and-pepper paste from Majorca. *Fuet* (literally, "whip," named for its slender shape) is Catalonia's best sausage, though the *botifarra* is the most popular spicy sausage, usually consumed with *secas* or *mongetes* (white beans), a popular Catalan dish.

The most elaborate poultry dishes are prepared in the Catalan province of Girona. These include *pollastre amb llangosta* (chicken with lobster), *gall dindi amb panses, pinyones, i botifarra* (turkey stuffed with raisins, pine nuts, and sausage), and *oca (anec) amb naps* (goose, or duck, with turnips). *Pollo al ajillo,* fried chunks of chicken smothered in chips of garlic, is beloved all over Spain. Rabbit (*conejo*) is another standard light meat, prepared either *al ajillo* (in garlic), a la brasa, or in stews and ragouts with peppers and assorted vegetables.

Fish, meat, and seafood meet exuberantly in paella, a saffron-flavored rice dish widely considered the most emblematic of Spanish dishes. Paella is actually comparatively new, having originated in Valencia and the Levante, Spain's rice-growing eastern coastal plain, in the early 19th century. Cooked in a wide, flat, round pan, it comes in several versions, including *marinera* (seafood), *conejo* (rabbit), *pollo* (chicken), and *mixta* (mixed). Chosen from a *menú del día,* paella will always be disappointing, little more than rice with some saffron and a few ingredients mixed in. Prepared on the spot and in the pan, however, with a caramelized crust around its edges, paella is delicious. The archetypal version is *paella a la marinera,* a seafood anthology including shrimp, crayfish, monkfish, and mussels on a bed of saffron rice cooked in a seafood broth with peppers and tomatoes. Related dishes include *arroz a banda,* paella with the seafood pre-shelled; *fideuà,* paella based on pasta rather than rice; and *arroz negro* (black rice), paella that takes its color and flavor from cuttlefish ink instead of saffron.

Iberian cheeses are many and varied. The sheep cheeses of La Mancha can be consumed *tierno* (soft and creamy, cured under three months), *semi-seco* (half-cured, for three to six months), or *seco* (dry, cured for more than six months). A mature *manchego seco* is nearly the equal of an Italian Parmesano. Cabrales, a powerful blue cheese from Asturias, makes Roquefort seem innocent. Other prominent northern cheeses include the soft and creamy breast-shape *tetilla gallega* and the sharper Asturian *pitu al' fuego.* The Basque country's smoky *idiazábal* is like a cedar-flavored sharp cheddar. Extremadura's *Torta del Casar* is widely considered the best Spanish cheese of all, a creamy sheep cheese that never hardens and needs to be scooped by spoon from the crust.

Spanish wines are rapidly emerging from the long shadow cast by their neighbors to the north. La Rioja, traditionally Spain's finest wine-growing region, is known for the deep, woody flavor of its celebrated reds, the result of aging in casks of American oak, traditionally preferred over French oak for its superior porosity and faster oxidating properties. This aging technique was introduced by French vintners from Bordeaux and Burgundy who moved to the Rioja in the 19th century to escape a phylloxera epidemic that was destroying the vines in their own country. Among time-honored Rioja labels are Rioja Alta, Viña Ardanza, Imperial, Muga, Marqués de Murrieta, Pomal, Ramón Bilbao, Marqués de Riscal, and Viña Tondonia. In response to competition from other regions producing wines of more complex structure, La Rioja is now producing a series of new wines that break with the traditionally smooth and oaky Rioja reds. Roda, Artadi, Pujanza, Vina Ijalva, Palacios Remondo, Alma de Tobla, Marqués de Riscal's Baron de Chivel, Señorlo de San Vicente, Sierra de Cantabria, Abel Mendoza, Ostatu, Solagüen, and Marqués de Vargas are among the leaders in this movement toward fruitier, more peppery brews.

Many Spanish oenophiles favor wines from La Ribera del Duero, north of Madrid. This increasingly prestigious region produces fine bottles of both young wine and wine that will improve with age. Vega Sicilia is the most famous winery in La Ribera del Duero. Pesquera, Protos, and Viña Pedrosa are other fine labels, as are Pago de Carraovejas, Mauro, and Abadia Retuerto.

Southwest of Valladolid, the Rueda winegrowing district produces some of Spain's most distinguished white wines, and Huesca's Somontano wines, especially the Enate and Señorío de Lazán labels, are rapidly gaining respect. The Valdepeñas wine country, 200 km (120 mi) south of Madrid, remains Spain's prime producer of simple table wines in unabashedly greater quantity than quality. That said, a pitcher of Valdepeñas with a meal or a round of tapas in and around Castile is never disappointing.

Catalonia's Penedès region specializes in *cava* (sparkling white wine). The most famous cavas are Codorniu and Freixenet, but many smaller outfits, such as Juvé i Camps, Augustí Torelló, Mascaró, and Gramona, actually produce better bubbly. Along with the Torres reds and whites and the Raventós cavas and whites, the Penedès produces Spain's greatest variety of wines overall. New artisanal wines, however, are steadily emerging from such unlikely places as the rugged hills of the Priorat area, west of Tarragona, where the Costers de Siurana labels Clos de l'Obac and Miserere are standouts. The Raimat wines from Costers del Segre are excellent, as are the Gran Caus, the Castillo Perelada, and the exciting new Oliver Conti wines from northern Catalonia's Ampurdán region.

Galicia's Ribeiro and Rías Baixas wines, especially the young green Albariños, are served in top restaurants throughout Spain with fish courses, and Albariño is gaining accolades overseas. The Basque country's *txakolí,* an even greener young white with a slight effervescence, has always been popular locally but is building a wider following as Basque restaurants and tapas bars flourish nationwide.

Sherry has always been popular abroad, especially with the British, who have dominated the sherry trade in Jerez de la Frontera since the 16th century. Indeed, many of the most famous labels are foreign—Domecq, Harvey, Sandeman. The classic dry sherry is the *fino. Amontillado* is deeper in color and flavor, and *oloroso* is really a sweet dessert wine, as are the even-sweeter creams. Another fortified Andalusian wine, often difficult for the inexperienced palate to distinguish from sherry, is *manzanilla,* from the coastal town of Sanlúcar de Barrameda. Manzanilla has a tangy, saline savor that comes from the cool Atlantic breezes at the mouth of the Guadalquivir River. With its faint taste of the sea, this wine does not travel well; there are even those who believe it tastes better in the lower part of Sanlúcar than in the upper town. Sherry and manzanilla are generally thought of as aperitif wines and are ideal with tapas—a Sanlúcar prawn with a glass of manzanilla is many a Spanish epicurean's idea of paradise. In England, sherry still has the genteel associations of an Oxbridge college, but Spain has a more robust attitude toward the beverage, especially during Sevilla's Feria de Abril, where more sherry and manzanilla are reputedly drunk in a week than in the whole of Spain the rest of the year.

Some of Spain's finest brandies, such as Osborne, Terry, Duque de Alba, and Carlos III, also come from Jerez. Málaga makes a sweet dessert wine that enjoyed a vogue with the English in the 19th century; look for the label Scholtz. *Aguardientes* (aquavits) are manufactured throughout Spain, with the most famous brands coming from Chinchón, near Madrid. A sweet and popular Jerez brandy, Ponche Caballero, is easy to identify by its silver-coated bottle, which looks like an amateur explosive. *Sangría,* a tourist potion imported from Mexico, is generally composed of cheap liquors and bad wine and should be avoided at all costs by those in search of Spanish delicacies.

Spain's top restaurants offer a selection of postprandial cheeses, but most meals end with dessert. Standard enticements are fresh fruit, such as strawberries with orange juice or vanilla ice cream, and *flan,* a caramel cream that comes close to being Spain's national dessert. In Catalonia, look for the ubiquitous *crema catalana,* a sort of crème brûlée, or the honey-and-fresh-cheese combination known as *mel i mató.*

The main problem with food and wine in Spain—perhaps an ironic one, in light of Spain's not-so-distant past—may be their very abundance. Dining heartily twice a day *and* making use of the tapas hour requires some management. The Spanish, looking forward to a substantial midday meal after having dined late the previous evening, breakfast on little more than coffee and a roll. Lunch, served between 2 and 4—preceded by an *aperitivo*—is generally considered the main meal of the day. The workday lasts until at least 8, after which it's time for the itinerant tapeo. Finally, often after 10, comes dinner, which can last until the wee hours. The traveler's key to surviving this delicious but demanding regimen is to partake zestily of tapas in the early evening—roam freely and you'll soon fill up on cleverly arrayed items from all four food groups. Above and after all, Spain is the ultimate moveable feast.

— George Semler and Michael Jacobs

BOOKS & MOVIES

Ernest Hemingway is the novelist most responsible for the world's image of 20th-century Spain. Read *The Sun Also Rises* (published in England as *Fiesta*) for a vicarious visit to Pamplona's running of the bulls. *For Whom the Bell Tolls* depicts the horrors of the Spanish Civil War, and *Death in the Afternoon* explores the technical, artistic, and philosophical aspects of bullfighting. Larry Collins and Dominique LaPierre's *Or I'll Dress You in Mourning* tells the rags to riches saga of El Cordobés, Spain's iconoclastic "ye-ye" matador.

A star contributor to this guide, George Semler has authored two guides of his own, *Barcelonawalks* and *Madridwalks,* each of which takes readers on five walking tours full of historic and literary detail. Jan Morris discusses Spanish history and culture via monuments and landscapes in a series of essays called *Spain,* while James A. Michener's *Iberia: Spanish Travels and Reflections,* though a Franco regime–informed and occasionally inaccurate view of Spain, still covers a lot of ground, some of it superbly well. Based on a long drive around mostly rural Spain, Cees Nooteboom's *Roads to Santiago* is a deeply personal meditation on Spain's history and resonance. Richard Ford's 1845 *Handbook for Travellers in Spain* was the first English-language guidebook on Spain. *Northern Spain: The Collected Traveler* includes essays by well-known contemporary writers, as well as practical and cultural information for travelers. Chris Stewart's hilarious *Driving Over Lemons* is a vivid, unromantic account of the tribulations of the former Genesis drummer who bought a farmhouse in Andalusia and moved there with his wife.

V. S. Pritchett (*The Spanish Temper*), H. V. Morton (*A Stranger in Spain*), George Orwell (*Homage to Catalonia*), and Washington Irving (*Tales of the Alhambra*) have all paid their respects to Spain. Gerald Brenan's works portray Spain before and during the Franco years: *The Face of Spain, The Spanish Labyrinth,* and *South from Granada,* released as a stunningly beautiful movie in 2003. *Moorish Spain,* by Richard Fletcher, details the cultural and intellectual riches of the Islamic era; *Farewell España,* by Howard M. Sacher, explores the lives and influence of the Sephardim, the Spanish Jews who were forced to flee after the 1492 expulsion decree. Jane Gerber's *The Jews of Spain* deals with the history of Sephardic Jews, from their first Roman settlements to their expulsion from Spain. Ronald Fraser's *Blood of Spain* is an oral history of the Spanish Civil War, woven from hundreds of interviews with survivors. (It's out of print, so check your library.) Journalist John Hooper examines the post-Franco era in *The New Spaniards.*

Ian Gibson's biographies of Federico García Lorca (*Federico García Lorca: A Life*) and Salvador Dalí (*The Shameful Life of Salvador Dalí*) are richly detailed accounts of the lives of two of Spain's greatest 20th-century artists.

Among Spanish texts, the story of the errant knight *Don Quijote,* by Miguel de Cervantes, will always be Spain's towering classic. For more modern works, try translations of the realism-drenched novels of Galician Camilo José Cela, the 1989 recipient of the Nobel Prize for Literature: his best-known books are *The Beehive* and *The Family of Pascual Duarte.* One of Spain's great 20th-century novels is Mercé Rodoreda's *The Time of the Doves,* the story of a woman buffeted by the misfortunes of the civil war. Federico García Lorca's play *Blood Wedding* is a disturbing drama of Spain's repressed yet powerful women of the early 20th century. Novelist Javier Marías has been hugely successful in several countries; among his best works in translation are *A Heart So White* and *Tomorrow in the Battle Think on Me.* Arturo Pérez-Reverte has written several popular and acclaimed mysteries, including *The Flanders Panel, The Club Dumas,* and *The Fencing Master.*

American Penelope Casas has written a number of cookbooks, including *Delicioso!* (regional dishes), *Paella!, The Foods and Wines of Spain,* and *Tapas,* as well as a guide: *Discovering Spain.* Colman Andrews' *Catalan Cuisine* is a wonderful collection of regional dishes from Catalonia, in northeastern Spain.

The tragic bullfighting novel, *Blood and Sand,* by Vicente Blasco Ibáñez, has three Hollywood adaptations: the first starring Rudolph Valentino; the second, Tyrone Power; the third, Sharon Stone. The last version shows quite a bit of Andalusia. Carlos Saura has directed several beautifully crafted classic films consisting mostly of dance—*Carmen, Bodas de Sangre* (*Blood Wedding*), and *El Amor Brujo* (*Love, the Magician*). Luis Buñuel's *Un Chien Andalou* is still a hallmark of surrealism, and *Belle de Jour, Tristana,* and *That Obscure Object of Desire* contain fascinating psychological studies. The last has lovely photography of Seville. Orson Welles's film *Don Quixote* was painstakingly finished in 1992, after his death, by Jess Franco and Patxi Irigoyen.

Set in 1931, *Belle Epoque* is a 1992 male-fantasy film about a man desired by four beautiful sisters. Set in 1930s Galicia, José Luis Cuerda's gorgeous *Butterfly* (released in the United Kingdom as *The Butterfly's Tongue*) shows how the civil war divided communities before the first shots were fired. Whit Stillman, an American married to a Catalan, directed *Barcelona,* a contemporary romantic comedy about three American men and three Barcelona women.

The current bad-boy darling of Spanish cinema is Pedro Almodóvar, whose *Women on the Verge of a Nervous Breakdown* (with some nice shots of Madrid), *Tie Me Up! Tie Me Down!,* and *All About My Mother* were greeted enthusiastically on both sides of the Atlantic. *All About My Mother* won the 2000 Academy Award for Best Foreign Film, while *Hable Con Ella* (Speak With Her) won the same award in 2003.

CHRONOLOGY

ca. 12,000 BC Paleolithic (Old Stone Age) settlement. Caves of Altamira painted.

ca. 2000 BC Copper Age culture. Stone megaliths built.

ca. 1100 BC Earliest Phoenician colonies, including Cádiz, Villaricos, Almuñecar, and Málaga. Native peoples include Iberians in south, Basques in Pyrenees, and Celts in northwest.

ca. 650 BC Greeks begin to colonize east coast at Empuries, in northern Catalonia.

237 BC Carthaginians land in Spain, found Cartagena circa 225 BC.

206 BC Romans expel Carthaginians from Spain and gradually conquer peninsula over next two centuries. Spain becomes one of Rome's most important colonies.

AD 74 Roman citizenship extended to all Spaniards.

380 Christianity declared sole religion of Rome and her empire.

409 First Barbaric invasions.

419 Visigothic kingdom established in northern Spain, with capital at Toledo.

Moorish Spain

711–12 Christian Visigothic kingdom destroyed by invading Muslims (Moors) from northern Africa. Moors create emirate, with capital at Córdoba, of Ummayyad Caliphate at Damascus.

756 Independent Moorish Emirate established by Ummayyad heir Abd al-Rahman I at Córdoba.

778 Charlemagne establishes Frankish rule north of Ebro.

813 Discovery of remains of St. James, following which the cathedral of Santiago de Compostela is built and becomes a major pilgrimage site.

912–61 Reign of Abd al-Rahman III: height of Moorish culture (though it flourishes throughout Reconquest).

The Reconquest

1085 Alfonso VI of Castile captures Toledo.

1099 Death of Rodrigo Díaz de Vivar, known as El Cid, who served both Christian and Muslim kings; buried at Burgos Cathedral (completed 1126), first Gothic cathedral.

1137 Aragón unites with Catalonia through marriage.

1209 Moors found first Spanish university, in Valencia.

1212 Victory at Las Navas de Tolosa by united Christian armies: Moorish power crippled.

1236–48 Valencia, Córdoba, and Seville fall to Christians.

1270 End of main period of Reconquest. Portugal, Aragón, and Castile emerge as major powers.

1435 Alfonso V of Aragón and Sicily conquers Naples and southern Italy.

1469 Isabella, princess of Castile, marries Ferdinand, heir to the throne of Aragón.

1478 Spanish Inquisition established.

1479–1504 Isabella and Ferdinand rule jointly.

1492 Granada, last Moorish outpost, falls. Christopher Columbus, under the sponsorship of Isabella, "discovers" America, setting off a wave of Spanish exploration. Ferdinand and Isabella, also known as the Catholic Monarchs, expel Jews and Muslims from Spain.

1494 Treaty of Tordesillas: Portugal and Spain divide the known world between them.

1499 Publication of *La Celestina,* by Fernando de Rojas, considered most important literary precursor to *Don Quijote.*

1516 Death of Ferdinand. His grandson and heir, Charles I, inaugurates the Habsburg dynasty and Spain's golden age.

The Habsburg Dynasty

1519 Charles I is elected Holy Roman Emperor as Charles V. From his father, Philip of Habsburg, he inherits Austria, the Spanish Netherlands, Burgundy, and nearly continuous war with France. Hernán Cortés conquers the Aztec Empire in Mexico.

1519–22 First circumnavigation of the world by Ferdinand Magellan's ships completed by Basque navigator Juan Sebastián Elkano.

ca. 1520–1700 Golden age. Funded by its empire, Spain's culture flourishes. Artists include El Greco (1541–1614), Velázquez (1599–1660), and Murillo (1617–82). In literature, the poet Quevedo (1580–1645), dramatists Lope de Vega (1562–1635) and Calderón (1600–81), and novelist Miguel de Cervantes (1547–1616) are known throughout Europe. Counter-Reformation Catholicism takes its lead from St. Ignatius of Loyola (1491–1556), founder of the Jesuit order (1540), and the mystic St. Teresa of Ávila (1515–82).

1531 Pizarro conquers the Inca empire in Peru.

1554 Charles's heir, Philip, marries Queen Mary of England ("Bloody Mary") circa 1558.

1556 Charles abdicates in favor of his son Philip II, who inherits Spain, Sicily, and the Netherlands. Holy Roman Empire goes to Charles's brother Ferdinand. Philip II leads cause of Counter-Reformation against Protestant states in Europe.

1561 Capital established at Madrid.

1571 Spanish fleet stops westward advance of Ottoman Empire in naval battle of Lepanto—afterward regarded as the high-water mark of the Spanish Empire.

1588 Philip attacks Protestant England with Spanish Armada, to no avail.

1598 Death of Philip II.

1605 Publication of first part of Miguel de Cervantes' masterpiece, *Don Quijote de la Mancha,* generally considered the first modern novel.

1609 Under Philip III, Moriscos (converted Muslims) expelled and independence of Netherlands recognized.

1618 Beginning of Thirty Years' War. Originally a religious dispute, it became a dynastic struggle between Habsburgs and Bourbons.

1621–65 Reign of Philip IV. Count-Duke Olivares reforms regime on absolutist model of France.

1640–59 Revolt in Catalonia; republic declared for a time.

1648 End of Thirty Years' War; Spanish Netherlands declared independent.

1659 Treaty of the Pyrenees ends war with France and Spanish ascendancy in Europe.

1665–1700 Reign of Charles II, last of the Spanish Habsburgs.

The Bourbon Dynasty

1701–14 War of the Spanish Succession: claimants to the throne are Louis XIV of France (on behalf of his eldest son Philip), Holy Roman Emperor Leopold I (on behalf of his son Archduke Carlos of Austria), and electoral prince Joseph Ferdinand of Bavaria. The Treaty of Utrecht, 1713, recognizes Philip as Philip V, first Bourbon king. By Treaty of Rastatt, 1714, Spain loses Flanders, Luxembourg, and Italy to Austrian Habsburgs; spends much of its energy in 18th century trying to regain them.

1756–63 Seven Years' War: Spain and France versus Great Britain. 1756: Spain regains Minorca, lost to Great Britain in 1709. 1762: Treaty of Paris in which Spain cedes Minorca and Florida to Great Britain and receives Louisiana from France in return.

1779 Spain supports rebels in American War of Independence, regains Florida and Minorca.

1793 Revolutionary France declares war.

1795 By Treaty of Basel, Spain allies with France against Great Britain.

Napoleonic Rule

1808 King Charles IV abdicates in favor of Joseph Bonaparte, Napoléon's brother. Napoléon takes Madrid in December.

The Peninsular War

1809–14 Napoleonic armies thrown out of Spain by a combination of Spanish resistance fighters and British and Portuguese troops under the command of Wellington.

Restoration of the Bourbons

1814 Bourbons restored under Ferdinand VII, son of Charles IV. Like other restored monarchs of the era, he was a reactionary and crushed all liberal movements.

1833 Ferdinand deprives brother Don Carlos of succession in favor of his infant daughter, Isabella; her mother, María Cristina, becomes regent.

1834–39 First Carlist War: Don Carlos contests the crown and begins an era of upheaval.

1840 Coup d'état: Gen. Baldomero Espartero becomes dictator, exiles María Cristina, and ushers in a series of weak and unpopular regimes.

1843 Espartero ousted; Isabella II restored to throne.

Period of Troubles

1868 Revolution, supported by liberals, topples Isabella II but ushers in the Period of Troubles: attempts to establish a republic and find an alternate monarch fail.

1873 First Spanish Republic declared; three-year Second Carlist War begins.

Restoration of the Bourbons

1874 Alfonso XII, son of Isabella, brought to throne.

1892 Peasant revolt, inspired by anarchist doctrine (to be repeated 1903).

1895 Revolution in Cuba, one of Spain's few remaining colonies. Spain moves to suppress it.

1898 Spanish-American War: United States annexes Spanish colonies of Puerto Rico and the Philippines. Cuba is declared independent.

1902–31 Reign of Alfonso XIII. Increasing instability and unrest.

1914 Spain declares neutrality in World War I.

1923 Coup d'état of Gen. Manuel Primo de Rivera, who models his government on Italian Fascism.

Republic, Civil War & Fascism

1930–31 Primo de Rivera is ousted. Republic is declared, and Alfonso XIII is deposed. Liberals attempt to redistribute land and diminish the power of the Church.

1936–39 Spanish Civil War: electoral victory of Popular Front (a coalition of the left) precipitates rightist military insurrection against the Republic, led by Gen. Francisco Franco. Europe declares neutrality, but Germany and Italy aid Franco, and the USSR and volunteer brigades aid (to a lesser extent) the Republic. More than 600,000 die, including the poet Federico García Lorca. Franco is victorious and rules Spain for the next 36 years.

1939 Fascist Spain declares neutrality in World War II.

1945 Spain is denied membership in the United Nations (but is admitted in 1950).

1953 NATO bases are established in Spain in return for economic and military aid.

1969 Franco names Prince Juan Carlos de Borbón, heir to the vacant throne, his successor.

1973 Franco's prime minister, Carrero Blanco, is assassinated by Basque separatists.

Restoration of the Bourbons

1975 Franco dies and is succeeded by Juan Carlos, grandson of Alfonso XIII.

1977 First democratic elections in 40 years are won by Center Democratic Union.

1978 New constitution restores civil liberties and freedom of the press.

1981 Attempted coup by Col. Antonio Tejero.

1982 Spain becomes a full member of NATO. Socialists win landslide victory in general election.

1985 Frontier with Gibraltar, closed since 1968, is reopened.

1986 Spain enters European Union. Socialists win for a second time.

1989 Camilo José Cela awarded Nobel Prize for Literature. Socialists lose majority but continue in office.

1992 Olympic Games held in Barcelona; Universal Exposition held in Seville.

1993 Socialists win victory in general election.

1996 Popular Party, Spain's conservative party, wins general election, ending 14 years of Socialist rule.

1999 Popular Party reelected with a clear majority, curtailing the power of the Catalonian nationalist party.

2000 Juan Carlos celebrates 25 years as Spain's king.

2002 Nobel prize-winner Camilo José Cela dies. Barcelona celebrates the 150th anniversary of the birth of Antoni Gaudí.

2003 Barcelona celebrates The Year of Design 2003. Socialists, led by José Luis Rodríguez Zapatero, win close victory overall in regional elections, buoyed by unpopularity of Aznar's support of Iraq war and mishandling of the Prestige oil spill.

2004 Universal Forum of Cultures Barcelona 2004 opens in August, in the Catalonian capital, a world symposium bringing together scholars, statesmen, philosophers, scientists, and Nobel Prize winners to exchange views on peace, diversity, sustainable development, and globalization within the ethical charters of the Universal Declaration of Human Rights and the United Nations.

VOCABULARY

	English	Spanish	Pronunciation
Basics			
	Yes/no	Sí/no	see/no
	Please	Por favor	pohr fah-**vohr**
	May I?	¿Me permite?	meh pehr-**mee**-teh
	Thank you (very much)	(Muchas) gracias	(**moo**-chas) **grah**-see-as
	You're welcome	De nada	deh **nah**-dah
	Excuse me	Con permiso/perdón	con pehr-**mee**-so/ pehr-**dohn**
	Pardon me/ what did you say?	¿Perdón?/Mande?	pehr-**dohn/mahn**-deh
	Could you tell me . . . ?	¿Podría decirme . . . ?	po-**dree**-ah deh-**seer**-meh
	I'm sorry	Lo siento	lo see-**en**-to
	Good morning!	¡Buenos días!	**bway**-nohs **dee**-ahs
	Good afternoon!	¡Buenas tardes!	**bway**-nahs **tar**-dess
	Good evening!	¡Buenas noches!	**bway**-nahs **no**-chess
	Goodbye!	¡Adiós!/ ¡Hasta luego!	ah-dee-**ohss/ ah**-stah-**lwe**-go
	Mr./Mrs.	Señor/Señora	sen-**yor**/sen-**yohr**-ah
	Miss	Señorita	sen-yo-**ree**-tah
	Pleased to meet you	Mucho gusto	**moo**-cho **goose**-to
	How are you?	¿Cómo está usted?	**ko**-mo es-**tah** oo-**sted**
	Very well, thank you.	Muy bien, gracias.	**moo**-ee bee-**en, grah**-see-as
	And you?	¿Y usted?	ee oos-**ted**
	Hello (on the phone)	Diga	**dee**-gah
Numbers			
	1	un, uno	oon, **oo**-no
	2	dos	dohs
	3	tres	tress
	4	cuatro	**kwah**-tro
	5	cinco	**sink**-oh
	6	seis	saice
	7	siete	see-**et**-eh
	8	ocho	**o**-cho
	9	nueve	new-**eh**-veh
	10	diez	dee-**es**
	11	once	**ohn**-seh

12	doce	**doh**-seh
13	trece	**treh**-seh
14	catorce	ka-**tohr**-seh
15	quince	**keen**-seh
16	dieciséis	dee-**es**-ee-**saice**
17	diecisiete	dee-**es**-ee-see-**et**-eh
18	dieciocho	dee-**es**-ee-**o**-cho
19	diecinueve	dee-**es**-ee-new-**ev**-eh
20	veinte	**vain**-teh
21	veinte y uno/ veintiuno	**vain**-te-oo-noh
30	treinta	**train**-tah
32	treinta y dos	train-tay-**dohs**
40	cuarenta	kwah-**ren**-tah
50	cincuenta	seen-**kwen**-tah
60	sesenta	sess-**en**-tah
70	setenta	set-**en**-tah
80	ochenta	oh-**chen**-tah
90	noventa	no-**ven**-tah
100	cien	see-**en**
200	doscientos	doh-see-**en**-tohss
500	quinientos	keen-**yen**-tohss
1,000	mil	meel
2,000	dos mil	dohs meel

Days of the Week

Sunday	domingo	doh-**meen**-goh
Monday	lunes	**loo**-ness
Tuesday	martes	**mahr**-tess
Wednesday	miércoles	me-**air**-koh-less
Thursday	jueves	hoo-**ev**-ess
Friday	viernes	vee-**air**-ness
Saturday	sábado	**sah**-bah-doh

Useful Phrases

Do you speak English?	¿Habla usted inglés?	**ah**-blah oos-**ted** in-**glehs**
I don't speak Spanish	No hablo español	no **ah**-bloh es-pahn-**yol**
I don't understand (you)	No entiendo	no en-tee-**en**-doh
I understand (you)	Entiendo	en-tee-**en**-doh
I don't know	No sé	no seh
I am American/ British	Soy americano (americana)/ inglés(a)	soy ah-meh-ree-**kah**-no (ah-meh-ree-**kah**-nah)/in-**glehs**(ah)

My name is . . .	Me llamo . . .	meh **yah**-moh
Yes, please/ No, thank you	Sí, por favor/ No, gracias	**see** pohr fah-**vor**/ no **grah**-see-ahs
Yesterday/today/ tomorrow	Ayer/hoy/mañana	ah-**yehr**/oy/mahn-**yah**-nah
This morning/ afternoon	Esta mañana/tarde	**es**-tah mahn-**yah**-nah/**tar**-deh
Tonight	Esta noche	**es**-tah **no**-cheh
This/Next week	Esta semana/ la semana que entra	**es**-tah seh-**mah**-nah/lah seh-**mah**-nah keh **en**-trah
This/Next month	Este mes/el próximo mes	**es**-teh mehs/el **prok**-see-moh mehs
How?	¿Cómo?	**koh**-mo
When?	¿Cuándo?	**kwahn**-doh
What?	¿Qué?	keh
What is this?	¿Qué es esto?	keh es **es**-toh
Why?	¿Por qué?	por **keh**
Who?	¿Quién?	kee-**yen**
Where is . . . ?	¿Dónde está . . . ?	**dohn**-deh es-**tah**
the train station?	la estación del tren?	la es-tah-see-**on** del **train**
the subway station?	la estación del metro?	la es-ta-see-**on** del **meh**-tro
the bus stop?	la parada del autobus?	la pah-**rah**-dah del oh-toh-**boos**
the bank?	el banco?	el **bahn**-koh
the hotel?	el hotel?	el oh-**tel**
the post office?	la oficina de correos?	la oh-fee-**see**-nah deh-koh-**reh**-os
the museum?	el museo?	el moo-**seh**-oh
the hospital?	el hospital?	el ohss-pee-**tal**
the bathroom?	el baño?	el **bahn**-yoh
Here/there	Aquí/allá	ah-**key**/ah-**yah**
Open/closed	Abierto/cerrado	ah-bee-**er**-toh/ ser-**ah**-doh
Left/right	Izquierda/derecha	iss-key-**er**-dah/ dare-**eh**-chah
Straight ahead	Todo recto	**toh**-doh-**rec**-toh
Is it near/far?	¿Está cerca/lejos?	es-**tah** **sehr**-kah/ **leh**-hoss
I'd like . . .	Quisiera . . .	kee-see-**ehr**-ah
a room	una habitación	**oo**-nah ah-bee-tah-see-**on**
the key	la llave	lah **yah**-veh
a newspaper	un periódico	oon pehr-ee-**oh**-dee-koh
a stamp	un sello	**say**-oh
How much is this?	¿Cuánto cuesta?	**kwahn**-toh **kwes**-tah
A little/a lot	Un poquito/ mucho	oon poh-**kee**-toh/ **moo**-choh
More/less	Más/menos	mahss/**men**-ohss
I am ill	Estoy enfermo(a)	es-**toy** en-**fehr**-moh(mah)

Please call a doctor	Por favor llame un médico	pohr fah-**vor ya**-meh oon **med**-ee-koh
Help!	¡Ayuda!	ah-**yoo**-dah

On the Road

Avenue	Avenida	ah-ven-**ee**-dah
Broad, tree-lined boulevard	Paseo	pah-**seh**-oh
Highway	Carretera	car-reh-**ter**-ah
Port; mountain pass	Puerto	poo-**ehr**-toh
Street	Calle	**cah**-yeh
Waterfront promenade	Paseo marítimo	pah-**seh**-oh mahr-**ee**-tee-moh

In Town

Cathedral	Catedral	cah-teh-**dral**
Church	Iglesia	**tem**-plo/ee-**glehs**-see-ah
City hall, town hall	Ayuntamiento	ah-yoon-tah-me-**yen**-toh
Door, gate	Puerta	poo-**ehr**-tah
Main square	Plaza Mayor	plah-thah mah-**yohr**
Market	Mercado	mer-**kah**-doh
Neighborhood	Barrio	**bahr**-ree-o
Tavern, rustic restaurant	Mesón	meh-**sohn**
Traffic circle, roundabout	Glorieta	glor-ee-**eh**-tah
Wine cellar, wine bar, wine shop	Bodega	boh-**deh**-gah

Dining Out

A bottle of . . .	Una botella de . . .	**oo**-nah bo-**teh**-yah deh
A glass of . . .	Un vaso de . . .	oon **vah**-so deh
Bill/check	La cuenta	lah **kwen**-tah
Breakfast	El desayuno	el deh-sah-**yoon**-oh
Dinner	La cena	lah **seh**-nah
Menu of the day	Menú del día	meh-**noo** del **dee**-ah
Fork	El tenedor	ehl ten-eh-**dor**
Is the tip included?	¿Está incluida la propina?	es-**tah** in-cloo-**ee**-dah lah pro-**pee**-nah
Knife	El cuchillo	el koo-**chee**-yo
Large portion of tapas	Ración	rah-see-**ohn**
Lunch	La comida	lah koh-**mee**-dah
Menu	La carta, el menú	lah **cart**-ah, el meh-**noo**
Napkin	La servilleta	lah sehr-vee-**yet**-ah
Please give me . . .	Por favor déme . . .	pohr fah-**vor deh**-meh
Spoon	Una cuchara	**oo**-nah koo-**chah**-rah

INDEX

N

O

P

NOTES

NOTES

NOTES

NOTES

NOTES

FODOR'S KEY TO THE GUIDES

America's guidebook leader publishes guides for every kind of traveler. Check out our many series and find your perfect match.

FODOR'S GOLD GUIDES

America's favorite travel-guide series offers the most detailed insider reviews of hotels, restaurants, and attractions in all price ranges, plus great background information, smart tips, and useful maps.

COMPASS AMERICAN GUIDES

Stunning guides from top local writers and photographers, with gorgeous photos, literary excerpts, and colorful anecdotes. A must-have for culture mavens, history buffs, and new residents.

FODOR'S CITYPACKS

Concise city coverage in a guide plus a foldout map. The right choice for urban travelers who want everything under one cover.

FODOR'S EXPLORING GUIDES

Hundreds of color photos bring your destination to life. Lively stories lend insight into the culture, history, and people.

FODOR'S TRAVEL HISTORIC AMERICA

For travelers who want to experience history firsthand, this series gives in-depth coverage of historic sights, plus nearby restaurants and hotels. Themes include the Thirteen Colonies, the Old West, and the Lewis and Clark Trail.

FODOR'S POCKET GUIDES

For travelers who need only the essentials. The best of Fodor's in pocket-size packages for just $9.95.

FODOR'S FLASHMAPS

Every resident's map guide, with 60 easy-to-follow maps of public transit, parks, museums, zip codes, and more.

FODOR'S CITYGUIDES

Sourcebooks for living in the city: thousands of in-the-know listings for restaurants, shops, sports, nightlife, and other city resources.

FODOR'S AROUND THE CITY WITH KIDS

Up to 68 great ideas for family days, recommended by resident parents. Perfect for exploring in your own backyard or on the road.

FODOR'S HOW TO GUIDES

Get tips from the pros on planning the perfect trip. Learn how to pack, fly hassle-free, plan a honeymoon or cruise, stay healthy on the road, and travel with your baby.

FODOR'S LANGUAGES FOR TRAVELERS

Practice the local language before you hit the road. Available in phrase books, cassette sets, and CD sets.

KAREN BROWN'S GUIDES

Engaging guides—many with easy-to-follow inn-to-inn itineraries—to the most charming inns and B&Bs in the U.S.A. and Europe.

BAEDEKER'S GUIDES

Comprehensive guides, trusted since 1829, packed with A–Z reviews and star ratings.

OTHER GREAT TITLES FROM FODOR'S

Baseball Vacations, The Complete Guide to the National Parks, Family Vacations, Golf Digest's Places to Play, Great American Drives of the East, Great American Drives of the West, Great American Vacations, Healthy Escapes, National Parks of the West, Skiing USA.

At bookstores everywhere. www.fodors.com/books